Human Sexuality

Human Sexuality

Second Edition

William H. Masters   Virginia E. Johnson
Robert C. Kolodny

LITTLE, BROWN AND COMPANY
Boston   Toronto

Library of Congress Cataloging in Publication Data

Masters, William H.
Human sexuality.

Bibliography: p.
Includes index.
1. Sex. 2. Sex (Psychology) 3. Sex (Biology)
4. Sexual disorders. I. Johnson, Virginia E.
II. Kolodny, Robert C. III. Title.
HQ21.M46157   1984   612'.6   84-17171
ISBN 0-316-54995-9

Library of Congress Catalog Card No. 84-17171

ISBN 0-316-54995-9

9 8 7 6 5 4 3 2

HAL

Published simultaneously in Canada
by Little, Brown & Company (Canada) Limited

Printed in the United States of America

CREDITS AND ACKNOWLEDGMENTS

Page viii   Scott F. Johnson (photos 1, 2, and 3); IU News Bureau (photo 4).
Chapter 1   p. 5 upper right-Visions, Donna Ferrato;   middle right-Christopher Brown, Stock, Boston;   bottom right-Michael O'Brien/Archive;   bottom left-Jill Freedman/Archive;   top left-Lily Solmssen, Photo Researchers.   p. 10 (left) Art Resource, Inc.;   (right) The Bettmann Archive.   p. 11 Art Resource/Sotheby Parke-Bernet/Harushige.   p. 15 The Bettmann Archive.   p. 17 The Bettmann Archive.   p. 18 The Bettmann Archive.
Chapter 2   p. 41 © David H. Barlow/State University of New York at Albany.

continued on page 638

Preface

OUR OBJECTIVES for the second edition of this text are fundamentally the same as those that guided our initial approaches to this project. We have tried to combine comprehensive coverage of the field of human sexuality suitable for an introductory college-level course with a lively, personalized, engaging style and a balanced approach that integrates biological, psychosocial, and cultural aspects of the subject. Throughout the preparation of this edition, we have also attempted to provide students with information that can contribute meaningfully to their knowledge, comfort, and choices regarding personal and interpersonal aspects of sexuality.

As in our first edition, we have drawn extensively on the literature of sex research as well as on our own published and unpublished work for insights and information. At the same time, we have made considerable use of personal quotes from ordinary people to give an authentic "real life" flavor to the book and to avoid the dryness and biases of the strictly academic approach. This approach is especially evident in the use of "Personal Perspectives" boxes interspersed throughout the text, a feature that is new to this edition.

The enthusiasm with which our first edition was received was gratifying, and we have retained many of the features of the original text. The outstanding illustrations of Robert Demarest have been retained, for example, with the addition of many new photographs, charts, graphs, and cartoons. Many new boxed items have been used to highlight topics throughout the text, including coverage of such areas as "If

You Have Ever Been Involved with Incest," "Practical Pointers on Educating Your Children About Sex," and other topics as diverse as sex-by-computer and telephone commercial sex services. And, as in the first edition, the attractive layout enhances the reader's use of the book.

NEW FEATURES OF THIS EDITION

This edition incorporates the suggestions of a substantial number of students and professors who have used the book, and generally provides expanded, updated coverage of the broad field of human sexuality. Some of the notable areas of additions are as follows:

– A new chapter on intimacy and communication skills

– Expanded coverage of childhood and adolescent sexuality, including an important section on unintended teenage pregnancy

– Expanded coverage of sexuality in mid-adulthood and geriatric years

– A separate, comprehensive chapter on sexually transmitted diseases, featuring the most detailed coverage on AIDS and genital herpes, from both biomedical and psychosocial perspectives, found in any college text

– A separate chapter on sex research, highlighting both the basic methodology and specific critiques of major sex research studies with which students need to be familiar

– New material on sexual harassment, mate rape, rape of men by women, pedophilia, divorce and remarriage, premenstrual syndrome, D.E.S. daughters and sons, the contraceptive sponge, and a host of other thought-provoking areas

— Expanded coverage of many controversies in the field, including research on the Grafenberg spot and the nature-nurture argument over formation of gender identity

— Expanded coverage of sex and various forms of disability, including spinal cord injury, blindness, deafness, and mental retardation.

In addition, Canadian research and statistics have been integrated into the text in many places with material provided by William Fisher, Ph.D.

ORGANIZATION

Human Sexuality begins with an introductory section consisting of two chapters. The first provides students with a basic orientation to the subject by discussing the various dimensions of sexuality and offering a synopsis of historical perspectives on sexual customs and thoughts, while the second gives students an overview of the methods of sex research and familiarizes them with the major sex research studies from Kinsey to the present. The remainder of the book is organized into five parts, each consisting of three to five chapters, that cover Biological Perspectives, Psychosocial Perspectives, Behavioral Perspectives, Clinical Perspectives, and Cultural Perspectives. This framework emphasizes different components of sexuality in a cohesive way. Each part, however, maintains a multidimensional view that highlights the interwoven complexity of the different perspectives.

LEARNING AIDS

As in the first edition, a number of special devices are used to bolster learning. Dozens of boxed items on timely, practical topics are used for special emphasis, and a new form of boxed item called *Personal Perspectives* has been added to this edition to allow for first person accounts of unusual topics — for example, what it feels like to participate in a sex research project, or what the elderly have to say about their sexual needs. *Research Spotlights* are used in many chapters to highlight important and sometimes controversial topics. *Chapter Summaries* and annotated *Suggested Readings* are also found in each chapter, and the detailed glossary, with its easy-to-use phonetic pronunciation guide, has been expanded. The reference list for this edition includes more than 1,300 items, making it uniquely useful to students searching for material on almost any topic covered in the book.

SUPPLEMENTARY MATERIALS

The valuable *Study Guide* has been revised and updated by Professor Marvin R. Levy of Temple University. It provides students with programmed-learning modules, well-defined sets of learning objectives, and review questions designed to reinforce key concepts and help students master technical material.

The detailed *Instructor's Manual* has also been revised by Nancy J. Kolodny, M.A., M.S.W., and provides a wide range of information to instructors including numerous test items, lists of audio-visual resources, and suggestions for class discussion questions.

ACKNOWLEDGMENTS

Throughout this project, superb editorial services were provided by a number of people at Little, Brown and Company. Special mention of the skills and insights of Jane Tufts is made with gratitude; her enthusiasm and hard work were matched by Victoria Keirnan, our Book Editor, whose talented touch is evident on every page of this book. Expert services were also provided by Kimberley Rieck Fisher and Shelley Roth (Editorial Assistants) and George McLean (Designer). In addition, the guidance of Molly Faulkner (Psychology Editor) and Chester C. Lucido, Jr. (Vice President and General Manager) materially helped our efforts from start to finish.

The entire manuscript was reviewed in draft form by Professor Marlene Tufts of Clackamas Community College who did an outstanding job of alerting us to inconsistencies and ambiguities. Likewise, Professor William Fisher of the University of Western Ontario provided us with extensive review comments on the entire manuscript as well as suggestions for adding coverage regarding Canadian perspectives on various sexual issues. We are also extremely grateful to the following college instructors who reviewed parts of our manuscript with meticulous attention to details of content, style, and accessibility: Wayne Anderson, University of Missouri; Richard L. Archer, Southwest Texas State University; Janice Baldwin, University of California – Santa Barbara; John Baldwin, University of California – Santa Barbara; Betsy Bergen, Kansas State University; Ruth C. Blanche, Montclair State College; Michael Campbell, Highline Community College; F. Scott Christopher, University of Nevada – Reno; Joseph S. Darden, Jr., Kean College of New Jersey; Richard Dienstbier, University of Nebraska – Lincoln; William Fisher, University of Western Ontario; Ronald Mazer, University of Southern Maine; David Newlin, Purdue University; Andrea Parrot, Cornell University; Randy Price, Richland College; William J. Serdahely, Montana State University; Marlene Tufts, Clackamas Community College; Donald Whitmore, University of Texas – Arlington; Edward Wickersham, Pennsylvania State University.

The following professors were helpful with their insightful comments regarding the first edi-

tion of this text: Marlene Tufts, Clackamas Community College; Hayden L. Mees, Western Washington University; Frederick Gault, Western Kalamazoo University; Ronald Mazur, University of Massachusetts—Amherst; Michael E. Walraven, Jackson Community College; B. E. Pruitt, University of Oregon; Susan Van Buskirk, North Texas State University; Robert DaPrato, Solano Community College; Kenneth L. Goodhue-McWilliams, California State University—Fullerton; Marvin R. Levy, Temple University; Elaine Baker, Marshall University; Alan G. Glaros, Wayne State University; Kay F. Schaffer, University of Toledo; Randy Price, Richland College; Barry Singer, California State University—Long Beach; Rae Silver, Barnard College at Columbia University; Roger N. Moss, California State University—Northridge; Helen J. MacAllister, Monmouth College; Gail Knapp, Charles Stuart Mott Community College; William L. Yarber, Purdue University; Richard Maslow, San Joaquin Delta College; John W. Petras, Central Michigan University; Joan DiGiovanni, Western New England College; Carol Rinkleib Ellison, Clinical Psychologist; Gertrude V. DiFrancesco, Bucks County Community College.

In closing, we will reiterate our final paragraph from the preface to the first edition of this book since it succinctly makes our point:

> Sexuality is an intensely personal subject, and we hope that this book reflects our view of each individual's potential to experience his or her sexuality in a unique way. We also hope that this book conveys our belief that today's knowledge may be short-lived when judged by the standards of time, so that we must all guard against assuming too certain a view of sexual matters.

William H. Masters
Virginia E. Johnson
Robert C. Kolodny

About the Authors

William H. Masters, M.D., is internationally acclaimed as one of the pioneer sex researchers and therapists of the twentieth century. Co-author of *Human Sexual Response* (1966), *Human Sexual Inadequacy* (1970), *The Pleasure Bond* (1975), and *Homosexuality in Perspective* (1979), among more than 200 publications, Dr. Masters has been instrumental in establishing the legitimacy of the scientific study of sex. Dr. Masters has been the recipient of more than a dozen awards from professional organizations in recognition of his outstanding career.

Virginia E. Johnson, D.Sc. (Hon.), is world-renowned for her innovative contributions to sex therapy and sex research. As Director of the Masters & Johnson Institute in St. Louis, she oversees clinical, research, and educational operations at this multidisciplinary organization, while continuing to maintain her own special interests in women's studies and the psychology of sexual behavior. Co-author of nine books and hundreds of journal articles, Dr. Johnson has been the recipient of more than a dozen awards from professional organizations during her remarkable career.

Robert C. Kolodny, M.D., is Medical Director and Chairman of the Board of the Behavioral Medicine Institute in New Canaan, Connecticut. He was previously Associate Director and Director of Training at the Masters & Johnson Institute, where he worked for over a decade, and where he continues to serve as a Consultant and member of the Board of Directors. In 1983, he was the recipient of the National Award from the Society for the Scientific Study of Sex. Dr. Kolodny's prior books include four co-authored with Drs. Masters and Johnson, including *Textbook of Sexual Medicine* (1979) and *Ethical Issues in Sex Therapy and Research* (1977 and 1980).

Guest-author Paul H. Gebhard, Ph.D., is well known as one of Alfred Kinsey's collaborators. After a distinguished career spanning five decades, Dr. Gebhard recently retired as Director of the Institute for Sex Research at Indiana University, where his leadership has continued the Kinsey tradition of research productivity.

Brief Contents

Contents

PART ONE **Biological Perspectives**   **47**

3   **Sexual Anatomy**   **49**

4   **Sexual Physiology**   **76**

5 Human Reproduction 107

Contents

PART THREE   Behavioral Perspectives   353

14   Solitary Sexual Behavior   355

15   Heterosexuality   374

16 Homosexuality and Bisexuality   407

17 The Varieties of Sexual Behavior   438

20   Sexual Disorders and Sexual Health   527

21   Sexually Transmitted Diseases   555

PART FIVE   **Cultural Perspectives**   581

22   **Sexual Themes in Popular Culture**   583

23   **Religious and Ethical Perspectives on Sexuality**   602

Introduction

1 Perspectives on Sexuality

E VERY PERSON has sexual feelings, attitudes, and beliefs, but everyone's experience of sexuality is unique because it is processed through an intensely personal perspective. This perspective comes from both private, personal experience and public, social sources. It is impossible to understand human sexuality without recognizing its multidimensional nature.

Sexuality has fascinated people in all walks of life from ancient times until the present. Sexual themes have been common in art and literature. Religions, philosophies, and legal systems — all concerned with shaping human behavior — have typically tried to establish sexual values and sexual taboos. At various times in history, illness, creativity, aggression, emotional disorders, and the rise and fall of cultures have all been "explained" as the result of too much or too little sexual activity or unusual sexual practices or thoughts.

While keeping in mind the private, public, and historical sources of our sexual heritage, we can broaden and deepen our understanding by studying sexuality from biological, psychosocial, behavioral, clinical, and cultural perspectives. In examining sexuality from these varied viewpoints, however, we must be careful not to forget that learning about sexuality, in all its forms, is really learning about people and the complexities of human nature.

WHY STUDY SEXUALITY?

While there are a number of different reasons for studying sexuality, many college students who enroll in sexuality courses do so for personal rather than academic reasons. This is because learning about sexuality — as contrasted to learning about physical chemistry or calculus — can provide people with knowledge that has a high potential for use in their everyday lives. This does not mean that there is no academic value to studying sexuality (since quite the opposite is true), but it does indicate that learning about sexuality has a number of practical applications that other subjects may not provide as easily.

Learning accurate information about sexuality can help prevent sexual problems and help us be better sex educators for our children. Becoming well-informed about sex can also help us deal more effectively with certain types of problems if they occur in our lives (e.g., infertility, sexual dysfunctions, sexually transmitted diseases, sexual harassment). Even more important, studying sexuality can help us become more sensitive and aware in our interpersonal relationships, thus contributing to the growth of intimacy and sexual satisfaction in our lives.

Unfortunately, it is also true that these results do not happen automatically. There is no guarantee that careful study of this text will make finding (or keeping) sexual partners any easier, nor that it will lead to sexual bliss. Instead, we believe that learning about sexuality in an objective fashion will enable our readers to examine important sexual issues — some intensely personal, some social, some moral — and emerge with deeper insight into themselves and others. We also believe that sexual knowledge can lead to reasoned, responsible interpersonal sexual behavior and can help people make important personal decisions about sex. In short, learning about sexuality is an invaluable preparation for living.

DIMENSIONS OF SEXUALITY: SOME DEFINITIONS

One would certainly think that there could be no doubt about what is to be understood by the term "sexual." First and foremost, of course, it means the "improper," that which must not be mentioned. (Freud, 1943, p. 266)

Sex is not a mere physiological transaction to the primitive South Sea Islander any more than it is to us; it implies love and lovemaking; it becomes the nucleus of such venerable institutions as marriage and the family; it pervades art and it produces its spells and its magic. It dominates in fact almost every aspect of culture. *Sex,* in its widest meaning . . . is rather a sociological and cultural force than a mere bodily relation of two individuals. (Malinowski, 1929, p. xxiii)

"Francie, you bloody fucker," I used to say, "you've got the morals of a clam." "But you like me, don't you?" she'd answer. "Men like to fuck, and so do women. It doesn't harm anybody and it doesn't mean you have to love everyone you fuck, does it?" (Miller, 1961, p. 262)

What is sexuality? As shown by the quotes above, there is no simple answer to this question. Freud saw sex as a powerful psychological and biological force, while Malinowski emphasized its sociological and cultural dimensions. Henry Miller used frank portrayals of sex in his novels to make a philosophical statement about the human condition. In everyday life, the word "sex" is often used to mean male or female (biological gender) or to refer to physical activity involving the genitals ("having sex"). The word "sexuality" generally has a broader meaning since it refers to all aspects of being sexual. Sexuality means a dimension of personality instead of referring to a person's capacity for erotic response alone.

Unfortunately, our language for talking about sex and sexuality is very limited.[1] We may

---

[1]Wardell Pomeroy, a leading sexologist, likes to ask an audience for a four-letter word ending in the letter "k" that means "intercourse" — and then pauses knowingly before he says, "talk."

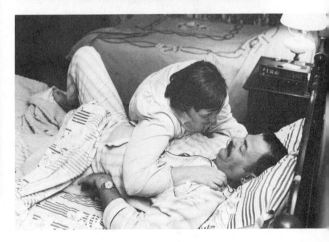

Sexuality is a part of everyone's life.

distinguish between sex acts (such as masturbation, kissing, or sexual intercourse) and sexual behavior (which includes not only specific sex acts but being flirtatious, dressing in certain ways, reading *Playboy,* or dating) without having yet scratched the surface of sexuality. We may describe different types of sex as *procreational* (for having children), *recreational* (for having fun, with no other goal), or *relational* (for sharing with a cared-for person), and find that our categories are still too few. While we cannot fully answer the question, "What is sexuality?" in this chapter, we can briefly introduce the dimensions of sexuality that are the subject of this book.

A CASE PROFILE

David and Lynn sat anxiously in the waiting room at a sex therapy clinic. Although feeling embarrassed and unsure, they were determined to seek a solution to the sexual problems that had troubled their relationship for the past three months. Although they had been living together for almost two years and had planned to marry after their graduation from college, the dissatisfactions that now rocked their lives had thrown these future plans into doubt.

Once inside the clinic, they told their story in a straightforward fashion. They had met three years ago, at age eighteen, during their freshman year at school. Romance blossomed as they discovered many shared interests and easily developed an intimate sexual relationship. Neither David nor Lynn was a virgin when they met, and they felt a strong sexual attraction to each other. Their first shared lovemaking experience was passionate and sensuous. As their relationship matured, their sexual interaction continued to be a major source of pleasure. Living together was a natural outgrowth of these feelings, and it had been fun — until recently.

Trouble first appeared during Christmas vacation when they visited Lynn's parents in Boston. David was upset because he and Lynn were not allowed to share the same bedroom. Lynn was put off by her parents' apparent coolness toward David. Their only sexual opportunity (on a Sunday morning while Lynn's parents were at church) was hurried and felt mechanical. They

were both relieved to return to school in time for a big New Year's Eve party with some friends.

The party lasted until 4:00 a.m. with great quantities of champagne consumed by all. Once back at their apartment, David and Lynn tried to make love but David was unable to get an erection. They laughed it off and fell asleep, happy to be "home."

The next morning David had a terrible hangover. He took some aspirin, ate a quick breakfast, and invited Lynn into their bedroom. She wasn't very enthusiastic, having a slight hangover herself, but didn't object. Once again David was unable to get an erection. Although Lynn was very understanding and supportive, David worried about his sexual performance (or lack of it) all day. He decided he needed some rest and relaxation before trying again, so he went to bed early that evening without any romantic overtures.

David awakened the next day feeling rested and refreshed and immediately turned to embrace Lynn.

Despite feeling good, he found himself having only a partial erection, and even that disappeared when they tried to have intercourse. From that point on, David was plagued by difficulties getting or keeping an erection, and Lynn — despite initial attempts at helping him — was getting increasingly upset. Whereas their relationship *had* been relaxed and comfortable, now they were becoming short-tempered and abrupt. They talked about splitting up but believed they still loved each other and that they could — with some expert help — overcome this problem.

This real-life example, drawn from our files, allows us to introduce the various perspectives on sexuality that we will examine in greater detail later in this book. By looking at David and Lynn's situation, we can see the importance of the different dimensions of sexuality that interact in all of our lives.

The Biological Dimension

David's problem with erections first occurred after he had consumed a lot of champagne. This is not very surprising, since alcohol is a depressant to the nervous system. Because the nervous system normally transmits physical sensations to the brain and activates our sexual reflexes, too much alcohol can block *anyone's* sexual response.

The biological dimension of sexuality is far more inclusive than this, however. Biological factors largely control sexual development from conception until birth and our ability to reproduce after puberty. The biological side of sexuality also affects our sexual desire, our sexual functioning, and (indirectly) our sexual satisfaction. Biological forces are even thought to influence certain sex differences in behavior, such as the tendency of males to act more aggressively than females (Olweus et al., 1980; Reinisch, 1981). And sexual turn-ons, no matter what their source, produce specific biological events: the pulse quickens, the sexual organs respond, and sensations of warmth or tingling spread through our bodies.

The Psychosocial Dimension

David and Lynn reacted to their situation in different ways. David became anxious and goal-oriented and lost his self-confidence, while Lynn, who started out being supportive and understanding, became irritated and aloof. Clearly, the nature of their relationship changed in response to the stress of their sexual problem. David and Lynn even began to doubt whether they were in love and wanted to marry, although while visiting Lynn's parents they were convinced this plan was "right."

These responses illustrate the psychosocial dimension of sexuality, which includes psychological factors (emotions, thoughts, and personalities) in combination with social elements (how people interact). In this case, David's concern about his first sexual "failure" led him into further difficulties even when the original biological "cause" — too much alcohol — was removed

from the situation. His anxieties led him into trying too hard to make sex work, with the result being exactly the opposite of what he and Lynn wanted.

The psychosocial side of sexuality is important because it sheds light not only on many sexual problems but also on how we develop as sexual beings. From infancy, a person's *gender identity* (the personal sense of being male or female) is primarily shaped by psychosocial forces. Our early sexual attitudes — which often stay with us into adulthood — are based largely on what parents, peers, and teachers tell us or show us about the meanings and purposes of sex. Our sexuality is also social in that it is regulated by society through laws, taboos, and family and peer group pressures that seek to persuade us to follow certain paths of sexual behavior.

The Behavioral Dimension

Talking with David and Lynn separately, we learned that the pattern of their sexual interaction changed considerably during the three months of their problem. The frequency of attempted lovemaking fell drastically, while in the past it had been four or five times per week. David masturbated several times a week (which he had not done for several years) after finding that he could easily get erections this way. On the other hand, Lynn masturbated only once, since she felt guilty about this activity. She also shied away from initiating sexual activity or even acting romantic with David because she thought this would put extra pressure on him.

These aspects of David and Lynn's situation reflect the behavioral dimension of sexuality. Sexual behavior is a product of both biological and psychosocial forces, yet studying it in its own right can be enlightening. The behavioral perspective allows us to learn not only *what* people do but to understand more about *how* and *why* they do it. For example, David may have used masturbation to boost his self-confidence by "proving" to himself that he could still get erections. Lynn's withdrawal from initiating physical intimacy may have been well-intended, but David may have interpreted it as rejection.

In discussing this topic, we should avoid judging other people's sexual behavior by our own values and experiences. Too often, people have a tendency to think about sexuality in terms of "normal" versus "abnormal." "Normal" is frequently defined as what we ourselves do and feel comfortable about, while the "abnormal" is what others do that seems different or odd to us. Trying to decide what is normal for others is not only a thankless task but one ordinarily doomed to failure because our objectivity is clouded by our values and experiences.

The Clinical Dimension

David and Lynn entered our sex therapy program and resolved their difficulties within two weeks. Not only did their sexual interaction return to its previously pleasurable state, but both felt that the therapy experience improved their relationship in other ways. As Lynn commented to us: "Overcoming the sexual problem was great, but we've also learned so much about ourselves. Our communication is about 1,000 percent better now, and we really feel like we have a solid relationship that can cope with any kind of problem that comes up."

Although sex is a natural function, many types of obstacles can lessen the pleasure or spontaneity of our sexual encounters. Physical problems such as illness, injury, or drugs can alter our sexual response patterns or knock them out completely. Feelings such as anxiety, guilt, embarrassment, or depression and conflicts in our personal relationships can also hamper our sexuality. The clinical perspective of sexuality examines the solutions to these and other problems that prevent people from reaching a state of sexual health and happiness.

Greatly improved results have been obtained in the treatment of a wide variety of sexual difficulties in the last two decades. Two key changes have contributed to this success: a better understanding of the multidimensional nature of sexuality and the development of a new discipline, called sexology, devoted to the study of sex. Doctors, psychologists, nurses, counselors, and other professionials trained in sexology can integrate this knowledge with training in sex counseling or sex therapy to help a high percentage of their patients.

The Cultural Dimension

David and Lynn's lives, like all of ours, reflect the input of the culture in which they live. For example, Lynn's parents refused to let them sleep in the same bedroom although they knew David and Lynn were living together. As another example, Lynn's sense of guilt toward masturbation stemmed largely from her religious upbringing. And David's anxiety over his sexual difficulties was partly a reaction to the prevailing American notion that men should be instantly erect at the first moment of a sexual encounter.

Our own cultural attitudes toward sexuality are far from universal. In some societies, a man's special obligations to guests or friends are discharged by an invitation to have sexual relations with his wife (Voget, 1961). Ford and Beach (1951, p. 49) listed eight cultural groups in which kissing was unknown, pointing out: "When the Thonga first saw Europeans kissing they laughed, expressing this sentiment: 'Look at them — they eat each other's saliva and dirt.'" While these cultural differences may shock or amuse us, they can also help us understand that our viewpoint is not shared by all people in all places.

Sexual topics are often controversial and

value-laden, but the controversy is often relative to time, place, and circumstance. What is labelled as "moral" or "right" varies from culture to culture, from century to century. Many of the moral issues pertaining to sex relate to certain religious traditions, but religion has no monopoly on morality. People who have no closely held religious creed are just as likely to be moral as those whose values are tied to a religious position. *There is no sexual value system that is right for everyone and no single moral code that is indisputably correct and universally applicable.*

In America, messages about sexual behavior that prevailed in the first half of this century now appear to be changing. Three trends deserve particular mention. The first is a loosening of gender role stereotypes. *Gender role* is the public expression of gender identity — that is, how an individual asserts his or her maleness or femaleness in social settings (Money and Ehrhardt, 1972).[2] Traditionally, women and girls were cast as sexually passive and unresponsive creatures while men were seen as virile sexual aggressors. According to this view, the male was expected to be the sexual initiator and expert, and the female who was aggressive or enjoyed sex too much was frowned upon. This notion has now been replaced for many people by a concept of mutual participation and satisfaction. A second trend is the greater degree of openness about sexuality. All forms of the media from television to cinema to the printed word reflect this change, and, as a result, sex has become less shameful and mysterious. The third trend is the growing acceptance of relational and recreational sex as opposed to reproductive sex. This shift, which has been especially evident in the past twenty years, is due

partly to improved contraceptive techniques and concern for overpopulation. The emergence of a positive sex philosophy is also tightly intertwined with the sexual emancipation of women and greater societal openness toward sex.

HISTORICAL PERSPECTIVES ON SEXUALITY

A major obstacle to understanding our own sexuality is realizing we are prisoners of past societal attitudes toward sex. (Bullough, 1976, p. xi)

To understand the present, it is helpful to begin by examining the past. In certain respects, we are bound by a sexual legacy passed on from generation to generation, but in other ways modern views of sex and sexuality differ drastically from past patterns.

Early Times

Although written history goes back almost 5,000 years, only limited information is available describing sexual behavior and attitudes in various societies prior to 1,000 B.C. Clearly, a prominent taboo against incest had already been established (Tannahill, 1980), and women were considered as property, with sexual and reproductive value (Bullough, 1976). Men were free to have many sexual partners, prostitution was widespread, and sex was accepted as a straightforward fact of life.

With the advent of Judaism, an interesting interplay of sexual attitudes began to emerge. In the first five books of the *Old Testament*, the primary source of Jewish laws, there are rules about sexual conduct: adultery is forbidden in the Ten Commandments (*Exodus* 20:13), for example, and homosexual acts are strongly condemned (*Leviticus* 18:22, *Leviticus* 21:13). At the same time, sex is recognized as a creative and

---

[2] Although the term "sex roles" is more widely used than "gender roles," we have chosen the second usage throughout this book to avoid the risk that "sex roles" implies an underlying biological mechanism (Unger, 1979).

pleasurable force, as depicted in the *Song of Songs*. Sex was neither considered inherently evil nor restricted to procreative purposes alone.

In ancient Greece, however, there was tolerance and even enthusiasm regarding male homosexuality in certain forms. Homosexual relations between an adult man and adolescent boy past the age of puberty were commonplace, usually occurring in an educational relationship where the man was responsible for the boy's moral and intellectual development (Tannahill, 1980; Karlen, 1980; Bullough, 1976). At the same time, exclusive homosexuality and homosexual acts between adults were frowned upon, and homosexual contact between adults and boys under the age of puberty was illegal. There was a strong emphasis on marriage and family yet women were second-class citizens, if they could

be considered citizens at all: "In Athens, women had no more political or legal rights than slaves; throughout their lives they were subject to the absolute authority of their male next-of-kin. . . . As everywhere else in the first millennium B.C., women were chattels, even if some of them were independent-minded ones. To the Greeks, a woman (regardless of age or marital status) was *gyne*, whose linguistic meaning is 'bearer of children' " (Tannahill, 1980, pp. 94-95).

As Christianity developed in its early forms, there was an intermingling of Greek and Jewish attitudes toward sexuality. In contrast to Judaism, which did not distinguish physical from spiritual love, Christian theology borrowed from the Greek and separated *eros*, or "carnal love," from *agape*, a "spiritual, nonphysical love" (Gordis, 1977). Bullough (1976) points out that the

Sexual themes have been shown in art since ancient times. This Greek dish, with its erotic scene, and Roman lamp, used to ward off evil spirits, are two interesting examples.

Perspectives on Sexuality

Hellenistic era in Greece (beginning in 323 B.C.) was marked by a denial of worldly pleasures in favor of developing the purely spiritual. Along with the *New Testament* portrayal of the imminent end of the world, this led to Christianity placing a high ideal on celibacy, although St. Paul allowed that while "It is good for a man not to touch a woman . . . it is better to marry than to burn" (1 *Corinthians* 7:1–12).

By the end of the fourth century A.D., despite small groups of Christians whose views of sexuality were less rigid and constrained, the Church's negative attitudes toward sex were dramatically presented in the writings of St. Augustine, a religious leader whose background included a vivid and varied set of erotic experiences before he renounced worldly ways. Augustine confessed in stark terms, "I muddied the stream of friendship with the filth of lewdness and clouded its clear waters with hell's black river of lust" (*Confessions*, Book III:I). He believed that sexual lust came from the downfall of Adam and Eve in the Garden of Eden and that

this sinfulness was transmitted to children by the inherent lust that separated humanity from God. Thus, sex was strongly condemned in all forms, although Augustine and his contemporaries apparently felt that marital procreative sex was less evil than other types.

EASTERN THOUGHT

Elsewhere in the world, sexual thinking varied remarkably from that just described. In particular, Islamic, Hindu, and ancient Oriental sexual attitudes were considerably more positive. Bullough states that "almost anything in the sexual field received approval from some segment of the Hindu society" and that in China "sex was not something to be feared, nor was it regarded as sinful, but rather, it was an act of worship" and even a path toward immortality (Bullough, 1976, pp. 275 and 310). The *Kama Sutra*, compiled at about the same time Augustine was writing his *Confessions*, is a detailed Indian sex manual; in ancient China and Japan, similar manuals were abundant and glorified sexual pleasure and vari-

Oriental art has a long tradition of explicitly depicting erotic scenes, as this work from the 18th century shows.

ety. These divergent patterns continued, although our focus for now will remain with the history of sex in the Western world. Other cultures will be examined in later chapters.

Medieval and Renaissance Thought

The early Christian traditions regarding sexuality became more firmly entrenched in Europe during the twelfth and thirteenth centuries as the Church assumed greater power. Theology often became synonymous with common law, and there was a generally oppressive "official" attitude toward sex except for the purpose of procreation. There was, however, a certain hypocrisy between professed Church policies and actual practices: "religious houses themselves were often hotbeds of sexuality" (Taylor, 1954, p. 19).

During this era, a new style of living emerged among the upper classes that brought about a drastic separation between actual practice and religious teachings. This style, called courtly love, introduced a new code of acceptable behavior in which women (at least high-ranking women) were elevated to an immaculate plane and romanticism, secrecy, and valor were celebrated in song, poetry, and literature (Tannahill, 1980). Pure love was seen as incompatible with the temptations of the flesh, and sometimes this concept was tested by lovers lying together in bed naked to see if they could prove the fullness of their love by refraining from sexual intercourse. Needless to say, it is unlikely that courtly love was always the unconsummated romantic ideal portrayed in story and verse.

Not too long after the era of courtly love began, chastity belts made their appearance. These devices allowed husbands to lock up their wives just as they would protect their money; while they may have been originally designed to prevent rape, they also served to guard "property":

The belt of medieval times was usually constructed on a metal framework that stretched between the woman's legs from front to back. It had two small, rigid apertures that allowed for waste elimination but effectively prevented penetration, and once it was locked over the hips the jealous husband could take away the key. . . . (Tannahill, 1980, p. 276)

The rebirth of humanism and the arts that subsequently engulfed Europe in the sixteenth and seventeenth centuries was accompanied by a loosening of sexual restrictions as well as less adherence to the formulas of courtly love. The Protestant Reformation, led by Martin Luther, John Calvin, and others, generally advocated less negative attitudes toward sexual matters than the Catholic Church did. For example, although Luther was hardly liberal in his sexual attitudes, he thought that sex was not inherently sinful and that chastity and celibacy were not signs of virtue. At the same time, Europe was caught in a massive epidemic of syphilis — possibly imported from the Americas — that might have worked to limit sexual freedom.

The Eighteenth and Nineteenth Centuries

When we speak of the attitudes of an historical era, we must keep in mind that there was variance among different countries, levels of society, and religious groups. Although evidence can be cited to show a rather broad tolerance toward sexuality in England and France in the 1700s (Bullough, 1976), the Puritan ethic reigned in colonial America. Sex outside of marriage was condemned and family solidarity was exalted; those giving in to the passions of adultery or premarital sex, if discovered, were flogged, put in pillories or stocks, or forced to make public confessions. Some readers may be familiar with Nathaniel Hawthorne's *Scarlet Letter* which presents an account of colonial times.

In America, the Puritan ethic was carried over into the nineteenth century with a curious schism. As American frontiers expanded and as large cities took on a more cosmopolitan flair, there was a corresponding loosening of notions about sexual propriety and prostitution became commonplace. This new development was met by the formation in the 1820s and 1830s of several groups whose primary mission was to combat the social evils of prostitution and rescue the "fallen women" who plied this trade (Pivar, 1973). Despite the organized resistance of such groups as the American Society for the Prevention of Licentiousness and Vice and the Promotion of Morality and the American Society for Promoting the Observance of the Seventh Commandment, prostitution flourished. During a three-year period in the 1840s, the government prosecuted 351 brothels in Massachusetts alone, and by the eve of the Civil War, a guidebook listing fashionable brothels in big cities described 106 establishments in New York, 57 in Philadelphia, and dozens of others in Baltimore, Boston, Chicago, and Washington, D.C. (Pivar, 1973).

By the mid-1800s, as the Victorian Era began, reserve and prudery emerged once again in Europe, although this time less connected to religious edict. The spirit of Victorianism was sexual repression and a strong sense of modesty necessitated by the presumed purity and innocence of women and children. Taylor points out, "So delicate did the sensibilities of the Victorians become, so easily were their thoughts turned to sexual matters, that the most innocent actions were taboo in case they might lead to lurid imaginings. It became indelicate to offer a lady a *leg* of chicken. . . ." and clothing styles, showing not even a glimpse of ankle or bare neck, mirrored this conservatism (Taylor, 1954, pp. 214-215). The prudishness of this period is astonishing to us today: in some Victorian homes, piano legs were covered with crinolines, and books by authors of opposite sexes were not shelved side by side unless the authors were married to each other (Sussman, 1976).

In America, although the influence of Victorianism was strongly felt, crosscurrents sent the mainstream of moral thinking into a dizzying spin. For example, in 1870 the St. Louis City Council found a loophole in state law that allowed it to legalize prostitution, causing an uproar across the nation. Groups were again formed to combat sexual immorality and managed to find allies in other organizations dedicated to the cause of temperance (abolishing the sale of alcoholic beverages). This movement achieved several legislative successes. In 1886, for example, twenty-five states fixed the age of consent at ten (thus permitting child prostitution to flourish), but by 1895, only five states retained this low age, and eight states had raised the age of consent to eighteen.

Although the mainstream of Victorianism was antisexual — pornography was first banned by law in this era — there was another side to the times. A sexual "underground" of pornographic writings and pictures was widely read (Marcus, 1967). Prostitution was common in Europe, and in the 1860s it was legalized and regulated by an act of the British Parliament. Furthermore, Victorian prudery in sexual behavior and attitudes was not standard for all social classes (Gay, 1983). The middle and lower classes did not practice the sexual pretensions of the upper class. Indeed, it was the abject poverty of the lower classes that forced many young women into prostitution, and the middle classes — despite the ideal of the docile, sexless Victorian lady — not only had sexual feelings and desires, but acted on them in much the same way women do today. Victorian women had (and enjoyed) marital sex and occasionally had torrid love affairs as seen in a number of diaries which detailed the number and quality of their orgasms (Gay, 1983). In fact, a female sex survey conducted by a woman named Clelia Duel Mosher in 1892 has recently come to light, providing additional evidence that viewing the Victorian period as strictly antisexual is incorrect. In addition, an interesting viewpoint has been advanced about female sexuality in Victorian times:

> Although it is obvious that many Victorians suffered from sexual repression, it appears on closer observation that those women who contributed to the concept of prudishness were far closer to today's feminists than most are willing to admit. . . . the Victorian woman sought to achieve a sort of sexual freedom by denying her sexuality . . . in an effort to keep from being considered or treated as a sex object. Her prudery was a mask that conveniently hid her more "radical" effort to achieve freedom of person. (Haller and Haller, 1977, p. xii)

Science and medicine reflected the antisexualism of the era thoroughly. Masturbation was variously branded as a source of damage to the brain and nervous system and a cause of insanity and a wide range of other illnesses (Bullough and Bullough, 1977; Haller and Haller, 1977; Tannahill, 1980). Women were thought to have little or no capacity for sexual response and were viewed as inferior to men both physically and intellectually. In 1878, the prestigious *British Medical Journal* printed a series of letters in which a number of physicians offered evidence supporting the idea that the touch of a menstruating woman would spoil hams. And even as eminent a scientist as Charles Darwin, the father of the theory of evolution, wrote in his *Descent of Man and Selection in Relation to Sex* (1871) that "Man is more courageous, pugnacious, and energetic than woman, and has a more inventive genius," and that "the average of mental power in man must be above that of women."

In the latter part of the nineteenth century Richard von Krafft-Ebing, a German psychiatrist, undertook a detailed classification of sexual disorders. The impact of his *Psychopathia Sexualis* (1886), which went through twelve editions, was profound and influenced subsequent public attitudes and medical and legal practice for more than three-quarters of a century (Brecher, 1975). There were positive and negative aspects to this influence: on the one hand, Krafft-Ebing advocated sympathetic medical concern for the so-called sexual perversions and reform in laws dealing with sex criminals, while on the other hand his book seemed to lump sex, crime, and violence together. Much of his attention was devoted to aspects of sexuality he considered abnormal, such as sadomasochism (sexual arousal from inflicting or experiencing pain), homosexuality, fetishism (sexual arousal by an object rather than a person), and bestiality (sexual contact with animals). Because he frequently used lurid examples (sexual murders, cannibalism, and intercourse with the dead, to name just a few) which he presented in the same pages with less frightening sexual variations, many readers were left with a general loathing for almost all forms of sexual conduct. Nevertheless, Krafft-Ebing is often considered the founder of modern sexology.

The Twentieth Century

By the turn of the new century, sexuality began to be investigated in a more objective manner. Although Victorian attitudes still prevailed in many circles, the work of serious scientists such as Albert Moll, Magnus Hirshfeld, Iwan Bloch, and Havelock Ellis combined with the dynamic theories of Freud to initiate a striking reversal in thinking about sex.

FREUD

Sigmund Freud (1856–1939) was a Viennese physician who, more successfully than any figure before or since, demonstrated the central importance of sexuality to human existence. Today

Messages from Sex Manuals

Throughout the ages, sex manuals of one sort or another have provided advice to people searching for a way to improve their skill as lovers. Here, we offer some excerpts from a number of these manuals showing the diversity of style and opinion that can be found.

From *The Kama Sutra of Vatsyayana* (Richard Burton, trans., 1862, p. 100):

It is said by some that there is no fixed time or order between the embrace, the kiss, and the pressing or scratching with the nails and fingers, but that all these things should be done generally before sexual union takes place, while striking and the various sounds generally takes place at the time of union. Vatsyayana, however, thinks that anything may take place at any time, for love does not care for time or order.

On the occasion of first congress, kissing and the other things mentioned above should be done moderately; they should not continue for a long time, and should be done alternately. On subsequent occasions, however, the reverse of all this may take place, and moderation will not be necessary; they may continue for a long time; and for the purpose of kindling love, they may be all done at the same time.

From T. H. Van De Velde, *Ideal Marriage*, first published in 1926:

The genital kiss is particularly calculated to overcome frigidity and fear in hitherto inexperienced women who have had no erotic practice, and are as yet hardly capable of specific sexual desire.

But – the husband must exercise the *greatest gentleness,* the *most delicate reverence!* …

The fact that in this particular form of caress more than any other, the man is generally the active partner, is because of his naturally greater initiative, and also because of the difference in the *tempo* of the respective erotic reactions, which is usual while the woman is still a novice.

On occasions where the man's reactions are less rapid, the woman may with advantage take the more active part during the second act of love-drama, and *herself, most successfully give – instead of receiving – the genital kiss.*

From Dr. J. Rutgers, *How to Attain and Practice the Ideal Sex Life,* 1937:

First of all, we must reflect that the proper satisfaction of all these finer stimulations demands much time; there should never be any undue haste. With machinery, if we wish to get tremendous rapidity we can do so, though the result is frequently some terrible accident. The intoxication of love, on the other hand, can no more be hurried than sleep when we go to bed.

As I have already said, it is the gentlest and most delicate caresses which, because they are so soft and ethereal, charm us the most. And this is a fundamental difference between the biological cell function on the one hand and mechanics on the other. In the latter case, the result is proportionate to the force expended, while the biological consequences of these caresses is not.

We must learn from massage. … We can indeed think of sexual love as the high school of massage; and vice versa a knowledge of the secrets of massage is the best method of perfecting our sexual relationships. Thus a well-informed man can always further refine and multiply his more delicate mental and physical feelings.

From *The Joy of Sex* (Comfort, 1972, pp. 116–118):

A woman who has the divine gift of lechery and loves her partner will masturbate him well, and a woman who knows how to masturbate a man – subtly, unhurriedly and mercilessly – will almost always make a superlative partner. … Some men can't stand really proficient masturbation to climax unless they are securely tied, and virtually none can hold still for slow masturbation. …

Clitoral rubbing can be as mind-blowing for her as slow masturbation is for him, but it can be painful if it is unskillful, repeated too often or straight after an orgasm achieved in this way. …

For preparation as well as orgasm, the flat of the hand on the vulva with the middle finger between the lips, and its tip moving in and out of the vagina, while the ball of the palm presses hard just above the pubis, is probably the best method.

From R. T. Trall, *Sexual Physiology and Hygiene,* 1897, p. 295:

The frequency with which sexual intercourse can be indulged without serious damage to one or both parties depends, of course, on a variety of circumstances – constitutional stamina, temperament, occupation, habits of exercise, etc. Few should exceed the limit of once a week; while many cannot safely indulge oftener than once a month. But as temperance is always the safe rule of conduct, if there must be any deviation from the strictest law of physiology, let the error be on that side.

Freud's genius is recognized as partly a matter of original discovery and partly a reflection of his ability to synthesize emerging ideas into a cohesive and persuasive theoretical framework (Sulloway, 1979). Freud believed that sexuality was both the primary force in the motivation of all human behavior and the principal cause of all forms of *neurosis,* a mild form of mental disorder in which anxiety is prominent and coping skills are distorted although a sense of reality is maintained. He clearly described the existence of sexuality in infants and children, expanding views expressed by other sexologists between 1880 and 1905 (Kern, 1973; Sulloway, 1979), and formulated a detailed theory of psychosexual development discussed in chapter 8.

Freud devised many innovative concepts related to sexuality. The best known, the *Oedipal complex,* refers to an inevitable sexual attraction of the young male child to his mother accompanied by an ambivalent mixture of love, hate, fear, and rivalry toward his father. Freud also believed that boys were concerned about the possible loss of their penis as a terrible form of punishment (*castration anxiety*) and that girls felt a sense of inadequacy and jealousy at not having a penis (*penis envy*). Freud saw these situations as operating primarily at the unconscious level — a level of the personality deeper than conscious awareness. From the rich theoretical tapestry of his thought, Freud wove a clinical method called psychoanalysis for assessing and treating the unconscious conflicts that lead to psychological problems. Although many modern sexologists disagree with Freud's formulations, as we will discuss in subsequent chapters, psychoanalysis remains a widely used method of treatment today.

ELLIS

At about this same time, an English physician named Havelock Ellis (1859–1939) was publishing a six-volume series called *Studies in the Psychology of Sex* (1897–1910). Ellis anticipated

much that Freud later wrote about childhood sexuality and had remarkably modern views in certain areas. For example, he recognized the common occurrence of masturbation in both sexes at all ages, took exception to the Victorian idea that "good" women had no sexual desire, and emphasized the psychological rather than physical causes of many sexual problems. His writings also focused on the varied nature of human sexual behavior and provided an important balancing influence to Krafft-Ebing's view of sexual variations as diseases (Brecher, 1969, 1975).

1920–1940

By the end of World War I, massive social changes were emerging in both Europe and America that differed drastically from Victorian

Havelock Ellis, through his prolific writings, became one of the most influential early sexologists.

practices. Influenced by increasing social and economic freedom for women and the availability of the automobile, sexual attitudes became increasingly less inhibited in the Jazz Age and were accompanied by corresponding changes in fashion, dance, and literature. Women had become involved professionally in the sexual revolution that was brewing. Margaret Sanger was a leader of the birth control movement in America. Katharine Davis conducted a survey of the sex lives of 2,200 women which was published initially as a series of scientific articles between 1922 and 1927 and then as a book (Davis, 1929). An Englishwoman, Marie Stopes, wrote an explicit marriage manual that sold well on both sides of the Atlantic.[3] By 1926, when a gynecologist named Theodore van de Velde published *Ideal Marriage*, providing specific details about a wide range of sexual techniques and endorsing such practices as oral-genital sex, his book became an instant international best-seller.

The Roaring Twenties came to a sudden end in 1929 with the stock market crash. In the Great Depression that followed, concern for sustenance, shelter, and survival seemed to take precedence over sex. In the 1940s, the world was quickly at war again, and the postwar era brought instant notoriety to another sexologist who was to leave an indelible mark on scientific history.

KINSEY

Alfred C. Kinsey (1894–1956), a zoologist at Indiana University, had been asked to participate

---

[3] It is interesting to note that Stopes, who had obtained a doctorate and was an accomplished scientific researcher, was very much a victim of Victorian prudishness about sex. Six months after her marriage to another scientist, Dr. Reginald Ruggles Gates, she "began to feel instinctively that something was lacking," and went to the British Museum to try to discover what it was. Finding out that her marriage had not been consummated, she successfully sued for divorce and later undertook the writing of her book to help others avoid such problems (Harrison, 1977).

Alfred Kinsey brought boundless enthusiasm to his career in sex research despite the considerable controversies that his methods and findings provoked.

in teaching a noncredit college course on marriage in the summer of 1938. Struck by the lack of scientific data about human sexual behavior, he used this opportunity to administer questionnaires to some of his students for the purpose of gathering information about their sexual histories. Soon thereafter, Kinsey decided that personal interviewing was a more promising technique for obtaining such case history material since it permitted greater flexibility and detail, and he embarked on a course of action that eventually led to interviews with thousands of men and women across the country. Joined by his coauthors and colleagues, Wardell Pomeroy and Clyde Martin, Kinsey published the monumental *Sexual Behavior in the Human Male* on January 5, 1948. Five years later, with Paul Gebhard, they published the companion volume, *Sexual Behavior in the Human Female*.

The Kinsey reports were based on extensive face-to-face interviews with 12,000 people from all segments of the population and the findings were often startling. For instance, 37 percent of American men were reported to have had at

Perspectives on Sexuality

least one homosexual experience to the point of orgasm after the age of puberty; 40 percent of husbands had been unfaithful to their wives; and 62 percent of the women studied had tried masturbation.

The publication of *Sexual Behavior in the Human Male* on January 5, 1948, instantly catapulted the Kinsey research into the public eye. By mid-March more than 100,000 copies had been sold, and the book remained on the bestseller list for twenty-seven weeks.

Although Kinsey and his colleagues attempted to describe how people behave sexually without moral or medical value judgments, their work was severely criticized on methodological and moral grounds. Prestigious *Life* magazine called it "an assault on the family as a basic unit of society, a negation of moral law, and a celebration of licentiousness" (Wickware, 1948). Margaret Mead criticized Kinsey for dealing with sex "as an impersonal, meaningless act" (*New York Times*, March 31, 1948), a charge that was echoed by many critics, including one professor from Columbia University who stated that "there should be a law against doing research dealing exclusively with sex" (*New York Times*, April 1, 1948). However, the Kinsey report was also praised as having "done for sex what Columbus did for geography" (Ernst and Loth, 1948).

All in all, the reception of Kinsey's first volume was fairly positive (Palmore, 1952), but the same cannot be said for his second book, *Sexual Behavior in the Human Female* (1953). Many newspapers denounced this report in editorials and refused to give it coverage in their news columns. For example, the *Times* of New Philadelphia, Ohio, justified this decision by saying "we believe it would be offensive to a large portion of our readers" (August 20, 1953). Church leaders and educators called Kinsey's findings amoral, antifamily, and even tainted with communism.

Kinsey died in 1956, embittered and disillusioned, but the impact of his energetic investigations was to be strongly apparent in the years ahead. In addition to the cultural and scientific legacy he left behind, he and his colleagues formed the Institute for Sex Research at Indiana University which continues as a major center under the leadership of June Reinisch.

THE 1950S

In the aftermath of Kinsey's studies, there was an era marked by quite a bit of sexual confusion. Premarital sex became more commonplace than it had been before, although it seems to have been restricted mainly to engaged couples. Popular descriptions of sex began to appear in books (such as the then-steamy *Peyton Place*) and movies (mostly imported from overseas), and even popular music began to present sexual themes. One observer, horrified by what he heard and saw, sourly noted that the "sexualization" of music made it "naked, seductive, . . . lusty and perverse," with performers whose "bleating is underscored by their gyrations, contortions, and bodily rhythms all too clear in sexual innuendo and undisguised meaning" (Sorokin, 1956).

At the same time, the 1950s were a time when females were expected to be glamorous but brainless creatures — something along the lines portrayed by Marilyn Monroe in her movies — whose primary ambitions should be directed toward marriage and motherhood. *Harper's Magazine* (January, 1950) noted, "If an American girl wears plain, unadorned eyeglasses, instead of highly colored and fancifully shaped specs, she might just as well be dead, for all the dating it will get her." And *See* magazine (January, 1950) solemnly advised readers: "It is quite legitimate for a girl to use falsies and not to tell her husband about them before marriage."

Albert Ellis (1959, p. 227) succinctly summarized the prevailing mores of the times this way:

"The fundamental law underlying all our sex, love, and marriage attitudes can be stated with absolute and appalling clarity in two simple statements: (a) If it's FUN you mustn't do it; (b) If it's DUTY you must."

THE 1960S

In the early 1960s, several factors influenced the start of a sexual revolution that was more visible than any America had previously seen. Many factors contributed to this revolution: (1) the availability of birth control pills; (2) the protest movement among adolescents and young adults; (3) the reemergence of feminism in modern form; and (4) greater openness in discussions and displays of sex. While it isn't possible to render any final historical judgment on the relative importance of each of these factors in fueling the sexual revolution, it appears certain that each had a strong influence.

The pill made premarital sex considerably safer and permitted millions to think of sex as relational or recreational rather than procreative, as we have already noted. Indeed, the availability of the pill provided a sense of freedom for many women and probably contributed more to changing sexual behavior than has generally been imagined. The protest movement among the young, which began with the civil rights movement and expanded with the growing disillusionment with the Vietnam war, led teens and young adults to challenge their parents' generation ("the establishment") in every way imaginable. This challenge was expressed not only in the younger generation's clothing, long hair, and music, but also in their recreational drug use and their support of sexual freedom ("Make love, not war").

With their consciousness raised at many levels to political and social injustices, young adults in the sixties also embraced the women's movement with enthusiasm. Since the pill had given women a new degree of control over their sexual destinies, it is not surprising that female sexuality was increasingly accepted as a natural fact of life.

In society at large, the initial reactions to the sexual revolution were mixed. While some sought to join the movement enthusiastically, many others seemed to regard it as a passing phase that would eventually fade away. And it's probably safe to say that a sizable segment of the population watched this upheaval with great distaste and alarm, concerned that the moral fabric of American society was disintegrating before their eyes. Nevertheless, sexuality became more talked about, shown, and studied, and the sixties saw the advent of "topless" bars, nudity in Broadway shows (first with "Hair," later with "Oh! Calcutta!"), and the publication of a revolutionary study of human sexual function.

MASTERS AND JOHNSON

Kinsey and his collaborators had investigated the nature of human sexuality by interviews designed to find out how, when, and how often people behaved sexually. Since then, sex research has expanded in various directions in an attempt to answer questions that had not previously been resolved. Among the first and most significant departures from Kinsey's methods were those used by William H. Masters and Virginia E. Johnson, a physician and a behavioral scientist at Washington University Medical School in St. Louis.

Masters and Johnson believed that to understand the complexities of human sexuality, people must understand sexual anatomy and physiology as well as psychological and sociological data. Unsatisfied with the relevance to humans of information gathered by studies of sexual response in animals, Masters and Johnson decided that only a direct approach to the problem would be illuminating. A laboratory investigation began in 1954 to observe and record the physical details of human sexual arousal. By 1965

20

FEIFFER®

THINKING ABOUT SEX.

THE MORE I READ ABOUT IT IN SEX MAGAZINES THE LESS APPEALING IT IS.

THE MORE I SEE IT IN X- RATED FILMS THE LESS EROTIC IT IS.

THE MORE I LEARN ABOUT IT IN SEX MANUALS THE MORE INTIMIDATING IT IS.

I WISH SCHOOLS WOULD TEACH SEX IGNORANCE COURSES.

THEN I COULD ENJOY IT LIKE MY FATHER.

more than 10,000 episodes of sexual activity by 382 women and 312 men had been observed, and the report that followed, *Human Sexual Response* (Masters and Johnson, 1966), drew rapid public attention. Although some health care professionals quickly grasped the importance of these findings, others were shocked by the methods employed. Amid the accusations of "too mechanistic an approach" and the cries of moral outrage, relatively few people recognized that the physiological information was not an endpoint but was instead a foundation on which a treatment method for people with sexual problems could be based.[4]

---

[4] It is noteworthy that all of medical science is based on understanding normal anatomy and physiology before meaningful advances can be made in treating abnormalities. In 1966, when *Human Sexual Response* was published, many physicians seemed to forget this fact, which would have been unquestionable in the study of heart disease or skin disorders. Our files from that year have many angry letters written by physicians criticizing the physiology work because of its impropriety and departure from traditional medical "respectability."

THE 1970S AND 1980S

In the seventies and eighties, the new openness about sexuality was readily apparent. In 1970, Masters and Johnson published *Human Sexual Inadequacy*, a landmark book that described a startlingly new approach to the treatment of sexual problems that had previously required lengthy treatments without very high rates of success. With a two-week treatment program and only a 20 percent failure rate, this work was soon to give rise to an entire new profession — sex therapy — with the eventual proliferation of thousands of sex clinics across the country before the end of the decade, and the development of other therapy approaches by doctors such as Helen Kaplan and Jack Anon.

Other less technical books about sex were published by the dozens, with Alex Comfort's *The Joy of Sex* (1972) probably being the most accomplished and certainly the most successful (with sales of over nine million copies). Television became a notable force in the sexual revolution, too, as a number of programs tackled previously taboo sexual themes. Not to be outdone, movies became more sexually explicit, and, in the early days of the home video market, pornographic films were the single best-selling category.

A number of other trends occurred in this time period that affected the ways Americans viewed sexuality: (1) The practice of nonmarital cohabitation — living together — began to assume increasing importance as a stage preceding marriage; (2) the legalization of abortion by the U.S. Supreme Court in 1973 made it possible to obtain safe abortions, but also provoked considerable controversy about the morality of this practice; (3) the 1974 decision by the American Psychiatric Association to remove homosexuality from classification as a mental disorder set the stage for advances to be made in the gay rights movement; (4) a growing awareness of the significance of all forms of sexual victimization — in part an outgrowth of the women's movement and in part a result of the work of scientists and scholars who effectively showed that rape is a crime of violence rather than a crime of passion (e.g., Brownmiller, 1975; Metzger, 1976; Burgess and Holmstrom, 1974) — led to major legislative changes aimed at modernizing procedures for trying rape cases, as well as the rapid growth in rape crisis centers across the country; (5) the appearance of new reproductive technologies encompassing the birth of the world's first "test tube baby" in 1978 (with more than 500 babies conceived by similar means now alive) has now proceeded to even more startling techniques, such as embryo transfer methods and the controversial "surrogate mother" practice.

The late 1970s and early 1980s were also a time for a backlash against what some perceived as overly permissive, even immoral sexual practices. The Moral Majority sought to block sex education in public schools and campaigned against "promiscuous" sexual behavior, which seemed to include anything other than marital sex. The "Right to Life" movement challenged the legality of abortion and unsuccessfully tried to pass a constitutional amendment that would have banned abortion under all circumstances. In 1983, the Reagan administration tried to implement a policy requiring notice to the parents of teenagers requesting contraceptives; this proposal, which became derisively known as the "Squeal Rule," fortunately never got off the ground.

Particularly alarming to some was the appearance in the late 1970s and early 1980s of seemingly new epidemics of sexually transmitted diseases: genital herpes, primarily among heterosexuals, and AIDS (acquired immune deficiency syndrome), primarily among homosexual men. Since cures were not available for these two diseases, and since they seemed to be linked incontrovertibly to promiscuous sexual behavior, some observers suggested that they were a form of punishment from God for sexual transgressions.

We cannot know, of course, if the changes and trends we see as significant today will have any lasting impact on our sexual behavior over time. Nor can we be certain that a century from now, historians won't label our era with a single word (like "Victorian") and reduce the many complexities of our sexual attitudes to a single notion. The only thing we can be sure of is that our attitudes and behaviors will continue to change — what directions those changes will take, however, is impossible to predict with any accuracy.

SUMMARY

1. Human sexuality is a multidimensional phenomenon having biological, psychosocial, behavioral, clinical, moral, and cultural aspects. No single dimension of sexuality is universally dominant.

2. History teaches us that sexual attitudes and practices vary considerably over time and place. For more than two thousand years, religion has been a principal force in shaping sexual thought. In the past century, the advent of sexology as a science — from the early approaches of Krafft-Ebing, Havelock Ellis, and Sigmund Freud, to the dramatic research studies of Kinsey and Masters and Johnson — has greatly influenced contemporary attitudes toward sex and sexuality.

3. We must guard against interpreting sexual behavior too simplistically. For instance, although the Victorian era was certainly a time of sexual prudishness in many respects, it was clearly also a time when prostitution flourished, pornography was widely read, and the middle and lower classes paid scant attention to the sexual pretensions of the upper class.

4. In our recent past, many observers have pointed to the 1960s as a time when a sexual revolution began. Four factors contributed to this phenomenon: the availability of birth control pills, the protest movement among teenagers and young adults, a renewed interest in feminism, and a greater openness to discussions and displays of sex.

5. Predicting the changes in sexual thinking and behavior that will occur in the future is difficult at best. All we can be sure of is that our attitudes and behaviors *will* change in one way or another.

SUGGESTED READINGS

Brecher, Edward. *The Sex Researchers*. Boston: Little, Brown, 1969. A collection of biographical sketches of the most influential sex researchers from Krafft-Ebing to Kinsey to Masters and Johnson.

Bullough, Vern, and Bullough, Bonnie. *Sin, Sickness and Sanity — A History of Sexual Attitudes*. New York: New American Library, 1977. A provocative study of how past attitudes to certain aspects of sexuality (e.g., masturbation, homosexuality, prostitution, pornography) have affected present sexual theorizing.

Gay, Peter. *The Bourgeois Experience: Victoria to Freud. Volume One: Education of the Senses*. New York: Oxford University Press, 1983. An in-depth reassessment of sexuality during the Victorian era that shows why viewing this period as a strictly antisexual time is incorrect.

Tannahill, Reay. *Sex in History*. New York: Stein and Day, 1980. A lively, opinionated survey of sexual customs and attitudes from prehistoric to modern times.

2 Sex Research: An Overview

*I*S IT POSSIBLE for a man to be raped by a woman? Does alcohol stimulate or inhibit sexual response? Is it normal to have sex fantasies while making love with your spouse? Do homosexuals differ from heterosexuals in the physiology of their sexual responses? Questions like these have always caused lively discussions and generated a number of answers, but, until recently, the answers that were given were simply opinions — in other words, guesses that had not been proven right or wrong. In the past two decades, these and many other questions about human sexuality have been approached in more scientific ways by professionals in the field of sex research.

Sex research is surrounded by an aura of mystery because it explores areas that are often considered forbidden, private, controversial, and exciting. But instead of being the titillating pastime the public imagines it is, research in human sexuality is like other types of scientific research. It involves hard work, long hours, careful attention to detail, and rigorous examination and evaluation of the information obtained.

Because so much is published about sex and sexuality, it can be difficult to distinguish research-based fact from one person's opinion or from an account of personal experiences. The distinction between a literary or journalistic report about some facet of sex and a sex research report is often blurred. Even when a fact is based on a research study, it should not always be taken at face value. Thus, it is important to understand how sex research is conducted — including its drawbacks and limitations — in order to intelligently evaluate its findings and apply them to our own lives. This chapter will describe a variety of sex research methods, discuss the designs of some major sex research reports, and provide guidelines for analyzing the reliability and significance of such studies.

GENERAL ISSUES IN SEX RESEARCH

Sampling Strategy

Researchers are almost never able to study the entire population of people that fit a category being investigated. Studies of female sexuality could not possibly include all women in the world, nor could they realistically expect to include all women in one country, state, city, or even school. Time, cost, and some individuals' unwillingness to participate in such studies are the key constraints. As a result, scientists choose a group of people (a *sample*) from a larger group with a particular characteristic (a *population*). This process is called *sample selection*. The degree to which the sample is similar to or different from the population from which it is taken has important implications about the research results.

If the sample closely matches the characteristics of the population, the research findings will also apply to the population. Applying the research findings from a sample to a larger group — either the population from which the sample was taken or a related population — is called *generalizing*. For example, if you studied a group of rape

victims in Michigan, the results would probably apply to rape victims in other states. However, if your study involved drug use patterns in southern California, your findings might not describe what was happening in the Midwest.

The size of the sample is another important factor in the confidence that can be placed in the research results. A very small sample, even if representative of the larger population, is an unreliable basis for major conclusions. Would you feel comfortable with a report on the attitudes of American college students toward premarital sex if the study involved a sample of only a dozen students? What would your reaction be if the sample size was twenty-five? One hundred? One thousand? When other aspects of two research designs are equivalent, the larger sample usually provides greater reliability. However, the more alike the members of a population are — a condition statisticians call *homogeneity* — the more the sample size can be reduced while still being representative of the population.

The sample is more likely to represent the larger population from which it is drawn if it is a *random sample*, chosen so that each person in the population has the same chance of being selected. Very few sex research studies have been conducted on national probability samples, which are random samples drawn systematically from the entire U.S. population (or the segment of the general population being studied, such as married women). This is unfortunate, since a true national probability sample provides the strongest possible basis for reaching conclusions about the generalizability of a study's findings.

Methods of Obtaining Data

In addition to making decisions about sampling, the researcher must consider how to obtain information required to elucidate the problem under study. Research data may be gathered by questionnaire, personal interview, direct observation, indirect observation (e.g., use of videotapes, film, or a remote microphone), examination of case records, laboratory testing, experimentation, and other techniques. Deciding which method (or methods) is most suitable for a given study is not always easy.

Sometimes ethical considerations preclude certain research approaches. For example, it would hardly be ethical to study incest by asking families to try it in order to observe its effects. Instead, questionnaires, interviews, or examination of case records would probably be used to study this controversial subject. Another factor that influences the choice of research method is the availability of reliable techniques for achieving a particular objective. For example, before the late 1960s, there was no way of accurately measuring sex hormones in the human body. Once these methods were developed, entirely new types of research were undertaken using analysis of blood samples to shed light on a wide range of sexual problems and behavior. A third set of influences on choosing a method of gathering data are matters of practicality: How much time and expense are involved, how likely is it that the method will produce useful information, and how likely is cooperation from the potential subjects? The advantages and disadvantages of various methods in sex research will be discussed shortly.

Measurement or Classification of Data

Scientific research generally requires quantification — turning observations into numbers. Certain types of data are easy to quantify (e.g., height, age, number of sexual partners) or to classify (marital status, occupation, type of contraception used). Measuring other types of data is much more complex: How does one quantify love, fear, happiness, or sexual satisfaction? The

researcher must devise specific strategies for quantifying or classifying data in order to process it or use it to make comparisons between groups. This is often done by constructing a scale or set of scales ("rate your sexual satisfaction on a scale from 0 to 10"), which is not quite as simple as it sounds. The adequacy of a measurement procedure depends on its *reliability*, or consistency and freedom from error, and its *validity*, the degree to which it measures what one is looking for. The complex ways of testing the reliability and validity of measuring techniques are beyond the scope of our discussion.

Data Analysis

After research information has been collected, it must be evaluated. This is usually accomplished by the use of statistics. Although a detailed discussion of statistical methods is unnecessary for our purposes, several points must be made. First, statistics may be used in a purely descriptive sense (e.g., "43 percent of the men and 55 percent of the women studied were married," or "the average frequency of sexual intercourse was 2.6 times per week"). Second, statistics also may be used to draw inferences. The inferences, or predictions, that statistical tests allow to be made about sets of data are not absolute but are simply probability statements. That is, inferential statistics lead to scientific guesses (sometimes very *good* guesses) about the likelihood that a particular set of observations could have occurred by chance alone. If you studied one hundred high school girls taking a sex education course and one hundred girls from the same high school who did not take this course and found that only two in the first group had unwanted pregnancies compared to twenty in the latter group, this difference would be statistically significant. That is, it is unlikely that the pregnancies could have occurred by chance alone, and you could thereby infer that sex education courses reduce unwanted teenage pregnancies. However, inferential statistics cannot *prove* this conclusion, and some artifact in the study of which you were not aware may have determined its outcome. Third, statistical methods can also be used to examine the relationship among several variables: correlational statistics and factor analysis help researchers sort out some aspects of the problem of how one variable interacts with another but do not allow researchers to determine cause and effect.

Ethical Concerns

When conducting any type of research, the investigators have a strong responsibility to respect the welfare and dignity of their subjects, a responsibility that involves attention to the following:

1. *Informed consent* — The purposes, procedures, and potential risks and benefits of participation in a research project should be explained to all potential subjects in an understandable manner. Prospective subjects must be free to choose whether or not to participate (without any coercion, force, or deceit) and once the study has begun, participants should be free to withdraw from participation at any time without being penalized in any way.

2. *Confidentiality* — Sex researchers must take every possible precaution to protect the confidentiality of their research subjects. In some cases, information provided by research subjects could be legally incriminating (e.g., information about use of illicit drugs or illegal sexual practices), while in other instances, a breakdown in confidentiality could expose participants to embarrassment, ridicule, or negative effects on their personal relationships. (Imagine, for instance, how you and your partner might feel if he or she

learned because of your participation in a sex research project that you have been involved in an incestuous relationship with your sister for several years.)

Sex researchers follow a number of procedures to ensure confidentiality, including: collecting data in ways that protect anonymity, such as assigning code numbers for identification and storing a masterlist linking the code numbers with names in a secure place, such as a bank vault; restricting access to research data to one person; destroying all identifiable research information as soon as a study has been completed.

3. *Honesty* — While deception may occasionally be necessary as part of a research design, we believe that it is appropriate only if subjects have previously consented to being deceived (although they do not need to know the exact nature of the deception) and if the risks of deception are minimal. Whenever deception is used by researchers, they have a major responsibility to correct the situation by describing the deception to each subject in a debriefing session after the experiment so that he or she can learn about the results of the study and pose questions about the experience.

A detailed code of ethical guidelines for sex research was recently developed (Masters et al., 1980) and similar codes govern research ethics for psychologists, psychiatrists, and other scientists. Most American colleges and universities now have committees known as Institutional Review Boards or Human Subject Committees that must evaluate all research planned within the institution before it is begun. If this committee discovers ethical problems in the study plan (for example, inadequate attention to obtaining informed consent), it will make recommendations for improving the project's attention to ethical matters and will withhold its approval of the research until the deficiencies are corrected.

PROBLEMS AND PITFALLS IN SEX RESEARCH

Sex research, like other forms of research, does not always provide a definitive answer to the question being addressed. Understanding the limitations of sex research methods can assist you in deciding how applicable a particular set of findings may be to your own life and can help you critically evaluate the quality of a given study.

Scientists often speak about *bias* in research, meaning that factors other than those being studied may affect the information collected and how the information is used to draw conclusions. Bias implies a systematic source of error that reduces objectivity.

Sampling Problems

One of the most frequent types of bias is *sampling bias*, which may take several forms. The size of the sample may be too small to deal with the number of variables being studied. Kinsey's research was criticized on these grounds, even though his surveys included 12,000 people. Even with a sample of adequate size, lack of similarity between the sample and the larger population it was selected to represent severely limits the research findings. An illustration of this type of sampling bias exists in studies of homosexuality prior to 1957. These studies usually involved subjects who were psychiatric patients or prisoners, thus leading to the faulty conclusion that homosexuals were maladjusted and mentally ill. Is it likely that valid conclusions about the nature of homosexuality would be drawn from these samples? Would studies of heterosexuals who were psychiatric patients or prisoners be useful in reaching conclusions about personality patterns in all heterosexuals? More recently, better sampling techniques in studies on homosexuality have avoided this systematic error (Hooker,

"According to the quiz I took in this mazagine, I discovered that my husband isn't having an affair, but I am."

Playboy, April 1983, p. 203. Reproduced by special permission of Playboy Magazine; Copyright © 1983 by Playboy.

1957; Saghir and Robins, 1973; Bell and Weinberg, 1978).

Another sampling problem is that of *volunteer bias,* meaning that there are often specific differences between people who agree to participate in a sex research project and those who decline. Statistically, a random sample is the ideal method of minimizing sampling biases because it avoids subjective errors the researcher might make in selecting study subjects. Unfortunately, truly random samples are seldom possible because of the ethical need to obtain informed consent: volunteer bias is thus automatically present. Although volunteer bias affects all methods of sex research, it is particularly evident in observational studies (Farkas, Sine, and Evans, 1978; Wolchik, Spencer, and Lisi, 1983). Would you agree to participate in studies requiring observation of your sexual behavior? People who agree probably have different attitudes toward sexual privacy than those who do not, and this unquestionably influences representativeness.

Erroneous Answers

Another source of research bias is the truthfulness of answers study subjects give. Questionnaires have an advantage if they are completed anonymously, since the respondent is relatively free from embarrassment. But questionnaires do not usually have a mechanism for checking to see if the subject understands each item; some answers may therefore be incorrect due to misinterpretation. Personal interviews usually allow explanation of questions and permit the gathering of more extensive data, but the presence of the interviewer may affect some of the answers. Certain people brag about or exaggerate their sexual experiences, while others may try to hide an embarrassing or uncomfortable fact.

Intentional falsification of answers may occur with either questionnaires or interviews, although the interviewer may be able to detect this phenomenon more easily. Lack of accuracy also occurs commonly because of faulty recall. Even in regard to recent events — those in the past month, for example — it may be difficult to remember how many times you felt a certain way or participated in a given activity. Recall of distant events (or feelings) is sometimes even more difficult. For instance, you may or may not be able to recall with certainty how old you were when you first learned "the facts of life." Try to remember the first time you masturbated or when your adolescent growth spurt occurred. Often, when married couples are interviewed separately about various aspects of their sexual relations, there are wide discrepancies in their answers about when, how often, and what they do. In such cases, how can an interviewer decide which person is being factually correct? If only one spouse is interviewed, how can an interviewer be certain that his or her answers are accurate?

Other sources of bias in sex research will be examined as we describe the various types of sex research and discuss specific studies that exemplify these methods. While it may seem that we are occasionally being repetitious in pointing out some of these limitations, we do so to emphasize that they are recurring problems that must be kept in mind in analyzing and interpreting a particular study's usefulness. Since the findings of these studies will be discussed frequently in later chapters, it is important to be aware of their strengths and weaknesses.

METHODS USED IN SEX RESEARCH

There are several different methods that can be used in sex research. Since each method has particular strengths and weaknesses, it is not usually possible to say that one approach is "best." Most often, the appropriateness of the method is determined by the nature of the subject to be studied. As we discuss each general method of sex research (surveys, observational research, case studies, clinical research, and experimental research) we will look at actual studies that used these methods and will examine the strengths and limitations of these investigations.

Survey Research

Surveys are used to gather information about a sample of a population by interviewing people or by having them fill out a questionnaire. Since the modern era of sex research was ushered in by the pioneering surveys of Kinsey and his colleagues, it is no surprise that this method has been the most commonly employed approach to the study of human sexual behavior. Furthermore, surveys offer many advantages compared to other research methods: they are comparatively economical, they permit flexibility in sampling, and they are generally free of significant risks to participants.

Given these facts, it is easy to understand why hundreds of sex surveys have been done. Unfortunately, many of these studies are of little use in reaching broad conclusions about human sexuality because of inadequate design, and even the better surveys must be interpreted with caution. In the following discussion of a number of major sex research surveys, we will point out some of the elements that can be used to evaluate the value of survey research.

THE KINSEY REPORTS: 1948 AND 1953

The two broad-based surveys published by Kinsey and his colleagues probably have been more widely discussed and criticized than any subsequent sex research studies. Aside from acknowledging their historical significance, it is instructive to review the manner in which these studies were carried out.

Kinsey's team gathered data solely by face-to-face interviews. They used highly sophisticated techniques for gaining the confidence of each volunteer subject and avoiding the use of leading questions. At the same time, they had to code answers and detect falsification or inconsistencies in the participants' histories. Since the basic interview used by the Kinsey team involved approximately 300 questions, with the exact number of questions partially dependent on the material uncovered as the interview progressed, considerable skill was required to do each survey. Details of the interview process have been thoughtfully described by Wardell Pomeroy, one of Kinsey's original collaborators, in a recent book called *Taking a Sex History* (Pomeroy, Flax, and Wheeler, 1982).

Even though the interviewing technique of the Kinsey team stands out as a model of excellence for other researchers to follow, the interview itself (originally designed for college students) was not updated and expanded sufficiently to keep up with new developments in the research. Paul Gebhard, another early Kinsey team

member, points out that Kinsey was reluctant to change the interview partly out of concern for consistency with the case histories already gathered and partly because of the time factor. The more complex the interview grew, the longer it would take; longer interviews cost more and fewer could be done each day (Gebhard and Johnson, 1979, p. 12).

Although the interview itself had minor problems — for example, extramarital sex activity was not routinely queried about "until well into the 1940s" (about five years after the research began) according to Gebhard — the major methodological criticisms of the Kinsey surveys were levelled at their sampling techniques. Despite the extensive size of the Kinsey samples (5,300 males were interviewed for the first study, while 5,940 females formed the sample for the second report), these samples were far from representative of the entire U.S. population. Data gathered from blacks were simply not published in the original studies because the black samples were comparatively small (this situation was rectified by Gebhard and Johnson in 1979); the samples heavily overrepresented prisoners, college graduates, and Protestants, while underrepresenting the elderly, people living in rural communities, and the poorly educated.

Kinsey said that he avoided any attempt at obtaining a random sample because he felt that such an effort would be doomed to failure. Instead, he tried to compensate in two ways. First, he hoped eventually to obtain a sample of 100,000 interviews that would be such a monumental mountain of data that it would overwhelm any and all objections to the sampling techniques. (While illustrating Kinsey's optimism, this belief did not reflect well on his understanding of the importance of sampling in the behavioral sciences.) His second way of getting partially around the problem of being unable to get a random sample was to devise a method he called "100 percent sampling," which involved

Reflections on Being in a Sex Research Project

The following passages are excerpted from a journal kept by a 22-year-old woman who participated in a study investigating the effects of the menstrual cycle on female sexual arousability.

*   *   *

I'm not sure what I got myself into today. As I was leaving the library, I saw a notice posted on the bulletin board asking for female volunteers for a sex research project. I guess it piqued my curiosity or something, because I wrote down the phone number and the information and then spent the next two hours trying to decide whether I should call. The problem was partly that I wasn't sure about what they'd want me to do, but since the study was being done at the medical school, I was pretty sure it was reputable and safe. So I finally called and made an appointment to go in tomorrow afternoon to hear a description of the project and fill out a couple of questionnaires. It was kind of simple at that – pretty much like

making an appointment at the dentist's.

Last night I sort of tossed and turned in bed before I fell asleep wondering about the project I had applied for. What'll I do if they ask me to *try out,* like an audition for the cheerleader squad, I thought. What's this project going to involve, anyway? (They didn't say much about it on the phone yesterday – was that being secretive or professional?) Then I started thinking, what if I'm *rejected?* The ultimate putdown! Finally, I managed to fall asleep, but I woke up real early, and I must admit that as I write this – it's an hour before I go in for my appointment – I'm nervous as can be.

Well, it was a big relief to get that appointment over with. As it turned out, there wasn't really much to be nervous about. First, after I got there, I filled out a brief questionnaire giving some identifying information about myself. Then I met with a woman connected with the research team (not the tall, dark doctor I fantasized about last night) who explained what the project involves and let me ask questions about it. Then I signed a consent form, agreeing to be in the project, and spent 45 minutes filling out a questionnaire about my health, my menstrual patterns, and my sex life.

It seems that the project will involve my being tested on four different days, at various phases of my menstrual cycle. I'll have to abstain from drinking or having sex for at least 48 hours before each test, and as far as I can tell now, the test seems to involve masturbating in a private room while I'm hooked up to a machine that measures sexual arousal with a small probe inside the vagina. I saw the machine today and didn't think it looked too complicated. I'll also be paid $100 for this experiment if I complete all the steps. That seemed like a classy touch.

Well, tomorrow's the big day. My first "study day," as they call it. I'm not exactly nervous about it, but I find myself wondering about a lot of things. What if I can't have an orgasm because I'm trying too hard? Will that probe interfere with my arousal? What if I don't even get aroused because of being uncomfortable? I guess that these sorts of jitters are pretty natural to have, but I hope that I won't run into any problems.

It was interesting to me that Larry got a little upset tonight because we couldn't have sex. I had told him weeks ago about the project, and he was really encouraging, but now he seems annoyed at the inconvenience factor. I'm not sure that's completely true, as I think about it, though – maybe he's jealous in some fashion (of the machine?) or just trying to be protective.

IT WAS A SNAP! After I got there, my nervousness was very apparent. My palms were sweaty, my heart was kind of racing a bit, and I was a little jumpy – especially when I was undressing in the testing room. I thought to myself, "Now's your chance to get out of this if you want to," but the research assistant was so easygoing and reassuring that I thought, why not give it a try. So I found myself lying there on a bed, listening to some soft music, with this small probe that I inserted inside my vagina (they showed me how to do this using a plastic model of a pelvis). Then I pushed a button to indicate that I was going to start masturbating. For a minute I wondered if they had a secret camera and were all watching me (making lewd jokes about my body or my masturbatory technique), but I quickly got into a favorite fantasy scene in my mind and I became really quite aroused. In fact, I was quite pleased with myself, because it was all so easy. I guess I masturbated for three or four minutes, had a nice orgasm, lay on the bed relaxing for a few minutes, and then got dressed. I came out in the hall, went to another room to fill out a few short questionnaires, made an appointment to come back in a week (around the time I'll be ovulating) and left. All in all, and despite my preliminary worries, it was much easier than I ever imagined it would be.

getting virtually all of the members of groups such as organizations, clubs, and college classes to agree to be interviewed. While he succeeded in getting about one-fifth of his subjects in this manner, it did not quell subsequent criticisms of his sample, as he had hoped.

On the other hand, the Kinsey team should be commended for choosing straightforward statistical methods that led to a fairly clear presentation of data. Although many quibbled about the statistical validity of their research (in what can now be seen as largely an attempt to discredit the credibility of Kinsey's "shocking" findings), a blue-ribbon committee of the American Statistical Association reviewed the Kinsey team's work and gave a critique that stated "our overall impression of their work is favorable" (Cochran, Mosteller, and Tukey, 1953, p. 674).

THE HUNT REPORT: 1974

One of the first large-scale sex surveys conducted in the post-Kinsey era was commissioned by the Playboy Foundation early in the 1970s. An independent research organization was hired to design and perform the study, with the primary objectives being to update Kinsey's data on sexual behavior and to improve on Kinsey's sampling technique. The results were written about by Morton Hunt in a series of articles in *Playboy* magazine and subsequently published in book form as *Sexual Behavior in the 1970s* (Hunt, 1975). Since this research was not a magazine survey or actually conducted by *Playboy* magazine, it is often referred to as the Hunt report.

Hunt's sample was obtained by random selection from telephone book listings in twenty-four American cities. Twenty percent of those contacted agreed to participate in small, private group discussions of trends in sexual behavior in America; after the discussions, participants were asked to complete a self-administered questionnaire on their sexual attitudes and experiences. Virtually all of the people who had taken part in

the small group discussions completed the questionnaire, giving a final sample of 982 males and 1,044 females aged eighteen and over. Although Hunt's sample mirrored the makeup of the national population in many ways (10 percent of participants were black, 71 percent were married, and the urban-rural mix was a close approximation of the actual distribution of the U.S. population), the sample has been faulted both for volunteer bias and for the more minor problem of underrepresenting people who are not listed in telephone directories (e.g., college students, institutionalized persons, people who don't have telephones, and people with unlisted phone numbers). Since it is uncertain how similar the 20 percent of people contacted who agreed to be in the study were to the 80 percent who declined participation, Hunt's findings must be interpreted with some caution. Nevertheless, this study provides valuable data that can be compared to that of Kinsey and his colleagues.

MAGAZINE SURVEYS

One of the more intriguing trends in research about sexuality in the past decade has been the proliferation of surveys conducted by major national magazines. Various surveys of this sort have been done by *Psychology Today* (e.g., Athanasiou et al., 1970; Rubenstein and Shaver, 1982; Rubenstein, 1983), *Redbook* (Levin and Levin, 1975; Tavris and Sadd, 1977; Sarrel and Sarrel, 1979), *Ladies' Home Journal* (Schulz, 1980), *Cosmopolitan* (Wolfe, 1980), and *Consumer Reports* (Brecher, 1983). Generally, these surveys produce samples far larger than those obtained in other sex research studies, sometimes drawing over 100,000 responses.

While it can certainly be useful to examine the sexual attitudes or experiences of such large numbers of people, it is important to realize that each sample consists of only a small fraction of the total number of readers of these magazines and cannot be considered to be representative of

Americans in general. Since it's not likely that the profile of the average *Redbook* or *Cosmopolitan* reader is the same as the profile of the average reader of *Family Circle* or *Good Housekeeping,* and since magazine readers as a group are probably more affluent and better educated than non-readers, it is easy to see why findings of these surveys are somewhat skewed. In addition, there is no way to tell why certain people have filled out these questionnaires while others have not. For instance, a distorted picture of sexuality might emerge if people who feel comfortable about their sexuality are more likely to respond to such surveys than people who are having sexual problems. Furthermore, there is no way to tell whether people have answered the questionnaires truthfully. In some cases, magazine readers who are annoyed or upset by seeing a sex survey in their favorite publication may vent their wrath by sending in intentionally false answers so as to interfere with the results of the study. How large an impact this source of distortion (and others, such as faulty recall) has on the conclusions of such reports is difficult even to guess at.

THE HITE REPORTS: 1976 AND 1981

Shere Hite conducted two surveys that have achieved best-seller status and provoked considerable controversy in the field of sex research. The first of these, *The Hite Report* (1976), was a study of female sexuality based on questionnaire responses from 3,019 women. The second study, *The Hite Report on Male Sexuality* (1981), describes the replies of 7,239 men to an essay-type questionnaire similar to the one in the first study.

Hite's research methods have been roundly criticized by a number of observers, with much of the criticism directed at her sampling technique. Despite the seemingly large number of people who completed her questionnaires, her actual response rates were quite small — only 3 percent in the female study and 6 percent in the male study — making it unlikely that her samples

were representative of the population at large. However, Hite makes a special point of the diversity of her sample, which was — for the male volume — accomplished in part by seeking out elderly respondents and others who statistically supplemented her main body of subjects. As Apfelbaum (1982, p. 85) notes, "This is a perfectly acceptable way to broaden one's pool of respondents, but to claim, as Hite does, that the result is proof of representativeness is a bit like passing a blood test by adding a few red cells to your sample." Additional evidence of the nonrepresentative nature of Hite's samples is shown in her female study, in which only 35 percent of participants were married (a rate approximately half that in the population at large).

Both of Hite's books are also handicapped by the failure to present data in clear, quantitative terms and the absence of a valid statistical analysis of her findings (Robinson, 1981; Gould, 1981). Thus, these studies are basically anecdotal impressions, which makes it difficult to judge the significance of her findings. However, this shortcoming also provides Hite's work with one of its major strengths: Readers encounter a rich lode of narrative descriptions of sexual thoughts and practices that are typically missing from more scientific studies. Thus, Hite's work can be seen as at least partly humanizing issues of sexuality rather than simply reducing them to numerical equations.

Another troublesome criticism of Hite's studies is that they frequently pose questions in a leading way. For instance, question number 132 of the male questionnaire asks: "Do you feel there is something wrong with your 'performance,' technique, or sensitivity if the woman does not orgasm from intercourse itself? That you're 'not *man* enough,' or at least that you did not do it right?" Most sexologists would shudder at this form of question, which is apt to elicit exactly the type of answers that characterize much of Hite's findings. (It would be preferable to ask the question in a more neutral manner, such as "How do you feel if the woman you're with doesn't have an orgasm from intercourse?" Then follow-up questions could be asked to see if the man feels that he's at fault, or that it's his partner's problem, and so on.) Thus, for a variety of reasons, the findings of the two Hite reports must be interpreted and applied very cautiously.

BLUMSTEIN AND SCHWARTZ: 1983

One of the most intriguing and sophisticated surveys of sexuality in relationships was conducted recently by two sociologists, Philip Blumstein and Pepper Schwartz, from the University of Washington. They recruited participants in a variety of ways, depending heavily on the use of newspaper, radio, and television announcements about their research to attract volunteers. Eventually, questionnaires were distributed to about 11,000 couples, with a return rate of about 55 percent. Their final sample consisted of 4,314 heterosexual couples, including more than 650 cohabiting, unmarried couples as well as more than 3,600 married couples, plus 969 gay male couples and 788 lesbian couples. In addition to analyzing the data provided by these questionnaires, Blumstein and Schwartz also conducted personal interviews with 129 heterosexual couples, 98 gay male couples, and 93 lesbian couples randomly chosen from their overall sample. Eighteen months later, they sent follow-up questionnaires to all the people who were interviewed and to more than 40 percent of their original sample.

The strengths of this study, which was published in 1983 in a book called *American Couples,* lie in four major areas: (1) A large, diverse national sample was obtained; (2) the research design allowed careful comparisons to be made between married couples, cohabiting heterosexual couples, gay male couples, and lesbian couples in a way that had not been done previously; (3) a well-planned questionnaire allowed the re-

searchers to gather information about many nonsexual areas of relationships (e.g., work and money) that shed light on sexual attitudes and behavior; and (4) follow-up studies were included in the research plan. The principal shortcoming of the study lies in the fact that the sample — despite its size and diversity — is not random or representative: the elderly, racial minorities, and working-class people were notably underrepresented, and couples who live apart were not studied at all. In addition, the research can be criticized for obtaining relatively superficial information in some areas and no information in other areas that might be considered important: For instance, no data was obtained about the use of sex fantasies by couples, or about sadomasochistic practices, or about rates of sexual dysfunctions. Nevertheless, the Blumstein and Schwartz study must be regarded as one of the most ambitious — and most successful — sex research studies yet carried out.

SURVEYS OF SPECIAL POPULATIONS

A number of studies have targeted particular research topics that are less broad than those of the surveys discussed above. We will consider several of these surveys both because of their innovative approaches to research design and because they will be referred to in later chapters.

TWO SURVEYS ON ADOLESCENT SEXUALITY. In 1973, social psychologist Robert Sorenson published the results of an important survey of adolescent sexuality in a book titled *Adolescent Sexuality in Contemporary America.* His sample randomly selected over 2,000 households in urban, suburban, and rural areas of the country. Although the final number of adolescents who participated in his study was only 411 — many parents objected to their teen's being interviewed and some adolescents whose parents gave consent were unwilling to volunteer — Sorenson was nevertheless able to obtain nearly a 50 percent response rate from a national probability sample, and this should be regarded as a major accomplishment. In interpreting Sorenson's findings, however, we must remember that the research does not apply to adolescents whose parents wouldn't permit them to participate in this type of research, nor to teens who themselves would decline participation in such a study. This probably means that Sorenson's findings are most applicable to adolescents from liberal, rather than conservative, backgrounds. Despite this drawback, Sorenson's study has been praised by many observers who believe that it, like the Hunt survey, represented a major advance in attention to sampling techniques. Furthermore, Sorenson's work was also strengthened by the use of an exceptionally comprehensive questionnaire that delved into issues of adolescent sexuality far more deeply than any prior study.

Further studies on adolescent sexuality have been done by two researchers from Johns Hopkins University, Melvin Zelnik and John Kantner, whose series of reports on sexual and contraceptive behavior of fifteen- to nineteen-year-old unmarried females embodies an even greater number of research strengths. On three different occasions — in 1971, 1976, and 1979 — they succeeded in obtaining a true national probability sample of notable size. Their 1971 survey included 4,392 females, while their 1976 survey included 1,886 females. Their 1979 sample was expanded to include 917 males aged seventeen to twenty-one as well as 1,717 females aged fifteen to nineteen, but the sampling was restricted to those living in metropolitan areas only.

Zelnik and Kantner's work is remarkable for the following reasons as well: (1) They used special sampling procedures to ensure the selection of large, representative populations of black females, so meaningful racial comparisons could be made (1,339 of the females in their 1971 study were black, for example, as were 654 females in their 1976 study); (2) they used a well-designed,

pre-tested research questionnaire; (3) they used highly sophisticated statistical techniques for data analysis; and (4) they included tests such as repeat interviews to substantiate the reliability of the information they obtained. In addition, by using essentially the same sampling technique on three different occasions over a decade, they were able to report on trends in adolescent sexual and contraceptive behavior more accurately than others had been able to.

Despite these strengths, the Zelnik and Kantner studies can be faulted in some areas. For example, their 1971 and 1976 surveys did not include teenage males, although researchers were certainly aware at those times of the importance of male sexual attitudes and behaviors in leading to unwanted teenage pregnancies. In addition, they gathered almost no information on sexual behavior other than intercourse, which places a surprising limitation on the overall usefulness of their findings. Finally, although they had originally planned to conduct a *longitudinal* study — that is, to resurvey the same population of subjects at various points over time — they dropped this plan because of lack of funds (Zelnik, Kantner, and Ford, 1981).

TWO STUDIES ON HOMOSEXUALITY. The Kinsey Institute returned to national prominence in 1978 with the publication of a major survey conducted by psychologist Alan Bell and sociologist Martin Weinberg in a book called *Homosexualities: A Study of Its Diversities Among Men and Women*. Several years later, a subsequent volume called *Sexual Preference — Its Development in Men and Women* (Bell, Weinberg, and Hammersmith, 1981) was published based on data collected in the same survey.

Working over nearly a decade with the financial support of the National Institute of Mental Health, Bell and Weinberg recruited a sample of homosexual men and women in the San Francisco Bay area through newspaper announcements, notices posted in gay bars and baths, mailings to membership lists of gay organizations, and similar strategies. From an initial pool of 4,639 people, they were able to conduct in-depth face-to-face interviews with 979 persons: 575 white homosexual males, 111 black homosexual males, 229 white homosexual females, and 64 black homosexual females. The researchers also interviewed a comparison group of 477 heterosexuals matched to their corresponding homosexual sample for age, race, gender, and education.

Each of the interviews, which were conducted in 1970, took from two to five hours to complete and covered 528 separate questions. Meticulous attention was devoted to training a team of interviewers so that the information gathered would be as reliable as possible. In addition, a substantial number of interviews were repeated six months after the original interview as a further check on accuracy.

While the Bell and Weinberg survey has many strengths, it is important to recognize that their sample is not very representative of homosexuals in America. By choosing to conduct their study in San Francisco, which is far more accepting of homosexuality than most other cities in the country, Bell and Weinberg made a deliberate trade-off between the possible representativeness of their sample in return for the relative ease (and, presumably, lower expense) in locating and recruiting subjects that San Francisco provided. Thus, their sample overrepresented homosexuals with liberal attitudes and a proclivity toward political activism while it largely overlooked those who are secretive about their sexual orientation. Furthermore, compared to homosexuals in other regions of the country, it is likely that this San Francisco-based sample was — at the time of the survey — more heavily involved in experimentation with illicit drugs, raising the possibility of unaccounted variables that might have distorted the research.

TWO SURVEYS ON SEXUALITY IN LATE ADULTHOOD. We will conclude this survey of surveys by briefly considering two different studies of the sexuality of elderly adults. *The Starr-Weiner Report on Sex and Sexuality in the Mature Years* (1981) was based on a rather haphazardly gathered sample of 800 adults over the age of sixty. Most of the subjects were recruited after hearing the authors of the study give a lecture; others were recruited by word-of-mouth, by referral from a colleague, or by other miscellaneous methods. While the findings of this study are of some interest because of the paucity of reliable data available on sex and the elderly, the poor sampling procedures and weak statistical analysis of this survey make it scientifically far from ideal. A particular problem of their sampling method was that subjects who heard them lecture may have been influenced to give answers that supported Starr and Weiner's already-stated views and to keep quiet about things that didn't match their philosophy.

In contrast, a more reliable survey of sexuality in middle and later life was also published in 1981 by George and Weiler. These researchers correctly pointed out that a true understanding of the effects of aging on sexuality would have to be based on longitudinal data. Thus, they surveyed a group of several hundred men and women chosen from a local health insurance program every two years over an eight-year period, and they reported on 278 individuals who remained married throughout the study period. The findings of their research, which are discussed in chapter 9, have considerably more validity than most studies of sex and aging because of the unique strategy they chose: using a longitudinal design.

Observational Research

Observational research involves the use of a human observer or an instrument to record the events being studied. Thus, it provides a means for avoiding dependence on subjects' self-reports. It can be done either in a laboratory setting or in the natural environment of study subjects. The latter technique is called *field study* and is a method commonly used by anthropologists and sociologists. Field studies can be done in almost any setting: sex research has been done on South Sea islands, in gay bars, at massage parlors, and on college campuses, to name just a few possible locations. Neither field studies nor other types of observational research require random samples for validity as long as they involve a reasonably diverse sample. A related type of research is the *participant-observer* method, in which the scientist is involved in the social setting while recording events. Two well-known examples of the participant-observer method can be found in studies of swinging (mate-swapping) done by Bartell (1970) and of impersonal homosexual sex in public places (Humphreys, 1970).

THE MASTERS AND JOHNSON STUDIES OF SEXUAL PHYSIOLOGY

As mentioned in the preceding chapter, *Human Sexual Response* (Masters and Johnson, 1966) was the first study to describe laboratory observations of the physical details of human sexual arousal. Masters began his research by interviewing 118 female prostitutes and twenty-seven male prostitutes in order to gather background information about the nature of sexual response. Next, a physiology laboratory was equipped with standard testing devices such as an electrocardiogram (to measure heart rate and rhythm) and an electromyogram (to measure muscle tension and contractions during the sexual response cycle). In addition, special devices were prepared such as the so-called artificial coital equipment, which consisted of a clear plastic penis-shaped object that permitted observation and filming of changes inside the vagina during sexual stimulation that simulated intercourse.

The device was designed so that a woman using this equipment could control the depth and tempo of thrusting herself. Masters and Johnson then tested their equipment on a small group of male and female prostitutes who served as their earliest research subjects.

Since they realized at the initial stages of their work that observing sexual responses among prostitutes would not suffice for a description of the sexual physiology of a normal population, Masters and Johnson began to recruit their actual research sample from the local academic community.[1] Over time, as news of the research quietly spread through the community, they obtained a broader array of volunteers, with the final sample consisting of 382 women (ranging in age from eighteen to seventy-eight) and 312 men (from twenty-one to eighty-nine).

It is important to realize that the people who volunteered to be watched and measured during sexual activity in a laboratory were certainly atypical in their willingness to be in such a study, and they may have been atypical in other ways as well. Both to guard against this factor as a major problem to the research and to protect the welfare of their subjects, Masters and Johnson conducted extensive interviews on several occasions with each potential subject in order to assess his (or her) psychological stability, motivations for volunteering, and other factors pertinent to the nature of the research.

Subjects were assured that all possible precautions would be taken to protect their confidentiality and anonymity, and as news spread around the medical center where the work was

---

[1] Prostitutes were unlikely to have had completely normal sexual anatomy because of frequent sexually transmitted infections and because many of the female prostitutes had had several abortions (at a time when abortions were both illegal and often unsafe). Furthermore, the high frequency of their sexual activity raised the possibility that their sexual physiology would have differed from other persons', much as the cardiovascular responses of trained athletes differ from those of nonathletes.

Sex Research: An Overview

being done, these precautions proved to be of considerable importance. Physicians and nurses began to congregate in the corridors near the research suite in an attempt to catch sight of those entering and leaving, and some even tried listening to what was happening inside by putting a stethoscope to the outer wall of the research area. Masters and Johnson had fortunately foreseen the need for stringent security measures and had thoroughly soundproofed their laboratory, but they were forced to switch many of their studies to evening hours in order to bypass traffic jams from curiosity seekers who "just happened to be passing by."

Once a couple was accepted for the study, and following the completion of their interviews, they were given one or more opportunities to become acclimated to the laboratory setting. This involved experimenters first showing them the equipment and testing room, and then asking them to have sexual activity in the laboratory without observers present or being hooked up to any machines. This "practice session" was used to help eliminate nervousness and discomfort, although admittedly a "practice session" was not exactly the same as the real thing.

Once actual participation began, subjects were measured in a broad range of sexual activities (including self-masturbation, genital stimulation by a partner, oral-genital stimulation, and intercourse), with most subjects studied on dozens of occasions to identify degrees of variability in their response patterns. Overall, over 10,000 orgasmic sexual response cycles were studied.

Although some critics have contended that Masters and Johnson's physiology research was flawed because their sample did not consist of a good cross-section of the population, most research on medical physiology assumes that normative processes (e.g., natural body functions such as vision, digestion, and so forth) do not require such a sample, as long as the sample is both diverse and healthy. Thus, exercise physiologists

don't worry too much about getting random samples in order to study the physiology of muscle, and physicians interested in the physiology of breathing aren't concerned with having a random sample to identify the anatomic events and physiologic details of respiration.

Another criticism levelled at Masters and Johnson's work is that the artificial setting of the laboratory may have distorted subjects' responses. Although there is no way of proving or disproving this criticism directly, the applicability of their findings to such areas as sex therapy, contraceptive technology, infertility counseling, and sex education weakens such criticisms.

Case Studies

Case studies are in-depth examinations of one or more people with a particular condition (such as alcoholism) or a specific characteristic (such as being a victim of sexual assault). Unlike survey interviews, which are usually done in a matter of hours, most case studies require weeks or months of assessment. Historically, the case study method was widely employed in the early days of sexology, as Krafft-Ebing, Ellis, and Freud made extensive use of this method. Even today, case studies are frequently published, although they are often of limited scientific value. In fact, a single, unreplicated case usually tells us nothing but an interesting story. Another problem with case studies is that not only is the accuracy of the subject's self-reports open to question, but the researcher's own biases strongly influence what he or she "sees" in the case. In addition, it is not uncommon for a patient to learn what type of information the researcher is most interested in and selectively cultivate this material so as to gain his or her praise. The researcher's biases may influence case reports in another way, as shown in the following example: a psychologist doing an in-depth study of the cause of erectile difficulties in a twenty-eight-year-old man spent many hours administering psychological tests and conducting interviews with the subject, his wife, and other family members, but neglected the medical side of the evaluation since this was not his major interest. The man's sexual dysfunction eventually turned out to be due to multiple sclerosis, and the psychologist had to withdraw a paper he had submitted on the case.

Recent case studies in the sex research literature include reports on men raped by women (Sarrel and Masters, 1981), studies of rare sexual practices (e.g., Stoller, 1982; Wise, 1982), reports on aspects of sex therapy, and studies relating sexual functioning to various health conditions.

Clinical Research

Clinical research usually consists of studies that test a type of treatment for a specific problem and assess how that treatment changed the underlying condition. This type of clinical research, which is sometimes known as an *outcome study,* is frequently done in conjunction with the use of a *control group* of subjects who receive no treatment. Clinical research also includes *epidemiological studies* that focus on the pattern of distribution of a phenomenon (such as the spread of a sexually transmitted infection, or the prevalence of sexual dysfunctions in a population), as well as studies of a series of cases of an illness to evaluate its natural (untreated) history, to gather diagnostic information about the illness, or to uncover information about what causes it.

One of the best-known examples of clinical research in the field of sexology is *Human Sexual Inadequacy* (Masters and Johnson, 1970), a report which described the results of sex therapy in 790 cases, with many of the cases followed for a five-year period after the conclusion of therapy. Although this study has been criticized on methodological grounds (Zilbergeld and Evans, 1980), it is accepted by most sexologists today as a major research accomplishment.

Experimental Research

Experimental research involves use of a method in which the investigator varies one factor under carefully controlled conditions to isolate its effect. In a sense, researchers using this approach create the specific situation they want to investigate. Among the many strengths of this research method is that it permits conclusions about cause-effect relationships which cannot generally be proven by any other means.

Experimental research has been used to study many aspects of sexual behavior and response, including the effects of viewing erotic materials (discussed in chapter 13), the effects of alcohol on sexual arousal (the box on page 41), and the effectiveness of various forms of sex therapy. The experimental method has also been used to evaluate gender role effects on behavior, the nature of the premenstrual syndrome, the effects of sex education on rates of unintended teenage pregnancy, and factors that might prevent people from developing sexual difficulties.

Although the experimental method can be used to study many situations, it has a number of disadvantages as well. One of the primary limitations of this method is that laboratory experiments often involve artificial situations, so their findings may not apply to spontaneous behaviors and feelings in real life. Another problem is that of volunteer bias. Finally, researchers can't always be sure that they have implemented proper controls over all of the variables that influence the phenomenon they are studying. For example, if an experiment to study sexual arousal patterns in men in response to an erotic movie is inadvertently conducted in a room where the air conditioning is blasting away, the results will likely be influenced by the temperature. If the researcher does not realize this problem, the conclusions reached on the basis of the actual results obtained will clearly be inaccurate.

Experimental Research in Action: Three Studies of the Sexual Effects of Alcohol

A practical glimpse at the way the experimental method is applied to sex research can be gained by considering three different studies designed to investigate the effects of alcohol on sexual response. Each study dealt with a different population of subjects and utilized different measures, yet their findings were remarkably similar.

The first study was an experiment conducted by Wilson, Lawson, and Abrams (1978) that was designed to demonstrate the effects of alcohol on sexual arousal in male alcoholics. Eight men who were chronic alcoholics were chosen from a larger sample who responded to a newspaper advertisement about the study. Each man was studied on four consecutive days, receiving a beverage to drink containing either a miniscule amount of alcohol or one of three graded doses of alcohol. An hour later, a blood sample was obtained to measure the amount of alcohol that had been absorbed,

and each man was asked to predict (by completing a questionnaire) what effect, if any, the alcohol he had consumed would have on his sexual arousal while watching erotic films. Measurements of the degree of penile enlargement that occurred while watching these films were then taken with a penile plethysmograph, a device (as shown in Figure A below) that measures circumference changes in the penis continuously over time. The study found that the higher the amount of alcohol consumed, the more sexual arousal was impaired. However, subjects consistently expected that alcohol either would have no effect on their sexual arousal or would actually increase it.

A second study of alcohol effects on sexual response in men, done by Malatesta and co-workers (1979), involved a sample of twenty-four non-alcoholic men. Each subject was given one of four doses of alcohol on four different test days, and then was escorted to a private, temperature-controlled, soundproof room in which he viewed sexually explicit videotapes while being monitored by remote control by means of an electromyographic device connected to his genital region. Each participant was instructed to masturbate to orgasm while viewing the erotic videotape. At the two highest blood alcohol levels, ten of the twenty-four men were completely unable to reach orgasm. As shown

FIGURE A

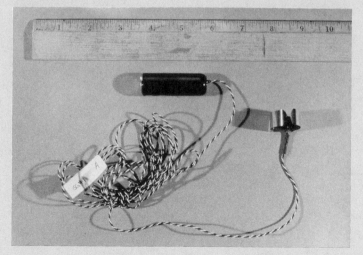

in the accompanying graph (see Figure B), for the entire research sample, the higher the amount of alcohol in the blood, the longer it took for the men to ejaculate.

The third experiment, also done by Malatesta and his colleagues (1982), examined the effects of alcohol on female orgasmic response utilizing a research design much like that described for the preceding study (four different alcohol doses, masturbating in privacy while watching erotic videotapes). Subjects in this experiment were eighteen non-alcoholic women aged twenty-two to thirty-four. The results showed that these women had considerably more difficulty reaching orgasm by masturbation with the two higher doses of alcohol than with low doses of alcohol or no alcohol at all. In fact, the more alcohol they consumed, the longer it took them to reach orgasm (as shown in Figure C) and the more their physiologic signs of sexual response were impeded. Despite these findings suggesting that the effects of alcohol on the female are entirely

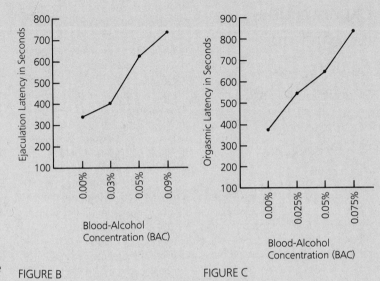

FIGURE B

FIGURE C

negative, the researchers discovered that the same women reported *more* sexual pleasure and *more* sexual arousal with the highest dose of ahcohol. Perhaps they viewed the sexual experience they had while intoxicated as more pleasurable than at other times because of socialization that teaches women that being "turned on" by

alcohol is expected and permitted, while being turned on under other conditions is less acceptable. Other explanations of the discrepancy between the objective physiological and subjective psychological reports of sexual arousal are possible, so it will require further experiments to clarify the explanation of this finding.

Research Limitations Revisited

Biases in sex research (and research in general) come from many other sources. The treatment success in an uncontrolled clinical trial may be due to the attention paid to subjects and the power of positive suggestion — scientifically known as the *placebo effect* — rather than to the treatment itself. The attitudes and preconceptions of the researcher influence the study methods, the specific questions asked, and the interpretation of data. Researchers may fail to "see" events that do not match their theoretical view of the problem or they may "see" nonexistent events that neatly fit their model of thought (Barber, 1976).

Individual characteristics of the researcher — personality, appearance, friendliness, age — may cause distortions in the data. For instance, a study of sexual function in young spinal-cord-injured men used female nurses as interviewers (Bors and Comarr, 1960), thus giving rise to the possibility that subjects might have exaggerated their reports of sexual ability to impress the nurse or not embarrass themselves. It is possible that different information might have been obtained if the interviewers were male. Another example: subjects interviewed by black experimenters give different answers to questions about racial prejudice than subjects interviewed by white experimenters (Summers and Hammonds, 1966).

Questionnaires are useful from an economic viewpoint and for reasons of time efficiency. However, they have several limitations. They can only be used with subjects who can read and write; they must be constructed in such a way that respondents do not lose interest or become fatigued; and there is no opportunity for in-depth examination of the meaning or nuance of answers (Labovitz and Hagedorn, 1976). Survey studies in general — whether done by questionnaire or interview — share another limitation: the questions asked usually elicit opinions, attitudes,

or *perceptions* of behavior, but these do not necessarily reflect the *actual* behavior under study. There is nothing wrong with studying attitudes or perceptions, but scientific accuracy is not served by confusing fact and feeling.

Observational and experimental studies are usually more expensive and time-consuming than surveys. In both of these methods, the setting of the study may influence the observed behavior. Even after subjects become acclimated to a laboratory environment and the equipment used to monitor or measure their responses, it is unlikely that they will be as relaxed and spontaneous as if they were at home. All observational research in which subjects know that they are being observed exerts some influences on subsequent behavior. The same is true for experimental research: subjects may try to respond in ways they believe the experimenter "wants" them to or in ways dictated by how they want the experimenter to perceive them. The change in people's behavior caused by knowing they are in an experiment is called the *Hawthorne effect*.

Significance and Replication

Although a detailed discussion of appropriate methods of statistical analysis is beyond the scope of this book, one point is important. Many reports use statistical tests of significance, with *significance* in this instance meaning a result not likely to have happened by chance. Most commonly, a probability level of 5 percent or less ($p \leq .05$) is chosen to define significance: this means that the probability of the research findings arising from chance alone is one in twenty or less. Although this formulation sounds impressive, results showing statistical significance are not infallible and absolute. More important than such statistics alone are the questions of whether the research design is appropriate, the types of bias minimized, and whether the findings have been independently replicated. When research findings are closely duplicated by a separate investigator using similar methods, it is much safer to conclude that the findings are valid.

One cautionary note about replication is important, however. If two independent researchers use the same methods and perpetuate the same biases, the conclusions they come to may be identical but still may be wrong. We already discussed research on homosexuality before 1957: by repeatedly studying poorly selected samples (prisoners and psychiatric patients), researchers concluded that homosexuals were often maladjusted and sick. Later studies, without the same sampling bias, came to very different conclusions about homosexuals.

There are many other potential pitfalls in research, but an exhaustive catalogue is not likely to be useful for our purposes here. It is helpful to remember that the research perspective is just one way of looking at the world — not the only way and not necessarily the best way. Remember, research is only an approximate way of getting at facts. Studying sex research can be informative but so is knowledge gained from clinical situations, personal experiences, literature, art, and culture. No single perspective on human sexuality has a monopoly on truth.

SUMMARY

1. Sex research, when properly conducted, follows the general scientific principles that also apply to research in other fields. These include paying adequate attention to obtaining a proper sample, and to employing the appropriate methods for obtaining and analyzing data.

2. Responsible sex research is conducted in an ethical manner, protecting the rights and welfare of the research subjects. This requires obtaining the informed consent of potential study subjects and taking precautions to protect the subjects' confidentiality.

3. Various types of bias (extraneous influences on the research) can affect the validity of any sex research study. Common examples of the types of bias that must be considered are volunteer bias, erroneous answers, sampling problems, the placebo effect, and biases of the researcher.

4. The most popular method of sex research has been the survey, which can be done with either questionnaires or personal interviews. While questionnaires are more economical and anonymous, interviews allow for a greater depth of material to be obtained. Surveys, however, are frequently troubled by such difficulties as obtaining a proper sample (for instance, very few studies have succeeded in obtaining true national probability samples), which may limit the generalizability of the survey findings. In addition, surveys are affected by the accuracy of information provided by subjects in answering questionnaires or interviewers' questions.

5. The original Kinsey studies, published in 1948 and 1953, exemplify both the problems and the strengths of the survey method. Despite having had very large sample sizes, their two samples were not random or representative, leading some to question the validity of their reported findings. Many sex researchers have subsequently improved the survey sampling techniques of Kinsey and his co-workers.

6. Observational research involves the use of a human observer or an instrument to record the events being studied. The landmark study using this method was conducted by Masters and Johnson, who observed and recorded the physical patterns of sexual response in a laboratory setting. Field studies and participant-observer studies have also been conducted by sex researchers. Observational research enables researchers to bypass their total dependence on the accuracy of subjects' self-reports. However, volunteer bias and the question of artificiality (that is, would subjects respond the same way in their

home environment as they do in a laboratory setting?) also pose some uncertainties and limitations on this method.

7. Case studies are in-depth examinations of one or more people having a particular condition or characteristic. These studies are usually not a good source of scientific "proof" because they have poor generalizability and because they are handicapped by the biases of the researcher probably more than in other forms of research.

8. Clinical research usually involves studies that test a type of treatment given for a specific problem and can include case studies, surveys, and experimental studies. Clinical research must be examined carefully to be certain that improvement is really a result of the treatment rather than a reflection of either the placebo effect or the passage of time. Clinical research done without the benefit of a control group must be viewed with a high degree of scientific skepticism.

9. Experimental research permits scientists to isolate the specific variables that affect a condition or behavior and may allow them to draw conclusions about cause and effect. Experimental research, however, is apt to be difficult and expensive to perform, and is not completely free of error. Volunteer bias, experimenter effects, and the artificiality of the experimental situation may limit the validity of this type of study.

10. In evaluating the overall quality of any sex research study, it is useful to look at such fundamental methodological issues as the size and nature of the sample, the means by which data were collected, the type of data analysis that was done, and the researcher's discussion of the study's limitations. In addition, it is useful to see whether a study has been replicated by others, since independent verification of a set of research findings is one of the most powerful tools science can offer for confirming the validity of a study.

SUGGESTED READINGS

Gebhard, Paul, and Johnson, Alan. *The Kinsey Data: Marginal Tabulations of the 1938-1963 Interviews Conducted by the Institute for Sex Research*. Philadelphia: W. B. Saunders, 1979. Expanded data from the original Kinsey studies, reorganized to include data from blacks and other special groups, such as a delinquent population. Although this book consists almost entirely of numerical tables, it is a valuable compendium of data for anyone interested in sex research.

Green, Richard, and Wiener, Jack (eds.). *Methodology in Sex Research*. Rockville, Maryland: U.S. Department of Health and Human Services (Publication Number [ADM] 80-766), 1980. A comprehensive, sophisticated "state-of-the-art" review. Difficult reading but filled with useful ideas.

Mason, Emanuel J., and Bramble, William J. *Understanding and Conducting Research*. New York: McGraw-Hill, 1978. A good primer on research methodology, with a clear and understandable treatment of statistical methods for data analysis.

Pomeroy, Wardell; Flax, Carol; and Wheeler, Connie. *Taking a Sex History: Interviewing and Recording*. New York: The Free Press, 1982. An invaluable guide to the interviewing methods used in the original Kinsey research, updated to apply to contemporary sex research. Particularly fascinating for revealing the intricate coding system used by the Kinsey team.

PART ONE

Biological Perspectives

3 Sexual Anatomy

Karen is a twenty-year-old college junior who generally avoided dating because she felt her breasts were too small. She wrote: "I hate looking in a mirror or wearing a bathing suit because I see how flat I am. I would be *mortified* to let a guy touch or see my breasts." (Authors' files)

Brad is an athletic seventeen-year-old who quit his school's basketball team because his breasts were large. He told us that his teammates kidded him mercilessly in the locker room and showers about when he was going to get a bra. He was afraid he might "turn into a woman." (Authors' files)

A married couple in their mid-twenties who were sex therapy patients said they frequently used stimulation of the clitoris as part of making love.

When asked to identify the clitoris during a physical exam, the husband pointed to a large freckle on the lower part of his wife's left labia majora. (Authors' files)

A class of eighty college sophomores was given a brief test on sexual anatomy the first day of their course on sexuality. The average student had more mistakes than right answers. (Authors' files)

As these examples show, many of us have inaccurate information or negative feelings about our sexual anatomy. This should not be surprising for a variety of reasons: we are taught to keep our sex organs covered by clothing; we are scolded or punished for touching our

49

"private parts"; we are not likely to be told the correct terminology to describe our sexual anatomy; we are discouraged from conversations or questions about sex; and the sexual images we are exposed to in movies and magazines are likely to present almost unattainable standards to measure ourselves against. It is no wonder that our sexual anatomy can be a source of anxiety, shame, guilt, mystery, and curiosity, as well as a source of pleasure.

The mixed feelings we have about our sexual body parts are mirrored in the words we use to talk about them: some words are "clean" and "proper," while others are "dirty" or "impolite." These differences are a result of how we interpret words, not an innate property of the words themselves. Consider, for example:

> In Nigeria, the moral taboos of sex were taught by missionaries and administrators who used only clean words. These were the words that became taboo. The dirty words used as part of the vernacular of sailors, traders, and the like, became part of Nigerian vernacular English, with no taboo attached. In consequence, today it is as forbidden to say sexual intercourse, penis and vagina on Nigerian television as it is to say fuck, cock, and cunt on the national networks in the United States. In Nigeria, the latter terms are considered normal and respectable. (Money, 1980, pp. 50-51)

In this book we will not use slang terms about sex because they convey a negative message to some people. As a matter of convenience, however, slang terms that describe sexual parts of the body are listed in Table 3-1. Sex organs in the pelvic region — in females, the outer sexual structures and the vagina, and in males, the penis, scrotum, and testes — are customarily called the *genitals*.

People of all ages have common concerns about sexual anatomy: What is the normal size of the penis? Is something wrong if one breast is smaller than the other? Does circumcision lessen sexual pleasure? Do large breasts indicate a pas-

---

TABLE 3-1
Some Sexual Terminology:
Science and Slang

Proper Name	Slang Terms
Vulva	Pussy, snatch, crotch
Pubic hair	Beaver, bush, pubes
Mons veneris	Love mound
Clitoris	Clit, button, joy button
Labia	—
Hymen	Cherry, maidenhead
Urethral meatus	
(urinary opening)	Peehole
Vagina	Cunt, box, pussy, hole, snatch, slit, twat, honeypot
Anus	Asshole
Breasts	Boobs, tits, knockers, bazooms
Buttocks	Ass, rear end, bottom, buns
Penis	Prick, cock, peter, tool, organ, meat (rod, boner, and hard-on usually refer to erect penis only)
Testes	Balls, nuts, jewels

---

sionate woman? Is it abnormal if one testicle hangs lower than the other? Where and what is the clitoris? The answers to such questions begin with learning about sexual anatomy. The basis for understanding the way our bodies function sexually will be discussed in the next chapter.

FEMALE SEXUAL ANATOMY

> We are encouraged to feel as if our bodies are not ours. Our "figure" is for a (potential) mate to admire. Our breasts are for "the man in our lives" to fondle during lovemaking, for our babies to suckle, for our doctors to examine. The same kind of "hands-off" message is even stronger for our vaginas. (The Boston Women's Health Book Collective, 1976, p. 24)

Anyone who has been around young children knows that baby girls play with their genitals just as they touch and explore all parts of their body. Although this activity seems pleasurable and interesting, most girls are quickly taught that it's "not nice" or "dirty," a prohibition that is probably reinforced during toilet training when the two- or three-year-old girl is urged to "wipe carefully" and "be clean." The sex-negative tone of these early childhood messages is consistently reinforced for most girls as they grow up, commonly creating anxieties and inhibitions about sex in general and their sexual anatomy in particular (Long Laws, 1979; Barbach, 1980; Hite, 1977). These difficulties are compounded by many people's perception of the female sex organs as unattractive and unclean.

Menstruation is one source of such negative attitudes: menstrual periods are sometimes called "the curse," menstrual flow is contained by "sanitary" napkins (which suggests an underlying condition of uncleanliness), sex during menstruation is often avoided by men and women because it may be messy, and in some societies, there are strong taboos surrounding menstruating women that isolate them so they will not contaminate food, plants, or people (Delaney, Lupton, and Toth, 1977). In our cosmetic-conscious society of perfumes, deodorants, and after-shave lotions, women have been told that their vaginal odors are unpleasant and should be hidden. As a result, "feminine hygiene deodorant sprays" were widely used until it became apparent that they frequently caused vaginal irritation and itching.

Many women have not taken a direct look at their own genitals or cannot accurately name and identify the parts of their sexual anatomy. While we cannot imagine a person unable to distinguish between eyes, nose, mouth, and chin, many men and women have no idea of the locaton of the female urethra, clitoris, or hymen.

The Vulva

The external sex organs of the female, called the *vulva* (meaning "covering"), consist of the mons, the labia, the clitoris, and the perineum (Figure 3-1). Although the vagina has an external opening (the *introitus,* or entrance), it is principally an internal organ and will be discussed separately.

THE MONS

The *mons veneris* (Latin: mound of Venus; Venus was the Roman goddess of love) is the area over the pubic bone which consists of a cushion of fatty tissue covered by skin and pubic hair. Since this region has numerous nerve endings, touch and/or pressure here may lead to sexual arousal. Many women find that stimulation of the mons area can be as pleasurable as direct clitoral touch.

THE LABIA

The *outer lips* (labia majora) are folds of skin covering a large amount of fat tissue and a thin layer of smooth muscle. Pubic hair grows on the sides of the outer lips, and sweat glands, oil glands, and nerve endings are liberally distributed in them. In the sexually unstimulated state, the outer lips usually are folded together in the midline, providing mechanical protection for the urethral (urinary) opening and the vaginal entrance.

The *inner lips* (labia minora) are like curving petals. They have a core of spongy tissue rich in small blood vessels and without fat cells. The skin covering the inner lips is hairless but has many sensory nerve endings. The inner lips meet just above the clitoris forming a fold of skin called the *clitoral hood* (see Figure 3-1). This portion of the inner lips is sometimes referred to as the female foreskin.

The labia are an important source of sexual sensations for most women since their many nerve endings serve as sensory receptors. When the skin of the labia is infected, sexual intercourse may be painful, and itching or burning may occur.

FIGURE 3–1
The Vulva

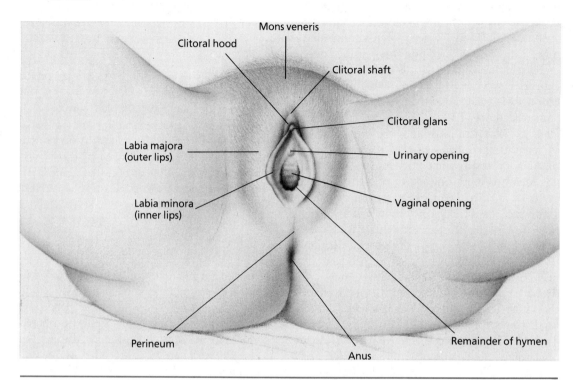

Women's external genitals may vary greatly in appearance. There are differences in the size, shape, and color of the labia (a few examples are shown in Figure 3-2), in the color, texture, amount, and distribution of pubic hair, and in the appearance of the clitoris, vaginal opening, and hymen. Sexual anatomy varies just as much as facial anatomy differs from one person to another.

Bartholin's glands lie within the labia minora and are connected to small ducts that open on the inner surface of the labia next to the vaginal opening. Although once thought to play a major role in the production of vaginal lubrication, it is now clear that the few drops of secretion usually produced by these glands during sexual arousal are not important contributants to vaginal lubrication, although they may slightly moisten the labia.

THE CLITORIS

The *clitoris*, one of the most sensitive areas of a female's genitals, is located just beneath the point where the top of the inner lips meet. The only directly visible part of the clitoris is the head or *clitoral glans*, which looks like a small, shiny button. This head can be seen by gently pushing

FIGURE 3-2
Some Variations in the Appearance of the Female Genitals

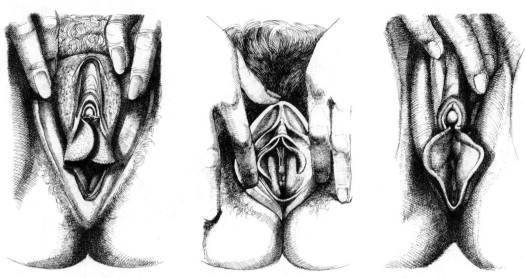

Betty Dodson's drawings of the female genitals reflect not only her artistic per-
spective, but also the feminist view of the importance of women accepting their
sexual anatomy as a positive attribute and a source of pleasure rather than shame.

Source: Betty Dodson, *Selflove & Orgasm* (1983), Box 1933 Murray Hill Station, New York, N.Y. 10156, $5. 50 pp.

up the skin or *clitoral hood* that covers it. The clitoral hood also hides the *clitoral shaft*, the spongy tissue that branches internally like an inverted V into two longer parts or *crura*. The crura lead to the bony pelvis (see Figure 3-3). The clitoris is richly endowed with nerve endings which make it highly sensitive to touch, pressure, and temperature. It is unique because it is the only organ in either sex whose only known function is to focus and accumulate sexual sensations and erotic pleasure (Masters and Johnson, 1970).

The clitoris is often regarded as a miniature penis, but this notion is sexist and incorrect. The clitoris has no reproductive or urinary function and does not usually lengthen like the penis when stimulated, although it does become engorged. The clitoris and the penis, however, are derived embryologically from the same tissues.

The size and appearance of the clitoris vary considerably among women, but there is no evidence that a larger clitoris provides more intense sexual arousal. Contrary to the opinion of some physicians, masturbation rarely causes enlargement of this organ.

Clitoral circumcision — surgical removal of the clitoral hood — has been said to improve female sexual responsivity by exposing the clitoral

FIGURE 3–3
Anatomy of the Clitoris

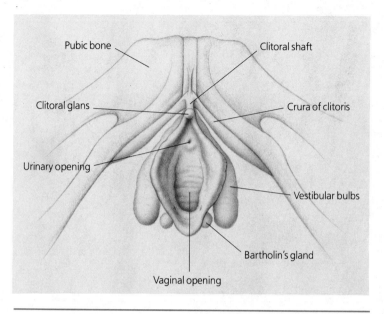

Pubic bone

Clitoral shaft

Clitoral glans

Crura of clitoris

Urinary opening

Vestibular bulbs

Bartholin's gland

Vaginal opening

glans to more direct stimulation.[1] We believe, however, that this procedure is rarely useful since it has two major drawbacks: (1) the clitoral glans is often exquisitely sensitive to direct touch, to the point of pain or irritation (in this sense, the clitoral hood serves a protective function),[2] and (2) during intercourse the thrusting of the penis indirectly stimulates the clitoris by moving the inner lips of the vagina, causing the clitoral hood to rub back and forth across the clitoral glans (Masters and Johnson, 1966). A less drastic procedure than circumcision is advocated by several sexologists to improve some women's sexual responsiveness. A probe is used to loosen adhesions or thickened secretions (*smegma*) between the clitoral hood and clitoral glans (Graber and Kline-Graber, 1979). In more than thirty years of practice, we have seen very few cases that re-

---

[1] Some tribes in Africa and South America practice surgical removal of the clitoris (clitoridectomy) as a ritual rite of puberty. And, according to one Egyptian physician, more than one-half of all young girls in Egypt are still undergoing this painful procedure today (*Sexuality Today,* Vol. 6, No. 3, June 6, 1983). Although this practice is sometimes called "clitoral circumcision," it is not at all the same. Clitoridectomy does not destroy the capacity for sexual arousal or orgasm, but it certainly does not help it at all. When a resolution was introduced at the Sixth World Congress of Sexology in 1983 to formally oppose this procedure, it was defeated because many delegates were concerned that they had no business meddling in the long-standing customs of other cultures.

---

[2] In masturbation most women stroke areas around the clitoral glans but avoid its direct stimulation for this very reason. Apparently, the advocates of clitoral circumcision (usually men, oddly enough) have overlooked this finding.

quired such an approach and remain skeptical about the use of this procedure on a routine basis.

THE PERINEUM

The *perineum* is the hairless area of skin between the bottom of the labia and the anus (the opening for evacuation of the bowels). This region is often sensitive to touch, pressure, and temperature and may be a source of sexual arousal.

The Hymen

The opening of the vagina is covered by a thin tissue membrane called the *hymen*. The hymen, which has no known function, typically has perforations in it that allow menstrual flow to pass from the body at puberty. The hymen usually stretches across some but not all of the vaginal opening and may vary in shape, size, and thickness as Figure 3-4 reveals.

FIGURE 3–4
Variations in the Hymen

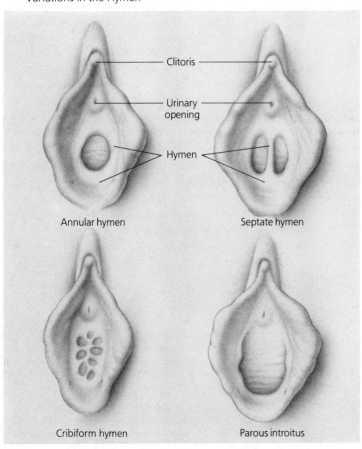

Clitoris

Urinary opening

Hymen

Annular hymen

Septate hymen

Cribiform hymen

Parous introitus

The annular hymen forms a ring around the vaginal opening; the septate hymen has one or more bands of tissue that cross the diameter of the vaginal opening; and the cribiform hymen stretches completely across the vaginal opening but has many small perforations. The parous introitus is the opening of the vagina in a woman who has previously given birth to a child by vaginal delivery; only small remnants of the tissue of the hymen are visible.

Historically, it has been important for a woman to have an intact hymen at the time of marriage as proof of her virginity. In some societies, a bride who does not have an intact hymen is returned to her parents, subjected to public ridicule, physically punished, or even put to death (Ford and Beach, 1951). Even in modern Japan and Italy, plastic surgeons are kept busy by reconstructing the hymens of many engaged women to create "neovirginity" for those who wish to conceal their sexual histories from their future husbands.

Contrary to the fears of some females, a doctor cannot usually tell if they are virgins by conducting a pelvic examination. The presence or absence of an intact hymen is not an accurate indication of prior sexual behavior. The hymen may be broken or stretched at an early age by various exercises or by inserting fingers or objects in the vagina. Some females are born with only a partial hymen or none at all. In addition, intercourse does not always tear the hymen; instead, it may simply stretch it. Under most circumstances, the first intercourse experience for a girl or woman is not painful or marked by a great deal of bleeding. The excitement of the moment is usually enough so that the pressure on the hymen is barely noticed.

The Vagina

The *vagina* is a muscular internal organ that tilts upward at a 45° angle diagonally pointed toward the small of the back (Figure 3-5). In the sexually unstimulated state, the vagina's walls are collapsed. In a woman who has never had a child, the back wall of the vagina averages 8 centimeters (about 3 inches) in length, while the front wall is approximately 6 centimeters (2½ inches) long.

The vagina functions as a potential space that like a balloon can change shape and size. It can contract and expand, accommodate the passage of a baby during childbirth or adjust in size to fit snugly around a finger.[3]

Many people wonder about the relationship between vaginal size and sexual gratification. Since the vagina adjusts equally well to a large or small penis, it is unusual for size differences between male and female sex organs to lead to sexual difficulties. Following childbirth, the vagina usually enlarges moderately and loses elasticity. Exercises to strengthen the muscles supporting the vagina are thought by some authorities to improve this condition and foster sexual responsiveness (Kegel, 1952; Kline-Graber, 1978).[4]

The inside of the vagina is lined with a surface similar to the lining inside the mouth. This *mucosa* is the source of vaginal lubrication. There are no secretory glands in the vagina, but there is a rich supply of blood vessels. The vagina has relatively few sensory nerve endings except near its opening. As a result, the inner two-thirds of the vagina are relatively insensitive to touch or pain.

Recently, there have been claims that a region in the front wall of the vagina midway between the pubic bone and the cervix has a special sensitivity to erotic stimulation. Called the G *spot* (or Gräfenberg spot, for the German physician who first suggested its presence in 1950), it

---

[3] Despite its ability to contract, the human vagina cannot "clamp down" on the penis during intercourse and make physical separation impossible. In dogs, there is a type of intravaginal "locking," but it occurs primarily because of expansion of the head of the penis.

[4] The "Kegel exercises" are done by contracting the pelvic muscles that support the vagina (most notably, the *pubococcygeus* and *bulbocavernosus muscles*). These same muscles are used when a woman stops the flow of urine or tightens the vagina against an inserted object such as a tampon, a finger, or an erect penis. The muscles are contracted firmly for one or two seconds and then released; this is repeated in a series of ten contractions several times a day for maximum results. In addition to strengthening muscular contractions, these exercises can improve a woman's sense of self-awareness. Whether they really improve sexual responsivity is less certain at present.

Sexual Anatomy

FIGURE 3–5
Internal Side View of the Female Reproductive System

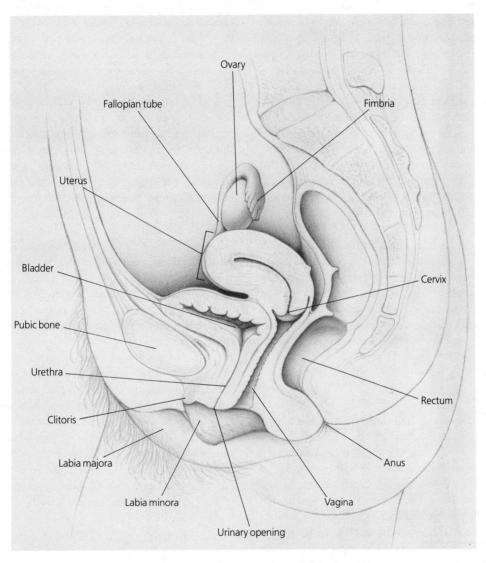

Ovary

Fallopian tube

Fimbria

Uterus

Bladder

Cervix

Pubic bone

Urethra

Rectum

Clitoris

Labia majora

Anus

Labia minora

Vagina

Urinary opening

has been described as a mass of tissue about the size of a small bean in the unstimulated state. When stimulated the tissue swells to the size of a dime or larger (Ladas, Whipple, and Perry, 1982).

Ladas, Whipple, and Perry (1982) state that examinations of more than 400 women identified the "G spot" in each one; they explain that it has generally been overlooked in the past because "in its sexually unstimulated state, it is relatively small and difficult to locate, especially since you can't see it." This explanation does not fit a research project in which Whipple herself participated in which the "G spot" could be found in only four out of eleven women (Goldberg et al., 1983), nor does it coincide with our studies at the Masters & Johnson Institute, where less than 10 percent of a sample of over 100 women who were carefully examined had an area of heightened sensitivity in the front wall of the vagina or a tissue mass that fit the various descriptions of this area. Another recent study also was unable to find evidence supporting the existence of the "G spot" (Alzate and Londono, 1984), although many of the women studied showed signs of erotic sensitivity in the front wall of the vagina. Thus, at the present time it seems that additional research is needed to establish whether the "G spot" exists as a distinct anatomic structure or whether, as Helen Kaplan (1983) says, "the knowledge that many women have erotically sensitive areas in their vaginas which contribute to pleasure and orgasm is not new or controversial."

The Uterus

The *cervix* is the bottom part of the uterus that protrudes into the vagina. Through the vagina, the cervix of a woman who has never been pregnant looks like a smooth pink button with a rounded face and a small central hole. At the mouth of the cervix (the *cervical os*), sperm cells enter the uterus and menstrual flow passes into the vagina. The *endocervical canal* (a thin tubelike communication between the mouth of the cervix and the cavity of the uterus) contains many secretory glands that produce mucus. The consistency of cervical mucus varies during different phases of the menstrual cycle in response to changing hormonal stimulation: just before or at the time of ovulation (when the egg is released

from the ovary), cervical secretions become thin and watery; at other times, these secretions are thick and form a mucus plug that blocks the entrance to the cervix.

The cervix has no surface nerve endings so it experiences little in the way of sexual feelings. If the cervix is removed surgically, there is no loss of sexual responsivity.

The *uterus* (womb) is a hollow muscular organ shaped like an inverted pear somewhat flattened from front to back. It is about 7.5 centimeters (3 inches) long and 5 centimeters (2 inches) wide. Anatomically, the uterus consists of several parts (Figure 3-6). The inside lining of the uterus (the *endometrium*) and the muscular component of the uterus (the *myometrium*) have separate and distinct functions. The inner lining changes during the menstrual cycle and is where a fertilized egg implants at the beginning of a pregnancy. The muscular wall facilitates labor and delivery. Both aspects of uterine function are regulated by chemicals called hormones, which also play a part in the growth of the uterus during pregnancy.

The uterus is held loosely in place in the pelvic cavity by six ligaments. The angle of the uterus in relation to the vagina varies from woman to woman; ordinarily, it is relatively perpendicular to the axis of the vaginal canal, but in about 25 percent, the uterus is tipped backward and in approximately 10 percent, it is tilted further forward. If the uterus is rigidly fixed in position by scar tissue or inflammation, it may be a source of pain during sexual activity requiring surgical correction.

The Fallopian Tubes

The *Fallopian tubes*, or oviducts, begin at the uterus and extend about 10 centimeters (4 inches) laterally (Figure 3-6). The far ends of the Fallopian tubes are funnel-shaped and terminate in long fingerlike extensions called *fimbria*, which

FIGURE 3–6
Front View of the Internal Female Reproductive System

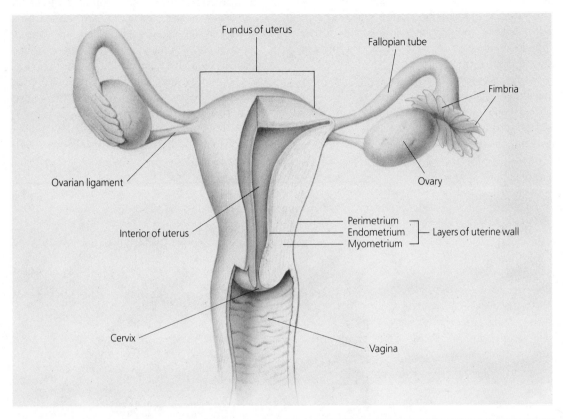

Fundus of uterus

Fallopian tube

Fimbria

Ovarian ligament

Ovary

Interior of uterus

Perimetrium
Endometrium — Layers of uterine wall
Myometrium

Cervix

Vagina

The uterus and vagina in this figure are shown partially cut away.

hover near the ovaries. The inside lining of the Fallopian tubes consists of long, thin folds of tissue covered by hairlike *cilia*. The Fallopian tubes pick up eggs produced and released by the nearby ovary and then serve as the meeting ground for egg and sperm.

The Ovaries

The *ovaries*, or female gonads, are paired structures located on each side of the uterus.

About the size of unshelled almonds (about 3 x 2 x 1.5 centimeters or 1.2 x 0.8 x 0.6 inches), they are held in place by connective tissue which attaches to the broad ligament of the uterus. The ovaries have two separate functions: manufacturing hormones (most notably, estrogen and progesterone) and producing and releasing eggs.

Before a baby girl is born, development of future eggs begins in her just-forming ovaries. About half-way through her mother's pregnancy, the girl's ovaries contain 6 or 7 million future eggs, most of which degenerate before birth. About 400,000 immature eggs are present in the newborn girl, and no new eggs are formed after this time. During childhood, continued degeneration reduces the number of eggs still further. The immature eggs are surrounded by a thin capsule of tissue forming a *follicle*.

When puberty arrives and girls begin to have menstrual cycles (see chapter 7), each cycle is marked by a process of maturation in which some immature eggs divide twice, splitting their genetic material in half. Through this process,

called *meiosis*, each young egg divides into four cells, only one of which is a mature egg (*ovum*). A mature egg is about 0.135 millimeters (1/175th of an inch) in diameter and is surrounded by a zone of jellylike material called the *zona pellucida* (Figure 3-7). A human egg is just barely visible, appearing as a speck smaller than the period at the end of this sentence. The other three cells, called *polar bodies* (Figure 3-8), have no known function, and eventually degenerate.

Although a number of different follicles begin growing in each cycle, usually only one devel-

FIGURE 3–7
Photomicrograph of a Human Egg in a Secondary Follicle

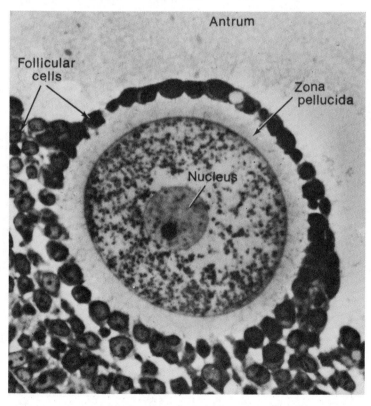

FIGURE 3–8
Development of Sperm Cells and Ovum

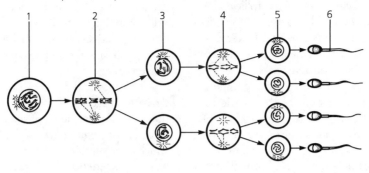

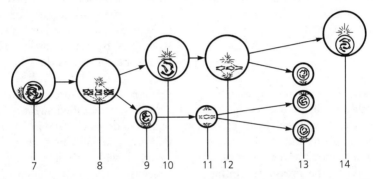

Development of sperm cells (upper diagram)

Stages 1 and 2: Primitive germ cell no. 1, the primary spermatocyte. At stage 1, the chromosomes in the nucleus double lengthwise. At stage 2, the chromosomal pairs are arranged in a plane for meiotic division. This will give rise to two new cells each with half the normal complement of chromosomes.

Stages 3 and 4: Primitive germ cell no. 2, the secondary spermatocyte. At stage 3, the chromosomes in the nucleus again double longitudinally. At stage 4, the chromosomes are aligned in a plane for ordinary cell division, not meiosis.

Stage 5: Four sperm cell precursors, or spermatids, are produced from the original spermatocyte.

Stage 6: Mature sperm cells.

Development of an ovum (lower diagram)

Stages 7 and 8: The primitive germ cell, or the primary oocyte. At stage 7, the chromosomes in the nucleus double lengthwise. At stage 8, the chromosomes are aligned in a plane for meiotic division. This gives rise to a secondary oocyte and the first polar body, each with half the number of chromosomes.

Stages 9 and 11: First polar bodies. At stage 11, the chromosomes of the first polar body are arranged for ordinary cell division.

Stages 10 and 12: The second primitive germ cell, or the secondary oocyte. At stage 10, the chromosomes in the nucleus double longitudinally. At stage 12, the chromosomes are aligned in a plane for ordinary cell division, not meiosis.

Stage 13: Three secondary polar bodies are produced.

Stage 14: Mature ovum.

Source: Copyright © 1973, by Albert Bonniers Forlag, Stockholm, under the title *Se Manniskan*. English translation: Copyright © 1974 by Albert Bonniers Forlag, Stockholm.

ops to the point where it moves to the surface of the ovary and ruptures, releasing the egg in a process called *ovulation*. For every follicle that ovulates, about a thousand undergo various degrees of growth and then degenerate. Fewer than 400 follicles are usually involved in ovulation during the female's reproductive years.

After the release of the egg, the *granulosa cells* that made up the capsule of the follicle begin to enlarge, forming a structure called the *corpus luteum*. The corpus luteum produces hormones and is destined to degenerate within two weeks if pregnancy does not occur, but with conception, the corpus luteum continues to develop and provides important hormonal support during early stages of pregnancy.

The Breasts

Although the breasts are not reproductive organs, they are clearly part of the sexual anatomy. In American society, the female breasts have a special erotic allure and symbolize sexuality, femininity, and attractiveness. Prominent attention is devoted to the breasts in clothing styles, men's magazines, advertising, television, and cinema. This attitude is not universal by any means, and in some cultures, little or no erotic importance is attached to the breasts. For example, in Japan women traditionally bound their breasts to make them inconspicuous. Today, however, the westernization process has brought about changes in Japan and the breasts have become rather fully eroticized.

As the big-breasted female has become an almost universal sex symbol — the image used to promote everything from car sales to X-rated films — men and women have been bombarded on a daily basis with the not very subtle suggestion that a woman with large breasts has a definite sexual advantage. This has led to a number of harmful misconceptions. For example, men

and women alike have come to believe that the larger a woman's breasts are, the more sexually excitable she is or can become. Another fallacy, still firmly subscribed to by many men, holds that the relatively flat-chested woman is less able to respond sexually and actually has little, if any, interest in sex.

The fact is that there is absolutely no evidence to suggest that breast size bears any relation to a woman's level of sexual interest, to her capacity for sexual response, or to the ease with which she attains orgasm. Actually, many women experience very little sexual sensation when their breasts are fondled or caressed, and this is as true of those with large breasts as it is of those with small ones. Furthermore, the woman who does become sexually excited when her breasts are stimulated does so regardless of their size.

For all their erotic significance, breasts are actually just modified sweat glands. The female breasts undergo changes in size and shape during puberty, gradually becoming conical or hemispherical with the left breast usually slightly larger than the right (DeGowin and DeGowin, 1976). Each breast contains fifteen to twenty subdivided *lobes* of glandular tissue arranged in a grapelike cluster, with each lobe drained by a duct opening on the surface of the nipple (Figure 3-9). The glandular lobes are surrounded by fatty and fibrous tissue, giving a soft consistency to the breast.

The *nipple* is located at the tip of the breast and mostly consists of smooth muscle fibers and a network of nerve endings which make it highly sensitive to touch and temperature. The dark wrinkled skin of the nipple extends 1 or 2 centimeters onto the surface of the breast to form the *areola*, a circular area of dark skin with many nerve fibers and with muscle fibers that cause the nipple to stiffen and become erect.

The sexual sensitivity of the breast, areola,

FIGURE 3–9
External and Internal Anatomy of the Female Breast

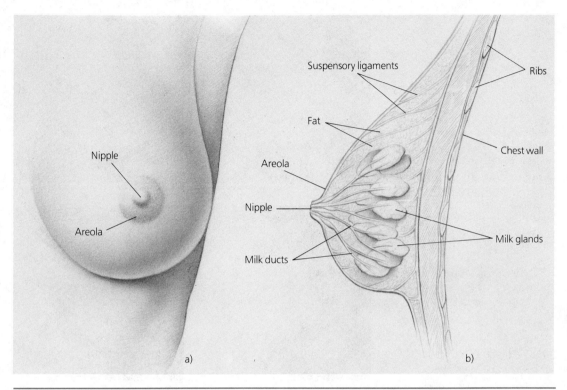

Suspensory ligaments

Ribs

Fat

Chest wall

Areola

Nipple

Milk glands

Milk ducts

Nipple

Areola

a)

b)

and nipple do not depend upon breast size or shape (Figure 3-10). Personal preference, learned habit, and biology all contribute to their responsiveness. Nevertheless, the American male's fascination with female breasts leads many women who consider themselves "flat-chested" or "underdeveloped" to seek to improve their sexual attractiveness and self-esteem by the use of exercises, lotions, or mechanical devices such as suction machines to enlarge their breasts. These methods, though widely advertised, do not work. For this reason, so-called breast augmentation surgery has become popular. In the past, liquid silicone was injected directly into the breasts to in-

crease their size, but this technique proved to be highly unsatisfactory since it led to many medical complications. Today, soft thin plastic pouches filled with silicone gel are implanted through a simple breast incision to increase breast size while retaining a natural appearing and soft feeling breast.

Conversely, some women are troubled by breasts that are too large. This condition, called *mammary hyperplasia* or *macromastia*, can be treated by reduction mammaplasty, a fairly simple operation to reduce breast size and weight. Other common breast problems include *inverted nipples* (the nipples are pushed inward), a harm-

FIGURE 3–10
Variations in Appearance of the Female Breast

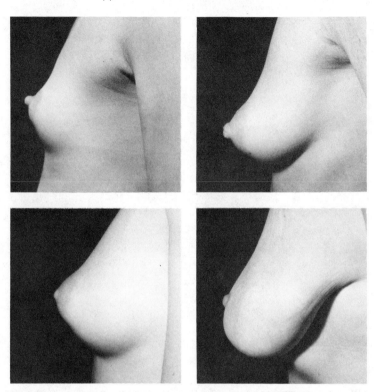

less anatomical variation that usually does not interfere with nursing, and *extra nipples*, which are minor errors of development that have no adverse health consequences but may be a source of embarrassment. Information on breast cancer and self-examination can be found in chapter 20.

MALE SEXUAL ANATOMY

It is not much of an exaggeration to say that penises in fantasyland come in only three sizes — large, gigantic, and so big you can barely get them through the doorway. . . .

Accepting your own merely human penis can

be difficult. You know it is somewhat unpredictable and, even when functioning at its best, looks and feels more like a human penis than a battering ram or a mountain of stone. But you do have one small advantage. You are alive and can enjoy yourself whereas the supermen of the model with the gigantic erections are unreal and feel nothing. (Zilbergeld, 1978, pp. 23 and 26)

The male sex organs are more visible and accessible than the female sex organs. Unlike the clitoris or vagina, the penis is involved directly in the process of urination so that boys become accustomed to touching and handling their penis at a relatively early age. The sexual aspects of the male organ are hard for a boy to miss. He learns about them by watching, touching, and playing with his penis as it becomes erect (a pleasurable experience) or by hearing stories and jokes that graphically portray the sexual and reproductive purposes of the penis. Despite such exposure, many males are not fully informed about the details of the anatomy and function of their sex organs.

The Penis

The penis is an external organ that consists primarily of three parallel cylinders of spongy tissue bound in thick membrane sheaths (Figure 3-11). The cylindrical body on the underside of the penis is called the *spongy body (corpus spongiosum)*. The *urethra* (a tube that carries urine or semen) runs through the middle of the spongy body and exits at the tip of the penis via the *urinary opening (urethral meatus)*. When the penis is erect the spongy body on the underside looks and feels like a straight ridge. The other two cylinders, called the *cavernous bodies (corpora cavernosa)*, are positioned side-by-side above the spongy body. All three consist of irregular spongelike tissue dotted with small blood vessels. The tissue swells with blood during sexual arousal causing the penis to become erect.

Internally, beyond the point where the penis attaches to the body, the cavernous bodies branch apart to form tips (*crura*) that are firmly attached to the pelvic bones. The penis has numerous blood vessels, both inside and apart from the cylindrical bodies; a pattern of veins is often visible on the outer skin of the erect penis. The penis also has many nerves, making it highly sensitive to touch, pressure, and temperature.

The tip of the penis, the *glans* or head, consists entirely of corpus spongiosum. This region has a higher concentration of sensory nerve endings than the shaft of the penis and is thus particularly sensitive to physical stimulation. Two

other areas particularly sensitive to touch are the rim of tissue that separates the glans from the shaft of the penis (the *coronal ridge*) and the small triangular region on the underside of the penis where a thin strip of skin (the *frenulum*) attaches to the glans (Figure 3-11). Many males find that direct stimulation of the glans may become painful or irritating and prefer to masturbate by rubbing or stroking the penile shaft.

The skin that covers the penis is freely moveable and forms the *foreskin* or prepuce at the glans. Inflammation or infection of the foreskin or glans may cause pain during sexual activity. Sometimes the foreskin sticks to the underlying glans when *smegma*, a naturally occurring substance of cheesy consistency made up of oily secretions, dead skin cells, dirt particles, sweat, and bacteria, is not regularly washed away from underneath the foreskin. This type of problem occurs only in uncircumcised men and is one argument in favor of routine circumcision.

Circumcision is the surgical removal of the foreskin. As a result of this minor operation, usually done shortly after birth, the glans of the penis is fully exposed. Circumcision is sometimes a religious practice, as in Islam or in Judaism, where it symbolizes the covenant with God made by Abraham. In the United States, it is often done routinely for nonreligious reasons, whereas it is less common in Canada and Europe.

The advantages of circumcision are primarily related to hygiene and health: smegma does not collect, the glans of the penis is easier to clean, conditions of inflammation or infection are less likely to occur, and cancer of the penis is less frequent. Although the rate of cancer of the cervix is considerably lower in the spouses of circumcised men (Green, 1977, p. 403), it is not certain that this is a cause-effect relationship (Rotkin, 1973). Opponents of routine circumcision see no clear reason for this operation and suggest that removing the skin protecting the

FIGURE 3–11
Anatomy of the Penis

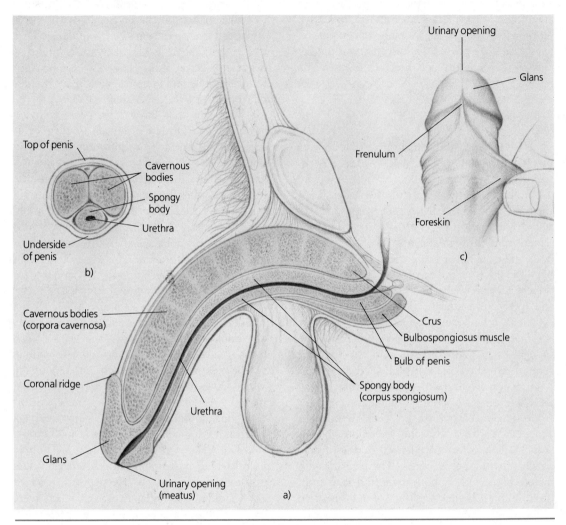

a) Internal side view of the penis. b) A cross-section of the penis. c) A view of the underside of the penis showing the location of the frenulum.

glans weakens the region's sexual sensitivity since it constantly rubs directly against clothing. Others believe that circumcision increases the risk of premature ejaculation (this is probably not true, since the foreskin of the erect uncircumcised penis retracts, exposing the glans, and researchers have not found a difference in the rates of premature ejaculation in circumcised vs. uncircumcised men). We are not aware of any believable evidence demonstrating that circumcision affects male sexual function one way or the other. In any event, uncircumcised men who practice routine hygenic care are unlikely to be at any major health disadvantage.

Recently, Greer and co-workers (1982) reported on a small number of men who were so dissatisfied with having been circumcised as infants that they underwent a complicated series of operations to reconstruct the foreskin. While the results were reported as uniformly pleasing to these men, it was also noted that the reconstructed foreskin (which was taken from the scrotum) has a noticeable difference in skin texture, color, and contour from the skin on the shaft of the penis. The series of operations takes up to a year to complete.

The appearance of the penis varies considerably from one male to another. These variations are due to differences in color, size, shape, and the status of the foreskin (circumcised or uncircumcised). Some examples of different male genitals are shown in Figure 3-12.

Concerns about penile size are common in males of all ages. Although the size of the nonerect penis differs widely from one male to another (the average length is approximately 9.5 centimeters or just under 4 inches), in adulthood this variation is less apparent in the erect state. Erection can be thought of as "the great equalizer" since men with a penis that is smaller when flaccid (nonerect) usually have a larger percentage volume increase during erection than men who have a larger flaccid penis (Masters and Johnson, 1966).

FIGURE 3–12
Some Variations in the Appearance of the Male Genitals
The middle drawing shows an uncircumcised penis.

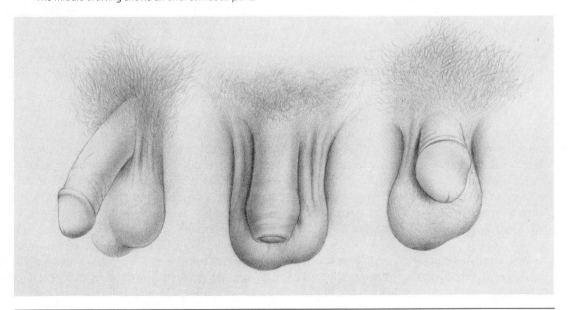

The Scrotum

The *scrotum* is a thin loose sac of skin underneath the penis that is sparsely covered with pubic hair and contains the testicles (testes). The scrotum has a layer of muscle fibers that contract involuntarily as a result of sexual stimulation, exercise, or exposure to cold, causing the testes to be drawn up against the body. In hot weather, the scrotum relaxes and allows the testes to hang more freely away from the body. These reflexes of the scrotum help to maintain a stable temperature in the testes, an important function because sperm production (occurring in the testes) is impaired by heat or cold. In response to cold, the scrotum lifts the testes closer to the body to provide a warmer environment. In hotter conditions, the scrotum loosens, thereby moving the testes away from the body and providing a larger skin surface for the dissipation of heat. Tightening of the scrotum with sexual arousal or physical exercise may be a protective reflex that lessens the risk of injury to the testes.

The Testes

The *testes* (the male gonads) are paired structures usually contained in the scrotum (Figure 3-13). The two testes are about equal in size, averaging 5 x 2 x 3 centimeters (2 x 0.8 x 1.2 inches) in adults, although one testicle generally hangs lower than the other. Most often, the left testis is lower than the right one, but in left-handed men the reverse is usually true. There is no significance attached to the relative height of the testes within the scrotal sac, but if one testis is considerably larger or smaller than the other there could be a medical problem and a doctor should be seen.

The testes are highly sensitive to pressure or touch. Some men find that light caressing or stroking of the scrotum or gentle squeezing of the testes during sexual activity is arousing, but many others are uncomfortable with touching in this region.

The testes have two separate functions: hormone and sperm production. The cells that manufacture hormones — most importantly, *testosterone,* which controls male sexual development and plays an important part in sexual interest and function — are called *Leydig cells.* Sperm production occurs in the *seminiferous tubules,* tightly coiled tubes of microscopic size that collectively measure almost 500 meters (more than a quarter mile) in length. The entire process of sperm production takes seventy days. Unlike the female who creates no new eggs after birth, the male produces sperm from puberty on, manufacturing billions of sperm annually.

A mature sperm is considerably smaller than the size of a human egg, being about 0.06 millimeter (1/500th of an inch) in length and thousands of times smaller than the egg in volume. Sperm are only visible with the aid of a microscope, which shows that they consist of three pieces: a head, a midpiece, and a tail (Figure 3-14). The head of the sperm contains genetic material (*chromosomes*) and a chemical reservoir (the *acrosome*). The midpiece contains an energy system that allows the sperm to swim by lashing its long tail back and forth.

The Epididymis and Vas Deferens

The seminiferous tubules (the tubes where sperm are produced) empty into the *epididymis,* a highly coiled tubing network folded against the back surface of each testis (Figure 3-13). Sperm cells generally spend several weeks traveling slowly through the epididymis as they reach full maturation. From here, sperm are carried into the *vas deferens,* long tubes (approximately 40 centimeters, or 16 inches) that leave the scrotum and curve alongside and behind the bladder.

FIGURE 3–13
Internal Side View of the Male
Reproductive System

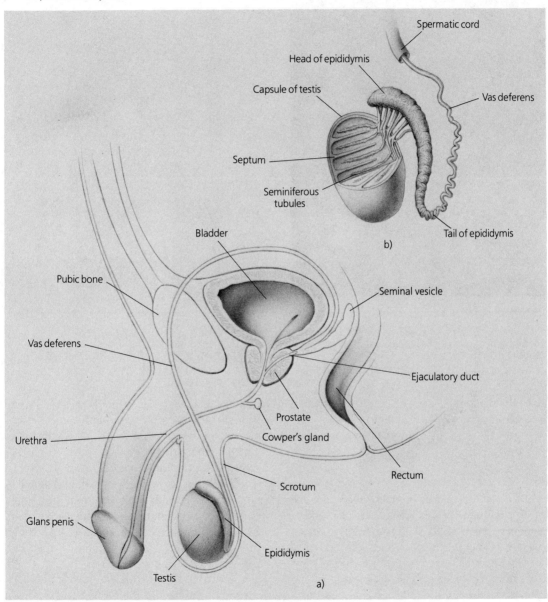

FIGURE 3–14
The Human Sperm

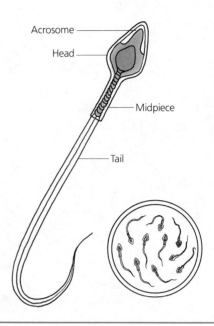

Acrosome

Head

Midpiece

Tail

The insert shows live sperm as seen under a microscope, where their active swim-
ming motion is apparent. The photograph of human sperm is taken with a
scanning electron microscope.

Both the right and left vas deferens are cut when a vasectomy is done (see chapter 6).

The Prostate and Accessory Organs

The *prostate gland*, normally about the size of a chestnut, consists of a muscular and a glandular portion. The prostate is located directly below the bladder and surrounds the urethra (the tube though which urine passes) as it exits from the bladder. The relationship of the prostate to the urethra is like a large bead (the prostate) on a string (the urethra). Because the

rectum (the lowest part of the bowels) is directly behind the prostate, the prostate can be examined by a physician during a rectal examination. This is important because the prostate can become infected or cancerous (chapter 20).

The prostate produces clear fluid that makes up about 30 percent of *seminal fluid*, the liquid that is expelled from the penis during ejaculation. The other 70 percent of seminal fluid comes from the *seminal vesicles* (Eliasson and Lindholmer, 1976; Spring-Mills and Hafez, 1980). These two small structures lie against the back portion of the base of the bladder and join with the ends of the vas deferens to form the *ejacula-*

Penis Size

We have already mentioned that many males are somewhat anxious about the size of their penis. More specifically, this concern is a comparative one: "How does *my* penis stack up against what others have?" This interest in penis size has several different components. First, it shows a concern for being "normal" – the same as everyone else. Second, it is related to a wish to be sexually adequate. Our society generally believes that "biggest is best," and the notion that a "big" penis will provide more sexual satisfaction to a woman is widespread. Actually, penile size has little physiological effect for the woman (although it may have positive or negative psychological significance) since the vagina accommodates its size equally well to an erect penis that is relatively smaller or larger in circumference. The length of the penis, which determines the depth of vaginal penetration, is also relatively unimportant, since the inner portion of the vagina and the cervix have few sensory nerve endings. Third, there is often an element of status-seeking in wishing to have a large penis. Finally, some males feel that a larger penis would make them more sexually attractive. Most of these points apply to both heterosexual and homosexual males.

In art and in the media (particularly erotic books, male magazines, and movies) there is a tendency to portray male genital size in "bigger than life" dimensions. This distortion reflects the triumph of anxious perception versus reality, literary and cinematic license (the use of particular camera angles or close-up shots, for example), and the deliberate selection of male subjects whose genital proportions are decidedly larger than average. Male readers

"Doris, I thought you told me size wasn't important!"

Playboy, April 1983, p. 182. Reproduced by special permission of *Playboy* Magazine; Copyright © 1983 by *Playboy.*

should remember, too, that there is a visual difference between the view you get of your own genitals (they appear shortened because of your viewing angle) and the view you get of someone else's penis size in the locker room or on the movie screen.

Recently, a team of Canadian researchers studied the psychological impact of penis size on sexual arousal. They found that reading erotic passages that differed only in the description of the size of the penis produced no differences in the levels of arousal of male or female undergraduates (Fisher, Branscombe, and Lemery, 1983). Thus, they concluded that "penis size may be as unimportant on a psychological level as it appears to be on a physical level."

There *is* a rare medical condition called *micropenis* in which the penis is formed properly but is miniature in size. This condition is marked by a penis length of less than 2 centimeters (approximately ¾ inch), and sometimes is due to a treatable deficiency of testosterone. In other circumstances, there is no means of increasing penis size by drugs, creams, gadgets, hypnosis, or hormones although there are advertisements for such "treatments" which exploit the myth that bigger is necessarily better.

Men who are preoccupied or extremely anxious about the size of their penis appear to be more likely to develop sexual difficulties than other men. These difficulties range from the avoidance of potentially sexual relationships because of embarrassment or worry to difficulty in obtaining or maintaining an erection due to poor self-confidence, tension, and anxiety. Fortunately, this type of problem can usually be overcome by brief sex counseling or therapy (see chapter 19).

tory ducts. These ducts in turn join the urethra, thereby creating a continuous tubing system that leads to the end of the penis.

On the average, there are 3 to 5 milliliters (5 milliliters = about one teaspoonful) of semen (seminal fluid plus sperm) per ejaculate. Although the concentration of sperm is highly variable, depending in part on the frequency of ejaculation, a count of 40 to 120 million per milliliter is considered normal. This means that there may be 120 to 600 million sperm in a single ejaculate.[5]

Seminal fluid ranges in color from whitish to tones of yellow or grey and has a creamy, sticky texture. Right after ejaculation, seminal fluid is rather thick but then liquefies quickly. It consists of water, mucus, and a large number of chemical substances that include sugar (providing an energy source for sperm), bases (for neutralizing the acidity of the male urethra and the female vagina), and prostaglandins (hormones that cause contractions in the uterus and Fallopian tubes, possibly aiding upward transit of sperm).

Cowper's glands are two pea-sized structures connected to the urethra just below the prostate gland. They produce a few drops of fluid which sometimes appear at the tip of the penis during sexual arousal but before ejaculation. Some men never notice this pre-ejaculatory fluid, while others may produce a teaspoonful or more of this slippery secretion. Although this pre-ejaculatory fluid may buffer the acidity of the urethra, there is no certainty about its function. Occasionally, the pre-ejaculatory fluid contains a small number of live sperm cells, accounting for at least some of the "failures" of withdrawal of the penis before ejaculation as a method of birth control.

---

[5] After a vasectomy, although there are no longer sperm in the ejaculate, the amount of fluid in the ejaculate remains the same.

The Breasts

The male breasts have a nipple and areola but have little underlying glandular tissue or fatty padding. The male nipple and areola seem to be less sensitive to touch and pressure than the same structures in adult females (Robinson and Short, 1977). Nevertheless, some males find that having their breasts or nipples stroked or licked is sexually arousing. Others do not notice any erotic pleasure from such practices.

Sometimes one or both of a male's breasts may become enlarged. This condition, called *gynecomastia,* occurs in 40 to 60 percent of boys during puberty but usually disappears within a year or two (Kolodny, Masters, and Johnson, 1979; Lee, 1975). In adulthood, it may be caused by alcoholism, liver disease, thyroid disease, drug ingestion, or certain forms of cancer. When gynecomastia is so severe that it creates major psychological problems, it can be corrected by relatively simple surgery.

The male breasts can also become enlarged if a man takes estrogen over a period of time. As we will discuss in chapter 10, most male-to-female transsexuals undergo such treatment. We have also seen a case in which a man unwittingly took birth control pills for several months, causing the same result.

OTHER EROGENOUS ANATOMY

Many parts of the body besides those involved in reproduction are potential sources of sexual arousal in both sexes. Surprisingly, the largest sensory organ for both females and males is the skin itself. The insides of the thighs, the neck, and the perineum are often sources of sexual pleasure. In our genitally oriented society, where sex is often thought of as synonymous with intercourse, it is easy to overlook the impor-

A view from behind is sometimes sexy, too.

tance of touching and body-to-body contact as a form of intimacy and gratification. Stroking, caressing, and massage can be forms of nonverbal communication, sensual pleasure, or invitations to further sexual activity.

Some people are well aware of the erotic sensations they can experience from touch, while others pay little attention to this component of their sexual arousal. However, there are wide differences from person to person in such matters: for some, the skin outside the genital region has relatively little sexual input or may actually dampen sexual feelings (what would happen to your level of arousal if a touch felt persistently ticklish or irritating?); at the other extreme, some women can be aroused to the point of orgasm by having the small of their back rubbed without any other stimulus (Masters and Johnson, 1966). (However, the likelihood of being or encounter-

ing a female capable of reaching orgasm by back-rubbing alone is less than one in a million.)

The mouth, including the lips and tongue, is an area of high erotic potential. Kissing is one practice that uses the sensitivity of this region in a sexually stimulating fashion. In addition to the sensory signals activated by kissing, it is also an act of intimacy that can symbolize passion and penetration (think of the form of kissing called "French kissing" or "soul kissing" in which one partner's tongue enters the other's mouth). Oral-genital contact — stimulation of one person's genitals in a licking or sucking fashion by the partner's lips or tongue — is another common form of sexual stimulation.

The anus, rectum, and buttocks are also potentially erogenous areas. The anus is highly sensitive to touch and the insertion of a finger, object, or penis in the anus and rectum is part of some people's sexual activity. Anal intercourse is often thought to be primarily an act of male homosexuals. However, numerically speaking, far more heterosexual couples engage in this activity than homosexuals and many homosexual men have not had experience with this type of sexual behavior (see chapters 5 and 6 for a more detailed discussion).

The buttocks are regarded in some cultures as symbolic of female sexuality in much the sense that our society regards the female breasts. The buttocks are bulky groups of muscles covered by fat and skin, with a relatively sparse distribution of nerves sensitive to touch. The underlying muscles are important in the mechanical process of pelvic thrusting during sexual intercourse. As a target for spanking, the buttocks are sometimes provocative for those of both sexes who find this activity erotically arousing. As a visible part of the anatomy, the buttocks (especially when displayed in tight jeans, swim trunks, bikinis, or similar apparel) commonly serve as a form of sexual enticement.

Many other parts of the body can also have erotic allure. For instance, hair can be sensual or sexual: some women are turned on by their partner's hairy chest and some lovers like to stroke each other's hair. Well-developed muscles make males more attractive to some females, whereas others are less impressed or actually turned off by this "he-man" appearance. Nibbling an earlobe, caressing the face, and touching fingertips can all be part of a sexual encounter and all may be a source of excitation. Our attempt here is not to provide an exhaustive catalogue, but to demonstrate the wide range of what can be sexual.

We each have a unique appearance to our sexual anatomy and an even more unique experience of sexual feelings and interactions. As we have repeatedly stressed, the variations — even

anatomically — from one person to another are considerable. Unfortunately, some people are preoccupied with the notion that "biggest is best" and others believe that sexual satisfaction is mainly a matter of "pushing the right buttons." Instead, we believe that a mechanical view of sex often leads to a mechanical experience, whereas a view of sex as a matter of comfort, mood, and feelings combined with physical sensations and response is more likely to be fulfilling and fun.

SUMMARY

1. Sexual anatomy includes the organs of reproduction and the parts of the body that are potential sources of sexual pleasure. Accurate knowledge about sexual anatomy can help people distinguish between fact and myth and can lead to a better understanding of one's self and one's sexual partner.

2. The female vulva consists of the mons, the inner and outer labia, the clitoris, and the perineum. The clitoris is not a miniature penis. It is a unique organ, richly endowed with sensory nerves, that serves solely as a receptor and transformer of sexual sensations.

3. The opening of the vagina is partially covered by a membrane called the hymen, which is sometimes mistakenly thought to be a foolproof indication of female virginity. The vagina itself is an internal organ, capable of expanding and contracting, with relatively few sensory nerve endings except near its opening. The vaginal lining is similar to that found inside the mouth, and vaginal lubrication originates from this surface. There is currently considerable controversy over the possible existence of the "G spot," which is claimed by some to be an anatomic area in the front wall of the vagina that has a high degree of erotic sensitivity.

4. The uterus is a hollow muscular organ

part of which protrudes into the vagina (the cervix).

5. The male sex organs include the penis, scrotum, testes, and various internal structures. The penis is made up of three cylinders of spongy tissue with a rich network of blood vessels. There is great variation from male to male in the size of the nonerect penis, but with erection size differences tend to diminish.

6. The glans, or head, of the penis is covered by foreskin in the uncircumcised male, but is exposed in a male who has been circumcised. Circumcision has not been proven to have any effect, positive or negative, on sexual feeling or responsivity.

7. The scrotum is a sac of skin underneath the penis that contains the testes. Muscle fibers in the scrotum move the testes closer to or further away from the body in response to temperature changes or exercise in order to facilitate sperm production.

8. Sperm made in the testes are carried by a long tubing system (the epididymis and vas deferens) inside the body. Sperm are mixed with seminal fluid from the prostate gland and seminal vesicles to make up semen.

9. The breasts are basically modified sweat glands, but in our society the female breasts have assumed major sexual importance. Not all women find that breast stimulation is a sexual turn-on, and many women are concerned about the size (or lack of size) of their breasts.

10. The mouth, tongue, lips, thighs, buttocks, anus, and skin are other parts of the body often involved in sexual activity and can be a source of erotic arousal.

SUGGESTED READINGS

Ayalah, D., and Weinstock, I. J. *Breasts*. New York: Summit Books, 1979. An informal and informative look at how women of all ages react to their breasts.

Boston Women's Health Book Collective. *Our Bodies, Ourselves*. 2d ed. New York: Simon & Schuster, 1976. A readable and practical collection of facts and insights into female sexuality and reproduction.

The Diagram Group. *Man's Body: An Owner's Manual*. New York: Paddington Press — Two Continents Publishing Group, 1976. Although there are no really good books on the subject of male sexual anatomy, this straightforward book includes some interesting material and diagrams.

Federation of Feminist Women's Health Centers. *A New View of a Woman's Body*. New York: Simon & Schuster, 1981. A profusely illustrated guide to female anatomy and health care. Excellent color photos of the cervix and vulva.

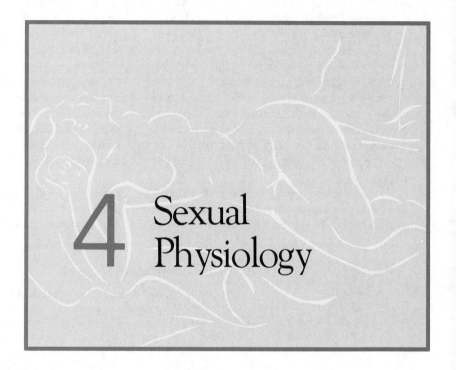

4 Sexual Physiology

An orgasm is like a rocket ride. First the ascent, then the blackout, and after that the burst of light as the golden apple turns into the golden sun and azure skies with a slow parachute until the earth appears below, streams and meadows or a city street. You slowly touch and bounce up again. ... Then you slowly touch once more, and then the afterglow and the deep refreshing sleep. (Berne, 1971, p. 233)

Orgasm can be a very mild experience, like a ripple or peaceful sigh; it can be a very sensuous experience where our body glows with warmth; it can be an intense experience with crying out and thrashing movements; it can be an ecstatic experience with momentary loss of awareness. (Boston Women's Health Book Collective, 1976, p. 45)

Sometimes I think orgasms are overrated. Getting there is more than half the fun. (Comment by a twenty-three-year-old woman, Authors' files)

P EOPLE INTERPRET their sexual responses in various ways, as these quotations show. But the basic details of how the body responds to sexual arousal are identical whether the stimulation comes from touching, kissing, intercourse, masturbation, fantasy, watching a movie, or reading a book. This statement does not imply that sex is just a mechanical process, any more than dancing or playing the violin are "only" mechanical because certain parts of the body are involved in these activities. Human sexual response is multidimensional, with input from feelings and thoughts, learning and language, personal and cultural values, and many other sources combining with our biological reflexes to create a total experience.

To understand the complexities of human sexuality, it is helpful to become familiar with the details of sexual physiology (the functions of our sexual anatomy). Learning about the various responses of the body during sexual arousal and about the forces that regulate them will increase your awareness of your own and your partner's responses and may clarify many misconceptions, myths, and questions about sex. It is also important to understand sexual physiology to comprehend many sexual disorders discussed later in the book.

SOURCES OF SEXUAL AROUSAL

When people talk about sexual arousal, they frequently say they are "turned on," "revved up," or "hot." Each phrase likens sexual arousal to an energy system, and as a starting point, this comparison is useful. From a scientific perspective, sexual arousal can be defined as a state of activation of a complex system of reflexes involving the sex organs and the nervous system. The brain itself, the controlling part of the nervous system, operates with electrical and chemical impulses "wired" to the rest of the body through the spinal cord and peripheral nerves. Signals from other parts of the body (like the skin, genitals, breasts) are integrated and focused in the brain, for without sexual thoughts, feelings, or images, sexual response is fragmentary and incomplete. At times, sexual arousal may be largely a cerebral event — that is, a person may be aroused while no visible physical changes are occurring elsewhere in the body. On other occa-

sions, genital sensations can be so intense that they block out awareness of almost everything else.

Sexual arousal can occur under a wide variety of circumstances. It may be the result of voluntary actions such as kissing, hugging, reading a sexy book, or going to an erotic movie. Sexual arousal can also be unexpected, unwanted, or even alarming. Consider, for instance, the following situations: (1) A twelve-year-old boy gets an erection while taking a shower in a crowded all-male locker room at school; (2) A female college student who is an ardent feminist becomes sexually aroused while watching a rape scene in a movie; (3) A female medical student is sexually excited when she examines an elderly male patient; (4) A male lawyer is sexually aroused by discussions with a female client who hires him to help her obtain a divorce. These people may be embarrassed or uncomfortable temporarily, but unexpected sexual arousal is normal and happens to most of us occasionally.

The sources of sexual arousal are also varied. The process of getting "turned on" may be triggered by direct physical contact such as a touch or a kiss, or may be activated by a verbal invitation ("let's make love"), a nonverbal message ("body language"), or a visual cue (such as nudity or a particular clothing style). It may also spring from fantasies or the most everyday occurrences — clothing rubbing against the genitals, the rhythm of a moving vehicle, or taking a bath or shower. Sexual arousal occurs in all age groups, from infants to the elderly, and it occurs when we are asleep as well as when we are awake. Men have about a half dozen erections during a night's sleep (the erections usually last five to ten minutes), and women have similar episodes of vaginal lubrication during sleep (Masters and Johnson, 1966; Abel et al., 1979). These reflex responses occur automatically and are not controlled by the specific content of dreams.

THE SEXUAL RESPONSE CYCLE

Before the 1960s, relatively little was known about the way the body responds during sexual arousal. Scientists were not convinced by Kinsey's claims that some women had more than one orgasm at a time (Pomeroy, 1966), and it was thought that vaginal lubrication was produced by glands in the cervix and Bartholin's glands. The mechanisms controlling erection and ejaculation in the male were incompletely understood. As a matter of propriety, sexual response was studied in animals, not people. In this climate, the results of an investigation of sexual physiology based on direct laboratory observation of more than 10,000 episodes of sexual activity in 382 women and 312 men first appeared (Masters and Johnson, 1966).

The findings of this study indicated that human sexual response could be described as a cycle with four stages: *excitement, plateau, orgasm,* and *resolution.* These stages correspond to varying levels of sexual arousal and describe the typical responses people have during sexual function. Although it is convenient to use the cycle as a model for descriptive purposes, remember that the stages are arbitrarily defined. They are not always clearly separated from one another and may vary considerably both in one person at different times and between people. Bear in mind also that the physiological processes of sexual response are not simply mechanical movements detached from thoughts or feelings but are part of the sexual involvement and identity of the whole person.

Although the sexual response cycle usually follows a consistent pattern of progression, the simplified schematic patterns of sexual response may vary widely, as Figure 4-1 reveals. Sometimes excitation is rapid and leads quickly to orgasm. On other occasions, excitement mounts slowly over a period of hours — while having a romantic, intimate meal, for example — and the rest of the cycle may seem brief in comparison. The plateau stage may not always lead to orgasm as the high levels of arousal that characterize this phase may dissipate; and a person may slip back to the excitement phase. If sexual stimulation stops, a person may also drift back into an unaroused state.

There are two basic physiologic reactions during human sexual response. The first is *vasocongestion,* an increased amount of blood concentrated in body tissues in the genitals and female breasts. The second is increased *neuromuscular tension* or *myotonia.* Here, tension does not refer to a negative physical state ("feeling tense") but to a build-up of energy in the nerves and muscles. Myotonia occurs throughout the body in response to sexual arousal, not simply in the genital region.

Although there are some differences in male and female sexual response, many details are similar. The physiology of sexual response is also the same for heterosexuals and homosexuals (Masters and Johnson, 1979).

Before we discuss the specific details of sexual response, a note of caution is in order. It is often tempting to equate the speed, size, and strength of sexual responses (such as erection, vaginal lubrication, or muscular contractions during orgasm) with the gratification a person experiences or with his/her proficiency as a lover. This is like saying that a bowl of chili is "better" than sirloin steak simply because chili causes a faster and larger secretion of digestive juices than steak. In both cases ("better" digestive response, "better" sexual response), the degree to which one experience is "better" than the other depends on your perspective *and* on your personal satisfaction.

Excitement

Excitation results from sexual stimulation which may be physical, psychological, or a com-

FIGURE 4–1
The Sexual Response Cycle

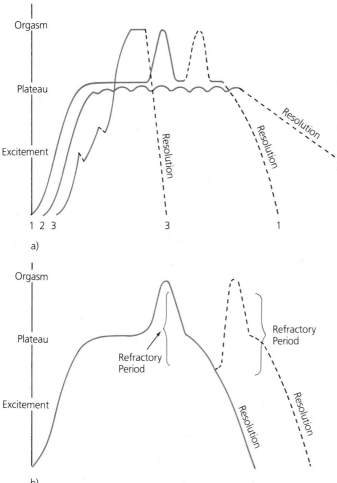

a) Three representative variations of female sexual response. Pattern 1 shows multiple orgasm; pattern 2 shows arousal that reaches the plateau level without going on to orgasm (note that resolution occurs very slowly); and pattern 3 shows several brief drops in the excitement phase followed by an even more rapid resolution phase.
b) The most typical pattern of male sexual response. The dotted line shows one possible variation: a second orgasm and ejaculation occurring after the refractory period is over. Numerous other variations are possible, including patterns that would match 2 and 3 of the female response cycle.

Source: From Masters and Johnson, 1966. © 1966 by William H. Masters and Virginia E. Johnson.

bination of the two. Sexual responses are like other physiologic processes that may be triggered not only by direct physical contact but by vision, smell, thought, or emotion. For example, thinking about food, smelling fresh baked goods, or watching a television commercial may prompt salivation and gastric acid production; and fear may activate a complex set of reflexes including sweating, a faster pulse rate, and increased blood pressure.

FEMALE

The first sign of sexual excitation in the female is the appearance of vaginal lubrication, which starts ten to thirty seconds after the onset of sexual stimulation. Vaginal lubrication occurs because vasocongestion in the walls of the vagina leads to moisture seeping across the vaginal lining in a process called *transudation*. Beads of vaginal secretion first appear as isolated droplets which flow together and eventually moisten the entire inner surface of the vagina. Early in the excitement stage the quantities of fluid may be so small that neither the woman nor her partner notices it. As vaginal lubrication increases, it sometimes flows out of the vagina, moistening the labia and the vaginal opening, but this depends on the woman's position and the type of sexual play going on.

The consistency, quantity, and odor of vaginal lubrication varies considerably from one woman to another and also varies in the same woman from time to time. Contrary to commonly held beliefs, the amount of vaginal lubrication is *not* necessarily indicative of the woman's level of sexual arousal, and the presence of vaginal lubrication does not mean the woman is "ready" for intercourse. Vaginal lubrication makes insertion of the penis into the vagina easier and smoother and prevents discomfort during intravaginal thrusting.

Other changes also occur in women during the excitement phase. The inner two-thirds of the vagina expand, the cervix and uterus are pulled upward, and the outer lips of the vagina flatten and move apart (see Figure 4-2). In addition, the inner lips of the vagina enlarge in diameter, and the clitoris increases in size as a result of vasocongestion. A woman's nipples typically become erect during the excitement phase as a result of contractions of small muscle fibers. Late in the excitement phase (again as a result of vasocongestion), the veins on the breasts become

more visible and there also may be a small increase in breast size.

MALE

The most prominent physical sign of sexual excitation in men is erection of the penis, which usually occurs within a few seconds after sexual stimulation starts (Figure 4-3). Although this response may seem very different from vaginal lubrication, they are parallel events that both occur because of vasocongestion. Erection results from the spongy tissues of the penis rapidly filling with blood. It is not certain at present whether engorgement occurs because the veins that drain the penis cannot keep up with this rapid filling or if special structures called "polsters" in the blood vessels of the penis limit outflow (Weiss, 1972; Krane and Siroky, 1981). Whatever the exact mechanism, the increased size and firmness of the erect penis are due to increased fluid pressure: erection can thus be viewed in simplest terms as a hydraulic event. Despite this seeming mechanical simplicity, a man may be physically and/or psychologically aroused and not have a firm erection, particularly under conditions of anxiety or fatigue. Contrary to some common misconceptions, there is neither a bone in the human penis (although erections are sometimes called "boners") nor a penis muscle that controls the process of erection.[1]

In addition to erection, the skin ridges of the scrotum begin to smooth out and the testes are partially drawn toward the body. Late in the ex-

---

[1] Many animals have a penis bone (*os penis*). The late Dr. Francis Ryan, a zoologist who taught a popular course on comparative anatomy at Columbia University, delighted in waving a large, baseball bat-sized bone in the air and asking, "Does anyone know what this is?" After no response from his all-male class, he would declare, "This, gentlemen, is the *os penis* of the Arctic Whale." He would pause then for effect before saying, "Life in the Arctic is a stiff proposition."

citement phase, the testes increase slightly in size. Nipple erection occurs during excitation for some men but not others.

Although many people think of male sexual response as nearly instantaneous and constant, in real life it does not always happen this way. Literary descriptions of a "pulsating," "throbbing," or "steel-hard" penis are common but often fictional. As Zilbergeld (1978, p. 24) observes, in our unrealistic expectations, "The mere sight or touch of a woman is sufficient to set the penis jumping, and whenever a man's fly is unzipped, his penis leaps out. ... Nowhere does a penis merely mosey out for a look at what's happening." In other words, a man is expected to be instantly erect at the drop of a bra, which of course creates a dilemma for anyone who finds that his arousal is not so dramatic or visible.

VARIATIONS IN EXCITEMENT

As we have seen, the physical changes of the excitement phase are neither constant nor always increasing for men and women. Mental or physical distractions can and often do decrease the build-up of sexual tension that is the hallmark of excitement. A honking horn, a knock on the door, an inopportune telephone ring, a shift in position, a muscle cramp, or a growling stomach are among the innumerable possible distractions. In addition, changes of tempo or manner of direct sexual stimulation can also temporarily disrupt sexual arousal, just as too much of a particular caress may temporarily cause a dulling of sensations.

Some people become upset or worried if their initial sexual arousal does not build steadily to a shattering peak. If a man's erection recedes even briefly, he may think "I'm losing it" or his partner may wonder "What am I doing wrong?" If a woman's vagina seems to get dry or her nipples lose their erection, she (or her partner) may have the same concerns. As a result, sexual spontaneity is likely to be lessened and awareness of body sensations is reduced. In such situations, the initial worry often becomes a self-fulfilling prophecy.

Vasocongestive mechanisms of sexual arousal wax and wane in everyone, just as most biological processes fluctuate a bit. An erection may be diminishing in firmness or size, or vaginal lubrication may seem to cease, although physical sensations and neuromuscular tension indicate that the man and woman are clearly nearing the plateau phase of the sexual response cycle. In this example, if the partners become alarmed or give up because they "see" that their physical response is less than what they want or expect it to be, they are not really giving themselves a chance.

Plateau

In the excitement phase, there is a marked increase in sexual tension above baseline (unaroused) levels. As Figure 4-1 shows, in the plateau phase high levels of sexual arousal are maintained and intensified, potentially setting the stage for orgasm. The duration of the plateau phase varies widely. For men who have difficulty controlling ejaculation, this phase may be exceptionally brief. In some women, a short plateau phase may precede a particularly intense orgasm. For other people, a long, leisurely time at the plateau level is an intimate and erotic "high" that may be a satisfying end in its own right.

FEMALE

During the plateau phase in women prominent vasocongestion in the outer third of the vagina causes the tissues to swell. This reaction, called the *orgasmic platform*, narrows the opening of the vagina by 30 percent or more (Figure 4-2). One reason penis size is not so important to a woman's physical stimulation during inter-

FIGURE 4–2
Internal Changes in the Female Sexual Response Cycle

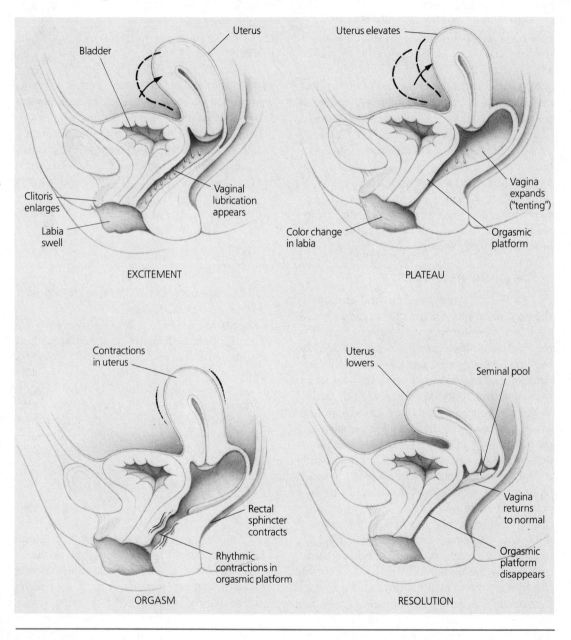

EXCITEMENT

- Bladder
- Uterus
- Clitoris enlarges
- Labia swell
- Vaginal lubrication appears

PLATEAU

- Uterus elevates
- Vagina expands ("tenting")
- Orgasmic platform
- Color change in labia

ORGASM

- Contractions in uterus
- Rectal sphincter contracts
- Rhythmic contractions in orgasmic platform

RESOLUTION

- Uterus lowers
- Seminal pool
- Vagina returns to normal
- Orgasmic platform disappears

FIGURE 4–3
External and Internal Changes in the Male Sexual Response Cycle

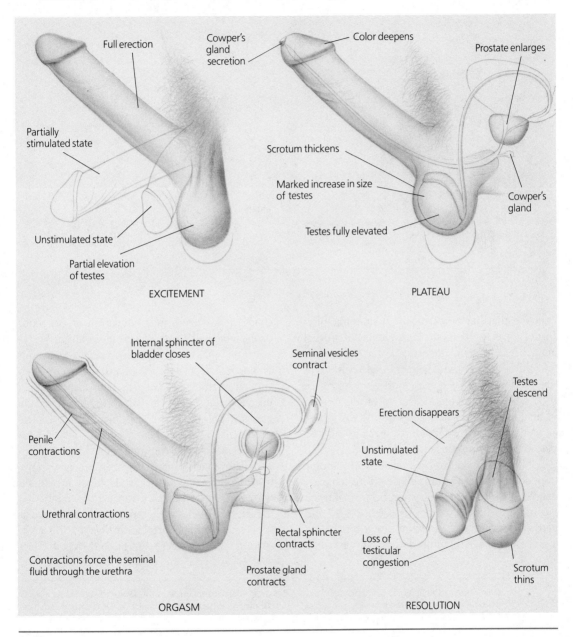

EXCITEMENT

- Full erection
- Partially stimulated state
- Unstimulated state
- Partial elevation of testes

PLATEAU

- Cowper's gland secretion
- Color deepens
- Prostate enlarges
- Scrotum thickens
- Marked increase in size of testes
- Testes fully elevated
- Cowper's gland

ORGASM

- Internal sphincter of bladder closes
- Seminal vesicles contract
- Penile contractions
- Urethral contractions
- Contractions force the seminal fluid through the urethra
- Rectal sphincter contracts
- Prostate gland contracts

RESOLUTION

- Testes descend
- Erection disappears
- Unstimulated state
- Loss of testicular congestion
- Scrotum thins

FIGURE 4–4
The Clitoris and Labia in the Female Sexual Response Cycle

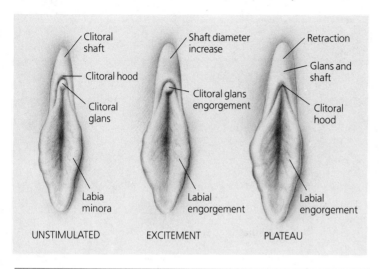

In the plateau phase, the clitoris seems to disappear beneath its hood, but it is actually quite engorged. The orgasmic phase is omitted because of lack of information.

course is that her outer vagina or orgasmic platform "grips" the penis if plateau levels of arousal are reached.[2] During the plateau phase, the inner two-thirds of the vagina expand slightly more in size as the uterus becomes more elevated in a process known as "tenting." The production of vaginal lubrication often slows during this phase as compared to excitation, especially if the plateau phase is prolonged.

The clitoris pulls back against the pubic bone during the plateau phase. This change, coupled with the vasocongestion occurring in the vaginal lips, hides the clitoris (Figure 4-4) and partially protects its head from direct touch. No loss of clitoral sensation occurs during these changes, however, and stimulation of the mons or the labia will result in clitoral sensations.[3]

The inner lips enlarge dramatically as a result of engorgement with blood, doubling or even tripling in thickness. As this happens, the inner lips push the outer lips apart, providing more immediate access to the opening of the vagina. Once this reaction has occurred, vivid color changes develop in the inner lips. The inner lips of women who have never been pregnant range from pink to bright red, while those in women who have been pregnant range from bright red to a deep wine color because of greater vascular supply delivering more blood flow to this area. Masters and Johnson (1966) noted that if effec-

---

[2] As we mentioned in chapter 3, some women may find a large penis to be important for *psychological* stimulation, and some women claim to receive more physical stimulation from a larger penis. As someone once said, "Different strokes for different folks."

[3] Marriage manuals in the 1950s all seemed to instruct the male that finding and stimulating the clitoris was the key to female sexual responsiveness. We wonder how many men panicked when this phase of clitoral retraction made the clitoris seem to disappear.

Sexual Physiology

FIGURE 4–5
Breast Changes During the Female Sexual Response Cycle

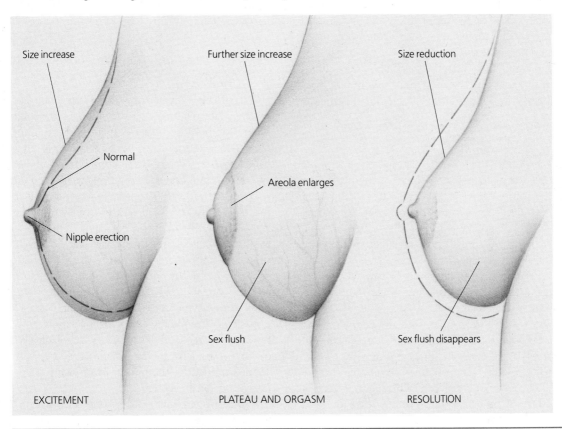

Size increase

Normal

Nipple erection

Further size increase

Areola enlarges

Sex flush

Size reduction

Sex flush disappears

EXCITEMENT

PLATEAU AND ORGASM

RESOLUTION

After orgasm, the rapid reduction in swelling of the areola often makes it appear as though the nipple has again become erect.

tive sexual stimulation continues once this "sex skin" color change appears, orgasm invariably follows. In more than 7,500 cycles of female sexual response, an orgasm never occurred without the preceding color change of the inner lips.

Late in the excitement phase, the areola of the female breast begins to swell. During the plateau phase, swelling continues to the point that the earlier nipple erection usually becomes obscured (Figure 4–5). Increases in breast size dur-

ing the plateau phase are striking in women who have not breast-fed a child, averaging 20 to 25 percent above baseline levels. For women who have previously nursed a child, this increase is much less pronounced or nonexistent because of their more developed venous drainage. However, this does not reduce erotic sensations in the breasts.

Late in the excitement phase or early in the plateau phase, a reddish, spotty skin color change resembling measles develops in 50 to 75 percent of women and about one-fourth of men. This "*sex flush*" generally begins just below the breast bone in the upper region of the abdomen and then spreads rapidly over the breasts and front of the chest. It may also appear on other parts of the body, including the neck, buttocks, back, arms, legs, and face. The sex flush results from changes in the pattern of blood flow just below the surface of the skin.

MALE

During the male's plateau phase (Figure 4-3), the diameter of the head of the penis near the coronal ridge increases slightly. This area often deepens in color due to pooling of blood. Vasocongestion also causes the testes to swell, becoming 50 to 100 percent larger than in the unstimulated state.

As sexual tension mounts toward orgasm, the testes not only continue to elevate but also begin to rotate forward so that their back surfaces rest in firm contact with the perineum (the area between the scrotum and the anus). Full elevation of the testes indicates that orgasm is imminent. In some men, particularly over age fifty, the testes elevate only partially. This seems to cause a reduction in ejaculatory pressure (Masters and Johnson, 1966).

Small amounts of clear fluid may sometimes appear from the male urethra during the plateau phase. This fluid is thought to come from Cowper's glands and, as mentioned in the previous chapter, occasionally carries live sperm. Many men experience a sensation of internal pressure or warmth during the plateau phase that corresponds to vasocongestion in the region of the prostate gland and seminal vesicles.

In addition to the sensations and changes just described, men and women experience several changes throughout their bodies during the plateau phase. A generalized increase in neuromuscular tension is particularly apparent in the buttocks and thighs. The heart rate increases, sometimes leading to a prominent awareness of heart thumping inside the chest. Breathing also becomes faster and the blood pressure increases, too.

Orgasm

If effective sexual stimulation continues late in the plateau phase, a point may be reached where the body suddenly discharges its accumulated sexual tension in a peak of sexual arousal called *orgasm*. Orgasm is sometimes called climax or coming. Eric Berne (1971, p. 3) observed, "Climax started off as a decent enough word, but it has been so overworked on the newsstands that it now sounds like the moment when two toasted marshmallows finally get stuck to each other." We also prefer the word orgasm. Biologically, orgasm is the shortest phase of the sexual response cycle, usually lasting for only a few seconds during which rhythmic muscular contractions produce intense physical sensations followed by rapid relaxation. Psychologically, orgasm is usually a time of pleasure and suspended thought — the mind turns inward to enjoy the personal experience.

Orgasms vary not only for one person at different times but also for each individual. Sometimes orgasm is an explosive, ecstatic avalanche of sensations, while others are milder, less intense, and less dramatic. While "an orgasm is an orgasm is an orgasm," one orgasm may differ from another just as a glass of ice water tastes better and is more satisfying if you are hot and thirsty than if you are cool and not thirsty at all. Different intensities of orgasms arise from physical factors such as fatigue and the time since the last orgasm as well as from a wide range of psychosocial factors, including mood, relation to partner, activity, expectations, and feelings about the experience.

For all these reasons, trying to define or

"Multiple? Are you kidding? It wasn't even fractional!"

describe orgasm is a difficult task because each individual's subjective experience includes a psychosocial as well as physiological dimension. Measuring intense muscular contractions during one orgasm does not mean that it is necessarily perceived as "better than" another orgasm with less intense bodily changes. A milder physiological orgasm may be *experienced* as bigger, better, or more satisfying than a physiologically more intense one.

FEMALE

Until the mid-twentieth century, many people (including some medical authorities) believed that women were not capable of orgasm. This belief undoubtedly reflected a cultural bias: sex was seen as something the man did *to* the woman for his own gratification. Women were told for centuries to "do their wifely duties" by making themselves available to their husbands for sex yet were also cautioned that "proper" women did not enjoy sex. Since a sign of physical

pleasure or orgasm was thought to be "unlady-like," it followed that women were not able to have orgasms. In other words, females were told "You can't have any physical sexual release, and even if you can, you shouldn't." It is now clear, however, that orgasm occurs in both sexes.

Orgasm in the female is marked by simultaneous rhythmic muscular contractions of the uterus, the outer third of the vagina (the orgasmic platform), and the anal sphincter (Figure 4-2). The first few contractions are intense and close together (at 0.8 second intervals). As orgasm continues, the contractions diminish in force and duration and occur at less regular intervals. A mild orgasm may have only three to five contractions, while an intense orgasm may have ten to fifteen.

Orgasm is a total body response, not just a pelvic event. Brain wave patterns show distinctive changes during orgasm (Cohen, Rosen, and Goldstein, 1976) and muscles in many different body regions contract during this phase of sexual response. In addition, the sex flush achieves its greatest intensity and its widest distribution at the time of orgasm.

Women often describe the sensations of an orgasm as beginning with a momentary sense of suspension, quickly followed by an intensely pleasurable feeling that usually begins at the clitoris and rapidly spreads throughout the pelvis. The physical sensations of the genitals are often described as warm, electric, or tingly, and these usually spread throughout the body. Finally, most women feel muscle contractions in their vagina or lower pelvis, often described as "pelvic throbbing."

Despite a popular misconception, most women do not ejaculate during orgasm. The erroneous belief that women ejaculate probably stems from descriptions in erotic novels of fluid gushing from the vagina as a woman writhes and moans at the peak moment of sexual passion. Such descriptions may sell books but are not particularly accurate.

Recently, however, it has been suggested that a somewhat different form of female ejaculation occurs. Various workers have claimed that some women expel semen-like fluid from the urethra at the time of orgasm (Grafenberg, 1950; Sevely and Bennett, 1978; Belzer, 1981; Perry and Whipple, 1981). It has been theorized that this fluid may come from a "female prostate," rudimentary glands (Skene's glands) around the urethra near the neck of the bladder that derive embryologically from the same tissues that develop into the prostate gland in males. In fact, some suggest that this "female prostate" is the anatomical site of the "G spot," but this idea — although stirring considerable controversy and conjecture — has not yet been proven scientifically (Bohlen, 1982; Kaplan, 1983). And, while a report on one woman with this ejaculation-like phenomenon indicated that the fluid was not urine (Addiego et al., 1981), another more detailed study of six other women who "ejaculated" showed that the fluid they expelled was indistinguishable from urine (Goldberg et al., 1983).

Further confusion in this area is caused by uncertainty over the number of women who have this ejaculation-like response. Perry and Whipple (1981) initially claimed that "perhaps 10 percent of females" had this response, but later reported that they were finding "closer to 40 percent" of women "had ever experienced" female ejaculation (Ladas, Whipple, and Perry, 1982, p. 60). In our own studies, a survey of approximately 300 women aged eighteen to forty revealed only fourteen who claimed to note any gushing or expulsion of fluid at orgasm. This observation is certainly more in keeping with our experience with well over a thousand women in our sex therapy program, where there have been only a handful of reports of fluid "ejaculated" by women with orgasm. However, we *have* observed several cases of women who expelled a type of fluid that was not urine (Masters, 1982).

Although it is clear that at least *some* women experience this ejaculation-like response, it should be realized that a number of these cases represent a condition called *urinary stress incontinence* in which urine is expelled from the urethra due to physical straining such as occurs with coughing, sneezing, or sexual arousal. Since this condition is usually correctable either by the use of Kegel exercises or minor surgery, medical evaluation is warranted if a woman is bothered by such a response.

MALE

Orgasms in men, unlike those in women, occur in two distinct stages. In the first stage of orgasm, the vas deferens (the two tubes that carry sperm) and the prostate and seminal vesicles begin a series of contractions that forces semen into the bulb of the urethra (Figure 4-3). The man experiences a sensation of *ejaculatory inevitability* — that is, the feeling of having reached the brink

Describing Orgasm

Previous research has shown that expert judges were unable to reliably distinguish between written reports of male and female orgasms (Proctor, Wagner, and Butler, 1974). The sex of the person describing orgasm in the following examples from our files may surprise you.

1. Like a mild explosion, it left me warm and relaxed after a searing heat that started in my genitals and raced to my toes and head.
2. Suddenly, after the tension built and built, I was soaring in the sky, going up, up, up, feeling the cool air rushing by. My insides were tingling and my skin was cool. My heart was racing in a good way, and breathing was a job.
3. Throbbing is the best word to say what it is like. The throbbing starts as a faint vibration, then builds up in wave after wave where time seems to stand still.
4. When I come it's either like an avalanche of pleasure, tumbling through me, or like a refreshing snack – momentarily satisfying, but then I'm ready for more.
5. My orgasms feel like pulsating bursts of energy starting in my pelvic area and then engulfing my whole body. Sometimes I feel like I'm in freefall, and sometimes I feel like my body's an entire orchestra playing a grand crescendo.
6. An orgasm feels like a dive, magnified many times over. First I feel my muscles tensing, then there's a leap into a cool lake, a sense of suspension and holding my breath, and

then my whole body feels relaxed and tingling.
7. Exhilaration is the best word I can find. I feel all pumped up and then, instead of exploding, I am one big wave of happiness and whooshing feelings.
8. Some orgasms feel incredibly intense and earth-shattering, but other times orgasms feel like small, compact, self-contained moments.
9. I feel like a cork popping out of a champagne bottle.
10. There is a warm rush from my toes to my head, with a strong, pulsing rhythm. Then everything settles down like a pink sunset.

1.M 2.F 3.M 4.F 5.F 6.M 7.F 8.M 9.F 10.M

of control — as these contractions begin. This sense of inevitability is quite accurate because at this point ejaculation cannot be stopped.[4] In the second stage of the male orgasm, contractions of the urethra and penis combine with contractions in the prostate gland to cause ejaculation or the spurting of semen out of the tip of the penis. The external appearance of semen does not occur until several seconds after the point of ejaculatory inevitability because of the distance semen must travel through the urethra.

During ejaculation, the neck of the urinary bladder is tightly shut to ensure that semen moves forward and to avoid any mixing of urine and semen. The rhythmic contractions of the prostate, perineal muscles, and shaft of the penis (creating the physical force that propels semen on its journey) occur initially at 0.8 second intervals, just as in women, and account for the spurting of the semen during ejaculation. After the first three or four contractions of the penis, the intervals between contractions become longer and the intensity of the contractions tapers off.

Male orgasm and ejaculation are not one and the same process, although in most men and under most circumstances the two occur simultaneously. Orgasm refers specifically to the sudden rhythmic muscular contractions in the pelvic region and elsewhere in the body that effectively release accumulated sexual tension and the mental sensations accompanying this experience. Ejaculation refers to the release of semen, which sometimes can occur without the presence of orgasm. Orgasm without ejaculation is common in boys before puberty (Kinsey, 1948) and can also occur if the prostate is diseased or with the use of some drugs. Ejaculation without orgasm is less common but can occur in certain cases of neurological illness.

In *retrograde ejaculation*, the bladder neck does not close off properly during orgasm so that semen spurts backwards into the bladder. This condition occurs in some men with multiple sclerosis, diabetes, or certain types of prostate surgery. There are no harmful physical effects, but infertility results and the man may have a different sensation during ejaculation.

The subjective experience of orgasm in men starts quite consistently with the sensation of deep warmth or pressure (sometimes accompanied by throbbing) that corresponds to ejaculatory inevitability. Orgasm is then felt as sharp, intensely pleasurable contractions involving the anal sphincter, rectum, perineum, and genitals which some men describe as a sensation of pumping. A different feeling, sometimes called a warm rush of fluid or a shooting sensation, describes the actual process of semen traveling through the urethra. In general, men's orgasms tend to be more uniform than women's, although all male orgasms are certainly not identical.

During the orgasmic phase in both sexes, there are high levels of myotonia evident throughout the body. Late in the plateau phase or during orgasm, the myotonia is often visible in facial muscles, where a grimace or frown may be seen. While this expression is sometimes viewed by a partner as an indication of displeasure or discomfort, it is actually an involuntary response that indicates high levels of sexual arousal. Muscle spasms or cramps in the hands or feet may also occur late in the plateau phase or during orgasm, and at the peak of orgasm, the whole body may seem to become rigid for a moment.

CONTROVERSIES ABOUT FEMALE ORGASM

While many controversies about the nature of female orgasms exist, there are several that de-

---

[4] Women do not have a consistently identifiable point of orgasmic inevitability that corresponds to the stage of ejaculatory inevitability in the male response cycle. Distractions can interrupt women's orgasms, whereas if the male has reached "inevitability," orgasm occurs no matter what.

serve special mention. The first controversy originated with Freud, who believed that there were two types of female orgasm, a clitoral and a vaginal orgasm. Freud stated that clitoral orgasms (those originating from masturbation or other noncoital acts) were evidence of psychological immaturity, since the clitoris was the center of infantile sexuality in the female. Vaginal orgasms (those deriving from coitus) were "authentic" and "mature" since they demonstrated that normal psychosexual development was complete. In his essay "Some Psychological Consequences of the Anatomical Distinction Between the Sexes," Freud wrote that "the elimination of clitoral sexuality is a necessary precondition for the development of femininity." Many women were considered neurotic or pushed into psychoanalysis because of this view (Schulman, 1971; Sherfey, 1972; LoPiccolo and Heiman, 1978).

Physiologically, all female orgasms follow the same reflex response patterns, no matter what the source of sexual stimulation. An orgasm that comes from rubbing the clitoris cannot be distinguished physiologically from one that comes from intercourse or breast stimulation alone (Masters and Johnson, 1966). This does not mean that all female orgasms feel the same, have the same intensity, or are identically satisfying. As discussed earlier, feeling and intensity are matters of perceptions, and satisfaction is influenced by many factors.

Some women prefer orgasms that occur as a result of intercourse, while others prefer masturbatory orgasms. Those who prefer coital orgasms often say that the overall experience is more satisfying, but the actual orgasm is less direct and intense. One recent study notes that many women find masturbatory orgasms to be more satisfying than coital ones, perhaps because the woman is not affected by her partner's style, needs, or tempo (Hite, 1977). In other reports, attempts have been made to differentiate between "vulval orgasm," "uterine orgasm," and "blended

orgasm" (Singer and Singer, 1972), or other classifications of orgasmic types (Fox and Fox, 1969; Clark, 1970; Fisher, 1973; Bohlen et al., 1982). Recently, Ladas, Whipple, and Perry (1982) have claimed that stimulation of the "G spot" produces a completely different type of orgasm than stimulation of the clitoris: one in which no orgasmic platform forms, and in which the uterus, instead of elevating and expanding the inner portion of the vagina, "seems to be pushed down and the upper portion of the vagina compresses." However, data to support these claims have not yet been published. Despite the continued controversy about "types" of female orgasms, the idea that one type is immature or less good than another has been generally discarded (Masters and Johnson, 1966; Sherfey, 1972; Hite, 1977; Barbach, 1982).

A second controversy about female orgasm is the question of whether or not all women in good health are able to experience a coital orgasm without any other type of simultaneous stimulation. While Masters and Johnson (1966) and others (Sherfey, 1972; Barbach, 1980) believe all women have this ability, some sexologists believe that there may be a group of women who do not. Helen Kaplan (1974, p. 374) seems to favor the latter view when she says "this pattern may represent a normal variant of female sexuality, at least for some women." And various studies show that the number of women who experience orgasm regularly during intercourse is about 40 to 50 percent (Kinsey et al., 1953; Fisher, 1973; Hite, 1977; Wilcox and Hager, 1980). Many authorities believe that lack of coital orgasm is usually caused by factors such as anxiety, poor communication between partners, hostility, distrust, or low self-esteem. However, if certain females are incapable of experiencing a sexual reflex due to physiological factors (Brindley and Gillan, 1982), it would have implications in diagnosing and treating some women's sexual problems as discussed in chapter 19.

Another controversial area has to do with the role of the muscles surrounding the vagina in orgasm. Both Arnold Kegel (a surgeon who was the inventor of the "Kegel exercises") and other workers (Perry and Whipple, 1981; Ladas, Whipple, and Perry, 1982; Graber, 1982) claim that the condition of the pubococcygeus muscle (PC muscle) is an important determinant of the occurrence of orgasms in women. However, other studies fail to document any correlation between PC muscle strength and female orgasmic responsiveness (Sultan and Chambles, 1982) and have also found that using the Kegel exercises did not improve orgasmic responsivity in nonorgasmic women (Trudel and Saint Laurent, 1983).

Finally, although many observers believe that most women don't feel that orgasm is a necessity for sexual satisfaction, a recent study by Waterman and Chiauzzi (1982) found that "orgasm consistency was significantly related to sexual satisfaction in females but not in males." While this doesn't mean that women who have the most frequent orgasms are happiest sexually, it does imply that not having orgasms (or not having them very often) may correlate with sexual dissatisfaction.

Resolution Phase

There is a major difference between male and female sexual response immediately following orgasm. Generally, females have the physical capability of being *multiorgasmic* — that is, they can have one or more additional orgasms within a short time without dropping below the plateau level of sexual arousal (Figure 4-1a, pattern 1). Being multiorgasmic depends on both continued effective sexual stimulation and sexual interest, neither of which is consistently present for most women. For this reason, some women never experience multiple orgasms, and others are multiorgasmic in only a small fraction of their sexual experiences. It is unusual for a woman to have multiple orgasms during most of her sexual activity.

Interestingly, multiple orgasm in females seems to occur more frequently during masturbation than intercourse. This may reflect several factors: (1) the relative ease of continuing sexual stimulation, (2) the lack of distraction by concerns about one's partner, and (3) the more frequent use of sexual fantasy by women during masturbation as compared to intercourse.

Men, on the other hand, are not able to have multiple orgasm if it is defined in the same way. Immediately after ejaculation, the male enters a *refractory period* (Figure 4-1b), a recovery time during which further orgasm or ejaculation is physiologically impossible. A partial or full erection may be maintained during the refractory period, but usually the erection subsides quickly. There is great variability in the length of the refractory period both within and between individual males, and it may last anywhere from a few minutes to many hours. For most males, this interval usually gets longer with each repeated ejaculation within a time span of several hours. In addition, as a man gets older, the refractory period gets longer. In 1978, Robbins and Jensen reported on 13 men who said they had multiple orgasms by withholding ejaculation (only one of whom they studied in the laboratory), but their claims have not yet been fully substantiated. However, it does appear that at least a few men have the capacity to have multiple orgasms before a true refractory period sets in, although it should be stressed that this does not happen once ejaculation has occurred.

The period of return to the unaroused state is called the resolution phase. In this phase, which includes the refractory period in men, the anatomic and physiologic changes that occurred during the excitement and plateau phase reverse. In females, the orgasmic platform disappears as the muscular contractions of orgasm pump blood away from these tissues. The uterus moves back into its resting position, the color changes of the labia disappear, the vagina begins to shorten in both width and length, and the clitoris returns to its usual size and position (Figure 4-2). If the breasts enlarged earlier in the response cycle, they decrease in size at this time, and their areolar tissue flattens out faster than the nipples themselves, giving the impression that the nipples are again erect (Figure 4-5). Stimulation of the clitoris, the nipples, or the vagina may be unpleasant or irritating during the post-orgasmic phase.

In males, erection diminishes in two stages. First, as a result of orgasmic contractions that pump blood out of the penis, there is a partial loss of erection. In the slower second stage of this process, genital blood flow returns to baseline (unaroused) patterns. The testes decrease in size and descend into the scrotum, moving away from the body, unless sexual stimulation is continued (Figure 4-3).

As both men and women return to their unaroused state, the "sex flush" disappears and prominent sweating is sometimes noticeable. A fast, heavy breathing pattern may be present just after orgasm, accompanied by a fast heart beat, but both recede gradually as the entire body relaxes.

If there has been considerable excitement but orgasm has not occurred, resolution takes a longer time. Although certain changes occur quickly (such as disappearance of the orgasmic platform in women and the erection in men), there is sometimes a lingering sensation of pelvic heaviness or aching that is due to continued vasocongestion. This may create a condition of some discomfort, particularly if high levels of arousal were prolonged. Testicular aching ("blue balls") in men and pelvic congestion in women may be relieved by orgasms that occur during sleep or by masturbation. Although *nocturnal emissions* ("wet dreams") in young males are well known, females also can experience orgasm during sleep (Kinsey et al., 1953).

COMMON MYTHS ABOUT SEXUAL RESPONSE

In the preceding chapter, we discussed a number of misconceptions related to sexual anatomy and sexual satisfaction (e.g., a bigger penis provides more stimulation to the female during intercourse). In light of the physiologic responses just considered, we can now debunk some other common myths about sex.

One commonly held belief is that males have a greater sexual capacity than females. The reverse is actually true. From the viewpoint of physical capability, females have an almost unlimited orgasmic potential, while men, because of the refractory period, are unable to have a rapid series of ejaculations. (While women do not have a true refractory period, orgasmic potential is undoubtedly restricted by fatigue. There may be other physiologic limitations not known at present.) Many males also find it difficult to obtain another erection shortly after ejaculation. From a mechanical perspective then, their capacity to participate in repeated intercourse usually does not match that of the opposite sex.

Another misconception about sexual response is that the male can *always* tell if his female partner had an orgasm. At times, the male may be unaware of his partner's orgasm because he is caught up in his own feelings of arousal or because he doesn't recognize the physical signs of female orgasm. This may occur either because his expectations are inaccurate, because he doesn't know what to expect, or because the accuracy of his sense of vision is lessened during high levels of sexual excitation. Some males are fooled by a partner who "fakes" orgasm by means of loud moans and groans, intense pelvic thrusting, heavy breathing, and voluntary contractions of the outer portion of the vagina.[5]

The notion that all orgasms are intense, earth-shattering, explosive events is another widespread sexual misconception that can probably be traced to the literary imagination. Although the reflex mechanisms of orgasmic response are fairly uniform, some orgasms are mild, fluttery, or warm, while others are blockbusters. These differences arise from variations in a person's physical state such as being tired, tense, having a sore throat or headache, or from variations in the emotions that accompany the sexual experience. The sensations of any physiologic process — drinking a glass of water, eating a meal, breathing, urinating, or sex — vary in different times and circumstances.

In the 1950s, the idea that "mutual orgasm" (both partners experiencing orgasm at the same time) was the ultimate peak in sexual pleasure became popular and was advocated enthusiastically in numerous marriage manuals. Many people tried to "fine tune" the timing of their responses, but working at sex usually resulted in a loss of spontaneity and fun. While mutual orgasm can be exhilarating, each person can be so wrapped up in his or her own response that the experience of the partner's orgasm is missed.

HORMONAL REGULATION OF SEXUAL FUNCTION AND BEHAVIOR

The physiologic processes of sex are not only vascular and neuromuscular. An important part of sexual physiology is under the control of the endocrine system, which consists of ductless glands that produce chemical substances called *hormones*. Hormones are secreted directly into the bloodstream where they are carried to tissues on which they act. Some hormones, such as cortisol (made in the adrenal glands, which lie just above the kidneys), are necessary for life itself and influence a wide range of body functions. Other hormones are required for reproduction or sexual development. Here, we will consider the hormones that influence our sexual function.

The Sex Hormones

The most important hormone in sexual function is *testosterone*. This hormone, sometimes called the male sex hormone, is actually present in both sexes. In a normal man, 6 to 8 mg of testosterone are produced per day, with more than 95 percent manufactured in the testes and the remainder in the adrenal glands. In a woman, approximately 0.5 mg of testosterone is made daily in the ovaries and the adrenals.

Testosterone is the principal biologic determinant of the sex drive in both men and women. Deficiencies of testosterone may cause a drop in sexual desire (Bancroft, 1978; Kolodny, Masters, and Johnson, 1979), and excessive testosterone may heighten sexual interest. In men, too little testosterone may cause difficulty obtaining or maintaining erections, but it is not certain whether testosterone deficiencies interfere with female sexual functioning apart from reducing sexual desire. However, there is no evidence whatsoever to suggest that because women have less testosterone than men, they have lower sexual interest. Instead, it seems that men and women have different levels of behavioral sensitivity to the effects of this hormone, with women actually being more sensitive to small quantities in their circulation (Persky et al., 1978; Kolodny, Masters, and Johnson, 1979; Bancroft, 1984).

---

[5] Men also sometimes resort to sexual fakery. For both women and men, this may be motivated by the wish to please their partner. For a fuller discussion, see chapter 19.

Estrogens, sometimes called female hormones, are also present in both sexes and are made primarily in the ovaries in women and in the testes in men. In women, they are important from a sexual viewpoint in maintaining the condition of the vaginal lining and in producing vaginal lubrication. Estrogens also help to preserve the texture and function of the female breasts and the elasticity of the vagina. In men, estrogens have no known function. It does not seem that estrogens are important determinants of female sexual interest or capacity, since surgical removal of the ovaries does not reduce the sex drive in women nor lessen sexual responsivity. Too much estrogen in males, however, dramatically reduces the sexual appetite and can cause difficulties with erection and enlargement of the breasts.

Progesterone, a hormone structurally related to both the estrogens and testosterone, is also present in both sexes. The effects of progesterone on sexual behavior and function have been studied primarily in animals, where it appears that large amounts suppress sexual interest. Some authorities speculate that it may also act as a sexual inhibitor in humans (Bancroft, 1984).

Regulatory Mechanisms

Two decades ago, it was thought that the "master gland" of endocrine function was the *pituitary*, an acorn-sized structure lying beneath the brain. It is now clear that the regulatory role of the pituitary is more like a relay station and that a portion of the brain itself — the *hypothalamus* — has primary control over most endocrine pathways.

The hypothalamus produces a substance called *gonadotropin releasing hormone* (GnRH) that controls the secretion of two hormones made in the pituitary gland which act on the gonads (ovaries and testes). *Luteinizing hormone* (LH) stimulates the Leydig cells in the testes to manufacture testosterone; in the female, LH serves as the trigger for ovulation (release of an egg from the ovary). *Follicle stimulating hormone* (FSH) stimulates the production of sperm cells in the testes; in the female, FSH prepares the ovary for ovulation.

The hypothalamus acts much like a thermostat in regulating hormonal function (Figure 4-6). Instead of reacting to temperature, as a thermostat does, the hypothalamus reacts to the concentrations of hormones in its own blood supply. For example, in adult males the amount of testosterone "registers" in the hypothalamus. If the amount is high, production of GnRH is turned off, leading to a drop in LH secretion by the pituitary. The decrease in LH in the bloodstream quickly results in reduced production of testosterone in the testes, and therefore lower amounts of testosterone are secreted into the blood. When the amount of testosterone reaching the hypothalamus drops below a certain level, it triggers the secretion of GnRH into the pituitary. The pituitary responds to this signal by sending more LH into the circulation, where it will soon reach the testes and cause an increased rate of testosterone production.

Hormones and Sexual Behavior

It is tempting to try to understand sexual behavior in terms of hormones. In many animal species, patterns of sexual interaction are tightly regulated by hormonal events which control both the sexual receptivity of the female (her willingness to mate) and the sexual interest (courtship behavior) of the male, as well as male mounting and penile thrusting (Hutchison, 1978). Testosterone and estrogen have been found in mammals, birds, reptiles, amphibians, and fish; in all of these groups, actions of sex hormones on the brain appear to be important determinants of sexual behavior (Kelley and Pfaff, 1978).

FIGURE 4–6
Endocrine Regulation in the Adult Male (a) and Female (b)

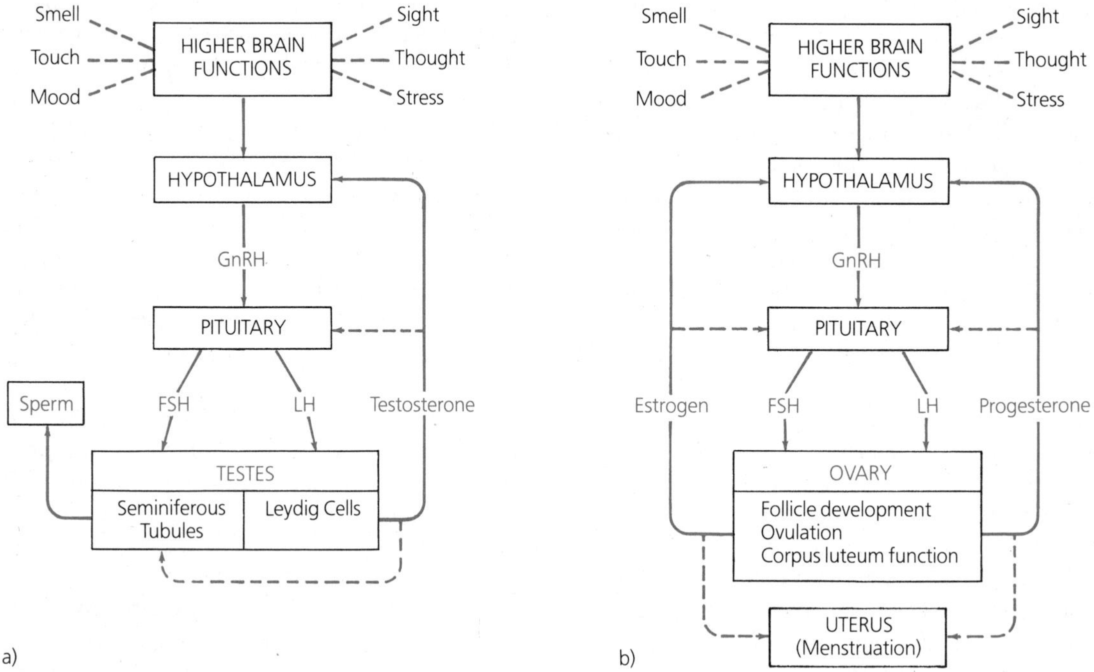

In humans, however, there is a more complicated relationship between hormones and sexual behavior. Although a marked testosterone deficiency usually reduces sexual interest in men or women, there are cases where this effect is not seen. Similarly, although many men with subnormal testosterone levels have difficulty with erection, others continue to have completely normal sexual function. Women who have low amounts of estrogen in their bodies do not usually lose their ability to be sexually aroused or to have orgasms. People's sex hormone levels do not "predict" their sexual behavior or interest.

Although there is no simple one-to-one relationship between sex hormones and human sexual behavior, fascinating questions about the role of hormones in sexuality abound. Later chapters will address such questions as: How do hormones influence sexual development (chapter 7)? Do hormones "cause" homosexuality (chapter 16)? What kinds of sexual disorders are caused by hormone imbalance (chapter 20)? We will now consider the hormonal patterns of the menstrual cycle and see whether they influence sexual behavior in women.

MENSTRUATION

Menstruation is a flow of blood that occurs about once a month in most women from approximately ages twelve to forty-eight. Although menstruation is a normal part of the female reproductive cycle, it is a subject of considerable misunderstanding and taboo. In ancient times, a menstruating woman was regarded as unclean and liable to pollute foods she handled, or as contagious and liable to cause illness or even death in others (Delaney, Lupton, and Toth, 1977). In the modern era, menstruation is sometimes seen as a physical and emotional handicap that makes women "inferior" to men (Koeske, 1976; Frieze et al., 1978; Sherif, 1980). Whether menstruation is called "the curse," "the monthlies," or "being on the rag," it is often referred to in negative terms. In this section, we will discuss the physiology of the menstrual cycle and consider the effects of menstruation on emotions and physical well-being.

Physiology of the Menstrual Cycle

The menstrual cycle is traditionally described as starting with the first day of menstrual flow (cycle day one) and ending the day before the next menstruation begins. The length of the cycle varies, normally ranging from twenty-one to forty days and averaging about twenty-eight days (Vollman, 1977). Very few women are so regular that they can accurately and consistently predict the length of each cycle on the basis of their past pattern of cycle lengths.

The menstrual cycle consists of three phases which we will describe in terms of an "average" twenty-eight day cycle (Figure 4-7). The *follicular phase* is the first portion of the menstrual cycle. Ovarian follicles, oval arrangements of cells around a young egg, begin to mature as FSH stimulates them. At the start of this phase, estrogen and progesterone levels are quite low and the uterus sheds its lining, resulting in three to six days of menstrual flow. Menstrual flow consists of a small amount of blood combined with tiny bits of tissue from the lining of the uterus, and the entire amount is usually only 2 or 3 ounces (4 to 6 tablespoons).

Midway in the follicular phase (around cycle days seven to ten), estrogen output from the ovaries increases, which acts with FSH to prepare the developing follicle for ovulation. Estrogen also causes the lining of the uterus to thicken, or proliferate, due to growth of glands, connective tissue, and blood vessels. Just before ovulation, estrogen levels reach a broad peak which acts on the hypothalamus to trigger the surge of LH and FSH released from the pituitary a day or two afterwards.

Ovulation, release of the egg from the ovary, typically occurs at about the fourteenth cycle day in most twenty-eight day cycles. However, we have studied cycles in which ovulation ranged from the ninth day to the nineteenth day of a cycle of this length, and in some menstrual cycles, ovulation does not occur at all (see chapter 5). Ovulation usually follows the LH peak by twelve to twenty-four hours. The ovulatory phase is the shortest phase of the menstrual cycle.

The third portion of the menstrual cycle is the *luteal phase,* which encompasses the time from immediately after ovulation until the start of the next cycle. This phase is named for the corpus luteum, the mass of cells left in the ovary after the follicle ruptures during ovulation. The corpus luteum produces large amounts of progesterone and estrogen, leading to increased levels of these hormones in this portion of the menstrual cycle (Figure 4-7). The progesterone causes the small blood vessels in the thickened endometrium to develop and produces coiling in the endometrial glands, changes that prepare the uterus to receive a fertilized egg if pregnancy occurs. The progesterone also registers in the hypothalamus, where it shuts off output of

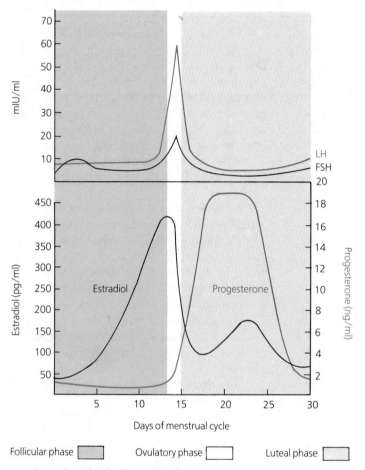

FIGURE 4–7
Hormone Changes During a Typical Menstrual Cycle

Follicular phase ☐   Ovulatory phase ☐   Luteal phase ☐

Source: Reproduced, with permission, from Benson, R. C. (editor), *Current Obstetric and Gynecologic Diagnosis and Treatment,* 3rd ed. Copyright 1980 by Lange Medical Publications, Los Altos, California.

GnRH, resulting in a rapid decline in LH and FSH from the pituitary. Unless the egg is fertilized, the corpus luteum degenerates ten to twelve days after ovulation and its hormone production drops drastically. The next menstrual flow occurs as the lining of the uterus sheds in preparation for regrowth in the next cycle. Menstruation is thus the result of abrupt withdrawal of hormone stimulation.

Menstrual Cycle Effects

Brief comments from three women who participated in studies of the menstrual cycle at the

If Men Could Menstruate

This excerpt from *Outrageous Acts and Everyday Rebellions,* by noted feminist author Gloria Steinem (1983), points out how perceptions might change if men had periods.

*　　　*　　　*

What would happen if suddenly, magically, men could menstruate and women could not?

Clearly, menstruation would become an enviable, boastworthy, masculine event:

Men would brag about how long and how much.

Young boys would talk about it as the envied beginning of manhood. Gifts, religious ceremonies, family dinners, and stag parties would mark the day.

To prevent monthly work loss among the powerful, Congress would fund a National Institute of Dysmenorrhea. Doctors would research little about heart attacks, from which men were hormonally protected, but everything about cramps.

Sanitary supplies would be federally funded and free. Of course, some men would still pay for the prestige of such commercial brands as Paul Newman Tampons, Muhammad Ali's Rope-a-Dope Pads, John Wayne Maxi Pads, and Joe Namath Jock Shields – "For Those Light Bachelor Days."

Statistical surveys would show that men did better in sports and won more Olympic medals during their periods. . . .

Male liberals or radicals, however, would insist that women are equal, just different; and that any woman could join their ranks if only she were willing to recognize the primacy of menstrual rights ("Everything else is a single issue") or self-inflict a major wound every month ("You *must* give blood for the revolution").

Street guys would invent slang ("He's a three-pad man") and "give fives" on the corner with some exchange like, "Man, you lookin' *good!*"

"Yeah, man, I'm on the rag!"

TV shows would treat the subject openly. (*Happy Days:* Ritchie and Potsie try to convince Fonzie that he is still "The Fonz," though he has missed two periods in a row. *Hill Street Blues:* The whole precinct hits the same cycle.) So would newspapers. (SUMMER SHARK SCARE THREATENS MENSTRUATING MEN. JUDGE CITES MONTHLIES IN PARDONING RAPIST.) And so would movies (Newman and Redford in *Blood Brothers!*).

Men would convince women that sex was *more* pleasurable at "that time of the month." Lesbians would be said to fear blood and therefore life itself, though all they needed was a good menstruating man.

Medical schools would limit women's entry ("they might faint at the sight of blood").

Of course, intellectuals would offer the most moral and logical arguments. Without that biological gift for measuring the cycles of the moon and planets, how could a woman master any discipline that demanded a sense of time, space, mathematics – or the ability to measure anything at all? In philosophy and religion, how could women compensate for being disconnected from the rhythm of the universe? Or for their lack of symbolic death and resurrection every month?

Menopause would be celebrated as a positive event, the symbol that men had accumulated enough years of cyclical wisdom to need no more.

Liberal males in every field would try to be kind. The fact that "these people" have no gift for measuring life, the liberals would explain, should be punishment enough....

In short, we would discover, as we should already guess, that logic is in the eye of the logician. (For instance, here's an idea for theorists and logicians: If women are supposed to be less rational and more emotional at the beginning of our menstrual cycle when the female hormone is at its lowest level, then why isn't it logical to say that, in those few days, women behave the most like the way men behave all month long?)

The truth is that, if men could menstruate, the power justifications would go on and on.

If we let them.

Source: From *Outrageous Acts and Everyday Rebellions* by Gloria Steinem. © 1983 by Gloria Steinem. Reprinted by permission of Holt, Rinehart & Winston, Publishers.

Masters & Johnson Institute show the great diversity in how women feel about menstruation:

> I have a rough time with my periods. First, I get irritable and depressed a day or two before my period starts — nothing seems to go right. Then, I have real bad cramps for two days. I have to stay in bed; it's sheer agony.

> A few days before my period, my breasts get swollen and tender, and I usually get a headache. Once my period starts, everything is back to normal.

> Menstruation is no big deal. One time when I was thirteen or so I had some cramping, but I really don't have any problems at all.

Mirroring this diversity, there is also considerable scientific controversy about the physiological and psychological effects of the menstrual cycle. In 1931 an American physician reported that estrogen causes "varying degrees of discomfort preceding the onset of menstruation," including "increased fatigability, irritability, lack of concentration, and attacks of pain" (Frank, 1931). High doses of X-rays were sometimes prescribed to knock out the ovaries in severe cases of this condition, which Frank called *premenstrual tension.*

More recently, Dr. Katharina Dalton conducted an extensive series of studies on the subject, reporting that female criminal acts, accidents, hospital visits, poor judgments, and suicides are more common in the premenstrual and menstrual phases than at other times (Dalton, 1959, 1960, 1964, 1966, 1968, 1970, 1980). Numerous reports also indicate that the menstrual and premenstrual phases are associated with negative moods (Moos, 1969; Golub, 1976; May, 1976; Rossi and Rossi, 1977).

These findings, however, are not universal or interpreted in the same way by all scientists. For example, Persky (1974) found that mood was fairly constant in college-aged women at three different points in the menstrual cycle. Dan

(1976) noted that mood changes were very similar in women and their husbands over time regardless of the menstrual cycle. Webster and her co-workers (1978) noted that "menstrual or premenstrual symptoms" were unrelated to hormone levels and occurred with some frequency throughout the cycle, even around the time of ovulation. More recently, another research group found no evidence of menstrual cycle effects on academic performance as shown by examination grades (Walsh et al., 1981). Many investigators have suggested that social expectations and stereotypes seem to influence the occurrences of menstrual or premenstrual distress (e.g., Paige, 1973; Parlee, 1973; Koeske and Koeske, 1975; Sherif, 1980; Brooks-Gunn and Ruble, 1980). For example, some observers note that the title of one of the questionnaires most frequently used in menstrual cycle research, the Menstrual Distress Questionnaire, is inherently biased, as are the preponderance of questions asked:

> If the questionnaire were called the *Menstrual Joy Questionnaire,* if the majority of items asked for responses such as "happiness" or "feeling great" or "able to plot effective strategy" or "increased creativity," the end results would inevitably be different. (Delaney, Lupton, and Toth, 1977, p. 84)

Others in the field point to the problems associated with a person's attempts at remembering past events (including the exact timing of the onset of menstruation) months after they have happened, although this type of retrospective self-reporting has been a mainstay of much of Dalton's research (Sherif, 1980). And, as Ruble, Brooks-Gunn, and Clarke (1980, p. 234) have noted, cultural factors influence both the anxiety about or acceptance of a biological event like menstruation: "If a woman believes that women normally experience a variety of premenstrual symptoms, she may report such symptoms in part to make herself appear normal."

While it is clear that women are not ruled

by their monthly hormone cycles, two kinds of menstrual problems are very common: *dysmenorrhea* (painful menstruation) and the *premenstrual syndrome* (PMS). Dysmenorrhea is usually marked by pelvic or lower abdominal cramping, backache, headache, and a feeling of being bloated. Although the cause of dysmenorrhea has been elusive, it now appears that excessive release of prostaglandins from the uterus is the trigger. Studies now reveal that drugs which inhibit prostaglandin production relieve menstrual discomfort (Henzl et al., 1977; Marx, 1979). Birth control pills also relieve dysmenorrhea by interrupting the hormone changes of the menstrual cycle and indirectly affecting prostaglandin production (see chapter 6). Some women find that having an orgasm relieves this discomfort by reducing pelvic heaviness (Masters and Johnson, 1966).

The premenstrual syndrome is usually de-

RESEARCH SPOTLIGHT

Premenstrual Syndrome

In Brooklyn, New York, attorney Stephanie Benson decided to defend a client who was accused of beating her four-year-old daughter by claiming that the woman was a victim of hormonal imbalances associated with her menstrual cycle, a condition called *premenstrual syndrome* (PMS). Although the idea of using PMS as a legal defense was eventually dropped in this case as part of a plea-bargaining agreement, in at least two murders in England the so-called PMS defense was used successfully to claim mitigating circumstances (*American Medical News,* Nov. 26, 1982, p. 14).

While some lawyers appear interested in pursuing this line of legal ground-breaking, many feminists feel they are uncomfortably caught in a paradoxical situation. On the one hand, as Susan Edmiston (1982) points out, "Throughout the 1970s, the feminist attitude toward menstruation was to deny that it made a difference and to minimize any effects women might feel. ... The reasoning was that to admit that menstruation mattered was to open the door to charges of biological inferiority." Now, however, increasing numbers of women (including many feminists) have become concerned about the realities of PMS, which they realize can be addressed only by open and intensive study. To pretend that PMS doesn't exist, or that it affects only a tiny fraction of women, they believe, is only going to slow much-needed research and make women who suffer from PMS feel lonely and abnormal. But, as well-known politician-lawyer-feminist Elizabeth Holtzman has pointed out, the PMS defense could backfire to harm women in divorce proceedings and custody battles and might even be used to justify violence against women (Allen, 1982).

The problem is an especially complicated one since researchers seem surrounded on all sides by disagreement, methodological difficulties, and uncertainty over what their findings mean. According to a recent news report in the *Journal*

fined as occurring in the two or three days before menstrual flow begins and is marked by feelings of tension and irritability (Delaney, Lupton, and Toth, 1977; Frieze et al., 1978; Money, 1980). Other variable findings include feeling sluggish, impatient, dizzy, nervous, depressed, and indecisive, as well as having physical symptoms such as breast tenderness, constipation, headache, bloating, and alcohol intolerance. It is uncertain how many women have such premenstrual difficulties

(estimates range from 20 to 75 percent). Researchers are also trying to determine whether a woman's attitudes toward menstruation or her physiological events, such as shifting hormones or fluid retention, induce these mood changes and discomfort (González, 1981). The specific cause of the premenstrual syndrome is unclear, although some researchers think it relates to the estrogen-progesterone ratio, the adrenal hormones controlling water retention, or the chem-

---

of the American Medical Association (June 3, 1983), scientists attending a PMS workshop sponsored by the National Institute of Mental Health agreed that PMS existed but "were hard-pressed to define the disorder precisely." Instead, noting that PMS doesn't seem to have a single pattern, they suggested using the plural term "premenstrual syndromes" rather than the singular form.

Disagreement in PMS research seems to apply up and down the line. While some workers such as England's Dr. Katharina Dalton champion the notion that progesterone deficiency causes PMS, no studies have actually measured this deficiency in a way that shows a cause-and-effect relationship. Although one research team claims that even in its severest forms, PMS is *not* a form of depression (Haskett et al., 1980), others say that exactly the opposite is true (Shuckit et al., 1975; Halbreich, Endicott, and Nee, 1983). Worst of all, research on the treatment of PMS – which now includes literally hun-

dreds of studies on dozens of different approaches – is often surprisingly slipshod, poorly designed, and difficult to interpret. As researcher Judith Green says, "No one approach has yielded consistent results, and no single agent has stood out as consistently useful."

Uncertainty among researchers is magnified, in a sense, by the large numbers of women who have read or heard about PMS and are now demanding treatment. Since progesterone use is not approved for treatment of PMS in the United States, many physicians are unwilling to prescribe it, particularly since it has been reported to cause cancer in animals. In addition, many of the most knowledgeable physicians in this field are aware that controlled, double-blind studies (in which neither the test subjects nor the investigators know whether a subject is taking progesterone or an inert look-alike pill called a placebo) have not been able to show that progesterone works better than a pla-

cebo in reducing premenstrual symptoms (Blume, 1983).

Despite this uncertainty, scores of PMS clinics have sprouted all over the country, with most of them offering progesterone therapy. Predictably, perhaps, they've been greeted by an avalanche of patients, partly because they've done a good job of selling American women on the idea that almost *any* symptom during the premenstrual week is a sign of PMS (Allen, 1982). In addition to offering the experimental hormone treatments, most of these clinics also prescribe dietary changes (e.g., avoiding salty foods, refined sugar, chocolate, and caffeine; eating six small meals a day), and they perform blood tests of dubious value. Not surprisingly, many of these centers charge high fees. The bottom line here seems to be "Let the buyer beware" – at least until the research community can provide better documentation for the causes and cures of this elusive but troublesome disorder.

---

ical substances in the brain influencing mood. Whatever the resolution of these interesting controversies, premenstrual symptoms are usually transient, do not always occur, and are often unobservable (Delaney, Lupton, and Toth, 1977). Moreover, most researchers agree that only 5 to 10 percent of women have premenstrual distress that is serious enough to interfere with their functioning (Keye, 1983). The severity of this problem may be as much a reflection of negative societal attitudes about menstruation as an indicator of physiological processes.

Sex and the Menstrual Cycle

As part of our evolutionary heritage, there is some basis for assuming that women should be most interested in sex around the time of ovulation, when pregnancy can occur. In most animal species, the female follows this pattern of behavior rather exclusively, avoiding sexual contact at all other times. Some studies document a pattern of increased sexual activity around the presumed time of ovulation and do not find such a "peak" in women using birth control pills, which block ovulation (Udry and Morris, 1968, 1970; Adams, Gold, and Burt, 1978), but these findings appear to have been a result of imprecise determination of when ovulation occurred (James, 1971; Kolodny and Bauman, 1979). Other reports find no evidence of heightened female sexual interest during ovulation (James, 1971; Persky et al., 1978; Bancroft, 1984).

A recent well-designed study by Schreiner-Engel and co-workers (1981) found objective laboratory evidence of higher levels of vaginal vasocongestion during the follicular and luteal phases of the menstrual cycle. Subjective reports of sexual arousal were also higher at these times than during the ovulatory phase, providing further confirmation that an ovulatory peak in female sexual responsivity is unlikely. Another recent study confirmed that female sexual activity

and sexual interest peak in the follicular phase well before ovulation (Bancroft et al., 1983). Nevertheless, individuals differ in unique ways, so that some women may well find themselves feeling sexier at mid-cycle while others are most interested in sex earlier or later in their cycles.

Taboos about sexual intercourse during menstruation are still a part of everyday life for many people. In some cases, avoiding sexual contact is a matter of religious practice. For example, Orthodox Jews are supposed to abstain from sex for seven days after the end of menstrual flow, and sex is resumed only after the woman has immersed herself in a ritual bath, called the *mikvah*. In other cases, abstinence seems to stem from cultural and psychological sources: "A man is as likely to be sexually aroused by a woman when she is menstruating as he is at any other time. But the blood of the menstruating woman is somehow dangerous, magical, and apparently not something he wants to get on his penis" (Delaney, Lupton, and Toth, 1977). The following comments illustrate the broad range of feelings people have about sexual activity during menstruation:

> I often find that I feel sexiest when I'm having my period, so making love is particularly enjoyable then. (Authors' files)

> I somehow feel like it's not right to have sex when my girlfriend is menstruating. I don't know why, but I just feel funny about it. (Authors' files)

> Jill and I love to have sex during her periods. It's a particularly passionate time because we don't need to use any birth control then. (Authors' files)

> In a word, I'm embarrassed about it. I feel like I'm not completely clean when I'm flowing, and tampons make me dry inside, so I really prefer waiting until my period is done. (Authors' files)

The notion that sexual activity, including intercourse, is "dangerous" to either partner during menstruation has no basis in fact (Masters and Johnson, 1966). Yet some people feel that intercourse is messy during menstruation and restrict their sexual experiences to noncoital options. It appears as though attitudes toward sex during menstruation are beginning to change, however, since younger people seem to be less affected by the negative attitudes concerning such activity than their parents' generation (Paige, 1978).

SUMMARY

1. Sexual physiology describes the functions and reflexes of sexual response. Sexual arousal is the activation of a complex network of reflexes that involves the sex organs and sensory, cognitive, and hormonal pathways in the brain.

2. The sexual response cycle of both sexes consists of four basic stages: excitement, plateau, orgasm, and resolution. The primary physical changes that occur during the cycle are a result of vasocongestion and the accumulation of neuromuscular tension.

3. Vaginal lubrication in the female and penile erection in the male are the most prominent signs of the excitement phase. This phase is also marked by internal vaginal expansion and nipple erection.

4. In the plateau phase of high sexual arousal, the outer portion of the vagina swells, forming the orgasmic platform, and the labia thicken and undergo a prominent color change. In the male, the testes increase in size and are pulled tightly against the body, and a pre-ejaculatory fluid may appear. A measleslike rash called the "sex flush" is seen in the majority of women and in about 25 percent of men.

5. Orgasm is a highly pleasurable reflex discharging neuromuscular tension via a total body response. In both sexes, a series of muscular contractions occur initially at 0.8 second intervals and then diminish in intensity and rapidity. In females, orgasm includes contractions of the outer portion of the vagina, the uterus, and the anal sphincter. In males, orgasm begins with contractions in the prostate and seminal vesicles, which initiates the process of ejaculation.

6. The resolution phase is a period in which the foregoing changes reverse, with a return to the unaroused state.

7. The male is limited in terms of physiologic response capacity by a refractory period immediately after ejaculation during which he cannot ejaculate again. Females do not have a refractory period. While women have the capacity to be multiorgasmic, this pattern of response has been noted in only a small number of men.

8. The old notion that there are two types of female orgasm — "vaginal" or "clitoral" — has been disproven. The physiologic patterns of female orgasm are identical no matter what the source of sexual stimulation.

9. The sex hormones — principally testosterone, estrogens, and progesterone — are present in both sexes and are controlled by the hypothalamus and pituitary gland. Testosterone is an important influence on sexual drive in males and females, but sexual behavior in humans cannot be thought of as tightly controlled by the sex hormones.

10. The menstrual cycle consists of three phases: the follicular phase, ovulation, and the luteal phase. The length of the entire cycle and its effects on mood and physical symptoms vary considerably.

11. Dysmenorrhea (painful menstruation), which is marked by cramping, backache, and feeling bloated, is now thought to be due to excessive release of chemicals called prostaglandins; it can usually be controlled by drugs that inhibit these substances.

12. PMS (premenstrual syndrome) affects a substantial number of women, typically causing irritability and tensions in the few days before the period begins. Many theories abound about the causes of PMS, but there is little agreement on this or on the proper treatment.

SUGGESTED READINGS

Brecher, R., and Brecher, E. *An Analysis of Human Sexual Response*. New York: New American Library, 1966. A readable and accurate examination of Masters and Johnson's physiology studies, with additional social and historical perspectives.

Delaney, J., Lupton, M. J., and Toth, E. *The Curse: A Cultural History of Menstruation*. New York: New American Library, 1977. A lively and authoritative account of taboos, myths, rituals, and contemporary research about menstruation and the menstrual cycle.

Hite, S. *The Hite Report*. New York: Dell, 1977. A detailed analysis of women's views of their own sexual responsivity, lacking in scientific precision but useful for women's descriptions of their sexual feelings.

Hite, S. *The Hite Report on Male Sexuality*. New York: Alfred A. Knopf, 1981. The male companion-piece to the original *Hite Report*; unscientific but clearly showing the great diversity of male sexual feelings and fears.

Norris, R. V., and Sullivan, C. *PMS — Premenstrual Syndrome*. New York: Rawson Wade, 1983. An opinionated and not too scientific approach, but with some useful pointers.

Sherfey, M. J. *The Nature and Evolution of Female Sexuality*. New York: Random House, 1972. A detailed discussion integrating sexual physiology with female psychology. Heavy reading in parts, but a classic.

Zilbergeld, B. *Male Sexuality: A Guide to Sexual Fulfillment*. Boston: Little, Brown, 1978. An insightful, well-written view of male sexuality, with a nice touch of humor.

5 Human Reproduction

THIS CHAPTER continues our look at sexuality in a biological perspective by focusing on one special aspect: how life begins. We will start our discussion of reproduction by examining the process of conception (the union of egg and sperm) and will then explore what happens during pregnancy, childbirth, and the first days of infancy. We conclude with a look at problem pregnancies and difficulties that prevent conception.

THE DYNAMICS OF CONCEPTION

In humans, pregnancy can result only when sperm meets egg. For this to happen, sperm must be deposited in the vagina close to the time of ovulation. In general, sperm retain their capability to penetrate the egg for twenty-four to forty-eight hours. In some cases intercourse one week before the presumed time of ovulation led to pregnancy, but the estimation of ovulation may have been inaccurate.

Although it may seem as though pregnancy happens almost instantaneously, fertile couples who are trying to have a baby or who have intercourse regularly without contraception take an average of 5.3 months for pregnancy to occur (Shane, Schiff, and Wilson, 1976). Only 25 percent of women conceive after one month of unprotected intercourse. Sixty-three percent conceive by the end of six months, and by the end of one year, 80 percent become pregnant. Clearly, even when intercourse in fertile couples is timed to be near ovulation, there is an element of luck in whether a pregnancy occurs.

The Union of Sperm and Egg

After ovulation, the egg is gently drawn from the surface of the ovary into the Fallopian tube where it is propelled toward the uterus by movement of cilia (tiny hairlike outgrowths). If fertilization occurs, it is usually in the upper portion of the Fallopian tube, not in the uterus.

After ejaculation in the vagina, healthy sperm swim rapidly into the female reproductive system in an arduous race which has few survivors. Although 200 million or more sperm are in the vagina, only a few thousand get to the Fallopian tubes and only about 200 actually get near the egg. Most sperm never reach the cervix because they spill out of the vagina or are immobilized by clumping together. Other sperm are damaged along the way, and about half the sperm that swim into the uterus take a wrong turn and enter the eggless Fallopian tube (except in rare circumstances, ovulation occurs on only *one* side each month). The difficult journey is nature's way of making sure that only the healthiest sperm have a chance to fertilize the egg.

Fertilization

Sperm spend several hours in the female reproductive tract undergoing a poorly understood process called *capacitation*, which enables them to penetrate the egg. Some sperm can reach the egg in an hour, but they must still wait to undergo this process. The race to penetrate the egg then is not always won by the swiftest; in fact, usually there are about 40 sperm clustered about the egg at fertilization. After capacitation, sperm secrete a chemical that dissolves the zona pellucida, the jellylike coating around the egg.

FIGURE 5–1
Human Egg Being Fertilized

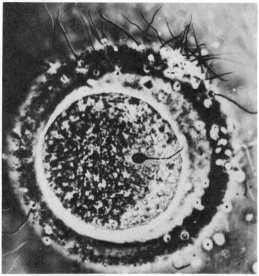

Source: Dr. Landrum B. Shettles

Note that only one sperm has penetrated the egg; the tails of many other sperm are visible at the border of the egg, where they have been blocked.

Recent research has shown that the egg is not just a passive participant in this process. The egg actually embraces the sperm by extending tiny outgrowths called microvilli up from its surface. Then, to avoid penetration by more than one sperm, the egg first produces a brief electrical block on its surface (lasting only about 30 seconds), followed by a hard outer protein coat. Schatten and Schatten (1983, p. 32) describe it this way: "The successful sperm is held down on the egg membrane in the tight grip of microvilli, while the coat rises above it, pushing all other sperm away. It is rather as if the egg had opened an umbrella, holding the crowd of spermatozoa at a distance." Next, the egg pulls the sperm inside itself and moves its nucleus to meet that of the sperm. Once a sperm enters the egg, the zona becomes impenetrable (Figure 5-1). The moment

Human Reproduction

FIGURE 5–2
Early Development after Fertilization

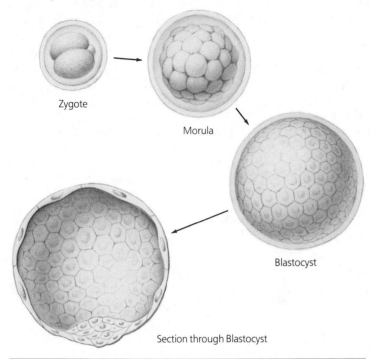

Zygote

Morula

Blastocyst

Section through Blastocyst

The blastocyst implants in the lining of the uterus.

at which sperm and egg combine is the moment of conception or fertilization — the beginning of embryonic life. If an egg is not fertilized, it disintegrates.

Fertilization produces a single cell called the *zygote* (Figure 5–2). This cell contains twenty-three chromosomes (strands of genetic material) contributed by the sperm and twenty-three chromosomes from the egg. These forty-six chromosomes provide programming for inherited characteristics such as blood type, height, skin color, and so forth. Two of the chromosomes, called the sex chromosomes, combine to determine the sex of the developing baby. All eggs and half of the sperm cells contain an X sex chromosome, while the remaining sperm have Y sex chromosomes only. A zygote with two X chromosomes will become a female; and a zygote with one X and one Y will become a male.[1] Since eggs always have X chromosomes, the sex of the baby is determined by the contribution of the father, whether it be an X or a Y chromosome.

Despite this biological reality, some men mistakenly believe that the woman is responsible for determining the baby's sex, and in some cultures divorces have occurred when a wife "couldn't" produce a male heir for her husband.

---

[1] Some exceptions and complications of this process of sex determination are discussed in chapter 7.

Sex Preselection

The desire to choose the sex of a baby before conception is probably as old as written history. In some cultures, folklore provides advice about various ways of selecting a child's sex: for instance, wearing boots to bed will produce boys, or eating sweet foods improves the chances of having a girl. In an age of greater scientific sophistication, most Americans are unlikely to believe these sorts of notions, yet interest in predetermining the sex of a child is so high that numerous other methods have been advanced with a more "plausible" scientific ring to them but without much more value than the boots or sweets theories.

One popular set of ideas proposed by Shettles and Rorvik (1970) suggested that having intercourse as close as possible to the time of ovulation, increasing the alkalinity of vaginal secretions by douching with a baking soda solution, using deep penetration during intercourse, and having the woman be orgasmic before the male ejaculates all favor conceiving boys. These suggestions — which were each rationalized on detailed scientific grounds — have not yet been supported by any secure research data; in fact, in one well-designed study of 3,658 births it was actually found that the proportion of male births was higher two days or more after ovulation than at or near ovulation (Harlap, 1979).

A more promising but still unproven method of sex preselection involves separating X and Y sperm in test tubes by passing them through liquid albumin, a protein found in blood that is similar to the thick material of an egg white. The faster swimming Y sperm migrate to the bottom of the tube in higher numbers than the somewhat slower X sperm, permitting their ultimate recovery and use via artificial insemination to increase the chances of conceiving a male (Glass and Ericsson, 1982).

If a sex preselection method is eventually found to work reliably, experts predict that it will lead to a substantially higher percentage of male births and possibly an overall decline in family size. However, some people are concerned about the ethics of using sex preselection techniques, which have been termed "one of the most stupendously sexist acts in which it is possible to engage" (Powledge, 1981). While many would disagree with this statement — including, for instance, couples who have several sons and would like to have a daughter — there is little question that past history strongly suggests that this practice might just become another form of discrimination against women.

Transport and Implantation

The single-celled zygote begins to divide about thirty hours after fertilization. It splits initially into two cells, then these two cells split into four cells, eight cells, and so on. As this division occurs, the size of each cell becomes progressively smaller. This collection of cells, resembling a mulberry, is called a *morula* (Figure 5-2). During the three or four days after fertilization, the morula travels down the Fallopian tube and enters the cavity of the uterus. The morula now has a hollow inner portion containing fluid and is called a *blastocyst* (Figure 5-2).

The blastocyst undergoes further growth inside the uterus, receiving oxygen and nourishment from secretions of the lining of the uterus (the endometrium). After a few days, the blastocyst begins to attach itself to the lining of the uterus in a process called *implantation*. The endometrium of the uterus thickens and becomes richly endowed with blood vessels as a result of hormone secretions. If fertilization does not occur, this hormonal stimulation ceases abruptly and the thickened tissue is shed during menstruation. However, if it does occur, the thickened, spongy endometrium becomes a "bed" for the blastocyst, which usually attaches to the upper portion of the back wall of the uterus. If implantation occurs outside the uterus (for example, in the tubes or in the abdomen), an *ectopic* (misplaced) *pregnancy* results.

Implantation is completed about five to nine days after fertilization. There are no physical sensations that accompany implantation, so it is impossible to know just when it has occurred. In some women, implantation is accompanied by bleeding that may be confused with a menstrual period. As a result, women sometimes miscalculate when pregnancy began, leading to a wrong estimation of the expected date of delivery.

PREGNANCY

Being pregnant is often thought of as a time of fulfillment and joy, but it can also be an unsettling surprise or a source of anguish and despair. Some couples actively plan for a pregnancy, while others try to avoid it or leave it to chance. A couple's attitudes and motivations certainly influence their reactions when learning that pregnancy has occurred.

The average pregnancy lasts for 266 days during which remarkable changes occur in both the developing baby and the mother. As a matter of convenience, the events of pregnancy are usually described in terms of three month periods or *trimesters*. The first trimester includes the first three months after conception, the second trimester spans the fourth to the sixth months, and the third trimester ranges from the seventh month to delivery. The unborn baby is called an *embryo* during the first eight weeks after fertilization and a *fetus* thereafter.

First Trimester

FETAL DEVELOPMENT

Parts of the tiny, spherical blastocyst that implants in the lining of the uterus develop into the *placenta* and the *fetal membranes*. The placenta is the organ through which the developing baby receives nourishment and oxygen from the mother's circulating blood. Waste products from the fetus are also passed through the placenta. The fetal membranes, an inner *amnion* and outer *chorion*, are thin sacs of tissue that enclose the developing baby. The fetus is suspended in a liquid called *amniotic fluid* that keeps the temperature constant and serves as a shock absorber to protect the fetus against physical injury.

At the time of implantation, the blastocyst-embryo is less than one millimeter (0.04 inch) in diameter. By the end of the first trimester, the fetus will be 9 centimeters (3.5 inches) long. This phenomenal rate of growth is accompanied by intricate patterns of organ formation that transform a small, undifferentiated mass of cells into an unmistakably human appearance.

By the end of the first month, the embryo has a primitive heart and digestive system and the beginnings of the brain, spinal cord, and nervous system have been established. The outlines of eyes can be seen on the large head, but distinct facial features have not appeared. In the fifth week, arm and leg buds become visible, the jaws begin to form, and indentations are seen in the region where the ears will develop. The *umbilical cord*, which contains two arteries and a vein connecting the embryo to the placenta, becomes a distinct structure.

In the sixth and seventh weeks (Figure 5-3), the eyes and ears develop more fully and teeth and facial muscles begin to form. A distinct neck becomes visible, and bone formation begins as well. Testicular tissue appears in male embryos at this point, but in a female embryo formation of the ovaries has not yet begun. Before this time, male and female embryos are anatomically indistinguishable (see chapter 7). By eight weeks, the embryo has distinct hands and feet and all major blood vessels are forming. At this point, the embryo weighs about one gram (0.04 ounces)

FIGURE 5–4
A Human Fetus Early in the Ninth Week of
Development

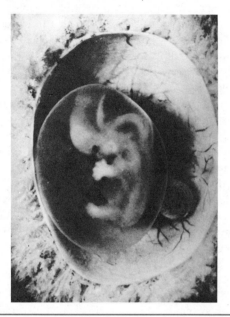

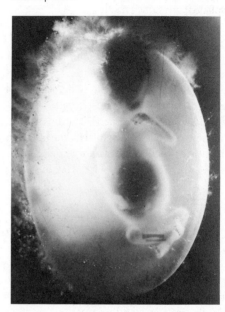

and is three centimeters (1.2 inches) in length (Figure 5–4).

In the third month, fetal development proceeds with the appearance of fingernails, toenails, hair follicles, and eyelids. The limbs become properly proportioned in relation to the rest of the body and recognizable male and female genital organs are seen. By the end of the twelfth week, all of the major organs are formed, although they are not all completed.

THE MOTHER

Early pregnancy is experienced in different ways by different women. Some have a strong sense of energy, radiance, and well-being even before they know they are pregnant. Others find the first months of pregnancy are marked by fatigue, loss of appetite, or humdrum emotions. More commonly, the pregnant woman's feelings vary from day to day in an unpredictable fashion.

Being tired is such a typical feature of the first trimester that it is considered a symptom of pregnancy. Another frequent symptom is nausea or vomiting which usually begins around the end of the first month. This "morning sickness" can occur at any time of day. Morning sickness usually disappears spontaneously a month or two after it begins. Frequent urination, irregular bowel movements, breast swelling and tenderness, and an increased amount of vaginal secretion are among the other physical changes that may be noticed by the pregnant woman in the first tri-

mester. However, the woman cannot feel the changes going on inside her uterus during this time.

Missing a period is not a sure sign of pregnancy (periods can be skipped because of stress or illness, among other reasons), but it raises a question in most women's minds. To find the answer, the woman can have a pregnancy test done by a physician, at a medical laboratory, or at a clinic, or she can purchase a kit for a self-administered home test.

In the past, biological tests using laboratory animals such as frogs, rabbits, or mice were employed to check for pregnancy, but these were cumbersome, time-consuming, expensive, and relatively inaccurate. Now there are many immunological tests that allow a diagnosis to be made in as short a time as two minutes. They work by detecting the presence of HCG (human chorionic gonadotropin), a hormone secreted by the placenta. A drop of urine is placed on a glass slide (or in a tube) and is mixed with several chemicals. If HCG is present, the mixture does not coagulate and the test is said to be positive, indicating pregnancy.

Immunological pregnancy tests are 95 to 98 percent accurate two weeks after a missed period, but before that time their reliability is not as high. A newer test, called the *beta-subunit HCG radioimmunoassay*, offers 99 percent accuracy as early as one week after conception but is not as widely available as other test methods. A negative pregnancy test, no matter what method is used, is *not* foolproof, and a repeat test done a week or two later may be in order. Women need to have an early knowledge of their pregnancy to begin proper health care (such as good nutrition and avoidance of drug use). Early diagnosis is also important so that those who want to terminate pregnancy can have an abortion in the first trimester, when this procedure is safest and simplest.

Pregnancy can also be detected in other ways. During a pelvic examination, a physician can note: (1) a softening of the cervix; (2) a bluish color of the vagina and cervix; (3) a softening of the uterus just above the cervix; and (4) an irregular increase in the size of the uterus. These signs of pregnancy may be present at about the sixth week, but are quite variable. The most conclusive physical signs of pregnancy — finding a fetal heartbeat, feeling the fetus move, and identi-

fying the fetus by X-ray or sound-wave tests —
cannot usually be done before the second trimester.

Once a woman knows that she is pregnant,
she may be happy, proud, ambivalent, fearful,
angry, or depressed. Her reaction reflects many
things — her age, marital status, economic resources, career objectives, personal values, and
expectations of parenthood. Most of all, her reaction will depend on whether or not she wanted
to be pregnant and how she feels about herself.

Negative feelings about a pregnancy, even
when it is planned, are similar to the second
thoughts we all have after taking a major step in
our lives. Did I choose the right college? Is this
really the person I wanted to marry? Why did I
buy this car when that other one looks so good?
Our initial uncertainties and hesitations are not
necessarily predictors of how we will feel later
on. The psychological impact of pregnancy and
the practical implications of bringing a child into
the world are immense and require time for
thought and acceptance.

THE FATHER

While often neglected as a participant in the
experience of pregnancy, men also have important feelings about this event. The man's initial
reaction on learning of his partner's pregnancy
may be elation, joy, surprise, uncertainty, or concern. Until he has time to adjust to the idea of
pregnancy as a reality, he is likely to be somewhat ambivalent toward his partner. He may be
anxious about her well-being and the developing
baby's health until he can see his partner's bulging abdomen or feel the baby's movement. His
anxieties may also relate to the additional responsibilities (financial and emotional) that the pregnancy presents. Some men even have morning
sickness along with their pregnant partners, perhaps a sign of their anxiety and wish to share in
the pregnancy experience. In fact, one study re-

cently found that 23 percent of a group of American expectant fathers had a condition called the
couvade syndrome in which husbands experience
physical symptoms that are related to their wives'
pregnancies and are not explained by other medical factors (Lipkin and Lamb, 1982).

Many men are uncertain about the effects of
sex during pregnancy (see pp. 122–123) and believe that the woman must refrain from exercise
or vigorous work so the baby will not be injured.
Other men do not understand why a pregnant
woman seems so sleepy and may become upset,
especially if they imagine that this tiredness will
progress relentlessly through the months ahead.
Both partners are likely to react to a pregnancy in
a more relaxed fashion if they have already had a
child and have some idea of what to expect.

In the early months of pregnancy, many
couples draw closer together, both emotionally
and physically. Pregnancy can be a very concrete
manifestation of commitment and sharing, and a
first pregnancy in particular provides good reason
for planning and dreaming about the future.

Second Trimester

FETAL DEVELOPMENT

In the fourth month, the fetus develops lips,
fingerprints, and hair on its head. Sucking motions begin, and the fetus swallows small
amounts of amniotic fluid. The fetus moves and
turns very actively within the amniotic sac (Figure 5-5). During the fifth month, the fetal heartbeat can be heard and the body becomes covered
with fine, downy hair. The fetus also responds to
sound and spends part of its time asleep and part
awake. In the sixth month, the fetus opens its
eyes and has long hair on its head. By the end of
the second trimester, the fetus is 30 centimeters
(12 inches) long and weighs 600 to 700 grams
(1.3–1.5 lbs.). If born at this time, the chances for
survival are extremely poor.

FIGURE 5–5
A Sixteen-week Fetus

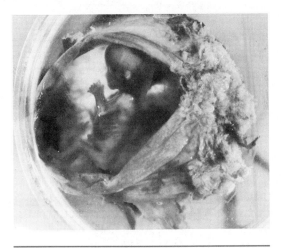

At this stage of development, although most major organs have formed, the fetus is unable to survive if born prematurely because the lungs are immature.

THE MOTHER

The second trimester is a time of many physical changes for the pregnant woman. Her waist begins to bulge, her abdomen protrudes, her bustline expands, and her regular clothes no longer fit very well. She may be troubled by these changes in her figure, or she may be happy with her body and anxious to let the whole world know that she is pregnant.

Late in the fourth month (between the sixteenth and eighteenth weeks), the woman can usually feel the fetus moving ("*quickening*"). This is often an exciting event and a moment of relief because the developing baby "signals" it is doing well. As the baby's kicks and twists become more vigorous in the following weeks, the novelty and wonder may wear off and the sensations may become annoying. The mother may alternate between feeling love and tenderness for her unborn, active child and feeling resentful of being controlled by the fetus.

In the second trimester, the uterus grows considerably larger and pushes up inside the abdomen. This commonly leads to indigestion and constipation. The skin over the abdomen is stretched and pink or reddish stretch marks may appear on its surface. The breasts increase prominently in size, the nipples become larger and more deeply pigmented, the areola becomes broader, and *colostrum*, a thin yellowish fluid which is a precursor of milk, may drip out of the nipple. These changes are a result of the hormones produced by the placenta and prepare the breasts for later milk production.

Other physical changes may lead to minor problems. Varicose veins in the legs and hemorrhoids can start to form or be worsened because of the pressure of the growing uterus. Nose bleeds may occur because of a larger blood volume. Fluid retention can cause *edema*, swelling of the hands, wrists, ankles, or feet. On the other hand, the morning sickness of the first trimester usually disappears and the woman's appetite is apt to become hearty.

Psychologically, the second trimester is often a time of relative tranquility and confidence. Most women have adjusted to being pregnant and feel more energetic than they did in the first few months. Heightened sensuality at this time is often a pleasant bonus; it is not unusual for some women to first experience orgasm in the middle months of pregnancy (Masters and Johnson, 1966).

THE FATHER

With the birth of the child still far away, the father is likely to be drawn more closely into the experience of pregnancy in the second trimester. He is able to see obvious changes in his partner's body, but these changes occur gradually and give him time to adjust. Feeling the baby kick or turn is likely to give him a greater sense of contact, of knowing that the baby is really there. His partner's renewed energy is also reassuring and gives the couple more time together — a pleasant interlude that will be gone all too soon when a newborn infant arrives. His earlier anxieties about the fragility of the developing baby in the first trimester are generally put to rest.

Third Trimester

FETAL DEVELOPMENT

During the seventh month, the brain and nervous system complete development, fatty tissue grows under the skin, and the downlike hair on the fetus disappears in most places. A baby born prematurely at the beginning of the seventh month has a 10 percent chance of survival, but by the eighth month this increases to 70 percent. In the eighth month, the baby's skin has lost its wrinkled appearance and is pink in color. If it has not done so earlier, the baby is likely to assume a head-down position in the uterus. In the ninth month, the fetus usually is less active than it has been, partly because of its size and cramped quarters. Its eyes are blue, because other eye colors develop only after a period of exposure to light. The fetus has acquired antibodies from its mother that will help protect it against infection during early infancy. The average full-term baby is 50 centimeters (20 inches) long and weighs 3,100 to 3,400 grams (6.8 to 7.5 lbs).

THE MOTHER

The increasing size and firmness of the uterus are quite obvious. When the woman stands it pushes forward, altering her center of gravity. To balance this, she may walk with her head and shoulders thrust backward and chest protruding, a posture sometimes called "the pride of pregnancy." Unfortunately, this position can result in backache, a common occurrence in the last months of pregnancy. The enlarged uterus also puts pressure on the blood vessels in the lower part of the body, which may partly explain the common discomfort of leg cramps. Other problems caused by pressure changes include a frequent need to urinate because of pressure against the bladder and shortness of breath since the diaphragm is pushed upwards.

Many women have difficulty controlling their weight gain during pregnancy, especially during the third trimester. Physicians generally suggest that weight gain be limited to about 25 pounds because larger increases in weight increase the odds of medical problems. On the other hand, too little weight gained is potentially harmful to the fetus, since a gain of almost 20 pounds can be expected from normal physiological changes. This gain includes the weight of the baby (7½ pounds), placenta and membranes (1½ pounds), and amniotic fluid (2 pounds), as well as increases in the weight of the uterus (2½ pounds), blood (3½ pounds), and breasts (1 pound). Normal fluid retention is likely to account for another 2 or 3 pounds of weight gain.

In the last months of pregnancy, the uterus has more frequent *Braxton-Hicks contractions*, painless short episodes of muscle tightening that are not a sign of labor. In women who have not had a baby before, the head of the fetus lowers into the pelvis in the last few weeks of pregnancy. When the largest diameter of the head has settled firmly into position against the pelvic bones, it is *engaged*. Engagement (also called "dropping" or "lightening") usually occurs during labor in women who have had children.

The end of the last trimester is apt to be a time of physical discomfort and awkwardness. Each day may seem longer than the last. Sleeping is frequently interrupted by trying to find a comfortable position, by the baby's movements, and by trips to the bathroom. Energy levels are low, irritability high. The first-time mother, especially, is likely to have anxieties about pain or problems with labor and delivery and may worry considerably about her baby not being normal. Her self-esteem may be on the wane as she seems, for now, to be at the mercy of her unborn child's whims and the requirements of a body that does not seem really hers.

THE FATHER

The last trimester is not without its tribulations for the male. His partner's changing shape and physical discomforts may lead to a loss of his sexual desire for her or his continued interest may not be matched by hers. Masters and Johnson (1966) found that for these reasons the last trimester is a time some men seek extramarital sex. Men may also feel aloof for other reasons. For example, the pregnant woman may become quite close to her own mother during pregnancy, with more discussions and time spent together as delivery nears. His partner's relation to her physician may also be a source of feeling "left out." So-cial events, recreation, and other details of everyday living are typically altered now, and the man may be understandably anxious for things to return to "normal."

At the same time, most men feel a strong sense of loyalty, closeness, and gratitude toward their very pregnant partner. They are usually glad not to be pregnant themselves, are concerned with making their partner comfortable, and, if a home delivery has not been chosen, are more than a little nervous about driving to the hospital once labor is underway. If this is their first child, and they have been asked to be present at the delivery, they may be somewhat queasy and unsure of "how they will do."

Prenatal Care and Planning

Most pregnancies progress smoothly for the mother and unborn child, but problems can also occur. *Prenatal* (prebirth) *care* not only increases the mother's chances of staying healthy but also protects the well-being of her developing baby.

Although most people think of prenatal care as something done by a doctor, it is a joint venture in which the mother and her physician or nurse collaborate. The mother's responsibilities are really more important than the doctor's, since she lives with the pregnancy day in and day out. Prenatal care is mainly a means for preventing problems; secondarily, it is a way to detect complications as early as possible in order to minimize their impact.

NUTRITION

Good nutrition during pregnancy is an essential part of prenatal care. The mother requires more calories and extra nutrients such as vitamins and minerals to meet the needs of her body and her developing baby. Poor maternal nutrition can lead to slower fetal growth, premature delivery, and low birth weight babies. Prematurity and low birth weight both cause higher infant death rates, and malnourished babies with low birth weights may have brain damage and retardation.

Obviously, the woman's nutritional state before pregnancy is an important consideration. If previous dietary habits were poor, special steps must be taken to provide extra amounts of needed nutrients. Even when this is not a problem, pregnant women need about 300 extra calories and extra amounts of protein, calcium, iron, and vitamins A, B, C, and D compared to their ordinary daily intake. Protein (found in meat, fish, eggs, and dairy products) is important for the growth of the placenta, uterus, and the blood supply in the pregnant woman's body. Calcium (obtained mainly from dairy products and vegetables) is necessary for growth of the fetal skeleton and tooth buds; too little calcium can also cause muscle cramps for the mother. Iron (found in red meats, dried fruits, eggs, and enriched cereals) is needed for the manufacture of red blood cells to prevent maternal anemia; folic acid (found in leafy green vegetables) also helps prevent anemia. Necessary vitamins are usually provided by a balanced diet that includes milk, bread, fresh fruits, and vegetables.

DRUGS

Almost every drug used by a pregnant woman will cross the placenta and enter the circulation of the developing baby. Because it is not always clear which drugs will affect the embryo or fetus, it is vital that drug use be restricted to situations of medical necessity, even for drugs that seem safe for the mother. Some drugs, called *teratogens*, produce malformations in the unborn child. The kind of effect a toxic drug produces depends partly on the time it is used. Certain drugs act selectively on the formation of a particular organ in the embryo or fetus and do not cause damage after its formation is complete. For this reason, drug use in the first half of pregnancy is particularly likely to damage the fetus, since this is when organ formation occurs. The effects also depend on the duration and amount of drug use — taking a single pill is unlikely to be harmful, while repeated use may be a problem.

MEDICATIONS. A wide variety of medicines can affect the fetus, including some that might surprise you. For instance, aspirin can cause fetal bleeding and, if used with large amounts of caffeine and phenacetin (in pills called APC's), can lead to low birth weight, prolonged pregnancy, anemia, and lower infant survival rates after birth (Collins and Turner, 1975). Tranquilizers have also been reported to cause a variety of fetal malformations, including cleft palate (Valium) and heart defects (Librium and Equanil). Thalidomide, a tranquilizer widely used in Europe in the early 1960s, resulted in severe malformations of the arms and legs of the fetus when taken during early pregnancy.

Hormones are also frequently teratogenic. Birth control pills used during pregnancy have been found to cause heart defects (Nora and

Choosing a Doctor

It's very important to see a doctor early in pregnancy for a general health check and to have regular medical exams to follow its course. The pregnant woman must choose among several options for care, which may vary depending on her locale and economic situation. She may select a private doctor, a medical group, a clinic, or a hospital. She must also decide whether to see a specialist (called an obstetrician) or a family physician who includes pregnancy care and delivery among other areas of his or her practice.

The choice of a doctor is important for many reasons. The pregnant woman's relationship with her physician greatly affects her knowledge about her pregnancy and her sense of security from knowing she is receiving competent, trustworthy advice and care. If she feels that her doctor is cold, distant, and difficult to talk with, she may be hesitant in raising important questions or telling the doctor about "little" problems that might be significant. If she feels talked down to or lightly regarded, she may be angry and less likely to follow otherwise sound medical advice. The doctor's philosophy about certain practices (for example, natural versus induced labor, the male partner's presence during the delivery) will also be important, as is the physician's ability to manage emergencies or complicated situations.

Unfortunately, the medical care system in the U.S. sometimes puts pregnant women in a position where passivity and dependence are expected and healthy curiosity, independence, and personal choices are frowned upon. Some physicians, including some women who are obstetricians, seem insensitive to the feelings and needs of their patients and have such busy schedules (and crowded offices with long waits) that the pregnant woman may rightfully feel rushed, ignored, or unimportant. The situation is not likely to be corrected quickly and easily, but it is not typical of the quality of available health care for most women who have a choice. The following pointers may assist pregnant women choosing a doctor.

1. Decide first if one or more of the following factors are highly important to you: the doctor's age, specialty, sex, location, hospitals (that is, where the doctor delivers babies), or willingness to do home deliveries (discussed later in this chapter).

2. Talk to friends and to your regular doctor (if you have one) to get recommendations. It can also be helpful to call your local medical society, which will usually provide you with names of obstetricians and family doctors if you want a larger "shopping list."

3. Call several offices to inquire about the doctor's background and training, fees, and philosophy. Arrange a personal visit to the doctor who sounds most suitable, taking into account all of the information gained in the previous steps.

4. Remember that choosing a doctor is not a popularity contest. While personality and style are important to your comfort, they are not a substitute for knowledge and skill.

5. If you are unhappy with your doctor, whatever the reason, try to discuss it with her or him face to face. If the response is unsatisfactory, switch doctors even if you have been seeing the same person for several months.

Finally, remember that the doctor is human too. The physician you see for prenatal care may be on vacation, doing another delivery, or in bed with a bad cold when you go into labor. Find out what arrangements your doctor has for such situations, since your baby might be delivered by someone else.

Nora, 1973; Heinonen et al., 1977) and abnormalities of the limbs, spinal column, windpipe (trachea), and kidneys (Janerich et al., 1974). Progesterone or testosterone can cause masculinizing changes in a female fetus and progestins or estrogens can cause improper formation of the penis in a male fetus. A form of estrogen called diethylstilbestrol (DES) which many mothers took to prevent miscarriage may cause cancer of the vagina in girls whose mothers used this drug during pregnancy (see chapter 20). Medications that can damage the fetus are listed in Table 5-1.

DRUG ADDICTION. Pregnant women who are addicted to drugs like heroin, barbiturates, and amphetamines expose the fetus to a large number of problems. Low birth weight and prematurity are characteristic of such pregnancies. The baby also becomes addicted, so the first days of life are likely to be a painful time of withdrawal symptoms. Convulsions and depressed breathing are commonly seen just after birth in infants born to addicted mothers. In addition, the mother's health may be compromised by poor nutrition, infections (particularly serum hepatitis), and other medical difficulties caused by drug addiction.

SMOKING

Dozens of studies show that cigarette smoking during pregnancy is associated with lower birth weights, shortened pregnancies, higher rates of spontaneous abortion, more frequent complications of pregnancy and labor, and higher rates of perinatal mortality (death of the fetus or newborn near the time of birth) (see detailed review by Coleman, Piotrow, and Rinehart, 1979). A study involving 28,000 children found that children of mothers who smoke heavily during pregnancy have almost twice the risk of having hyperactive-impulsive behavior at age seven than children born to nonsmoking mothers and also

have lower IQs, grade placement, and motor skills (Dunn et al., 1977).

The effects of marihuana smoking on fetal development are not clear. The active chemical ingredients of marihuana are known to cross the placental barrier (Harbison and Mantilla-Plata, 1972) and some animal studies have shown fetal damage and miscarriages with heavy marihuana use. However, these studies may not be applicable to humans. Because chronic, frequent marihuana smoking has been found to lower blood prolactin levels in women (Kolodny et al., 1980), it is possible that nursing might be affected by marihuana use.

ALCOHOL

Heavy use of alcohol by a pregnant woman can cause considerable damage to the developing baby. The *fetal alcohol syndrome* includes growth deficiencies before and after birth, damage to the brain and nervous system, and facial abnormalities especially affecting the eyes (Ouellette et al., 1977; Clarren and Smith, 1978). Mental retardation is sometimes found in the children of alcoholic mothers. There are also behavioral effects of the fetal alcohol syndrome with irritability noted in infancy and hyperactivity in later childhood (Smith, 1979).

Moderate use of alcohol and "binge" drinking by pregnant women are viewed by some scientists as risky, although the evidence here is not complete. At the present time, it seems safest for pregnant women who are not willing to abstain from drinking to limit their use of alcoholic beverages to not more than one or two drinks every few days.

PHYSICAL ACTIVITY

Pregnancy should not be regarded as a time of incapacity and fragility. In healthy women, patterns of work and play do not usually need to change significantly during pregnancy. Many

TABLE 5–1
Medications that May Affect the Fetus If Taken During Pregnancy

Drug	Fetal Effect
Antibiotics (used to treat infections)	
Streptomycin	Deafness
Tetracycline	Stained teeth (common), cataracts (rare)
Chloramphenicol	Vomiting, respiratory problems, circulatory collapse in newborns
Anticancer drugs	
Aminopterin, Busulfan, Chlorambucil, Cyclophosphamide, Mercaptopurine, Methotrexate	Abortion, various malformations
Anticoagulant drugs (blood thinners)	
Dicumarol	Fetal bleeding or death
Warfarin	Facial deformities, mental retardation, fetal death or bleeding
Anticonvulsant drugs (used to treat epilepsy)	
Dilantin	Cleft palate, heart defects
Paramethadione	Growth retardation
Trimethadione	Multiple defects
Phenobarbital	Bleeding
Hormones (various treatments)	
Birth control pills	Limb defects, genital malformations, possible heart or windpipe defects
Progestins	Masculinization of female fetus
Estrogens	Genital defects in male fetus
Diethylstilbestrol (DES)	Delayed effects: vaginal cancer in adolescent and young adult women; reproductive tract abnormalities in men
Testosterone	Masculinization of female fetus
Miscellaneous drugs	
Aspirin	Bleeding
Lithium	Heart defects
Tranquilizers (Librium, Valium, Equanil)	Various defects
Quinine	Deafness

Source: Data primarily from Wilson, 1977; and Benson, 1978.

women continue working and engaging in some sports activities until the last month of pregnancy, when fatigue and physical discomfort may make such activity difficult. Common sense is the best guide to follow, since avoiding excessive fatigue is largely a matter of self-judgment. Activities that might be physically dangerous (skiing, diving, roller skating, mountain climbing, and so on) must be considered carefully by each woman in terms of her health and the length of her pregnancy. Proper amounts of sleep are also important but vary considerably from person to person. Women with health complications during pregnancy such as high blood pressure or vaginal bleeding will find these conditions respond best to rest.

Sexual Activity During Pregnancy

Pregnancy has no uniform effect on sexual feelings or function. For some women, pregnancy is a time of heightened sexual awareness and sensual pleasure, while for others no changes are noticed or sexual feelings decline. Some couples find that late in pregnancy the awkwardness of a bulging belly and concern about the baby lead to voluntary abstention from sex. For others, adjustments in sexual positions or the use of non-coital sex play solves these problems fairly easily.

Masters and Johnson (1966) found marked variation in patterns of sexual behavior in the first trimester of pregnancy. Not surprisingly, women with morning sickness and high levels of fatigue reported losing interest in sex and a lower frequency of sexual activity, but other women experienced just the opposite effects. In the second trimester, however, 80 percent of the women noted heightened sexuality both in terms of desire and physical response. In the last trimester, there was a pronounced drop in the frequency of intercourse. The women thought this was because they were less physically attractive, but their husbands generally denied this explanation and instead voiced concern about injuring the fetus or their wife.

These findings have been verified in other studies that also showed an increased frequency of sexual activity in the second trimester (Falicov, 1973; Tolor and DiGrazia, 1976). One study, however, found a gradual, persistent decline in sexual behavior as pregnancy progresses (Solberg, Butler, and Wagner, 1973). This difference may be partly due to different research methods, since Solberg's study relied on interviews of women after delivery whereas Masters and Johnson interviewed women from the early stages of pregnancy on.

A few practical guidelines about sex during pregnancy are in order. Women with a history of previous miscarriages or whose pregnancy is in danger of miscarriage should abstain from any type of sexual activity that might result in their having orgasms, since contractions of the uterus during orgasm could be risky. If vaginal or uterine bleeding occurs during pregnancy, it is also wise to avoid all forms of sexual activity until receiving a medical okay. Air blown forcefully into the vagina during oral-genital contact can be dangerous for the pregnant woman, if it causes air embolism (air bubbles in the bloodstream). Cunnilingus *without* air blown into the vagina is not risky. If the membranes have ruptured, intercourse or cunnilingus should be prohibited because of the danger of fetal infection. *Aside from these few cautionary notes, sex during pregnancy is quite safe for the fetus and the mother.*

A few doctors have voiced concern about orgasms causing premature delivery. While it is possible that uterine contractions resulting from orgasm late in the third trimester may start labor in a small number of pregnant women (or that the prostaglandins contained in semen may trigger the same response), a recent report documents no statistical correlation between orgasm or intercourse and premature birth (Perkins, 1979). In fact, being orgasmic by intercourse or masturbation was associated with lower rates of prematurity.

BIRTH

Preparing for Childbirth

For the woman who has never had a baby, the process of childbirth may seem mysterious and frightening. Much of the mystery and fear can be relieved by attending childbirth classes held in hospitals or clinics and by obtaining accurate information from readings and discussions with her physician. Because friends and family are as likely to recite gruesome stories or incorrect "facts" as they are to be informative, what is heard from these sources must be taken with a large grain of salt. To get the most out of the experience, the pregnant woman and her husband or partner should attend childbirth classes together whenever possible.

Childbirth classes usually combine lectures and discussions with movies or slides showing a typical delivery. Participants are familiarized with medical terminology, labor room routines, and the operation of the hospital nursery. Most classes take a guided tour of the maternity ward and the nursery as well, so these rooms and their equipment will not seem unfamiliar to them during their labor, delivery, and hospital stay. In addition, most courses provide instruction in specific types of physical exercises designed to make labor and delivery easier.

Labor

Labor consists of rhythmic, regular contractions of the uterus that result in delivery of the child, the placenta, and membranes. Labor is usually preceded by several related events. As already mentioned, a few weeks before labor begins, women who are pregnant for the first time experience lightening. *Effacement,* or thinning of the cervix, and *dilatation,* opening of the mouth of the cervix, are also likely to begin about two weeks before the onset of labor. A very dependable sign of imminent labor is "show" (or "bloody show"), the discharge of a small amount of blood-tinged mucus.[2] Generally, labor begins a few hours or a few days after this occurs. About 10 percent of women experience a premature rupture of their membranes (the amniotic sac or "bag of waters") before labor starts. They will usually feel a gush of warm fluid from the vagina either running down their legs (if standing) or wetting the bed (if lying down). Labor typically begins within a day after this occurs. If it does not, the doctor may want to start labor artificially to protect the baby from infection since it is no longer isolated from the outside world.

HOW LABOR BEGINS

The exact biological forces that start labor are not clearly understood. For many years, it was thought that a rapid drop of progesterone at the end of pregnancy might stimulate the beginning of regular contractions of the uterus, but recent studies in humans do not support this explanation. *Oxytocin,* a hormone made in the pituitary gland, has also been thought to play a role, but women whose pituitaries have been surgically removed are still capable of normal, spontaneous labor. At present, evidence indicates that prostaglandins may be involved because (1) they can cause strong uterine contractions at any time during pregnancy, (2) the fetal membranes have

---

[2] "Show" is not a reliable indication of labor if a pelvic exam was done in the preceding day or two, since this may have caused a slight amount of internal bleeding and disrupted the mucus plug guarding the cervix.

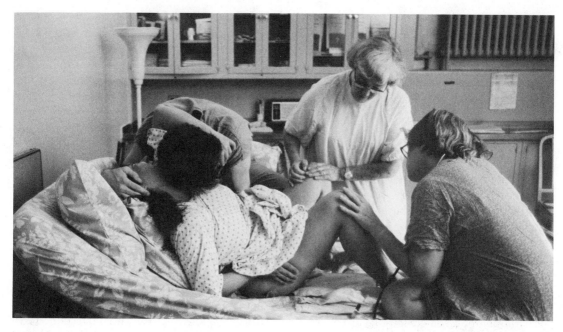

Labor can be a shared experience between wife and husband. Here, two midwives are assisting.

high concentrations of the substances necessary for the manufacture of prostaglandins, and (3) drugs such as aspirin that inhibit prostaglandin formation can delay the onset of labor (Pritchard and MacDonald, 1980).

THE STAGES OF LABOR

For descriptive convenience, labor is divided into three stages. The length and experience of these stages varies from woman to woman and for different pregnancies of the same woman.[3]

The *first stage of labor* begins when uterine contractions are strong enough, long enough, and frequent enough to begin effacement and dilatation of the cervix. In first pregnancies, complete effacement occurs before dilatation starts; in later pregnancies the two occur simultaneously.

When the cervix is completely effaced, its thickness has decreased from about 2 centimeters (0.8 inch) to the thickness of a piece of paper. This process is measured in percentages. If the doctor tells a pregnant woman that she is 50 percent effaced, that means the thickness of the cervix is about 1 centimeter (0.4 inch).

When the opening of the cervix is 10 centimeters (4 inches), a width that must be reached

---

[3] *False labor*, contractions that are simply an exaggeration of Braxton-Hicks contractions, may mimic the start of true labor. Although false labor can be convincing enough to result in a trip to the hospital, it can usually be differentiated from true labor. Its contractions tend to be irregular, the interval between them does not shorten, and the woman feels discomfort mainly in the lower abdomen and groin. True labor produces back and abdominal pain. Furthermore, false labor does not result in progressive effacement and dilatation.

Human Reproduction

for a baby to be born, dilatation is complete. Dilatation is caused by pressures from uterine contractions pushing the amniotic sac or the baby's head in wedgelike fashion into the cervix.

The first stage of labor is by far the longest: in first pregnancies, it averages 13 hours, and in later pregnancies, 8 hours. Early in first-stage labor, when dilatation is minimal, contractions are mild (lasting 20 to 40 seconds) and far apart, occurring at intervals of 10 to 20 minutes. The woman is usually comfortable and can be out of bed if she wishes. She may be discouraged by the length of time it takes to get even a little dilatation, but once she has gotten to 4 or 5 centimeters she has usually completed more than half of the time in this stage. At this more active part of the first stage, contractions are typically 30 to 60 seconds long and occur every 2 to 4 minutes.

The woman may obtain treatment to help deal with pain at this time, since medications given any earlier might slow the progress of labor. Various types of pain relief are available (see Table 5-2), and the woman should become familiar with them and discuss her options with her doctor well before labor starts. Although all medications have potential risks — including some negative effects on the baby — careful use under medical supervision can be important in allowing the mother to go through labor and delivery with only mild discomfort. This relief can have obvious psychological and physical benefits. Regrettably, some women feel guilty if they want pain relievers during childbirth. They may feel inadequate for needing such help, especially if a friend or relative had an easy delivery *without* drugs and is sure everyone else's experience should be the same. Others have been told that the medical "establishment" pushes medications primarily for its own convenience and income. While some doctors do this, most have the welfare and comfort of their patient and her baby uppermost in their minds.

The last part of the first stage of labor (8 to 10 centimeters dilatation) is usually the most uncomfortable. The woman's contractions last 45 to 60 seconds or longer, are only about 2 minutes apart, and are very strong. In first pregnancies, this part of labor usually lasts about 40 minutes and in later pregnancies it averages 20 minutes. Most often, the membranes rupture at this time. The first stage of labor ends when dilatation is complete; at this point, the mother is usually moved to the delivery room.

The *second stage of labor*, which goes from full dilatation to birth of the baby, is shorter (average length, 80 minutes in first pregnancies, 30 minutes in others) and is usually less stressful for the mother. She can now assist the baby's descent by pushing down with her contractions. Before *crowning*, the appearance of the head at the opening of the vagina, the doctor or midwife may perform an *episiotomy*, an incision in the perineum that gives the baby's head more room to emerge (see p. 130).

Once the baby's head is delivered, blood and mucus are wiped off and the nose and mouth are suctioned to aid breathing.[4] As soon as the rest of the baby is out (a process that is surprisingly quick in an uncomplicated birth), the newborn is held below the level of the mother's body and suctioning of the mouth and nose repeated. The umbilical cord is clamped and cut about 3 centimeters (1¼ inches) from the baby's body (the stub dries up in a few days and falls off, leaving the navel behind as a souvenir). Although often shown in movies or television dramas, doctors

---

[4] The baby's head is the first part to be delivered in about 95 percent of pregnancies. These are called *occiput, vertex,* or *cephalic presentations. Breech presentations* occur about 4 percent of the time; in this position, the buttocks or feet are delivered first. In the rarer cases called *transverse positions,* the baby lies across the uterus and a shoulder or arm will present first. This requires either turning the baby or a cesarean section.

TABLE 5–2
Medications for Pain Reduction in Labor and Delivery

Method	Effects on Mother	Effects on Fetus
Analgesics		
Tranquilizers Valium, Vistaril, Sparine	Physical relaxation and reduced anxiety; takes the edge off pain but does not eliminate it entirely	Minimal
Barbiturates Nembutal, Seconal, Amytal	Drowsiness and reduced anxiety; may slow the progress of labor	Can depress nervous system and breathing
Narcotics Demerol, Dolophine, Nisentil	Reduce pain and elevate mood, but may inhibit uterine contractions and cause nausea or vomiting	Can depress nervous system and breathing
Amnesics Scopolamine ("Twilight")	Does not reduce pain but causes the woman to forget her experience after it is over; may cause physical excitation and wildness	Minimal
Anesthetics		
Local Paracervical	Blocks pain in the uterus and cervix, but relatively short-lasting and ineffective late in labor; can lower mother's blood pressure	Causes a slowing of fetal heartbeat in about 20 percent of cases
Pudendal	Blocks pain from the perineum and vulva in about 50 percent of cases	Minimal
Regional Spinal, Epidural, Caudal	Blocks pain from the uterus, cervix, and perineum; highly effective, but can cause serious drop in blood pressure or seizures	Generally does not affect fetus but requires forceps delivery more often than other methods
General Nitrous Oxide (laughing gas), Halothane, Thiopental	Usually used only in the last few minutes of labor to eliminate pain completely, but may cause vomiting or other complications and is a leading cause of maternal death	Can depress nervous system and breathing

rarely have to spank a baby to induce crying and breathing, since this usually happens spontaneously. As the baby takes his or her first breaths, the skin will become pink unless there is a medical problem.

The baby is shown to the mother and usually given to her to hold. To prevent eye infections after the passage through the vagina, the baby is almost always given eye drops (usually silver nitrate) or an antibiotic ointment. The baby is also given a vitamin K shot to prevent bleeding, since this vitamin cannot be manufactured in newborns immediately after birth. Finally, the baby is given an identification bracelet, footprints are taken, and a medical exam is done to check for birth defects or other health problems.

The *third stage of labor* follows the baby's birth. At this point, the placenta separates from the wall of the uterus, and the placenta and membranes (the "afterbirth") are delivered. This usually requires only 10 to 12 minutes. If even small pieces of the placenta or membranes are retained in the uterus, bleeding problems may result. If an episiotomy was done, or if any tears in the vagina occurred, the doctor repairs it at this time.

Delivery

Over the years, many different schools of thought have emerged concerning the details and style of labor and delivery, and pregnant women and doctors are often bombarded with information "proving" that one way is undeniably the best. Usually, it is a matter of personal preference (or health considerations) between a woman and her doctor. Here, we will discuss some of the more popular methods.

HOSPITAL DELIVERY

A hospital delivery usually begins once the first stage of labor is underway. A nurse or doctor asks a series of questions to outline the history of the pregnancy and the sequence of events near the time of labor, and a vaginal examination is done to see how much dilatation and effacement has occurred. A blood sample and urine specimen are usually taken for a general health check, and a physical exam is performed to evaluate the mother's condition and that of the baby.

After this point, hospital procedures vary considerably. In some locales, the pregnant woman is "prepped" (prepared) by having her pubic hair shaved, either entirely or just around the vagina, and having the vulva washed with an antiseptic solution to reduce the risk of infection to the newborn baby. She also may be given an enema to clear her bowels. In many hospitals, sophisticated electronic equipment is used to check the progress of the baby (*fetal monitoring*) as well as the frequency, intensity, and duration of the mother's contractions. Watching the fetal heart rate is particularly important because a sustained drop in rate may indicate fetal distress.

In some cases, a woman may be admitted to the hospital at or near the end of her pregnancy to have labor started artificially. This procedure, called *induction* or *induced labor,* is usually done so that a well-rested woman can begin labor under planned conditions with her doctor present; this technique is also used in certain types of problem pregnancies where it can protect the health of mother and child alike. Labor is usually induced by giving the mother oxytocin. Inducing labor is not without risk to the mother and fetus, but most physicians feel that the benefits outweigh the risks substantially. Some feminists claim the issue is really a matter of medical chauvinism, however, believing that induction is mainly done for the doctor's convenience (Hahn and Paige, 1980).

The woman's husband or partner is usually encouraged to be present in the labor room, and sometimes the delivery room, so that he can

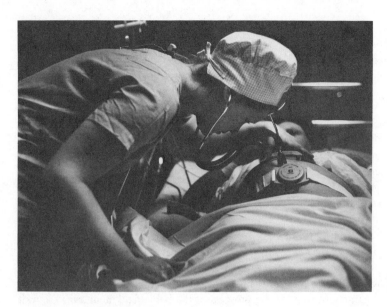

Monitoring the progress of labor and the heartbeat of the unborn child.

share the experience, give encouragement and support, and help make her comfortable. In most hospitals, other family members are not permitted to be present. However, obstetrical nurses can provide close, continuing attention and information.

Doctors sometimes rupture the membranes to stimulate the progress of labor. An intravenous solution of sugar and water may be started to prevent dehydration and to allow for rapid administration of anesthesia or blood transfusions if something goes wrong. During the delivery, the baby's head may be assisted out of the vagina by the use of *forceps* if there is fetal distress, if the umbilical cord is wrapped tightly around the baby's neck, if the cord is being compressed so that the blood supply to the baby is cut off (*prolapsed cord*), or if anesthesia interferes with the mother's ability to push out her baby.

At the time of crowning, many American physicians routinely perform an *episiotomy* to enlarge the opening for the baby's head. An episiotomy is an incision made through the skin

and muscle of the perineum, the area between the vagina and the anus (see Figure 5-6). The episiotomy has several purposes: (1) it reduces the pressure against the baby's head, lessening the trauma of delivery; (2) it reduces the risk of tearing the perineum, which might cause more extensive tissue damage and might be ragged-edged and difficult to repair; and (3) it permits the use of forceps if needed to assist in delivering the baby's head. Most women do not feel the incision being made because the perineum is numbed from the pressure of the baby's head.

Many feminists and some physicians are opposed to routine episiotomies, noting that fewer than one-third of deliveries in Europe use this technique (Arms, 1975; Lake, 1976). Furthermore, they point out that the vaginal opening has the capacity to stretch widely without tearing in most circumstances, and suggest that episiotomy should be done only in selected cases (Boston Women's Health Book Collective, 1976). Repairing an episiotomy has sometimes been called sewing "husband's stitches" since the vagi-

Human Reproduction

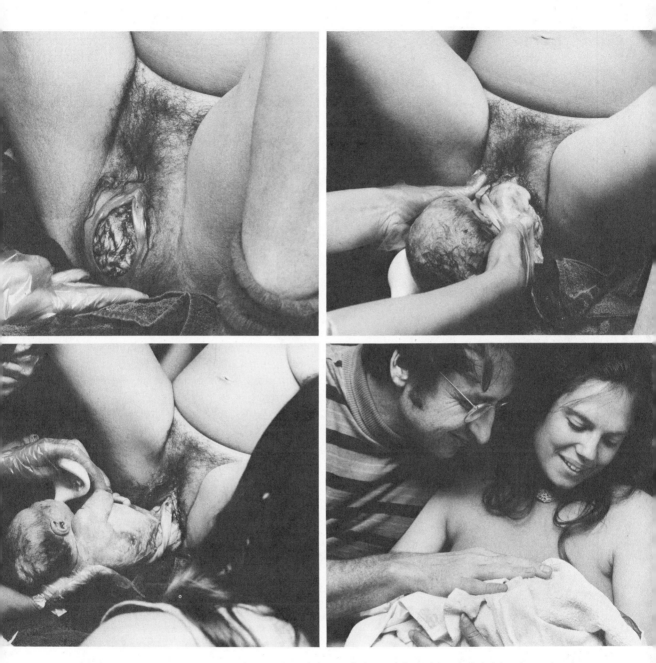

This sequence of photos of a home delivery shows the baby's head crowning, the first shoulder being delivered, the baby's mouth and nose being suctioned clear of mucus, and the proud parents with their child.

Birth

FIGURE 5–6
An Episiotomy Done during Labor

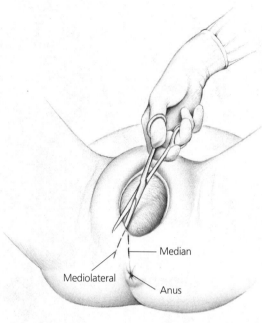

Median

Mediolateral

Anus

breech presentation, transverse lie, maternal illness), others are not discovered until labor is far along.

NATURAL CHILDBIRTH

Natural childbirth refers to a method described by a British obstetrician, Grantly Dick-Read, in 1932 in a book titled *Childbirth Without Fear*. He objected to much of the medical intervention in delivery and believed that culturally imbued fear and tension were the principal causes of pain and difficulty in the childbirth experience. He felt that fear and anticipation of pain led to psychological and muscular tension which opposed dilatation of the birth canal and became, in effect, a self-fulfilling prophecy.

To break the fear-tension-pain reaction, Dick-Read suggested eliminating fear through education and reducing tension by the use of relaxation techniques such as breathing and physical exercises. Prenatal classes were used to stress the positive side of childbirth and teach exercises to increase elasticity in the pelvic muscles, flexibility in the joints of the pelvis and back, and improve circulation. Special breathing patterns to reduce pain and increase the effectiveness of contractions were taught.

Although some consider childbirth to be truly "natural" only if no painkilling medications are used at all, Dick-Read felt that painkillers were permissible but to be avoided if possible.

LAMAZE

A similar approach to that of Dick-Read was advocated by Fernand Lamaze, a French obstetrician who travelled to Russia to study obstetrical practices. The Lamaze method, first publicized in this country in a book called *Thank You, Dr. Lamaze* (Karmel, 1959) and later described in *Painless Childbirth* (Lamaze, 1970), also depends on

nal opening is tightened. For this reason, some feminists believe that episiotomies are done primarily to protect the man's future sexual pleasure during intercourse (Hahn and Paige, 1980).

Although 80 percent of deliveries are straightforward and uncomplicated, there are specific advantages to hospital delivery. Sophisticated equipment is available for rapid diagnosis of problems affecting either mother or child, facilities for surgery are close at hand if emergency cesarean section is needed, blood is available for transfusion if maternal bleeding cannot be controlled, and the personnel and equipment of the nursery are specially geared to problems of the newborn infant. While some problems of labor and delivery are detectable in advance (e.g.,

education and exercises to allow a woman to gain control over her labor.

The Lamaze method, taught in prenatal classes to both the wife and husband (or to the woman and another friend acting as her "coach" if she is unmarried or her husband is not available), shows women how to relax all the muscles in their bodies and how to position themselves and breathe during different stages of labor. Other techniques are used to distract the woman from awareness of pain: these include *effleurage*, a light, circular stroking of the abdomen used when active labor begins, pressure on the front of the hip bones to reduce abdominal discomfort, and massage techniques to lessen backache. Both the coach and the mother are active participants in the process of labor, with a prearranged set of exercises to follow.

Neither natural childbirth nor childbirth by the Lamaze method is completely painless. Both approaches depend on personal awareness through education to reduce fear of the unknown and physical relaxation techniques that reduce tension and the anticipation of pain. In both methods, there is some distraction from the perception of pain, but pain is not eliminated.

LEBOYER

The French physician Frederick Leboyer described his approach to delivery in his book, *Birth Without Violence* (1975). Leboyer believes that birth is a traumatic event for the baby and suggests ways of minimizing the shock of the experience. He feels that the ideal birth should occur in a quiet, dimly lit, warm room to avoid frightening or overstimulating the baby. After delivery, the baby should be placed on the mother's abdomen and the cutting of the umbilical cord should be delayed for a while, to maintain contact between mother and infant. Leboyer

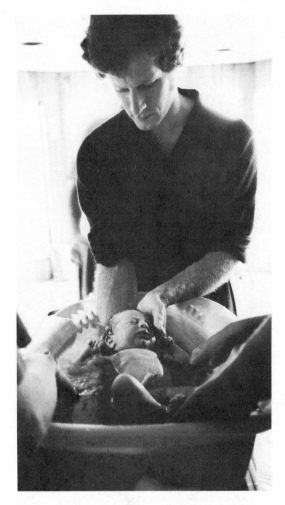

A father giving a Leboyer bath to a newborn. Whether this technique is mostly a matter of making the parents feel soothed or whether it actually benefits the baby is uncertain, but it certainly is a poignant time.

also recommends calming the baby with a gentle, sensuous, warm bath after birth.

Although Leboyer claims that children delivered by his method grow up to be healthier and more free of conflict than those born in traditional fashion, a recent report found no differences in infant behavior in the first hour of life, one or two days after birth, or at eight months between children born by the Leboyer method and conventional delivery (Nelson et al., 1980).

CESAREAN SECTION

Cesarean section (C section) is an operation to remove the fetus through an incision in the walls of the abdomen and uterus. Cesareans are done when the woman cannot deliver vaginally without endangering her or the baby's life or health. Among conditions that usually require cesarean delivery are: (1) a size difference between the baby's head and the mother's pelvis that makes it difficult or impossible for the baby to pass through the birth canal, (2) transverse position of the baby or other difficult presentations, (3) fetal distress from any cause (for example, prolapsed cord), (4) premature separation of the placenta or abnormal positioning of the placenta so it blocks the opening to the cervix from within the uterus, and (5) long, difficult labor that is not progressing properly.

The cesarean birth rate in America has tripled in the last decade, from 5.5 to 15 percent (Kolata, 1980a). Although cesarean births have a low rate of complications, the maternal death rate (1 in 10,000) is double the rate for vaginal deliveries. Recently, a task force sponsored by the National Institute of Health recommended that many women who had cesarean deliveries can safely have subsequent normal vaginal deliveries, although in the past, 99 percent were automatically given cesareans in their future deliveries (Kolata, 1980a). Confirming this, one recent study found that approximately one-third of women who had previously had a cesarean were able to have successful vaginal deliveries (Gellman et al., 1983). Some couples who were not expecting a cesarean birth may feel cheated or disappointed, while others actually prefer cesarean delivery as an "easier" way of having a baby.

HOME DELIVERY AND BIRTHING ROOMS

Not everyone views the hospital, with its authoritative atmosphere, complex rules, impersonality, and association with illness, as an ideal setting for childbirth. In some countries, such as France and Holland, some women go to special childbirth centers that are separate from hospitals (a few can now be found in the U.S.). In many societies, home delivery supervised by a midwife is common (Cavero, 1979). While two decades ago there were only 300 nurse-midwives in the United States, there are now more than 2,500, with several hundred new nurse-midwives graduating annually from certified training programs. Although many work in hospitals, others are in private practice either in association with physicians or independently. Nurse-midwives generally emphasize prenatal counselling, family-centered childbirth, and a limited degree of intervention in the natural process of labor and delivery. Unlike most physicians, nurse-midwives typically stay with a woman throughout her labor and often encourage the woman to get up out of bed and move around through most of her labor. Today, a number of states (including New York, Pennsylvania, Alaska, Maryland, Mississippi, New Mexico, and Utah) have laws requiring that insurance companies provide coverage for the services of certified nurse-midwives who work under the guidance of physicians or hospitals, but in other states there is considerable resistance to the use of nurse-midwives, especially those who practice independently of hospitals.

Having a baby at home offers a chance for a more relaxed experience in familiar surroundings, freedom from hospital routines, contact with the whole family (including children who can share in the process), and a less expensive bill. In addition, there is preliminary evidence that home delivery may be as safe as hospital delivery for un-

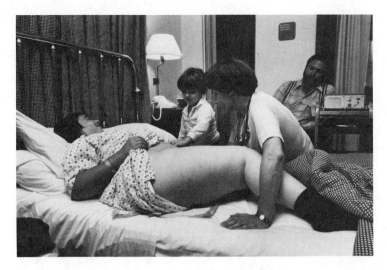

Birthing rooms have been added at many hospitals to provide a more home-like environment for labor and delivery while permitting the entire family to participate in the experience.

complicated pregnancies (Wertz and Wertz, 1977; Hahn and Paige, 1980).

Although many doctors are opposed to home births, some are willing to cooperate and a few are even enthusiastic about the practice. In any case, careful prenatal screening must be done to identify potential problem pregnancies or difficult deliveries, provisions must be made for appropriate supervision by an experienced midwife or doctor, and emergency access to a hospital must be available since prenatal screening is not infallible.

A relatively recent compromise development designed to overcome the image of hospital austerity is the opening of so-called birthing rooms at hundreds of hospitals across America. In these rooms, which are typically furnished in a comfortable, home-like fashion but are also equipped with oxygen and anesthesia, labor and delivery are possible in a more relaxed climate in which other family members, including children, can be part of the childbirth experience. If something goes wrong, however — for example, if a blood transfusion is needed — all necessary re-

sources are at hand to take care of the emergency, thus circumventing what many see as the primary risk of home delivery. Use of these birthing rooms usually costs about the same as a more traditional delivery in the hospital.

Psychological Aspects of Childbirth

Each woman brings her own personality style and ways of dealing with a new experience to the process of childbirth. Her initial anxieties may reflect concerns for her safety and the status of her baby, fear of the unknown, uncertainty about her capacity to love and care for a child, and a host of other questions (How will my husband react? What if the baby is not normal? Will I make a fool of myself?). The childbirth experience is also colored by the woman's relationship to her doctor, her feelings about the use of medications, the support she receives from her husband or partner, and the expectations she has of what it will all be like. The relatively high rate of cesarean deliveries and other obstetrical complications means that childbirth is frequently not the idealized experience it is expected to be (Grossman, Eichler, and Winickoff, 1980). No wonder it is difficult to talk about a "typical" experience.

In some cases, a woman may sacrifice personal choice about aspects of childbirth to medical routine or philosophical principles. For example, a woman may prefer to be given pain-killers but may not if friends or relatives discourage this practice. Or a woman may reluctantly agree to having a fetal monitor although she finds it annoying and artificial. Certainly, competent obstetrical service with high standards must be available but it should not preclude personal expression in having a baby. Childbirth is an intensely personal experience. The culmination of pregnancy in labor and delivery is ideally a time of intimacy, sharing, and fulfillment.

THE POSTPARTUM DAYS

The *postpartum period,* the time after the baby's birth, requires many adjustments for all concerned. Physical changes occur as the mother's body adjusts to no longer being pregnant. Both parents must also psychologically adjust to the new baby, parental roles and responsibilities, changes in family relationships, and looking ahead to the future. This is a complex time of ups and downs, new experiences, frustrations and joys.

Physiologic and Anatomic Processes

After delivery, the uterus will shrink back to its normal size gradually, going from about 1,000 grams (2.2 pounds) just after delivery to 50 to 70 grams (1.8 to 2.5 ounces) at the end of the sixth postpartum week. Once the placenta separates from the uterus, the levels of certain hormones in the mother's body (most notably, estrogen and progesterone) decline abruptly. It usually takes the woman several weeks to adjust to this rapid change, and some authorities believe that the emotional ups and downs of the early postpartum period are related to this phenomenon.

Immediately after childbirth, the cervix is collapsed and flabby but it quickly regains its tone, tightening so that by a week after delivery there is an opening of less than 1 centimeter (0.4 inch). During the first few postpartum weeks, as the lining of the uterus regrows, there is a discharge called *lochia* that changes in color from dark red to pinkish-brown to yellowish-white. The vagina, which was stretched considerably during birth, gradually gets smaller but usually does not return to the exact size it was before childbirth.

Psychological Reactions

The first day or two after childbirth is often a time of happiness and relief. The woman enjoys a feeling of accomplishment, family and friends congratulate her, and people around her attend to her needs without great demands on her time and energy. By the third or fourth day after delivery, many women experience a turn in their mood — feeling "down," being tearful, or having frightening thoughts or dreams — a phenomenon called "baby blues" or *postpartum depression.*

The irritability and vulnerability that also mark this emotional letdown probably stem from many sources: the hormonal changes previously mentioned, the effects of fatigue and physical stress, a sense of loneliness and separation, the strangeness of being in the hospital, and mixed feelings about the mother's role and viewing herself in a new light. In most cases, postpartum depression lasts for only a few days.

Some women may feel guilty or troubled in the early postpartum period. Not all pregnancies result in normal children, and the mother of an infant with a birth defect or serious illness (as well as a woman whose child was stillborn) may try to "explain" what happened on the basis of something she thinks she did wrong. Women might also worry over their partner's welfare, over particular decisions such as nursing versus bottle-feeding, or over their ability to care for their child. For other women, there may be a personal sense of failure if, for example, they were unable to deliver vaginally and required a cesarean section. A woman who has previously decided to put her child up for adoption may have second thoughts at this time or may have a profound sense of loss even though she feels she's doing the right thing.

A new set of circumstances and a new set of adjustments occur immediately after leaving the hospital. The demands of the new infant (nighttime feedings, diaper changes, and so on) are thrown into the demands of everyday living. Older children and husband want attention, friends and family want to visit and talk, and the mother is apt to feel fragmented, confused, and exhausted. Some women receive considerable help during this time from their own mother, another relative, a friend, or someone they have hired. Husbands can help out too, but usually seem a less reliable source of comfort than an "outsider." The postpartum adjustment beyond the first week or two is primarily a reflection of the adjustment to parenting, a process that will now be considered.

PARENTING

The first days after delivery can play a critical role in the development of an emotional link between parent and child, a process called *parent-child bonding*. Physical contact, cuddling, cooing, and eye contact in this period of the infant's life seem to have a major impact on the child's later behavior and psychological health (Trause, Kennel, and Klaus, 1977). One experiment showed that babies who received more early postnatal contact with their mothers were more attentive to them at four weeks of age (Klaus et al., 1972). Another study demonstrated that newborns were able to recognize differences in adult voices and to show a preference for their mother's voice within the first three days of life (DeCasper and Fifer, 1980). Although studies have not yet explored the importance of father-child bonding in the early postpartum period, it may also have long-range significance.

As already mentioned, arriving at home with a new baby is apt to be a trying time. One aspect of this dilemma is neatly described in this comment from a first-time mother:

> I don't think I was prepared at all because you read in books and you talk with people and you think that all of a sudden there is going to be this motherly surge of love which is not true. In my case it wasn't. I had this colicky baby that spit up and we had to stay home. It took me a long time [to adjust]. . . . I don't think motherly love is automatic as a lot of times you are led to believe. I think you should be prepared for this because you think you're unusual. There is a lot of guilt. (Shereshefsky, Liebenberg, and Lockman, 1974, p. 175)

Adjusting to the state of parenthood, with its restrictions on freedom, privacy, and self-indulgence, is not easy. No one can be the perfect parent — always patient, never angry, constantly available, forever exercising good judgment, and never making a mistake — but new parents often need a while to gain this perspective.

Nursing

Milk production (*lactation*) occurs two or three days after birth, replacing the colostrum previously secreted by the breasts. The breasts are prepared for lactation by large amounts of prolactin secreted by the pituitary during the second half of pregnancy. In response to the stimulus of suckling, which further increases prolactin secretion, the breasts become more distended until finally there is a milk flow reflex (ejection of milk from the breast) which is controlled by oxytocin. In the first day or two of nursing, the breasts may be uncomfortable because of congestion; the nipples may also be sore because the hungry baby's sucking grip is surprisingly powerful.

While nursing has a number of advantages over bottle feedings, it has disadvantages as well. Breast milk has natural ingredients that strengthen the baby's resistance to disease, is instantly available, does not require sterilization or heating as bottles do, and is self-replenishing. Nursing also provides a closeness that may have psychological benefits for both child and mother. On the negative side, drugs taken by the mother are usually secreted in her milk (Platzker, Lew and Stewart, 1980), breast-feeding may be inconvenient if the mother works outside the home, and in some cases, if milk flow does not prove adequate to meet the baby's nutritional needs, the mother may experience a sense of failure.

Women often become sexually aroused during nursing; some women even have orgasms in this fashion. Erotic arousal in this context can create reactions ranging from pleasure to guilt or fear. Interestingly, Masters and Johnson (1966) found that women who breast-feed their babies have considerably higher sexual interest in the first three postpartum months than women who do not.

In the United States, there has been a definite trend toward breast-feeding in the past decade. Breast-feeding in hospitals after childbirth increased from 25 percent in 1971 to 58 percent in 1981, and the number of breast-fed five and six month olds increased from 6 percent to 27 percent (Martinez and Dodd, 1982). While highly educated, relatively affluent mothers are most apt to nurse their babies, the greatest rate of increase in breast-feeding was found among less well-educated mothers.

The individual woman's decision to nurse or to bottle-feed is influenced by many different factors. Jelliffe (1976) identified several social biases in this decision-making process: the Western world's tendency to overvalue manufactured products, overemphasis on the sexual rather than nurturing role of the breasts, the changing role of women in terms of work outside the home, and pressures from the food industry via advertising. On the other hand, in recent years the arguments of breast-feeding advocates have often made women feel that bottle-feeding is a crime against nature and is a shirking of their duties as "good" mothers. Our suspicion is that if breast-feeding is undertaken out of a sense of obligation, the emotional benefits to mother and child probably diminish considerably. Bottle-feeding allows both parents to interact with the baby more freely and can certainly foster a close, loving relationship just as breast-feeding can.

Returning to Sexual Interaction

Most doctors advise women to abstain from coitus for a number of weeks after childbirth to allow healing of the episiotomy and restoration of the vagina and uterus. The exact timing of when sex can be resumed is an individual matter, influenced by both medical factors (e.g., persistent bleeding, fatigue) and psychological considerations (e.g., postpartum depression). By three to four weeks after delivery, most women find their sexual desire returning and can comfortably resume sexual activity. In circumstances where intercourse is still uncomfortable, alternate means of sexual expression can be used until full recovery takes place.

PROBLEM PREGNANCIES

Not all pregnancies go as planned or as described in textbooks. There are several common problems, which we will discuss here.

Prematurity

A premature baby is one born any time before the thirty-sixth week of pregnancy. Babies born prematurely are more likely to have health difficulties than full-term babies; as a result, prematurity is a leading cause of newborn death. "Preemies" have a high rate of respiratory problems, seizures, and infections which may lead to brain damage or other long-range handicaps. Premature births are associated with maternal illness, malfunction of the placenta, heavy smoking, and pregnancies in young teenagers; but in many cases no underlying cause can be found. Modern methods of caring for premature infants have significantly improved survival rates from just a few years ago (Hack, Fanaroff, and Merkatz, 1979). Recently, a drug called ritodrine that inhibits labor by relaxing the muscles of the uterus has been found to be effective in stopping premature labor.

Toxemia

Toxemia of pregnancy is a disease marked by the sudden appearance of high blood pressure, severe edema, and protein in the urine after the twentieth week of pregnancy (*preeclampsia*) which in some cases progresses to convulsions and coma (*eclampsia*). Although 6 percent of pregnancies have this complication, its cause is not known. Toxemia is most frequent in first pregnancies, especially in the very young or women over the age of thirty-five. In later pregnancies, it may be associated with diabetes or vascular disease. Toxemia is most commonly found in women of low socioeconomic standing, and some evidence suggests that a tendency to this disorder is inherited. Untreated, toxemia can cause maternal or fetal death, but if properly treated it can often be controlled.

Birth Defects and Their Detection

Birth defects occur in approximately 3 percent of all live births and at a substantially higher rate in miscarried pregnancies. About 20 percent of birth defects are inherited, 3 to 5 percent reflect chromosome abnormalities, 2 to 3 percent are due to infections, and 5 percent are due to maternal drug use or exposure to environmental chemicals; but in the majority of cases no specific explanation can be discovered (Wilson, 1977).

Only two examples of birth defects will be mentioned here. *Down's syndrome* (also called *trisomy 21* or *mongolism*) is a chromosome disorder that causes severe mental retardation and defects of the heart, kidneys, and intestines. Its incidence increases with advanced maternal age. In young mothers, the frequency is about 1 in 1,500 births, but by age thirty-five it is 1 in 300 births and at age forty-five it is 1 in 30 to 50 births. Maternal infection with the virus that causes German measles (*rubella*) can also be dangerous to the developing baby. German measles causes serious defects in about half of exposed embryos during the first month of pregnancy, but this rate decreases to 25 percent in the second month and less than 15 percent in the third month. The fetal damage caused by rubella includes deafness, cataracts, heart defects, mental retardation, and retarded growth.

Having a child with a birth defect can be

frightening and disheartening. Our society emphasizes success and physical appearance, and the parents of a child with a defect may see their baby as a sign of a defect within themselves or as "punishment" for something they did wrong. Some parents react by rejection and denial, while others cope by bringing extra love and care to their newborn and accepting the infant as a full-fledged family member. Some families find new strength and closeness after the birth of a child with a defect.

Fortunately, there are now several ways of detecting the presence of certain types of defects in the developing fetus. Using a procedure called *amniocentesis*, a sample of amniotic fluid is obtained by inserting a needle into the uterus after first deadening the abdominal wall with a local anesthetic (Figure 5-7). Analysis of the fluid can

FIGURE 5-7
Amniocentesis

Amniocentesis involves removing a small amount of amniotic fluid from inside the pregnant uterus. The fluid is then analyzed in a laboratory to provide information about many types of birth defects or genetic conditions that may affect the fetus.

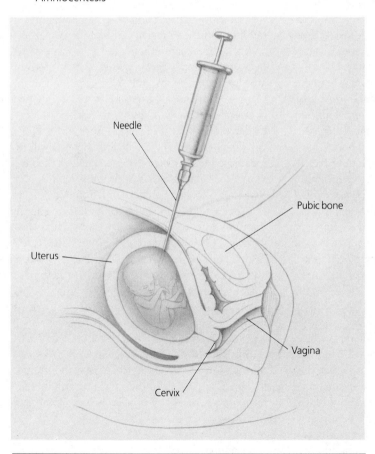

Needle

Pubic bone

Uterus

Vagina

Cervix

Human Reproduction

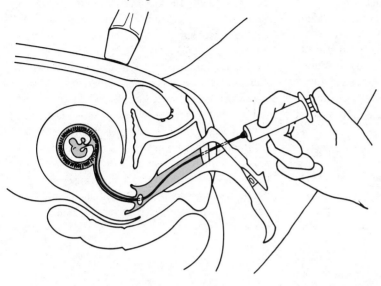

FIGURE 5–8
Chorionic Villi Sampling

identify a variety of genetic disorders (for example, Down's syndrome, muscular dystrophy) as well as the sex of the fetus. One recent study found that amniocentesis identified significant chromosome abnormalities in 1 out of 200 women at age thirty-five, 1 in 67 women at age forty, and 1 in 20 women at age forty-five (Hook, Cross, and Schreinemachers, 1983). If a serious abnormality is uncovered, the parents can consider terminating the pregnancy by abortion if this choice is consistent with their personal values. There is about a 1 percent risk that amniocentesis may result in loss of the fetus, but this risk must be balanced with the benefits of a highly reliable means of identifying serious genetic problems.

A newer technique, called *chorionic villi sampling* (CVS), is seen by some authorities as having even greater usefulness. This method, which involves insertion of a thin catheter through the vagina and cervix into the uterus (see Figure 5–8), takes a small sample of tissue from the chorionic villi — tiny thread-like protrusions on the chorion membrane that surrounds the fetus. But unlike amniocentesis, which cannot be done until the sixteenth week of pregnancy, CVS can be done at the eighth week — almost as soon as a woman knows she's pregnant. Furthermore, the results from CVS are available in two days, whereas it usually takes three to four weeks to get the results of an amniocentesis. Thus, if a birth defect is detected, a first trimester abortion can be done, which is much safer than having an abortion after 20 or more weeks of pregnancy.

Another technique used to detect many birth defects (although it does not check for most genetic diseases that can be detected by amniocentesis or CVS) is the use of ultrasound examination. Ultrasonic waves are used to form a picture of the fetus. If a birth defect is detected it can sometimes be treated while the baby is still developing within the uterus, or this information may be used to plan for early delivery so the baby can receive corrective treatment (Hill, Breckle, and Gehrking, 1983). Although ultrasound studies are now done in more than half of all pregnancies (both for diagnostic purposes and to check the sex of the developing fetus), some have questioned this since there is no longer term data proving the safety of this procedure.

Ectopic Pregnancy

Ectopic pregnancy (a pregnancy occurring outside the cavity of the uterus) occurs approximately once in every hundred pregnancies (Breen, 1970; Franklin and Zeiderman, 1973; Rubin et al., 1983) (see Figure 5-9). About 97 percent of ectopic pregnancies occur in the Fallopian tubes (tubal pregnancy); in the remainder of cases, the fertilized egg implants in the ovary, the abdomen, or the cervix. Ectopic pregnancies are usually caused by conditions that block or slow the passage of the fertilized egg into the uterus such as anatomical abnormalities, scar tissue resulting from surgery or infections, or tumors. The presence of an IUD (intrauterine device: a means of contraception) is also associated with an increased chance of ectopic pregnancy.

Most ectopic pregnancies abort at a relatively early stage, but when growth of the embryo, placenta, and membranes occurs, there is a substantial risk of rupture and bleeding. Because it is difficult to diagnose this condition, ectopic pregnancy is the seventh leading cause of maternal death. The recurrence rate of an ectopic pregnancy in subsequent pregnancies is about 20 percent.

Rh Incompatibility

Rh incompatibility refers to a condition in which antibodies from the mother's bloodstream destroy red blood cells in the fetus causing fetal anemia, mental retardation, or death. This problem occurs only when a mother whose blood does not have the Rh factor (Rh negative) has a fetus with the Rh factor (Rh positive), a combination that can occur only if the father is Rh positive. Even in this circumstance, the risk is usually not in the first pregnancy (since antibodies have not yet formed in the woman's circulation to the Rh factor) but applies to later pregnancies with an Rh positive fetus.

The development of Rh sensitivity can be prevented by the use of a medication called RhoGAM which neutralizes antibody formation. This must be given within seventy-two hours after delivery (or abortion) of an Rh positive fetus to an Rh negative mother. If sensitivity is already present, either from a blood transfusion or an earlier pregnancy, the fetus can be given a special blood transfusion while still inside the uterus.

FIGURE 5–9
Ectopic Pregnancy Rates per 1,000
Reported Pregnancies

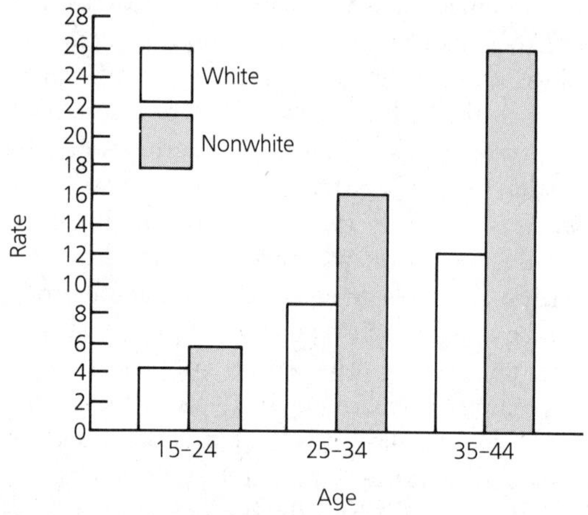

Source: From Rubin, 1983. *Journal of American Medical Association,* April 1, 1983, Vol. 249, No. 13, p. 1727. Copyright 1983, American Medical Association.

INFERTILITY

People usually assume that reproduction happens almost automatically, but 10 to 15 percent of couples trying to have a baby do not succeed after a year or more of sexual intercourse without the use of contraception. This condition, known as *infertility*, has been greatly misunderstood. Often the source of considerable anguish and embarrassment, it rarely poses a direct threat to nonreproductive health or longevity.

Causes

Although the woman typically seeks medical help first, both partners in an infertile couple often have conditions that contribute to their inability to conceive. Thus, it is important that both the man and woman be seen by a physician, since proper treatment and an optimal chance for pregnancy depend on accurate testing. In about 85 percent of couples with infertility, a specific cause can be found.

FEMALE INFERTILITY

The two major causes of female infertility are failure to ovulate and blockage of the Fallopian tubes. Lack of ovulation (or infrequent ovulation) can be caused by ovarian disorders, hormone abnormalities, certain types of chronic illness, drug addiction or abuse, and poor nutrition. Rarely, ovulation is blocked by psychological stress.

Failure to ovulate may be detected by the use of *basal body temperature* (BBT) charts, hormone testing, or scraping the lining of the uterus to examine tissue under a microscope. The BBT chart is obtained by the woman's daily measurement of her temperature immediately after awakening and before getting out of bed. During the first portion of the menstrual cycle the BBT is low, but as progesterone production in the ovary increases just after ovulation, the temperature shifts upward and remains higher for ten to sixteen days (Figure 5-10). BBT increases just after ovulation; if no temperature shift is seen, it is an indication that ovulation did not occur.

Blocked Fallopian tubes may be caused by scarring after an infection in the pelvic tissues or abdomen and can be checked for obstruction by either *Rubin's test,* which involves inserting carbon dioxide into the uterus and seeing if this gas passes into the abdomen, or by X-rays of the uterus and tubes using a dye which outlines these structures. The X-ray method is preferred by most physicians because it is more accurate.

Other less frequent causes of female infertility include abnormal cervical mucus that impedes the passage of sperm, birth defects of the reproductive organs, tumors, infections (see chapter 21), and allergy to sperm. In some cases, not having intercourse close to the time of ovulation may be a problem, and in other instances, the use of artificial lubricants like Vaseline or K-Y Jelly may be killing the sperm.

MALE INFERTILITY

The primary cause of male infertility is a low sperm count. Less than 40 million sperm per cubic centimeter is below normal, but pregnancy is often possible with sperm counts of 20 million per cubic centimeter. With lower counts, the chances of impregnation are considerably reduced. Other factors that determine male fertility include the ability of sperm to swim, the number of abnormal sperm, and the volume of seminal fluid.

Low sperm counts can be caused by testicular injury, infection (especially mumps occurring after childhood, when it can spread to the testes), radiation, endocrine disorders, varicose veins in the scrotum, undescended testes, and birth defects. Drug use can also impair sperm production, with alcohol, cigarettes, narcotics, marihuana,

FIGURE 5–10
Basal Body Temperature (BBT) Patterns

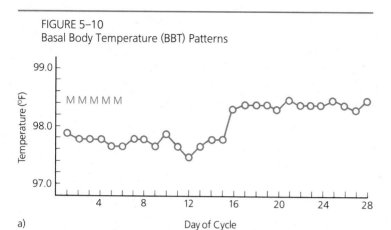

a)

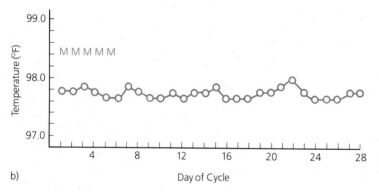

b)

Source: From Kolodny, Masters and Johnson, 1979. © 1979 by Robert C. Kolodny, William H. Masters, and Virginia E. Johnson.

a) The pronounced, sustained temperature rise from day 16 on indicates ovulation occurred. b) The absence of a sustained temperature rise suggests that ovulation did not occur in this cycle. (Days of menstrual flow are indicated by M.)

and some prescription medications potential sources of such a problem (Kolodny, Masters and Johnson, 1979). Some reports indicate that long distance bicycle riding or tight-fitting underwear can lower sperm counts (Shane, Schiff, and Wilson, 1976). Since sperm production is sensitive to temperature, prolonged and frequent use of saunas, hot tubs, and steam baths may have a negative effect. A high frequency of ejaculation can also lower the sperm count (but not enough to be reliable as a contraceptive method!).

In the male, just as in the female, the reproductive tubing system may be blocked as a result of infection or birth defect. If the blockage is complete, no sperm will be in the ejaculate, even though sperm production in the testes is normal. Infertility can result if the male is unable to ejaculate, if he ejaculates outside the vagina, or if he is

Test-Tube Babies

Late in the evening of July 25, 1978, a slightly premature 5 pound, 12 ounce baby girl was born by cesarean section to Lesley and John Brown of Oldham, England. They named their healthy, normal baby Louise and since then her name and picture have made the pages of nearly every major newspaper in the Western world. The sperm and egg that united to conceive Louise met not in Lesley Brown's Fallopian tube, but in a test tube, *in vitro,* outside the mother's body. Louise Brown was the first baby ever born from *in vitro* fertilization techniques.

The British doctors responsible for this remarkable achievement were Patrick Steptoe and Robert Edwards. Steptoe had been experimenting with *in vitro fertilization* (IVF) for more than a decade before meeting Lesley Brown, who was unable to conceive because of blocked Fallopian tubes. She had undergone surgery to unblock the tubes before coming to Steptoe. The surgery was not only unsuccessful, but when Steptoe did his exploration of her reproductive organs, he found the tubes so badly damaged ("mere remnants," he said) that they were removed.

Lesley was first given hormones to stimulate the maturation of eggs in her ovaries. Steptoe and Edwards then made a small incision near her navel and by using an instrument which magnifies and illuminates the tiny ovum, they withdrew a ripe egg and placed it in a laboratory dish. The dish contained a carefully mixed culture of nutrients designed to resemble the environment of the Fallopian tubes. As quickly as possible, John Brown's sperm (obtained through masturbation) were added to the culture and the doctors waited for one of the sperm to impregnate the egg.

Meanwhile, Lesley was given more hormones to insure that her uterus would accept a fertilized egg. After the sperm and egg united in the laboratory dish and the embryonic cells began to divide, the blastocyst (a hollow sphere of about sixty separate cells) was inserted into Lesley's uterus. In about a week, the doctors knew the embryo had attached itself to a wall of the uterus and Lesley Brown was pregnant.

Steptoe and Edwards had made over thirty attempts to implant eggs fertilized outside the mother before their success with the Browns. Two pregnancies had

Louise Brown and her baby sister, both IVF babies

143

resulted, but both were spontaneously aborted – one because the membrane around the embryo ruptured and the other because of a genetic abnormality. This second case is a cause of concern by doctors working in this area. Who is responsible for a child born with genetic damage? Did the damage result from handling the embryo outside the uterus, or would it have occurred even during normal fertilization? Is destroying a fertilized egg in a test tube an abortion?

Since the initial breakthrough by Steptoe and Edwards, a number of IVF clinics have opened around the world, including forty-four in the United States alone (*American Medical News,* May 27, 1983). The first American test-tube baby was Elizabeth Jordan Carr, born December 28, 1981, at Norfolk General Hospital under a program run by the Eastern Virginia Medical School. At the end of 1983, more than 200 IVF babies had been born world-wide (including a sister for pioneering baby Louise Brown), with even larger numbers still to come.

One aspect of this burgeoning activity that distresses some onlookers is the danger of commercialism. Patients are typically charged $3,000 to $5,000 for each attempt at pregnancy, and it generally takes at least three or four attempts before a successful pregnancy occurs. Yet, despite this high cost, some clinics report long waiting lists for their services. At Norfolk General Hospital – which is certainly not typical – there were 3,000 to 4,000 couples on a waiting list for IVF as of mid-1983 (Kolata, 1983). It's little wonder, then, that experts estimate that more than 150 additional clinics may open in America by the end of 1984.

To be sure, the costs – which one scientist likened to the expense of buying a car – are not outrageous considering how important having a child is to some couples. Given improvements in techniques that may soon propel IVF to success rates equalling natural pregnancy, perhaps doing these procedures on a larger scale may lower these costs, as well. At the present time, however, since most insurance companies won't pay for IVF procedures and there is no government support available to defray these costs, there is some concern that these methods are only within reach of a select group.

Even more troubling to others are certain controversial practices sometimes connected with IVF. In Australia, for example, some sterile IVF patients have received eggs donated by other women. In another case, a successful pregnancy was attained using an embryo that had been frozen for four months in liquid nitrogen (*American Medical News,* May 13, 1983). And in various countries where IVF is used, concern has been voiced over the matter of what to do with multiple fertilized eggs, since some contend that discarding or destroying these eggs is tantamount to abortion. As a result of this outcry, in some programs several fertilized eggs are reimplanted in the uterus each cycle so that several sets of twins and at least one set of triplets have now been born after IVF. Where this will all lead is unclear today, but it is certain that guidelines will need to be developed carefully for these and other unasked or unimagined questions about difficult ethical decisions.

impotent (unable to have intercourse). These conditions are discussed in chapter 19.

Treatment

Women who do not ovulate can frequently be helped by treatment with *clomiphene*, a pill which induces ovulation by stimulating the pituitary to secrete LH and FSH. About half of the women given this medication become pregnant. There is a modestly increased chance of having a multiple pregnancy (twins, triplets, etc.), which occurs about 8 percent of the time with clomiphene compared to 1.2 percent in routine pregnancies. Women who do not achieve a pregnancy with clomiphene may be treated with HMG (human menopausal gonadotropins), which is given in a series of injections. This medication acts directly on the ovaries, bypassing the pituitary gland, and will induce ovulation in more than 90 percent of women with functioning ovaries. Pregnancy is achieved by 60 to 70 percent of women receiving this treatment, and 20 percent of these pregnancies are multiple (15 percent are twins, and 5 percent are triplets, quadruplets, quintuplets, or sextuplets). Neither clomiphene nor HMG causes a greater risk of abortion or birth defects than in naturally occurring pregnancies. These drugs, however, can overstimulate the ovaries, causing them to enlarge (sometimes to the size of grapefruit) and to leak fluid into the abdomen. This condition, which is more common with HMG than clomiphene, usually requires hospitalization because there is a danger that the ovaries may rupture.

Blocked Fallopian tubes can sometimes be treated by microsurgery. Using a microscope for visual guidance, a surgeon removes the obstruction, then sews together the healthy portions of the tubes with tiny needles and suture material. Microsurgery is successful in only 30 to 50 percent of women with tubal problems at the present time. Women who have tubal damage beyond surgical repair or women without Fallopian tubes now have the possibility of being treated by *in vitro fertilization*, the dramatic "test tube baby" procedure.

The treatment of male infertility is considerably less developed. Surgical repair of varicose veins in the scrotum can improve the sperm count substantially, but most other conditions respond poorly to treatment. The use of testosterone to achieve a "rebound effect" after first suppressing sperm production is sometimes useful, but the results obtained from using clomiphene in men have been inconclusive. Proper medical management of infections, anatomical defects, or hormonal disorders is definitely helpful, but such cases are relatively few. In men with borderline sperm counts, daily ejaculation can actually lower fertility by reducing the number of sperm, and the chances for a pregnancy can be improved by decreasing the frequency of ejaculation to a minimum of forty-eight hours from one time to the next.

Two recent Canadian studies raise some important questions about the results currently attained in treating infertility. In the first, a two- to seven-year follow-up of 1,145 infertile couples showed that the pregnancy rate in the treated couples (41 percent) was just slightly better than that in untreated couples (35 percent) (Collins et al., 1983). The second study showed that the cumulative pregnancy rate in untreated couples with unexplained infertility was 65 percent (Rousseau et al., 1983). Thus, since many cases of infertility achieve pregnancy spontaneously, it appears important for physicians to perform careful diagnostic testing to determine whether, and if, treatment is required. Likewise, couples contending with infertility should realize that pregnancy is quite possible in many cases even if medical treatment initially doesn't seem to be effective.

Artificial Insemination

Artificial insemination means placing semen in the vagina or uterus by a means other than sexual intercourse. There are two basic types of artificial insemination: using semen from the husband (AIH) or using semen from a donor (AID). For either method, the woman's fertility status must be relatively normal.

AIH can be tried if the husband's count is low but not zero. For practical reasons, successful AIH is infrequent if the count is less than 10 million per cubic centimeter or if the sperm motility is low. AIH is best done by inserting a fresh semen specimen in the vagina at the mouth of the uterus. Using frozen, thawed specimens reduces sperm motility, and combining several frozen specimens does not seem to improve the outcome. Injecting the semen into the uterus causes severe cramping and poses a risk of infection. AIH works by concentrating the husband's sperm at the mouth of the cervix; with coitus, only a small fraction of sperm get to this location.

AID is used when the husband's sperm count is zero or very low. A donor, selected on the basis of excellent health, good intelligence, and closeness of physical characteristics to the husband, provides a masturbated semen specimen (for which he is paid). The donor's identity is unknown to the couple. The legal status of AID is uncertain in many states, although in California once the husband signs a consent form agreeing to AID, he is the legal father of the baby. The pregnancy rate for AID is about 75 percent if fresh donor sperm is used and about 60 percent using frozen semen obtained from a sperm bank.

The decision to undergo AID must be made jointly by husband and wife; clearly this type of treatment is not psychologically right for everyone for whom it might be used. Some people equate this procedure with adultery, others have conflicts with their religious values, and some fear that the husband will reject or dislike the baby because it is not "his." Despite the latter concern, almost all couples who achieve a pregnancy by AID find that the experience brings them very close together and that the husband's excitement at fatherhood is genuinely felt. In some locations, AID is also being used by single women who want to become pregnant.

Adoption and Infertility

Adopting a child is another way of becoming a parent, although this option is far less available today than it was twenty years ago. Adoption is the only route to having a child if both partners are infertile. It is a common misconception that many women of infertile couples conceive shortly after adopting a child — presumably because the couples' pressure to reproduce is lessened (Lamb and Leurgans, 1979). While the conception certainly attracts attention, the couple was obviously not infertile.

The Impact of Infertility

Infertility is rarely an expected problem. Not being able to have a child when you want to can be frustrating, confusing, and depressing. Pressures may be felt from peers and family, spouses may blame each other for the failure to conceive, and sex may become work rather than fun as a couple "tries harder" to achieve a pregnancy. Many women feel empty and unfulfilled as they deal with a situation of infertility, and men often experience anxiety or depression because they incorrectly equate virility with the ability to father a child. Many men are so unwilling to deal with the issue of possible infertility (or afraid of what might be discovered) that they refuse to participate in medical testing. It is no wonder that marital tensions often flare up in this situation.

Surrogate Parents

In the previous edition of this text, we mentioned in a footnote the small number of instances in which a couple composed of an infertile wife and fertile husband hired a woman to act as a "surrogate mother." Such a stand-in is artificially inseminated using the husband's sperm and carries the pregnancy to term, at that point giving the baby to the couple who had hired her for adoption. Since that time, the practice of surrogate parenting has attracted considerably more attention and prompted the founding of the nonprofit Surrogate Parent Foundation (in Los Angeles) as well as an attempt by at least one state legislature (Michigan) to ban the practice entirely. It is currently estimated that hundreds of surrogate mothers have contracted with couples to bear a child for them for pay (ranging from $2,000 to $20,000), with legal fees in the neighborhood of $5,000.

In January 1983, the public's attention was drawn to this previously little-known practice by headlines announcing "Surrogate Infant Left Unclaimed." As the complicated story unravelled, what became clear was that the twenty-six-year-old surrogate mother, Judy Stiver of Michigan, had given birth to a deformed and probably mentally retarded baby, only to have forty-six-year-old Alexander Malahoff of New York, who had contracted for the child, reject him on grounds that he was not the father. Although medical tests eventually supported Mr. Malahoff, the entire episode was an unsavory one in many respects, including a tasteless, prearranged television confrontation between the Stivers and Malahoff in which accusations seemed more important than the welfare of the child. Although the Stivers eventually agreed to keep the baby, who may need to be institutionalized, this case raises a number of difficult issues about the ethical implications of our new reproductive technologies.

What would have happened if Malahoff, or some future Malahoff, had proved to be the infant's father? Could he, as one journalist suggested, try to send the child back and demand a refund?

> Technological parenthood may have the trappings of a business, but it is not a business; it is the answer to someone's most personal prayers. So it should be seen and handled. If the answer to a particular prayer happens to emerge deformed, it is no less the prayer's answer; and, as so many parents of such "damaged goods" have discovered, they sometimes give more contentment to a family than whole and healthy children and thus provide answers to different prayers entirely. (Rosenblatt, 1983, p. 90)

This viewpoint seems laudable, but in the real world people don't always behave in such kindhearted ways. What will become of deformed children born not only to surrogate mothers but to unmarried women using the services of a sperm bank? If a baby conceived by *in vitro* methods turns out to be physically or mentally defective, will lawsuits follow and financial repercussions ensue? Or are we on the verge of an era of government regulation of reproductive decisions along the lines envisioned by George Orwell in *1984* or Aldous Huxley in *Brave New World?*

Some observers see the surrogate mothering issue as analogous to the process of being a sperm donor, while others see it as a form of baby selling, which is clearly an illegal act. Although legal precedents in this area are remarkably few, in one case (Doe v. Kelley, 1980) it was decided that if money changed hands, the inherent commercialism of the situation would "strike at the very foundation of human society" and would be "injurious to the community." While more legal opinions are sure to come, it is quite certain that the complexities of new advances in reproductive technology – gene splicing and other forms of cell manipulation, sex preselection, and so on – raise important questions that must be answered before our scientific advances outpace our ethical thoughtfulness.

Being treated for infertility is frequently a source of sexual problems, since there are time pressures ("the doctor says to have intercourse Monday, Wednesday, and Friday this week"), restrictions ("not tonight, dear, I have to have my sperm count checked tomorrow"), and pressures to perform ("I'm ovulating today and we *have* to have intercourse. *Why* can't you get an erection?"). When sex becomes highly focused on the goal of reproduction, couples often dispense with aspects of sexual play that they previously enjoyed in an effort to "get down to business," thereby creating a hurried, unimaginative, and often emotionally detached experience. Under these circumstances, it is not surprising that sexual pleasure and responsivity both diminish.

SUMMARY

1. Conception occurs when sperm and egg meet in the Fallopian tube. This leads to a single fertilized cell called the zygote, which has forty-six chromosomes including two sex chromosomes (XY = male, XX = female). The zygote divides into a blastocyst that implants in the uterus.

2. The development of the embryo or fetus depends on the placenta, which transmits nourishment and filters wastes between the mother's body and her unborn child's. The embryo is protected by two membranes (the amnion and chorion) and the amniotic fluid. In the first trimester, all major organs develop in the fetus; in the second and third trimesters, these organs mature and the fetus undergoes considerable growth.

3. Early pregnancy is usually marked by missing a period, nausea, breast tenderness, and fatigue. Pregnancy tests, which are 95 to 98 percent accurate, depend on detecting HCG in urine. The emotional reactions to pregnancy vary considerably from person to person, and even when a pregnancy is wanted it may be a source of uncertainty or worry.

4. The second trimester is a time of prominent physical changes for the pregnant woman — the uterus enlarges, making the abdomen bulge, and quickening occurs. It is usually a time of emotional tranquility and heightened sexual interest.

5. Mechanical problems become prominent in the third trimester, as the abdomen is occupied by a growing "resident" who kicks and turns a lot. Back ache, leg cramps, shortness of breath, and frequent urination are common.

6. Proper prenatal care is important to the health of mother and fetus alike. This includes regular medical check-ups, proper nutrition, avoidance of unnecessary drugs, and prompt treatment of pregnancy complications such as toxemia. Attendance at childbirth classes and appropriate reading can help familiarize the parents-to-be with what lies ahead.

7. Sexual activity during pregnancy usually is possible without difficulty or risk. Although controversial, one study shows that sexual activity may reduce the frequency of premature labor.

8. Labor is divided into three stages. In the first (and longest) stage, the cervix effaces and dilates as a result of regular contractions of the uterus. In the second stage, the baby passes though the birth canal, and in the third stage, the placenta and membranes are delivered.

9. Different styles of childbirth are possible, including hospital or home delivery, induction of labor versus spontaneous labor, and use of natural childbirth, Lamaze, or Leboyer's techniques. None of these methods can guarantee a "painless" childbirth. In certain situations, cesarean section may be required to protect the child's or the mother's health.

10. The postpartum period, marked by an abrupt drop in hormone levels, is a time of adjustment. Postpartum depression is common but

usually transient; adjusting to parenthood takes a while longer. Early parent-child bonding is thought to be of special significance to the child.

11. Lactation occurs because of hormone actions on the breasts. Nursing provides an opportunity for a satisfying psychological experience as well as health benefits to the newborn child, but bottle-feeding has advantages of convenience and flexibility.

12. Problem pregnancies — prematurity, toxemia, birth defects, improper implantation, and Rh incompatibility — were outlined briefly.

13. Approximately one out of seven couples is affected by infertility, with the majority of cases due to failure to ovulate and blocked Fallopian tubes in women and low sperm count in men. While treatment with drugs can often induce ovulation, treating the other two problems is less successful at present. Artificial insemination using a donor's semen may be done if the husband's sperm count is poor; in vitro fertilization techniques are now being used increasingly to treat women with infertility due to blocked Fallopian tubes.

SUGGESTED READINGS

Arms, Suzanne. *Immaculate Deception*. Boston: Houghton Mifflin, 1975. A thought-provoking critical survey of childbirth practices in America.

Ashford, Janet. *The Whole Birth Catalog: A Sourcebook for Choices in Childbirth*. Trumansburg, N.Y.: The Crossing Press, 1983. A most impressive collection of material about the various options for different styles of childbirth available today. Lots of diagrams, lists of suggested readings, and practical pointers throughout.

Brown, Judith. *Nutrition for Your Pregnancy*. Minneapolis: University of Minnesota Press, 1983. A well-done, practical guide to nutrition during pregnancy and in the first three postpartum months. Answers almost every imaginable question in a readable but authoritative style.

Glass, Robert, and Ericsson, R. J. *Getting Pregnant in the 1980s*. Berkeley, Calif.: University of California Press, 1982. A lucid, nontechnical discussion of a range of interesting topics including infertility, pregnancy after age thirty-five, test-tube babies, and sex preselection.

Grad, Rae; Bash, Deborah; Guyer, Ruth; Acevedo, Zoila; Trause, Mary Anne; and Reukauf, Diane. *The Father Book — Pregnancy and Beyond*. Washington, D.C.: Acropolis Books, 1981. A fine forum for answering questions and clearing up uncertainties for the expectant father.

Grossman, Frances; Eichler, Lois; and Winickoff, Susan. *Pregnancy, Birth and Parenthood*. San Francisco: Jossey-Bass, 1980. A systematic research study on pregnancy and the first postpartum year in eighty-four couples. Technical but interesting.

Hales, Diane, and Creasy, Robert. *New Hope for Problem Pregnancies*. New York: Harper & Row, 1982. Sparkling clarity and readable, accurate advice in a comprehensive book on high-risk pregnancies and medical complications of pregnancy.

Messenger, Maire. *The Breastfeeding Book*. New York: Von Nostrand Reinhold, 1982. The best book we've ever seen on this topic.

Nillson, Lennart, et al. *A Child Is Born*. New York: Delacorte Press, 1977. Incredible color photographs of fetal development make this short book fast and fascinating reading.

Pritchard, J. A., and MacDonald, P. C. *William's Obstetrics*. 16th ed. New York: Appleton-Century-Crofts, 1980. The standard medical reference, highly accurate but *heavy* reading and not for the squeamish.

Silber, Sherman. *How to Get Pregnant*. New York: Charles Scribner's Sons, 1980. A lucid, practical discussion, including an excellent section on infertility.

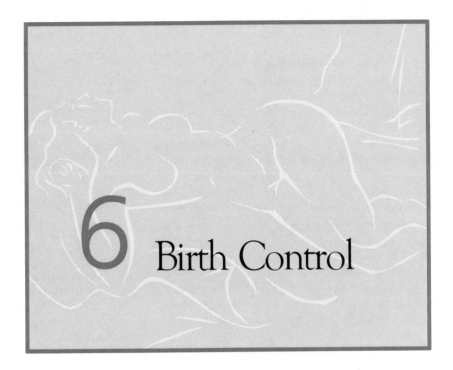

6 Birth Control

Young American women are now delaying childbirth until later ages than their mothers did, but in many cases this delay is achieved by aborting an unintended pregnancy — almost two-thirds of the million and a half abortions in the United States in 1980 were obtained by women under age 25 (U.S. Bureau of the Census, 1983; Henshaw and O'Reilly, 1983).

Currently, about 4.9 million couples of reproductive age in the United States (about 9 percent of couples in this age group) rely on vasectomy for contraception. Statistics from Canada indicate that at least 10 percent of couples there are also protected by this safe and simple contraceptive method (Liskin, Pile, and Quillin, 1983). Nevertheless, there are few reversible methods of contraception available for use by males, so that females are generally left to shoulder the burden of contraceptive responsibility.

If current rates of world population growth continue for the next five years, the world population will increase by about 375 million people, which is about the same as the current population of all the cities of Latin America and Africa combined (Kols and Lewison, 1983).

As these facts show, methods for preventing unwanted or unintended pregnancy are either not used, misused, or used sporadically by many people. Those who rely on "faith" and "hope" as their primary contraceptives are playing a risky form of reproductive roulette, as many discover to their surprise. Others depend on unreliable contraceptive techniques like douching, using astrological charts, or using tampons. Contrary to common misbelief, female orgasm is not a requirement for conception, and making love while standing up or crossing your fingers doesn't prevent sperm from reaching the egg.

Not too long ago, contraceptive products could not be displayed or sold in certain states, abortions were illegal, and birth control methods were not very reliable. Although times have changed remarkably, people are now faced with a vast number of birth control products or methods, each with its own advantages and disadvantages (Table 6-1). In trying to make a personal choice, people may have a number of questions: Why use contraception? How does each method work? How well does it work? What are the medical risks? How might each method affect my sexuality? What possibilities do I have if I'm already pregnant? In the following pages, we will examine the currently available methods of birth control in an effort to answer some of these questions.

WHY USE CONTRACEPTION?

An individual's or couple's decisions about birth control can depend on many factors including age, future plans, marital or relationship status (including trust and cooperation), finances, religious beliefs, sexual attitudes, health, and prior experiences. *Not* using birth control if you are sexually active is a specific kind of personal decision, just as choosing to use birth control, whatever the reason, is a personal decision.

The main reason for using birth control is to prevent an unwanted pregnancy. Not only is an unwanted pregnancy likely to cause emotional turmoil and health risks, it also may present financial burdens. Often, unwanted pregnancies occur in young teenagers or women over thirty-five, times when health risks during pregnancy are highest. The social and economic costs may also be high at these same ages, as these two quotations show:

A twenty-two-year-old woman: I got pregnant when I was fifteen and had my baby the day before my sixteenth birthday. My parents wanted me to finish school, and they took care of my son for a while when he was little, but then my father died and I had to drop out to go to work. Now, it doesn't look like I'll ever marry — who'd want to have me? (Authors' files)

A thirty-seven-year-old woman: I'd been married for fifteen years when I got pregnant again at thirty-five. My two other kids were fourteen and twelve, and I was finishing a two-year course to be a court stenographer. I had to change my plans completely and become a mother again, and it was no cup of tea, believe me. Now my husband has filed for divorce, and I'm sure the baby was part of the cause. (Authors' files)

TABLE 6–1
Contraceptive Methods Used by Sexually Active Women Aged 15–44 in the United States

Method	Percent
Pill	27
Sterilization, female	19
Sterilization, male	13
Condom	12
IUD	6
Diaphragm	5
Spermicide	4
Withdrawal	3
Rhythm	2
Other	less than 0.5
None	8

Source: Modified from Forrest and Henshaw, 1983, Table 5.

Birth Control

Of the 1.2 million teenagers who become pregnant in the United States each year, more than 400,000 obtain abortions (Henshaw and O'Reilly, 1983). Many others drop out of school and enter into hasty marriages where the odds of divorce are high, the chances of getting a good job are low, and ending up on welfare is common (Furstenberg, 1976; Fielding, 1978). Others try to raise a child alone or with the assistance of relatives, but this plan often proves more difficult than it might at first seem. An unplanned pregnancy at any age may also disrupt career plans, and economic costs are created by terminating the pregnancy or raising the child. There is also an emotional cost to an unwanted pregnancy. Feelings of foolishness, guilt, anger, or helplessness may strain or break a relationship ("It was *all your fault!*"), or may create later sexual problems.

Of course, there are other reasons for using contraception, including the wish to space pregnancies, limit family size, avoid potential genetic disorders or birth defects, protect the mother's health, and allow women more control over planning their lives. Contraception also permits people to enjoy a sexual relationship without making commitments to marriage or parenthood. Limiting reproduction also has major social and philosophical consequences in a world of limited natural resources where overpopulation exerts political and psychological effects and environmental issues are of prominent concern.

EVALUATING CONTRACEPTIVE EFFECTIVENESS AND SAFETY

The decision to use contraception and the choice of one method over another depend primarily on two practical matters: how well it works (its effectiveness) and its health risks (its safety).[1] Evaluating these two issues is complicated. *No one contraceptive method is always best or safest.*

When evaluating effectiveness and safety, remember that information from various sources may be biased. The popular media, for instance, are eager to report the latest "news" about the real or suspected hazards of a contraceptive method. Yet the story is usually condensed to a few paragraphs in the newspaper or is crammed into less than sixty seconds of TV or radio broadcast time. Scientific accuracy or caution is often lost in a process of oversimplification, misinterpretation, and unwarranted conclusions. In addition, much of the research on the effectiveness and safety of birth control methods is paid for by the drug companies that manufacture them. These companies have an obvious interest in presenting their merchandise in a way that will boost sales. Finally, all scientific studies are not equivalent in their applicability to *you*. In general, studies about people close to your age, cultural background, and socioeconomic status are more meaningful than studies about other groups. For example, if you are a twenty-two-year-old single American woman, you cannot put much faith in the findings of a study about thirty-five-year-old married women in Lapland.

Understanding some other aspects of evaluating effectiveness can also be helpful. First, it is important to distinguish between two factors: theoretical versus actual effectiveness. The *theoretical effectiveness* of a particular method is how it *should* work if used correctly and consistently, without human error or negligence. The *actual effectiveness* is what occurs in real life, when in-

---

[1] The choice of method may also depend, in individual cases, on factors such as cost, availability without a prescription, aesthetic preferences, and sometimes even the ease of concealment.

consistent use or improper technique ("user fail-ure") combines with failures of the method alone ("method failures"). For example, if a couple runs out of condoms on a week-long camping trip yet continues to have intercourse, the woman's sub-sequent pregnancy is not counted as a method failure. But if she conceives even though she has used a contraceptive foam exactly according to instructions each time she had intercourse, her pregnancy qualifies as a method failure.

Second, for most types of contraception, the longer a person uses a particular method, the more effective it becomes. The reason is that people improve their technique and become more accustomed to using the method regularly.

Third, effectiveness rates for almost every nonsurgical contraceptive method vary depend-ing on whether a couple uses the method to *pre-vent* pregnancy or to *delay* (space) pregnancy. Failure rates are generally 50 to 100 percent higher for delay compared to prevention, since there seems to be less consistency in method use (Ryder, 1973).

There are other difficulties in assessing the safety of contraceptive methods. Firstly, there are often wide differences in the frequency of side ef-fects reported by different investigators. Their re-sults reflect differences in research design, choice of control groups, different characteristics in the populations studied (such as age, health, socio-economic status), and the methods investigators use to identify a problem (self-administered ques-tionnaire, personal interview, laboratory testing). Secondly, there are some relative aspects to the safety question. How important is avoiding preg-nancy? Are the side effects of a contraceptive method more or less serious than the risks of pregnancy and childbirth? How do the risks of a contraceptive method compare to other health risks (such as the risk of getting cancer or having high blood pressure) or to risks of everyday life? These questions will be addressed in more detail

as we review the safety and side effects of each method of contraception.

METHODS OF CONTRACEPTION

Birth Control Pills (Oral Contraceptives)

The introduction of birth control pills in 1960 revolutionized contraceptive practices around the world. Millions of women turned en-thusiastically to this convenient and effective method of preventing pregnancy, but within a decade reports of serious side effects of the pill began to appear and the popularity of this method declined substantially. Now, after twenty-five years of observation, what are the facts about the pill?

There are two types of oral contraceptives currently in use: a *combination pill,* which con-tains a synthetic estrogen and a progesterone-like synthetic substance called "progestogen," and a *minipill* with progestogen only in low dosage. This discussion will focus on combination pills (unless otherwise specified) because they are most commonly used.

HOW BIRTH CONTROL PILLS WORK

Birth control pills prevent pregnancy primar-ily by blocking the normal cyclic output of FSH and LH by the pituitary, thus preventing ovula-tion (Figure 6-1). In addition, the progestogen makes implantation difficult by inhibiting the de-velopment of the lining of the uterus, and also thickens the cervical mucus, decreasing the possi-bility that sperm can get through.

USE AND EFFECTIVENESS

Birth control pills are taken one per day for twenty-one days beginning on the fifth day of the menstrual cycle (that is, four days after a pe-riod begins). Some brands of birth control pills

FIGURE 6–1
Serum Gonadotropin Levels During the
Menstrual Cycle

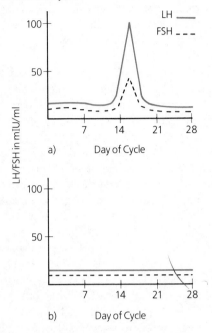

a) Women not using oral contraceptives. b) Women using
combination oral contraceptives.

are packaged with seven inactive pills (usually of another color) which the woman takes on a daily basis to complete the cycle, whereas with other brands the woman must remember to resume her pills one week later.

If a pill is missed, *two* pills should be taken the next day. If two pills are missed, it is likely that the pill will not work properly and an *alternate* form of contraception must be used to prevent pregnancy.

Birth control pills are the most effective nonsurgical method of contraception. Among women who use the pill consistently, only one

pregnancy will occur among 200 women during a year. Among all women using the pill — including those who sometimes forget to use it — two or three pregnancies will occur in 100 women annually.

The minipill, which is taken every day, even during menstruation, is less effective than the combination pill. If used perfectly, one or two pregnancies will occur in one hundred women during a year. In actual use conditions — including the occasional forgotten pill — five to ten pregnancies occur in one hundred women using the minipill for a year.

SIDE EFFECTS AND SAFETY

Birth control pills have now been used by more than 150 million women around the world and have probably been studied more intensively than any other medication in history. Despite scare stories that appear regularly in the press, the evidence shows that the pill has more health benefits than risks for many users. For example, there is no reliable evidence that birth control pills cause cancer (Drill, 1975; Lipsett, 1977; Rinehart and Piotrow, 1979; Kols et al., 1982), and they actually protect against cancer of the ovaries (Newhouse et al., 1977; Centers for Disease Control, 1983) and of the uterine lining (Weiss and Sayvetz, 1980; Kaufman et al., 1980; Centers for Disease Control, 1983a).[2] Furthermore, women who use birth control pills are only one-fourth as likely to develop benign (noncancerous) breast tumors as non-users, one-fourteenth as likely to develop ovarian cysts,

---

[2] Two points should be made: (1) An earlier type of birth control pill, the *sequential pill*, was banned because it *was* found to cause cancer of the uterus; (2) As it may take decades for certain types of cancer to develop, it cannot be concluded that the combination pill *does not* cause cancer. However, it has recently been estimated that more than 2,000 cases of endometrial cancer are prevented each year by use of the pill (Centers for Disease Control, 1983a).

Birth control pills come in different brands and packages, each accompanied by a package-insert describing their use and potential side effects.

nausea, constipation, breast tenderness, minor elevations in blood pressure, edema (swelling), and skin rashes (including brown spots on the face called *chloasma*). Other relatively minor side effects include weight gain or loss, an increased amount of vaginal secretions, and an increased susceptibility to vaginal infections.

Less common but more troublesome side effects caused by the pill include high blood pressure (4 percent of users), diabetes (1 percent of users), migraine headaches and/or eye problems (0.5 percent of users), and rarely jaundice or liver tumors (Rinehart and Piotrow, 1979). Because the pill causes alterations in liver function, women with hepatitis or other forms of liver disease should avoid it. If taken during pregnancy, the pill may cause birth defects (Heinonen et al., 1977; Nora and Nora, 1978; Kasan and Andrews, 1980), but if used before pregnancy, the pill does not have this effect (Harlap and Davies, 1978). Some reports have linked the pill to depression (Royal College, 1974) while others have not (Kutner, Phillips, and Hoag, 1974).

The most serious risks to women using birth control pills are disorders of the circulatory system: the overall death rate from circulatory diseases is approximately four times higher in users than nonusers (Royal College, 1977). However, to put this finding in perspective, only one in 27,000 women using the pill annually dies from this cause (Ory, Rosenfeld, and Landman, 1980).

There are three different types of circulatory problems involved. The most common, affecting about one in 1,000 users each year, is the formation of a blood clot in a vein (usually in the legs). Most often this clot results in only minor discomfort caused by inflammation and swelling, but there is a risk that a piece of the clot may break off and cause serious damage in the lungs or brain. These problems, called *thromboembolic diseases,* are two to four times more common

one-half as likely to develop rheumatoid arthritis, and two-thirds as likely to develop iron deficiency anemia (Ory, Rosenfeld, and Landman, 1980).

Other beneficial side effects of the pill have been noted. Many women find that the pill reduces the amount of menstrual flow and produces more regular cycles with less menstrual cramping (Mishell, 1982). Acne can be improved by the pill (although sometimes it is worsened), premenstrual tension can be reduced, and pelvic inflammatory disease — a serious cause of infertility — is only half as common in pill users as nonusers (Senanayake and Kramer, 1980; Kols et al., 1982).

The most common bothersome side effects of the pill mimic those encountered in pregnancy:

Birth Control

among pill users than nonusers but account for only two or three extra deaths per 100,000 users annually (Rinehart and Piotrow, 1979). Birth control pills also increase the risk of heart attacks, but the excess risk is almost entirely found in users who smoke and/or users older than thirty-five (Mann and Inman, 1975; Arthes and Masi, 1976; Jick et al., 1978; Rosenberg et al., 1980). Women in their thirties who smoke and use the pill are about seven times more likely to have a heart attack than users who do not smoke, but pill users who do not smoke are less at risk than smokers who do not use the pill (Horwitz, 1977). Finally, an association between pill use and strokes has also been found (Royal College, 1977; Petitti and Wingerd, 1978; Jick et al., 1978a), but even with an increased risk, stroke is a rare disorder in women under 45.

A few final words about the safety of oral contraceptives are in order. Safety is a relative matter, not just a statistical equation (Figure 6-2). For example, a woman who has intercourse frequently receives more contraceptive protection from the pill than one who does not. While other contraceptive methods may seem "safer," she may choose to risk certain health problems to be more certain of not becoming pregnant. Another example applies to women in developing countries, where maternal death rates during pregnancy and childbirth are much higher than in countries with advanced medical care systems. In this situation, oral contraceptives are far safer than no birth control even over age thirty-five. The safety of birth control pills should also be looked at in comparison to risks of everyday living such as auto accidents or sports injuries. In this case the figures may seem somewhat different: only one pill-related death occurred in 46,000 women under thirty-five who were nonsmokers in 200,000 *woman-years* (one woman-year is equivalent to a woman using a particular

"Oh, I know all that stuff about the birds and the bees. What I want to know is whether, in your opinion, the possible hormonal side-effects of the Pill outweigh the inconvenience of using mechanical contraceptives."

contraceptive method for 12 calendar months) of use of the pill (Royal College, 1977). By contrast, nine deaths from auto accidents would be expected in a group of this size over this period of time.[3] Confirming this view, the largest prospective American study of pill users found that overall, the risks of oral contraceptive use appear to be minimal (Ramcharan, 1981).

SEXUAL EFFECTS OF BIRTH CONTROL PILLS

Evaluating the effects of birth control pills on sexuality is tricky for a number of reasons. First of all, the pills used during the 1960s had much higher amounts of estrogen than today's pills, and different effects seem to relate to the

---

[3] Careful studies on the side effects of the minipill have not yet been concluded, and it is not certain if the circulatory risks are present or not.

FIGURE 6–2
Annual Number of Deaths in Women Associated with Use or Nonuse of Birth Control

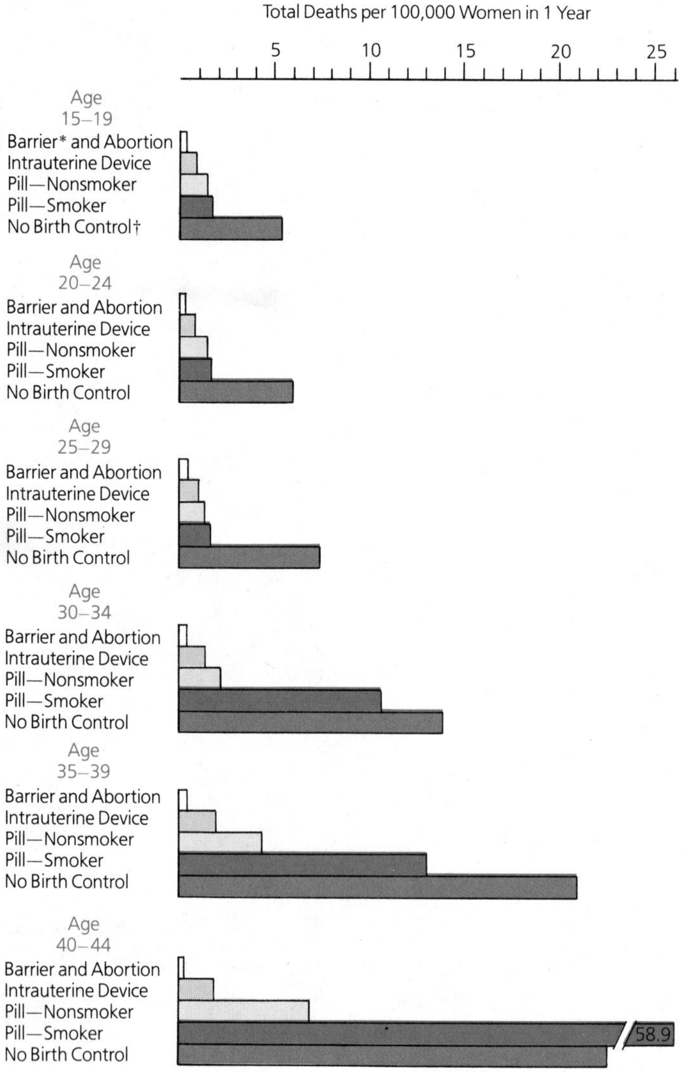

Total Deaths per 100,000 Women in 1 Year

Age 15–19
Barrier* and Abortion
Intrauterine Device
Pill—Nonsmoker
Pill—Smoker
No Birth Control†

Age 20–24
Barrier and Abortion
Intrauterine Device
Pill—Nonsmoker
Pill—Smoker
No Birth Control

Age 25–29
Barrier and Abortion
Intrauterine Device
Pill—Nonsmoker
Pill—Smoker
No Birth Control

Age 30–34
Barrier and Abortion
Intrauterine Device
Pill—Nonsmoker
Pill—Smoker
No Birth Control

Age 35–39
Barrier and Abortion
Intrauterine Device
Pill—Nonsmoker
Pill—Smoker
No Birth Control

Age 40–44
Barrier and Abortion
Intrauterine Device
Pill—Nonsmoker
Pill—Smoker
No Birth Control

58.9

*Barrier = Diaphragm or Condom
†Deaths in women not using birth control = Deaths from pregnancy complications

Source: Modified from C. Tietze, 1977. Reprinted with permission from Family Planning Perspectives, Volume 9, Number 2, 1977. Note: Abortion here is during the first trimester.

The deaths are expressed as a rate per 100,000 nonsterile women in various age groups.

level of estrogen. Older research generally noted that long-term use of the pill had negative sexual effects (Masters and Johnson, 1970; Herzberg et al., 1971) but more recent studies do not support this view (Gambrell et al., 1976; Bragonier, 1976). Second, there are many individual reasons that the pill helps or hinders a woman's sexual feelings and function. Some reasons are biological: a woman who develops a vaginal infection may have sexual problems as a result, or a woman who has less premenstrual and menstrual cramping may feel better physically and thus may be more sexually receptive and responsive. Some reasons are psychological. If a woman expects to have sexual side effects from the pill, her prophecy becomes self-fulfilling. Some women may feel guilty about using the pill because of religious beliefs or conflicts between wanting children and using contraception. Alternatively, the psychological security of using a highly effective method of contraception reduces the fear of pregnancy and may therefore improve sexual interest and enjoyment (after all, it is harder to enjoy something when you are afraid). One woman told us, "After switching to the pill, I found that sex became more fun. I had my first orgasm during intercourse less than two months later" (Authors' files). Since the pill also requires no interruptions at the time of sexual activity, it permits a degree of spontaneity and intimacy that other methods may not.

Most women using oral contraceptives today do not report significant changes in sexual interest, behavior, or enjoyment. Approximately 10 percent experience improved sexuality, which is about the same as the percent who note decreased sexual interest or responsiveness.

IUDs

The IUD, or *intrauterine device,* is a small plastic object that is inserted into the uterus through the vagina and cervix and then continuously kept in place. There are many different models of IUDs (Figure 6-3) which vary in shape, size, and composition. For example, some contain copper filaments (the Copper 7 and the Copper T) and some contain a hormone (the Progestasert T slowly releases a synthetic form of progesterone into the uterus).

While IUDs became popular in this country only in the last twenty years, they are a modern application of an ancient concept. For centuries, Arab and Turkish camel drivers put a large pebble into the camel's uterus for contraceptive purposes, since a pregnant camel on a long desert trek would not be very helpful. The first IUD designed for humans, a ring made of silkworm gut, did not gain much attention when introduced in 1909. In the late 1920s a ring of gut and silver wire was developed by Grafenberg, a German physician, and enjoyed some popularity. Early models of the IUD, however, were condemned because of the risk of pelvic infection and fell into disrepute.

By 1978 about 6 percent of married women of reproductive age in America used the IUD, while about 20 percent did in Scandinavia and approximately half of all women using contraceptives adopted it in China (Piotrow, Rinehart, and Schmidt, 1979). On a worldwide basis, approximately 60 million women use the IUD.

HOW IUDs WORK

The exact way the IUD works is not known. The most plausible explanation is that it interferes with implantation of the fertilized egg in the lining of the uterus. This outcome may result from a local inflammatory reaction or from interference with chemical reactions inside the uterus that affect implantation. IUDs containing progesterone also alter the development of the lining of the uterus so that implantation is unlikely.

FIGURE 6–3
The IUD

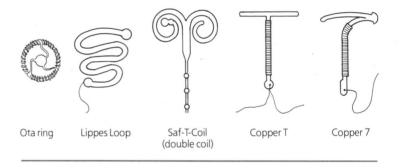

a) Carrier with Lippes Loop
inserted beyond internal os

b) Lippes Loop inserted

c) Carrier removed

Ota ring   Lippes Loop   Saf-T-Coil
(double coil)   Copper T   Copper 7

*Insertion of an IUD (a–c) and several
models of IUDs currently in use.*

USE AND EFFECTIVENESS

The IUD must be inserted into the uterus (Figure 6–3) by a trained health care professional after determining that the woman is not pregnant and does not have gonorrhea or other pelvic infections. Inserting an IUD can cause abortion in a pregnant woman and can push bacteria from an infection into the uterus or Fallopian tubes. Insertion is usually done during a menstrual period, since it is a fairly reliable sign that the woman is not pregnant, but it can be done at other times.

Inserting an IUD usually causes only brief discomfort, but some women prefer to be given a short-acting painkiller. Taking two or three aspi-

rin tablets about an hour before insertion provides some pain relief and may theoretically decrease cramping because it blocks release of prostaglandins. The woman must be shown how to check the plastic thread that comes through the mouth of the cervix to be sure the IUD is in place. If this thread cannot be located, or if it seems longer than it was before, the woman must return for a check-up.

IUDs are sometimes expelled from the uterus so that they no longer provide contraceptive protection. Expulsion rates are lower in women who use copper or progesterone containing devices (about six or seven per one hundred women during a year) compared to a rate of approximately fifteen per one hundred women during a year for other IUDs (Piotrow, Rinehart, and Schmidt, 1979). Expulsion rates are higher in younger women, in women who have had no children, and during menstruation. One-fifth of expulsions go unnoticed and this accounts for one-third of the pregnancies among IUD users (Mishell, 1974).

Even though they may be expelled, IUDs are highly effective, with only one to six pregnancies occurring in one hundred women using IUDs for one year. One study showed that women using IUDs to *prevent* pregnancy had a failure rate of 2.9 percent, whereas women using IUDs to delay or space pregnancy had a failure rate of 5.6 percent (Vaughan et al., 1979).

SIDE EFFECTS AND SAFETY

Perforation of the uterus (puncturing the wall of the uterus) is the most serious risk of using an IUD. If it occurs, it is almost always at the time of insertion. This problem, which occurs in about one in 1,000 insertions, can cause sudden pain and bleeding or, more rarely, may be without immediate symptoms. Perforation usually requires surgery to prevent damage to the intestines, since the IUD usually perforates through the uterus into the abdomen. Recently, it has been found that inserting an IUD while a woman is breast-feeding causes a ten-fold increase in the risk of perforation of the uterus (Merz, 1983), so it seems advisable to choose a different method of birth control during this time.

The most common side effects of the IUD are increased bleeding from the uterus and cramping pain. Menstrual periods are typically heavier and longer (except in women using IUDs with progesterone, which decreases menstrual flow), and there is more likely to be spotting between periods. This increased blood loss can cause anemia. Cramps and bleeding can be serious enough to have the IUD removed (about

10 percent of women find this necessary) but usually lessen after the first three months.

IUD users have about a four times higher risk of pelvic infection than other women. This risk is present not only at the time of insertion but also with continued use of the device. Bacteria, viruses, or fungus infections may enter the uterus by "climbing" the tail of the IUD, and there is a chance that the infection will spread to the Fallopian tubes and ovaries, which can cause permanent scarring and infertility (Vessey et al., 1981; Beerthuizen et al., 1982).

If a pregnancy occurs in a woman with an IUD, there is about a 5 percent chance that the pregnancy is ectopic or misplaced (Green, 1977). As described in the preceding chapter, this poses a major threat to the woman's health if not properly detected. Uterine pregnancies in IUD users have a 30 percent risk of spontaneous abortion if the IUD is removed, compared to a 50 percent abortion risk if the device is left in place (Alvior, 1973; Vessey et al., 1974). IUDs, however, do not cause any birth defects.

The IUD is well suited to women who want a highly effective contraceptive method that requires no active participation on their part and is easily and promptly reversible. It may be particularly appropriate for women who cannot use birth control pills for medical reasons and for the mentally retarded who may not be able to remember to take a pill or use a mechanical method of birth control. IUDs should not be used by women who are pregnant or who have active pelvic infection, bleeding disorders, anatomical abnormalities of the uterus or cervix, or abnormal pelvic bleeding. Women who have had an ectopic pregnancy, severe menstrual disorders, or any disease that suppresses normal immunity to infection should not use IUDs.

SEXUAL EFFECTS OF IUDs

Like birth control pills, the IUD is effective in preventing pregnancy and does not interfere with sexual spontaneity or mood. Yet the IUD can cause pain during intercourse. The woman may experience pain if the IUD is not in the right position or if there is pelvic infection or inflammation; the man may have pain at the tip of the penis or along the shaft because of irritation from the tail of the IUD in the vagina. Both abdominal cramping and persistent bleeding can lessen a woman's interest in sexual activity, but these side effects occur in only about 10 percent of users. Infrequently, women who use IUDs find that orgasm may cause intense, unpleasant cramping because of uterine contractions around the IUD.

Diaphragms

The diaphragm is a round, shallow dome of thin rubber stretched over a flexible ring (Figure 6-4). After a spermicidal (sperm-killing) jelly or cream is applied inside the dome and around the inner part of the rim, the diaphragm must be inserted inside the vagina and positioned so that it completely covers the cervix. Before the introduction of birth control pills, the diaphragm was the most widely used method of contraception, and it is still popular today.

HOW DIAPHRAGMS WORK

The diaphragm is a mechanical barrier that blocks the mouth of the cervix so that sperm cannot enter. Because this blocking effect is not very reliable by itself, the use of a spermicide is required to kill sperm that manage to swim inside the rim of the diaphragm.

USE AND EFFECTIVENESS

Diaphragms come in different sizes and must be properly fitted by a trained health care professional to match the anatomy of the user. The size and position of the cervix and the size and shape of the vagina must be taken into account

to achieve a proper fit; the actual fitting is done using a set of graduated flexible rings to select the right size. After the fitting, the woman is shown how to insert the diaphragm either manually or with a plastic inserter (see Figure 6-4).[4]

The diaphragm can be inserted up to two hours before intercourse and should remain in place at least six hours afterward. If it is worn for more than two hours before intercourse, the effectiveness of the spermicide may drop. For this reason, a full application of spermicidal jelly, cream, or foam should be placed in the vagina before intercourse in these circumstances. If the diaphragm is removed less than six hours after intercourse, it is possible that live sperm in the vagina may reach the cervix and swim up into the uterus.

The effectiveness of this method is not as high as birth control pills or IUDs, with failure rates in most reports ranging from six to twenty pregnancies in one hundred women using this device during a year (Sherris, Moore, and Fox, 1984). Yet since the effectiveness of this method depends on the regularity of its use, the woman's motivation and memory are important factors. A woman who leaves her diaphragm at home and finds herself unexpectedly in a sexual situation might have a "user" failure rather than a "method" failure. In one study with a highly motivated, experienced population of users, the failure rate was only 1.9 per one hundred woman-years (Vessey, Lawless, and Yeates, 1982). Another problem that influences effectiveness is that the diaphragm may slip out of po-

---

[4] Some clinicians recommend that a woman be refitted if she gains or loses ten pounds. However, a recent study found that more women whose weight was stable needed refitting (Fiscella, 1982), so the matter is not a clear one. We recommend that women be refitted for a diaphragm after a pregnancy or on an annual basis. If there is a weight change of 15 pounds or more, it also may be advisable to be refitted.

FIGURE 6–4
The Diaphragm

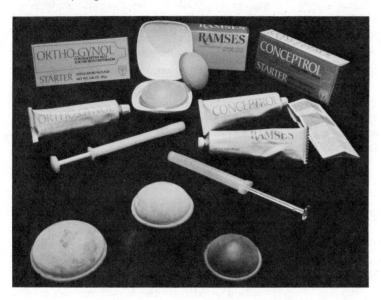

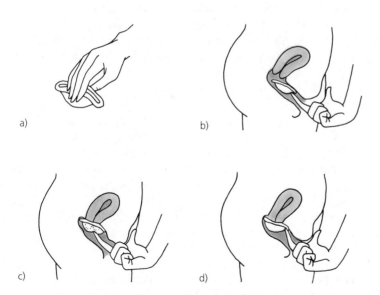

a)

b)

c)

d)

Proper use of a diaphragm: a) After inserting spermicidal jelly or cream, the rim of the diaphragm is pinched between the fingers and thumb. b) The folded diaphragm is gently inserted into the vagina and pushed downward and backward as far as it will go. c) To check for proper positioning, feel the cervix to be certain it is completely covered by the soft rubber dome of the diaphragm. d) A finger is hooked under the forward rim to remove the diaphragm.

sition during sexual play because of improper insertion, a poor fit, or expansion of the inside of the vagina and movement of the uterus during sexual excitation. Johnson and Masters (1962) found that even a well-fitted and properly inserted diaphragm can become dislodged during intercourse when the woman is on top of the man or if the penis is removed and reinserted into the vagina during plateau levels of arousal. Even a tiny hole in the dome of the diaphragm will permit sperm to enter, so it is important to inspect it carefully and to avoid use of Vaseline on it, since this can cause deterioration of the latex. Despite these problems, consistent use of the diaphragm with a condom provides a rate of effectiveness comparable to birth control pills. In addition, the diaphragm seems to offer protection against cervical cancer (Wright et al., 1978) and against some sexually transmitted diseases (Sherris, Moore, and Fox, 1984).

SIDE EFFECTS AND SAFETY

The only potential side effects are: (1) possible allergic reactions to the rubber in the diaphragm or to the spermicide itself, and (2) the chance of introducing infection into the vagina if the diaphragm is not clean. Both problems are infrequent. In addition, it is not advisable to wear a diaphragm for more than twelve hours at a time because this seems to cause an overgrowth of bacteria in the vagina and cervix that is linked to the toxic shock syndrome (see chapter 20). The diaphragm has no effects on hormones or physical processes of the body and poses no danger to later fertility.

Women who have pelvic disorders affecting the vagina or cervix or who do not like to touch their genitals should not use the diaphragm.

SEXUAL EFFECTS

The primary sexual difficulty with use of the diaphragm is inconvenience. For example, either partner may experience loss of sexual arousal while the woman takes time to insert and check the diaphragm if she did not insert it before sex play began. Some couples solve this problem by making the insertion of the diaphragm a part of their sexual play preliminary to intercourse. Either partner may find the diaphragm or the process of its insertion unaesthetic. In addition, a diaphragm that is too large may cause pain during intercourse and some men complain that intercourse feels "different" with the diaphragm in place. There is a sexual advantage, however: during menstrual periods, the diaphragm can be used to provide a "reverse barrier" that contains flow during sexual activity.

The Cervical Cap

A device related to the diaphragm is the *cervical cap*, which fits snugly over the cervix and stays in place by suction (see Figure 6-5). This method of birth control is now enjoying an upsurge of interest in the United States, although it has had greater popularity in England in the last twenty years. The cervical cap can be worn either for short periods like the diaphragm or for several weeks at a time (McBride, 1980). Currently, a custom-molded cervical cap that contains a small valve that permits the release of menstrual flow and cervical secretions is being studied; if found to be safe and effective, this type of cap would have the advantage of being able to be worn continuously for months at a time without having to be removed.

The effectiveness of the cervical cap has not been extensively studied but it seems to be somewhat lower than the diaphragm (Zodhiates, Feinbloom, and Sagov, 1981). In one recent study of women at a university clinic, the pregnancy rate was 19.6 per 100 woman-years (Boehm, 1983). In some cases, the cap has reportedly caused discomfort to the male during intercourse and has dislodged from the cervix during intercourse.

FIGURE 6–5
Cervical Caps

Three different types of cervical caps currently used for contraception.

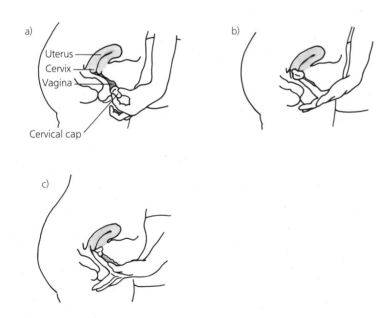

a)
Uterus
Cervix
Vagina

Cervical cap

b)

c)

Condoms

The condom (also called a rubber, safe, or prophylactic) is a thin sheath of latex rubber or tissue from a lamb's intestine that fits snugly over the penis. Currently, it is the only effective non-surgical birth control method for males and it does not require a prescription. Condoms can be purchased in drug stores, by mail-order, at family planning clinics, and, in some locations, from coin-operated vending machines in men's rooms of bars and gas stations.

Condoms are usually rolled up into plastic or foil packets (Figure 6-6) and come in many different styles. Some are lubricated, some come in a variety of colors, and some have tiny ribs or bumps on their surface that supposedly provide more stimulation to the female as intravaginal thrusting occurs. One of the more recent innovations in condom design is the introduction of a condom coated with a spermicide combined with a lubricant. Condoms are designed with either a round end or a reservoir end, a small receptacle to catch the semen.

The condom has been relatively ignored as a method of contraception for a number of reasons:

> Physicians rarely recommend the condom because its use requires no medical expertise; researchers rarely undertake to study or improve it because they see no challenge in such a simple device; and the media rarely accept advertisements or even provide news coverage because they are still reluctant to associate contraception with sexual intercourse. (Dumm, Piotrow, and Dalsimer, 1974)

USE AND EFFECTIVENESS

The condom, which works by preventing sperm from entering the vagina, must be unrolled onto the erect penis shortly before intercourse. If it is put on too early, it may tear if rubbed against the sheets (or dirt, sand, or car seat) or it may be accidentally punctured by a fingernail. If put on shortly before ejaculation, some drops of pre-ejaculatory fluid containing live sperm might have already entered the vagina. If a round-end condom is used, a little extra space should be left at the tip to catch the ejaculate. After ejaculation, the condom should be held at the base of the penis so it does not slip or spill while being withdrawn. If leakage occurs for any reason it is wise to put a spermicidal foam or cream in the vagina immediately. A condom should not be tested before use by inflating, stretching, or being filled with water. It is impossible to detect microscopic holes that would be large enough to allow sperm to pass through, and you *may* inadvertently damage the condom while you are trying to check it.

In theory, the condom is a very reliable method of birth control — when used properly and consistently. Note that condoms are *not* reusable, and homemade condoms of saran wrap *do not work!* Fewer than five pregnancies occur in one hundred couples using condoms for a year. Furthermore, if condoms are consistently used in combination with a vaginal spermicide, the effectiveness is even better, becoming almost as good as the pill. In actual practice, however, couples using the condom as their only method of contraception often have unwanted pregnancies — overall failure rates of ten to twenty per one hundred couple-years are commonly reported. The main problem is not defective condoms (they must meet rigorous testing standards of the Food and Drug Administration) or improper use, but *inconsistent* use. Many people using this method sometimes "take chances" instead of using condoms during every act of intercourse.

One other aspect of condom use that is increasingly important today is that it provides considerable protection against many sexually transmitted diseases (Sherris, Lewison, and Fox, 1982).

FIGURE 6–6
The Condom

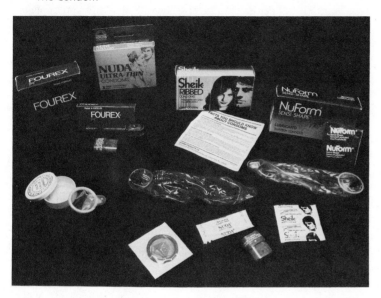

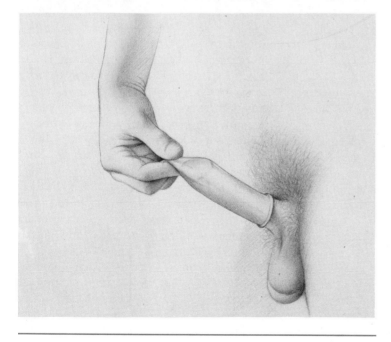

The photo shows an assortment of condoms and their packages. The drawing shows the proper method of pinching the tip of a condom without a reservoir end to leave some room for the semen.

SIDE EFFECTS AND SAFETY

Very infrequently, the material the condom is made from can cause burning or irritation to the genitals. Otherwise, condoms have no health risks at all.

SEXUAL EFFECTS

There are several sexual disadvantages to using condoms. Putting the condom on may interrupt sexual spontaneity, although some couples make this a shared moment of sexual play. Many men complain of lessened sensations in the penis while wearing a condom (one student told his class "It's like playing the piano wearing mittens"), and some men have difficulty maintaining an erection while trying to put on the device. The condom is a poor contraceptive choice for a man having problems with erection, since it calls attention to the degree of erection and may seriously increase "performance anxiety" (see chapter 19). Also, unless the penis is removed from the vagina soon after ejaculation, loss of the erection makes spillage of semen more likely. This can certainly interfere with the intimacy and mood of the moment.

There are also some sexual advantages to the condom. The female may be pleased because her partner is not leaving the responsibility for birth control to her. Lubricated condoms can make intercourse more comfortable if vaginal lubrication is a problem. There is little or no postcoital drippiness for the woman whose partner uses condoms. And use of a condom may help many men who have difficulty controlling ejaculation.

Spermicides

Spermicides, or vaginal chemical contraceptives, come in many varieties, including foams, jellies, creams, and tablets or suppositories. They do not require a prescription and are available at drug stores and family planning clinics. Spermicides should not be confused with feminine hygiene products, often displayed beside them, which have no spermicidal effectiveness.

HOW SPERMICIDES WORK

Spermicides work in two ways: their active chemical ingredient kills sperm, while the material containing this ingredient provides a mechanical barrier that blocks the entrance to the cervix.

USE AND EFFECTIVENESS

Because of the individual differences in the many products on the market, the manufacturer's instructions regarding use and effectiveness must be consulted. This information is given in the package insert that comes with each product. *These products are not identical in how they are used or in their reliability in preventing pregnancy.* In general, foams and suppositories are much more effective than creams or jellies, which should be used only with another method of birth control such as a diaphragm or condom. All spermicides require proper placement in the vagina, as shown in Figure 6-7. If used properly and regularly, some spermicidal products can be very effective. In several studies, less than five pregnancies occurred for every one hundred couples using these methods for one year (see Coleman and Piotrow, 1979). Failure rates tend to be about three times higher than this in actual use as a result of inconsistent use of the method and improper following of the manufacturer's instructions. Failures occur when a couple inserts the spermicide in the vagina incorrectly, has intercourse a second time without using more of the product, or overlooks the time limits of product effectiveness. In addition, failures can occur if the spermicide has become outdated; for this reason, users should check the expiration date stamped on the spermicide package prior to use.

FIGURE 6–7
Vaginal Spermicides

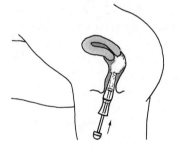

a) Correct foam placement

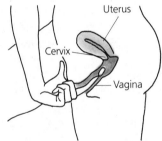

b) Correct suppository placement

Use of vaginal spermicides: a) When contraceptive foam is inserted with a plastic applicator, it must be placed well within the vagina so it completely covers the cervical mouth. b) Spermicidal suppositories must be removed from their wrapper and inserted high in the vagina; the manufacturer's instructions on the timing of intercourse must be followed carefully since these products may require up to ten minutes to dissolve.

SIDE EFFECTS AND SAFETY

Burning or irritation of the vagina or penis occurs in about one in twenty people using spermicides, but this problem can often be alleviated by changing to a different product. Although one study found a higher rate of birth defects in the infants of women who had used a spermicide in the ten months before conception, the researchers stressed that these results were not conclusive (Jick et al., 1981), and a more recent investigation found no evidence supporting the existence of such a problem (Shapiro et al., 1982). However, it now appears that women who use spermicides after becoming pregnant are more likely than other women to have miscarriages (Scholl et al., 1983).

On the positive side, there is mounting evidence that spermicides provide some protection against sexually transmitted diseases such as gonorrhea and also protect against pelvic inflammatory disease (Jick et al., 1982; Cates, Weisner, and Curran, 1982; Sherris, Moore, and Fox, 1984).

SEXUAL EFFECTS

The use of spermicides may require interrupting the spontaneous flow of sexual activity, but insertion can be made a part of sexual play. With spermicidal suppositories, unlike aerosal foams, ten to fifteen minutes must elapse before vaginal distribution of the product has occurred (depending on the brand) and intercourse is "safe" — so these should not be used if you are in a hurry! Vaginal chemical contraceptives may discourage cunnilingus (oral stimulation of the vulva and vagina) because most products do not have a very pleasant taste. Finally, some people find that these products are messy and provide too much vaginal lubrication (one woman described the sensation as "sloshy").

The Contraceptive Sponge

The newest type of birth control device to become widely available (approved by the Food and Drug Administration in April 1983) is a soft, disposable contraceptive sponge which is inserted into the vagina. Now sold exclusively under the "Today" brand name, the two inch by one inch round product is made of polyurethane permeated with the commonly used spermicide, nonoxynol-9 (see Figure 6-8). The contraceptive sponge is sold over the counter in drugstores and doesn't require a prescription or need to be fitted by a physician. Its early reception by consumers has been enthusiastic.

HOW THE SPONGE WORKS

There are three different ways in which the sponge functions. First and most important, it carries the spermicidal effect of nonoxynol-9 (which is the active chemical ingredient in many contraceptive creams, foams, and gels). Second,

the sponge also functions as a mechanical barrier, partially preventing sperm from entering the mouth of the cervix. Finally, the sponge is also thought to trap and absorb sperm, although the importance of this action is uncertain.

USE AND EFFECTIVENESS

The contraceptive sponge is inserted into the vagina before intercourse. The sponge is first dampened with about two tablespoons of water and then squeezed gently until foam appears (this activates the spermicide in the sponge). Many users report that it is considerably easier to insert than a diaphragm and, since it can be inserted up to eighteen hours before intercourse, it is convenient as well. (Insertion can be done either manually or with an applicator.) As another major advantage, the sponge retains its contraceptive effectiveness for twenty-four hours without any need for the reapplication of spermicide, so it provides contraceptive protection regardless of how many times the user has intercourse. The sponge is removed by pulling on a small ribbon attached to one of its sides.

The sponge has been found to have an actual failure rate of about 15 percent, according to the F.D.A., which makes it approximately equivalent to a diaphragm in this regard. As with the diaphragm or spermicides, many of the failures are due to improper use — such as removing the sponge too soon after intercourse — and the user's motivation also seems to play a role. The effectiveness rate can be materially improved by combining use of the sponge with use of a condom.

Women who have used the sponge report a number of distinct advantages compared to the diaphragm. In addition to mentioning how easy it is to insert (which is nearly a universal reaction), many women are pleased to have an inexpensive, disposable contraceptive method available that is unobtrusive, tasteless and odor-

FIGURE 6–8
The Contraceptive Sponge

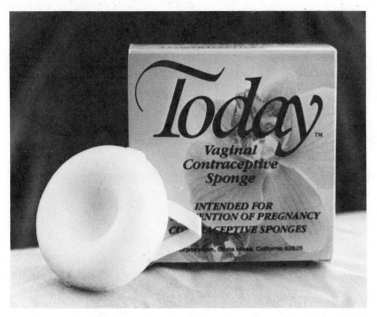

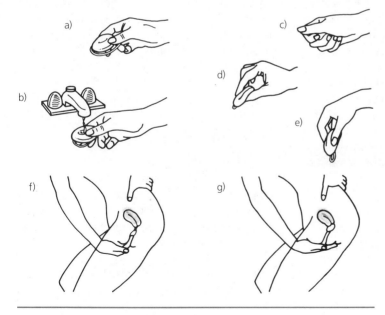

Proper insertion of the sponge: a) Remove the sponge from the inner pack and hold with dimple side up. The loop should dangle under the sponge. b) The sponge will feel slightly moist. Wet it further with a small amount of clean water (about two tablespoons). c) Squeeze the sponge gently to remove excess water. It should feel moist and soapy, but not dripping wet. d) Fold the sides of the sponge upward with a finger along each side to support it. The sponge should look long and narrow. Be sure the string loop dangles underneath the sponge from one end of the fold to the other. e) From a standing position, squat down slightly and spread your legs apart. Use your free hand to spread apart the lips of the vagina. You may also stand with one foot on a stool or chair, sit cross-legged, or lie down. The semi-squatting position seems to work best for most women. Slide the sponge into the opening of the vagina as far as your fingers will go. Let the sponge slide through your fingers, deeper into the vagina. Now use one or two fingers to push the sponge gently up into your vagina as far as it will go. Be careful not to push a fingernail through the sponge. Check the position of the sponge by sliding your finger around the edge of the sponge to make sure your cervix is not exposed. You should be able to feel the string loop.

less, and lasts for twenty-four hours. In addition, the sponge reportedly isn't as messy or drippy as some spermicidal products.

SIDE EFFECTS AND SAFETY

The commonest side effect of the sponge is mild irritation of the vagina or penis, which occurs in about 3 to 5 percent of users. Although the sponge hasn't been in widespread use for a long enough time to assess its safety fully, the only serious health risk to come to attention at the time of this writing is the rare occurrence of toxic shock syndrome in a few women who used the sponge. Whether this was a coincidental finding or a direct relationship isn't clear at present; thus, users should read the package insert carefully to determine if any new information arises on this (or other) health effects.

SEXUAL EFFECTS

Because the sponge can be inserted either hours before sexual activity or at the last moment before intercourse, convenience makes it especially advantageous from a sexual viewpoint. In addition, men and women who have tried the sponge almost invariably say they don't feel it during intercourse, and many couples also report that it doesn't interfere with cunnilingus. But the sponge's most noticeable sexual benefit may be that once it is inserted, it provides protection for multiple acts of intercourse. As one woman told us, "That means we can make love at night and then again in the morning without my having to get up and get ready all over again."

Rhythm

Rhythm methods of contraception depend on periodic abstinence from intercourse during times of the menstrual cycle when fertility is most likely. These methods are the only meth-

ods of birth control approved by the Roman Catholic Church, which considers them "natural" rather than "artificial."

CALENDAR METHOD

The *calendar method* involves identifying "safe days" in the menstrual cycle (days where intercourse will not lead to pregnancy) based on the lengths of previous cycles. The underlying assumption is that ovulation will occur approximately fourteen days before the start of the next menstrual period. Careful hormone studies of the menstrual cycle, however, indicate that this assumption is not always correct (Kolodny and Bauman, 1979).

To calculate the "unsafe" (fertile) period, a record must be kept of the length of each menstrual cycle for a minimum of six months. The first day of the unsafe period is determined by subtracting 18 from the length of the shortest cycle, and the last day of the unsafe period is found by subtracting 11 from the number of days in the longest cycle. For example, if a woman's shortest cycle is 26 days and her longest is 32 days during her "record keeping" time, she must abstain from intercourse beginning on cycle day 8 (26 − 18 = 8) and continue abstention until day 21 (32 − 11 = 21). Thus, the unsafe days would be days 8 to 21, inclusive, a time of 14 days when intercourse would not be permitted.

THE TEMPERATURE METHOD

The *temperature method* involves daily recording of the basal body temperature (BBT) to pinpoint the time of ovulation. Intercourse is not allowed from the day menstrual flow stops until two to four days after the temperature rise. (If no temperature rise is detected in a full menstrual cycle, which sometimes happens, users of this method must observe total abstinence from sexual intercourse.)

THE OVULATION METHOD

The *ovulation method,* also known as the Billings method, depends on changes in cervical mucus to indicate the probable days of fertility during the menstrual cycle. The start of the fertile time is signalled by the appearance of a mucus discharge within the vagina which is whitish or cloudy and of tacky consistency. A day or two before ovulation, greater amounts of mucus are produced in a clear and runnier form with a stretchy consistency very similar to egg white. Intercourse is thought to be "safe" four days after the clear mucus begins, when the mucus has returned to a cloudy color.

EFFECTIVENESS OF THE RHYTHM METHODS

The overall effectiveness of the rhythm methods leaves a great deal to be desired. The calendar method is unquestionably the least reliable among this group (failure rates are approximately 15 to 45 per 100 woman-years; Ross and Piotrow, 1974), and unless the woman's cycle is very regular, long periods of abstinence from intercourse will be required. Temperature methods are inaccurate because they are difficult to interpret (Lenton, Weston, and Cooke, 1977; Bauman, 1981), and in about 20 percent of ovulatory cycles, the BBT chart does not indicate ovulation (Moghissi, 1976; Bauman, 1981). The World Health Organization (1978) found that the ovulation method was "relatively ineffective for preventing pregnancy" based on carefully designed studies done in five different countries, with an overall failure rate of 19.4 per 100 woman-years. This is probably because many women have difficulty noting the cyclic changes in their cervical mucus, and women who have a vaginal infection (which may itself create a discharge) usually cannot use this method. In a more recent study of 725 women, an overall failure of 22.3 per 100 woman-years was noted (World Health Organization, 1981).

SEXUAL EFFECTS OF THE RHYTHM METHODS

Most couples using the rhythm methods do not experience major sexual difficulties. However, some couples may develop sexual problems because the need for abstinence creates unusual pressures to have intercourse on "safe" days regardless of whether they feel like it or not. Fear of pregnancy may also lead to sexual difficulties.

Sterilization

The highest degree of contraceptive protection currently available short of absolute abstinence is found in the use of surgical procedures to prevent pregnancy (*sterilization*). The popularity of these operations for both men and women has increased considerably in America in the last fifteen years. One recent estimate indicates that among all married American couples, about one-quarter will use sterilization within two years after the birth of their last wanted child and by ten years after their last child, more than half will undergo sterilization (Westoff and McCarthy, 1979).

Sterilization procedures are appealing because they are safe, effective, and permanent. Their permanence can be a drawback, however, if there is a change in feelings or circumstances (e.g., death of a child or spouse, divorce) that leads a person to want more children. Although there is some possibility of reversing the sterilization, these procedures are far from guaranteed. Anyone thinking about sterilization as a method of birth control should thoroughly consider its probable irreversibility. One way of retaining the option to reproduce after male ster-

FIGURE 6–9
Two Types of Tubal Ligation

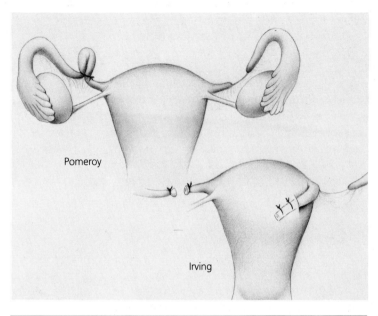

Pomeroy

Irving

ilization is to use a sperm bank to store several samples of frozen semen produced before sterilization. If reproduction becomes desirable at a later time, the semen samples are thawed and used in artificial insemination.

FEMALE STERILIZATION

More than one hundred different types of operations can be used to achieve female sterilization. Almost all block the Fallopian tubes to prevent the union of sperm and egg. *Tubal ligation* (tying the tubes) is rarely done by itself today, since it is not as effective as other methods that also cut, clip, or otherwise block the tubes (Figure 6-9). Many of these operations are still called "tubal ligation" even though more is done.

Tubal ligation is frequently achieved by us-

ing a *laparoscope,* a tubelike instrument with lights and a viewer that is inserted through the abdominal wall. The tubes are cut and cauterized (burned) through this instrument. If laparoscopy can be done through the navel, no scar is visible; as only a one-inch incision is required for this operation, it is often called "band-aid sterilization." A similar instrument can be inserted through the back end of the vagina or through the vagina and uterus to perform a tubal ligation.

Laparotomy, an operation involving a four- or five-inch incision through the abdomen, can also be used to perform a tubal ligation. It is rarely used for sterilization unless there is another reason for abdominal surgery, a technical difficulty, or a danger to the woman because of a medical problem. Female sterilization also results from *hysterectomy* (removal of the uterus) or *ovariectomy* (removal of the ovaries), but these operations are generally done for other reasons with sterility occurring as a byproduct.

Female sterilization by most techniques offers almost foolproof protection against pregnancy. In rare instances, the cut ends of the tubes may rejoin, leading to a pregnancy, but the most common cause for "method failure" is when the woman is already pregnant (but no one knows it) when the operation is done (Wortman and Piotrow, 1973). Side effects are infrequent (less than 5 percent) and are usually limited to the first few days after surgery, when infection or bleeding may be a problem.

Most women have no sexual difficulties after sterilization, which affects neither their hormones (since their ovaries are intact) nor their sexual anatomy. A few women may run into problems. If a woman undergoes sterilization involuntarily (e.g., if it was a decision she was pushed into by her husband or by health or economic circumstances), she may develop a reduced interest in sex for psychological reasons. Some women find that after sterilization they no longer feel the same way about sex (or have lowered sexual responsiveness) because they feel "incomplete" or "less than a woman." This reaction is particularly possible in a woman whose religious background considers sex unnatural or sinful if it is separated from its reproductive potential. On the other hand, some women show increased sexual interest after sterilization due to no longer fearing pregnancy.

MALE STERILIZATION

Vasectomy is a simple surgical procedure that consists of cutting and tying each vas deferens (the tube that carries sperm) (see Figure 6-10). The operation is usually done using local anesthesia in a doctor's office or clinic and requires only about fifteen or twenty minutes. The man can then go home, although it is usually advisable to avoid strenuous physical activity for a day or two afterward.

Vasectomy does not stop sperm production; it blocks the passage of sperm from the testes to the upper part of the vas deferens. Sperm then accumulate in the epididymis (a mass of tubes at the back of each testis), where they are engulfed and destroyed by cells called phagocytes. Some sperm appear to leak out into the scrotum, where they disintegrate. Because some sperm are already above the point where the vasectomy was done, it usually takes six to eight weeks (about a dozen ejaculations) after this operation before the ejaculate is sterile (contains no sperm). For this reason, the man and his sex partner should use another method of birth control until at least two consecutive semen exams show that no sperm are present.

Vasectomy does not affect hormone production and does not interfere in any way with erection or ejaculation. The amount of the ejaculate is almost unchanged, since secretions from the testis and epididymis account for less than 5 percent of the volume of seminal fluid. There are no long-range health risks created by vasectomy.[5]

Vasectomy is the simplest and safest form of surgical contraception: the failure rate is a very low 0.15 percent. Failures occur either because of unprotected intercourse before all sperm have disappeared from the ejaculate, mistakes in performing the operation, or, very rarely, because

---

[5] Research in monkeys has found hardening of the arteries years after vasectomy (Clarkson and Alexander, 1980), but there is no evidence of this complication in humans (Wallace et al., 1981). In fact, a recent study of about 20,000 men found no signs of increased health risks (including heart disease and cancer) in vasectomized men compared to men who hadn't had this operation (*American Medical News*, Nov. 25, 1983, p. 3).

FIGURE 6–10
The Vasectomy

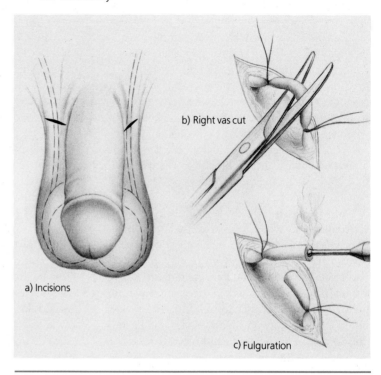

b) Right vas cut

a) Incisions

c) Fulguration

A vasectomy must completely prevent sperm from traveling out of the scrotum higher into the male reproductive system. Drawing a) shows the site of the small incisions in the scrotum used to perform a vasectomy; b) shows the vas being cut with surgical scissors; and c) shows the cut ends of the vas being burned with a controlled electric current so that scar tissue forms to block the passage of sperm.

the cut ends of the vas have grown back together. The rate of medical complications such as bleeding or infection is less than 5 percent, although minor swelling, pain, and temporary skin discoloration due to bruising occur in about half of men after this procedure. Postoperative ice packs and a well-fitted athletic supporter can reduce discomfort.

Less than one man in twenty reports decreased sexual pleasure after a vasectomy, while close to half claim increased pleasure and about a quarter report an increased frequency of intercourse (Wortman, 1975). In fact, many couples find that sex is more spontaneous and fun after a vasectomy since they don't need to worry about becoming pregnant or using other contraceptive methods. Men who have a history of sexual problems are not always good candidates for vasectomy, since they may be more prone to developing psychological impotence or other difficulties after such surgery. For some couples, there may be a drop in marital harmony after a vasectomy, because the man expected special recognition or gratitude from his wife in return for having the surgery (Rodgers and Ziegler, 1973) or because the wife resents not being able to have additional children. Occasionally, a man who has been well adjusted to a vasectomy may

Comparison of Vasectomy and Female Sterilization

VASECTOMY	FEMALE STERILIZATION
Effectiveness	**Effectiveness**
Very effective, but slightly higher rate of spontaneous recanalization and pregnancy.	Very effective; slightly lower failure rate.
Effective 6 to 10 weeks after surgery.	Effective immediately.
Complications	**Complications**
Procedure involves almost no risk of internal injury or other life-threatening complications.	Procedure involves slight risk of serious internal injuries and other life-threatening complications.
Very slight possibility of serious infection.	Slight possibility of serious infection.
No anesthesia-related deaths.	Few anesthesia-related deaths.
Acceptability	**Acceptability**
Minute scar.	Scar can be small but still visible.
Slightly more reversible.	Slightly less reversible.
Less expensive.	More acceptable in many cultures.
Personnel	**Personnel**
Can be performed by one trained person with or without an assistant.	Team needed, including one doctor, one trained anesthetist, and at least two assistants with more training than needed for vasectomy assistant.
Safely performed by trained paramedics.	More difficult for paramedics to learn and to perform.
Can usually be performed in half the time of most female sterilizations.	Usually only physicians with training in gynecology can perform laparoscopy and laparotomy. Minilaparotomy is simpler.
Equipment	**Equipment**
Requires no specialized equipment. Equipment readily available.	Laparoscopy requires expensive, complex equipment, which needs to be carefully maintained. Minilaparotomy requires only simple standard surgical instruments.
Can usually be performed under local anesthesia.	Systemic sedation necessary as well as local anesthesia.
Back-Up Facilities	**Back-Up Facilities**
No back-up facilities needed for immediate complications.	Back-up facilities needed in case of damage to abdominal organs and blood vessels or other complications that require laparotomy.
Possible Long-Term Side Effects	**Possible Long-Term Side Effects**
None demonstrated. Uncertainty about effect of increase in sperm antibodies.	Slight risk of ectopic pregnancy.

Source: POPULATION REPORTS, Series D, Nov.–Dec. 1983

become impotent (usually temporarily) if he divorces and then remarries, particularly if he and his new wife would like to have children. More typical, however, is this comment from a thirty-year-old man six months after his vasectomy: "It was simple and quick and did the trick. Now sex is *really* making love, without worrying about 'accidents' " (Authors' files).

Other Methods of Contraception

Withdrawal (coitus interruptus) is the removal of the penis from the vagina before ejaculation occurs. This is a difficult form of birth control in which even perfect timing (which is not always possible) does not give perfect results. If ejaculation occurs before the penis is withdrawn completely, or if drops of semen spurt into the opening of the vagina, pregnancy can occur. As live sperm can also be in the pre-ejaculatory fluid long before ejaculation (or even if the male doesn't ejaculate), this method is chancy at best, with a failure rate of 20 to 25 percent. This method can also be a frustrating form of birth control for both parties, who may find that it seriously interrupts the spontaneity of the sexual interaction. However, it is clearly better than not using any contraceptive when nothing else is available.

Douching, using a liquid to flush the vagina, is a poor method of contraception, since sperm can quickly penetrate the cervical mucus, where they are unaffected by douching. The failure rate is more than 40 percent.

Breast-feeding inhibits ovulation in some women (possibly via the effect of high prolactin levels on the ovaries) but this method of birth control is very unreliable. Women who do not want to become pregnant soon after childbirth should begin using a more effective means of contraception right away. Some studies of nursing mothers not using any other method of birth control indicate pregnancy rates of over 50 percent (Buchanan, 1975).

Abstinence from intercourse is, needless to say, a highly effective way to prevent pregnancy if practiced consistently. Some couples voluntarily limit their sex lives to noncoital acts, but this does not seem to be a very popular choice for most heterosexual couples.

POSTCONCEPTION METHODS OF BIRTH CONTROL

The "Morning After" Pill

Various types of estrogen used in high doses shortly after conception can prevent implantation and provide a form of "after the fact" birth control. This approach can be useful in special situations (such as rape or leakage of a condom) but it is not suitable for routine contraceptive use. Most commonly, diethylstilbestrol (DES) is given to the woman for five days, beginning as soon after unprotected intercourse as possible and within seventy-two hours. The effectiveness of using this timetable is extremely high: the pregnancy rate is less than one percent (Rinehart, 1976). The primary side effects are nausea (sometimes accompanied by vomiting), breast tenderness, and alterations in the menstrual cycle. Used on a short-term basis, as just outlined, DES or other forms of estrogen are unlikely to have any lasting effect on the woman or on a fetus if a pregnancy occurs. Although DES used during later stages of pregnancy has been linked to abnormalities in the reproductive systems of children of mothers receiving this drug, there is no indication that this effect applies to its use in preventing pregnancy. Nevertheless, the risks of "morning after" pills are not entirely known at present, and it should not be assumed that they are completely safe.

Menstrual Extraction

This technique has been pioneered by the women's self-help movement. Just when a period is expected, a thin, flexible plastic tube is inserted through the cervix into the uterus, and suction (using either a syringe or a pump) is applied to draw out the endometrial lining. If the woman is pregnant, the tiny embryo is easily withdrawn. There may be mild cramping, but no anesthetic is usually used. Although further research is required, there do not seem to be any major side effects when done under proper conditions by a health care professional.

Abortion

Abortion is the termination of pregnancy before the fetus is able to survive outside the uterus (Tietze, 1977). Abortion can be either *spontaneous*, that is, when a medical problem ends a pregnancy, or *induced*, when the contents of the pregnant uterus are removed intentionally. On a worldwide basis, it has been estimated that 30 to 55 million induced abortions are performed annually (Tietze and Lewit, 1977).

Abortion has been practiced since early times. In ancient Greece, where it was thought the fetus had no soul, Plato suggested in *The Republic* that abortion be used in cases of incest or older parents, and Aristotle recommended abortion as a way to limit family size (Babikian, 1975). In 1800, there were no laws against abortion in America, and by the mid-1800s, advertisements for abortion services appeared in respectable newspapers, journals, and religious magazines (Mohr, 1978).

In 1869 Pope Pius IX issued a decree declaring abortion sinful and banning it entirely, thus providing support for an antiabortion campaign that had been already started by the newly formed American Medical Association. By 1900 abortion was illegal all over America. Although an illegal abortion trade flourished, with incredibly high rates of bleeding, infection, and death among women getting such "help," it was not until the late 1960s that a few states changed their abortion laws. In January 1973 a decision by the U.S. Supreme Court established the legal right of women to choose whether or not to have an abortion, although in Canada the legal issues are somewhat different (see the boxed item on page 181).

Today, the abortion issue is argued heatedly by various groups. The "Right-to-Life" movement opposes abortion on the grounds of protecting the rights of the unborn fetus, while "Pro-Choice" advocates want women to have freedom of choice in controlling their own bodies and futures. Public opinion on these issues is divided, as shown in Table 6-2. The complex aspects of rights and responsibilities as they affect individuals and society are not simple or easily summarized; they are discussed more fully in chapter 23.

ABORTION METHODS

The abortion method chosen depends mainly on the length of the pregnancy. During the first trimester, the most common method is called *vacuum aspiration* or *suction*. After widening the mouth of the cervix, a small plastic tube is inserted into the uterus. The tube is connected to an electric pump that removes the fetal tissue, placenta, and membranes from the uterus by suction (Figure 6-11). The procedure usually requires only ten to fifteen minutes.

During the fourth and fifth months of pregnancy, the safest method for abortion is *dilatation and evacuation* (D&E), a method that is similar to vacuum aspiration. After the mouth of the cervix is widened (dilated), vacuum suction is applied to partly remove the contents of the uterus. However, because at this later stage of pregnancy not all of the tissue can be removed by

TABLE 6–2
Percentage of U.S. Adults Approving of Legal Abortion in Various
Circumstances, 1965–1980

Circumstance	1965	1975	1980
Please tell me whether *you* think it should be possible for a pregnant woman to obtain a *legal* abortion:			
If the woman's health is seriously endangered by the pregnancy	73%	91%	90%
If she became pregnant as a result of rape	59	84	83
If there is a strong chance of a serious defect in the baby	57	83	83
If the family has a very low income and cannot afford any more children	22	53	52
If she is not married and does not want to marry the man	18	48	48
If she is married and does not want any more children	16	46	47
For any reason	na	na	41
Average approval for the six specified reasons	41	67	67

Source: Adapted from Granberg and Granberg, 1980. Reprinted with permission from *Family Planning Perspectives,* Volume 12, Number 5, 1980.
Note: All percentages are based on the number of respondents answering yes or no. Those who said they did not know or who did not give a yes or no answer were excluded from the analysis.
    na—question not asked in that year.

suction alone, a forceps is used to remove additional material until the uterus is completely empty. In addition, a metal instrument called a curette may be used to gently scrape the walls of the uterus to ensure that all remnants of extra tissue have been removed.

Second trimester abortions are also sometimes done by using chemicals to stimulate contractions of the uterus, causing expulsion of the fetus and membranes. *Prostaglandin-induced* abortions are done by injecting prostaglandins into the amniotic sac, dripping them slowly into a vein, or placing them in the vagina. In *saline-induced* abortions, 7 ounces of a saline (salt) solution are injected into the amniotic fluid. Both methods require hours before completion, have the disadvantages of physical and emotional discomfort during contractions of the uterus, and require vaginal delivery of the dead fetus.

Less commonly, surgical procedures are used for abortion. *Dilatation and curettage* (D&C) involves dilating the cervix and then gently scraping the lining of the uterus with a metal instrument (the curette) to extract the fetal tissue, placenta, and membranes. A D&C can be done until about fifteen weeks after the last menstrual period and, unlike the previously mentioned methods, requires the use of general anesthesia.

Abortion in Canada

The United States is not the only country where opinions are divided and controversy exists about abortion. In Canada, abortion has been legal since 1969, but only under highly specific circumstances that are spelled out in the Criminal Code:

> 251.(1) Every one who, with intent to procure the miscarriage of a female person, whether or not she is pregnant, uses any means for the purpose of carrying out his intention is guilty of an indictable offense and is liable to imprisonment for life.

There is an exception to this rule, however: *if* a committee of at least three physicians approves a woman's request for abortion; *if* the abortion is to protect the "life and health" of the woman; and *if* the abortion is performed at an accredited hospital – then the abortion will technically be legal. In actual practice, these complicated provisions create many problematic situations for the woman seeking an abortion. First, although a committee of three physicians must approve an abortion, *no hospital is under any obligation to have such a committee.* Many hospitals (estimates go as high as 80%) simply sidestep the abortion issue by not having an abortion committee, but this makes abortion inaccessible to many women in large geographic areas that are not served by hospitals with abortion committees. Second, abortion may only be performed to protect the "life and health" of the woman, but the law does not define "life or health." Some committees may interpret this broadly (i.e., psychological health), others more strictly, but many women resent the fact that the decision is being made by three unfamiliar doctors, not by the woman (who will have to bear the consequences) herself. Third, abortions must be performed only in accredited hospitals, and free-standing abortion clinics – which may be more convenient, approachable, etc. – are forbidden. The abortion committee procedure is time-consuming and may delay an abortion until the second trimester, when it is more likely to result in complications, and a sizable number of Canadian women choose to cross the border and get an abortion in the United States.

One Canadian physician, Dr. Henry Morgentaler, has been an activist in seeking abortion reform in Canada. In 1973, Dr. Morgentaler publicly announced that he had performed more than 5,000 technically illegal abortions, and was televised performing an abortion in his Montreal clinic. Morgentaler was arrested, tried, and acquitted by the jury. This verdict was appealed, however, and the Court of Appeals not only overturned the verdict but – *without even ordering a new trial* – sentenced Morgentaler to 18 months in jail (Watters, 1976). Morgentaler served time in prison, but is again active in establishing free-standing abortion clinics in Toronto and Winnipeg. The police have raided his clinics in both cities, and Morgentaler and his associates are on trial for his abortion activities at this time.

FIGURE 6–11
Vacuum Aspiration Abortion

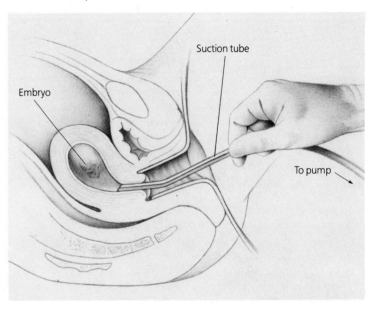

Suction tube

Embryo

To pump

Vacuum aspiration for abortion involves suctioning the embryo and membranes from within the uterus.

A *hysterotomy* is an operation like a cesarean section which can be used throughout the second trimester. It also requires general anesthesia and is rarely used.

Although some people believe that eating certain foods, vigorous exercise, or other "do it yourself" techniques will lead to abortion, this is not true. Attempts at inducing abortion by inserting objects such as a wire coathanger or knitting needle into the uterus are *extremely dangerous* and can lead to fatal infections or bleeding.

SAFETY

Modern abortion techniques are less risky to the mother than a full-term pregnancy: less than four deaths occur per 100,000 induced abortions compared to approximately twenty deaths per 100,000 pregnancies (Grimes and Cates, 1980). In fact, among healthy women (those with no serious pre-existing medical problems) the risk of dying from a legal abortion in the United States is less than one per 100,000 procedures (LeBolt, Grimes, and Cates, 1982). Abortions done during the first trimester are simplest and safest, as shown in Table 6-3; after this, complications such as bleeding, infection, and perforation of the uterus are more common. There is no solid evidence that having a properly done abortion causes later infertility. Recent reports do indicate that having two or more induced abortions leads to a higher rate of miscarriages in subsequent pregnancies (Harlap et al., 1979; Levin et al., 1980; Madore et al., 1981) and may increase the rate of prematurity and low birth-weight infants (World Health Organization, 1978).

TABLE 6–3
Safety of Legal Abortions, by Weeks of
Pregnancy, United States 1972–1978

Weeks of Pregnancy	Number of Deaths per 100,000 Abortions
Up to 8	0.5
9–10	1.4
11–12	2.3
13–15	6.7
16–20	13.9
21 or more	17.5

Source: Centers for Disease Control, *Abortion Surveillance 1978,* issued November 1980, p. 48.
Note: Eighty-eight percent of all legal abortions in the United States during these years were done before the thirteenth week of pregnancy.

PSYCHOLOGICAL ASPECTS OF ABORTION

The emotional benefits of abortion outweigh the psychological risks for most women (Osofsky et al., 1971; Niswander, Singer, and Singer, 1972; Nadelson, 1978). Serious problems requiring psychiatric referral occur in less than 3 women in every 100,000 who have had an abortion and, for many women, "the decision to terminate an unwanted pregnancy represents a healthy coping with reality, a maturing experience culminating in feelings of relief" (H. David, 1978). Nevertheless, short-lived feelings of guilt, sadness, and loss are common in women who have had abortions; preabortion and postabortion counseling is often effective in helping women deal with these reactions.

One relatively neglected aspect of the abortion experience is the *male's* reaction. A recent survey of the impact of abortion on men shows that many men try to approach the abortion decision in an abstract, intellectual way but later find themselves having to deal with feelings of hurt, guilt, or anger (Shostak, McLouth, and Seng, 1984). Few abortion centers offer counseling services for men, perhaps reflecting the view of one abortion counselor who told us: "The imperial male attitude is just too hard to deal with in many cases. It's the woman who's pregnant, and it's her feelings I worry about. Let the men go find a psychiatrist on their own if they need to." While not all abortion counselors share this view, many point out that men don't seem interested in their services.

THE PSYCHOLOGY OF CONTRACEPTIVE USE

Why do some people who do not want a pregnancy avoid the use of contraception or misuse the form of birth control they have selected? One common reason is inadequate knowledge. Illustrating this point, Zelnik and Kantner (1979) found that about half of sexually active teenage women aged fifteen to nineteen thought they could not become pregnant (see Table 6–4). Similarly, a survey of urban mothers showed that only one-third knew when during the menstrual cycle a woman is most likely to become pregnant, and for mothers under age twenty-one, only 10 percent were correct in their knowledge (Presser, 1977).

Inadequate knowledge does not explain why many people who understand the mechanics and risks of conception still do not use birth control or use it haphazardly. This phenomenon raises a fundamental question about personal motivation and contraceptive practice. Clearly, some people avidly want to avoid pregnancy, while others only want to delay the timing of a pregnancy or do not mind if they happen to conceive (in this discussion, we will not deal with couples wanting a pregnancy, since contraceptive use does not

TABLE 6–4

Percentage Distribution of Women Aged 15–19 in 1976 Who Had
Premarital Intercourse More than Once without Contraception

Intention and Reason for Last Nonuse	Total	White	Black
All Nonusers	(N = 590)	(N = 339)	(N = 251)
Pregnant	15.0	15.0	15.2
Trying to become pregnant	5.2	4.1	9.2
Not pregnant or trying	79.8	80.9	75.6
Total	100.0	100.0	100.0
Not Pregnant or Trying	(N = 452)	(N = 261)	(N = 191)
Thought they could become pregnant	49.0	46.7	58.4
Did not expect to have intercourse	20.3	19.3	24.3
Wanted to use something but could not under the circumstances	7.2	7.7	5.2
Partner objected	1.9	1.4	4.2
Believed it was wrong or dangerous to use contraception	4.9	4.4	6.9
Did not know about contraception, or where to get it	3.1	3.2	2.7
Sex was not much fun with contraception or contraception was too difficult to use	3.8	2.6	8.5
Other	7.8	8.1	6.6
Thought they could not become pregnant	51.0	53.2	41.6
Had intercourse at time of month when could not become pregnant	22.6	24.3	15.7
Too young to become pregnant	5.3	5.3	5.2
Had intercourse too infrequently to become pregnant	4.1	3.4	6.7
Other	19.0	20.2	14.0
Total	100.0	100.0	100.0

Source: Zelnik and Kantner, 1979, p. 292. Reprinted with permission from *Family Planning Perspectives,* Volume 11, Number 5, 1979.

really apply). In general, the more motivated a person is to avoid pregnancy, the more likely he or she will choose and consistently use a highly effective birth control method. But this motivation may also be affected by other factors, such as forgetfulness, denial ("it can't happen to me"), dissatisfaction with a particular method, wanting to please a partner, or concern about medical risks. This comment from a twenty-three-year-old woman illustrates a commonly encountered situation:

I'd been using the pill for about two years, but I read about its risks so I decided to switch. I got pregnant the third time I used a diaphragm. I'm back on the pill now, older but wiser. (Authors' files)

Not using contraception is sometimes a sign of personal embarrassment about sexuality in general or about a particular method. One twenty-four-year-old woman told us that she had tried to insert a diaphragm for a half hour and finally just gave up because she felt foolish about it. Other people worry that someone may discover their contraceptive devices, giving away that they are, or plan to be, sexually active. While this concern obviously affects teenagers who may be afraid of a parent finding out that they use contraception, it may also apply to a woman whose date accidentally discovers a container of foam in her purse. She may have no intention of having intercourse or *any* sexual activity with him, but the "discovery" may be taken to mean that she is willing or even expecting to.

For other people, it is okay to have sex in the heat of passion, but *planning* for it makes it immoral, mechanical, or unromantic (these people are often called parents). Many people also use contraceptives on a fairly regular basis with only occasional lapses into sexual brinksmanship. In these instances they decide to indulge their soaring sexual feelings (and not call Time Out) or to forgo contraception to "have more fun" or "make it more natural." Couples using rhythm methods sometimes have a particular problem with sexual brinksmanship, since sex may seem more enticing on the days when abstinence is expected.

In some cases hostility, power struggles, or differences in the reproductive goals of two sexual partners may lead to disuse or misuse of contraception. The man who insists on using withdrawal may make sex unpleasant and even threatening to his partner. The woman can attempt to manipulate her partner by limiting her sexual availability ("My IUD is cramping" or "I have an infection"), or by seeking a pregnancy to entrap her partner in marriage or to prevent separation or divorce (Sandberg, 1976). Who assumes responsibility for contraception may be a heated issue, particularly if the woman has done so for a long while and then wishes to turn this job over to her partner.

One last aspect of the psychology of contraceptive use will be mentioned. When sexual problems exist in a relationship, couples frequently become sloppy in their attention to birth control or stop using contraception altogether. Sometimes they believe their sexual difficulty results from or is worsened by their contraceptive method. In other cases, they think that when sex is a problem, conception is unlikely (of course, they *may* be mildly shocked to discover how wrong they are). In yet other instances, discontinuing the use of birth control may be used as a psychological ploy to symbolize that "sex really is not so important" or, conversely, to attempt to make sexual contact more intimate and exciting.

FUTURE TRENDS IN CONTRACEPTION

There is general agreement that currently available contraceptive methods are less than perfect from the viewpoints of safety, reversibility, effectiveness, and ease of use. To improve the range of choices, considerable research is underway.

New Directions in Male Contraception

Not surprisingly, the most intense interest focuses on the possibility of developing a male birth control pill. In theory, this could be accomplished by using drugs to: (1) block sperm production in the testes, (2) interfere with sperm maturation in the epididymis, (3) impair sperm transport at any point along their journey from testis to epididymis to vas deferens to urethra, or (4) reduce sperm motility or ability to undergo capacitation. Various drugs have already been found to accomplish each task, but so far they have either proved to have incomplete effects or to have unacceptable side effects. For example, combinations of estrogen and progestogen (as used in the "female" pill) are effective in blocking sperm production but cause a profound drop in sexual interest in most males and frequently lead to impotence. Pills combining testosterone and a progestogen are currently under investigation, since they do not seem to cause the circulatory side effects estrogen does and do not usually interfere with sexual function. However, these pills are not highly effective in inhibiting sperm production for long periods of time (Segal, 1979).

A recent report from China indicates that an extract from cottonseed oil called gossypol suppresses sperm production (National Coordinating Group for Male Contraceptives, 1978). Gossypol acts on sperm metabolism, either immobilizing sperm cells or killing them (Tong, Zhou, and Zhou, 1982). While the incidence of side effects with gossypol seems to be acceptable, with only about 10 percent of men developing minor problems such as dizziness, fatigue, dry mouth, and digestive tract difficulties, and only 5 percent reporting decreased libido or potency problems, it is not clear if gossypol's effects on sperm production are completely reversible (Liskin, Pile, and Quillin, 1983).

An even more promising recent development has been the creation of a synthetic form of inhibin, a protein substance made in the testes that provides feedback to the hypothalamus and pituitary gland controlling the production of FSH (Sairam et al., 1984). Since it is thought that inhibin suppresses sperm production without affecting sexual function, clinical trials with this substance may provide the ultimate breakthrough in the search for an effective, reversible male contraceptive.

The search for additional methods of male contraception also includes several other possibilities:

1. Developing a vaccine or drug to block production of FSH in the pituitary, since this hormone controls sperm production but has no known effects on sexual function;

2. Developing a vaccine to impair the enzymes released by the acrosome (chemical reservoir) of the sperm, since these enzymes are required for the sperm to penetrate the egg;

3. Using ultrasound to produce temporary sterility by blocking sperm production.

New Directions in Female Contraception

Improvements in methods of female fertility control are being studied currently by many groups of scientists. One of the most promising approaches is the attempt to develop an antipregnancy vaccine that is activated only in the event of conception and that works in a reliable and unobtrusive fashion. Vaccines directed against HCG, a hormone secreted by the placenta (and the hormone detected by pregnancy tests), are being tested at the present time (Greep, Koblinsky, and Jaffe, 1976) and seem to prevent pregnancy without interfering with ovarian or menstrual cycles (Segal, 1979).

An attempt is also underway to identify a compound that could block progesterone production by the corpus luteum (the part of the ovarian follicle that produces hormones in early pregnancy). This compound would prevent implantation and induce menstruation whether or not pregnancy occurs. Research is also being conducted to develop a pill, liquid, or vaginal tampon that could be self-administered at the expected time of menstruation to induce menstrual flow and evacuate the contents of the uterus. Various synthetic analogues of prostaglandins that cause uterine contractions are being investigated for this purpose, but while they appear to be at least 90 percent effective, they are typically accompanied by an unacceptably high rate of negative side effects. Another idea is to block signals from the hypothalamus to the pituitary gland that trigger LH release. An important step in the initiation of ovulation would thereby be disrupted. Theoretically, blocking tubal transport of the fertilized egg could also reduce the chances of implantation, but this possibility has not been thoroughly studied.

Attention has also been focused on improving hormonal methods of female birth control. These include developing pills without estrogen (to avoid unwanted side effects) and using long-acting forms of contraceptive hormones. These hormones would be either injected or placed in small implants under the skin or in plastic vaginal rings which slowly release hormones. In fact, it will soon be possible for a woman wishing long-term contraceptive protection to carry a five-year supply of hormonal birth control with her all the time in an implant placed under the skin in the upper arm. This implant, called the NORPLANT system, actually consists of six small silastic capsules packed with the hormone levonorgestrel — the same progestogen used in many minipills — which are thought to provide about the same degree of contraceptive effectiveness as the pill. The contraceptive, which is slowly released from the capsules, doesn't always block ovulation but instead prevents pregnancy in two ways: by thickening the cervical mucus (making it difficult for sperm to swim up the Fallopian tubes) and by blocking implantation. The major drawback at this time is that many users experience abnormal menstrual bleeding (but this problem generally decreases after about one year of use).

A synthetic form of progesterone called *medroxyprogesterone acetate*, or MPA, is currently used as a long-acting contraceptive in other countries. (In the United States, its trade name is Depo-Provera.) It is given by injection once every three months (so the woman does not need to remember to use it) and is about as effective as combination birth control pills. Its drawbacks include possible infertility after long-term use, reported toxicity in animal studies, and the newly reported finding that MPA may cause cancer of the uterus (Maine, 1978; Family Planning Perspectives, 1979). However, two recent studies found no evidence to support a definite link between MPA and any form of cancer in humans (Liang et al., 1983; Rosenfield, 1983).

Various techniques for developing a non-surgical method of female sterilization are also being explored. These methods, which are irreversible, involve plugging up the place at which the Fallopian tubes open into the uterus. Material that causes thick scar tissue to form at the tubal openings is inserted through the vagina and cervix with a special instrument that doesn't require making an incision or using anesthesia. Studies of the effectiveness of this approach are now underway (Atkinson et al., 1981).

Finally, a pocket-size electronic device that flashes a red light when a woman is fertile may be useful to those interested in practicing natural family planning. The device consists of a thermometer and a microcomputer that keeps track of a woman's temperature changes during her menstrual cycle, displaying a green light on "safe" days and a red light on days near the time of ovulation. While there are no published studies as yet on the accuracy of this device (or similar devices that claim to detect ovulation by a litmus paper test, measuring the thickness of cervical mucus, and other similar means), this type of approach bears further investigation, particularly since its use would be acceptable to the Roman Catholic Church.

SUMMARY

Table 6-5 on page 188 summarizes the various contraceptive methods that we have discussed in this chapter.

TABLE 6-5
Summary of Contraceptive Methods

Method	Effectiveness Rating	Ideal Failure Rate	Actual Failure Rate	Advantages	Disadvantages
Birth Control Pills (combination)	Excellent	0.5%	2-3%	Highly reliable; coitus independent; has some health benefits	Side effects; daily use; continual cost
Minipill	Very Good	1-2	5-10	Thought to have low risk of side effects; coitus independent	Breakthrough bleeding; daily use; continual cost
IUD	Excellent	1-3	5-6	No memory or motivation required for use; very reliable	Cramping, bleeding, expulsion
Condom and Diaphragm	Excellent	1	3-5	Highly reliable with no major health risks	See separate discussions of condom and diaphragm below
Condom and Foam	Excellent	1	3-5	Highly reliable with no major health risks	See separate discussions of condom and foam below
Diaphragm and Cream or Jelly	Good-Very Good	3	15-20	No major health risks; inexpensive	Aesthetic objections
Condom	Very Good	3	10	Protects against VD; simple to use; male responsibility; no health risks; no prescription required	Unaesthetic to some; requires interruption of sexual activity
Sponge	Good-Very Good	3	15	24-hour protection; simple to use; no taste or odor; inexpensive; effective with several acts of intercourse	Aesthetic objections
Cervical Cap	Good	3	10-20	Can wear for weeks at a time; coitus independent; no major health risks	May be difficult to insert; may irritate cervix
Spermicides	Good	3	18-22	No major health risks; no prescription required	Unaesthetic to some; must be properly inserted
Rhythm	Poor to Fair	13	20-40	No cost; acceptable to Catholic church	Requires high motivation and periods of abstinence; unreliable
Withdrawal	Fair	9	20-25	No cost or health risks	Reduces sexual pleasure; unreliable
Douching	Poor	?	40+	Inexpensive	Extremely unreliable
Breast-Feeding	Poor	15	50+	No cost; acceptable to Catholic church	Extremely unreliable
Vasectomy	Excellent	0.15	0.15	Permanent and highly reliable	Expensive; relatively irreversible; possible complications
Tubal Ligation	Excellent	0.04	0.04	Permanent and highly reliable	Expensive; relatively irreversible; possible complications

Source: Based on data from Hatcher et al., 1982, and *Population Reports* research reviews (see Suggested Readings).

SUGGESTED READINGS

Djerassi, C. *The Politics of Contraception*. New York: W. W. Norton & Co., 1979. One of the inventors of the pill provides an authoritative look at the ethical, social, and political sides of birth control.

Dornblaser, C., and Landy, U. *The Abortion Guide: A Handbook for Women and Men*. New York: Berkley, 1982. A readable, comprehensive guide to all aspects of abortion, including its aftereffects.

The Alan Guttmacher Institute. *Safe and Legal: 10 Years' Experience with Legal Abortion in New York State*. 1980. A concise and information-packed report, including an interesting afterward by the Episcopal Bishop of New York.

Hatcher, R. A., et al. *Contraceptive Technology 1982–1983*. New York: Irvington Publishers, 1982. A complete and thoroughly referenced guide to contraception.

Population Reports. Published by the Population Information Program, Johns Hopkins University, Hampton House, 624 North Broadway, Baltimore, Maryland 21205. A series of in-depth review articles on all aspects of contraceptive technology and policy, with major subjects updated annually.

Interested persons may also find useful literature at any Planned Parenthood office.

Developmental Sexuality: A Biological View

7

S EXUAL development is a complex process that starts at conception and continues thoughout the life cycle. Before birth, in the *prenatal period,* sexual development is controlled mainly by biological forces. But from the moment the doctor says, "It's a girl" or "It's a boy," the rest of our sexual development is profoundly influenced by psychosocial factors interacting with our biological heritage.

In this chapter, we will consider developmental sexuality from a biological viewpoint. Some behavioral observations will be discussed when they help to clarify biological principles, but the influences of learning on our sexual development will be considered in more detail in chapter 8.

PRENATAL DEVELOPMENT

At the moment of conception, the combination of genetic material from each parent starts a process called *sexual differentiation* which leads to the specific physical differences between females and males. The process of prenatal sexual differentiation is largely controlled by genetic and hormonal mechanisms. We will examine these mechanisms and the events they control in two ways. First we will examine normal development patterns of prenatal sexual differentiation, and then we will consider several examples of altered or abnormal development that can occur.

Normal Prenatal Differentiation

At fertilization, when the male sperm and female egg unite to form a zygote, the initial programming for sexual differentiation is set in place. Remember that the sperm carries an X or Y sex chromosome while the egg always has an X sex chromosome. When the 23 chromosomes of the sperm combine with the 23 chromosomes of the egg, the zygote has a total of 46 chromosomes. Under ordinary circumstances, a 46,XX chromosome pattern is the genetic code for a female and a 46,XY pattern programs for a male.

Regardless of the genetic coding, during the first weeks of development male and female embryos are anatomically identical (Table 7-1).

TABLE 7-1
Homologous Sex Organs

Male	Female
Testes	Ovaries
Penile glans	Clitoral glans
Penile shaft	Clitoral shaft
Foreskin	Clitoral hood
Scrotum	Labia majora
Underside of penile shaft	Labia minora
Cowper's glands	Bartholin's glands

Note: Homologous structures are those that develop from the same embryonic tissue.

Two primitive gonads form during the fifth and sixth weeks of pregnancy, first as ridges of tissue and then as more distinct structures. At this point, the gonads are bipotential, meaning that depending on events to come, they can differentiate into either testes or ovaries. There are also two paired primitive duct systems that form in both male and female embryos during this time, the *Müllerian* ducts and the *Wolffian* ducts (Figure 7-1).

For the testes to develop, there must be one further step in genetic control. A chemical substance called *H-Y antigen* (controlled by the Y chromosome) starts the transformation of the primitive gonads into testes (Wachtel, 1979; Haseltine and Ohno, 1981). If H-Y antigen is not present, the primitive gonads will always develop into ovaries.

From this point on, sexual differentiation occurs at three different levels — the internal sex structures, the external genitals, and the brain — and is largely controlled by hormones. Even if the sex chromosome pattern is 46,XY, without enough testosterone produced at the right time, anatomic development will be female rather than male (Jost, 1953; Jost, 1972; Money and Ehrhardt, 1972; Wilson, George, and Griffin, 1981).

INTERNAL SEX STRUCTURES

If the embryo is a male, the newly formed testes begin secreting two different products by the eighth week after conception. A chemical called *Müllerian duct inhibiting substance* causes the Müllerian ducts to shrink and practically disappear instead of forming female internal sex organs. At the same time, testosterone is also produced, stimulating the development of the Wolffian ducts into the epididymis, vas deferens, seminal vesicles, and ejaculatory ducts (Figure 7-1). In addition, testosterone is converted in some tissues to another form, called *dihydrotestosterone*, which stimulates development of the

FIGURE 7–1
The Stages of Internal Fetal Sex Differentiation

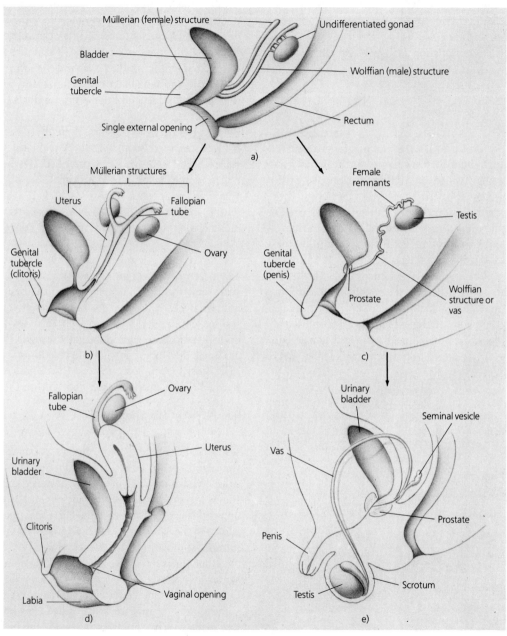

penis, scrotum, and prostate gland (Imperato-McGinley and Peterson, 1976). Testosterone and dihydrotestosterone are both *androgens*, hormones that cause masculinization.

In contrast, female sexual differentiation does not depend on hormones. Ovaries generally develop at about the twelfth week after conception, but even if they do not, the Müllerian duct system will proceed to develop into the uterus, Fallopian tubes, and inner third of the vagina (Money and Ehrhardt, 1972). Without high amounts of testosterone to stimulate its growth, the Wolffian duct system in the female shrinks into tiny remnants. By the fourteenth week of development, there is a clear difference in the internal sex structure of a male and female fetus (Figure 7-1 b&c).

EXTERNAL GENITALS

In the seventh week of development, the external genitals look the same in both sexes. If there is little androgen present, as we expect in a female embryo, a clitoris, vulva, and vagina will form in six to eight weeks (Figure 7-2). In the male, androgen stimulation causes the folds that would develop into the inner vaginal lips in the female to grow together, forming the cylindrical shaft of the penis. The genital tubercle, which develops into the clitoris in the female, becomes the glans of the penis in the male. The labioscrotal swellings differentiate into the outer vaginal lips in the female and the scrotum in the male.

Both ovaries and testes first develop inside the abdomen during fetal life. Later, the ovaries move into the pelvis and the testes migrate down into the scrotum.

a) The undifferentiated stage at approximately six to seven weeks of development. b) The pattern of female internal differentiation at approximately fourteen weeks. c) Male differentiation at approximately fourteen weeks. d) Female differentiation at approximately forty weeks. e) Male differentiation at approximately forty weeks.

BRAIN DIFFERENTIATION

Intriguingly, hormones in the blood of the fetus also affect the development of the brain and pituitary gland. The best documented structural differences between male and female brains are in the number and location of certain types of nerve cell connections (*synapses*) in the hypothalamus (Goldman, 1978; Carter and Greenough, 1979). As in other aspects of prenatal sex differentiation, with androgen stimulation the brain develops in a male pattern; without it, the brain develops in a female direction (Plapinger and McEwen, 1978; McEwen, 1981; MacLusky and Naftolin, 1981). This prenatal hormone programming determines the pattern of function of the hypothalamus and pituitary gland during and after puberty. As a result, girls have cyclic sex hormone production and menstrual cycles, while boys have a relatively constant level of sex hormone production. Female fertility is also cyclic whereas male fertility is not. Prenatal hormone effects on the brain may also influence later behavior patterns, including sexual behavior and aggressiveness, but the exact nature of these effects remains uncertain (Reinisch, 1974; Hutchison, 1978; Rubin, Reinisch, and Haskett, 1981).

Abnormal Prenatal Differentiation

Abnormal prenatal sexual development has three major causes: sex chromosome disorders, other genetic conditions, and exposure of the fetus to drugs given to the mother. A complete catalogue of such abnormalities would require an entire book, so we will briefly discuss only a few conditions that illustrate important principles of sexual development. Table 7-2 is a summary.

SEX CHROMOSOME DISORDERS

We have already pointed out that normally there are 46 chromosomes, including two sex

FIGURE 7–2
The Stages of External Fetal Sex Differentiation

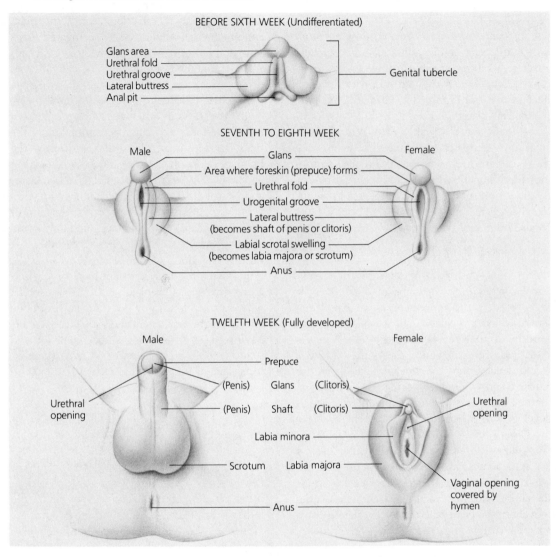

BEFORE SIXTH WEEK (Undifferentiated)

Glans area
Urethral fold
Urethral groove
Lateral buttress
Anal pit

Genital tubercle

SEVENTH TO EIGHTH WEEK

Male   Female

Glans
Area where foreskin (prepuce) forms
Urethral fold
Urogenital groove
Lateral buttress
(becomes shaft of penis or clitoris)
Labial scrotal swelling
(becomes labia majora or scrotum)
Anus

TWELFTH WEEK (Fully developed)

Male   Female

Prepuce
(Penis)   Glans   (Clitoris)
Urethral opening
(Penis)   Shaft   (Clitoris)
Urethral opening
Labia minora
Scrotum   Labia majora
Vaginal opening covered by hymen
Anus

chromosomes (XX or XY). Sometimes, however, a person may be born with extra sex chromosomes or one sex chromosome may be missing. These conditions have variable effects on a person's physical appearance, health, and behavior. Two of the most common sex chromosome abnormalities are described below.

Klinefelter's syndrome occurs when a genetic

TABLE 7–2
Summary of Abnormalities of Prenatal Sex Differentiation

	Chromosome Pattern	H-Y Antigen	Gonads	Genitals	Internal Sex Structures	Fertility	Comments
Klinefelter's syndrome	47,XXY	Yes	Testes	Male	Normal male	Sterile	Low testosterone (80%); Impotence is common
Turner's syndrome	45,X	No	Streak ovaries	Female	Uterus and Fallopian tubes	Sterile	No spontaneous menstruation or breast development due to estrogen deficiency
True hermaphroditism	46,XY or 46,XX	Yes	Testes and ovaries	Variable	Variable male and female combinations	Usually sterile	Exceedingly rare
Pseudohermaphroditism: Female Adrenogenital syndrome	46,XX	No	Ovaries	Ambiguous male	Normal female	Fertile	Requires medical management and surgical revision of genitals; tomboy pattern in childhood; increased rate of lesbian fantasy
Testicular Feminization syndrome	46,XY	Yes	Cryptorchid Testes	Female (short vagina)	No uterus or tubes; no prostate	Sterile	Spontaneous breast development at puberty but no menstruation; female psychosexual orientation
Dominican Republic syndrome	46,XY	Yes	Cryptorchid Testes	Ambiguous female	Vas deferens, epididymis, and seminal vesicles, but no prostate	Fertile but unable to inseminate	At puberty, voice deepens, muscles develop in male pattern, penis grows, testes descend and enlarge, male gender identity is assumed

male has an extra X chromosome (a 47,XXY pattern). This condition occurs about once in every 500 live male births but is usually not detected until adulthood. As a result of the extra X chromosome, the microscopic structure of the testes is abnormal and no sperm production occurs, leading to infertility. Testosterone production is also usually reduced. These men tend to be tall and may have poor muscular development and enlarged breasts. Low sexual desire and impotence are common in this condition but are likely to improve if the man is given regular injections of testosterone (Kolodny, Masters, and Johnson, 1979). Of particular interest is the observation that men with Klinefelter's syndrome tend to be passive and have relatively low ambition or drive, which may be related to their testosterone deficiency.

Turner's syndrome is an example of a missing sex chromosome: the pattern is 45,X. Because one X chromosome is missing, the ovaries of a woman with Turner's syndrome never develop properly. The external genitals, however, are normal. The usual features of Turner's syndrome, which occurs in about one in 2,500 live female births, include: shortness, absence of menstruation, infertility, and a variety of abnormalities that may involve facial appearance and internal organs such as the heart and the kidneys. Girls with Turner's syndrome who do not have any physical limitations usually develop normally as children. Yet when other girls begin to menstruate, develop breasts, and have an "adolescent growth spurt," these girls do not because of their nonfunctioning ovaries. Although menstruation and breast development can be induced by hormone treatments, the problems of height and infertility cannot be solved by any currently known approach.

GENETIC CONDITIONS

A true *hermaphrodite* is a person born with both testicular and ovarian tissue. In some cases, there is one ovary and one testis; in others, the gonads are mixtures of ovarian and testicular tissue. In this rare condition, a uterus is almost always present. There is either a Fallopian tube on one side of the body and a vas deferens and/or epididymis on the other, or male and female duct systems are on both sides. The *pseudohermaphrodite* is born with gonads that match their sex chromosomes but a genital appearance that resembles the opposite sex. A female pseudohermaphrodite has ovaries, a uterus, and Fallopian tubes, and a 46,XX chromosome pattern but masculinized genitals. The appearance of the genitals can range from mild enlargement of the clitoris to the formation of a penis-like phallus, and the labia may be fused together, looking like a

scrotum. Sometimes the genitals seem so obviously male that the gender of the newborn child is misidentified by the physician.

The most common cause of female pseudohermaphroditism is the *adrenogenital syndrome* (AGS), an inherited disorder in which excessive amounts of androgens are produced during fetal development. Although babies with this condition may look like boys, their internal sex structures are completely female, with normal fertility potential. When proper medical treatment is begun in early childhood, the abnormal androgen output of the adrenals can be brought under control, and plastic surgery can correct the appearance of the genitals.

Untreated female with adrenogenital syndrome. This severe case has resulted in the fusion of the labia and marked enlargement of the clitoris.

Photo courtesy of Clifford C. Snyder, M.D.

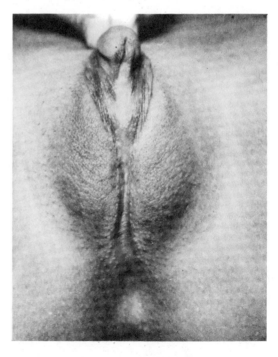

Developmental Sexuality: A Biological View

There is some evidence that girls with AGS treated at an early age show a high rate of tomboyishness, a preference for having boys instead of girls as playmates, and little interest in doll play, grooming, attractiveness, caring for infants, or rehearsing adult roles of mother or wife (Money and Ehrhardt, 1972). (Of course, many girls *without* AGS would also rather climb trees or play ball than play house or mother.) Girls with AGS, however, are not at all ambivalent about their female gender identity. In adolescence, their dating behavior is often delayed and they commonly have difficulty in forming close erotic relationships (Money and Schwartz, 1977). In addition, there are reports that bisexual and lesbian fantasy or experience is relatively common in this syndrome (Ehrhardt, Evers, and Money, 1968; Money and Schwartz, 1977). However, it is not clear whether these findings are solely the result of prenatal androgen effects on the brain.

Male pseudohermaphrodites have testes and a 46,XY chromosome pattern, but female genitals. The most common form of this disorder is the *testicular feminization syndrome,* an inherited condition in which testosterone and other androgens have no effect on body tissues. Thus, even though normal levels of testosterone are produced, differentiation proceeds as if no androgen were present at all: a clitoris, labia, and vagina develop. Yet since the fetal testes also produce Müllerian duct inhibiting substance (which is not impaired in this syndrome), the Müllerian ducts shrink and no uterus or Fallopian tubes develop. Because the inner third of the vagina normally is formed from the Müllerian system, the vagina in this syndrome is short and ends in a blind pouch.

A newborn baby with testicular feminization looks like a normal baby girl unless the testes have descended into the labia or can be felt in the groin. These children are raised as girls and their development proceeds in a normal feminine pattern. This condition is usually not diagnosed until age sixteen or later, when the lack of menstrual periods is investigated medically. Interestingly, at puberty female breast development occurs because some testosterone is broken down into estrogen (as it is in all males). Although there is a male chromosome pattern, normal testes, and no ovaries or uterus, these girls are quite feminine in appearance and behavior (Money and Ehrhardt, 1972). Their sexual behavior is also that of a normal female, although fertility is not possible.

In cases of complete testicular feminization, the child must be raised as a girl even if the diagnosis is made at birth. Neither surgery nor hormone treatment can create a functioning penis or alter the female appearance of the body. This syndrome is contrasted with another type of male pseudohermaphroditism in the Research Spotlight, *The Nature-Nurture Argument.* The comparison raises some intriguing questions about prenatal hormone effects.

PRENATAL DRUG EXPOSURE

Hormones given to a pregnant woman for medical reasons cross the placenta and enter the circulation of the developing fetus. Depending on when in the pregnancy the drug is taken and how much is taken, such hormones may affect sexual anatomy. As examples, androgens can enlarge the clitoris, creating a condition very similar to AGS, and synthetic female hormones can cause malformation of the penis (Aarskog, 1979). Research interest at present, however, centers on the behavior of children exposed to synthetic hormones during their prenatal development.

One report found that teenage boys born to diabetic mothers who had received estrogen and progesterone during pregnancy were rated as lower in general masculine behavior, assertiveness, and athletic ability than other boys of the same age (Yalom, Green, and Fisk, 1973). In another study, adolescent males sixteen to nineteen years old who had been exposed prenatally to high levels of progesterone were found to have less physical activity and participation in heterosexual activity than control group subjects (Zussman, Zussman, and Dalton, 1975, 1977). Another study investigating adolescents who received lower hormone doses did not find such effects (Meyer-Bahlburg, 1978). And in girls exposed prenatally to estrogens or progesterone, there seems to be a mild "enhancing effect" on femininity (Ehrhardt, Grisanti, and Meyer-Bahlburg, 1977).

Although these studies are far from conclusive, they suggest that in certain cases prenatal hormone exposure may influence later patterns of behavior. The relative importance of such prenatal influences is still a matter of controversy (Ehrhardt and Meyer-Bahlburg, 1981; Rubin, Reinisch, and Haskett, 1981).

RESEARCH SPOTLIGHT

The Nature-Nurture Argument

Scientists have argued for years about the relative importance of nature (biological forces) versus nurture (learning and the environment) in controlling human development. The complexity of this issue can be highlighted by reviewing two fascinating situations.

The first is one of the most famous cases in the annals of modern sexology, which was reported by John Money (Money and Ehrhardt, 1972; Money, 1975). When identical twin brothers underwent circumcision at seven months of age, an operating error led to the loss of the penis of one twin. After considerable anguish and consultation with various medical experts, the parents were finally referred to Johns Hopkins University, and a joint decision was made that the twin missing a penis would be raised as a girl. At seventeen months, the child's name, clothing, and hairstyle were changed, and four months later the first of a series of surgical procedures designed to reconstruct the genitals as female was started. Family members were provided with the best available advice about ways of coping with this gender reassignment.

The parents took great care to treat their twins as son and daughter even while knowing that both were biologically male. As a result, the daughter quickly began to prefer dresses to slacks and showed other "typical" signs of femininity, such as a desire for neatness. When the twins were 4½, the mother remarked: "One thing that really amazes me is that she is so feminine. ... She just loves to have her hair set; she could sit under the drier all day long to have her hair set" (Money, 1975). The twins were encouraged to develop play patterns and interests in toys along traditional lines – dolls for the girl, cars and tools for the boy. The mother also reported that her son and daughter imitated their parents' behavior differentially, the son following his father's example and the daughter imitating what the mother did. According to Money, these two children achieved normal (and different) gender identities and gender roles although they both had identical chromosomal, anatomic, and hormonal sex during prenatal development and for the first seven months of life.

The case has now taken a new twist, however, and the "girl" twin's adjustment to a female gender identity may not be as straightforward as Money previously suggested. According to interviews with the girl's psychiatrist conducted by the British Broadcasting System, she is having many problems as a teenager and is so unfeminine in appearance and behavior that classmates taunt her by calling her "cavewoman" (Dia-

INFANCY AND CHILDHOOD

From birth on, learning is ordinarily more important than biology in shaping sexuality. However, it is impossible to completely separate learning and biology. For instance, a baby "learns" about the physical sensations of various body parts, but this type of learning is impossible without biological responses. For any learning to oc-cur, events and their meanings must register in the brain, where they are probably coded and stored in chemical form (Parsons, 1980; Money, 1980). Individuals grow and change throughout their lives in a fashion determined by an inter-action between biology and experience.

There is a surprisingly full range of physical sexual responsiveness in the first year of life. Kinsey and his colleagues reported orgasm during

---

mond, 1982). While a final picture of her psychosexual development may not emerge for another decade – and while the current problem may reflect a need to adjust her estrogen dose properly – it is now difficult to use this case to support the position that gender development depends primarily on learning.

Another research study claims to support just the opposite conclusion. In 1974 thirty-eight male pseudohermaphrodites were discovered in four rural villages of the Dominican Republic. Although these subjects have normal sex chromosomes, an inherited enzyme defect causes improper formation of the external genitals, even though prenatal testosterone production is normal. The testes and internal sex organs are completely male. But at birth, the affected babies have an incompletely formed scrotum that looks like labia, a very small penis that looks like a clitoris, and a partially formed vagina. As a result, many of them are raised as female. Then, during puberty, normal male testosterone production starts, and

definite masculine changes occur. The voice deepens, male-pattern muscles develop, the "clitoris" grows into a penis, and the testes descend into the scrotum. Normal erections occur and intercourse is possible.

Of the eighteen genetically male children with this condition who were raised as girls, seventeen changed to a male gender-identity and sixteen of eighteen shifted to a male gender-role during or after puberty (Imperato-McGinley et al., 1979). The authors of this report believe that these findings show that when sex of rearing is contrary to the biological sex, the biological sex will prevail if normal hormone production occurs during puberty.

So far it all sounds very neat and convincing. Biology is "obviously" more important than learning, since these "girls" seem to easily discard the gender-roles they learned in the first ten or twelve years of life in order to become boys. A closer look at some of the reasons that may be behind this switch may give us a different message, however.

First, girls in these rural areas have to stay at home after age seven and do chores, while boys have "freedom to romp and play." After age eleven or twelve, the boys can go to bars or cock-fights, which girls are not permitted to do. Adult women are also supposed to stay home and be faithful, while men can seek entertainment and enjoy the services of prostitutes. Given these social restrictions, why wouldn't a young teenager with a choice choose to be the free and fun-seeking male? In addition, people usually define who or what they are by the reality of their physical appearance. Seeing a penis grow and a scrotum form and *knowing* that other such cases have occurred in the same village, the child would probably choose to live as a male. If he were to continue to live in a female role, he probably would not attract any male sex partners. Thus, this study does not "prove" anything about nature versus nurture, except that our sexual development is probably determined by an interaction of the two.

masturbation in nine baby boys under a year old, describing the physiologic changes as "development of rhythmic body movements with distinct penis throbs and thrusts, an obvious change in sensory capacities, a final tension of muscles . . . a sudden release with convulsions, including rhythmic contractions — followed by the disappearance of all symptoms" (Kinsey, Pomeroy, and Martin, 1948, p. 177). Orgasm has also been noted in girls during infancy and childhood (Kinsey et al., 1953; Bakwin, 1974). Although boys do not ejaculate prior to puberty, it appears that all other mechanisms of sexual response are present from infancy on.

There are only minor hormone differences between young girls and boys. In childhood, the gonads are relatively nonfunctional, and the major source of testosterone and estrogen is the adrenal glands. Because the adrenals are the same in both boys and girls, sex hormone production is the same too. The pituitary gland is, sexually speaking, not yet active because it receives no major signals from the hypothalamus.

In approximately 3 percent of newborn males (and 30 percent of premature male babies), the testes have not descended into the scrotum and are said to be *cryptorchid* (hidden). In most cases, descent occurs automatically within the first few months of life. If this does not happen, medical treatment with hormones or corrective surgery is advisable, since prolonged positioning of one or both testes in the abdomen can damage their sperm-producing capacity and creates an increased risk of cancer (Lattimer et al., 1974).

PUBERTY

Puberty is a period of change from biological immaturity to maturity. In this transition, dramatic physical changes occur such as the adolescent "growth spurt," the development of secondary sex characteristics, the onset of menstruation (*menarche*), and the ability of the male to ejaculate. In addition, this is a time when fertility for both sexes is achieved and important psychological changes occur.

Some people think that puberty happens overnight — as a student put it, "One morning, you wake up with pimples" — but actually, the maturing process lasts anywhere from one and one-half to six years (Grumbach, 1980). The blueprint for the physical changes that occur during puberty was actually established before

BLOOM COUNTY   by Berke Breathed

Bloom County, July 2, 1983. © 1983 Washington Post Writers Group; reprinted by permission.

Developmental Sexuality: A Biological View

birth, when the hypothalamus and pituitary gland were programmed by hormones for a later "awakening."

Hormonal Control of Puberty

Before puberty begins, there is a change in output of LH and FSH levels during sleep, due to increased production of the releasing factor from the hypothalamus that controls these hormones. Gradually, the gonads begin to enlarge as they slowly respond to this stimulation (imagine the finetuning you might have to do to start up a complicated piece of machinery that had not been used for eight or ten years). Shortly thereafter, sex hormone output begins to rise. During puberty, testosterone levels in boys increase ten to twenty times, while in girls they stay fairly constant. In girls, estrogen levels gradually increase eight to ten times above those found in childhood. Rising levels of adrenal hormone output before and during puberty triggers not only growth of pubic hair and axillary (underarm) hair but the increase in skin oil production that often leads to acne. These hormone changes account for many of the physical changes of puberty, as the next section describes.

Physical Growth and Development

CHANGES IN BODY SIZE

Everyone probably remembers a teenage friend who went away over a summer and came back much taller. This was not a result of sunshine, exercise, or clean living — it was simply the *adolescent growth spurt*. The explanation of this explosive growth rate is simple — it occurs because rising sex hormone levels in puberty temporarily cause bone growth.

The adolescent growth spurt typically occurs two years earlier in girls than in boys (on average,

The adolescent growth spurt often creates dramatic height differences between the sexes at around age twelve.

age twelve versus fourteen) (Marshall, 1977). As a result, girls are usually taller than boys of the same age from about age eleven to fourteen. (Remember those seventh-grade dances where girls seemed to tower over their partners, especially if they wore high heels?) The self-consciousness this may cause fortunately lessens by mid-adolescence as males "catch up" and usually go on to become somewhat taller than females.

The adolescent growth spurt does not always start at the same time in all parts of the body. For example, growth of the foot typically begins about four months before growth in the lower leg, so an adolescent's feet may seem disproportionately large (Marshall, 1975). Not realizing that more harmonious relative proportions will be restored, some teenagers are upset at this pattern.

There is no correlation between an "early" growth spurt and final adult height (which is partly controlled by genetics). This finding should comfort a young teenager who is the class "shrimp"; by age sixteen or seventeen the "shrimp" may be as tall as or taller than his or her classmates.

SEXUAL MATURATION IN GIRLS

The first physical sign of puberty in girls is usually the beginning of breast development, which occurs as early as age eight or as late as age thirteen. In the earliest stage of breast growth, there is only a small mound of tissue (the "breast bud"), but gradually the nipple and areola enlarge and the contour of the breast becomes more prominent (see Figure 7-3). Some girls have fully mature breasts before their twelfth birthdays, but others do not reach this stage until age nineteen or even later. Breast growth is controlled by estrogen levels and heredity.

The appearance of pubic hair (first lightly pigmented and sparse, gradually becoming darker, coarser, curlier, and more abundant) usually starts shortly after breast growth begins. By this time, the vagina has already begun to lengthen and the uterus is slowly enlarging. Menarche usually occurs as breast growth nears completion, and almost invariably comes after the peak growth spurt (Marshall and Tanner, 1969).

In the United States, the average age at menarche is 12.8 years for whites and 12.5 for blacks U.S. DHEW, 1973). It is interesting to note that a

FIGURE 7–3
Stages of Female Breast Development During Puberty

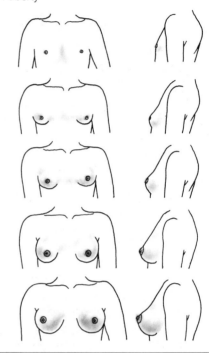

century ago, menstruation first occurred at an average age of sixteen or older; since then, the age at menarche has been consistently decreasing on a decade-by-decade basis (Zacharias and Wurtman, 1969) (Figure 7-4). Socioeconomic factors, climate, heredity, family size, and nutrition all influence the age of menarche. Most recently, this decrease has levelled off, perhaps reflecting more uniform nutritional conditions.

An interesting idea has been proposed by a research team studying the onset of menstruation. They believe that menarche occurs only when a minimum percentage of body fat is present (Frisch and McArthur, 1974). In support of this theory, female long distance runners and ballet dancers have been noted to have delayed

Developmental Sexuality: A Biological View

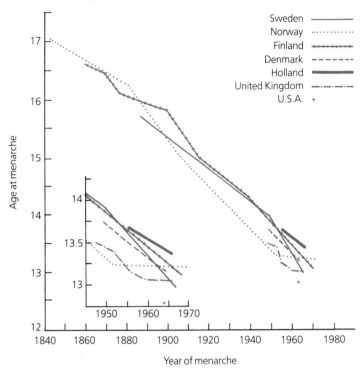

FIGURE 7–4
Declining Age of Menarche in Various Countries

Source: From J. M. Tanner, in *Endocrine and Genetic Diseases of Childhood and Adolescence* (L. I. Gardner, Ed.) W. B. Saunders, 1975, pp. 14–64.

menarche or to actually stop having periods when they are in rigorous training (Frisch, Wyshak, and Vincent, 1980).

The age of menarche varies widely from one girl to another, occurring as early as age eight and as late as sixteen or later. In the first year after menarche, menstrual cycles are frequently irregular and ovulation usually does not occur. It is possible, however, to begin ovulating with the very first menstrual cycle, and young adolescents who engage in intercourse need contraception.

One other aspect of female puberty not mentioned often is that vaginal secretions are likely to increase because of the changing hormone status. Some vaginal lubrication occurs because of sexual excitation whether this results from daydreams, reading, or sexual activity. But vaginal lubrication can also appear spontaneously, without a direct connection to sexual thoughts or acts. The sensations of vaginal wetness may be curious, pleasing, shameful, or alarming to the young teenager.

SEXUAL MATURATION IN BOYS

The physical signs of puberty in boys are also controlled by hormone changes, but puberty usually starts one to two years later than in girls. The earliest change during puberty is growth of the testes, resulting from LH stimulation and subsequent testosterone production. The increasing levels of testosterone also stimulate growth of the penis and the accessory male sex organs (prostate, seminal vesicles, and epididymis). Ejaculation is not possible before puberty because the prostate and seminal vesicles do not begin to function until they receive appropriate hormone signals.

Boys begin to undergo genital development at an average age of 11.6 years and the genitals reach adult size and shape at an average age of 14.9 (Marshall and Tanner, 1970) (Figure 7-5). In some boys, genital development occurs rapidly (in about a year), while in others it may take up to five and one-half years (Tanner, 1974). Sperm production (which begins in childhood) becomes fully established during puberty so fertility is present.

There is no exact counterpart in male puberty to menarche, but wet dreams seem to have a parallel degree of psychological importance. Kinsey and his colleagues (1948) reported that one-quarter of fourteen year olds and nearly two-

FIGURE 7-5
Stages of Male Genital Development During Puberty

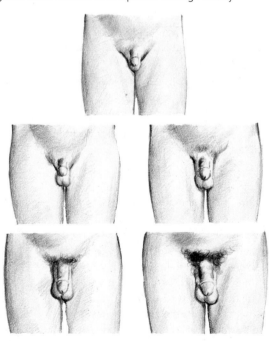

Developmental Sexuality: A Biological View

thirds of seventeen year olds had this experience, yet many pubertal boys are not told about the possibility of nocturnal emissions and are surprised, puzzled, or frightened upon discovery of the event. The ejaculatory experience itself or the resulting sensation of wetness or stickiness may awaken the boy having a nocturnal emission, and — just as uninformed girls may view their initial menstrual flow as a sign of illness — he may become anxious about disease or injury. Whether informed or not about this experience, the pubertal boy may attempt to "hide the evidence" of a stained sheet or pajamas to avoid embarrassment or questioning by his parents.

Growth of pubic hair begins around the time of genital development and is usually followed a year or two later by the appearance of facial and axillary hair. Facial hair growth is an important event because the earlier changes of male puberty are usually less visible than breast development in the female and beard growth is a visible sign of "becoming a man." Facial hair growth begins at the corners of the upper lip with a fine, fuzzy appearance, and then spreads to form a mustache with coarser texture. Hair next appears on the upper cheeks and just below the lower lip, and last of all develops on the chin. Body hair also appears during puberty, and chest hair continues to grow for a decade or more after this time.[1]

Deepening of the voice is another change of puberty and is caused by testosterone stimulation of the voice box, or *larynx*. As the larynx grows, the boy's voice may go through an awkward period of breaks and squawks, which may be a source of embarrassment. Like age at menarche, the average age of this voice change in boys has decreased, from eighteen years in 1749 to about 13.5 years today (Grumbach, 1980). The transient breast enlargement or gynecomastia, as previously discussed, is commonly seen in male puberty.

Hormone differences between adolescent boys and girls also cause differences in body shapes. For instance, the average seventeen- or eighteen-year-old boy has a leaner body and more muscle mass than his female counterpart. This is because estrogens cause accumulation of fat under the skin, while testosterone stimulates muscle growth. The structure of pelvic bones is also different in males and females, with the wider female pelvis creating a properly sized birth canal.

Pubertal Hormones and Sexuality

During puberty, rising hormone levels contribute to an activation of sexual sensations and erotic thoughts and dreams for boys and girls. John Money has described the role of hormones as follows: "the correct conception of hormonal puberty is that it puts gas in the metaphorical tank and upgrades the model of the vehicle, but it does not build the engine nor program the itinerary of the journey" (Money, 1980, pp. 36-37).

The relationship between pubertal hormones and sexual behavior is shown in the finding that boys who undergo "late" puberty (around ages fifteen or sixteen) generally have less and later teenage sexual activity — including masturbation and intercourse — than boys who have "early" puberty (around ages twelve or thirteen). Kinsey and his colleagues pointed out this pattern (Kinsey, Pomeroy, and Martin, 1948), and

---

[1] The degree of facial and body hairiness in both sexes is controlled by genetic factors in addition to hormones. As a result, some people are hairier than others. This is often a source of embarrassment to women who compare themselves to the apparently "hairless" women in *Playboy* or *Vogue*, or to men who are exposed to macho figures of heavily mustached men with an abundant crop of chest hair in various advertisements.

we have some preliminary data showing it is probably true. If testosterone levels of the pubertal boy increase the frequency or intensity of erections, for example, he may possibly have a heightened awareness of sexual sensations. Increased testosterone in the blood may also influence the brain itself to activate sexual feelings or thoughts or to lower the threshold for external triggers that activate such feelings or thoughts. Boys with higher testosterone levels, then, are more likely to be more physically developed and sexually active. Shorter, less muscular, later-maturing boys may experience a social handicap. While having sexual feelings, they may feel less confident about their abilities and therefore "lag" in sexual behavior.

In parallel fashion, girls who undergo "late" puberty seem to have a lower rate of early adolescent sexual activity than girls who complete puberty at ages twelve or thirteen. Although a lower frequency or later age of participation in sexual activity might be explained by purely psychological or social factors (e.g., less physically developed girls may be more shy or self-conscious about sex with a partner), it appears that masturbation is less frequent and occurs later in late-maturing compared to early-maturing adolescent girls. Recently, a large cross-cultural study found similar evidence. According to Udry and Cliquet (1982), data from five different countries show that girls who are younger at menarche tend to have intercourse and to give birth at earlier ages than girls with later menarche.

In contrast to the findings linking sexual activity to "early" puberty, when pubertal changes occur before age nine — a condition called *precocious puberty* — there is usually no accompanying change in sexual behavior (Kolodny, Masters, and Johnson, 1979). This is probably because the hormonal stimulation alone is not enough to initiate new behavior patterns without

a state of psychosexual readiness that the younger child simply hasn't attained.

While precocious puberty is usually a rare condition, occurring in about one in 10,000 children, there has recently been an epidemic of early sexual development among children in Puerto Rico (Zamichow, 1983). Premature breast development in infants and preschoolers, sometimes accompanied by the onset of periods, is the most common problem, with an estimated 3,000 Puerto Rican children (about one in fifty) having been affected between 1972 and the end of 1983 (Laino, 1984). Many physicians suspect (but have been unable to prove) that the problem is caused by eating chicken that contains estrogen. Despite the fact that the Food and Drug Administration banned the use of estrogen to stimulate growth of food animals over a decade ago, tests have shown that some chickens raised in Puerto Rico contain high levels of this hormone. In addition, a majority of the children who stop eating chicken (a relative staple of the Puerto Rican diet) have had a major reduction of their abnormal anatomical development.

SUMMARY

1. Sexual development begins before birth and continues throughout the life cycle. Sex chromosomes (XY = male, XX = female) provide the initial programming for sex differentiation.

2. Growth of the testes (induced by H-Y antigen) begins at about the sixth week after conception. The testes then produce testosterone (stimulating growth of the Wolffian ducts) and Müllerian duct inhibiting substance, which causes the structures which would develop into a female reproductive system to shrink. *For male*

sexual differentiation to occur, both H-Y antigen and testosterone must be present in adequate amounts at the right time of development.

3. Female sexual differentiation does not require hormone stimulation. The ovaries develop at the twelfth week of pregnancy, and the Müllerian duct system gives rise to the uterus, Fallopian tubes, and inner third of the vagina.

4. Prenatal sex differentiation in both sexes involves the genitals, the internal reproductive structures, and the brain itself.

5. Disorders of prenatal sex development include sex chromosome problems (47,XXY = Klinefelter's syndrome; 45,X = Turner's syndrome); conditions of male or female pseudohermaphroditism (such as adrenogenital syndrome and the syndrome of testicular feminization); and problems caused by hormones given to a pregnant woman.

6. In infancy and childhood, the sexual reflexes for males and females are all present except for the ability of the male to ejaculate. Sex hormone levels are low.

7. With puberty, as sex hormone levels are activated, there is a growth spurt, maturation of the gonads and genitals, and development of secondary sex characteristics. Girls begin menstruation and have breast and pubic hair growth; boys become able to ejaculate and have voice-deepening, growth of facial and body hair, and development of muscle mass. There is great variability to the timing and duration of puberty.

SUGGESTED READINGS

Golub, Sharon, ed. *Menarche: The Transition from Girl to Woman*. Lexington, Mass.: Lexington Books (D. C. Heath), 1983. The first book-length treatment of this important developmental event is an excellent, multidimensional collection of essays.

Katchadourian, H. *The Biology of Adolescence*. San Francisco: W. H. Freeman and Company, 1977. A fine review of all biological aspects of puberty. Numerous charts, tables, and diagrams aid the reader in using this book.

Money, J., and Ehrhardt, A. E. *Man & Woman, Boy & Girl*. Baltimore: Johns Hopkins University Press, 1972. A comprehensive, readable account of the principles of sex differentiation amply illustrated and filled with intriguing case reports.

Zamichow, Norma. "Is It Something in the Food?" *Ms. Magazine*, October 1983, pp. 92–93, 141–143. A fascinating description of the epidemic of precocious puberty among Puerto Rican children.

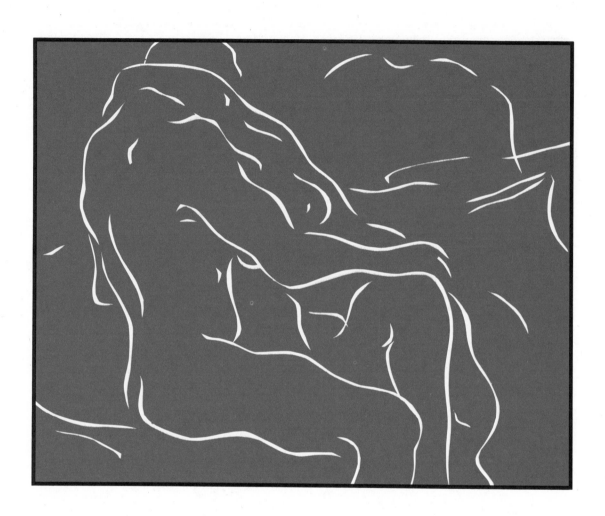

PART TWO

Psychosocial Perspectives

8 Childhood and Adolescent Sexuality

TRYING TO UNDERSTAND developmental sexuality from a biological viewpoint alone is like trying to understand music solely in terms of sound waves: while the information available to you is factual, it is also incomplete. To complement the information on the biology of sexual development just presented, this chapter will examine the psychological and social factors that influence our sexual development throughout childhood and adolescence. In addition, the chapter will include a discussion on a number of related topics, such as sex education for children and the causes and societal impact of unintended teenage pregnancy.

GENDER IDENTITY

In the preceding chapter we saw that from a biological viewpoint, the sex of an individual is determined by sex chromosomes, sex hormones, sexual anatomy (both external and internal), and secondary sex characteristics. These biological aspects of being male or female merge in important ways with psychological and social factors that begin to operate at birth and continue throughout life. *Gender identity* is an individual's private and personal perception of being male or female. *Gender role*, by contrast, is an individual's outward expression of maleness or femaleness in social settings. Gender role will be discussed more fully in chapter 10.

Gender identity formation occurs early in childhood and influences sexual development in many ways. As the preceding chapter stated, there is some controversy as to the forces that shape gender identity. Here, we will briefly summarize several current viewpoints.

Learning Theory

Learning theory suggests that gender development is shaped by personal models and cultural influences to which the young child is exposed. In a child's earliest years, parents are the most important models for the child to observe and imitate. The child learns to model the same-sex parent's behavior because imitation of that parent is rewarded. In addition, it is known that parents treat boys and girls differently from the moment of birth because of different expectations of them. This process, known as *differential socialization,* is thought to influence both gender identity and gender roles (Kagan, 1976; A. Petersen, 1980).

Cognitive-Developmental Theory

According to this viewpoint, gender development parallels the intellectual development of the child (Kohlberg, 1966). Very young children have an oversimplified view of gender which corresponds to an oversimplified view of the world at large. Just as a three year old may think there is a man inside a TV set, a three year old is likely to believe that by putting on a wig and dress, a man "changes" into a woman. A three-year-old girl, when asked what she wants to be when she grows up, may say "a daddy." It is only at ages five or six, when children understand that gender is constant, that they are able to form a firm gen-

der identity. Once this consistent self-concept is developed, children learn by observation and imitation that certain behaviors are appropriate for each gender. Cognitive-development theory, contrary to learning theory, proposes that children mimic adult behavior *not* to gain rewards but to achieve self-identity (Kaplan and Sedney, 1980).

Biosocial Interaction

Many researchers view one's emerging gender identity as an interaction between biological and psychosocial factors. In other words, prenatal programming, psychology, and society's norms all influence subsequent patterns during childhood and adolescence. The extent to which prenatal programming determines gender development is controversial. Milton Diamond believes that prenatal hormones organize sex differences in the brain that are important determinants of later behavior (Diamond, 1977). John Money and his colleagues agree that prenatal programming of sex differences occurs but emphasize that for most individuals, gender development is mainly influenced by social learning (Money and Ehrhardt, 1972; Money, 1980; Money and Wiedeking, 1980). The basic pathways from conception to adulthood that these workers see as contributing to gender development are summarized in Figure 8-1.

In general, the biosocial viewpoint stresses that there are certain *critical periods* in the overall process of sexual development. Just as there is a critical period for fetal androgen action (weeks six to fourteen of pregnancy; see chapter 7), Money believes there is a critical period for the formation of gender identity. He and his colleagues have found that in most instances, "core" gender identity — the fundamental establishment of a sense of one's self as male or female — is set in place by age three. After this time, the gender

FIGURE 8–1
Development of Gender Identity and Gender Role

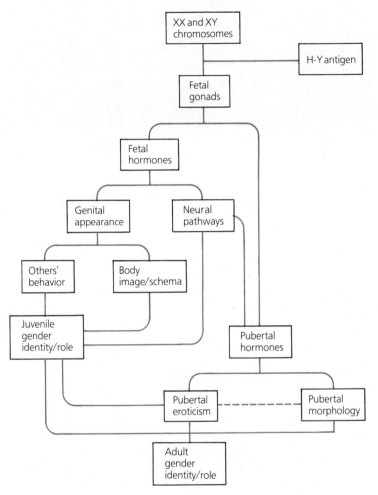

Source: Modified from Money and Wiedeking, "Gender Identity Role: Normal Differentiation and its Transpositions," in *Handbook of Human Sexuality,* ed. by Benjamin Wolman and John Money, © 1980, p. 270. Reprinted by permission of Prentice-Hall, Inc., Englewood Cliffs, N.J.

This schematic flowchart shows the sequence and cumulative interrelations of important factors in the development of gender identity/role.

identity gate seems to be tightly closed and locked and attempts at changing a child's gender orientation are thought to be fraught with psychological difficulty.

Money and his coworkers believe that the most important influences on gender development are learned rather than biologically controlled (Money and Ehrhardt, 1972; Money and

Ogunro, 1974; Money, 1980). This conclusion results from their studies of matched pairs of pseudohermaphrodites (people with ambiguous external genitals). Briefly summarized, they found that if two babies with the same biological sex (as shown by their chromosomes and gonads) were assigned opposite sexes at birth so that one was raised as a boy and the other was raised as a girl, in almost all cases the sex of assignment proved dominant over the biological sex in determining gender identity and gender role. In other words, biologically female babies brought up as boys thought of themselves as boys, played with boys' toys, and preferred boys' sports and clothing styles. Similarly, biologically male babies raised as girls developed female gender identity and gender role. The extensive evidence Money and his colleagues gathered suggests that the biological programming of prenatal development and the control of genetic forces are usually not enough to overcome the impact of postnatal learning.

This is a very interesting body of research, but its actual relevance to the question of what controls gender identity development for normal people is unclear. It might be that it is only those individuals who experience the unusual biological development of pseudohermaphrodites who have the flexibility to accept equally the gender identity of either sex. When all the measures of biological sex are in the same direction, it may be that learning cannot successfully reverse the gender identity programming that has occurred prenatally. The fact that the identical twin who was reassigned to be reared as a girl apparently has not made a successful personal or social adjustment is supportive of this possibility (see page 198).

Today, it is no longer useful to think of sexual development as rigidly controlled by "nature" (biology) or "nurture" (learning). Biological processes do not unfold in a cultural vacuum, and learning does not occur without the biological apparatus of the brain itself. Although additional research is needed to clarify details of the process, it appears that the biosocial interaction theory is the most comprehensive way of looking at all phases of sexual development.

CHILDHOOD SEXUALITY

Childhood has been called "the last frontier in sex research" (Money, 1976) because there is little reliable data about sexual behavior during this formative time. Studies based on interviewing adults about what they did or how they felt during childhood are distorted by faulty recall, exaggeration, and omissions due to embarrassment or the wish to seem "normal." Attempts to interview children or administer questionnaires to them about their sexual attitudes and behavior have often been thwarted by community outrage about "putting nasty ideas in children's minds" and accusations of undermining the moral fabric of our society. Except for some limited cross-cultural data from primitive societies in which childhood sex play is permitted and data from a few instances of direct observation, we are forced to rely on guesswork and inference in this important area.

Prior to the work of Freud and some early sexologists around the turn of the century, childhood sexuality was seen as either nonexistent or as something to be repressed because of its sinful and dangerous nature (Sulloway, 1979). These contradictory views still exist, but at least some parents today have come to regard the developing sexuality of their children in a more matter-of-fact, accepting way. Other parents are uncomfortable with any form of sexual interest or behavior in their children for several reasons. They worry that it is abnormal; they are uncertain about how to deal with it; or they are dealing with sexual conflicts within themselves.

Freud's Theories of Sexual Development

Freud was one of the first theorists to recognize that sexuality exists throughout the life cycle. Freud believed that the sex drive, or *libido,* an instinctual striving for sensual pleasure, was one of the key forces motivating behavior. Although Freud asserted that libido existed from infancy on, he did not say that infantile or childhood sexuality was identical to sexuality in adults. Instead he proposed that early unfocused sexual feelings pass through a predictable series of developmental stages that are necessary for the formation of mature adult personality and behavior. He saw this development occurring in five stages.

In the first year of life, called the *oral stage,* the mouth is the primary focus of sexual energy and sensual gratification. Infants not only get obvious pleasure from sucking but also put things (*any* things) into their mouths in order to explore them, to see what they are like.

In the *anal stage,* from ages one to three, sensual pleasure shifts to the anal region. In the process of toilet training, the child has his or her first real opportunity to assert some independence from parental control. Deliberately holding back bowel movements or letting them go produces both physical and psychological pleasure, but gradually the child learns to follow socially acceptable behavior regarding bathroom functions.

In the *phallic stage,* from about ages three to five, erotic interest shifts to the genitals. Here, Freud suggested separate developmental pathways for boys and girls. As a boy experiences erotic pleasure from masturbation, he develops fantasies of possessing his mother sexually. (This is quite understandable, since his mother is likely to be already loved and loving.) This fantasy wish leads to the *Oed-*

ipus complex (named after the Greek story in which Oedipus unknowingly killed his father and married his mother); the boy becomes jealous of his father whom he sees as a rival for his mother's affection. At the same time, the boy fears the anger of his powerful father and becomes especially afraid that his father will punish him by removing his penis. This *castration anxiety* is supported by two bits of logic in the young boy's mind: (1) he expects that his penis will be "punished" because it is the source of his pleasure and guilt, and (2) he knows by now that girls do not have penises, and this suggests that a penis can be taken away. The problem is resolved by a creative compromise. The boy gives up his sexual desire for his mother and his hostility toward his father and instead *identifies* with his father. In this way he tries to become as much like him as possible so that he too will one day be powerful and able to satisfy his sexual cravings.

The female counterpart of the Oedipus complex (the *Electra complex*, named after a Greek legend about a princess who helped kill her mother) is more complicated. Essentially, it is based on the view that after discovering that she does not have a penis, the girl feels envious and cheated. This so-called *penis envy* results in the girl's wanting to possess her father and to replace her mother, who she blames for her dilemma. Freud believed that this situation is less adequately resolved than the Oedipus complex because the girl is not so powerfully motivated by fear – after all, she has already "lost her penis." Freud thought that this less successful resolution of a childhood conflict led women to be less mature psychologically than men because penis envy persists throughout life.

After the resolution of the Oedipus or Electra complex, which is usually achieved by age six, the child enters a *latency stage* where sexual impulses presumably recede in importance. Here, the child becomes involved in non-sexual interests such as intellectual and social pursuits. This stage ends at the time of puberty when the *genital stage* is activated by internal biological forces. The adolescent gradually learns to focus his or her sexual interest on heterosexual relations in general and sexual intercourse in particular, finally expressing mature adult genital sexuality.

A brief outline of Freud's theories of sexual development does not adequately explain the richness of his work or the complexity of his viewpoints. The Freudian influence on modern sexology has been profound and continues to be felt today. Several criticisms of Freud's ideas, however, are relevant to our discussion here. First, many authorities (including some of Freud's own followers) believe that he largely overlooked the importance of cultural input on sexual development. For example, it has been suggested that the anal stage is really a result of our culture's emphasis on bowel-training rather than a reflection of erotic pleasure (Marmor, 1971). Similarly, cross-cultural anthropology provides evidence that the Oedipus complex is not encountered universally and that latency is primarily a function of a sexually restrictive society rather than being determined by inner psychological forces alone. Second, many critics have suggested that Freud's views on female sexuality were extremely biased (Sherfey, 1972; Millet, 1970; Tennov, 1975; Frieze et al., 1978). Finally, Freud himself acknowledged that many of his ideas were incomplete and indicated that they should be revised as new knowledge became available.

By learning about the typical patterns of sexual development during childhood, parents (or prospective parents) can become more effective in helping their children learn about sexuality in a comfortable, unthreatening way.

Sex in Infancy

Ultrasound studies have provided some evidence that reflex erections occur in developing baby boys for several months before birth, while they are still within the uterus (see Figure 8-2) (Masters, 1980; Calderone, 1983). Many newborn baby boys have erections in the first few minutes after birth – often, even before the umbilical cord is cut. Similarly, newborn baby girls have vaginal lubrication and clitoral erection in their first twenty-four hours (Langfeldt, 1981), so it is clear that the sexual reflexes are already operating at the very start of infancy and probably even before birth.

An important phase of infantile sexuality comes from the sensuous closeness of parent and child through holding, clinging, and cuddling (Higham, 1980). As mentioned in chapter 5, this parent-child bonding begins at birth and extends to include nursing, bathing, dressing, and other physical interactions between parents and their newborn child. A child who is deprived of warm, close bonding during infancy may experience later difficulties forming intimate relationships or, more speculatively, in being comfortable with his or her sexuality (Harlow and Harlow, 1962; Ainsworth, 1962; Trause, Kennell, and Klaus, 1977; Money, 1980).

Very young infants respond quite naturally to a variety of sources of physical sensation with signs of sexual arousal. For example, it is common for baby boys to have firm erections while they are nursing. While this is alarming to some parents, who see it as somehow abnormal or perverse, the fact is that the sensation of cuddling close to the warmth and softness of the mother's

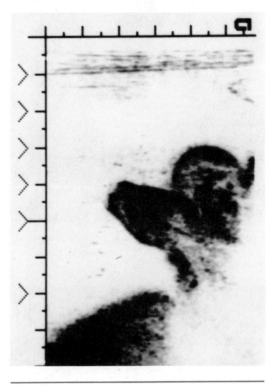

FIGURE 8–2
Ultrasound Image of Male Fetal Erection

body and having the intense neurological stimulation of suckling (the lips are well endowed with sensory nerve endings) combine to send messages to the brain that are interpreted as pleasurable and that activate sexual reflexes. Clitoral erection and vaginal lubrication in baby girls also occur commonly during nursing, indicating that this pattern is not restricted to one gender (although penile erection is more visible and thus more likely to be noticed). Similar signs of reflex sexual activation may occur when babies are bathed, powdered, diapered, or playfully bounced around. It is important to recognize, however, as Martinson (1981, p. 26) points out, that "the infant is too young to be consciously aware of the

In the first months of life, parent-child bonding through eye contact and touch is an important way the child learns about intimacy.

encounter, and therefore no sociosexual erotic awakening can be said to occur." How parents respond to observing these sexual reflexes during infancy may be part of the child's earliest sexual learning: The parent who is shocked or disapproving is apt to react in a manner that conveys discomfort, while parents who react calmly give children a message of acceptance regarding sex.

As any observant parent knows, baby boys and girls begin to touch or rub their genitals as soon as they develop the necessary motor coordination. As we noted in chapter 7, Kinsey and others reported that this sometimes leads to orgasm in infants less than one year old. The question is, what meaning does this behavior have? Is the infant simply exploring his or her body, with an equal likelihood that equally accessible parts (elbow, tummy, genitals) will be touched? Or is there a sexual component to such behavior, with a genuine sense of pleasure leading to repeated self-stimulation?

Although infants cannot answer these questions for us, the evidence seems to support the latter view. Helen Kaplan notes that babies "express joy when their genitals are stimulated" (Kaplan, 1974, p. 147). Bakwin points out that "infants show extreme annoyance if efforts are made to interrupt them" during masturbation and adds that self-stimulation is done "many times during the day" (Bakwin, 1974, p. 204). By the third or fourth month of life, genital stimulation is accompanied by smiling and cooing (Martinson, 1980). By one year of age, genital play is commonly observed when the infant is naked or bathing. Genital play is more common in infants reared in families than in infants reared in nurseries (Spitz, 1949), suggesting that parent-child bonding plays a major role in the development of subsequent sexuality.

The parents of very young children react to these displays of sexual behavior in a variety of ways. Some are amused, some are surprised, and

Childhood and Adolescent Sexuality

Learning Theory and Sexual Development

In contrast to the Freudian viewpoint, later theorists have developed the position that learning is the primary determinant of behavior. Learning occurs as a result of the interaction of a person with his or her environment.

The origins of modern learning theory may be traced back to the turn of the century when Ivan Pavlov (1849–1936), a Russian physiologist, elucidated the principles of classical *conditioning*. In studying the digestive responses of dogs, Pavlov found that a natural reflex (salivation in response to food) could be produced by an unrelated stimulus, such as a musical tone, if the sound repeatedly occurred just before the presentation of food. Once this pairing took place a number of times, the dog learned to associate the sound with the food, and the sound alone (the *conditioned stimulus*) would produce salivation (the *conditioned response*) even when the food was not present.

Pavlov's model of classical conditioning does not take us very far in understanding human sexual behavior. People may be "conditioned" in the Pavlovian sense to respond with sexual arousal when smelling a perfume or aftershave lotion their sex partner always wears or when hearing a particular recording they usually play during sex. Such stimulus-response connections, however, are not powerful enough in most cases to override other influences on sexual behavior such as mood, needs, and circumstance. But learning theory was broadened considerably through the work of several American psychologists, including Edward Thorndike, John B. Watson, and B. F. Skinner, who showed the importance of positive or negative consequences in shaping later behavior. According to the principles of *operant conditioning*, behavior followed by a reward or pleasurable result, or the removal of an unpleasant stimulus, is likely to be repeated, while behavior followed by unpleasant consequences or the removal of rewarding stimuli is likely to become less frequent.

Positive reinforcement has an obvious and direct effect on sexual behavior. For example, children who find that rubbing their genitals produces pleasure are likely to engage in this behavior again and again. Punishment also influences sexual behavior. Consider, for example, a person who has pain during sexual intercourse. If this happens repeatedly, the person will learn that coitus leads to pain and will be likely to avoid the behavior or engage in it less frequently. Punishment has been used in treating sex offenders such as child molesters. The treatment process, called *aversion therapy,* might involve showing a child molester pictures of children – if he becomes sexually aroused, he is given an electric shock (Barlow, 1973). This treatment process is carried out over a series of sessions until the undesired response (sexual arousal to children) is eliminated.

Negative consequences are usually a less powerful influence on behavior than positive consequences. Punishment is not as likely to eliminate a behavior as it is apt to lead to secrecy and attempts to avoid punishment. This is particularly true when there is a conflict in a given situation between positive and negative consequences (an *approach-avoidance conflict*). The threat of punishment may actually heighten pleasure: the forbidden becomes more exciting so that the threat becomes part of the positive reinforcement.

Learning theory has been expanded into a still broader framework by Albert Bandura (1925–   ) in a model called *social learning theory*. Bandura believes that people model their social behavior according to their observations of the behavior of others. What is learned depends in part on the prestige or power of the other person: a five year old might imitate a seven-year-old brother or sister but not a younger one. People tend to identify with and imitate others they admire or respect. Television or movies can therefore be an important source of learned behavior or a source of learned attitudes, just as social learning also occurs from friends, teachers, and parents.

Social learning theory has many direct applications to psychosexual development. Children develop their sexual attitudes not only from what their parents say to them about sex, but also from what attitudes they see expressed in their parents' behavior. Later attitudes or behaviors are strengthened or inhibited by observations of classmates, older friends, and nonfamily members. Watching a torrid seduction scene in a movie may provide a form of observational learning for a young, sexually inexperienced teenager who "learns" about how other people behave in such a situation. Social learning is also undoubtedly important to the development of gender identity and gender role.

some are alarmed — particularly if they do not realize that this is a completely normal developmental pattern.

Sex in Early Childhood (Ages Two to Five)

By age two, most children have begun to walk and talk and have established a sense of being a boy or girl. There is unquestionable curiosity about body parts, and most children discover (if they have not already) that genital stimulation is a source of pleasurable sensations. Genital play first occurs as a solitary activity and later in games like "show me yours and I'll show you mine" and "doctor." In addition to rubbing the penis or clitoris manually, some children

stimulate themselves by rubbing a doll, a pillow, a blanket, or some other object against their genitals.

Conversations with three-year-old boys and girls indicate that they are well aware of the sensual feelings of genital stimulation, although these feelings are not labelled by them as erotic or sexual (concepts the child does not yet understand). The following comments from our files illustrate this point:

> A three-year-old girl: When I rub my 'gina it's nice and warm. Sometimes it tickles. Sometimes it gets real hot. (Note: this child referred to her entire genital area as her "gina" and was specifically describing manual rubbing of the mons and clitoris which she practiced at least a half-dozen times a day. From age 2½ to age 3½, she preferred to go bottomless so she could have easy access to her genitals and frequently took off her underpants to achieve this goal.)

> A three-year-old boy: Look at my weiner! I can make it stand up. I rub it and it stands up and it feels good. Sometimes I rub it a lot and it feels very, very good. Sometimes I just rub it a little. And then it feels a little good. (This boy was very proud of his "weiner," which he liked to show to visitors. His parents told us that he stimulated his penis "several times a day" that they knew of and were pretty certain that he also pursued this activity in private.)

At about this same time, children also become aware of parental attitudes of disapproval of genital play and may be confused by parents who encourage them to be aware of their bodies but exclude the genitals from such awareness. While it is important for parents to educate their children about socially appropriate behavior (e.g., it is not acceptable to show or fondle your genitals in public places), some parents try to stop all forms of their child's sexual experimentation by saying, "That's not nice" or "Don't touch yourself down there," or by nonverbal communications such as pushing the child's hand away. The negative message that the child gets in such situations may be among the earliest causes of later sexual difficulties (Masters and Johnson, 1970; Calderone, 1978; Money, 1980). This attitude is compounded by many children's assumption that their genitals are "dirty" from messages received during toilet training. The emphasis on cleanliness in the bathroom ("wipe yourself carefully," "wash your hands after you go") conditions the child to see genital function in negative terms, even though it actually represents a legitimate health concern of parents.

By age four, most children in our society begin asking questions about how babies are made and how birth occurs (Martinson, 1980). Some parents respond with matter-of-fact answers, while others are obviously uncomfortable and reluctant to discuss this information at any length. Children have a pretty good idea of what bothers mommy or daddy, so they may react either by not asking such questions at all *or* by bombarding one or both parents with questions to see them squirm.

Four year olds generally have vague and somewhat magical notions about sex. They often believe the "stork-brings-the-baby" explanation without any further questioning, or, if given a more accurate explanation of reproductive facts, interpret them in unique ways. For example, four year olds are quite literal in thinking that the mommy's egg from which a baby grows is just like the ones bought by the dozen in the grocery store. Similarly, some four year olds presented with a "daddy-plants-a-seed-in-mommy's-body" explanation of conception and pregnancy are convinced that there is a patch of dirt inside the mother's body that must be periodically watered and weeded for the baby to grow. This way of viewing sexual matters reflects the four year old's concrete, literal view of the world in general.

Children who attend nursery school or day care centers before reaching school age are apt to confront many situations with sexual overtones. For instance, Billy and Peter, each four years old, have to be told repeatedly that it's not appropriate to kiss each other while they're playing. In the same nursery school class, Gerry amuses himself by sneaking up behind a girl and pulling up her skirt ("So I can see her underpants," he explains with a lot of giggling). Both girls and boys express considerable interest in bathroom functions and bathroom etiquette, and both sexes are very willing to try out new "dirty" words, a common practice that tends to alarm parents more than teachers.

At age five, when most children enter kindergarten, the opportunity to relate to age-mates in a structured environment leads to modesty, and sex games decrease in frequency (Martinson, 1980). Children of this age become fascinated with learning words about sexual parts that they have not heard before, and jokes about sex and genital function begin to make their rounds, often heard first from a slightly older child and then repeated. The five year old may not understand the joke but laughs heartily (sometimes at the wrong line) to cover this up. As Money (1980) observes, when frank, direct information about sex is not available to a child, sexual jokes become the most important source of sex education for both girls and boys. Since even young children quickly learn the difference between a "clean" and "dirty" joke, this leads to the attitude that sex is dirty.

At this age children also begin to form ideas about sex based on their observations of physical interactions between parents — seeing mommy and daddy hugging and kissing, and obviously enjoying it, is a pretty good advertisement for the pleasures of physical and emotional intimacy. On the other hand, seeing parents constantly fighting or hearing one tell the other "don't touch me" can have just the opposite effect on the child's view of intimacy.

Sex and the School-Age Child

Six- and seven-year-old children have usually acquired a clear understanding of basic anatomic differences between the sexes and typically show a strong sense of modesty about body exposure. Parental attitudes and practices regarding nudity in the home undoubtedly influence the child's self-consciousness, but at the same time the natural curiosity of childhood is likely to emerge in games like "hospital" or "playing house" that permit sexual exploration. These games may involve simply inspecting each other's genitals or may include touching, kissing, rubbing, or inserting objects into the rectum or vagina.

Sexual experimentation includes activities with children of the same sex and the opposite sex. One purpose of this behavior is seeking knowledge: "How different am I from others who are like me?" and "How different are members of the opposite sex from me?" Another purpose is testing the forbidden to see what happens: who finds out, how they react, what can I get away with, and so on. These two components are interrelated, since forbidden knowledge is usually more alluring than easily available knowledge.

Childhood participation in such games is probably nearly universal, although available studies (mainly based on recall data) give much lower estimates. For example, Kinsey found that about 45 percent of adult women recalled participating in some form of sex play by age twelve, and 57 percent of adult males recalled similar experiences (Kinsey, Pomeroy, and Martin, 1948; Kinsey et al., 1953). In a survey of children aged four to fourteen, 35 percent of the girls and 52 percent of the boys reported some homosexual play (Elias and Gebhard, 1969). In a more recent survey, parents of six- and seven-year-old children noted that 76 percent of their daughters and 83 percent of their sons had participated in some sex play, with more than half of their

known experiences involving play with siblings (Kolodny, 1980). One explanation for this relatively low rate of recalling childhood sex play is suggested by a theory of Austrian sex researcher Ernest Borneman. According to Borneman, puberty characteristically is accompanied by a form of amnesia — blocked memories — about prior sexual experiences. Borneman suggests that this selective amnesia might explain why so many parents are shocked when they find their children playing sexual games: The adults have no recollection of such experiences in their own lives, even though they probably occurred. While there is as yet no substantiation of Borneman's thesis by others, it is an intriguing suggestion.

Childhood sex play is not psychologically harmful under ordinary circumstances and is probably a valuable psychosocial experience in developmental terms (Jensen, 1979; Money, 1980). However, psychological harm *can* come from harsh parental reaction. When children are discovered in sex play, either solitary or with others, negative parental reaction may be difficult to understand but easy to perceive. From the child's viewpoint, play is play, but for the parent who discovers a child masturbating or engaging in sex play with others, SEX in capital letters flashes across the scene. The parent who reacts with ominous predictions or threats that continuing such "bad" behavior will lead to dire consequences is frightening the child. The parent who says "that's dirty" may be interpreted very literally by the child, sowing the seeds of an attitude that may persist into adulthood.

Parental reactions to the discovery of sex play in school-age children frequently operate on a double standard. Girls are often cautioned strongly against sexual play, especially with boys. Boys, on the other hand, tend to get mixed messages from their parents; they may be warned or even punished for such activity, but there is a hint of resignation or even pride in the attitude that "boys will be boys." One father described the sexual escapades of his seven-year-old son and a female classmate by saying "Good for him, he's getting an early start." The unspoken permission for boys to follow their sexual curiosity (except in homosexual situations, where parents consistently react in a negative way) is only rarely found directed to school-age girls in American society. With the arrival of puberty, parents seem to react with even more of a double standard toward the sexual behavior of their sons and daughters.

Freud's concept of a period of sexual latency during late childhood — a time when sexual interests and impulses are diverted into nonsexual behaviors and interests — is no longer accepted by many sexologists. Money (1980) says that this is a time of sexual prudery when participation in sex play simply goes underground. Cross-cultural studies clearly show that if a society is not repressive toward childhood sex rehearsals, such play continues and may even be more frequent during the preadolescent years (Ford and Beach, 1951; Marshall and Suggs, 1971; Currier, 1981). Kinsey's data also shows that sexual experimentation does not stop or even slow down during this period (Kinsey, Pomeroy, and Martin, 1948; Kinsey et al., 1953). A detailed study of childhood sexuality involving interviews with over 800 children ages five and over in Australia, North America, Britain, and Sweden also provides no indication of a phase of childhood development where sexual development is suspended (Goldman and Goldman, 1982). In fact, these researchers note: "Discrediting Freud's latency period theory, overwhelming evidence was produced which reveals children from age five to fifteen to be increasingly interested in exploring sexual topics in linear progression with age" (Goldman and Goldman, 1982a, p. 7). Perhaps the available evidence is best summed up in the following passage:

Children pursue the course of their psychosexual development in blithe disregard of an expected sexual latency. Their only nod in the direction of the theoretical expectations is that they have learned to play according to adult rules. They learn to fulfill the letter of the law, even as they proceed secretly in their own ways. (Gadpaille, 1975, p. 189)

The sexual experiences of older children may be infrequent and less important than other events in their lives but may include the entire range of possible sexual acts, including attempts at intercourse that are sometimes successful. Masturbation occurs in private as well as in heterosexual or homosexual pairs or groups; sexual play with animals and objects has been noted; and oral or anal sex has been reported (Gadpaille, 1975; Martinson, 1976, 1980, 1981). By ages eight or nine, there is little question that children have awareness of the erotic element of such activities, and it is no longer accurate to think of these as "play" only. Sexual arousal is more than a byproduct of these deliberate activities and is willfully sought, not just an accidental happening. Erotic arousal may be accompanied by sexual fantasies, and in some instances, falling in love occurs (Gadpaille, 1975; Tennov, 1979; Money, 1980). These encounters can help children learn how to relate to others, with important consequences for their adult psychosexual adjustment (Broderick, 1968; Gadpaille, 1975; Martinson, 1976; Money, 1980).

Many parents are unaware that homosexual play among children, as well as heterosexual play, is a normal part of growing up. Homosexual play does *not* usually lead to adult homosexuality, although many parents worry unnecessarily on this point.

Another common form of childhood sexual behavior is sexual contact between siblings. While technically such behavior may be called *incest* — sexual activity between relatives — it seems unnecessarily pejorative to label the "look-

224

Sex Education

In the last decade, there has been an unusual amount of controversy on the topic of sex education. While almost everyone seems to agree that teaching children about sex is necessary, there is much disagreement about what should be taught, *where* it should be taught, and who should do the teaching.

The background can be summarized as follows. A number of studies indicate that only a minority of parents provide meaningful quantities of sex education for their children. American teenagers, for example, report that they learned most of what they know about sex from their friends, not their parents (Gebhard, 1977; Kirby, Alter, and Scales, 1979; Kallen, Stephenson, and Doughty, 1983). Until relatively recently, this problem seemed to polarize communities into two groups: those who favored sex education in schools to prevent lack of knowledge and those who insisted that sex education in the schools was unnecessary and unwise. Opponents of sex education in the schools argued that: (1) exposing children to information about sex would liven their sexual curiosity and draw them prematurely into sexual behavior; (2) teaching about sex is so closely linked to moral and religious values that it should be done at home or in a religious setting; and (3) the quality of materials and teaching in public school sex education was uneven at best, and quite poor in many cases.

Today, although opposition to sex education in the schools continues, its tone is somewhat muted. Seventy-seven percent of American adults believe sex education should be taught in schools, and when such courses are given, fewer than 5 percent of parents ban their children from attending (Kirby, Alter, and Scales, 1979; Alan Guttmacher Institute, 1981). An increasing number of school systems have some form of sex education (often called "Family Life Education") offered in the curriculum, and three states – New Jersey, Maryland, and Kentucky – as well as the District of Columbia now require it. Perhaps even more encouraging is a broad coalition of community-oriented programs, including the Y.M.C.A. and Y.W.C.A., the Girls Clubs of America, the Salvation Army, Four-H, Campfire, Inc., and a number of other youth-serving groups who have now begun to implement sex education programs geared to both children and parents (Gregg, 1982).

Despite these signs of progress, there are still a number of problems with sex education today. Certainly one of the most pressing dilemmas is that relatively few American fathers play an active role in providing their children with age-appropriate sex information. Another aspect that requires attention is the fact that sex education, beyond the most rudimentary "birds and bees" facts of anatomy and reproduction, is often ignored by parents and schools alike until a child reaches adolescence. Since children are exposed to a great deal of information about sex at an earlier age – through television shows, movies, books, and a host of other sources – parents run the risk of allowing them to interpret what they see as accurate depictions of what sex is all about, which may have unfortunate consequences. Put another way, this is education by default.

We believe that waiting until a child's teenage years to provide him or her with sex education is waiting too long. Educating *all* children in an age-appropriate fashion about sexuality will ultimately help them make informed, responsible sexual choices in their lives and play an important role in the long-term prevention of sexual problems.

see" games of a five-year-old boy and his six-year-old sister in so heavy-handed a fashion. Nevertheless, it can be difficult to decide when factors such as age differences between siblings, aggressive components of the sexual behavior, or exploitive or coercive elements should lead sexual contacts between siblings to be viewed as innocent play, a form of childhood learning, or a matter for parental action.

Finkelhor's data (1980, 1981) on sex between siblings is the most detailed non-clinical sample available. In brief, he found that 13 percent of college students surveyed admitted to childhood sexual activity with a brother or sister (a figure he considered an underestimate). Approximately three-quarters of these relationships were heterosexual (brother-sister), while one-quarter were homosexual (brother-brother or sister-sister). Additional findings from this survey included:

1. Sexual contact between siblings was not restricted to young children only; 73 percent of the experiences reported occurred when at least one sibling was over age eight.
2. The most common type of sexual activity between siblings was genital touching; only 4 percent included intercourse. Among younger children, looking at one another's genitals was the primary form of sex play.
3. There was considerable variability in the duration of these activities. One-third were single occurrences, while 27 percent continued off and on for at least one year.
4. In a quarter of the experiences, some type of force was involved (with girls being victimized most often).
5. Almost one-quarter of the experiences involved siblings who were at least five years apart in age.

These findings suggest that it may be necessary for sexologists to rethink previous notions about sexual contact between siblings as an innocent form of play. A situation where one sibling is much older than the other (by four years or more) or where force is used (which may be much more common than previously realized) is almost invariably exploitative and thus is cause for concern. However, parents must use their judgment in dealing with such situations: One episode of genital touching between an eleven-year-old girl and her consenting seven-year-old brother is not the same as a pattern of forced sex between siblings. Furthermore, it is important to realize that parental displays of alarm and horror on learning of their children's incestuous activities are not only inappropriate but may sometimes be harmful to the children. Finally, if an exploitative incest situation is discovered, obtaining psychological counseling for the victim may be advisable.

Since there is now considerable evidence that incest victimization often has negative long-term psychological consequences, including sexual problems in adulthood, parents may want to consider ways to minimize the risk of such an occurrence. For example, it may be helpful to discourage siblings who are more than two years apart from bathing together, and it also is advisable to avoid having an older sibling share a bedroom with a much younger one. A more detailed discussion of incest, including information about parent-child incest, appears in chapter 18.

As long as aggressive or coercive behavior is not involved, it is unlikely that isolated instances of childhood sexual activity are abnormal. It is not very helpful for parents to react to the discovery of childhood sex play with alarm or punishment. A matter-of-fact approach that includes understanding and age-appropriate sex education (while maintaining the parents' right to set limits) is likely to be more effective than threats and theatrics in helping the child undergo healthy psychosexual growth.

Childhood and Adolescent Sexuality

Practical Pointers on Educating Your Children about Sex

Despite the fact that some parents are vigorously opposed to sex education for children, parents don't really have a choice about whether their children get sex information: they can only choose whether or not to participate in the sex education that is already taking place. Realizing this, and wanting to do a good job in providing sex education at home, many parents approach this task with great trepidation, being at once unsure of how to begin, uncertain of what to say, and worried that they'll overload or frighten a child with inappropriate detail.

The truth of the matter is that teaching children about sex need not be different from teaching them about lots of other things; you don't need to have a Ph.D. in agriculture to teach children about gardening, for example. And just as you wouldn't wait for a child to ask you about the alphabet before exploring the A-B-C's, don't wait to talk about sex, either — take the initiative in talking about this topic.

Here are some straightforward suggestions for parents to keep in mind when it comes to sex education:

1. When you discuss sex with your child, try to do it in a matter-of-fact manner, the way you'd talk about anything else.
2. Avoid lecturing about sex. While it may relieve your anxiety to cover the whole topic in a 15-minute talk, young children don't usually have a long enough attention span for this approach and also need to ask questions about what they're learning.
3. Be sure that your discussions include more than just biological facts. Children need to learn about values, emotions, and decision-making, too.
4. Don't worry about telling a child "too much" about sex. Children will almost always tune out what they don't understand; in most cases, it will just go over their heads.
5. When your child uses four-letter words, calmly explain their meaning, and then explain why you don't want him or her to use those words. For example, you might say, "Other people get upset if they hear those words," or "I don't think that's a very good way of explaining how you feel." Remember that laughing or joking about your child's four-letter words will usually encourage repeat performances.

6. Try to use correct terminology for sexual body parts instead of using terms like "pee pee" for penis or "bottom" for vagina.
7. Even preschool-age children should know how to protect themselves from sexual abuse. This means that you need to let them know that it's okay to say "No" to an adult. Here's a good example of how this might be discussed with a four or five year old:

   You know, there are big people out there who have a hard time making friends with other big people. So sometimes they make friends with kids. And *that's* OK, but sometimes they ask kids to do things big people shouldn't ask kids to do. Like, they ask them to put their hands down their pants, or to touch each other sexually. I love you a lot, and if anyone ever asks you to do that, or asks you to do something you think is funny and asks you to keep it a secret, I want you to say "No" and come tell me right away. (Sanford, 1982, p. 13)

8. Don't wait until your child hits the teenage years before discussing puberty. Physical changes like breast development, menstruation, and wet dreams commonly occur before age ten.
9. Be sure to discuss menstruation with boys, as well as girls, and be sure that girls understand what an erection is. Also, don't leave topics like homosexuality and prostitution

out of your discussions. Most children see and hear these subjects mentioned on television or read about them and have a natural curiosity about what they are.

10. Help your child feel comfortable in coming to ask you questions about sex. Don't embarrass a child or tell him or her "you're too young to understand that now." If a child is old enough to ask questions, he or she *needs* to understand it at some level.

11. If you don't know the answer to a question your child has asked, don't be afraid to say so. Then either look it up or call on someone, such as your family doctor, who can help you with the necessary facts.

12. After you've tried to answer your child's question, check to see if your answer is understood. Also see if you've told him or her what he or she really wanted to know and give a chance to ask more questions that may arise from the answer you've provided.

ADOLESCENT SEXUALITY

Adolescence, the period from ages twelve to nineteen, is a time of rapid change and difficult challenge. Physical maturation is only one part of this process because adolescents face a wide variety of psychosocial demands: becoming independent from parents, developing skills in interacting well with their peers, devising a workable set of ethical principles, becoming intellectually competent, and acquiring a sense of social and personal responsibility, to name just a few. At the same time this complex set of developmental challenges is being met, the adolescent must also cope with his or her sexuality by learning how to deal with changing sexual feelings, deciding whether to participate in various types of sexual activity, discovering how to recognize love, and learning how to prevent unwanted pregnancy. It is no wonder that the adolescent sometimes feels conflict, pain, and confusion.

On the other hand, adolescence is also a time of discovery and awakening, a time when intellectual and emotional maturation combine with physical development to create increasing freedom and excitement. Adolescence is not simply a period of turmoil, as older theory states, but is just as likely to be a time of pleasure and happiness as a turbulent, troubled passage to adulthood (Offer and Offer, 1975). The paradoxical nature of adolescence is particularly visible in the sexual sphere.

Psychosexual Aspects of Adolescence

In the previous chapter, we considered the biological side of puberty. Here, we will try to link some of the social and psychological reactions that accompany these biological changes.

SEXUAL FANTASIES

Sexual fantasies and dreams (which will be discussed at length in chapter 13) become more common and explicit in adolescence than at earlier ages, often as an accompaniment to masturbation (Hass, 1979). One study found that only 7 percent of adolescent girls and 11 percent of adolescent boys who masturbated never fantasized, and about half reported using fantasy most of the time during masturbation (Sorenson, 1973). Fantasy seems to serve several different purposes in adolescence: it can add to the pleasure of a sexual activity, be a substitute for a real (but unavailable) experience, induce arousal or orgasm, provide a form of mental rehearsal for later sexual experiences (thus increasing comfort and anticipating possible problems just as rehearsing any other kind of activity can), and provide a safe, controlled, unembarrassing means of sexual experimentation. Each of these functions of fantasy is a forerunner of ways in which sexual imagery will continue to be used in adulthood by most people. For this reason, the adolescent's experience in and exploration of the range and uses of fantasy is important to her or his later sexual existence and confidence.

INDEPENDENCE

As adolescents struggle to establish a sense of personal identity and independence from parents and other authority figures, interactions with their peer group (other people of about their same age) become increasingly important. Teenagers look to each other for support and guidance, vowing to correct the mistakes of the older generations, but quickly discover that their peer group has its own set of expectations, social controls, and rules of conduct. Thus the adolescents' need for freedom is usually accompanied by a need to be like their friends, even though these two needs sometimes conflict.

Peer group pressures vary from one community to another and also reflect the ethnic and economic subcultures within each community. In one group, the code of sexual conduct may be very traditional with a high premium on female virginity and almost all sexual activity limited to "meaningful" relationships. If this code is not followed by females, they will get a "reputation" which may tarnish their futures and make them prey for boys looking for an "easy lay." In another group, sex may be viewed as a status symbol — the "uninitiated" versus "those in the know." This view often motivates members of the group to participate in sexual activity to be accepted. The suggestion has been made that a new tyranny of sexual values is emerging; teenagers are expected by their peers to become sexually experienced at an early age and those who are not comfortable with this pressure are viewed as old-fashioned, immature, or "uptight" (Sarrel and Sarrel, 1979; Chilman, 1979; Burkhart, 1981).

The teenager's sexual decision-making reflects individual psychological readiness, personal values, moral reasoning, fear of negative consequences, and involvement in romantic attachments. These personal factors are often not compatible with peer pressures and seem to be felt as

Although sex is a fact of life for many teenagers, some adolescents feel they are on the outside looking in.

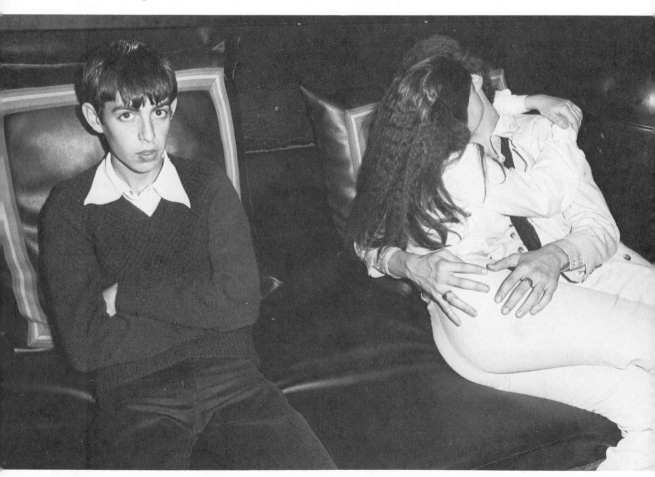

Childhood and Adolescent Sexuality

limits more strongly by adolescent females than by males in our society. It appears that teenagers who engage in sexual intercourse and those who are close to doing so place a high premium on personal independence, have loosened family ties in favor of more reliance on friends, and are more apt to experiment with drugs or alcohol and to engage in political activism than their contemporaries (Jessor and Jessor, 1975; I. Reiss, 1980).

In seeking to become free from parental or adult control, some adolescents see sex as a way of proving their ability to make independent decisions and of challenging the values of the older generation. Their freedom is not achieved so easily: adolescents manage to acquire a sizeable sexual legacy from the older generation complete with a persistent double standard and a strong sense of sexual guilt. Teenage *attitudes* have changed more rapidly than behavior, since an attitude of equality between the sexes is now fairly widespread; yet the old double standard persists in certain ways. The male is still expected to be the sexual initiator; if the female assumes this role, she is likely to be viewed as "aggressive" or "oversexed." Adolescents have not rid themselves of all sexual conflict, misinformation, and embarrassment; instead, it seems they have sometimes traded one set of problems for another (Sarrel and Sarrel, 1979; Burkhart, 1981).

PARENTAL REACTIONS

While adults generally encourage adolescents to develop independence, our society puts teenagers in a double-bind. No longer children, not yet adults, adolescents are expected to act grown up in many ways, but this attitude usually does not extend to their sexual behavior. Many adults seem threatened by adolescent sexuality and try to regulate it in illogical ways: ban sex education in schools (it would "put ideas in their heads"), limit information about contraceptive methods ("keep them afraid of getting pregnant"),

censor what teenagers read or can see in movies ("pure minds think pure thoughts"), invent school dress codes ("modesty conquers lust"), or simply pretend that adolescent sexuality does not exist.

Fortunately, not all parents adopt such a negative view of teenage sexuality, and in some instances parents take a much more liberal stance. Not only are there some parents who discuss sex very openly and assist their teenage daughters and sons in obtaining contraception, a few parents actually pressure their adolescent children into becoming sexually experienced. This attitude sometimes reflects the parents' desire to relive their own teenage years through the experiences of their children.

It is also important to realize that teenagers may create pressure for their parents by their sexual behavior. Most parents are concerned about the possibility of an unwanted teenage pregnancy, realizing that even if their son or daughter has access to contraception, that does not mean it will be effectively used whenever needed. Parents are also realistically worried about venereal disease. In addition, many parents are caught in a double-bind of their own: they do not want to seem old-fashioned and unduly restrictive but they genuinely believe in traditional values about sexual behavior that the teenager may have a hard time understanding. Interestingly, some parents become worried if their teenage child *does not* show any interest in the opposite sex, since they interpret this as a possible sign of homosexuality.

Most parents, regardless of their own sexual lifestyles, have a tendency to be less permissive about premarital sex for their own children (I. Reiss, 1967; 1980). Perhaps as a result, when parents are the primary source of sex education, adolescents have more traditional sex values and have higher rates of virginity (Lewis, 1973).

One additional aspect regarding parental reactions to teenage sexuality should be mentioned because it has been a matter of some controversy

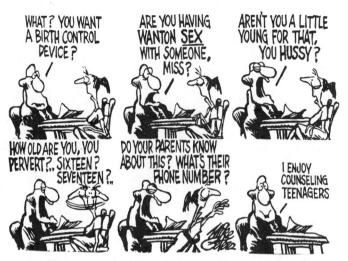

Mike Peters, February 11, 1983. Reprinted by permission. © 1983 United Feature Syndicate.

for the past few years. In 1982, the federal government proposed regulations (derisively referred to in the press as the "squeal rule") that would have required that federally funded clinics notify parents in writing whenever a teenager wished to receive a prescription contraceptive. Although this regulation was overturned by several judicial rulings in 1983, before it went into effect, the Reagan administration is seeking to reactivate it as of mid-1984. For additional discussion of this issue, see the Personal Perspectives box on the facing page.

Patterns of Sexual Behavior

Discussing patterns of sexual behavior during adolescence depends on interpreting the data available from various researchers who collected information in different times and places using widely different sampling methods. The findings of Kinsey and his colleagues will be mentioned in each section on sexual behavior as a reference point, but readers should remember that these statistics are now more than thirty years old.

MASTURBATION

Kinsey and his colleagues (1953) found a marked difference in the incidence of masturbation between adolescent females and males. While 82 percent of fifteen-year-old boys had masturbated to orgasm, only 20 percent of fifteen-year-old girls had done so, and this pronounced difference persisted through the rest of the teenage years. More recently, Sorenson (1973) found that 39 percent of adolescent girls and 58 percent of adolescent boys had masturbatory experience, and it appears that by age twenty, this figure rises to about 85 percent of males and 60 percent of females (Abramson, 1973; Hunt, 1975; Arafat and Cotton, 1974). Most recently, data from interviews with 580 women aged eighteen to thirty indicated that more than three-quarters had masturbated during adolescence (Kolodny, 1980), confirming indications of a trend to a higher incidence of masturbation in female teenagers since Kinsey's time.

In spite of this behavioral trend, guilt or anxiety about masturbation continues to plague teen-

Childhood and Adolescent Sexuality

The "Squeal Rule"

A regulation proposed by the U.S. Department of Health and Human Services would have required all family planning clinics funded under Title X of the Public Health Service Act to notify parents when teenagers received prescription contraceptives from the clinic. At the height of the ensuing controversy, the following article written by an anonymous Harvard law school student appeared in *The New York Times* (February 11, 1983):

*　　*　　*

I didn't plan to fix the day so indelibly in my mind, but I can pinpoint exactly the first time I went to the doctor to see about birth control.

It was my 17th birthday, a milestone that entitled me to that most important of suburban rites of passage, a driving permit. Spurred, perhaps, by that one small step into adulthood to venture another, I took a drive with my boyfriend to the Planned Parenthood office in a neighboring town, my novice driving skills made even shakier by the nature of our trip.

My recollection of that day, now more than seven years ago, is prompted by a new regulation of the Department of Health and Human Services that is to take effect later this month. Under that regulation, the so-called squeal rule, any federally subsidized clinic that dispenses prescription birth control to a patient under 18 will also have to send a registered letter to her parents informing them of that fact.

The supposed rationale of the rule is to encourage family communication about sex and birth control, and to "protect the health and safety of minor adolescents," according to departing Secretary Richard S. Schweiker.

If the squeal rule had been in effect when I was 17, I never would have driven to the clinic. It wouldn't have stopped me from having sex; I was already doing that, stupidly, unprotected, in the blind belief that "it" could not happen to me. The rule simply would have prevented me from receiving a reliable method of contraception.

Why couldn't I just tell my parents that I loved my boyfriend, thought I was old enough to have sex, and wanted to take the responsibility that accompanies it?

It wasn't that my parents had unshakeable religious or moral convictions opposed to premarital sex, or to birth control. It wasn't that they were unable even to discuss the issue: My mother had explained all the technical details long before. It wasn't that my father was going to beat me, or lock me in my room or forbid me to see my boyfriend. But I knew my parents would disapprove. I knew that their disapproval wasn't going to make me stop, no matter how much "family communication" we had. And I didn't see any reason to throw my actions in their faces, to create the discord that would have followed such a revelation. There was also the matter of my privacy: I didn't want my sex life to become a matter of dinner table debate.

Perhaps in the best of all possible worlds we would have talked about it. Family communication is the sort of thing, like apple pie, that no one is against. But it is a rare adolescent who lives in an ideal world, at least where parents are concerned. I didn't. I wasn't going to tell my parents, no matter whether that decision was wise or not. And I wasn't going to have that decision forced on me by some Government regulation.

Neither are the teenagers who will be subject to the squeal rule. There I was, supposedly smart – at the top of my high school class, on my way to a prestigious Ivy League college, perfectly aware of the importance of contraception – still having sex without any protection. What of teenagers with less knowledge of birth control, or a more abiding trust that beginners' luck will protect them from pregnancy? If my mother had found my diaphragm, the worst consequence that would have ensued would probably have been a nasty fight. What of teenagers with more to risk than mere disapproval if a clinic had to notify their parents?

The squeal rule is going to backfire. It is going to promote pregnancy, not family communication. Instead of encouraging teenagers to use birth control, the rule will force them to turn away from clinics and to use less reliable methods, or none at all.

Supporters of the squeal rule may like to comfort themselves with the belief that teenagers denied access to reliable birth control will do the rational thing, and simply abstain. But sex is not a subject that provokes the most rational decisions at any age. A 1981 study of 1,200 teenagers visiting family planning clinics found that 86 percent were already sexually active; the average time before coming in for birth control was one year. Teenagers affected by the rule are not going to stop having sex because of it. And some of them – too many of them – are going to get pregnant.

There were more than one million teenage pregnancies last year; more than 450,000 of those teenagers had abortions. Those numbers are a tragedy that the government should be doing something about. Instead, it has issued the squeal rule, which will push the numbers even higher. And contributing to the problem, rather than working to solve it, is the greatest tragedy of all.

*   *   *

Shortly after this letter appeared, the attempt to implement the "squeal rule" was dropped in the face of several court decisions that prohibited its use.

agers. Fifty-seven percent of adolescent girls and 45 percent of adolescent boys reported such negative feelings "sometimes" or "often" according to Sorenson (1973), and other workers have confirmed this finding (Abramson and Mosher, 1979; Hass, 1979). On the other hand, masturbation fulfills some important needs for adolescents: relieving sexual tension, providing a safe means of sexual experimentation, improving sexual self-confidence, controlling sexual impulses, combating loneliness, and discharging general stress and tension (Sorenson, 1973; Clifford, 1978; Barbach, 1980; Kolodny, 1980). The interplay of guilt and pleasure is shown in the following comment from a nineteen-year-old female college student:

> I began to masturbate in a very fumbling, uncertain way when I was about 14. At first, it didn't do much for me, and I started to think that maybe it was wrong, like they taught me in Sunday school. Then one night I was reading a really sexy book and I started rubbing myself as I read. Suddenly I had this gigantic orgasm — it really took me by surprise I guess — and from then on I found masturbation a lot more enjoyable. I was glad to see that I could come like that and it gave me a lot of self-confidence. Now I never feel guilty about masturbating, and I use it to relax or just feel good. (Authors' files)

PETTING

Kinsey and his colleagues defined petting as physical contacts between females and males in an attempt to produce erotic arousal without sexual intercourse. Most authorities would narrow this definition a bit and not include kissing as a form of petting, and some define petting as sexual touching "below the waist" while any other sexual touching is called "necking."

Kinsey's team reported that by age fifteen, 39 percent of girls and 57 percent of boys had engaged in petting and that by age eighteen, these figures had risen to over 80 percent for both sexes. Only 21 percent of boys and 15 percent of girls, however, had petted to orgasm before age nineteen. Sorenson (1973) found that 22 percent of his sample had no sexual experience other than kissing, and 17 percent had some petting experience without having intercourse. More recently, interviews with sixty first-year college students about their high school sexual experiences showed that 82 percent had experience in genital stimulation with a partner; 40 percent of the women and half of the men reported having been orgasmic during petting (Kolodny, 1980).

"Necking" and "petting" must be looked at in terms of the changing trends in teenage sexual behavior discussed more fully in the next section. Along with engaging in most forms of sexual behavior at an earlier age (Chilman, 1979; Hass, 1979), many of today's teenagers have moved away from older rituals of dating and "going steady" in favor of less structured patterns of social interaction (Murstein, 1980). Widespread use of illicit drugs such as marijuana may have contributed to this change, and evidence from several sources indicates that adolescents who use such drugs are more sexually experienced than adolescents who do not use marijuana or other drugs (Sorenson, 1973; Jessor and Jessor, 1975, 1977; Kolodny, 1981a).

SEXUAL INTERCOURSE

> The first time I had intercourse I was 17 years old. I was a senior in high school and I'd been going with a guy I really thought I loved. We had done just about everything else and it seemed kind of silly to stay a virgin any longer so one night we just went ahead. No big planning or discussion or lines, it just happened. I was nervous at first but it turned out really nice. From then on, we had intercourse two or three times a week and it was great sex. I have no regrets at all. (Authors' files)

> I was 16 the first time I tried to have intercourse. My girlfriend was younger but had done it before. I was so nervous I couldn't get it in, and then when she tried to do it it went soft. We

TABLE 8–1
Percent of Unmarried American Teenage Females with Coital Experience

AGE	STUDY			
	Kinsey et al. (1953)	Sorenson (1973)	Zelnik and Kantner (1980) [1971]	[1979]
13	1	9	–	–
14	2	15	–	–
15	3	26	14	23
16	5	35	21	38
17	9	37	26	49
18 }	14	45	40	57
19	17		46	69

tried for hours but no luck. I was really down. A few days later, we tried again, and it was smooth as silk. I felt really good then, like everything was okay. (Authors' files)

My first time was very unpleasant. The boy I was with rushed and fumbled around and then came so fast it was over before it started. I thought, 'What's so great about this?' For weeks afterward, I was afraid I had V.D. and had bad dreams about it. (Authors' files)

The first experience of sexual intercourse can be a time of happiness, pleasure, intimacy, and satisfaction, or it can be a source of worry, discomfort, disappointment, or guilt as these descriptions show.

According to the available research data, the age of first sexual intercourse has declined in the last few decades, particularly for teenage girls (Table 8-1). In 1953 Kinsey and his colleagues reported that only 1 percent of thirteen-year-old girls and 3 percent of fifteen-year-old girls were nonvirgins; by age twenty, this figure had only increased to 20 percent. In contrast, Sorenson (1973) found that nearly one-third of thirteen- to

fifteen-year-old girls and 57 percent of sixteen- to nineteen-year-old girls were nonvirgins. Jessor and Jessor (1975) found that 26, 40, and 55 percent of girls in tenth, eleventh, and twelfth grades were no longer virgins. Even more recently, Zelnik and Kantner (1980) found that the prevalence of sexual intercourse among never-married American teenage women increased by nearly two-thirds between 1971 and 1979.

Statistics concerning the age of adolescent males' first sexual intercourse show less change over time. Kinsey and his colleagues (1948) reported that 15 percent of thirteen-year-old boys and 39 percent of fifteen-year-old boys were nonvirgins; by age twenty, this figure had increased to 73 percent. Sorenson (1973) found that 44 percent of thirteen- to fifteen-year-old boys and 72 percent of sixteen- to nineteen-year-old boys were coitally experienced. According to Zelnik and Kantner (1980), 56 percent of never-married seventeen-year-old males and 78 percent of never-married nineteen-year-old males were nonvirgins. A study of different racial groups in a large northeastern city showed that black teenage

TABLE 8–2

Percentage Distribution of Women Aged 15–19 and of Men Aged 17–21, by Relationship with Their First Sexual Partner, According to Race

Relationship with first partner	Women			Men		
	Total (N=936)	White (N=478)	Black (N=458)	Total (N=670)	White (N=396)	Black (N=274)
Engaged	9.3	9.6	8.2	0.6	0.5	1.0
Going steady	55.2	57.6	46.5	36.5	39.2	21.9
Dating	24.4	22.2	32.6	20.0	20.2	19.0
Friends	6.7	6.0	9.4	33.7	30.2	52.4
Recently met*	4.4	4.6	3.3	9.3	9.9	5.7
Total	100.0	100.0	100.0	100.0	100.0	100.0

*Among women, this category includes a small number who reported some other relationship.

Source: Zelnik and Shah, 1983, p. 65. Reprinted with permission from Family Planning Perspectives, Volume 15, Number 2, 1983.

males were sexually active at a younger age than white teenage males (Finkel and Finkel, 1975) and this finding has been verified by others (Zelnik and Kantner, 1980).

The types of relationships generally found between teenagers and their first coital partners are shown in Table 8-2. It is a mistake, however, to regard the lower age of first sexual intercourse as a sign of teenage promiscuity because many teenagers restrict themselves to one sex partner at a time. Many adolescents who are no longer virgins have intercourse infrequently (Shah and Zelnik, 1980). For some teenagers, particularly those who "tried" intercourse as a kind of experimentation, once the initial mystery is gone, the behavior itself is far less intriguing. As a result, they may have little or no sexual intercourse for long periods of time — sometimes waiting to meet the "right person." Teenagers in long-term romantic relationships are more likely to participate in coitus fairly regularly.

In the last few years, it has become apparent that among sexually experienced teenagers, a group is emerging who are disappointed, dissatisfied, or troubled by their sex lives. Given the name "unhappy nonvirgins" by Kolodny (1981), this group includes an estimated 30 percent of adolescents who have had coital experience. In some cases, these are teens who had such high expectations of what sex "should" be that they feel like either failures or dupes when their actual experience is less than earthshattering ecstasy. In other instances, these teenagers have experienced sexual dysfunctions which have prevented them from enjoying sex. Still others in this group enjoy sexual activity initially but become disillusioned when sex dominates their relationship ("That's all he ever wants to do now") or when their relationship breaks up and they feel that they've been used or manipulated. Many of these "unhappy nonvirgins" revert to abstinence as a means of coping, hoping that when they're older — or when they meet the right person — things will be different. Others continue to be sexually active while deriving little, if any, enjoyment of sex.

HOMOSEXUAL EXPERIENCE

The Kinsey studies showed that it was fairly common for males to have at least one homosexual experience during adolescence, while considerably fewer adolescent females engaged in sex with another female. More recently, there seems to have been a moderate decline in adolescent homosexual experience. Sorenson (1973) found that 5 percent of thirteen- to fifteen-year-old boys and 17 percent of sixteen- to nineteen-year-old boys had ever had a homosexual experience, and 6 percent of all adolescent females he surveyed had at least one episode of homosexual activity. Hass (1979) reported that 11 percent of the teenage girls and 14 percent of the teenage boys he studied had at least one sexual encounter with a person of the same sex, but noted that this was probably an underestimate because many respondents did not regard preadolescent "games" as sexual acts.

It is important to realize that an isolated same-sex encounter or a transient pattern of homosexual activity does not translate into "being homosexual." Most adolescents who have had some experience with homosexual activity do not see themselves as homosexuals and do not go on to homosexual orientation in adulthood. Nevertheless, some adolescents develop guilt or ambivalence about their sexual orientation as a result of a single same-sex episode and may experience emotional turmoil.

The teenager who is worried about being homosexual may deal with it in a variety of ways. Some avoid homosexual contacts while trying to reaffirm their heterosexual identity through dating and heterosexual activity. Others withdraw from all sexual situations. Still others look on themselves as bisexual, consider homosexual arousal a passing phase which they will outgrow, or seek help from a professional.

Some adolescents intuitively "feel" that they are homosexual or work through their initial confusion about sexual identity to accept their homosexuality in a positive way. These teenagers may seek out readings on the subject, contacts with other homosexuals, and a social introduction to the homosexual subculture. As we will discuss in chapter 16, these persons face some difficulties because of current attitudes toward homosexuality, and they may not choose to announce their sexual preferences to family or friends (referred to as "coming out") until a later time, if at all.

Unintended Teenage Pregnancy

More than one million pregnancies occur each year among American teenage females, which is equivalent to one adolescent pregnancy beginning every 35 seconds. Since the majority of these pregnancies are unplanned and unwanted, it is no surprise that they frequently create considerable psychological anguish, serious economic consequences, and even health risks that are too often ignored or misunderstood.

A few background statistics can highlight the scope of this epidemic (Alan Guttmacher Institute, 1981; Zelnik, Kantner, and Ford, 1981):

- 30,000 pregnancies occur annually among girls under fifteen years of age.
- 400,000 American teenagers have abortions each year, accounting for more than one-third of all abortions performed in this country.
- Six out of ten teenage females who have a child before age seventeen will be pregnant again before age nineteen.
- With one out of twenty adolescent females having a baby each year, America's teenage birth rate is the highest in the western hemisphere, double the rate of Sweden, and is an astonishing seventeen times higher than Japan's (Figure 8-3).
- Four out of ten girls now fourteen years old will get pregnant in their teens.

FIGURE 8–3
Number of Births per 1,000 Women Younger Than 20, Selected
Countries, Middle-to-Late 1970s

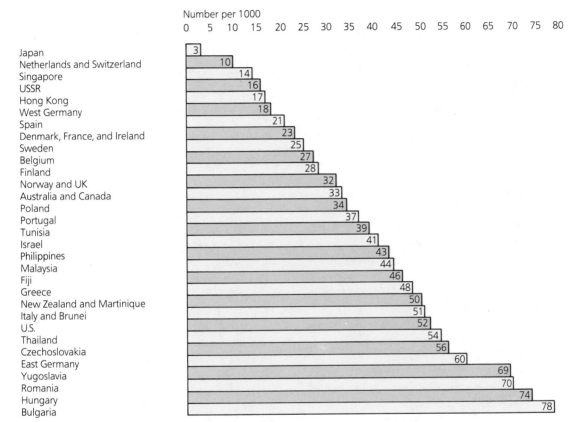

Number per 1000

0	5	10	15	20	25	30	35	40	45	50	55	60	65	70	75	80

Japan — 3
Netherlands and Switzerland — 10
Singapore — 14
USSR — 16
Hong Kong — 17
West Germany — 18
Spain — 21
Denmark, France, and Ireland — 23
Sweden — 25
Belgium — 27
Finland — 28
Norway and UK — 32
Australia and Canada — 33
Poland — 34
Portugal — 37
Tunisia — 39
Israel — 41
Philippines — 43
Malaysia — 44
Fiji — 46
Greece — 48
New Zealand and Martinique — 50
Italy and Brunei — 51
U.S. — 52
Thailand — 54
Czechoslovakia — 56
East Germany — 60
Yugoslavia — 69
Romania — 70
Hungary — 74
Bulgaria — 78

Source: Reprinted with permission from *Teenage Pregnancy: The Problem That Hasn't Gone Away,* published by The Alan Guttmacher Institute, New York, 1981.

About 5 percent of U.S. teenagers give birth each year. A higher proportion of adolescents become mothers in the United States than in any developed country, except for Czechoslovakia, East Germany, Yugoslavia, Romania, Hungary, and Bulgaria.

These statistics show how widespread the problem of unintended teenage pregnancy is, but to understand *why* it is a problem, we need to examine some additional aspects of the consequences of teenage pregnancy. To begin with, there are increased health risks associated with teenage pregnancy, particularly among younger teens (those in the thirteen to sixteen year age group). For example, babies of teenage mothers have an increased chance of being underweight and are nearly twice as likely to die in infancy as those born to women in their twenties (Smith and Mumford, 1980; McCormick, Shapiro, and Starfield, 1981). In addition, teenagers tend to have more medically complicated pregnancies — including miscarriages, toxemia, and hemorrhage — as well as a higher risk of maternal death than women in their twenties (Fielding, 1978; Hellman, 1981).

Possibly even more alarming than these medical risks are the socioeconomic consequences of unintended teenage pregnancy. Even though it is now illegal to expel students who are pregnant or who are mothers from public schools, most teenage mothers who keep their babies drop out of school and don't return (Bolton, 1980; Furstenberg, Menken, and Lincoln, 1981; McGee, 1982). Largely as a result of this abrupt withdrawal from formal education, women in this group are far less likely than their peers to enter the job market or to gain regular employment (McCarthy and Radish, 1982). It is no surprise, then, that these teenage mothers are overrepresented in poverty statistics and are apt to become largely dependent on government services and support (Moore et al., 1979; Alan Guttmacher Institute, 1981; McGee, 1982).

Unmarried teenage girls who find themselves pregnant are confronted by a series of psychologically complicated choices, as well. They often get little or no support — either emotionally or financially — from the child's father. They must decide whether to abort the pregnancy (which sometimes produces intense feelings of guilt and anguish) or have the baby. If they have the baby, they then must decide to keep it or put it up for adoption; today, fewer than 5 percent of unwed teenage mothers choose adoption as a course of action (McGee, 1982). In other cases, their partners may pressure them to do something they don't want to, thus creating additional pressures and uncertainties. Here's how one seventeen year old described her dilemma:

> When I found out I was pregnant, my boyfriend insisted that we get married and have the baby. I had no interest in marrying him or in being sad-

dled with an infant at age eighteen, so I refused. But his parents hired a lawyer to try to stop me from having an abortion, and the whole thing wound up being a nightmare for me and my parents. Fortunately, I got the abortion and dumped my so-called boyfriend, so I'll be going to college next year instead of playing mommy. (Authors' files)

Some teenagers, unlike the one quoted above, find themselves rushed into unanticipated marriage as a result of a pregnancy. Unfortunately, these marriages are much likelier than most to end in divorce or desertion, and there is a suicide risk among these young women that is considerably higher than in the general population (Cvetkovitch et al., 1975; Bolton, 1980; Furstenberg, Menken, and Lincoln, 1981).

There is relatively little research describing the consequences of unintended teenage *fatherhood*. This may be partly because it is difficult to identify these individuals for study and partly because they are not socially or economically linked to the pregnancy outcome in the same ways mothers are. However, the available evidence shows that males who become fathers while in their teens tend to have lower income and less educational attainment than peers who postpone fatherhood until their twenties (Baldwin and Cain, 1980; Alan Guttmacher Institute, 1981; McGee, 1982). Nevertheless, the impact of teenage pregnancy is considerably less on males than on females.

Clearly, many adolescent males continue to regard the ultimate responsibility for contraception as the female's, generally feeling that an unintended pregnancy could have been prevented and thus is the "fault" of the female — in other words, that it is "not their worry." Others feel a joint responsibility that extends only to offering to share (or perhaps pay entirely) for the cost of an abortion; to them, this gesture is an honest acknowledgment of their involvement and willingness to help, but it is involvement of the most limited sort. In fact, as noted sex educator Sol

Childhood and Adolescent Sexuality

Gordon (1982) points out, "almost 90 percent of all teenage boys who make a teenage girl pregnant abandon her."

While there are no easy solutions to the problem of unintended teenage pregnancy, it appears that misinformation or complete lack of information is a key factor. At present, only one-third of American junior and senior high schools offer sex education courses, and many of those offered are remarkably incomplete (Orr, 1982). Since many of the sex education courses are given only to older teenagers, their preventative function is lessened considerably. Those people who believe that sex education should be taught in the home — while voicing a fine idea — overlook the reality of the situation today. Research indicates that only about 10 percent of parents discuss sexuality with their teens beyond simply saying "don't." On the other hand, a recent study by Zelnik and Kim (1982) demonstrates that among unmarried sexually active teenage women, those who have had sex education courses have fewer pregnancies than those who haven't (see Table 8-3).

Almost all authorities agree that greater responsibility for contraceptive use by the adolescent male is a major element in the effort to reduce the rate of unintended teenage pregnancy.

First, educating males about contraceptive options at an early age seems warranted since studies suggest that this information leads to better contraceptive use (Cvetkovitch and Grote, 1983). Although teenage males are generally unwilling to admit to ignorance or misinformation about sex, it is not unusual to find fifteen- or sixteen-year-old boys who believe that a diaphragm should be removed right after intercourse, or who don't know the fertile days in a female's menstrual cycle. Such education need not be restricted to schools — it can be done at home, in church-affiliated programs, or as part of community projects. Education must be practical, too, explaining how and where to purchase contraceptives, why it's important to discuss birth control with a partner, and why consistent contraceptive use is necessary.

Another important step is to provide males (as well as females) with a better view of how birth control practices relate to their own lives. For instance, teens must recognize how rigid sex roles or the risk of parental disapproval can influence their contraceptive behavior. In addition, teens need to be aware that the risk of contracting a sexually transmitted disease is materially reduced by use of certain contraceptive methods. This is important not only because it

TABLE 8-3
Percent of Never-Married, Sexually Active Teenage Women Who Have Been Pregnant, by Whether They Had Previously Had a Sex Education Course in School

	WHITE		BLACK	
	Age 15-17	Age 18-19	Age 15-17	Age 18-19
Had Sex Education	15.4%	25.0%	28.7%	48.2%
No Sex Education	25.0%	31.9%	49.2%	54.0%

Source: Modified from 1979 survey data of Zelnik and Kim (1982).

encourages the teenage male to use contraception, but because the male's expression of interest and concern about contraception encourages his partner to find and use an appropriate method as well (Gilgun, 1983). In addition, teenagers need incentives to engage in responsible birth control practices.

Some authorities suggest public campaigns geared at urging teens to say "no" to having intercourse (Gordon, 1982; Howard, 1983). This approach might be effective with some adolescents, but would probably not be realistically effective with the majority of teenagers, given today's patterns of sexual behavior in our culture: It is hard to put a genie back in a bottle. Also, such an approach runs the risk of being repressive — it is, after all, an attempt to frighten teens into abstinence — and this may produce a backlash. Indeed, anti-drug and anti-cigarette campaigns have often been discredited by teens on this basis. In any case, since it is unlikely that the majority of sexually experienced teenagers will become celibate *en masse,* it is necessary to provide teens with positive role-models toward appropriate contraceptive use and a more effective view of the ways in which responsibility in sexual behavior is important to their welfare.

SUMMARY

1. Gender identity is usually shaped by an interaction between biological and psychosocial forces in the first few years of life.

2. There is now evidence that erections occur in the later months of fetal development, which, together with other data showing that newborn babies of both sexes show signs of sexual responsivity, indicates the innate naturalness of sexuality from the very beginning of life. It is also common to see young babies rubbing or stroking their genitals.

3. Children typically show considerable curiosity about sexual matters and are likely to engage in sexual games with others at one time or another. (These activities may include same-sex contacts or sexual contact between siblings.) Although some parents are alarmed and upset by such behavior, it is unlikely to be harmful as long as it is not exploitative.

4. During adolescence, sexual behavior is likely to become a greater focus of attention. Although not all adolescents are sexually experienced, and about 30 percent of non-virgins seem dissatisfied with their sex lives, a majority of American teenagers become coitally experienced by age 18 or 19.

5. Unintended teenage pregnancy is a major social and public health concern in America today, with more than one million pregnancies occurring annually among teenage females. These pregnancies are often problematic because of increased health risks (particularly among younger teens) and adverse socioeconomic consequences for both the parents and child. While no easy solutions are available to resolve this problem, effective sex education programs and involvement of the male (as well as the female) in the contraception decision process may be important steps in the right direction.

SUGGESTED READINGS

Alan Guttmacher Institute. *Teenage Pregnancy: The Problem That Hasn't Gone Away.* New York: Alan Guttmacher Institute, 1981. An eighty-page monograph with attractive visual format that covers an immense amount of data on teenage pregnancy in easy-to-grasp graphics and concise, to-the-point text. Highly recommended, nontechnical.

Childhood and Adolescent Sexuality

Bryne, Donn, and Fisher, William, eds. *Adolescents, Sex, and Contraception.* Hillsdale, N.J.: Lawrence Erlbaum Associates, 1983. Comprehensive discussion of teenage sexuality principally in terms of factors that govern contraceptive attitudes and behavior. Difficult reading in spots, but worth the effort for its thorough and thoughtful coverage.

Burkhart, Kathryn. *Growing into Love.* New York: Putnam, 1981. Interviews with teenagers on sexuality presented with wit, insight, and sensitivity. Although this is not a research study in the scientific sense, it is highly useful nontechnical reading.

Calderone, Mary, and Ramey, James. *Talking with Your Child about Sex.* New York: Random House, 1982. A practical, easy-to-read how-to book for parents to help them be more accessible and less anxious in talking about sexual issues with their children.

Constantine, Larry, and Martinson, Floyd, eds. *Children and Sex: New Findings, New Perspectives.* Boston: Little, Brown, 1981. A multidisciplinary collection of essays and research reports on childhood sexuality that is uneven in its coverage in spots, often highly opinionated, and certain to provoke controversy. Nevertheless, it is informative reading that is generally presented without too much technical jargon.

Goldman, Ronald, and Goldman, Juliette. *Children's Sexual Thinking.* Boston: Routledge and Kegan Paul, 1982. An impressive study of the sexual thinking of over 800 children in four different countries, based on direct interviews. Although parts of this book are sometimes dry and bogged down in statistical detail, the conclusions are quite fascinating.

9 Adult Sexuality

Traditionally, developmentalists have studied childhood and adolescence as a means of understanding adulthood. This viewpoint is useful in many ways, but it has inadvertently created the impression that development stops at a precise moment, leaving the adult a relatively static creature. Another view that can be traced back to the writings of psychologists Carl Jung and Erik Erikson stresses the developmental aspects of adulthood. According to this perspective, adulthood is a continuing pattern of learning, crisis, and choice. Daniel Levinson (1978) has suggested that the life cycle is a kind of journey:

Many influences along the way shape the nature of the journey. They may produce alternate routes or detours along the way; they may speed up or slow down the timetable within certain limits; in extreme cases they may stop the developmental process altogether. But as long as the journey continues, it follows the basic sequence. (Levinson, 1978, p. 6)

Gail Sheehy has added to the view of adult developmental stages by conceptualizing them as a series of passages through fairly predictable crises that contribute to our growth. She observes:

During each of these passages, how we feel about our way of living will undergo subtle changes in four areas of perception. One is the interior sense of self in relation to others. A second is the proportion of safeness to danger we feel in our lives. A third is our perception of time — do we have plenty of it, or are we beginning to feel that time is running out? Last, there will be some shift at the gut level in our sense of aliveness or stagnation. These are the hazy sensations that compose the background tone of living and shape the decisions on which we take action. (Sheehy, 1976, p. 21)

We will only take an abbreviated look at adult sexuality here as the rest of this book is largely about the sexual experiences and sexual problems of adults. The notion of adulthood as a time of transition and development is a useful one to retain while reading subsequent chapters.

EARLY ADULTHOOD

The phase of early adulthood, from approximately ages twenty to forty, is a time when people make important life choices (marriage, occupation, lifestyle) and move from the relatively untested ambitions of adolescence to a personal maturity shaped by the realities of the world in which they live. For most people, it is a time of increasing responsibility in terms of interpersonal relations and family life.

In recent years, both in the United States and abroad, there has been a definite trend toward marriage at a later age than in past decades (U.S. Bureau of the Census, 1978a). As a result, many young men and women face an extended period of being single after adolescence that unquestionably changes patterns of sexual behavior from Kinsey's day. Today, most people in their twenties believe that becoming sexually experienced rather than preserving virginity is an important prelude for selecting a mate. Erikson (1968) remarks that developing the capacity for intimacy is a central task for the young adult.

Young adults are generally less subject to "sexual peer pressure" than adolescents but more driven by an internal need to become sexually knowledgeable. Freedom from parental limits is accompanied by easier access to private surroundings (an apartment, a motel room, a vacation spot) which also creates more sexual opportunity. In this state of singlehood, several common patterns of sexual behavior can be seen. The *experimenter* seems to judge sexual experiences in terms of frequency, variety, and performance proficiency. She or he seems to view the world as a sexual smorgasbord and generally has the attitude that "now's the time to play, because later I'll settle down." The *seeker* strives to find the ideal relationship (and perfect marriage partner) by developing sexual relationships and hoping for the best. Living together can be a proving ground for a relationship begun on this basis. The *traditionalist* participates willingly and joyously in sex, but reserves intercourse for "serious relationships." The traditionalist may have several sexual partners before ultimately marrying, but does so one at a time. There are undoubtedly other patterns that can be identified, but these three seem to be most common.

The early years of adulthood are a time of sexual uncertainty for some and sexual satisfaction for others. Conflict can arise because of attitudes of sexual guilt or immorality carried over from earlier ages. The adolescent's concern with sexual normality has not fully disappeared, and the young adult continues to worry about his or her physique, sexual endowment, and personal skill in making love. Sexual identity conflicts may not yet have been resolved, and even for those who have come to accept themselves as homosexual or bisexual, social pressures and prejudices may cause some difficulty.

Despite the existence of such problems, young adults are more sexually active today than in the past (Robinson and Jedlicka, 1982). A major factor contributing to this change has been the relative disappearance of the old double-standard that regarded premarital sexual experience as permissible for men but not for women (DeLamater and MacCorquodale, 1979). Thus, it is not surprising to see that the gender gap in premarital sexual experience has narrowed considerably from what it used to be, as shown in Table 9-1.

Although the popular notion is that being young and single automatically leads to sexual happiness, the reality may be somewhat different. In one recent survey of 250 college students, for instance, 43 percent stated that they were concerned about being unable to find time for sexual relations, and 40 percent had problems with lack of privacy for sex (Koch, 1982). This survey also found relatively high rates of sexual dysfunctions: 37 percent of the students had difficulty becoming vaginally lubricated or getting erections at least half of the time; 30 percent of the females had trouble reaching orgasm; and 23 percent of the males ejaculated too quickly. College students are not the only ones who have these sorts of problems, either. A 1983 *Psychology Today* survey found that 28 percent of men and 40 percent of women complained of lack of sexual desire, while almost 20 percent of both sexes admitted to fears about sexual adequacy (Rubenstein, 1983).

Today's young adults are faced with some additional sexual conflicts that may represent a sort of backlash against the "anything goes" banner of the sexual revolution of the 1960s and 1970s. For example, while attitudes toward premarital sex have changed dramatically in the last three decades, having sex with a large number of

TABLE 9-1
Percentage of College Students Having Premarital Intercourse

Year	Males		Females	
	%	N	%	N
1965	65.1	129	28.7	115
1970	65.0	136	37.3	158
1975	73.9	115	57.1	275
1980	77.4	168	63.5	230

Source: From Robinson and Jedlicka (1982).

partners is still somewhat frowned on (Robinson and Jedlicka, 1982). Furthermore, although most singles don't believe that love is necessary for good sex, there seems to be increasing disillusionment with casual sex or one-night stands (Simenauer and Carroll, 1982; Rubenstein, 1983).

This trend seems to be at least partly the result of increased awareness of the possibility of exposure to a sexually transmitted disease, such as the much-publicized genital herpes. Among young adult homosexual men, who have — as a group — typically participated in casual sex much more than their heterosexual age-mates, fear of contracting AIDS has also led recently to a reduction in the number of sexual partners and more interest in establishing "monogamous" relationships. Fear is not, however, the only element operating here. Many of the young adults we have interviewed are concerned with another aspect of casual sex: its relatively impersonal nature. The following remarks are typical of what we have been told:

A *twenty-six-year-old man*: Having one-night stands was fun at first because there were no demands attached, no one's expectations to fulfill. But after a year or so I began to realize that something was missing from these encounters —a sense of caring about the person I was making it with, or a feeling that she cared about me. (Authors' files)

A thirty-year-old woman: You just can't compare the quality of sex with someone you hardly know and feel nothing for with the quality of sex in a caring relationship. Casual sex is just mechanical, one-dimensional release. Sex with someone I care about is warmer and psychologically far more satisfying. (Authors' files)

Why are a number of young adults becoming disillusioned with having only casual sexual encounters? Peter Marin, in an article titled "A Revolution's Broken Promises," offers one interesting analysis of what may be occurring: he suggests that while loosening restraints on sexual behavior creates a climate of sexual freedom and choice, this freedom is not unequivocally positive. Sexual freedom can lead to disappointment, pressure, and conflict as well as satisfaction, so that "To the extent that it diversifies and expands experience, it also diversifies and multiplies the pain that accompanies experience, the kinds of errors that we can make, the kinds of harm we can do to one another" (Marin, 1983, p. 53).

Similarly, Susan Washburn claims that the commercialization of sex in our society leads to completely unrealistic expectations of what sex should be:

When sex is treated as a commodity, the consumerist credo, "more is better" is extended to sexual interactions. If one partner is good, two are better, and an orgy the ultimate sexual experience; if one orgasm is good, a Chinese firecracker string of multiple orgasms is better. . . . We collect sexual experiences with the same compulsiveness that marks our accumulation of material goods. We're afraid that we won't get ours before the supply runs out. (Washburn, 1981, p. 230)

To be sure, sexual experiences in early adulthood are often warm, exciting, gratifying, and untroubled. Even casual sex can serve a number of useful purposes, psychologically as well as physically, and there is certainly no reason that having fun is to be frowned on. But the prevailing trend is clearly toward sex in the context of caring relationships, and one place this is particularly evident is in the relatively recent growth of cohabitation — unmarried heterosexual couples living together — which is discussed in detail on page 249.

In contrast to single life, marriage, which will be discussed in greater detail in chapters 11 and 15, presents different sexual development patterns. For better or for worse, a majority of young adults eventually marry, which can itself create certain sexual difficulties. As the novelty of early marital bliss dissolves in the process of learning to live with one another's quirks and habits, as early dreams of conquering the world give way to a more practical focus on details of everyday life, sex is likely to become less exciting and sometimes less gratifying for one or both partners. Reflecting this, the frequency of sexual activity generally declines in the early years of marriage, as shown in Table 9-2. Parenthood leads to less privacy, more demands, and even exhaustion. It is hard to get excited about sex if you have been running after a two year old all day long, just as sex is apt to lose its attraction if you have worked a fourteen-hour day at the office.

TABLE 9–2
Frequency of Intercourse in Early Marriage

	N	Mean frequency of intercourse per month
1st year	12	14.8
2nd year	10	12,2
3rd year	19	11.9
4th year	7	9.0
5th year	18	9.7
6th year	8	6.3

Source: Modified from Greenblatt, 1983.

For most young married adults, sex is no longer the frantic secret activity of adolescence or the stylistic *tour de force* of singlehood. While sexual pleasure is not sacrificed or lost, it is balanced with other needs and responsibilities — an important developmental task in this phase of the life cycle. Those who do not succeed in this process of integration are more likely to become sexually dissatisfied. As a result, they may turn to extramarital sex, professional counseling, or divorce. Each of these paths seems well-travelled at the present time.

Some couples fulfill the American dream of marital bliss by staying together, raising children, remaining faithful, and loving one another all along the way. Others live out a modified version of this script in which love disappears but the other features are retained. Still others modify the script in different ways: no children, no faithfulness, or no bliss. The appearance to outsiders and the reality within the relationship do not always match.

One concrete bit of evidence that bliss is often missing from marriages can be found in the divorce rate in our society. Since the early 1960s, the annual number of divorces has climbed steadily (Figure 9-1), reflecting the change in attitudes toward divorce (less stigmatization and

sense of failure) and in divorce laws (which make it possible to obtain "no fault" divorces in most states). Recent projections based on statistics gathered by the U.S. Census Bureau suggest that approximately one out of five couples marrying now will divorce before their fifth anniversary, while a third won't make it through a decade of marriage (National Center for Health Statistics, 1982). Four out of ten will divorce before their fifteenth anniversary. Thus, as you might infer from these projections, the majority of divorces involve spouses who have not yet reached middle age.

It is not clear how frequently sexual dissatisfaction is a primary cause of divorce, but marriage counselors are well aware that sexual problems are common between couples whose marriages are troubled. Whether the sexual difficulties precede and contribute to other marital problems, or whether the reverse is more typically true, is simply not known.

Relatively little has been written about sexuality in the aftermath of divorce. It might be expected that the new sense of personal freedom that would follow a divorce would lead to increased rates of sexual activity, and in fact one study of 367 divorced singles has partially confirmed this (Simenauer and Carroll, 1982). The

CATHY   by Cathy Guisewite

Adult Sexuality

Cohabitation

Only twenty years ago, the typical female college student had an 11:00 P.M. curfew (extended to midnight on Fridays and Saturdays) and had to sign in and out of her dormitory. Male visitors were often not allowed above the ground floor level, and only a few daring campuses permitted female visitors in male dorms – usually for one or two hours per week, with the door wide open, and "monitors" to enforce these regulations. Today, many college campuses have mixed dorms (men and women living side by side) and unrestricted visiting policies.

Perhaps even more striking than these revolutionary changes is the rapid acceptance of unmarried couples living together in heterosexual arrangements formally called "cohabitation." Current estimates suggest that more than two million people (4 percent of unmarried American adults) are cohabiting, while in Sweden more than 90 percent of the populace has tried this pattern (Reiss, 1980). Although cohabitation is *not* a practice limited to college students (Clayton and Voss, 1977), about one-quarter of college students have had the experience and another 50 percent would like to (Bower and Christopherson, 1977).* Actually, about half of the people now cohabiting have previously been married, although the majority of cohabitants appear to be under age thirty-five.

What factors led to the popularity of cohabitation? One psychologist suggests that the women's movement, loosening of restrictive college housing regulations, and the radical political climate of the late 1960s combined with other social changes to promote this practice (Macklin, 1978, pp. 199–200):

> The increase in divorce, and the changing conception of the function of marriage, caused many young single people and divorcees to move cautiously into that state. The increased acceptance of sexuality outside marriage and improved contraception made it easier for nonmarried persons to engage openly and comfortably in a sexual relationship. And the increased emphasis on relationships and personal growth called into question the superficiality of the traditional dating game, and led to a search for styles of relating that allowed for change, growth, and a high degree of total intimacy.

The majority of college students apparently believe that no long-term commitment between partners is necessary to undertake a cohabitation relationship (Macklin, 1978, Table 3). Generally, there are three basic forms of cohabitation – casual or temporary involvement, preparation or testing for marriage, and substitute for or alternative to marriage. Most college students who begin cohabitation see their relationship as affectionate but uncommitted (Petty, 1975; Macklin, 1978). In one study, however, 96 percent of the students who had cohabited said that they wanted to marry in the future (Bower and Christopherson, 1977). Often, cohabitation serves as an added step in the courtship process. In fact, given the current trend of delaying the timing of marriage, cohabitation for a period of several years or more may be becoming something of a cultural fixture.

In their recent study of relationships, Blumstein and Schwartz (1983) included 653 cohabiting heterosexual couples who had lived together an average of 2.5 years. They found that while cohabitants had more frequent sex than married couples, as cohabitants stayed together longer their frequency of sexual relations de-

*Cohabitation is legally distinguished from common-law marriage in how the partners present themselves to the world. While cohabitors may live much as husbands and wives, they must advertise themselves as single if they do not want to take the risk of running afoul of laws pertaining to common-law marriage.

clined. Other key findings included:

1. As with married couples, when there were problems in non-sexual areas of the cohabitants' lives, their sex lives suffered.
2. Cohabiting women initiate sex more often than married women, but in older cohabiting couples the male often resents this.
3. Only about one-third of people who are cohabiting have sex with other people outside their relationship.

Blumstein and Schwartz believe that it will be difficult for cohabitation to become a viable permanent institution as long as the traditional marriage model exists, since "As long as marriage retains its image as the highest form of commitment, it acts as a lure to cohabiting couples who want to prove their love for each other" (1983, p. 321).

According to Cherlin (1981), however, not only are people in America now becoming more tolerant of cohabitation, there is some evidence that it is being institutionalized as part of the family system. "Far from being a threat to the primacy of marriage," Cherlin says, "cohabitation is becoming more and more like the first stage of marriage." Since even expert sociologists can't agree it will probably take more studies to discover the trends.

What effects does cohabitation have on the participants? Generally, cohabitants have given very positive ratings to their experience, describing it as "maturing," "fostering emotional growth and personal understanding," and "improving skills in heterosexual relationships" (Peterman, Ridley, and Anderson, 1974; Macklin, 1976). The great majority of college students surveyed who have

had prior experience with cohabitation say they would never marry without living with the person first (Bower, 1975; Macklin, 1976). Although critics are concerned that cohabitation leads to erosion of the family and a reduced marriage rate, there is little reason to believe that many people are permanently substituting living together arrangements for marital relationships (Macklin, 1980). Although there is not enough current data, it is possible that cohabitation may actually lower the divorce rate by allowing couples a closer premarital look at each other.

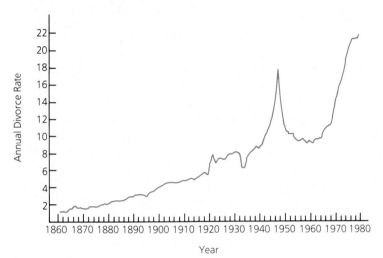

FIGURE 9–1

Annual Divorce Rates in the United States, 1860–1978
(Divorces per 1,000 Married Women)

Source: Reprinted by permission of the publisher. From *Marriage, Divorce, Remarriage* by Andrew J. Cherlin, Harvard University Press, 1981.

same study, however, found that 27 percent of the men and 36 percent of the women reported decreased amounts of sexual activity. Similarly, a separate survey found that lack of sexual desire was more prevalent among divorced men than among those who were married (Rubenstein, 1983). To understand why this divergence occurs, we should realize that the reality of life after divorce is not always one of freedom and happiness. These comments illustrate what may be going on:

A *thirty-two-year-old woman:* Sure I wanted to have new sexual experiences, but someone had to take care of my kids, and the guys I met were all pretty grubby, and I spent a lot of time feeling sorry for myself. Looking back, I guess I wasn't very good company. (Authors' files)

A *thirty-three-year-old man:* It wasn't at all what I thought it was going to be. I sort of expected to find being single again a blessing, sexually speaking. I had visions of myself living out fantasies

from *Playboy*, but it didn't really work like that at all. At the beginning, I was so nervous and embarrassed I couldn't function properly; then, I got an infection from a girl I really was beginning to like. Being single is no cup of tea. (Authors' files)

A *twenty-six-year-old woman:* Every guy who asked me out expected that because I had been married, I'd be happy to have sex with him on our first date. It just wasn't comfortable for me, but I don't think many of them cared. (Authors' files)

The recently divorced man or woman may be delighted with a new-found sexual freedom, but the initial thrill is likely to be dampened by one of several difficulties. Returning to the rituals of dating and courtship may be annoying or embarrassing, especially to those who have been out of circulation for a decade or longer. Self-consciousness about sex with someone who is almost a stranger may be distressing. Concerns about the adequacy of sexual performance and personal attractiveness may be combined with remorse or guilt over lack of commitment and morality. To all of this, we must also add that there is frequently a sense that time is running out: "I'd better get a partner while I can."

Statistics show that about five out of six men and about three out of four women remarry after a divorce — about half within three years — apparently deciding that a second marriage will give them a chance to do things differently (Cherlin, 1981). Often, this is more illusion than reality: statistical projections suggest that more than half of *second* marriages for women born between 1945 and 1954 are expected to fail, with men trailing closely behind with a projected 40 percent second marriage divorce rate (Hegger, 1983). In addition, there is no evidence that divorced persons who remarry have an increased sense of well-being compared to those who remain single (Spanier and Furstenberg, 1982).

The problems encountered in second marriages are apt to be complex, including, for example, how to deal with children of earlier marriages, the financial strain of alimony, and relations between the new spouse and the "ex." In addition, many of the same problems that plagued a first marriage tend to reappear in a second one: selfishness, alcohol abuse, lack of communication, and other similar problems don't disappear easily.

One research survey of couples in second marriages suggests that the same sexual problems often reappear as well (Kolodny, 1983). These problems are not always apparent before the remarriage since sexual problems, such as low sexual desire, may be temporarily overcome by the excitement of a new romance and by the special attentions that each partner pays to the other. When the romance dies down to a low flickering flame and sex is attempted not in romantic circumstances, but after bathing three kids, washing the dishes, paying the bills, and arguing about

who is going to take the garbage out, it is no surprise that sexual feelings are not at an ecstatic peak. In addition, some couples may decide to marry even when they realize that a sexual problem is present. They may either hope that the problem will disappear with time — which is generally unlikely — or they may adopt a "who cares" attitude that deliberately deemphasizes the role of sex even before the marriage begins.

Despite the fact that divorce doesn't always provide as neat a solution to problems as many people think it will, there are certainly many instances in which divorce is the soundest option available. Knowing when to put an end to an unpleasant or painful relationship is often a key step toward creating the chance for a new start.

By their mid- to late thirties, most married people have moved beyond the demands of early parenthood and have acquired a sense of maturity and security in their own world. Individuals who have chosen not to marry have typically worked through whatever uncertainty may have surrounded this lifestyle choice at an earlier age. For both men and women, this is a time of becoming one's own person (Levinson et al., 1978; Frieze et al., 1978) and making decisions about future life directions. Women with teenage children begin to look ahead toward establishing life goals outside the home. Others who have postponed childbearing face final decisions about whether to proceed with having a family. Although this might seem to be, at last, the attainment of equilibrium and stability, it is often just the lull before the storm.

MIDDLE ADULTHOOD

At around forty, people enter a period of transition from their younger years to what has traditionally been called "middle age." It is a time when the visions and energy of youth begin to give way to hard realities and when most people first confront their own mortality and sense that time is running out. Some feel alarmed because their physique has folded and their youth "has flown the coop," never to be regained (despite attempts at fancy diets, jogging, hair dye, and face-lifts). For most people, life must be reappraised in terms of goals, accomplishments, and experiences. As a result, a midlife crisis sometimes begins to take shape (Howells, 1981).

From a sexual perspective, the male seems to be particularly vulnerable to the midlife crisis. Since rumor has it that after age forty a man is "over the hill" sexually, many men begin to check their sexual performance for signs of wear and tear. This is well-described in the following:

> He notes that it takes more time to become aroused. Where it used to be a matter of seconds and a mere glance at the orbs of flesh colliding beneath a pair of tennis shorts, he may take minutes or more to reach erection as he gets older. He also notices, correctly, that he is slower on the comeback. In the sweet agonies of teen age he may have walked about with an erection all day, seldom completely losing it even after he made love or masturbated — a virtual prisoner of his hormones and tight-fitting pants. But now each sexual act has a definite beginning and end, and it may be a matter of hours or all day before he can reach erection again. Comparisons, stinging comparisons . . . he is not the boy he once was. (Sheehy, 1976, p. 305)

Once a man begins to question his sexual capabilities, the odds are that he will experience difficulty getting or keeping an erection. This, of course, "proves" the correctness of the underlying concern, and a vicious cycle is set in motion.

Some men turn to younger sexual partners to heat up their passion and others succeed, at least to a certain degree, in blaming the problem on their wives. But the middle-aged male is in a precarious position of sexual vulnerability. If he goes to a physician to discuss the problem, he may be told (as several of our patients have been), "At your age, you shouldn't worry about it anymore."

The woman's midlife crisis is less apt to include concern about her sexual capacity. For women who have chiefly been mothers, it is a time for an emerging identity, a freeing of the inner self as children reach a relative stage of greater independence. It is a bittersweet time in which a woman who has not established a career or nonfamily interests may mourn the passing of her offspring into their own maturity and may simultaneously look at available options for redirecting her talents and energy. As children leave home, the "empty-nest syndrome" may strike, causing depression and listlessness as the woman tries to deal with too much unstructured time and few sources of rewarding or interesting activities (Frieze et al., 1978). Since these vulnerable feelings may be followed by or coincide with the menopausal years, it may be a particularly trying period for such women. Interestingly, recent research suggests that it is not only women who may be affected by the empty-nest syndrome. Roberts and Lewis (1981) point out that men are also sometimes distressed by their children's departure from home, "discovering that their marriages and friendships had become empty shells about the same time that loved children were leaving." Of course, having children leave home can have positive effects on a marriage, too — for instance, it gives couples a chance to focus on their own interaction and can create opportunities for freer, more relaxed sex as well.

There are more and more variations on the midlife transition today. Career-oriented women who postponed motherhood (and time off from work) until their mid-thirties may be anxious to reconfirm their work identity, but may have trouble finding a job or getting back on the "fast track." Other mothers who refused to restructure their lives around childrearing and continued to work outside the home — either by choice or by economic necessity — may feel considerable guilt or exhaustion. Still other women find their lives complicated by divorce and face childrearing as a single parent; alternatively, if they remarry a man with children of his own, the family interactions may become particularly complex.

Another component of the midlife crisis for both sexes that has been generally overlooked is the phenomenon of sexual burnout, which may affect as many as 20 percent of people in this stage of the life cycle (Kolodny, 1983). Unlike occupational burnout which occurs largely in reaction to a person's intense investment of time and energy in his or her work coupled with chronic, unrelenting emotional pressure (Pines, Aronson, and Kafry, 1981), sexual burnout stems from tedium and satiation with the same sexual routines. More than simply boredom, which can certainly be one of its precursors, sexual burnout is typically marked by a sense of physical depletion, emotional emptiness, and a negative sexual self-concept. Caught in the throes of sexual burnout, the middle-aged adult develops a feeling of sexual helplessness and hopelessness, as though nothing can be done to rekindle erotic passion or pleasure. Sexual burnout occurs not only in married couples but also in singles who have previously been very active sexually.

Sexual burnout is not the same as the sexual disinterest that often accompanies depression. Depression is typically marked by disturbances in sleep and appetite and by a general loss of pleasure in all or almost all usual activities or pastimes. People experiencing sexual burnout do not have these symptoms. While the prognosis for sexual burnout is generally good since most people recover spontaneously from this syndrome over time, about 10 percent of those affected remain sexually inactive on a relatively permanent basis. Perhaps this indicates that they are happier with celibacy than with cultural stereotypes that prescribe sexual participation as obligatory for a "healthy" adulthood, or perhaps it shows their inability to overcome the negative effects of the sexual burnout syndrome.

Of course, not everyone experiences a full-blown midlife crisis, and for some, the forties and fifties are a time of happiness and sexual satisfaction. One woman told us, "I'd never want to be twenty-one again — being forty-five is more fun!"

Most men have "discovered" their sexuality in a joyous way by their twenties, but — at least in past generations — a sizeable number of women did not awaken from their socially programmed sexual dormancy until their thirties or forties. Given the traditional limits set on female sexual behavior and feelings ("nice girls don't . . .") and given the traditional division of marital responsibilities (domestic and child-bearing duties are "female," career orientation is "male"), this pattern should come as no surprise. As a result, many women undergo a process of sexual self-discovery in mid-adulthood, perhaps including being orgasmic for the first time. Although not written about extensively, the woman in this phase of the life cycle is just as likely as her mate to seek out extramarital sexual opportunities (Fuchs, 1978; Wolfe, 1980; Grosskopf, 1983).

In a survey of 160 midlife women, Rubin (1982) found that the most characteristic pattern was one of *improving* sexuality. She noted that although these women had to overcome sexual inexperience and cultural prohibitions against female sexuality when they were younger (and then had to deal with raising young children), by midlife women were better able to relate sex to their own wishes and needs rather than participating in sexual activity principally to please their partners. Thus, Rubin found that midlife women take the sexual initiative more often than they previously had done (although, paradoxically, some of these women became concerned with putting sexual pressure on their husbands or partners by initiating sex too often).

One intriguing finding has been noted about sex differences in the psychology of middle adulthood. Among those forty to fifty-five, men are apt to exhibit a strong sense of self-confidence and control and typically engage in behavior geared to show their power and proficiency, while women tend to be more dependent, passive, and lacking in confidence. By the late fifties, however, a decided shift occurs. Men seem to move away from their need to demonstrate power and mastery and begin to show more concern for emotional sensitivity and interpersonal relations. At the same time, women frequently begin to show more self-confidence and assertiveness, in effect reversing the earlier roles that had been observed (Chiriboga, 1981). While the implications of this observation for sexual behavior are not entirely clear, it appears to lend support to the notion that some postmenopausal women become more sexually assertive than they had been previously, while men may become more interested in sharing tenderness and affection as they become less preoccupied with career concerns.

A few additional aspects of middle adulthood deserve mention. Some people who were content with being single as young adults begin to yearn for the commitment and long-term companionship that marriage can offer. These individuals may have a difficult time finding a potential mate who fits their expectations. For many in this situation, an increasingly acceptable alternative to the singles bar scene has been the "personal classified" ad section of a newspaper or magazine. It is intriguing to note that a substantial number of these ads run by women in their forties mention marriage as the objective, whereas in a recent review of more than a thousand personal classifieds we uncovered only two males in their forties advertising for a potential spouse. What we found, instead, were many ads from men in mid-adulthood looking for women twenty-five to forty years old to share "fun times" together. Since a recent survey found that ads placed by women get an average of 49 responses, while ads placed by men only draw 15

replies (Dullea, 1984), it is unclear what the exact meaning of this finding is.

While society has long accepted the practice of middle-aged men seeking younger women in an effort to find rejuvenation, friends and family and society in general often view a middle-aged woman's romance with a younger man as improper or shocking (Derenski and Landsburg, 1981). Today, perhaps in part because of higher divorce rates and a larger number of women gaining status and independence through career pursuits, it is no longer rare to see a middle-aged woman dating a man five to ten years or more her junior. There is, however, one typical difference between these relations and those of the middle-aged (or older) male with a younger female partner. The physical attractiveness of the older male seems to be of only minor importance to his desirability compared to his status or power, while the middle-aged woman generally needs to be relatively good-looking in order to attract a younger male.

Contrary to popular misconceptions, there has not been a sudden upsurge in the divorce rate for people in mid-adulthood (Cherlin, 1981). In fact, most of the boring or unhappy marriages that survive to middle age will continue to old age rather than be dissolved by a midlife crisis (Friedman, 1981). For those caught in such marital inertia, there is apt to be a decline in sexual ardor at home, which can express itself in a variety of ways. Decreased sexual desire frequently first appears at this time, as earlier pretenses of enjoying sex together are shed in favor of more behavioral honesty. Sexual dysfunctions can also appear as a reflection of marital stresses or of the pent-up hostility of one spouse for another (Kaplan, 1974; Clifford and Kolodny, 1983). Extramarital involvement is another sexual possibility that can provide a sense of escape from a stagnant relationship along with the excitement of getting to know a new partner on intimate terms; this topic is discussed more fully in chapter 15.

Mary Tyler Moore (age 46) and her husband Dr. Richard Levine (age 32) are a well-known example of a middle-aged woman involved with a younger man. Relationships of this type (older woman–younger man) have become more common in recent years.

One recent study of middle-adult couples engaged in marital or sex therapy found that spouses placed little emphasis on committing time or psychological energy to their marital or sexual relations (McCarthy, 1982). In this sample, 80 percent of marriages had experienced an extramarital affair. The likelihood of stress in the marital relationship was somewhat higher when the wife was having an affair. McCarthy observed that this might be because the women in his sample tended to become more emotionally involved in their affairs than did the men, who generally focused on the sexual interaction.

Another revealing aspect of this study had to do with husband-wife differences in expectations about sex:

> Men's expectations tended to be extreme, either extremely high in terms of frequent, high-intensity sex (the "every sex is dynamite" myth) or an extremely low expectation — after having sex with someone for six months there is just no excitement (the "sex is not for marriage" myth).

The woman's views ran the gamut from romanticism to seeing sex as a duty. Many women had an underlying disappointment about their husband's attitudes toward marital sexuality and with their skills as lovers. Yet, the women were reluctant to initiate discussions about sexuality and even more hesitant to experiment sexually and explore with their spouses. (McCarthy, 1982, p. 10)

The sexual problems of mid-adulthood are not restricted to heterosexuals, although little attention has been given to the middle-aged homosexual population in America. Here, too, a wide variety of patterns is seen. Gay men in their forties may find that it becomes more difficult to attract younger partners on physical grounds alone. As a result, some homosexual males turn to paid male prostitutes, others become relatively celibate, and still others form long-term relationships that provide companionship and emotional support as well as sexual opportunity. Gay men who were previously in heterosexual marriages — including many who were fathers — often decide

Adult Sexuality

to divorce and change to an exclusively homosexual life.

It has been noted that some gay males who have put an emphasis on conquests, techniques, and the ideals of the youth culture develop much anxiety about aging (Levy, 1981). These men sometimes resort to face lifts or hair transplants to retain the illusion of their youthfulness (as some heterosexual men do, too) and they often develop depression or become alcoholic as a reflection of the negative sense of self they experience as their aging becomes more apparent (Gagnon and Simon, 1973; Saghir and Robins, 1973; Smith, 1982; Harry, 1982). However, most homosexual men do not encounter such difficulties; generally, they have the same types of problems as they grow older that heterosexuals have (Berger, 1982).

Lesbians are often able to make an easier transition into middle-adulthood because of the fact that more of them are in lasting, one-to-one relationships (Tripp, 1975; Bell and Weinberg, 1978; Kimmel, 1978). Nevertheless, while concern over physical attractiveness may not be quite as strong an issue as it is for some gay males, there can be intense jealousy that arises in these relationships "whenever the relationship is threatened by other women who might intrude and attempt to disrupt the coupling" (Levy, 1981, p. 125).

THE MENOPAUSE

With aging, all women reach an end to their fertility. First, there is a gradual decline in female reproductive capacity from age thirty on, reflecting both a drop in fertility and a higher rate of miscarriages (Schneider, 1978; Schwartz, 1982). In addition, abnormalities of the menstrual cycle become more frequent over thirty-five as the aging ovaries respond less efficiently to LH and FSH from the pituitary gland. After age forty,

the frequency of ovulation generally begins to decrease, and around age forty-eight to fifty-two, menstrual flow stops entirely in a process called the *menopause*.[1] However, since deciding when the menopause has occurred can only be done retrospectively — by convention, after one year without further menstrual flow — women who are sexually active at this stage of their lives should continue to practice birth control until it is certain they cannot become pregnant.

The timing of the menopause and the symptoms that accompany it vary greatly from one woman to another. Although the ovaries stop producing all but a minute amount of estrogen, and ovarian progesterone production ceases entirely, small amounts of these hormones are still present because of continued activity of the adrenal glands. LH and FSH levels typically become elevated after menopause.

Symptoms

Although about 80 percent of women experience symptoms due to their changing hormone levels, only a minority of menopausal women seek treatment for symptom relief (Weideger, 1977; Perlmutter, 1978). This is probably because the majority of symptoms are of a relatively minor nature and tend to disappear with time.

The most common symptom in the menopause is the *hot flash*, which affects 75 to 80 percent of menopausal women (Bates, 1981; Erlik et al., 1981). Typically, the hot flash appears suddenly as a feeling of warmth over the upper part of the body (very much like a generalized blush-

---

[1] The term "menopause" correctly refers only to a woman's last natural menstrual period. Many people incorrectly use the word menopause to refer to a time more correctly called the *climacteric* or the *perimenopausal years*, that is, the several years immediately before and after the menopause.

ing) and is accompanied by reddening, sweating, and, occasionally, dizziness. In some women, hot flashes are infrequent (once a week or less) but others have them every few hours. Hot flashes may last just a few seconds and be quite mild, or they may last for 15 minutes or more in the most severe cases (experienced by less than 10 percent of women). One particularly disturbing feature of the hot flash is that it occurs more often during sleep than in the daytime, in which case it is liable to awaken the woman abruptly and contribute to insomnia.

Current evidence suggests that hot flashes are due to a malfunction of temperature control mechanisms in the hypothalamus (Casper, Yen, and Wilkes, 1979; Bates, 1981; Erlik et al., 1981). Although estrogen deficiency seems to be a necessary condition for hot flashes to occur, and estrogen therapy effectively combats this symptom, hot flashes generally disappear spontaneously within a few years after the menopause even without treatment. In approximately 20 percent of affected women hot flashes persist for at least five years beyond the onset of this time (Perlmutter, 1978). Since this symptom is sometimes severe enough to interfere with everyday functioning and there is no test that can predict when hot flashes will disappear spontaneously, deciding whether to obtain treatment or not is very much a subjective decision for the woman.

Other changes also reflect prolonged estrogen deficiency (Soules and Bremner, 1982; Speroff, Glass, and Kase, 1983). Lowered levels of circulating estrogen predispose women to shrinking and thinning of the vagina, a loss of tissue elasticity, and lessened vaginal lubrication during sexual arousal, all of which may sometimes lead to painful intercourse. Other physical changes that may occur in the postmenopausal years include thinning of the breasts and the vulva and loss of mineral content in bones, resulting in a more brittle structure (a condition that is called *osteoporosis*).

TREATMENT

Although there has been considerable controversy in the last decade about the risks and benefits of estrogen replacement therapy (E.R.T.) in the menopause and postmenopausal years, strong scientific evidence shows that the symptoms we have discussed can be significantly alleviated by its use (Schiff and Ryan, 1980; Soules and Bremner, 1982; Council on Scientific Affairs, 1983). In fact, E.R.T. plays a preventative role in slowing the occurrence of osteoporosis, rather than just alleviating symptoms once they occur. Because there is also considerable evidence that E.R.T. increases the risk of cancer of the uterus (Mack et al., 1976; Greenblatt and Stoddard, 1978; Antunes et al., 1979), and an unsubstantiated but realistic concern that it may increase the risk of breast cancer (Ross et al., 1980; Jick et al., 1980; Gambrell, 1982), caution is certainly in order. The consensus of medical opinion seems to favor E.R.T. for several different reasons:

1. Adding a progestin to the latter part of the estrogen cycle materially reduces the increased risk of cancer of the uterus that arises from estrogen use (Gambrell et al., 1979; Council on Scientific Affairs, 1983);

2. Osteoporosis has now been recognized as a disorder of great seriousness, since it often leads to hip fractures in elderly women, and in 20 to 30 percent of cases, these women die due to the fracture or its complications (Miller, 1978; Paganini-Hill et al., 1981; Speroff, Glass, and Kase, 1983);

3. E.R.T. may provide protection against certain forms of heart disease.

Most authorities caution that E.R.T. should not be used indiscriminately and that it should be employed in the smallest effective dose for the shortest period of time compatible with the therapeutic need.

258

Psychological Aspects

In the past, just about every problem that could befall a woman was inaccurately attributed to the menopause. In eighteenth- and nineteenth-century Europe, for instance, physicians thought women decayed at menopause (Stearns, 1975), and "nervous irritability" was diagnosed in nine out of ten menopausal women (Ballinger, 1981). Mistakenly blaming emotional instability, depression, and other psychological problems on the hormonal changes of the menopausal years has not just been a practice of ancient history; it is a relatively common error in modern times that continues even today.

Ballinger (1981) finds no evidence for an increased rate of depression or major psychiatric disorders in the years following the menopause and points out that "emotional symptoms at this time of life, as at any other time, are influenced by a multitude of environmental and personality factors." Others contend that menopausal discomfort has been greatly exaggerated, that the menopause may actually be an adaptive, positive event, and that "the mythology surrounding the menopause is based less on the reality of the female experience than on the sexist interpretations of the female experience" by male physicians (Alington-MacKinnon and Troll, 1981).

Bart and Grossman (1978) also point out that much of the research on the menopause is methodologically flawed, particularly the portion related to psychological aspects of the menopausal years. They suggest that a woman's response to the menopause is in large part a function of her "premenopausal personality and life patterns" and note that menopausal depression (when it occurs) is far more a result of lack of meaningful roles for women and poor self-esteem at this stage in their lives than a reflection of hormonal changes.

While there is some disagreement about the impact of the menopause on female sexuality, several studies suggest there is characteristically a decline in sexual interest and possibly a loss of female orgasmic responsivity in the immediate postmenopausal years (Pfeiffer, Verwoerdt, and Davis, 1972; Zussman et al., 1981; Dennerstein and Burrows, 1982). Hallstrom (1979) studied 800 women in Sweden and found considerable evidence to support this premise; for example, the prevalence of weak or absent sexual interest increased progressively from ages thirty-eight to fifty-four, and a declining capacity for orgasm was reported for these same ages. However, Hallstrom also found that some postmenopausal women showed increased sexual interest and capacity for orgasm (see Table 9-3). On the other

TABLE 9-3
Incidence of Increased Sexual Interest and Capacity for Orgasm During Preceding Five-Year Period, by Age

Age (years)	Increase in Sexual Interest		Increase in Capacity for Orgasm	
	%	N	%	N
38	16	93	21	91
46	12	225	18	215
50	4	204	13	188
54	2	62	6	52

Source: Modified from Hallstrom, 1979, Table 2, p. 167.

hand, several reports (Masters and Johnson, 1966, 1970; Kaplan, 1974; Starr and Weiner, 1981) have noted that sexual interest may increase in the postmenopausal years. The discrepancy in these findings may be the result of inadequate research design that does not take into account factors such as the health status of study subjects and their spouses or sexual partners.

LATE ADULTHOOD

In America, sex is generally regarded as something for the young, healthy, and attractive. Thinking of an elderly couple engaging in sexual relations usually provokes discomfort. The idea of sexual partners in a nursing home seems shocking and immoral to most people. Despite these cultural myths, the psychological need for intimacy, excitement, and pleasure does not disappear in old age, and there is nothing in the biology of aging that automatically shuts down sexual function.

Biological Considerations
FEMALE AGING

Aging alone does not diminish female sexual interest or the potential of the woman to be sexually responsive if her general health is good. Specific physiological changes do occur, however, in the sexual response cycle of postmenopausal women. These changes do not appear abruptly or in exactly the same fashion in each woman (Masters and Johnson, 1966).

Typically, there is little or no increase in breast size accompanying sexual arousal, although breast sensitivity to stimulation continues. The sex flush occurs less often and less extensively than at younger ages, but this change has absolutely no effect on sexual feelings or functioning. Less muscle tension develops during sexual arousal, particularly in the plateau phase, which is not surprising since this corresponds to the usual decrease in muscle size and strength that occurs with aging. This reduced muscular tension may account (at least in part) for the re-

Bloom County, December 11, 1983. © 1983 Washington Post Writers Group; reprinted by permission.

duced intensity of orgasm that is sometimes experienced by women in late adulthood.

While clitoral response is not affected by aging, vaginal function changes in two different ways. First, reduced elasticity in the walls of the vagina leads to less expansion during sexual arousal. Second, vaginal lubrication generally begins more slowly than at younger ages and vaginal dryness may create some problems as the quantities of lubrication are somewhat reduced. This condition can be overcome if it causes discomfort either by estrogen replacement therapy or by the use of an artificial lubricant such as K-Y jelly.

Recent research has shown that the decrease in vaginal lubrication in postmenopausal women is the direct result of diminished vaginal blood flow that, in turn, is caused by low estrogen (Semmens and Wagner, 1982). In another recent investigation, Leiblum and co-workers (1983) found that sexually active postmenopausal women had less shrinkage of the vagina and higher levels of androgens and pituitary gonado-

tropins (LH and FSH) than sexually inactive women. This suggests that regular sexual activity may provide at least some protection against the physiologic changes of aging in relation to female sexual anatomy.

MALE AGING

The normal pattern of reproductive aging in men is quite different from women because there is no definite end to male fertility. Although sperm production slows down after age forty, it continues into the eighties and nineties. Similarly, while testosterone production declines gradually from age fifty-five or sixty on, there is usually no major drop in sex hormone levels in men as there is in women.

About 5 percent of men over sixty experience a condition called the *male climacteric*, which resembles the female menopause in some ways. (Using the term "male menopause" to describe the male climacteric is incorrect since men do not have menstrual periods.) This condition is marked by some or all of the following features:

weakness, tiredness, poor appetite, decreased sexual desire, reduction or loss of potency, irritability, and impaired ability to concentrate (Kolodny, Masters, and Johnson, 1979; Greenblatt et al., 1979). These changes occur because of low testosterone production, and they can be reversed or improved by testosterone injections. It should be stressed that *most* men do not have a recognizable climacteric as they age.

The physiology of male sexual response is affected by aging in a number of ways. The following changes have been noted in men over 55:

1. It usually takes a longer time and more direct stimulation for the penis to become erect;
2. Erections tend to be less firm, on average, than at earlier ages;
3. The testes elevate only part-way up to the perineum, and do so more slowly than in younger men;
4. The amount of semen is reduced, and the intensity of ejaculation is lessened;
5. There is usually less physical need to ejaculate;
6. The refractory period − the time interval after ejaculation when the male is unable to ejaculate again − becomes longer (Masters and Johnson, 1966).

In addition, the sex flush usually does not occur in aging men, and muscle tension during sexual arousal is reduced, as in women, since muscle mass and strength generally decreases with aging.

Although the changes in male sexual physiology described above do not usually occur abruptly or represent an impairment of function, men who are uninformed about these patterns may be frightened into thinking something is wrong with them. In other instances, a man's partner may be the one to become alarmed. For example, while many men find that they enjoy sex in their later years without ejaculating at every opportunity, partners who don't realize this may think it reflects poorly on their attractiveness or skill as lovers.

Some men have completely unrealistic expectations about what their sex lives *should* be as they age. While they wouldn't expect to run a mile as fast at age sixty-five as they did at age twenty-five (or to recuperate from their exertion as quickly), they expect to get rock-hard erections instantly in all sexual situations and are worried when they can't make love twice in one evening. The aging male, by misinterpreting these changes, is particularly vulnerable to performance anxiety.

Psychosocial Considerations

In part, our cultural negativism about sex and romance in the geriatric years is a reflection of an attitude called *ageism*, a prejudice against people because they are old, that is similar to the more familiar prejudices of racism and sexism in our society. As Butler and Lewis (1976, p. 4) point out: "The ageist sees older people in stereotypes: rigid, boring, talkative, senile, old-fashioned in morality and lacking in skills, useless and with little redeeming social value." These same authors observe that ageism in relation to sexuality is the ultimate form of desexualization: "if you are getting old, you're finished" (Butler and Lewis, 1976, p. 5).

Ageism is not restricted to heterosexuals, either, as this quote from *Gay and Gray: The Older Homosexual Male* (Berger, 1982, p. 191) shows:

> Many older gay men believe that younger gays react negatively to them. Most older gays feel that young people sometimes take advantage of them, do not welcome their company in bars, clubs, and bathhouses, do not care to associate or form friendships with them, and think they are dull company.

It is interesting to note that in a recent study, college students estimated that average married couples in their sixties had intercourse less than once a month and expected that married couples in their seventies had intercourse even less often (Zeiss, 1982). As we will see, these are underestimates of actual behavior, showing that young adults are susceptible to ageism in their thinking — at least when it comes to sex.

Kinsey and his colleagues (1948, 1953) were the first to examine systematically the effect of aging on sexual behavior. Although their studies indicated that sex continued well into late adulthood, they also described a general decline in the frequency of sexual activity for both men and women across the adult age range. A number of other studies confirmed these overall trends (Newman and Nichols, 1960; Pfeiffer and Davis, 1972; Martin, 1977), with most reports suggesting that the decrease in sexual activity is partly due to diminished health and partly a reflection of cultural attitudes and expectations.

More recently, a longitudinal study done at Duke University has found that patterns of sexual activity actually remain relatively stable over middle and late adulthood, with only a modest decline appearing in most individuals (George and Weiler, 1981). For example, men who were sixty-six to seventy-one years old at the start of this study had no overall decline in sexual activity scores over the next six years, and a majority of men and women in the fifty-six to sixty-five age bracket at the beginning of the study had stable rates of sexual activity during this same time period. However, in those over age sixty-five, 18 percent of the men and 33 percent of the women completely stopped sexual activity with their partners over a six-year period.[2]

Various studies of sexual behavior in late adulthood indicate that the male's declining interest seems to be the major limiting factor to continued sexual activity (Kinsey et al., 1953; Pfeiffer and Davis, 1972; Martin, 1977; George and Weiler, 1981). This declining interest, however, may say more about cultural expectations which become self-fulfilling prophesies than anything else. While the pattern of sexual activity among aged people varies considerably, coital frequency in early marriage and the overall quality of sexual activity in early adulthood correlate significantly with the frequency of sexual activity in late adulthood (Masters and Johnson, 1966).

It is interesting to note that most researchers who claim to be studying sexual activity rates in the elderly have actually restricted themselves to studying coital behavior, as though other forms of sexual activity "don't count." As Table 9-4 shows, many adults over sixty continue to masturbate (Kinsey et al., 1948, 1953; Rubin, 1965; Christenson and Gagnon, 1965; Catania and White, 1982), although these are almost entirely individuals who masturbated when they were younger. Not surprisingly, elderly people without sexual partners tend to masturbate more frequently (Catania and White, 1982). In couples over sixty, other forms of sexual stimulation continue to be utilized (for example, oral sex and manual stimulation); they not only provide some variety, but also can be a source of pleasure and

---

[2] The George and Weiler (1981) study was particularly well designed in ways that represent an important advance over prior studies of geriatric sexuality. In addition to being longitudinal rather than cross-sectional (so that each person's behavior could be tracked over time), they also included only married subjects, since marital status is a determinant of sexual opportunity and sexual behavior in old age.

TABLE 9-4
Current Incidence of Masturbation in Older Adults

Age	Male	N	Female	N
60–69	52.6%	152	47.1%	281
70–79	29.5%	95	49.1%	161
80–91	45.8%	24	34.5%	29

Source: Adapted from Table 15B, Starr and Weiner, 1981, p. 263.

closeness even if the male is unable to obtain or maintain erections (Starr and Weiner, 1981). Here is what one seventy-eight-year-old man told us:

> In my mid-sixties, I had a real problem getting it up. Sexual intercourse became impossible and I got very upset over it at first. But my wife just found other ways to excite me, and after a while — when I relaxed more, I guess — my problem disappeared. Now, even though she doesn't always want to have intercourse when I do, we still use our mouths and tongues on each other, and we plan to keep doing it, too. (Authors' files)

In late adulthood, the longer lifespan of women combined with their tendency to marry men who are their age or slightly older frequently creates a situation of widowhood. At the same time that fewer men of the same age are available as new sexual partners, younger men tend to focus their attentions on women under forty. Thus, sexual opportunities and social contacts with men are often extremely limited for these mature women who might otherwise be enthusiastic sexual partners.

In the last few years, a new trend is emerging in which not all women in the sixties or older who find themselves widowed or divorced are passively accepting their fate. Some women in this situation are using their ingenuity to find new partners, as shown by the following ad from the personal classified section of a well-known magazine:

> Tall, handsome intelligent man sixty to sixty-five, wanted for attractive, lively sixty-two-year-old widow with fantastic figure and modern values. If you're interested in romance more than golf, send a photo and your phone •. Box xxx.

Although a sixty-five-year-old widow (or widower) may have an interest in sexual activity, social pressures may prevent sexual opportunities or belittle their meaning via snide jokes (e.g., only "dirty old men" are interested in sex, and "dirty old women" should "act their age"). As prolonged abstention from sexual activity in old age leads to shrinking of the sexual organs (just as a healthy arm loses strength and coordination if put in a sling for four months), the older adult is truly faced with a sexual dilemma — "use it or lose it."

An often-neglected aspect of aging in our society is that many elderly persons are relegated to nursing homes or other long-term care facilities for health reasons, to "protect" themselves, or for the convenience of their children. Although research on sexual behavior in this population is understandably sparse, a number of authorities have spoken out in favor of making provisions in such facilities (such as making private rooms available) for those who desire sexual interaction (Kassel, 1976; McKinley and Drew, 1977; Miller, 1978; Wasow and Loeb, 1979). While most nursing home administrators seem opposed to this notion, and some facilities actually insist on segregating men and women even if they're married, both ethical considerations for protecting the rights of the elderly and more practical considerations having to do with maintaining self-esteem and personal well-being lead us to advocate change in this area. However, it should be noted that permitting sexual expression in the institutionalized elderly is not the entire solution to their plight. Additional steps must be taken to overcome loneliness and boredom in the nursing home environment so that these facilities are not unintentional prisons for our older adults.

In the United States, where there is little preparation or education for aging, it is not surprising that many people are uninformed about the physiological changes in their sexual function in their sixties and seventies. They may mistakenly view these normal "slowing down" processes as evidence that loss of function is imminent. Brief preventive counseling during middle age might result in significant change in this area, but changed attitudes toward sex and aging seem

Sex after Sixty

Contrary to the popular notion that sexual interest and prowess disappear in aging adults, research shows that many members of the over-sixty set continue to lead active sex lives. Here are some excerpts from personal observations offered in group discussions that were conducted in a retirement community after the participants saw a film on sexuality and aging.

A sixty-eight-year-old married man: I have to admit that I used to think that older people didn't have sexual relations. I never really thought about it in personal terms, though, so when I got to my sixties and found my needs were still there, I wasn't all that surprised.

A seventy-two-year-old woman: I think that the thing that surprises people is that we even think about sex, but why shouldn't we? If sex is still fun, and doesn't cost anything, and you've got a person you love to be with, it's no sin.

A seventy-six-year-old widow: I say that you're as young as you think you are. If you think you're over the hill, you will be in a hurry. If you leave all the fun to younger people, you'll just sit in a rocking chair feeling old.

An eighty-one-year-old man: To me, it's like knowing how to ride a bicycle. Once you learn, you never really forget. Even though my friends don't talk much about sex except to make jokes, I still think about sex and even have dreams about it. And a couple of years ago, when I was having trouble with my prostate, my doctor was certainly surprised when I told him I still have sex twice a week.

A seventy-one-year-old widow: I think it's perfectly alright to stop having sex whenever you want to. When my husband was still alive, we continued to love one another long after we stopped having sex.

A seventy-year-old married woman: You have to admit that sex isn't exactly the same when you get older. I enjoy myself, and I know my husband does, but the passionate responses simmered down years ago, and sometimes I think we respond more out of memory than excitement.

A sixty-nine-year-old widower: One thing that nobody ever talks about is the pressure you get from women if you're an eligible man who is reasonably healthy and secure. They flirt, they hint, they make outright propositions – and I don't always like it, although I must admit that sometimes I do. But it's embarrassing to find that you've got a willing partner and you're not capable.

even more necessary. What people must recognize is that given good health and the availability of an interested and interesting partner, there is no reason that sexual enjoyment should have to come to an end in late adulthood. Perhaps the ultimate test of whether we have lived through a sexual revolution will be if attitudes toward sexuality in old age are transformed.

SUMMARY

1. Young adults are more sexually active today than they were two or three decades ago, although there has been a general trend toward marriage at a later age. This has been accompanied by the relative disappearance of the double-standard regarding premarital sexual experience and a marked upsurge in the number of cohabiting couples.

2. Young adults are not completely free of sexual problems despite this shift in attitudes and behavior. Sexual dysfunctions and low sexual desire are common, sexual pressures abound, and there are signs of a growing disillusionment with casual sex.

3. Marriage tends to complicate sexual behavior in some ways (while simplifying it in others) and requires an integration of sex with other aspects of life. However, the climbing divorce rate in our society, with divorces occurring primarily among young adults, suggests that marriage is no longer regarded as a life-long commitment. And, while most divorced people remarry, they often find problems in their second marriages that are similar to those they had experienced before.

4. Middle adulthood is often initiated by a midlife crisis in which the male is particularly vulnerable in sexual terms. In some cases, the fe-

male's midlife crisis may coincide with her children leaving home and the onset of menopause. But for other women, mid-adulthood is a time of sexual self-discovery.

5. The menopause, which typically occurs around age 48 to 52, is the cessation of menstrual periods. Dramatic decreases in estrogen production in the ovaries in the perimenopausal years can cause a variety of symptoms, including hot flashes, shrinking and thinning of the vagina, decreased vaginal lubrication during sexual arousal, and osteoporosis. These symptoms can generally be prevented or alleviated by estrogen replacement therapy combined with cyclic use of a progestin (to minimize the risk of cancer of the uterus).

6. Although many psychological problems have been attributed to the menopause, current research finds no evidence of an increased rate of emotional problems in the postmenopausal years.

7. About 5 percent of men over sixty have a male climacteric, marked by symptoms such as decreased sexual desire, weakness, tiredness, and poor appetite. This condition is the result of a testosterone deficiency that can be corrected by testosterone injections.

8. In late adulthood, there are a number of biological changes in the sexual response cycle, such as decreased vaginal lubrication in women and slower erectile response in men. In both sexes, muscle tension is reduced. However, these changes do not generally prevent sexual functioning.

9. Sexuality in late adulthood is profoundly influenced by ageism and other cultural stereotypes that deny the normality of sexual feelings and capabilities at this stage of the life cycle. While health problems and lack of a partner may complicate sexual functioning, there is no inherent reason most elderly persons must stop enjoying sex.

SUGGESTED READINGS

Anderson, Barbara Gallatin. *The Aging Game: Success, Sanity and Sex After 60*. New York: McGraw-Hill, 1979. Straightforward facts about
the needs of aging individuals presented in a sensitive manner.

Berger, Raymond M. *Gay and Gray: The Older Homosexual Male*. Urbana, Ill.: University of Illinois Press, 1982. A humanistic, thought-
provoking study of a much-neglected topic.

Fuchs, Estelle. *The Second Season: Life, Love and Sex for Women in the
Middle Years*. Garden City, N.Y.: Anchor Books, 1978. A well-written, thoughtful commentary including valuable insights on menopause, divorce, and widowhood.

Gadpaille, Warren J. *The Cycles of Sex*. New York: Charles Scribner's Sons,
1975. A well-balanced life-cycle view of sexuality and sexual development from birth to old age.

Howells, John G., ed. *Modern Perspectives in the Psychiatry of Middle
Age*. New York: Brunner/Mazel, 1981. A useful collection of excellent review articles on topics such as the empty nest syndrome, divorce and middle age, and the psychology of the widow and widower.

Starr, Bernard D., and Weiner, Marcella B. *The Starr-Weiner Report on Sex
and Sexuality in the Mature Years*. New York: Stein and Day, 1981.
Results of a survey of 800 people over age sixty, presented clearly and
nontechnically.

10 Gender Roles

ON A TELEVISION soap opera, a self-confident, smooth-talking businessman seduces a beautiful but not too bright female secretary. A children's book describes a warm, caring, stay-at-home mother while depicting father as an adventuresome traveller. A newspaper advertisement for cigarettes shows a husky young man enthusiastically dousing a shapely, squealing female companion with water, her wet T-shirt clinging to her bust — the headlined caption reads "Refresh Yourself." Each of these messages tells us something about stereotypes and sexism.

In the past twenty-five years, there has been considerable scientific interest in studying differences and similarities between the sexes for a number of reasons. First, various beliefs about sex differences in traits, talents, and temperaments have greatly influenced social, political, and economic systems throughout history. Second, recent trends have threatened age-old distinctions between the sexes. In 1981, for instance, more than half of American women worked outside the home. Unisex fashions in hairstyles, clothing, and jewelry are now popular. Even anatomic status is not fixed in a day where change-of-sex surgery is possible. Third, the women's movement has brought increasing attention to areas of sex discrimination and sexism and has demanded sexual equality.

As a result of these trends, old attitudes toward sex differences, childrearing practices, masculinity and femininity, and what society defines as "appropriate" gender role behavior have undergone considerable change. Many of today's young adults have been raised in families where a progressive attitude toward gender roles has been taught or where parents struggled to break away from stereotyped thinking. Thus, there is a continuum of types of socialization today that ranges from old, traditional patterns to more modern versions. This chapter will examine these issues and trends as they influence the experience of being male or female.

MASCULINITY AND FEMININITY

Before you read any further, you might take a few minutes to write out a list of the traits you would use to describe a typical American man and woman. If your descriptions are similar to most other people's, you probably listed characteristics like strong, courageous, self-reliant, competitive, objective, and aggressive for a typical man, while describing a typical woman in terms like intuitive, gentle, dependent, emotional, sensitive, talkative, and loving.

Most people not only believe that men and women differ but share similar beliefs about the ways in which they differ (Broverman et al., 1972). Beliefs of this sort, held by many people and based on oversimplified evidence or uncritical judgment, are called *stereotypes*. Stereotypes can be harmful because they lead to erroneous judgments and generalizations and can thus affect how people treat one another.

Because many stereotypes about sexuality are based on assumptions about the nature of masculinity and femininity, it is difficult to offer a concise definition of these two terms. In one usage, a "masculine" man or a "feminine" woman is a person who is sexually attractive to members

of the opposite sex. Advertisements for clothing and cosmetics constantly remind us of this fact. In another sense, masculinity or femininity refers to the degree a person matches cultural expectations of how males and females should behave or look. In the not too distant past, some segments of our society were upset when long hair became fashionable among young men or when women applied for admission to West Point because these patterns did not "fit" prevailing expectations about differences between the sexes. In still another meaning, masculinity and femininity refer to traits measured by standardized psychological tests that compare one person's responses to those of large groups of men and women.

According to traditional assumptions, it is highly desirable for males to be masculine and females to be feminine. If behavior matches cultural expectations, it helps to preserve social equilibrium and allows for a certain amount of stability in the details of everyday living. Conformity to cultural norms presumably indicates "adjustment" and "health," while straying too far from expected behavior patterns indicates abnormality or even disease. Finally, "masculine" men and "feminine" women are relatively predictable and behave in ways that are fairly consistent and complementary. Fortunately (or unfortunately, depending on your viewpoint), it now appears that masculinity and femininity are unlikely to tell us much about personality, sexual preferences, or lifestyle, and old stereotypes are now giving way to more useful and dynamic scientific views.

The traditional approach to studying masculinity and femininity looked at these traits as opposites. According to this view, if you possess "feminine" characteristics you cannot have "masculine" characteristics and vice versa (Spence and Helmreich, 1978). It was assumed that people who scored high on certain traits judged as masculine (e.g., independence, competitiveness) would also have a general lack of femininity. As a result, most psychological tests designed to measure masculinity and femininity were set up as a single masculinity-femininity scale (Kaplan and Sedney, 1980). Furthermore, men and women whose masculinity or femininity scores differed substantially from group averages were judged to be less emotionally healthy and less socially adjusted than others with "proper" scores.

Recent research findings have changed this approach. Instead of viewing masculinity and femininity as opposites, various behavioral scientists now look at them as separate characteristics that coexist to some degree in every individual (Bem, 1972; Spence and Helmreich, 1978). Thus, a woman who is competitive can be quite feminine in other areas; a man who is tender and loving may also be very masculine. As we discuss the ways in which gender roles are learned and the impact they have on our lives, it will be helpful to keep this viewpoint in mind.

PATTERNS OF GENDER-ROLE SOCIALIZATION

Even before a baby is born, parents are likely to have different attitudes about the sex of their child. In most societies, male children are clearly preferred over female children (Markle, 1974; Coombs, 1977), and having a son is more often seen as a mark of status and achievement than having a daughter (Westoff and Rindfuss, 1974). This preference probably stems from the belief that men are stronger, smarter, braver, and more productive than women, and that "it's a man's world" (certainly true in the past) — meaning that there are more and better educational, occupational, political, and economic opportunities open to males than to females.

Parents often try to guess the sex of their unborn child and may construct elaborate plans and ambitions for the child's life. If the child is thought to be a boy, the parents are likely to think of him as sports oriented, achievement oriented, tough, and independent. If the child is thought to be a girl, parents are more apt to envision beauty, grace, sensitivity, artistic talents, and marriage. These different attitudes are nicely shown in lyrics from the Broadway musical *Carousel* as a father-to-be dreams about his unborn child:

> I'll teach him to wrassle, and dive through a
>   wave,
> When we go in the mornin's for our swim.
> His mother can teach him the way to behave,
> But she won't make a sissy out o' him . . .
> He'll be tall and as tough as a tree, will Bill!
> Like a tree he'll grow, with his head held high
> And his feet planted firm on the ground,
> And you won't see nobody dare to try
> To boss him or toss him around! . . .
>
> Wait a minute! Could it be —
> What the hell! What if he is a girl? . . .
>
> She mightn't be so bad at that,
> A kid with ribbons in her hair!
> A kind o' neat and petite
> Little tin-type of her mother! What a pair!
> My little girl, pink and white
> As peaches and cream is she.
> My little girl is half again as bright
> As girls are meant to be!
> Dozens of boys pursue her,
> Many a likely lad does what he can to woo her.*

This sort of prenatal thinking is one form of stereotyping, as is guessing that the baby will be a boy because "he" kicks a lot inside the uterus. It is not surprising then to find that the earliest in-

---

* "Soliloquy," by Richard Rodgers & Oscar Hammerstein, II. Copyright © 1945 Williamson Music, Inc. Copyright renewed. Sole selling agent and manager of all rights: T. B. Harms Company c/o The Welk Music Group, Santa Monica, CA 90401. International Copyright secured. All rights reserved; Used by permission.

Children's play patterns often contradict cultural gender-role stereotypes, although parents and teachers sometimes become uncomfortable when this occurs.

teractions between parents and their newborn child are influenced in subtle ways by cultural expectations.

Birth and Infancy

At the moment of birth, the announcement of the baby's sex ("It's a boy" or "It's a girl") sets in motion a whole chain of events such as assigning a pink or blue identification bracelet, choosing a

name, selecting a wardrobe, and decorating the baby's room, each of which involves making distinctions between males and females.[1]

As friends, relatives, and parents discuss the newborn's appearance, gender stereotypes are everywhere: "Look at his size — he'll be a football player, I bet." "She has beautiful eyes — she's a real doll." "See how intelligent he looks!" "She's got great legs already! You'll have to work to keep the boys away." Informal banter about the child's future is also likely to be gender-linked: if friends remark, "You better start saving for the wedding," you can bet they are not talking about a baby boy.

Parents of newborn infants describe daughters as softer, smaller, finer-featured, and less active than sons, although no objective differences in appearance or activity level were noted by physicians (Rubin, Provenzano, and Luria, 1974). In early infancy, boys receive more physical contact from their mothers than girls do, while girls are talked to and looked at more than boys (Lewis, 1972) — a difference in treatment which tends to reinforce a female's verbal activities and a male's physical activity. Walum (1977) reports an exploratory study in which two groups of young mothers were given the same six-month-old infant dressed either in blue overalls and called Adam or wearing a pink frilly dress and called Beth: the results showed that "Beth" was smiled at more, given a doll to play with more often, and viewed as "sweet" compared to "Adam." Another recent study confirms the fact that both mothers and fathers behave differently toward unfamiliar infants on the basis of perceived sex,

---

[1] In the song "A Boy Named Sue," written by S. Silverstein and recorded by Johnny Cash, the father reversed usual gender distinctions in name selection in order to achieve the paradoxical effect of improving his son's masculinity. By giving him the name Sue, the father forced the boy to fight frequently to defend himself from ridicule, thus becoming "tough."

although the parents were unaware of this differential treatment (Culp, Cook, and Housley, 1983).

Parents respond differently to infant boys and girls in other ways. They react more quickly to the cries of a baby girl than a baby boy (Frieze et al., 1978) and are more likely to allow a baby boy to explore, to move further away, or to be alone, thus fostering independence. In contrast, the baby girl seems to be unintentionally programmed in the direction of dependency and passivity (Weitzman, 1975; Long Laws, 1979).

Gender differences in socializing children occur for reasons that are not fully understood at present. Certainly, cultural influences are important, but biological factors may also be involved. For example, boys' higher rates of metabolism, greater caloric intake, and higher rates of activity may prepare them for earlier independence, or parental encouragement of independence may reflect cultural expectations (Walum, 1977). Furthermore, the different prenatal hormone exposures of males and females may possibly account for behavioral differences in infancy. Often, parents are unaware of how their actions with their children are different depending on the child's sex. Nevertheless, differential socialization seems to occur even in parents who are philosophically committed to the idea of avoiding gender stereotypes (Scanzoni and Fox, 1980).

Early Childhood (Ages Two to Five)

By age two, a child can determine in a fairly reliable way the gender of other people and can sort clothing into different boxes for boys and girls (Thompson, 1975). However, two year olds do not usually apply correct gender labels to their own photographs with any consistency — this ability usually appears at around 2½ years. As already mentioned, core gender identity, the personal sense of being male or female, seems to solidify by age three. This process is probably assisted by the acquisition of verbal skills which allow children to identify themselves in a new dimension and to test their abilities of gender usage by applying pronouns such as "he" or "she" to other people.

At age two or three, children begin to develop awareness of gender roles, the outward expression of maleness or femaleness, in their families and in the world around them. It might seem that the child forms very sketchy impressions at first — "Mommies don't smoke pipes" or "Daddies don't wear lipstick" — but the toddler's understanding is greater than his or her ability to verbally express it. It is likely that impressions of what is masculine and feminine form across a broad spectrum of behaviors.

The serious business of young childhood is play, so by examining the objects used in play activities we may be able to learn something about gender-role socialization. Walk through the toy department of a large store and you will quickly see the principle of differential socialization at work. Boys' toys are action-oriented (guns, trucks, spaceships, sports equipment) while girls' toys reflect quieter play, often with a domestic theme (dolls, tea sets, "pretend" make-up kits, or miniature vacuum cleaners, ovens, or refrigerators). Where a particular toy is marketed to both girls and boys, the version for girls is usually feminized in certain ways. For instance, a boys' bicycle is described as "rugged, fast, and durable." The girls' model of the same bike has floral designs on the seat and pretty pink tassels on the hand-grips and is described as "petite and safe." A detailed analysis of the content of ninety-six children's rooms showed that boys were given more toy cars and trucks, sports equipment, and military toys, while girls received many more dolls, doll houses, and domestic toys (Rheingold and Cook, 1975). Although many boys today play with "E.T." or

Gender Roles

Nonsexist Childrearing

Letty Pogrebin, founder of *Ms.* magazine, offers straightforward advice to parents concerned with nonsexist childrearing in her book *Growing Up Free: Raising Your Child in the 80's.* Here are some of her suggestions for raising a parent's consciousness of gender role stereotypes and subsequent behavior.

Parents are children's chief role models and should set strong examples of nonsexist behavior. Both parents, for example, should share equally in basic childcare (changing diapers, feeding, bathing) as well as fun activities (going to the park, playing, teaching). Parents should also banish preconceptions about how baby boys and girls act. Do you expect boys to move more or cry more? Do you always describe male infants as strong or tough and female infants as pretty?

Avoid sexism in selecting furniture, decor, and toys for your child. Choose neutral colors like green and yellow for children's bedrooms instead of pink for girls, blue for boys. Pick sturdy furniture that children are not afraid to *live* in. French Provincial, with its whites and golds, delicate carvings and canopy, can make a girl feel trapped into a forced daintiness. Scenes of cowboys slaughtering Indians on your little boy's bedspread can help produce an indifference to violence. Would a boy *or* girl feel equally comfortable in your child's room? Be sure to provide lots of creative toys either sex can enjoy, such as paints, crayons, clay, or a box of old clothes for make-believe dress-up. Could you give your child's toy box to a child of the opposite sex? Which toys would not work?

Pay attention to how you deal with discipline and praise. Do you use more verbal punishment for girls and more physical punishment for boys? Are both sexes scolded for the same things, or is Tommy allowed to get dirty and Sally allowed to cry longer when she is hurt? Do you compliment girls more on their appearance and boys more on their achievements?

Do not forget that television provides your child with role models and "information." Monitor your children's programs to stay in touch with the kinds of shows they watch and the amount of time spent in front of the TV. Teach your children how to be critics. Point out what you consider good and bad in a program. When all else fails you can always turn the TV off or give it away and hope your children do not spend their afternoons watching a friend's TV.

Stay abreast of your child's school experience to detect signs of sexism. Review your children's school books for "noticeably absents," like whole history texts with no references to significant females or minority figures. Push for sex integrated classes in home economics and industrial arts. Teaching children only "traditional" gender-linked skills reinforces traditional gender role behavior because of unfamiliarity. Also ascertain teachers' attitudes, realizing that this is a difficult task because sexist teaching can be subtle and unconscious. Teachers may expect (and thus receive) a better performance from boys in math and from girls in English. A close relationship with the teacher, fostered by parent/teacher conferences and attendance at school board meetings, can help uncover and correct sexist attitudes.

Discuss occupational opportunities with your child in a nonsexist way. Children should be *shown* that males and females can successfully handle jobs that were traditionally "male" or "female." Visit a female pediatrician. Find pictures of men who are nurses. Point out the men in an opera or ballet and the women who are plumbers, construction workers, and athletes. Discuss men who tend to the children and the house while their wives work.

These suggestions are not infallible blueprints to control your child's development, but they *can* help you create an atmosphere that fosters gender role flexibility.

"Star Wars" dolls or other action-oriented figures, most parents of boys are likely to become concerned if their sons develop a preference for frilly, "feminine" dolls (Collins, 1984).

Picture books are another important source for learning gender roles. As Weitzman (1975, p. 110), observes, "Through books, children learn about the world outside their immediate environment: they learn what is expected of children of their age." Although in recent years some changes have occurred, an analysis of award-winning books for preschoolers showed marked evidence of gender role bias (Weitzman et al., 1972). First, males were shown much more frequently than females (there were 261 males and 23 females pictured, a ratio of eleven to one). Second, most males were portrayed as active and independent, while most females were presented in passive roles. Third, adult women shown in these books were consistently identified as mothers or wives, while adult men were engaged in a wide variety of occupations and professions. It is no wonder that girls get a strong message that "success" for them is measured in terms of marriage and motherhood. Fortunately, this imbalance is beginning to change today, with many recent books aimed at preschoolers showing women in a more favorable light.

Television is also a powerful force in the gender-role socialization of young children because it provides a window to the rest of the world. The fictionalized world of Saturday morning children's cartoons is filled with gender stereotypes: the heroes are almost all males and females are shown as companions or as "victims" needing to be rescued from the forces of evil. Even award-winning children's shows such as Sesame Street have been criticized because women were seldom shown as employed outside the home and male figures predominated (Vogel, Broverman, and Gardner, 1970). Advertisements geared at preschoolers perpetuate the same patterns: boys are shown as tough, action-oriented people, while girls are portrayed as more domestic, quieter, and refined.

The School-Age Child

By the time children enter elementary school, gender-role expectations are applied with some unevenness. A seven-year-old girl who likes sports and climbs trees is generally regarded as "cute" and is affectionately, even proudly, called a tomboy. A seven-year-old boy who prefers playing with dolls and jumping rope to throwing a football is labelled a "sissy" and may be the source of great parental consternation. Although child psychiatrists regard tomboyishness in girls as a "normal passing phase" (Green, 1974), "effeminate" boys are thought by many researchers to require treatment to prevent them from becoming homosexual or having later sexual problems (Lebovitz, 1972; Green, 1974; Newman, 1976; Rekers et al., 1978).

Different patterns of gender-linked play continue during the school years and are now reinforced firmly by peer group interactions. School-yard and neighborhood play is noticed by other boys and girls, and children whose play preferences do not match everyone else's are thought to be "weird" and are often the butt of jokes. Since there is a powerful motivation to be like everyone else in order to have friendship and group acceptance, this teasing can have a negative influence on a child's sense of self-esteem.

At this age, boys are generally expected to show their masculinity by demonstrating physical competence and competitive spirit in sports activities, which becomes the primary focus of boyhood play. They are rewarded for bravery and stamina and criticized for showing fear or frustration ("Big boys don't cry"). Girls, on the other hand, although physically more mature than boys at corresponding ages in childhood, have traditionally been steered away from highly competitive sports and sheltered from too much exertion. (Today, this pattern is changing considerably as girls are encouraged to enter competitive swimming, gymnastics, soccer, and Little League baseball just as much as they are encouraged to take ballet or music lessons.) Girls are expected to stay clean and be neat, to avoid fighting, and to avoid dangerous activities ("Be a lady"). Young girls often seem to be programmed to cry to show hurt or frustration and find that crying (at least in the presence of adults) often elicits comforting. Thus, males are encouraged to solve problems in an active, independent way, whereas females are more likely to be shown that *their* best way of solving problems is to act helpless and to rely on someone else to take care of them.

Even for the children of relatively "liberated" parents, sexism sometimes inadvertently looms:

> Take my friend Irene, a vice-president of a Fortune 500 company, who at a recent dinner party bemoaned the stiff resistance of male executives to women in senior management. Not ten minutes later, she proudly regaled us with tales of her eight-year-old son who struts around the house shouting, "Boys are the best, boys are the best."
>
> In Irene's mind, forty- or fifty-year-old executives practice sexist oppression. But when her Jonathan shuts girls out, he is cute, natural ("It's the age," she told me), and turning out to be a "real boy." (Rommel, 1984, p. 32)

There are also, of course, instances where parents react differently to a child's seemingly sexist behavior. In one case, a mother who encountered her eight-year-old son telling his friends that girls are poor athletes took her son on successive weekends to watch the U.C.L.A. women's basketball team and to a women's weight-lifting contest. The boy apparently gained a different perspective on female athletic capac-

ity, because he was seen soon thereafter playing softball with a nine-year-old girl from down the street.

While these sorts of situations are of concern to some parents who want to raise their children in a nonsexist fashion, other well-meaning parents feel that since many young girls "shut boys out" and believe that "girls are best," this is not really sexist at all. They point out that while these responses aren't appropriate for adults, such attitudes foster self-esteem in children.

Much of the child's time is spent in school, where gender role stereotypes still exist in many classrooms. Elementary school readers show many more male figures than females (Saario, Jacklin, and Tittle, 1973). History lessons portray a view of the world as male-dominated; in the few instances when women are mentioned, they are usually in a subservient or domestic role (recall how Betsy Ross served the cause of the American Revolution by sewing). Girls are usually assigned different classroom "chores" than boys are (for example, boys might be asked to carry a stack of books, while girls are asked to "straighten up the room"), and teachers often assign activities to boys and girls based on their presumptions about gender role preferences. In one school, third-grade girls were asked to draw a mural while the boys were asked to build a fort. A girl who said she would rather work on the fort was told by her teacher, "That's not a job for young ladies."

School-age children are also exposed to obvious gender role stereotypes on television. From commercials children learn that most women are housewives concerned about important decisions like which detergent to use, which soap does not leave a bathtub ring, and which brand of toilet paper is softest. Men, on the other hand, are concerned about health issues ("Four out of five doctors recommend. . . ."), economics, automobiles, or recreation (most beer commercials play upon themes of masculinity, for example). With a few notable exceptions, the lawyers, doctors, and detectives on TV are all men, and women — even when cast in adventurous occupations — are shown as emotional, romantic sex objects who cannot make up their minds. It is no wonder that stereotypes about masculinity and femininity continue: children are exposed to them so widely that they come to believe they are true. Supporting this observation, McGhee and Frueh (1980) found that children who watched television more than twenty-five hours per week had more stereotyped gender role perceptions than age-matched children who watched less than ten hours of television weekly.

Adolescence

Adhering to gender-appropriate roles is even more important during adolescence than at younger ages. What was earlier seen as rehearsal or play is now perceived as the real thing. The rules are more complicated, the penalties for being "different" are harsher, and future success seems to hinge on the outcome.

Adolescent boys have three basic rules to follow in relation to gender roles. First, succeed at athletics. Second, become interested in girls and sex. Third, do not show signs of "feminine" interests or traits. Teenage boys who disregard these rules too obviously are likely to be ridiculed and ostracized, while those who follow them closely are far more likely to be popular and accepted.

The traditional prohibition of feminine traits in male adolescents probably relates to two separate factors. The first is the view of masculinity and femininity as complete opposites that was discussed earlier in the chapter. For a teenage boy to "fit" the male stereotype, he must be achievement-oriented, competitive, rational, independent, self-confident, and so on. If the op-

posite traits emerge, his masculinity is subject to question. Second, a teenage boy who shows "feminine" interests or traits is often regarded suspiciously as a potential homosexual. In a variation on this theme, in schools where home economics courses were opened to male enrollment, some parents have voiced concern that it would "rob" boys of their masculinity and lead to "sexual deviance" (Spence and Helmreich, 1978). However, in communities where boys take home economics and girls take shop courses, it is remarkable that an easy equilibrium has been reached, with no one "harmed" psychologically by the experience.

The adolescent girl is confronted by a different set of gender role expectations and different socialization pressures. In keeping with the traditional expectation that a female's ultimate goals are marriage and motherhood rather than career and independence, the prime objective seems to be heterosexual attractiveness and popularity. As a result, the adolescent girl's school experience may push her toward learning domestic or secretarial skills instead of orienting her toward a profession, and the message she gets — from peers and parents — is that academic achievement may lessen her femininity (Weitzman, 1975; Frieze et al., 1978; Long Laws, 1979). However, it appears that this pattern is now undergoing considerable change. As it has become more culturally "permissible" for women to enter professions such as medicine and law, or to enter the business world at the management level, more and more teenage females have become comfortable with maintaining a high level of academic success.

For many women, the high value that society places on both achievement and popularity poses a problem. One factor that seems to influence female nonachievement is fear of success, that is, being anxious about social rejection and loss of perceived femininity if success is achieved (Horner, 1972; Shaffer, 1981). This fear is not entirely irrational, as studies show that in adulthood, men often seem to be threatened by a woman who is more successful than they are, resulting in lower rates of marriage for high-achieving women (Frieze et al., 1978). Interestingly, a recent report notes that females who are masculine sex-typed have lower fear of success scores than those who are feminine sex-typed (Forbes and King, 1983).

Female adolescents also get mixed messages about the relationship between femininity and sexuality. While the traditional message about sexual behavior has been "nice girls don't," or should feel guilty if they do, the primary allure of femininity is sexual, and the "proof" of femininity is sexual desirability. But if femininity is to be valued, why not be sexually active? The dilemma lies partly in the cultural double standard that sanctions varied male sexual experience but regards the female with more than one partner as promiscuous.

To be certain, the traditional gender role stereotypes related to sexual behavior have been set aside by many adolescents. Teenage girls are much more apt to ask boys out today than they were twenty-five years ago and often take the initiative in sexual activity. This is seen as a major relief by some adolescent males, who feel freed from the burden of having to be the sexual expert, but is frightening to others who feel more

Public schools are now providing many opportunities for nontraditional gender-role activities. These teenage girls are taking a class in industrial arts.

comfortable with traditional sexual scripts. As one seventeen-year-old boy put it, "I don't like the feeling of not being in control. What am I supposed to do if a girl wants to make love and I'm not in the mood?" (Authors' files)

In many ways, the old "quarterback-cheerleader" idea of masculine and feminine gender roles during adolescence has broadened into newer, more complex, and less clearly defined patterns. Athletic, educational, and career aspirations have become less compartmentalized, styles of dress have been altered, and many colleges that were previously restricted to one sex have now become coeducational. Nevertheless, it is important to realize that the influence of traditional gender role attitudes continues to affect today's adolescents, showing that the present is still very much the product of the past.

Adulthood

Before proceeding any further with our overview of gender role socialization, two points must be made. First, our discussion has deliberately highlighted common denominators of this process while ignoring many sources of variability. To believe that children in Beverly Hills, Detroit, and rural Vermont are exposed to identical messages about gender roles is obviously incorrect. Differences in religion, socioeconomic status, family philosophies, and ethnic heritage all influence the socialization process: for instance, researchers have found that gender role distinctions are sharper in the lower class than in the middle or upper classes (Reiss, 1980). Second, to think that gender roles are entirely shaped in childhood or adolescence implies that adults cannot change. In recent years, however, many young adults have moved away from the traditional gender role distinctions with which they were brought up and have chosen alternate patterns with which they can live more comfortably. How this trend will ultimately affect future generations is not known.

Despite differences in upbringing and changing attitudes, our culture's gender role stereotypes usually come into full bloom in the adult years, although the patterns change a little. For men, although heterosexual experience and attractiveness continue as important proofs of masculinity, strength and physical competence (as in hunting, fighting, or sports) are no longer as important as they once were. Occupational achievement, measured by job status and financial success, has become the yardstick of contemporary masculinity for middle- and upper-class America.

For women, marriage and motherhood remain the central goals of our cultural expectations, although this stereotype is now beginning to change significantly. As more and more women join the work force, as more and more women are divorced, as more and more people choose childless marriages, the notion that femininity and achievement are antithetical is slowly beginning to crumble away.

Marriage is a fascinating social institution in which gender roles play out in some unexpected ways. Tavris and Offir (1977, p. 220) observe:

> The irony is that marriage, which many men consider a trap, does them a world of good, while the relentless pressure on them to be breadwinners causes undue strain and conflict. Exactly the reverse is true for women. Marriage, which they yearn for from childhood, may prove hazardous to their health, while the optional opportunities of work help keep them sane and satisfied.

Married men are physically and mentally healthier than single men (Weissman, 1980; Gurman and Klein, 1980; Scanzoni and Fox, 1980), but married women have higher rates of mental and physical problems than single women (Knupfer,

Clark, and Room, 1966). Gove (1979, pp. 39-40) suggests several aspects of gender roles and marriage that conspire to cause such problems:

1. Women usually have their "wife-mother" role as their only source of gratification, whereas most men have two sources of gratification — worker and household head.
2. Many women find raising children and household work to be frustrating and many others are unhappy with the low status of their "wife-mother" role.
3. The relatively unstructured and invisible role of the housewife is a breeding-ground for worry and boredom.
4. Even when a married woman works outside the home, she is generally expected to do most of the housework (and thus is under greater strain than her husband) and typically has a low-status, lower-paying job and must contend with sex discrimination at work.
5. The expectations confronting married women are diffuse and unclear; uncertainty and lack of control over the future often conspire to create problems and low self-esteem.

Fortunately, there are some positive indications that change is not just on the horizon but actually here in our midst today. Dual-career families are becoming common and more and more men are willingly participating in ordinary household tasks that were previously regarded as strictly "women's work." A small but growing number of men are staying home to be house-husbands while their wives pursue outside careers (Beer, 1983).

Adult gender roles hinge on areas other than marriage, of course. It is fascinating to see how the same status inconsistency found in many marriages also applies to situations outside the home. In the business world, very few companies have substantial numbers of women as executives (and the secretarial pool is unlikely to have many men). Although a young man who is successful in business is pegged as a "boy wonder," a young woman who achieves corporate success is sometimes accused of having "slept her way to the top." Medical schools and law schools only began to admit sizeable numbers of women in the last decade, and even then it took some prodding from the federal government. Furthermore, changes in admissions policies do not necessarily reflect an open-armed embrace. As one woman attending medical school put it:

> From the beginning, I could notice great astonishment that I was attractive *and* bright. My teachers seemed to think that only ugly women have brains. Then, there was a constant sense of being singled out for "cruel and unusual punishment." From the anatomy labs to the hospital wards, the female medical students were gleefully given the dirtiest assignments and made the butt of jokes. I never did understand why a woman physician examining a penis is so different from a male physician doing a pelvic exam, but this seemed to be a constant source of humor. (Authors' files)

Complicating matters even more, and showing how widespread sexism remains in our society, is the indisputable fact that many women who enter even the most prestigious professions are also subjected to sexual harassment. For instance, a recent report found that 25 percent of female students and faculty at Harvard Medical School had encountered varying forms of sexual harassment ranging from leering, sexually oriented remarks to instances of unwanted touching and requests for sexual favors (*American Medical News*, Nov. 11, 1983, p. 1). At Atlanta's old-line law firm of King & Spaulding, where a former female associate had filed a sex discrimination law suit to protest against being denied

Gender Roles

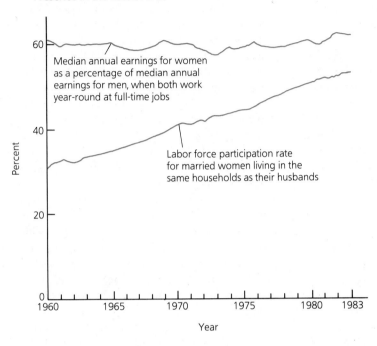

FIGURE 10–1
The Proportions of Women's Earnings and Their
Presence in the Work Force

Median annual earnings for women
as a percentage of median annual
earnings for men, when both work
year-round at full-time jobs

Labor force participation rate
for married women living in the
same households as their husbands

*Earnings figure for 1983 not available.

Source: The New York Times, Oct. 3, 1983. Reprinted by permission. Copyright © 1983 by The New York Times Company.

partnership, a summer outing for law students working at the firm featured a bathing suit contest for women at which one male partner proclaimed, "She has the body we'd like to see more of" (*Wall Street Journal,* Dec. 20, 1983, p. 1).

Not only do women have difficulty gaining access to nontraditional occupations, they are also frequently penalized by lower salaries than those for men and face more obstacles to advancing on the job (Figure 10–1). Furthermore,

when women are successful in their achievements at work, the results are more likely to be attributed to luck than to skill, dedication, or effort (Walum, 1977; Heilman, 1980). Another form of prejudice that women often have to overcome is shown in a recent research study that had 360 college students — half of them male, half of them female — evaluate academic articles that were presented as written by either "John T. McKay" or "Joan T. McKay." Although the same articles were used for the evaluations, with only the first name of the author varying, the articles supposedly written by a male were more favorably evaluated by both sexes than the articles supposedly written by a female (Paludi and Bauer, 1983).

Clearly, sex discrimination is a problem of today's world that will not disappear overnight (Heilman, 1980). However, there are certainly signs of changing times as women now enter "male" occupations like welding and making telephone repairs and as men increasingly infiltrate traditionally "female" occupations. One report estimates that from 1972 to 1978, the number of male secretaries rose 24 percent, telephone operators 38 percent, and nurses 94 percent (Hymowitz, 1981).

ANDROGYNY

While reading this chapter, you may have decided that your own personality reflects certain traits socially labelled as "masculine" and others viewed as "feminine." If so, you are like many other people; relatively few individuals are 100 percent one or the other.

In the recent past, as psychologists have discarded some older assumptions about the nature of masculinity and femininity, the concept of *androgyny* has attracted considerable attention. Androgyny refers to the combined presence of both stereotypical feminine *and* masculine characteristics in one person (Kaplan and Sedney, 1980). The word itself comes from two Greek roots: *andro,* meaning male, and *gyn,* meaning female.

Just what does it mean to say a person is androgynous? There is no firm agreement on this point among researchers. First, masculine and feminine traits could coexist but be expressed at different times. Kaplan and Sedney (1980, pp. 7-8) explain this dualistic model of androgyny as

follows: "She or he might disagree forcefully and assertively with a colleague on a major issue of program development, but act comfortably and caringly toward that same person's distress over a personal problem." In other words, he or she acts typically male then female. Or, feminine and masculine traits may exist in a fully integrated way within a person. Instead of alternating between feminine and masculine characteristics, the individual blends the two together. For example, an androgynous woman may initiate sexual activity (traditionally regarded as a "masculine" role) but do so in a style that is warm and sensitive (traditionally viewed as "feminine" traits). Thus, becoming androgynous does not imply losing the qualities associated with one's gender and taking on those associated with the opposite sex. It involves developing those opposite-sex qualities that already exist within us and manifesting them in ways determined by our own-sex qualities (Washburn, 1981, pp. 254-255).

Several recent studies by psychologists show that about one-third of college and high school students are androgynous (Bem, 1975; Spence, Helmreich, and Stapp, 1975; Spence and Helmreich, 1978). Spence and Helmreich (1978) found that androgynous individuals display more self-esteem, achievement orientation, and social competence than people who are strong in either masculinity or femininity, or those who have low scores in both areas. Furthermore, Bem's research has shown that androgynous individuals seem to have more flexible behavior than people with more traditional masculine or feminine patterns (Bem, 1972; Bem, 1975; Bem, Martyna, and Watson, 1976). Likewise, there is evidence that androgynous females may have fewer psychological problems than masculine- or feminine-stereotyped persons (Burchardt and Serbin, 1982).

However, androgyny may also have some disadvantages. A recent study of college assistant professors found that being androgynous was associated with greater personal satisfaction but an increased amount of work stress (Rotheram and Weiner, 1983). Jones, Chernovetz, and Hansson (1978) found that masculine males, rather than androgynous males, showed better overall emotional adjustment. Androgynous males had more drinking problems, while masculine males were more creative, less introverted, more politically aware, and felt more in control of their behavior. Furthermore, androgyny does not necessarily lead to more effective behavior or problem-solving (Spence and Helmreich, 1978; Kaplan and Sedney, 1980). In fact, a recent study of 236 college students found that androgyny does not help a person to be more versatile or adaptable; instead, it was found that for both sexes, the presence of "masculine personality characteristics, rather than the integration of masculinity and femininity, appears to be critical" (Lee and Scheurer, 1983, p. 304).

Confusing the issue even more is the fact that depending on how one measures self-esteem, different results may be obtained in studies of androgyny (Dorgan, Goebel, and House, 1983). With this research still in its infancy, it is too early to know if androgyny is a desirable goal for the future or a potential source of trouble. However, it does provoke many interesting questions about "traditional" male/female roles.

THE PSYCHOLOGY OF SEX DIFFERENCES

The controversy over the psychological differences between the sexes has long been steeped in myth. Some of the early researchers who determined which sex possessed "superior" skills are now being accused of using sloppy methods and male bias to insure the results affirmed male superiority. Times have changed, and a landmark study published in 1974 dispels many of these myths by concluding that the sexes are more alike than different.

Eleanor Maccoby and Carol Jacklin spent three years compiling and reviewing over 2,000 books and articles on sex differences in children to find which beliefs were backed by hard evidence and which had insufficient experimental support. Their study did not try to explain why these differences and similarities exist; Maccoby and Jacklin wanted only to describe the present state of the research — without bias.

To rate your own biases, take the following true/false quiz:

T F 1. Girls are more social than boys.
T F 2. Boys have higher self-esteem than girls.
T F 3. Girls are better than boys at simple, repetitive tasks.
T F 4. Boys have greater mathematical and visual-spatial abilities than girls.
T F 5. Boys are more analytical than girls.
T F 6. Girls have greater verbal ability than boys.
T F 7. Boys have a stronger motivation to achieve.
T F 8. Girls are less aggressive than boys.
T F 9. Girls can be persuaded more easily than boys.
T F 10. Girls are more alert to auditory stimulation; boys are more alert to visual stimulation.

The answers, based on the Maccoby and Jacklin research, are surprising.

Question 1 — There is no evidence to suggest that girls are more social than boys. In early childhood, both sexes choose to play in groups with equal frequency, and neither sex is more willing to play alone. Boys do not prefer inanimate objects over playmates, and at certain ages boys spend more time with playmates than girls do.

Question 2 — Psychological tests show that girls and boys are very similar in self-esteem throughout childhood and adolescence, but they pick different areas in which they feel they have greatest self-confidence. Girls believe they have more social competence; boys see themselves as dominant and powerful. These beliefs have no experimental support and probably spring from early social learning rather than an accurate assessment of their own abilities.

Questions 3 and 4 — Both sexes perform equally well at simple, repetitive tasks. Boys excel in mathematical ability from about age twelve and have an increased ability to perceive relationships among objects in space. Boys, for example, are better able to mentally rotate a picture of an object and to correctly describe its hidden side. This difference is not evident until adolescence, suggesting it may arise either from environmental factors (perhaps boys are given more opportunities to perfect this skill) or from hormonal influences.

While some authorities have questioned whether male mathematical superiority is a byproduct of cultural expectations (Kolata, 1980), the evidence seems to be somewhat divided. A study by researchers at the University of Chicago found no sign of sex differences in the ability to solve geometry problems among 1,366 tenth graders. Two other reports suggest, however, that biological influences may be important. In one study, researchers found that men with severe lifetime androgen deficiency had impaired spatial abilities compared to men with normal hormone levels or men who developed androgen deficiencies after puberty (Hier and Crowley, 1982). In another study, researchers have found additional evidence linking exceptional mathematical talent to hormonal status, suggesting that prenatal programming of the brain by androgens may predispose to later sex differences that may be magnified at the time of puberty by rising levels of the male hormone (Kolata, 1983). It is important to realize, however, that the sexes overlap considerably in their mathematical abilities, so this minor sex difference should not be used to counsel boys or girls in regard to courses or careers.

Question 5 — Boys are not more analytical than girls. To analyze, one must be able to recognize the important information in a situation uninfluenced by context or surroundings. Both boys and girls are as likely to respond to the unimportant elements in analyzing a problem.

Question 6 — Girls' verbal abilities mature more rapidly than boys'. Boys and girls remain about equal from infancy to early adolescence, but in high school and possibly beyond, females take the lead. Girls score higher on tests requiring the understanding of complex language, creative writing, analogies, fluency, and spelling. As with the boys' greater mathematical abilities, the girls' later increase in verbal ability may result more from socialization encouraging girls to perfect language skills.

Question 7 — Boys and girls can be equally motivated to achieve but by different factors. Girls are motivated to achieve when neither competition nor social comparison is stressed. Boys need direct appeals to their ego and a sense of competition to reach the girls' level of motivation.

Question 8 — Girls are less aggressive than boys, a difference exhibited as early as age two, when social play begins. Boys are more aggressive physically and engage in mock fighting and verbal forcefulness. Their aggression is usually directed at other male playmates rather than at the less aggressive girls. There is no evidence, however, that parents encourage boys to be more aggressive than girls — they actually discourage aggression in both sexes.

Question 9 — Boys and girls are both as likely to be persuaded by others and to imitate the behavior of people around them. Both sexes are equally affected by social pressure to conform. The only verifiable difference is that girls are slightly more likely to adapt their own judgments to those of the group, while boys are able to accept peer group values without changing their own values even when the two conflict.

Question 10 — Male and female infants respond alike to aspects of their environment that require hearing and sight. They are similarly skilled in identifying speech patterns, various noises, objects, shapes, and distances. This equality persists throughout adulthood.

An alternative approach for detecting differences between the sexes is the "brain-based" study. Neurologists and psychologists measure brain size and use tests such as the electroencephalograph (the "brain wave" test) to measure the brain's electrical response to stimuli. These studies reduce the possibility of experimenter bias because they do not rely as heavily on interpretations of observed behavior.

Major findings of these brain-based studies (published after the Maccoby and Jacklin research) point toward a neurological basis for some sex differences. Dianne McGuinness and Karl Pribram (1978), using an approach similar to Maccoby and Jacklin's, summarized the findings of a majority of these studies. They found that women have more sensitive taste, touch, and hearing. A woman's hearing in the higher ranges is so much better than a man's that a sound at 85 decibels seems twice as loud to her as to him. McGuinness and Pribram also concluded that women have better manual dexterity and fine coordination, are more interested in people, and are more attentive to sounds as infants. Since evidence is beginning to emerge showing some structural anatomic differences between the brains of men and women (Lacoste-Utamsing and Holloway, 1982), it seems that more brain-based studies will be required to clarify the current controversies in this area.

THE TRANSSEXUAL PHENOMENON

In 1953 the world was startled to learn about Christine Jorgensen, an American ex-Marine who underwent surgery in Denmark to convert his anatomical appearance from male to female. Since then transsexualism has achieved considerable notoriety. Jan Morris's autobiography, *Conundrum*, provides some fascinating details into her own transsexual odyssey. Renee Richards, an accomplished eye doctor and tennis player as a male, provoked quite a stir when she insisted on joining the woman's pro tennis circuit as a converted female.

Transsexual individuals persistently feel an incongruity between their anatomical sex and gender identity. They frequently describe their dilemma as "being trapped in the wrong body." Their psychological sense of existence as male or female (their gender identity) does not match the appearance of their genitals and secondary sex characteristics. Looking and being biologically male, the male transsexual wishes to change to female anatomy and live as a woman. Conversely, looking and being biologically female, the female transsexual wishes to change to male anatomy and live as a man.

Precise statistics on the prevalence of this gender identity variation are not available, but one estimate suggests the figure as one in 100,000 for male transsexuals and one in 130,000 for female transsexuals (Pauly, 1974). Among persons who contact gender identity clinics and request change-of-sex surgery, there are many more men than women (American Psychiatric Association, 1980). Although there has been considerable speculation about the possible cause(s) of transsexualism (Benjamin, 1966; Green and Money, 1969; Stoller, 1972, 1975; Green, 1974; Hunt, Carr, and Hampson, 1981), there is little agreement on this matter among re-

Well-known author James Morris, who underwent sex-change surgery in mid-adulthood, wrote about the experience in a book called Conundrum *and now uses the name Jan Morris. These photos were taken before and after the sex-change process was completed.*

searchers in the field. Both biological and psychological factors have been suggested as causes.

In the best defined cases of transsexualism, the person has a life-long sense of being psychologically at odds with his or her sexual anatomy. Typically, this psychological discomfort is partially (but only temporarily) relieved by pretending to be a member of the opposite, desired sex. Many transsexuals describe having had great interest in cross-dressing (i.e., wearing clothes of

the "other" sex) during childhood or adolescence. Transsexuals, however, should not be confused with *transvestites,* who cross-dress to become sexually aroused but usually do not want a permanent change of anatomy or appearance (see chapter 17). In at least some cases, discovery of transsexual impulses does not occur until adulthood.

Psychotherapy has been generally unsuccessful in resolving the transsexual's basic distress of feeling trapped in the wrong body (Tollison and Adams, 1979). As a result, those judged to be authentic transsexuals have been treated in programs designed to lead to change-of-sex surgery — in effect, redoing the body to match the mind. Since such surgery is irreversible, responsible practitioners take a cautious approach and require a one- to two-year trial period beyond the initial evaluation during which the transsexual patient lives in a cross-gender role (Meyer and Hoopes, 1974; Money and Wiedeking, 1980). During this time, the transsexual begins living openly as a person of the opposite sex, adopting hairstyles, clothing, and mannerisms of that sex, and also assuming a name that "matches" the new gender.

The transsexual male is given estrogens on a daily basis to produce a certain degree of anatomic feminization: breast growth occurs, skin texture becomes softer, and muscularity decreases, for example. However, treatment with estrogens does not remove facial or body hair (electrolysis is required) or raise voice pitch (some male-to-female transsexuals take voice lessons to learn to speak in a more feminine fashion). Estrogen therapy also reduces the frequency of erections and causes the prostate gland and seminal vesicles to shrink.

Transsexual women are treated with testosterone to suppress menstruation, increase facial and body hair growth, and deepen the voice. Surgery is required to reduce breast size. For both male and female transsexuals, hormone treatments are given throughout the trial period of cross-dressing and adjusting to a new set of gender roles. At the same time, the patient's progress is periodically evaluated by a psychiatrist or psychologist. Attention is also directed to achieving legal recognition of the sex-change and to personal matters, such as family or religious counseling.

If all goes fairly smoothly in the trial period and the transsexual is judged to be psychologically stable and able to adjust socially to the conversion, the final stage of treatment is surgery to change the sexual anatomy. At present, it is much simpler to perform male-to-female conversion surgery than the reverse. The male-to-female operation requires removing the penis and testes and creating an artificial vagina and female-appearing external genitals. The more difficult female-to-male procedure involves creating a "penis" from a tube made from abdominal skin or from tissue from the vaginal lips and perineum. While the artificial vagina created in the male-to-female transsexual often looks authentic and may allow a fairly full range of sexual response (e.g., vaginal lubrication and orgasm have both been claimed but not scientifically verified), female-to-male transsexual surgery creates an artificial penis that cannot become erect or feel tactile sensation.

In female-to-male transsexual surgery, it is sometimes possible to attain a degree of sexual function by implanting a mechanical inflatable device inside the penis to produce an artificial erection. Experience with this method is limited at the present time, and in any event, ejaculation is not possible. Many female-to-male transsexuals choose to have hormone therapy and surgical removal of their breasts and uterus but do not opt for an artificial penis.

Transsexual surgery is not a cure for this disorder but is only a procedure that may foster a sense of emotional well-being. Recently, the wisdom of surgery for transsexuals has been questioned by researchers who claimed to find no significant psychological benefits in patients who had undergone such operations compared to those who did not (Meyer and Reter, 1979). The matter is unresolved at present, although several prominent medical centers stopped doing transsexual surgery in 1980 because of the lack of solid evidence that the surgery is beneficial.

GENDER ROLES AND SEXUAL BEHAVIOR

The gender roles in most societies have a strong impact on sexual attitudes and behavior. For example, in America it is still widely thought that males are innately more interested in sex than females, that males characteristically assume an active role in sex while females are characteristically passive, and that male sexual arousal occurs quickly and automatically, while females require sweet talk and special handling and even then have only a precarious degree of arousability. Each of these stereotypes has some behavioral consequences: in general, men try to measure up to the cultural expectations and women often accept the notion of being second-class citizens from a sexual viewpoint.

By looking at a culture that has a very different set of expectations about sexual interaction, we can see how limiting these stereotypes are. In Mangaia, a tiny Polynesian island in the South Pacific, the cultural message is that sexual pleasure is for everyone. As a result: "Less than one out of a hundred girls, and even fewer boys — if, indeed, there are any exceptions in either sex — have *not* had substantial sexual experience prior to marriage" (Marshall, 1971, p. 117). Female sexual passivity is frowned on among Mangaians, and sexual intimacy does not require prior establishment of personal affection. Girls are expected to learn to be orgasmic at a young age, and although their first sexual experiences are likely to be with boys of their own age, older and more experienced partners soon become desirable because they can give more sexual pleasure (Marshall, 1971). One particularly interesting observation: "upon hearing that some American and European women cannot or do not achieve the climax, the Mangaian immediately asks (with real concern) whether this inability will not injure the

married woman's health" (Marshall, 1971, p. 162). On Mangaia, all women learn to be orgasmic.

The Double Standard

We have previously mentioned the double standard that applies to sexual behavior in our society. According to the traditional double standard, males are permitted to have premarital sexual experience while females are expected to remain virgins. After marriage, while fidelity is "officially" expected, it is acknowledged that men might roam and women are expected to remain faithful. In recent years, the double standard has undergone some subtle changes. Many teenagers have discarded the belief that female virginity is necessary or desirable (Sorenson, 1973; Hass, 1979) but it now seems that a young woman must wait for a "serious relationship" to have intercourse, while young men are not so strongly saddled with this expectation.

The double standard also assigns responsibility for being the sexual "expert" to the male. The male is expected to initiate sexual interaction, to control the timing and tempo, to select the proper activities to bring about his partner's arousal, and to bring his partner to orgasm. While this version of the double standard (the idea that sex is something a man does "for" a woman) may be an improvement on the older belief that "good" women had no sexual feelings (in this view, sex was something a man did "to" a woman for his own release), it hardly encourages flexibility and sharing.

The double standard and its variations can create a number of sexual problems. The female, for example, may develop a narrow view of sexual interaction. Feeling that she must prevent the male from "trying to get all he can," her potential pleasure is decreased by her need to set limits.

The male, on the other hand, may feel compelled to prove his masculinity by making sexual advances even when he is not particularly in the mood or attracted to his companion.

It now appears that the sexual double standard, like many other gender role stereotypes, is beginning to be replaced by concepts of equal opportunity and mutual interaction. To conclude this chapter, we will examine what lies ahead in this direction.

Sex and Equality

What a great many men and women are learning is that they cannot achieve the pleasure they both want until they realize that sex is not something a man does to or for a woman but something a man and woman do together as *equal participants*.

The woman who honors her sexuality learns that she can, when she chooses, express openly the full range of her excitement and involvement — the delight of wanting and being wanted, touching and being touched, seeing and being seen, hearing words and uttering them, of fragrances and textures, silence and sounds. The man who appreciates her as a partner can enjoy letting go of responsibility for her satisfaction and can savor her varying moods and desires in conjunction with his own.

The responsiveness of both partners is based on acceptance of each other as vulnerable human beings with unique needs, expectations, and capabilities. Both can express their creative impulses without fear of violating the gender role expectations of ladyhood or chivalry. Emotional needs, which vary with the mood, time, and place, are not labeled "masculine" and "feminine." Each partner can appreciate the other's sexual urges. If their sexual needs conflict at times, they can gently negotiate a solution — not as representatives of two different sexes but as two separate partners united by a mutual concern.

Sexual emancipation grows out of a sense of self-respect and personal freedom. If you are nothing to yourself, you have nothing to give and expect nothing in return. Sexually perhaps you might consider yourself useful, as an object is useful, but that is all. Before a true partnership is possible, both individuals must have pride in themselves and feel happy in being male or female.

At least half the potential pleasure of the sexual experience comes from how a partner responds. If there is virtually no reaction, or at best passive acceptance, the emotional current steadily weakens and eventually flickers and goes dead. However, with an actively involved partner, one individual's spontaneous feelings, spontaneously communicated, stimulate the other and heighten his or her tensions, impelling that person to act on his or her own impulses. Whatever she gives him returns to her and whatever he gives her comes back to him.

The relationship between the sexes is often conceived in terms of a misleading image: two on a seesaw. Power is the pivot, and if one sex goes up, the other must come down. What women gain, men lose. But the sexual relationship itself shows the analogy to be false. What men and women achieve together benefits both — the quality of life, as it is *individually* experienced, can be greatly expanded by a fully shared *partnership*.

SUMMARY

1. Masculinity and femininity are difficult to define concisely but can be looked at in terms of how closely a person's behavior or appearance conforms to cultural expectations of males and

females. Contrary to older views that looked at masculinity and femininity as mutually exclusive opposites, it is now clear that masculine and feminine traits coexist in many people. Persons having the greatest combination of masculine and feminine traits are called androgynous.

2. Gender role socialization patterns in our society provide many examples of ways in which boys and girls are exposed to different role models and receive different messages about what is appropriate to each gender. Clothes, toys, books, television, and school each provide different input to the child's socialization.

3. By adolescence, it becomes very clear that males are expected to "achieve" while females are expected to marry and raise children. Many females are led to believe that achievement detracts from their femininity and popularity. On the other hand, males are conditioned to equate their masculinity with their sexual proficiency and experience.

4. Gender role expectations in adulthood affect marriage, work, politics, and play. Sexual behavior has been strongly influenced by gender role stereotypes such as the double standard and the idea that men should be the sex experts. Cross-cultural evidence indicates that many male-female differences found in our society derive from stereotypic expectations.

5. Studies in the psychology of sex differences show that males and females are far more similar than different.

6. The transsexual has a persistent, life-long feeling of being trapped in the "wrong" body. The cause of transsexualism is unknown. Currently, there is a disagreement among sexologists about whether change-of-sex surgery is the optimal treatment for this disorder.

SUGGESTED READINGS

Kaplan, Alexandra G., and Sedney, Mary Anne. *Psychology and Sex Roles: An Androgynous Perspective*. Boston: Little, Brown, 1980. A well-balanced look at gender differences and gender roles from an androgynous viewpoint.

Long Laws, Judith. *The Second X*. New York: Elsevier, 1979. An opinionated but scholarly feminist view of female gender role socialization and the problems of women in today's society.

Maccoby, Eleanor E., and Jacklin, Carol. *The Psychology of Sex Differences*. Stanford: Stanford University Press, 1974. The definitive work on this topic. Tough reading but exhaustive in coverage.

Pleck, Joseph H. *The Myth of Masculinity*. Cambridge, Mass.: The MIT Press, 1981. A thoughtful, research-based view of the dilemmas of masculinity in our society.

Pogrebin, Letty. *Growing Up Free: Raising Your Child in the 80's*. New York: McGraw-Hill Book Company, 1980. A thorough, entertaining overview of current research on gender and childraising, with advice on how to decrease the effects of gender role stereotypes on your children.

Tavris, Carol, and Offir, Carol. *The Longest War: Sex Differences in Perspective*. New York: Harcourt Brace Jovanovich, 1977. A readable, often humorous, account of gender role socialization and its results.

11 Loving and Being Loved

WHEN William James wrote his classic *Principles of Psychology* in 1890, he devoted only two pages to "love." While noting the connection between love and "sexual impulses," James observed "these details are a little unpleasant to discuss" (James [1890] 1950, vol. 2, p. 439). D. H. Lawrence, the English novelist, was much less timid in dealing with this topic. In *Lady Chatterley's Lover* (1926), he suggested that love depends on being uninhibited in all respects, as illustrated in this bit of dialogue between Lady Chatterley and Mellors, her lover:

> "But what *do* you believe in?" she insisted.
> "I don't know."

"Nothing, like all the men I've ever known," she said.

They were both silent. Then he roused himself and said: "Yes, I do believe in something. I believe in being warm-hearted. I believe especially in being warm-hearted in love, in fucking with a warm heart. I believe if men could fuck with warm hearts, and the women take it warm-heartedly everything would come all right. It's all this cold-hearted fucking that is death and idiocy." (Lawrence, *Lady Chatterley's Lover*, p. 266)

Until very recently, the topic of love was more in the province of writers, poets, and philosophers than in the minds of psychologists and scientists. Even though it has been said that "love makes the world go round," few sexologists (including ourselves) have addressed this subject in any detail. Nevertheless, we have all felt love in one way or another. Many of us have dreamed of it, struggled with it, or basked in its radiant pleasures. It is also safe to say that most of us have been confused by it too. In this chapter, we will focus our attention on the complicated relationships between love, sex, and marriage in an effort to reduce at least some of this confusion.

WHAT IS LOVE?

Trying to define love is a difficult task. Besides loving a spouse or boyfriend or girlfriend, people can love their children, parents, siblings, pets, country, or God, as well as rainbows, chocolate sundaes, or the Boston Red Sox. Although the English language has only one word to apply to each of these situations, there are clearly different meanings involved.

Loving and Being Loved

When we talk about person-to-person love, the simplest definition may be one given by Robert Heinlein in the book *Stranger in a Strange Land:* "Love is that condition in which the happiness of another person is essential to your own" (Heinlein, 1961, p. 345). This is certainly the love that Shakespeare described in *Romeo and Juliet,* that popular singers celebrate, and that led Edward the VIII to abdicate the throne of England to marry the woman in his life.

In any type of love, the element of caring about the loved person is essential. Unless genuine caring is present, what looks like love may be just one form of desire. For example, a teenage boy may tell his girlfriend "I love you" just to convince her to have sex with him. In other cases, the desire to gain wealth, status, or power may lead a person to pretend to love someone to reach these goals.

Because sexual desire and love may both be passionate and all-consuming, it may be difficult to distinguish between them in terms of intensity. The key feature is the substance behind the feeling. Generally, sexual desire is narrowly focused and rather easily discharged while love is a more complex and constant emotion. In pure, unadulterated sexual desire, the elements of caring and respect are minimal, perhaps present as an afterthought, but not a central part of the feeling. The desire to know the other person is defined in only a physical or sensual way, not in a spiritual one. This end is easily satisfied. While love may include a passionate yearning for sexual union, respect for the loved one is a primary concern. Without respect and caring, our attraction for another person can only be an imitation of love. Respect allows us to value a loved one's identity and integrity and thus prevents us from selfishly exploiting them.

The importance of caring and respect was central to the thinking of Erich Fromm, whose classic book, *The Art of Loving* (1956), influenced all subsequent study of this subject. Fromm believed that people can achieve a meaningful type of love only if they have first reached a state of self-realization (being secure in one's own identity). Thus, Fromm defined mature love as "union under the condition of preserving one's integrity, one's individuality," and noted that the paradox of love is that "beings become one and yet remain two" (Fromm, 1956, p. 17). In speaking about the respect inherent in all love, Fromm suggested that a lover must feel, "I want the loved person to grow and unfold for his own sake, and in his own ways, and not for the purpose of serving me" (Fromm, 1956, pp. 23-24).

Fromm's insistence that people must be self-realized before having a "meaningful" type of love overlooks that love itself can be a way of attaining self-realization. We believe that people have a great capacity to learn about themselves from a love relationship, although we also agree with psychologist Nathaniel Branden's observation that love cannot be a substitute for personal identity (Branden, 1980).

Peele and Brodsky (1976) have an interesting viewpoint on what happens when respect and caring are missing from a love relationship. They believe that some relationships of this variety serve the same needs that can lead people to alcohol abuse or drug addiction. The resulting "love" is really a dependency relationship:

> When a person goes to another with the aim of filling a void in himself, the relationship quickly becomes the center of his or her life. It offers him a solace that contrasts sharply with what he finds everywhere else, so he returns to it more and more, until he needs it to get through each day of his otherwise stressful and unpleasant existence. When a constant exposure to something is necessary in order to make life bearable, an addiction has been brought about, however romantic the trappings. The ever-present danger of withdrawal creates an ever-present craving. (Peele and Brodsky, 1976, p. 70)

Peele and Brodsky (pp. 83-84) suggest specific criteria for distinguishing between love as a healthy relationship with growth potential versus love as a form of addiction:

1. Does each lover have a secure belief in his or her own value?
2. Are the lovers improved by the relationship? By some measure outside of the relationship are they better, stronger, more attractive, more accomplished, or more sensitive individuals? Do they value the relationship for this very reason?
3. Do the lovers maintain serious interests outside the relationship, including other meaningful personal relationships?
4. Is the relationship integrated into, rather than being set off from, the totality of the lovers' lives?
5. Are the lovers beyond being possessive or jealous of each other's growth and expansion of interests?
6. Are the lovers also friends? Would they seek each other out if they should cease to be primary partners?

These questions are not listed to suggest that there is only one "right" way to love. While most people in love probably can not answer "yes" to all six questions, thinking about these issues may give you some ideas for present or future relationships.

As a practical matter, it is often difficult to draw a line between loving and liking. Although various researchers have tried to measure love (Rubin, 1970; Pam, Plutchik, and Conte, 1975; Dion and Dion, 1976), we agree with the observation: "The only real difference between liking and loving is the depth of our feelings and the degree of our involvement with the other person" (Walster and Walster, 1978, p. 9).

ROMANTIC LOVE

The great loves of fiction and verse have been romantic loves marked by a whirlwind of emotions from passion to jealousy to anguish. In romantic love, unlike any other type of love, we immerse ourselves almost completely in another person (Pope, 1980). When Chaucer wrote that "love is blind," he was acknowledging that the intensity of romantic love distorts our objectivity. In our craving for our loved one, we may overlook flaws, magnify strengths, and lose all sense of proportion.

The puzzles and paradoxes of romantic love are many. We will address them by first discussing some psychological theories about the nature of romantic love and then presenting a conceptual model of the romantic love cycle.

Psychological Perspectives

It should be no surprise that there is little agreement among psychologists on a valid definition of romantic love. Branden (1980) says that it is "a passionate spiritual-emotional-sexual attachment between a man and a woman that reflects a high regard for the value of each other's person." Since we believe that romantic love is not restricted to heterosexual relationships, this definition is too restrictive. Fromm did not define romantic love specifically, but it appears that he used the term "erotic love" to mean the same thing. In contrast, other definitions of romantic love do not include a sexual component as a requirement, as shown in this example:

> A preoccupation with another person. A deeply felt desire to be with the loved one. A feeling of incompleteness without him or her. Thinking of the loved one often, whether together or apart. Separation frequently provokes feelings of genuine despair or else tantalizing anticipation of reuniting. Reunion is seen as bringing feelings of euphoric ecstasy or peace and fulfillment. (Pope, 1980, p. 4)

Recently, psychologist Dorothy Tennov (1979) coined the word "*limerence*" to describe the particularly powerful form of romantic love in which a person is said to be "love-struck" or "head-over-heels" in love. Limerence is marked by preoccupation with thoughts of the loved one

Infatuation

Infatuation (sometimes called "puppy love," "adolescent love," or "pseudo-love") is a superficial, short-lived emotional state based on wishful thinking more than reality. While its powerful attraction may be just as strong as love in its early stages, infatuation does not have the staying power or the depth of commitment of love.

Although there is general agreement that infatuation is a counterfeit version of love, it is usually not possible to distinguish between infatuation and love while they are happening; a distinction can only be reliably made in retrospect (Walster and Walster, 1978). As a practical matter then, you cannot always trust your emotions when you seem to be falling in love. Infatuation and romantic love both result in a blurred objectivity that overlooks the faults or weaknesses of the person to whom you are drawn. Infatuation and romantic love both involve an emotional high, a sense of being "on top of the world." However, infatuation is more likely than love to flourish without being returned and to be directed to a person you don't really know very well. Only when a relationship has stood the test of time, successfully dealing with everyday problems and pressures, can you be reasonably sure you're in love rather than caught in a pleasant interlude of infatuation.

While psychologists seem unable to differentiate between love and infatuation, a suggestion inspired by Judith Viorst ("What Is This Thing Called Love?," *Redbook*, February 1975, p. 12) offers a humorous view that just may do the trick:

> You can tell that it's infatuation when you think that he's as sexy as Paul Newman, as athletic as Pete Rose, as selfless and dedicated as Ralph Nader, as smart as John Kenneth Galbraith, and as funny as Don Rickles. You can be reasonably sure that it's love when you realize he's actually about as sexy as Don Rickles, as athletic as Ralph Nader, as smart as Pete Rose, as funny as John Kenneth Galbraith, and doesn't resemble Paul Newman in any way – but you'll stick with him anyway.

"When I fell in love with you, suddenly your eyes didn't seem close together. Now they seem close together again."

From *New Yorker,* March 15, 1976, p. 28. Drawing by Wm. Hamilton; © 1976 The New Yorker Magazine, Inc.

and the certain knowledge that only this person can satisfy your needs. The limerent lover's mood depends almost totally on the actions of the loved one; that person's every gesture or word is doted on in hope of approval and in fear of rejection.

Limerence, like other forms of romantic love, is an affliction as well as a joy because it is almost completely outside rational control. The consuming emotional ups and downs of limerence can interfere with other relationships, reduce the capacity for work or study, and disturb a person's peace of mind. According to Tennov, many people never experience limerence (although they may experience love), while other people pass through a series of limerent episodes.

HOW DO I LOVE THEE?

According to a love survey conducted by sociologist John Alan Lee (1973, 1976), there are six primary types of romantic love. Lee assigned Greek and Latin names to these categories, pointing out that many love relationships are composites of two or more of these patterns.

Eros describes a love based on physical attraction — an intense, sexual magnetism. Erotic love, according to Lee, is often quick to ignite and quick to flicker out and infrequently turns into a deep, lasting relationship.

Ludus refers to a playful, casual variety of love. Ludic lovers are apt to engage in gamesmanship and usually do not show high levels of

Loving and Being Loved

commitment to each other. They may date several partners and preserve their options by avoiding dependence on their lover. In this form of love, sex is more "fun and games" than intimacy or commitment.

Storge is warmth and affection that slowly and imperceptibly turns into "love without fever, tumult, or folly." Storge emerges from friendships, but it has no identifiable starting point where people realize they fell in love. Storge is a solid, stable type of love that can withstand crises, but it lacks dramatic passion.

Mania, in contrast, is a stormy, topsy-turvy kind of love. Mania connotes madness and agitation, and the manic lover is driven by powerful urges — the "need for attention and affection from the beloved is insatiable." The manic lover is either climbing a mountain of ecstasy or sliding into a valley of despair. Manic love is like a roller-coaster ride: the thrilling dizziness and ups and downs usually come to an abrupt and rapid ending.

Pragma is a more level-headed practical love. The pragmatic lover is searching for the proper match with a mental checklist of desirable features for the loved one. Once a likely candidate is found, if there is some degree of mutual agreement, pragmatic love may develop into more intense feelings.

Agape, Lee's final category of love, is based on the traditional "Christian" view of love as undemanding, patient, kind, and everpresent. It is interesting that Lee admits to never having found an unqualified example of agape, so this type of love remains an ideal more than a reality.

Lee believes that the most satisfying love relationships are between lovers who share "the same approach to loving, the same definition of love." A manic lover who demands intensity and commitment, for example, would be tormented by the ludic lover's playful approach to love. While Lee endorses the idea that two lovers of the same type are most likely to be compatible,

there is no guarantee that a person's "lovestyle" is unchangeable and the same in all relationships. The style of any love relationship probably emerges out of the personalities, needs, and prior experiences of the lovers. People may even avoid a style of love that did not work out for them previously — after all, we can learn from our mistakes.

The Romantic Love Cycle

Research on romantic love has not been exhaustive, but we will summarize the current data and present our clinical observations in terms of a "romantic love cycle." The model shown in Figure 11-1 does not imply that all romantic loves are identical or that each romantic love passes through the phases of this cycle in a predictable, sequential fashion. Instead, it gives us a way to organize our thinking about romantic love.

LOVE READINESS

Although there is no certifiable proof that people can be in a state of love readiness, we believe such a state of mind exists. Love readiness does not always result in falling in love, but it does seem to increase its probability.

Love readiness consists of several different elements. First, love is seen as something that is desirable and rewarding rather than as troublesome or encumbering. People who look at romantic love as a sign of weakness or as a distraction from career development are unlikely to permit themselves to fall in love (as far as anyone can control such emotions). But people who believe that love is ennobling and brings out their best may actively search for a suitable love object. Second, there is a longing for interpersonal intimacy and companionship. This longing may be motivated by loneliness, jealousy for someone else's love relationship, or a desire to replace a past love. Third, sexual frustration often contributes to the state of love readiness (Walster and

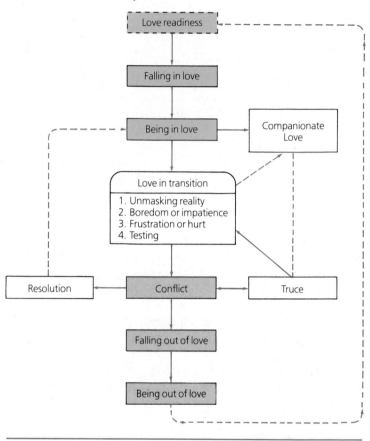

FIGURE 11–1
The Romantic Love Cycle

Love readiness

Falling in love

Being in love

Companionate Love

Love in transition
1. Unmasking reality
2. Boredom or impatience
3. Frustration or hurt
4. Testing

Resolution

Conflict

Truce

Falling out of love

Being out of love

Walster, 1978). This frustration may result from sexual deprivation or from a wish for sex as part of a passionate, committed relationship. Casual sex may be accessible but less fulfilling. Finally, love readiness may reflect the hopefulness people have about being loved; if this is so, the frequency of romantic love may decline as people get older because their expectations of having their feelings returned are reduced (Tennov, 1979).

Some people always seem to be in a state of love readiness but never succeed in getting any farther. While they may eventually make concessions and enter into relationships that don't really qualify as romantic love, their mental quest doesn't seem to end. Other people never experience love readiness or pass beyond it after a brief time. In trying to evaluate love readiness, remember that no one has ever measured it, and that it's not unusual for people who don't match

Loving and Being Loved

the description given here to find themselves falling in love. As we said before, love is neither rational nor completely predictable.

FALLING IN LOVE

Like everybody who is not in love, he imagined that one chose the person whom one loved after endless deliberations and on the strength of various qualities and advantages. (Marcel Proust, *Cities of the Plain*, C. K. Scott Moncrieff, transl. New York: Random House, 1970)

What triggers love is still the subject of guesswork. But the process of experiencing romantic love begins with a stage of falling in love that ranges from the instantaneous "love at first sight" to a gradual process that requires months or years of development.

A sudden flash of love is unlikely to occur unless a person is in a state of love readiness. In real life, instantaneous love is the exception not the rule, and falling in love is a process that can start out in many ways. Dating provides an opportunity for discovering if two people like each other, are compatible, and can meet one another's needs. Being physically near a person is another pathway: by close association, you can come to some preliminary conclusions about a person's desirability without announcing even

the possibility of a romantic interest. Friendships sometimes blossom into love, although it may be difficult to pinpoint exactly when the falling in love occurs. The trusting atmosphere of an intimate friendship may make passion seem out of place, and love, if it develops, may be a low-keyed rather than fiery emotion.

Two aspects of falling in love are particularly likely to ignite passion — the excitement of getting to know someone intimately and the excitement of sex (Walster and Walster, 1978). Both types of arousal intensify the push toward love by positive reinforcement.

BEING IN LOVE

Being in love, like falling in love, can occur whether or not love is returned. If there is no indication that reciprocal love might develop, the probability of a person's staying in love begins to decrease rapidly. But a person who has reached the "being" phase of romantic love is usually inventive, hopeful, and willing to accept even the flimsiest signs of reciprocation.

The romantic lover at this stage may be head-over-heels in love (caught in the grips of limerence) or in a more tranquil, self-satisfied, secure, and objective state. Sexual attraction is almost invariably strong, although it may not lead to action because of shyness, sexual problems, or moral constraints (Tennov, 1979). In some situations, people may try to defuse their sexual impulses by masturbation or strenuous exercise either to keep their love "pure" or if their loved one shows no interest in a sexual relationship. Whatever form being in love assumes, it is usually a passing phase, lasting an average of one to two years (Hill, Rubin, and Peplau, 1976; Tennov, 1979). Most of the time, romantic love either changes into another form of love called companionate love or gradually dissolves because of conflicts, boredom, or disinterest.

LOVE IN TRANSITION

The transitional phase of romantic love is a pivotal time. Here, the initial excitement of getting to know someone and the passion of a new sexual relationship begin to lessen and the thrill is going if not gone. Lovers begin to notice imperfections in each other that were previously unobserved or ignored, and boredom or impatience begins to set in. Frustration occurs when love does not measure up to our fantasies, when we realize that all our problems are not "cured," or when we discover that the ecstasy cannot go on forever without intermissions.

Characteristically, lovers in this transitional phase begin to test one another — and the presumed strength of their love — in various ways. Each lover is likely to try to force or trick the other into becoming what they were thought to be or what he or she would like them to become. Power struggles and competitive strivings emerge (Coleman, 1977). Testing becomes a means of making a rational decision about the future of the relationship: "Do I want to stay with this person, or should I get away now, while I can?" Jealousy may rear its ugly head, anger may erupt, and conflict is almost unavoidable.

The transition stage of love is basically a time for testing reality. In a sense, love pulls its head down from the clouds, and the conflicts and doubts that arise may lead to a stage of falling out of love or measures may be taken to push the relationship into a temporary state of truce. The truce may either lead things back to the "love in transition" stage (with the probability being high that further conflicts will occur), or may lead directly to a companionate love relationship.

If, on the other hand, given the ingredients of motivation, flexibility, cooperation, and a little bit of luck, the conflicts are resolved, the

Loving and Being Loved

Researchers on Love

No one is completely certain about what causes the feeling of love. Although the image of Cupid practicing his archer's skills is clearly not a satisfactory explanation, no good alternative has really been proposed. Much of the research on love has addressed this issue from the perspective of social psychology, looking at interpersonal attraction as a possible source for some answers. Let's see what findings from these studies might apply.

Physical appearance seems to be an important element in determining how attracted one person is to another. Nursery school children (Dion and Berscheid, 1974), teenagers (Dermer and Thiel, 1975; Dion, Berscheid, and Walster, 1972), and adults (Adams and Huston, 1975) all regard good looking people with more favor than their less attractive peers. People tend to be more socially responsive and more willing to provide help to attractive individuals (Barocas and Karoly, 1972; Benson, Karabenick, and Lerner, 1976). There is fairly solid evidence that despite sayings like "you can't tell a book by its cover," or "beauty is only skin deep," the physical attractiveness of females has a strong influence on their dating frequency – a finding that is far less true for males (Berscheid et al., 1971; Krebs and Adinolfi, 1975).

In a thought-provoking experiment, Dion, Berscheid, and Walster (1972) found that physical attractiveness also influences our expectations about other people's personalities and behavior. On the basis of photographs, both men and women rated good looking people as more sexually warm and responsive, interesting, poised, sociable, kind, strong, and outgoing than less attractive people. The group judged as physically attractive was also seen as more likely to attain high occupational status, to make better husbands or wives, and to have happier marriages than the less attractive group. And a recent study involving college-age couples matched by computer found that both sexes reacted most positively to their dates if they were good looking; intelligence, personality, and social charm had little to do with the romantic chemistry.

Physical attractiveness seems to be more important for females than for males in affecting interpersonal relationships. A man's occupational status or financial success is generally more important in rating his "social desirability" (Rubin, 1973; Walster and Walster, 1978). Physicians, lawyers, and other professionals are consistently rated by women as more desirable dates or marriage partners than men with low-status occupations such as janitor or waiter.

Here are a few other salient findings by "love researchers":

1. The notion of "love at first sight" may in many cases be only a myth that fulfills our need for instant acceptance and rationalizes our feelings of sexual arousal by giving them a "dignified" label (Murstein, 1980), but in some cases it proves to be real (Solomon, 1981). Unfortunately, only the passage of time will show which is which.
2. The old bit of folklore that men prefer "hard-to-get" women just is not true (Walster et al., 1973).
3. College-age women fall in love more frequently than college-age men (Dion and Dion, 1973 and 1975), but college-age men fall in love more quickly (Hill, Rubin, and Peplau, 1976).
4. Men hang on longer in a dying love affair than women (Walster and Walster, 1978), and women end more romances than men (Hill, Rubin, and Peplau, 1976).

Although research on love has become more fashionable in recent years, the following observation by a prominent psychologist still applies: "So far as love or affection is concerned, psychologists have failed in their mission. The little we know about love does not transcend simple observation, and the little we write about it has been written better by poets and novelists" (Harlow, 1958, p. 673).

relationship returns to the "being in love" stage. If this occurs, the new version of the relationship may actually be stronger, strengthened by the ability to successfully survive its conflicts. Mutual trust is no longer just a matter of faith but a byproduct of experience.

FALLING OUT OF LOVE

Just as people falling in love delight in learning everything about their partners and revealing much about themselves, people falling out of love are less open, intimate, and interested in their partners. Concern for the partner's happiness becomes a second priority rather than a guiding light and eventually becomes an incidental thought. Communications may be strained because the two lovers are no longer "on the same wavelength," and whatever troubles occur at this point in the relationship hardly seem worth the effort to overcome.

Love relationships come apart in different ways, most of which are painful. Only about 15 percent of love relationships end by mutual consent (Hill, Rubin, and Peplau, 1976). Many times one person pulls out of a love relationship while the other is still "in love." Here, the falling out of love stage occurs at different times for the two lovers. The heartbreak and sorrow of the deserted lover are sometimes very similar to a grief reaction, passing through a period of tearful mourning and shock followed by a time of persistent, haunting memories before there is a return to happiness. At other times, the jilted lover becomes angry, vengeful, or determined to avoid future love at any cost.

BEING OUT OF LOVE

Once having fallen out of love, some people quickly revert to a state of love readiness, no worse for wear and perhaps even wiser and wealthier from their love experience. There is a kernel of truth to the notion that a person "on the rebound" may be more open (and more vulnerable) to a new love relationship. On the other hand, there often seems to be a "refractory period" early in the "being out of love" phase during which it simply is not possible to fall in love again.

COMPANIONATE LOVE

It is rare for the passion and excitement of a romantic love relationship to last for more than a few years. Usually, romance is replaced (except for occasional brief flickers) by another kind of love which comes to a new state of equilibrium. This is called *companionate love,* which can be looked at as a steadier love based on sharing, affection, trust, involvement, and togetherness rather than passion.

Companionate love is not just a sorry substitute for romantic love, although it can deteriorate into drabness and routine if not sustained by continued caring and respect. Many companionate love relationships include an exciting, satisfying sexual side, and in many ways the partners may find that their pleasure in each other increases. Companionate love is less turbulent and more predictable than romantic love, so many people find it to be a soothing, secure kind of relationship.

Companionate love is most characteristic of marriage and other long-term committed relationships. Because it is less possessive and consuming than romantic love, it allows two people to carry on their lives — working, raising children, having hobbies, relaxing with friends — with a minimum of interference. It is a reality-based and steadier love, as opposed to romantic love, which is all too often based merely on ideals and fantasies.

Loving and Being Loved

THE BIOLOGICAL SIDE OF LOVE

So far we have discussed love as though it is solely a product of the mind. Some scientists suggest that there may be a biological component as well. Two types of evidence can be cited in favor of this idea.

First, evolutionary biologists point out that reproductive success may be at least partly linked to love. Hundreds of centuries ago, successful reproduction hinged on two factors: (1) genetic diversity to ensure the health of offspring, and (2) the man's closeness to his sexual partner during pregnancy and the infancy of their newborn child to provide protection and food, and to help in childrearing. Love might have created more stable attachments than sexual attraction could accomplish by itself (E. Wilson, 1978; Rizley, 1980). Love also drew genetically unrelated persons together to engage in mating, thus diversifying the gene pool and contributing to the survival of the species.

A second type of evidence that may shed light on the biological side of love also relates to sex. In 1964 psychologist Stanley Schachter devised a theory based on the physiological responses that accompany many emotions — a pounding heart, sweaty palms, heavy breathing, and so on. According to Schachter, how we distinguish between love, anger, jealousy, nervousness, and other emotions is not based on our bodily reaction only (since the responses may be identical) but rather on the way we interpret or label what we are experiencing. In Schachter's sense, love is a matter of physiological arousal interpreted in a certain way. Recent studies have shown, however, that Schachter's theories are only partly correct. It now appears that there are some specific differences in the reactions of the autonomic nervous system to various types of emotions (Ekman, Levenson, and Friesen, 1983), raising the possibility that the feeling we call love may be accompanied by a unique set of physiological responses.

One plausible explanation is suggested by psychiatrist Dr. Michael Liebowitz, who contends that the excitement and arousal of romantic love are a direct result of surging levels of two neurotransmitters, dopamine and norepinephrine, that carry chemical messages that bridge the gap between nerve cells in the brain. In his 1983 book, *The Chemistry of Love,* Liebowitz argues that these neurotransmitters are activated by visual cues — noticing someone who fits our ideal of attractiveness, for example — and then bathe the pleasure center of the brain in a sea of chemical messages. Liebowitz also believes that intense, transcendent love experiences may involve a separate neurotransmitter called serotonin, which can produce an almost psychedelic high, while companionate love may rely more on the brain's production of narcotic-like substances called endorphins that give a sense of tranquility.

LOVE AND SEX

The relationship between love and sex in our society is complicated. Traditionally, females were taught that love is a requirement for sex, while males were urged to obtain sexual experience whether or not love was present. Gradually in the 1960s and 1970s, premarital sex became more acceptable for females, at first if they were engaged to be married and later if they were involved in a "significant relationship" (one usually defined by love). Today, although restrictions have loosened even more for some, many heterosexual couples still need a statement of love before they feel morally comfortable with the idea of "going all the way."

Sex Without Love

It is tempting to categorize sex involving people who are not in love as casual sex, distinguishing it from relational sex. But people who do not love one another can have a strong relationship, and lovers can sometimes have casual sex in the sense that there's not much thinking about it or interpersonal communication going on. Sex can be mechanical, impersonal, and hurried whether or not two people love each other.

There is nothing inherently bad about impersonal sex if it is clearly consented to by all parties. Under certain circumstances and for some people, impersonal sex may be enjoyable in its own right. Others are offended or distressed by impersonal sex and could never consider participating in a group sex scene or having sex with a stranger or prostitute.

Some people enjoy a more personal, intimate brand of sex, hoping that it may develop into love. There are no guarantees that this will happen, so if this is the only reason for sexual participation, these people are liable to feel disappointed, cheated, or angry. It is probably easier for those who engage in casual sex to view sex without love as an experience valued for its own pleasures and unique returns. If nothing more is expected, disappointment is less likely.

Some moralists would be happier if it could be proven that sex without love does not work. There is no evidence, however, that sex is always or usually better if you are in love. We have worked with hundreds of loving, committed relationships where the sexual interaction was in shambles and with hundreds of people who deeply enjoyed sex without being in love.

Another aspect of this topic deserves mention. A love relationship, unless it's on the rocks, offers some protection against being used sexually. As we pointed out earlier, love is marked by caring and respect that buffers this risk. Sex without love is probably more likely to create misunderstandings and involves a greater risk of being used for the purposes of your partner without much regard for your own feelings and needs. It is harder to gauge the trust in a nonloving relationship, so "proceed at your own risk" (Figure 11-2).

Love Without Sex

There are a variety of circumstances in which a love relationship exists without sex. Parent-child love, brotherly love, and so-called platonic (friendly, nonsexual) love are some obvious examples. There are also forms of romantic and companionate love in which there is no sexual component. In the purest forms of love without sex, both partners agree to abstain from physical intimacies. They may make this choice because of religious beliefs, a disinterest in sex, or a desire to wait until marriage. This comment from a twenty-five-year-old man shows another motive for abstaining from sex:

> My partner and I became so caught up in our sexual activity that the rest of our relationship was neglected. After we decided not to have sex, we found more time and energy to love each other in ways that meant more to us. (Authors' files)

There are also unavoidable circumstances that may prevent or limit sexual interaction in a love relationship, such as serious illness or geographic separation. Sometimes the decision is one-sided rather than mutual, in which case one lover may be left in a sexually frustrating situation.

Personal Values and Sexual Decisions

Many people are troubled by questions about what's "right" and "wrong" sexually. Adolescents and young adults are often uncertain

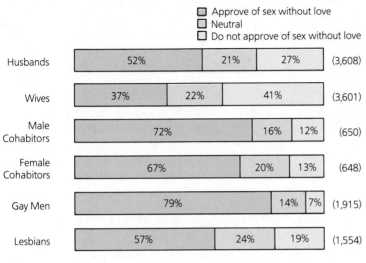

FIGURE 11–2
Feelings About Sex Without Love

☐ Approve of sex without love
☐ Neutral
☐ Do not approve of sex without love

Husbands	52% 21% 27%	(3,608)
Wives	37% 22% 41%	(3,601)
Male Cohabitors	72% 16% 12%	(650)
Female Cohabitors	67% 20% 13%	(648)
Gay Men	79% 14% 7%	(1,915)
Lesbians	57% 24% 19%	(1,554)

Numbers in parentheses are the number of people on which the percentages are based.

Source: From *American Couples,* p. 255, by Philip Blumstein, Ph.D. and Pepper Schwartz, Ph.D. Copyright © 1983 by Philip Blumstein and Pepper W. Schwartz. By permission of William Morrow & Company.

American adults' attitudes toward the propriety of sex without love are shown in this recent survey. Note that married women are least approving of this practice.

about the pros and cons of premarital sex. Others are puzzled about the morality and propriety of extramarital sex. When love is added into the equation, even more complex questions arise: Does sexual attraction to someone other than your lover mean that love is dying? Does "extra-relational" sex undermine the quality of love or trust in a primary love relationship? Should the presence or absence of love be the major determinant of our sexual decisions?

There is no simple formula for answering such questions. Each person approaches sexual decision-making from a framework of personal values, beliefs, and experiences that tip the balance one way or another. Some love relationships will wither and die if sex is "off limits." In other relationships, premature leaps toward the bedroom may jeopardize the foundations of love. For one person, abstaining from premarital sex is a matter of deep moral conviction, with potentially negative consequences if these convictions are set aside. For someone else, the same act of abstention prevents them from learning that there is poor sexual compatability with their future mate, creating a difficult problem to be faced early in marriage.

The dimensions of sexual decision-making can be appreciated better if we recognize some of the sources of potential conflict. It is easy to see how our society encourages us to adhere to a particular set of sexual values. Our religious beliefs — and the strength of these beliefs — may also guide us. But at the personal level of decision-making, we must deal with the tensions between our various needs. For instance, there is built-in conflict between the following pairs of values: commitment versus freedom, privacy versus intimacy, sexual novelty versus permanence, independence versus sexual fidelity (Meyners and Wooster, 1979). A person's sexual decisions are outgrowths of how she or he judges the relative importance of such personal values.

Sexual decisions are unfortunately sometimes made on the basis of guilt, ignorance, or impulse. This creates a different kind of decision-making process that is more likely to be second-guessed later on. Since we must live with our sexual decisions, we should take an active role in making sexual choices instead of just letting the choices "happen."

LOVE AND MARRIAGE

To discuss love without discussing its relationship to marriage would be like discussing free enterprise with no mention of money. Love and marriage are certainly not synonymous, but they are linked in important ways.

While marriage, unlike love, can be defined in legal terms, its psychosocial dimension is most closely related to love. We do not believe that marriage is the only way to go, the "best" choice, or a perfect solution to life's problems. We recognize that some couples who live together without a marriage certificate are more meaningfully wedded, more committed to each other, than other couples whose marriage is legally sanctioned. But we agree with the idea that:

> For all the books and preaching and counseling and psychological knowledge we have today, for all our new ideals of freedom and our emphasis on personal growth and fulfillment, marriage is still basically two people trying to love each other and answer each other's needs. (N. O'Neill, 1978, p. 4)

Selecting a Mate

Our culture is unique in the emphasis it places on love *before* marriage (Reiss, 1980). Unlike societies in which marriages are traditionally arranged by parents, with courtship following tightly controlled etiquette, we are led to believe that "love conquers all" and live our lives accordingly. In India, China, Japan, and parts of Africa and the Arab world, arranged marriages are common. Often, these matches preserve social and economic order and create a stable setting for family living. The partners in an "arranged" marriage — who may be "pledged" to each other during childhood — are not expected to begin their marriage *because* of love. Instead, devotion and responsibility are expected to grow as the marriage develops, and love may or may not occur.

Paradoxically, in America, where our strong sense of freedom and democracy carries over into mate selection processes, we have an extraordinarily high rate of divorce. This may tell us something about the lack of love education we receive while growing up. We are expected to recognize love and to select a marriage mate " 'til death do us part" largely on the basis of love. The odds are strong, however, that most of us have gotten more training in learning how to drive than in learning how to love.

Those caught in the throes of romantic love are drawn to thoughts of marriage like moths to light. The desire to be one with your loved one, especially when the love is mutually felt, fits neatly into our expectations of marriage as a form of intimate, lasting romance. But the irrational nature of romantic love often causes us to overlook potential problems and to minimize what will happen when and if the passion dies down.

This doesn't mean that you must adopt a scientific, calculating analysis of likely marriage candidates. Despite the success some computer dating services claim in finding the "perfect" match, no one has succeeded in devising a foolproof formula for marital success. Like many things in life, the process of selecting a mate is largely a matter of common sense combined with an element of luck.

At the common sense level, it helps to realize that men and women tend to be happiest in equitable relationships. People feel most comfortable when they are getting from a relationship what they believe they deserve: too much or too little (inequity) leads to discomfort and dissatisfaction (Murstein, 1976; Walster, Walster, and Berscheid, 1978). Research on "equity theory" shows that men and women generally marry someone with similar physical attractiveness, intelligence, and attributes (Walster and Walster, 1978). Marrying someone with a markedly different socioeconomic, educational, or cultural background is likely to be riskier than marrying someone more closely matching your own characteristics, but this is where personal choice comes into play. A general set of statistics is not an infallible guide, and sometimes you're better off following your heart than your head. Since people tend to change over the years, even the most impressive statistics may be invalid ten years later.

One way of assessing someone's marriage potential is to stay in a long-term relationship to see what happens. After the initial luster of love wears off you can see how problems are solved, how interactions change in times of stress and with the passage of time, and if boredom or dissent become commonplace. You can be fairly certain that premarital problems are likely to intensify rather than disappear, once the honeymoon is over. One way of accomplishing this type of assessment is by living together, a route chosen by about one-quarter of present United States undergraduates (Macklin, 1980).

One last note on mate selection. While sex is not the most important ingredient in most marriages, it does help to know if you and your spouse-to-be are sexually compatible or have considerable difficulty getting things together sexually. This doesn't mean that you should rush into a sexual relationship (again, your own values must be applied here) or that you need to have a performance checklist (a tactic which could boomerang in unexpected ways), but you do need to decide how to deal with the sexual side of your relationship and to think about how important sex is (or isn't) to *you.*

Love in Marriage

Marriage is rarely a faithful replay of the fairy tale ending "and they all lived happily ever after." Living in a marriage and making it work is no easy matter. It's easier to be loving when you aren't awakened by kids at 3:00 a.m., when you're not squabbling with the in-laws, or when your sexual advances aren't repelled by a headful of curlers, a facial mask, cigar breath, or Monday night football.

In the real world, few marriages maintain a perpetually loving relationship. Even companionate love shifts its intensity from time to time as a married couple reacts to the ordinary stresses and strains of life together. At any given moment, a husband and wife may dislike each other or even hate each other, yet still spring back into a love relationship.

Researchers have found that marital dissatisfaction tends to increase the longer people have been married (Blood and Wolfe, 1960; Wills, Weiss, and Patterson, 1974; O'Neill, 1978). While it is possible to speculate on its many causes — lessened sexual interest, the responsibilities of parenting and occupation, failure to share time together, poor communications, and changes in personal attractiveness, to name just a few — many marriages suffer from a kind of benign neglect that relegates the relationship to a low priority, thus removing the very elements that usually sustain love.

To maintain love or help it grow, marriage partners must invest emotions and energy on a continuing basis. Spouses who succeed in "giving" to one another — in communications, physical warmth, shared interests, and shared responsibilities — are also likely to succeed in staying in love.

While some marriages succeed quite well in keeping love alive, others evolve into business relationships or a sort of "roommate" status in which love fades away completely. Partners in marriages that become strained over time may stay together to protect the children or to adhere to a philosophy that simply will not allow for separation or divorce. Although these marriages may be loveless, they are not necessarily "bad." Even good marriages are susceptible to a disappearance of love.

In an essay called "The Future of Marriage," Morton Hunt (1977) observed: "Formal promises to love are promises no one can keep, for love is not an act of will; and legal bonds have no power to keep love alive when it is dying." The nature of marriage in the 1980s may have changed considerably from earlier times, but the nature of love has not. A major challenge facing any marriage is to preserve the spark of love — a task that requires hard work and creativity.

SUMMARY

1. Interpersonal love can be defined as a state in which someone else's happiness is essential to your own. The elements of caring and respect are important aspects of love and can help one distinguish between love as a growth relationship and love as a form of addiction or dependency.

2. Openness and sharing and desire (sexual or otherwise) are usually part of but not the same as love. The degree to which each of these characteristics is found in any love relationship is highly variable and does not define which love is automatically "best."

3. Romantic love is the dramatic, passionate form of love that has been celebrated in story and verse throughout history. Lee distinguished six types of romantic love — *eros, ludus, storge, mania, pragma,* and *agape* — and believed that the most rewarding and comfortable love relationships are between two people with similar love styles. Tennov coined the word *limerence* to describe the most intense forms of romantic love.

4. The romantic love cycle often, but not always, begins with a stage of receptivity toward love or *love readiness*. The *falling in love* stage usually flows into a stage of *being in love*, marked by optimism, elation, and a sense of permanency. This stage is usually short-lived, giving way to a *transitional period* in which lovers first notice imperfections and faults, encounter boredom, impatience, or frustration, and begin testing each other. This phase generates conflict, which may either be resolved (maintaining the relationship), temporarily shelved (in an uneasy truce), or be the cause of *falling out of love*.

5. Companionate love is a reality-based love without the passions of romantic love but with a better durability.

6. Love may have some biological bases as shown by evolutionary evidence and the interaction between physiological arousal states and emotions; but love is most importantly a psychosocial phenomenon.

7. In our culture, love is closely linked to sex and marriage, but either can exist without love. Sex without love isn't necessarily less good than sex with love, just as love without sex is most comfortable for some people. Personal decisions about sex are best made on the basis of individual values and beliefs, including examining and establishing a priority between two values that may conflict.

8. Love is not an automatic accompaniment to marriage, nor is marriage an automatic outgrowth of love. Our society has an unrealistic set of expectations about love in marriage (possibly because we do not think much about education to prepare for loving or being loved), and people are often disappointed or surprised when their own relationship does not hold its love in an effortless fashion. Keeping love alive requires active participation from two people — in order to "get" love, it helps to start by "giving."

SUGGESTED READINGS

Fromm, Erich. *The Art of Loving*. New York: Harper & Row, 1956. Although a bit dated, this short, classic book was the bible of love for many Americans.

Liebowitz, Michael R. *The Chemistry of Love*. Boston: Little, Brown, 1983. A provocative look at the biological mechanisms possibly involved in the feelings and experience we call "love."

Pope, Kenneth S., ed. *On Love and Loving*. San Francisco: Jossey-Bass, 1980. A comprehensive, balanced set of essays on the nature of romantic love from a wide variety of theoretical perspectives. Particularly useful is its life-cycle approach to the study of love.

Tennov, Dorothy. *Love and Limerence*. New York: Stein and Day, 1979. A fast-paced book that will hold your attention from start to finish. Tennov's theories present important ideas on the many faces of love.

Walster, Elaine, and Walster, G. William. *A New Look at Love*. Reading, Mass.: Addison-Wesley, 1978. In a marvelous synthesis of research findings and practical insights, these authors explore the similarities and differences between romantic and companionate love.

Wanderer, Zev, and Cabot, Tracy. *Letting Go*. New York: Putnam, 1978. Practical advice for dealing with the pain of breaking up or broken love relationships.

12 Intimacy and Communication Skills

Intimacy. We hunger for it, but we also fear it. We come close to a loved one, then we back off. A teacher I once had described this as the "go away a little closer" message. I call it the approach-avoidance dance. (Rubin, 1983, p. 65)

*T*HE SEARCH for intimacy is a familiar part of our lives, yet finding and sustaining satisfying intimate relationships seem to be difficult undertakings for many people. This might be surprising at first, since the benefits we derive from sharing warm, trusting relationships — like enjoyment, acceptance, comfort, support, and companionship — have an obviously self-fulfilling role in our lives. Yet despite the fact that most

people agree that intimacy is desirable, there is no clearcut path to follow for establishing an intimate relationship, and preserving intimacy, or helping it grow, seems to be a major problem today if we consider current divorce statistics or the tens of thousands of couples seeking marriage counseling.

Understanding the nature of intimacy — what it is, how to achieve and sustain it — while also recognizing the potential pitfalls and problems of intimacy is the subject of this chapter. In addition, since effective communications are, in many ways, essential to developing and maintaining intimacy, we will also discuss communication skills as they apply to intimate relationships.

310

INTIMACY AND INTIMATE RELATIONS

The word *intimacy* comes from the Latin *intimus*, which means innermost or deepest. Intimacy can be defined as a process in which two caring people share as freely as possible in the exchange of feelings, thoughts, and actions (Macionis, 1978; Levinger and Raush, 1977; Hatfield, 1982). As we will use the term in this discussion, intimacy is generally marked by a mutual sense of acceptance, commitment, tenderness, and trust.

This definition allows us to see that intimacy is not precisely the same as romance or even strong affection. Friends may work or play together and enjoy each other's company but have little or no exchange of their inner thoughts and feelings, and a person may fall in love with someone without expressing that feeling to the loved one.

In much the same way, intimacy as a temporary condition (in contrast to an ongoing process) is sometimes situation bound: It is defined by a particular set of circumstances that leads to openness with no commitment or tenderness necessarily present (Wong, 1981). For example, two people sitting next to each other on a long flight might engage in a very personal conversation, but if they later meet accidently at a cocktail party, they might be quite uncomfortable about their disclosures. In much the same way, two people who have engaged in casual sex together without any real exchange of feelings may have "been intimate" sexually but they have not experienced the sharing and caring of intimacy as we have defined it.

Thus, we can see that there is much variety and complexity in intimate relations; they are not all alike by any means. In particular, we can expect that intimacy without romance or sexual interaction (where this status is agreeable to both persons involved) is apt to be quite different from the intimacy that accompanies love or romance or sexual passion. But before we go on to examine the nature of interpersonal intimacy in more detail, it is helpful to take a brief look at another component of intimacy that undoubtedly influences a person's relationships with others: intimacy with self.

Intimacy with Self

> I used to think that intimacy was something I'd get, like a present, when I met "Mr. Right," but now I realize intimacy begins within *me*. (Authors' files)

A number of psychologists have stressed that a person's ability to form intimate relationships with others depends in part on having a firm sense of self based on realistic self-knowledge and a reasonable degree of self-acceptance (Erikson, 1963; Rogers, 1972; Levinger and Raush, 1977; Wolf, 1982). Such self-awareness helps us identify our needs and feelings and thus enables us to share them with others. Self-acceptance is also an important building-block for interpersonal intimacy because it allows people to be themselves without pretending to be something other than who and what they are.

People who don't like themselves very much or who feel ashamed of who they are often have a difficult time establishing and maintaining intimacy because they are preoccupied with trying to prove themselves to others or with trying to gain recognition or respect. Even if they are successful in these efforts, their feelings about themselves usually don't change in a lasting way. Others who are anxious or depressed about themselves may deal with these feelings in ways that block self-awareness: by using drugs (including alcohol) for escape, by sitting passively in front of a television set to distract themselves from themselves, or by becoming immersed in their work. Still others who are unhappy with themselves try to find personal satisfaction in relationships in which someone else cares for them, protects them, provides for them, or entertains them, but this is often only a short-term solution.

This does not mean that a person must be totally happy with him- or herself in order to be capable of intimacy with others. When we look within ourselves, we may not always like what we see. Generally, we separate what we like from what we don't like and use this process to try to change. If we are honest in our self-appraisals, the intimate knowledge we develop helps us relate to others. At the same time, a person who *never* looks inward (whether out of fear, laziness, or self-hatred) has such distorted self-perceptions that it is unlikely he or she can contribute fully to a relationship with someone else.

One useful caution should be added here: It is important to retain our sense of self even while involved in an intimate relation with another and not to become so preoccupied with a relationship that we lose touch with our sense of self. An intimate relationship that absorbs most of your time and emotional energy can be exhilarating, but it can also leave you little time for knowing yourself. Such an all-absorbing relationship can be draining or damaging rather than fulfilling. In contrast, intimate relations that enhance your self-acceptance and self-knowledge are likely to be positive elements in your life.

Components of Interpersonal Intimacy

A *twenty-two-year-old single woman:* What I really want most from a relationship is the privilege of being honest all the time. I don't know if that's possible, though. (Authors' files)

A *twenty-nine-year-old married man:* To me, intimacy means sharing. You share the good and the bad, the joys and pain, and through all the sharing you know your partner cares about you. (Authors' files)

A *thirty-five-year-old single woman:* It comes as a shock to some people to realize that lesbians can

have committed, lasting relationships, but that's exactly what Sallie and I have. To us, that commitment is a life-time bond. (Authors' files)

Because the joys of intimacy are numerous and varied, it is a mistake to think of it as a single, unchanging condition. Not only does intimacy exist in various degrees of intensity and in different types of relationships — between friends, between lovers, between family members, and so on — intimacy as a process fluctuates within any given relationship over time. This is partly because each partner's expectations and hopes influence how they evaluate what they're getting from the relationship (Stuart, 1980; Margolin, 1982). People who feel that an intimate relationship is consistently unfair or one-sided generally are more likely to end the relationship (or look for another to take its place). In contrast, those who view their relationships as equitable and balanced are likely to be happiest and stay together for longer times (Walster, Walster, and Berscheid, 1978; Hatfield, 1982). In addition, the intensity of intimacy in a particular relationship is influenced by external circumstances, such as geographic separation or work pressures, which can temporarily divert a person's energy and attention from the relationship to other aspects of his or her life.

In order to better understand the process of intimacy, we will examine its basic components: caring, sharing, trust, commitment, honesty, empathy, and tenderness. To get the most out of this discussion, however, it is important to recognize that these components do not usually exist separately from each other but instead are blended in a unique amalgam in which each strengthens and solidifies the others.

CARING AND SHARING

Caring is an attitude or feeling you have for another person which is generally related to the intensity of your positive feelings toward them. Although you might have positive feelings about

The sharing and caring of intimacy are not lessened by a disability.

someone with whom you have no personal in-volvement — on the basis of good looks alone, for instance, you might feel positively about a person sitting across the table from you in the li-brary — the mutual caring characteristic of in-timacy occurs only when two people share and interact together.

The sharing of thoughts, feelings, and expe-

riences that accompanies the growth of intimacy requires spending time together without the ordi-nary barriers with which people protect their pri-vacy in order to learn about each other. Thus, one of the key steps in developing an intimate relationship is *self-disclosure*, the willingness to tell another person what you're thinking and feeling. Because there is no certainty that the other person will be interested in what you have to say, and because it takes some time to establish the trustworthiness of the other person, most people begin the process of self-disclosure gradually. Instead of revealing their fondest dreams and deepest fears all at once, people generally develop personal openness in a relationship as they find it reciprocated and as they see signs of the other person's continuing interest (Altman, Vinsel, and Brown, 1981).

This process of intimate sharing is not limited to superficial or pleasant things alone, but should extend across a broad spectrum. According to noted psychologist Carl Rogers, saying " 'I want to share myself and my feelings with you, even when they are not all positive,' almost guarantees a constructive process to communications" (1972, p. 203). Sharing uncertainties, worries, and other personal problems with an intimate partner is essential for the growth of intimacy.

Although sharing thoughts and feelings is important to intimacy, it is important that experiences be shared also. Research has shown that people who share mutually rewarding experiences are most likely to develop and sustain a warm, caring relationship (Gottman, 1979; Hatfield, 1982). Such shared experiences can include many things. Sharing hard times and good times, sharing childrearing or a dual career, sharing recreational activities, or sharing in planning for the future are all examples of how intimate couples interact.

Sharing experiences does not necessarily mean that intimate partners should do everything together. Although such a system might work well for a few couples, most people would find total sharing difficult. This is partly because a particular activity or experience doesn't always provide equal rewards to each partner. You might love jogging, for instance, while your partner prefers to play bridge. Forcing each other into activities that are *not* mutually enjoyable just for the sake of togetherness is unwise. Furthermore, constant and complete sharing is not necessarily a measure of a couple's intimacy. Indeed, maintaining an identity independent of an intimate relationship is also important to the longevity of the relationship (Laurence, 1982). Pursuing individual interests and maintaining a circle of friends gives a person a chance to process the feelings generated in intimate interactions. Such efforts help to prevent partners from becoming psychologically overloaded with too much one-to-one togetherness. In addition, such independence allows people to bring new experiences and thoughts to their primary relationship, which can also help it grow.

TRUST

The process of self-disclosure we mentioned above doesn't occur in a vacuum but depends on the degree to which you trust the person to whom you are making disclosures about yourself. Thus, trust is another necessary ingredient for intimacy, and, like caring and sharing, trust develops over time. While people trying to form an intimate relationship usually have to make some initial assumptions about trusting each other, trust solidifies when a partner's behavior matches his or her words. If he promises to help and be there and his behavior confirms those words, she comes to trust him. If she promises never to laugh at his personal secrets and she doesn't, he comes to trust her. Once trust grows strong, two people are able to share even more information about their thoughts and feelings without fear that this will be used against them in some way.

COMMITMENT

Another component of intimacy, commitment, is generally an outgrowth of the caring, sharing, and trust that develop in the early stages of an intimate relationship (Levinger and Raush,

1977). Commitment requires both partners to work willingly to maintain their intimacy through periods of crisis, boredom, frustration, and fatigue, as well as through times of joy, prosperity, and excitement. Intimacy that surfaces only when life is on the upswing is a fleeting, unreliable form of closeness rather than the more encompassing interaction most people would like it to be. Here, too, Carl Rogers has nicely captured the essence of the commitment of intimacy: "We each commit ourselves to working together on the changing process of our present relationship, because our relationship is currently enriching our love and our life and we wish it to grow" (1972, p. 201).

Realistically, it is important to recognize that the degree of one's commitment to an intimate relationship may change over time. Those who pledge themselves to each other "forever and ever" on the basis of a passionate relationship that has lasted only a few weeks may find that as they get to know each other better their desire to stay together lessens. Even couples who have shared years of satisfying intimacy may find that they later grow apart or develop problems that undermine their relationship. Thus, commitment should be regarded as an attitude that states current intentions without being an irrevocable guarantee of the future. Nevertheless, commitment that is backed up by a willingness to work to overcome problems that might develop in a relationship is an important ingredient for a durable future.

OTHER COMPONENTS OF INTIMACY

Honesty is another necessary part of intimacy, although total honesty in the sense of full self-disclosure is not necessarily good for a relationship. Too much honesty can be devastating to any relationship if it is not tempered with an understanding of how a given message might affect one's partner. But there is a decided difference between keeping some things private – that is, setting limits on the self-disclosure that occurs – and deceit. When deliberate deception occurs in friendships or romances, it generally undermines the quality of information exchange that can occur, and therefore undermines intimacy. Indeed, the presence of deceit in a relationship usually is a warning sign that manipulation of one form or another is occurring.

If a person engages in deceit in an intimate relationship, even with the best of intentions, the discovery of that deceit almost inevitably leads to a loss of trust. Thus, telling lies (a sin of commission) is usually more harmful to intimacy than keeping something private (a sin of omission). This means that if your partner asks about something that you don't feel you can discuss truthfully, you can always say "I don't want to discuss this particular subject" without violating your partner's trust. Of course, putting too many topics "off limits" can lead your partner to wonder what you're hiding and may also result in your partner's pulling away from openness, too; as in most aspects of intimate relations, partners tend to parallel each other's behavior.

Empathy is the ability to understand and relate to another person's feelings and point of view. In order for self-disclosures to occur between intimate partners, each must feel that he or she is listened to and understood (or at least accepted) by the other person. Such empathy enables each person in an intimate relationship to act in ways that support and help the other and to avoid or limit destructive, irritating, or alienating attitudes.

One of the most neglected aspects of intimacy is the expression of tenderness, which can be achieved either by spoken messages or by physical contact (e.g., hugging, cuddling, holding hands), as well as by direct behavior. This ingredient of intimacy often seems to be particularly difficult for men who have been socialized to be purely rational, action-oriented beings: they seem bewildered by tenderness, or afraid that it is an "unmanly" way of acting. On the other hand, some of these men are able to be physically tender, but lack comfort or familiarity with the verbal side of tenderness. Both components — verbal and physical tenderness — are usually necessary for romantic intimacy. In fact, much of the time that people complain about intimacy disappearing from their relationships they are actually acknowledging that the amount of tenderness they receive from their partners has noticeably declined. Thus, paying attention to ways to express your tenderness to your partner, by both words and actions, is one of the best ways of keeping intimacy fresh and satisfying over time.

Finally, it is important to recognize that unless intimate partners are willing to set aside many of the ordinary defenses they use in everyday life, it can hardly be said that the intimate relation is a special one. It is hard to be intimate with a person who continually denies the reality

Intimacy is not bound by time or place.

Intimacy and Communication Skills

of his or her inner feelings (for example, some-one who always pretends that everything's great). It is equally difficult to have satisfying intimacy with a person whose behavior is based on pre-tense (for instance, a partner who is always look-ing for "status" and ways of impressing others). On the other hand, people who are able to relinquish such defenses in favor of being them-selves, authentically and spontaneously, are apt to find intimacy more rewarding.

Sex Differences in Intimacy

A twenty-eight-year-old woman: Whenever I go out with a guy, it seems like all he's interested in is sex. We sleep together once or twice and sud-denly he disappears. I think all the men I know are afraid of a really intimate relationship. (Au-thors' files)

A twenty-five-year-old man: It's sad to hear women condemning men for being unwilling to get into close, loving relationships. Many of my friends value intimacy highly, although admit-tedly it's not easy to find. (Authors' files)

The two opinions quoted above about sex differences in intimacy highlight a much-debated topic. Currently, there aren't any reliable data on whether men and women have different levels or types of motivations for intimacy. Thus, the best we can do is review current research evidence on sex differences in particular aspects of intimate behavior, such as self-disclosure.

A number of studies show that women seem more adept at self-disclosure than men (Markel, Long, and Saine, 1976), and that girls and women disclose more intimate information to their friends than boys or men (Rivenbark, 1971; Chelune, 1976; Fischer and Narus, 1981). In ad-dition, girls tend to have more intimate friend-ships than boys (Maccoby and Jacklin, 1974), and women show a higher correlation between friendship and intimate disclosures than men (Booth, 1972; Rubin and Shenker, 1978; Bell,

1981). Furthermore, women have an easier time building "genuine, deep, loyal, noncompetitive" friendships with other women than men do with other men (Sheehy, 1981).

However, the research evidence does not uniformly support the view that there are major sex differences in self-disclosure. Rubin and his co-workers (1980), who conducted a study of 231 dating college couples, found few differences in the levels of self-disclosure that men and women made to each other. Fifty-seven percent of each sex had made full disclosure of their pre-vious sexual experiences to their current partner, 73 percent of the men and 74 percent of the women had fully disclosed their feelings about their sexual relationship together, and 48 percent of the men and 46 percent of the women had given their partner their honest views on the fu-ture of the relationship. Although some differ-ences were found (e.g., women revealed more about their greatest fears, their feelings toward their parents, and their feelings about their clos-est friends, while men revealed more about the things they were proudest of, the things they liked best about their partners, and their political views), the researchers noted that overall, their sample of college students generally adhered to a norm of "full and equal disclosure." Other stud-ies have also found that men confide more in their girlfriends than in anyone else (Komarovsky, 1976) and that sex differences in self-disclosure are minimal (Hacker, 1981).

Other research indicates that intimacy is somewhat easier for women than men and/or that intimacy is more rewarding to or ingrained in women. For example, lesbians are more likely to pair off in intimate relationships than gay men (Saghir and Robins, 1973; Tripp, 1975; Bell and Weinberg, 1978; Peplau and Gordon, 1982). Similarly, sex therapists have noted that fear of intimacy is relatively common in men but less frequent in women (Sager, 1977; Kaplan, 1979;

Schwartz, 1983). Furthermore, men seem to want "instant intimacy" more often than women, an attitude that indicates a fundamental misperception of how intimacy actually develops.

How can we explain such differences? First, we should realize that the existing research only focuses on intimacy in a limited way, particularly emphasizing verbal self-disclosure. This approach necessarily avoids a more comprehensive view of intimacy as an ongoing experience in which time together, physical contact, and shared activities may outweigh the importance of the verbal exchanges that occur. Thus, it is possible that with more sophisticated studies, male-female intimacy differences would prove to be minor or nonexistent. However, it may be that early differences in the socialization of males and females in our society (discussed in detail in chapter 10) account for later differences in intimacy skills. Generally, females in our culture have been socialized to show their feelings, while males have been taught to keep their feelings hidden and to show no signs of weakness or fear. (As Kate Millett [1975] succinctly put it, "Women express, men repress.") In addition, females tend to be touched more during infancy and early childhood than males (Montagu, 1977), something that might lead to later sex differences in intimacy. Similarly, the competitive, aggressive behaviors that are generally encouraged in males in our society do not, in turn, encourage intimacy, while the nurturance and sensitivity usually encouraged in females do enhance intimate behavior.

Whatever differences in intimacy preparation exist because of childhood socialization, men are certainly fully *capable* of intimacy: some of them simply seem to need a while to learn how to find it. In fact, men seem to become increasingly concerned with intimacy from age forty on (Sheehy, 1981), although many men certainly develop a great deal of intimacy at much earlier ages. Perhaps the real dilemma of the sex-differences-in-intimacy problem has been aptly described by Rubenstein and Shaver (1982), who point out that although "men and women need intimacy to the same degree . . . fewer women than men get their needs met, despite women's expertise, because so many men are intimacy-takers rather than givers."

Intimacy Problems

Although most people readily express a need for intimacy in their lives, it often seems to be elusive. In this section, we will examine several different types of problems people have with intimacy, including common barriers to intimacy, fear of intimacy, and pseudo-intimacy.

BARRIERS TO INTIMACY

Some people seem to be able to forge close relationships easily, while others have a difficult time getting past the "social acquaintance" stage. The fortunate few who can comfortably develop closeness and rapport with others in a seemingly effortless way are a distinct minority. Most of us have to work at developing intimacy, and most of us, at one time or another, find that our intimacy overtures are ignored or rejected. Here is a list of common reasons for difficulty initiating or maintaining intimate relations.

1. *Shyness.* People whose shyness causes them to avoid social interactions or to isolate themselves in social settings are unwittingly restricting their opportunities for intimacy. Paradoxically, shy people often long for intimacy and companionship in their lives, but they seem unwilling or unable to take the risks necessary to overcome their shyness.

2. *Aggressiveness.* People who behave aggressively often scare others away or cause them to adopt a defensive posture. The typical concern seems to be, "I'll be overpowered by this person," and few people look for relationships in

Loneliness

Loneliness is a profound problem in America today. Many sociologists and psychologists say that literally millions of Americans are affected, yet loneliness is one of the least discussed and studied conditions of our time. Contrary to first impression, the silent epidemic of loneliness doesn't just involve the elderly, the divorced, the widowed, the abandoned, and the handicapped – although these are prime target groups for this unwanted, even dreaded, condition. Loneliness is increasingly a problem of young adults, who often go to singles bars or join computer dating services in attempts to find companionship. Adolescents, too, are among the loneliest people in our society (Weiss, 1981; Peplau and Peplau, 1982). Rising rates of teenage suicides and runaways

lend credence to this finding. Even mid-life adults, whose careers often call for geographic upheavals every two or three years (Gordon, 1976), are prime targets for a sense of loneliness and isolation.

Other people are lonely despite being part of a group. A twenty-year-old college student sitting with classmates at a party can feel just as lonely as a ten-year-old who's just gone off to sleep-away camp for the first time. Anyone who has visited nursing homes knows that many of the residents, though living in close proximity to each other, feel lonely and isolated by their age and physical frailty.

Loneliness and being alone are not the same thing. Some people prefer a life of solitude, finding that privacy energizes them and frees them from the "nuisance" of interpersonal relations. Loneliness, on the other hand, is a feeling of emptiness and longing, of anxiety tinged with sadness, of wanting an attachment to someone or something (a pet, for example) but not having it. Temporary loneliness is bearable, if unpleasant, as long as it seems destined to end soon. Thus, many people who are temporarily lonely are usually motivated into social actions (such as calling friends, joining a new group or club) that are geared at overcoming the loneliness. The chronically lonely person, however, is far more likely to be in a state of sad passivity marked by activities that won't overcome the lone-

liness, such as crying, watching a lot of television, drinking or using drugs, excessive sleeping, and overeating (Rubenstein and Shaver, 1982). In fact, this attitude may be a hallmark of those who are permanently lonely: they tend to blame their loneliness on themselves by seeing their own personalities and attractiveness in a negative light, which dooms them to half-hearted efforts to overcome their isolation (Weiss, 1981; Jones, Freeman, and Goswick, 1981; Peplau and Peplau, 1982).

Beyond the self-blaming attitudes and low self-esteem of many lonely people, specific elements of their behavior often make it difficult for them to form friendships. For example, the lonely tend to be both shy and self-conscious. In communicating with others, they are often either extremely self-centered (or seem this way out of bashfulness in asking about the other person) or unable to give a sense of caring. In addition, the lonely often have unrealistic expectations about their interpersonal relationships that prevent them from working at building up intimacy.

Experts agree that the best time to deal with loneliness is early in its course. A variety of different strategies can be used to overcome loneliness, but they all have two common features: they are action oriented (that is, don't wait for someone to come along and rescue you from your solitude) and they require attention to communication skills. In addition, it can also be useful to develop activities or hobbies that make being alone more tolerable – thus reducing the fear of loneliness – and to identify the primary sources of loneliness in your life and then set out to overcome those that you can do something about.

Loneliness probably exists at two different levels: social loneliness, marked by a lack of friends and support networks; and emotional loneliness, characterized by the lack of an intimate relationship (Weiss, 1981). While the social loneliness may be easier to overcome, both social and emotional attachments are usually required to ensure that a person doesn't feel lonely. Since intimacy doesn't "just jump up at you and grab you," as one student of ours put it, it's likely that most of us will encounter loneliness at some time or another in our lives.

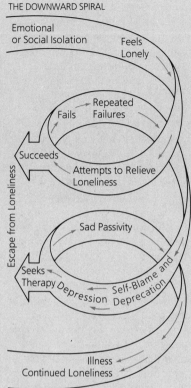

THE DOWNWARD SPIRAL

Emotional or Social Isolation

Feels Lonely

Repeated Failures

Fails

Succeeds

Attempts to Relieve Loneliness

Escape from Loneliness

Sad Passivity

Seeks Therapy

Depression

Self-Blame and Deprecation

Illness
Continued Loneliness

From "Common Errors in Times of Intimacy." First printed in *Esquire* Magazine, February 1984.
© 1984 Lynda Barry.

which they'll be dominated by someone else. Toning down aggressive language and behavior can improve a person's chances for intimacy.

3. *Self-centeredness.* Being preoccupied with one's self commonly turns others off. We all know people who insist on being center-stage all the time, who ignore the needs of others (not out of malice but because of lack of awareness), who monopolize conversations, and who are generally unwilling to do what a partner wants

unless it coincides with their own needs. These people frequently initiate intimacy by telling others a great deal about themselves, but they tend to have a more difficult time maintaining long-term relationships.

4. *Selfishness.* Going beyond self-centeredness, selfishness is apt to be far more damaging to the development of genuine intimacy. Selfish people are often manipulative and try to gain a tactical advantage over others to get their own way. The selfish person doesn't care much about what's best for the relationship or best for the other person; instead, he or she seeks to exert control for personal gain.

5. *Lack of empathy.* The person who is unwilling or unable to accept and understand another's views, thoughts, or feelings has a difficult time in intimate relationships. Often, these people seem to have difficulty listening: either they block out what their partner says or they fail to internalize the message and look at the situation from the partner's point of view. Empathetic people do not just sympathize with the feelings and needs of others, they try to respond to these feelings and needs as well.

6. *Conflicting or unrealistic expectations.* Many people are so idealistic about intimacy that they expect the impossible, creating a situation that frequently leads to disappointment, frustration, or, possibly, to giving up. In other intimate relationships, the partners' goals may be so different that the relationship fails. For instance, if one person is looking primarily for companionship and entertainment in a friendship, while the other is looking for a deeply philosophical, intellectual relationship, they are not likely to find a pleasing intimacy together.

Needless to say, this is not a complete list of all possible barriers to intimacy. There are other conditions, such as depression, drug abuse, or severe physical illness, that may make intimacy extremely difficult even when the other ingredients seem to be in place. But it is also important to re-alize that intimacy is often extraordinarily resilient, making its own way in the face of unforeseen obstacles. Perhaps that's one reason why so many of us are concerned with finding and keeping intimacy in our lives.

FEAR OF INTIMACY

Fear of intimacy is a common problem. People with such a fear are typically anxious about intimacy because of distrust, fear of rejection, and fear of losing control. In addition, many people who fear intimacy have negative self-images; they believe that they have nothing of value to bring to an intimate relationship and doubt the judgment of someone who seems interested in them because they consider themselves unworthy and uninteresting.

People who are untrusting and fear rejection sometimes avoid forming intimate relations entirely, preferring to have many superficial relationships instead of a relationship that calls for taking risks and making a commitment to someone else. These people guard themselves from hurt, but they also isolate themselves emotionally. Others enter into intimate relations but protect themselves by regulating the degree of closeness. Whenever the relationship threatens to become too intimate, they pick a fight, become distracted, or bury themselves in work; in short, they construct a buffer against the demands of the relationship and thus calm their fears by keeping the intimacy under control. Helen Kaplan notes that sometimes *both* partners in a relationship have intimacy conflicts:

> Such couples long for closeness with each other, but when they achieve a certain point of contact they become anxious. Then one or the other will behave in such a manner as to create distance. When distance reaches a certain point, anxiety and longing for closeness will be evoked in the couple. They miss each other and move closer to each other again — but not too close. Then the see-saw will move in the other direction. (Kaplan, 1979, p. 184)

Intimacy and Communication Skills

In some cases, fear of intimacy is a life-long condition. Sometimes such a fear reflects traumatic relations with parents during early childhood; in other cases it develops after a painful experience in an intimate relationship in which a person was not only hurt but intensely disappointed. While most of us survive the breakups of intimate relationships none the worse for wear, this isn't true in all cases — and if the emotional scars are thick enough, the fear of intimacy is most understandable.

PSEUDO-INTIMACY

It is possible to distinguish between genuine intimacy, which is a positive, self-enhancing process, and pseudo-intimacy, which is more pretense than openness, more manipulation than sharing. The latter form of intimacy is marked by the following features, which, while far from comprehensive, convey the key elements of pseudo-intimacy:

1. One person looks to the other to meet most or all of his or her needs rather than taking the responsibility to meet these needs.
2. There is a big gap between what is said and what is done.
3. Mutual trust is missing from the relationship

or has been deliberately and repeatedly violated by one of the partners.
4. The commitment in the relationship is either one-sided or illusory.
5. One person in the relationship persistently acts in a selfish fashion and shows little interest in giving.
6. Communication is one-sided (one partner monopolizes the talking or has little to say).
7. One or both partners order each other about and criticize each other for not following these demands.
8. Conflicts and arguments consume much of the time and energy of the partners with little or no resolution of key issues typically occurring.

This doesn't mean that genuine intimacy is present only if there is perfect tranquility and affection in a relationship. Commitment to a relationship and caring about one's partner do not ensure that intimacy always produces positive, happy feelings, or mutual agreement on all issues. People who are very much in love, for instance, can have moments when they hate each other just as people who feel tenderness toward each other sometimes act in cruel ways (Tennov, 1979; Stuart, 1980; Rubin, 1983). This variation

BLOOM COUNTY

by Berke Breathed

Bloom County, May 9, 1984. © 1984 Washington Post Writers Group; reprinted by permission.

Intimacy and Intimate Relations

of feelings doesn't mean that a couple doesn't have a meaningful intimacy: It simply shows that intimate relationships are highly complex. And in the final analysis, it is exactly this complexity that gives intimacy its greatest value — the strength that bonds us together, one to one, in a unique relationship of mutual giving and getting.

COMMUNICATIONS

As we said in the introduction to this chapter, it is through effective communication that intimacy is established and can grow. Thus, understanding how to communicate effectively is a cornerstone of interpersonal and sexual relations, yet few of us are taught the skills of intimate communications. In schools we learn to write essays and term papers and sometimes even the fundamentals of public speaking or debate, but when it comes to developing intimate communication skills, we are left alone. The following discussion provides some practical, common-sense suggestions for developing your ability to communicate effectively in personal relationships.

The Communication Process

Communication usually begins with the intent to convey information to someone else. The sender must convert the intent into an actual message that is presented to the intended recipient. The message may be verbal (words, sounds) or nonverbal (consisting of a look, a touch, or an action). The recipient must not only receive the message but also understand and interpret its meaning. At each one of these seemingly simple steps, things can and do go wrong.

In many cases, the sender doesn't succeed in saying what he or she really means. Sometimes, for example, people can't find the right words to convey what they're feeling, or what they need, so the messages they send are inaccurate. Even if the message has been accurately formulated, something may go wrong in the sending process so it's never received at all or is received in a garbled fashion. How often has someone missed the main point of your message, and after you explained yourself (perhaps with some exasperation) said, "Oh, that wasn't what I thought you said."

Next, the receiver may not be turned on and so may miss the message (that is, a person may not be listening to what you're saying), or he might hear what he would like or expect to hear, rather than what is actually said.

Possibly the single greatest source of communication trouble, however, is in the way messages are interpreted by those who receive them.

> *Man:* I told you earlier this evening I didn't want to make love tonight.
> *Woman:* I thought you just meant you didn't want to *then*, I didn't realize you meant for the whole night.

Although the seemingly simple art of communication can often be difficult and complex, there are steps we can take to ensure that our messages are sent as clearly as possible *and* that we are open to receiving messages as efficiently as we can. We examine these steps in the following sections.

SENDING SIGNALS CLEARLY

Effective communication begins with the message sent from one person to another. If an unclear message goes out, even an attentive listener is likely to be confused and forced to guess about the intended meaning. There seem to be three main reasons for this lack of clarity:

1. *Not saying what you mean.* When people aren't able to find the right words to express their feelings, they may not be fully in touch

with their feelings. People may also avoid saying what they really mean so they won't hurt someone they care about, so they won't be embarrassed, or so they won't risk being rejected.

2. *Sending mixed messages.* Mixed messages carry contradictory meanings. This can happen when body language or a person's tone of voice contradicts the spoken words. For instance, if someone says "That's lovely," but grimaces while speaking, the listener is apt to be confused. Likewise, a person who says "I am *NOT* upset" in a forced, slowly articulated voice is indicating just the opposite. Mixed messages also occur when there's an inconsistency in the content of a message, as when one part of the message negates the other: "I love it when you're rough with me, but I wish you'd be more gentle," or "I really don't want to worry you, but I think I may be pregnant" are examples of this type of problem.

3. *Not being specific.* Vague statements leave a listener frustrated and wondering "What did he/she mean?" For instance, being told "We should really have more romance in our lives" by your partner might lead you to ask yourself: Does this mean there's something wrong with our relationship? Am I being criticized? Should I be doing something new? Is my partner unhappy? What does my partner want? A more specific statement such as, "I'd love it if you would read me some love poems once in a while to help me feel romantic," wouldn't leave those loose ends.

Clarity in communications can be enhanced in a number of different ways. Here are some general suggestions to think about:

1. Think through what you want to say and how you'll say it particularly if it's an important or emotionally charged message.

2. Let your partner know what your priorities are; try not to crowd in so many requests and instructions that it's difficult to grasp your key points.

3. Be concise. Long-winded discussions are more likely to confuse than clarify. On the other hand, being concise doesn't mean being simplistic or superficial. Don't leave out important information about your feelings or desires in order to be brief.

4. Don't talk *at* your partner. Give him or her a chance to respond and interact.

5. Try not to begin communications by criticizing or blaming your partner. Starting on a negative note puts your partner on the defensive and makes objective listening difficult.

6. Don't be afraid to put what you need to say in a letter if you're having trouble saying it face-to-face. Writing it down shows that you cared enough to take the time to say it carefully.

7. Ask for feedback from your partner to be sure you've been understood and to get his or her reactions.

NONVERBAL COMMUNICATIONS

After a love-making session one night, Cathy withdrew into a stubborn silence. When George asked her what was wrong, she said "Nothing at all," but the firm set of her lips and the way she rolled away to avoid his touch told George how to interpret these words — that in fact something *was* bothering her. With some patience and encouragement, George was finally able to find out what had upset Cathy. She hadn't had an orgasm, and she felt the reason was that he had stopped stroking her clitoris too soon. (Authors' files)

As this example shows, the nonverbal side of communication is often at least as important as the words that are spoken. In fact, one psychologist suggests that of the total feeling expressed by a spoken message, only 7 percent is verbal feeling, 38 percent is vocal feeling, and 55 percent is conveyed by facial expression (Mehrabian, 1972). Posture and positioning (body language) also are powerful forms of nonverbal messages, sometimes saying "Keep away" and sometimes inviting intimacy and closeness (Fast, 1972). Sitting in a relaxed fashion sprawled out next to your partner usually conveys a sense of comfort and warmth, while sitting rigidly on the edge of your chair at a deliberate distance from your partner usually conveys a sense of withdrawal, annoyance, or preoccupation. Unspoken messages can also be powerfully transmitted by touch, which can suggest an attitude of caring and accessibility (Montagu, 1977).

It's important to recognize that inconsistencies between nonverbal cues and verbal content are usually resolved in favor of the former: in this sense, nonverbal messages are more "powerful" than spoken words alone (Stuart, 1980). For this reason it's useful to communicate in ways that maintain consistency between the verbal and nonverbal messages you send to your partner, taking care to avoid sending mixed messages by saying one thing with your words and something different with your body language or vocal tone. Thus one way to improve the chances of communicating effectively is to be aware of your own nonverbal language — an aspect of communicating to which many people never pay attention. It also helps to actually practice ways of sending positive nonverbal messages that express trust, commitment, and caring rather than suspicion, rejection, or impatience. You can do this by yourself, with the aid of a mirror or tape-recorder, or with your partner's help. Together you can discuss the nonverbal communication patterns in your relationship and see how they can be improved.

Not surprisingly, nonverbal messages apply in a special way to sexual interactions. At times, they indicate displeasure or resentment. For instance, if your partner's body tenses up whenever you stimulate the genital area with your tongue, you may begin to think that he or she is uncomfortable with this caress no matter what is said.

Likewise, if your partner usually moans with passion as you make love together, the sudden absence of such sounds may make you feel like you're doing something wrong. At other times, nonverbal messages convey a sense of pleasure, involvement, warmth, or similar feelings. In addition, nonverbal communications during sex can help your partner see what you like without breaking the mood by words. And taking your partner's hand and guiding it on your body, or showing your partner exactly how you'd like to be touched, can be a true gift of sexual intimacy.

Although touch can be used as an effective means of nonverbal communication in a variety of ways, intimate partners often seem to talk too much and touch too little, missing many opportunities to convey feelings of tenderness or affection to each other. In many situations, a long, tight hug says more about the way people feel about each other than a ten-minute dialogue. Likewise, stroking a partner's hair or face, or leisurely kissing, or performing a sensual massage can convey a sense of caring and pleasure that goes beyond words. On the other hand, if people confine their touching to sexual situations, they compartmentalize the physical side of their interaction, sometimes making sex seem like a bartered commodity used to attain closeness.

VULNERABILITY AND TRUST

Communicating in an intimate relationship differs in certain ways from communicating with other people in your life. This is partly because partners in a truly committed, intimate relationship can make the very basic assumption that neither one of them deliberately intends to hurt the other, an assumption that can't always be made in our dealings with the rest of the world. While this doesn't mean that emotional hurts will never occur, it does provide a safety-net of trust and support that allows each person to be-

Intimacy and Communication Skills

Nonverbal communication, such as body language, can be a powerful way of conveying a message. An open expression or gesture can mean comfort and interest, whereas a closed posture can convey annoyance, discomfort, or withdrawal.

come uniquely vulnerable in an intimate, caring relationship.

The willingness to risk being vulnerable, which is at the essential core of intimacy, and the trust that makes it possible encourage people to say what they're feeling or thinking. They feel free to reveal things about themselves — including fears, shortcomings, and failures — without worrying that this information will be used against them at any time. Thus, while trust and vulnerability are not methods of communication, they are necessary preconditions for intimate communications to occur.

"I" LANGUAGE

One of the most direct ways to communicate clearly and to avoid mind-reading games in a relationship is to use a highly effective style of communicating called "I" language. The basic premise of this approach is that a person should take responsibility for him- or herself, since no one knows better than the individual what he or she is feeling or needs at any given moment. By beginning as many statements as possible with the pronoun "I," a person takes responsibility for his or her self-expression. "I" sentences tell what you feel, what you need, or what you want. "I'd love it if we could cuddle and kiss," "I'm feeling restless now," or "I wish we could spend more time talking to each other" are examples of "I" language. To some people, "I" language sounds selfish because we're taught from an early age that it's not polite to talk about ourselves excessively. Intimacy, however, requires that a person open up and express his or her feelings without beating around the bush.

In contrast, sentences that begin with "you" are apt to be demanding or accusatory, provoking defensiveness in the other person: "You don't kiss me much anymore" or "You don't spend enough time talking to me" have a very different tone than the "I" messages previously listed.

"We" sentences are potentially problematical because they compel one person to speak for both. This requires that the person make assumptions or guesses about his (or her) partner's moods, preferences, and needs — and while a charming sense of togetherness may result when the "we" assumptions prove accurate, on many occasions they are actually annoyingly off-target.

"We" messages can also encourage imbalanced communications: one partner may monopolize the talking by speaking for both almost all the time. In this situation, the less assertive partner won't say much of anything and is liable to submerge his or her requirements beneath the flood of directives from the outspoken partner. Such lopsided communication is not conducive to close, intimate relations.

"I" language, then, provides an excellent means for one partner to put his or her emotional cards on the table in intimate dialogues instead of coyly fencing around. This openness, in turn, invites the other person to speak openly as well. Consider the following contrast in styles and content:

Without "I" language

Eileen: What do you want to do tonight?
John: Oh, I don't know. What would you like to do?
Eileen: Well, I wanted to do something we'd both enjoy.
John: Don't you have any ideas? [The conversation is apt to continue in this wheel-spinning mode for awhile, since Eileen and John are trying not to pressure or offend each other by making the first suggestion.]

With "I" language

Eileen: I'm feeling a bit lazy tonight, so I'd like to stay home and relax.
John: I was kind of looking forward to getting out — I thought maybe we'd go dancing.
Eileen: I don't think I'd really enjoy that the way I'm feeling. I'm just too tired to handle that right now.
John: Well, there's a ball-game on TV I can watch, so maybe we'll get out this weekend.

If John and Eileen hadn't agreed on what to do, "I" language could be used to reach a negotiated solution that would be mutually satisfactory. Here's an example of how it might be achieved:

Eileen: I really wasn't planning to go out tonight, I was hoping to stay in and take it easy. Would that bother you?

John: Well, I don't have my mind set on dancing, but I certainly wanted to get out and do *something.*

Eileen: I guess I can handle something that doesn't involve exerting much energy. How about a movie? How does that sound to you?

John: Oh, that'd be great. I wanted to see that new Woody Allen flick and we could catch the 9:00 show.

Eileen: That's fine with me. I'll take a nap if you make dinner, and then we can get going.

John: Sounds good to me. I'll wake you up in a half hour, okay?

When a satisfactory compromise can't be found via this sort of negotiation, the next step is for both partners to examine the relative strength of their different needs. Some couples find that this is easiest if each person rates the intensity of his or her needs on a quantitative scale (for instance, using a scale from -10 to $+10$, where 0 represents a neutral feeling). Other couples compare their needs by discussion that doesn't involve exact quantification. In either case, the basic premise of such negotiations is that it will usually be in the best interests of the relationship to go in the direction of the person whose need is greatest, as long as the other person isn't hurt by this process. It is also possible to negotiate so that each partner does something separately from the other; being in an intimate relationship doesn't mean always doing things together.

A word of caution about "I" language: Phony "I" sentences, such as ones that begin "I think that you . . . ," or "I feel that you . . . ," are really just "you" sentences camouflaged by the addition of the "I think" or "I feel." These should be avoided since it's not the grammatical construction of the sentence that's the key; the essence of "I" language is to speak for yourself without accusing or blaming.

The most complete, functional "I" messages should not simply announce what or how you're feeling (especially if it's negative) but should go on to say what you think you need to try to maintain (or change) the feeling. This prevents your partner from the often frustrating task of having to conjure up a remedy for whatever ails you. In sexual situations, this principle is particularly true. Instead of saying, "I don't like it when you dive for my crotch," you might rephrase the message to say "I really get uncomfortable when I feel sex is rushed and hurried, but a slow leisurely tempo turns me on." This type of communication avoids the trap of sending half a message — what you *don't* like — by completing the message and saying what you'd prefer. Here again, by assuming responsibility for stating your own needs and preferences, you relieve your partner of having to figure out what will please you.

It is also important to realize that "I" language is not the only way of communicating effectively in an intimate relationship. In fact, since intimacy generally produces a sense of thinking about a partnership as "we" or "us" rather than simply "you" and "me" (Hatfield, 1982), there is nothing wrong with using language that emphasizes this viewpoint. Similarly, "you" sentences that offer positive rather than critical content — for example, "You're so kind and sensitive" — are certainly welcome in any relationship. Thus, "I" language should be seen as a potential way of achieving clarity in intimate communication instead of as the only correct way of communicating with your partner.

EXPRESSING AFFECTION

While it might seem that expressing affection in an intimate relationship ought to be the easiest thing in the world, marriage counselors and sex therapists frequently find that even loving couples often neglect this side of their relationship. Although affection is expressed in actions more meaningfully than words, never hearing words of affection can be troubling and can lead people to question whether their partners really care for them.

> I know deep inside me that she really loves me, but she never says it anymore. I feel a little stupid about it, because I can't exactly say to her, "Laura, please tell me you love me" — then I wouldn't be sure if she really meant it or if she was just saying it to make me happy. (Authors' files)

Similarly, when affection is expressed only during sex, and not at any other time, it can lead a person to feel as though it's a limited or conditional affection — in other words, "I love having sex with you" rather than "I love you."

Some couples find creative ways of expressing their feelings for each other. These can be as varied as a note stuck inside a jacket pocket, a poem written by one person for the other, or a quick telephone call that says "I just wanted to say how crazy I am about you." Whatever style is chosen, being sure that your intimate partner knows of your affection (as long as it's real) is an important key to the durability of any relationship.

EXPRESSING ANGER

Anger at its raging peak is almost certain to distort communications, and it makes any real dialogue quite difficult. Postponing serious discussions about the source of your anger and its possible solutions until you have simmered down is usually a wise thing to do if at all possible. If not, it's best for both partners to recognize that much of what is said in anger may be regretted later on, since it may not be meant (it may just be said to hurt).

We believe it is important to recognize that anger is usually not a primary emotion. In most cases anger develops from preceding feelings of hurt, resentment, or frustration. If these can be identified and discussed while they're in their early stages, *before* they grow into anger, there is a much better chance of dealing with them successfully and avoiding the harm that anger can produce. However, when anger does occur, it is often better to release it quickly, in small doses, and in appropriate ways than to let it simmer in continuing resentment and hostility until it boils over or explodes. As social psychologist Carol Tavris points out, "Couples who are not defeated by rage and the conflicts that cause it know two things: when to keep quiet about trivial angers, for sake of civility, and how to argue about important ones, for the sake of personal autonomy and growth" (1982, pp. 222-223).

Some authorities believe that an outburst of anger can help people discharge pent-up tensions and can "clear the decks" to allow for a return to a relative state of emotional equilibrium (Bach and Wyden, 1968; Rubin, 1970; Bry, 1977). Others have concluded that anger is generally "constructively motivated" (not intended to hurt someone, but to bring about change) and have conducted research showing that anger is usually beneficial to both the person expressing the anger and the person who is its target (Averill, 1982). Thus, it is important to realize that getting angry with your partner occasionally is certainly no sign that your relationship is doomed. As Carol Tavris observes: "In the final analysis, managing anger depends on taking responsibility for one's emotions and one's actions: on refusing the temptation, for instance, to remain stuck in blame or fury or silent resentment" (1982, p. 226).

THE ART OF LISTENING

Many people have the mistaken notion that being a good listener simply means sitting back in a chair and keeping your mouth closed. But the ability to listen accurately and empathically is actually a complex process. Here are some specific pointers about what it takes to be an effective listener:

1. *Effective listening requires your undivided attention.* Trying to listen while you're doing something else, like watching TV or reading, tells your partner that you don't think that what he or she has to say is very important. In addition, listening with "half an ear" increases the chance that you'll miss a detail or nuance of your partner's message (verbal or nonverbal) that may be crucial to its overall meaning.

2. *Effective listening is an active rather than passive process.* The best listeners show the speaker that they are involved in the communication process even though they are temporarily silent. This can be done by eye contact, nodding your head, or asking an occasional question to clarify a point without disrupting your partner's message.

3. *Effective listeners are patient in their listening style.* People don't always plunge right in to intimate discussions without first establishing that their partner is receptive and willing to talk. If they feel rushed, they'll either skip the conversation entirely (and probably feel angry about your inaccessibility) or be forced to convey their message in a choppy, incomplete version. The patient listener realizes that a bit of encouragement early in a conversation can set the stage for a more meaningful dialogue later on. At the same time, patient listeners refrain from the temptation to barge in with their own comments before the other person has completed his or her message.

4. *Effective listeners avoid putting undue emphasis on one word or phrase in a message and wait for the message to be completed before they react to it.* This is particularly true in sexual matters, where many key words (such as "orgasm" or "satisfaction") can trigger an emotional response. One man became so agitated and annoyed when his wife mentioned the frequency of their sexual relations that he missed her actual message — that she was enjoying sex now more than ever before — as he mentally rushed to defend himself from criticism.

5. *Effective listeners pay attention to what the speaker is actually saying instead of approaching conversations with preconceived notions of what might be said.*

6. *Effective listeners are attuned to their partners even when there's been no request for a discussion.* Sometimes the most important communications occur in odd, off-hand moments rather than in planned, formal dialogues. Unless you're tuned in to this possibility and receptive to what is being said, you seriously cut down the chances of spontaneous communications, which are often the most valuable.

7. *You don't have to agree in order to listen — in fact, it can be useful to agree to disagree.* The point of being a good listener is to understand what the speaker is saying; this doesn't mean you have to endorse the message. Recognize that your partner is expressing his or her feelings, which may be very different from your own.

In addition to these points, it is also a good idea to realize that the listener's role is not a totally silent one. Most often, intimate communications invite some form of dialogue, with the listener making some acknowledgment of having heard the message, checking out any areas of uncertainty by asking for further clarification, and paraphrasing the overall gist of the message to be sure it has been correctly understood. The following exchange at the end of a longer conversation illustrates how this might be done:

> *Dan:* I hear your concern about our sex life. I don't know quite what to say right now — it's taken me by surprise.

Jane: That's okay, I just want you to think about it a while, not to have an answer tonight.

Dan: Is the major thing that's bothering you that sex has gotten too mechanical for us?

Jane: Well, that's part of it, but I'm also getting a little bored.

Dan: So you want us both to think about how we can get more creativity and tenderness in our sex?

Jane: That's it exactly.

Notice, in this dialogue, that when Dan checks out Jane's meaning and then paraphrases her earlier comments, he doesn't use "I" language. Dan isn't talking about himself here; instead, since he's trying to clarify Jane's "I" messages, he uses sentences that are focused on her rather than himself. Part of the art of listening is deciding when to listen and when to respond.

Talking About Sex

Although communicating about sex doesn't always involve words, letting a partner know what is important or pleasing to us sexually often requires verbal statements. Yet many people are particularly hesitant when it comes to talking about sex, perhaps because of embarrassment, fear of rejection, or concern that talking about it will cause sexual spontaneity to disappear.

As children, most of us were discouraged from saying much about sex and many never learned the terminology to describe their sexual anatomy. So, part of the hesitancy people have in talking about sex with a partner is actually a carry-over from these childhood taboos.

Our difficulties in talking about sex with even an intimate partner also are related to the sexual scripts our society has written, particularly the one that casts the male as the sexual expert and the female as the passive, naive participant.

I'd been dating Larry for three or four months when I finally decided that I had to talk to him about sex. I just wasn't enjoying his style, which was much too fast and rough for me. But every time I tried to bring up the topic, my vocal cords seemed to freeze and I backed off. Finally, I wrote him a letter that broke the ice, and we worked it out pretty easily. (Authors' files)

Nancy and I were having some problems with our sex life about a year after we got married, but I somehow couldn't bring myself to say anything to her about it. I figured that I was supposed to know what was wrong and how to fix it because I was the male — and because I was more experienced. It took us three years before we saw somebody who helped us straighten things out. (Authors' files)

Many couples have difficulty talking about sex (Sarrel and Sarrel, 1979; Barbach, 1982), so it's not surprising that people frequently put up with awkward or frustrating sexual patterns or don't openly express their desires. Yet talking about sex, like any other form of communication, can be facilitated by some thought and practice. Here are some pointers that may prove useful:

1. *Talk with your partner about how and when it would be most comfortable to discuss sex.* You may be surprised to find that your partner is also hesitant about sexual discussions and that simply bringing the topic out in the open provides you both with a good opportunity for defusing tensions. You may also be able to determine when it will be easiest to talk about sex. Some people prefer avoiding the "instant replay" analysis right after making love, but others feel this is the perfect time for talking since events and feelings are fresh in your minds. Whatever you decide about this, the important thing is to let your partner know that you're interested in feedback about your sexual interaction. Armed with this knowledge, your partner won't be worried that you'll react to anything that's said as though it was criticism.

2. *Consider the possibility of using books or other media sources to initiate discussions.* This

Intimacy and Communication Skills

approach allows partners to discuss what they've read or seen and relate it to their personal preferences or dislikes. The advantage is that the discussion is more abstract — in effect, a discussion of sexual ideas as much as sexual action — and thus doesn't sound so much like "When you touched me here I didn't feel good." The disadvantages are that the books you read may not fit your own styles and needs and that some of the suggestions you read about may be offensive or uncomfortable.

3. *Use "I" language as much as possible when talking about sex together, and try to avoid putting blame on your partner for your own patterns of response (or lack thereof).*

4. *Remember that if your partner rejects a type of sexual activity that you think you might enjoy, he or she is not rejecting you as a person.*

5. *Be aware that sexual feelings and preferences change from time to time.* It's very tempting, on hearing that your partner likes to have his or her earlobe licked, to do this automatically every time you make love. That way, you might think, you can't be accused of forgetting. The problem is that doing the same things over and over tends to get boring and sometimes becomes downright unpleasant. The other side of this coin is that a partner who doesn't generally like a particular form of sexual stimulation, such as oral sex, may develop a yen for that activity on any given occasion. Be flexible in translating your talks about sex into action; be prepared to change when necessary or advisable.

6. *Don't neglect the nonverbal side of sexual communications, since these messages often speak louder than words.* Don't be afraid of showing your partner just how you like to be touched: with firm or feathery stroking, with vigorous or slow rubbing, with alternating intensity to the touch, or with a consistent pattern held for some time. Since it's often difficult to express your precise preferences in words, put your hand on your

partner's and demonstrate. Not only is this a perfect "I" message, it also relieves your partner of the need to guess at what you like.

7. *Don't expect perfection.* Intimate relations can stumble if partners expect that sex should always be a memorable, passionate experience. Realize that just as your mood can change, or your physical feelings ebb and flow, so too can sexual experiences range from ecstatic peaks to fizzled-out fiascos. It isn't necessary to analyze what went wrong whenever sex wasn't superlative; instead, it's useful to talk with your partner to be sure that you both have realistic expectations about sex rather than impossible dreams that can only lead to disappointment.

It's important to realize that talking about sex with your partner isn't something to do once and then put aside. Like all forms of intimate communications, this topic benefits from an ongoing dialogue that permits a couple to learn about each other and resolve confusions or uncertainties over time.

If your partner doesn't communicate very openly about your sexual interaction, and you've tried to draw him or her into discussions a number of times only to be shut out, you need to examine your options. If you are generally happy with your sex life together, there may not be a pressing reason to talk about sex. As long as you feel that you can make your needs known, respecting your partner's silence on the subject can be the wisest course. If, on the other hand, your sex life is unsatisfactory (whatever the reason), attempting a candid conversation by stating your feelings and concerns and asking your partner to respond in kind certainly seems in order. Some couples find that a visit to a sex therapist or counselor is helpful if talking about sex together is difficult; the therapist or counselor may be able to pinpoint the source of reluctance for such discussions and suggest ways of solving this type of problem.

SUMMARY

1. Intimacy is an ongoing process in which two caring people share as freely as possible in the exchange of their feelings, thoughts, experiences, and actions in an atmosphere of mutual acceptance, commitment, and trust.

2. Developing intimate relationships with others is easier if a person first has a reasonable degree of self-knowledge and self-acceptance. (However, intimate relationships can also help people gain insights into themselves.)

3. In general, people disclose more of themselves to others as the intimacy of their relationship increases. However, too much self-disclosure, or self-disclosure offered too fast, can sometimes scare people away from a relationship rather than enhance intimacy.

4. The evidence available today (which may be limited somewhat by how we evaluate intimacy) generally shows that females are more comfortable and accomplished in intimacy skills than males. However, there doesn't seem to be any difference between the sexes in the need for intimacy.

5. Intimacy can be difficult to attain because of certain types of barriers, including shyness, aggressiveness, self-centeredness, selfishness, lack of empathy, or unrealistic intimacy expectations. Fear of intimacy is another common problem in which people have difficulties forming intimate relationships entirely or need to set limits on the closeness that develops in an intimate relationship. This condition is often related to distrust of others, fear of rejection, or fear of not being in control.

6. Pseudo-intimacy masquerades as the real thing but is closely marked by manipulation, dependency, lack of commitment, deceit, or other negative elements that prevent the relationship from being satisfying to both partners.

7. Communication is essential to the development and maintenance of intimacy. Effective communication requires that a clear message be sent and accurately received. Communication includes both verbal (words) and nonverbal (touch, body language) messages.

8. Ambiguity in communications commonly arises because of not saying what you mean, sending mixed messages, and not being specific. Unclear or ambiguous messages force the listener to guess what is meant, and they often lead to erroneous conclusions.

9. Nonverbal messages such as voice inflections, facial expressions, body language, and posture are particularly powerful forms of communication. When there is an inconsistency between the spoken word and the nonverbal messages that accompany it, people typically give more weight to the nonverbal cues and discount the spoken message.

10. Communicating in intimate relationships is best done as a form of self-expression and self-responsibility. Starting sentences with the word "I" can help to keep this focus and avoid the pitfalls of "you" sentences, which tend to be blaming or accusatory, and "we" sentences, which are often incorrect in their content and assumptions.

11. A much-neglected aspect of intimacy is the need to express affection on a regular basis to your partner. Not hearing affection expressed can lead some people to feel that they're taken for granted, or even unloved, and can undermine the solidity of a relationship.

12. Anger is an emotion that usually grows out of hurt or resentment. While it's sometimes useful to get anger out in the open, it's often even better to prevent it from occurring by recognizing and doing something about the things that lead to the early stages of resentment or hurt. Anger generally distorts communications.

13. Being an effective listener (a large part of effective communication) depends on several different things, including: giving the speaker your undivided attention; being patient; not taking something out of context; being receptive. It isn't necessary to agree with your partner in order to listen effectively, but your role as a listener can be enhanced by giving feedback to your partner, checking out anything you're uncertain about, and using paraphrasing to be certain you've understood correctly.

14. While talking about sex isn't inherently different from other kinds of intimate communications, many people have a difficult time in this area because of taboos carried over from childhood, embarrassment, or other concerns. Couples in intimate relations should try to talk openly and honestly with each other about sex using whatever approaches they are most comfortable with. Through talking and nonverbal messages, couples can learn to enhance their sexual communications, which will often enhance their sexual intimacy.

SUGGESTED READINGS

Branden, Nathaniel. *If You Could Hear What I Cannot Say.* New York: Bantam Books, 1983. A self-help book that uses sentence-completion techniques to help explain many of the principles of intimate communication.

Fisher, Martin, and Stricker, George, eds. *Intimacy.* New York: Plenum Press, 1982. A rich collection of papers on the nature of intimacy from a remarkably multidisciplinary group of contributors. Highly recommended reading.

Gottman, John; Notarius, Cliff; Gonso, Jonni; and Markman, Howard. *A Couple's Guide to Communication.* Champaign, Ill.: Research Press, 1976. A practical guide to the intricacies of couple communications, including useful advice on how to rescue yourself from damaging communication patterns.

Rubenstein, Carin, and Shaver, Philip. *In Search of Intimacy.* New York: Random House, 1982. A thought-provoking look at intimacy and loneliness based on extensive survey research. Well-written, nontechnical, and insightful.

Rubin, Lillian. *Intimate Strangers — Men and Women Together.* New York: Harper Colophon Books, 1983. A clearly written, insightful look at the relations between men and women, including much material on intimacy and communications.

13 Sexual Fantasy

FANTASY ALLOWS us to escape from the frustrations and limits of our everyday lives. Through fantasy, a person can transform the real world into whatever he or she likes, no matter how briefly or improbably. Although it is only a make-believe excursion of the mind, fantasy can help people find excitement, adventure, self-confidence, and pleasure.

From childhood on, most people have sexual fantasies that serve a variety of functions and elicit a broad range of reactions. Some are pleasant or exhilarating; others are embarrassing, puzzling, or even shocking. In this chapter, we will discuss the functions of sexual fantasies and then provide a classification for describing the most common types of fantasy patterns. For purposes of clarity, we will restrict our use of the term "sexual fantasy" to refer only to wakeful thoughts as distinguished from sleep-associated dreams.

FACTS ABOUT FANTASIES

Although every child learns that pretending is an important type of play, sexual fantasies after childhood are usually not thought of as playful.

This attitude may exist because sex is usually regarded as a serious matter, even in the imagination. Furthermore, some religious traditions regard a thought as equivalent to an act; thus, a person who has "immoral" sexual daydreams or desires is as sinful as a person who acts upon these impulses. Fantasies have also been viewed as having implications for mental health. Psychoanalysts were the only group for half a century to study fantasy in any depth. They viewed "deviant" sexual fantasies — those portraying anything other than heterosexual acts that led to intercourse — as immature expressions of the sex drive and as blocks to the development of more mature sexuality (Hollender, 1963). Many psychoanalysts also believed that such fantasies were likely to be forerunners of "deviant" sexual behavior (Freud, 1946; Eidelberg, 1945; Yalom, 1960).

Generally, imagination, creativity, and playfulness are part of the act of fantasizing. However, if a fantasy becomes a controlling force in a person's life, the play element may be completely eliminated. This situation isn't very different from the person who becomes addicted to gambling (which also begins as a form of play) or the person who gets so caught up in a competitive sport, such as long-distance running, that the playful side of the activity is lost.

At times, it may be difficult to distinguish sexual fantasy from sexual desire. Just as your awareness of hunger and thinking about what kind of food you'd like to eat may blend together, your sexual appetite may merge with thoughts about how sexual satisfaction may be obtained. Although a fantasy may be valued strictly as a piece of fiction as opposed to a preview of an expected reality, this distinction does not always hold. In some cases, a sexual fantasy expresses sexual desire, while in others it *provokes* sexual desire that does not necessarily require the fantasied act for fulfillment.

THE CONTEXT OF SEXUAL FANTASIES

Sexual fantasies occur in an astonishingly wide variety of settings and circumstances. Sometimes these imaginative interludes are intentionally called forth to pass the time, to enliven a boring experience, or to provide a sense of excitement. At other times, sex fantasies float into our awareness in a seemingly random fashion, perhaps triggered by thoughts or feelings of which we have little awareness.

Preferential Patterns

Among the most common varieties of sexual fantasies are those that can best be described as old familiar stories. The origin of such a fantasy, if it can be traced at all, might have been a book, a movie scene, or an actual experience. The person using this fantasy finds it to be particularly pleasing and comfortable and returns to it again and again. On different occasions, minor variations may be played out in the fantasy, but the fantasizer almost invariably occupies a central role in the story line.

How a particular fantasy comes to be preferred and repeated over and over again is not entirely clear. Sometimes the primary fascination with this sort of fantasy lies in its sexual arousal, while at other times the pleasure may be more related to the "director's role" — being able to control the scene, plot, and actors. In many instances, the complexity of this fantasy makes it more suitable for use in solitary situations than during sexual activity with a partner.

In another form of the preferential fantasy pattern the person repeatedly uses a particular *type* of fantasy — group sex, for example — but no characters or story line connect one fantasy to another. The first pattern described is like playing a specific record again and again, while this pattern is more like playing a certain type of record — country and western or classical music — repeatedly.

There are at least two situations in which preferential fantasies may become troublesome. For some people, the repeated and exclusive use of such a fantasy may lead to a situation in which the fantasy becomes necessary for sexual arousal. The person no longer responds sexually to his or her partner since sexual arousal depends on the fantasy alone. Infrequently, preferential fantasies can become obsessions that may interfere with thinking or behavior. Obsessional fantasies will be discussed more fully in chapter 17.

Curiosity and Creativity

Just as children exercise both their curiosity and creativity when they pretend, people who use sexual fantasy also draw on these elements. The desire to know about something not yet experienced, forbidden, or seemingly unattainable is often a key feature of sexual fantasies. For instance, a married woman who has always been faithful to her husband may fantasize about an extramarital liaison, or a fifteen-year-old boy may fantasize about making love to a woman pictured in a *Playboy* centerfold. In both examples, the fantasy does not necessarily mean that the person wants to actually participate in the fantasied behavior.

Fantasy in the context of curiosity may be highly arousing and intriguing but it may also include scenes that seem outlandish, preposterous, disgusting, fearful, or silly to the fantasizer if examined in a detached, rational moment. This discrepancy is not surprising because most of us enjoy things under some circumstances that would be unpleasant, embarrassing, or even frightening in others.

The creative side of sexual fantasies is not only linked to curiosity. Just as there is a creative aspect in an artist painting a scene from memory or an author writing in vivid detail about a past event, there is also a creative element in sexual fantasies that draw on memories of past sexual experience. The fantasizer embellishes the memories and molds them into new forms while retaining the essence of the remembered experience. The fantasy can be smoothed out or improved in comparison with the real-life experience; in the world of fantasy, blemishes, fatigue, and distractions disappear while passion mounts and the action is unencumbered by trivial details.

In creating a sexual fantasy, the fantasizer not only programs the action but also orchestrates the emotions of the principal fantasy figures. If a woman wants her fantasy lover to be strong and silent, he is; if she prefers a verbal, gentle partner, she instantly has such a person at her command. If a man wants a passionate, aggressive woman in his sexual imagery, she is immediately there; if he prefers a reserved, unwilling partner to force into submission, this is easily achieved. In this sense, fantasy provides a dimension that is relatively unattainable in real life because even if your partner is willing to try whatever sexual acts you suggest, you have no way of controlling his or her character or emotions.

Solitary or Shared

Many people regard their fantasies as private property and keep them to themselves. In recent years, it has been suggested that sharing fantasies between partners fosters intimacy and understanding. The implication is that not sharing your sexual fantasies may be selfish or immature. Those who believe in sharing fantasies point out that after a long time in a relationship, many couples discover that they each have fantasies

This block print by Harunobu, done in the late 1760s, shows a young girl fantasizing about her lover while she masturbates.

about the same activity (for instance, having anal intercourse). Fearing that their partner may be embarrassed, offended, or unwilling to "play," many couples do not share their fantasies. Sometimes the fantasies of two people in a relationship are quite complementary, as when one person wants to be spanked during sexual activity, while his or her partner fantasizes about spanking someone.

People who suggest that keeping fantasies private reflects immaturity do so for a number of reasons, some of which are at least partially incorrect. They believe that being embarrassed or ashamed of one's fantasies is in and of itself a mark of immaturity. They also feel that intimate relationships should have no barriers to communication because open communication is a mark of maturity and commitment. A third reason they give to "prove" that sharing sexual fantasies is best is that sharing fosters a deeper degree of understanding between partners and so is likely to improve the relationship. Finally, they often point out that sexual fantasies are more likely to be kept private by people who are sexually inhibited or "uptight." By bringing these fantasies out into the open, a person can become less inhibited (therefore, more "mature") and may attain more sexual satisfaction.

Such arguments are oversimplified in many ways. To begin with, there is nothing wrong or immature about having private thoughts or feelings. If private fantasies give a distorted view of a

"I think you're being silly. Would you like it better if I was thinking of you and sleeping with Robert Redford?"

Playboy, November 1977. Reproduced by special permission of *Playboy* Magazine; Copyright © 1977 by *Playboy.*

person's preferences, sharing the fantasy with a partner may result in misperception of what that person needs or wants instead of better understanding. For instance, if a woman occasionally fantasizes about being raped and enjoys the fantasy, this does not mean that she wants to be raped or would enjoy being raped. The same can be said of a person who fantasizes about robbing a bank: he or she can hardly be said to have a criminal mind or to be "dangerous" because of this type of fantasy.

A partner may not only misunderstand a fantasy, but may also believe that he or she is in some way expected to play it out in real life. Although the partner can say "no," there may be a subtle pressure, whether intentional or unintentional. Having learned that your partner is turned on by a particular sexual fantasy, do you agree to try it, even if it is a bit uncomfortable, in order to be open-minded and sensitive to your partner's needs? What if you mistakenly decide to "try out" the fantasy when your partner doesn't really want to? Sometimes, once a fantasy has been shared with a partner, it provokes jealousy, guilt, or self-doubt. This is particularly true when one partner assumes that the other's fantasy indicates dissatisfaction or a desire to try someone else.

Many people find that after telling a partner about their most highly charged sexual fantasy, the turn-on value of the fantasy fizzles. While this does not always happen — as sometimes the erotic stimulus of the fantasy increases — it is a potential pitfall. Unfortunately, there is no way of knowing beforehand if partners will benefit from sharing details of their sexual fantasies or if problems will result.

Other Viewpoints on Sexual Fantasies

While we believe that most sex fantasies are natural, creative experiments that help combat loneliness or boredom and that defuse forbidden urges, some experts have different views. Here is a sampling of their thoughts on the subject.

In a paper titled "Why We Should *Not* Accept Sexual Fantasies," California psychologist Bernard Apfelbaum (1980a) describes fantasies as "cut-off parts of us signalling wildly to get back in." He believes that sex fantasies stem from dissatisfaction with reality and have a high potential for creating relationship conflicts. For example, if one partner feels that the other's turn-on comes from a fantasy rather than from personal involvement, an instinctive sense of being ignored intrudes and blocks sexual responsiveness (he assumes, of course, that fantasy and involvement do not mix). Apfelbaum also suggests that having private, unshared fantasies lessens intimacy and trust in a relationship, and says: "Sexual fantasies always offer us precious clues about what needs to be done to strengthen our relationships."

A somewhat different approach is taken by Avodah Offit, a psychoanalyst in New York, who believes that sex therapists overemphasize the acceptability of sex fantasies: "Whether the object of the fantasy is a rhinoceros, a mutilated geriatric specimen, or a cloven-hoofed hermaphrodite, the injunction is to enjoy freely. ... The measure of psychological truth is an erect penis or a lubricated vagina. Pleasure is where you find it . . ." (Offit, 1977, p. 189). Offit thinks that if reality and fantasy are closely matched, this indicates a "well-integrated personality," a sort of psychological togetherness. If fantasy strays too far away from our personal realities, the inconsistencies point to potential personality problems. Finally, Offit regards sex fantasies as "a pale substitute for the complexities of joy and pain which are requisites for loving a real person" (Offit, 1977, p. 201).

Another psychoanalyst-sex researcher, Robert Stoller (1979), believes that sex fantasies are a private pornography that allow us to gain revenge over a previously painful situation. He suggests that there is a flame of hostility at the core of all sex fantasies (and all sexual excitement).

Psychiatrist Natalie Shainess (1971) takes an even stronger position. She says that fantasies during intercourse are "symptomatic of sexual difficulty" and "signs of sexual alienation." She also believes that healthy women do not fantasize very much except when they are young and inexperienced, and if fantasies persist "you can assume there's greater pathology."

Finally, Alan Rapaport, a clinical psychologist, takes the viewpoint that *any* fantasy that occurs during person-to-person sex is debasing because it reduces personal involvement. "If a person is caught up in a private fantasy while making love ... it interferes with a more sharing and intimate relationship" (Goleman and Bush, 1977).

Intruding Fantasies

Not all sexual fantasies are willfully conjured up or pleasing. Some fantasies recur over and over again despite being unwanted; other fantasies flood into a person's awareness in a frightening fashion, producing inner turmoil, guilt, or conflict. Fantasies of this sort either may result in sexual arousal or may be so distressing that they shut off sexual feelings.

Usually, intruding fantasies that depict sexual situations or conduct that the fantasizer considers abnormal or bizarre (yet also arousing) include some imagined form of punishment or injury as the price to be paid for the sexual indulgence. The punishment within the fantasy may range from physical afflictions (such as venereal disease or cancer) to being discovered by others in the midst of sexual activity, being arrested and jailed, or being deprived of sexual satisfaction via one calamity or another. Other intruding fantasies may result in real-life problems such as avoidance of sexual activity, profound sexual guilt, or sexual dysfunction.

It is not difficult to imagine how distressing it might be for a forty-year-old married woman with conservative religious and sexual values to find that during sexual activity with her husband she repeatedly has fantasies about having sex with a group of men. Similarly, a man who prides himself on his *macho* image and is strongly anti-homosexual may be alarmed to find himself fantasizing about performing oral sex on another man. If distressing fantasies recur regularly, counseling may be required. Psychologists, psychiatrists, or sex therapists can help a person troubled by such fantasy patterns learn how to "switch the channel" (as you would switch from a disturbing TV show to a more pleasant one), or can teach thought-blocking techniques to deal with the situation (Wolpe, 1969; Abel and Blanchard, 1974).

FUNCTIONS OF SEXUAL FANTASY

Our use of the sexual imagination is quite varied. Fantasies function at many different levels to boost our self-confidence, provide a safety valve for pent-up feelings, increase sexual excitement, or to let us triumph over the forces that prove troublesome in the everyday world, to mention just a few. Some of the most common functions of sexual fantasies will now be described.

Inducing or Enhancing Arousal

We have already said that fantasy and sexual desire often merge together. People with low levels of sexual desire typically have few sexual fantasies (Kolodny, Masters, and Johnson, 1979; Kaplan, 1979; Nutter and Condron, 1983) and will often benefit from treatment that helps them form positive fantasies (Wish, 1975; Byrne, 1977; LoPiccolo, 1980).

Many times, sexual fantasies are used to induce or enhance sexual arousal, and while fantasies are often combined with masturbation to provide a source of turn-on when a partner is not available, fantasies are also extremely common during sexual activity with someone else (Friday, 1973 and 1980; Hunt, 1975; Hariton and Singer, 1974).

For some, the use of fantasy provides an initial boost to getting things underway. Others use fantasy to move from a leisurely, low-key sexual level into a more passionate state. One of the most frequent patterns we have encountered is the use of a particularly treasured fantasy to move from the plateau phase of arousal to orgasm. Some men and women report that they are unable to be orgasmic unless they use fantasy in this way.

Sexual fantasies can enhance both the psychological and physiological sides of sexual response in many ways: counteracting boredom, focusing thoughts and feelings (thus avoiding distractions or pressures), boosting our self-image (in our fantasies we can assume our desired physical attributes and need not worry about penis size, breast size, or body weight), and imagining an ideal partner (or partners) who suits all our needs.

Safety with Excitement

Sexual fantasies also provide a safe, protected environment for engaging the imagination and letting our sexual feelings roam. They are safe because they are private and fictional: privacy ensures that fantasies are undiscoverable, while the fictional makeup of our fantasies relieves us of personal accountability. Another safety feature of fantasies lies in having the "director's role," even to the point of being able to end the fantasy abruptly if it becomes uncomfortable or threatening. Without such safety, the erotic value of most people's fantasies would probably decrease substantially.

If you consider that most sexual fantasies involve situations, partners, and/or behavior that might be judged improper or illegal if they were real, the importance of safety as a backdrop for excitement becomes apparent. A mild-mannered, genteel college professor can fantasize about orgies with the three attractive coeds in the first row of his classroom without risking his tenure or reputation. A young woman lawyer can fantasize about raping one of her clients without jeopardizing her standing before the bar. A teenage boy can construct elaborate sexual fantasies about ravishing his best friend's mother without risking parental punishment or losing a friend. Clearly, the element of safety ensures the appeal and power of these erotic images.

Releasing Anxiety or Guilt

Fantasies of all types function as psychological safety valves that discharge inner tensions or needs in a relatively painless way (Byrne, 1977). In our fantasies, we can get even with others for real or imagined injustices, conquer fears by carefully controlling the action and emotions, and compensate for any personal shortcomings that are troublesome in real life. Consider the following examples from our files:

A thirty-two-year-old married woman: My husband and I had a lousy sex life for years, and it mirrored a lousy relationship. During this time, my sex fantasies almost always involved making it with other men while he was forced to watch me with great humiliation. It was sweet revenge, I guess. . . .

Once we started marriage counseling, things began to improve. We learned how to talk together, and our sex life improved too. The interesting thing was, my fantasies began to change. I guess I no longer had a need to retaliate.

A twenty-two-year-old unmarried male medical student: I've always been very uptight about sex. I suppose one reason is that I'm embarrassed about the size of my penis, which seems very small. In my fantasies, the woman I'm with always remarks on how big my penis is and seems in awe of its power. I found that if I used this fantasy while I was really with someone, I was much less nervous. It sounds silly, but I really felt better about myself.

Since we live in a society with a strong tradition of sexual restrictions and taboos and we learn not to discuss sexual behavior, fantasy often provides an important means of clarifying and dealing with sexual conflicts or confusion.

Controlled Rehearsal

For most people, fantasy provides a way to preview an anticipated experience and to prepare themselves for what to expect and how to act.

While this function of sexual fantasies may be most prominent during adolescence or with any people who have only limited sexual experience, it is very important. The opportunity to visualize oneself in a certain form of erotic activity — oral-genital sex, for example — allows one to anticipate some problems that may occur. By replaying a scene several times, fantasizers can develop a better idea of how to minimize difficulties and can also partially desensitize themselves to feelings of awkwardness, embarrassment, or surprise. Of course, if and when the fantasy is transformed into fact, the actual event may be considerably different from the imagined one in feelings, tempo, and other details. Nevertheless, a sense of comfort usually results from using fantasy as rehearsal.

Fantasy and Sexual Values

Many people misunderstand the nature of sexual fantasy and think that it expresses an actual desire to participate in or experience a given situation. This is like saying that a person who daydreams about being a war hero wants to go to war or that a person who fantasizes about having children is ready or willing to be a parent. Professionals are not immune to confusing the issues still further, as Lonnie Barbach (1980, p. 119) explains:

> I worked with a group of feminist therapists who argued that it is sexist to derive pleasure from rape fantasies or fantasies that portray male domination. It was difficult for them to separate the sexual pleasure the fantasy provided from its political interpretation. I also knew a lesbian therapist who nearly panicked when she found herself having heterosexual fantasies, fearing that she might be a "latent heterosexual."

In an ongoing study of sexual fantasies being done at the Masters & Johnson Institute, we have found that most women who are aroused by fantasies that portray "unusual" sex practices such as rape, incest, sex with animals, or sado-masochistic sex indicate that they have no interest whatsoever in acting out the fantasy. In contrast, men appear to be somewhat more adventuresome. About two-thirds of the men we have interviewed who have such fantasies declare that they would be willing to try them under the right circumstances.

A study of the sexual fantasies of married women during intercourse with their husbands stressed that fantasy content does not indicate sexual problems, psychological problems, or personality flaws (Hariton and Singer, 1974). Masters and Johnson (1979) have shown that most people with recurrent sexual fantasies feel neither the desire nor the need to act on them in real life. They also found that the content of the most common fantasies of heterosexuals and homosexuals are remarkably similar. Homosexuals frequently fantasize about heterosexual situations and heterosexuals commonly fantasize about homosexual encounters (see Table 13-1).

While most people realize that a fleeting fantasy is not an in-depth revelation of the inner psyche, it is tempting to assume that a favorite fantasy theme says important things about our psychological makeup. There are no research data showing that this is true for all people (although it may be true in individual instances). Our sexual and personal values may differ considerably from our fantasy lives, just as an actor's true identity may vary greatly from the dramatic roles he plays.

Fantasy as Fact

Although many people say that they have no wish to transform their sexual fantasies into reality, for some the opposite is true. What motivates a person to lean one way or the other is uncertain, but some of the relevant factors may be:

TABLE 13–1
Comparative Content of Fantasy Material by Frequency of Occurrence

Heterosexual male
1. Replacement of established partner
2. Forced sexual encounter with female
3. Observation of sexual activity
4. Homosexual encounters
5. Group sex experiences

Heterosexual female
1. Replacement of established partner
2. Forced sexual encounter with male
3. Observation of sexual activity
4. Idyllic encounters with unknown men
5. Lesbian encounters

Homosexual male
1. Imagery of male sexual anatomy
2. Forced sexual encounters with males
3. Heterosexual encounters with females
4. Idyllic encounters with unknown men
5. Group sex experiences

Homosexual female
1. Forced sexual encounters
2. Idyllic encounter with established partner
3. Heterosexual encounters
4. Recall of past sexual experience
5. Sadistic imagery

Source: Based on Table 9–1 in Masters and Johnson, 1979. © 1979 by William H. Masters and Virginia E. Johnson.
Data from interviews with thirty persons in each group collected between 1957 and 1968.

(1) how powerful an erotic turn-on is involved, (2) how receptive, trustworthy, and understanding the partner is perceived to be, (3) how a person feels about himself or herself, and (4) how unusual or bizarre a fantasy appears.

Reliable statistics on how many people act out their sexual fantasies in real life are not available. For some couples, the acting out involves a limited dramatization, playing roles in a carefully controlled way — a rehearsal of the fantasy instead of the entire experience. For example, a woman who fantasizes about being spanked may ask her partner to give her a gentle spanking which is more symbolic than real, or a man who fantasizes about having sex with a young teenage girl may ask his partner to dress and act like a thirteen year old. In such situations, the fantasy comes to life in the sense of being "in the flesh" rather than imaginary, but it is still not the real thing. The limited dramatization form of acting out fantasies is particularly appealing to many people because of its safety and control, but it is often less psychologically satisfying than the purely imaginary fantasy since it is "only an act."

Some people go further in transforming a sexual fantasy into real life. A married couple may respond to an ad in a "swinger's magazine" to try out a fantasy of switching partners. A person with fantasies about being tied up (bondage) may convince his or her partner to do so. In some cases, the fantasy becomes more fulfilling, more meaningful, and a part of the continuing sexual relationship. Very often, however, the result is less than expected: sexual fantasies that are tried in real life often turn out to be disappointing, unexciting, or even unpleasant. Nancy Friday, who has studied male and female sex fantasies for almost a decade, says: "I think that for every person who has written to me about the joys of performing their sexual dreams in reality, there have been three or four who knew in advance that it wouldn't work, or who tried it and were disappointed" (Friday, 1975, p. 280). Our research also indicates that for many people, transforming fantasy to fact is unsatisfactory, resulting at times in a complete loss of the erotic value of the fantasy. A twenty-two-year-old female college student told us:

> I used to have one particular fantasy that never failed to work. It was almost an electric thing, like flipping a switch and then "Zowie." I almost always had my best orgasms, and most exciting sex, when I flashed this fantasy through my

mind. Then, unfortunately, I decided to try it out with my partner. We were both interested in this, I wasn't embarrassed or uptight, but it just didn't click together for me. After we had tried it two or three times, the fantasy itself became less exciting and less reliable and finally just didn't work at all. It was like losing a best friend.

A similar point is made by Karen Shanor (1977, pp. 162–163) in a book called *The Fantasy Files:*

> Often when a fantasy is finally acted out, it does not occur again with any frequency as a fantasy. Only if the acting-out experience is amazingly good does the thought remain prominent. . . . Most of the time reality does not live up to the excitement of the fantasy, and the fantasy is therefore modified or significantly lessened in its importance.

One other aspect of the fantasy-as-reality topic deserves mention. Men have often turned to prostitutes to assist them in living out a sexual fantasy because the prostitute-client situation is apt to be psychologically safe for a number of reasons. First, the prostitute is a sexually experienced person who has probably "seen it all" and is therefore unshockable. Second, the encounter with the prostitute is protected in a social sense — privacy is ensured and the experience is isolated from everyday relationships. Third, the transaction is primarily sexual rather than personal. Finally, a man requesting unusual sexual services from a prostitute risks no loss of self-esteem or personal repute — if he can afford the price, his fantasy is implemented without much ado. In newspapers across the country that carry sexually explicit classified ads, it is not unusual to see escort services (usually fronts for commercial sex) advertising "Try out your fantasies, whatever they may be" or to find female and male consorts marketing a particular fantasy angle, as shown by a poetic prostitute whose forbidding picture, black cape and all, was captioned, "My

whips and chains will thrill your veins. Call Mistress _____."

CONTENT OF SEXUAL FANTASY

The range of the erotic imagination is almost limitless. One person fantasizes about animals, another about movie stars, another about enemas, diapers, or South Sea islands. The action may be explicit and detailed or shifting and vague. The stylistic variations of sexual fantasies reflect the richness of the human mind.

In this section, we will briefly examine some of the more common types of sexual fantasies, realizing that many fantasies are difficult to pigeonhole neatly in a classification system.

Experimentation

One popular type of fantasy is to visualize experiences that have never been tried in real life. The content may focus on novel circumstances like being the star of a porno movie, having sex in a public place, or being a prostitute. The fantasy may also explore unusual forms of sexual activity such as sex with an animal or incest. In some cases, the thrill of the forbidden is important; in others, the desire for the unique or the untried is more relevant. For this reason, experimentation fantasies are often used to overcome sexual boredom.

Conquest

At the core of all conquest fantasies is an element of power. The power may be expressed in the ability to command, to force, or to seduce someone else into sexual relations. Assuming the imaginary role of ruling monarch or slave-owner

As these ads show, telephone fantasy sex has become a big business in the 1980s.

can set the stage for commands to be obeyed. Nonphysical force used to coerce someone into sex can be conjured up in roles such as prison warden, school principal, boss, or blackmailer. If physical force is involved, the fantasy is classified as rape or sadomasochism. Of course, the power to seduce others can be written into almost any fantasy script.

The flip side of the conquest fantasy is the idea of being conquered — of being commanded, forced, or seduced by someone else. The variety of roles that can be assumed to orchestrate such a fantasy is immense. The key element is being

powerless to resist, whether for reasons of fear, resignation to one's fate, blind obedience, economic difficulties, or protecting another person.

A subtype of the conquest/conquered fantasy is one version of the domination/humiliation theme. Here, power is not only used to obtain sexual activity, but circumstances must be degrading or embarrassing. The victim might be forced by the power-figure to grovel, to wear unusual items of clothing (diapers, see-through clothes, shackles), or to engage in humiliating acts. The turn-on comes from the debasement, from being "reduced to a state of abject humiliation" (Friday, 1973).

Switching Partners

Imagining sex with a different partner is one of the most common varieties of sexual fantasies. Sometimes the imagined partner is a previous partner (an old boyfriend or girlfriend, for example). More often, the fantasized partner is simply someone considered desirable: a friend, a neighbor, a relative, a teacher, a salesclerk, or an imaginary ideal.

Some people are uncomfortable when they have a fantasy of a different partner during sex with their lover or spouse. Guilt feelings can result if the person views such a fantasy as a sign of infidelity. If you have ever felt this way, you might be interested in knowing that replacing an established partner with another person in fantasy is so common that the chances are quite high that you and your own partner have both had this vision (Crépault et al., 1977; Crépault and Couture, 1980).

A subtype of the "switching partners" fantasy is the version that can be called "celebrity sex." Here, the fantasied partner is chosen from the public roster of celebrities: movie stars, television personalities, sports figures, politicians, musicians, artists, authors, and faces in the news. Just as past generations incorporated images of celebrities like Clark Gable, Humphrey Bogart, Marilyn Monroe, and Jayne Mansfield into their sexual fantasies, people continue this practice today.

We find the following story to be particularly intriguing, since it demonstrates a fairly consistent finding about sex fantasies, even those involving "celebrity sex."

> One young woman developed an elaborate fantasy of having intercourse with Mick Jagger, a member of the Rolling Stones. When she began having intercourse regularly as a "groupie" following different bands around, she always reverted, during the act itself, to images of her childhood fantasy of Mick. In the course of her travels as a "groupie," she actually finally encountered the real Mick Jagger. In bed with him at last, she still found it necessary to resort to her *fantasy* Mick Jagger because the real one, after all, was not as prodigiously gifted in bed as she had long fantasized him to be. (Singer, 1980, p. 187)

Group Sex

Another common type of fantasy that is related to the "switching partners" pattern is the group sex scene. The details of group sex fantasies vary from elaborate orgies involving friends to images of ancient Rome or being on a Hollywood movie set where the evenings turn into sexual olympic games. At the other end of the spectrum are group sex fantasies where a man imagines himself making love to two women or a woman visualizes herself with two men. In some group sex fantasies the action is bisexual, while in other imaginary scripts the action is strictly heterosexual although there may be dozens of arms, legs, and sex organs in motion at any given time. Interestingly, many people who enjoy this type of fantasy tell us they might be willing to try it out if given the right set of circumstances.

Watching

Some people become particularly aroused by fantasizing scenes in which they are watching others engage in sex. In the purest form of this fantasy type, the observer never actually enters the action, although he or she may be either visible or hidden from the sexual participants. In variations on this theme, the observer reaches high levels of sexual excitement from watching and then joins in the physical festivities. "Watching" fantasies are not unusual among married couples, where one person fantasizes a scene in which he or she watches their spouse having sex with someone else. "Watching" fantasies, however, are not equivalent to actual voyeurism, discussed in chapter 17.

Rape

Fantasies about rape are possibly the most misunderstood of all sex fantasies. Some people think that women who fantasize about rape are really yearning for such an event to occur and suggest that the fantasy represents an unrealized wish. This distorted interpretation has no basis in fact. It is more useful to look at rape fantasies as providing reassurance to some women that they are being sexually passive rather than aggressive, since this conforms to our cultural stereotypes about sexual behavior (Barclay, 1973). In addition, rape fantasies absolve the "victim" of personal responsibility for enjoying sex. As Nancy Friday (1973, p. 109) observes: "By putting herself in the hands of her fantasy assailant — by *making* him an assailant — she gets him to do what she wants him to do, while seeming to be forced to do what he wants. Both ways she wins, and all the while she's blameless, at the mercy of a force stronger than herself."

Rape fantasies have a variety of forms. A woman may visualize herself as the rapist or a man may envision himself as the victim or victimizer. Some heterosexual men occasionally have fantasies about being raped homosexually: as in the woman's situation discussed earlier, the man's fantasy frees him of "responsibility" for the homosexual act since he has been forced into it.

Idyllic Encounters

In sharp contrast to rape fantasies are those with strong overtones of romance and tranquility. "Idyllic encounter" scripts usually involve meeting a stranger under near perfect conditions — a quiet garden, a secluded, moonlit beach, a tropical paradise — where instant romantic attraction blossoms forth and an ecstatic sexual interlude takes place. Then the characters usually go on their way, happy but unencumbered.

One famous literary rendition of the idyllic encounter fantasy appeared in *Fear of Flying* (Jong, 1974, pp. 11, 14), where it was described as the "zipless fuck":

> The zipless fuck was more than a fuck. It was a platonic ideal. Zipless because when you came together zippers flew away like rose petals, underwear blew off in one breath like dandelion fluff. . . .
>
> For the true, ultimate zipless A-1 fuck, it was necessary that you never get to know the man very well. . . . [A]nother condition was brevity. And anonymity made it even better.
>
> The zipless fuck is absolutely pure. It is free of ulterior motives. There is no power game. The man is not "taking" and the woman is not "giving." . . . No one is trying to prove anything or get anything out of anyone. The zipless fuck is the purest thing there is. And it is rarer than the unicorn.

Sadomasochism

Inflicting pain (sadism) or receiving pain (masochism) may be a source of sexual arousal. Sexual fantasies with sadomasochistic themes invoke images of being beaten, tied, whipped, chained, tickled, teased, handcuffed, contorted, gagged, burned, spanked, or otherwise victimized or doing the victimization. Physical force or pain is vividly present and usually the turn-on value of the fantasy is in direct proportion to the protests of the victim. Here again, as with many other fantasies, there is often no desire to live out the fantasy. One research volunteer told us, after describing a favorite masochistic fantasy in some detail, "I really can't stand physical pain and I don't know why this turns me on."

GENDER DIFFERENCES IN SEXUAL FANTASIES

It used to be thought that men had more frequent sex fantasies than women and that the sexual fantasies of women were "tamer" than those of men. This viewpoint reflected the idea that women were less interested in sex than men but were more interested in interpersonal relations. For example, Barclay (1973) believed that female sexual fantasies usually dwelled on emotional, romantic elements, while male sexual fantasies sounded like pornographic books: explicit in sexual detail, with little regard to emotions. Similarly, John Money suggested that women have only two predominant "core" fantasies — masochistic fantasies and fantasies of soft objects and touch — whereas men have a much larger fantasy repertoire (J. Petersen, 1980). Morton Hunt (1975), who conducted a survey for *Playboy*, found that 75 percent of men and 80 percent of women fantasized about intercourse with a loved person during masturbation. Yet men reported fantasies of intercourse with strangers twice as often as women did, while women reported more frequent masturbatory fantasies about being forced to have sex and homosexual activities.

Our impression is that men and women are more similar than different in their sexual fantasy patterns. The idea that women do not have sex fantasies is now clearly recognized as outmoded (Friday, 1973; Hariton and Singer, 1974; Hunt, 1975; Sue, 1979). In studies conducted three decades ago, Kinsey and his colleagues (1953) found that 64 percent of women who masturbated used erotic fantasies. More recently, it was reported that 94 percent of women used sexual fantasies (Crépault et al., 1977), which is quite consistent with our finding that 86 percent of 300 women aged eighteen to thirty-five had erotic fantasies at various times (Masters, Johnson, and Kolodny, 1980). For both men and women, sexual fantasies are more common during masturbation than during intercourse (Hunt, 1974; Masters and Johnson, 1979; Crépault and Couture, 1980). In addition, a recent study found that 71 percent of men and 72 percent of women used fantasy to enhance sexual arousal (Zimmer, Borchardt, and Fischle, 1983). On the other hand, several studies have shown that the sex fantasies of women tend to be more passive than those of men (women tend to visualize their role in the fantasy as having something done to them by someone else, rather than being the active "doer"), perhaps reflecting an innate psychological difference but more likely accounted for by the way in which most females are socialized to see their roles in sexual interaction as essentially following the lead set by males.

The similarity of fantasy content between the sexes shown in Table 13-1 has been supported by our continued research findings. At least in recent years, the sexual fantasies of women are quite explicit and sexually detailed (Crépault et al., 1976; Masters, Johnson, and Kolodny, 1980). While changing sexual attitudes and the greater availability to women of sexually explicit materials have undoubtedly led to some changes in the acceptability of fantasy in the last decade, we suspect that male-female differences in fantasy patterns were never quite as large as they were thought to be.

SUMMARY

1. Sexual fantasies begin in childhood and serve important functions in our lives, such as combating boredom, providing or enhancing excitement, releasing inner tensions, and permitting safe, imaginary rehearsals of untried behavior.

2. A person's use of a particular type of sexual fantasy does not necessarily mean that he or she wishes to act it out. Many times, fantasies conflict with our personal values and beliefs, but their imaginary nature allows us to accept and deal with them.

3. Deciding whether to keep fantasies private or to discuss them with a partner is a complicated matter. Although such a discussion may be valuable in certain ways, it also has some risks — including the risk that the fantasy will lose its erotic value.

4. Similar difficulties apply to the question of whether to try out a fantasy in real life. While implementing the fantasy may be made easier by a trusting, accepting, willing partner, many people find that reality just doesn't measure up to the private experience of the fantasy itself.

5. The most common types of sexual fantasies include the following categories: experimentation, conquest, switching partners, group sex, watching, rape, idyllic encounters, and sadomasochism.

6. Contrary to older viewpoints, both women and men commonly have sexual fantasies. There is no convincing evidence that there are substantial sex differences in the content of these fantasies.

SUGGESTED READINGS

Crépault, Claude, and Couture, Marcel. "Men's Erotic Fantasies," *Archives of Sexual Behavior* 9 (1980): 565–581. A detailed research report on the sex fantasies of men.

Friday, Nancy. *My Secret Garden*. New York: Trident Press, 1973. A nonscientific but intriguing collection of women's sexual fantasies, showing the diversity and inventiveness of the erotic imagination.

Friday, Nancy. *Men In Love*. New York: Delacorte Press, 1980. A compilation of sex fantasy patterns from men that provides provocative reading if you disregard the author's interpretations of their "meanings."

Goleman, Daniel, and Bush, Sherida. "The Liberation of Sexual Fantasy," *Psychology Today* 11 (October 1977): 48–53 and 104–107. A balanced discussion of current professional views on sex fantasies.

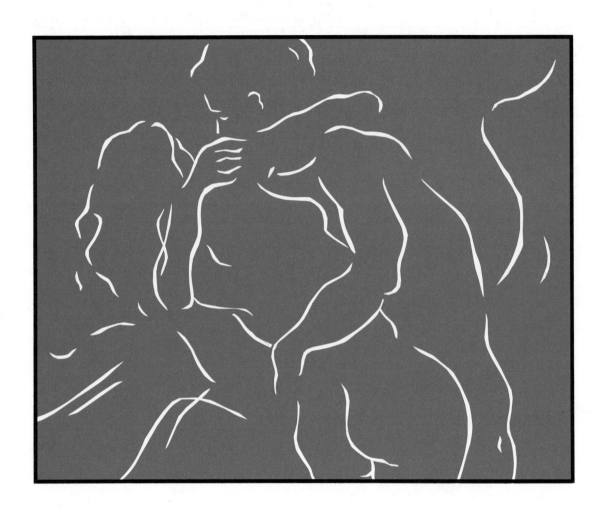

PART THREE

Behavioral Perspectives

14 Solitary Sexual Behavior

A twenty-eight-year-old man: My first clear memory of sexual arousal was at age twelve or thirteen while I was reading a sexy book. I kept the book hidden from my parents, and I marked all the "good parts" with paper clips. I must've read that thing a thousand times. (Authors' files)

A thirty-year-old woman: I went to see an X-rated movie with my boyfriend, and I liked it so much I went back to see it again by myself. (Authors' files)

A twenty-one-year-old woman: When I was thirteen, I discovered that rubbing my genitals against a pillow was sexually arousing, and I had lots of orgasms that way. I didn't learn that that was masturbation until I got to college. (Authors' files)

THE subject of solitary sexual behavior is surrounded by misconceptions and prohibitions. Most people have been taught that it isn't polite to talk about masturbation, and the activity itself is usually pursued with some fear about the possibility of discovery. As a result, people lack accurate information on the subject, and many are uncertain about how masturbation might affect their physical health or emotional stability.

Despite these concerns resulting from our cultural conditioning, new attitudes toward solitary sex (often called autoerotic activity) in its various forms have been emerging. Instead of labelling masturbation as an inferior or improper type of sexual behavior, many authorities now see it as a normal part of sexual development (Kinsey, Pomeroy, and Martin, 1948, 1953; Brashear, 1974; Gadpaille, 1975; DeMartino, 1979). Feminist Betty Dodson (1974, p. 55) takes an even stronger position: "Masturbation is our primary sex life. It is *the sexual base*. Everything we do beyond that is simply how we choose to socialize our sex life." The use of erotic readings, pictures, or movies by men and women has become accepted more widely than in the past. In a sense, solitary sexual behavior has come out of the closet: it has even been celebrated as the ultimate source of our sexual self-awareness. In this chapter, we will discuss several pertinent aspects of sexual behavior without a partner.

MASTURBATION

Masturbation can be defined as sexual self-pleasuring that involves some form of direct physical stimulation. Most often, masturbation is done by rubbing, stroking, fondling, squeezing, or otherwise stimulating the genitals, but it can also be carried out by self-stimulation of other body parts such as the breasts, the inner thighs, or the anus. The term masturbation refers to the act of self-stimulation without regard to the outcome; that is, sexual self-stimulation need not lead to orgasm to be masturbation.

In this book, we have deliberately used the term masturbation to refer only to sexual *self*-stimulation. Stimulation received from a partner, although similar in many ways, involves an interactional element that makes it helpful to maintain this distinction. While masturbation can occur as part of sexual activity with a partner, our focus in this chapter is primarily on masturbation as a private act.

As we have already pointed out, masturbation often begins during childhood and occurs

"Why do they call it self-abuse? I happen to love it."

Playboy, March 1984, p. 174. Reproduced by special permission of *Playboy* Magazine; Copyright © 1984 by *Playboy*.

commonly in both males and females throughout the life cycle. Masturbation is also found elsewhere in the animal kingdom. Ford and Beach (1951) noted that many species of apes and monkeys "form habits of self-stimulation," and other mammals also practice masturbation:

> Sexually excited male porcupines, for example, walk about on three legs while holding one forepaw on the genitals. . . . Male elephants sometimes manipulate their semi-erect penis with the trunk. . . . Male dogs and cats regularly lick the phallic organ, often showing convulsive pelvic movements which indicate the stimulatory value of the resulting sensations. . . . One [captive] male [dolphin] had a habit of holding his erect penis in the jet of water intake, and other [dolphins] characteristically rubbed the tumescent organ against the floor of the tank. . . . (Ford and Beach, p. 160)

Despite this apparent "naturalness" of masturbation from an evolutionary viewpoint, Ford and Beach noted that most human societies consider masturbation by adults to be undesirable. For an understanding of how a negative attitude toward masturbation developed in our own society, a glimpse back in history is revealing.

Historical Perspectives

The origins of the word masturbation are not entirely clear, although it seems to have been coined in Roman times. While it was previously thought that the term derived from the Latin *manus* (hand) and *stupro* (to defile), scholars now believe it has a Greek root, *mezea* (genitals), with the original meaning, "to arouse the genitals" (Bullough and Bullough, 1977).

The ancient Greeks and Romans were relatively silent on the subject of masturbation, although Hippocrates (a Greek physician commonly regarded as the "Father of Medicine") believed that excessive loss of semen caused spinal consumption (Haller and Haller, 1977). Even though the *Bible* has no clear-cut prohibitions against this sexual activity, both traditional Judaism and Christianity generally regarded masturbation as sinful. (The story of Onan [*Genesis* 38:9-11], which had been thought of as an edict against masturbation, is now thought by modern scholars to describe *coitus interruptus,* a very different act. Nevertheless, masturbation was referred to as "onanism" well into the twentieth century.)

The attitude of the Catholic Church has not changed in recent years; in a Vatican *Declaration on Sexual Ethics* (December 29, 1975), it was noted that "masturbation is an intrinsically and seriously disordered act." The Declaration went on to say, "Even if it cannot be proved that Scripture condemns this sin by name, the tradition of the Church has rightly understood it to be condemned in the *New Testament* when the latter speaks of 'impurity,' 'unchasteness' and other vices contrary to chastity and continence."

Masturbation was sometimes referred to as an "unnatural act" by church leaders because it had no reproductive goal, but later it was described as "self-abuse," "defilement of the flesh," and "self-pollution." In large part, the credit for giving masturbation such a bad reputation belongs to a Swiss physician, S. Tissot (1728-1797), who brought the matter into the scientific arena and transformed masturbation from a simple sin to an illness that had to be cured.

Tissot believed that all sexual activity was dangerous because it forced blood to rush to the head, leaving too little in the rest of the body, so that nerves and other vital tissues slowly degenerated. In keeping with the scientific knowledge of his time, he was certain that this form of nerve damage caused insanity. Tissot was convinced that masturbation was a particularly "dangerous" form of sex because it was convenient and could be started during the vulnerable years of childhood, and because the masturbator's guilt over his or her sinfulness further irritated the nervous system and made it more susceptible to damage.

The "proof" of Tissot's theory could be seen in mental asylums, where patients were either observed in the process of, or openly admitted to, masturbating. By the time Tissot's notions had crossed the Atlantic to America, the average doctor was quite willing to believe that masturbation caused insanity, epilepsy, acne, weight loss, decreased mental capability, weakness, lethargy, and — the ultimate punishment — early death. Benjamin Rush, one of the signers of the Declaration of Independence and a leader in early American medicine, published several pamphlets supporting Tissot's attitude toward masturbation (Bullough and Bullough, 1977). Fortunately, American physicians rejected Tissot's belief that sexual intercourse between married people was harmful.

Parents searched desperately for ways to keep their children from being stricken. Physicians were happy to oblige; after all, it was the conscientious doctor's duty to put an end to masturbation. Much energy and money was spent on cures ranging from elaborate belts, locks, and cages — to protect the genitals from roving hands — to surgical "cures" which left little for the patient to fondle.

The nineteenth-century medical profession in America attacked masturbation with zest. The battle was fought on two main fronts — diet and physical constraint. Gravies, alcohol, oysters, salt, pepper, fish, jelly, chocolate, ginger, and coffee were forbidden to masturbators (both male and female) as it was thought that they irritated the nerves and increased sexual desire. Dr. W. F. Morgan (1896) told readers of the *New York Medical Times* that cheese, eggs, and asparagus should not be eaten by young men as an evening meal because they increased the chance of nocturnal emissions.

Other doctors blamed tight britches, the friction of sheets, handling of the genitals during urination, and the touching of children's genitals by nursemaids or parents during bathing. If "irritants" were removed from the diet and tight britches removed from the wardrobe but masturbation still continued, drastic steps became necessary. Doctors prescribed such remedies as straightjackets at bed time, wrapping the child in cold, wet sheets to "cool" desire, and tying the hands to the bed posts. The U.S. Patent Office granted several patents to variations of the medieval chastity belt that shielded the genitals from fondling. Parents could padlock their children into these elaborate "genital cages" and tuck away the key (Figure 14-1). (One particularly torturous version constructed for adolescents and adults consisted of a tube lined with metal spikes into which the penis was inserted. If the penis became erect — it would be pricked.) By the early part of this century, metal mittens were being sold to deter the evil wanderings of little children's hands as well as an alarm that rang in the parents' bedroom if their child's bed was moving (LoPiccolo and Heiman, 1978).

For those seeking a more permanent solution to their problem (cages, belts, and metal mittens had to be removed for bathing, leaving the wearer vulnerable to temptation), doctors prescribed other treatments: leeches could be applied to the genital area to suck away blood and relieve the congestion that caused sexual desire; cautery (burning of genital tissue by an electric current or hot iron) was believed to deaden the nerves and decrease feeling and desire. The extreme cures — castration and removal of the clitoris — were most popular in the 1850s and 1860s. American medical journals of the mid-1800s also reported that castration was often a successful treatment of insanity. Our modern belief in immediate circumcision of newborn males is partly a carryover from the Victorian conviction that this surgery discouraged masturbation. Foreskin made the penis difficult to wash; removal of the foreskin thus lessened the amount of time the genitals had to be handled (Bullough and Bullough, 1977).

Slowly, beginning in the early 1900s, the American medical community began to realize that masturbation caused neither acne nor insanity. A few brave doctors even recommended that females masturbate to relieve hysteria and that males masturbate instead of picking up prostitutes (and venereal disease). As recently as 1930, however, a medical authority continued to warn of the dangers of "onanism" which could lurk in activities like rope-climbing, bicycle riding, or running a sewing machine. He argued that "the path leads to imbecility and premature senility," "loss of spirit, weakness of memory, dependency," "apathy," "languor, irritability, headaches, neuralgias, dimness of vision" and so on (Scott, 1930, p. 424).

Solitary Sexual Behavior

FIGURE 14–1
Antimasturbation Devices of the Nineteenth Century

Contemporary Attitudes

As the twentieth century neared its midpoint, medical authorities relied on research instead of speculation and slowly moved away from the notion that masturbation caused illness or insanity. For example, the 1940 edition of the respected pediatric textbook, Holt's *Diseases of Infancy and Childhood*, removed its discussion of masturbation from a chapter called "Functional and Nervous Disorders" and rejected the use of surgery, mechanical restraints, threats, or punishment to deal with this type of sexual behavior. The new edition took the position that masturbation caused no physical harm and defined the problems of masturbation as primarily the worry and guilt that a child may feel.

By the time of the Kinsey reports (1948 and 1953), both public and professional thinking about masturbation had shifted significantly from the early part of the century. But carryovers remained: even today, some people half-jokingly believe that masturbation will lead to "hair on the palm of your hand" or misshapen genitals, while others are convinced masturbation causes sterility, sexual dysfunction, fatigue, or memory loss. Unfortunately, some physicians are no better informed on this subject than the public.

A number of studies in the last fifteen years indicate that attitudes toward masturbation have relaxed considerably compared to earlier times. Morton Hunt (1975), reporting on the *Playboy* survey of sexual attitudes and behavior, found that only one out of six men or women between the ages of eighteen and thirty-four felt that masturbation is wrong. In the forty-five and over age groups he studied, approximately one-third of the women and men viewed masturbation as wrong. Arafat and Cotton (1974), reporting on a questionnaire administered to 230 college males and 205 college females, found that most of those who did not masturbate refrained due to lack of desire. Of the nonmasturbators, 32 percent of the males versus 14 percent of females thought of masturbation as a waste of energy, immoral, and producing cheap feelings. Only a small fraction of those who did not masturbate cited guilt, inhibition, or religious beliefs as their reasons.

As we mentioned in chapter 8, many teenagers are still troubled by masturbation and continue to have concerns over the possible effects of masturbation on their health. This belief was humorously described by novelist Philip Roth in *Portnoy's Complaint:*

> It was at the end of my freshman year of high school — and freshman year of masturbating — that I discovered on the underside of my penis, just where the shaft meets the head, a little discolored dot that has since been diagnosed as a freckle. Cancer. I had given myself *cancer*. All that pulling and tugging at my own flesh, all that friction, had given me an incurable disease. And not yet fourteen! In bed at night the tears rolled from my eyes. "No!" I sobbed. "I don't want to die! Please — no!" But then, because I would very shortly be a corpse anyway, I went ahead as usual and jerked off into my sock. (Philip Roth, *Portnoy's Complaint* [New York: Random House, 1969], p. 19)

Today, masturbation is a more accepted form of sexual behavior than it has ever been in the past, but there are still some lingering doubts. These doubts center on the following sorts of issues:

1. *Masturbation is sinful.* This, of course, is a matter of moral or religious conviction that each person must deal with in his or her own way. Several studies have found that people who are strongly religious masturbate less often than those who are not religious or who have less strongly held religious beliefs (DeMartino, 1979).

2. *Masturbation is unnatural.* The logic of this statement is hard to grasp. If naturalness refers to what occurs in nature, then this statement is incorrect since masturbation has been observed in many animal species. Furthermore, the numerous reports of masturbation during infancy or early childhood also refute the notion that it is unnatural.

3. *Masturbation may be a part of growing up, but adults who masturbate are psychologically immature.* Freudian theory generally supports this viewpoint, suggesting that adult masturbation is a symptom of psychosexual immaturity except when it is used as a substitute for heterosexual intercourse when no partner is available (Marcus and Francis, 1975). Today most authorities believe that adult masturbation is a legitimate type of sexual activity in its own right (see, for example, Fisher, 1973; Dodson, 1974; Hunt, 1975; Barbach, 1975; Miller and Lief, 1976; Hite, 1977; and DeMartino, 1979). The tension between these two positions is created by different theories of psychological maturity; yet no studies show that adults who masturbate are less mature than those who do not. Some experts believe that masturbation is "immature" only when it is *exclusively* and *compulsively* practiced even though other outlets are easily available (Ellis, 1965).

4. *Masturbation tends to be habit-forming and may prevent the development of healthy sexual functioning.* Most sexologists and psychotherapists see this claim as a throwback to nineteenth-century thinking. There is mounting evidence that *lack* of masturbatory experience may lead to psychosexual problems such as impotence or anorgasmia (Barbach, 1975; Hite, 1977; De-

Martino, 1979; Money, 1980), and learning about masturbation is a central feature of many sex therapy programs (LoPiccolo and Lobitz, 1972; Kaplan, 1974; Barbach, 1975 and 1980; Leiblum and Pervin, 1980).

In addition, it is now clear that masturbation may have a number of additional benefits. For example, it can provide a viable (and pleasurable) sexual outlet for people without partners, including the elderly. It can also be beneficial to persons whose sex drives are greater than their partners' at a particular moment. Finally, it is often a gratifying way of releasing tension, thus helping a person relax.

Techniques of Masturbation

People use a wide variety of methods of sexual self-pleasuring. For some, a single approach to masturbation, with only minor variations on the theme, is used over and over again. Other people experiment with a number of different masturbatory methods, sometimes selecting a few favorites for consistent use, and sometimes preferring continued inventiveness to repeat performances.

Masters and Johnson (1966) noted that no two women they studied had been observed to masturbate in exactly the same way. Even if the general pattern of physical self-stimulation was similar, the timing, tempo, and style of each individual's approach were unique. While men, in general, have less diversity and more "sameness" in their masturbation patterns, individual embellishments or idiosyncrasies exist here too.

A complete catalogue of the varieties of techniques used in masturbation could fill a full-length book and would probably be boring reading. Thus, we will restrict our discussion to common patterns of masturbation with brief mention of a few interesting variations.

FEMALE MASTURBATION

The most common form of female masturbation is to stimulate the clitoris, mons, or vaginal lips by stroking, rubbing, or applying pressure by hand (Masters and Johnson, 1966, 1979; Fisher, 1973; Hite, 1977). Clitoral stimulation may be accomplished by rubbing or stroking the clitoral shaft or may result from applying pressure to the mons or tugging on the vaginal lips. The clitoral glans, or tip, is rarely rubbed directly during masturbation because of its sensitivity. If clitoral stimulation is concentrated in one area for a long time, or if intense stimulation is applied to one spot, pleasurable sensations may lessen because the area can become partially numb (Masters and Johnson, 1966).

Interestingly, only a few women masturbate by inserting a finger or object into the vagina: Kinsey and his associates (1953) found that about 20 percent of women used this approach, and Hite (1977) found that only 1.5 percent of women masturbated by vaginal insertion alone. Similarly, only a small percentage of women routinely include breast stimulation as a part of masturbation (Kinsey's group found that 11 percent of women who masturbate incorporated breast play into self-stimulation).

Most women masturbate while lying on their backs, but some prefer a standing or sitting position. Hite (1977) found that 5.5 percent of her sample usually applied clitoral/vulval stimulation lying face down, with a hand placed between their legs. Other women prefer to masturbate by rubbing their genitals against an object such as a pillow, chair, bedpost, or doorknob. (A few years ago, one of our research subjects insisted on bringing her own pillow to our offices for a study involving masturbation since she couldn't masturbate without it). In variations on this theme, the woman may rub her genitals with fur, velvet, silk, or any soft material.

Female masturbation.

About 3 percent of women usually masturbate by pressing their thighs together rhythmically (Hite, 1977), and some women prefer to masturbate using some form of water massage of the genital region or perineum. The use of oils or lotions during masturbation is a fairly common practice but is usually only a secondary part of the masturbatory experience.

As women have become more informed and liberated in their attitudes toward masturbation, they have increasingly used hand-held vibrators to enhance sexual sensations. Almost half of the young women in our studies who masturbate have tried a vibrator at least once, and one-quarter of these women prefer the vibrator over other methods of self-stimulation (see Table 14-1). Vibrators come in many sizes, shapes, and styles. Some are cylindrical or shaped to anatomically resemble a penis, and others have changeable attachments that permit a variety of stimulatory modes. A few are discreetly designed and

are sold in fashionable stores without any hint of their possible sexual utility.

Vibrators are usually applied to the external genitals, but some women prefer to insert the vibrator into the vagina and move it slowly in and

TABLE 14–1
Preferred Types of Female Masturbation

Manual stimulation of clitoral/vulval area	48%
Vibrator stimulation of clitoral/vulval area	26
Rubbing against an object	6
Thigh pressure	4
Water massage	4
Vaginal insertion	10
Miscellaneous methods	2
Breast stimulation only	0

Data from 265 women, aged 18 to 35, who completed a detailed sex history questionnnaire and personal interview as part of the screening process for a research project at the Masters & Johnson Institute. Data collected from 1977 to 1980.

Solitary Sexual Behavior

What's Good and Bad About Vibrators

In the 1970s, the use of electric vibrators as a source of sexual stimulation became widely popular. Women were told by friends, the media, and professional counselors that the vibrator provided an almost foolproof means of experiencing orgasm, and vibrators began to be touted as "a woman's best friend." Although the vibrator is a relatively innocuous gadget, it also has some drawbacks that are less thoroughly advertised than its advantages. Let's look at both sides of the issues.

The vibrator's intensity helps many women reach orgasm quickly and easily during self-stimulation. For this very reason, the vibrator has become a popular teaching aid for women who have never experienced orgasm. Even for women who have no difficulty reaching orgasms on their own, the reliable and rather effortless use of the vibrator is often a matter of convenience and satisfaction.

However, the "instant orgasm" of the vibrator-induced variety may create problems. If a woman consistently uses intense mechanical means to achieve orgasm quickly, she will not appreciate the various stages of build-up to her release of sexual tension. Her pleasure may actually diminish, leaving her with a sense of restlessness or frustration.

A woman who fails to be orgasmic with a partner the first time she tries, after long and continued success with a vibrator, could incorrectly interpret that failure as evidence of her own sexual inadequacy. She may not realize that another person cannot duplicate the focused physical stimulation of the vibrator, and she may overlook other possible explanations of this situation – not relating well to her partner (or vice versa), being self-conscious or nervous, or trying too hard. In addition, some women seem to feel that orgasms resulting from vibrators are "artificial" and are therefore not as good as the "authentic" version.

Some people have asked if a woman can become "addicted" to a vibrator. It seems more accurate to say that she can become dependent on it, especially if she has tried and failed to reproduce the experience by any non-mechanical means or if for other reasons she feels insecure in her own ability to respond and so is reluctant to give up the dependable results of the vibrator.

The vibrator's intensity (especially when used to induce multiple orgasms) can give ecstatic sexual pleasure to one woman, but it may produce a painful uterine spasm for another. When the vibrator is used to relieve menstrual cramps it may be effective for some women, but it can increase menstrual flow to an uncomfortable level for others or it may even create more severe cramps. If applied to the same favorite area with great frequency, the vibrator may actually deaden the feelings temporarily. There are other highly individual reactions that should be considered before using this instrument freely, such as the presence of genital infections or skin disease.

The sensual high that can be produced with a vibrator is pleasurable, fast, and reliable for those women who are free of emotional or physical problems connected with its use. but the vibrator should be seen objectively *for what it is for each individual:* a toy, a bridge, a crutch – the means to a desired response or a substitute for an absent partner in a time of need. Objectivity is the key, perhaps because overindulgence with a vibrator, like overindulgence in food, can so easily become a way of masking real needs and genuine feelings.

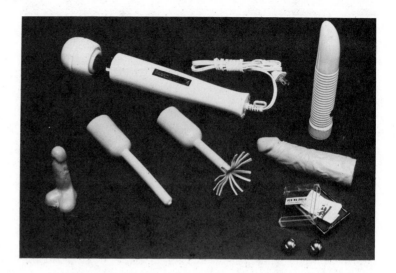

Vibrators, dildos, and ben-wa balls.

out. Other objects may be inserted into the vagina during masturbation, including dildos (artificial penis-shaped objects usually made of rubber), ben wa balls (two metal balls that are put inside the vagina and provide stimulation as they roll against each other), and a variety of other objects such as candles, soda bottles, and cucumbers. Among little-used but novel approaches to this type of female masturbation we've encountered are: an electric toothbrush, a dildo made of ice, and a lucky rabbit's foot.

MALE MASTURBATION

Most males masturbate by rubbing, stroking, or pumping the shaft of the penis with one hand. Scrotal stimulation or direct stimulation of the head of the penis is relatively infrequent (Masters and Johnson, 1966, 1979), although men sometimes stroke the whole penis in an up-and-down motion. A few men focus their self-stimulation on the raised area (the frenulum) just below the head on the underside of the penis, and a few masturbate primarily by pulling their foreskin back and forth.

The typical male masturbatory episode begins with a comparatively slow, deliberate touch. As sexual arousal increases, the tempo also increases, and by the time of impending orgasm, the stroking motion becomes as rapid as possible (Masters and Johnson, 1966). During ejaculation, penile stimulation is variable: some men slow down, others grip the penis firmly, and others stop all stimulation.

During adolescence, some males participate in group masturbation (commonly referred to as "circle-jerks") where there may be a contest to see who can ejaculate most quickly or farthest.

TABLE 14–2
Preferred Types of Male Masturbation

Manual stimulation of the penis	82%
Lying on stomach, rubbing against bed	15
Thigh pressure	1
Water massage	0.5
Self-fellatio	0.5

Data compiled from *The Hite Report on Male Sexuality*, by Shere Hite, p. 1106. Copyright © 1981. Reprinted by permission of Alfred A. Knopf, Inc.

Solitary Sexual Behavior

Other adolescents (and some older men, too) may be more concerned about catching the ejaculate in tissues, a washcloth, or something else. Because of concern for the "evidence" of masturbation — dried semen leaves a tell-tale stain — many males masturbate in the bathroom, where a little soap and water will remedy this problem.

A relatively small percentage of males employ some type of friction against an object such as a bed or a pillow as a preferred form of masturbation (Kinsey, Pomeroy, and Martin, 1948). Other "hands-off" varieties of male masturbation depend on thrusting the penis into something — the neck of a milkbottle, a cored apple, or modelling clay, for example — in a form of simulated coitus.

Gadgets assisting male masturbation abound and are widely advertised in sex tabloids, magazines, and direct mail catalogues. They include: numerous models of "artificial vaginas" made of rubber or other soft, pliable material; "inflatable life-size dolls" variably equipped with vagina, breasts, open mouth, and anus; suction devices (manually and electrically operated) that promise to deliver the ultimate forms of sexual ecstasy for the male without a partner. These devices can be used with lubricating lotion or cream and may also have features that add vibration or heat to the experience.

It should be pointed out that these devices are not always carefully manufactured and may pose some physical risk if they go haywire. Several years ago, some cases of severe penile injury were caused by inserting the penis into a vacuum cleaner hose (Mannion, 1973).

Statistically rare varieties of male masturbation include the two or three males per thousand who perform oral sex on themselves (Kinsey, Pomeroy, and Martin, 1948) as well as males who masturbate by inserting objects into the urethra or the anus. Breast stimulation is rarely included as a regular feature of male masturbation.

Male masturbation.

Separating Fact from Fiction

Data about masturbation are a bit tricky to interpret. You may recall that Kinsey and his colleagues (1948, 1953) found a wide discrepancy in the incidence of masturbation between male and female adolescents, but some recent studies suggest that this difference may be narrowing (see chapter 8). A similar trend may also be occurring in regard to masturbatory behavior in adulthood.

The Kinsey reports stated that 92 percent of the males and 62 percent of the females queried had masturbated at least once in their lives. More recently, two separate studies came up with very similar statistics: the *Playboy* survey (Hunt, 1975) found that 94 percent of 982 adult males and 63 percent of 1,044 adult females had masturbated, and Arafat and Cotton's study (1974) of 435 college students found masturbatory experience in 89 percent of males and 61 percent of females.

However, Miller and Lief (1976) reported that 78 percent of young adult women indicated having masturbated. Levin and Levin (1975), summarizing data from a *Redbook* questionnaire survey answered by 100,000 women, found that almost three-quarters of the married women had masturbated since marriage. Providing additional evidence that more women seem to have tried masturbation today than in past decades, Hite reported that 82 percent of her sample of 3,000 women had masturbatory experience.

There are several possible explanations for this rise of female masturbation:

1. Negative attitudes toward female masturbation seem to have softened, although some women continue to feel guilty or ashamed of this activity.
2. Women have learned about masturbation at an earlier age and in more explicit detail than in the past, primarily through the media (books, magazines, movies). As a result, masturbation is less likely to be discovered only accidentally.
3. Both men and women have become more aware that sexuality is a positive aspect of being female. Acting upon sexual feelings is thus a legitimate activity for women, who

are sometimes encouraged to first try masturbation by a sexual partner.

Although the number of females who masturbate seems to be increasing, research data do not suggest that females as a group masturbate as often as males. While there is wide individual variability and some females masturbate several times a day, it appears that males masturbate about twice as often as females (Simon and Gagnon, 1967; Sorenson, 1973; DeMartino, 1979).

Kinsey and his colleagues (1948) found that among individuals who masturbate, the average frequency for single 16- to 20-year-old males was 57 times a year, dropping to 42 times a year in the 21- to 25-year-old group. In contrast, the average frequency for single females aged 18 to 24 was about 21 times a year (Kinsey et al., 1953). The *Playboy* survey suggests a contemporary increase in female masturbatory activity: the 18- to 24-year-old sample comparable to Kinsey's had an average masturbatory frequency of 37 times a year (Hunt, 1975).

Many people assume that once someone has married, his or her use of masturbation should all but disappear. This generally doesn't happen, though — in the *Playboy* survey, 72 percent of young married husbands masturbated, with an average frequency of about 24 times per year, and 68 percent of young married wives were actively involved in masturbation, averaging approximately 10 times per year (Hunt, 1975). The *Redbook* survey came up with similar findings. Even among older married couples, masturbation continues as a common type of sexual behavior (Masters and Johnson, 1966; DeMartino, 1979).

Most of the old myths about masturbation causing health problems have now been laid to rest. Physical tolerance for masturbation (or any sexual stimulation) in fact has a built-in safety valve: once the system has reached a point of overload, it temporarily shuts down and does not respond to further stimulation. There is no evi-

Solitary Sexual Behavior

dence that masturbation causes physical problems other than the rare cases of genital injury stemming from overly vigorous stimulation.

Nevertheless, a few authorities caution against "excessive" masturbation although they rarely define the term. Men almost always see "excessive" masturbation as somewhat more than their own rate (Masters and Johnson, 1966). Very few people we have seen as either research subjects or as patients feel they masturbate too much. Of those who do, the concern is often, "It's excessive because I'm married," or, "It's excessive for my age." Rather than count masturbatory episodes, it is probably more useful to consider whether masturbation involves anxiety, conflict, guilt, or an overwhelming compulsiveness. If it does, a person may benefit from professional help, but if masturbation leads to satisfaction and pleasure, it's unlikely to be a problem.

At the opposite end of the spectrum, in the rush to legitimatize masturbation, there is often a built-in implication that everyone *should* masturbate. People who have *never* masturbated, while in a statistical minority, should certainly not be made to feel abnormal. People who choose not to masturbate — whether or not they've tried it, whether or not their choice is based on religious conviction, personal preference, or some other consideration — have every right to their decision without any intellectual browbeating by self-proclaimed experts in sexual health. Sexual decisions, in the final analysis, must be personal.

SEXUAL AROUSAL AND SLEEP

We have already mentioned that sexual reflexes function in a rhythmic fashion during sleep (see chapter 4). In addition to having sleep-associated erections or vaginal lubrication, people can experience orgasm during sleep. While it may not be entirely accurate to call this a type of sex-

ual behavior, this form of solitary sex deserves discussion too.

Nocturnal Ejaculation

Kinsey and his coworkers (1948) found that 83 percent of all males experience nocturnal ejaculation at one time or another, with the highest incidence and frequency of this phenomenon occurring during the late teens. The average frequency of about once a month during this period declines substantially during the twenties, and few men over the age of thirty continue to ejaculate during sleep. Kinsey's group pointed out, however, that several cases of nocturnal ejaculation in older males up to age eighty had been verified.

Nocturnal ejaculation provides a physiologic "safety-valve" for accumulated sexual tension that has not been released in another fashion. Men who have reached high and sustained levels of sexual arousal without ejaculating, no matter how the arousal came about, are thus able to discharge this physiologic tension in a completely natural reflex.

Female Orgasm and Sleep

Kinsey's group (1953) also found that women can experience orgasm during sleep. They noted: "As with the male, the female is often awakened by the muscular spasms . . . which follow her orgasms" (p. 192). Thirty-seven percent of their sample reported orgasm during sleep by age forty-five, but only about 10 percent of females had such an experience in any given year. Eight percent of their sample had sleep-associated orgasms more than five times per year and only 3 percent averaged more than twice a month.

We have found that almost all women who report sleep-associated orgasms have previously been orgasmic by other means. A small number of women are distressed by orgasms occurring during sleep because they fear they either may have been unknowingly masturbating or are "oversexed." One married woman told us:

> One month I was awakened by orgasms four or five different times. I have a good sex life with my husband, and I hardly ever masturbate, so I couldn't figure out why this was happening to me. I started to think that perhaps I was becoming a nymphomaniac, a person who could never get enough sexual satisfaction. Fortunately, I was able to discuss this with a woman who's a psychiatrist, and she set my mind at ease.

Until more people become aware of the natural occurrence of female orgasms and periodic vaginal lubrication during sleep, it is likely that similar reactions will occur.

Sexual Dreams

Explicitly sexual dreams, like wakeful sexual fantasies, are quite common. Seventy percent of females and nearly 100 percent of males have erotic dreams (Kinsey et al., 1953) The content of sexual dreams may sometimes be alarming because behavior is depicted that might be objectionable as an actual event. While most people realize that dreams are not equivalent to action, others are distressed because they fear the impulse that the dream represents. Persistently disturbing sexual dreams may in some cases be a sign of an underlying sexual conflict that might benefit from professional counseling.

OTHER FORMS OF SOLITARY SEX

Interest in reading sexually explicit materials or in looking at pictures of sexual acts or organs is hardly new. The erotic art of ancient Greece, India, Africa, and Japan is one indication of the cultural universality of such interest. Throughout the centuries, books about sex have been widely and eagerly read. While the legal aspects of pornography and obscenity and a historical overview of depictions of sexuality in everyday life (in the form of literature, media, advertising, art, and music) will be discussed in chapter 22, we will look briefly here at the behavioral side of using erotic materials for solitary sexual arousal.

The Use of Erotica

Today, it is practically impossible to find a high-school student in America who has not come across some form of sexually explicit material (erotica). Although there are bookstores, movie theatres, and videotape clubs catering to the "twenty-one or older" crowd, there are ample supplies of so-called soft-core erotica in men's and women's magazines, bestselling novels, advertising campaigns, comic books, and general-release movies to guarantee that anyone remotely interested in viewing such materials can have the opportunity.

There are many reasons why people show an interest in the use of erotica. Erotica provides a source of knowledge and comparative information about sexual behavior. These materials often produce sexual arousal which can be prolonged or abbreviated depending on a person's appetite at a particular moment. Like sexual fantasies, erotica triggers the imagination and so helps people deal with forbidden or frightening areas in a controlled way. Erotica gives people an opportunity to imaginatively rehearse acts that they hope to try or are curious about. Finally, just like Westerns or spy thrillers, erotica can provide a kind of pleasurable recreation or entertainment separate and apart from its sexual turn-on effect.

There seem to be few differences in the sexual arousal induced by words, photographs, or movies (Byrne, 1977). Some people prefer the more vivid, real-life action of cinema, whereas others prefer to let their imaginations expand on a drawing or photograph or find that the printed word offers a greater ease in erotic interest. Such differences are matters of style and preference in just the same way that one person prefers a concert to a movie while someone else likes seeing a play, no matter what the subject matter. In contrast, the content of erotica, rather than its style of presentation, does have a specific effect. People are more likely to be sexually aroused by content to which they relate, rather than by portrayals of sexual acts which they find uncomfortable or offensive.

The sexual arousal that occurs with the use of erotic materials is not simply psychological. Many investigators have noted specific physiologic changes in people who watch erotic pictures or movies (Schmidt and Sigusch, 1970; McConaghy, 1974; Geer, Morokoff, and Greenwood, 1974; Wincze, Hoon, and Hoon, 1976; Henson, Rubin, and Henson, 1979), read erotic passages (Bahm, 1972; Englar and Walker, 1973), or listen to tape recordings of erotic stories (Heiman, 1977, 1980; Schreiner-Engel and Shiavi, 1980). Men often experience penile erection while women undergo changes in vaginal blood flow or lubrication. Although one study suggested that viewing a sexually explicit movie elevated circulating testosterone in men (Pirke, Kockott, and Dittmar, 1974), other studies have not found any evidence of hormone changes (Lincoln, 1974; Kolodny, 1981).

In the past, it was generally assumed that men responded more frequently and powerfully to erotic readings, pictures, and films than women did. Research evidence, however, indicates that this is not the case: both sexes respond to erotica in similar ways (Englar and Walker, 1973; Byrne, 1977; Athanasiou, 1980). To be certain, some females — having been taught that it is not "ladylike" to allow oneself to be intrigued or excited by such materials — avidly avoid any exposure to erotica or do their best to block their own spontaneous responses by an act of will. The same reaction may occur among women who object to pornography on political grounds as exploitive of females. Other females may be more open to the opportunity but have difficulty noticing mild sexual arousal even when physiological changes such as increased vaginal blood flow can be detected. The male, in contrast, usually has more obvious external evidence of his arousal.

Another consideration is that while both males and females have a similar capacity to respond to erotica, the *type* of erotica (content, style, plot) may also be important in determining the response pattern. In the past, it was thought that males tend to be more "object" oriented and respond to stark close-ups of sexual action, while females pay more attention to the style, setting, and mood. Recent studies, however, show that males and females are actually quite similar in what they find erotically arousing (Fisher and Byrne, 1978; Fisher, 1983).

Some of the time — exactly how often no one knows — people use erotic readings, pictures, or movies to accompany masturbation. This is certainly what springs to mind when we think of a teenager and his collection of *Playboy* centerfolds or a businessman who has slipped out of his office in midafternoon to watch a skin flick at the local theatre. At other times, erotica is used primarily to stimulate sexual desire — heightening the appetite but not providing the main course. Erotic materials are also used to try to turn on a partner, turn someone into a partner, or to otherwise enrich an interpersonal sexual experience. We will not dwell on this aspect here since our discussion is about solitary sex.

The Effects of Erotica on Behavior

How the use of erotica affects behavior is a complicated question that provokes much controversy at present, with no single answer readily apparent. In the United States, President Lyndon Johnson established a special Commission on

Obscenity and Pornography in 1968, which reviewed a large body of research over the next two years. The Commission (1970, pp. 28-29) noted:

> When people are exposed to erotic materials, some persons increase masturbatory or coital behavior, a smaller proportion decrease it, but the majority of people report no change in these behaviors. Increases in either of these behaviors are short lived and generally disappear within 48 hours. . . .
>
> In general, established patterns of sexual behavior were found to be very stable and not altered substantially by exposure to erotica.

In addition, in Denmark after hard-core pornography became widely available (and legal) in 1965, the rates of many sex crimes decreased substantially (Kutchinsky, 1970, 1973), while studies in America showed that rapists, child molesters, and other sex offenders actually had less exposure to sexually explicit materials during adolescence than other adults (Goldstein, 1973). Furthermore, repeated heavy exposure to erotica seems to lead to satiation and boredom rather than changes in sexual behavior (Lipton, 1983). Thus, a number of authorities have concluded that reading pornographic materials or viewing sexually explicit pictures or films doesn't turn people into sexual maniacs (Money, 1980) or incite men to rape or act in sexually impulsive ways

---

RESEARCH SPOTLIGHT

Violent Pornography and Aggression

Although most researchers agree that the use of erotica in and of itself doesn't lead to negative social consequences (Green, 1982), many feminists have suggested that there is a profound debasement of women found in most pornographic materials (Faust, 1980; Griffin, 1981; Steinem, 1983). Recently, attention has focused on a particular form of pornography – violent pornography, defined as depictions of sex in which force or coercion is used against women. In the past decade, violent pornography has become more prominent in films such as "Maniac," "Texas Chainsaw Massacre," and "Tool Box Murders," and has been shown graphically in issues of *Hustler* and similar men's magazines. Now evidence linking the viewing of such violent pornography to aggression against women is beginning to emerge.

Neil Malamuth and Edward Donnerstein have been in the forefront of researchers studying this relationship. Their work has shown that it is the violence, rather than the sexual content, of such materials that produces negative effects. For instance, Donnerstein recently conducted a set of experiments that showed that exposure to X-rated depictions of sexual violence against women often increases the acceptance of myths about rape (such as the notions that women secretly want to be raped and enjoy the experience) and lead many men to say that they would commit rape if they were certain they wouldn't be caught (Donnerstein, 1983). In addition, viewing X-rated violent films increases men's aggressive behavior against women in laboratory settings and decreases male sympathy and sensitivity toward rape victims when the subjects are viewing videotapes of simulated rape trials (Donnerstein and Linz, 1984). Specifically, Donnerstein (1983) observed:

Solitary Sexual Behavior

(W. Wilson, 1978; Money, 1980; Athanasiou, 1980; Lipton, 1983; Green, 1982).*

There is another aspect to this question, however, since a number of observers believe that in recent years there has been a considerable increase in the appearance of violence in pornography (Eysenck and Nias, 1978; Malamuth and Spinner, 1980; Lederer, 1980; Stock, 1983; Donnerstein and Linz, 1984). Since both a 1960s

---

* The studies cited all have methodological flaws — as all research does — and their findings have not been universally accepted. For an alternate view of these and other studies on the effects of pornography, see Diamond (1980) and Bart and Jozsa (1980).

---

presidential commission and a more recent task force of the National Institute of Mental Health have found clear evidence linking pictorial portrayals of violence in the media to increased aggressive behavior by observers, there is now much concern about whether this fusion of violence and pornography may have specific negative effects on behavior (see the Research Spotlight, "Violent Pornography and Aggression"). In addition to other uncertainties about violent pornography, many people are also concerned with the ways in which pornography debases and "objectifies" women, portrayals which they feel may contribute to sex discrimination by showing women as "mindless" sex objects. Thus,

---

Most startling, the men by the last day of viewing graphic violence against women were rating the material as significantly less debasing and degrading to women, more humorous, more enjoyable, and claimed a greater willingness to see this type of film again.

Malamuth's studies have previously shown that hostility toward women predicts rape-related attitudes, motivations, and behaviors (Malamuth and Donnerstein, 1984). In addition, he has found that men who score high on the likelihood-to-rape scale have more arousal fantasies after exposure to slides and tapes depicting rape than after exposure to mutually consenting coitus (Malamuth, 1981). However, some of the research findings are confusing, since "even men who score low on the likelihood-to-rape scale are

sometimes highly sexually aroused by portrayals of rape" (Cunningham, 1983), and women themselves are also sometimes highly aroused by eroticized depictions of rape (Stock, 1983). On the contrary, women who listened to a description of rape that was realistic, emphasizing the victim's fright and pain without any attempt at eroticizing the scenario, generally registered lower genital responses and lower levels of subjective sexual arousal (Stock, 1983).

Although these studies are thought-provoking, they must be interpreted cautiously at present for several different reasons. Thus far, for example, they have involved relatively small samples and have been conducted primarily in college student populations. Furthermore, these studies have involved experimental methods that lead to

somewhat artificial judgments of attitudes and (potential) behaviors; for ethical reasons, a true field-study of the effects of violent pornography has not yet been conducted. Despite these limitations, however, the findings described above are particularly noteworthy because they have been based on the effects of viewing relatively brief amounts of violent pornography. Since loss of sensitivity to violence and even a proclivity toward violent behavior may well be a cumulative effect, studies are now underway examining aggressive behavior and attitudes toward violence after repeated, prolonged exposure (Donnerstein and Linz, 1984).

---

even if such materials do not directly affect behavior, by reinforcing existing stereotypes and prejudices about men and women they may strengthen or even create types of attitudes that are ultimately expressed in behavior.

There are several other sides to the question of the long-range effects of erotica. There is evidence that sexually explicit materials can sometimes help people to overcome sexual problems or can lessen their sexual inhibitions (W. Wilson, 1978; Money, 1980). Sometimes, however, these materials provoke anxiety — particularly when people compare their physical attributes or sexual response patterns to the stars of erotica. These heroes and heroines are not only highly attractive but engage in instantaneous, endless passion (the hallmark of erotica). Some people understandably respond to these images with guilt, embarrassment, or self-doubt.

Given the trend of the last fifteen years toward a greater acceptability and accessibility of sexually explicit items — and the recent boom in uncensored cable TV and home video systems — it seems important to gather more complete data on the effects of erotica. We should not overlook the possibility that use of erotica is sometimes accompanied by problems; neither should we be frightened by old negative attitudes reborn in the guise of modern morality.

SUMMARY

1. Masturbation, or sexual self-pleasuring involving some form of direct physical stimulation, is a normal form of sexual behavior in people of all ages.

2. Negative attitudes toward masturbation can be traced, at least in part, to eighteenth- and nineteenth-century preoccupation with the erroneous notions that masturbation caused illness and insanity. As a result, the medical profession engaged in a fervent crusade to stamp out what was called "self-abuse." Religious viewpoints that have labelled masturbation as sinful also have made some people view masturbation with disdain.

3. Current surveys indicate that more than 90 percent of males and 70 percent of females have masturbated at one time or another; the available data also show that males generally masturbate more often. However, there is considerable individual variation in this regard.

4. Females use a greater diversity of masturbatory techniques and styles than males. Contrary to general belief, few women prefer to masturbate by inserting an object into the vagina; most commonly, clitoral/vulval stimulation is chosen. Males generally masturbate by stroking the shaft of the penis.

5. There is no objective evidence supporting views that masturbation is inherently immature, unhealthy, or sexually harmful. Masturbation plays an important role developmentally in helping people learn about their bodies and their sexual preferences. In addition, masturbation may help discharge tension, makes no demands on sexual partners, and may increase sexual self-confidence.

6. Orgasms occur spontaneously during sleep in both males and females. In males, nocturnal ejaculations are most common in adolescence and early adulthood, but in women sleep-associated orgasms (occurring less frequently than men's) appear in all age groups.

7. The use of various types of erotica — sexually explicit books, pictures, or movies — is widespread and generally harmless. The most potent and direct effect of these materials is an increase in sexual arousal, which can be measured either physiologically or phychologically.

8. Contrary to a popular misconception, women are just as able to "turn on" in response to erotica as men.

9. There is no evidence that exposure to sexually explicit materials *per se* results in antisocial or criminal behavior. However, a number of recent studies suggest that exposure to violent pornography may have negative effects on behavior.

SUGGESTED READINGS

DeMartino, Manfred F., ed. *Human Autoerotic Practices.* New York: Human Sciences Press, 1979. A lively collection of essays and papers on masturbation providing exceptionally thorough coverage of the topic from a variety of viewpoints.

Malamuth, Neil, and Donnerstein, Edward, eds. *Pornography and Sexual Aggression.* New York: Academic Press, 1984. A thorough review of the most recent research on the behavioral effect of pornography.

The Report of the Commission on Obscenity and Pornography. New York: Bantam Books, 1970. Written by government-appointed experts, this lengthy but enlightening study on erotica in its many forms has something for everyone. Although it is not easy reading, it is important for its depth and breadth.

15 Heterosexuality

I love the idea of there being two sexes, don't you?*

Most people would agree with James Thurber's sentiment, since a great majority of the population is heterosexual, that is, they choose a sexual partner of the opposite sex instead of the same sex. In this chapter, we will examine the most common forms of heterosexual behav-

ior, beginning with a discussion of sexual techniques and then looking at certain aspects of heterosexual behavior in a variety of contexts: premarital, marital, extramarital, and nonmarital.

TECHNIQUES OF HETEROSEXUAL ACTIVITY

There is always a danger that any discussion of sexual technique will sound like a mechanical checklist that implies that good sex is simply a matter of pushing the right buttons at the right time. Fortunately, sex usually involves more than

---

mechanical coupling. It draws upon feelings, moods, desires, and attitudes that are expressed in the physical interaction and that contribute significantly to the quality of the shared experience. At the risk of saying the obvious, there is not just one way of having good sex — sexual technique is, as much as anything else, a matter of communication between partners in which each person conveys to the other a sense of what feels good and what doesn't. As we discuss sexual techniques with some attention to their physical (and practical) details, keep the preceding thoughts firmly in mind.

Noncoital Sex Play

Many people describe all sexual activity between partners other than intercourse by the term "foreplay," which implies that these acts are (or should be) preliminary to intercourse, making intercourse the "main event." However, foreplay is a misleading term because intercourse is not always the focal point of sex; some people prefer other forms of sexual activity instead of coitus. Furthermore, if coitus is first and other sexual acts follow, should these then be called "afterplay?" To avoid such problems, we prefer to discard the term foreplay entirely and talk instead about noncoital sex play.

TOUCHING AND BEING TOUCHED

Touching can be many different things. At one level, it is primarily a wordless way to communicate a willingness, a wish, or a demand to make love. At another level, while touching serves the same communicative purpose, it is valued and enjoyed for its sensual pleasures almost as much as intercourse or orgasm. At still another level, touching is a source of comfort and security — an affirmation of togetherness, commitment, and trust. Touching can also be a me-

chanical, unemotional way of manipulating another body. In this approach, the essence of sexual interaction seems to be in knowing how to move a hand, where to place a mouth, or when to use a tongue in a joining of separate, almost disembodied anatomical parts. This mechanical kind of touching turns persons into objects, regardless of gender.

Touching another person satisfies the human need not to feel alone, while being touched satisfies the need to be desired as a physical presence. In touching and being touched by a trusted and trusting person, one experiences not only the pleasure of being alive but also the joy of being a sensual creature.

Touching need not involve the hands only. Many varieties of skin-to-skin contact lead to feelings of warmth, tenderness, and closeness. Kissing is a fine example of a touch that can be immensely sensual or more important as a symbol of affection and intimacy. Some people enjoy passionate, almost continuous kissing during sex, while others prefer only an occasional kiss or no mouth-to-mouth kissing at all. Psychiatrist Marc Hollender (1971) theorizes that women have a greater need for being held and cuddled than men do, although he emphasizes that this does not mean that sex is less important to women. He does speculate, however, that sometimes a woman's need to be held leads her to participate sexually in exchange for cuddling and affection from her partner.

The act of touching can be unstructured and exploratory, or it can be focused in a more stimulative fashion. While touch as a vehicle for sexual arousal will be discussed in some detail in just a moment, it is also relevant to point out that many people find that touch in the form of a massage — with or without sexual stimulation — permits them to relax and to develop an awareness of their bodies that enhances the quality of a sexual experience.

TOUCHING THE GENITALS

Many forms of genital stimulation can result in sexual pleasure and arousal. The genital regions in both sexes are highly sensitive to touch, and this sensitivity tends to increase as erotic excitation mounts. A touch that might be unarousing or even uncomfortable to a person who is not sexually excited can be pleasurable or electrifying as physical passion rises; conversely, a touch that is "just right" in the beginning moments of sexual play may be "too little" or "too slow" or otherwise out of sync at a later moment.

During genital touching, many people presume that their partner would like just the same type of stimulation they enjoy. As a result, men often stimulate the clitoris vigorously, mimicking the rapid, forceful stroking typical of male masturbation (Masters and Johnson, 1979). In contrast, women are often worried about stroking the penis too vigorously, or touching or squeezing the scrotum too roughly, not wishing to hurt their partner. In addition, men and women often rely on erroneous assumptions about what would or would not turn their partner on; probably the most common example is that many men routinely insert a finger or fingers deeply into the vagina early in genital play although relatively few women find this arousing and some find it distracting or uncomfortable (Masters and Johnson, 1966, 1979).

These observations underscore the importance of clear communication between sexual partners not only to enhance sexual pleasure but to protect your partner from making you uncomfortable physically or psychologically. One person can't know with any real accuracy what another is feeling or wants at a given moment without some form of communication. Since none of us is an infallible mind-reader, it is helpful to develop open lines of information exchange. But since words may disturb a beautiful mood, nonverbal messages — conveyed by a touch, a move, a look — are often best-suited to the occasion unless they don't succeed in getting the message across, in which case words become necessary.

Not only does the type of genital play that a woman prefers vary from one woman to another, the same woman may have different preferences at different times. Many women enjoy firm, sustained rubbing of the shaft of the clitoris (as we mentioned in chapter 3, direct stimulation of the tip of the clitoris is frequently uncomfortable), while others prefer clitoral stimulation alternated with caresses of the vaginal lips, the mons, or the perineum. Some women enjoy insertion of a finger into the mouth of the vagina, or gentle, teasing stroking just outside the vaginal opening. Deep vaginal penetration is usually not pleasurable unless a woman is highly aroused and even then she may get little out of this form of stimulation, permitting it to occur primarily because she feels that it excites her partner (Masters and Johnson, 1966, 1979; Hite, 1977). There are wide individual differences in this matter, as the following comment from a twenty-four-year-old woman shows:

> The thing that I like best of all about sex is when I'm really turned on and Tom is finger-fucking me. If he can get three or four fingers crammed inside, I have my biggest and best orgasms. (Authors' files)

The tissues of the vulva and vagina may be irritated by too much touching or too much pressure if there is not enough lubrication present. Since the clitoris and the vaginal lips have no lubrication of their own, bringing some lubrication from the vagina to these areas is often helpful. Saliva or artificial lubricants such as K-Y Jelly, hypoallergenic lotions, or baby oil can also be used to reduce friction and to provide another dimension to genital touching.

In the last chapter, we mentioned that many

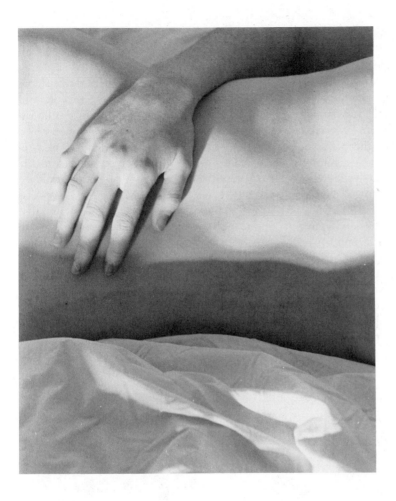

women enjoy using a vibrator during masturbation. A vibrator can be incorporated into partner sex as well, but it is important to talk this through together. Some men feel that the vibrator is a kind of mechanical intruder; others worry that the vibrator is desired only because they can't do the job properly; yet many men are perfectly happy to share in a variety of sexual stimulation that increases their partner's pleasure. Some couples have made their vibrator an integral part of their sex lives, even taking it with

them on vacations, while others use it only from time to time.

There are many similarities between male and female sexuality, as we have noted before, and genital touching preferences are no exception. Men do not only want one kind of touch, and there is variability between men and in the same man at different times regarding the genital touches that create pleasure or arousal.

When the penis is not erect, most men prefer a light, playful stroking or caressing of the penis, the inner thighs, and the scrotum. If touching is restricted to the penis (or if penile stimulation is too vigorous) while the penis is flaccid, it is unlikely to be very arousing and may actually be somewhat threatening since the man may begin to worry that he isn't responding swiftly enough. Once erection begins to occur, the firmness of touch applied to the penis in stroking or squeezing motions can be comfortably (and arousingly) increased. One of the most common complaints we have heard from men is that their female partners don't grasp the penis firmly enough once it is erect (Masters and Johnson, 1979). Men usually prefer an up-and-down stroking of the penis with the fingers encircling the shaft; direct manual stimulation of the head of the penis may be uncomfortable or irritating.

Some men enjoy having the scrotum gently squeezed or lightly stroked or cupped in their partner's hand, while other men prefer not receiving any direct scrotal stimulation. If the testes are "rubbed the wrong way," it may be quite uncomfortable and a real dampener to sexual feelings. Many men enjoy some form of tactile stimulation focused at the frenulum (the small fold of skin just below the coronal ridge on the underside of the penis), although relatively few women seem to be aware of this fact. Men may also enjoy having saliva, lotion, or oil applied to the penis to enhance their arousal. Care should be taken (in either sex) that the lotion or oil applied to the genitals is not too cold or too hot and that it contains no alcohol, since alcohol tends to irritate the male urethra and female genital tissues.

It may be surprising, but relatively few heterosexual men and women have taken the time to show their partners how they like to have their genitals touched (Masters and Johnson, 1979). Of course, this can be accomplished partly in conversation alone ("I really liked how you did that

The preferred pattern of genital touching varies considerably from person to person and from time to time.

Heterosexuality

tonight — would you try that again another time?"). But conversation sometimes leaves a few doubts ("What does he mean by a firmer touch?"), and a "hands-on" demonstration is often the simplest way of conveying an accurate message. One person can place a hand on top of his or her partner's hand, showing them what they mean by "firm" and "light" or just *where* to stroke, since small differences in positioning may make all the difference in the world.[1] You can also show your partner exactly what you like by doing it yourself in his or her view. For a variation on this theme, ask them to put their hand on top of yours so they can actually feel the rhythm of the movement.

ORAL-GENITAL SEX

Stimulation of the male genitals by the use of the tongue, lips, and mouth is called *fellatio*, and oral stimulation of the female genitals is called *cunnilingus*. Fellatio or cunnilingus can be used to induce or heighten sexual arousal or to produce orgasm. Either form of oral-genital sex can be done with one partner stimulating the other individually or with simultaneous reciprocal stimulation (the simultaneous version is sometimes called "69" because the inverted, side-by-side position of the numbers is similar to the position commonly used for this form of sex play).

There are a vast number of techniques and combinations of techniques for oral-genital stimulation that can be pleasurable and arousing. No one way is the "right" way to do it. Licking, sucking, kissing, and nibbling can feel good anywhere on the genitals; the pressure (light, firm, or in be-

tween), speed (fast, slow, or changing), and type of motion employed can be varied considerably to attain different effects. The moistness and warmth of oral-genital contact is highly erotic for many people. Some enjoy a teasing, stop-start approach; others prefer a more direct, sustained type of stimulation. Here too, finding out what your partner likes is a matter of open communication.

In cunnilingus, many women are highly aroused by oral stimulation of the clitoris. This can take the form of gentle tongue movements over the shaft and tip of the clitoris, more rapid, focused licking, or sucking the clitoris either gently or in a rougher fashion. During high levels of arousal, a few women enjoy having the clitoris bitten gently. Other techniques some women enjoy are: oral stimulation of the clitoris combined with manual stimulation of the vagina; oral stimulation of the minor lips (the area just outside the vagina); having the tongue thrust in and out of the vaginal opening; having the clitoris stimulated manually (either by their partner or by themselves) while oral stimulation is directed at other parts of their genitals; and having their partner blow into the vagina or on the clitoris.

In fellatio, methods of stimulation include sucking the glans or shaft of the penis by engulfing it in the mouth, licking various parts of the penis or scrotum, and nibbling or kissing anywhere along the genitals. Although fellatio is often referred to as a "blow job," most men don't enjoy a real blowing motion (it's not like playing a saxophone). The frenulum is often particularly sensitive to oral stimulation and most men find that the glans of the penis is also exquisitely sensitive to warm, moist caresses. Many men enjoy having the scrotum lightly stroked during fellatio and the area just beneath the scrotum is often quite sensitive to manual or oral massage.

Some women are uncomfortable with fellatio because they have a sensation of gagging if

---

[1] This point is readily apparent to anyone who has had an itch on their back that they couldn't reach themselves. Trying to direct someone else to just the right spot — "A little higher . . . to the left . . . now up a little . . . no, back down a little lower and toward the middle . . ." — can be terribly frustrating. Just the same is sometimes true of telling someone in words what feels good sexually.

Simultaneous oral-genital stimulation in the "69" position.

they take the erect penis into their mouth. This sensation is often due to a reflex response called the "gag reflex" which can be triggered by pressure at the back of the tongue or in the throat; it is a real physiologic event, not an imaginary happening. Even when a woman can comfortably accommodate part of the penis in her mouth, if her partner thrusts in the throes of his own excitation, it may push the penis so far in that the gag reflex takes over. There are two solutions to this problem. First, the woman can grasp the shaft of the penis so that she has full control over the depth of penile penetration into her mouth, preventing sudden thrusts or jabs. Second, the gag reflex can be fairly easily reconditioned in most people by gradually inserting the penis a bit more deeply over a number of occasions until the reflex is minimized, or even practicing by inserting a cylindrical object (or some fingers) into the mouth.

Another difficulty a woman may have with

fellatio is not wanting the man to ejaculate in her mouth. A couple can agree in advance that the man will withdraw before ejaculation; alternately, many women have found that with a little experience they can overcome this concern. Some women prefer to rinse the ejaculate out of their mouth promptly because they don't like the taste of semen; others don't mind it much; and still others swallow the ejaculate. While there are no health risks to swallowing semen, it is unlikely that this has beneficial health effects (preventing acne or preserving youthfulness) either.

While many people are enthusiastic about the pleasures of oral-genital sex, others consider it "dirty," perverted, sinful, embarrassing, or simply unappealing. Among those with reservations about this type of sexual activity, many find that with a little effort (and practice) they can easily develop a personal comfort level for oral-genital sex. This comment from a twenty-eight-year-old man illustrates some of the dilemmas:

At first, when I thought about oral sex on a woman I was scared — scared that I would be turned off by the smell and the flavor, and scared that I wouldn't know how to do it right. I was also into this trip where I didn't think it was a very "manly" thing to do, although I can't really remember where I got that idea. But then I got involved with a beautiful woman who sort of eased me into it, helping me take my time and all. After just a few tries, my fears disappeared and I sort of threw myself into the action. (Authors' files)

Although many people have been taught to think of the genitals as unclean, routine bathing or showering that includes carefully washing the genitals with soap and water will ensure cleanliness. From a scientific viewpoint, oral-genital contact is no less hygenic than mouth-to-mouth kissing. The natural secretions of the genitals are relatively clean and each person's genital odors partly reflect the type of foods they eat. Many couples like to shower or bathe together before engaging in oral sex, and some people who consider oral sex the most intimate form of sex will only engage in this activity with a partner to whom they are particularly close. For others, oral sex is a stopping point to prevent the intimacy (and reproductive risk) of coitus, as shown by this comment from a twenty-two-year-old woman:

> While I was in high school I learned that if I gave a guy a good blow-job he wouldn't pressure me into screwing. So I stayed a virgin — except for my mouth — for five years of a very active sex life. Everyone was happy! (Authors' files)

One last word about oral-genital sex: some people incorrectly think that fellatio or cunnilingus are homosexual acts, even if experienced by heterosexual couples. While many homosexuals engage in oral-genital sex, so do a majority of heterosexual couples. The activity itself is neither homosexual nor heterosexual.

ANAL SEX

Stimulation of the anus during sexual activity can be done in several different ways: manually, orally, or by anal intercourse. Although anal sex is sometimes thought of as a strictly "homosexual" activity, a large number of heterosexual couples occasionally incorporate some variety of anal stimulation into their noncoital sexual play.

Anal stimulation can be the primary focus of sexual activity or an accompaniment to other types of stimulation. For instance, many couples sometimes include manual stimulation of the anus (either lightly rubbing the rim or inserting a finger into the anus) during coitus, and others use this technique during oral-genital sex. Anal sex in any of its forms can be highly arousing and lead to male or female orgasm. But many people have strongly negative attitudes toward anal sex, an act which they may regard as being unclean, unnatural, perverted, disgusting, or simply unappealing.

Although anal intercourse can be pleasurable, it can also be a source of discomfort in both a physical and emotional sense. The anal sphincter tightens ordinarily if stimulated, and attempts at penile insertion may be distressing even if done slowly and gently. If the penis is forced into the anus, injury is possible. To minimize risk, it is wisest to use an artificial lubricant liberally and to dilate the anus gently by manual stimulation before attempting insertion.

One final note about anal stimulation. Anything that has been inserted into the anus should not be subsequently put into the vagina unless it has been thoroughly washed. Bacteria that are naturally present in the anus can cause vaginal infections, so moving from anal intercourse (or finger insertion) to vaginal intercourse (or finger insertion) is unwise.

Coital Sex

For many people, the hallmark of heterosexuality is penile-vaginal intercourse, or coitus. Hundreds of marriage manuals have offered instruction in the "how-to's" of coital connection; although many of these books speak of "making love," they usually wind up conveying the message that the best sex is attained by following their mechanical blueprints. As Germaine Greer put it in *The Female Eunuch*, (1972, p. 37):

> The implication that there is a statistically ideal fuck which will always result in satisfaction if the right procedures are followed is depressing and misleading. . . . Real satisfaction is not enshrined in a tiny cluster of nerves but in the sexual involvement of the whole person.

We have talked about the individuality of sexual responsivity in many places in this book. Each person is a unique sexual being with personal preferences and idiosyncracies molded by past experiences, current needs, mood, personality, and a host of other variables. Each of us may also find that our body responds in different ways at different times, even if external circumstances are almost the same. When we add a partner into this equation, it's no wonder there is no way of describing the ideal type of coitus. We will discuss selected aspects of techniques of coital sex first in terms of coital positions and then in terms of styles.

MAN-ON-TOP, FACE-TO-FACE

The most common coital position in the United States is with the woman lying on her back, legs spread somewhat apart, with the man lying on top of her. This position, which is sometimes called the "missionary position," offers a relative degree of ease of penile insertion and also permits as much eye contact and kissing as de-

Man-on-top, face-to-face intercourse position.

sired. If the woman wishes, she may raise her legs in the air or wrap them around the man's back or shoulders, which causes deeper penetration of the penis in the vagina. This position also gives the best chance of conception, since the semen pools in a position in the vagina closest to the mouth of the cervix.

Despite its popularity, the man-on-top position has some disadvantages. Many women feel "pinned" underneath the weight of their partner and find it difficult to do much pelvic movement. The woman also has little control over the depth of penetration, and if her partner is lying against her body it may be difficult for either person to stimulate the clitoris manually. While the man has maximum freedom of movement, he may find it tiring to support his weight on his elbows and knees and, as his muscles fatigue, he may "tense up" physically. In addition, men tend to have less control over ejaculation in this posi-

tion than in many others. This position is also apt to be uncomfortable if the man is considerably heavier than the woman or if the woman is in the later stages of pregnancy.

WOMAN-ON-TOP, FACE-TO-FACE

Another popular coital position is for the woman to be on top. In this position, the woman either can be sitting up to a degree or can lie down against her partner. In contrast to the man-on-top position, in this position the woman has considerable control over coital movements, thrusting, and tempo. The woman is free to caress her partner's body with her hands, and the man has his hands available for stroking her breasts, genitals, or other body parts. The visual stimulation of this position and the man's freedom from supporting his weight may encourage his stroking. The woman-on-top position is generally the best one to use for a man who wants to

One variation of the woman-on-top, face-to-face intercourse position.

Another variation of the woman-on-top, face-to-face intercourse position.

gain greater control over ejaculation and is also the position used most often in sex therapy when a woman has difficulty reaching orgasm, since either partner can stimulate the clitoris manually in this position. It is also well-suited to the later stages of pregnancy.

A few drawbacks to the woman-on-top position should be mentioned. Some couples feel uncomfortable with this position because they believe the man should "always" be on top. Since the woman may seem to be the "aggressor" by being above the man, and since she has greater control over pelvic movements, a few men feel that their masculinity is threatened in this position. At a more practical level, some men find it difficult to engage in active pelvic thrusting in this position.

When the woman-on-top position is used, it is important to insert the penis properly. The woman should never hold the erect penis at a 90 degree angle to the man's body and try to sit down on it, as this can be uncomfortable to either partner. Instead, the penis should be held at a 45 to 60 degree angle (pointed in the direction of the man's head) since this matches the angle of the vagina when the woman is in a forward-leaning position; the woman can then slide back onto the penis. With a little bit of practice, this maneuver becomes simple.

REAR-ENTRY

In rear-entry positions, the man faces the woman's back and the penis is placed into the vagina from behind. Coitus can be accomplished with the woman on her hands and knees in the "doggy style"; the woman may lie face down with her hips propped up by a pillow; or the couple may lie on their sides, with the man's front to the woman's back in the "spoon position." Rear-entry can also be done in a sitting or standing position. In most of these positions, the man can usually reach around his partner's body to stimulate her

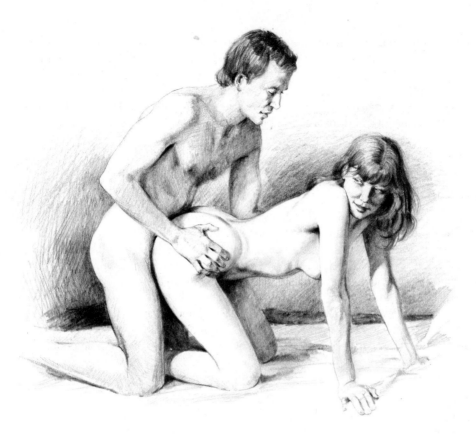

Rear-entry intercourse, "doggy style" (above) and "spoon position" (below).

clitoris or breasts, but mouth-to-mouth kissing is difficult and eye contact is lost. Many couples feel that rear-entry coitus is less intimate for these latter reasons, and some couples object to this position because it seems too much like anal intercourse. However, the sensations of thrusting against the buttocks can be pleasurable, and when the woman's legs are close together more stimulation of the penis is possible.

SIDE-TO-SIDE, FACE-TO-FACE

In this position, the partners are facing each other but lying on their sides. Since neither person is burdened by the other's weight, this is often a relaxed position where a lot of leisurely caressing and cuddling can be included. Both partners have at least one free hand. The primary drawback of this position is that inserting the penis in the vagina can be tricky. Thus, many couples begin in a different face-to-face position

and then roll onto their sides. There are two other disadvantages in the side-by-side position: first, the penis is a bit more likely to slip out of the vagina than in other positions, and second, there is less mechanical leverage to achieve vigorous pelvic thrusting.

TIMING, TEMPO, AND OTHER THEMES

Above and beyond the countless embellishments in coital positioning that are possible, there are many stylistic variations that affect coital sex. The surroundings chosen for a sexual encounter can range from a bedroom to an automobile to an outdoor setting. People can make love in the dark, with dim lighting, or in broad daylight. Some people like to have background music for sex, others like to use a water bed or lots of pillows, and still others prefer sex in a hot tub or in front of a crackling fire.

Timing and tempo are also important in-

Side-to-side, face-to-face intercourse position.

Heterosexuality

gredients. Just as a person's appetite for food can be met in a variety of ways — a quick snack, an elegant gourmet meal, or a simple, satisfying steak — sexual appetite can also be served by a "quickie," by a long, leisurely episode of love-making, or by a technically straightforward sexual encounter. One version is not always better than another — its quality and enjoyment depend on the needs and responses of the people involved.

Many heterosexual couples approach coitus in a businesslike fashion — sex is always at the same time (usually late at night), with the same "routines," the same position, and sometimes identical dialogue. Although this can lead to boredom for some people, for others it is a perfectly comfortable and satisfying situation — predictability is not always a liability. On the other hand, many couples enjoy a more creative approach to their sex lives, varying not only the positions and stimulatory techniques they use but also the time when sex occurs, the setting, and who plays the most active role.

Although it was the traditional view of our culture that women should be relatively passive sexually and let men initiate, set the tempo, and end the activity (by ejaculating), this pattern has undergone considerable change in the last decade. Our impression from thousands of research and clinical interviews is that many women are now playing a far more active role in sexual interactions in general and in coital sex in particular. Being less bound by old gender role stereotypes means that many women now feel freer to show or tell their partners what they like and do not like sexually. This openness benefits both sexes by improving the chance that the woman will enjoy sex and by relieving the man of the responsibility of having to be the expert who knows just what to do to satisfy his partner.

A few specific examples can illustrate how this works. It is often easier for the woman to insert the penis in the vagina than for the man because: (1) the woman knows when she's "ready"; (2) the woman knows precisely where the opening to the vagina is; and (3) the woman can adjust the angle of insertion to whatever feels most comfortable. If the man tries to control insertion, he is far more likely to have to hunt for the vagina (in contrast, women have little difficulty locating the position of an erect penis!);[2] he also frequently proceeds to intercourse before his partner is ready (Masters and Johnson, 1966, 1970, 1979). Another example of an active role a woman may take during lovemaking is to communicate what tempo of penile thrusting she prefers. Many men automatically start deep, vigorous thrusting during intercourse, but most women become more stimulated by slower, shallower thrusting at least in the early stages of coitus (Masters and Johnson, 1966, 1970; Hite, 1977).

We cannot conclude this section about sexual techniques without stressing again that sexual enjoyment usually relates less to mechanical proficiency than to how two people relate to one another. This does not mean that good sex requires a meaningful long-term relationship, but it most often depends on effective communications between partners. Working at sex — trying to develop erotic artistry through diligence, practice, and having a single-minded purpose — is more likely to interfere with the spontaneous enjoyment of sexual experiences than to produce a memorable sexual encounter.

---

[2] A simple experiment can document this point fairly well. In a dark room compare the difference in feeding your partner and feeding yourself. You should have no problem placing food in your own mouth — you know instinctively just where it is — but when you try to guess where your partner's mouth is, you are liable to deliver the food to the chin, the nose, or some other slightly-off-target area. A similar problem can occur when the man tries to always insert the penis — it can lead to some stumbling and fumbling, which can be an annoying distraction.

PERSPECTIVES ON
HETEROSEXUAL BEHAVIOR

Now we will shift our attention from matters of sexual technique to an examination of heterosexual behavior and attitudes toward such behavior. As we have pointed out, the descriptive information about sexual behaviors and attitudes available from various survey studies has methodological shortcomings. Nevertheless, it is useful to become acquainted with some of the findings of these surveys as long as we recognize that they are all approximations of the actual patterns of behavior they seek to measure.

Premarital Sex

Premarital sex is often talked about as synonymous with premarital intercourse, but people can be sexually active prior to marriage without having coital experience. Another problem with the term "premarital sex" is its implication that marriage is the goal of each and every person in our society.

Statistics about age at first sexual intercourse and experience with other types of sexual behavior during adolescence were given in chapter 8, but a few other facts about premarital intercourse are intriguing. Kinsey and his colleagues shocked many people in 1953 when they reported that half of the women they studied had sexual intercourse before marriage. Among men studied, 68 percent of men with a college education, 85 percent of men with a high-school education, and 98 percent of men with only an elementary school education had premarital coitus (Kinsey, Pomeroy, and Martin, 1948).

Two of the more recent sex surveys indicate that, at least among younger women, there has been a sizable increase in premarital coital experience. Hunt's data (1975) showed that 81 percent of married women between the ages of eighteen and twenty-four had premarital inter-

course (Table 15-1). The *Redbook* survey (Levin, 1975) reported that 90 percent of women under twenty-five said they had premarital intercourse and among all women in their survey who were married between 1970 and 1973, 89 percent had such experience. While these major differences from the Kinsey findings may reflect some sampling biases (for instance, the 100,000 women who answered the *Redbook* survey were younger, better educated, and more financially secure than the population as a whole), there is no question that premarital intercourse among women is more widespread today than it once was and that the age at first intercourse is declining (for additional observations on these points, see also Hopkins, 1977; Barrett, 1980; Wolfe, 1980; and Zelnik and Kantner, 1980).

These changes seem to reflect a shift in attitudes toward premarital sex between 1963 and 1975 in America: the percentage of adults who thought that premarital intercourse was always wrong dropped from 80 to 30 percent during this time as shown by three national surveys (Reiss, 1980). Data from the *Playboy* study, while supporting this finding, also put it in a slightly different perspective — even among eighteen to twenty-four year olds, premarital coitus for a man in circumstances other than a strongly affectionate relationship was thought to be wrong by 29 percent of the men and 53 percent of the women queried. Premarital coitus for a woman in the same circumstances was thought to be wrong by 44 percent of the men and 71 percent of the women (Hunt, 1975).

Thus, it appears that approval of premarital coitus for many teenagers and young adults is still restricted to love relationships or relationships with strong caring and affection (Hunt, 1975; Reiss, 1980). Recreational or casual sex, as opposed to relationship sex, is far less common, although it is written about so extensively that many young adults are convinced that most of their contemporaries have "freer" sexual attitudes

TABLE 15–1
Premarital Coitus: Total Married Sample, by Age

	18-24	25-34	35-44	45-54	55 and over
Percent of Men	95	92	86	89	84
Percent of Women	81	65	41	36	31

Source: Reprinted with permission of PEI Books, Inc. from *Sexual Behavior in the 1970's* by Morton Hunt. Copyright © 1974 by Morton Hunt.

than they do. The fact that most young adults see premarital coitus as justified when it occurs in a legitimate, committed relationship but less so when it is purely casual and sensuous shows that older cultural values have not been discarded but have changed (Hunt, 1975; Hopkins, 1977).

Not all adolescents or young adults are comfortable with the idea of nonvirginity, although the reasons for their concerns vary considerably. One useful framework for examining the diversity of sexual philosophies among the unmarried has been described by D'Augelli and D'Augelli (1977). According to these authors, *inexperienced virgins* are individuals who have had little dating experience until college and usually have not thought much about sex; *adamant virgins* are people who firmly believe that intercourse before marriage is improper (and often have a strong religious basis for this belief); *potential nonvirgins* are individuals who have not yet found the right partner or the right situation for coital sex and often seem to have a high fear of pregnancy; *engaged nonvirgins* are those whose coital experience has usually been only with one partner (typically someone they love or care deeply about) and only in the context of a committed relationship; *liberated nonvirgins* are people who have more permissive attitudes toward premarital intercourse and value the physical pleasures of coitus without demanding love as a justification; and *confused nonvirgins* are those who "engage in

sex without real understanding of their motivation, the place of sex in their lives, or its effects on them" (D'Augelli and D'Augelli, 1977, p. 53). People in the latter category often use sex as a way of attempting to establish a relationship and after the relationship terminates usually feel ambivalent about having had intercourse.

A number of other notable changes have occurred in premarital sexual behavior in the last three decades. First, relatively few young men today are sexually initiated by prostitutes or have premarital intercourse with prostitutes (Hunt, 1975; Sarrel and Sarrel, 1979), although Kinsey and his colleagues (1948) found that more than one-quarter of college-educated men who had not married by age twenty-five and 54 percent of high-school-educated men had premarital intercourse with a prostitute. Second, use of oral-genital sex among young unmarried men and women has increased dramatically compared to Kinsey's day, with the percent of people using fellatio more than doubling and the percent trying cunnilingus rising from 14 to 69 percent (Hunt, 1975). Third, there seems to be a greater degree of premarital sexual experimentation in recent years compared to Kinsey's time. People are more willing to try a wider range of coital positions, drugs (especially marihuana) to enhance sexual and sensual feelings, and anal intercourse (Hunt, 1975; Levin, 1975; Hite, 1977; Sarrel and Sarrel, 1979). The trend toward experimentation is also shown by recent evidence that women are having premarital sex with more partners than in the past (Levin, 1975; Wolfe, 1980). Finally, the average frequency of premarital coitus has increased, particularly among women. Kinsey and coworkers (1953) reported that one-third of twenty-one- to twenty-five-year-old women had premarital intercourse, averaging a frequency of once every three weeks, while Hunt (1975) found that two-thirds of his eighteen- to twenty-four-year-old sample had premarital coital experience with an average frequency of just over once a week. The percentage of women who are orgasmic with premarital coitus has increased substantially too (Hunt, 1975; Wolfe; 1980).

Another change in premarital sex behavior has been the greater acceptance of *cohabitation* — unmarried heterosexual couples living together. The implications of this development for sexual behavior are discussed on page 249.

Although the research is not sophisticated enough to draw firm conclusions about the effects of premarital intercourse on marital relationships, some studies have indicated potential problems. Many studies in the 1960s concluded that marriages tend to be rated as more successful when premarital chastity has been maintained (Muus, 1960; Reiss, 1966; Shope and Broderick, 1967). This view, however, was challenged by some who suggested that the findings might only show that the same people who are ashamed or afraid of having premarital intercourse might also be ashamed or afraid of admitting that their marriages were unhappy (Ellis, 1965). One large-scale survey in 1969 found that people with extensive premarital sexual experience tend to have numerous extramarital affairs and also noted that the more premarital coital partners a person had, the greater the tendency to have less happy marriages (Athanasiou and Sarkin, 1974).

We suspect that better designed studies might show more positive effects of premarital sex — for example, better sexual communication and less sexual inhibition. We also want to point out that couples who break up premaritally because of lack of sexual compatability (a group that has not yet been studied at all) may be actually doing each other a favor.

Marital Sex

More than 90 percent of Americans have married by their early thirties. By ages forty-five to fifty-four, only about 4 percent of women and 6 percent of men in the United States have never been married (U.S. Bureau of the Census, 1978a). In this section, we will examine patterns of marital sex behavior in terms of coital frequency, orgasm, techniques, and satisfaction in traditional marriages and then look briefly at the sexual implications of alternative marriage styles.

FREQUENCY OF MARITAL COITUS

The average American married couple has intercourse two or three times per week in their twenties and thirties, after which the frequency slowly declines. Past age fifty, coital frequency averages once a week or less. The survey data that provide the basis for this overview (Kinsey et al., 1948, 1953; Bell and Bell, 1972; Hunt, 1975; Levin and Levin, 1975; Trussell and Westoff, 1980) must be interpreted as less than precise information because of methodological limitations (see Figure 15-1).

"Average" frequencies do not tell the whole story, however. In each study on the frequency of marital coitus, a broad range of individual variation was found. Some young married couples have no coital activity, while other couples have intercourse several times a day. While, in general, coital frequency rates decline with the length of marriage, some couples clearly develop better sexual relationships as time goes by and may be more coitally active after fifteen or twenty years of marriage than they were early in their marital lives. There does not seem to be any correlation between the frequency of coitus in marriage and educational or occupational status (Kinsey, Pomeroy, and Martin, 1948, 1953; Hunt, 1975). The effects of strong religious feelings on marital sexuality are uncertain. Kinsey and his co-workers (1948) found that less religious husbands had higher marital coital rates but such an effect was not found for women (Kinsey et al., 1953); according to the *Playboy* survey (Hunt, 1975), churchgoing wives had lower rates of marital coitus than less religious women. In the *Redbook* survey (Levin, 1975), the frequency of marital

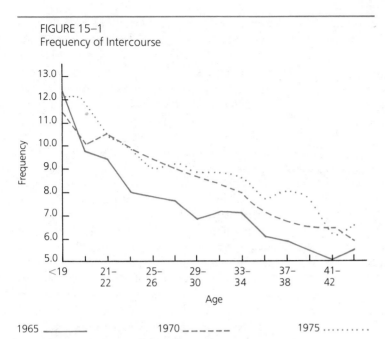

FIGURE 15–1
Frequency of Intercourse

Age

1965 ——————   1970 — — — — —   1975 · · · · · · · · ·

Source: From Trussell and Westoff, 1980, p. 248. Reprinted with permission from *Family Planning Perspectives,* Volume 12, Number 5, 1980.

The average frequency of intercourse in the four weeks before interview for married white American women, by age.

coitus was virtually identical for strongly religious and nonreligious women, although strongly religious wives were more likely to report that they always play an active role in lovemaking.

ORGASM

Although Kinsey and his colleagues (1948) reported that men reached orgasm in essentially all of their marital coitus, Hunt (1975) found that 8 percent of husbands in the forty-five and older age group did not have orgasm anywhere from occasionally to most of the time, and 7 percent of the twenty-four- to forty-four-year-old married men did not have orgasm in at least one-quarter of their coital experiences. These statistics do not mean that a man who doesn't ejaculate during intercourse necessarily has a problem: in some cases, the man may have already ejaculated in an-

other type of sexual play, and in other cases, the man simply may not feel the need.

Kinsey and his co-workers (1953) reported that marital coital orgasm had not been experienced by one-quarter of women after one year of marriage, but by the end of twenty years of marriage, this figure had fallen to 11 percent. In the same study, it was found that 45 percent of wives reported orgasms in 90 to 100 percent of coital experiences in their fifteenth year of marriage. Hunt (1975) found that 53 percent of wives reported coital orgasms "all or almost all the time" in marriages of fifteen years median duration. In the *Redbook* survey, 63 percent of wives reported coital orgasms all or almost all of the time, and only 7 percent had never experienced coital orgasm.

For some married couples, lack of orgasmic

responsiveness in coitus can be a major problem, as shown by this comment from a thirty-nine-year-old woman:

Although I feel like I am pretty open sexually, willing to try things and fairly easily turned on, after eighteen years of marriage I still haven't had an orgasm with intercourse. Years ago, it didn't bother me all that much, but for the last five years I've felt worse and worse about it. My husband and I have tried everything possible, all to no avail. After awhile, I started to lose interest in sex and to get very depressed. Our marriage has been badly hurt by this problem and I don't know what to do. (This woman and her husband subsequently entered sex therapy with us and were able to correct the lack of coital orgasm quite easily. Sometimes with long-standing problems, it is easier to get objective help from others than to try to "do-it-yourself.") (Authors' files)

For other couples, lack of female coital orgasm poses no problem or threat, as a thirty-one-year-old woman explained:

I've never had an orgasm during intercourse, but that's never really bothered me. In fact, I think my husband was more concerned about it than I was. I enjoy the closeness and touching of sex, and I get aroused, too — it's just the orgasm that's missing. If I need the release of an orgasm I can masturbate, but orgasm just isn't the most important part of sex for me. (Authors' files)

SEXUAL TECHNIQUES

Marital sexual techniques have undergone some remarkable changes in the last forty years if data from available surveys are to be believed. For example, while oral-genital sex was avoided by large numbers of the married men and women who participated in the Kinsey studies, a majority of married people today include fellatio and cunnilingus in their sexual repertoires (Table 15-2). Eighty-seven percent of wives in the *Redbook* survey reported using cunnilingus often or occasionally, and 85 percent reported fellatio with a similar frequency (Tavris and Sadd, 1977). Similarly, although Kinsey and his colleagues did not report

statistics on anal intercourse in marriage in their initial volumes, an updated report (Gebhard and Johnson, 1979) showed that less than 9 percent of married respondents had experience with this type of sexual act. In contrast, nearly one-quarter of the married women in Hunt's study (1975) and 43 percent of the wives in the *Redbook* survey had tried anal intercourse. (Most women indicated, however, that this was the least liked type of sexual activity.)

The other major changes in marital sexual technique include an increased amount of time in sexual play and the use of a wider variety of coital positions. While Kinsey and his co-workers found that precoital play was often limited to a few kisses among those with a grade-school education and averaged about twelve minutes among the college-educated, Hunt found that at both educational levels the time spent in sexual play before intercourse averaged fifteen minutes. Similarly, while Kinsey believed that three-fourths of married men ejaculated within two minutes after inserting the penis in the vagina, Hunt's data indicate that marital coitus now lasts an average of ten minutes. This change may reflect a greater awareness by married men and women today that women are more likely to enjoy sex more and to be orgasmic if intercourse is unhurried.

Greater use of a diversity of coital positions in marriages today may be due to an increased awareness that the "missionary position" often limits the sexual options available to the woman. Table 15-3 shows the percentage of married couples using other coital positions on a frequent basis.

SEXUAL SATISFACTION

How does the quality of a couple's marriage contribute to their sexual satisfaction? And how does the nature of a married couple's sex life relate to their overall marital satisfaction? Since relatively little research has been done on these sub-

TABLE 15–2
Oral-Genital Foreplay in Marital Sex Relations

	Percents of Marriages in Which Fellatio Is Used		Percents of Marriages In Which Cunnilingus Is Used	
	1938-1946 (Kinsey)	1972 (Present survey)	1938-1946 (Kinsey)	1972 (Present survey)
High-school males	15	54	15	56
College males	43	61	45	66
High-school females	46	52	50	58
College females	52	72	58	72

Source: Reprinted with permission of PEI Books, Inc. from *Sexual Behavior in the 1970's* by Morton Hunt. Copyright © 1974 by Morton Hunt.

TABLE 15–3
Marital Coital Positions

		Hunt	
Position	Kinsey et al.	18-24 (age)	35-44 (age)
Female-on-top	16%	37%	29%
Side-by-side, Face-to-face	12	21	15
Rear-entry	4	20	8
Sitting	–	4	2

Kinsey data adapted from Gebhard and Johnson, 1979, showing frequent use among college-educated, white, married couples.

Hunt data adapted from Hunt, 1975, Table 33, for white, married sample reporting the frequency of using a specific coital position as "often," given for two different age groups.

jects, these questions can only be partially answered.

The original Kinsey reports did not evaluate the relationship between sexual adjustment and marital happiness, but a later analysis of the data led Gebhard (1966) to conclude that women were much more likely to be orgasmic in "very happy" marriages (rated by self-report) than in other marriages. It is not clear whether the very happy marriages led to a better sexual climate or vice versa.

Data from the *Playboy* survey indicate that a large majority of married men and women who described their marital sex as very pleasurable rated their marriages as very close (Hunt, 1975). Among those who rated their marital sex as displeasing or lacking in pleasure, almost no one rated their marriage as very close and just a few thought their marriages were fairly close. Interestingly, in people rating their marriages as not close or fairly distant, 59 percent of the men still reported that marital sex was "mostly" or "very" pleasurable, as compared to 38 percent of the women. Apparently more men than women are able to enjoy sex when their marriage is strained.

The *Redbook* survey found a strong correlation between the frequency of intercourse and satisfaction with marital sex for women. It also noted that 81 percent of the women who were orgasmic all or most of the time in marital coitus rated the sexual side of their marriage as good or very good, while only 52 percent of women who were occasionally orgasmic and 29 percent of women who were never orgasmic (or who did not know if they were) felt that their sexual relationship was good. A strong correlation was also found between a wife's ability to communicate her sexual desires and feelings to her husband and the quality of marital sex.

More recently, Blumstein and Schwartz (1983) also found a correlation between the frequency of marital sex and sexual satisfaction (Figure 15-2). Among those having sex three times a week or more, 89 percent of husbands and wives were satisfied with the quality of their sex lives, while only 53 percent of those having sex between once a week and once a month were satisfied. In marriages with a sexual frequency of once a month or less, the satisfaction rate dropped to only 32 percent. Another important factor that was linked to sexual satisfaction was equality in initiating or refusing sex. Eighty percent of husbands and wives who reported that sexual initiation in their relationship was equal were satisfied with the quality of their sex lives, versus 66 percent of those who said that sexual initiation was one-sided. Similarly, 80 percent of married men and women who reported being able to refuse sex on an equal basis were satisfied with the quality of their sex lives, compared to 58 percent of husbands and 61 percent of wives who reported that sexual refusal was not equal.

Intriguingly, it appears that heterosexual men who receive and give oral sex are happier with their sex lives and with their relationships than those who do not (Blumstein and Schwartz, 1983). Performing or receiving oral sex, however, does not seem to be linked to sexual satisfaction for heterosexual women, possibly because many of them see both fellatio and cunnilingus as a form of submissiveness or degradation. Instead, it appears that intercourse is more essential to sexual satisfaction for heterosexual women than for heterosexual men (Blumstein and Schwartz, 1983).

Research surveys are not the only way of elucidating the relationship between sexual and marital satisfaction, and attempts to categorize just what satisfaction is may be misleading. One person may be satisfied with a marriage that provides economic security and freedom from major conflict, while another person considers that kind of marriage as tolerable but unsatisfactory. Likewise, one person may judge how satisfying a sexual relationship is primarily in terms of coital frequency, while to someone else a variety of forms of sex play and the quality of both partners' sexual responses may be the basis for making a judgment. If both spouses largely agree on what they require for sexual and marital happiness, the chances seem to be higher that they will be able to attain it. On the other hand, many marriage counselors and sex therapists can attest to the fact that many marriages are troubled by some major form of sexual distress (Masters and Johnson, 1970; Kaplan, 1974; Frank, Anderson, and Rubinstein, 1978; LoPiccolo and LoPiccolo, 1978). It has also been suggested that the high prevalence of extramarital sex may also relate to a lack of marital sexual satisfaction since, as Reiss (1980, p. 307) says, if other things are equal, "the more marital sexual satisfaction, the less the desire for extramarital relationships." We will return to this point shortly.

ALTERNATIVE MARRIAGE STYLES

Although marriage may be defined by legal criteria that strictly regulate who the spouses can be, there are many types of marriage that differ in various ways from the traditional one man–one woman (monogamous) marriage. In the following paragraphs, we will briefly describe certain aspects of alternative (nonlegal) marriage styles as they relate to heterosexual behavior.

Triads, or three partner marriages, can consist of one man and two women or two men with one woman, with the latter form being less

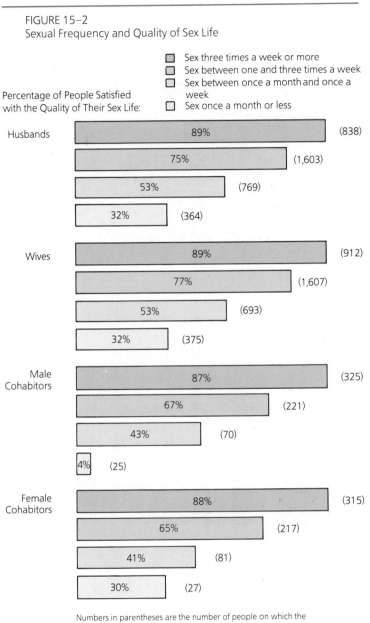

FIGURE 15–2
Sexual Frequency and Quality of Sex Life

☐ Sex three times a week or more
☐ Sex between one and three times a week
☐ Sex between once a month and once a week
☐ Sex once a month or less

Percentage of People Satisfied with the Quality of Their Sex Life:

Husbands
89% (838)
75% (1,603)
53% (769)
32% (364)

Wives
89% (912)
77% (1,607)
53% (693)
32% (375)

Male Cohabitors
87% (325)
67% (221)
43% (70)
4% (25)

Female Cohabitors
88% (315)
65% (217)
41% (81)
30% (27)

Numbers in parentheses are the number of people on which the percentages are based.

Source: From *American Couples* by Philip Blumstein, Ph.D. and Pepper Schwartz, Ph.D. Copyright © 1983 by Philip Blumstein and Pepper W. Schwartz. By permission of William Morrow & Company.

"It's especially tough when the magic goes out of a group marriage."

frequent. Triads tend to form more naturally than larger group marriages, which usually require some design and planning, and seem more likely to be motivated by existing friendship or love (Constantine, 1978). Triads are also likely to be formed on the basis of pre-existing sexual relationships, although sex is often not the primary reason behind this choice of alternative marriage style. Here's how one twenty-six-year-old woman involved in a triadic marriage with another man and woman explained it:

> Most people think our marriage is just an excuse for freewheeling sex, but that's not true at all. If sex was what we wanted, why go to all the trouble of marrying in a threesome, which makes almost everyone think we're weird? The real reason we married is that we all love each other, and we want to stay together, sharing our lives. Sex is just one part of that sharing, although it's a part we usually enjoy. (Authors' files)

Group marriages consist of four or more partners who genuinely regard themselves as married to each other although they do not all have a legally recognized relationship. To date, there has only been a limited amount of research on group marriage, with the work of Constantine and Constantine (1973) providing the best overview of the subject. The participants in group marriages tend to be in their twenties or early thirties and many of them have previously been legally married and have one or two children (Constantine, 1978). The most common form of group marriage in America consists of two men and two women; in some widely publicized cases one man has had five to ten wives. Individuals in group marriages tend to have liberal nonreligious backgrounds, an unconventional outlook, and a high need for change and autonomy, but they enter group marriages for just the same reasons that two people might get married (Constantine and Constantine, 1973; Ramey, 1976). The potential advantages of a group marriage are both economic and emotional: it can satisfy a need for variety (including sexual variety) and it can present opportunities for interpersonal growth. On the other hand, most group marriages do not survive very long (Macklin, 1980): sexual jealousy is fairly common and arranging sexual attention and combinations can be difficult. As Murstein (1978, p. 132) notes, "In a six-person group there are nine possible heterosexual pairings for the night and fifty-seven different relationships of from two to six people." In general, men appear to have greater difficulty adapting to group marriages than women (Constantine, 1978).

A few other types of nontraditional marriage styles will be discussed in the next section, while celibacy as a choice for heterosexual marriage will be considered in chapter 17.

Extramarital Sex

Extramarital sex can be defined as any form of sexual activity between a married person and someone other than his or her spouse. Although considered sinful, criminal, or immoral through most of the history of the Western world — and sometimes punished by whippings, fines, brandings, and even death (Murstein, 1974) — the practice has both persisted and become fairly commonplace.

In 1948 Kinsey and his co-workers estimated that half of all married males in their sample had had extramarital coitus (this figure was approximate because many men were reluctant to discuss this area openly). Kinsey's group (1953) also noted that by age forty, 26 percent of married women had had extramarital sex. In 1975 Hunt believed that these estimates were still accurate, but the *Redbook* survey found that among thirty-five- to thirty-nine-year-old wives, 38 percent

had extramarital sexual experience (Levin, 1975). In the *Cosmopolitan* survey (Wolfe, 1980), half of married women eighteen to thirty-four years old and 69.2 percent of married women thirty-five or older had had extramarital sexual activity. While some other recent surveys have also reported higher figures for extramarital sex — for example, Hite (1981) found that two-thirds of the married men in her sample had extramarital experience, and the *Playgirl* survey found a 43 percent incidence in married women (Grosskopf, 1983) — these numbers contrast sharply with the data of Blumstein and Schwartz (1983) which show that only 26 percent of husbands (N = 3,591) and 21 percent of the wives (N = 3,606) they studied had any form of extramarital sex involvement.

Unfortunately, much of the research on extramarital sex is methodologically limited and the reasons that motivate people to engage in extramarital sex are only poorly understood at the present time (Reiss et al., 1980; Atwater, 1982; Thompson, 1983).

THE EXTRAMARITAL EXPERIENCE

While most people believe that extramarital sex is always wrong (Singh, Walton, and Williams, 1976), there has been a traditional double standard that rationalizes to a certain degree extramarital sex for men while more strongly condemning it for women. In some European countries, for instance, having a mistress is regarded as a privilege of wealthy married men. Similarly, many societies permit female heterosexual prostitution (a sort of temporary "rent-a-mistress") as a means of providing for a presumed male need for sexual variety while protecting against destruction of the bonds of matrimonial relationships. Since prostitution is seen by most people as extramarital sex at a purely physical level, it is not as threatening as other types of extramarital sex that carry the risk of emotional involvement that might eventually lead to the break-up of a marriage.

Perhaps for this same reason, some married people feel most comfortable with extramarital sex that is purely and directly aimed at physical pleasure: the "one-night stand." The background circumstances that lead to this brief encounter of extramarital sex vary tremendously — a lonely businessman on an overnight trip, a bored housewife who feels the walls are closing in on her at home and makes the rounds of the city bars, men or women trying to prove to themselves that they're not really getting old or that they still have sex appeal — the list could go on indefinitely. The extramarital one-night stand is often so impersonal that the participants don't know each other's names. No commitment is made and none is intended; it's really sex with "no strings attached."

How do people react to having such an experience? Some people find exactly what they're looking for: a release of pent-up tension, a means of getting even with their spouse for something, a way of satisfying their curiosity, a change of pace from their ordinary sexual diet, or a temporary form of escape. Others find the experience to be empty, guilt-provoking, awkward, or frightening. These comments illustrate the types of reactions we've frequently heard:

A thirty-one-year-old woman: I'd been married for almost ten years and had always been faithful, but I kept wondering what it would be like to have sex with someone else. One night I was out with some friends, and we met a few guys who bought us drinks and talked with us awhile. One of them was real good-looking and flirting with me, and I sort of flirted back. We went off to a motel for three or four hours, and it was beautiful sex, fantastic sex, just like in a novel. But that was the end of it, and it just felt good to know that I'd had the experience. I never told my husband and I don't plan to. (Authors' files)

A thirty-six-year-old man: My wife and I have very old-fashioned values and we both took our marital vows seriously, meaning no screwing around with anyone else. I never worried about it too much, since I wasn't the type to be running around anyway. But one night when I was working late a secretary asked me for a ride home, and then invited me in for coffee. Well, she was just divorced a few months, and she wanted more than coffee, and I was perfectly happy to oblige. But it was a stupid thing to do — not much fun, and lots of guilt about it afterwards — and I don't think I'd do it again. (Authors' files)

The extramarital affair contrasts sharply with the one-night stand in that there is a continued sexual relationship over time. The affair may be relatively short-lived (lasting just a few weeks) or may go on for years. A popular Neil Simon play, *Same Time Next Year,* tells the story of an extramarital affair that occurred once a year on the same weekend for decades. An extramarital affair can be mainly for sex or it can blossom into a relationship on its own with sex playing a relatively minor part and companionship and conversation being more important (see Table 15-4).

Affairs are probably less frequent than one-night stands for both practical and personal reasons. Unless a person's spouse knows about, and approves of, a continued extramarital liaison (a statistically unlikely possibility at present), the partners in the affair must create time to be together, find a place to meet (and preserve their anonymity), and explain their absence to their spouses.[3] For these reasons, many affairs involve

---

[3] Extramarital sex between a married man and a single woman or a married woman and a single man is likely to offer greater convenience than an affair between two married persons. They have a place to go (the single partner's residence) and less of a scheduling problem, since the single partner is not as likely to be tied down by home and family responsibilities. But these types of affairs can create their own brand of problems: the single person may press the married one to divorce and remarry, for example.

TABLE 15–4
Reasons Given By Women for Having an Extramarital Affair

Reason	Percent
Emotionally dissatisfied with husband	72
Sexually dissatisfied with husband	46
Seduced by lover	39
Feel naturally polygamous	39
Found out husband had an affair	35
To gain revenge against husband	23
Have an open marriage	14
Don't know why	30

Source: Modified from data in Grosskopf, 1983, p. 195; based on replies from 516 married women.

secretive (and hurried) get-togethers during the day, since it may be easier to get an hour or two away from work than a similar time away from home at night.

At the personal level, many people feel that having an affair is like "playing with dynamite." Although it may be sexually satisfying and emotionally fulfilling, they are cautious about letting the affair take over their lives or pose a threat to their marriage. Many people who have had affairs state that they loved their spouse during the time of their extramarital involvement and did not want to jeopardize that relationship.

Lacking thorough research, it is difficult to say how frequently extramarital sex contributes to divorce. Clearly, some men and women are so upset at discovery of their spouse's infidelity that this leads to a broken marriage. On the other hand, it is not likely that many solid marriages break up for this reason alone. It is also impossible to know how often an affair occurred because the marriage was already weak or troubled or how often an affair was simply "the straw that broke the camel's back." The experience of many marriage counselors indicates that it isn't so much

the notion of a spouse having sex outside the marriage that causes the rift (we've never encountered a marriage that broke up because a man visited a prostitute, for instance) as the idea of an emotional involvement with someone else along with the sex. In other words, for some couples, extramarital sex poses a threat to the intimacy of marriage in both a physical and psychological sense. For other couples, extramarital involvements are no source of concern — they judge their marriage primarily in terms of how they interact together and how adequately their relationship meets their needs.

The *Redbook* survey uncovered another interesting aspect of extramarital sex. Married women who work outside the home seem to have a higher likelihood of extramarital sex: 27 percent of full-time housewives have had extramarital sex, but 47 percent of wives who work part-time or full-time outside the home have had extramarital intercourse (Levin, 1975). It is not clear whether these statistics mean that women who work outside the home have more liberal attitudes to begin with, or have extramarital sex more often because of greater opportunity, or if some other explanation applies.

Although extramarital sex offers excitement, variety, and the thrill of the forbidden, the available data show that the overall pleasure of extramarital sex is somewhat lower for men and women in general than their overall sexual pleasure in their marriages (Hunt, 1975). While extramarital sex may release sexual inhibitions for some people and help them to become fully responsive for the first time in their life, it may lead other people to sexual problems (Masters and Johnson, 1970, 1976).

CONSENSUAL EXTRAMARITAL SEX

When two spouses agree that one or both of them is free to engage in extramarital sexual activity, there may be many reasons behind the decision. They may be looking for a way to preserve their personal freedom, hoping to improve the quality of their marriage, seeking to live by a particular personal philosophy, or simply trying to add variety and excitement to their lives.

Both partners may be interested in extramarital sex or one person may agree to let the other do as he or she pleases without any intention of participating themselves. For one couple, talking about the extramarital experience in vivid detail may be a source of turn-on, while another couple decides that extramarital sex is okay for them only if they don't discuss it together.

Consensual (i.e., with consent) extramarital sex can take many forms. A decade ago, Nena and George O'Neill wrote a best-selling book called *Open Marriage* in which they suggested that traditional marriages often presented few options for choice or change. Their "open marriage" concept — as opposed to the "closed," or traditional, marriage — envisioned a flexible relationship in which both spouses were committed to their own and their partner's fulfillment and growth. The O'Neills stressed that an open marriage involved a willingness to negotiate change and to discard the expectations of a closed marriage, particularly the idea that one partner is able to meet all of the other's needs (emotional, social, economic, intellectual, and sexual). The O'Neills emphasized role equality and flexibility between spouses, but many people presumed that their book was primarily an endorsement of consen-

---

RESEARCH SPOTLIGHT

Non-Monogamy

In *American Couples*, Blumstein and Schwartz use the term "non-monogamy" to describe sexual activity outside a couple's relationship so that they can examine such behavior in married couples, cohabiting heterosexual couples, and homosexual and lesbian couples. Here is a summary of their major findings:

1. Monogamy is strongly held as a moral ideal even by those who don't practice what they preach.
2. Sex differences in monogamy are most apparent among homosexual women and men (82 percent of gay men versus 28 percent of lesbians are nonmonogamous), but while similar numbers of husbands and wives have had extramarital sexual experiences, the men have had more partners.
3. Couples never can be completely sure their relationships will remain monogamous even after they've been together a decade or longer.
4. One episode of non-monogamy doesn't mean that a person has begun a "career" of infidelity — in fact, for some people an act of sex outside the relationship may be more to satisfy curiosity than anything else.
5. Men are more likely to seek

Heterosexuality

sual extramarital sex as a growth experience. However, the O'Neills later wrote:

> While some benefits were noted, it was observed that by and large these [extramarital sex] experiences did not occur in a context where the marital partners were developing their primary marriage relationship sufficiently for this activity to count as a growth experience. Frequently it obscured relationship problems, became an avenue of escape, and intensified conflicts. (O'Neill and O'Neill, 1977, p. 293)

Nevertheless, the open marriage approach to discarding the notion of sexual exclusivity and restrictiveness seems to work well for some couples. It should be noted, however, that an open marriage does not need to involve outside sexual relationships (Knapp and Whitehurst, 1978).

Swinging is another form of consensual extramarital sex. Here, married couples exchange partners with other couples, with all parties agreeing to the arrangement. Most surveys indicate that only 2 to 4 percent of married couples have ever engaged in swinging, and less than half of these couples have done it on a regular basis (Spanier and Cole, 1972; Athanasiou, 1973; Hunt, 1975; Murstein, 1978a).

The husband usually first brings up the idea of swinging, and the wife's reaction is typically one of shock (Murstein, 1978a). Only a few couples who discuss the idea ever attempt to put it into reality, and even here many get cold feet and don't go through with their plans at the last minute.

Although a couple will occasionally be in-

casual sex outside their relationships, while women seek to form emotional attachments.

6. People who attend church or synagogue regularly are as likely as anyone else to have extramarital sex.

7. Heterosexuals who have non-monogamous sex are just as happy with their relationships as monogamous people, but they are somewhat less sure their relationships will last.

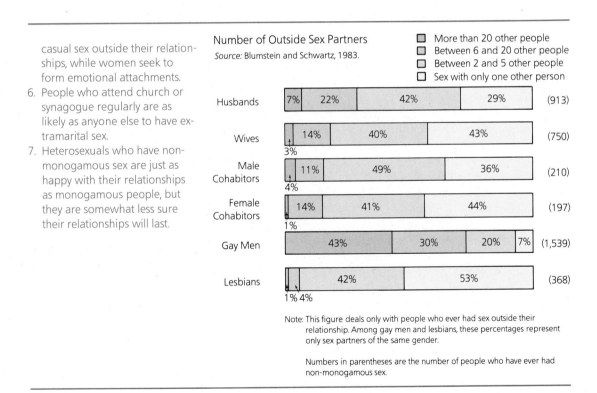

Number of Outside Sex Partners
Source: Blumstein and Schwartz, 1983.

- ☐ More than 20 other people
- ☐ Between 6 and 20 other people
- ☐ Between 2 and 5 other people
- ☐ Sex with only one other person

	More than 20	Between 6 and 20	Between 2 and 5	Sex with one	(n)
Husbands	7%	22%	42%	29%	(913)
Wives	3%	14%	40%	43%	(750)
Male Cohabitors	4%	11%	49%	36%	(210)
Female Cohabitors	1%	14%	41%	44%	(197)
Gay Men	43%	30%	20%	7%	(1,539)
Lesbians	1% 4%	42%	53%		(368)

Note: This figure deals only with people who ever had sex outside their relationship. Among gay men and lesbians, these percentages represent only sex partners of the same gender.

Numbers in parentheses are the number of people who have ever had non-monogamous sex.

troduced to swinging by people they already know, this is generally an "underground" activity. The interested couple usually must turn to swingers' magazines or sexually explicit newspapers to either answer an ad or place one themselves. Here are several examples of ads from swingers' publications:

Attractive Couples. He, mid-30s, muscular, virile. She, mid-20s, shapely, sexy. Desire open-minded couples under 35 for relaxed get-togethers.

Sensual Black Couple, male 32 and hung, female 28 and 36-24-36. Into partying and fun. Photos required for reply.

Super Attractive Couple — she bi, 28, beautiful, natural redhead; he, 30, 6'1", 175 lbs., handsome and good build. Seeking extremely attractive couples for friendship and fun. Both educated, sincere, gentle, with sense of humor. Photo, phone a must.

Swingers may either get together for a two-couple "party" or may meet in groups with many couples. There are usually drinks served and pornographic movies may be shown to get people in the mood. The sexual activity may take place entirely in heterosexual twosomes, with each couple retreating behind a closed bedroom door ("closed swinging") or, if the door is left open, it's a signal for anyone who wishes to come in and join the fun (Murstein, 1978a). While "open swinging" commonly involves two women having sex together, male homosexual contact is less frequent and in some groups of swingers it is entirely barred. Several factors account for female homosexual relationships among swingers: most men are hardly matches for sexually aroused multiorgasmic women. While the men rest, they often experience sexual restimulation if they watch women make love to each other. Presumably the sight of other men making love to their spouses (while they are not similarly occupied) can be too ego-threatening while the sight of two women making love usually is not.

Variations on the swinging theme include group sex in private clubs such as the now defunct Sandstone in California (Talese, 1980) or in clubs that charge admission, such as Plato's Retreat in New York City. Swinging can also be an activity with a prominent social side: groups of swingers occasionally vacation together, organize picnics, or go for a day at the beach.

Different studies have defined the backgrounds and personalities of swingers in different ways. In some studies, swingers appeared to be conservative, traditional, and religious (Bartell, 1971; Walshok, 1971). In others they were portrayed as liberal, nonreligious (or even antireligious), and antiestablishment (Gilmartin, 1974). All studies agree that swingers as a group tend to have more premarital experience, more premarital partners, and more (and earlier) interest in sex than "nonswingers" (Murstein, 1978a). Although there is no evidence that swingers have abnormal personalities, two studies found that swingers are more likely to have had counseling or psychotherapy than nonswingers (Smith and Smith, 1970; Gilmartin, 1974).

The positive side of swinging includes having a shared activity that truly eliminates the double standard. Couples may feel pleased by having a variety of sexual partners without deceiving each other; some couples find that their own sex lives are improved. But the other side of the coin bears examining too, especially since most couples withdraw from swinging after brief experimentation (Murstein, 1978a). They may find that swinging has led to jealousy, feelings of inadequacy, guilt, rejection, and even to sexual dysfunction and divorce (Masters and Johnson, 1976).

Nonmarital Sex

Despite the popularity of marriage in our society, there are still many people who remain single by choice or by lack of marital opportunity. Current statistics indicate, for example, that almost 2 million Americans are now living in cohabitation relationships (see chapter 9). Others become single after once having been married by divorce or death of a spouse. Although largely neglected by researchers, these individuals also have sexual needs which they act on in various ways.

THE NEVER-MARRIED SINGLE

Although in the past it was often presumed that a man or woman who reached age thirty without marrying was flawed in one way or another, today it is clear that many people choose to be single as a creative option in their lives. The choice may be a rejection of the restrictions and responsibilities of marriage or it may be based on other factors, such as economic independence. Increasing numbers of women are placing career objectives ahead of marriage as a goal today (Frieze et al., 1978), and men are also reconsidering whether being married is really the way they want to live. Some of these people decide to marry after a long period of singlehood while others remain single throughout their lives.

Relatively few people choose to be single to preserve a particular sexual lifestyle, but the image of the "swinging singles scene" — freely accessible sex with little or no interpersonal responsibility beyond the requirements of the moment — has been burned into the public mind by the media. While singles bars continue to flourish in many locales, many people dislike the impersonal nature of sexual shopping around as these two comments reveal:

> A twenty-eight-year-old woman: I spent much of last year making the rounds at the singles bars looking for fun. After awhile, the "lines" and faces all blurred together — every guy claimed he was a doctor, a lawyer, or a corporate vice president — and the deceptiveness got to be too much. Even the sex wasn't very good . . . it certainly wasn't worth the agonies of trying to find someone to make it with. (Authors' files)

> A thirty-four-year-old man: I tried the dating bars for a month or so, but I couldn't really bring myself to continue. Sure there was lots of sex available — by 11:00 at night a lot of gals got desperate — but it was all a phony scene, one that had no real humanity to it. (Authors' files)

On the other hand, some people find the freedom and variety of the singles bars exciting and fulfilling.

> A twenty-nine-year-old woman: I'm a lawyer, and all day long I've got to think, to use my brain. Sometimes at night I just like to throw away that identity and go out for a good time. If I meet an attractive guy, I invite myself to his place — that way I don't have to worry about throwing him out, I can get up and leave when I'm ready. And sometimes it just feels good to make contact with someone else, with no commitments or obligations. (Authors' files)

The singles bars are populated by several different groups of people. The under-twenty-five-singles are generally in a "premarital" stage. Most of the over-thirties are divorced people and married men or women on the prowl for extramarital sex. The twenty-five to thirty year olds include both the not-interested-in-marriage-now group, the younger divorced crowd, and some people looking for the perfect mate.

Other nonmarried singles choose different approaches to their sexual needs, meeting prospective partners at work, through their families, or in other social settings. In recent years, computer dating services have become a popular means of trying to meet someone with similar interests where a sexual opportunity may develop. Some nonmarried people form relatively exclusive long-term sexual relationships in which neither partner has marriage as an objective. Others maintain nonexclusive long-term sexual relationships with a small number of partners who they see on a rotating basis. Others avoid lasting relationships in favor of a series of one-night stands, and others choose celibacy as best for themselves.

One infrequent but interesting aspect of nonmarital singlehood is *communal living,* where a group of people pool their economic resources and personal energies into a cooperative venture of sharing that sometimes includes sexual sharing but always includes some degree of emotional sharing and support (David, 1978). Communal living can be seen as a form of group cohabitation, and communes are certainly not new — in the mid-1800s hundreds of communes existed, some of which included rather free and open sex as a central theme. Some communes are organized on the basis of political or religious beliefs, while others are far less structured and seem to exist mainly on the philosophy of "do your own thing." Most communes have relatively short life spans, perhaps because sexual jealousy and possessiveness crop up fairly frequently.

THE PREVIOUSLY MARRIED SINGLE

People who have been married and then become single through divorce or death of a spouse remarry at extraordinarily high rates, as we mentioned in chapter 9. Most divorced men and women become sexually active within a year following their divorce (Hunt, 1975), although older divorced people are somewhat slower in this regard than those under age forty.

Since almost half of all marriages end in divorce, there is less stigma toward divorce now than in the past. The divorced woman is no longer viewed as "used goods" by men, and people are not regarded as being "failures" if their marriages don't last forever. The person who becomes divorced, however, may find it somewhat difficult at first to adjust to the idea of nonmarital sex, to work out the specific details of how to meet people, and to handle the logistics of sexual activity (where to go, what to tell the kids, and so on).

Widowed men and women sometimes choose to abstain from sexual activity after their spouse's death but a large majority of widowers

and 43 percent of widows engage in postmarital coitus (Gebhard, 1968; Hunt, 1975). The widow over sixty is sometimes handicapped by a lack of available male partners. Interestingly, the widower at any age is likely to have a wider selection of partners as women outlive men and men are relatively free to choose from women of all ages. Widows, conversely, are expected to choose partners close to their own age or older. As previously stated, many people think that the elderly have no sexual needs or feelings, but this is far from true: sexual interest is often maintained and sometimes improves with age. Among divorced or widowed persons, it is common to hear that postmarital sex is more pleasurable and fulfilling than in their prior marital experience.

SUMMARY

1. Sexual activity is not just a matter of good technique; interpersonal communication is usually an important component of the sexual experience. Finding out what your partner likes and dislikes and informing your partner about your own stylistic preferences are important aspects of any sexual relationship.

2. Among the many varieties of physical stimulation couples can use during lovemaking, certain practices such as oral-genital sex or anal stimulation can be anxiety-provoking for some people while acceptable and highly arousing for others. In one recent survey, it was found that almost 90 percent of married couples had oral-genital sex often or occasionally.

3. There are an almost infinite number of positions for intercourse, but most are variations on four basic methods: man-on-top, face-to-face (the "missionary" position); woman-on-top, face-to-face; rear-entry; and side-by-side. Although the missionary position is most commonly used, other positions can offer the woman more freedom of movement and some people enjoy chang-

ing positions from time to time for variety's sake alone.

4. In general, men and women today are less bound by old sexual stereotypes that limited the woman's role in initiating or participating actively in sex. More traditional views on other aspects of sexual behavior – particularly premarital sex – have also undergone substantial change in the last thirty to forty years.

5. There is solid research evidence that premarital sex is more common among women today than in the past, but for most people it still occurs in the context of an affectionate or love relationship. Cohabitation has become one fairly widespread form of premarital sex which permits a close-up view of what day-to-day living together is like, with its plusses and minuses.

6. Most Americans marry and have coitus two to three times a week during their twenties and thirties, after which the average coital frequency declines. There are wide individual differences in the frequency of marital sex and the activities that married couples include in their sexual interaction. The amount of time spent in noncoital play and the average duration of intercourse among married couples both seem to have lengthened since Kinsey's day.

7. There is no simple one-to-one relationship between good sex and good marriage, but marriages that are most satisfying sexually tend to stay together longer and have less extramarital sex than marriages marked by sexual dissatisfaction. Communication between partners seems to be a key element influencing the quality of a couple's sexual relationship.

8. Although extramarital sex has been strongly condemned in the past, many people seem to be doing it today. In the last few decades, more married women have become involved in this behavior as a result of shifting attitudes (e.g., a fading double standard, the advent of women's liberation), contraceptive availability, and more time spent outside the home.

9. Extramarital sex can take many forms: secretive versus consensual, one-night stands versus long-term affairs, recreational or relational, and so on. Although swinging is a relatively infrequent type of extramarital involvement, it is similar to the other varieties in that all of these behaviors can lead to pleasure or distress. It is not clear at present how often marital infidelity contributes to divorce, but our guess is that it is a fairly important factor in many cases.

10. Nonmarital sex includes the sexual behavior of the never-married single, the widowed, and the divorced. There is relatively little research about this area, but it generally appears that there are no major surprises. Sexual behavior is not all that different inside or outside of marriage.

SUGGESTED READINGS

Blumstein, Philip, and Schwartz, Pepper. *American Couples*. New York: William Morrow and Company, 1983. A monumental study of American couples – married, cohabiting, and homosexual – that includes unique data on sexual relations. One of the best research studies of the last thirty years.

Comfort, Alex. *The Joy of Sex*. New York: Crown Publishers, 1972. A beautifully illustrated, comfortably written book about sexual techniques that has been a long-time best-seller. Equally applicable for the beginner or more advanced student of the subject.

Hunt, Morton. *Sexual Behavior in the 1970's.* New York: Dell Publishing Co., 1975. A readable, crammed-full-of-facts report on the Playboy Foundation's national survey of sex in America. Particularly valuable for its contrasts with the Kinsey reports and its numerous tables.

Levin, Robert J. "The Redbook Report on Premarital and Extramarital Sex," *Redbook,* October 1975, pp. 38-44, 190-192.

Levin, Robert J., and Levin, Amy. "Sexual pleasure: the surprising preferences of 100,000 women," *Redbook,* September 1975, pp. 51-58. These two magazine articles summarize the most important statistics from a survey of the sexual preferences of 100,000 women. Fascinating reading, although not a scientific sample.

Murstein, Bernard I., ed. *Exploring Intimate Life Styles.* New York: Springer Publishing Co., 1978. A lively, readable overview of alternative marriage styles, swinging, cohabitation, creative singlehood, and other aspects of sexual and relationship behavior.

Heterosexuality

16 Homosexuality and Bisexuality

I N all known societies heterosexual behavior is the preferred pattern of most people most of the time (Beach, 1977). However, homosexual behavior has existed throughout history, and in many societies homosexuality in certain forms is accepted or even expected (Ford and Beach, 1951; Carrier, 1980).

In Western society, the subject provokes strong reactions from many people. Homosexuality has been described, for example, as "loathsome and disgusting," "grossly repugnant," "degenerate," "foul," and "immoral, indecent, lewd, and obscene." These statements were not made in a public opinion poll: they can each be found in judicial decisions from important court cases in the 1970s (Knutson, 1979/80). Similarly, a psychiatrist writing in the *Journal of the American Medical Association* called homosexuality "a dread dysfunction, malignant in character, which has risen to epidemic proportions" (Socarides, 1970).

Despite such strongly negative attitudes toward homosexuality, the last decade also provided a remarkable set of counterbalancing events. In 1974 the American Psychiatric Association officially decided that homosexuality was not an illness. Increasing numbers of courts began to uphold the civil rights of homosexuals on the basic premise that discriminating against people

407

on the basis of their sexual preferences was illegal (Vetri, 1979/80; Slovenko, 1980; Altman, 1982). Homosexual men and women in many walks of life — sports, science, government, the arts — publicly announced their sexual orientation and began using slogans such as "gay is beautiful" to raise the consciousness of the country and combat stereotypes. Homosexuals in the United States have also recently emerged with substantial political power (Clendinen, 1983). In early 1984, for example, a top aide to Democratic presidential-hopeful Walter Mondale said that gays "may be the most important new force in American politics" (Hume, 1984).

In this chapter, after first offering some definitions of homosexuality and bisexuality and briefly examining their history, we will discuss a number of complex and often controversial issues relating to these sexual orientations.

DEFINING TERMS

The word "homosexual" comes from the Greek root "homo," meaning "same," although the word itself was not coined until the late nineteenth century (Karlen, 1971). It can be used either as an adjective (as in: a homosexual act, a homosexual bar) or as a noun that describes men or women who have a preferential sexual attraction to people of their same sex over a significant period of time. While most homosexuals engage in overt sexual activity with members of the same sex and generally do not find themselves particularly attracted sexually to people of the opposite sex, neither of these two conditions is required to fit the definition we have offered. It is clear that a person with no sexual experience whatever may still consider himself or herself homosexual; also, many homosexuals are able to be aroused by heterosexual partners or heterosexual fantasies (Bell and Weinberg, 1978; Masters and Johnson, 1979).

Bisexuals, in contrast, are men or women who are sexually attracted to people of either sex. Usually, but not always, the bisexual has had overt sexual activity with partners of both sexes.

To clarify that heterosexuality, bisexuality, and homosexuality exist along a continuum in real life, Kinsey and his colleagues (1948) devised a 7-point rating scale to describe the overt sexual experiences and the inner psychological reactions of an individual (see Table 16-1). The bisexual man or woman would be rated as a Kinsey 2, 3, or 4.

TABLE 16–1
Kinsey's Heterosexual-Homosexual Rating Scale

0	Exclusively heterosexual
1	Predominantly heterosexual: only incidentally homosexual
2	Predominantly heterosexual: more than incidentally homosexual
3	Equally heterosexual and homosexual
4	Predominantly homosexual: more than incidentally heterosexual
5	Predominantly homosexual: only incidentally heterosexual
6	Exclusively homosexual

Source: Adapted from Kinsey, Pomeroy, and Martin, *Sexual Behavior in the Human Male* (Philadelphia: Saunders, 1948). Reprinted by permission of The Kinsey Institute for Research in Sex, Gender & Reproduction, Inc.

Homosexuality and Bisexuality

The best statistics available on the numbers of homosexuals in the U.S. are from the Kinsey reports, which found that 10 percent of white American males were more or less exclusively homosexual for at least three years of their lives between ages sixteen and fifty-five; 4 percent were exclusively homosexual on a life-long basis. Thirty-seven percent of the white male population had at least one homosexual experience in adolescence or adulthood which led to orgasm. In their female sample, Kinsey and his associates found that by age forty, 19 percent had experienced some same-sex erotic contact, but only 2 or 3 percent of women were mostly or exclusively homosexual on a life-long basis.

Many homosexuals today prefer the term "gay" as a synonym for homosexual, believing either that it sounds less harsh or judgmental or that it makes a social-political statement of pride in this sexual orientation. Other homosexuals feel uncomfortable with the word "gay" and reject its use completely. To provide appropriate background for a contemporary look at homosexuality and bisexuality, we will first look back in history.

HISTORICAL PERSPECTIVES

Homosexuality was clearly condemned in the earliest Jewish tradition. In the *Bible* we are told: "And if a man lie with mankind, as with womankind, both of them have committed abomination: they shall surely be put to death; their blood shall be upon them" (*Leviticus* 20:13).

Yet in ancient Greece, homosexuality and bisexuality in certain forms were widely accepted as natural in all segments of society (Hoffman, 1980). Plato's *Symposium* praised the virtues of male homosexuality and suggested that pairs of homosexual lovers would make the best soldiers. Many of the Greek mythological heroes, such as

Zeus, Hercules, Poseidon, and Achilles, were linked with homosexual behavior (Boswell, 1980). Although some Greek literature and art portrayed sexual relations between two women or two adult men, most of the homosexual relations seemed to occur between grown men and young adolescent boys (Karlen, 1980). Clearly, most Greek men married; yet homosexual activity was not seen as shameful or sinful.

In the early days of the Roman Empire, homosexuality was apparently unregulated by law, and homosexual behavior was common. Marriages between two men or between two women were legal and accepted among the upper classes, and several emperors, including Nero, reportedly were married to men (Boswell, 1980).

Although most historians who have written on the subject suggest that Christianity more or less from its beginnings strongly condemned and persecuted homosexuality, a new study states that this was not the case at all. In a book called *Christianity, Social Tolerance, and Homosexuality,* John Boswell (1980) argues that for many centuries Catholic Europe showed no hostility to homosexuality.

The primary ammunition for the church's position against homosexuality came from the writings of St. Augustine and Thomas Aquinas, who both suggested that any sexual acts that could not lead to conception were unnatural and therefore sinful. Using this line of reasoning, the church became a potent force in the regulation (and punishment) of sexual behavior. While some homosexuals were mildly rebuked and given prayer as penitence, others were tortured or burned at the stake.

In the Middle Ages, accusations of homosexuality became one of the weapons of the Inquisition, whose dedicated investigators rarely failed to extract an appropriate "confession" from their suspect, whether guilty or not. These "confessions" were used to portray purported homo-

Homosexuals have been increasingly visible in political circles and in organized public demonstrations seeking support for their civil rights.

sexuals not only as sexually deviant but as heretic and treasonous (Karlen, 1980).

The negative attitudes toward homosexuality that stemmed from religious beliefs dominated Western thought until the medical view of sexuality began to emerge in the eighteenth and nineteenth centuries (Bullough, 1978). This was hardly a sign of progress, however, since the medical view simply substituted the word "illness" for "sin." For example, Krafft-Ebing's *Psychopathia Sexualis* linked homosexuality to genetic flaws and a predisposing weakness of the nervous system. By the start of the twentieth century, it was generally agreed that homosexuality was an illness with which a person was born.

Although there is still a lively scientific debate on the origins of homosexuality, it appears that tolerance for homosexuality is once again on the upswing. In 1957 the *Wolfenden Report* in England recommended that laws against any form of private sexual behavior between consenting adults be repealed. In 1969 a few nights of summertime demonstrations on Christopher Street in Manhattan's Greenwich Village protesting police raids on a homosexual bar marked the beginning of an era of gay political activism that expanded into a full-fledged gay rights movement. By 1979 thirty-nine American cities, towns, and counties had enacted ordinances that banned discrimination against homosexuals in housing and jobs. In Canada, as in the U.S., homosexuals continue to face a number of legal and

Homosexuality and Bisexuality

social problems. For example, Toronto's gay community was enraged when 150 police officers — some wielding crowbars and hammers — raided four gay baths simultaneously in February of 1981 and arrested 266 persons on a variety of charges. Furthermore, many observers believe that the former mayor of Toronto's bid for re-election was lost because of his open support for homosexual issues (*Maclean's*, 1981; Fulford, 1981). The new visibility of the gay community has activated political and social opposition from many quarters, including the so-called Moral Majority, and tensions exist not only between heterosexuals and homosexuals, but within the homosexual community itself.

In his book, *The Homosexualization of America*, Dennis Altman (1982, p. 35) pointed out:

> No longer sinners, criminals, perverts, neurotics, or deviants, homosexuals are being slowly redefined in less value-laden terms as practitioners of an alternative lifestyle, members of a new community. In a self-proclaimed pluralistic society like the United States, this is probably the most effective way to win tolerance, if not acceptance.

However, Altman's view, which was undoubtedly correct at the beginning of the 1980s, is rapidly being undermined by a new development that may ultimately disrupt much of the social progress made by gays in the last two decades. This new development comes in the form of a deadly disease known as AIDS (for acquired immune deficiency syndrome, discussed in detail in chapter 21), which predominantly affects homosexual males, and which has alarmed much of the country because of its mysterious nature, apparent sexual transmission, and high fatality rate. If the number of AIDS cases continues to grow at the alarming pace seen from 1980 to 1984, it may give people an excuse once again to view homosexuality as a form of disease and provide ammunition to those who want to discriminate against gays.

THEORIES ON THE ORIGINS OF HOMOSEXUALITY

Why do some people become homosexual? Is it a life-long condition over which a person has no control? Is it an entirely voluntary choice, consciously and deliberately made at a certain phase in life? Is it mainly a response to the role models a child is exposed to at home or at school?

Each of these questions has important implications for political, legal, and religious interpretations of homosexuality, but unfortunately, the basic problem is that no one really knows what "causes" heterosexuality either. It may simply be that so far the wrong research questions have been asked. Nevertheless, it is useful to understand some of the viewpoints on the origins of homosexuality.

Biological Theories

Many homosexuals claim that their sexual orientation is the result of biological forces over which they have no control or choice. Several types of evidence have been examined to see if this might be so.

GENETIC FACTORS

One investigator reported findings that supported the earlier viewpoint that homosexuality was a genetic condition (Kallman, 1952). This study examined the sexual orientations of sets of identical and fraternal male twins where one twin was homosexual. Its underlying assumption was that since both twins were exposed to the same prenatal and postnatal environments, a genetic cause for homosexuality would show up as a high *concordance rate* among identical twins, since they have identical genes; that is, both twins would be homosexual rather than one being homosexual and one heterosexual. A lower concordance rate would be expected among fraternal twins, since their genetic make-up is different. Astonishingly, Kallman found 100 percent concordance in identical twins for male homosexuality and only 12 percent concordance in fraternal twins. This finding is astonishing because very few phenomena in biological research show 100 percent outcomes or matching. Subsequent studies have failed to replicate these results (Zuger, 1976; Heston and Shields, 1968), and the genetic theory of homosexuality has been generally discarded today.

HORMONAL FACTORS

Several different types of research have led many to speculate on the possibility of hormonal factors causing or predisposing to homosexuality. First, it has been well documented that prenatal hormone treatments of various types can lead to male or female homosexual behavior patterns in several different animal species (Dörner, 1968, 1976; Money and Ehrhardt, 1972; Hutchison, 1978). Second, some scattered findings show that prenatal sex hormone excess or deficiency in humans may be associated with homosexuality. For example, some preliminary studies of human females with the adrenogenital syndrome — a prenatal androgen excess — indicate that these individuals may be more likely to develop a lesbian orientation (Ehrhardt, Evers, and Money, 1968; Money and Schwartz, 1977). Similarly, there are a few reports of homosexuality in men with Klinefelter's syndrome, which is usually marked by a prenatal androgen deficiency, although the statistics are far from comprehensive.

Third, a great deal of attention has focused on a comparison of hormone levels in adult homosexuals and heterosexuals. While several studies have found either lower testosterone or higher estrogen in homosexual men, and one study found higher blood testosterone in lesbians than in heterosexual women, other studies have failed to replicate these findings (Meyer-Bahlburg, 1977, 1979; Tourney, 1980).

This body of research has major limitations. For example, treating adult homosexuals with sex hormones does not alter their sexual orientation in any way. The experimental animal models of homosexuality do not appear to be a good parallel to homosexuality in humans. The relatively rare instances of prenatal hormone excess or deficiency linked to homosexuality in humans may be special cases without much relevance to sexual development in general. And the conflicting reports on the sex hormone status of adult homosexuals leave many questions unanswered. Most notably, there may possibly be many "types" of homosexuality (and heterosexuality) which — until discovered — will confound attempts at pinpointing the biological influences on sexual orientation (Masters and Johnson, 1979).

Despite the interest in possible hormone mechanisms in the origin of homosexuality, no serious scientist today suggests that a simple cause-effect relationship applies. Instead, the possibility that prenatal hormones may influence brain development in ways that could predispose individuals to certain adult patterns of sexual behavior is being considered.

Psychological Theories

FREUD'S VIEWS

Freud believed that homosexuality was an outgrowth of an innate bisexual predisposition in all people. Under ordinary circumstances, the psychosexual development of the child would proceed smoothly along a heterosexual course. Under certain circumstances, however, such as improper resolution of the Oedipal complex, normal development might be arrested in an "immature" stage, resulting in adult homosexuality. Furthermore, since Freud thought that all people have latent homosexual tendencies, he believed that under certain conditions — such as continuing castration anxiety in males — overt homosexual behavior might occur for the first time in adulthood.

Freud's views on homosexuality are difficult to pin down, because he wrote relatively little on the subject. Although psychoanalysis seems to have reinforced the notion of homosexuality as a form of mental illness, Freud took a fairly neutral stance on the subject in a letter to the mother of a homosexual son:

> Homosexuality is assuredly no advantage, but it is nothing to be ashamed of, no vice, no degradation, it cannot be classified as an illness; we consider it to be a variation of the sexual development. Many highly respected individuals of ancient and modern times have been homosexuals, several of the greatest men among them (Plato, Michelangelo, Leonardo da Vinci, etc.). It is a great injustice to persecute homosexuality as a crime and cruelty, too. (Historical Notes: A Letter from Freud, 1951)

While it is not clear whether Freud was simply trying to reassure this distraught mother or genuinely held to the sentiments shown in this letter, it is clear that many later psychoanalysts took positions strongly opposed to homosexuality (see reviews by Karlen, 1971; Green, 1972; Tripp, 1975).

BIEBER'S MODEL

Since Freud had suggested that disordered parent-child relations might lead to homosexuality, psychoanalyst Irving Bieber and his colleagues (1962) evaluated the family backgrounds of 106 homosexual and 100 heterosexual men seen as patients. They found that many of the homosexual men they saw had overprotective, dominant mothers and weak or passive fathers, whereas this family constellation was infrequently seen in their heterosexual subjects. Bieber discarded the Freudian notion of psychic

bisexuality and suggested that homosexuality results from fears of heterosexual interactions.

Further research on this apparent "cause" of male homosexuality has had mixed results. Bene (1965) found that homosexual men had relatively poorer relationships with their fathers than did heterosexual men, and described their fathers as "ineffective," but there was no indication of maternal overprotection. Greenblatt (1966), however, found that fathers of homosexual men were good, generous, dominant, and underprotective, while mothers were free of excessive protectiveness or dominance. Siegelman (1974) reported that for groups of heterosexuals and homosexuals who were well adjusted psychologically, there were no apparent differences in family relationships. Likewise, Bell, Weinberg, and Hammersmith (1981) found no support for Bieber's theory in their important study discussed in the Research Spotlight on pages 414-415.

Reviewing such findings, Marmor suggests that although there seems to be "a reasonable amount of evidence that boys exposed to this kind of family background have a greater than average likelihood of becoming homosexual," not all people who have this background become homosexual (Marmor, 1980, p. 10). As Marmor also notes:

> Homosexuals can also come from families with distant or hostile mothers and overly close fathers, from families with ambivalent relationships with older brothers, from homes with absent mothers, absent fathers, idealized fathers, and from a variety of broken homes. (p. 11)

Pursuing this same line of research, Wolff (1971) found that among one hundred lesbians compared to heterosexual women, the most prominent parental characteristics were a rejecting or indifferent mother and a distant or absent father. Thus, she believed that female homosexuality arises from a girl's receiving inadequate love from her mother — leading her to continually seek such love from other women — combined with her poor relationship with her father that prevented her from learning to relate to men. To these observations we must add that many homosexuals come from perfectly well-adjusted family backgrounds (Tripp, 1975; Gagnon, 1977; Masters and Johnson, 1979). Unfortunately, many parents assume the blame for a child turning out gay and agonize over "What did we do wrong?" The present evidence simply does not show that homosexuality only or usually results from improper parenting.

BEHAVIORAL THEORIES

Psychosocial theories emphasize that homosexuality is primarily a learned phenomenon (McGuire, Carlisle, and Young, 1965; Gagnon and Simon, 1973; Masters and Johnson, 1979). In this view, the psychological conditioning associated with the reinforcement or punishment of early sexual behavior (and sexual thoughts and feelings) largely controls the process of sexual orientation. Thus, people's early sexual experiences may steer them toward homosexual behavior by pleasurable, gratifying same-sex encounters, or by unpleasant, dissatisfying, or frightening heterosexual experiences.

Sexual fantasies can also be conditioned. A positive sexual encounter with a homosexual partner can become the raw material for fantasy during masturbation, which is positively reinforced when it is followed by orgasm. In addition, a variety of other factors may influence a person's early sexual conditioning. Currently, attention has focused on children who show atypical gender-role behavior ("sissy" boys and

---

RESEARCH SPOTLIGHT

How Sexual Preference Develops

Tackling the complex question of how people become heterosexual or homosexual is not an easy task. A new level of methodological sophistication in approaching this topic was shown by Bell, Weinberg, and Hammersmith in a two-volume study entitled *Sexual Preference: Its Development in Men and Women* (1981). The sample that they examined consisted of 686 homosexual men, 293 homosexual women, 337 heterosexual men, and 140 heterosexual women, all of whom underwent an extensive face-to-face interview requiring three to five hours to complete.

In addition to developing what is probably the most extensive collection of data in existence on such a sizeable sample, Bell and his co-workers were careful to draw on a variety of different theories about the "causes" of homosexuality in order to examine their validity. Thus, they gathered information that might support the psychoanalytic viewpoint of how homosexuality develops, as well as information that might "prove" the social learning theory view or tie in with various sociological theories.

The researchers tested their data by using a complicated statistical method called "path analysis" that attempts to fit the observed findings in a study to a causative chain of linked events or conditions in a given theoretical model. On the basis of their analyses, they reached the following conclusions:

"tomboyish" girls) who are thought by some researchers to have a greater likelihood of becoming homosexual (Green, 1974; Rekers, 1978; Money and Russo, 1979).

The behavioral view also suggests why some heterosexuals change their sexual orientation to homosexuality in adulthood. According to Feldman and MacCulloch (1971), if a person has unpleasant heterosexual experiences combined with rewarding homosexual encounters, there may be a gradual shift in the homosexual direction. Although some homosexuals who have "switched" after an earlier period of heterosexual life do not fit this picture exactly, it is common to find many who do (Masters and Johnson, 1979). The observation that some female rape victims shift to lesbianism also supports this viewpoint (Grundlach, 1977).

A CONCLUDING NOTE ON "CAUSES"

We have already indicated that there is no firm agreement about what "causes" homosexuality or heterosexuality. When discussing a few of the best-known theories, we cautioned in almost every instance that the data are not complete and that current thinking must be left open, subject to better studies and research questions. Several of these theories may be correct and may account for a certain percentage of homosexuals in our society. Yet some years from now, all these ideas may also appear terribly foolish and outdated. Although we now believe that homosexuality is primarily a byproduct of postnatal events, we are open to the possibility that prenatal programming may yet be proven to play an important role.

---

1. There is little evidence that male homosexuality is caused by a dominant mother and a weak or inadequate father.
2. There is no support for the theory that female homosexuality is caused by girls choosing their fathers as role models.
3. The stereotype that homosexuality is frequently caused by being seduced by an older person of the same sex is untrue.
4. Sexual preference is strongly established by adolescence; sexual feelings rarely undergo major directional changes in adulthood.
5. As children and adolescents, homosexuals have as many heterosexual experiences as their heterosexual counterparts, but they find these encounters ungratifying or less gratifying.
6. Gender nonconformity (e.g., boys avoiding sports like baseball and football, while enjoying more "girlish" activities like playing house, hopscotch, or jacks) in childhood is a significant (but not absolute) predictor of the later development of homosexuality.

The most surprising conclusion of this study was the researchers' speculation that since they could not find solid support for any of the theories they tested, there is probably a biological basis for homosexuality. In fact, Bell, Weinberg, and Hammersmith say that hormonal influences during the prenatal period could produce patterns consistent with the data they found. However, since they conducted no hormone or genetic studies of their subjects, and made no attempt to gather information concerning their mothers' pregnancy histories (e.g., drug use, illness), it seems that their research leaves us pretty much back at square one in understanding what causes homosexuality. And their contention that homosexuality is probably biological in its origins requires that further research must be done if we hope to understand more fully how sexual preference develops.

THE PSYCHOLOGICAL ADJUSTMENT OF HOMOSEXUALS

Through most of the last hundred years, the prevailing notion was that homosexuality was an illness. Recalling Krafft-Ebing's belief that homosexuality resulted from hereditary defects and the psychoanalytic notion that homosexuality resulted from incapacitating fears of castration, it is not difficult to see how this viewpoint was so logically accepted.

Further "proof" of the psychological maladjustment of homosexuals was provided by a fair number of enterprising scientists. Some who conducted studies of homosexuals in prisons concluded, not surprisingly, that these individuals were less emotionally healthy than heterosexuals chosen from everyday life. By the 1950s, the trend was to select homosexuals being seen by psychiatrists, ignoring the basic sampling error this strategy introduces: since people usually go to psychiatrists because of emotional difficulties, it was almost preordained that this type of sampling would lead to the (unwarranted) conclusion that homosexuals are mentally ill.

Fortunately, a more sophisticated line of research was undertaken by psychologist Evelyn Hooker (1957). Hooker selected a group of sixty men — thirty homosexuals and thirty heterosexuals — who were neither psychiatric patients nor prisoners and who were matched for age, education, and IQ. She gave them all personality tests and obtained detailed information about their life histories, and then had a group of expert psychologists evaluate the tests without knowing which belonged to the homosexual or heterosexual men. The results showed that the "raters" could not distinguish between the two groups, providing the first objective indication that homosexuality is not necessarily a form of psychological maladjustment.

In an important series of studies Saghir and Robins (1973) extended the work begun by Hooker. They not only chose nonpatient populations but also decided to compare male and female homosexuals to unmarried heterosexuals, since the rate of certain psychiatric illnesses is higher in single persons. Their overall conclusion was straightforward: the majority of homosexuals studied were well-adjusted, productive people with no signs of psychiatric illness. Relatively few differences were observed between the homosexual and heterosexual groups, although an increased rate of alcoholism was found in lesbian subjects.

For the last fifteen years, many research studies have evaluated the performance of homosexuals and heterosexuals on a variety of psychological tests. A recent review of data from dozens of these studies concluded that there are no psychological tests that can distinguish between homosexuals and heterosexuals and there is no evidence of higher rates of emotional instability or psychiatric illness among homosexuals than among heterosexuals (B. Reiss, 1980).

These results do not imply that homosexuals are *always* emotionally healthy any more than similar results could prove that heterosexuals never get depressed or become anxious. But the underlying fact is that homosexuality, by itself, is not a form of mental illness nor is it typically associated with other signs of mental illness (Green, 1972; Hoffman, 1977; Marmor, 1980a).

HOMOPHOBIA

The hostility and fear that many people have toward homosexuality is called *homophobia*. The origins of homophobia are just as uncertain as the origins of homosexuality, but some psychologists believe that it is partly a defense that people use to insulate themselves from something that strikes too close to home. Thus, in

Homosexual Teachers

Some people worry about the possible effects of homosexual school teachers on their students, and in recent years a number of teachers have been fired because their homosexual orientation was discovered. The primary concerns voiced by parents and self-proclaimed public protectors of education are that homosexual teachers might molest the children, provide poor role models that contaminate the sexual development of the young, and might actively try to "recruit" students to their sexual preference.

What are the facts? First, there is no indication that homosexual teachers seduce or molest students more frequently than heterosexual teachers. If anything, it looks as though the opposite is true: examining reports of teacher-student sex and adjusting for the relative incidence of homosexuality in our society, heterosexual teachers are proportionately more likely to be sexual transgressors in this sense (Newton, 1978). Second, as a noted psychiatrist has pointed out, having a homosexual teacher as a role model can never "cause" homosexuality in a child whose biological and developmental programming has been heterosexual: "The only effect that exposure to homosexual teachers can have on heterosexual children (assuming the teachers' sexual orientations become known) is to create more tolerance and understanding toward homosexuals as people, and to dispel the widespread pre-judicial myths about them, thus reducing potential homophobia" (Marmor, 1980, p. 20).

Third, homosexual teachers could no more propagandize their students to "recruit" them into same-sex experiences than any teacher could propagandize for a specific religion. Jewish or Catholic teachers (both minorities in our society) do not try to "convert" Protestant students to their own religious preferences. If they did, in either case, it would be grounds for dismissal. Yet the hysteria over homosexuality in the schools sometimes reaches such a volume that simple facts like this are ignored.

Most students have probably had at least one homosexual teacher by the time of high-school graduation, although they will most likely be unaware of this fact. Yet such teachers generally must "stay in the closet" to protect their jobs, which can lead to tensions that may reduce their effectiveness as teachers. As a gay elementary school teacher pointed out, "The irony is that only by going public will gays in teaching eventually gain respect" (Trent, 1978, p. 136).

cases of brutal beatings or murders of homosexuals — perhaps the ultimate expression of homophobia — the motivation may be partly to stamp out any inherent homosexual impulses that may lurk in the attacker's heart.

Homophobia is expressed in many ways in our society. Homosexuals are ridiculed by jokes or by derogatory terms like "fairy," "faggot," or "queer." Parents are fearful that any "feminine" interest shown by a boy may lead to a homosexual life, so they are quick to provide footballs, toy guns, and model airplanes even if their son is not very interested in those items. Police use a variety of techniques to apprehend men engaging in homosexual acts, including entrapment (having a policeman pose as a willing homosexual partner) and use of hidden cameras in public restrooms; if these forms of law enforcement were to be directed at heterosexual activity, the hue and cry would be deafening!

Homosexuals have been banned from the military and the ministry (although not in all church denominations). Homosexuals have been denied housing, jobs, and bank loans. To many people, the homosexual is seen as a sick or even "contagious" individual who may "infect" others and so propel them to a life of homosexual depravity. This view was suggested by an attorney who stated that most male homosexuals find sex partners by walking up to a man standing at a bathroom urinal and grabbing hold of the man's penis (*Gay Liberation* v. *University of Missouri*, 1977).

In light of such homophobia, it is not surprising that much of the straight world thinks homosexuals should be treated to convert them to heterosexuality. While such treatment is often possible with homosexuals who are highly motivated and desire such a change (Hatterer, 1970; Masters and Johnson, 1979; Marmor, 1980), it is unwarranted and unethical for homosexuals who have no wish to *be* converted.

TECHNIQUES OF HOMOSEXUAL AROUSAL

The sexual techniques used by homosexual men and women generally mirror those of heterosexual partners, but homosexuals seem to be more willing to experiment and to be more attentive to style. This is partly because heterosexuality is more subject to convention and partly because heterosexual variations are regarded as "abnormal" by many people; since *no* techniques of homosexual stimulation are socially approved, there are fewer automatic restrictions that limit the behavior of homosexual partners (Tripp, 1975).

The physical approaches to erotic arousal used by homosexual men and women must be viewed in context, since there are wide differences in the styles and techniques employed depending on time, place, and circumstance. Although individuality is primary, a few general observations are useful: sexual openness is likely to be greater in a committed relationship rather than in anonymous sex; a leisurely, relaxed approach to sex depends on privacy and environmental comfort; and much homosexual interaction is a matter of mutual agreement and doing what feels good at the moment rather than following a preordained script.

One other fact is pertinent to this section. It has been shown that the physiological responses of homosexual men and women are no different from those of their heterosexual counterparts (Masters and Johnson, 1979). Laboratory observation of the sexual responses of 94 homosexual men and 82 homosexual women in more than 1,200 sexual response cycles involving masturbation, partner manipulation, or oral-genital sex showed that more than 99 percent of these cycles resulted in orgasm. This percent almost exactly matches the earlier observations of heterosexual men and women studied under identical conditions. Of course, equivalent physiology does not suggest equivalence in all other ways, but it is helpful to realize that the ways in which our sexual responses work are not controlled by our individual sexual orientation, whether it is homosexual or heterosexual.

Lesbian Sex

Kinsey and his co-workers (1953) found that two-thirds of homosexual women had orgasms in 90 to 100 percent of their lesbian contacts, while only two-fifths of women in their fifth year of marital intercourse had this high a rate of orgasmic frequency. They also found that among women with extensive lesbian experience, 98 percent had used genital touching, 97 percent had manually stimulated the breasts, 85 percent had orally stimulated the breasts, 78 percent had experience with cunnilingus, and 56 percent had

used a genital apposition technique (rubbing the genitals together).

Manual stimulation of the genitals is the most widespread and frequent form of lesbian sex. Saghir and Robins (1973) found that all of the fifty-seven lesbians in their study had used this technique, while Bell and Weinberg (1978) noted that approximately 80 percent of their sample had used it in the past year, with more than 40 percent reporting a frequency of once a week or more.

In contrast to married heterosexual couples — where the "action-oriented" man seems to hurriedly reach for the breasts or move directly to genital stimulation — committed lesbian partners usually share full body contact, with holding, kissing, and general caressing for some while before they make a specific approach to breast or genital touching (Masters and Johnson, 1979). Furthermore, when a committed lesbian couple

begins breast play, the two women usually give it lengthier and more detailed attention than heterosexual couples. Masters and Johnson (1979, p. 66) noted that for committed lesbian couples:

> The full breast always was stimulated manually and orally with particular concentration focused on the nipples. Interestingly, almost scrupulous care was taken by the stimulator to spend an equal amount of time with each breast. As much as 10 minutes were sometimes spent in intermittent breast stimulation before genital play was introduced.

The lesbian caressing her partner's breasts seems to do so with more attention to her partner's responses, while men often approach heterosexual breast stimulation more for their own arousal than for their partner's pleasure. This concern is also shown by the fact that lesbian lovers realize that breast touching can be painful just before a period, while many men seem oblivious to this fact.

During genital stimulation in lesbian couples, the clitoris is rarely approached first, in contrast to the pattern shown in marital sex, where direct clitoral stimulation was the first form of genital contact in about half of the observed episodes (Masters and Johnson, 1979). Besides starting with more relaxed genital play, lesbians do not usually insert a finger deeply into the vagina. When vaginal stimulation occurred, it was usually in the form of play around or just inside the mouth of the vagina. In spite of the common belief that lesbians usually use a dildo or object inserted in the vagina to simulate heterosexual intercourse, a distinct minority of lesbians employ this technique (Kinsey et al., 1953; Saghir and Robins, 1973).

Two patterns of genital play are most common in lesbian encounters: (1) a prolonged, nondemanding approach of repeatedly bringing the partner to a high level of arousal which is then allowed to recede, in a "teasing" pattern; and (2) stimulation involving more continuity and rapidly increasing intensity until orgasm is reached. Although these two approaches are sometimes combined, most lesbian couples seem to prefer and consistently use one or the other (Masters and Johnson, 1979).

Cunnilingus is the preferred sexual technique among lesbians for reaching orgasm (Bell and Weinberg, 1978; Califia, 1979). Lesbians generally are more effective in stimulating their partners via oral-genital sex than heterosexual men are and usually involve themselves with more inventiveness and less restraint than heterosexual couples (Masters and Johnson, 1979). This is probably because a woman is more apt to know what feels good to another woman on the basis of her own personal experiences; lesbian lovers may also be less embarrassed about genital tastes and odors than their heterosexual counterparts. In keeping with these points, it was noted that committed lesbian couples characteristically used a leisurely, less demanding approach to cunnilingus than married heterosexuals.

While lesbians who have oral sex most frequently seem happiest with their sex lives and their relationships, about one-quarter of lesbians say they rarely or never use this form of stimulation (Blumstein and Schwartz, 1983).

Body rubbing techniques involving total body contact and specific genital-to-genital rubbing are also enjoyed by some lesbians but seem to be a less important source of attaining orgasm (Bell and Weinberg, 1978; Califia, 1979). Relatively few lesbians use techniques of anal stimulation.

A recent survey that included 772 lesbian couples and 3,547 married heterosexual couples found that lesbians had genital sexual activity considerably less often than married heterosexuals (Blumstein and Schwartz, 1983). However, another study that involved individuals rather than couples found that lesbians had sex more often than heterosexual women and also had more frequent orgasms, a greater number of partners, and a higher degree of sexual satisfaction (Coleman, Hoon, and Hoon, 1983).

Gay Male Sex

Like their lesbian counterparts, male homosexuals in committed couples tend to take their time in whatever form of sexual interaction they are involved in instead of hurrying along in a goal-oriented effort as many married heterosexual couples do. Male homosexuals also tend to deliberately move more slowly through excitement and to linger at the plateau stage of arousal, using more freeflowing, inventive styles of sexual play than married heterosexuals. This general description has its exceptions. Some committed homosexual couples are completely goal-oriented and push ahead with the sexual action at a frenzied pace while some married heterosexuals enjoy a much more leisurely, unstructured pattern of sex. But the overall contrast between the two groups is striking (Masters and Johnson, 1979).

In the initial stages of sexual interaction, most committed homosexual male couples begin with a generalized approach of hugging, caressing, or kissing. Nipple stimulation — either manually or orally — is frequently incorporated into the early touching, almost invariably leading to erection for the man being stimulated. (Interestingly, few wives stimulate their husbands' nipples as part of sexual play.)

A "teasing" pattern of genital play is frequently used in gay male sex. This often involves selective attention to the frenulum of the penis and the use of a variety of touches or caresses to enhance erotic arousal. Many of the men in committed homosexual relationships studied by Masters and Johnson said that they stimulated their partners the way they liked to be stimulated. Others said that they had discussed genital stimulation techniques directly with their partners and had learned in this fashion what was most pleasing. In contrast, very few heterosexual married couples have specifically discussed the man's preferences in techniques of penile stimulation, and the "teasing" approach is infrequently employed.

There are no major differences in the techniques used for fellatio between homosexual or heterosexual couples, presuming that there are equivalent amounts of experience with this type of sexual play. Fellatio seems to be the most common form of gay male sexual activity, with more than 90 percent having experience in giving and receiving such stimulation (Saghir and Robins, 1973; Bell and Weinberg, 1978).

Anal intercourse is another common male homosexual practice. Saghir and Robins (1973) found that 93 percent of the homosexual men they studied had experienced anal intercourse with a male partner. However, Bell and Weinberg (1978) found that 22 percent of the gay white males in their study had not performed anal intercourse in the preceding year, and the frequency of anal intercourse was considerably less than for fellatio.

Some authorities have suggested that male homosexuals be classified as "active" or "passive" depending on whether they prefer to be the "insertor" or the "insertee" in anal intercourse. The fact is, most gay men who participate in anal sex enjoy both roles; other gay men find the idea of anal sex discomforting or repulsive.

Recently, another form of anal sex has become popular in certain gay communities. This practice, known as "fisting" or "handballing," involves the insertion of the hand into the rectum (usually after prior cleansing with an enema) followed by movement geared at producing sexual stimulation (Morin, 1981; Lowry and Williams, 1983). While this type of sexual activity is not unique to homosexual males, having been reported both in heterosexuals and lesbians, it appears to be predominantly a practice of the gay male community. Devotees of this form of sexual stimulation, which is often combined with the use of illicit drugs, point out that it requires considerable trust, slowness, and gentleness, and sometimes describe it as an ecstatic, transcendent type of experience (Lowry and Williams, 1983). There are substantial health risks associated with "fisting," including the risk of damaging the anus or rectum and the risk of contracting hepatitis B.

PERSPECTIVES ON HOMOSEXUAL BEHAVIOR

Although it is just as foolish to suppose that all homosexuals are alike as it would be to imagine that all vegetarians behave the same way, dress similarly, and fit a general personality profile, many people in our society have made just such an assumption. The resulting stereotypes tell us that we can identify a homosexual by appearance (e.g., the limp-wristed, lisping, mincing male or the short-haired, "butch" female), by profession (the male hairdresser or interior decorator), by personality (maladjusted, overly emotional and impulsive), and by lifestyle (unmarried men or women over thirty are "suspect"; if they live with another person of the same sex, they are *doubly* suspect).

These stereotypes are largely inaccurate. While it is true that a small number of homosexual men carry themselves in an effeminate way, this group amounts to no more than 15 percent of the homosexual population (Voeller, 1980). There are also many men who are totally *heterosexual* who speak in an effeminate voice or whose other mannerisms appear effeminate. The number of gay women who have a "masculine" appearance is also very small, and a woman who looks "masculine" is not necessarily homosexual. Similarly, there are homosexual doctors, lawyers, truck drivers, professional athletes, and politi-

cians as well as gay hairdressers or designers. No occupational group is purely heterosexual or homosexual.

There is no evidence that most homosexuals are emotionally maladjusted — a fact that is particularly remarkable when one considers the anti-homosexual prejudices of our society. Finally, there is no such thing as a "homosexual lifestyle" that would accurately describe how most gays live. This is not surprising, since there are people who are exclusively homosexual on a lifelong basis while others are exclusively homosexual for just a few years. There are also "closet" homosexuals who try to pass as straight in the everyday world (including many homosexuals who are in heterosexual marriages) and others who have openly announced their homosexuality. There are militant homosexuals and more conservative ones; there are homosexuals who remain in long-term, committed relationships while others prefer independence and a more casual approach to sex — there are endless examples of homosexual diversity.

Recognizing these facts, it is nevertheless possible to discuss certain common aspects of homosexual behavior as they apply to the lives of many gay people just as we examined heterosexual behavior patterns.

Discovering Homosexuality

Some homosexuals say that they were aware of being gay as early as age five or six, while others don't make the discovery until sometime in adulthood. However, it is not very likely that the young child has a real sense of homosexual orientation. The sense of being "different" during childhood that some homosexuals recall as adults is not always an accurate barometer of later sexual orientation, since many "straight" adults also felt "different" as children. Furthermore, adult recollections of childhood feelings and behaviors may possibly be influenced by social expectations of what homosexuals "should" have felt (Ross, 1980).

Most of the available research on self-discovery of a homosexual identity suggests that this process is most likely to occur during adolescence for males and at a somewhat later time for females (Dank, 1971; Weinberg, 1978; Cass, 1979; Troiden and Goode, 1980; Stanley and Wolfe, 1980). At earlier ages, the child is exposed to role models that are exclusively heterosexual (at least in a visible sense) whether at home, at school, on television, or in children's books. This fact, combined with the automatic assumption in our society that everyone is heterosexual unless "proven" otherwise, means that children are almost invariably conditioned to think of themselves as heterosexuals destined to live a heterosexual life.

How do people "discover" that they are homosexual? No single pattern fits everyone. Many gay males report having first had some type of sexual contact with another boy as young teenagers which led them to initially suspect that they were homosexual. Only after a period of identity confusion did they begin to actually think of themselves as homosexual, to seek out other homosexuals, and to devise ways of dealing with their homosexuality in a heterosexual world (Cass, 1979).[1] Others suspect that they may be homosexual *before* having any same-sex sexual activity and confirm their suspicion by positive responses to sexual experiences with male partners or by feeling more comfortable with homosexual friends than heterosexual ones (Weinberg, 1978). For some homosexuals, the process of self-discovery occurs only after much effort is spent trying to fit the expected heterosexual mold but finding that it just isn't comfortable.

Although some lesbians come to a firm discovery of their sexual identity in adolescence, more typically whatever homosexual feelings they have during this time are pushed aside as "a passing phase" (Stanley and Wolfe, 1980). There may be close emotional attachments formed with other females that never progress to the stage of physical contact, or specifically sexual experiences may not be labelled as homosexual. A large number of lesbians do not adopt this sexual orientation until after a heterosexual marriage.

There is, of course, a big difference between *discovering* homosexuality and *accepting* it. Some gay men and women have no difficulty at all in this sphere, but much more often there is conflict and uncertainty over the implications of being homosexual in a heterosexual society. Some who have labelled themselves as homosexual seek therapy to "cure" themselves of this self-perceived problem; others feel enthusiastic and even energized by their homosexuality. Although only one out of twenty homosexual men and women studied by Bell and Weinberg (1978) expressed a great deal of regret over being homosexual, approximately one in three had considered giving up their homosexual activity. These authors also noted that gay men are more likely than lesbians to have difficulty accepting their homosexuality, which they speculated might be because homosexuality is more often seen by males "as a failure to achieve a 'masculine' sexual adjustment," whereas lesbians "more often experience their homosexuality as a freely chosen rejection of heterosexual relationships" (Bell and Weinberg, 1978, p. 128).

A Typology of Homosexuals

Bell and Weinberg (1978) studied 979 homosexual men and women who were recruited by personal contacts, public advertising, use of mailing lists, and special recruitment cards distributed in gay bars, gay baths, and by gay orga-

---

[1] It is important to remember that homosexual and heterosexual experimentation is very common in childhood or adolescence. The fact that someone finds pleasure in a sexual act with another person of the same sex does *not* necessarily mean that he or she is homosexual.

nizations. Although their sample is neither truly cross-sectional nor representative of all homosexuals in America, it provided a broad-based opportunity for analyzing important information about homosexual feelings and behavior. One of the more interesting findings to emerge from this study was the existence of a typology of sexual experiences that allowed for comparisons between groups. Approximately three-fourths of their sample could be assigned to one of these types on the basis of statistical criteria (Table 16-2).

Close-coupled homosexuals lived in one-to-one same-sex relationships that were very similar to heterosexual marriages. They had few sexual problems, few sexual partners, and infrequently engaged in cruising (deliberately searching for a sexual partner).

Open-coupled homosexuals lived in one-to-one same-sex relationships but typically had many outside sexual partners and spent a relatively large amount of time cruising. They were more likely to have sexual problems and to regret their homosexuality than close-coupled homosexuals.

Functional homosexuals were those who were not "coupled," who had a high number of sexual partners and few sexual problems. These individuals tended to be younger, to have few regrets over their homosexuality, and to have high levels of sexual interest.

Dysfunctional homosexuals were not "coupled" and, while scoring high in number of partners or amount of sexual activity, had substantial numbers of sexual problems.

Asexual homosexuals were low in sexual interest and activity and were not "coupled." They tended to be less exclusively homosexual and more secretive about their homosexuality than others.

These types also proved to have important connections to a person's social and psychological adjustment. In general, close-coupled homosexuals tended to be at least as happy and well-adjusted as heterosexual men and women. The dysfunctionals and asexuals, on the other hand, tended to be worse off psychologically than heterosexuals and had considerable difficulty coping with life. Male dysfunctionals were "more lonely, worrisome, paranoid, depressed, tense, and unhappy than any of the other men," and dysfunctional lesbians were more likely than other women "to have needed long-term professional help for an emotional problem" (Bell and Weinberg, 1978, p. 225). The asexuals were generally loners who, despite being lonely, had little inter-

TABLE 16–2
Percent of Homosexuals in Each
Group of the Bell-Weinberg Typology

	Close-coupled	Open-coupled	Functionals	Dysfunctionals	Asexuals
Male Homosexuals	10%	18	15	12	16
Lesbians	28%	17	10	5	11

Twenty-nine percent of male homosexuals and 28 percent of lesbians could not be classified into one group or another.

Source: Data from Alan P. Bell and Martin S. Weinberg, *Homosexualities.* Copyright © 1978 by Alan P. Bell and Martin S. Weinberg. Reprinted by permission of Simon & Schuster, Inc. and Mitchell Beazley Pub., Ltd., London.

Homosexuality and Bisexuality

Contrary to popular misconceptions, many homosexuals have children and function well as parents.

est in becoming involved with friends or socializing in the gay community. Asexual homosexual men had the highest incidence of suicidal thoughts.

The existence of these homosexual types *"proves"* nothing — there are probably corresponding "types" of heterosexuals that could be identified, with some showing better social and psychological adjustment and others being more troubled. The point we want to reinforce is that

all homosexuals are not alike; there is just as much diversity among homosexuals as among heterosexuals.

Coming Out

"Coming out" is a process in which homosexuals inform others of their sexual orientation. It can be a long process of self-disclosure that begins cautiously with telling a best friend (and waiting to see the reaction that is provoked), then progresses to include a group of close friends, and finally — in its most complete form — lets family members, colleagues at work, and more casual acquaintances know as well. Coming out can also be accomplished in a remarkably brief time, although a great deal of thought and planning may have gone into the decision.

Many homosexuals find that it is considerably easier to come out in the gay world than to their heterosexual friends and family. They may choose to live a life of "passing" as heterosexual to avoid social disapproval, economic repercussions, or other potential problems while they are still known to other gays as "out of the closet" in a limited sense. Here is what one twenty-six-year-old homosexual man said about this issue:

> Philosophically, I'd love to announce my gayness to the world. But it'd probably cost me my job, and it would cause so many problems for my family (especially my father, who's a minister) that I just don't see the point. I lead one life at night, and another during working hours or family get-togethers, and it's really no big deal. (Authors' files)

Others consider such a solution unsatisfying, dishonest, or lacking in trust or conviction. However, coming out to a hostile world can create tremendous agony in a person's life. On the other hand, finding support from family and friends can be reassuring and gratifying, as this explanation from a twenty-four-year-old woman makes clear:

> For my whole college career I was afraid to let my parents know I was gay. I talked about coming out, and worried about it tremendously, but I couldn't really bring myself to do it. Then, just before I graduated, something clicked in my head that said I had to come out NOW. I just couldn't believe how accepting my parents were. It certainly helped me feel better about myself. (Authors' files)

"Coming out" doesn't usually work out this easily, however. Most parents are terribly upset at finding out that their son or daughter is homosexual, and many of them urge the child to seek therapy to "correct the problem." In some cases, parents refuse to see or speak to a gay child; in other cases, while taking a less severe attitude of reproach, parents (or other family members) clearly remain very uncomfortable with the idea of having a homosexual relative.

Despite a current push for homosexuals to "come out of the closet" to indicate pride in their sexual orientation and to work for political gains, most homosexual men and women remain secretive. It appears that homosexuals with lower social status are somewhat more likely to be open about their sexual orientation, while those who are better educated or who have more income are more likely to keep their homosexuality hidden (Bell and Weinberg, 1978).

Partners and Relationships

Not all homosexuals engage in sexual activity on a frequent basis, but in general homosexual men tend to be more sexually active than homosexual women (Figure 16-1). Most research has also shown that homosexual men tend to have many more sexual partners than lesbians (Table 16-3) or heterosexual men and women (Saghir and Robins, 1973; Tripp, 1975; Bell and Weinberg, 1978).

While many homosexual males engage in quick, impersonal sex with strangers, others prefer to enter into long-term affectionate homosexual relationships. Tripp (1975) suggests that these ongoing homosexual relationships seem to be rare because they are far less visible than either long-term heterosexual relationships or short-lived homosexual liaisons. Bell and Weinberg (1978) note that the relative instability of long-term homosexual relationships may be partly be-

FIGURE 16–1
Frequency of Sexual Activity

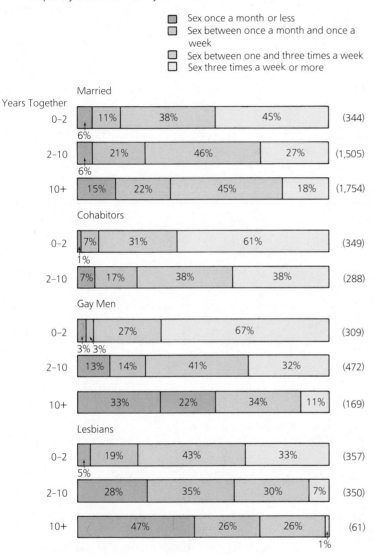

- ▦ Sex once a month or less
- ▨ Sex between once a month and once a week
- ▤ Sex between one and three times a week
- ☐ Sex three times a week or more

Married

Years Together

0–2 | 6% ↑ 11% | 38% | 45% | (344)

2–10 | 6% ↑ 21% | 46% | 27% | (1,505)

10+ | 15% | 22% | 45% | 18% | (1,754)

Cohabitors

0–2 | 1% ↑ 7% | 31% | 61% | (349)

2–10 | 7% | 17% | 38% | 38% | (288)

Gay Men

0–2 | 3% 3% ↑↑ 27% | 67% | (309)

2–10 | 13% | 14% | 41% | 32% | (472)

10+ | 33% | 22% | 34% | 11% | (169)

Lesbians

0–2 | 5% ↑ 19% | 43% | 33% | (357)

2–10 | 28% | 35% | 30% | 7% | (350)

10+ | 47% | 26% | 26% | 1% ↑ | (61)

Note: Very few of our cohabitors had been together more than 10 years.

Numbers in parentheses are the number of couples on which the percentages are based.

Source: From *American Couples* by Philip Blumstein, Ph.D. and Pepper Schwartz, Ph.D. Copyright © 1983 by Philip Blumstein and Pepper W. Schwartz. By permission of William Morrow & Company.

TABLE 16–3
Sexual Partnerships Among Homosexuals

	Homosexual Males		Homosexual Females	
	White (N=574)	Black (N=111)	White (N=227)	Black (N=64)
Lifetime Number of Homosexual Partners				
1	0%	0%	3%	5%
2	0	0	9	5
3–4	1	2	15	14
5–9	2	4	31	30
10–14	3	5	16	9
15–24	3	6	10	16
25–49	8	6	8	11
50–99	9	18	5	8
100–249	15	15	1	2
250–499	17	11	1	2
500–999	15	14	0	0
1,000 or more	28	19	0	0
Proportion of Partners Who Were Strangers				
None	1%	5%	62%	56%
Half or Less	20	43	32	38
More than Half	79	51	6	6
Proportion of Partners with Whom Sexual Activity Occurred Only Once				
None	1%	4%	38%	41%
Half or Less	29	59	51	55
More than Half	70	38	12	5

Source: Adapted from Alan P. Bell and Martin S. Weinberg, *Homosexualities.* Copyright © 1978 by Alan P. Bell and Martin S. Weinberg. Reprinted by permission of Simon & Schuster, Inc. and Mitchell Beazley Pub., Ltd., London.

cause they are not encouraged socially or sanctioned legally. In addition, some observers believe that one effect of the recent AIDS epidemic has been to encourage monogamy and close-coupled relationships among gay men.

Coleman (1981/82) believes that male homosexuals are at a disadvantage in learning intimacy and relationship skills because they have few role models to follow and because there has traditionally been "a lack of public support for these relationships." He also points out that "lingering negative attitudes about homosexuality can sabotage efforts to establish or maintain a relationship." Extending this view, McCandlish (1981/82) states that "society's homophobia and resulting social isolation" and lack of family support often produce such stresses on stable relationships that "what might have been minor and even growth-producing difficulties, instead overwhelm the couple and force a premature end to the relationship."

Another perspective on this topic can be gained by recalling the differences in socialization that typically affect males and females in Western society. As Bell and Weinberg (1978) suggest, socialization tends to orient males (straight or gay) to sexual variety, whereas females (straight or gay) are more oriented to monogamy. As a result, many young males want a number of sexual partners, while most females want the intimacy that they are more likely to find in a one-to-one relationship. When heterosexual males form relationships with females, they are socialized by the female to become more monogamous (Gagnon and Simon, 1973), but this is less likely to happen for males in homosexual relations. Thus, many gay males are promiscuous because they've had few social learning experiences to help them to develop intimacy skills.

We have worked with homosexual couples who have been together for decades in relationships that were every bit as close and committed as heterosexual marriages. We have also seen homosexuals who passed through a series of medium-term relationships lasting a few years each. In general, these patterns mirror the descriptions of love discussed in chapter 11, suggesting that there may not be that many major differences between heterosexual and homosexual committed relationships.

This view is now supported by a good deal of research that shows that homosexual couples are generally well adjusted and indistinguishable from heterosexual couples (Mendola, 1980; Silverstein, 1981; Cardell, Finn, and Marecek, 1981; Peplau, Padesky, and Hamilton, 1982; Blumstein and Schwartz, 1983; McWhirter and Mattison, 1983).

THE GAY WORLD

The gay world, like the heterosexual world, is not simply or easily described in a few paragraphs. In large urban areas, the gay community may exist as a full-fledged entity, complete with places for social and sexual contacts (bars and baths), gay merchants, gay churches, gay clinics, and gay recreational groups. In other areas, there is no organized homosexual community, and sexual contacts may be hurriedly made in public restrooms, parks, and pick-up bars.

Although in the past homosexuals were often forced to go to gay bars or to "cruise" in certain designated locations, today there are mushrooming numbers of homosexual organizations that provide new meeting-grounds without the stigma of "being on the prowl." Cities like Washington, San Francisco, and New York have dozens of support organizations for gay physicians, lawyers, teachers, and parents (a sizeable number of homosexuals have had children in heterosexual marriages). Other organizations aim at providing various forms of counseling services for homosexuals ranging from religious advice to help in dieting to finding nonjudgmental medical care. On many college and university campuses, gay students have formed groups to provide peer support and acceptance. Homosexually oriented newspapers and magazines, both national and regional, provide additional information about the homosexual subculture in America and also carry personal advertisements that allow interested parties to get together for sexual purposes.

However, the emerging pride of the homosexual community is a complex phenomenon — all is not happiness and tranquility (just as there are problems with the heterosexual world). Karlen (1978, pp. 232-233) describes the other side of the coin:

No one knows better than homosexuals that gay is a euphemism. There is a squalid side of the life

— lavoratory gropings, prostitution, rampant venereal disease, play-acting, promiscuity, mercurial and crisis-ridden romances, abuse of alcohol and drugs, guilt, suicide. Almost all homosexuals except gay militants have said to me that the causes are as much inherent in homosexuality as in the antihomosexuality of the rest of society.

The gay world has a bruising, predatory quality that gives many in it a far grimmer view than their heterosexual sympathizers hold.

In addition, gay males and lesbians have often had political clashes in the past decade due to their different priorities for the homosexual ac-

Many gay baths went out of business because of widespread publicity about the AIDs epidemic in 1983 and 1984.

Homosexuality and Bisexuality

Bisexuals and Gays in Heterosexual Marriages

Although many people who identify themselves as bisexual or gay choose to enter conventional heterosexual marriages, this phenomenon has received relatively little attention until recent years. Yet various research surveys have found that about one-fifth of homosexual men and one-third of homosexual women have been married at least once (Bell and Weinberg, 1978; Masters and Johnson, 1979), and it's quite possible that these numbers are underestimates, since many married homosexuals – by their own admission – are extremely secretive and have no desire to reveal themselves.

Although understanding how marriage might appeal to a bisexual person is not overly difficult, many people cannot envision why some homosexual men and women choose to enter heterosexual marriages. No single answer, of course, fits each person's motivations. However, it appears that there are several explanations that are almost universal in their applicability. First, our society pushes people toward marriage as though it were an expected condition of responsible adulthood. Parents and other relatives often exert strong pressures on their young adult children to "marry and settle down," and people with same-sex preferences are not immune from these entreaties. Second, most of the homosexuals (or bisexuals) who choose to marry have negative feelings about "gay life" (Coleman, 1981/82). Not wanting to be labelled homosexual (by themselves or others) and not wanting to be part of a life they often view as sordid or sinful, they turn to marriage as "proof" that they're really not gay. In effect, these individuals seem to be fighting one myth by embracing others: that marriage can "prove" a person's masculinity or femininity and that having children makes you a card-carrying heterosexual.

It should also be recognized that most of the homosexual men or women who marry genuinely love their chosen spouse and many of them want to have children (Coleman, 1981/82). In addition, it is important to realize that some of these individuals marry without consciously seeing themselves as bisexual or homosexual, only coming to recognize this orientation at a later time.

Interestingly, relatively few of the people who are aware of their same-sex feelings prior to marriage disclose them to their prospective spouse (Masters and Johnson, 1979; Coleman, 1981/82). While some marriages seem none the worse for this situation – at least in terms of the sexual relationship and overall marital satisfaction – others are strained by sexual problems and other types of interpersonal difficulties. Gay or bisexual men, in particular, are quite likely to seek extramarital same-sex contacts that may create a highly explosive situation if discovered by the unsuspecting wife.

Recently, Dr. Jean Gochros has studied what is likely to happen when a husband reveals his homosexuality to his wife. She finds that most wives in this situation react "in a stunned but positive fashion. ... [seeing] the disclosure as a confirmation of trust that spelled a challenge or opportunity" (*Sexuality Today,* December 19–26, 1983). Our own experience is not quite so optimistic, since we have seen many instances where a married person's announcement of his or her previously hidden same-sex preference to a spouse led to bitter fighting, accusations, and ultimate rejection. In fact, husbands seem to be particularly threatened by the discovery of their wife's lesbian preferences, perhaps because they see them as a negative reflection on their own prowess as a lover. (Realistically, we should acknowledge that husbands may find it easier to divorce their wives in these situations because they are apt to be in a better position financially and can often gain child custody; wives may be more inclined to stay with their husbands under unpleasant conditions for fundamental economic reasons.) In other cases where one spouse's homosexuality is brought out in the open, the other spouse agrees to continue the relationship only if a promise of monogamy is made.

Coleman (1981/82) has listed a number of factors that seem necessary for successful adjustment in a marriage where the husband has disclosed his same-sex feelings to his wife:

1. Both people love each other and want to make the relationship work.
2. There is a high degree of communication in the relationship.
3. Feelings of guilt, blame, and resentment need to be resolved and set aside by both people.
4. There has to be regular physical contact between husband and wife.
5. The wife should have a sense of worth apart from the marriage.
6. Both partners must agree to work on and accept the husband's same-sex feelings.
7. If the husband has outside sexual contacts, the wife doesn't need to be told about it unless they have both agreed to an open-marriage arrangement. (To this, we would add a balancing statement that if the wife has outside sexual contacts, the husband doesn't need to be told about it, either.)

There are, of course, other ways of proceeding – including the possibility of seeking treatment to assist the husband in developing his heterosexual desires more fully, if that is what he wants – but until further work is done in this area, we can simply acknowledge that there is a great deal yet to be learned.

tivist movement (Altman, 1982). The AIDS epidemic is leading to further dissent, with some homosexual men saying that monogamy is a sign of sanity and gays who are still having sex with numerous partners are really "homophobic" (Meredith, 1984).

HOMOSEXUALITY AND THE LAW

Laws in our society have been strongly anti-homosexual for the last few centuries. Underlying this legal posture was the notion that if homosexuals were allowed to function as freely as heterosexuals do, they would undermine the moral fabric of our society and possibly recruit large numbers of people into homosexual acts.

In the last ten years, however, the law has been turning somewhat from foe to friend of homosexuals (Knutson, 1979/80; Slovenko, 1980). Although homosexual acts are still illegal in most places, ordinances banning "crimes against nature" — which usually apply equally to heterosexual and homosexual noncoital acts — are now rarely enforced if the acts involve consenting adults in private. Even when a conviction is obtained, the usual sentence is to seek psychiatric counseling.

Homosexuals are still banned from being employed by the FBI, the CIA, or the military (McCrary and Gutierrez, 1979/80). A representative of the Defense Department's Office of Manpower told a group of Harvard students that the military believed homosexuals "harmed military discipline, morale, and effectiveness" (*The New York Times*, April 19, 1983), and in fiscal 1983, the U.S. Navy alone discharged 1,167 homosexuals from its ranks (*The New York Times*, December 2, 1983).

Gay organizations have generally been denied tax-exempt status by the Internal Revenue Service. Even in San Francisco, which probably has the largest homosexual population in America, when county supervisors approved a law in 1983 giving homosexuals partnership rights similar to those of married heterosexuals (for instance, coverage of partners by city health and pension plans), it was vetoed by the mayor. Legal advances, however, have been made as well.

Gay parents — particularly lesbian mothers — have been slowly but increasingly successful in winning child custody cases in the courts (Green, 1978; Hitchens, 1979/80). Employment discrimination against homosexuals has been banned in most federal agencies (Hedgpeth, 1979/80; Slovenko, 1980), and gay people may now leave the military with honorable discharges (Vetri, 1979/80). While in the past the U.S. Immigration and Naturalization Service barred homosexuals from visiting this country or becoming citizens (Reynolds, 1979/80), a recent ruling by the Ninth Circuit U.S. Court of Appeals declared that since homosexuality was no longer considered a mental disorder, this practice could no longer continue (*The New York Times*, September 8, 1983). Discrimination in housing and against homosexual prisoners has also been banned in many states.

These advances, which have been part of a general movement to protect the civil rights of minority groups, still have a long way to go to eradicate legal inequities against homosexuals in a society that is still "antigay." But the loosening of harsher practices is being viewed by some as promising a more equitable treatment under the law in future times.

BISEXUALITY

Although homosexuality has been extensively studied and written about in the last fifteen years, bisexuality has received far less attention. It is difficult to estimate the incidence of bisexuality in our society today. Kinsey found that 9 percent of single thirty-year-old women could be classified between 2 and 4 on the heterosexual-homosexual rating scale while about 16 percent of single thirty-year-old men fit the same description. However, these numbers may exaggerate the active incidence of bisexuality, which we suspect is actually less than 5 percent in our society if it is defined in terms of sexual activity with male and female partners in the past year.

Bisexuals are sometimes called "AC/DC" (based on terminology used to describe two types of electric current), "switch-hitters" (borrowed from baseball lingo for a person who bats from either the right or left side of home plate depending on who's pitching), or people who "swing both ways" (this too is a baseball phrase that might also relate to "swinging" as a type of sexual behavior). In the last few years, bisexuality has become stylish in certain circles where it is regarded as a sign of sexual sophistication and being "open-minded."

People move into bisexuality in a number of different ways. For many, it is a form of experimentation which adds spice to their sex lives but doesn't become the main course. For others, it represents a deliberate choice that permits participation in whatever feels best at the moment. Some men and women seem to alternate their choice of sex partners randomly, depending on availability and circumstances to dictate which gender is involved at a particular time. Most often, whichever of these patterns applies, people with bisexual experience have a decided preference for one gender, but this is not always true.

Masters and Johnson (1979) recently described a subgroup of bisexuals they called *ambisexuals* who were men or women who had no preference whatsoever over the gender of their sex partners, had never become involved in a committed sexual relationship, and had frequent sexual interaction with both men and women. The ambisexuals accepted or rejected any sexual opportunity primarily on the basis of their physical need, with the personality or physical attractiveness of a potential partner having much less to do with their choice.

In some instances, the bisexual has had a long-term heterosexual relationship which is then followed by a long-term homosexual relationship (or vice versa). After such a sequence, the person involved may develop new views on traditional notions that limit sex-object choice (Blumstein and Schwartz, 1976). Another pattern sometimes seen is concurrent involvement in heterosexual and homosexual relationships, as described in this comment from a twenty-three-year-old woman:

> I had been dating a guy I was very friendly with for about a year with a good sexual relationship. Then I suddenly found myself making it with my roommate, who slowly but expertly introduced me to how two women can make love. I really enjoyed both kinds of sex and both personal relationships, so I continued them for some while until my graduate school career was over and I moved to a new town. (Authors' files)

Research on female bisexuality has shown that some women who identify themselves as bisexual say that they have different emotional needs, some of which are best (or exclusively) met by men, and others by women (Blumstein and Schwartz, 1976). We have occasionally come across this same explanation from bisexual men, but much more often the male bisexual explains his sexual lifestyle in terms of a need for variety and creativity. Some bisexuals of either gender say that their sexual openness is a sign that they aren't biased against homosexuality and that they aren't sexist.

Three different sets of circumstances seem to be particularly conducive to bisexuality (Blumstein and Schwartz, 1977). Sexual experimentation in a relationship with a close friend is quite common among women and can also occur with two male friends or with a male homosexual who develops a casual but friendly relationship with a woman. Group sex also is another avenue for bisexual experimentation; while males usually initiate the group activity, females often feel more comfortable engaging in same-sex contact. Finally, some people come to adopt a bisexual philosophy as an outgrowth of their personal belief systems. For instance, some women who have been active in the "women's movement" find that they are drawn closer to other women by the experience and translate this closeness into sexual expression. This same process can be a form of subtle intellectual coercion, however:

> I was an ardent feminist but also as straight as I could be. As I worked extensively with women's groups, I began to feel more and more pressure to "try" a sexual experience with another woman, with the implication being that if I didn't, I really wasn't into sisterhood and was enslaved by male cultural propaganda. I finally gave in to this pressure and had an awful time. Shortly after that, I began drifting away from the movement because it hit too raw a nerve in me. (Authors' files)

A few other circumstances of bisexual behavior are notable because they are usually not labelled as bisexual by the participants. Under conditions of prolonged sexual segregation, heterosexual people often turn temporarily to same-sex experiences. This is true of both male and female prisoners (Kirkham, 1971; Giallombardo, 1974; Money and Bohmer, 1980) and members of the military. Similarly, many men who participate in brief homosexual encounters in public restrooms (euphemistically called the "tearoom trade") are heterosexually married and do not think of themselves as bisexual (Humphreys, 1970). Young male prostitutes who cater to a homosexual clientele generally see this as a detached, depersonalized act done "for the money,"

thus their self-perception remains strongly heterosexual (A. Reiss, 1967).

The nature of bisexuality remains very much a puzzle at the present time. There are no good leads on what "causes" bisexuality, and the varied pattern of bisexual biographies wreaks havoc with many theories about the origins of sexual orientation. It is very possible that as more is learned about this subject our understanding of the complexities of human sexuality will be improved.

SUMMARY

1. Although attitudes toward homosexuality in the past have varied from acceptance to strong condemnation, homosexuals in our society today are clearly a minority faced with social, religious, and legal prejudices. Homophobia — a fear of homosexuality — is widespread and difficult to reduce in light of prevailing stereotypes.

2. There are many theories about the "causes" of homosexuality. Some suggest biological origins such as genetic factors, prenatal hormone exposure, or a hormone imbalance. Others stress faulty childhood development, such as Freud's idea of homosexuality arising from a fixation at an immature stage of psychosexual development or Bieber's theory that male homosexuality results from having a weak, passive father and a dominant, overprotective mother. According to learning theory, sexual orientation is partly dependent on the nature of early sexual experiences. There is no firm support for any of these theories, which may be because there are different types of homosexuality, each of which originates in a different way.

3. Homosexuality is neither an illness nor a form of poor psychological adjustment. Much of the early research that attempted to show that

homosexuals were "sick" suffered from poor research design, and more research studies have generally shown that homosexuals are as well-adjusted as properly matched groups of heterosexuals. Recognizing this, the American Psychiatric Association no longer considers homosexuality an illness.

4. The sexual techniques of gay men and women are generally similar to heterosexual techniques, but homosexuals in committed relationships seem more attuned to their partner's responses and somewhat less goal-oriented than most heterosexual married couples.

5. In general, self-discovery of homosexuality in males occurs at an earlier age than in females. The decision on whether or when to "come out" is a difficult one for many homosexuals, regardless of their age.

6. Homosexuals are not usually recognizable by their appearance, mannerisms, or occupational choice. The diversity of homosexual lifestyles is considerable, but most homosexual men are more active sexually than lesbians (i.e., engage in sex more frequently) and have more sex partners than lesbians or heterosexuals. However, many gay men and women have lasting committed same-sex relationships.

7. The gay world has its visible and invisible components. Today, in addition to gay bars and baths, there are also gay churches, organizations, newspapers, and — in larger cities — full-scale gay business and social communities. But homosexuality is not always "gay": there is a less pleasant side to homosexuality, with impersonal, hurried sex, fear of police entrapment, high rates of sexually transmitted disease, alcoholism, and personal guilt or fear of discovery. Reflecting this, mounting fear of AIDS has apparently led to changes in sexual behavior within some segments of the gay male community.

8. Bisexuality is a form of sexual experimentation or a deliberately chosen sexual style that is currently fashionable in some circles. Relatively little research has been done on this subject, but it appears to be a comfortable option for some people while being unthinkable to many others.

SUGGESTED READINGS

Altman, Dennis. *The Homosexualization of America.* Boston: Beacon Press, 1982. A thought-provoking analysis of the influences the gay minority has had on "mainstream" American society during the 1970s.

Bayer, Ronald. *Homosexuality and American Psychiatry: The Politics of Diagnosis.* New York: Basic Books, 1981. The definitive account of how the American Psychiatric Association changed its view of homosexuality in the 1970s; a fascinating depiction of the interplay of science and politics.

Bell, Alan P., and Weinberg, Martin S. *Homosexualities.* New York: Simon & Schuster, 1978. A detailed and revealing examination of the range of lifestyles and sexual practices of homosexual men and women.

Fairchild, Betty, and Hayward, Nancy. *Now That You Know: What Every Parent Should Know About Homosexuality.* New York: Harcourt Brace Jovanovich, 1979. An informative, sensitively written guide for parents of homosexuals.

Homosexuality and Bisexuality

Marmor, Judd, ed. *Homosexual Behavior*. New York: Basic Books, 1980. A thought-provoking group of essays on homosexuality by a well-balanced group of experts in fields such as law, history, sociology, anthropology, psychology, psychiatry, and religion.

Masters, William H., and Johnson, Virginia E. *Homosexuality in Perspective*. Boston: Little, Brown, 1979. A detailed report on the physiology of homosexual response as observed in the research laboratory and clinical aspects of treating homosexuals in sex therapy.

McWhirter, David, and Mattison, Andrew. *The Male Couple*. Englewood Cliffs, N.J.: Prentice-Hall, 1983. An intriguing look at the ways in which gay male relationships develop and stabilize over time.

Silverstein, Charles. *Man to Man: Gay Couples in America*. New York: William Morrow and Company, 1981. Detailed, insightful commentary on love relationships among gay men written poignantly by the founding editor of the *Journal of Homosexuality*.

17 The Varieties of Sexual Behavior

S EXUAL behavior, like human behavior, is varied and complex, and defies simple schemes of classification. In this chapter, we will shift our focus from the more common patterns of sexual behavior considered in the last three chapters and look at the diversity shown in less typical sexual variations. Considering these variations can be intriguing and instructive: besides learning more about the nature of sexuality, we also increase our tolerance for others. To accomplish these goals of learning and tolerance in a reasonably objective manner, we will start out by discussing the concepts of normality, labeling, and stigmatization.

DEFINING NORMALITY

It isn't very difficult to decide that a person who is sexually aroused only when riding a camel is abnormal or that a couple whose sex life consists primarily of intercourse several times a week at night in the privacy of their bedroom seems almost "too normal." Most people believe they know intuitively how to rate sexual behavior as normal or abnormal. Nevertheless, trying to define what is sexually normal and what is not is one of the more perplexing problems in sexology today. Let's see where the difficulties arise.

Most dictionary definitions of "normal" say

438

that it is primarily a matter of conforming to a usual or typical pattern. What is unusual or atypical not only varies from culture to culture (as discussed in chapter 24) but also varies over time, as we have noted throughout this book. But there is still more complexity in establishing what is normal. From a sociological perspective, behavior that falls outside the accepted customs and rules of a particular society is considered deviant. From a biological viewpoint, normality implies natural and healthy. A psychological view of abnormality stresses that it produces a personal, subjective sense of distress — such as excessive nervousness, depression, or guilt — or that it interferes with a person's ability to function adequately in ordinary social and occupational roles. Statistically, normality becomes a matter of numbers: what is rare is abnormal, what is common is not.

The point we are making is two-fold: first, defining normality is not as simple as it seems; second, the distinction between normal and abnormal is somewhat arbitrary because it generally involves value judgments of one type or another. Thus, it is important to note that in many instances there is no clear-cut separation between normal and abnormal. While it is easy to say that a person who masturbates twice a week is not exhibiting abnormal sexual behavior and that a person who compulsively masturbates a dozen times a day *is*, where do you draw the line? Once a day? Three times a day? Six times a day? Is the behavior abnormal only if it is compulsive? Is it abnormal only if it continues persistently over time?

Given these potential difficulties in determining just what normality means, we suggest that you be aware of your own feelings about the topics we'll be discussing and try to determine how those feelings color your reaction to understanding these different forms of sexual behavior.

LABELING AND STIGMATIZATION

Using words like normal or abnormal to describe people or behavior, or using other word combinations that may sound scientific or "official" (such as healthy, well-adjusted, and law-abiding versus diseased, pathological, deviant, sick, or criminal) is called *labeling*. Labels affect how we view other people and how they view us in return; labels may also affect how we feel about ourselves. In general, labels that identify a person as "different" are likely to lead people to cautiously distance themselves from or perhaps reject that person; labels that indicate sameness or familiarity (in association with something viewed as "normal" or "good") tend to foster acceptance.

Stigmatization refers to the negative effects labeling can produce, such as branding people as undesirable or discrediting them in various ways with social, legal, and economic consequences. For instance, people labeled as forgers may be picked up by the police as suspects if bad checks are being passed in their community even if they have reformed completely. A veteran with a dishonorable discharge may have a hard time getting a job. Stigmatization operates very strongly in terms of sexual labels, too — how would you react to being told that someone was a child molester?

In the past, some of the forms of sexual behavior discussed in this chapter were called sexual deviations, perversions, or aberrations. These labels inevitably led to stigmatization and were also applied in a somewhat arbitrary fashion, since their underlying concept was based on a notion of cultural conformity (Tallent, 1977). To avoid these problems as much as possible, we prefer to speak about sexual variations and to use the relatively neutral term *paraphilia* — derived from Greek roots meaning "alongside of" and "love" —to describe what used to be called sexual deviations. While this strategy serves our purpose fairly well at this time, it is possible that in the future this term will also become a source of stigmatization and a new, unstigmatized alternate will be needed.

THE PARAPHILIAS

A *paraphilia* is a condition in which a person's sexual arousal and gratification depends on a fantasy theme of an unusual sexual experience that becomes the principal focus of sexual behavior. A paraphilia can revolve around a particular sexual object (e.g., children, animals, underwear) or a particular sexual act (e.g., inflicting pain, making obscene telephone calls). The nature of a paraphilia is generally specific and unchanging, and most of the paraphilias are far more common in men than in women (Money, 1980).

A paraphilia is distinguished from sporadic sexual experimentation just as drug dependence is different from episodic, recreational drug use. The person with a full-blown paraphilia typically becomes preoccupied with thoughts of reaching sexual fulfillment to the point of being seriously distracted from other responsibilities. In addition, types of sexual activity outside the boundaries of the paraphilia generally lose their turn-on potential unless the person supplements them with the paraphilic fantasy.

While some of the paraphilias may seem so foreign to you that it's hard to see how they could be arousing to anyone, paraphilic acts, often in watered-down versions, are commonly used by sex partners wishing to add a little variety to their ordinary techniques. For example, some people get turned on by very explicit sexual language, others want to be bitten, scratched, or slapped during sex, and others find that watching their partner undress is highly arousing. Each of these innocuous acts if magnified to the point of psychological dependence could potentially be transformed into a paraphilia.

With this general background, we will now discuss some of the major types of paraphilias.

Fetishism

In *fetishism*, sexual arousal occurs principally in response to an inanimate object or body part that is not primarily sexual in nature. The fetish object is almost invariably used during masturbation and is also incorporated into sexual activity with a partner in order to produce sexual excitation. Fetishists usually collect such objects and may go to great lengths, including theft, to add just the "right" type of item to their collection. One man we encountered who had a fetish for women's high-heeled shoes had gradually accumulated a hoard of more than a thousand pairs, which he catalogued and concealed from his wife in his attic.

Among the long list of objects that have served as fetishes, the most common are items of women's clothing such as panties, brassieres, slips, stockings or panty-hose, negligees, shoes, boots, and gloves. Other common fetish objects include specific materials such as leather, rubber, silk, or fur or body parts such as hair, feet, legs, or buttocks. While a few fetishists are aroused by drawings or photographs of the fetish object, more commonly the fetishist prefers or requires an object that has already been worn. This object, however, does not function as a symbolic substitute for a person (the former owner). Rather it is *preferred* to the owner because it is "safe, silent, cooperative, tranquil and can be harmed or destroyed without consequence" (Stoller, 1977, p. 196). In the great majority of cases, the person with a fetish poses no danger to others and pursues the use of the fetish object in private.

The Varieties of Sexual Behavior

"I don't know if my fetish is better or worse. A pair of shoes used to turn me on to you, but now you turn me on to shoes."

© 1984 by Sidney Harris.

In some cases, the fetishist can become sexually aroused and orgasmic only when the fetish is being used. In other instances, sexual responsiveness is diminished without the fetish but not completely wiped out. In the second set of circumstances, the fetishist often engineers sexual arousal by fantasizing about the fetish. For a small number of fetishists, the fetish object must be used by a partner in a particular way for it to be effective: for instance, the genitals must be rubbed by silk, or a partner must wear black garters and high heel shoes.

There is a thin line of distinction between fetishism and certain types of sexual preferences. A person is not described as a fetishist if sexual arousal is dependent on having an attractive partner; a man who is turned on by a woman in black, lacy lingerie is also not labeled as a fetishist

as long as this is not the primary focus of his arousal. Deciding exactly when individual preference blends into too much dependency is not always easy.

Transvestism

A transvestite is a heterosexual male who repeatedly and persistently becomes sexually aroused by wearing feminine clothing (cross-dressing).[1] Although many transvestites are married and are unremarkably masculine in everyday

---

[1] It is interesting to note that women who cross-dress (wear male clothing) are often regarded as fashionable and are not diagnosed as transvestites. While cross-dressing among women is not rare, it has not generally been associated with sexual excitement.

life, their cross-dressing may be accompanied by elaborate use of make-up, wigs, and feminine mannerisms in a masquerade that sometimes can fool even the most skilled onlooker.

Transvestism must be distinguished from male transsexualism, where the person wants an anatomical gender change and wants to live as a woman (see chapter 10). Transsexuals usually are not sexually aroused by cross-dressing, but in a few cases, transvestism may evolve into transsexualism (Stoller, 1977; Person and Ovesey, 1978; Wise and Meyer, 1980). Transvestites can also be distinguished both from female imper-

sonators (who are entertainers) and from male homosexuals who occasionally "go in drag" (cross-dress). These types of cross-dressing are not associated with sexual arousal, and there is no psychological dependence on wearing feminine clothing as a form of tension release.

Cross-dressing usually begins in childhood or early adolescence, with the histories of many transvestites indicating that as children they were punished by being dressed in girl's clothes (Stoller, 1977). In one of the cases we have seen, a six-year-old boy was deliberately "taught" to cross-dress by his transvestite father, who in turn had been guided into this behavior by his father when he was a child. In adulthood, most transvestites confine their cross-dressing to the privacy of their own homes, although a few may

Many men who are cross-dressers prefer to do so in private, but this man appears to be enjoying the attention he is receiving.

The Varieties of Sexual Behavior

A Case Synopsis of a Fetishist

Mr. Z was a twenty-seven-year-old lawyer who contacted us because of occasional bouts of impotence in his four-year marriage. A personal interview revealed that Mr. Z had a striking fetish for women's panties; without such a prop, his sexual excitement was marginal, and even fantasizing about panties did not always permit him to maintain an erection. Furthermore, it was not just any pair of panties that would do – only used panties with a female odor would excite him.

Mr. Z was a middle child, with an older sister and younger brother. He recalled his childhood as happy and described his family as close-knit and well-to-do. At around age six or seven he was occasionally involved in sex games with a few neighborhood children, but there was nothing remarkable that he could recall about these experiences.

At age twelve he began to masturbate. From time to time he tried to spy on his older sister (who was then fifteen) when she was showering or in the bathroom, but he was generally unsuccessful in these attempts. One day, however, his sister left her panties on the bathroom floor – he recalled vividly their appearance and the distinctly musky odor of the crotch – and he used these as a prop in his masturbation, with an accompanying fantasy of ravishing his sister while she was asleep.

Following this, his masturbatory fantasies sometimes revolved around female undergarments, while at other times they did not. At age thirteen, he stole a pair of his cousin's panties, which he kept hidden in his room and used from time to time for autoerotic stimulation. At age fourteen, when he began having a sexual relationship with a girlfriend, their activity consisted primarily of petting while wearing their clothing, which meant that his genital touching was done either through her panties or by slipping a finger just inside them. On one occasion, he talked his date into letting him have her panties, giving a reason he couldn't recall.

By age sixteen, he had begun to visit laundromats where he could conveniently "borrow" panties from a load of soiled clothing waiting to be put in the wash. His erotic turn-on was generally proportionate to the odor of the panties. On the few occasions when he could only manage to steal panties from a drier, he found that they produced little sexual arousal.

This pattern persisted through college and law school. By his own estimate, he had stolen more than 500 pairs of panties over an eleven-year period. His thievery had not slowed down at all after his marriage, and even on his honeymoon in Honolulu he had managed to slip away from his wife, visit a laundromat, steal some panties, masturbate with them, and discard the evidence.

Although he claimed to love his wife and professed a close relationship with her, she had no inkling of his fetish. In her view, his sexual difficulties were primarily a result of too much pressure at work. Mr. Z had no desire to eradicate his fetish; he simply wanted to be able to function sexually with his wife. After a few days of therapy, he terminated treatment because he became fearful that his "secret" would be unveiled.

wear women's panties under their usual masculine clothing throughout the day. In many cases, the transvestite's wife is fully aware of her husband's cross-dressing and may actually help him perfect his use of make-up or select attractive clothing styles (Stoller, 1977). In other cases, the wife may be confused and upset by discovering her husband's passion for cross-dressing and may insist that he seek treatment or may simply file for divorce. Other wives reluctantly tolerate the cross-dressing but don't give it their approval, as this forty-two-year-old woman explains:

> I can't really understand why John enjoys this bizarre business, and I live in constant fear that he'll be discovered by our children. But he doesn't hurt anyone with his dressing up, and it doesn't take anything away from our love, so I really can't complain too much — I just have to accept things as they are. (Authors' files)

While most transvestites are exclusively heterosexual (the majority of married transvestites have children), a small percentage cross-dress while cruising heterosexual bars or social clubs. Their prospective male partners may be completely unaware that a masquerade is going on and may become involved in limited varieties of sexual activity. The transvestite, for example, may perform fellatio on them or masturbate them manually, claiming to be genitally "indisposed" because of menstruation or some other reason. Obviously, the "truth-in-advertising" laws are not being met here, or to paraphrase a Flip Wilson line, "What you get is not exactly what you see."

Voyeurism

In our society, looking at nude or scantily clad women is an acceptable male pastime, as shown by attendance at topless bars, Las Vegas revues, and the binoculars that are trained on the Dallas Cowboy Cheerleaders instead of the action on the football field. Recently, there has been a corresponding phenomenon among women who can view the nude or seminude male in "women-only" clubs that feature attractive male go-go dancers or in women's magazines that show male frontal nudity. The social acceptability of such interests illustrates our earlier point about the continuum between normality and abnormality because the pleasures of "looking" can be transformed into another form of paraphilia.

The *voyeur*, or Peeping Tom, is a person who obtains sexual gratification by watching others engaging in sexual activity or by spying on them when they are undressing or nude. Voyeur comes from the French verb meaning "to see." Peeping Tom comes from the legendary nude ride of Lady Godiva; Tom the Tailor was the only townsman who violated Lady Godiva's request for privacy by "peeping." In *voyeurism*, "peeping" (or fantasizing about peeping) is the repeatedly preferred or exclusive means of becoming sexually aroused. While women may be "voyeuristic" in the sense of becoming sexually excited by seeing others nude or watching others in sexual acts, cases of female dependency on voyeurism for sexual response are very rare.

Voyeurism is mainly found among young men and often seems to burn out by the middle-age years. Voyeurs frequently have a great deal of trouble forming heterosexual relationships (Tollison and Adams, 1979), and many have only limited amounts of heterosexual experience. In fact, being a voyeur allows such a man to avoid social and sexual interaction with women; many voyeurs confine their sexual activity to masturbation while peeping or while fantasizing about previous peeping escapades.

The voyeur prefers to peep at women who are strangers, since this confers a novelty and forbidden quality on the act (Gebhard et al., 1965). The voyeur is often most sexually excited by situations in which the risk of discovery is high, which may also explain why most voyeurs are not particularly attracted to nudist camps, burlesque shows, nude beaches, or other places where observing nudity is accepted (Tollison and Adams, 1979).

While it might be thought that peepers are harmless individuals because they avoid personal contact, this is not always the case. Some voyeurs have committed rape, burglary, arson, or other crimes (Yalom, 1960; Gebhard et al., 1965; MacNamara and Sagarin, 1977).

Exhibitionism

Exhibitionism is a condition in which a person repeatedly and preferentially exposes the sex organs to unsuspecting strangers to obtain sexual arousal. While exhibitionism is found almost exclusively in males (Mohr, Turner, and Jerry, 1964; Smukler and Schiebel, 1975; Stoller, 1977), a few cases of female exhibitionism have been reported (Evans, 1970; Hollender, Brown, and Roback, 1977). Many exhibitionists are impotent in other forms of heterosexual activity and seem to be pushed by an "uncontrollable urge" which leads to their impulsive behavior.

The peak occurrence of exhibitionism is in the twenties, with relatively few cases after age forty (Mohr, Turner, and Jerry, 1964). (This probably indicates that most exhibitionists gradually stop exposing themselves as they become middle aged.) According to one study, the typical exhibitionist is married, above average in intelligence, satisfactorily employed, and without evidence of serious emotional problems (Smukler and Schiebel, 1975). Most exhibitionists also tend to be passive, shy, and sexually inhibited men. In many instances, a particular episode of exhibitionistic behavior is triggered by a family conflict or a run-in with an authority figure (Tollison and Adams, 1979).

Although an act of exhibition usually produces sexual excitation in the performer, it is not always accompanied by erection or ejaculation even if the man masturbates while exposing himself. For some men, the primary intent of exhibitionism is to evoke shock or fear in their victims; without such a visible reaction, they derive little pleasure from the act. Apparently such men are trying to "prove" their masculinity by an unmistakable anatomical display.

More exhibitionists are caught by the police than any other category of paraphilia. The need to risk being caught may be an important element of the turn-on (Stoller, 1977), leading some exhibitionists into behavior almost guaranteed to result in arrest. The exhibitionist may repeatedly "perform" at the same street corner or use a parked car (which can be easily identified) as the theater for his "act."

It is generally agreed that the exhibitionist is unlikely to rape or assault his victims (Tollison and Adams, 1979; American Psychiatric Association, 1980), but there are apparently a few exceptions to this finding (Gebhard et al., 1965; MacNamara and Sagarin, 1977). In one case, an exhibitionist who was unsatisfied with his victim's response slapped her in the face; in another instance, an exhibitionist became so enraged at being ignored by his victim that he ran after her, dragged her into an alley, and forced her to perform fellatio (authors' files).

Just as observing nudity or sexual activity is relatively acceptable in our society under certain conditions, displaying one's body in sexually provocative garb (low-cut dresses, open-necked shirts, "see-through" blouses, tight-fitting pants) is acceptable too.

Obscene Telephone Calling

Twentieth-century technology has contributed at least one new type of paraphilia through the widespread availability of the telephone in our society: some people repeatedly make obscene telephone calls as a means of obtaining sexual excitement.

The obscene telephone caller is almost always male and typically has major difficulties in interpersonal relationships. The relative safety and one-sided anonymity of the telephone — the caller usually knows the name and phone number of the person to whom he is speaking — allows an idealized masturbatory experience with no need to worry about a face-to-face confrontation.

There are three different types of obscene telephone calls. In the first (and probably most common), the caller boasts about himself and describes his masturbatory action in explicit detail. In the second type, the caller directly threatens his victim ("I've been watching you," "I'm going to find you"). In the third type, the caller tries to get the victim to reveal intimate details about her life. This is often done by the caller claiming to be conducting a "telephone research survey" about a subject such as women's lingerie, menstruation, or contraception. More than a few obscene telephone callers announce themselves to their victims as sex researchers.[2]

Sometimes the obscene telephone caller repeatedly calls the same victim; more often, unless the "victim" shows a willingness to stay on the phone and play his game (and a surprising number of women do), the caller moves on to other victims. The compulsive obscene phone caller must be distinguished from the adolescent who occasionally indulges in the same activity as a prank without giving much thought to the distress caused to others (MacNamara and Sagarin, 1977).

The victim can report obscene phone calls to the telephone company and the police, but

the chances of catching the caller are fairly low unless the call can be traced by keeping the caller on the line or the caller can be trapped into "meeting" the victim under police supervision. Obtaining an unlisted telephone number may help stop obscene telephone calls, and some women prefer to list their names in the phone book with last name and first initial only in order to make themselves a less obvious target.

Sadism and Masochism

Sadism is the intentional, repeated infliction of pain on another person to achieve sexual excitement. It is named after the Marquis de Sade (1774-1814), a French author who wrote extensively about cruelty as a means of obtaining sexual gratification. *Masochism* is a condition in which a person derives sexual arousal from being hurt or humiliated. It is named after an Austrian novelist, Leopold Baron Von Sacher-Masoch (1836-1905), whose *Venus in Furs* (1888) gave a detailed description of the pleasure of pain.

The exact incidence of sadism and masochism is not known, but several surveys indicate that 5 to 10 percent of men and women describe such activities as sexually pleasurable on an occasional basis (Kinsey et al., 1953; Hunt, 1975; Barbach and Levine, 1980). Many of these people have probably engaged in mild or even symbolic sadistic or masochistic behavior, with no real physical pain or violence involved. Judging from our research, sadomasochism is only infrequently a full-fledged paraphilia. Giving or receiving physical suffering is thus infrequently the preferred or exclusive means of attaining sexual excitement. And, contrary to the mistaken notion that most women are masochists, both sadism and masochism occur as paraphilias predominantly in men.

Forms of sadism run the entire gamut from "gentle," carefully controlled play-acting with a willing partner to assaultive behavior that may

---

[2] We have had many complaints over the years from women who received phone calls inquiring about their sex lives from men who claimed to be representatives of the Masters & Johnson Institute. Incredibly, many of these women talked at great length to the bogus "interviewer" and had second thoughts only after the call was completed. Readers should be aware of the fact that *no* legitimate sex research is conducted by telephone surveys.

The Varieties of Sexual Behavior

include torture, rape, or even lust-murder. Some sadists require an unconsenting victim to derive pleasure; others become sexually aroused with a consenting partner only if the suffering is obvious.

Similarly, masochism can range from mild versions to extremes. In the mild forms of masochism, activities like bondage (being tied up for the purpose of sexual arousal), being spanked, or being "overpowered" by physical force are mainly symbolic enactments under carefully controlled conditions with a trusted partner. At the opposite end of the spectrum are genuinely painful activities such as whippings, semistrangulation, being trampled, and self-mutilation. The masochist who desires "heavy" pain or bondage may have great difficulty in finding a cooperative partner. For this reason, some masochists resort to inflicting pain on themselves in bizarre ways, including burning themselves, hanging themselves (which causes several dozen deaths annually [Walsh et al., 1977]), or searching out the services of a prostitute who will provide the necessary stimulation.

Although sadomasochistic activities in their extreme forms can be physically dangerous, most people who try these varieties of sex do so with a common-sense understanding of the risks involved and stay within carefully predetermined limits. The allure of sadomasochistic sex, for many people, seems to lie in its erotic nature and its sense of "breaking the rules" of ordinary sexual conduct. In sharp contrast is the relative handful of people whose sexual arousal is dependent on sadomasochism, whose preoccupation with pleasure derived from giving or receiving pain becomes almost all-consuming. As one man told us, "In the heat of my sexual passions, I would stop thinking about the real world and its consequences" (Authors' files).

The psychological meaning of sadomasochism is unclear at present. Noting that many masochists are men who occupy positions of high status and authority (such as executives, politicians, judges, and bankers), some experts theorize that private acts of submissiveness and degradation provide the masochists with an escape valve from their rigidly controlled public lives (Leo, 1981). Seeking sexual pain or humiliation may also be a way of atoning for sexual pleasure for a person who was raised to believe that sex is sinful and evil. Conversely, sadists either may be seeking a means to bolster their self-esteem (by "proving" how powerful and dominant they are) or may be venting an internal hostility that they cannot discharge in other ways.

An entire industry has evolved in support of sadomasochistic sex (often abbreviated as S-M). There are equipment supply catalogues that advertise shackles, whips, nail-studded chains, mouth gags, and other devices of torment. There are magazines with picture spreads on S-M activities and detailed "how-to" articles. In some large cities, S-M bars have opened, and "private" clubs featuring dungeons and regular "social" hours exist. Sexually explicit newspapers usually carry ads like these:

> "Mistress Alexandra" — I was born to dominate men. My perfect, young sensuous body brings men to their knees. . . . Slaves desire so much to please me that they will submit to penis torture, nipple discipline, rectum stretching, enemas, whichever entertains me. I will, if necessary, enforce obedience with my cat-of-nine-tails or other dungeon devices. Mon.-Sat. Noon 'til 10 p.m. Call _____ .

> MISTRESS INGA'S WORLD — Come visit her dungeon room built out of 7″ solid stone, equipped with everything from a whipping post to a suspension system. Call _____ .

> "Submissive Cherry" — Most girls grow up needing to be touched gently "like China dolls." Ever since I was a little girl I wanted to be dominated and put in my place. Now I am a big girl with a luscious bottom that needs to be spanked. I would like to be your total body slave. Reasonable Rates. Call _____ .

As we pointed out in chapter 13, sadomasochistic fantasies are very common, but most people who find such fantasies arousing have no desire to have the real-life experience.

Zoophilia

Engaging in sexual contact with animals is known as *bestiality*; when the act or fantasy of sexual activity with animals is a repeatedly preferred or exclusive means of obtaining sexual excitement, it is called *zoophilia*.

Kinsey and his colleagues (1948, 1953) found that 8 percent of the adult males and 3.6 percent of the adult females they studied reported sexual contact with animals. For the females, this usually involved sexual contact with household pets, while for males, this often involved farm animals such as sheep, calves, or burros (animal sex contacts were two to three times as common in rural males as in city dwellers according to Kinsey's findings). Male bestiality generally included vaginal intercourse, while female bestiality was more likely to be limited to having the animal perform cunnilingus or masturbating a male animal. A few adult women have trained dogs to mount them and regularly engage in intercourse with their pet.

Bestiality usually involves curiosity, a desire for novelty, or a desire for sexual release when another partner is unavailable (Tollison and Adams, 1979). Zoophilia sometimes involves sadistic acts that may harm the animal.

Pedophilia

Pedophilia (literally, "love of children") describes adults whose preferred or exclusive method of achieving sexual excitement is by fantasizing or engaging in sexual activity with prepubertal children (American Psychiatric Association, 1980). While some authorities state that pedophilia occurs only in males (Stoller, 1977), there are specific cases of women having repeated sexual contact with children (Kolodny, Masters, and Johnson, 1979; Tollison and Adams, 1979). About two-thirds of the victims of pedophiles are girls (most commonly, between ages eight and eleven).

The pedophile, or child molester, is a complete stranger to the child in only 10.3 percent of cases (Mohr, Turner, and Jerry, 1964), showing that the popular stereotype of the child molester as a stranger who lurks around schools and playgrounds with a bag of candy is generally incorrect. In about 15 percent of reported cases, the pedophile is a relative, making the sexual contact a form of incest. The actual percentage of cases involving relatives may be higher than this, since fewer cases of this type may be reported to the police out of concern for "protecting" the family member. (Incest will be discussed in more detail in chapter 18.) Most pedophiles are heterosexual and many are married fathers; a substantial number have marital or sexual difficulties and alcoholism figures prominently in these cases, too (Gebhard et al., 1965; Rada, 1976; Kolodny, Masters, and Johnson, 1979).

MacNamara and Sagarin (1977, p. 73) caution that it is hard to know how often pedophiles who have been caught say they were drunk as an excuse to reduce the stigma and lessen the chances of punishment: "By claiming drunkenness, a man is saying in effect that he is not the sort of person who in a sober state would become involved in an act of this type." Thus, he may convince others that instead of needing punishment, psychiatric care, or rehabilitation, he simply needs to stop getting drunk.

There are three distinct age groups where pedophilia is common: over age fifty, in the mid-to-late thirties, and in adolescence. Strictly speaking, the person who has only isolated sexual contacts with children is not a pedophile (American

Psychiatric Association, 1980) and may be expressing sexual frustration, loneliness, or personal conflict.

Several different types of pedophiles have been distinguished. According to Cohen, Seghorn, and Calmas (1969), the most common is the *personally immature pedophile* — a person who has never succeeded in developing interpersonal skills and is drawn to children because he feels in control of the situation. His victims are usually not strangers and the sexual contact is not impulsive, often beginning with a drawn-out "courtship" in which he befriends the child with stories, games, and disarming companionship. In contrast, the *regressed pedophile* usually has developed strong heterosexual relationships without much difficulty; during some point in adulthood, however, he begins to develop a sense of sexual inadequacy, has problems dealing with everyday stresses, and often becomes alcoholic. His sexual contact with children is apt to be impulsive and with strangers, sometimes reflecting a sudden, uncontrollable urge that comes over him. The *aggressive pedophile* (the least common version) often has a history of antisocial behavior and may feel strong hostility toward women. They are most likely to assault their victims and may cause severe physical harm.

According to psychologist Nicholas Groth, who works extensively with sex offenders, 80 percent of pedophiles have a history of being sexually abused when they were children. Exactly why these men who were themselves sexually victimized should in turn victimize others is uncertain at present, but the tendency may relate to defects in personality development partly caused by the trauma of sexual victimization.

There is no single pattern of sexual activity that fits all pedophiles. While fondling the child's genitals or having the child touch his own genitals may be the most common pedophilic act,

there are many instances of intercourse, fellatio, and other varieties of sexual stimulation.

Most societies take a dim view of pedophilia, and laws against sexual contacts between adults and children are strongly enforced. But the sexual abuse of children has become another "big business" today, with numerous instances of children being pushed into prostitution or being used for the production of pornography. The *Chicago Tribune* (May 16, 1977) reported that a nationwide homosexual ring had been discovered which shipped young boys around the country for prostitution. In Los Angeles, the Rene Gunyon Society is working to decriminalize sex between children and adults, using the slogan "Sex by age eight, or else it's too late!" (Tollison and Adams, 1979). The North American Man-Boy Love Association, which argues for the right of adults to have sex with underage boys, recently accused the FBI of conducting a "witch hunt" when arrests involving two of their group's members were made in connection with kidnapping charges (Leo, 1983). Even more recently, charges of child sexual abuse have been levelled at school and day-care personnel in various parts of the country (including some women as well as men). A strong public outcry against such practices has occurred in the past few years as the dimensions of this problem have become more widely publicized.

Other Paraphilias

There are a number of other paraphilias that are relatively rare and about which fairly little is known. *Apotemnophilia* refers to persons with a sexual attraction to amputations, who may sometimes try to convince a surgeon to perform a medically unnecessary amputation on them to increase their erotic satisfaction (Money, Jobaris, and Furth, 1977). Persons with this type of paraphilia seek out sexual partners who are amputees.

Coprophilia and *urophilia* refer, respectively, to sexual excitement deriving from contact with feces and urine. *Klismaphilia* is sexual excitement preferentially or exclusively resulting from the use of enemas. *Frotteurism* is sexual arousal that results from rubbing the genitals against the body of a fully clothed person in crowded situations such as subways, buses, or elevators.

Necrophilia is sexual arousal from viewing or having sexual contact with a corpse. This bizarre paraphilia has sometimes led people to remove corpses from cemeteries, or seek jobs in morgues or funeral homes (Tollison and Adams, 1979).

Causes and Treatment of the Paraphilias

There is very little certainty about what causes a paraphilia. Psychoanalysts generally theorize that these conditions represent "a regression to or a fixation at an earlier level of psychosexual development resulting in a repetitive pattern of . . . sexual behavior that is not mature in its application and expression" (Sadoff, 1975, p. 1539). In other words, an individual repeats or reverts to a sexual habit arising early in life. Castration anxiety and Oedipal problems are seen as

---

RESEARCH SPOTLIGHT

Is There a Positive Side to Pedophilia?

A report by Dutch psychologist Theo Sandfort (1983) is stirring up a great deal of controversy because of its claims that boys enjoy and benefit from their involvement with adult pedophiles. Sandfort bases this contention on interviews with twenty-five boys aged ten to sixteen who were in ongoing sexual relationships with adult men. The boys were recruited for his study by older friends who were participants in the Dutch League for Sexual Reform. Among Sandfort's findings:

1. "The partner and the relationship, including sexual aspects, were experienced in predominantly positive terms; evidence of exploitation or misuse was absent." (p. 164)
2. The boys tend to see the pedophile as someone they can "talk to easily and with whom they can discuss their problems," as well as a teacher.
3. Very few negative feelings were reported.

However, the methodology of Sandfort's study leaves a lot to be desired. To begin with, his sample was completely unrepresentative, since his "recruiters" apparently deliberately sought out "better" pedophile relationships. What does "better" mean? Possibly these were relationships in which the boys were so intimidated by the pedophile that they were afraid to say anything against him. In addition, Sandfort never defines what "negative" effects on the boys would be and gives no evidence of having asked appropriate questions to discover if these effects were present or not. Unlike standard practice in research of this sort, no psychological tests were

---

The Varieties of Sexual Behavior

central issues. According to Robert Stoller (1975a; 1977), these conditions are all expressions of hostility in which sexual fantasies or unusual sexual acts become a means of obtaining revenge for a childhood trauma usually related to parents inhibiting their child's budding sexuality by threats or punishment. The persistent, repetitive nature of the paraphilia is caused by an inability to completely erase the underlying trauma.

Behaviorists, instead, suggest that the paraphilias begin via a process of conditioning. Nonsexual objects can become sexually arousing if they are frequently and repeatedly associated with pleasurable sexual activity (most typically, masturbation). Particular sexual acts (such as peeping, exhibiting, bestiality) that provide an especially intense erotic response (often heightened because of their "forbidden" nature) can, under certain circumstances, lead the person to prefer this sexual behavior. However, this is not usually a matter of classical conditioning alone: there must usually be some predisposing factor, such as difficulty forming person-to-person sexual relationships or poor self-esteem (Tollison and Adams, 1979).

---

administered to evaluate the boys' emotional stability or self-esteem, and no attempt was made to examine records of the boys' school performances. Even more unbelievably, each boy was interviewed in the home of "his" pedophile with the pedophile present, without any apparent regard for the fact that the adult's presence would have almost assuredly prevented the boy from voicing complaints about the way he was treated because of fear of punishment. Finally, no follow-up of these boys and their relationships was attempted to discover what the long-range impacts might be.

The inadequacies of Sandfort's research design should remind you to be cautious in accepting whatever "research findings" you read about. For instance, even in twenty-five well-adjusted marriages, an objective researcher

conducting reasonably detailed interviews would discover many instances of inequities, manipulations, and other sources of unhappiness. Sandfort's unqualified endorsement of these man-boy relationships is also puzzling because it overlooks a fundamental question: is an inherently abusive, exploitive relationship "positive" under any circumstances? Although we think the answer is no, and we are opposed to adult-child sexual relations no matter how "beneficial" either party may claim them to be, we realize that other researchers have also concluded that pedophilia often provides positive experiences for children (see, for example, Bernard, 1981, and Ingram, 1981). It is our contention that claims of this sort require far more rigorous research that must include long-term follow-up studies before it can be

shown that pedophilia is usually harmless to children or possibly even beneficial. In fact, we agree with Dr. Suzanne Sgroi, co-director of the St. Joseph College Institute for the Treatment and Control of Child Sexual Abuse, who believes that these relationships are always negative ones. "The sexually abused child may not feel abused initially, but as the child learns what society thinks of what he has done, the child feels betrayed," she points out. "He feels he cannot trust adults or family members . . . [and] has a sense of danger, of being violated, a sense that he is not as good as he was before" (Nelson, 1983).

Whatever the cause, it is apparent that paraphiliacs rarely seek treatment unless they are trapped into it by an arrest or discovery by a family member. Most of the time, the paraphilia produces such immense pleasure that giving it up is unthinkable (Money, 1980). Among paraphiliacs in therapy, there may be deliberate attempts to lull the therapist into believing the behavior has been eradicated when it continues in full force.

The literature describing treatment approaches is fragmentary and incomplete. Traditional psychoanalysis has not appeared to be particularly effective with the paraphilias and generally requires several years in treatment. Therapy with hypnosis has also had mixed results. Current interest is focused primarily on a number of behavioral techniques that include: (1) *aversion therapy* which attempts to reduce or extinguish behavior by conditioning; for example, electric shocks may be given to a person while he views photographs of the undesired behavior (Bancroft, 1974; Kilmann et al., 1982); (2) *desensitization procedures* which neutralize the anxiety-provoking aspects of non-paraphiliac sexual situations and behavior by a process of gradual exposure; (3) *social skills training,* generally used in conjunction with either of the other approaches, and aimed at improving a person's ability to form interpersonal relationships (Zilbergeld and Ellison, 1979); for example, a man may be coached in how to talk with women, how to overcome his fear of rejection, and how to express affection; and (4) *orgasmic reconditioning,* wherein a person might be instructed to masturbate using his paraphilia fantasy and to switch to a more appropriate fantasy (for example, intercourse with his wife) just at the moment of orgasm. With this reconditioning process, the person is gradually taught to become aroused by more acceptable mental imagery, and other appropriate techniques, such as fading or satiation, are used to reduce substantially the arousal of the undesirable fantasy (Schwartz and Masters, 1983).

Recently, drugs called antiandrogens that drastically lower testosterone on a temporary basis have been used in conjunction with these forms of treatment (Van Moffaert, 1976; Walker, 1978; Money, 1980). The antiandrogens lower sex drive in males and also reduce the frequency of mental imagery of sexually arousing scenes. Thus, these drugs usually lessen the compulsiveness of the paraphilia, allowing concentration on counseling without as strong a distraction from paraphiliac urges (Berlin and Meinecke, 1981). MPA (medroxyprogesterone acetate, also known by its trade name, Depo-Provera) has been the main antiandrogen used in this country.

Ethical questions have been raised about the propriety of aversion therapy and the use of antiandrogens. The primary issue is that men who enter treatment only because they are caught may be faced with the choice of treatment or jail; they are not really giving a *free* consent to these treatment methods (Kolodny, 1978a).

HYPERSEXUALITY

People with extraordinarily high sex drives, which are insistent and persistent but rarely lead to more than fleeting gratification or release despite numerous sex acts with numerous partners, are considered to be *hypersexual,* or "over-sexed." In women, this condition has been called *nymphomania;* in men, it is called *satyriasis* or *Don Juanism.*[3]

---

[3] The satyrs were half-human, half-animal creatures in Greek mythology; they led carefree, lusty lives with orgies and other types of partying perpetually occupying their attention. Don Juan was a fictional character who seduced women in prodigious numbers without regard for their feelings and without obtaining real satisfaction from these brief encounters.

The Varieties of Sexual Behavior

There has been little scientific study of these conditions, which often seem to be considered more of a joke than anything else. There are no absolute criteria for defining hypersexuality. The central features of most studied cases are: (1) sexual activity is an insatiable need, often interfering with other areas of everyday functioning; (2) sex is impersonal, with no emotional intimacy; and (3) despite frequent orgasms, sexual activity is generally not satisfying.

To many men, the idea of a woman with a greater sex drive than their own is somewhat threatening, so they may use the label of nymphomania to preserve their own egos: the label "proves" that the woman is abnormal. Similarly, men with sexual dysfunction sometimes accuse their wives or partners of being "oversexed" in an effort to hide their own fears and sense of inadequacy, just as some women who do not enjoy sex or who object to the frequency of their husband or partner's amorous desires accuse him of being oversexed. In our society, a man who is highly sexed and who has many sexual partners is generally (often enviously) called a "stud," while a woman with the same characteristics is often called a "nympho," which carries a negative connotation.

CELIBACY

A very different form of sexual behavior is *celibacy* or abstention from sexual activity. Celibacy can be a conscious and deliberate choice, or it can be a condition dictated by circumstance (poor health, unavailable partner, etc.).

In some religions, a vow of lifetime celibacy is expected of those who join the clergy.[4] Vari-

ous religions also exalt the purity and holiness of celibacy for their lay members. Celibacy can also be practiced on a temporary or periodic basis, where it can allow some people to have more of a sense of control over their lives, to devote more attention to nonsexual aspects of their relationships, or to take a "rest" from the pressures of sexual interaction.

In the last few years, celibacy has become more talked about as a sexual alternative. An article in *The Village Voice* (January 23, 1979) reported that "coming out" as celibate is the latest sexual vogue. In 1980 a book appeared titled *The New Celibacy: Why More Men and Women Are Abstaining From Sex — And Enjoying It,* suggesting:

> Celibacy is a way of breaking boundaries, old patterns of behavior that exist between mind and body, between the self and others. It enables one to be free of sexuality in order to evaluate and experience the joys of life without sex. If the results of being celibate for some time lead to becoming sexual once again, fine; it will be bringing about an even more sexually alive state than before. If one chooses to remain celibate because other nonsexual experiences turn out to be very fascinating, then too there will be clear benefits resulting from the celibate exploration. (Brown, 1980, p. 29)

For people who get no pleasure out of sex, celibacy may be a welcome relief, like being released from imprisonment. Others may choose celibacy even though they enjoy sex because they find that abstinence rejuvenates their lives or creativity. Of course, some people find celibacy to be a frustrating and unfulfilling choice and may quickly reject it.

There are no health risks known to result from celibacy. As mentioned in chapter 14, if physical sexual tensions mount to a critical level, they are discharged by orgasms during sleep. But it is clear that while celibacy is a positive sexual alternative for some people, it is not right for everyone.

---

[4]The vows are not always followed, however. In an interesting research study, it was shown that a sizeable number of Catholic priests and nuns engage in sex (Halstead and Halstead, 1978).

At this legalized house of prostitution in Nevada, customers under age 17 must be accompanied by a parent or guardian.

PROSTITUTION

Prostitution is difficult to define since humans have always used sex to obtain desirables such as food, money, valuables, promotions, and power. For practical purposes it is best to define a prostitute as a person who for immediate payment in money or valuables will engage in sexual activity with any other person, known or unknown, who meets minimal requirements as to gender, age, cleanliness, sobriety, ethnic group, and health. Some societies lack prostitution while in others, particularly urban societies, prostitution is tolerated or exists in spite of efforts to eliminate it.

The major reason for the existence and extraordinary persistence of female prostitution is that it is an easy solution to the problem faced by economically disadvantaged women. Virtually all the prostitutes in Europe and America today entered their occupation for economic reasons; they were not captured by "white slavers" nor motivated by pathological sexual needs. Some needed money for an emergency or a drug habit, others drifted into it through accepting gifts and finally money from boyfriends who gradually became more numerous and less known; some were beguiled by a pimp's promises; and still others simply realized — as one said — "I was sitting on a fortune."

The section on prostitution was written in collaboration with Paul Gebhard, Ph.D., formerly Director of the Institute for Sex Research at Indiana University.

The Varieties of Sexual Behavior

A group of male hustlers on a New York City street corner.

Here are two different stories that show how a woman finds her way into "the life."

A *nineteen-year-old call girl:* I was one of six children in a poor family with nowhere to go. I was having sex regularly by the time I was 13, and at age 17 I realized I might as well get paid for it. Everyone knew who the pimps were, and I just connected with a guy who set me up in his stable. Now I make plenty of money and I help my family out. (Authors' files)

A *twenty-four-year-old massage parlor attendant:* I was divorced at twenty-one with a kid and no talent. The only legitimate work I could find was at the minimum wage and that was the pits. A friend told me about this place, and now I get about $500 a week for locals [masturbating the male customer] and blow jobs. If a guy wants to get laid, that'll cost him $50 extra. In another couple of years I'll quit this job, but I'll have some money saved. (Authors' files)

Female prostitutes can be classified as house girls who work in brothels, street girls who solicit in public, B-girls who meet their clients in bars, and call girls who accept appointments, usually via telephone and often only with recommended clients. To this list, one must now add massage parlors and other not so subtly disguised cover-ups such as "escort services." Many, but by no means all, have pimps with whom they share their income. The pimp provides affection and protection, arranges for bail, is available for an occasional loan, and often helps obtain customers. A pimp generally (depending on one's viewpoint) is supported by, or manages, several prostitutes.

Female prostitutes seldom have orgasm in their business contacts but are normally orgasmic in private life. Some will engage in certain sexual techniques with a customer but never with a husband or boyfriend and vice versa. Prostitution may be a regular occupation or an occasional source of extra income, but age ultimately reduces attractiveness and forces retirement.

Although Xaviera Hollender's famous book, *The Happy Hooker* (1972), presents a generally rosy picture of prostitution, there is another side to it too. The detrimental side of female prostitution is not the sexual activity itself but the evils that often accompany prostitution: exploitation by organized crime and/or pimps, sexually transmitted disease, drug addiction, the physical risks of "kinky" sex or assault by a customer, and the inability to save money for future needs. These evils can be eliminated or at least minimized, as in Denmark where organized prostitution and pimping are strictly prohibited and where the prostitutes are required to have regular employment in addition to their prostitution. Most nations, however, content themselves with futile attempts to wholly suppress prostitution or to confine it to specific areas.

While female prostitution is almost exclusively heterosexual (men paying women), male prostitution is almost exclusively homosexual (men paying men). In male prostitution, there are no pimps; large-scale organization is absent; the price is much less; male brothels are extremely rare (although call boys exist); and the relationship with the customer is not the same. In the United States the male prostitute often presents himself as a "straight" (heterosexual) male who has orgasm as a result of the customer's activities and who often does nothing to the customer. Elsewhere in the world, the male prostitute is active rather than passive and seeks to provide the customer with an orgasm.

Male prostitutes are often known as "hustlers" since "hustling" (by male or female prostitutes) is the act of soliciting a prospective customer. As with female prostitutes, customers are referred to as "Johns," "scores," or "tricks." Male prostitutes sometimes assault and rob their customers knowing that there is almost no likelihood their crime will be reported to the police. A recent study found that about seven out of ten young male prostitutes are only "part-timers"

who continue to pursue conventional educational, vocational, and social paths while earning money by selling sex (Allen, 1980). Male prostitutes who sell their services to women are generally known as gigolos. However, gigolos primarily cater to wealthy, older women.

Prostitution exists primarily because men are willing to pay for sex. Men seek out prostitutes for a variety of reasons. Some men are temporarily without sexual partners because they are traveling or in military service; others with a physical or personality handicap cannot easily obtain partners. In some societies sex with nonprostitutes is very difficult to arrange. Some males seek special techniques that their usual partner will not provide; others do not want to invest the time, emotion, and money in an affectional relationship and simply prefer to buy physical sex. While the increase in nonmarital sexual intercourse in the United States has diminished the prevalence of prostitution, there will always be some customers such as the men just described.

LEGAL ASPECTS OF SEXUAL BEHAVIOR

Most laws pertaining to sexual behavior in the U.S. and in most of the Western world can be traced back to sexual prohibitions from the Judeao-Christian tradition. The original intent of these prohibitions was to preserve moral order as defined by particular sets of religious values. Today, our Constitution demands that our legal system function apart from any religious influence, but this does not totally alter the body of law that has been passed down through the centuries.

Most laws about sexual behavior in America are found at the state or local level. Since these laws vary incredibly from one state to the next and undergo considerable change from year to year (based on both new legislation and new judi-

The Varieties of Sexual Behavior

cial decisions), it is not possible to provide a comprehensive, up-to-date listing of what is legal and what is not on a state-by-state basis. Instead, we will provide an overview of some controversies related to laws about sexual behavior, illustrating our discussion with several specific areas of interest. Legal aspects of rape and incest will be considered separately in chapter 18.

Private Sex with Consenting Adults

It's safe to say that in any twenty-four hour period, millions of ordinary Americans unwittingly engage in sexual acts that are defined as criminal and could lead to imprisonment. In most states, oral-genital sex is illegal — even between husband and wife — and extramarital sex, premarital sex, homosexual acts, and prostitution all fall within the long arm of the law.

Laws that regulate private sexual behavior between consenting adults are a source of dismay to many who argue that these are "victimless" crimes: no one is hurt by the activity, and the government should not be poking its nose in the bedrooms of the nation. Others note that laws pertaining to sexual behavior are no more arbitrary than laws pertaining to business, sports, taxes, or education and point out that many laws depend on first making a moral judgment that gets transformed into legislation.

While most people agree that there are indeed "victimless" crimes, not everyone agrees on just what "victimless" means. The prostitute is regarded as a victim by many (see the boxed item); women may be victimized by an unintended pregnancy; anyone can be victimized by sexually transmitted disease. Defining victimization broadly, some people believe that unrestricted sexual permissiveness may lead to the downfall of our civilization.

Despite these philosophical and political disputes, if current laws regulating sexual behavior

were enforced in a strict and uniform manner, our prisons would have to accommodate the great majority of our population. Recognizing this dilemma and recognizing that the greater common good could be better served if our criminal justice system turned its attention to crimes of violence and of a serious nature, the American Law Institute drafted a Model Penal Code that recommends abolishing laws that regulate the private sexual behavior of consenting adults. The major provisions of this code have now been adopted by a number of states (including Illinois, Connecticut, Colorado, Oregon, and Hawaii), although political pressures have prevented it from becoming more widespread. The basic problem is that most politicians need to run for reelection and do not want to be accused by ultra-conservative groups or fundamentalist religious organizations of being "soft on crime" or "soft on sex."

Here are some examples of the ways in which sex laws categorize and criminalize private, consensual adult sexual acts.

NONMARITAL HETEROSEXUAL INTERCOURSE

The law usually differentiates between *fornication* (intercourse between unmarried heterosexual adults) and *adultery* (extramarital intercourse), with adultery being the more serious crime. In a few states, cohabitation is illegal. The statutes pertaining to fornication and adultery are infrequently enforced today; when they are, people on welfare or members of minority groups are usually involved. Not too long ago, in some states these laws applied only to biracial sexual couples, but such laws have now been abolished as discriminatory and unconstitutional. Punishment for those convicted of fornication or adultery is generally a fine, but in a handful of states, a jail sentence may be given, depending on the discretion of the judge.

An interesting subcategory of fornication is

called *seduction,* which is legally defined as a situation in which a woman is enticed into sexual intercourse by a promise of marriage. Only the male can be prosecuted under this statute (who said the law was always fair?). Although laws against seduction are rarely enforced, they can carry prison sentences of five years or longer.

The laws pertaining to nonmarital heterosexual coitus have an interesting past. Adultery was orginally frowned on because it violated the sanctity of the family and made it difficult to determine a child's paternity (complicating inheritance decisions) (MacNamara and Sagarin, 1977). In addition, a married woman was considered the property of her husband; so if she engaged in extramarital sex, her husband's property rights were violated. A similar line of reasoning held in cases of seduction: the male who seduced a woman violated a verbal contract (his promise to marry her) just as surely as if he had pulled out of a business venture. The result of his broken promise was judged to be "damaged" or "used" property, which no longer had the value of the original, unsullied merchandise. His punishment? Take delivery of the "used" property (that is, marry her, thus fulfilling the original "contract") or go to prison.

NONCOITAL ACTS

In many states, most forms of noncoital sexual activity are considered illegal even if they are done in private by consenting adult partners. As astonishing as it may seem in an age when oral sex is statistically the norm rather than the exception, a pleasant interlude of cunnilingus or fellatio can, theoretically, lead to arrest and imprisonment. Anal sex is similarly banned. In general, the statutes refer to these acts as "crimes against nature," going back to the view that heterosexual intercourse (with its reproductive potential) is the only "natural," healthy, nonsinful way of having sexual relations.

While a few states permit these sexual practices in legally recognized marriages, many states do not. Needless to say, homosexual acts are banned by most states on the same grounds, and the likelihood of prosecution for gay men or women is substantially higher than it is for heterosexuals. Most arrests of homosexuals, however, are for public solicitation and not for specific sexual acts.

PROSTITUTION

Although prostitution is legal in many countries across the world, where it is generally regulated by some form of government licensing and health check-ups, it is illegal in all U.S. jurisdictions except for several counties in Nevada. Since prostitution often involves private sex acts between consenting adults, we have chosen to discuss it in this context. This discussion does *not* apply to prostitutes who are minors, since they may not have the capacity for giving true consent to their behavior; nor does it apply to females who are forced into prostitution by one means or another.

The laws dealing with prostitution vary considerably from state to state. In some jurisdictions, the customer of a prostitute is technically not engaging in any illegal act, although he may be violating another statute by participating in a "crime agivst nature" or fornication. In some areas, however, patronizing a prostitute is a legal violation that can result in a fine. In states such as New York, where this type of law is in effect, it has been justified on the grounds that it is unfair to penalize the prostitute but not her customer.

In a number of cities, including Dallas and St. Louis, the police regularly use policewomen "decoys" on street corners where prostitution abounds. An unwary male approaches the decoy (usually by car), engages her in conversation, and — once he offers money in return for a sexual act

One Woman's View of Prostitution

The following comments were transcribed from a tape-recorded interview with a twenty-three-year-old women we'll call Jane who works part-time for an expensive "escort service" that is actually a sex-for-sale operation (Authors' files).

Interviewer: How did you first get started in this business?

Jane: I guess it began when I was working as a waitress when I was eighteen. This nice looking guy from out of town had been joking with me and talking real friendly, and then near closing time he asked me if I'd go back to his hotel with him for forty bucks. I needed the money, so I said yes. Actually, I was turned on to this guy, or I never would have gone with him, but the money made it especially nice.

Interviewer: How did you feel after that first time? Did you think "Now I'm a prostitute"?

Jane: I actually felt pretty good. I had fun, I got some money for it, but I didn't think of it as getting paid – I sort of looked at it as a gift. It was only after I started doing this more often – going with men after work, or a few

times just going out to a guy's car in the parking lot while I was on break – that I finally began to see it was a business.

Interviewer: Did you have a pimp?

Jane: When I started, I was just an amateur and I didn't know too much about it. The guy who owned the restaurant where I worked eventually caught on to what I was doing and he wanted to get in on the deal. He threatened to fire me and tip off the cops unless I had sex with him and gave him half of what I made. I was scared, so I gave in to him for a while. But after a couple of weeks I realized that it was a losing proposition, so I quit my job. That was the only time I ever had a pimp, and that guy didn't really qualify.

Interviewer: Why did you start working for an escort service?

Jane: Free-lancing got a little slow. There was a lot of competition in town, and the escort service became a good way of getting customers – they do the advertising, screen the calls, and so forth. I still have a few private customers I see at my place. I thought about quitting last year, but I really still need the money.

Interviewer: What made you think about quitting?

Jane: A bunch of things, I guess. I got gonorrhea three times in one year, which was no fun at all, and I got beaten up pretty badly twice by weirdo Johns. So I started to think, "Is this really how you want to be spending your life?"

Interviewer: How do you feel about it now?

Jane: I'm doing two things differently now. First, I'm going to college part-time. I like business, and I'm a business major, so maybe in a few years I'll be able to open my own fashion boutique. Second, I've been saving money. I realize that my earnings won't mean anything if I spend it all now, so I'm careful about that. One of my regulars is a stockbroker who helps me invest. So I guess I see my work as a temporary arrangement for just a few more years.

Interviewer: Do you know many of the other women who work for the escort service? Are most of them planning as carefully as you are?

Jane: Well, it's hard to say. Two of the girls I know are pretty strung out on drugs. But one other friend of mine is doing it pretty much like I am – she works for a modelling agency and has gotten some pretty good assignments. She uses the escort work to supplement her income, if you know what I mean.

Interviewer: What benefits are there to working as a prostitute besides the money?

Jane: Not many, I guess. Oh, independence. And you get to meet some nice guys – and some creeps. But it's scary, too. You never know if a John is going to try to strangle you or cut your throat. I won't be sorry to leave this life behind.

— the decoy signals to her hidden police confederates who move in to make the arrest.

The prostitute is liable to arrest, although it is primarily the street girl and the male hustler who are vulnerable. This is because many laws against prostitution are actually directed against loitering in a public place for purposes of prostitution or solicitation; the call girl or call boy doesn't usually risk violating these statutes.

In most cases of women arrested for prostitution, conviction leads to a minimal fine which is simply one of the expenses of doing business. Pimps often have a service contract with a lawyer who promptly arranges bail for any of their arrested "girls" so that their time off the streets is limited.

It is a tried but true political fact of life that in many cities, major campaigns to "wipe out prostitution" are primarily carried out to generate favorable publicity for the police and a mayor seeking reelection. These campaigns also result in a prominent surge in arrest statistics, making it look as though the war against serious crime is nearing a victorious conclusion. However, it is unlikely that prostitution — the "oldest profession" — will be wiped out soon. It seems equally unlikely that prostitution will be either decriminalized or legalized in the United States at any time in the near future since public opinion still runs strongly against this reform.

Sex Between Adults and Minors

In sharp contrast to the variations in law regarding sex between consenting adults, sex between an adult and a child is strongly condemned in all jurisdictions in the United States, Canada, Europe, and most other countries. Sexual activity between an adult and a child is now widely regarded as a form of child abuse. The specific crime may be rape, statutory rape, sexual assault, child molestation, impairing the morals of a minor, or incest, depending on the precise circumstances. (These will be defined in chapter 18.)

For the purpose of this discussion, we should point out that adults who have sexual contact with children or who exploit them in other sexual ways (by forcing them into prostitution or by using them in the production of pornographic materials) are generally dealt with harshly by our criminal justice system. The severity of sentencing depends, to some extent, on the age of the child and the nature of the sexual act. As a general rule of thumb, an act with an older teenage child is not judged as harshly unless force or injury were involved. The convicted sex offender is likely to receive a stiff prison term, particularly if it is a repeat conviction. In some jurisdictions, the offender may be given an indeterminate (open-ended) sentence. Depending on subsequent behavior and willingness to participate in treatment, the offender may be paroled in a shorter or longer time, or may be imprisoned indefinitely.

The Paraphilias

Many paraphilias involve sexual acts that violate the law in one form or another. For example, exhibitionism falls under laws against "indecent exposure" and, if genital exposure is accompanied by masturbation, it also violates statutes prohibiting sex acts done in public (Sherwin, 1977). Peeping involves an unwanted invasion of privacy. The cross-dressing of the transvestite is sometimes criminal under "public nuisance" laws (although females in male clothing are not arrested on these grounds). Sadistic acts may violate laws on assault; the fetishist may steal to enlarge his fetish collection; and bestiality is generally illegal as a "crime against nature."

The Varieties of Sexual Behavior

People with a paraphilia are in an unusual state of limbo in a legal sense today. Often, they will be categorized as *sexual psychopaths*, a term that is not a psychiatric diagnosis but a legal label. This designation permits them to be given an indeterminate sentence and also suggests that they are a menace to society. While this may be true of some paraphiliacs, it is difficult to see how someone with zoophilia is menacing or what danger is posed by the ordinary transvestite. Similarly, the majority of voyeurs, fetishists, and exhibitionists are unlikely to endanger others. The problem is that there is no way to predict what subsequent behaviors will occur after treatment or after "successful" prison rehabilitation. With every case of a sexual psychopath who is arrested a second or third or fifteenth time, the public demands better protection, stricter law enforcement, and harsher sentencing. Until more reliable information is developed to understand the nature of these conditions, there is no effective answer to such concerns.

SUMMARY

1. Defining abnormal behavior consists of several different components: social deviance, frequency and persistence, psychological dependence, and how the behavior affects psychosocial functioning. Labeling something as abnormal affects how we view ourselves and others; stigmatization refers to the negative effects labeling can produce.

2. The paraphilias (previously called "sexual deviations") are conditions where sexual arousal becomes dependent on an unusual type of sexual behavior or fantasies of that behavior. The paraphilias are much more common in men than in women and often do not cause any sense of personal distress.

3. Specific examples of paraphilia include: fetishism (inanimate objects), transvestism (cross-dressing), voyeurism (peeping), exhibitionism (displaying the sex organs), obscene telephone calling, sadism (pleasure from inflicting pain), masochism (pleasure from experiencing pain), zoophilia (sex with animals), and pedophilia (sexual contact with children by an adult).

4. The origins of paraphilias are obscure at present. Many different treatment approaches have been tried, but none of them works in a completely satisfactory way.

5. Hypersexuality (nymphomania in females, satyriasis in males) is also of obscure origins and is a difficult condition to define. The core features seem to be an insatiable sexual appetite, fairly impersonal sex, and low or nonexistent sexual satisfaction.

6. Celibacy, or sexual abstinence, is a viable choice for some people but an unappealing option for others.

7. Prostitution — engaging in sex for pay — takes many different forms, from the lowly street walker to the more stylish call girl. Most prostitutes choose "the life" for economic reasons. While female prostitution is almost entirely heterosexual, male prostitution is primarily homosexual.

8. In the United States, there are numerous laws that attempt to regulate sexual behavior. While some of these laws seem outdated today and are rarely enforced (e.g., laws prohibiting heterosexual acts between consenting adults in private), other sex laws are still quite visible in many jurisdictions (e.g., antiprostitution laws, statutes banning adult-child sex). There has been a gradual trend to move in the direction of the Model Penal Code, but political pressures have maintained the status quo in many areas.

SUGGESTED READINGS

Allen, Donald M. "Young male prostitutes: a psychosocial study," *Archives of Sexual Behavior* 9 (1980): 399-426. A comprehensive report based on personal interviews with ninety-eight male prostitutes.

Brown, Gabrielle. *The New Celibacy*. New York: McGraw-Hill, 1980. The whys and wherefores of abstinence as a sexual option.

MacNamara, Donald E. J., and Sagarin, Edward. *Sex, Crime and the Law*. New York: Free Press, 1977. An outstanding discussion of the interface between sex and the law.

Sheehy, Gail. *Prostitution: Hustling in Our Wide-Open Society*. New York: Delacorte Press, 1973. A journalistic look at many sides of prostitution, including the role of the pimp.

Stoller, Robert J. "Sexual Deviations." In *Human Sexuality in Four Perspectives*, ed. Frank A. Beach, pp. 190-214. Baltimore: The Johns Hopkins University Press, 1977. A psychoanalyst-sex researcher presents his ideas on the paraphilias concisely and readably.

18 Coercive Sex: The Varieties of Sexual Assault

A FIFTEEN-YEAR-OLD female hitchhiker is kidnapped by a truck driver and raped repeatedly over an eighteen-hour period. She is stabbed eight times and left in a field for dead. She is a victim of sexual assault.

A seventy-five-year-old widow is returning to her apartment from the grocery store, struggling with a heavy bag of food. A teenage boy on her street offers to carry it for her. When she unlocks her apartment door, he pushes her inside, rips off her clothes, and rapes her. She is a victim of sexual assault.

A twenty-two-year-old secretary is repeatedly pinched and ogled at work. Invitations are made for sexual trysts at lunch time, with a

veiled threat that "if you don't do what I want, I'll find someone else who will." The secretary *is* finally fired by his boss, and files a law suit against her. He is a victim of sexual assault.

A twenty-six-year-old man is being held in the county jail on marihuana charges. Before his hearing, he is gang raped by six other prisoners who stuff a towel in his mouth and hold him down by force. The prison guards refuse to remove him from the cell. The next day, he is found hanging from the ceiling, an apparent suicide. He, too, is a victim of sexual assault.

These true cases provide a glimpse of the types of coercive sex in our society. Other aspects of sexual victimization include a child trapped in an incestuous situation, a teenager pushed into prostitution, the thousands of women who are sexually harassed and intimidated at work, and the wives who are beaten if they are not ready for sex when their husbands demand it. This chapter provides some historical, legal, social, and psychological perspectives about coercive sex.

RAPE

Rape is an emotion-laden subject surrounded by myths and misunderstandings. While it is defined as a sexual act, it is primarily an expression of violence, anger, or power. Its victims can be male or female, very young or very old, rich, poor, mentally retarded, disabled, or able-bodied. The victimizers — those who rape — are also a diverse group that defies neat classification or description.

Although there are many definitions of rape, it is legally defined in most jurisdictions as sexual assault with penile penetration of the vagina without mutual consent (Brownmiller, 1975; Warner, 1980). Strictly speaking, penile penetration of the mouth or anus without mutual consent is not rape but falls under other basic laws against sexual assault.

Historical Perspectives

The word rape comes from a Latin term (*rapere*) which means to steal, seize, or carry away (Warner, 1980). In ancient times, rape was one way to procure a wife — a man simply overpowered a desirable woman and then brought her into his tribe. The man then had to protect his property and his honor by preventing others from seizing or raping his wife. This appears to have provided the origins for the first laws against rape in which rape was viewed as a crime against property or honor but not against women (Brownmiller, 1975).

According to the Code of Hammurabi, a set of laws established in Babylonia about 4,000 years ago, a man who raped a betrothed virgin was to be put to death. If a man raped a married woman, however, both the rapist and his victim were regarded as guilty and were executed by drowning. A similar distinction with a slightly different twist was found in biblical injunctions about rape (*Deuteronomy* 22: 22-28): a married woman who was raped was seen as a willing accomplice, so she and her rapist were killed; a virgin was considered guilty only if she was raped in the city, since it was assumed that her screams would have led to her rescue. In contrast, a virgin who was raped in a field outside the city walls was spared, since no one could hear her screaming. If she was betrothed to someone, her rapist was stoned to death — if not, he had to marry her (whether or not she liked this arrangement didn't seem to matter).

Later laws against rape continued to specify varying circumstances by which rape was judged as more or less serious. Penalties were highest if the woman was a virgin or of high social class. Under William the Conqueror (1035-1087), a man who raped a virgin of high social standing was punished by castration and blinding. Guilt, however, was determined by trial by combat, so unless the victim had a champion willing to risk his life by fighting the accused rapist, she had no way of establishing her case.

By the twelfth century, jury trials replaced combat as a means of determining guilt or innocence. Yet all were not equal in the eyes of the law — a nobleman or knight could easily blame a rape he committed on one of his men and save his vision and chances for fatherhood. At the end of the thirteenth century, two additional changes appeared in English law concerning rape: the distinction between raping a virgin or a married woman was dropped, and the old custom of penitence through marriage was permanently banned (Brownmiller, 1975). The essential elements of defining rape and its punishment had fallen into place. Seven centuries later, not too many changes have been made.

Despite the legal system, rape has not always been regarded as bad. In wartime, from thousands of years ago until today, victorious soldiers have raped enemy women. In literature, rape has sometimes been presented in heroic terms, as Ayn Rand did in *The Fountainhead*. In society, rape has often been practically defined in terms of the social positions of victim and victimizer: in the 1940s and 1950s, for example, a white male was rarely charged with raping a black woman in the South, but a black male charged with raping a white woman was dealt with swiftly and harshly. Even today, in most jurisdictions, a man is unlikely to be charged with raping a prostitute, and forced intercourse between husband and wife does not "count" as rape in thirty-eight of the fifty American states.

The last decade has seen a great increase in public awareness of rape. The women's movement played a major role in this process, raising issues and demanding improvement in services to rape victims. Today, almost all metropolitan police departments have specially trained teams (including policewomen) to work with rape victims; there are hundreds of rape hotlines and rape crisis centers for emergency and long-term assistance; many hospital emergency rooms have developed special procedures for treating rape victims; and trial procedures and laws about rape have been changed in important ways.

Myths About Rape

The most devastating myths about rape have cast women in the role of being responsible for the rapist's act (Metzger, 1976; Gager and Schurr, 1976). According to this view, women secretly "want" to be raped and really enjoy the experience. This nonsensical notion has led at least one rapist to give his name and phone number to his victim, so she could "get together" with him again. His conceit led to his immediate arrest. Lurking beneath the surface of this myth are some commonly held misconceptions: women find overpowering men irresistible; women's rape fantasies indicate a real-life sexual desire; and women dress and act provocatively to "turn on" men, who somehow are the hapless victims of their own reactions to this deliberate provocation.

Closely allied to this view of women as instigators is the idea that "she was asking for it, and she got what she deserved." Susan Brownmiller comments on this "explanation" of rape:

> The popularity of the belief that a woman seduces or "cock-teases" a man into rape, or precipitates a rape by incautious behavior, is part of the smoke screen that men throw up to obscure their actions. The insecurity of women runs so deep that many, possibly most, rape victims agonize afterward in an effort to uncover what it was in their behavior, their manner, their dress that triggered this awful act against them. (Brownmiller, *Against Our Will*, 1975, pp. 312-313)

Most research shows that rapists look for targets they see as vulnerable (e.g., walking by themselves, appearing unfamiliar with where they are) rather than women who are dressed in a certain way or who have a certain manner of appearance (Grossman and Sutherland, 1982/83). The "provocation" myth loses its believability when it is recognized that many rape victims are elderly women or young children (Davis and Brody, 1979; Burgess et al., 1978). Furthermore, it is a little like believing people should dress in old, worn-out clothes in order to prevent being mugged, thus misplacing responsibility from the criminal to the victim.

Despite this, the woman is still frequently "blamed" for being raped. This view is based not only on her possible role as instigator but on the incorrect notion that a woman who resists *cannot*

A nighttime vigil by women protesting after a rape at Big Dan's Cafe in New Bedford, Massachusetts. According to the trial proceedings, which were nationally televised on cable TV, patrons in the bar stood by and watched while several men repeatedly raped the victim on a pool table.

be raped. According to two old saws: "A girl can run faster with her skirts up than a man can with his pants down," and "You can't thread a moving needle." These bits of attempted "common sense" humor completely overlook the terror of the rape victim, her fear of physical injury, mutilation, and death, and her shock and disbelief. Even when no weapon is in view, can a woman be certain that one is not hidden? In rape situations, many women hope that by seeming to co-operate with their assailant, they can avoid injury and get it over with more quickly (Burgess and Holmstrom, 1976). But, in an irony of our legal system, this intelligent way of coping is penalized — the case against her attacker depends in part on "proving" her physical resistance by cuts, bruises, and other signs that she put up a struggle. No such evidence is required to "prove" that a robbery occurred.

The last myth we will mention here (al-

Coercive Sex: The Varieties of Sexual Assault

though there are many others) is the idea that women frequently make false accusations of rape. This view is so common that it has even found its way into contemporary literature: in *Rabbit Redux* (Updike, 1972, p. 41) a woman observes, "You know what rape is? It's a woman who changed her mind afterward." While there have certainly been cases where a false cry of rape was made for some ulterior motive, the belief that most women are capable of such an act is the ultimate view of women as emotional, vengeful "bitches." Yet the law in some states quietly upholds this view: unlike cases of assault or robbery, where the victim's word and evidence are enough to prove that a crime occurred, in rape cases another person's testimony or evidence — called *corroboration* — is required as proof (Gager and Schurr, 1976; Lasater, 1980).

Rape Patterns

Forcible rape is far and away the most common form of rape reported. Here, the act of penile penetration is achieved by force or the threat of force. Several subcategories of forcible rape can be distinguished, although most of these are not legally defined terms. The *solo rape* is carried out by one man, acting alone. The *pair rape* or *gang rape* — often a particularly terrifying form of rape — involves either two men or a group of men, sometimes with a female accomplice, who take turns raping the victim. An apparently rare form of gang rape involves several women raping a man (Groth, 1979; Sarrel, 1980; Sarrel and Masters, 1981). In another, more common version, a group of men rape another man rectally. This rape of men by men is infrequent among homosexuals and usually involves heterosexual men in prison (Groth, 1979; Braen, 1980).

Two other types of forcible rape should be mentioned: *date rape* and *mate rape*. In interviews with 300 women between the ages of eighteen and thirty, we found that about one woman in five had been forced into some form of unwanted sexual activity on a date or at a party. One woman in twenty-five had been raped in these circumstances, although very few of these cases were reported to the police (Kolodny and Masters, unpublished data). The following brief account from a twenty-one-year-old woman is typical of the explanations we have been given of these situations:

> I was out on my second date with Jerry and we'd been drinking and dancing and having fun. I agreed to go back to his apartment with two other couples. We drank some more, and the other people left, and we were messing around a little on his bed. When I said I had to get home, it was late, he got mad and pushed me down and raped me. I wasn't really hurt, but I was forced to do something I didn't want to. But I couldn't see that anything would be gained by reporting it. (Authors' files)

Similar patterns of date rape were reported by Kanin (1969).

One of the primary problems of date rape is that many males believe the idea that women are so coy and illogical that "when they say no they mean maybe, and when they say maybe they mean yes." Thus, the male rejects his date's messages about sex partly because he wants to interpret them "his" way, rather than in their literal meaning. Furthermore, the male is often primed into forcing himself sexually on his date through the prior use of alcohol, which lowers his ordinary social inhibitions and may increase his sense of urgency to "score" and fulfill his "macho" self-image without recognizing that what he is doing is actually a form of criminal behavior. In addition, some men think they've paid for sex by picking up the tab on a date — they see women who refuse their sexual advances as backing down from their side of the bargain. Thus, one of the best ways of avoiding potential date rape situations is for women to be prepared to pay their own way and not drive anywhere with a man who has been drinking too much. Brownmiller (1975, p. 257) notes that date rapes "look especially bad for the victim in court, if they ever get to court."

Mate rapes are probably even more common but can be charged in only 12 states at present because rape laws generally exempt a husband from raping his wife on the assumption that their marriage provides firm evidence of her consent to sexual relations. It is interesting to note that marriage does not exempt people from conviction for other acts of physical violence against their spouse.

Marital rape is estimated to be a far more common form of family violence than had previously been realized. In one study, rape by a husband reportedly occurred more than twice as often as rape by a stranger, with one out of eight married women saying that they had been victimized in this manner (Russell, 1982). Other researchers suspect that the real incidence of mate rape is much higher, noting that many women are either unwilling to report being forced to have sex by their husbands or don't think of this as a "real" form of rape. While some cases of forced sex in marriage might not qualify as rape according to a court of law, in other instances the victim (usually, but not always, the wife) is beaten and battered or otherwise abused. A recent study of marital rape found that there is little evidence that wives who have been raped by their husbands provoke these assaults by refusing reasonable sexual requests. Instead, it ap-

---

RESEARCH SPOTLIGHT

Rape of Men by Women

To fully examine the spectrum of coercive sex, we must acknowledge that men can be rape victims, too. That males can be raped by other males — in the form of anal rape — has been reported as occurring in community settings (Groth and Burgess, 1980) and, more commonly, in prisons (Sagarin, 1976; Money, 1981; Scacco, 1982). Until very recently, however, not many realized that men could actually be raped by women.

Sarrel and Masters (1982) documented eleven cases in which men were sexually assaulted by women, including a number of cases in which the men were forced to have intercourse by the female rapists. Here are brief descriptions of several of these cases:

– A twenty-three-year-old medical student was tied up and then forced to have intercourse with a woman who threatened him with a scalpel.

– A thirty-seven-year-old white married man was forced to have intercourse by two black women who accosted him at gunpoint. The man was terrified during the entire experience.

– A twenty-seven-year-old truck driver who fell asleep in a motel with a woman he had just met in a bar awoke to find himself gagged, blindfolded, and tied to the bed. He was forced to have intercourse with four different women who threatened him with castration if he didn't perform properly – he could feel

---

Coercive Sex: The Varieties of Sexual Assault

peared that the husbands liked violent sex and used physical force to intimidate and control their wives (Frieze, 1983).

One of the most troublesome aspects of mate rape, of course, is that the victim not only must live with the memory of her traumatic experience but also must live with her rapist, never being sure when she will be assaulted again. One thirty-three-year-old woman thus described it:

> If he's mad at me, he loves to drag me into the bedroom and force me to have sex. It's a punishment session, he says. I learned a long time ago that physically resisting just goaded him on and left me bruised and bloody. So I don't fight back now, but I don't see how anyone could call this violence a form of making love. (Authors' files)

In addition to forcible rape, there is also a somewhat smaller category of *nonforcible rape*. Included here is *statutory rape*, defined as intercourse with a girl below the age of consent (even if she agreed to or initiated the sexual contact). While a woman could theoretically be charged with statutory rape, cases of intercourse between a woman and an underage boy are generally prosecuted under charges such as "contributing to the delinquency of a minor" or "carnal abuse." Also included in the category of nonforcible rape are rapes where the woman's capacity to consent is impaired because of mental illness or retardation, drugs or alcohol, or deceit. Other varieties of nonforcible rape involve some form of coercion: a blackmailer who extracts sexual payment,

---

the blade of the knife being held against his genitals – and he was held captive and repeatedly assaulted for more than twenty-four hours.

In many ways, of course, these cases mirror the circumstances in which women are raped by men. One of the more notable findings to emerge from these case examples is that even though these males were extremely frightened – indeed, in a near-panic state – they were still sexually responsive. This may shed some light on the fact that some women who are raped respond with signs of physical sexual arousal (e.g., vaginal lubrication, orgasm). In either case, the physical response does *not* mean

the victim is enjoying the experience – yet victims who respond physically during a sexual assault are apt to feel tremendous guilt.

Another similarity between male and female rape victims is that the males had a post-rape trauma reaction, and most of them also developed sexual difficulties after the traumatic sexual experience. Understandably, perhaps, given the lack of information on this type of rape, most of these victims also saw themselves as abnormal for responding in the circumstances of assault and thought of themselves as inadequate in their masculinity.

Because men who have been raped by women may be embarrassed by what happened to them

or convinced that the police won't believe their stories, few cases of this type of violent crime are ever reported. While some of these men seek treatment for ensuing sexual problems, others harbor their feelings of guilt and anguish, which is why we believe it is important for the public to become more aware of this form of sexual assault.

---

a professor who demands sex in return for a better grade, a sex therapist who "diagnoses" or "treats" his female patients by having sex with them, a prospective employer who makes it clear that a job offer depends on sexual submission.

Rape Victimology

Rape is an act of violence and humiliation in which the victim experiences overwhelming fear for her very existence as well as a profound sense of powerlessness and helplessness which few other events in one's life can parallel. (Hilberman, 1976, p. 437)

Rape is a crime against the person, not against the hymen. (Metzger, 1976, p. 406)

You have to stop being a victim of the rape. The person who raped you didn't do it for sexual pleasure; he did it to have power over you. And if you let him have power over you for the rest of your life, he's really won. A lot of women remain victims the rest of their lives. (Anonymous rape victim, quoted in the *St. Louis Globe-Democrat,* March 20, 1983)

According to FBI statistics, there were 82,000 forcible rapes reported in the United States in 1981 (FBI Uniform Crime Reports, 1982). Most researchers and law enforcement authorities believe that reported rapes are only a small fraction of actual rapes, so it is possible that the number of annual rapes is over one-half million (Brownmiller, 1975; Gager and Schurr, 1976; Nadelson, 1977). A recent estimate suggests that one woman in six will be the victim of an attempted rape in her lifetime and one in twenty-four will be the victim of a completed rape (Nelson, 1980). In light of these statistics, it is particularly important to understand the effects of rape on the victim.

MEDICAL CONSIDERATIONS

The rape victim, whether female or male, young or old, emotionally composed or in a terri-

fied state of shock and disbelief, needs careful medical attention. Physical injuries are common — and not always visible or obvious — and some are so serious that they present a life-threatening emergency.

In addition to the detection and treatment of physical injuries, the victim should be provided with information about testing for and possibly treating sexually transmitted diseases to which she or he may have been exposed. Female rape victims who could become pregnant should also undergo a pregnancy test and should be informed of the pregnancy prevention options available to them. These include the use of DES (diethylstilbestrol), insertion of an IUD (which prevents implantation), menstrual extraction, and abortion.

Finally, if the victim consents, the medical examination may be used to gather evidence for possible legal proceedings. For this reason, it is advisable that the woman not bathe or shower (or otherwise clean herself up) before being examined if she wants to report the rape to legal authorities.

LEGAL CONSIDERATIONS

For many rape victims, a major question is whether to report their rape to the police or not. While reporting a rape may seem logical, many women have hesitated or decided against it for any or all of the following reasons: (1) fear of retribution by the rapist who may get out on bail; (2) an attitude of futility — "the police probably won't catch him, and even if they do, he'll probably get off"; (3) fear of publicity and embarrassment; (4) fear of being mistreated by the police or trial lawyers; (5) pressure from a family member against reporting; and (6) occasionally, unwillingness to ruin a friend or relative's life by sending him to prison. In addition, the victim of a date rape may be afraid of facing the adverse judgment of mutual friends if she reports the in-

Rape and Self-Defense

A woman who is approached by a man threatening to rape her must make several quick decisions. She can scream, try to run, fight the attacker, or use a weapon. She can passively endure the attack, hoping she won't antagonize the rapist into seriously injuring her. Or she can use psychological ploys and tell him she is pregnant, menstruating, or has a contagious disease.

No course of action guarantees a safe result. Some rape victims chose a passive response which angered the rapist to further physical violence. Some victims who tried to defend themselves with a weapon had that weapon turned against them. Psychological ploys may not be believed and may cause the rapist to punish the woman for lying.

Recent studies funded by the National Center for the Prevention and Control of Rape found that women who fought back by kicking, screaming, hitting, biting, and attempting to flee had the greatest chance of escaping their attacker and were less likely to be seriously injured. In the first study, 94 women from the Chicago area who had been approached by

Self-defense classes are offered nationwide to teach women to defend themselves from attack.

attackers were interviewed. Fifty-one of them had escaped the attack without harm (Bart, 1980). In the second study, 320 rape attempts were analyzed of which 120 of the women were able to flee (McIntyre, 1980). Bart and McIntyre found that resistance did not increase the risk of serious bodily harm but did increase the risk of minor injuries such as bruises and black eyes. The assailant's possession of a weapon was of minor importance in determining the outcome of the rape attempt, but the women who escaped tended to be taller and heavier than those who were raped (*St. Louis Globe-Democrat*, "Fighting Back," 1 December 1980).

Resistance need not be confined to physical measures after the attack has begun. Verbal assertiveness or verbal aggression when a woman is initially approached may deter the attack (Warner, 1980). Rape centers in many cities train women in awareness and preparation for a possible attack to help decrease a woman's panic during an actual attempt. Another possible deterrent is for the woman to repulse her attacker by forcing herself to vomit, urinate, or defecate. Pretending to faint when being forced toward a car or an abandoned area can cause a sufficient delay for the attacker to give up and leave. Of course, attempting any or all of these defensive behaviors may not work, and the woman may still wind up being raped despite her efforts to escape the situation.

Lists of general safety tips are available through many police sexual assault units and through local rape centers. Some groups are opposed to these suggestions since they can encourage a woman to live in fear, installing extra locks on doors and windows, never walking alone at night, and staying very alert to (and perhaps anxious about) her surroundings. Many people feel the solution to rape is *not* for every woman to change her lifestyle but in encouraging our society to reexamine the values that seem to give rise to many rapes and other violent crimes.

Here are a few common sense tips which we hope will increase awareness – not fear:

1. Don't rely on a door chain for identification of strangers.
2. Don't advertise living alone. You can put a fictitious name on your mailbox or use only your first initial and last name so strangers will not know you are female and living alone.
3. Have the key to your auto or home in hand before reaching the door so you can make a quick entrance.
4. If accosted yell "FIRE!" instead of "HELP!" because the word "fire" will draw more attention (Warner, 1980).
5. Aerosol cans of a chemical irritant (such as Mace or deodorant) should not be solely relied on for protection. The attack may happen too quickly to find and use the spray (Boston Women's Health Book Collective, 1976). Whistles suffer from the same drawback and in a noisy area they might not be heard.
6. Self-defense classes in the martial arts are often of limited benefit to the average person. Classes tend to be expensive and can take years of training to attain proficiency. Even when skilled in techniques such as judo or karate, a person who is attacked by surprise may be too flustered to employ these to advantage. Nevertheless, overall physical conditioning is recommended (Warner, 1980).

cident, and victims of marital rape may fear the social and economic consequences if their husband is convicted and sent to jail.

These concerns are, by and large, founded in fact. In the past, police often scoffed at a woman's story and asked humiliating questions like "Did you enjoy it?" or "Do you like sex a lot?" As Gager and Schurr (1976, p. 68) comment, "Such questions have little to do with finding the rapist and much more with human curiosity or satisfying the officers' vicarious sexual urges." Similarly, in many instances a report of rape never gets to trial, even if the rapist is identified — the district attorney can simply decide that the case is unfounded or unprovable (Brownmiller, 1975; Gager and Schurr, 1976).

Even when reporting a rape leads to identification and arrest of a suspect, the trial itself may be an anguishing ordeal for the victim. Typically, the woman is made to feel that *she* is on trial rather than the accused man. The defense lawyer may try to show that she consented to sexual activity; if she waited for more than a few hours to report the rape, her motivation and truthfulness may be questioned; if she showered or changed her clothes, there may be insufficient evidence; and in some instances, her past sexual behavior may be questioned on the presumption that a woman with many sexual partners is likely to have consented rather than have been raped (Slovenko, 1973; Brownmiller, 1975).

Fortunately, there have been some major advances in police investigations of rape cases (Moody and Hayes, 1980) as well as in the legal process (Lasater, 1980). In many states, for example, it is no longer permissible for a defense attorney to introduce the woman's past sexual behavior into the trial and women are not required to "prove" that they attempted to resist the rape by signs of physical injury. Police have also generally improved their sensitivity toward dealing with rape victims. In most American cities, police departments now have specially trained teams for dealing with victims of sexual assault.

One additional point should be noted about legal aspects of rape. Although a criminal case can only be filed and prosecuted by the city, county, or state, the rape victim herself may choose to file a civil action in which she sues her assailant for personal injury, pain and suffering, or punitive damages. In a civil suit, unlike criminal proceedings, the woman can hire her own attorney. In addition, since civil proceedings require that the suspect be proven guilty only by "a preponderance of evidence" rather than the more stringent standard of guilt used in criminal proceedings ("beyond a reasonable doubt"), there may be a greater likelihood of winning the case (Grossman and Sutherland, 1982/83). However, a civil suit will not succeed in putting even a convicted rapist in prison: it will only obtain a monetary judgment.

THE AFTERMATH OF RAPE

The psychological impact of rape can be profound from the first moments of the attack and for years afterward. The rape victim reacts with a sense of isolation, helplessness, and total loss of self (Metzger, 1976; Hilberman, 1978). How the victim handles the severe stress of this crisis usually falls into a recognizable pattern (Sutherland and Scherl, 1970; Burgess and Holmstrom, 1974; Notman and Nadelson, 1976; Warner, 1980).

The *acute reaction phase* usually lasts for a few days to a few weeks. The victim typically reacts with shock, fear, disbelief, and emotional turmoil. Guilt, shame, anger, and outrage are commonly seen in those women who are able to talk about their feelings. Other women, who adopt a more controlled style, have an apparent calmness that may indicate that they are forcing an attitude of control or are denying the reality or impact of the experience.

This phase is usually followed by a *post-traumatic "recoil" phase* which can last weeks or months. The victim undergoes a limited degree of coming to grips with herself and her situation. Superficially, she may seem to be over the experience. She tries to relate to her family and friends. She returns to her everyday activities and tries to be cheerful and relaxed. But deep down inside, she has not really grappled with her fears, her self-doubts, and her feelings about the experience.

The final phase, a *long-term regrowth and recovery process,* varies considerably depending on the victim's age, personality, available support systems, and how she is treated by others. Frightening flashbacks and nightmares are common. Fears about being alone, suspicious men, and sexual activity surface with distressing frequency. Proper counseling or psychotherapy may be needed to deal with these fears and the depression that often occurs.

One recent study of women interviewed an average of twenty-two months after being raped found that three-quarters of the women reported changes in their lives that they directly attributed to the rape experience (Nadelson et al., 1982). Almost half of the women reported some form of fear, anxiety, or symptoms of depression; many also had trouble sleeping, feelings of vulnerability, and fear of walking alone, even during the day. The most common symptom still present almost two years after the rape was a generalized suspiciousness of others.

After a rape, some women avoid any type of involvement with men in sexual or social situations. Other women take just the opposite approach, with mixed results.

> After I was raped, I had intercourse with my husband as a ritual gesture. (I had learned as a child to get back on my bike after falling, lest I never mount again.) Intercourse was easy. It didn't matter. I was an abandoned house. Vacated. Anyone or anything could enter. (Metzger, 1976, p. 406)

Women who have been raped may face a number of sexual problems as a consequence (Masters and Johnson, 1970; Becker et al., 1983). Sexual aversion or vaginismus are the most dramatic responses to the trauma of rape, but other women have difficulty with decreased sexual desire, impaired vaginal lubrication, loss of genital sensations, pain during intercourse, and anorgasmia (Kolodny, Masters, and Johnson, 1979). One study indicates that even though rape victims may have the same *frequency* of sexual activity one year after their rape as nonraped women, their sexual satisfaction is significantly reduced (Feldman-Summers, Gordon, and Meagher, 1979). Another study found that more than half of a group of women who were victims of either rape or incest had post-assault sexual dysfunctions, with fear of sex, lowered sexual desire, and difficulty becoming sexually aroused accounting for the majority of problems (Becker et al., 1983). The husband or sexual partner of the rape victim may also encounter sexual difficulties. Erectile dysfunction is not unusual, and *his* sexual desire may be affected by anger or disgust.

The male partner of a rape victim often experiences a psychological crisis, too, in which shock, blame, and a sense of guilt emerge (Orzek, 1983). This may cause him to become overprotective or to try to take charge of the legal and medical decisions that his partner faces. In some instances, the male may become preoccupied with thoughts of vengeance as a means of dealing with his own turmoil and discomfort. In other cases, the male may try to show that his love for his partner is still intact by pushing for sexual intimacy, not recognizing that the woman needs to be the one to decide — based on her own feelings and reactions, and not his — when to resume sexual activity (Burgess and Holmstrom, 1979).

What is most helpful is a willingness on the male's part to allow for open communication,

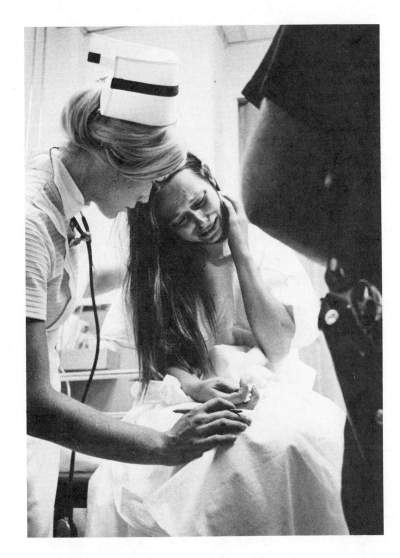

A distraught rape victim at the hospital emergency room. Many hospital personnel and police officers have undergone special training in sensitively assisting victims in such cases.

giving his partner a chance to express her anger, anxieties, or other feelings in an atmosphere of acceptance and empathy. This openness should also include his being able to accept her silence, if that is what she requires. In addition, if the couple has children, they also will be likely to sense that something significant has happened. As Grossman and Sutherland (1982/83, p. 32) point out: "What children imagine is usually more frightening to them than knowing the facts. It is helpful if they are given the opportunity to deal with their feelings."

As the couple adjusts to the post-rape period, the male may benefit from counseling, too. In fact, the long-term process of recovery from rape often can be facilitated by counseling for the couple, since there is some evidence that in stable, committed relationships, the male is a

Rape

prime source of support for his partner (Crenshaw, 1978; Orzek, 1983).

How a rape victim resolves all of these problems is not well understood at present. For many, the counseling experience provides a useful opportunity for working through feelings of anger, worthlessness, depression, or fear. Others seem to handle things most comfortably on their own; although until more information is available, it is not certain that their adjustment is as satisfactory.

The Rapist

Information about men who commit rape almost exclusively depends upon studies of convicted rapists. The information obtained from these studies cannot be applied to all rapists because the less intelligent, less affluent rapist is most likely to be arrested and found guilty. Many of these studies are also done many months or even years after the rape was committed, and the rapist may not be accurate in recalling the details of his act.

Summarizing findings from a number of sources (Amir, 1971; Rada, 1978; Groth, 1979; Wolfe and Baker, 1980), it is possible to outline some general facts about convicted rapists:

- Eighty-five percent have a prior criminal record.
- Eighty percent never completed high school.
- Seventy-five percent are under thirty years old.
- Seventy percent are unmarried.
- Seventy percent are strangers to their victims.
- Sixty percent are members of racial minorities.
- Fifty percent were drinking heavily or drunk when they committed the rape.
- Thirty-five percent have previously been convicted of rape.

However, convicted rapists are not all alike.

Their motivations for raping vary considerably, and their methods of finding a victim, overpowering her, and sexually tormenting her are not the same.

In some cases, the rapist methodically commits a long string of carefully planned assaults. Such rapists are not always deranged outcasts from society: in 1983, for example, Dr. Edward F. Jackson, a respected practicing physician and hospital board member, was convicted of twenty-one rapes over a seven-year period and pleaded guilty to an additional fifteen rapes in a separate case (*Facts on File*, November 18, 1983, pp. 879-880). Jackson, who had kept a list in his car of the names of the women he had assaulted and the dates of his attacks, was sentenced to 191 to 665 years in prison. The much-publicized case of Ted Bundy, a one-time law student who was convicted of the rape and murder of a number of women, also shows how "respectable" some rapists may seem (Michaud and Aynesworth, 1983).

Other rapists act impulsively, with no apparent premeditation of their act. In Colton, California, a forty-year-old man who discovered four teenage boys raping a twelve-year-old girl in a shed in his backyard "apparently got in line and participated," according to police (*The New York Times*, March 23, 1983). And, in a case that received major national publicity in 1983, a twenty-one-year-old woman who stopped in a bar in New Bedford, Massachusetts, for some cigarettes and a drink was grabbed by a group of men and brutally raped for several hours while the bar's other patrons stood by watching, laughing, and cheering without attempting to call the police (*The New York Times*, March 17, 1983).

One of the key advances of the last decade in studying rapists has been the realization that rapists are not oversexed men and that rape is usually an expression of power or anger and not an act of sexual desire (Burgess and Holmstrom, 1974; Brownmiller, 1975; Hilberman, 1976; Groth, Burgess, and Holmstrom, 1977). Notably,

476

most rapists do not lack available sexual partners (Groth, 1979). This is not to say that rape has no sexual meaning or motivation; in most rapes, however, the aggressive components are so predominant that the sexuality of the act becomes secondary (Tollison and Adams, 1979).

Groth, Burgess, and Holmstrom (1977) — a psychologist, nurse, and sociologist — studied 133 rapists and 92 rape victims to better understand the dynamics of the rape situation. They found that forcible rape could be classified as either power rape or anger rape. None of their rape cases showed sex as the dominant motive. According to these researchers, *power rape* occurs when the rapist tries to intimidate his victim by using a weapon, physical force, and threats of bodily harm. The power rapist is usually awkward in interpersonal relationships and feels inadequate as a person. Rape becomes a way for him to reassure himself about his strength, identity, and sexual adequacy.

In *anger rape*, the rapist brutalizes his victim and expresses rage and hatred by physical assault and verbal abuse. The motive behind this type of rape is often revenge and punishment against women in general and not the victim specifically. The anger rapist usually gets little or no sexual satisfaction from the rape and may have difficulty getting an erection or being able to ejaculate with his victim.

Groth, Burgess, and Holmstrom later described a third pattern, *sadistic rape,* where sexuality and aggression are fused together and the suffering of the victim is the primary source of the rapist's satisfaction (Groth, 1979). The victim of a sadistic rape may be tortured or deliberately injured by cigarette burns, bites, or whipping. Sex murders, with grotesque mutilations of the victim's body, are extreme cases of sadistic rape. Groth (1979) estimates that about 5 percent of rapes are sadistic rapes, 40 percent are anger rapes, and 55 percent power rapes.

Two separate studies shed additional light on the psychological makeup of the rapist (Abel et al., 1977; Barbaree, Marshall, and Lanthier, 1979). In each study, a group of rapists was compared to a group of nonrapists in terms of erection measurements while listening to taped descriptions of rape and of mutually consenting sexual scenes. Both studies showed that rapists developed erections while listening to descriptions of rape, but nonrapists did not. In response to descriptions of mutually consenting intercourse, the erection responses of rapists and nonrapists were similar. Interestingly, the rapists did not show greater sexual arousal to forced or violent sex than to consenting sex. These findings suggest that nonrapists may have internal controls, such as fear or empathy for the victim, that inhibit their sexual arousal to descriptions of rape situations, while rapists either lack such internal controls or have learned to overcome them. It should be noted, however, that these studies involved only a small group of rapists, and it is uncertain if these findings apply more widely.

It is also not clear if the patterns described above apply to the motivations and dynamics of date rape. In this situation — which may actually be the most common form of rape — the sexual anticipation component may be a primary factor, although the power issue is also involved. Further research is required in this area.

Male Sexual Dysfunction During Rape

A fascinating study of 170 convicted rapists showed that sexual dysfunction during rape attempts is a frequent occurrence (Groth and Burgess, 1977). After eliminating 69 cases where no data were available or where an evaluation of sexual function was inapplicable because of successful resistance by the victim, an interrupted assault, or no attempt made at penile penetration, 101 cases were left. Of these cases, erectile difficulties occurred in 27 men, premature ejaculation occurred in 5 men, and ejaculatory incompetence was seen in 26 cases.

These findings have two important implications. First, they confirm the view that rape is not primarily an act of sexual desire. Fifty-eight percent of the rapists in this study were sexually *dysfunctional,* indicating that either desire or arousal had gone awry. Ejaculatory incompetence is a particularly infrequent male dysfunction in the general population, and its high rate of occurrence in rapists may signify that their preoccupation with expressing power or anger inhibits their sexual responsiveness. Second, a very practical point arises from this study. In some rape cases, the woman's testimony has been discredited if no sperm were detected on her body. Now two new findings will prove useful in prosecuting rapists who in the past may have been acquitted — many men do not ejaculate during a rape and others may ejaculate prematurely before touching their victim.

Treatment of the Rapist

Since rape is a crime, rather than a medical diagnosis, most convicted rapists are sent to prison. Often, there is little attempt at rehabilitating the rapist; instead, the prison term is regarded purely and simply as punishment. Given this practice, it is not surprising that approximately three-quarters of convicted rapists become repeat offenders.

Various past attempts to provide psychological counseling to men convicted of rape have not improved the situation very much. One of the problems with these "psychotherapy only" programs has been that they have not succeeded, by and large, in quelling the inner compulsion to rape that some of the rapists claim they feel. Recently, this has been approached (in a limited number of cases) by the combined use of the drug medroxyprogesterone acetate (MPA; also known by its trade name, Depo-Provera) and

psychotherapy. The use of MPA results in a sizeable reduction in circulating testosterone, which in turn causes a marked drop in the man's sex drive. This enables psychotherapists to be more effective in helping a man to reorient his sexual and aggressive impulses, although the effect is a temporary one that lasts only for as long as the drug is taken.

Dr. Fred Berlin of Johns Hopkins University, who has pioneered in the use of MPA for rapists and other sex offenders, states that 17 out of 20 men treated with this drug were able to self-regulate their sexual behavior while receiving the medication (*American Medical News,* August 26, 1983). However, almost all of the men who stopped taking the drug subsequently relapsed, and it is not as yet clear how this experimental treatment could be monitored effectively even if it ultimately proves useful. Another, more compelling criticism is that MPA is hardly the answer to what is basically a crime of violence. Since there is no guarantee that MPA will prevent a man from functioning sexually, nor that it would reduce a rapist's hostility toward women, it is even possible that the use of MPA might make some rapists more hostile, and thus more likely to break the law, than they may have been before. In any event, it is clear that more information is required on the long-term effectiveness of the use of MPA in treating rapists before this method will be widely accepted.

INCEST

Incest (from the Latin word for "impure" or "soiled") refers to sexual activity between a person and a close relative, such as a parent, a brother or sister, a grandparent, or an uncle or aunt. Although brother-sister incest is probably most common, most cases of incest reported to the authorities involve an adult-child interaction. Therefore, we will discuss this form of incest in most detail. All states require the reporting of such cases of suspected incest under child abuse laws, with the underlying assumption that a child is unable to consent in a meaningful way to a sexual interaction with an adult.

The incidence of incest can only be guessed at since reported cases make up only a small fraction of the overall number. Estimates suggest that perhaps 50,000 children are abused sexually by their parents or guardians each year (Finkelhor, 1978; Burgess et al., 1978; Summit and Kryso, 1978), with an even larger number victims of rape or molestation at the hands of other family members. In one study, in 32 percent of rapes involving children, the offender was a relative (Peters, 1976).

Research on incest has been plagued by the limitations of working with clinical samples (those seeking treatment) or samples drawn from prisons. One distortion that this has introduced is the idea that father-daughter incest is the most frequent pattern. In reality, father-daughter incest seems to be far less common than brother-sister incest, but sexual activity between siblings is almost never reported or brought into treatment. The Playboy Foundation survey (Hunt, 1975) found that about 4 percent of men and women had ever had sexual contact with a sibling, but only 0.5 percent of the women had sexual contact with their fathers and an even smaller percent of men described participation in parent-child sex. The Kinsey surveys (1948, 1953) also found that brother-sister incest was far more common than parent-child sexual relations. Recent data from a sex-therapy clinic confirm this finding (Renshaw, 1983).

Myths About Incest

Several myths about incest continue to be widely believed. The origins of these myths are not entirely clear but they continue to influence people's thinking about incest.

Myth: *Incest occurs primarily in poor, uneducated families.*

Fact: Incest is not bound by family wealth or education. While incest in middle-class or well-to-do families may be handled privately without being reported to the courts or social agencies, solid evidence shows that families in all walks of life can be affected (Meiselman, 1978).

Myth: *Incest is usually committed by a father who is a sexual degenerate.*

Fact: Most studies show that fathers who commit incest are neither "oversexed" nor fixated on children as sex objects (Gebhard et al., 1965; Finkelhor, 1979).

Myth: *Claims of incest by a child are usually made up.*

Fact: This myth can be traced back to Freud who suggested that reports of sexual activity with a parent were actually based on fantasies due to Oedipal desires (Peters, 1976). Unfortunately, most children's reports of incest — no matter how shocking and unbelievable they may seem — are likely to be true.

Patterns of Incest

Incest occurs in a wide variety of forms, and it would be foolish to regard them all as equivalent. Some cases of incest, for example, are one-time occurrences producing so much guilt or anxiety for either participant that they are never repeated. Other cases involve long-term interactions in which both parties seem to be interested (with no physical force used), one party is overtly coerced and terrorized, or multiple incest occurs, as when a father molests several daughters.

Other variables to consider when defining the incest situation include the child's age at the outset of the relationship, the openness or secrecy of the activities, the types of sexual activity involved, and the impact of the interaction on family dynamics. Often, the incest behavior begins as a kind of teasing, playful activity with prolonged kissing, wrestling, and surreptitious genital touching. Over time, these activities can develop into overt genital sexuality, without any physical force being used.

> Commonly, the daughter is made to feel that the father and mother's happiness, their love for her, and the stability of the family rests on her willingness and her silence. Unlike many other forms of sexual abuse, incest often leads to very complex, ambiguous feelings in the daughter. It is not uncommon for the daughter to experience some sexual pleasure and a feeling of importance and power in her family. Often these feelings are intertwined with negative feelings such as sexual displeasure, pain, and guilt. (Gottlieb, 1980, pp. 122-123)

At other times, incest begins abruptly and forcefully. The father may be drunk or may have had a vicious argument with his wife, or decides to use sex to "punish" his daughter or to "teach her what she needs to know." The child is likely to fight back and may be physically injured.

Interestingly, most men who become involved in incest are shy, conventional, and devoted to their families (Summit and Kryso, 1978; Meiselman, 1978). Their wives, who were often themselves the victims of sexual abuse as children, tend to be dependent, disenchanted women who withdraw from the family either through depression or outside diversions (Summit and Kryso, 1978; Gottlieb, 1980). The mother may actually force the daughter into assuming her role, relieved at having the daughter as a "buffer" between her and her husband and sometimes pleased to no longer have to deal with her husband's sexual advances (Browning and Boatman, 1977; Herman and Hirschman, 1977; Meiselman, 1978). Even after incest is discovered by a mother, in more than two-thirds of cases she does not try to help or protect her child

(Stoenner, 1972; Herman and Hirschman, 1977). Yet the mother is not the primary culprit in most cases of incest: she may be defenseless to stop her husband, unable to control her daughter, fearful of her husband's physical retaliation, and worried about having her family break up if her husband is put in jail.

Recent evidence has begun to show that incest is particularly common in reconstituted families, those in which remarriage occurs after divorce or the death of a spouse (Sager et al., 1983; Renshaw, 1983). Statistics gathered by researcher Diana Russell support this view: in interviews of 930 San Francisco women Russell found that only one out of forty was sexually abused by her biological father, but one out of six reared in reconstituted families had been sexually abused by a stepfather (*Sexuality Today*, Vol. 7, No. 1, October 24, 1983). The explanation for this difference may be that there is less of an incest taboo between non-blood relatives. In addition, in many reconstituted families the stepfather is thrust into close daily contact with an adolescent stepdaughter, a situation possibly contributing to sexual arousal. Lacking proper internal controls that ordinarily arise from the protectiveness of parenting a child from infancy on, the new father may find less to prevent such arousal from being translated into behavior. In fact, it appears that in at least some instances men have married divorced women primarily so they could gain sexual access to their children (Schwartz, 1983).

There is almost no research information available on brother-sister incest. Reported cases usually involve an older brother (in his late teens or early twenties) and a considerably younger sister (Gebhard et al., 1965), but most cases probably involve siblings who are close in age (Finkelhor, 1980). The brother is usually the dominant partner in sibling incest (Meiselman, 1978), but we have seen almost a dozen cases where the reverse relationship was true. Although most cases of brother-sister incest seem to involve mutual consent, in a few instances one sibling blackmails the other into providing sexual gratification, as shown by this description of her experiences given to us by a twenty-six-year-old woman:

> When I was fourteen, my older brother (who was sixteen) found out that I was doing drugs. Apparently he snuck around for awhile and got a whole set of "evidence" together, and then he confronted me with it one night when our folks were at a movie. He told me I had two choices: either give him a blow-job, or he'd tell my parents what I was doing.

A recent survey of 796 college students found that of those who reported sibling incest experiences (15 percent of females and 10 percent of males), one-fourth of the experiences were categorized as exploitive (Finkelhor, 1980).

Mother-son incest is rare. In one sample of 203 cases of incest in the nuclear family (that is, mother, father, and children — not other relatives), only two cases of mother-son sexual activity were described (Weinberg, 1955). According to Meiselman (1978, pp. 299-300), "In the great majority of reported cases in which the son initiates incest with his mother, the son is schizophrenic or severely disturbed in some other way prior to incest." In cases of mother-initiated incest, the mother is usually psychologically disturbed. Mother-son incest typically involves genital fondling without intercourse if the child is young, but with boys over age ten, coitus is the most typical activity.

Mother-daughter incest seems to be the rarest form of nuclear family sex. While father-son incest is encountered more frequently, it too is exceptionally rare and accounts for less than one percent of cases overall.

In an effort to prevent child molestation, Senator Paula Hawkins of Florida revealed that she herself was a victim of sexual abuse as a child.

The Aftermath of Incest

Most researchers and clinicians agree that incest is an intensely damaging psychological experience. It can lead to drug abuse, prostitution, suicide attempts, and a host of other problems (Herman and Hirschman, 1977; Meiselman, 1978). One research team concisely summarizes this viewpoint:

> There is a striking similarity in the reported reactions of incest participants: The children take over the responsibility and the blame from the initiating parent. The betrayal of parental responsibilities and the failure of responsible adults leads the child to feel he or she is fundamentally bad and unworthy of care or help. Sexuality, tainted with guilt and fear, becomes exaggerated as the only acknowledged aspect of attraction or power. (Summit and Kryso, 1978, pp. 248-249)

Perhaps the most striking, but not surprising, finding in incest victims is the long-term persistence of a variety of sexual problems (Masters and Johnson, 1970; McGuire and Wagner, 1978; Meiselman, 1978). Sexual difficulties usually bring an adult woman into psychotherapy, where she finally is able to reveal a childhood incest situation ten to twenty years after the fact. In many cases, the woman has been unable to form close, intimate, trusting relationships with men because she expects betrayal, rejection, or punishment (Summit and Kryso, 1978).

There are a few studies, however, that suggest that incest victims may not be harmed by their experience and can become healthy, well-adjusted adults (Bender and Blau, 1937; Yorukoglu and Kemph, 1966). If such cases exist in any numbers, they would be the last to be identified or reported by traditional means. Nevertheless, it seems likely that an incestuous relationship between an adult and a child will create major conflicts for the child, even if these are eventually overcome. In addition, and perhaps of even more importance, is the fact that even in cases where incest has no demonstrably harmful effects on the child, it is still morally wrong because the child is not capable of truly giving a free and informed consent to such behavior. As Finkelhor (1979) points out, children are not knowledgeable enough about sexuality and its personal and social meanings to give a valid consent to sexual contact with an adult; furthermore, children don't have the freedom, either legally or psychologically, to give a meaningful consent to such behavior. While these remarks do not apply to cases of adult-adult incest, we believe that adults are morally and ethically bound to refuse to have sexual contacts with children and that failure to follow this ethical imperative should be regarded as an act of serious consequences.

SEXUAL HARASSMENT AT WORK

Many women who work outside the home have been victimized by another sort of sexual coercion. Although sexual harassment at work is less shocking to most people than rape or incest, it is a social problem of considerable size. Traditionally joked about or viewed as trivial, it has now become an important issue of sex discrimination in both a legal and practical sense. Although there has been relatively little research on the subject, cases of male sexual harassment at work have also come into view.

Sexual harassment at work can appear in a number of different forms. One version is in the attempt to seek employment. Here, the prospective employer makes it clear that hiring the applicant depends on her sexual availability — and a "sample" is requested as a sign of "good faith." Jokes about the "Hollywood casting couch" as a means for aspiring starlets to gain entry to the world of entertainment are based on fact. Even

If You Have Ever Been Involved in Incest

Reading about incest can stir up old, hidden memories for anyone who has been involved in sexual contact with a relative. The descriptions of incest presented here may or may not match your own feelings and experiences; for example, you might be surprised to learn that others were harmed by such involvement if you never felt you were, or you might not have realized that incest is illegal. Certainly, no two people cope with an incest experience in exactly the same way. However, since current studies show that many people who were involved in incest as children never told anyone about their situation and have residual feelings of guilt, resentment, anger, or poor self-esteem that seem to be linked to the incest experience, it may be helpful to consider the following options.

Some people feel completely comfortable with a "forgive and forget" attitude and have no desire to talk about this topic with anyone. Others who feel they were in consensual, nonexploitive incest relationships may not even see a need to forgive or forget, since they may view the entire experience as a positive one.

On the other hand, people with a background of incest who are having sexual problems or difficulty forming intimate relationships are likely to benefit from professional help in dealing with these issues. Even though the incest may have occurred decades ago, even if it was a single episode rather than a recurring pattern, consulting a psychologist, psychiatrist, social worker, or sex therapist can help you determine whether counseling on this issue can help. In fact, in these circumstances many people discover that the opportunity to bring the incest experience and their long-range reactions to it out in the open is a key step in gaining more control over their lives.

If you fall in between these two groups – those who are most comfortable leaving things as they are and those who seek professional help – there are two other options you can also consider:

1. Some incest victims have felt tremendous relief in confronting the person who initiated the incest behavior years later, in adulthood, to explain how they felt and to obtain an acknowledgement or even an apology. This approach can help you feel more in control and less a victim, but it can backfire if you let your anger drown out all your other feelings, or if the person you confront denies your accusations or even asserts that *you* initiated the sexual contact.

2. Short of confrontation, which may not always be possible (for instance, if the other person has died or is mentally incapacitated), it can be helpful to confide in someone else – a spouse, sibling, parent, lover, best friend, or member of the clergy, for example – so that you're not forced to bottle up your feelings and carry around this burdensome "secret" for the rest of your life. In many instances, the very act of disclosure to someone you trust can be a tremendous relief. But only you can judge whether you are comfortable with this approach.

One other aspect of incest should be mentioned here. If your child ever tells you that he or she has been approached sexually by a family member, do *not* dismiss it as a "misunderstanding" or something that the child "imagined." Realize that younger children usually won't have a vocabulary to describe just what happened – so they may say something like, "Uncle Joe was trying to do funny things to me." All children should be taught that they have the right to say "No" to adults who ask them to do something they don't want to do; they should also know that any form of genital contact with adults is strictly off limits.

with far less glamorous jobs, the person doing the hiring has economic power to assist him in making such a request. To a woman who has been unable to find a job and needs to support her family, economic realities may make giving in the simplest and most logical thing to do.

A more common situation for sexual harassment occurs when a boss or supervisor makes sexual compliance a condition for keeping a job, getting a promotion, or obtaining other work-related benefits. Again, the person who does the hiring and firing has economic power. The coercion is even stronger than the pre-employment situation because if the woman is fired for her unwillingness to cooperate sexually, her boss will have to make up a reason "for the record," and this may hurt her chances for future employment. In some situations, the request for sexual interaction is direct, blatant, and threatening. In other cases, while the sexual invitation may be direct, the threat is unspoken — the woman is left to decide what will happen to her if she refuses to play along.

Sexual harassment can occur in virtually any setting (Brewer, 1982). A recent survey of nurses found that more than 60 percent had experienced sexual harassment in the preceding year (Duldt, 1982), and surveys of female law students, medical students, and military personnel have also reported alarmingly high rates of sexual harassment. A survey of twenty thousand federal employees found that 42 percent of the women and 15 percent of the men reported having been sexually harassed at work in the preceding 24 months (Tangri, Burt, and Johnson, 1982). In many places little significance is attached to this issue and victims have no formal path for voicing grievances or having a full investigation con-

Mrs. Phyllis Schlafly, president of the Eagle Forum—a conservative organization opposed to most feminist goals—told a U.S. Senate Labor subcommittee in April 1981 that women who are sexually harassed at work usually bring it on themselves by their bearing or behavior. "Virtuous women," she testified, "are seldom accosted by unwelcome sexual propositions or familiarities, obscene talk or profane language." Mrs. Schlafly's opinionated testimony provoked a considerable furor, with many newspaper editorials decrying her insensitive view.

484

Child Pornography

The most recent variety of sexual abuse of children to attract national attention has been the use of children in the production of pornographic photographs, movies, or videotapes. While the number of children involved in such activities is unknown, it is certain that thousands are exploited in this fashion every year. In some instances, very young children apparently have no idea they are posing for pornographic purposes – they may actually be posed with teddy bears or dolls. In other cases, what begins as nude modeling quickly escalates to posing in nude scenes staged to resemble sexual activity to finally enacting "live" sex so that movies can be shot or photographs can become more realistic. The allure of payment for such work is usually the principal motivating factor, but in some cases "cooperation" is obtained by threats, blackmail, or kidnapping.

There are also cases where an adolescent seeks out a chance to "be in the movies," where not only the money but the thirst for adventure and "stardom" comes into play.

Many of the "stars" and "starlets" for such productions come from the ranks of the estimated 700,000 to one million children who run away from home each year (Baker, 1980). Usually, the runaway child has no realistic plan of survival and only limited financial resources; lacking friends, family, lodging, and the ordinary restraints of everyday routine, such children are perfect victims for the porn recruiters and pimps who prowl bus depots and hamburger stands looking for their victims. In addition to money, drugs are often provided as enticement or pay.

The effects of participation in child pornography are serious and lasting. A psychoanalyst warns, "Children who pose ... begin to see themselves as objects to be sold. They cut off their feelings of affection, finally responding like objects rather than people" (*Time*, April 4, 1977, p. 56). As with other victims of sexual coercion, they are prone to sexual problems as adults. Worst of all is that "sexually exploited children tend to become sexual exploiters of children themselves as adults" (Baker, 1980, p. 304).

Recently, a government report recommended the following legislative steps to combat the problem of child pornography:

1. Require film processors and laboratories that receive what appears to be child pornography to turn the material over to local law enforcement bodies or to the State's attorney.
2. Require photographers wishing to film a child nude or semi-nude to receive and maintain possession of a signed release from the child's parent or guardian authorizing such photography.
3. Amend the civil code to provide for licensing of all children used in commercial modeling or performing, with carefully worded prescriptions and substantial sanctions against the use of such children in sexually explicit activities. (General Accounting Office, 1982)

ducted, although some employers have issued directives to combat this problem. The U.S. Navy, for example, has ordered commanders to deal with sexual harassment with "swift and appropriate" discipline (*The New York Times*, December 30, 1982, p. 7). Because there are few, if any, effective safeguards against reprisal, however, the victim of sexual harassment may have too much to lose to report the problem.

According to Catherine MacKinnon, a lawyer who has written the most detailed book on the subject, when a woman refuses the sexual advances of her boss, retaliation may come in any number of ways. She may be demoted or have her salary cut, unfavorable reports may be put in her personal file, she may be denied requests for vacations, she may be passed over for promotion, she may be given tedious or unpleasant assignments, or her work conditions may be made undesirable (MacKinnon, 1979). In the last category,

> She may be constantly felt or pinched, visually undressed and stared at, surreptitiously kissed, commented upon, manipulated into being found alone, and generally taken advantage of at work — but never promised or denied anything explicitly connected with her job. . . . Never knowing if it will even stop or if escalation is imminent, a woman can put up with it or leave. . . . Most women are coerced into tolerance. (MacKinnon, 1979, p. 40)

Although a survey by *Redbook* in 1976 answered by more than 9,000 working women revealed that almost nine out of ten experienced some form of sexual harassment at work, the impact of this type of sexual coercion has only been studied to a limited degree. The experience seems to be a degrading, humiliating one in which the woman usually feels a sense of helplessness similar to the feeling reported by rape victims (Safran, 1976). As one woman explained:

> I'd heard before about women being told to "put out or get out." But when my boss, who was my father's age, tried to get me to sleep with him, I

thought at first it was a nice compliment. Nothing too shocking, and something I assumed would pass. I wasn't prepared for his change in behavior. Suddenly, nothing I did was right. I was constantly pressured to change my mind. He began to grab at me, and one day he pulled me down on his lap. I felt cheap, confused and used — although I hadn't done anything wrong. Later, I felt anger, and I went to see a lawyer. (Authors' files)

A 1981 survey of almost 2,000 business executives done by *Redbook* and the *Harvard Business Review* found that men and women in top management positions disagree considerably on the extent of the problem of sexual harassment at work, with two-thirds of the men believing the scope of the problem "is greatly exaggerated" while only one-third of the women agreed with this statement (Safran, 1981). Male and female executives, however, were nearly unanimous in feeling that "unwanted sexual approaches distract people from the job at hand" and nearly three-quarters were in favor of management issuing a statement to all employees disapproving of sexual harassment.

The legal definition of sexual harassment is now quite specific:

> Unwelcome sexual advances, requests for sexual favors, and other verbal or physical conduct of a sexual nature constitute unlawful sexual harassment when (a) submission to such conduct is made either explicitly or implicitly a term or condition of an individual's employment, (b) submission to or rejection of such conduct by an individual is used as the basis for employment decisions affecting such individual, or (c) such conduct has the purpose or effect of unreasonably interfering with an individual's work performance or creating an intimidating, hostile, or offensive working environment. An employer is responsible for sexual harassment by its agents or supervisory employees regardless of whether the employer knew or should have known of their occurrence. An employer is responsible for acts of sexual harassment in the workplace committed by "non-supervisory employees" where the employer knows or should have known of

the conduct and no immediate and appropriate corrective action was taken. (Source: *EEOC Rules and Regulations,* 1980)

As more and more women have become aware of their legal rights in situations of sexual harassment, a large number of law suits have been filed with claims based primarily on sex discrimination under Title VII of the Civil Rights Act of 1964. Since few states have laws banning (or defining) sexual harassment at work, many of these cases have not been decided favorably for the woman even when it was clear that sexual harassment did occur. Here, the situations were viewed as "personal" instances of harassment rather than

sex discrimination (MacKinnon, 1979). Some landmark cases in the last few years, however, have now been decided in the woman's favor, and it may be anticipated that such judgments will become more realistically decided in the future. Recently, a male employee of the Wisconsin Department of Health and Social Services won a major sexual harassment suit against his female superior; a federal jury of five women and one man awarded him $196,500 (*Time,* August 2, 1982, p. 19). New regulations published by the U.S. EEOC in 1980 state that employers now have an "affirmative duty" to prevent and eliminate sexual harassment at work.

Sexual Harassment at Work

SEXUAL HARASSMENT AT SCHOOL

Sexual harassment is not confined to the workplace, of course. Examples of sexual harassment are common in many situations in which there is a hierarchy of power. Even the halls of academe are not immune from this form of abusive behavior, as these examples show:

> A *twenty-two-year-old woman:* My economics professor kept asking me to schedule meetings with him to review the work I was doing on my senior thesis. Whenever he could, he would drape his arm on my shoulder while we were talking and he would remind me that I needed his support to get an honors grade and to get into grad school. One day, he tried to rub my breasts — and when I pulled away from him, he just came out and said, "Look, either you put out for me or I won't put out for you." When I went to the dean to complain, I was told that without proof of my accusation, nothing could be done.

> A *twenty-seven-year-old woman:* One of my professors seemed to take a strong interest in my work and asked if I would help him grade some exam papers from his intro course. While I was working in his office, he calmly peeled off his clothes and said, "Let's take a break." I made a fast retreat, believe me, but I was shaken up by the experience. Then he called me at home to say that I shouldn't have been upset, he was only trying to be friendly. (Authors' files)

The scope of sexual harassment on college campuses is not known for certain, but Bernice Sandler of the Association of American Colleges estimates that one out of five college coeds is subjected to sexual harassment (*Time*, November 14, 1983, p. 109). A 1983 survey done at Harvard University found that one-third of female undergraduates and 41 percent of female graduate students had encountered some form of sexual harassment, although outright assaults accounted for only a small fraction of these in-

cidents. Whatever the precise numbers may be, it is clear that sexual harassment of students is a problem of considerable magnitude that has not attracted much publicity (or action) to date (Somers, 1982).

DEALING WITH SEXUAL HARASSMENT

Deciding how to handle sexual harassment in its various forms is not an easy task. As the preceding discussion shows, victims of sexual harassment are typically in a precarious position because they have less power than the person who is harassing them. Because of this, they may worry about whether their accusations will be believed and whether the harasser will be able to get back at them in some manner. Thus, as with other forms of sexual coercion, it appears that the overwhelming majority of cases of sexual harassment are never reported, leaving the harasser free to victimize others repeatedly. Being informed about options for handling this problem can help turn things around. Here, then, are a number of practical pointers:

1. If you have been the victim of actual or attempted sexual assault or rape by a boss, supervisor, or co-worker, you can file either civil or criminal charges against the offender.

2. In cases of sexual harassment that have not included an actual assault, you can confront the person who is harassing you in a number of different ways.

a. Consider writing a letter to your harasser telling him (or her): (1) what the facts are as you see them (e.g., "On March 14, 1983, when we met in your office to go over my draft of the Smith contract, you put your arm around me and tried to kiss me, and then asked me to come to your apartment so we could 'work more intimately together.'"),

Coercive Sex: The Varieties of Sexual Assault

(2) how you feel about what happened (e.g., "Now I am upset when I see you and worried that you won't evaluate my work objectively."), and (3) what you want to happen next (e.g., "I am willing to forget what happened if our relationship is a purely professional one from this point on.").

b. An alternate approach would be to confront the person who is harassing you, either in person or by telephone, although this is more likely to produce an emotional response than a letter.

c. Another possibility is to have an attorney write to your harasser for you, telling him to immediately stop such behavior or to run the risk of a subsequent law suit. (An attorney's letter may be more effective than your own in letting the harasser know you mean business.)

3. Keep careful documentation of each incident of harassment, including memos that include the dates, times, and specific details of offensive actions. Note the names of any witnesses, since they may be of considerable help in substantiating your case.

4. File a grievance with the appropriate person (for example, someone at the dean's office at school, or the personnel office at work, or with a union representative, if you're a union member).

5. If confronting the offender and filing a grievance doesn't work, seek help from sympathetic co-workers. You may discover others who have been victims of sexual harassment at the hands of the same person. Consider forming a group to discuss and deal with issues of sexual harassment.

6. If you aren't able to remedy the situation by the above steps, or if you have been unjustly fired or discriminated against in any other way, you can file a complaint with the Equal Employment Opportunity Commission (EEOC). You may be entitled to unemployment compensation and back pay, in addition to damages.

7. Don't let yourself feel guilty. As Backhouse and Cohen (1981, p. 165) put it: "The most important consideration in dealing with sexual harassment is to protect yourself, to refuse to feel guilty or in any way responsible for your problems. . . . You are a victim and are in no way to blame for being the target of this heinous behavior."

THE CULTURAL UNDERPINNINGS OF SEX VICTIMOLOGY

We live in a society that trains and encourages females to be victims of sexual coercion and males to victimize females. This statement is harsh but true, and it has important implications for what must be done to prevent sex victimization in its many forms.

Without repeating the detailed discussion of gender roles presented in chapter 10, we can summarize the situation by saying that females are generally socialized for passivity and dependence, while males are programmed for independence and aggressiveness (Frieze et al., 1978; Long Laws, 1979). This fundamental difference lies at the heart of sexual victimization, which is primarily an act of power and control.

> The fact is that families generally are given the job of socializing children to fill prescribed roles and thus supply the needs of a power society. . . . Ingrained in our present family system is the nucleus of male power and domination, and no matter how often we witness the devastatingly harmful effects of this arrangement on women and children, the victims are asked to uphold the family and submit to abuse. (Rush, 1974, p. 72)

The teenage boy is quick to learn that he is expected to be the sexual aggressor. For him, it is acceptable — even "manly" — to use persuasion or trickery to seduce his prey. He is also taught (by our society, if not in his home) that females do not really know what they want, that when they say "no" they mean "maybe," and when they say "maybe" they mean "yes." He may also have heard that bit of male folk-wisdom that says — in reference to some "uppity" or unhappy female — "What she needs is a good lay." Given this background, it's not surprising that what men see as being an "active, aggressive (and desirable) lover" may quickly be transformed into sexual assault in its various forms.

Most women have been taught as children not only to be passive ("nice," "polite," "ladylike"), but also to be seductive and coy. They are usually not trained to deal with physical aggression (unlike boys, whose play activities develop this capacity), but *are* trained to deal demurely with sexual situations. Thus, the female in a situation of sexual coercion is ill-prepared to act against it. Faced with a physical threat, she often becomes psychologically paralyzed (Brownmiller, 1975). Faced with unwanted sexual demands, she is likely to question what it was about her manner, dress, or behavior that produced the attention — she blames herself and feels guilt instead of taking more positive action. This hesitancy is frequently misread by the male who sees it as a sign of weakness and a chance that she will give in. His past experience may prove him right — how many women "give in" in various undesired sexual situations just is not known.

There are no perfect solutions that can wipe out sexual coercion, but a significant part of the problem can be addressed in two fundamental ways. First and foremost, as this discussion implies, is to change traditional gender role socialization that puts females in the position of being vulnerable to sexual abuse. Second, in-depth attention is required to identify the conditions that push men into the "victimizer" role. Only when a clear understanding of the causes and motiva-

tions underlying coercive sex is at hand will it be possible to develop effective strategies for dealing with this problem on a large-scale basis.

SUMMARY

1. Coercive sex takes many different forms, with the key element being an abuse of physical or social power. Females are victimized by coercive sex far more often than males.

2. Rape is a form of sexual assault in which penile penetration of the vagina occurs without mutual consent. It affects victims from all age groups and all walks of life; males can be victimized (either by women or via rectal rape by other men) as well as females.

3. Rape victims require attention to their medical needs, legal choices, and psychological reactions. Many women are reluctant to report rapes based on deficiencies in the police and legal systems. In many locations these deficiencies have been improved or overcome by the availability of "victim advocates" and specially trained police and lawyers.

4. The psychological impact of rape is usually profound; the typical victim feels isolated, helpless, and frightened. Three stages of psychological reaction to rape have been described by researchers — the acute reaction phase, the posttraumatic "recoil" phase, and a long-term regrowth and recovery phase. Sexual difficulties after rape are very common.

5. Information about rapists is very incomplete because it is based mainly on studies of men convicted for this crime. These men tend to be young and poorly educated, often having a prior criminal record.

6. Rape is not primarily a sexual act. Research studies show that most rapes are an expression of power, anger, or sadistic impulses through sexual assault.

7. Incest, or sexual contact between relatives, can occur in families in all walks of life and is not usually associated with diagnosable mental illness. Father-daughter incest is most frequently reported to authorities, but brother-sister incest is probably far more common. Incest with adults is generally thought to be psychologically harmful to children, but research in this area is limited. It is clear that some incest victims have a variety of later sexual problems.

8. Sexual harassment at work or school is a less recognized but widespread form of sexual coercion. Like the rape victim, the victim of sexual harassment may feel helpless, degraded, used, and angry. Increasingly, this form of sexual coercion has led to legal action from victims.

9. As long as our culture enforces gender role stereotypes that train females to be sexual victims and program males to see sexual aggression as "manly," we will probably continue to have major problems with sexual coercion in its many forms.

SUGGESTED READINGS

Brownmiller, Susan. *Against Our Will*. New York: Simon & Schuster, 1975. One of the key books responsible for shifting public attitudes toward rape, this volume is actually the definitive history of rape, discussed from a strong (sometimes strident) feminist perspective.

Grossman, Rochel, and Sutherland, Joan, eds. *Surviving Sexual Assault*. New York: Congdon & Weed, 1982/83. An outstanding, concise discussion of the rights and options for rape victims. Nontechnical, practical, and authoritative.

Groth, A. Nicholas. *Men Who Rape*. New York: Plenum Press, 1979. A definitive look at the motivations and psychological makeup of rapists.

MacKinnon, Catherine A. *Sexual Harassment of Working Women*. New Haven, Conn.: Yale University Press, 1979. An important, thoughtful treatment of a little-studied problem. Particularly rich in its legal perspectives and extensive footnotes.

Meiselman, Karin C. *Incest*. San Francisco: Jossey-Bass, 1978. A comprehensive, well-written review that includes extensive information based on a detailed study of fifty-eight cases.

Renshaw, Domeena. *Incest — Understanding and Treatment*. Boston: Little, Brown, 1983. A thorough, thoughtful summary of clinical insights into incest, including a chapter on the anthropological aspects of this form of behavior.

Russell, Diana E. H. *Rape in Marriage*. New York: Macmillan, 1982. An eye-opening treatment of an important but largely overlooked topic.

Schultz, Leroy G., ed. *The Sexual Victimology of Youth*. Springfield, Ill.: Charles C. Thomas, 1980. A good collection of papers on incest, kiddie porn, and the sexual abuse of children.

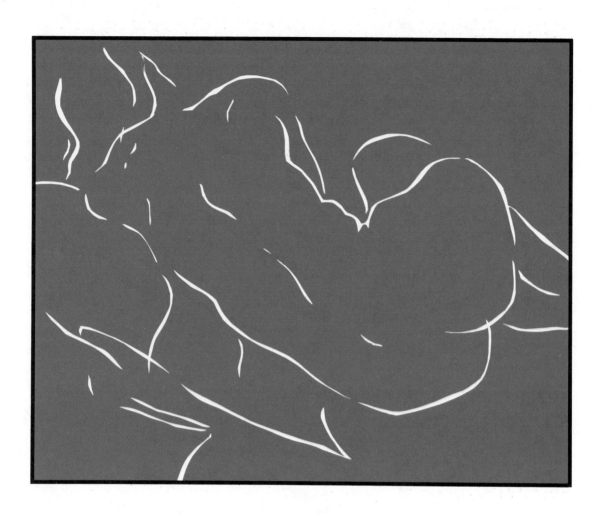

PART FOUR

Clinical Perspectives

19

Sexual Dysfunctions and Sex Therapy

_L_IKE MANY other body processes, when sexual function goes along smoothly, it is usually taken for granted and given little thought. But if sexual function is a problem in one way or another, it can be a source of anxiety, anguish, and frustration that often leads to general unhappiness and distress in personal relationships.

This chapter begins with a description of sexual dysfunctions — conditions in which the ordinary physical responses of sexual function are impaired. Our attention then turns to the causes of these dysfunctions. The concluding portion of the chapter discusses the methods and effectiveness of sex therapy in dealing with these problems.

MALE SEXUAL DYSFUNCTION

For most men in most societies, sexual adequacy is considered a yardstick for measuring personal adequacy. The man who does not "measure up" sexually is often embarrassed, confused, or depressed over his plight which he regards as reflecting poorly on his manhood. The sexually dysfunctional male may change his behavior to avoid sexual situations (fearing in advance that he will fail); he may cope with his dilemma by inventing excuses (blaming the dysfunction on his partner, for example); or he may try to overcome his problem by diligently "working" at sex, which usually makes the situation worse instead of better. We will now describe the various forms of male sexual dysfunction.

Erectile Dysfunction (Impotence)

Erectile dysfunction, or *impotence,* is the inability to have or maintain an erection that is firm enough for coitus. Erectile dysfunction is classified as either primary or secondary: the male with *primary erectile dysfunction* has never been able to have intercourse, whereas the male with *secondary erectile dysfunction* has succeeded in having intercourse once, twice, or a thousand times before his dysfunction began. Secondary erectile dysfunction is about ten times more common than primary erectile dysfunction (Kolodny, Masters, and Johnson, 1979).

Erectile dysfunction can occur at any age and can assume many different forms. Total absence of erection is infrequent except in certain medical conditions. More typically, the male with erectile dysfunction has partial erections that are too weak for vaginal insertion (or anal intercourse). Sometimes, there are firm erections that quickly disappear if intercourse is attempted. In other instances, a man with erectile dysfunction may be able to have normal erections under some circumstances but not others. For example, some men with erectile dysfunction have no problem during masturbation but cannot get erections during sexual activity with a partner. Other men have solid erections during extramarital sex but only feeble erections with their spouses. The reverse of this pattern is also common: some men who have no sexual difficulty with their wives are unable to function during attempts at extramarital sex.

Isolated episodes of not having erections (or of losing an erection at an inopportune time) are so common that they are nearly a universal occurrence among men. (For this reason, Masters and Johnson [1970] classified a man as secondarily impotent only if his erection problems occurred in at least 25 percent of his sexual encounters.) Such isolated episodes do *not* mean that a man has a sexual dysfunction; they may reflect a temporary form of physical stress (having the flu, being tired, having overindulged in food or drink), or may relate to other problems like tension, lack of privacy, or adjusting to a new sexual partner. If the man does not take such incidents in stride and becomes deeply upset by his "failure" to respond the "right" way physically, he may set the stage for difficulties in later sexual situations because he is worried about his ability (or inability) to perform.

Fears of sexual performance — "Will I lose my erection?" "Will I satisfy my partner?" — are likely to dampen sexual arousal and cause loss of erection. The stronger and more insistent such fears become, the greater is the likelihood that they will become self-fulfilling prophecies, and the man will experience an actual inability to get and keep an erection. On a long-term basis, performance fears may lead to lowered interest in sex (avoidance), loss of self-esteem, and attempts to control the anxiety by working hard to overcome it (which usually reduces sexual spontaneity and causes sex to be even more of a "performance" instead of just being *fun*). In addition, fears of performance often cause one or both partners to become spectators during their sexual interaction, observing and evaluating their own or their partner's sexual response. By becoming a spectator, a person usually becomes less involved in the sexual activity because of the distraction of watching and evaluating what is going on.

The spectator role, which can affect men and women, is not only found in cases of erectile dysfunction. When a person slips into the spectator role because of performance fears, the reduced intimacy and spontaneity of the situation combined with pre-existing fears usually stifle the capacity for physical response. This cycle tends to feed on itself: erectile failure leads to performance fears which lead to the spectator role, which results in distraction and loss of erection, which heightens the fears of performance. Unless this cycle is broken, there is a strong possibility that sexual dysfunction will be firmly established.

Men react to erectile dysfunction in various ways, ranging from great dismay (probably the most typical response) to studied nonchalance (the least typical). While there are some men and women who see sex as more than a throbbing, erect penis and do not judge the satisfaction of a sexual encounter on the basis of having intercourse alone, for most people the practical limitations of erectile dysfunction are bothersome. One thirty-four-year-old man relates his personal feelings in dealing with it:

> After a while, the problem becomes so predictable that you start to make excuses in advance. It's as though you lose any chance of having sexual pleasure because you become preoccupied with the notion of failure. And that failure hits you right in the gut — you don't feel like much of a man. (Authors' files)

The partner of a man with erectile dysfunction may blame herself for not being attractive enough to turn him on or not being skilled enough to arouse his passion, or she may fear that she is pressuring him and causing his difficulties. On the other hand, the partner may blame the man in various ways for his sexual problems. We have encountered women who accused their husbands of extramarital sex, being homosexual, or not being in love with them as explanations of erectile dysfunction. Sometimes the impact of erectile dysfunction can alter the fabric of a close relationship by introducing strain, doubt, irritability, and frustration, all of which have effects outside the bedroom.

Premature Ejaculation

Premature ejaculation, or rapid ejaculation, is a common sexual dysfunction but difficult to define precisely. Older definitions that used a specific duration of intercourse as the dividing line ("less than two minutes," for example) or that specified a minimum number of penile thrusts before ejaculation have now been discarded. This is fortunate because some men actually tried to time themselves with a stopwatch to determine if they were normal, and others tried to hurry their thrusting ("just four more thrusts, dear") although this usually speeds up ejaculation instead of delaying it.

In *Human Sexual Inadequacy,* an attempt was made to define premature ejaculation in terms of the interaction between sexual partners, not just the male alone. (Prior to 1970 premature ejaculation had frequently been classified as a form of impotence, a belief that reflected a poor understanding of the underlying physiology.) A man was considered to ejaculate prematurely if his partner wasn't orgasmic in at least 50 percent of their coital episodes, but it was acknowledged that this definition was still lacking (Masters and Johnson, 1970). Specifically, it couldn't be applied to situations in which a woman was infrequently orgasmic or never had orgasms during intercourse, and it was an arbitrary way of estimating normality at best. Later, Helen Kaplan (1974) suggested that premature ejaculation occurred if the male didn't have voluntary control over when he ejaculated — although most sex therapists agree that total voluntary control over the timing of ejaculation is the exception rather than the rule.

The American Psychiatric Association has recently side-stepped this issue by defining premature ejaculation in terms of "reasonable voluntary control." "The judgment of 'reasonable control' is made by . . . taking into account factors that affect duration of the excitement phase, such as age, novelty of the sexual partner, and the frequency and duration of coitus" (American Psychiatric Association, 1980, p. 280). Another view suggests that premature ejaculation does *not* exist if both partners "agree that the quality of their sexual encounters is not influenced by efforts to delay ejaculation" (LoPiccolo, 1977, p. 1234).

Despite the shortcomings of these definitions (or the definitions of this shortcoming), it is usually not too difficult to decide when rapid ejaculation is problematic in a sexual relationship. Although Kinsey and his co-workers suggested that rapid ejaculation was a sign of biological competence, noting that "It would be difficult to find another situation in which an individual who was quick and intense in his responses was labeled anything but superior . . . however inconvenient and unfortunate . . . from the standpoint of [the] wife" (Kinsey, Pomeroy, and Martin, 1948, p. 580), today most sexologists disagree with this idea. Kinsey's belief may have influenced his finding that 75 percent of men ejaculated within two minutes of vaginal entry, but it now seems unlikely that this figure is accurate (Hunt, 1975). While it is certainly true that some people see sex as primarily for the male's pleasure — and some females may actually be grateful to "get it over with" quickly — these ideas, which were once widespread, seem to have been replaced today by a more egalitarian view of sexual interaction except among the least educated and lowest socioeconomic levels.

Clearly, the male who persistently ejaculates unintentionally during noncoital sexual play or while trying to enter his partner has a problem. While this extreme situation is found in fewer than 10 percent of cases, it is likely to be particularly distressing. More typically, the premature ejaculator is able to participate in a variety of sexual activities and only loses his ejaculatory control soon after intercourse begins. Premature ejaculation may occur in some situations and not in others. For example, a man may have this problem only during extramarital sex.

Some men are not bothered at all by ejaculating rapidly. Many others question their masculinity and have low self-esteem (Perelman, 1980). Fears of performance often seem to heighten the lack of ejaculatory control and can occasionally lead to erectile dysfunction by the "fears-spectator-failure-greater fears" cycle described earlier (Kolodny, Masters, and Johnson, 1979). Erectile difficulties can also occur if a premature ejaculator struggles to control his sexual arousal by using distraction (thinking about the office or counting backwards from 1,000): if he succeeds too well in distracting himself from involvement in the sexual interaction, he may lose his erection as well as the urgency to ejaculate.

While many of the female partners of men with premature ejaculation are understanding and accepting of the involuntary nature of the problem, others "feel angry and 'used,' leading them to seek professional guidance, to seek another lover, or to avoid sex" (Perelman, 1980, p. 201). Because most males have a tendency to ejaculate more quickly if it has been a long time between sexual opportunities, avoidance is likely to worsen the problem and may worsen the relationship too. Similarly, if the man tries to reduce his arousal by shortening the time of noncoital play, his tactic is not only ineffective but also may backfire by further convincing the woman of her partner's selfishness (Kolodny, Masters, and Johnson, 1979).

Although premature ejaculation is less frequent than erectile dysfunction among male patients at the Masters & Johnson Institute (Masters and Johnson, 1970; Kolodny, Masters, and Johnson, 1979), we believe it is probably the most common sexual dysfunction in the general population. We estimate that 15 to 20 percent of American men have at least a moderate degree of difficulty controlling rapid ejaculation, but less than one-fifth of this group consider it to be enough of a problem to seek help. Some men find that they can overcome premature ejaculation on their own by using a condom to cut down on genital sensations; others discover that a glass or two of an alcoholic beverage may reduce their ejaculatory quickness; and others find that controlling ejaculation is no problem "the second time around" — that is, once they have already had one orgasm and attempt intercourse within the next two or three hours. Over-the-counter creams and ointments that "desensitize" the penis deaden sensations. If they help control rapid ejaculation at all, they do so at the cost of not feeling very much or by the power of suggestion.

Ejaculatory Incompetence and Retarded Ejaculation

Ejaculatory incompetence is the inability to ejaculate within the vagina despite a firm erection and relatively high levels of sexual arousal. It must be distinguished from *retrograde ejaculation*, which is a condition where the bladder neck does not close off properly during orgasm so that the semen spurts backwards into the bladder, where it is mixed with urine. *Retarded ejaculation* can be thought of as the opposite of premature ejaculation; here, although intravaginal ejaculation eventually occurs, it requires a long time and strenuous efforts at coital stimulation, and sexual arousal may be sluggish.

Ejaculatory incompetence is an infrequent disorder mainly seen in men under age thirty-five. The most common pattern (about two-thirds of patients) is *primary ejaculatory incompetence* or never having been able to ejaculate in the vagina. *Secondary ejaculatory incompetence* refers to men who have lost the ability to ejaculate intravaginally or who do so infrequently after a prior history of normal coital ejaculation. In either the primary or secondary versions of this dysfunction, ejaculation is usually possible by masturbation (about 85 percent of patients in our series) or by noncoital partner stimulation (about 50 percent of patients in our series). In about 15 percent of our cases, men with ejaculatory incompetence had never experienced ejaculation except through nocturnal emissions. Rarely, ejaculatory incompetence can be situational, occurring with one partner but not another (Munjack and Kanno, 1979).

Ejaculatory incompetence can be a source of sexual pleasure because it permits prolonged periods of coitus. A few of our patients have told us that they were regularly able to sustain an erection for one or two hours of intercourse — much to the delight of their partners, many of whom marvelled at this staying power. However, once the woman discovers that her partner is unable to ejaculate intravaginally, a new reaction most likely sets in. She may assume that the man does not find her attractive, is not enjoying the experience, or is "withholding" orgasm as a sign of selfishness (Munjack and Oziel, 1980). If reproduction is a goal of the sexual partners, ejaculatory incompetence can be even more frustrating and may lead to accusations and arguments that can threaten even the best of relationships, as this example from our files shows:

> A *twenty-seven-year-old married man:* I'm sick and tired of being psychoanalyzed by my wife because of this problem we're having. I want a baby just as much as she does, but my penis doesn't seem to understand. But that's no reason to accuse me of being homosexual.

Retarded ejaculation is seen in all age groups from adolescence on and is probably two or three times more common than ejaculatory incompetence. Although it may also be a source of sexual enjoyment, sometimes the prolonged periods of coital thrusting required to bring about ejaculation are uncomfortable both physically and psychologically for the female, whose own sexual needs may have been amply met in a briefer time frame. The woman may become resentful of the sexual demands placed on her by her partner. Her feeling corresponds to the male whose female partner needs to be stimulated coitally for a long time to reach orgasm.

Here again, it is important to distinguish between the fairly consistent pattern of sexual dysfunction and the occasional episodes when a man cannot ejaculate intravaginally or requires a long period of vaginal containment and thrusting to ejaculate. Occasional difficulty with ejaculation is *not* a sign of sexual disturbance and is often related to fatigue, tension, illness, too much sex in too short a time, or the effects of alcohol or other drugs (see chapter 20). In addition, a male may be unable to ejaculate with a partner he's not very emotionally involved with (e.g., when he's just having sex because he feels it's expected of him).

Painful Intercourse

Painful intercourse, or *dyspareunia,* is generally thought of as a female dysfunction but it also affects males. Most typically, the pain is felt in the penis but it can also be felt in the testes or internally, where it is often associated with a problem of the prostate or seminal vesicles. Causes of painful intercourse in males are discussed later in this chapter.

FEMALE SEXUAL DYSFUNCTION

Until fairly recently, it was presumed that women were less sexual than men. Females with a sexual dysfunction were therefore not seen as incomplete or "unable to measure up" as men with sexual problems were. In the past two decades, traditional views of female sexuality were all but demolished, and women's sexual needs became accepted as legitimate in their own right. But as part of this process, female sexual responsivity became something of an expected accomplishment, with women — helped along by numerous magazine articles, how-to books, and TV talk shows — suddenly put on the spot with performance pressures of their own.

As a result, females began to develop more awareness of the existence of sexual dysfunctions. The woman who sees herself as "unresponsive" in one way or another often becomes embarrassed, confused, or depressed just as men do. She too may try to cope by avoidance, inventing excuses, or studiously "working" at sex to find the "right" technique to unlock her sexual potential. We will now describe the various forms of female sexual dysfunction.

Vaginismus

Vaginismus is a condition in which the muscles around the outer third of the vagina have involuntary spasms in response to attempts at vaginal penetration (Figure 19-1). Females of any age can be affected, and the severity of the reflex is highly variable. At one extreme, vaginismus can be so dramatic that the vaginal opening is tightly clamped shut, preventing not only intercourse but even insertion of a finger. Less severe, but still considerably distressing, is when any attempts at coitus — no matter how gentle, relaxed, and loving — result in pelvic pain. In its milder versions, vaginismus may allow a woman to have intercourse but only with some discomfort. The frequency of vaginismus in the general population is unknown, but judging from our patients, it accounts for less than 10 percent of cases of female sexual dysfunction. We estimate that 2 to 3 percent of all postadolescent women have vaginismus.

FIGURE 19–1
Vaginismus

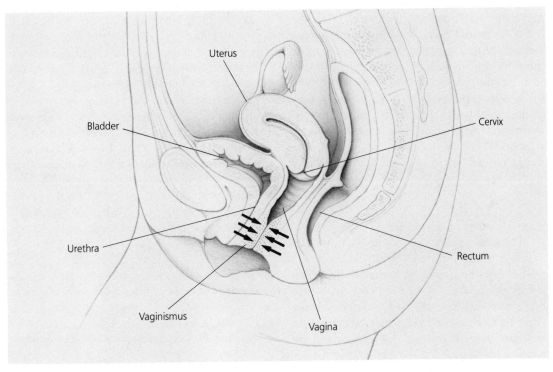

The involuntary muscular spasms of vaginismus at the outer third of the vagina are shown by the arrows.

Although some women with vaginismus are very fearful of sexual activity, which may impair their sexual responsiveness, most women with this dysfunction have little or no difficulty with sexual arousal. Vaginal lubrication occurs normally, noncoital sexual play may be pleasurable and satisfying, and orgasm is often unaffected (Kolodny, Masters, and Johnson, 1979). Women with vaginismus usually have normal sexual desire and are upset by their inability to enjoy intercourse. Vaginismus can be particularly troubling to a couple who wants to have children, and it is

often this consideration that pushes the couple to seek help.

The male partner of the woman with vaginismus may be completely baffled about why sexual difficulties arise. Often, he has no specific knowledge of the involuntary muscle spasms involved and either thinks that he is doing something that hurts his partner or sees her as deliberately avoiding intercourse by "tensing up." If he thinks he is hurting her, he may become more and more passive in sexual situations. Erectile dysfunction may develop, especially if he assumes the blame for the situation. If, instead, he blames the woman, he may lose patience after awhile and become resentful or openly hostile or may simply seek other sexual partners.

Vaginismus may be suspected from a woman's history (e.g., the woman may have had difficulty using a tampon or a diaphragm), but identification of this dysfunction can only be made with certainty by a careful pelvic examination. Unfortunately, not all physicians are well-versed in detecting sexual problems, and women are sometimes mistakenly told "everything's normal" when vaginismus is unquestionably present.

Anorgasmia

Before the publication of *Human Sexual Inadequacy* in 1970, the term *frigidity* was generally used to describe a number of female sexual difficulties ranging from not having orgasms to not being interested in sex to not becoming sexually aroused. As this term lacked diagnostic precision and was increasingly used in a negative, disparaging way, portraying women as "cold" or "rejecting," many sexologists abandoned its use. Masters and Johnson (1970) and Kaplan (1974) substituted the term *orgasmic dysfunction* to describe women who have difficulty reaching orgasm; *anorgasmia* is currently used as a synonym.

As with many sexual dysfunctions, there are several categories of anorgasmia. *Primary anorgasmia* refers to women who have never had an orgasm. *Secondary anorgasmia* refers to women who were regularly orgasmic at one time but no longer are. *Situational anorgasmia* refers to women who have had orgasms on one or more occasions but only under certain circumstances — for example, women who are orgasmic when masturbating but not when being stimulated by their partner. Women who are orgasmic by a variety of means but do not have orgasms during intercourse are described in a subcategory of situational anorgasmia called *coital anorgasmia*. Finally, *random anorgasmia* refers to women who have experienced orgasm in different types of sexual activity but only on an infrequent basis.

As indicated by these definitions, there are many forms of anorgasmia. Within these classifications, the diversity is even greater. Some anorgasmic women get little pleasure out of sex and see it as an obligation of marriage or a means of maintaining a relationship. Other anorgasmic women find that sex is stimulating and satisfying. One woman told us, "Since I've never had an orgasm, I don't really know what I'm missing, but I certainly know when I'm having fun." Many women with orgasmic difficulties voice opinions somewhere between these extremes, as shown by these comments from our files:

> *A twenty-two-year-old single woman:* I enjoy sex, but I keep pushing to reach for an orgasm, and the worry that it won't be there keeps gnawing away inside me. I'd feel a lot better if I knew I could come every time.

> *A thirty-one-year-old married woman:* I've always been able to have orgasms when I masturbate, but it's never happened with my husband. After eight years of marriage this has really become a strain on our relationship — for him, because he feels he's inadequate; for me, because I'm missing a special kind of sharing.

> *A nineteen-year-old college student:* There's so much talk about orgasms that I've been wondering what's wrong with me, that I don't have them. I used to enjoy sex a lot, but lately it's a bad scene because I just get reminded of my own problems.

Not having orgasms can create fears of performance that propel a woman into the spectator role, dampening her overall sexual responsiveness, just as is true for a man. Anorgasmia can also lead to less self-esteem, depression, and a sense of futility.

It must be stressed that the stimulation of intercourse *alone* is not always sufficient for female orgasm to occur. Many women usually require

502

additional stimulation (e.g., stroking the clitoris) during intercourse to have coital orgasms. Unfortunately, some people believe that "genuine" coital orgasms are only the result of penis-vagina contact, which is simply not the case.

There is some controversy today about the number of women who are anorgasmic during intercourse. A number of studies, viewed as a group, suggest that about 10 percent of women have never experienced coital orgasm (Kinsey et al., 1953; Chesser, 1956; Fisher, 1973; Hunt, 1975; Levin and Levin, 1975). Perhaps another 10 percent have coital orgasms on an infrequent basis. Kaplan (1974) suggests that these women should not necessarily be thought of as having a problem, since she believes that not having orgasms during intercourse is within the normal range of female sexual response. Hite (1977) voices a similar opinion, pointing out that many of the women she surveyed preferred noncoital orgasms to those occurring during intercourse. To us, their approaches are flawed for several reasons: (1) If the same line of reasoning was applied to males, premature ejaculation would be viewed as "within the normal range," since it appears to affect a similar number of men; (2) Many coitally anorgasmic women are easily able to begin having orgasms during intercourse with the aid of short-term sex therapy; and (3) There is no reliable research evidence that a sizeable fraction of women are incapable of coital orgasm. Furthermore, since many women who have coital anorgasmia are distressed by their situation, what is gained by telling them that everything is normal and it's no cause for concern?

We would like to make it clear that we believe that people should seek sex therapy with attainable goals and a genuine sense of need. A woman who is content not to have orgasms or who is unconcerned about how she reaches her orgasms should not be pushed into sex therapy, and we would be the first to tell her this directly. We also believe that it is usually a mistake to undertake sex therapy for female anorgasmia when the primary motivation is to satisfy the male partner.

Anorgasmia in its different forms is far and away the largest category of female sexual dysfunction, accounting for about 90 percent of cases in most large studies. Many women, however, are not orgasmic during every sexual encounter yet do *not* have a sexual dysfunction. Lack of orgasm must be viewed in terms of the individual's desires, the skill and sensitivity of her partner (as well as his attractiveness, cooperation, etc.), the circumstances of sexual activity (privacy, timing, comfort, and so on), and other factors too numerous to mention here. A woman who sometimes has orgasms should be classified as having orgasmic dysfunction only if her orgasmic frequency is so low that it is a source of distress or dissatisfaction.

The male partner of an anorgasmic woman may feel sympathetic while also feeling threatened, since many men assume it's their responsibility to make their partner orgasmic. If he sees his role as "tutor" or "coach," he may become impatient or angry if his partner doesn't reach orgasm in response to his attentions. If he concentrates on romance and carefully orchestrated sexual technique, he may become resentful if the female does not achieve orgasm. Some men give up trying and become resigned to the situation, while others are convinced that their partners are deliberately withholding orgasm. If a man discovers that his partner has been faking orgasm, he is particularly likely to be upset or angered.

Rapid Orgasm

Although premature ejaculation in men has been widely discussed, its female counterpart — rapid orgasm — has been almost completely ignored by sexologists. This is probably because this condition is relatively rare. In more than two decades of our research, we have encountered only a handful of women who complained of reaching orgasm too quickly. The primary problem for these women is that once orgasm occurs they have little interest in further sexual activity and often find that it is physically uncomfortable. In contrast, most women who have rapid orgasms remain sexually interested and aroused (often going on to additional orgasms) and thus consider it an asset, not a liability. The male partner of a woman who reaches orgasm rapidly is also likely to view it in a positive light, either seeing it as a sign of a very responsive partner or giving himself a pat on the back for his lovemaking skills.

Painful Intercourse

Dyspareunia, or painful intercourse, in women can present a major stumbling block to sexual satisfaction. In this condition, which can occur at any age, pain can appear at the start of intercourse, midway through coital activities, at the time of orgasm, or after intercourse is completed. The pain can be felt as burning, sharp, searing, or cramping; it can be external, within the vagina, or deep in the pelvic region or abdomen.

The incidence of dyspareunia is unknown. We have found that about 15 percent of adult women experience coital discomfort on a few occasions per year. We estimate that 1 to 2 percent of adult women have painful intercourse on more than an occasional basis.

Dyspareunia detracts from a person's sexual enjoyment and can interfere with sexual arousal and orgasm. The fear of pain may make the woman tense and decrease her sexual pleasure; in many cases, the woman may avoid coital activity or abstain from all forms of sexual contact. The partner of a woman with dyspareunia may either be very understanding and sensitive to her feelings, or resentful and demanding in spite of her discomfort.

CAUSES OF SEXUAL DYSFUNCTION

It is customary to classify the causes of sexual dysfunction as either *organic* (physical or medical factors such as illness, injury, or drug effects) or *psychosocial* (including psychological, interpersonal, environmental, and cultural factors). The precise cause of a specific dysfunction in a given person cannot always be identified, and in some instances, it may be a combination of several different factors.

Organic Factors

It is generally estimated that 10 to 20 percent of sexual dysfunction cases are caused primarily by organic factors (Kolodny, Masters, and Johnson, 1979; Munjack and Oziel, 1980; Kaplan et al., 1983). In another 15 percent of cases, organic factors may contribute to the sexual difficulty, although they may not be the direct or sole cause of the disorder. Given these facts, it is important for a person seeking treatment for a sexual dysfunction to have a thorough physical examination as well as appropriate laboratory testing of blood and urine samples to identify or rule out organic conditions that might be affecting sexual function. We will now review each sexual dysfunction to examine organic factors that may be important. Many of these disorders are discussed more fully in the next chapter.

MALE SEXUAL DYSFUNCTION

Erectile dysfunction can result from many medical conditions. *Diabetes* (a condition in which the body improperly handles blood sugar regulation) and *alcoholism* are the two most prominent organic causes of erectile dysfunction. Together, they probably account for several million cases in the United States alone. Other organic causes of erectile dysfunction include spinal cord injury, multiple sclerosis, or other neurological disorders; infections or injuries of the penis, testes, urethra, or prostate gland; hormone deficiencies; and circulatory problems. Both prescription medications (such as drugs for high blood pressure) and street drugs like uppers (amphetamines), downers (barbiturates), and narcotics sometimes cause difficulty with erection.

Premature ejaculation rarely results from organic causes. In over 500 cases of premature ejaculation seen at the Masters & Johnson Institute, we have found only one instance where an organic condition proved to be of importance.

With *ejaculatory incompetence,* organic causes can be eliminated as a possibility if ejaculation occurs in noncoital situations. In cases of complete inability to ejaculate, drug use and neurological disorders are sometimes found, accounting for about one out of twenty cases. Drug use and alcoholism account for about 10 percent of cases of retarded ejaculation.

Painful intercourse in males can be due to several different organic problems, although psychosocial factors appear to cause at least half of such cases. Inflammation or infection of the penis, the foreskin, the testes, the urethra, or the prostate are the most likely organic causes of male dyspareunia. A few men experience pain if the tip of the penis is scratched or irritated by the tail of an IUD (the stringlike portion that protrudes through the cervix into the vagina). Other men develop painful penile irritation when exposed to a vaginal contraceptive foam or cream.

FEMALE SEXUAL DYSFUNCTION

Vaginismus is most frequently a psychosocial problem rather than an organic one. However, any of the organic causes of female dyspareunia can condition a woman into vaginismus as a natural protective reflex (Kolodny, Masters, and Johnson, 1979). Even when the underlying organic problem is detected and successfully treated, the vaginismus may remain, particularly if it has been present for a long period of time.

Anorgasmia is linked to organic causes in less than 5 percent of cases. Severe chronic illness of almost any variety can impair female orgasmic response. Specific disorders that sometimes block orgasm include diabetes, alcoholism, neurological disturbances, hormone deficiencies, and pelvic disorders such as infections, trauma, or scarring from surgery. Drugs such as narcotics, tranquilizers, and blood pressure medications can also impair female orgasm. *Rapid orgasm* in women has no known physical causes.

Female dyspareunia can be caused by dozens of physical conditions, although psychosocial factors may be as frequent as organic ones (Lazarus, 1980). Any condition that results in poor vaginal lubrication can produce discomfort during intercourse. The chief culprits here seem to be drugs that have a drying effect (e.g., antihistamines — used to treat allergies, colds, or sinus conditions; certain tranquilizers; and marihuana) and disorders such as diabetes, vaginal infections, and estrogen deficiencies. Other causes of female dyspareunia include:

1. *Skin problems* (blisters, rashes, inflammation) around the vaginal opening or affecting the vulva
2. *Irritation or infection of the clitoris*
3. *Disorders of the vaginal opening,* such as scarring from an episiotomy, intact hymen or remnants of the hymen that are stretched during intercourse, or infection of the Bartholin glands
4. *Disorders of the urethra or anus*
5. *Disorders of the vagina,* such as infections, surgical scarring, thinning of the walls of the vagina (whether due to aging or estrogen deficiency), and irritation due to chemicals that are found in contraceptive materials or douches.
6. *Pelvic disorders* such as infection, tumors, abnormalities of the cervix or uterus, and torn ligaments around the uterus.

Psychosocial Factors

It has been much more difficult to develop a clear understanding of how psychosocial factors "cause" sexual dysfunction. Much of the research to date has found *associations* between factors such as developmental traumas, psychological traits, behavior patterns, and relationship difficulties and the existence of a sexual dysfunction, but research of this sort cannot prove what *causes* sexual dysfunctions. Furthermore, many people whose histories are loaded with potentially devastating psychosexual events have completely normal sexual function, while others who have unremarkable histories turn up with sexual dysfunctions.

Despite these problems, we can identify some psychosocial factors that are currently thought to contribute to the orgins of sexual dysfunction. Since many of these are nonspecific — that is, they may lead to a number of dysfunctions in either men or women — we will consider them in terms of several broad categories.

DEVELOPMENTAL FACTORS

Many authorities have suggested that troubled parent-child relationships, negative family attitudes toward sex, traumatic childhood or adolescent sexual experiences, and gender identity conflicts may all predispose one toward developing later sexual dysfunctions, either singly or in combination (Masters and Johnson, 1970; Kaplan, 1974; Leiblum and Pervin, 1980). For example, a child who is brought up believing that sex is sinful and shameful may be handicapped in later sexual enjoyment. Children who have been repeatedly and severely punished for touching their genitals or for innocent sex play with other boys or girls are also liable to become fearful about sex in any form and may have difficulty developing a positive view of sex as an intimate, pleasurable, desirable activity.

A traumatic first coital experience — either physically or psychologically painful — is another common problem found in the backgrounds of many people with sexual dysfunctions. Such an experience can raise fear about sexual encounters, lead to avoidance, or cause considerable guilt. Another variation is shown in this comment from one of our patients:

> A *forty-eight-year-old coitally anorgasmic woman:* When I was twenty-one and still a virgin I had been looking forward to my wedding night in a romantic, idealized way. But the wedding day was exhausting, my husband and I both had too much to drink, and when we tried to make love for the first time, instead of being blissful and tender, it was hurried and disastrous. It seems as though we were never able to catch the spark of loving sex after that — it's always been disappointing and unpleasant for me. (Authors' files)

One other developmental factor will be mentioned briefly. In *Human Sexual Inadequacy,* it was noted that a rigid religious background during childhood seemed to be associated with many sexual dysfunctions. What was striking about these cases was not the specific set of religious teachings (since these did not always condemn sexuality) but that sex was strongly regarded as evil and dirty in these rigidly religious families. Since 1970, when these findings were published, we have gathered more information in this area. We can now say that rigid religious upbringing seems to be a common factor only in certain dysfunctions: vaginismus and primary anorgasmia in women, and ejaculatory incompetence and primary impotence in men. Furthermore, by interviewing many individuals from similar backgrounds who did *not* have sexual dysfunctions, we have become even more confident in stressing that it is generally *not* the religious beliefs that are troublesome, but the severely antisexual attitudes that are forced upon the child.

Sexual Fakery

A twenty-eight-year-old married woman tells her husband that for six years of marriage she's been "faking" orgasms. He gets so angry at her that he kicks her off the end of their bed. Later, with professional counseling, he admits that his anger was self-directed – he couldn't believe he didn't see through her act.

A twenty-four-year-old man who's been having problems with erections finds himself with an intimate invitation from a girl he's just begun dating. "Look," he tells her, "I'm not feeling so good tonight, so don't expect too much." (Authors' files)

No one knows how many people lie to their partners by faking sexual responsivity or personal satisfaction. When one partner tenderly asks another, "How was that for you?," the usual answer ("terrific!") may be more a matter of tact than truth. Although there are certainly times when sexual deception may seem the better part of valor by allowing a person to save face or by protecting a partner's feelings, many problems may arise if it becomes habitual. This can be illustrated by considering what seems to be the most common form of sexual fakery: a woman who fakes orgasms.

The woman who "fakes" is sabotaging communication rather than doing her partner a favor. Although she may succeed in temporarily massaging his ego by making him feel like a great lover, her pretense convinces him that he's doing everything "just right."

As a result, he will probably continue doing what he thinks she enjoys, having no reason to change his style and being unaware of her need for anything different.

While men have an impossible time trying to fake erections and while male orgasm usually produces unmistakable external evidence, "faking" can still occur. This usually takes the form of trying to hide an inability to achieve erection, using fatigue or illness as an excuse. In other instances, a man may try to hide his own difficulties by convincing his partner that he wants only to please her – that *he* is satisfied when *she* is satisfied – although this pretense works only with noncoital acts. In a few cases of ejaculatory incompetence, men have faked intravaginal ejaculation successfully for years without their partner's detection. Whatever the particular deception, the result is very similar to the female version of sexual fakery. By undermining effective communication, the man cuts off an opportunity to gain his partner's understanding and thus lessens his chances of being able to change the situation.

Sexual fakery has no long-lasting advantages. It may save a partner's feelings temporarily, but this is usually at the cost of the other person's pleasure. The sexual lie is all too likely to become a barrier between partners. If the barrier becomes thick enough, it can dissolve the relationship.

PERSONAL FACTORS

People's feelings obviously have a lot to do with how they function sexually. We have already noted that fears of performance often suppress sexual function. Other types of anxiety, including fears of pregnancy, venereal disease, rejection, losing control, pain, intimacy, and even success can also block the pathways of sexual response.

Other feelings can also affect sexual responsiveness. Guilt, depression, and poor self-esteem are encountered frequently in association with sexual dysfunctions. Sometimes, though, it is difficult to know which came first, the feeling or the dysfunction. It is natural for people who have sexual problems to become depressed about them or to feel less good about themselves. Thus, identifying such a feeling does not always mean it caused the dysfunction.

Other personal factors that can play a part in sexual dysfunction are lack of sexual information and blind acceptance of cultural myths. Uncertainty about the location of the clitoris or lack of awareness of its importance in female sexual response are prime examples of lack of sexual information. Believing that the capacity for sexual function disappears with aging or that the pace of sexual activity must be set by the male are examples of how cultural myths can translate into personal attitudes and behavior.

Although a number of different studies have attempted to correlate sexual dysfunctions with particular types of personalities, no solid evidence exists documenting such a relationship.

INTERPERSONAL FACTORS

Interpersonal factors are of tremendous importance in most sexual dysfunctions. The most common problem is poor communication, both in sexual and nonsexual areas of the relationship. Communications problems either can lead directly to a sexual dysfunction (through misunderstandings or defensiveness) or can play a key role in perpetuating a dysfunction. As we have stressed throughout this book, sex is a form of communication and effective communication is extremely important in sexual relationships. Other interpersonal factors frequently involved in sexual dysfunctions include power struggles within a relationship, hostility toward a partner or spouse, preference for another partner, distrust or deceit, lack of physical attraction to a partner, and gender role conflicts (which often become power struggles). Conflicts in the sex value systems of partners or widely different sexual preferences in terms of timing, frequency, or type of sexual activity may also contribute to dysfunctions.

It must be recognized, however, that such problems do not *always* lead to sexual difficulties. Some couples find that sex is most enjoyable when they are angry at each other. Other couples with terrible communications have fantastic sexual relationships. As always, we must be careful not to oversimplify.

ADDITIONAL CONSIDERATIONS

Until the detailed studies of Masters and Johnson were released, it was generally thought that sexual dysfunctions were invariably due to deep-seated personality problems that originated in childhood (Kaplan, 1974; LoPiccolo and Heiman, 1978; Apfelbaum, 1980). Today, most sexologists recognize that many people with sexual dysfunctions have completely normal personalities, no signs of emotional illness, and simple, straightforward explanations for their problem.

Yet there are still some major differences between how psychoanalysts and behaviorists explain sexual dysfunction. The traditional psychoanalytic viewpoint has been that the dysfunction is not the primary problem but is instead a symptom of a deeper psychological disturbance. Analysts have suggested that ejaculatory incompetence, erectile dysfunction, and premature ejaculation result from castration anxiety and unresolved Oedipal wishes that are usually present at the unconscious level. Similarly, the analytic viewpoint generally suggests that vaginismus and anorgasmia also reflect unresolved Electra conflicts, as well as unconscious hostility toward men because of penis envy. In essence, old fears of being punished for sexual play that were supposedly learned in early childhood are reawakened (in the unconscious) by adult sexual encounters and cause psychological conflict, anxiety, and dysfunction.

In sharp distinction, the learning theory viewpoint sees sexual dysfunction as a conditioned, or learned, response. A man may develop erectile dysfunction if his partner constantly criticizes his performance or if he feels guilty after every sexual encounter. A woman may be anorgasmic because she was conditioned to believe that sex was "wrong" or shameful, or because she was taught that "nice" girls don't enjoy sex. Premature ejaculation may originate from early sexual experiences in which ejaculating quickly was desirable. Such experiences might include situations with a risk of being discovered by someone else, as in sex in a parked car; sex with a prostitute who typically encourages speed so she can see more customers; or group masturbation, where ejaculatory speed was seen as a sign of virility. If the conditioning is powerful enough, it cannot be easily "unlearned" even when circumstances change.

The learning theory model also points out that some dysfunctions are maintained by positive reinforcement. That is, the dysfunction may result in increased tenderness or attention from a partner, or it may give a person the upper hand in a power struggle. Furthermore, behaviorists generally believe that a precise understanding of causation is less important in treating a sexual dysfunction than recognizing the conditions that *maintain* the difficulty, since these are the ones that need to be changed.

Perhaps as sex research becomes more sophisticated it will be possible to approach the question of causation with more certainty. At present, the understanding of this area remains limited.

DISORDERS OF SEXUAL DESIRE

Since the mid-1970s, sex therapists have become increasingly aware of a new category of sexual problems that are not, strictly speaking, sexual dysfunctions. In these conditions, which are collectively referred to as disorders of sexual desire, the capacity for physical sexual response is usually preserved, and the problem is one of lack of willingness to participate in sexual relations due to either disinterest or fear. If lack of interest in sex is the predominant problem, it is classified as *inhibited sexual desire* (ISD). If lack of participation in sex is mainly due to overwhelming fear it is classified as *sexual aversion*.

In deciding when a disorder of sexual desire is present, it is necessary to remember that while some people seem to be interested in sex at almost any time, others have low or seemingly nonexistent levels of sexual interest. Only when lack of sexual interest is a source of personal or relationship distress, instead of voluntary choice, is it classified as ISD. Schover et al. (1982) suggest that ISD is present if there is both a low rate of sexual activity and "a subjective lack of desire for sexual activity; desire here includes sexual dreams and fantasies, attention to erotic materials, awareness of wishes for sexual activity, noticing attractive potential partners, and feelings of frustration if deprived of sex."

People with ISD characteristically have low interest in initiating sexual behavior and are generally unreceptive to a partner's sexual advances, although they may reluctantly "give in" to their partner's wishes from time to time in order to preserve peace in the relationship. Generally, people with ISD are sexually functional (in physiological terms) but this disorder can also coexist with one or more sexual dysfunctions. ISD can be primary (lifelong) or secondary, and it can be either generalized (occurring all of the time) or situational. Although the exact incidence of this problem is unknown, it has been appearing frequently in sex therapy clinics around the country in the recent past, accounting for as many as three out of ten cases in some clinics (Lief, 1977; Schover and LoPiccolo, 1982).

The causes of inhibited sexual desire include both organic and psychosocial conditions. Hormone deficiencies, alcoholism, kidney failure, drug abuse, and severe chronic illness may each play a role. Ten to 20 percent of men with this disorder have pituitary tumors that produce excessive amounts of prolactin; the prolactin suppresses testosterone production and sometimes causes impotence as well as ISD (Schwartz and Bauman, 1981). A majority of cases of ISD appear to be psychosocial in origin, reflecting problems such as depression, prior sexual trauma, poor body image or self-esteem, interpersonal hostility, and relationship power struggles. In some cases, ISD seems to develop as a means of coping with a pre-existent sexual dysfunction. For instance, a man with erectile dysfunction who develops a low interest in sex finds that this allows him to avoid the unpleasant consequences of sexual failure such as embarrassment, anxiety, loss of self-esteem, and frustration.

Women or men with ISD may be sexually functional or may have difficulties with sexual arousal and orgasm. In many cases, they seem to not be able to recognize early signs of sexual arousal in themselves and use a limited set of cues to define a situation as sexual (LoPiccolo, 1980). For example, such persons may ignore warmth and tenderness as possible signs of sexual feelings while waiting to be swept off their feet by a tidal wave of sexual passion. In addition, many people with ISD believe their initial desire is a good predictor of their ultimate response to a sexual situation, so if they are not feeling "turned on" at the first touch or kiss, they give up all hope of enjoying themselves.

ISD is not a source of difficulty in all marriages or relationships where it occurs. Sometimes a couple reaches an acceptable accommodation to the situation: for example, a person with ISD may agree to participate in sex when his or her partner requests it, regardless of personal interest. Alternatively, some couples reach a workable solution by allowing — or even encouraging — the partner with an intact sex drive to seek sexual activity outside the relationship. Most frequently, however, when only one person in the relationship has low sexual desire, it poses a major strain.

Sexual aversion is a severe phobia (irrational fear) to sexual activity or the thought of sexual activity which leads to avoidance of sexual situations. It, too, affects both males and females. The intense fear or dread found in sexual aversion is sometimes expressed in physiological symptoms such as profound sweating, nausea, diarrhea, or a racing, pounding heartbeat. But in many cases, the phobia expresses itself in purely psychological terms: simply put, the person is terrified of sexual contact.

Perhaps surprisingly, people with sexual aversion are likely to be able to respond fairly naturally to sexual encounters — if they can get past the initial dread. Some patients with this disorder have told us they have more difficulty with undressing and touching in a sexual context than they do with participation in intercourse.

Between 1972 and 1980, we have seen 143 cases of sexual aversion at the Masters & Johnson Institute. The primary causes seem to be: (1) severely negative parental sex attitudes; (2) a his-

510

tory of sexual trauma (e.g., rape, incest); (3) a pattern of constant sexual pressuring by a partner in a long-term relationship; and (4) gender identity confusion in men. In the typical case of sexual aversion, the frequency of sexual activity drops to only once or twice a year — if that often. This can obviously become a major source of relationship stress, and the partner of the person with sexual aversion often becomes extremely angry and considers leaving the relationship. Fortunately, the success rate for treating sexual aversion is over 90 percent even in cases of long duration (Kolodny, Masters, and Johnson, 1979). Schover and LoPiccolo (1982) have also reported that cases of ISD and sexual aversion usually have successful treatment outcomes.

SEX THERAPY

Prior to 1970 the treatment of sexual dysfunctions and problems was generally the province of psychiatry (Levine, 1976). Treatment usually took a long time and successful reversal of the sexual distress was very uncertain. The traditional psychiatric model of individual treatment (one therapist working with one patient) was almost always used.

Today, sex therapy is a field that includes practitioners of many different backgrounds — psychology, medicine (both psychiatry and other specialities), social work, nursing, counseling, and theology, just to name a few. There are also many approaches to sex therapy, some of which are described below.

The Masters and Johnson Model

Beginning in 1959, Masters and Johnson began their revolutionary program for treating sexual dysfunctions. It is considerably different from prior approaches in a number of ways. For example, they work only with couples (instead of individuals) because they feel that there is no such thing as an uninvolved partner in a committed relationship in which there is any form of sexual distress. This does not mean that the partner always *causes* the problem, but points out that he or she is *affected* by it, as the relationship is affected. This strategy shifts the therapeutic focus to the relationship instead of the individual. Furthermore, it provides a more effective means of identifying the full dimensions of a problem. Masters and Johnson found that the input of both partners usually proved more useful than the one-sided view that an individual provided. Finally, this strategy provides an opportunity to gain the cooperation and understanding of both partners in overcoming the distress.

A logical extension of this approach is the use of *two* therapists — a man and woman working together as a *cotherapy team*. This team increases therapeutic objectivity and balance by adequately representing male and female viewpoints and gives each partner a same-sex therapist to whom he or she can (theoretically) relate more easily. The cotherapy team also provides a model for the patient couple in important ways: for example, they can easily demonstrate effective communication skills.

Another important element of the Masters and Johnson approach is the integration of physiologic and psychosocial data in assessment and treatment. In the past, many psychiatrists never examined their patients because they feared that this might trigger unwanted sexual feelings that could complicate the treatment relationship. Masters and Johnson recognized that it was important to identify organic conditions that might require medical or surgical treatment instead of sex therapy. They also found that explaining the anatomy and physiology of sexual response to patients often had important therapeutic benefits of its own.

Finally, the Masters and Johnson model in-

In therapy sessions at the Masters & Johnson Institute, wide-ranging discussions cover much more than sexual issues only. In some cases, questions about sexual positions are answered using wooden artist's dolls for "demonstration" purposes.

Sexual Dysfunctions and Sex Therapy

volves a rapid, intensive approach to treating sexual problems. Couples are seen on a daily basis for a two-week period (the average duration of therapy is actually just under twelve days). This format permits a day-to-day continuity that appears to be beneficial in certain aspects of sex therapy, such as reducing anxiety or helping patients overcome mistakes. Couples are also urged to free themselves from their ordinary work, family, and social activities during the two weeks of therapy to be able to devote their undivided attention to their own relationship without outside distractions.

Against this general background, some additional treatment concepts of the Masters and Johnson approach are important:

1. *Therapy is individualized to meet the specific needs of each couple.* The couple's values and objectives are the primary determinants of exactly what is done. Therapists must avoid imposing their own values on their patients.

2. *Sex is assumed to be a natural function, controlled largely by reflex responses of the body.* Although many different factors can interfere with sexual function by disrupting these natural reflexes, sex therapy does not generally involve "teaching" the desired sexual response. Masters and Johnson focus instead on identifying obstacles that block effective sexual function and on helping people remove or overcome these obstacles. When this happens, natural function usually takes over promptly.[1]

3. *Because fears of performance and "spectatoring" are often central to cases of sexual dysfunction, therapy must be approached at several levels.*

---

[1] Sometimes removing the obstacles to natural function is not enough, particularly for people who have a lifelong pattern of sexual dysfunction. They may also need specific therapeutic attention to facilitate arousal or to improve sexual techniques. In this situation, there is some "teaching" going on.

Pressures to perform are removed initially by banning direct sexual contact. Couples are then helped to rediscover the sensual pleasures of touching and being touched without the goal of a particular sexual response (the "sensate focus" exercises). The therapists also help couples relabel their expectations so they do not judge everything they do as "success" or "failure." They also give people "permission" to be anxious, which helps them to talk about their anxiety more openly. This open communication often reduces the severity of the anxiety.

4. *Determining who's "to blame" for a sexual problem is discouraged as a counterproductive exercise.* Instead, couples are assisted in finding out what makes them feel comfortable and relaxed as opposed to tense or nervous. In this approach, each person is urged to take responsibility for himself or herself rather than waiting for his or her partner to provide the "right" mood, the "right" touch, or the "right" style of making love.

5. *Helping couples see that sex is just one component of their relationship is stressed.* Often, when a sexual problem occurs in people's lives, it causes them to worry about sex so much that they devote a disproportionate amount of time to thinking and talking about this topic. One typical objective of therapy is to help couples achieve a balanced perspective toward sex in which it is neither the totality of their relationship nor the most neglected part of their relationship. In fact, a general truism of sex therapy is that when a couple's relationship improves outside the bedroom, it is apt to have positive results inside the bedroom, too.

THE MASTERS AND JOHNSON THERAPY FORMAT

On the first day of therapy, the couple begins by briefly meeting with their cotherapists who introduce themselves and explain the events of the next few days. Following this overview, the patients are separated and a detailed history is taken from each partner by the same-sex therapist. After a break for lunch, when the cotherapists get together to discuss what they have learned, a second history is taken but this time on a cross-sex basis — that is, the male therapist interviews the female patient and the female therapist interviews the male patient. Rounding out a busy day, each patient has a complete physical examination. Blood samples are obtained the following morning for laboratory evaluation of general health.

The second day of therapy is the time of the "roundtable session" in which the couple and both cotherapists meet together. Here, the therapists present their assessment of the sexual *and* nonsexual problems that the couple is facing and give an honest opinion of the chances of successful treatment. The patients are encouraged to comment on the therapists' impressions and to correct any factual errors that have been made. The therapists try to explain the most plausible causes of the sexual dysfunction(s) or problem(s) and begin to outline the type of approach for treatment. Generally, there is some discussion of sex as a natural function, how fears of performance originate, the effect of spectatoring, and the importance of communication skills. The roundtable usually concludes with suggestions to try the "sensate focus" exercises (described soon) in the privacy of their own home or hotel room.

Each initial history-taking session usually lasts one and one-half to two hours, and the cross-sex histories average about forty-five minutes apiece. The roundtable generally lasts about ninety minutes, although any of these times are quite variable, depending in part on how talkative the couple is. Daily sessions after the roundtable average about an hour in length.

From the third day, the patient couple and the cotherapists continue to meet in a four-way interaction, although occasionally the therapists may see each patient separately to discover if there are any individual concerns that one partner is hesitant to discuss in the presence of the other. Each partner is asked to describe the events of the previous twenty-four hours, with particular attention to communication patterns and interaction during the sensate focus assignments.

Interestingly, a majority of time in the therapy sessions is usually spent on nonsexual issues (such as dealing with anger, self-esteem, or power struggles), although there is a direct attempt to provide information about sexual anatomy and physiology while attending to the couple's other needs. Couples who have negative sexual attitudes are encouraged to adopt new viewpoints.

SENSATE FOCUS

At the beginning of therapy, each couple is asked to refrain from direct sexual interaction involving genital contact. This approach helps to remove performance pressures and provides a framework for breaking the fear-spectatoring-failure-fear cycle that is often deeply ingrained. To learn more effective ways of sexual interaction, the idea of sensate focus is introduced.

In the first stage of sensate focus exercises, the couple is told to have two sessions in which they will each have a turn touching their partner's body — with the breasts and genitals "off limits." The purpose of the touching is *not* to be sexual but to establish an awareness of touch sensations by noticing textures, contours, temperatures, and contrasts (while doing the touching) or to simply be aware of the sensations of being touched by their partner. The person doing the touching is told to do so on the basis of what interests them, *not* on any guesses about what their partner likes or doesn't like. It is emphasized that

Sexual Dysfunctions and Sex Therapy

this touching should not be a massage or an attempt to arouse their partner sexually.

The initial sensate focus periods should be as silent as possible, since words can detract from the awareness of physical sensations. However, the person being touched must let his or her partner know — either nonverbally (by body language) or in words — if any touch is uncomfortable.

Although many people say, "Oh, we've touched lots of times before — can't we just skip this and go on to a more advanced level?", this first stage of sensate focus is critical in several ways. For example, it allows the therapists to find out additional information about how a couple interacts that supplements their histories in important ways. This stage also has a specific treatment value of its own, as shown by the fact that many times, men who have not had erec-

tions for years in attempts at sex suddenly discover a kingsize erection probably because the performance demand was removed. After all, they were told that sexual arousal was not expected but even if it occurred, it was not to be put into action. Finally, it provides an excellent means for reducing anxiety and teaching nonverbal communication skills.

In the next stage of sensate focus, touching is expanded to include the breasts and genitals. The positions shown in the drawings are recommended but not required. The person doing the touching is instructed to begin with general body touching and to not "dive" for the genitals. Again, the emphasis is on awareness of physical sensations and not on the expectation of a particular sexual response.

At this stage, the couple is usually asked to try a "hand-riding" technique as a more direct

The "hand-riding" technique for conveniently giving nonverbal messages.

means of nonverbal communication. The couple takes turns with this exercise. By placing one hand on top of her partner's hand while he touches her, the woman can indicate if she would like more pressure, a lighter touch, a faster or slower type of stroking, or a change to a different spot. The male indicates his preferences when the situation is reversed. The trick is to integrate these nonverbal messages in such a way that the person being touched doesn't become a "traffic cop" but simply adds some additional input to the touching, which is still primarily done based on what interests the "toucher."

In the next phase of sensate focus, instead of taking turns touching each other, the couple is asked to try some mutual touching. The purpose of this is twofold: first, it provides a more natural form of physical interaction (in "real life" situations, people don't usually take turns touching and being touched); and second, it doubles the potential sources of sensual input. This is a very important step in overcoming spectatoring, since one thing the spectator can try is to shift attention to a portion of his or her partner's body (getting "lost" in the touch) and away from watching his or her own response. Couples are reminded that no matter how sexually aroused they may feel, intercourse is still "off limits."

The next stages of sensate focus are to continue the same activities but at some point to shift into the female-on-top position without attempting insertion. In this position, the woman can play with the penis, rubbing it against her clitoris, vulva, and vaginal opening regardless of whether there is an erection or not. If there is an erection, and she feels like it, she can simply slip the tip of the penis a bit inside the vagina, all the while focusing on the physical sensations and stopping the action or moving back to simple nongenital touching or cuddling if she or her partner becomes goal-oriented or anxious. When comfort is developed at this level, full intercourse can usually occur without difficulty.

As simple as these techniques may sound, it is important to realize that they are used as part of a detailed program of psychotherapy, not just as a grab-bag of "gimmicks." The remarkable thing is how dramatically and effectively these techniques work, even in cases where severe sexual dysfunctions have been present for ten, twenty, or thirty years.

SOME SPECIFIC TREATMENT STRATEGIES

The general features of the Masters and Johnson treatment model just described are supplemented by some additional methods used in the treatment of various dysfunctions.

In *erectile dysfunction*, it is important to help the man understand that he cannot "will" an erection to occur on demand anymore than he can "will" his blood pressure to drop or his heart rate to increase. He *can* set the stage for his own natural reflexes to take over by not trying to have erections and by moving out of his performance fears. Not surprisingly, the man with erectile dysfunction often finds himself having firm erections during the early stages of sensate focus experience. While this can be reassuring to him, it is also important for the man (and his partner) to realize that losing an erection is *not* a sign of failure; it simply shows that erections come and go naturally. For this reason, the woman may be instructed to stop stroking or fondling the penis when an erection occurs, so the man has an opportunity to see that it will return with further touching. A related problem is that many men with erectile dysfunction try to rush their sexual performance once they get an erection out of fear that they will promptly lose it. The "rushing" adds one more performance pressure, and the usual result is a rapid loss of erection.

When intercourse is attempted (only after the man has gained considerable confidence in his erectile capacity *and* has been able to reduce his spectatoring behavior), the woman is advised

These positions are suggested to couples for the sensate focus exercises at the stage that includes genital exploration. When the man is touching his partner, the position in the top drawing is used; when the woman is touching her partner, the position in the bottom drawing is used. Couples are urged to modify these positions to whatever they find comfortable and to experiment with other positions, too.

FIGURE 19-2
The Squeeze Technique Used in Treating Premature Ejaculation

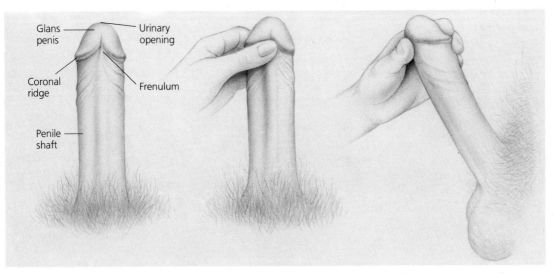

to insert the penis. This reduces pressures on the man to decide when it is time to insert and removes the potential distraction of his fumbling to "find" the vagina.

In treating *premature ejaculation*, the couple approach is particularly important since the condition may actually be more distressing to the woman than the man. In addition to discussing the physiology of ejaculation, the therapists introduce a specific method called the "squeeze technique" that helps recondition the ejaculatory reflex. When genital touching is begun, the woman uses the "squeeze" periodically. As shown in Figure 19-2, the woman puts her thumb on the frenulum of the penis and places her first and second fingers just above and below the coronal ridge on the opposite side of the penis. A firm, grasping pressure is applied for about four seconds and then abruptly released. The pressure is

always applied front to back, never from side to side. It is important that the woman use the pads of her fingers and thumb and avoids pinching the penis or scratching it with her fingernails. For unknown reasons, the squeeze technique reduces the urgency to ejaculate (it also may cause a temporary, partial loss of erection). It should not be used, however, at the moment of ejaculatory inevitability — instead, it must begin at the early stages of genital play and continue periodically, every few minutes. The "squeeze" can be used whether the penis is erect or flaccid, but the firmness of the pressure should be proportionate to the degree of erection.

When the couple begins having intercourse, the woman is asked to use the squeeze three to six times before attempting insertion. Once the penis is fully inside her, she should hold still for a fifteen- to thirty-second period, with neither part-

Sexual Dysfunctions and Sex Therapy

FIGURE 19-3
The Basilar Squeeze Technique Used in Treating Premature Ejaculation

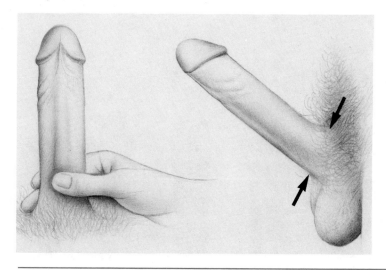

Unlike the squeeze at the coronal ridge, the basilar squeeze can be applied by either the woman or man. Firm pressure is applied for about four seconds and then released; the pressure should always be from front to back (as shown by the arrows), never from side to side.

ner thrusting, and then move off the penis, apply the squeeze again, and reinsert. This time a slow thrusting pattern can begin. Once the man improves his ejaculatory control both partners are taught the "basilar squeeze," another version of the squeeze technique (Figure 19-3), so that intercourse need not be interrupted by repeated dismounting to apply a squeeze.

Ejaculatory incompetence is treated by in-depth attention to the underlying psychological components combined with sensate focus experiences that seek to lead the man through a sequence of: (1) ejaculating by masturbation while alone, (2) ejaculating by masturbation in the presence of his partner, (3) ejaculating by manual stimulation received from his partner, and (4) having the partner stimulate the penis vigorously to the point of ejaculatory inevitability and then quickly inserting it in the vagina. In most cases,

when the man has ejaculated in the vagina once or twice, the fears or inhibitions about this act disappear completely. In some cases where the treatment sequence has not worked, it may be helpful to have the man ejaculate (via manual stimulation) externally onto the woman's genitals. After he becomes used to seeing his semen in genital contact with his partner, intravaginal ejaculation may occur more easily.

Vaginismus is treated by explaining the nature of the involuntary reflex spasm to the couple and demonstrating the reflex in a carefully conducted pelvic examination with the male partner present and the woman urged to watch by use of a mirror. After this is done, the physician teaches the woman some techniques for relaxing the muscles around the vagina. The most effective method seems to be having her first deliberately tighten these muscles and then simply

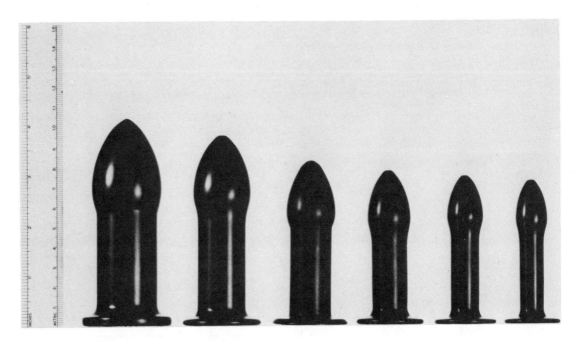

Plastic dilators used to treat vaginismus to allow the woman to learn how to recondition the reflex response of the muscles surrounding her vagina. Treatment begins with the smallest dilator and progresses gradually to the larger sizes.

let go. It is much more difficult to relax on command. Next, the woman is given a set of various sized plastic dilators. The smallest of these, slightly thinner than a finger, is gently inserted in the vagina by the physician — often to the amazement of the woman, who may have never been able to insert *anything* in her vagina. She is then shown how to insert the dilator herself, using plenty of sterile lubricating jelly, and is asked to practice this at home several times a day, keeping the dilators in place for ten to fifteen minutes at a time. Most women with vaginismus find that within five or six days they are able to use the largest dilator in the set which is similar in thickness to an erect penis. If relationship issues have been dealt with adequately (often a key part of therapy), the transition to successful intercourse

is usually easy at this point. At this time, it is particularly important for the woman to insert the penis so she feels in control.

The strategies used in treating *anorgasmia* depend greatly on the nature of the dysfunction. Different approaches are needed for a woman who has never had an orgasm as compared to a woman who is easily orgasmic with masturbation, manual stimulation, or oral-genital sex. Similarly, depending on the cause(s) of the anorgasmia, treatment strategies will vary widely from case to case. For example, a woman with a poor body image may be helped to find various ways of regarding her body more positively. A woman who is distracted from high levels of arousal by disturbing fantasies might be taught thought-blocking techniques, while another woman who

Sexual Dysfunctions and Sex Therapy

cannot get beyond plateau may be encouraged to experiment with fantasies as an aid to boosting her into orgasm.

Common techniques used in treating anorgasmia include: (1) encouraging a woman to explore her own body, especially focusing on genital exploration and stimulation in a relaxed, undemanding fashion; (2) dealing with performance anxieties and spectatoring, with particular attention to reducing performance pressures from her partner; (3) fostering sexual communications so that the woman is able to let her partner know what type of touch or stimulation she prefers at a given moment; and (4) reducing inhibitions that limit the woman's capacity for arousal or that block orgasm. A woman helped by this last technique is often given "permission" to have sexual feelings and learns to overcome fears that orgasm involves losing consciousness or losing control of her bladder. In most cases, these strat-

egies make it fairly simple for the woman to reach orgasm via masturbation or partner stimulation. To make the transition to have orgasms during intercourse, a "bridging" technique is used in which either partner stimulates the clitoris manually during coitus with active thrusting.

These methods have now been used for more than twenty years in the treatment of sexual dysfunctions, with approximately four out of five patients successfully treated. Between 1959 and 1973, patients were followed for five years after therapy to evaluate the permanence of treatment results. More recently, a two-year follow-up period has been used. About one couple in twenty returns to the Masters & Johnson Institute for additional therapy sometime after their two-week course of treatment. Statistics describing the Masters & Johnson Institute's experience for the various categories of dysfunction are shown in Table 19-1.

TABLE 19-1
Results of Sex Therapy at the Masters & Johnson Institute

	N*	Failures	Successes**	Success Rate
Primary Impotence	51	17	34	66.7%
Secondary Impotence	501	108	393	78.4
Premature Ejaculation	432	17	415	96.1
Ejaculatory Incompetence	75	18	57	76.0
Male Totals	1,059	160	899	84.9
Primary Anorgasmia	399	84	315	79.0
Situational Anorgasmia	331	96	235	71.0
Vaginismus	83	1	82	98.8
Female Totals	813	181	632	77.7
Combined Totals	1,872	341	1,531	81.8

*Cases seen between 1959 and 1977. (Adapted from Masters and Johnson, 1970, and Kolodny, Masters, and Johnson, 1979.)

**A case was categorized as successful only if the change in sexual function was unequivocal and lasting. For all patients seen before 1973, follow-up lasted five years. From 1973, the follow-up period was reduced to two years. If a patient was successful during the two-week sex therapy program but then slipped back into dysfunction, the case was listed as a failure.

Other Approaches to Sex Therapy

Important contributions to sex therapy have been made by a number of other workers using treatment methods that differ from Masters and Johnson's model. Most therapists, for example, see patients on a once a week basis rather than daily (Schmidt and Lucas, 1976; Caird and Wincze, 1977; Schiller, 1981). Many therapists believe that a single therapist can work as effectively as a cotherapy team (H. Kaplan, 1974, 1979; Annon, 1976; Ellis, 1980; Schiller, 1981; Arentewicz and Schmidt, 1983), which reduces the expense of sex therapy. Others have experimented successfully with group therapy formats or individual therapy (Kaplan, 1974; Barbach, 1980; Zilbergeld, 1980; Cotten-Huston and Wheeler, 1983). Hypnosis has also been reported to be useful in treating sexual difficulties (Alexander, 1974; Fuchs et al., 1975; Fabbri, 1976; Brown and Chaves, 1980). Here, we will consider some of the most common approaches used by other therapists.

HELEN KAPLAN: THE NEW SEX THERAPY

Psychiatrist Helen Kaplan (1974, 1979) has written extensively on the treatment of sexual dysfunctions, integrating many of the methods of Masters and Johnson with principles of psychoanalytic therapy. In her view, human sexual response is best seen as *triphasic* or consisting of three separate but interlocking phases: desire, arousal, and orgasm. She believes that desire phase disorders are most difficult to treat, because they tend to be associated with deep-seated psychological difficulties (H. Kaplan, 1979). She also states that "the standard sex therapy methods seem to be effective primarily for those sexual problems which have their roots in mild and easily diminished anxieties and conflicts" (H. Kaplan, 1979, p. xviii). To deal with more complex cases, she uses a lengthened form of sex therapy which seeks a deeper level of insight and addresses unconscious conflicts. One of her underlying theories is that a sexual disorder usually results from multiple levels of causes — some more immediate and accessible, some more remote and hidden.

The details of Kaplan's treatment methods differ considerably in some ways from the Masters and Johnson methods. In the treatment of premature ejaculation, for example, she advocates use of the "stop-start" technique instead of the squeeze. In the "stop-start" method, introduced by James Semans in 1956, the female partner stimulates the penis manually until the man feels that he is rapidly approaching ejaculation, at which time she stops all stimulation until the sense of ejaculatory urgency disappears. Stimulation then begins again, and the stop-start cycle is repeated several times before the man is allowed to ejaculate (Kaplan, 1974).

BEHAVIORAL THERAPY

Modern behavioral methods for treating sexual difficulties are generally traced back to Joseph Wolpe (1958) and enjoy widespread acceptance today (LoPiccolo, 1977; Bancroft, 1977; Leiblum and Pervin, 1980). While many methods used by Masters and Johnson are very similar to behavioral techniques, there are some theoretical and practical differences in approach.

The operant approach to behavioral therapy is to carefully analyze the problematic behavior (e.g., the sexual dysfunction) and to use positive and negative reinforcers best suited to the individual case. Gradual exposure to imaginary scenes of sexual activity may be used before exposure to real-life sexual situations in sensate focus exercises. These techniques are both forms of *desensitization*, in which the controlled exposure to limited amounts of anxiety helps to eliminate the anxiety. *Relaxation training* (learning specific breathing and muscle exercises to reduce tension) and *assertiveness training* (learning how to say what you feel and what you need) are other methods used to reduce anxiety. *Directed masturbation* (LoPiccolo and Lobitz, 1972), which is used in the treatment of anorgasmia, is a nine-step program for helping a woman learn to masturbate to orgasm and then include her partner in her orgasmic response, first in manual stimulation and then during intercourse.

An interesting and logical way of approaching sexual problems has been suggested by behavioral psychologist Jack Annon (1976). He uses a four-level model, represented by the acronym PLISSIT, to go from the simplest to more advanced levels of treatment. The four levels are: P = permission, LI = limited information, SS = specific suggestions, and IT = intensive therapy. This model makes use of the fact that in simple cases of sexual difficulties, reassurance and education are sometimes enough to solve the problem. Specific suggestions might include instruction in the squeeze technique or in sensate focus, without dealing with major psychosocial issues. Intensive therapy goes beyond these steps to deal with relationship conflicts, psychological problems, and other complex issues that may be present.

ADDITIONAL METHODS

There are now so many different approaches to sex therapy that it is practically impossible to describe them all. Only brief mention of a few other notable methods can be made here due to space limitations. Lonnie Barbach (1975, 1980) has pioneered in the use of women's groups for treating anorgasmia. These groups have the particular advantages of being useful for women without partners and being relatively inexpensive and quite successful. Psychologist Albert Ellis has developed Rational-Emotive Therapy (R.E.T.) as a useful approach to sexual and nonsexual problems. R.E.T. helps people overcome irrational beliefs and unrealistic expectations that feed into

their sexual dysfunction. Blending behavioral methods with unique strategies for dealing with emotional discomfort (such as shame-attacking exercises, risk-taking exercises), R.E.T. principles can be applied in individual, couple, or group therapy.

Some sex therapists follow the controversial practice of "body work therapy" in which the therapist has sexual activity with the patient (Apfelbaum, 1980). Many ethical objections have been raised to this practice (Marmor, 1980a).

A different approach, still controversial but more widely accepted, is the use of a "surrogate partner" in sex therapy. The surrogate is usually a trained woman who is paid to participate in therapy and sexual activity with a single male to improve his chances of success; there are also a few male surrogates who work with female partners. The surrogate does not function as a cotherapist but usually makes periodic reports to the therapists on the patient's progress and follows their instructions closely (Masters and Johnson, 1970). Although some people have criticized this practice as being only a thinly veiled form of prostitution, others see it as an important means of helping people who are unable to find a partner who will accompany them in sex therapy.

THE EFFECTIVENESS OF SEX THERAPY

As there are many different models of sex therapy and the specialty is still fairly young, evaluating the effectiveness of these approaches is difficult. Most studies to date have not had control groups, and many reports are based on a small number of cases. Other problems are: (1) lack of uniform definitions of the dysfunctions, (2) differences in selection of patients, (3) differences in defining success or failure, and (4) lack of adequate follow-up (checking the results periodically after therapy is over). Additional methodological issues have been raised in several detailed reviews (Schumacher, 1977; Kilmann, 1978; Hogan, 1978; Kilmann and Auerbach, 1979).

Psychologists Bernie Zilbergeld and Michael Evans (1980) have criticized Masters and Johnson's data on the effectiveness of sex therapy on a variety of methodological grounds. Specifically, they have questioned the criteria Masters and Johnson used to rate treatment outcomes, suggesting that the results obtained may have reflected undue leniency in deciding how to classify cases. In addition, they suggested that Masters and Johnson's results may have been artificially inflated by selecting only the best candidates for treatment (and rejecting fairly large numbers of cases that appeared "difficult"). In actuality, however, fewer than one out of fifty couples who apply to the Masters & Johnson Institute are turned down for therapy, and the criteria used to evaluate the outcome of sex therapy at the Masters & Johnson Institute are relatively stringent (Kolodny, 1981; Masters et al., 1983). These criticisms also seem to lose sight of the fact that other sex therapy programs are reporting rates of success that are similar to those of the Masters and Johnson program (Rachman and Wilson, 1980; Schover and LoPiccolo, 1982; Apfelbaum, 1983; Arentewicz and Schmidt, 1983).

Some critics of sex therapy have suggested that it is a dehumanizing, mechanistic process. Psychiatrist Natalie Shainess (1973), for example, argues that sex therapy "debases" sex and that Masters and Johnson "have tended to detach the sex act from the moods, feelings, and emotions of desire and love." In her view, sex therapy is a kind of "coaching that reduces one partner to a push-button operator" (Cadden, 1978, p. 487). Psychiatrist Thomas Szasz (1980, p. xvi) sees sex therapists as "determined to conceal moral values and social policies as medical diagnoses and treatment."

As most sex therapists agree, success or failure is a subjective commodity. Some sex therapy patients who are classified as "failures" may see their treatment as very beneficial. Others, who attained enough change in their sexual function to be called "successes" by their therapists, may continue to feel unhappy or anxious. Sometimes two partners disagree about whether therapy was helpful. In all these situations, it is impossible to say that one viewpoint is right or wrong.

Although sex therapy offers no instant, magical cures, a variety of studies show that it can be of significant help to many people. Furthermore, the gains made in sex therapy tend to be long-lasting rather than short-lived (Leiblum and Pervin, 1980). Thus, while sex therapy is no cure-all and some people admittedly require a different type of professional help, sex therapy has managed to improve the lives of thousands of people with sexual distress.

CHOOSING A SEX THERAPIST

Unfortunately, sex therapy is an unregulated profession today. People can call themselves sex therapists even if their "training" consists only of watching a movie or reading a book. Judging from letters received at the Masters & Johnson Institute and from situations we have encountered with our patients, there are many sex therapists who are quacks, and there are hundreds of well-meaning persons who try to do sex therapy but simply are not qualified. The hapless victim of these self-proclaimed "therapists" may be bilked out of thousands of dollars. Worse yet, emotional problems may be created by improper therapy, sexual problems may worsen, and the lack of success may discourage a person from seeking further care.

To minimize the risk of falling prey to unqualified sex therapists, the following guidelines may be of assistance.

1. Turn first to sex therapy centers that are

affiliated with universities, medical schools, or hospitals. Alternately, your local medical society, psychological association, or your family physician may be able to provide a list of qualified therapists. Two professional organizations, the Society for Sex Therapy and Research (New York, NY) and the American Association of Sex Educators, Counselors, and Therapists (Washington, DC) publish national directories. AASECT has a sex therapist certification program; SSTAR has tougher membership requirements which it believes are equivalent to certification.

2. Ask about the education and training of the sex therapist. Unless he or she is willing to discuss this with you, do not continue any further. In addition to having a genuine graduate degree from a recognized university, be sure to verify that the therapist has received post-graduate training in sex therapy that included personal supervision. Attendance at a weekend seminar isn't the same as in-depth training.

3. Avoid therapists who make unrealistic promises or guarantees of cure and therapists who tell you that part of your "treatment" includes having sexual relations with them.

4. Be sure the therapist is willing to discuss treatment costs, schedules, and plans in an open, straightforward fashion. (Many sex therapy clinics have a sliding scale fee arrangement where charges are adjusted to the client's ability to pay.)

PREVENTING SEXUAL DYSFUNCTION

The prevention of sexual dysfunctions probably begins in the parenting role by providing children with sex information appropriate for their age and by permitting them to discuss sexuality in an open, honest fashion. Severely negative family attitudes about sex may predispose a child to later sexual difficulties. After childhood, the following pointers apply:

1. Approach sex as an opportunity for exploration and intimacy instead of as a job to be done. Goal-oriented sex creates performance demands, which can lead to spectatoring and impaired responsivity. Remember that there's no "right" way of having sex; it's a matter of personal interest and comfort.

2. Try to develop open, effective lines of communication with your partner. Guessing about what your partner wants is difficult at best; making your partner guess about your needs is equally problematic. Effective communications include being able to say "no" just as well as "yes" — if you never say "no," your partner can't be sure if your "yes" is genuine or not.

3. Don't believe everything you read or hear about sex. Many books and articles about how people "should" respond are oversimplified at best and may be inaccurate and misleading. It's easy to talk yourself into a problem by comparing yourself to what "others" say.

4. If you're having a sexual problem of any sort, discuss it with your partner instead of pretending it doesn't exist. Often, by using some of the sensate focus methods or the self-help readings listed at the end of this chapter, a solution can be found. *However, if the problem doesn't go away fairly quickly, seek professional help.* It's usually much easier to treat recent problems than problems that have solidified over a long time.

SUMMARY

1. Sexual dysfunctions are conditions in which the physical responses of sexual function are impaired. In males, the principal sexual dysfunctions are erectile dysfunction, premature ejaculation, ejaculatory incompetence, and retarded ejaculation; in women, they are anorgasmia, vaginismus, and dyspareunia.

2. Overall, about 10 to 20 percent of cases of sexual dysfunction have organic causes such as

diabetes, alcoholism, infection, neurologic disease, and drugs. Psychosocial causes can be classified as developmental (e.g., negative sex attitudes, sexual trauma), personal (e.g., anxiety, depression, guilt), or interpersonal (e.g., poor communication, relationship conflicts, hostility).

3. Inhibited sexual desire and sexual aversion are examples of sexual problems that do not necessarily cause dysfunction but can lead to considerable emotional distress.

4. Sex therapy as a distinct specialty originated with the work of Masters and Johnson. Their approach involves a cotherapy team working with couples on a daily basis over a two-week period emphasizing integration of physiologic and psychosocial information. Sex is seen as a natural function; sensate focus exercises are used to reduce anxiety and improve spontaneity; and methods such as the "squeeze" technique (for premature ejaculation) and use of vaginal dilators (for vaginismus) are sometimes employed along with careful attention to relationship dynamics.

5. Other approaches to therapy include Helen Kaplan's work (integrating sex therapy and psychoanalytic methods), behavioral models, Rational-Emotive Therapy, and group therapy.

6. Although sex therapy is not foolproof, it has been shown to be highly effective in most studies. Many so-called sex therapists, however, have little or no formal training in the field, so it is important to choose a sex therapist carefully.

SUGGESTED READINGS

Belliveau, Fred, and Richter, Lin. *Understanding Human Sexual Inadequacy*. New York: Bantam, 1970. A translation into nontechnical language of *Human Sexual Inadequacy*, accurately summarizing the content in easily readable form.

Heiman, Julia; LoPiccolo, Leslie; and LoPiccolo, Joseph. *Becoming Orgasmic: A Sexual Growth Program for Women*. Englewood Cliffs, N.J.: Prentice-Hall, 1976. A personal sensitively written book designed to help women overcome sexual difficulties.

Kaplan, Helen. *The Illustrated Manual of Sex Therapy*. New York: Quadrangle/New York Times, 1975. A beautifully produced book with tasteful illustrations and clear, concise explanations of Kaplan's approach to sex therapy.

Kelly, Gary F. *Good Sex: A Healthy Man's Guide to Sexual Fulfillment*. New York: Harcourt Brace Jovanovich, 1979. A readable "self-help" book emphasizing a common sense but creative approach to sex.

Ambitious students who are willing to wade through more technical terminology might also be interested in Helen Kaplan's *Disorders of Sexual Desire* (Brunner/Mazel, 1979), Lonnie Barbach's *Women Discover Orgasm* (Free Press, 1980), Leiblum and Pervin's *Principles and Practice of Sex Therapy* (Guilford Press, 1980), and the original *Human Sexual Inadequacy* (Little, Brown, 1970), by Masters and Johnson.

Sexual Dysfunctions and Sex Therapy

20 Sexual Disorders and Sexual Health

S EXUAL health is tightly interwoven with total health: both depend on freedom from physical and emotional limitations. The preceding chapter emphasized emotional causes of sexual distress and ways of dealing with these problems. In this chapter, we will consider the physical conditions that affect sexuality. Our discussion will cover four major topics: sex and disability, the impact of illness on sexuality, drugs and sex, and infections involving the sex organs. Learning about these problems is important because it increases our understanding of the physiology of sex and helps us better grasp the emotional dimension of such situations.

SEX AND DISABILITY

A number of common myths and stereotypes about the sexuality of disabled people have been identified by the Sex & Disability Project of George Washington University. These myths, which "can drastically and unnecessarily curtail the sexual expression of disabled people" (Chipouras et al., 1979), are as follows:

1. Disabled people are asexual.
2. Disabled people are dependent and childlike, so they need to be protected.
3. Disability breeds disability.

The joy of loving and being loved is shared fully by disabled people. Despite popular misconceptions, the disabled also have sexual feelings and needs which can be expressed in a multiplicity of ways.

Sexual Disorders and Sexual Health

4. Disabled people should stay with and marry their own kind.
5. Parents of handicapped children don't want sex education for their children.
6. Sexual intercourse culminating in orgasm is essential for sexual satisfaction.
7. If a disabled person has a sexual problem, it's almost always the result of the disability.
8. If a non-disabled person has a sexual relationship with a disabled individual, it's because he or she can't attract anyone else.

These myths collectively show how uncomfortable our society is with the idea of disabled persons as sexual beings. Somehow, many people seem to think, the disabled should worry about more important things in their lives and not concern themselves with an area that is obviously intended for healthy, "normal" people to enjoy. Fortunately, many of those who are disabled have refused to be intimidated by this line of reasoning and have joined forces with a number of workers in the health care professions as activists in seeking more attention to the sexual needs and feelings of people who have one form of disability or another. In fact, this movement has led to the development of a sexual bill of rights for the disabled (Chipouras et al., 1979) that covers the following items:

1. The right to sexual expression.
2. The right to privacy.
3. The right to be informed.
4. The right to have access to needed services such as contraceptive counseling, medical care, genetic counseling, and sex counseling.
5. The right to choose one's marital status.
6. The right to have or not have children.
7. The right to make decisions which affect one's life.
8. The right to develop to one's fullest potential.

Although we are not yet in an era when the disabled are totally free to exercise these rights, we have made considerable progress in this direction in the last decade. Hopefully, as attitudes toward the disabled continue to change and as our society accepts sexuality as a positive, enhancing aspect of all of our lives, we may finally see the disappearance of myths and stereotypes and a more tolerant, open, and informed attitude taking their place.

Spinal Cord Injuries

A dramatic example of the impact of a disability on sexuality can be seen in people who have had injuries of the spinal cord. These injuries occur in a variety of circumstances, such as auto or motorcycle accidents, stab or bullet wounds, crushing industrial accidents, diving accidents, and serious falls. The injury usually results in *paraplegia* (paralysis of the legs) or *quadriplegia* (paralysis of all four limbs) and loss of all sensations in the body below the level of the injury. Normal bowel and bladder control is usually lost, and persons with spinal cord injuries are apt to have a significant loss of sexual function as well.

Most spinal-cord-injured (SCI) men lose the ability to have normal erections in response to psychological arousal, although they may be able to have brief reflex erections (which they cannot feel) in response to mechanical stimulation such as pinching or rubbing close to the genitals. Most (but not all) SCI males also become infertile and lose the ability to ejaculate. Those who are still able to ejaculate generally do so with no pelvic sensations of orgasm, and in many of the cases retrograde ejaculation (a backflow of semen into the bladder) occurs. On the other hand, intercourse may be possible for about four out of five men with incomplete spinal cord injuries. Even when erections do not occur, a technique called "stuffing" can be used. This involves tucking the soft or semi-firm penis into the vagina, with the woman thrusting with her hips, taking care not to move so the penis falls out.

Women with spinal cord injuries generally have normal fertility and can have children. While they usually retain their interest in sex, they typically lose their genital sensations and orgasmic responsiveness, and their vaginal lubrication is greatly reduced. Some SCI women — as well as SCI men — report experiencing "phantom" (non-genital) orgasms which include both psychological feelings of orgasm (e.g., intense pleasure) and physical sensations in some unaffected areas of the body that resemble prior patterns of orgasmic response.

Many people cannot understand why a spinal-cord-injured person who has no genital sensations would want to have intercourse. While the motivations of all cord-injured people are not the same, the following reasons are commonly given by people in this situation:

1. Having intercourse is a special act of sharing and intimacy quite apart from genital feelings.
2. Having intercourse can be intensely *psychologically* arousing.
3. Being able to engage in intercourse can provide a boost to a person's self-concept.

In addition, many cord-injured males mention that being able to have intercourse makes them feel more like a man, while some cord-injured females note that having intercourse enhances their sense of femininity. There are also some cord-injured persons who have intercourse primarily to please their partner (just as some people *without* cord injuries do, too).

While a number of people have pointed out that the SCI woman is less handicapped sexually than the SCI man because she is still able to have intercourse, this is an oversimplification of a complex issue and perpetuates a view of females as sexually passive. Many cord-injured women are distressed by their sexual limitations and require counseling to help them reaffirm their sexuality (Thornton, 1979). Unfortunately, as Zwerner (1982) points out, sexuality counseling is not included in many rehabilitation programs for SCI women, forcing many to seek out such services on their own or to do without their potential benefits.

The sexual abilities of the spinal-cord-injured and their ways of coping with their situation vary greatly. While some adopt a completely defeatist attitude and avoid all sexual opportunities, others have a continuing interest in sex which they express through active involvement with a partner. What must be stressed is that there are many methods of sexual interaction besides intercourse (Mooney, Cole, and Chilgren, 1975). Oral-genital sex, kissing, use of a vibrator (which a quadriplegic can sometimes apply by holding the base with his or her teeth), massage, and cuddling are only a few of the available options for having intimacy and sexual pleasure. In addition, many SCI people find that unaffected regions of their body become extraordinarily sensitive and erotic, so that stimulation above the region of sensory loss can produce arousal and sometimes orgasm. It is now possible for the SCI man with permanently impaired erections to have a device implanted surgically that will permit him to have erections and to participate in intercourse (see the boxed item).

Blindness and Deafness

If a person is blind or deaf from birth (or from a very young age), the sexual learning that occurs during childhood and adolescence can be seriously hindered. The person who has been blind since birth, for instance, is deprived of the ability to see the various shapes of human bodies

Penile Implants

When injury or illness causes complete inability to have erections, sexual functioning can now be restored to a significant degree thanks to modern technology. Several types of devices are available for surgical implantation in the penis. Although these devices can provide firm enough erections for intercourse to take place, they cannot restore sensation to the penis or normal ejaculation if these have been lost due to organic causes.

There are two basic types of penile implants. The simplest is a pair of fixed, semirigid rods which are placed inside the shaft of the penis. These rods produce a permanent state of semierection, so they may be embarrassing to some men. More complicated and expensive, but more realistic in appearance and function, is an inflatable device that also requires surgical placement. Two tapered inflatable cylinders are inserted into the penis and are connected by a tubing system to a fluid storage reservoir implanted in the lower abdomen. By pinching a simple pump and valve in the scrotum, fluid moves into the cylinders, causing a natural looking erection. Releasing the valve moves the fluid out of the cylinders back to the reservoir (returning the penis to the flaccid state).

Either device may seem somewhat "artificial" to the man or his partner – in some cases, this feeling is so problematic that after surgery, the man only uses his implant a few times (Renshaw, 1979). For many men facing a "hopeless" situation, however, penile implants can restore a sense of manhood and improve self-esteem considerably.

It is important to remember that erections are not all there is to sex. Some thought-provoking comments about sexuality and the physically impaired provide an interesting counterpoint to the seemingly "mechanical" approach of the penile implants:

– A stiff penis does not make a solid relationship, nor does a wet vagina.
– Absence of sensation does not mean absence of feelings.
– Inability to move does not mean inability to please.
– Inability to perform does not mean inability to enjoy.
– Loss of genitals does not mean loss of sexuality. (Anderson and Cole, 1975)

Inflatable penile implant shown deflated and inflated.

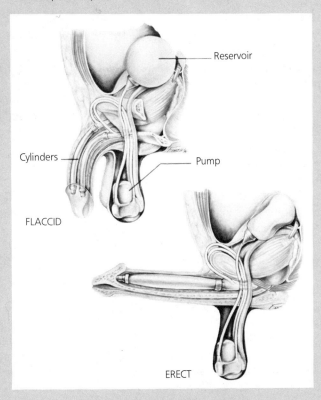

Reservoir

Cylinders

Pump

FLACCID

ERECT

both clothed and undressed that most of us silently notice and learn from. As a result, the person with lifelong blindness may be quite uncertain about the anatomic relation of one part of the body to another. (One fifteen-year-old boy was quite surprised to learn finally that the female breasts weren't located just above the waist, where he imagined them to be.) The person who has been deaf since birth often has difficulty understanding abstract concepts like maleness, parenting, and intimacy (FitzGerald and FitzGerald, 1977). Since very few parents of deaf children can communicate with them effectively with sign language, any semblance of sex education in the home is difficult if not impossible.

Neither blindness nor deafness produces any physical limitations on the body's sexual responsivity in and of itself. However, the sexual ignorance of many deaf or blind persons, coupled with their all-too-common lack of social skills, may create a predisposition toward sexual and relationship problems. In addition, the distorted body-image and poor self-esteem that many deaf or blind persons experience can also contribute to later sexual difficulties. Since blind persons do not have the visual cues surrounding sexual behavior that most of us depend on, and deaf people are apt to have significant problems in communicating with others, it's not surprising that such difficulties might occur.

Fortunately, sex education curricula have been devised for the deaf and blind. Most of these programs emphasize both social and biological aspects of sexuality and make good use of innovative methods of teaching, as well. For instance, blind students may be given sex-related articles like condoms, tampons, birth control pill packages, and vibrators to handle, so they develop familiarity with these products by touch. In fact, in Europe the touch method is sometimes used for anatomy lessons with live nude models (Helsinga, 1974). Many deaf students are

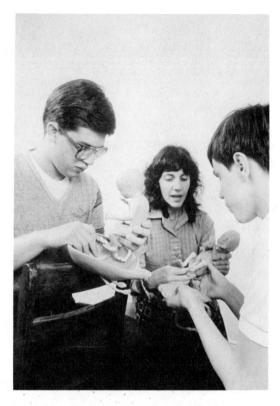

Two blind students are being educated about pregnancy by an instructor using lifelike plastic models. This type of sexual education is invaluable to persons with sensory disabilities.

now being taught by sex educators trained in sign language, and special visual materials have been prepared to make sex education easier despite the existence of hearing impairment.

Mental Retardation

Until very recently, people who are mentally retarded have been viewed as either asexual (in a state of child-like innocence) or as totally impulse-ridden and unable to control their primitive sexual urges. These myths, along with the general public's distaste for seeing the retarded as persons in their own right, have combined to make the topic of sexuality and the retarded a threatening one that arouses indignation and sometimes anger. One reflection of this attitude that has recently been changed was the involuntary sterilization that was often performed on young retarded adults or even adolescents to ensure that they couldn't reproduce (even though there is no evidence that most forms of retardation are genetically transmitted).

It is important to recognize that not all mentally retarded people are alike in their learning capacity, emotional stability, social skills, or capacity for independent living. The mildly retarded, for example, are educable and often lead productive lives, holding jobs, marrying, and raising families. Their lives are often indistinguishable from the lives of "normal" people, and they are usually capable of learning responsible sexual behavior without difficulty (Monat, 1982). The moderately retarded do not fit into our society so easily and are more apt to behave in a child-like manner both sexually and in other areas of living. They may alarm people by masturbating or disrobing in public or acting in a fashion that appears to be reckless or aggressive when showing affection for others, and they often require a protected or restricted environment in order to live their lives as comfortably and safely as possible. Yet they, too, are capable of learning much about sexuality and reproduction; for example, they can be taught how babies are conceived, what menstruation is (and how to deal with it), how to channel their sexual impulses into appropriate (i.e., non-public) masturbation. They also can learn how to avoid taking advantage of others and how to avoid sexual abuse. The severely or profoundly retarded, who must generally be institutionalized for their own safety, present a different range of problems since they are much more difficult to teach and are often capable of only the most rudimentary forms of communication.

The primary way of helping retarded people learn to handle their sexual feelings and express their sexual desires is through appropriate sex education. Kempton notes: "The retarded need sex education more than anyone else because they cannot readily learn about sexuality from friends, books, or from observing the behavior of others, and they have more than usual difficulty with sorting out reality from unreality" (1978, p. 138). In addition, cause-and-effect relationships are not always clear to the retarded; for instance, they may not realize that having intercourse can cause pregnancy. While some parents of retarded children have worried that sex education simply puts ideas into their children's heads, the available evidence suggests that withholding sex information does not deter sexual behavior and providing sex education does not lead to irresponsible sexual acts — in fact, just the opposite is likely to happen (Kempton, 1978; Monat, 1982).

A number of specific issues regarding sex and the mentally retarded are too complex to discuss meaningfully here. These issues include:

1. Providing privacy for the institutionalized retarded.
2. Providing appropriate contraceptive protection for the retarded. (In general, the IUD seems to be the best option for retarded women who are sexually active. Birth control pills are appropriate for use by the mildly retarded, but condoms, diaphragms, and foams are usually not practical since they are too easily forgotten and too difficult for many to use.)
3. Providing opportunities for long-term relationships and marriage, if desired.

Further information about these and related topics can be found in several books listed at the end of this chapter.

SEX AND ILLNESS

A wide variety of medical illnesses cause sexual problems. Until fairly recently, these situations were generally overlooked by health care professionals because they were often: (1) uncomfortable discussing sexuality; (2) uninformed about sexual aspects of illness; and (3) untrained in providing useful ways of dealing with these problems. Fortunately, this situation is rapidly changing today because fundamental research in this area is increasing and most health care schools include specific education about sexuality in their curricula.

Illnesses affect sexuality in direct and indirect ways. Physically, an illness can disrupt the normal reflexes of sexual response, as seen in persons with multiple sclerosis. Sometimes the treatment of an illness creates a sexual problem: medications that cause sexual side effects or surgery that results in sexual impairment are common examples. In other instances, sexual problems arise from the general effects of illness such as weakness, fatigue, or pain. There is an emotional side too: people with an illness may assume that it is "wrong" for them to have sexual feelings or may believe erroneously that their illness will prevent them from enjoying sex or from functioning sexually.

Now we will describe the sexual problems encountered in some specific types of medical disorders.

Neurologic Conditions

Sexual behavior and sexual function are both controlled in important ways by the nervous system. The brain itself is the ultimate synthesizer of sensory input (touch, sight, sound, taste, smell) and transforms electric impulses sent to it by nerve fibers into perceptions of pleasure,

pain, and human emotion. Similarly, impulses sent from the brain to other organs, including the genitals, translate sexual desire into sexual response. For these reasons, it is easy to see why many diseases or injuries of the nervous system can lead to sexual difficulties.

Multiple sclerosis (M.S.) is a disease that typically affects young adults and involves patchy damage to the protective covering of nerves throughout the body. Loss of erections and ejaculation eventually affects more than half of men with M.S., while difficulty reaching orgasm (or complete anorgasmia) affects a similar fraction of women (Lilius, Valtonen, and Wikström, 1976). Early in the disease there may be a partial numbness in the genitals, and sometimes any type of touch to the affected body region produces irritating, unpleasant sensations (Lundberg, 1977). For this reason, painful intercourse is another common problem. The sexual effects of M.S. tend to vary over time, so a person may have difficulties for several weeks or months and then go through a period of relatively normal sexual function.

People with *brain tumors* are somewhat less likely to encounter sexual difficulties. Although pituitary or hypothalamic tumors commonly cause erectile dysfunction and decreased sexual desire (Lundberg and Wide, 1978), tumors in other regions of the brain do not usually lead to sexual problems. *Epilepsy* is another neurologic disorder with little physical effect on sexual function. Some people with epilepsy, however, feel inferior because of their condition and may avoid sexual opportunities in the mistaken fear that arousal will cause a seizure. Although *polio* can cause spinal cord damage, it affects muscular function, not sensations. For this reason, most people with paralysis from polio are not impaired in their sexual function, although their inability to move may create problems in coital thrusting.

Sex and Disability

Understanding the impact of a major disability on a person's sexuality is not simply a matter of understanding sexual physiology or even the medical side of the disability. The following candid observations explain, in their own ways, other aspects of the disability that may be eye-opening.

First, Don Smith talks about his reactions after a spinal cord injury at age nineteen:

> I felt asexual for a long time because a man's sex was supposed to be in his penis, and I couldn't feel my penis. So that contributed to my feeling of being asexual; it didn't occur to me that it felt good to have the back of my neck licked, or that it felt good to have my arms stroked lightly. Stroking the wrists, then to the arms, then up the arms is a sequence that I've since learned can be very exciting.
>
> A lot of my first sexual contacts were just to gain experience. I wanted to find out what was going on and what I liked. With the help of two really excellent lovers, I learned about my body. I learned to take goals out of my lovemaking; I don't have to have intercourse or any kind of penetration if I'm going to have sex. I don't even have to do anything with the genitals if I'm going to have sex. I can take my time; I feel less pressure and less performance anxiety. That's not to say it's all gone, because it's there; I want to be there for my partner. (Bullard and Knight, 1981, p. 16)

Next, a spinal-cord-injured woman discusses some aspects of her relationships with men:

> I find that I am often suspicious of the motives of men who are attracted to me sexually. That is, some men want to be caretakers; some men can't find able-bodied partners (and assume that disabled women are also unable to find partners). Other men are sexually intrigued with disabled women, believing they will have a "kinky" experience; some men want a "strong mother confessor" figure they can depend on or want a woman who will be totally dependent on them. I don't intend to do a general indictment of the whole male race, but I do believe disabled women must be very selective in choosing partners.
>
> Many of my relationships have matured into strong relationships with sexual dimensions, some of my partners have been "affairs," flings, one-night stands, etc. During my sexually active years, I have had several different partners; among them three long-term relationships. I have had one sexual experience with a gay woman. (Becker, 1978)

A twenty-five-year-old woman with cerebral palsy talks about her sexual feelings:

> When I was a teenager, I was intensely jealous of the beautiful, able-bodied women I saw on television and in the movies. I thought that sex was for them, not me, and I was angry because I knew I'd never have a baby. In fact, I was pretty much resigned to never finding a husband, and being celibate all of my life.

Fortunately, I learned how to masturbate at age twelve or thirteen. I figured out a way of getting a rubber hose attachment from the faucet near my genitals while I was bathing, and I quickly found myself looking forward to baths for reasons quite apart from cleanliness. The almost electric, tingly feelings of sexual excitement began to build up for me slowly for hours before bath time, and the sudden surge of a climax was sheer joy. Even now, years later, I still get excited thinking about this wonderful way of stimulating myself, or having a partner do it for me. But what was most important was that my discovery of the joys of masturbating let me know that I was a sexual being, that it was legitimate to have these feelings. (Authors' files)

Finally, consider the comments of a man remembering his reactions after a spinal cord injury resulting in quadriplegia at age sixteen:

At home I felt like the town eunuch for a few years. I saw a lot of the women I had been dating before I broke my neck, but now there was nothing sexual going on between us. I kept secretly blaming them for not giving me a chance, not treating me as needing or wanting or even being capable of having a sexual relationship. Now I realize that I wasn't *acting* like I needed or wanted or was capable of having a sexual relationship. The simple truth was that I was just plain scared. I didn't know what I could do, how I could pleasure or be pleasured, and I sure didn't want to look like a jerk while trying to find out, or worse yet, find out I was a failure and face the eventual rejection.

My eunuch years also included a lot of martyrdom. I remember deciding that if I ever really fell in love with someone, I would end the relationship because I thought, being in a wheelchair, I could never really make anyone happy. (Bullard and Knight, 1981, pp. 65–66)

As these heartfelt recollections show, the disabled are very much interested in and able to have sexual feelings and relationships. It is the mistaken assumptions of an able-bodied society that impose an asexual image on these individuals, which is equivalent to denying the very core of their humanity.

Endocrine Conditions

The most common type of endocrine disorder is *diabetes,* which affects approximately 4 percent of the U.S. population. About 50 percent of diabetic men have erectile dysfunction, which can either be an early symptom of this disorder or may not occur for many years after the diagnosis (Podolsky, 1983). Retrograde ejaculation occurs in about 1 percent of diabetic men, but sex drive is usually unaffected. Although the sexual difficulties of diabetic men had been well known for at least two centuries, sexual problems in diabetic women were not identified until the 1970s. It is now known that about one-third of diabetic women have secondary anorgasmia, which usually occurs four to six years after the disease is discovered (Kolodny, 1971). In addition, some diabetic women have problems with vaginal lubrication.

The primary cause of these sexual problems in both diabetic men and women is a form of nerve damage that is a complication of diabetes. In a smaller fraction of cases, these dysfunctions are due to circulatory problems. Unfortunately, both types of problems tend to be permanent and untreatable (except for the possibility of using penile implants to overcome erectile dysfunction). In cases where diabetics have sexual difficulties for other reasons, such as anxiety or poor communication, sex therapy can be beneficial (Kolodny, Masters, and Johnson, 1979).

Disorders of the pituitary, thyroid, or adrenal glands are also commonly associated with sexual difficulties. In each of these conditions, sex drive is likely to be altered along with sexual function. About 40 percent of women with an underactive thyroid or adrenal glands have orgasmic difficulties, and a similar percentage of men have problems with erections (Kolodny, Masters, and Johnson, 1979). Sexual dysfunction is even higher in people with underactive pituitary

glands. Fortunately, these conditions are easily treatable by giving the proper amount of the "missing" hormone in pill form.

Heart Disease

In severe forms of chronic heart disease, the capacity for sexual activity is likely to be greatly limited. In milder types of heart problems, however, there may be no physical limitation on sexual activity. Nevertheless, several studies of men who had heart attacks have shown that six months to a year after recovery, sexual difficulties are common (Tuttle, Cook, and Fitch, 1964; Singh et al., 1970; Green, 1975; Mehta and Krop, 1979). The primary factor here is not a physical one but a mental one: anxiety, misconception, and avoidance conspire to create sexual difficulties. The man may be worried that his heart attack will cause sexual problems or that sexual excitement will cause another heart attack. This worry is also expressed in stories about men dying from a massive heart attack in the midst of a passionate sexual episode. There is no solid evidence to support this as a meaningful risk for most heart patients, and the cardiac cost of sexual activity — including intercourse and orgasm — seems to be about the same as walking up two flights of steps (Masur, 1979; McLane, Krop, and Mehta, 1980). Women who have had heart attacks seem to be less likely to develop subsequent sexual problems than men (Kolodny, Masters, and Johnson, 1979).

Cancer

Until the last few years, most people have automatically assumed that a person with cancer could not possibly have sexual feelings or sexual needs. Now it is clear that this view is incorrect, and increasing attention is being paid this area (Derogatis and Kourlesis, 1981). We will briefly examine several types of cancer and their impact on sexuality.

BREAST CANCER

An American woman has about a one-in-eleven chance of developing breast cancer, the most frequent female cancer and the leading cause of cancer death in women (Silverberg, 1981). More than 100,000 new cases are discovered each year, and late detection seriously lowers the chances of survival.

Breast cancer is usually treated by *mastectomy,* surgical removal of the affected breast. This operation typically creates psychological conflicts for the woman, with concerns about physical attractiveness and possible rejection by her husband or sexual partner ranking high on the list (Witkin, 1975; Notman, 1978). Perhaps this response is not surprising in light of the degree to which our society emphasizes the breast as a symbol of sexuality and femininity. As a result, the woman who has a mastectomy is likely to feel "incomplete" and unfeminine.

Although surgical removal of a breast does not "cause" sexual problems in a direct, physical sense, the psychological impact of mastectomy can be profound. Women react in a variety of ways ranging from relatively easy adjustment, to depression, loss of sexual desire, or sexual dysfunction. Following mastectomy, a few women avoid all forms of sexual activity. More typically, the frequency of sexual activity declines and women initiate sexual activity less often than they did before (Frank et al., 1978).

Nudity may be a matter of self-consciousness for the woman or discomfort for her partner. The couple may shift away from intercourse in the female-on-top position, since the male looks directly at the area of the surgical scar. Women who are without a partner at the time of the mastectomy may be particularly worried about dating and what to tell a prospective sexual partner; they may also be afraid that no man could possibly fall in love with a woman with one breast. For women in ongoing relationships, how their partner responds is an important ingredient of their overall adjustment (Wellisch, Jamison, and Pasnau, 1978). In many cases, it is possible to use plastic surgery techniques for breast reconstruction as a way of helping a woman adjust to mastectomy most comfortably. Currently, some physicians favor removal of the tumor without removing the entire breast (a procedure called "lumpectomy") and radiation therapy as treatment options for the breast cancer patient (Calle et al., 1978; Harris, Levene, and Hellman, 1978). These alternative treatments result in less disfigurement and less profound psychological effects, and in many cases they are just as effective as mastectomy.

CANCER OF THE CERVIX AND UTERUS

Cancer of the cervix accounts for slightly more than 60,000 new cases of cancer annually and cancer of the lining of the uterus is found in another 38,000 women (Silverberg, 1981). There are two forms of cervical cancer: carcinoma in situ (CIS) and invasive cancer of the cervix (ICC). Although neither form is likely to cause symptoms, both can be detected by Pap smears during routine pelvic exams. CIS is really a precancerous condition involving cells on the surface of the cervix that do not invade other tissues. On average, it takes eight years or more for CIS to progress to true cancer, or ICC (Eddy, 1980; Richart and Barron, 1980). Treatment of CIS while it is still precancerous results in virtually 100 percent long-term survival. Treatment of ICC depends on whether the cancer cells have spread beyond the cervix: either surgical techniques or radiation therapy can be used. Sexual difficulties are common but depend on the amount of pelvic scarring that occurs (Abitbol and Davenport, 1974; Lamberti, 1979). One recent report suggests that surgery is less disruptive

Self-Examination of the Breasts

It is important for women to examine their own breasts on a regular basis because most breast lumps are self-discovered rather than found by a doctor or nurse. Although some women feel uncomfortable about this type of self-exam, two specific facts should be noted: (1) about nine out of ten breast lumps are *not* cancer; and (2) women who examine their own breasts on a monthly basis have significantly higher survival rates after breast cancer than women who do not (Foster et al., 1978). The best time for a breast self-exam is right after your period ends because estrogen levels are low. Women who do not have periods should still examine their breasts once a month. The following technique should be used.

1. *Stand in front of a mirror with good lighting.* Inspect your breasts visually in the mirror, with your arms relaxed at your sides. Then raise your hands above your head. Finally, put your hands on your hips and push down. Look for flattening or bulging in one breast but not the other, puckering of the skin, dimpling or redness, or one nipple being unusually drawn up into the breast. Squeeze each nipple gently to see if there is any discharge.

2. *Lie flat on your back, with one arm beyond your head.* Feel every part of your breast using the flat part of your fingertips. Move your hand in small circles so the breast tissue slides underneath the skin. Cover the entire area of each breast (using any pattern that you wish) and also feel over the ribs to the side of each breast and up under each arm.

3. *Repeat step two in the sitting or standing position.* The position change redistributes the breast tissue and may allow you to feel a lump that was hidden when you were lying down. You may want to do this in the bath or shower, since hands glide more easily over wet skin.

Sources: The Boston Women's Health Book Collective, 1976; Stewart et al., 1979; American Cancer Society, 1980.

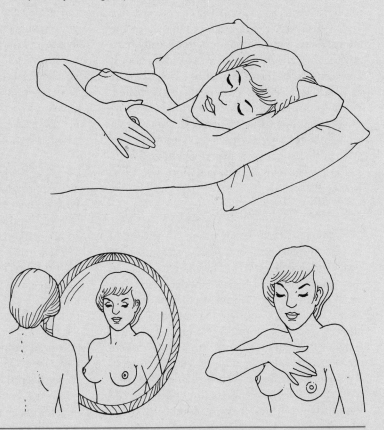

to sexual function than radiation therapy (Seibel, Freeman, and Graves, 1980).

Cancer of the lining of the uterus is rare before age forty and is usually marked by abnormal bleeding early in its course. Later symptoms include cramping, pelvic discomfort, bleeding after intercourse, or lumps in the groin. Pap smears are *not* a foolproof way of detecting this form of cancer; usually a D & C (dilation and curettage; scraping the inside of the uterus) is done to establish the diagnosis. Depending on the findings, treatment ranges from surgery (removal of the uterus and ovaries) to radiation therapy, drug therapy, or hormone therapy. If the cancer has not spread beyond the uterus, the patient has an 83 percent chance of being cured — that is, of not having the cancer recur within the next five years (Silverberg, 1981). Surgical removal of the uterus, called *hysterectomy*, does not usually have any negative effects on female sexual function. It may actually be beneficial since physical problems such as bleeding or cramping are corrected. However, some women have impaired sexual responsiveness and/or decreased sexual interest after a hysterectomy because they see the operation as a lessening of their femininity (Utian, 1975; Dennerstein, Wood, and Burrows, 1977; Roeske, 1978).

CANCER OF THE PROSTATE

Prostate cancer accounts for 17 percent of cancers in men, or about 70,000 new cases annually (Silverberg, 1981). The disease is rare in men under forty and is generally diagnosed by a rectal examination. Treatment consists of surgical removal of the prostate (*prostatectomy*), radiation therapy, or hormone therapy. Prostatectomy for prostate cancer frequently causes erectile dysfunction because nerves that supply the penis are damaged. When the prostate is removed for reasons other than cancer, erectile dysfunction is a less frequent complication, al-

though a high percentage of men develop retrograde ejaculation.

CANCER OF THE TESTIS

Cancer of the testis is a relatively rare condition that is most common in the twenties and thirties. Since only about half of these cancers are accompanied by pain, it is important for males to learn a method of testicular self-examination (see the boxed item on page 547) and to seek prompt medical attention if a testicular lump or swelling is noticed.

Treatment of testicular cancer (surgery, drugs, radiation) is sometimes a cause of sexual dysfunction and generally results in infertility. It is common to find that men with this form of cancer develop considerable guilt over their previous sexual practices, often blaming the problem incorrectly on masturbation, venereal disease, or an "overactive" sex life. Other men with this problem feel that the surgical removal of one testis makes them "less than a man." They may also develop fears of sexual performance and spectatoring, leading to difficulty with erection for strictly psychological reasons.

DES DAUGHTERS AND SONS

Approximately six million people — pregnant women and their daughters and sons —were exposed to the synthetic estrogen DES (diethylstilbestrol) and other DES-like drugs from 1940 to 1971, when it was widely used to treat so-called high-risk pregnancies — those with a threatened miscarriage or those complicated by a medical problem such as diabetes. In 1971, physicians found evidence of a rare form of cancer of the vagina or cervix (technically called clear cell adenocarcinoma) in daughters whose mothers had taken DES and related drugs during pregnancy (Herbst, Ulfelder, and Poskanzer, 1971). Subsequently, a number of reproductive abnormalities were found in some of the sons of

Men's Fears after Mastectomy

The husband or male partner of a woman who has a mastectomy may have many worries that influence his sexual feelings or behavior. Some men are afraid that they may have been partly responsible for "causing" the breast cancer by favoring one breast more than the other during sex or by overstimulating the breasts. These men may be reluctant to touch the remaining breast during lovemaking out of fear it, too, will become cancerous. Other men avoid breast stimulation so they won't upset their partner by "reminding" her that she only has one breast – but this may be an even harsher reminder of her loss. Infrequently, a man may be worried that he can "catch" cancer from his female partner and so avoids all physical intimacy. This belief is, of course, totally untrue.

A more common problem is that some men – who have been conditioned by our culture into equating female breasts and female sexuality – mistakenly believe that mastectomy automatically reduces a woman's sex drive or her ability to enjoy sex. Such men, although perhaps well-meaning in their behavior, inadvertently convey a message to their partners that surgery has made them "less of a woman," and may thus play a role in undermining the woman's self-image and self-esteem.

The range of problems that a man may encounter in adjusting to his wife's or partner's mastectomy are best prevented by including him in counseling about the facts of mastectomy (before the surgery takes place, whenever possible), and by encouraging open discussion between sexual partners regarding this sensitive topic at the earliest possible opportunity. As one man explained to us:

> When my wife was discharged from the hospital after her mastectomy, no one had talked with us about our sexual relationship, and I think we both assumed it was a matter best avoided. Our first attempts at sex, some weeks later, were embarrassed and uncomfortable for us both – but for different reasons. It seems now, in retrospect, that I was my wife's biggest problem. If someone had only provided us with a few simple facts, some words of encouragement, and "permission" to talk to each other about our concerns, we never would have had such difficulty. Fortunately for both of us, we were able to work things out together, but it was an emotionally painful process that I hope others can avoid. (Authors' files)

women given DES during pregnancy, including incomplete development of the testes, undescended testes (cryptorchidism), anatomical abnormalities of the penis, and preliminary evidence of infertility (Gill, Schumacher, and Bibbo, 1977). Still more recently, there is some preliminary concern about cancer of the testis in DES-exposed sons, although this finding requires further substantiation.

While the cancer found in DES daughters is relatively infrequent (it is estimated to occur in about one of every 800 exposed women), noncancerous abnormalities are found in the vagina in one-third of these individuals and abnormalities of the cervix are present in almost every case (Robboy et al., 1981). It is not certain if a higher rate of vaginal/cervical cancer (or other forms of cancer, such as cancer of the breast or uterus) will emerge as this population of women ages, so that long-term medical follow-up is important. In fact, evidence suggests that there is an increased risk of cancer in the mothers who took the drug during pregnancy (Hoover, Gray, and Fraumeni, 1977; Meyers, 1983). It also appears that there is a higher rate of ectopic pregnancies and miscarriages in DES daughters (Herbst, 1981).

If you were born after 1940, you should ask your mother whether she had any drugs prescribed for her during pregnancy — especially to prevent miscarriage or to treat a problem pregnancy associated with diabetes. If she did (or thinks she might have), go to your physician for evaluation. While it would be helpful to try to find out the dosage of the DES-type drug received, when in the pregnancy it was first administered, and for how long a period, such information is not always available. Nevertheless, a medical examination is in order if you (or your child) had such an exposure or think you may have.

DES daughters should undergo a pelvic examination including a Pap smear and also should have a test using an iodine solution to stain the lining of the vagina temporarily. The physician may also use a special magnifying instrument called a colposcope for this examination, and if there are areas of the vagina that appear abnormal, a biopsy (removal and examination of tissue specimens) may be taken. Usually this type of biopsy causes relatively little discomfort, although a slight amount of bleeding (less than during menstrual flow) may occur for 12 to 24 hours after this procedure is done.

The situation for DES sons is not yet completely understood, but we suggest that until more information is available, they undergo a medical examination on an annual basis.

Generally, treatment is *not* required for DES-related abnormalities, and over 98 percent of exposed individuals will be found to be cancer-free. Nevertheless, follow-up examinations (advisable at least every six months if abnormalities are found, or once a year if not) are important because the success of treating the types of cancer that can develop is partly dependent on detecting it in its earliest stages.

Needless to say, knowledge of DES exposure can lead to anger, guilt, fear of cancer, and concerns about fertility and sex. One twenty-four-year-old nurse summarizes her reactions:

> When I first learned that my mother had used DES while she was pregnant with me, I didn't fully comprehend what it meant. Now that I realize that the risk of cancer is remote, I'm less afraid, but I'd be dishonest if I didn't say that I consider myself abnormal and I constantly worry about what will happen. Statistics mean very little when you're on the line yourself. (Authors' files)

Other DES daughters voice dismay at being advised not to use birth control pills (it is possible that the pill might aggravate the DES-induced changes, although whether or not this actually

Sexual Disorders and Sexual Health

Pelvic Exams and Pap Smears

One aspect of sexual and reproductive health care that often seems shrouded in mystery is the pelvic exam, sometimes called a vaginal or internal exam. Many women are embarrassed or anxious about having a "female checkup" done, yet the information gained from such an exam is important in many ways. For instance, the pelvic exam can be used to diagnose such diverse conditions as pregnancy, vaginal infections, cancer of the cervix, certain causes of infertility, and tumors of the uterus. It is also needed to fit a diaphragm or to insert an IUD.

The pelvic exam is done with the woman lying flat on her back on an examination table with her knees bent, legs apart, and heels in

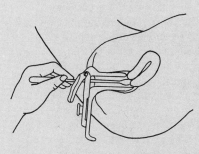

special foot-rests called stirrups. The physician or nurse conducting the exam begins by inspecting the outer genital structures, checking the labia, clitoris, and vaginal opening for signs of infection, irritation, rashes, swellings, sores, or other problems. Next, wearing thin

rubber gloves, the examiner gently inserts a finger just inside the vagina to check for vaginismus or other abnormalities. Following this, an instrument called a speculum is slipped into the vagina in order to spread the vaginal walls apart. (If the speculum is metal, it should be warmed first so it won't be shockingly cold.) Although some women find that insertion of the speculum may be a bit uncomfortable, it is generally not painful if properly positioned. Since this instrument comes in different sizes, a woman who has a lot of discomfort should ask the examiner to try a narrower or shorter instrument.

With the speculum in place, the cervix is visually inspected and a Pap smear is taken. The Pap smear (or, officially, the Papanicolaou smear, named for its inventor) is done by gently scraping the area around the mouth of the cervix with a thin wooden spatula. Contrary to what many people believe, this is a painless procedure – most women don't even realize when it's been done (it only takes about two seconds). The scraping is then smeared on a glass microscope slide for later evaluation. The Pap smear shows early changes in cervical cancer or other abnormalities of the cervix. Generally, a second smear is also taken to examine vaginal secretions for microscopic signs of infection.

The speculum is then withdrawn slowly and gently from the vagina while the examiner carefully looks

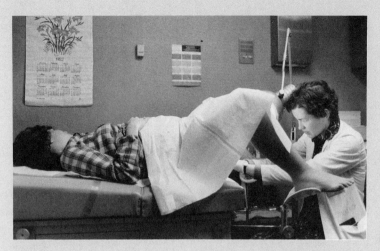

at the lining of the vagina for any unusual signs. Next, a bimanual exam is done. This involves inserting two gloved fingers into the vagina and pressing downward on the lower abdomen with the other hand. By this maneuver, the examiner can feel the size, shape, and position of the ovaries, uterus, and Fallopian tubes. Although there is often a sense of dull pressure during this part of the exam, it is not usually painful. The final step in the pelvic exam is the recto-vaginal exam in which the examiner puts one finger into the vagina and one finger into the rectum to check for weakness in the muscular wall of the vagina or other problems.

Not all health care professionals are equally adept or sensitive to women's feelings when it comes to pelvic exams. It's important for a woman to find a doctor or nurse with whom she feels comfortable and is able to communicate. If a woman is tense and anxious before her pelvic exam it can cause tenseness in her pelvic muscles so that it is more likely that the examination will be uncomfortable. A good health care professional can help in this situation by teaching the woman several relaxation techniques and by using an unhurried approach. In addition, many women find that if each part of the exam is explained to them in advance and they are told at each step what is being done, they are less apprehensive. Finally, many women appreciate the opportunity to watch the exam in a hand-held mirror.

We strongly suggest that all women who are sexually active have a pelvic exam and pap smear done once a year. Women who are using birth control pills or who have a history of genital herpes should have a pap smear twice a year. The most recent recommendations of the American Cancer Society (1980) are: (1) all women age twenty or over should have a Pap smear annually for two negative exams and then at least every three years until age sixty-five; (2) pelvic exams should be done as part of a general physical exam every three years from age twenty to forty and annually thereafter; (3) any of the following factors suggest the need for more frequent tests: early age at first intercourse, multiple sexual partners, infertility, abnormal uterine bleeding, obesity, or use of estrogens.

happens is not currently clear) or worry about their future childbearing risks. Fortunately, there are several groups available to help them deal with such concerns, including DES Action (Long Island Jewish Hospital, New Hyde Park, NY 11040); National Women's Health Network (2025 I Street, N.W., Suite 105, Washington, DC 20006); and the National Cancer Institute (Department DES, Office of Cancer Communications, Bethseda, MD 20205).

Alcoholism

Since many authorities regard alcoholism as an illness, we will discuss its sexual effects here. The alcoholic man or woman has a high chance of having sexual problems. Not all of these problems result from the alcoholism, however: in more than a few cases pre-existing sexual difficulties may have played an important role in starting a person on a path toward heavy drinking. Here, the use of alcohol may help people cope with feelings of sexual inadequacy by making them less interested in sex or less critical of their own performance. Given the popular notion that drinking is "manly" and that liquor can be used to seduce a woman by lowering her resistance (both "facts" being subtly reinforced by the advertising industry), it is easy to see how drinking seems to be "beneficial" from a man's sexual viewpoint. Women who feel guilty or inhibited about sex may find that drinking loosens these restraints and lets them feel more comfortable.

We have found that about 40 percent of alcoholic men have problems with erections and 5 to 10 percent have retarded ejaculation. Thirty to 40 percent of alcoholic women have difficulties in sexual arousal, and 15 percent have problems being orgasmic (Kolodny, Masters, and Johnson, 1979; Murphy et al., 1980). Sexual desire is also apt to be low in alcoholics.

There are several reasons behind these problems. Alcoholism directly affects hormone production and lowers testosterone in men (Van Thiel, 1976; Lindholm et al., 1978) and estrogen in women (Ryback, 1977). Shrunken testes and breast enlargement are common in alcoholic men. Other medical complications of alcoholism include liver damage, nerve damage, lowered resistance to infection, and poor nutrition, all of which may provide a biological basis for sexual impairment. Relevant psychosocial factors include fears of performance and spectatoring, marital conflicts, low self-esteem, guilt, and depression.

Even when an alcoholic has stopped drinking completely, there is no guarantee that his or her sexual difficulties will disappear. About half of the time these problems continue, requiring professional counseling to be resolved.

DRUGS AND SEX

For many centuries, there has been an avid search for *aphrodisiacs* — substances that could increase a person's sexual powers or desire. The long list of substances that have been claimed to have such an effect includes oysters, ginseng root, powdered rhinoceros horn, animal testicles, and turtles' eggs, but there is no evidence that an actual aphrodisiac response occurs. "Spanish fly," the most famous supposed aphrodisiac, is made from beetles found in southern Europe. The beetles are ground into a powder and when taken internally, it irritates the bladder and urethra and can also cause ulcers, diarrhea, and even death. The burning sensation in the penis due to irritation of the urethra has been interpreted by some men as a sign of lust.

Aphrodisiacs aside, both prescription drugs and drugs used recreationally (or illicitly, depending on your viewpoint) have some specific effects on sexuality.

Prescription Drugs

Many of the medications used to treat high blood pressure cause sexual difficulties for men and women. For example, Aldomet (alpha-methyldopa), the drug most commonly used to treat this condition, causes erectile dysfunction in 10 to 15 percent of men at low doses and in up to half of men in high doses (Kolodny, 1978a). Decreased libido and impaired sexual arousal is found in similar proportions of women using this drug. A different type of problem is found with Ismelin (guanethidine), which inhibits ejaculation in more than half of the men using it. Usually these difficulties will disappear within a week or two after stopping the medication, but in some cases the sexual dysfunction may persist because of anxiety. Fortunately, there are many medications available to treat high blood pressure. Some have low rates of sexual side effects, and it is almost always possible to find a combination that will leave sexual function intact while simultaneously controlling high blood pressure.

Tranquilizers such as Librium (chlordiazepoxide) and Valium (diazepam) can sometimes cause erectile dysfunction, anorgasmia, or decreased sexual desire but in other instances may be beneficial by reducing sexual anxiety. Barbiturates and related drugs such as Quaalude (methaqualone) have also been reported to cause a variety of sexual problems (Gay et al., 1975; Bush, 1980), although Quaalude has developed a street reputation as an aphrodisiac. Our research has shown that some people using Quaalude temporarily lose some of their sexual inhibitions, which they translate as a sexual "stimulant" effect. The problem, as a number of experienced drug users confirm, is that Quaalude also depresses the functions of the nervous system and can actually impair sexual performance (Gay et al., 1975).

Antihistamines, used in allergy pills and sinus medications, can affect sexuality in two ways. Drowsiness is a prime side effect and one not likely to improve the quality of sex. In women, these drugs often cause a reduction in vaginal lubrication so they may sometimes cause painful intercourse.

The effects of hormones on sexual function were discussed in chapter 4. A more detailed discussion of the sexual effects of prescription drugs is given in several references listed at the end of this chapter.

Nonprescription Drugs

ALCOHOL

The effects of alcohol on sexuality have fascinated people throughout history. In *Macbeth*, Shakespeare reported that "it provokes the desire but it takes away the performance" (Act 2, scene 3, line 34), and recent research has shown that this view is fairly accurate. In one study, college men were given alcohol in three different doses while watching erotic movies (Farkas and Rosen, 1976). Amounts of alcohol well below the legal levels of intoxication suppressed erections. Similar studies in women showed that alcohol had a negative impact on physiologic signs of sexual arousal (Wilson and Lawson, 1976, 1978). Alcohol has also been shown to weaken male masturbatory effectiveness and to decrease the pleasure and intensity of male orgasm (Malatesta, 1979), and alcohol, even in moderate amounts, makes it more difficult for women to reach orgasm (Malatesta et al., 1982).

Despite the *physical* inhibition of even two or three drinks of an alcoholic beverage (due to a depressant effect on the nervous system), most people believe that alcohol *increases* their sexual responsiveness. This is partly because alcohol has a "disinhibiting" effect — it lowers the sexual inhibitions a person may ordinarily have, thus making it possible for sexual desire to emerge. The belief that alcohol enhances sex also stems from advertising and cultural myths.

Self-Examination of the Testicles

After a twenty-nine-year-old film projectionist showed a movie about testicular self-examination to a group of doctors, he decided to take the film's recommendations and found a bean-sized lump in his right testicle. This simple act probably saved his life because he had a fast-growing cancer that required immediate surgery (P. Smith, 1980).

Men are not usually told about the importance of self-examination of the testes even though women are advised about checking their own breasts. This may partly reflect that cancer of the testis is statistically infrequent, with fewer than 5,000 cases annually (Silverberg, 1981). It is the most common cancer in men between the ages of twenty and thirty-four, however, and in many cases it does not produce pain or other symptoms.

The self-examination procedure is a simple one. After a warm bath or shower, when the scrotum is relaxed and loose, each testis should be felt individually. The surface of each testis should be covered, using the fingertips and thumb to feel for lumps, irregularities, hardening, or enlargement. If any suspicious areas are found, see your physician *immediately*.

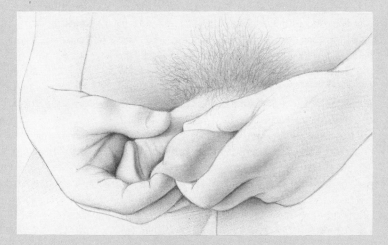

NARCOTICS

Addictive drugs such as heroin and morphine produce many sexual problems (Cushman, 1973; Mintz et al., 1974; Cicero et al., 1975). One large survey found that in 162 male addicts, erectile dysfunction occurred in 48 percent, retarded ejaculation in 59 percent, and low sexual interest in 66 percent; in 85 female addicts, 27 percent had orgasmic dysfunction and 57 percent had low sexual interest (Kolodny, 1983). This is a complex area to evaluate, however, because drug addiction may be a means of trying to escape from pre-existing sexual difficulties or may be a substitute for sex. Factors such as hormone problems (Azizi et al., 1973; Santen et al., 1975; Mirin et al., 1980), infections, and poor nutrition, which occur as a result of addiction, also play a role in causing sexual difficulties.

Narcotic addicts are also likely to have other problems that complicate their sex lives. Rosenbaum (1981) has noted that: (1) female addicts usually have partners who are also addicted; (2) many addicts find that the "hit" of mainlining heroin is far more pleasurable, intense, and easy to get than an orgasm (in fact, many ex-addicts say the feeling is like dozens of orgasms rolled up into one); and (3) the sensuality and sharing that accompany narcotic use become a replacement for the sharing and sensuality of sex. Furthermore, since most female addicts must turn to prostitution to raise money for their habit, it is not surprising that sex becomes less appealing to them.

AMPHETAMINES AND COCAINE

Amphetamines ("speed," "uppers," "pep pills") reportedly increase sexual responsiveness when used in low doses but have the opposite effect in high doses or when used on a long-term basis.

Cocaine ("coke," "snow") has a street reputation as a strong sexual stimulant, but there are also reports of sexual dysfunction with its use (Gay et al., 1975; Bush, 1980). Kolodny (1983) found that 17 percent of 168 male cocaine users had episodes of erectile failure when they used this drug, and 4 percent had experienced priapism (painful, persistent erections) at least once during or immediately after the use of cocaine. Similarly, Wesson (1982) found evidence of male erectile difficulties during the use of cocaine, and Siegel (1982) reported that the dangerous practice of "free-basing" cocaine consistently leads to sexual disinterest and situational impotence (twenty of twenty-three men were affected in his study).

Cocaine use as a purported sexual stimulant is interesting for several other reasons. For one thing, many users believe that rubbing cocaine on the tip of the clitoris increases female sexual sensitivity and arousal, but how this could occur is difficult to understand since cocaine is used medically as a topical anesthetic, that is, to deaden nerve endings. The continued use of this practice may indicate how powerful expectations are in interpreting our experiences.

A second interesting point is that cocaine clearly acts as a sexual facilitator in a social sense. Because of its status and expense, as well as its reputation as a sexual stimulant, when a man offers cocaine to a woman (or vice versa) there is usually a sexual invitation implied. As Kolodny (1985) notes:

> Widely available at singles bars and in the economically advantaged "just-got-a-divorce" crowd, cocaine literally opens the doors of sexual access for many males and provides a convenient excuse for many females who otherwise might pass on having "instant sex" with a partner they hardly know.

MARIHUANA

Marihuana ("pot," "dope," "grass") is generally reported to enhance sexual feelings. In our own research with more than 1,000 men and women aged eighteen to thirty-five who had used this drug as an accompaniment to sex, 83 percent of the men and 81 percent of the women said that marihuana improved their sexual experience (Kolodny, Masters, and Johnson, 1979). Most users, however, denied that marihuana led to more sexual desire, quicker sexual arousal, or more intense orgasms. Instead, they indicated that marihuana gave them an increased awareness of touch all over their bodies, led to greater relaxation (both mentally and physically), and put them more in tune with their partners. These are highly subjective judgments which cannot be fully verified in experimental research. However, generally similar findings have been reported by others; for example, Halikas, Weller, and Morse (1982) described self-reports of enhanced touch awareness and physical closeness in a majority of both male and female users.

In nonsexual situations, it has been shown that instead of *increasing* touch sensitivity, marihuana actually produces no change or *lessens* touch perception (Reese, 1977). There is also considerable documentation that marihuana use slows reflex reactions (Klonoff, 1974; Manno et al., 1974; Jones, 1976; Jaffe, 1980). The fact that marihuana users say that if *they* are "high" but their partner is not, the sexual experience is unpleasant (disjointed?) also indicates that there is a strongly subjective element to the reported effects.

Some other research findings also bear examination. Erectile dysfunction has been found to affect about 20 percent of men using marihuana on a daily basis, although no association between marihuana use and sexual dysfunction in women has been noted (Kolodny, 1981). However, some women who use marihuana report that it causes temporary vaginal dryness which can sometimes cause painful intercourse. Furthermore, heavy marihuana use has been reported to lower testosterone production in animals and men (Collu et al., 1975; Harmon et al., 1976; Smith et al., 1976; Kolodny et al., 1974, 1976, 1979) and to disturb sperm production as well (Kolodny et al., 1974; Hembree, Zeidenberg, and Nahas, 1976).[1] Although these effects are reversible once the drug is stopped, they may sometimes contribute to sexual problems. One study of chronic, frequent marihuana use in women showed menstrual cycle abnormalities and hormone changes but no negative sexual effects (Bauman et al., 1979).

SOME MISCELLANEOUS DRUGS

Lysergic acid diethylamide (LSD, "acid") and related psychedelic drugs have not been studied extensively from a sexual viewpoint. The few bits of research that exist indicate that these drugs are not used primarily for their sexual effects and that they generally lead to preoccupation with mental imagery during a "trip."

In contrast, drugs such as *amyl nitrite* ("snappers," "poppers"), which are inhaled, are widely used to prolong or intensify the sensation of orgasm (Lowry, 1979; Cohen, 1979) especially among homosexual men (Goode and Troiden, 1979). Severe headaches are a common side effect and fainting sometimes occurs.

In concluding it is important to note that all of these drug effects vary considerably from one person to another depending on health, age, body size, and many other factors. We have tried to describe the *most typical* sexual effects encountered.

---

[1]One carefully designed research study found that three weeks of daily marihuana smoking under controlled conditions did *not* lower testosterone in men (Mendelson et al., 1974). However, a similar study, using the same carefully controlled conditions, but administering marihuana daily over a three-*month* period found that the testosterone-lowering effect did not show up for five to six weeks (Kolodny, Masters and Johnson, 1979, Figure 13-2).

INFECTIONS

Certain types of infections that affect the sex organs are not usually transmitted through sexual intercourse, unlike the conditions called sexually transmitted diseases that we will discuss in the next chapter. These infections, which *can* be sexually transmitted, can produce troublesome symptoms that interfere with sexual pleasure or cause considerable emotional turmoil. Fortunately, the most common of these infections are easily treatable and have no major health risks. We discuss them here to avoid the implication that they are always or usually of sexual origin.

Vaginitis

Vaginitis refers to any vaginal inflammation, whether caused by infection, allergic reaction, estrogen deficiency, or chemical irritation. Vaginitis can create sexual problems by causing tenderness or pain during intercourse or by causing disagreeable odors that embarrass the woman or reduce her partner's enthusiasm for intimacy. Here, we will consider only the most common forms of vaginal infection.

TRICHOMONAS INFECTIONS

Trichomonas (pronounced "trick o moan' ess") *vaginitis* is caused by a one-cell microorganism called *Trichomonas vaginalis*, ordinarily present in small numbers in the vagina (Green, 1977). If these organisms multiply rapidly or are transmitted by sexual contact, the resulting infection produces a frothy, thin, greenish-white or yellowish-brown, foul-smelling discharge which usually causes burning and itching of the vagina and vulva. The diagnosis is made by examining the discharge under a microscope. The most effective treatment is a prescription drug called Flagyl (metronidazole), which should be given to the woman and her male sexual partner. Flagyl should not be used by nursing mothers because it appears in breast milk, and there is currently some concern about its safety because it has been found to produce tumors in mice.

MONILIA INFECTIONS

Monilial vaginitis is a type of fungus or yeast infection caused by an overgrowth of *Candida albicans*, a microorganism that is normally found in the vagina. The discharge is usually thick, white, and cheesy, and is accompanied by intense itching. Diabetic women, pregnant women, and women using birth control pills or antibiotics have an increased incidence of this infection. Treatment involves use of special vaginal creams or suppositories, such as these prescription medications: Monistat (miconazole), Mycostatin (nystatin), or Vanobid (candicidin) for one or two weeks.

Because yeast infections can mask the presence of gonorrhea or syphilis, specific testing should be done to see if any STDs are also present. In two studies of women with STDs, more than 25 percent were found to have genital yeast infections (Oriel et al., 1972; Thin, Leighton, and Dixon, 1977).

HEMOPHILUS INFECTIONS

Hemophilus vaginalis is a small bacteria that commonly causes another troublesome vaginitis. The brownish-white or greyish discharge usually has a foul odor and is accompanied by burning or itching. Treatment possibilities include ampicillin or tetracycline pills and various vaginal creams or suppositories. Because there is a high likelihood that the male sexual partner of a woman with hemophilus vaginitis has this bacteria in his urethra, he should also undergo treatment.

PREVENTING VAGINITIS

The vagina normally contains a number of different microorganisms. Some of these seem to play a specific role in vaginal physiology, such as maintaining the proper degree of acidity, while others can produce symptoms and infection if they multiply disproportionately. According to a recent review by Larsen and Galask (1982), an average of seven different species of bacteria are found in the vagina, and other microorganisms such as yeasts and viruses are also present.

Why some women develop vaginal pain or itching without having any detectable infection is unclear (Osborne, Grubin, and Pratson, 1982). It is also uncertain why many women with documented infections don't have any discharge or other symptoms. However, the fact remains that vaginitis is often an annoying condition that women and their partners would like to prevent if they can. Here are several suggestions for minimizing the risk of developing vaginitis:

1. Wear cotton underpants; nylon or synthetic fiber underpants retain heat and moisture, creating a good environment for bacteria to grow.
2. Avoid frequent douching, since this can irritate the vagina and remove important "natural" microorganisms that protect you. (Many medical authorities believe routine douching is unnecessary and only advise it under specific conditions.)
3. After going to the bathroom, always wipe with a front-to-back motion. This way, bacteria from the rectum will not be brought forward to the vagina.
4. Avoid the long-term use of antibiotics which can reduce the number of bacteria normally present in the vagina, allowing yeast forms to overgrow.
5. Maintain good habits of personal hygiene, including regular washing of the genital and anal regions with mild soap and water. Avoid so-called feminine hygiene sprays that can be irritating to the skin.
6. If your partner has an infection of the genitals, avoid sexual contact. (Using a condom may be of some help in this situation.)

7. Do not put the penis in or near the vagina after anal intercourse since this can directly introduce "foreign" bacteria into the vagina.
8. Avoid forms of sexual activity that produce any vaginal discomfort.

Cystitis

Cystitis, or infection of the bladder, is closely related to sexual activity in women. Sexual intercourse leads to an increase in bacteria in the urine (Buckley, McGuckin, and MacGregor, 1978) presumably because of inward pressure on the urethra during coital thrusting. Because the female urethra is short (about 2.5 cms, or 1 inch) compared to the male urethra (usually more than 15 cms, or 6 inches), cystitis is far more common in women than men (the bacteria have a shorter distance to travel).

The symptoms of cystitis include burning during urination, frequent urination, cloudy or bloody urine, and lower abdominal pain. The diagnosis can be made by examining a urine sample under the microscope and by taking a culture to identify the specific bacteria involved. Broad-spectrum antibiotics such as tetracycline or ampicillin are often prescribed.

One special variety of this infection is the so-called honeymoon cystitis that can occur either when a woman first becomes coitally active (not always on her honeymoon) or when coital activity is resumed after a prolonged period of inactivity.

Toxic Shock Syndrome

Toxic shock syndrome (TSS) first came to public attention in 1980 when it was widely reported as a serious, sometimes fatal illness suddenly striking healthy menstruating women who used tampons. Although TSS was named in

1978 by Todd and co-workers, who reported on a small number of cases appearing in children, it now is clear that it is actually a rare form of scarlet fever that was initially described in 1927 (Stevens, 1927; Reingold, 1983).

TSS is marked by high fever, vomiting, diarrhea, muscle pain, and a skin rash that resembles a severe sunburn. Fainting spells, low blood pressure, and dizziness are other common symptoms. TSS is caused by a toxin, or poison, produced by a bacteria called *Staphylococcus aureus,* and it occurs primarily in menstruating women who use tampons. Most of the cases encountered in 1980 were associated with the use of Rely tampons, which were subsequently found to have a relative risk for developing TSS eleven times greater than Playtex tampons, twenty-eight times higher than OB tampons, thirty-eight times higher than Kotex tampons, and seventy-seven times higher than Tampax (Schlech et al., 1982). After Rely tampons were withdrawn from the market, the number of cases of TSS linked with tampon use dropped (Reingold et al., 1982), and by 1983, approximately 15 percent of the cases being reported were unrelated to menstruation (Reingold, 1983). It is now clear that TSS can affect men as well as women and all age groups — including infants and the elderly — but the group at highest risk still seems to be tampon-using white females aged fifteen to twenty-five.

While women using tampons have the greatest risk of TSS, and a few cases have been linked to use of the contraceptive sponge as well as to use of a diaphragm, the chances of developing this illness are very low. Preventive measures that can be taken to reduce this risk still further include: (1) switching to sanitary napkins or minipads entirely; (2) alternating the use of tampons and minipads or sanitary napkins several times each day; or (3) changing tampons three or four times daily. If you develop symptoms suggestive of TSS while you are menstruating, you should immediately see a physician since TSS is a rapidly progressive illness that is fatal in about 4 percent of cases. Fortunately, with proper medical management — including hospitalization, treatment of shock, and aggressive antibiotic therapy — it is now clear that TSS is not as frightening as it first seemed to be.

Prostatitis

Prostatitis, or inflammation of the prostate, can be either acute (sudden) or chronic (long-lasting). The infecting organism is usually *E. coli,* a normal inhabitant of the intestines. Acute prostatitis is marked by fever, chills, perineal or rectal pain, painful urination, and urinary frequency and is likely to interfere with sexual function (painful ejaculation is common). Chronic prostatitis may involve no symptoms at all, or low back pain or perineal discomfort may be present. Chronic prostatitis has sometimes been thought to cause premature or bloody ejaculation (Davis and Mininberg, 1976). Antibiotic treatment usually clears up acute prostatitis but may be ineffective in curing the chronic form of this disease.

SUMMARY

1. A number of myths exist about the sexuality of disabled people that present obstacles to their freedom of sexual expression. In recent years, these myths have been countered by a better understanding of the fact that being disabled does not prevent a person from having sexual feelings and needs, and by recognition that a broad range of sexual expression is possible even if a disability partially interferes with sexual functioning.

2. Although spinal cord injury (SCI) commonly causes a variety of sexual problems (in-

cluding erectile difficulties and disruption of ejaculation in men and impairment of vaginal lubrication and anorgasmia in women), as well as loss of sensations in the genitals, many SCI persons are able to be sexually active. In addition to non-coital options for intimacy and sexual sharing (such as oral-genital sex, massage, and cuddling), some SCI men can have intercourse using a "stuffing" technique and others choose to have a penile implant.

3. People who have been blind or deaf since birth are often hampered in learning about sex. While these conditions do not impair the physical reflexes of sexual response, they may at times create interpersonal problems that make sexual relationships difficult.

4. Many mildly or moderately mentally retarded persons are able to learn the basic facts necessary for responsible sexual behavior if this information is presented to them in a manner geared to their learning level.

5. A number of medical conditions can interfere physiologically with sexual function. For example, neurologic problems such as multiple sclerosis commonly cause erectile dysfunction and female anorgasmia. Erectile dysfunction occurs in 50 percent of diabetic men and 40 percent of male alcoholics; anorgasmia is found in about one-third of diabetic women and 15 percent of female alcoholics.

6. Other illnesses may be closely associated with anxiety about sex that limits sexual enjoyment. Heart attacks, breast cancer, and conditions that require hysterectomy are examples of such health problems.

7. DES (diethylstilbestrol), which was widely used over three decades to treat problem pregnancies, is now known to cause a variety of problems in the children of women who took this drug while pregnant. Although cancer of the vagina or cervix is infrequent in DES-exposed daughters, noncancerous abnormalities are common and should be followed closely by a physician. DES-exposed sons have an increased rate of reproductive abnormalities and may also have a heightened risk of cancer of the testis (although this has not been proven as yet).

8. No true aphrodisiac has ever been found, although many people claim that alcohol, marihuana, cocaine, or amphetamines enhance their sexual experiences. Others report that these same substances lower their sexual desire or impair their sexual responses.

9. Prescription medications that can cause sexual problems include drugs used to treat high blood pressure, tranquilizers, barbiturates, and antihistamines.

10. Vaginitis is most commonly caused by trichomonas, monilia, or hemophilus. Vaginitis is not always sexually transmitted, and it is often a reflection of an overgrowth of microorganisms that normally reside in the vagina. Although preventive measures are able to minimize the chances of developing vaginitis, and most cases are easily treated, some women have long-term difficulty with this annoying but minor health problem.

11. Toxic shock syndrome (TSS) is a serious disorder caused by a toxin produced by the *Staphylococcus aureus* bacteria. Marked by an abrupt onset of fever, vomiting, muscle pain, skin rash, and low blood pressure, about 85 percent of TSS occurs in menstruating women. Although the TSS outbreak has slowed now compared to what it was in 1979-80, it is advisable for women to change their tampons three or four times daily while they are menstruating or to switch to the use of sanitary napkins or minipads so as to minimize the risk of this illness.

12. Cystitis is an infection of the bladder that can occur in either sex, while prostatitis is an infection of the prostate. Either condition may cause pain or burning with urination and can make sexual functioning uncomfortable.

SUGGESTED READINGS

Bullard, David, and Knight, Susan, eds. *Sexuality and Physical Disability.* St. Louis: C. V. Mosby, 1981. The first half of this book provides an extraordinary collection of personal reflections on the sexual needs and experiences of the disabled. The second half of the book, which is less engaging, consists of a number of papers of uneven quality discussing professional issues in this field.

Bush, Patricia. *Drugs, Alcohol and Sex.* New York: Richard Marek Publishers, 1980. Broad coverage of the physical and psychological effects of drugs and alcohol on sex, conveyed with a sense of humor.

Chipouras, Susan; Cornelius, Debra; Daniels, Susan; and Makas, Elaine. *WHO CARES? A Handbook on Sex Education and Counselling Services for Disabled People.* Washington, D.C.: George Washington University, 1979. A practical and comprehensive survey of the field of sex and disability, including extensive annotated bibliographies and lists of resources.

Gregg, Charles. "Toxic Shock." In *A Virus of Love and Other Tales of Medical Detection,* by Charles Gregg, pp. 93-112. New York: Charles Scribner's Sons, 1983. A superb recounting of the whole toxic shock syndrome story including a scientific viewpoint and a revealing look at the commercial side of the issues involving Proctor & Gamble, the makers of Rely tampons.

Kolodny, Robert; Masters, William; and Johnson, Virginia. *Textbook of Sexual Medicine.* Boston: Little, Brown, 1979. A comprehensive but sometimes technical discussion of the impact of illness, drugs, and surgery on sexuality.

Meyers, Robert. *D.E.S. — The Bitter Pill.* New York: Putnam, 1983. The story of DES and its effects on millions is told with accuracy, insight, and compassion. Nontechnical but scientifically sound, this book is must reading for those who have been DES-exposed.

Monat, Rosalyn. *Sexuality and the Mentally Retarded.* San Diego: College-Hill Press, 1982. A thoughtful overview of a much-neglected topic.

Rabin, Barry. *The Sensuous Wheeler: Sexual Adjustment for the Spinal Cord Injured.* San Francisco: Multi Media Resource Center, 1980. A thoughtful, creative approach to a difficult subject, written in an informal tone. Deserves an award for its title!

Stewart, Felicia; Stewart, Gary; Guest, Felicia; and Hatcher, Robert. *My Body, My Health: The Concerned Woman's Guide to Gynecology.* New York: John Wiley & Sons, 1979. A clearly written, well-illustrated book loaded with practical explanations of women's health problems. Especially good chapters on infections, the pelvic exam, Pap smear results, and cancer.

21 Sexually Transmitted Diseases

*I*NFECTIONS that are spread by sexual contact are referred to as *sexually transmitted diseases,* or STDs. STDs include infections that were formerly known as venereal diseases (VC) — those almost always transmitted by sexual contact — as well as various other infections that are sometimes transmitted by nonsexual routes. In addition to describing a broader category of infections, the term STD has not yet acquired the stigmatizing sound that the label VD carries. The following sections will describe the symptoms, diagnosis, and suggested treatment of sexually transmitted diseases.

GONORRHEA

Gonorrhea is the oldest and most common form of STD. In the Old Testament, Moses spoke about its infectivity (Leviticus 15); it was also mentioned in the ancient writings of Plato, Aristotle, and Hippocrates. Its modern name was coined by Galen, a Greek physician in the second century A.D. In 1879 Albert Neisser discovered the bacterium that causes it, which was named after him (*Neisseria gonorrheae*).

Although the discovery of penicillin as an effective treatment for this disease slowed its spread in the 1940s and 1950s, the incidence of gonorrhea has grown tremendously in the last twenty years and has reached epidemic proportions today (Figure 21-1). Gonorrhea is among the most frequent infectious diseases in America: more than a million cases are reported annually, and these probably represent only a quarter of the actual cases that occur each year.

Gonorrhea is transmitted by any form of sexual contact, ranging from sexual intercourse to fellatio, anal intercourse, and infrequently, cunnilingus or even kissing (Robertson, McMillan, and Young, 1980; Barlow, 1979). A woman who has intercourse once with an infected man has a 50 percent chance of getting gonorrhea (Platt, Rice, and McCormack, 1983), while a man who has intercourse once with an infected woman has a lower risk, probably around 20 to 25 percent, of becoming infected (Rein, 1977; Hooper et al., 1978). The old excuse, "I caught it from a toilet seat," which was previously laughed at by scientists has now been shown to be at least theoretically possible since the infective bacteria can survive for up to two hours on a toilet seat or on wet toilet paper (Gilbaugh and Fuchs, 1979). However, it is unlikely that this form of transmission is more than a rare occurrence.

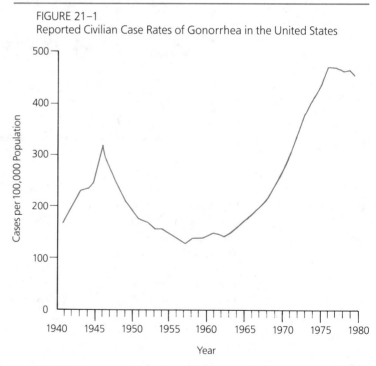

FIGURE 21-1
Reported Civilian Case Rates of Gonorrhea in the United States

Source: From Centers for Disease Control, *Morbidity and Mortality Weekly Report,* 1979 Annual Summary.

Sexually Transmitted Diseases

Symptoms

Most men with gonorrhea develop a yellowish discharge from the tip of the penis and painful, frequent urination as the first indications of gonorrhea. These symptoms usually appear within two to ten days after infection but may sometimes start as much as a month later (Schofield, 1979). The symptoms are produced by infection in the urethra which leads to inflammation (urethritis). The puslike discharge (which often stains the underwear) is part of the body's reaction to this infection. In about 10 percent of cases in men, there may be no symptoms from the infection, which means that the man can spread gonorrhea without realizing it.

Men with symptoms from gonorrhea usually seek treatment promptly and are cured. For men who do not receive treatment, the infection may move up the urethra to the prostate, seminal vesicles, and epididymis, and can cause severe

Gonorrhea discharge from the penis.

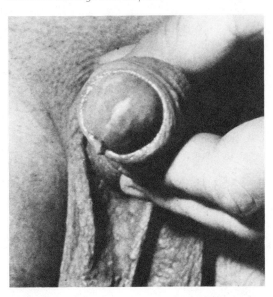

pain and fever. If untreated, gonorrhea can lead to sterility (Schofield, 1979), but this is a relatively infrequent complication in men.

Since less than half of the women with gonorrhea have any visible symptoms, they are likely to have their infection for a longer time before treatment is begun. This delay exposes women to a greater risk of complications. In addition, symptomless women may unknowingly spread their infections to their sexual partners. Many women do not find out they are infected until their partner's penile discharge or burning appears.

Even when symptoms occur in women, they may be very mild and tend to go unnoticed or are misdiagnosed. The symptoms include increased vaginal discharge, irritation of the external genitals, pain or burning with urination, and abnormal menstrual bleeding. In women, infection is most commonly found in the cervix (90 percent of cases) but can also be present in the urethra (70 percent), the rectum (30 to 40 percent), the throat (10 percent), or any combination of these sites.

Women who are untreated may develop serious complications. Gonorrhea commonly spreads from the cervix to the uterus, Fallopian tubes, and ovaries, causing pelvic inflammatory disease (PID). PID, although not always caused by gonorrhea, is the most common cause of female infertility because it can produce scarring that blocks the Fallopian tubes. The early symptoms of PID are lower abdominal pain, fever, nausea or vomiting, and pain during intercourse.

In both sexes, gonorrhea can spread through the bloodstream to other organs, causing infection and inflammation of the joints (gonococcal arthritis), the heart (gonococcal endocarditis), or the covering of the brain (gonococcal meningitis). Fortunately, these complications are rare and treatable. Eye infections with gonorrhea occur (rarely) in adults, where they are caused by touching the eye with a contaminated hand.

Newborn children may develop eye infections during birth if their mother's cervix is infected. Because this can produce blindness, infection-preventing drops are routinely put in every newborn baby's eyes.

Diagnosis and Treatment

Gonorrhea in men is diagnosed by examining the urethral discharge under a microscope after staining it with a specially colored dye. As this method is only about 90 percent accurate, it may also be necessary to try to grow the infecting bacteria in a laboratory by a culture test that takes several days. Men who have had homosexual contacts should have cultures of the throat and rectum, as well as the urethra.

In women, culture tests are the only reliable means of establishing the diagnosis. Swabs should *always* be taken from the mouth of the cervix *and* the rectum, even if the woman has never had anal intercourse, because a vaginal discharge may drip onto the anus and cause infection there. If the woman has experience with fellatio, a throat swab should also be taken. There is no blood test that can identify gonorrhea reliably at the present time.

The most effective treatment for gonorrhea is a large dose of penicillin G divided into two shots, one given in each buttock. It is recommended that a medicine called probenecid be taken in pill form at the same time to block excretion of the penicillin in the urine, keeping high levels of this antibiotic in the body (Centers for Disease Control, 1979). For people who are allergic to penicillin, tetracycline pills can be used effectively when taken over five days.

Unfortunately, a form of gonorrhea that is resistant to penicillin treatment (because it produces an enzyme that breaks down and neutralizes penicillin) has been encountered with growing frequency since 1976. Although this penicillin-resistant form of gonorrhea can be suc-cessfully treated with other antibiotics such as spectinomycin, if a widespread outbreak of this gonococcus occurs, control would be much more difficult.

In *any* case of gonorrhea, it is important to abstain from sexual activity with a partner until you have been rechecked after treatment to be certain you are cured. *It is also extremely important to notify anyone with whom you had sexual contact, including the person you know or suspect gave you the infection, to insist that they see a doctor for proper diagnosis and treatment.*

SYPHILIS

Syphilis first came to public attention at the end of the fifteenth century, when it swept across Europe, decimating armies and towns as it travelled. The source of this widespread outbreak is unclear. Some authorities believe that a particularly infectious type of syphilis was imported from America by Columbus and his crew, while others believe that it was already present in Europe (Catterall, 1974). The spiral-shaped microorganism that causes syphilis, *Treponema pallidum*, was identified in 1905.

Syphilis is far less common than gonorrhea today. In 1983 there were about 2,000 new cases reported in America, with a male-female ratio of two to one. Half of the men with syphilis are homosexual or bisexual.

Syphilis is usually transmitted by sexual contacts but it can also be acquired from a blood transfusion or can be transmitted from a pregnant mother to the fetus.

Symptoms

The earliest sign of syphilis in its *primary stage* is a sore called a *chancre* (pronounced "shanker"). The chancre generally appears two to four weeks after infection. The most common locations for the chancre, which is painless in 75 percent of cases, are the genitals and anus, but chancres can also develop on the lips, in the mouth, on a finger, on a breast, or on any other part of the body where the infecting organism entered the skin. The chancre typically begins as a dull-red spot which develops into a pimple. The pimple ulcerates, forming a round or oval sore usually surrounded by a red rim. The chancre usually heals within four to six weeks, leading to the erroneous belief that the "problem" went away.

Secondary syphilis begins anywhere from one week to six months after the chancre heals if effective treatment was not received. The symptoms include a pale red or pinkish rash (often found on the palms and soles), fever, sore throat, headaches, joint pains, poor appetite, weight loss, and hair loss. Moist sores called *condyloma lata* may appear around the genitals or anus and are highly infectious. Because of the diversity of symptoms, syphilis is sometimes called "the great imitator." The symptoms of the secondary stage of syphilis usually last three to six months but can come and go periodically. After all symptoms disappear, the disease passes into a *latent stage*. During this stage, the disease is no longer contagious, but the infecting microorganisms burrow their way into various tissues, such as the brain, spinal cord, blood vessels, and bones. Fifty to 70 percent of people with untreated syphilis stay in this stage for the rest of their lives, but the remainder pass on to the *tertiary stage*, or late syphilis. Late syphilis involves serious heart problems, eye problems, and brain or spinal cord damage. These complications can cause paralysis, insanity, blindness, and death.

Syphilis can be acquired by an unborn baby from its mother if the infecting microorganisms are in her bloodstream, since they cross the placenta. The resulting infection, called *congenital syphilis,* produces bone and teeth deformities, anemia, kidney problems, and other abnormalities. Congenital syphilis can be prevented if a pregnant woman with syphilis is treated adequately before the sixteenth week of pregnancy (Holmes, 1980).

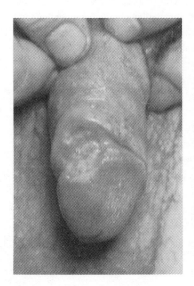 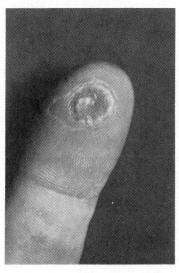

On the left is a primary stage syphilis chancre on the penis. On the right is a primary chancre on a finger.

Diagnosis and Treatment

Syphilis is usually diagnosed by a blood test. Several different tests are available, including some that are most suitable for screening purposes and others that are more time-consuming and expensive but also more accurate. Although none of these tests is completely foolproof in detecting the primary stage of syphilis, secondary syphilis can be diagnosed with 100 percent accuracy. Diagnosis also depends on a carefully performed physical examination looking for signs of primary or secondary syphilis. Chancres of the cervix or vagina may only be detected by a pelvic examination, since they are usually painless. An examination under a special microscope of the fluid taken from a chancre will usually show the characteristic spiral-shaped organisms.

Syphilis can be easily treated with one injection of penicillin in its primary or secondary stages. Latent, tertiary, or congenital syphilis requires larger doses over a period of time. Patients who are allergic to penicillin can be given tetracycline or erythromycin.

GENITAL HERPES

The herpes family of viruses and the infections they cause, such as chicken pox, shingles, and cold sores, are widespread today, as they have been for thousands of years. First named by ancient Greek physicians from the word *herpein,* meaning "to creep," because of the appearance of their characteristic skin rashes, and described in some detail by Roman physicians of the first and second centuries A.D., herpes infections have recently been the subject of considerable public attention.

Genital herpes currently affects some 15 to 20 million Americans, with an additional 500,000 cases occurring annually. Viewed by some as a relatively minor skin infection with annoying but brief symptoms and by others as a life-threatening disease or even a heaven-sent directive against loose morals, the genital herpes epidemic of the 1980s has received almost as much media coverage as a presidential campaign.

Genital herpes is caused by two different but related forms of the herpes simplex virus, known as herpes virus type 1 and herpes virus type 2. In the past, herpes virus type 1 was almost exclusively a cause of cold sores and fever blisters, while genital herpes infections were almost invariably caused by the type 2 virus. Today, this distinction no longer holds true: In the United States, 10 to 20 percent of cases of genital herpes are now caused by the type 1 virus (Peter, Bryson, and Lovett, 1982), while in Japan 35 percent of first episodes are due to the type 1 virus (Corey et al., 1983). While some researchers have suggested that this crossover phenomenon may be a result of more frequent oral-genital sex in recent years than in the past, it is not clear that this explanation is correct.

Genital herpes is generally transmitted by sexual contact. Direct contact with infected genitals can cause transmission via sexual intercourse, rubbing the genitals together, oral-genital contact, anal intercourse, or oral-anal contact. In addition, normally protected areas of skin can become infected if there is a cut, rash, or sore, so that infections of the fingers, thighs, or other areas of the body are also possible. In some cases, genital herpes can be spread by less direct means. For example, transmission of the herpes simplex virus can occur by kissing alone, and if herpes of the mouth develops, it can then be spread by auto-inoculation, that is, touching your genitals after putting your fingers in your mouth. Recently, several reports have noted that the herpes virus can live for at least several hours on toilet seats, plastic, and cloth, raising the possibility of genital herpes infection occurring by nonsexual

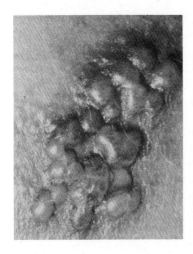

Genital herpes blisters before treatment (left) and after four days of treatment (right).

transmission (Larson and Bryson, 1982; Turner et al., 1983; Nerurkar et al., 1983). It is unlikely, however, that this mode of transmission is a very common one.

Symptoms

Genital herpes is marked by clusters of small, painful blisters on the genitals. After a few days, these blisters burst, leaving small ulcers in their place. In men, the blisters occur most commonly on the penis but they can also appear in the urethra or rectum. In women, blisters appear on the vaginal lips most often, but the cervix or anal area can also be affected.

The first episode of genital herpes is accompanied by fever, headache, and muscle soreness for two or more consecutive days in 39 percent of men and 68 percent of women (Corey et al., 1983). Almost all cases are marked by painful burning at the site of blister formation. Other relatively common symptoms include pain or burning during urination, discharge from the urethra or vagina, and tender, swollen lymph nodes in the groin, but these all tend to disappear within one to two weeks. More serious complications of first episodes, which occur more often in women than men, include the following: aseptic meningitis (an inflammation of the covering of the brain), estimated to occur in 8 percent of cases; eye infections, which occur in 1 percent of cases; and infection of the cervix in 88 percent of women with primary herpes type 2 infection (Peter, Bryson, and Lovett, 1982; Corey et al., 1983; Langston, 1983).

A typical first infection of genital herpes involves the appearance of ten to twenty painful blisters on the genitals. If generalized symptoms such as fever or headache appear, they are usually most prominent within the first four days after the blisters occur, and then they diminish gradually over the first week of the infection. After the blisters burst, they may form larger reddish wet sores or ulcers, which usually heal in one to two weeks. Sores on the penis or on the mons become crusted before they heal, whereas those on the vaginal lips do not. Skin lesions last an average of 16.5 days in men and 19.7 days in women during first episodes of genital herpes (Corey et al., 1983), but if the sores become secondarily infected with bacteria, healing may be somewhat delayed.

Genital Herpes

Although the blisters disappear and the ulcers heal spontaneously within one to three weeks, the herpes simplex virus invades nerves in the pelvic region and continues to live in a dormant state near the base of the spinal cord. In about 10 percent of cases there are no further attacks, but many people have recurrent episodes of genital herpes varying in frequency from once a month to once every few years.[1] Repeat attacks are sometimes brought on by emotional stress, illness, sunburn, physical exhaustion, or extreme climates, or they may occur for no apparent reason. Generally, these recurrences are less severe than the original episode because the body is able to mobilize appropriate antibodies to counteract the infecting virus. Fortunately, many who suffer from herpes find that repeat attacks tend to die out after a few years (Gillespie, 1982).

Recurrences are sometimes preceded by warning symptoms that occur up to thirty-six hours before blisters appear. These include itching or tingling sensations in or near the genitals, tenderness or achiness in the groin area, and burning or pain with urination or defecation. While these symptoms are not invariably followed by active outbreaks, and while some repeat episodes of genital herpes are totally symptom-free, when such symptoms occur they deserve attention. First, they indicate the possibility that a person may be infectious *even before blisters appear*. This is possible because live herpes virus may be carried in semen or cervical or vaginal secretions even when no rashes or blisters can be seen. Second, it may be possible to prevent a flare-up of herpes by taking steps that reduce stress (e.g., getting more sleep, eating well, and avoiding substances like alcohol or drugs that might suppress the body's immunologic response system) (Gillespie, 1982; Langston, 1983).

Scientists are still puzzled by many aspects of genital herpes and they do not understand clearly why some people never have recurrences while others have a number of repeat attacks. Certainly no one leads a completely stress-free life, nor can most people completely avoid the types of physical illnesses — like the flu — that often trigger recurrences. It is possible that there may be different strains of the herpes simplex virus, types 1 and 2, that partly account for this variability, and the individual's resistance (as determined by the body's immunologic defenses) may play a role, too. However, it would be a mistake to assume that people who experience recurrences of genital herpes aren't taking care of themselves properly or are being reinfected by another sexual partner, since such things usually aren't true.

There are two special problems with genital herpes. First, like syphilis, genital herpes in a pregnant woman can cause birth defects in the developing baby since the virus can cross the placenta. Fortunately, this is a rare occurrence. Spontaneous abortion and premature labor were also thought to be common in pregnant women with genital herpes (Nahmias et al., 1971), but the validity of this finding has recently been questioned (Vontver et al., 1982). More worrisome is the fact that the baby can be infected from the cervix or vagina during delivery, with such infections causing death or serious damage to the brain or eyes more than 50 percent of the time (Binkin and Alexander, 1983). Recent evidence also suggests that the rate of herpes infections in newborns has increased considerably in the last fifteen years (see Figure 21-2), with 11.9 cases occurring per 100,000 live births in 1978 to 1981 (Sullivan-Bolyai et al., 1983). While the risk of infecting the baby may be as high as 50 percent with vaginal delivery during a first attack of genital herpes in the mother, the risk is estimated at about 5 percent during recurrent episodes (Corey et al., 1983). Compounding

---

[1]If the first episode of genital herpes is caused by the type 1 virus, recurrences occur in only 55 percent of cases (Corey et al., 1983).

Sexually Transmitted Diseases

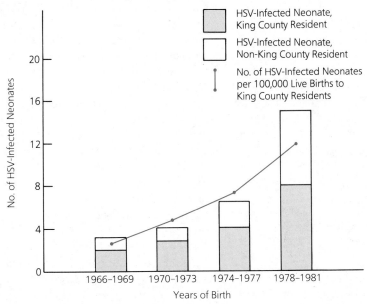

FIGURE 21–2
Incidence of Neonatal Herpes per 100,000 Live Births to King County Residents, 1966–1981. HSV Indicates Herpes Simplex Virus

Legend:
HSV-Infected Neonate, King County Resident
HSV-Infected Neonate, Non-King County Resident
No. of HSV-Infected Neonates per 100,000 Live Births to King County Residents

Y-axis: No. of HSV-Infected Neonates
X-axis: Years of Birth (1966–1969, 1970–1973, 1974–1977, 1978–1981)

Source: Sullivan-Bolyai, 1983. From the *Journal of American Medical Association,* December 9, 1983, Vol. 250, No. 22, p. 3060. Copyright 1983, American Medical Association.

the difficulties of this situation is the fact that newborns may be infected even when the mother has no symptoms at the time of delivery. In one recent study, almost three-quarters of the babies with neonatal herpes infection were born to mothers who had no symptoms of infection when they gave birth (Whitley et al., 1980). For this reason, Cesarean section is often recommended to pregnant women with genital herpes, whether active or latent (Langston, 1983), but this is an individual matter that each woman should discuss with her physician. In addition, infection can occur after birth if the mother or father has oral lesions or if the virus is transmitted in breast milk.

The second serious issue regarding complications of genital herpes is that there appears to be an association between the herpes simplex type 2 virus and both cervical cancer (McDougall et al., 1980; Kessler, 1979; Graham et al., 1982) and cancer of the vulva (Schwartz et al., 1981). Because these forms of cancer are easily treated if detected early, it is advisable for women who have had genital herpes to have a Pap smear and pelvic exam every six months.

The Emotional Impact of Herpes

Just as the physical severity of genital herpes varies greatly from person to person, the emotional response to the discovery of herpes varies considerably, too. Most victims first experience a sense of shock, anger, and disbelief: "It can't really be happening to *me*." Their initial anger is usually (and understandably) directed at the partner who caused the infection, but it can be self-directed anger, as well. One man told us, "I suppose this is the price I have to pay for not being more careful about who I slept with."

Not surprisingly, herpes sometimes causes conflict and suspiciousness in marriages or other long-term relationships. If one partner infects the other, it is taken as a sign of sexual infidelity, but this is not always true; for instance, a person may have reactivation of herpes that has been dormant for years and that preceded the relationship. Nevertheless, the discovery of herpes in a relationship can lead to so much discord and strife that the partners become combatants rather than lovers.

> *A twenty-eight-year-old woman:* When I found out I had herpes, I was scared out of my wits. I knew my husband would be outraged, but I also knew that trying to hide it was hopeless. So I told him about it, hoping that he'd understand that what was done was done. I wasn't really prepared for what happened, though. He suddenly refused to come near me. He questioned me in minute detail about everywhere I went. He was jealous and angry and rejecting, and it led us to a painful divorce. (Authors' files)

As might be expected, genital herpes is at least as emotionally troublesome to singles. On college campuses across the country, many students admit that they have altered their patterns of sexual behavior out of fear of contracting herpes. Here are some typical comments we've heard in interviews: "I couldn't stand the thought of having this infection for the rest of my life — having casual sex may be fun, but it's just not worth it." "To me, it's like playing Russian roulette, only it's my peace of mind at stake." "How could I ever find a husband if I had herpes? I'd have to marry someone else who had it too."

Some herpes sufferers have turned to dating services that provide a means of meeting others with this STD. Others feel such profound shame and depression over their affliction that they withdraw from the social scene completely.

Those who continue to date face a difficult dilemma: whether and when to tell a date that they have herpes. Some people feel a moral obligation toward candor but are dismayed by how quickly their honesty scares off potential mates. (Not everyone shares this reaction, though. One woman told us: "At least I knew if they were interested in ME if they stayed around.") Others unfortunately feel it's alright to deceive their partners, perhaps deciding to make up excuses for abstinence whenever an outbreak occurs (which will *not* always prevent transmission) or convincing themselves that there is so much herpes around that it just doesn't matter. One morally obtuse thirty-year-old lawyer told us, "I've probably given this to twenty-five women in the last two years, and it serves them right — because one of them gave it to me."

Those who find themselves in the throes of emotional anguish over having genital herpes — and even well-adjusted, psychologically stable people can find themselves in this position — can often obtain assistance from support groups composed of people with the same disease. Organizations such as HELP (Herpetics Engaged in Living Productively), initiated by the National Herpes Resource Center of the American Social Health Association, which has chapters in over forty cities nationwide, provide valuable information and perspective (as well as many practical pointers) for people with herpes. In a few cases, particularly if sexual problems develop as a result of herpes or if guilt or depression becomes overwhelming, psychotherapy may be helpful. Most people, however, once past the initial anger and shock at discovering they have herpes, manage to adjust fairly easily to the disease and find that it rarely interferes with their lives. Unfortunately, media discussions of genital herpes have often presented such distorted or alarming "facts" about this disease that they have frightened many people rather than reassured or enlightened them (see the box on the facing page).

Herpes Hysteria and Media Hype

While there is no question that genital herpes poses a major public health problem and affects people in unpleasant ways, some scientists are concerned that there has been too much ballyhoo about the herpes epidemic in popular media sources. For example, Dr. Harry Keyserling of Emory University points out that "The medical consequences of genital herpes for most people are relatively inconsequential. ... The vast majority of patients have a few blisters that don't bother them very much and heal quite rapidly" (1982, p. 32). Similarly, Dr. Oscar Gillespie, cofounder of New York HELP, writes "Herpes ... is rarely life-threatening in a physical sense, nor terribly life-disturbing in most any other respect for individuals who contract it" (1982, p. 5). But *Time* magazine didn't see things this way when it ran a cover story on herpes.

According to *Time* (August 2, 1982), genital herpes sends "thousands of sufferers into months of depression and self-exile," causes wives to give "smiling lectures on the ravages of the disease" to their husbands "to keep them faithful," and leads many to "compulsively change towels and sheets and wash their hands dozens of times a day." And, as *Time* sees it, "With vi-

sions of herpes sores clouding each new encounter, would-be lovers who used to gaze romantically into each other's eyes now look for the telltale blink or averted glance of the dissembling herpetic."

Phyllis Schlafly, a staunch anti-feminist who opposed the Equal Rights Amendment, was quick to jump on the bandwagon. Her con-

servative organization, Eagle Forum, printed 100,000 pamphlets warning of the dangers of herpes and blaming sex educators and birth control clinics for the rise in the disease. The pamphlet's principal bit of advice seems to be "Remain a virgin until you marry, marry a virgin, and remain faithful to each other" (quoted in *St. Louis Post-Dispatch,* October 7, 1982). Mrs. Schlafly is hardly alone in her views: both Jerry Falwell (head of the Moral Majority) and the Reverend Billy Graham have asserted that the herpes epidemic is God's punishment for the sexual immorality of modern-day America.

Television hasn't been immune to herpes hysteria, either. Not only have various talk-shows featured self-appointed experts on this disorder who have sometimes offered misleading or inaccurate advice, but millions have heard comments such as Johnny Carson's monologue query: "What's the difference between herpes and true love? (pause) Herpes is forever." And a national television network showed a hastily made-for-TV movie called "Intimate Agony" about the effects of an outbreak of herpes on a resort community that *The New York Times* called "unabashed soap opera" (O'Connor, 1983).

Perhaps as an outgrowth of these and other frightening portrayals of genital herpes, a rash of lawsuits have arisen claiming damages for contracting herpes. On December 29, 1982, the *St. Louis Post-Dispatch* reported that the wife of a bank president in Kansas City sued her husband for six million dollars, claiming he had caused her "permanent and progressive injury" by giving her herpes. On April 15, 1983, the *American Medical News* noted that a California woman in her fifties was suing her husband for five million dollars for "intentionally, unlawfully, and harmfully" infecting her with herpes. In another case, a single woman sued a sexual partner for lying to her about herpes: allegedly, when she asked him about a sore on his body, the man said it wasn't contagious – but two days later she developed a first herpes attack.

Clearly, genital herpes is nothing to dismiss lightly, and we make no claims about the merits of the type of lawsuits mentioned above. But to let your life be controlled by herpes, or the fear of herpes, is a mistake. Unfortunately, the type of scarlet letter rhetoric that has been prominent in the media has predictably led to unnecessary panic and alarm.

Diagnosis and Treatment

The diagnosis of an active infection generally can be made with accuracy by a physician on the basis of a physical examination of the genital blisters and/or ulcers. However, other STD's can mimic genital herpes, and sometimes genital blisters or ulcers are a result of inflammation rather than infection. Thus, making a proper diagnosis is not always a simple matter. Various laboratory tests can establish the diagnosis with more certainty. These include (in increasing order of accuracy): (1) Pap smears in women; (2) blood tests to measure antibodies against herpes viruses; and (3) cultures to grow the virus in the laboratory (these are usually taken by touching a cotton swab to a blister or ulcer; the procedure is generally painless).

There is no known cure for genital herpes, although much research is being done. A new drug called acyclovir is of some usefulness in lessening the severity of symptoms, especially in first attacks. One study found that acyclovir ointment reduced the time of shedding virus in secretions by more than 50 percent, lessened the time of itching from eight days to four days, and also shortened the time it took for healing to occur (Corey et al., 1982). Acyclovir ointment is not recommended presently for use in recurrent attacks because it doesn't seem to work very well and because there is some concern that using it indiscriminately may cause resistant strains of herpes to emerge (Hirsch and Schooley, 1983), but studies are now underway examining the use of this drug in pill form and by injection (Reichman et al., 1984). Other anti-viral medications are also being studied for treating genital herpes, and a concerted effort is being made to develop a vaccine that would prevent this infection in the first place.

General measures such as taking aspirin (or an aspirin-substitute) and using cold, wet compresses to relieve pain are often helpful during an initial herpes episode or recurrent flare-ups. In addition, avoiding tight underwear or clothing can reduce skin irritation, and keeping the genitals clean and dry by washing with warm water and soap several times a day can also be benefi-

Support groups for people with genital herpes can help bolster self-esteem.

cial. The skin should be dried with clean towels and a patting, rather than vigorous rubbing motion, and hand-to-eye contact should be avoided after touching the genitals. Towels and washcloths should be kept separately, since they may be contagious to others. In fact, it's wisest to use a separate towel for the face to avoid inadvertent spread of the virus from the genital region to the eyes.

Sexual contact should be completely avoided from the time symptoms of genital herpes first begin until ten days after healing is complete (for a first attack) or until two days after complete healing in recurrent episodes. Unfortunately, a few people seem to shed virus all the time — whether they have visible skin lesions or symptoms or not — so it's impossible to guarantee that there is no risk of contagion. While use of a condom can help prevent transmission of genital herpes, it is not a foolproof method (both because it doesn't cover all lesions and because it isn't always worn from the start of genital contact) and it may actually irritate the condition.

ACQUIRED IMMUNODEFICIENCY SYNDROME (AIDS)

The newest and most frightening STD to come to public awareness was first documented in 1981. Now known by the acronym *AIDS* — for *acquired immunodeficiency syndrome* — this devastating illness is marked by a breakdown of the immune system that protects the body against infections. Because of the relative collapse of these immune defenses, AIDS victims fall prey to a variety of rare infections that are usually found only in cancer or transplant patients whose resistance is lowered by drugs that impair their immune responses.

According to the Centers for Disease Control, 3,646 cases of AIDS had been reported in

America as of March 1, 1984, and hundreds of other cases have been reported in more than thirty other countries. Although this number may not seem very imposing at first, it is particularly alarming for two reasons. First, current evidence suggests that the number of new cases is doubling every six months. If this rate of increase continues, there would be one million *new* cases of this disease in the last six months of 1988! Second, AIDS appears to be an unusually fatal disease; in fact, some researchers believe that no one survives a full-blown case. These two facts — a high rate of increase and a high fatality rate — combine to produce a public health threat almost without parallel in recent times.

Of the first thousand cases of AIDS in the United States, 73 percent occurred in homosexual or bisexual men, 16 percent were in intravenous drug abusers (both men and women), 5 percent were in Haitian men (only a few of whom admitted to homosexual or bisexual behavior), and about 1 percent were in hemophiliacs (Jaffe, Bregman, and Selik, 1983). Overall, 94 percent of these cases were in men, and almost half occurred in those between ages 30 and 40.

It appears that AIDS is spread primarily through sexual contact, although the infectious agent responsible, generally thought to be a form of virus, has not yet been conclusively identified. The evidence for AIDS as a sexually transmitted disease comes primarily from a number of clusters of cases in which it has been possible to trace outbreaks occurring in sexual partners who had essentially no other activities together (Darrow, 1983). Sexual transmission of AIDS apparently occurs not only between gay men; there are documented cases of AIDS in at least five women who were long-term sexual partners of male drug addicts (but who did not use drugs intravenously themselves) and in female prostitutes (Wallace et al., 1983). Nonsexual transmission can also occur: sharing needles (among drug addicts) or receiving transfusions of contaminated blood products point to a blood-borne route of infection,[2] while a small number of cases reported in infants and children who are household contacts of AIDS victims or persons at high risk for AIDS suggest that transmission may also occur by other routine, close contact (Fauci, 1983).

One of the more troubling aspects of AIDS is that the incubation period, or time from exposure to appearance of symptoms, is as long as twelve to eighteen months. During this time, a person is probably contagious to others (Curran, 1983; Darrow, 1983). Thus, there may be little, if any, way of telling whether a person has AIDS by the presence of physical symptoms until the disease has been brewing for some time, leaving a potentially large number of sexual partners unknowingly exposed, and possibly contagious themselves. Currently, studies are being conducted to evaluate tests for the early detection of AIDS — one such test involves the laboratory measurement of a substance called acid-labile alpha interferon — but it is not certain as yet how accurate such testing will be.

It appears that homosexual men who develop AIDS are more likely to have had very large numbers of sex partners in the past than non-AIDS homosexual controls (sixty-one versus twenty-six partners in the past year according to Jaffe et al., 1983). In fact, a sizeable number of gay AIDS victims report sexual contact with more than 100 men each year, and many of these contacts are of the brief, anonymous form that occur in bath-houses, gay bars, and public rest rooms (Darrow, 1983). Other factors that may explain in part why certain homosexual men develop AIDS include: (1) relatively high rates of abuse of illicit drugs that may disrupt the immune system; (2) the practice of frequent anal intercourse and "fisting" — insertion of the hand into a sex partner's rectum — which may cause bleeding in the rectum that transmits the infection; and (3) higher rates of prior STDs such as syphilis and hepatitis B.

Symptoms

No single pattern of symptoms fits all cases of AIDS. The principal findings are progressive, unexplained weight loss, persistent fever (sometimes accompanied by night-sweats), swollen lymph nodes, and reddish-purple coin-sized spots on the skin. These skin lesions often turn out to be a form of cancer called Kaposi's sarcoma that has been previously quite rare in America, although it is common in equatorial Africa. (Kaposi's sarcoma in Africa has been linked to the cytomegalovirus, a member of the herpes virus family, which is also found in many urban homosexual men [Drew et al., 1981].)

When symptoms first appear they may remain unchanged for months or they may be quickly followed by one or more opportunistic infections, that is, infections that occur when immunity is compromised. These infections include an unusual form of pneumonia caused by *Pneumocystis carinii*, fungal infections, tuberculosis, and various forms of herpes. Although treat-

---

[2] Although AIDS can develop in *recipients* of blood transfusions from donors with this disease, there is absolutely no evidence that *giving* blood causes AIDS. Blood banks across the country are worried about this common misperception because many of them have experienced a drop in blood donations because of the AIDS scare. Hemophiliacs are at heightened risk for AIDS because the plasma concentrate used to control their bleeding is made from the blood of thousands of donors. Since a person may be entirely symptom-free when donating blood and develop AIDS months or even years later, the American Red Cross and U.S. Public Health Service have adopted a policy of turning away would-be blood donors from what they term "high risk" groups: people who have AIDS and their sexual partners, people with symptoms of AIDS, homosexual or bisexual men with multiple sex partners, Haitian entrants to the U.S., and current or past abusers of intravenous drugs (*The New York Times*, March 7, 1983).

ment may sometimes fend off these infections, the typical course is for one after another overwhelming infection to occur until the victim finally succumbs because the depressed condition of the immune system never returns to normal. At present, it appears that AIDS is almost invariably fatal within a matter of two or three years, although there is certainly the possibility that only the most severe cases were recognized at first and that milder forms of AIDS may exist that are not generally fatal.

The immune deficiency in AIDS seems to result from a decreased number of certain white blood cells called T-helper lymphocytes that assist antibodies and the cells that make antibodies in fighting off infection. Furthermore, the T-helper cells that *are* present are less efficient than normal. In addition, suppressor cells that impede antibody formation are not reduced in number, so the normal immune response is partially suppressed. T-cell abnormalities have been found in high percentages of symptom-free homosexual men who don't have AIDS (Kornfeld et al., 1982; Lane et al., 1983), but the significance of this finding is uncertain.

As of early 1984, no successful treatment for AIDS has emerged. It is most likely that finding effective treatments will depend first on discovering the cause of AIDS. Once this is accomplished, it may become possible to develop a vaccine to prevent this disease, but at present it appears that prevention depends on educating the public (especially those in high-risk groups) about how to avoid person-to-person and blood transmission (Curran, 1983).

Social and Emotional Reactions

The AIDS epidemic has produced a number of different reactions. In the gay community, which has been most directly affected, pervasive fear and dismay are rampant. Worry about possible exposure to AIDS has apparently led to widespread changes in sexual behavior in this group: as a result, many gay bath-houses have shut down due to lack of clients and a large number of gay men have cut back to having sex with only a handful of partners who are well known to them. This is not a universal change, however; there are still some homosexual men who seem bent on proving how "macho" they are by ignoring warnings from many gay organizations and continuing their lifestyles of frequent sex with anonymous partners. At the opposite extreme are homosexual males who are so paralyzed by fear of AIDS that they decide to be completely celibate until a cure is found, as well as a small number of male homosexuals and bisexuals who have switched to heterosexual partners, at least temporarily.

Gay males who discover that one of their previous sex partners has AIDS have particular reason to be fearful, although the actual risk of transmission is not known at present. Other homosexual men have become so anxious about the possibility of contracting this disorder that they become unduly preoccupied with every minor physical symptom they experience. To these gay men, a sore throat, a skin rash, or a fever is a sign of impending doom, and they may even mistakenly tell their partners that they have AIDS before it has been diagnosed. Needless to say, among the very fearful it is common to see a sharp decline in sexual interest and activity.

There has been some resentment in the gay community that not enough money was spent on AIDS research initially. Donald Currie, manager of a San Francisco Kaposi's sarcoma hotline, was quoted in *Time* (March 28, 1983, p. 55) as saying, "If the same number of Boy Scouts had been dying of this, there would have been a hell of a lot more money for research." By mid-1983, however, increasing responsiveness by the federal government, private foundations, and the

An AIDS Victim's Reaction

The following letter, which has been edited only to remove identifying information, was written by a thirty-one-year-old man who had been found to have AIDS approximately three months earlier.

My first reaction to the news, as you might imagine, was one of absolute shock and disbelief. I had been all too well aware of the mysterious plague that was haunting us all, yet I hardly imagined it could affect me, of all people. After all, I generally was rather fastidious in my choice of sexual partners. After a few bleak, disheartening visits to the baths years ago, I had sworn off the faceless, nameless, passionless groping that others have only given up recently out of fear. My choice was made for aesthetic reasons, not because of the danger of lurking microbes, yet apparently I should have thought more about those evil microbial beings, for it seems they were searching for me, looking for a moment of weakness to spring in and seize my soul.

I spent weeks trying to decide who had betrayed me. In my mind, I had decided on three likely candidates, but eventually I realized the futility of this cerebral detective game. Instead, I became more concerned with practical matters. I wrote a will, spoke to my best friends, and tried to come to grips with the knowledge that I probably had – at best – two years to live.

I must be honest with you and tell you that the thought of suicide crossed my mind. I told my parents that I had an unusual form of leukemia, since news of the true diagnosis would have probably killed them both. . . .

When I was in the hospital, I began to notice that people avoided me in a variety of ways. Not only did the nurses and orderlies and people delivering food rush in and out of my room as though pausing to talk might infect them, too, even my doctor kept a determined distance between us. This distance, which I've now come to accept, was perhaps most apparent in the fact that very few people, including my friends, could bear to have eye contact with me. When I looked directly at them, they diverted their gaze, as though ashamed or afraid.

I'm not a religious person, as you know, but I've been praying a lot lately. There's little else to do except hope for a medical miracle, because right now it looks like the odds are a million to one against my making it. If that honesty is too brutal for you to bear, think how it makes me feel. Now I know how a prisoner on death row must feel as he awaits his execution date.

I suppose that my brothers in the gay world are rightfully distraught because this gruesome epidemic is turning back the clock. But it's hard for me now to think about equal rights and the movement. For me, equal rights would mean being able to live. If that's selfishness, I suppose I have a terminal case.

The author of this letter died in late 1983, less than a year after the original diagnosis was made.

medical community led to a near-maximum effort to combat this disease, and more money had been earmarked for AIDS research in one year alone than had been spent over an eight-year period on toxic shock syndrome and Legionnaire's disease combined (*Science, 1983*).

Of somewhat more concern to many leaders of the gay community is the effect AIDS publicity is having on the general public in terms of increasing homophobia. Having made considerable progress in the last decade in attaining civil rights for homosexuals in employment and housing situations, gays are distressed that a disease which is not understood very well may be pushing heterosexuals toward intolerance of homosexuals once again, this time, out of fear for their personal safety. Fundamentalists who proclaim that AIDS is an expression of the wrath of God

against homosexual acts further fuel this type of reaction. A similar anti-AIDS reaction has led to the near-total collapse of the tourism industry in Haiti, and almost any product made in Haiti has been tinged with suspicion (Simons, 1983).

Fears about AIDS and subsequent discrimination are not restricted to the general public. Some hospitals have found that their personnel have refused to care for AIDS patients, and a number of nursing homes have turned AIDS patients away even when funds were available for their care. Even within the gay community, some AIDS victims have found themselves deserted by former friends and lovers, left alone to deal with an overwhelming disease.

The long-term implications of the current AIDS epidemic probably will not be fully apparent for some years to come. If the current trend

Sexually Transmitted Diseases

of the spread of AIDS continues, it may dissuade some adolescent males from becoming actively homosexual and may keep many others from "coming out." It is also possible that pronounced behavioral changes within the gay male community will emerge, in particular, a trend to more close-coupled relationships. It is also possible that AIDS may increasingly spread to the heterosexual community, thus altering — at least partly — its stigmatization of homosexual men. On the brighter side, many scientists believe that intensive study of AIDS may ultimately provide important breakthroughs in cancer research that will benefit all of humanity.

PUBIC LICE

Pubic lice, or "crabs," are parasites that invade the pubic region (Figure 21-3). Although "crabs" are usually transmitted by sexual contact, they may also be inadvertently picked up from sheets, towels, or clothing used by an infested person. The lice attach themselves to pubic hair and require fresh blood at least twice a day to survive. Eggs laid by female lice are cemented onto the pubic hairs and cannot be washed off.

The crab louse (known officially as *Phthirus pubis* and called "papillon d'amour," or "butterfly of love" by the French) causes intense itching which is mainly felt at night. A few people have no real symptoms; others develop an allergic rash which can be infected by bacteria after a lot of scratching. The lice can be killed by gamma benzene hexachloride, marketed in cream, lotion, or shampoo form under the trade name Kwell. Although pubic lice can only survive for twenty-four hours once they leave the human body, eggs that fall off into sheets or onto clothing can survive for six days. For this reason, fresh bedding and clean clothing should always be used to avoid reinfestation.

FIGURE 21-3
The Crab Louse

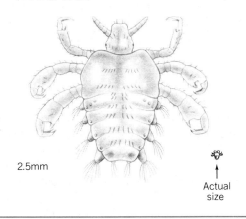

2.5mm

Actual size

The crab louse can be transmitted by sexual or nonsexual contact and typically causes intense itching in the pubic region at night.

NONSPECIFIC URETHRITIS

Nonspecific urethritis (NSU) is any inflammation of the male's urethra that is not caused by gonorrhea. Among male college students, 80 to 90 percent of cases of urethritis are due to causes other than gonorrhea (Holmes and Stamm, 1979). NSU has been increasing in incidence at a faster rate than gonorrhea in the last ten years and may now be twice as common (Hjorth, Schmidt, and Maibach, 1979; Felman and Nikitas, 1981), but the exact cause cannot always be found. The organisms most frequently isolated are *Chlamydia trachomatis* and *T. myco-plasma* (Holmes et al., 1975); however, the inflammation can also be of chemical or allergic origin (Barlow, 1979).

Chlamydia trachomatis is found in about 30 to 50 percent of women who are sex partners of men with chlamydia-positive NSU (Schacter, 1978), and it is also frequently found in women with the so-called acute urethral syndrome marked by painful, frequent urination (Stamm et al., 1980). Chlamydial infections in women, which have been estimated as five to ten times more common than gonorrhea in college and middle-class populations, can also cause cervical inflammation and PID (Holmes and Stamm, 1979; Holmes, 1981). In addition, 30 to 60 percent of women with gonorrhea also have chlamydia infections, and chlamydia during pregnancy causes an increased risk of prematurity and death of the baby around the time of delivery (Holmes, 1981). There is a sizeable risk of the newborn developing an eye infection or pneumonia if the mother has chlamydia.

The symptoms of NSU are similar to gonorrhea but are usually milder. The urethral discharge is generally thin and clear. Treatment of NSU with tetracycline will usually clear it up, but other antibiotics may be required (Felman and Nikitas, 1981). Penicillin is usually *not* effective in treating NSU. One important aspect of treatment that is often overlooked is that if a chlamydia infection is identified, the sex partner(s) of the infected person should be examined and treated. This is particularly important since untreated persons can be long-term carriers of this infection, reinfecting their partners who may not always recognize what has happened because the symptoms do not always occur.

VIRAL HEPATITIS

Viral hepatitis is an infection of the liver that can vary in severity from a completely symptomless state to mild gastrointestinal symptoms (poor appetite, indigestion, diarrhea) to an acute debilitating illness with fever, jaundice (yellowish appearance of the skin), vomiting, abdominal pain, and — occasionally — more serious medical complications. There are three main types of viral hepatitis: hepatitis A, hepatitis B, and non-A, non-B hepatitis.

Hepatitis A (formerly known as infectious hepatitis) has an incubation period of fifteen to forty-five days. The hepatitis A virus is mainly spread by the fecal-oral route, with person-to-person transmission, foodborne epidemics (usually caused by infected foodhandlers), and the consumption of raw or poorly cooked shellfish from contaminated waters accounting for most cases in industrialized nations. Recent data show that homosexual males have a higher incidence of hepatitis A than heterosexuals (Corey and Holmes, 1980; Fawaz and Matloff, 1981). It appears that oral-anal contact is the primary explanation for this finding, so that at least within the homosexual population hepatitis A may sometimes be sexually transmitted. (Oral-anal contact by heterosexual partners also can transmit this infection, but this is relatively uncommon.)

Hepatitis B, previously called serum hepatitis, is usually spread by blood or blood products but it can also be transmitted by saliva, seminal fluid, vaginal secretions, and other biologic fluids (Zuckerman, 1982). Many of the approximately 200,000 annual cases of hepatitis B in the United States are sexually transmitted (Brandt, 1982), and recent evidence suggests that homosexual men have the highest rates of previous or current infection with this disorder (Schreeded et al., 1982; Reiner et al., 1982). It is thought that trauma to the rectal mucosa from anal intercourse, manual stimulation of the rectum, or frequent use of enemas may predispose to the spread of this infection. Whether transmission occurs only when infected saliva is introduced into the rectum (either from oral-anal stimulation or from the use of saliva as a lubricant for anal intercourse) or whether seminal fluid can transmit the infection rectally is not clear at present. Although male homosexuals may have the highest past and current prevalence of this infection, there are many more cases of hepatitis B that are sexually transmitted between heterosexual partners because heterosexuals outnumber homosexuals by approximately ten to one.

Hepatitis B persists in a carrier state in approximately 5 to 10 percent of infected adults, with an estimated 400,000 to 800,000 carriers in this country and 150 to 200 million worldwide. This condition, in which the person is still infectious although not generally ill, can persist for months, years, or a lifetime. Carriers of hepatitis B have an increased risk of developing liver cancer in their lifetime.

Non-A, non-B hepatitis, which is the most common form after blood transfusions, is not thought to be sexually transmitted.

Hepatitis is diagnosed on the basis of laboratory tests (for instance, blood tests show abnormalities in liver enzymes) and the specific type of hepatitis is determined by immunologic testing of blood samples. Treatment is generally symptomatic, with hospitalization required only in the more severe cases.

Persons in intimate contact with someone with hepatitis A can obtain partial immunity by getting a shot of immune serum globulin, but as a practical matter, they have often been exposed for weeks before the diagnosis has been made. Viral hepatitis B vaccines are now being tested (including large-scale testing in the homosexual community), but results do not yet show how useful they will be in preventing the disorder.

OTHER SEXUALLY TRANSMITTED DISEASES

Venereal warts (*condylomata acuminata*) are dry, usually painless warts that grow on or near the genitals and around the anus. They are caused by a sexually transmitted virus and are usually greyish-white with a cauliflowerlike surface. Venereal warts are more of a nuisance than a health problem, but they may coexist with other STDs. They can be treated by applying a podophyllin ointment or liquid, by using liquid nitrogen, or by "burning" them off with an electric current.

Molluscum contagiosum is caused by a pox virus that typically produces raised skin lesions

 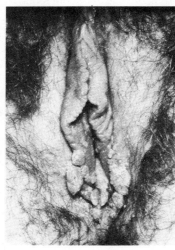

Venereal warts in the male (left) and female (right).

on the external genitals or on the thighs, buttocks, or lower abdomen. The painless lesions, which usually appear three to six weeks after exposure, vary from one millimeter to one centimeter in diameter and have a pinkish-orange color with a pearly top. If the lesion is squeezed, the cheesy plug of material within it can be expressed, much like a blackhead. Since the infection usually causes little trouble and often disappears spontaneously in a period of about six months, treatment is not always necessary. Local applications of liquid nitrogen or frozen carbon dioxide have been used to remove the skin lesions.

Chancroid, granuloma inguinale, and *lymphogranuloma venereum* are other STDs that are rare in the United States but more common in tropical climates. If you have traveled to these areas or had sexual contact with a partner who has, there may be some risk of these infections.

PSYCHOSOCIAL ASPECTS OF STDs

We have already mentioned that most people react to the news of having an STD with disbelief and anger. Unfortunately, some people are so unwilling to admit that they might have an STD that they delay going to see a physician as a means of denying the reality of the situation — as though pretending an infection isn't there will make it go away. Since most symptoms of STDs disappear within a matter of a few weeks, these individuals fool themselves into thinking that "It was nothing after all"; they continue to harbor the infection in their bodies and expose their sex partners to the risk of infection, as well.

Some people are reluctant to go to a physician when they have symptoms of a possible STD because they're worried about getting a lecture or they're concerned about the confidentiality which will be extended to them. Physicians are legally bound to keep information they learn about patients strictly confidential, so problems in this area are unlikely, but some physicians continue to treat STD patients with Sunday school lessons and unwanted "personal" advice. If you encounter such a physician, don't be intimidated: it would generally be in your best interests to switch to someone else as soon as possible since this doctor won't be an effective health-care provider for you if you are uncomfortable and worried in his or her presence.

What is the impact of an STD on a person's sexuality? In most cases, assuming the infection is properly detected and treated, there will be little if any physical effect. During the acute phase of many STDs some people have little interest in sex because it's painful, while others continue functioning sexually without noticing that anything is wrong. Even when an STD has been untreated and has become chronic, it is not likely to depress libido or interfere with sexual functioning (genital herpes is the major exception, since sex can be quite painful during flare-ups). But even though STDs don't typically interfere with the *physical* component of sexual functioning, some people find themselves having sexual difficulties due to the psychological effects of finding out that they have an STD. Often, these individuals are guilty and embarrassed about what has happened. They sometimes decide that their infection was God's way of warning or punishing them for sexual transgressions. Since they equate sex with sin it is no wonder that such people occasionally develop subsequent sexual inhibitions.

Others develop obsessive concerns about sexual cleanliness and worry constantly about the possibility of being reinfected or catching another form of STD. Some men who fall in this category find themselves having erectile problems, while women who are exceptionally fearful about STDs may develop vaginismus as an unconscious way of protecting themselves from infection. Needless to say, such major concerns about sexual cleanliness may lead people to change their patterns of sexual behavior, too — for instance, not participating in oral-genital sex.

When one partner in an intimate relationship develops an STD which the other person doesn't have, it immediately implies that the infected person has been sexually active outside the relationship. While this isn't always true, and some types of STD (such as hepatitis B) are also commonly transmitted by nonsexual means, doubt and suspiciousness may affect even a stable, loving relationship under these circumstances. If one partner infects the other with an STD, there may be even more conflict and hostility. This hostility may be expressed in sexual terms (that is, by rejecting sexual activity with the other person) and may spill over into the entire relationship. This type of reaction can infect a relationship far more destructively than an STD and, fortunately, most people soon return to a better state of relating to their partners.

STDs are no longer as frightening as they once were, but for many people they remain somehow "different" from other infections because they are transmitted by sexual contact and generally affect the sex organs. Until people are able to think about sex as naturally as they think about breathing or eating, it is likely that this form of stigmatization will continue as a fact of life.

PREVENTING SEXUALLY TRANSMITTED DISEASES

The People's Republic of China apparently has managed to practically wipe out syphilis and many other STDs by enforcing rigid codes of sexual behavior and stopping prostitution, but most other countries must contend with the STDs as a price for social and sexual freedom.

Even so, some practical guidelines can be offered to help minimize the chances of contracting an STD or spreading it once you've caught it.

1. *Be informed.* Knowing about the symptoms of STDs can help protect you against exposing yourself to the risk of infection from a partner and help you know when to seek treatment.

2. *Be observant.* Knowledge alone is not enough. Looking is the best way of discovering if you or your partner has a genital discharge, sore, rash, or other sign of sexual infection. (This can't be done with the lights out or in a moonlit back seat of a car). If you see a suspicious sore or blister, don't be a hero about it — refrain from sexual contact and insist that your partner be examined. While "looking" may seem clinical and crass, you don't have to announce *why* you're looking, and often a good, close look can be obtained in the sexual preliminaries (getting undressed, giving your partner a massage). A step beyond looking is commonly used by prostitutes (and doctors) to check for gonorrhea and NSU in men. The penis is gently but firmly "milked" from its base to its head to see if any discharge is present; the "exam" is sometimes called a "short-arm inspection."

3. *Be selective.* Having numerous sex partners greatly increases the risk of developing an STD. Likewise, anonymous sex is risky, too: you don't know if you can trust your partner or who he or she has been with in the recent past. Being selective in your choice of sex partners will improve your chances of avoiding STDs.

4. *Be honest.* If you have (or think you *may* have) an STD, tell your partner (or partners). This can avoid spreading the infection and will alert your partner to watch for her or his own symptoms, or to be examined or tested. Similarly, if you are worried about your partner's status, don't hesitate to ask. It's foolish to jeop-

ardize your health to protect someone else's feelings.

5. *Be cautious.* Use of a condom will significantly lower the chances of getting or spreading STDs. Using an intravaginal chemical contraceptive (foams, jellies, creams) reduces the woman's risk of getting gonorrhea. Urinating soon after sexual activity helps flush invading organisms out of the urethra and so limits risks to a small degree. *If you think you've been exposed, promptly contact your doctor for advice.* If you *know* that you've been exposed, also abstain from sexual activity until your tests show everything is okay.

6. *Be promptly tested and treated.* A quick diagnosis and an effective course of treatment will help you prevent some of the serious complications of STDs. Treatment can be obtained from your private doctor, hospital clinics, or public health service clinics. After treatment, you must be rechecked to be certain that the disease has been eradicated. In addition, be sure to urge your partner to be tested (and treated if necessary) so as to avoid reinfection.

SUMMARY

1. Sexually transmitted diseases (STDs) is now the preferred term for what were previously called venereal diseases to minimize stigmatization and broaden the scope of infections included in this group.

2. STDs today are occurring in epidemic numbers in the United States, with estimates suggesting that there are, annually, more than 4 million new cases of gonorrhea, 2.5 million cases of nonspecific urethritis, 500,000 new cases of genital herpes, 200,000 new cases of hepatitis B, and 80,000 cases of syphilis.

3. Gonorrhea in men is usually marked by a thick discharge from the penis and burning with urination. In women, gonorrhea often has no noticeable symptoms but can cause serious damage to the Fallopian tubes (PID). Gonorrhea is treated with high doses of penicillin.

4. Syphilis is caused by *Treponema pallidum,* a corkscrew-shaped organism. The first symptom is a chancre two to four weeks after the infection. If untreated, syphilis goes through a secondary stage (rash, fever, aches and pains), a latent stage, and sometimes a tertiary stage where brain damage or heart problems occur. Diagnosis usually requires a blood test and treatment is by a shot of penicillin.

5. Genital herpes is caused by both herpes virus type 1 and herpes virus type 2. It usually begins with painful blisters on or around the genitals that typically heal in two to three weeks in first attacks. The herpes virus remains dormant in the body and periodically may be reactivated, causing flare-ups of genital herpes that are usually milder than the first episode. Although there is no cure at present for this viral infection, a drug called acyclovir is useful in lessening the symptoms of first attacks.

6. AIDS, or acquired immunodeficiency syndrome, predominantly affects homosexual men, intravenous drug abusers, Haitians, and hemophiliacs. The cause of AIDS is currently unknown but it is suspected to be a virus. Prominent features of AIDS include weight loss, fever, and a rare form of skin cancer called Kaposi's sarcoma. Malfunctioning of the body's immune defense system makes AIDS victims susceptible to the occurrence of opportunistic infections with a high fatality rate. There is no present cure for AIDS.

7. Pubic lice are crab-like parasites that attach themselves to pubic hair and cause intense itching. They are relatively easy to treat with a medicated shampoo or lotion called gamma benzene hexachloride (Kwell).

8. Nonspecific urethritis (NSU) is now

thought to be more common than gonorrhea in many populations. This condition, which is frequently caused by *Chlamydia trachomatis,* has symptoms that mimic gonorrhea (e.g., urethral discharge, painful urination) but are generally milder. Chlamydia can be treated effectively with tetracycline.

9. Hepatitis A and B (both caused by viruses) now appear to be sexually transmitted at times, with the highest rates of infection occurring in the male homosexual population. Hepatitis B can produce a carrier state that has a heightened risk of subsequent liver cancer.

10. Other sexually transmitted diseases include venereal warts, molluscum contagiosum, chancroid, granuloma inguinale, and lymphogranuloma venereum.

11. To prevent STDs (or minimize the risk of complications), be informed, observant, selective, honest, cautious, and promptly tested and treated when symptoms appear or exposure is suspected.

SUGGESTED READINGS

Barlow, David. *Sexually Transmitted Diseases — The Facts.* New York: Oxford University Press, 1979. Written with a touch of British humor (and illustrated with cartoons as well as photos), this compact book presents the best treatment of the subject we have ever seen.

Chase, Allan. *The TRUTH About STD.* New York: Morrow, 1983. A quick-reading, somewhat opinionated book that provides a good overview of a difficult subject. Although this is a nontechnical discussion, the author occasionally goes out on a speculative limb or overstates negative evidence in a somewhat frightening fashion. Nevertheless, a book of many insights.

Gillespie, Oscar. *Herpes: What To Do When You Have It.* New York: Grosset & Dunlop, 1982. Somewhat less complete than Langston's book (listed below), this is nevertheless a useful compilation of commonsense advice for herpes sufferers. Emphasis is on a self-help approach.

Langston, Deborah. *Living with Herpes.* Garden City, N.Y.: Doubleday, 1983. This is an exceptionally thoughtful, scientifically accurate, detailed, yet readable book on all forms of herpes. If you have herpes, or you're close to someone who does, you should make this book number one on your reading list.

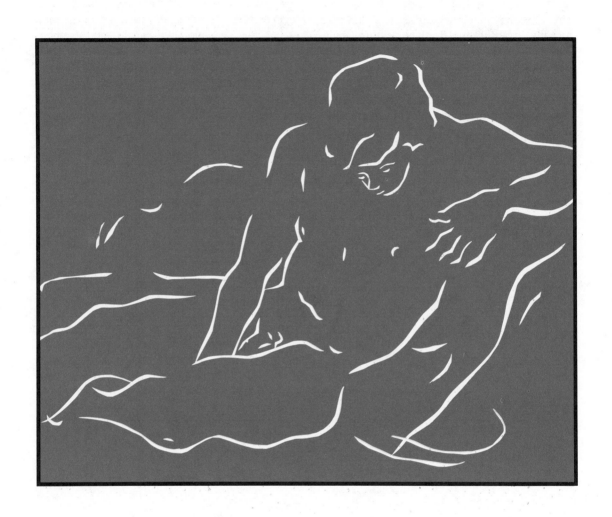

PART FIVE

Cultural Perspectives

22 Sexual Themes in Popular Culture

From the lyrics of many rock 'n' roll hits to the flickering images of today's television shows, sexuality is all around us. Dozens of magazines compete for readers with explicit nude photography and stories about sexual technique. Modern artists deal with erotic themes in styles that range from the surrealistic work of Salvador Dali to paintings that approach photography in their attention to accuracy and detail. Advertisements for a variety of products are largely based on sexual innuendo. The best-seller lists — both fiction and nonfiction — are heavily peppered with books about sex. And the Hollywood movie industry shows sex in dazzling technicolor productions in every imaginable way.

This openness and high visibility of erotic themes in everyday life tells us something about our culture's collective attitudes toward sexuality. Today, in sharp contrast to earlier times, sex has become a legitimate subject for discussion, reading, or viewing. This change mirrors the belief that sex is a valued, important, and interesting part of life for the majority of people who make up our society.

By examining how sexual themes appear or are prohibited in a particular culture, we learn

---

The original version of this chapter was written in collaboration with Cheryl Deep, M.A., a Research Assistant at the Masters & Johnson Institute.

583

something about that culture's sexual identity. In cultures that are strongly antisexual, censorship is prominent, and sexuality is hidden from view. In cultures that have an accepting attitude toward sex, sexuality is likely to be shown in art, literature, dance, and other forms of public expression. In some cultures with a "split personality" on sexual matters, there may be different levels of sexual openness in different levels of the society.

The degree to which the erotic environment *reflects* the attitudes found in that society and the degree to which it helps *shape* those attitudes are not always apparent. Furthermore, a particular cultural trend (such as frank discussions of sex in literature) is rarely endorsed by all groups within a society: whether in political, economic, or sexual matters, the conflicts between opposing groups also reveal an important side of the culture's identity.

In this chapter, we will begin with a brief overview of pornography and obscenity and then examine some of the ways that sexual themes permeate our lives. In this discussion, we hope to show how our current cultural attitudes and uncertainties about sex are mirrored in these everyday presentations.

PORNOGRAPHY AND OBSCENITY

Webster's New Collegiate Dictionary (1980) defines *pornography* (from a Greek term meaning writings of or about prostitutes) as any form of communication intended to cause sexual excitement, while *obscenity* refers to anything that is "disgusting to the senses," "abhorrent to morality or virtue," and/or specifically designed to incite "lust or depravity." According to U.S. law, pornography is not illegal but obscenity is.

U.S. obscenity laws date back to Massachu-setts in the 1600s where obscenity was first punishable by death and later by boring through the tongue with a hot iron. But obscenity meant something different then: it was an offense against religion — a blasphemy — and had nothing to do with sexual content or material. Obscenity did not encompass sexual materials until 1815 when a Pennsylvania court found several men who exhibited a painting of a nude couple in an "indecent posture" guilty of a common-law offense. In 1821 Massachusetts became the first state to convict booksellers of selling obscene literature. The book was John Cleland's *Fanny Hill*, and although the upper courts did not discuss the issue directly, the book seems to have been assumed to be obscene (Rembar, 1969, p. 15). By the mid-1800s several states had broadened their obscenity statutes to include sexual materials that "corrupted public morals."

In spite of the proliferation of obscenity laws and statutes during most of the nineteenth century, there was little enforcement at either a state or federal level. A young grocery clerk named Anthony Comstock changed all that when he decided to personally check on the enforcement of an 1868 act that prohibited the distribution of obscene literature. Comstock, obsessed with the issue, joined forces with the YMCA, lobbied in Washington, and finally got Congress to broaden its federal mail act (later dubbed the Comstock Act) to prohibit the mailing of obscene literature and to allow the post office to confiscate it (Talese, 1980). The mailing of birth control information particularly riled Comstock and his crusade temporarily ended the practice.

In the first part of the twentieth century, obscenity laws in America were applied to a wide range of materials. Margaret Sanger's pioneering work advocating birth control for women ran afoul of these laws, Havelock Ellis' scholarly *Studies in the Psychology of Sex* was banned, and many books now recognized as literary classics

"SALACIOUS, NAUGHTY, PRURIENT, DISGUSTING, TASTELESS, VULGAR."
--U.S. COURT OF APPEALS

X RATED

Cartoon Source: From the *Wall Street Journal,* January 31, 1983 – permission, Cartoon Features Syndicate.

were prohibited (Rembar, 1969; Bullough and Bullough, 1977).

The first breakthrough came in 1933 when Judge Woolsey of the New York District Court lifted the ban on importing *Ulysses*, a novel written by the Irish author James Joyce. Woolsey's famous decision noted that although *Ulysses* included many explicit sexual passages, its main purpose was not to incite lust. In addition, Woolsey's decision found that a work with serious artistic, literary, political, or scientific value could not be banned as obscene.

For the next two decades obscenity trials followed the guidelines of Woolsey's decision. However, in 1957 the U.S. Supreme Court established new standards for judging obscenity. The test now became whether the "average person, applying contemporary community standards" found the "dominant theme of the material taken as a whole appeals to prurient interest" (*Roth* v. *U.S.*, 1957). This decision was expanded in 1966 when the Supreme Court handed down

a three-part definition of obscenity that is still used today: the material must appeal to a prurient interest in sex, offend contemporary community standards, *and* be "utterly without redeeming social value" (Rembar, 1969; Wilson, 1973).

These judicial opinions seem to make obscenity judgment more objective and fair, but they led to a number of problems. For example, Supreme Court Justice Potter Stewart admitted that defining hard-core pornography was difficult, but said "I know it when I see it" (*Jacobelis* v. *Ohio*, 1965). Charles Rembar, who argued several important obscenity cases before the Supreme Court, also pointed out this subjective element when he noted that the difference between literature and pornography lies in the groin of the beholder (Rembar, 1969).

Other problems of these judicial decisions further complicate the issue. For instance, the Supreme Court has never defined what it means by "community." Does this refer to a geographic location or a group of people sharing similar cultural, political, or religious beliefs? On what basis is social value to be judged? Is the "average person" a man or a woman? Is it necessary for juries deciding obscenity cases to have equal numbers of males and females in order to strike an average?

In 1973 the Supreme Court ruled that *local* community standards could be used to obtain obscenity convictions (*Miller* v. *California,* 1973). Following this decision, publishers of national newspapers and magazines and actors in pornographic movies have been convicted in some communities for criminal violations of obscenity statutes although they had never been in those communities. Civil libertarians — concerned with protecting the constitutional rights of freedom of speech and freedom of the press — worried that the threat of such lawsuits would create a stifling climate of censorship. While this has not yet come to pass, further rulings from the Supreme Court are needed to clarify the ambiguities of current obscenity standards.

Our country has been aware for more than a decade of the social and legal inadequacies of our obscenity and pornography definitions. In 1967 Lyndon Johnson appointed a President's Commission on Obscenity and Pornography to study the question. The Commission spent three years collecting data, researching pornography in other countries, assessing U.S. attitudes toward the issue, and working on recommendations for legislative and nonlegislative changes. Of key importance was its study of Denmark which repealed legislation in 1967 that had limited the availability of pornography. Between 1967 and 1970, not only was there no increase in sex crimes in Denmark, the rates of several sex offenses actually declined.

The Commission concluded that Denmark's experience and other data had indicated that there was no significant link between adult exposure to sexual material and subsequent harmful or destructive behavior. Thus, it recommended the repeal of all existing pornography and obscenity laws, the inclusion of sex education in the public schools, and a general atmosphere of freedom to communicate about sexuality.

> Failure to talk openly and directly about sex has several consequences. It overemphasizes sex, gives it a magical, non-natural quality, making it more attractive and fascinating. It diverts the expression of sexual interest out of more legitimate channels, into less legitimate channels. . . . The Commission believes that interest in sex is normal, healthy, good. (*The Report of the Commission on Obscenity and Pornography,* 1970, p. 53)

The Commission's report was rejected by President Richard Nixon, but its findings and recommendations foreshadowed general attitudes of U.S. culture toward sexuality in the last decade.

New evidence is beginning to emerge, however, that questions the harmlessness of all forms of pornography. Specifically, violent pornography, showing women victimized by force or coercion, has been linked to attitudinal and behavioral changes in experimental settings that suggest the possibility of negative effects (Donnerstein and Linz, 1984; see also the Research Spotlight in chapter 14). While this research has not yet had any discernible impact on judicial decisions regarding pornography, in 1983 the Minneapolis City Council passed an ordinance that would have defined pornography as a form of sex bias if it included "sexually explicit subordination of women, graphically depicted" and also portrayed women as "objects" or "commodities," or showed women enjoying rape or physical abuse, or portrayed women in sexual situations involving degradation or torture (*The New York Times,* January 6, 1984). Minneapolis Mayor Donald Fraser vetoed the City Council action, saying that research showing that such material had negative effects was not yet proven, and noting that "when in doubt, I probably err on the side of the First Amendment."

SEX IN LITERATURE

Contemporary literature is filled with sexual themes in works of great artistic merit as well as in thousands of pulp novels seemingly written with more of an eye to sales potential than literary style. But sex in literature is not an invention of the twentieth century — examples can be found throughout history.

In ancient Greece, sexual themes were prominent parts of theater and poetry. Aristophanes, writing in the fifth century B.C., provides a good example in his play, *Lysistrata,* about a group of women who end the Peloponnesian War by withholding sex from their husbands and lovers until they vote for peace. The abstinence pushes the women's willpower to its limits, but the men

"Sex Talk" Telephone Service

When AT&T advertised "Reach out and touch someone" to boost the use of long-distance telephone lines, it wasn't likely that the company envisioned the problems that would occur when the publishers of *High Society,* a men's magazine, initiated a telephone service that allows callers to listen to recordings of women moaning and groaning in an ecstatic fashion meant to simulate the sounds of passionate sex. Not only was the "sex talk" service an instantaneous financial success, attracting up to 500,000 calls per day (with the publisher earning two cents per call), it has also been the source of considerable controversy.

Among the more intriguing revelations to emerge about users of this service were the following items: (1) A nine-year-old boy in the Midwest chalked up a $400 phone bill in one month (Ma Bell bills for ordinary long-distance service for callers outside New York City) before his parents discovered what was happening. (2) Officials in the Pentagon said that 136 calls were made from the Defense Intelligence Agency to the "sex talk" service in the first three months of 1983, leading them to put an electronic block on their telephones to prevent such calls. (3) The Justice Department, when asked to put a stop to the practice under criminal statutes banning obscene phone calls, referred the matter back to the Federal Communications Commission (*The New York Times,* September 11, 1983, p. 59).

Much consternation and outrage followed. A lawyer for the Federal Communications Commission (FCC) indicated that existing laws regarding obscene phone calls were designed to protect innocent victims rather than people who wanted to listen (and paid for the privilege). Even if obscenity laws were to be used to regulate such a call-in service, which local community standards would be used to determine what was obscene: those of New York, where the service originated, or those in, say, Ames, Iowa, where a caller might live? And, since children could call in as easily as adults, were special regulations warranted?

On December 8, 1983, President Reagan signed a law authorizing the FCC to declare any commercial telephone service "using obscene or indecent" language illegal if it was available to people under age eighteen (*The New York Times,* December 15, 1983, p. 25). However, by early 1984 the legal questions had not yet been resolved, and *High Society* went to court aiming to overturn the new regulation as unconstitutional.

fare even worse. A magistrate teases a herald about the erection he tries to hide. "But look, you are hiding a lance under your clothes, surely. . . . Then why do you turn away like that, and hold your cloak out from your body? Have you gotten swellings in the groin from your journey?" The war ends quickly and the play concludes with an orgiastic reunion of the men and women. Many early Roman writers also took an open, bawdy approach to sex, as can be seen in Petronius' *The Satyricon* (100 A.D.) and *The Golden Ass of Apuleius* (200 A.D.). This openness about sex in literature corresponds to a general acceptance of sexuality that characterized these cultures.

Interestingly, there is no similar period of cultural openness about sex in the history of the Western world until well into this century. This does not mean that sexuality was censored from literature completely, as any reader of Chaucer, Shakespeare, Rabelais, or Swift certainly knows, but it does show that sexual themes were submerged by a number of social and religious factors, as we discussed in chapter 1.

The Victorian Era (1837–1901) would seem an unlikely period in which to find sexually explicit literature, but it has been said that the society most fanatical about repressing sex is also most obsessed with indulging in it. An underground world of erotic literature originated in the Victorian Era, some of which has only recently been uncovered (Marcus, 1967).

During the same decades in which publishers printed expurgated editions of Shakespeare for family reading, an anonymous Englishman published an eleven-volume sexual autobiography which he called *My Secret Life*. As he recounts his frantic sexual activity with an X-rated vocabulary and a sex-as-a-series-of-adventures format, he describes in detail his encounters with prostitutes, lesbians, rapists, and children. Similar, though less ambitious Victorian novels

were widely circulated and can be seen as forerunners of today's pornography. Concern with character development and literary style was negligible; the plot, such as it generally was, rose and fell with the hero's erections.

America's native contribution to erotic literature during the Victorian Era began with Walt Whitman's poetic masterpiece *Leaves of Grass* (1855). This collection of poems describes not only Whitman's exploration of America's cities, forests, and people but also his long and arduous self-exploration. In the preface to the second edition, Whitman rationalized the book's abundance of sexual imagery by stressing that sex must be openly examined so that healthier attitudes can develop toward this important phase of life. Shortly thereafter, bawdy essays by Mark Twain were privately printed but enthusiastically received.

In the first part of the twentieth century, sexual themes in literature were artfully presented by the English author D. H. Lawrence (quoted in chapter 11) and James Joyce, an Irish writer. Joyce completed *Ulysses* in 1922, and though its beginnings were fraught with scandals and censorship, modern scholars recognize it as an unquestionable turning point in literary history. The entire novel takes place on June 16, 1904, centering on the physical and mental actions — and interactions — of the young scholar Stephen Dedalus, advertising salesman Leopold Bloom, and Leopold's voluptuous and adulterous wife, Molly. *Ulysses,* which includes many passages about masturbation, prostitution, voyeurism, and adultery, concludes with Molly Bloom's long soliloquy. This is one of the most famous and erotic passages in modern literature and is unbroken by paragraph indentations and punctuation to mimic her continuing flow of thought:

> . . . and how he kissed me . . . and then I asked him with my eyes to ask again yes and then he

asked me would I yes . . . and first I put my arms around him yes and drew him down to me so he could feel my breasts all perfume yes and his heart was going like mad and yes I said yes I will Yes. (*Ulysses*, 1961, p. 783)

Where Joyce and Lawrence led, other writers followed. In 1934, an ex-telegraph company personnel manager named Henry Miller published his first book in Paris. *Tropic of Cancer* was almost immediately banned in all English-speaking countries. Like Whitman, Miller hails sex as a joyous part of life, an affirmation of ecstasy. Like Joyce and Lawrence, he often describes it in coarse, frank terms, preferring realism to romance. Realism, as depicted in Miller's novels, seems synonymous with alienation and cynicism.

Tropic of Cancer and its sequel, *Tropic of Capricorn*, are vaguely autobiographical, depicting the harried life of the personnel manager of Cosmodemonic Telegraph Company. All of humanity seems to pass the narrator's desk looking for employment as a messenger.

The best thing about the new day was the introduction of female messengers . . . At the end of the day I always had a list of five or six who were worth trying out. The game was to . . . promise them a job but to get a free fuck first. Usually it was only necessary to throw a feed into them in order to bring them back to the office at night and lay them out. . . . (*Tropic of Capricorn*, pp. 21-22)

Although *Ulysses* became available in the United States after Judge Woolsey's decision in 1933, *Lady Chatterley's Lover* and *Tropic of Cancer* were banned until the late 1950s. At about this same time, popular fiction contributed much to the liberation of literature from sexual prudishness. In the U.S., Grace Metalious wrote *Peyton Place* (1957) about the torrid passions beneath the placid surface of a small New England town. In 1958 Vladimir Nabokov's *Lolita* shocked readers by describing the schemes of a middle-aged man named Humbert Humbert who seduces a twelve-year-old nymphet.

In the last fifteen years, most fiction bestsellers contain at least some sex, and authors such as John Updike, Philip Roth, and Erica Jong have written about sex while turning out high quality literature. Other authors (the most successful of whom is probably Harold Robbins) turn out less "literary" novels that usually describe in detail the highly erotic and sensual lives of a large cast of characters. Other popular romances (marketed primarily for women) and novels such as those by Janet Dailey and Judith Krantz avoid the explicitly sexual while teasing their readers, although many more modern romances feature highly sensual (but no more explicit) love scenes.

Not even children are exempt from the pervasive increase of sex in literature. Once upon a time, authors of children's books wrote of choo-choo trains that successfully climbed hills, and young girls who won medals for horseback riding. But beginning in the sixties, authors began to broach subjects like divorce, alcoholic parents, drugs, and teenage sex. The first innovative books sold well, and it became obvious to publishers that preadolescents and teenagers were hungry for knowledge about *real* life. An example of the distance children's books have traveled in the past twenty years is *Steffie Can't Come Out to Play* (1978) by Fran Arrick and marketed for ten to twelve year olds. The fourteen-year-old heroine leaves home for the big city, falls in love with a handsome man who talks her into prostitution and becomes her pimp, has a bad experience with LSD, seeks help at a rehabilitation center, and finally returns to her home and family. Not exactly "Snow White and the Seven Dwarfs."

Despite the trend to present realistic, somewhat bleak sexual themes in contemporary literature and to trivialize sex by presenting it as an acrobatic competition, a more humane, intimate side of sex has also emerged, as shown by this quote from Doris Lessing:

> Sex was the slow building up, over hour after hour, from the moment of meeting the woman he was to make love with, a power, a force, which, when held and controlled, took both up and over and away from any ordinary consciousness into — an area where no words could be of use. (*The Four-Gated City*, 1970, p. 61)

SEX IN THE MEDIA

Although erotic themes and explicit sex in literature were hardly inventions of the twentieth century, the "popular" media — newspapers, magazines, cinema, and television — were exceedingly quiet about sex in any form until fairly recent times. The transformation, when it came, was shocking to some and welcomed by others. We will trace just a few of the highlights of this process in the following pages.

Sex in Newspapers and Magazines

The family newspaper hardly seems like a logical starting point for our discussion, yet newspapers have played an important role in transmitting — even shaping — popular attitudes. In 1948 and again in 1953, many newspapers such as the *Philadelphia Bulletin* refused to discuss the Kinsey reports, while others ran harsh editorials alongside their news coverage making it clear they disapproved of both the subject and the findings. For example, the Chicago *Tribune* called Kinsey a "menace to society." These editorials were usually written in oblique language because concerns for propriety did not allow many of the papers to use words such as "masturbation," "orgasm," or "homosexual." Through the

1950s and into the early 1960s, most family newspapers remained pure (or prudish, depending on your viewpoint). Sexual matters were discussed, if at all, only in vague terminology, with the possible exception of sex crime reports, where the word "rape" would sometimes be used.

Gradually in the mid-1960s newspapers became more daring. For example, the words "penis," "vagina," and "clitoris" first appeared in many papers in April of 1966, when *Human Sexual Response* was published. By the 1970s, stories and feature articles discussed sex from every conceivable angle. Even the advice columns of Ann Landers and "Dear Abby" (Abigail Van Buren) frequently discuss sexual issues with remarkable candor.

Another type of "newspaper" — decidedly *not* family-oriented — came into being in the late 1960s. These papers either were devoted entirely to sex (as with Al Goldstein's still controversial *Screw*, begun in 1968) or featured prominent "classified ads" for sexual services mixed in with other news coverage (e.g., the *Berkeley Barb*, the *Los Angeles Free Press*). Goldstein ran regular reviews of current pornographic movies, giving them ratings on a "Peter Meter" scale; other weekly features in *Screw* included Sexitems, Sex Scene, Smut from the Past, Dirty Diversions, and Mail Order Madness.

Unlike the newspapers' gradual response to a changing society, in magazine publishing there was one specific event that signalled the start of a new era. In 1953 Hugh Hefner — a young man with a background in magazine promotion at *Esquire* and *Modern Man* — went against the advice of numerous consultants and brought out the first issue of *Playboy*. *Playboy* became one of the greatest success stories in the history of publishing, and Hefner parlayed his original investment of $600 into a multimillion dollar fantasy empire.

Playboy was not simply a sign of changing times — it was a forerunner of these changes. By

Sexual Themes in Popular Culture

Sex-Bytes

Now that we've entered the computer age, there's a whole new dimension of sexuality opening before our eyes: sex on the computer screen. That your disk drive can be compatible with your sex drive is shown in many different ways, including X-rated computer games, computer dating services, and computer-based electronic bulletin boards that cater to special sexual interests.

The newest, and perhaps most popular, sexual interlude available via computer requires a device called a "modem," which allows one computer to hook up with another via the telephone. With such an arrangement, you can dial a high-capacity computer service that provides an electronic network much like a national Citizens Band radio. One channel of this service, in which messages are printed out on a screen rather than heard, is restricted to "adult conversation." As with CB radio, users identify themselves with a self-chosen "handle," including names like Studly Hungwell, Cherries Jubilee, Sweet Buns, Spanker, Flasher, and Sultry Lady. And in part with a courage that comes from the anonymity provided by their computer, users of-ten choose to play what's called CompuSex. Here's how one writer described her daughter's introduction to this practice:

It was CompuSex that my two prepubescent daughters were itching to try. Within minutes after logging on, they were dragooned into private talk mode by a fellow who seemed delighted to be talking to Compusexers of the female persuasion. After a cursory chat about their careers (he was an electronics engineer; the girls described themselves as "students"), "Anthony" asked, "Are you ladies cute?" Then he asked about the length and color of their hair. The kids found this line of inquiry fascinating, and went on in detail about their shoulder-length blond and chestnut tresses. From there the conversation went something like this:

HE: HAVE YOU BEEN INTRODUCED TO COMPUSEX YET?
THEY: No we haven't, but introduce us.
HE: JUST RESPOND WITH WHATEVER YOU FEEL LIKE. (pause)
THEY: When does it start?
HE: I LOVE YOU DARLING [LONG FRENCH KISS] (pause)
THEY: Phtoooey!
HE: [CARESSING YOUR HAIR]
THEY: I haven't washed it for ten weeks!
HE: [FONDLING YOUR BREASTS]
THEY: Get the hell off!
HE: DON'T LIKE IT, HUH?
THEY: Anthony, we have a confession to make. You happen to be talking to a twelve- and nine-year-old kid. We just are very sophisticated because we come from New York. (pause)
THEY: Hello? … Hello?

Poor Anthony's come-on brought a new dimension to the concept of "touch typing." But at the time, I assumed he was a lone CompuPervert lookin' for love in all the wrong databases. In the weeks and months that followed, however, I learned that CompuSex — along with its less flashy but equally sought after sibling, compufriendship – is a staple out there in the global village. "Whoever would have thought," as one of my CB pals, Changeup, typed one night during a bemused discussion of the phenomenon, "that sexual technique would depend on spelling!" (Van Gelder, 1983, p. 426)

In some ways CompuSex mirrors real life, but in other ways it does not. According to Robert Lindsey, writing in *The New York Times* (December 2, 1983), "For many people the computer has become a new kind of singles' bar, accompanied by the same kind of boasting, posturing, and lying that occurs in the real thing." Computer-based "romances" can also cause jealousy between spouses. In other instances, erotic dalliances that began on the computer screen have led to real-life meetings and even marriage. While computer-sex may not be for everyone, and certainly is no substitute for the real experience, you might want to give it a try someday. After all, computers don't kiss and tell.

combining an open and honest attitude toward sexuality with high quality photographs and humor, Hefner was able to appeal to the average American male with attractively packaged "good, clean sex." Although *Playboy* has come under attack from some feminists as an exploitive venture that belittles women, others believe that *Playboy* — especially in its strong support of civil liberties — is gravely misread if judged as antifemale.

As a number of *Playboy* imitators (such as *Penthouse*, *Chic*, and *Hustler*) tried to grab a share of the market, increasingly explicit nude photography was used as the main attraction. The famous *Playboy* "centerfolds" of the late fifties and early sixties look tame indeed compared to the "crotch shot" explicitness of dozens of men's glossies today.

Women's magazines also had one visionary publisher who changed their orientation toward sexual themes. Helen Gurley Brown at *Cosmopolitan* correctly predicted the sexual changes of the 1960s and began featuring regular articles on sex from the woman's perspective. Since then, other women's magazines have followed *Cosmopolitan's* lead. Now, it is rare to find a single issue of *Redbook*, *McCall's*, *Ladies Home Journal*, or *Mademoiselle* without at least one article on sexuality.

Two other developments in women's magazines and sex are of interest. First, *Playgirl*, *Viva*, and others tried to duplicate *Playboy's* success in marketing a glossy, sex-oriented magazine featuring opposite-sex nudity. Although moderately successful, sales have not reached the peaks that were first anticipated. Second, several feminist magazines — most notably, *Ms.* — appeared that dealt with gender role issues and female sexuality in a more serious and in-depth fashion. Read by men as well as women, the thoughtful, well-researched articles often caused people to question many assumptions they had been socialized to accept.

Sex in Cinema

Sex has always been found in visual entertainment, but censors have usually tried to regulate the way it is presented. In 1935 the motion picture industry in America was banned from using erotica. Therefore, the films of that era relied on sexual innuendo instead of sex, although actors and actresses like Clark Gable, Cary Grant, Jean Harlow, and Marlene Dietrich learned to make one kiss look like an orgy.

By the 1960s moviemakers and the Motion Picture Association of America (MPAA) realized that a little sex could sell a lot of tickets. Directors and producers who couldn't get backing in the States for scripts with a sexual theme went abroad where their production costs dropped (nonunion labor) and censors weren't breathing down their lenses. In the early sixties several major censorship boards were eliminated when courts ruled them unconstitutional. New York, Chicago, and Maryland censors disappeared and moviemakers began, albeit tentatively, to explore the borders of sexual license. Gradually, box office success and not censorship alone began to determine the acceptability of sex on the screen.

Although the times were changing, the changes in films in the 1960s were more of a superficial, visual tribute to sex than an artistic investigation into human sexuality. The trend in the seventies was toward more social comment, with a prime example being "Coming Home," in which Jane Fonda and Jon Voight sensitively portrayed the fact that a paraplegic was capable of sexual feelings and sexual function. Other films dealt in depth with issues like homosexuality, child prostitution, male prostitution, pornography, and female sexuality.

A new style of X-rated theater catering to a new clientele also appeared in the 1970s. For decades, underground stag films and blue movies had been produced and sold for private viewing,

Brigitte Bardot, the French actress, was a prominent figure in European films in the late 1950s and early 1960s when these films were more visibly erotic than their American counterparts.

but the camera work, sound, and acting in these films had usually been of poor quality. Relaxed censorship regulations permitted better productions and relaxed cultural attitudes made it more acceptable for couples, rather than just men, to view such movies. Popular movies like "Deep Throat," "The Devil in Miss Jones," and "Behind the Green Door" were greeted by long lines at many box offices. More recently, the advent of cable TV and home video cassette players has produced another change. A wide range of pornographic films can now be rented or purchased for home viewing, allowing interested persons to avoid the potential embarrassment of being seen at an X-rated theater. This has resulted in an amazing drop-off in attendance at pornographic theaters.

One ironic twist in censorship pressures came in 1978 with the protest of "Hardcore," starring George C. Scott as a distraught father searching for his teenage daughter last seen in a porno movie. The Adult Film Association of America (AFAA), whose members include directors, script writers, producers, and distributors of sexploitation films, complained that the movie unrealistically depicted their industry and they almost stopped its production.

By the beginning of the eighties, sex was more than titillating bait to dangle before potential viewers. For example, movies portrayed the many facets of homosexuality, from the seamy side of leather bars and murder in "Cruising" to the elegant wealth and fame of "Nijinsky" the ballet star. In 1982, movies like "Personal Best," starring Mariel Hemingway, dealt matter-of-factly with the lesbian experiences of a young female athlete; "Making Love" told the story of a young Los Angeles doctor who leaves his wife for a homosexual lover; and the humorous "Victor, Victoria," starring Julie Andrews as a woman playing a man pretending to be a woman, was squarely in the tradition of "La Cage Aux

Folles," which made it successfully to the Broadway stage. The next year, an artful comedy called "Risky Business" did excellent box office business, telling the story of an ingenuous teenager whose future is transformed when he inadvertently runs a brothel from his parents' posh suburban home and makes a great deal of money. Less financially successful was a little-known 1983 film called "Lianna" that dealt with lesbianism in an open, direct way: it may only be remembered for a scene in which the heroine, having just separated from her husband, meets another tenant in the basement laundry room of her apartment. "I'm gay," she announces happily. The other woman, slightly distracted from her business, replies, "I'm Sheila."

Sex in the movies of the seventies and early eighties is no longer either the center or noticeably absent. It seems, finally, to be taking its rightful place in the cinema, woven into the stories as intricately as it is woven into our lives.

Sex on Television

The television industry through the 1950s and 1960s was even more heavily censored than the movie industry. Since televisions were located directly in the home, and since even small children could turn on the set or switch the channel, many authorities agreed that its "capacity for evil" was high (Cowan, 1979). When Elvis Presley first appeared on The Ed Sullivan Show in 1956, it was only with a strict agreement that cameras would not show his famous pelvic gyrations. Even in the late 1960s, the most explicit television mentions of sex were carefully whitewashed innuendos in comedy shows.

All of this changed on January 12, 1971, when the first episode of Norman Lear's "All in the Family" appeared. Starring Archie Bunker, a bigoted, hard-headed buffoon, played by Carroll O'Connor and his wife, Edith, played by Jean

Stapleton, the show portrayed the life of the lower-middle-class, white family. The very first show made references to marital sex and featured Archie's daughter and her husband (Gloria and Mike) coming downstairs after a mid-morning lovemaking session. (When Archie realized what they had been up to he bellowed "Eleven o'clock on a Sunday morning!") Later episodes of "All in the Family" dealt with topics such as impotence, homosexuality, the menopause, and extramarital affairs.

The frankness of "All in the Family" opened the gates, and sexual themes became commonplace on TV in a variety of settings. Comedies like "M*A*S*H*," "Maude," and "Good Times" dealt openly with topics like venereal disease, teenage pregnancy, abortion, prostitution, and having your son turn out gay. Network talk shows began to feature factual discussions of sex complete with explicit terminology. The popular morning national TV show, The Phil Donahue Show, even aired a live at-home childbirth, with a full view of the baby's head emerging from the mother's vagina. Other shows such as "Charlie's Angels" relied mainly on visual titillation by featuring attractive women in tight-fitting or revealing garb — these shows became so common they were collectively referred to as "T & A" (for "Tits and Ass") or "jiggle" programming. More recently, so-called "beefcake" programming, featuring handsome, macho-appearing stars like Tom Selleck, have enjoyed some popularity.

This upsurge in sexually oriented programming was by no means an easy process. Network leaders fought at first to limit sex on the screen; by the late 1970s there were several attempts by conservative religious groups and other "citizen action committees" to ban such programs by write-in campaigns to large advertisers like Sears and General Motors. However, it now seems that network television is unlikely to return to its earlier days of rigorous censorship, especially in light

Sexual Themes in Popular Culture

of the competition now coming from cable TV. Daytime soap-operas with increasing sexual frankness and prime-time made-for-TV movies like "Sessions" (about a prostitute), "Something About Amelia" (dealing with the family traumas of father-daughter incest), and "Intimate Agony" (a forgettable film about genital herpes) all demonstrate the willingness of the networks to air shows that depict sexual themes in an open, direct fashion. However, although commercial television permits advertisements for hemorrhoid remedies, acid indigestion, tampons, enemas, and pregnancy test kits, ads for contraceptives are still banned. According to a poll conducted by the National Association of Broadcasters, most Americans would find such ads "embarrassing and distasteful" (Mayer, 1982).

SEX IN ADVERTISING

To be successful, an ad must sell its product by attracting the audience's attention and imbedding the product's name in the potential customer's consciousness. Since sex attracts attention, many ads use nudity, sexual innuendo, and physically attractive men and women to catch the eyes and ears of an audience. Even people who respond negatively to sex in advertising often aid product sales by stirring controversy that circulates the product's name.

A well-endowed, attractive woman lightly touches the chin of a well-developed, attractive man as the man brags that he "got stroked" last night and again this morning. In addition to amusing and stimulating the audience with sex-

Phil Donahue often features frank discussions of sexual issues on his nationally syndicated talk show.

ual double entendre, this ad provokes its audience into wanting to be like the people they see in the ad. The couple's life seems exciting (at least erotic); perhaps by buying the product, the consumer's life will be more like the actors'. Adpersons call this "identification." If I shave with your brand of razor, wash my hair with your shampoo, and dress in your designer jeans, I will look like you and lead the appealing lifestyle the ad projects.

Why does everyone want to be sexy? In our culture, sexy has become synonymous with attractive, desirable, and worthy of the most intimate of actions. (Everyone wants to be at least moderately wealthy, too, which is why most ads show upper-middle-class home owners using the product.) Fragrances, vacations, apparel, and sports cars often make sexuality the prime motivation for purchase. For example, a Paco Rabanne cologne ad was refused certain prime time TV spots. This ad shows a man lounging in bed, naked from his waist up (and probably down). He is speaking on the phone with his female companion of the previous night who confesses to stealing his cologne to rub on her body when they are separated and "remember every little thing about you . . . and last night." The packaging of certain products also reflects this sexuality. Several men's cologne bottles are in the shape of a phallus, some with a rounded base resembling testicles.

Of course some products (e.g., pet foods, children's toys, laxatives) don't lend themselves to "sexy" advertising. But generally where sex is possible, it's used. For instance, who would have thought a sexual commercial for traveler's checks would increase sales? A Citicorp subsidiary claims their humorous "Japanese Public Baths" ad did just that. The ad shows a naked American couple and a naked Japanese man up to their necks in water in a communal Japanese bath. After uneasy introductions, the polite Japanese man

starts to rise and bow to the lady. "Oh no," she embarrassedly assures him, "don't get up!" Citicorp says its market share has grown substantially since they scrapped their old ads featuring bank tellers.

Ads that do not rely on blatant sexuality to push their product may still rely on stereotypical gender roles (see chapter 10). The women are usually young and slender with flawless complexions; "typical housewives" are dull and matronly; blondes are innocent and a bit dumb, brunettes are seductive and worldly. Rugged, virile men have an abundance of hair on their chests and faces; sophisticated, wealthy businessmen are clean-shaven with a refined bone structure. Women promote household and childcare items; men advertise automobiles, tools, and business-related products. But traditional gender roles have also been jostled occasionally. A woman calls a man to ask him over for Harvey's Bristol Cream sherry, and the advertising world's idea of a liberated woman sings the praises of Enjoli Cologne: "I can bring home the bacon, fry it up in a pan, but never, never let you forget you're a man . . . Enjoli."

Critics of the upsurge of sex in advertising say that too much sex detracts from the product. The audience ogles the model's breasts or buttocks instead of the advertised product. Sex still causes setbacks with censors. Is it worth the risk of spending tens of thousands of dollars shooting a commercial only to have it rejected by half of its potential markets? And identification can work in reverse. The audience may think of the model as vulgar or silly and say "I don't want to be like that man shaving in his underwear or that woman advertising her cleavage along with her lipstick, so I'm not going to buy that product."

It would seem those people are in the minority, though. Even the California Avocado Commission advertises its green, nubby-skinned fruit as "Love food."

Sexual Themes in Popular Culture

The unmistakable sexual innuendo of these ads is commonplace in today's competition to sell many products.

Sex in Advertising

SEX IN ART

Art, even more than literature, has had an abundance of sexual themes from its earliest beginnings. Primitive art from many cultures shows a fascination with the genitals, with particular attention to the penis as an object of mystery, magic, and power. Ancient Greek and Roman art is replete with detailed scenes of heterosexual and homosexual interactions. Later European painters turned to exquisite scenes of sex in every imaginable form, with contributions from many famous masters such as Rembrandt, Titian, Rubens, and Degas. But the heyday of erotic art has unquestionably been in the twentieth century. Interested readers might want to consult Bradley

Etching by Picasso: 347 Series; No. 77, 1968.

Smith's *20th Century Masters of Erotic Art*, listed in the suggested readings.

SEX IN ROCK 'N' ROLL

In the mid-1950s many adults thought rock 'n' roll music was evil and full of lust and that its performers were mindless seducers of America's youth. While many pre-rock 'n' roll records had clear sexual connotations — "I Want to Play House With You" (1951), "Sixty Minute Man" (1951), "Make Love to Me!" (1954), and "Sexy Ways" (1954), to mention just a few — it was the King of Rock, Elvis Presley, who symbolized to many adults sex in this new form of music.

"Elvis the Pelvis" (so nicknamed because of his gyrating hip movements) sang music that had a driving, sexual beat but remarkably tame lyrics. While Elvis sang of love in a sultry, sexy voice, with hits like "Heartbreak Hotel" (1956), "Love Me Tender" (1956), and "Let Me Be Your Teddybear" (1957), other early rock singers took to sexuality in a more direct way. One fascinating example was Little Richard (Richard Penniman), whose affected, camp antics (wearing mascara, lipstick, and a pompadour hairdo) foreshadowed things to come. "Tutti-Frutti" (1955), his earliest hit selling over 500,000 copies, was based on an obscene ditty that caught his fancy, slightly revised for "lyrical purity." As *The Rolling Stone Illustrated History of Rock & Roll* notes, "Even though the words had been cleaned up, the pure sexual excitement of the song comes through as plain as day — everyone knew that behind all that foolishness lurked a turn-on somewhere" (Miller, 1980, p. 50).

Chuck Berry, one of the giants of early rock whose influence on later musicians was immense, scored his biggest success with a song about sex called "My Ding-a-Ling" (1972) — "a fourth grade wee-wee joke that used to mortify true believers at college concerts," as *Rolling Stone* described it

Sexual Themes in Popular Culture

(Miller, 1980, p. 54). Jerry Lee Lewis, another early giant, had a clearly sexual message to send in hits like "Whole Lot of Shakin' Going On" (1957), "Great Balls of Fire" (1957), and "Breathless" (1958). Lewis' career plummeted when he married his fourteen-year-old third cousin.

While the Beatles took the rock 'n' roll world by storm in the 1960s, the real sexual revolutionaries of this time were the Rolling Stones, whose musical talents and blatant sex appeal combined perfectly with direct sexual messages. Their best-selling hits, "(I Can't Get No) Satisfaction" (1965) and "Let's Spend the Night Together" (1967) (which was banned on most U.S. radio stations), and their albums such as "Get Yer Ya-Ya's Out" (1970), "Sticky Fingers" (1971), "Hot Rocks" (1972), and "Black and Blue" (1976) captured the attention of rock fans all over the world. Unlike the Beatles (whose sex was more in their appearance than their songs), the Stones sang about sadomasochism, masturbation, and "straighter" sex.

In the mid- to late 1960s the Motown scene — with the Temptations, the Supremes, Gladys Knight and the Pips, Smokey Robinson and the Miracles, and Diana Ross — presented laundered love songs with few sexual connotations. Other groups like the Jefferson Airplane, Country Joe and the Fish, and the Grateful Dead extolled the drug scene and the hippies' spirit of communion more than sex. Blues singer Janis Joplin juggled both themes — drugs and sex — in albums like "Cheap Thrills" (1968), and her live concerts featured lots of sexual banter with her audience.

Recently, there has been a noticeable resurgence of sexual themes in rock music. This trend may have reached a pinnacle of sorts in 1982 with the Pointer Sisters' hit song "(I Want a Man with a) Slow Hand," whose lyrics intoned, "I want a man with a slow hand, I want a lover with an easy touch, I want somebody who will spend some time, not come and go in a heated rush." Shortly thereafter, Marvin Gaye rose to

During the fifties and sixties, Elvis Presley captured the adoration of young women with his pouty sexuality and seductive voice.

the top of the charts with one of the ultimate songs of male chauvinism, "Sexual Healing," in which he admonished his partner, "Wake up, wake up, wake up — I'm hot just like an oven . . . I need some lovin' . . . and when I get that feeling I need some sexual healing."

The androgynous look, pioneered previously by Mick Jagger and David Bowie, became

Boy George (left) and Annie Lennox (right) are two of a long line of rock 'n' roll stars sporting an androgynous look, including such other talents as Little Richard and David Bowie.

even more popular with the meteoric rise of Michael Jackson, and was taken a step further with the cross-dressing of Boy George, who was facetiously named one of the 10 worst-dressed women of 1983. Mick Jagger and the Rolling Stones continued their remarkable career with a 1984 album ("Undercover") whose cover and lyrics were filled with images of debauchery and S&M sex, including cuts like "She Was Hot, Tie You Up (The Pain of Love)" and "Pretty Beat Up."

OVERVIEW

In tracing some of the ways that sexual themes are found in everyday life in America today, the contrast with earlier times becomes quickly apparent. The exact meanings of these contemporary displays may be better judged by later historians than speculated on right now, but it is clear that the overall trend reflects a remarkable change in cultural attitudes.

There are many groups in America today

who are alarmed by this climate of permissiveness. Objections to sexual openness are raised on moral grounds as well as for other reasons. For example, many fundamentalist religious groups ardently oppose the widespread availability of pornography, but many feminist groups object to pornography for entirely different reasons, claiming that it debases women and programs men toward coercive sex.

Although those who object to sexual openness often say that it is pushed onto an unwilling public, the public pretty much gets what it wants in a democratic society. People who decry sexually explicit themes on television should recognize that the ratings mainly determine what stays on TV; when 20 million sets are tuned to a program with obvious sexual content, the sponsoring network is not likely to drop the show. When a sexually oriented advertising campaign increases sales by 15 percent, a company isn't likely to drop that style of selling its product. Popularity also determines trends in publishing, record sales, and other related areas. Needless to say, no one is forced to watch a particular TV show or to buy a product whose advertising or content they find objectionable.

It's impossible to predict how these trends will change as our cultural attitudes toward sex and sexuality evolve in the years ahead. The sexual themes in our everyday lives are not simply byproducts of our culture but become a part of that culture, the themes themselves actually influencing how the culture's sexual identity develops.

SUGGESTED READINGS

Cowan, Geoffrey. *See No Evil: The Backstage Battle Over Sex and Violence On Television.* New York: Simon & Schuster, 1979. Entertaining and informative, this is a detailed look at how network TV reacted to the "sexual revolution" — at least on its own turf.

DeGrazia, Edward, and Newman, Roger. *Banned Films — Movies, Censorship, and the First Amendment.* New York: R. R. Bowker Co., 1982. The definitive history of movie censorship in America. Interesting, informative reading.

Faust, Beatrice. *Women, Sex and Pornography.* New York: Macmillan, 1980. A balanced, thoughtful discussion of a difficult subject.

Key, Wilson B. *Media Sexploitation.* New York: Signet, 1977. An examination of sex in advertising and other media sources.

Miller, Jim, ed. *The Rolling Stone Illustrated History of Rock & Roll.* New York: Random House, 1980. The definitive work, joyfully produced, crammed with facts, insights, and memories.

Rembar, Charles. *The End of Obscenity.* New York: Bantam Books, 1969. A fascinating journey through the trials of *Lady Chatterley's Lover, Tropic of Cancer,* and *Fanny Hill* written by the lawyer who defended these books before the U.S. Supreme Court.

Smith, Bradley. *20th Century Masters of Erotic Art.* New York: Crown Publishers, 1980. A colorful, high quality collection of reproductions of a representative sample of modern erotic art, this book is both provocative and (sometimes) unnerving.

Religious and Ethical Perspectives on Sexuality

23

T HE IMPORTANT role of personal and cultural values in sexual decision-making has been mentioned in many places throughout this book. We have also suggested that there is no single set of values and rules that fits all people in all societies all of the time. This chapter will address the two major ways in which individuals and societies approach questions of values: through religious beliefs and ethical analysis. The intent is not to present "yes" or "no" answers to difficult sexual choices but to examine ideas that have been important historical influences on sexual attitudes and practices and that continue to affect contemporary cultural patterns.

RELIGIOUS VIEWS OF SEXUALITY

Many books have been written about religion and sex, and it would be naive to think that thorough and detailed coverage is possible in these few pages. Instead, we will highlight some of the similarities and differences in the ways

This chapter was written in collaboration with J. Robert Meyners, Ph.D., who is Associate Director of the Masters & Johnson Institute. Previously, Dr. Meyners was Professor of Theology and Urban Culture at the Chicago Theological Seminary from 1966 until 1979.

that certain religions have dealt with sexual issues, remembering that these views have changed over the course of time. While our discussion will focus on Jewish, Catholic, and Protestant thought, we will also mention the sexual values found in several other religious traditions.

Judaism

Jewish views of sexuality stem from both the Hebrew Bible (called the Old Testament by Christians) and from the Talmud, a collection of writings interpreting the Bible and applying its teachings to everyday matters. Throughout these writings, the basic attitude of Judaism is that sexuality is a positive force, a gift of God the crea-

tor. This attitude is clearly expressed in the Song of Songs, supposedly written by King Solomon. This brief excerpt shows its decidedly erotic tone:

> Oh may your breasts be like clusters of the vine
>   and the scent of your breath like apples
> And your kisses like the best wine. (Song of Songs 7:8-9)

Judaism teaches that it is irreverent to regard the sex organs or their functions as obscene (Gordis, 1978) since God created Adam and Eve in his own image and since he saw that all of his creations were good (Genesis 1:27, 31). Furthermore, although one purpose of sex is reproduction — as stated by the first positive command in the Bible, "Be fruitful and multiply" (Genesis

In Orthodox Judaism, women are always segregated from men in the synagogue (the house of worship).

1:28) — sex is also meant to be enjoyed (Franzblau, 1975; Rosenheim, 1977; Fertel and Feuer, 1979). Judaism teaches that the joy of sexual activity is good in and of itself, apart from its procreative potential. However, sexual activity is seen as proper only within a marriage, a view reflecting that the Jewish family has "a supreme religious significance" (Rosenheim, 1977).

As indicated by many writings, the Jewish tradition has never believed that marriage exists only for the purpose of having children. Instead, companionship and mutuality between spouses are of major importance. For this reason, Jewish law urges that *all* people marry — including those who are infertile or elderly. Furthermore, Jewish law has always seen sexual activity between husband and wife as mandatory. The Talmud suggests how often sexual intercourse ought to take place according to the husband's occupation: for example, laborers should have intercourse at least twice a week and scholars should have intercourse at least once a week, preferably on Friday evening (the eve of the Jewish Sabbath), since intercourse is sacred. The Talmud also declares, however, that a woman has the right to reject her husband's sexual advances, in which case he is forbidden to pressure her to try to change her mind (Gordis, 1978). Jewish wives have always been encouraged to take an active role in lovemaking. This active role includes the opportunity to initiate sex if they wish. Needless to say, this view of female sexuality was relatively unique 2,000 years ago. Although the family structure of ancient Jews has often been regarded as male-dominated, this is certainly not the case today (in some branches of Judaism, women have been ordained as rabbis).

Sexual relations between husband and wife are relatively unrestricted. Oral and anal sex are both permissible (although the male is expected to ejaculate only within the vagina), no limits are placed on the frequency of sexual activity, and both partners are expected to derive pleasure from their sexual interaction. Celibacy is not only valueless as a virtue, it is actually regarded as sinful. Since each spouse has an obligation to provide for the sexual fulfillment of his or her partner, a woman is permitted to divorce an impotent man or a man who is uninterested in sex, and a man may divorce a woman who refuses to have intercourse with him.

Although it supports the joy and pleasure of sexual activity within marriage, Judaism also condemns certain forms of sexual behavior. Adultery is forbidden (Leviticus 20:10). Premarital intercourse is strongly discouraged, although a child born out-of-wedlock is not regarded as illegitimate (Rosenheim, 1977). Incest is prohibited (Leviticus 18:6–18). Forcing daughters into prostitution is outlawed (Leviticus 19:20), although prostitution itself seems to be tolerated. Male homosexual acts are condemned (Leviticus 18:22 and 20:13), but female homosexual behavior is not mentioned in the Bible. Bestiality and pedophilia are also outlawed. However, Judaism generally takes the view that sex is good and has no concept to parallel the Christian notion of original sin.

In America today there are three basic categories of Judaism: Orthodox, Conservative, and Reform. Orthodox Jews, who follow the teachings of the Old Testament with a literal interpretation that has changed very little over the centuries, are strongly opposed to abortion (except in cases of grave danger to the mother's life) and observe the Laws of Niddah, which prohibit sexual contact between husband and wife during menstruation and for one week after menstrual flow has stopped (Fertel and Feuer, 1979). Orthodox Judaism also prohibits male masturbation if it leads to ejaculation, although female masturbation is not specifically banned. Reform Jews have discarded many of the rituals described in the Old Testament and Talmud — such as the

dietary (kosher) laws and the Laws of Niddah —
to adapt to changing times. Reform Judaism generally takes a liberal stance on matters such as
abortion, masturbation, and premarital sex. Conservative Jews, on the other hand, fall midway
between these positions, modifying the Orthodox tradition less drastically than the Reform
movement.

Orthodox Judaism has been criticized by
many people as a sexist religion. An Orthodox
Jewish man must recite a prayer each morning
that thanks God for not creating him as a
woman; females are segregated from males in the
synagogue during services (supposedly so as not
to distract the men's attention from spiritual matters by the sight of tempting flesh); and women
are not counted in calculating the minimum
number of ten worshippers (called a *minyan*)
needed for a service. Orthodox Jewish laws on
marriage and divorce also treat women as second-class citizens, and the Laws of Niddah
strongly proclaim menstruation as unclean
(Priesand, 1975).

Christianity

Christian teachings have often been silent or
negative about sexuality. In fact, many people
thought (and continue to think) that the principal Christian word about sex was "don't." As you
may recall from chapter 1, the earliest Christians
were Jews and their views about sexuality came
primarily from Judaism. However, the early disciples of Jesus seem to have been strongly influenced by Greek ideas that separated physical
from spiritual love. This outlook contrasted
sharply with the Jewish view that body and soul
are complementary parts of human nature and
not antagonistic opposites. Since the disciples
also believed that Jesus would return to earth in
the near future to bring salvation (1 Thessalonians 5; 1 Corinthians 7:29ff), some of the early

Christian teachings about sex that seem negative
today were probably meant as temporary measures (Kosnik et al., 1977; Nelson, 1978). A few
centuries later, St. Augustine's belief that sex was
contaminated by original sin led him to view
every sexual act — even marital intercourse — as
sinful (see chapter 1). With these historical points
in mind, we will now turn our attention to contemporary Christian viewpoints on sex.

CATHOLICISM

The position of the Catholic church on sexuality is based not only on the Old and New Testaments but also on the teachings of the Popes.
While sexual activity in marriage is considered
good as long as it has the potential for reproduction, all other forms of sexual behavior are condemned. The traditional Catholic views on sex
for the unmarried are summarized in this passage
from a Catholic textbook on morals:

> It is grievously sinful in the unmarried deliberately to procure or to accept even the mildest degree of true venereal pleasure; secondly, it is
> equally sinful to think, say or do anything with
> the intention of arousing even the smallest degree of this pleasure . . . (Murphy, 1981, p. 44)

The "Declaration on Certain Questions
Concerning Sexual Ethics," a position paper issued by the Sacred Congregation for the Doctrine of the Faith in 1976 and approved by the
Pope, spelled out the Catholic position on sexuality in more detail: "In the present period, the
corruption of morals has increased, and one of
the most serious indications of this corruption is
the unbridled exaltation of sex." The declaration
went on to make the following points: (1) It is incorrect to regard biblical writings about sex as
"expressions of a form of a particular culture at a
certain moment of history." Thus, the centuries-old teachings of the church still apply in full
force today even though societies may have
changed. (2) Even in engaged couples where both

An engraving by Albrecht Dürer showing Adam and Eve in the Garden of Eden.

persons have strong affection for each other, sexual activity is sinful, for "every genital act must be within the framework of marriage." (3) All homosexual acts are "intrinsically disordered," although a homosexual orientation unaccompanied by homosexual acts is not in and of itself sinful. (4) Masturbation, even though not specifically condemned in the Bible, is a "grave moral disorder." (5) Chastity (either virginity or celibacy) is virtuous not only because it avoids sin but also because it attains a higher spiritual good.

In addition to these viewpoints on sexual matters, the Catholic church does not permit divorce except under special circumstances and prohibits the use of all artificial methods of contraception (that is, any methods other than abstinence or rhythm).

Within the modern day church, many Catholic clergymen believe that some of these teachings are outdated and have expressed serious mis-

Religious and Ethical Perspectives on Sexuality

Sexual Viewpoints in Other Religions

The perspectives found in the Judaeo-Christian tradition are not the only ways in which religions view sexuality. Every known religion has teachings that relate to sexual ethics, although some of these religions express viewpoints that seem quite foreign to most Westerners. In this section, we will briefly mention three of these other religious perspectives.

Islam was the third major religion, along with Judaism and Christianity, to be born in the Middle East. Although its early followers (called Moslems) were Arabs, Islam has spread to many non-Arabic peoples across the world. Muhammad, who founded Islam in the seventh century A.D., influenced his followers on sexual matters both through his life and his teachings as recorded in the Koran (the Islamic holy scriptures). Muhammad had several wives and concubines, and Islam takes a very positive view of most forms of sexuality. Celibacy is discouraged, Moslem men may have up to four wives, and sexuality is regarded as a gift from God. While adultery is punishable by death (a penalty that is still sometimes enforced in countries such as Saudi Arabia and Iran), Islam takes a fairly tolerant position on other sexual issues. The institution of "mut'a," or temporary marriage, is one indication of this approach. Divorce is also permitted but is subject to many detailed regulations. Although generally tolerant on sexual issues, to Westerners Islam seems biased against women for several reasons: women must wear veils in public (except in Egypt and Turkey), harems still exist, and clitoridectomy (surgical removal of the clitoris) and other forms of female genital mutilation are still practiced in some sects.

In the oldest religion of India, *Hinduism,* sex is treated as a form of spiritual energy. Because Hinduism is a collection of many different approaches to life, it encompasses a number of different sexual philosophies. For example, those taking the path of Karma (the pursuit of pleasure) have very open and accepting attitudes toward sex, as shown by the *Kama Sutra,* a book written by a Hindu priest in the fourth century A.D. that provides a detailed discussion of sexual technique and coital positions. Others who choose the paths of Dharma (the moral life) or Moksha (liberation from the continuing cycle of rebirth by renunciation of physical pleasures and passions) may strive for celibacy at certain times in their lives in order to devote their attention to finding inner knowledge or peace. However, celibacy does not play a central role in Hinduism, and most Hindu priests marry.

Buddhism was founded in India in the fifth century B.C. and stresses a philosophy that sees suffering as a basic part of earthly life. Liberation from worldly suffering comes from mental and moral self-purification; thus, celibacy is highly desired. In actual practice, while celibacy is demanded of priests and encouraged for monks and nuns, other followers of this faith are usually married and not restricted from sexual enjoyment. Interestingly, although Buddhism regards prostitution as lowly, it is not condemned because of the conviction that prostitutes are working out their "karma," the force which determines their destiny in their next existence.

While these three religions differ in many ways from Jewish or Christian teachings about sexuality, they provide a source of guidance for millions of people across the world.

givings about the church's positions. For example, in 1970 Father John L. Thomas decried the Catholic view of everything connected with sex "as somehow tainted with moral evil, or, at least, as somehow dirty" and expressed a hope that new attitudes toward female sexuality would evolve (Thomas, 1970). In 1977 a study on human sexuality commissioned by the Catholic Theological Society of America recommended that all sexual behaviors be judged to see if they are self-liberating, other-enriching, honest, faithful, socially responsible, life-serving, and joyous. "Where such qualities prevail," the authors said, "one can be reasonably sure that the sexual behavior that has brought them forth is wholesome and moral" (Kosnik et al., 1977, p. 95).

United States and Canadian bishops attending a 1981 meeting on the subject of sexuality pointed out that although sexual union produces children, its primary role is "enabling the person to reach fulfillment." Furthermore, the Reverend Benedict M. Ashley criticized the church for having "failed to meet the actual problems of human beings in realistic compassionate ways," and suggested that the inseparable linkage between human sexuality and procreation "is by no means evident" (Schaeffer, 1981).[1] However, when Pope John Paul II held a bishops' synod in Rome in the fall of 1980, "the Vatican-dominated synod reaffirmed the precedence of laws over compassion" (Murphy, 1981, p. 44) despite hopes that the church would reform its positions on some crucial sexual issues.

In 1983, Pope John Paul II repeated his admonitions to Americans to adhere to the church's teachings on a number of different occasions. On September 5, 1983, he reminded a group of twenty-five visiting United States bishops that premarital sex and homosexuality are incompatible "with God's plan for human love" and he reemphasized the church's doctrine regarding the indissolubility of marriage (*The New York Times*, September 6, 1983). Later the same month, the Pope spoke out against cohabitation without marriage and condemned all forms of artificial birth control, saying "Couples must be urged to avoid any actions that threaten a life already conceived, that denies or frustrates their procreative power, or violates the integrity of the marriage act." In the same talk, the Pope also denounced what he described as the "trivialization or desecration of sexuality," noting that "Sexual love is truly human only if it is an integral part of the love by which a man and a woman commit themselves totally to one another until death" (*The New York Times*, September 25, 1983).

A few months later, the Vatican issued a set of guidelines on sex education that generally repeated the prohibitions voiced in the 1976 declaration, once again calling masturbation "a grave moral disorder" and speaking of extramarital sex as "a grave disorder" (*The New York Times*, December 2, 1983). Although the new guidelines specify that parents have the primary responsibility for providing sex education for their children, they do allow schools to assist and complete this education.

Protestantism

Protestantism as a separate branch of Christianity developed in the sixteenth century when Martin Luther led a split from the Catholic church. Luther rejected many elements of Catholic faith because he believed that salvation is freely available to the sinner and does not depend on human righteousness. He described this process as "salvation by faith through grace." Ac-

---

[1] A few months before this meeting, Pope John Paul II created quite a stir when he said that a man is guilty of committing "adultery in the heart" if he looks at his wife in a lustful manner (*New York Times*, Oct. 10, 1980). Although the Pope later explained that he was trying to free women from the role of being sex objects, his remarks were widely taken to mean that even healthy sexual desire between spouses is sinful in the eyes of the church.

Religious and Ethical Perspectives on Sexuality

"It was hard bargaining — we get the milk and honey, but the antiadultery clause stays in."

Source: Punch, September 21, 1977, © *1977 Punch/Rothco.*

cordingly, the most conspicuous change in sexual attitudes was Luther's rejection of celibacy as a way to Heaven. He encouraged priests and nuns to marry because they did not possess special divine authority, because there was no religious meaning to trying to be especially holy, and because he saw sex as a natural part of human life.

In other respects, the Protestant Reformation followed traditional Christian ideals in sexual matters. Adultery, masturbation, and homosexuality were seen as sinful, and marriage was regarded as a life-long commitment. Although these rules were thought to be necessary to restrain the outbreak of sin and lawlessness, obedience was not thought of as contributing to individual salvation. John Calvin (1509–1564) originated another tradition in which the orderly development of social life, including sexual behavior, glorified God in grateful response to the gift of salvation.

The individualism that Luther and Calvin represent provided the basis for a number of divisions and wide differences of opinion within Protestantism. Today, therefore, there are many Protestant denominations with extremely diverse positions on sexual matters. In addition, the differences of opinion *within* the denominations are almost as great as those *between* denominations.

Protestant perspectives are usually classified into conservative, moderate, and liberal. In the conservative group are "fundamentalists" who believe that a Christian must accept a specific set of beliefs (what they see as the fundamental teachings of the Bible) in order to be saved. Also in this group are "evangelicals" who, along with fundamentalists, emphasize the necessity of a personal experience of Jesus Christ as Lord and savior but do not require the same degree of adherence to a specific set of beliefs. The sexual beliefs of such groups — including the opposition to

Religious Views of Sexuality

abortion, rejection of premarital sex, skepticism about contraception, very negative judgments about divorce, and condemnation of homosexual behavior — are hardly distinguishable from those of the Catholic church. Moderate or mainline Protestantism places greater emphasis on Christian nurture in which children are educated to be Christians and to experience the power of faith in Christ. The sexual values of this group are somewhat more diverse. Moderate Protestants generally accept abortion, are no longer willing to condemn premarital sex outright, regard contraception as a social and individual good, believe that divorce is often the lesser evil to a tormented marriage, and are more tolerant of homosexuality.

Liberal Protestants understand Christian faith as a perspective on the world and on human life that is guided by human reason in combination with the traditions of historic faith. They do not regard the Bible as an infallible source of truth but as the record of the human struggle to find meaning in life. Thus, liberal Protestants are likely to be open to completely new understandings of many aspects of human sexuality.

Some Protestant denominations are completely traditional in their sexual views. The Jehovah's Witnesses, for example, seek to follow the Bible literally and to find biblical rules for sexual behavior. At the other extreme is the Unitarian-Universalist Association that affirms humanistic values and reveres religious tradition only to the extent which it fosters human fulfillment. For them, sexual values must be continually reinterpreted in the light of modern knowledge and contemporary experience.

Very few denominations fit neatly into the conservative, moderate, or liberal categories. There are conservative and liberal Presbyterians, conservative and liberal Quakers. Some fundamentalist Baptists have joined with the Roman Catholic church in the right-to-life movement.

Some liberal Baptists are in the forefront of the struggle for the rights of homosexuals. Both groups believe their sexual perspective is rooted in the history of their faith, yet they are poles apart.

Nearly a generation ago the Quakers released a study which defined a measure for sexual morality as the integrity of the relationship between the people involved. Since then other denominations also have attempted to reexamine their traditional religious viewpoints in light of new developments in moral thinking and new knowledge about human nature, with the goal of enhancing relationships between people. In this struggle to reevaluate and redefine a contemporary moral perspective, it is no wonder that many Protestant denominations are embroiled in controversy about sexual matters, while other denominations are slowly evolving an openness to new sexual options. No one can now predict the conclusion of all these struggles and changes, but one thing is certain: the divisions of opinion will continue for decades to come.

Religion and Sex in Perspective

Many people who consider themselves religious find that in real life they make sexual decisions in ways that conflict with the teachings of their church or synagogue. While this dilemma has undoubtedly occurred for many centuries, the problem seems to be more pressing today in light of changing cultural attitudes toward various types of sexual behavior.

This tug-of-war between traditional teachings and contemporary cultural attitudes affects people in many different ways. Some devout believers experience great guilt as a result of their sexual behavior. Others, who begin with a genuine desire to follow their religious orientation, decide that the teachings of their religion are so outdated in regard to sex that they either dis-

Religious and Ethical Perspectives on Sexuality

regard them entirely or drop their participation in organized religion. There are also many people who feel completely comfortable with the sexual values of their religion and endorse their views in theory and practice.

The uneasiness with traditional religious viewpoints on sexuality is not only found among the laity (that is, members of the churches, not the leaders). For instance, there is a movement in today's Catholic clergy that advocates permitting priests and nuns to drop their vows of celibacy and marry. In each religion, there are members of the clergy who respond to the sexual problems of their congregants with flexible and inventive counseling, taking into account the relative merits of all the various issues (religious, social, psychological, etc.) in each individual situation. Overall, there seems to be much discussion among American clergy about the needs to avoid cut-and-dried pronouncements on the morality or immorality of sexual behavior and to develop a dialogue about sex (Wynn, 1970; Kosnik et al., 1977; Nelson, 1978; Gordis, 1978).

SEXUAL ETHICS AND SEXUAL DECISIONS

Clearly, people base their sexual decisions on a variety of considerations in addition to their religious perspective. For example, some sexual decisions are mainly based on personal taste and preference. In reaching such decisions people may ask themselves questions like: "Is this person (or act) attractive and pleasing?" "Am I in the mood?" "Is this the right time and place?" Questions of this sort are ethically value-free; that is, they are not a matter of "right" and "wrong" in a moral sense, any more than the question of whether to order a vanilla milkshake or to see a particular movie is morally "right" or "wrong."

Other sexual decisions are based on personal and social values or the priorities that we assign to these values. Here, people may ask questions like: "Am I doing the right thing?" "Am I being honest?" "Is there a chance I'll hurt my partner?" These value-loaded questions *are* ethical questions, since they have to do with the moral quality (rightness or wrongness) of a particular course of action. Unlike making moral decisions based solely on religion, a process which requires faith, ethical decision-making requires a process of rational thought. This is particularly important because the most difficult ethical problems are those that do not present black and white choices but involve choosing between several conflicting values. Of course, some people deal with ethical dilemmas on the basis of a mixture of faith and reason.

There is considerable variety in the way people resolve ethical conflicts, just as there is considerable variety in the sexual activities in which people engage. For example, Kinsey and his colleagues found that in the 1940s and 1950s, people generally judged what was "proper" sexual behavior in different ways depending on their educational background. People with only a grade-school education generally believed that permissible sexual acts were those that were "natural." Thus, intercourse was approved but masturbation, oral-genital sex, and homosexual acts were questioned or rejected. In contrast, people with junior-high-school or high-school educations generally used respectability as the standard of right and wrong sexual behavior. College-educated people tended to regard sexual behavior in still another way: the primary standard was whether two people really loved each other. Kinsey concluded that educational level influenced people's views of sexual morality more than their formal religious affiliations did (Kinsey, Pomeroy, and Martin, 1948; Kinsey et al., 1953).

More recently, as more people are completing high school and college than in the 1950s, three other ways of judging the moral appropriateness of a sexual act have become widespread. First, some argue that any private sexual activity between consenting adults is moral. Second, others believe that good sexuality is anything that enhances interpersonal relationships and personal growth and development. Third, still others suggest that there are no absolute rules to follow and that decisions should be made on the basis of all the facts of a given situation. This approach, called "situation ethics," was extensively developed by Joseph Fletcher.

Whatever the attitudes toward sexuality, choices are always made in terms of some values. Even if the terms right and wrong and good and bad are not used, similar distinctions are often made between healthy and unhealthy, neurotic and normal, inhibited and free. To what extent these attitudes are ethical must be decided by each person on the basis of the standards and values to which he or she is committed.

The concluding portion of this chapter discusses three sexual issues that are a continuing source of ethical and religious controversy. Because these are particularly complicated matters, this brief discussion should be seen as an outline of several perspectives on each issue rather than the final word. No matter how strong your own feelings may be, it is helpful to recognize that many intelligent, thoughtful, honest people hold opposing views on these issues.

Abortion

Historical references to abortion go as far back as China 4,600 years ago, with attitudes ranging from harsh penalties in Assyria to encouragement in Greece. However, throughout most of recorded history abortion was generally disapproved of because it was a health risk. Abortion did not become a major moral issue until modern medicine made safe abortions possible.

In the last decade, the discussion over abor-

tion has exploded into a strident public controversy. There are three primary positions that people seem to take on this matter. At one extreme are those who wish to ban abortion under all circumstances (the "Pro Life" group); at the other are those who believe that abortion should be available to all pregnant women at their request (the "Pro Choice" group). The middle ground is occupied by people who would restrict abortions to certain situations such as pregnancies that threaten the health of the mother or that result from rape or incest.

People who hold these positions debate about the appropriate role of legislation regarding abortions. The liberal view assumes that the state has no right to limit the freedom of the mother's choice. The conservative view assumes that the state has no right to endorse destruction of the embryo or fetus by legalizing abortion. The middle position seeks to impose certain legal safeguards against "irresponsible" abortions.

The "Pro Life" movement, which is highly organized and politically active, is largely supported by the Catholic church. However, Orthodox Jews, Eastern Orthodox followers, some nonreligious persons, and many conservative Protestants have also taken this position. The four central propositions of this viewpoint have been pointed out by Daniel Callahan (1970):

1. Every human being, even the child in its mother's womb, receives its right to life directly from God.
2. Human beings do not have the right to take the lives of other innocent human beings.
3. Human life begins at the moment of conception.
4. Abortion at whatever stage of development is the taking of innocent human life.

In the Catholic view, human life can be taken only when it is not innocent, as in capital punishment, or when it is the unintended effect of some other action, as in the "just war." This is the principle of double effect. If, for example, a malignancy is removed from the uterus of a preg-

Abortion and the Famous Violinist

The debate over legalized abortion often revolves around a question of rights: the woman's right to decide what happens to her body versus the fetus' right to live. Like many ethical issues, this choice is not nearly as simple as its summary. The complexities of the abortion issue are well illustrated by considering a provocative analogy used by Judith Jarvis Thomson (1971) to focus on certain aspects of the morality of abortion.

Imagine waking up one morning to find yourself in a hospital bed, your back against a strange man. The hospital director explains that the man is a world famous violinist whose kidneys have failed and who will die without your help. The Society of Music Lovers had canvassed the country for someone whose blood type perfectly matched the violinist's, and you are that person. The Music Lovers kidnapped you, and while you were unconscious they attached your circulatory system to the violinist's so his blood could be filtered through your kidneys. The hospital director apologizes and says that he not only opposes kidnapping but would have prevented this event had he known about it in advance. Yet he also tells you that you cannot leave because your exit would mean the death of the violinist – and the violinist has a right to life.

The director then informs you that you must remain attached to the violinist until his kidneys recover sufficiently to sustain him – about nine months. Also, there may be considerable risk to your own life because of the added strain on your kidneys. Are you morally obliged to sacrifice nine months of your life – and perhaps your entire life – so the violinist can live? Does his right to life outweigh your right to decide the use of your body?

In creating this farfetched situation for discussion, Thomson recognizes that pregnancy, unlike the attachment to the violinist, does not always occur by kidnap or force, nor does pregnancy always entail a significant risk to the mother's health. Some people, however, are opposed to abortion even in cases of rape or danger to the life of the mother. Others, who feel abortion is justified under those circumstances but not for the average uncomplicated pregnancy, believe a woman voluntarily engaging in sexual intercourse thereby agrees to take responsibility for the consquences.

What if the woman *knows* she does not want a child and faithfully uses an intelligent method of contraception? Suppose the contraceptive fails – no method other than hysterectomy is 100 percent effective – must she then allow the unwanted child to develop inside her? Should she have had a hysterectomy, thus giving up the chance to ever have children, to insure against an unwanted pregnancy?

Thomson believes the abortion issue has been unreasonably clouded by people who confuse "rights" with "shoulds." If the hospital director had said you need to stay attached to the violinist for only nine *minutes* with a very minimal risk to your own life and that this was the only way to keep the violinist alive, moral decency would probably persuade you to pass the nine minutes and save another person's life. But neither the violinist nor the Society of Music Lovers has the right to demand this of you. As a Good Samaritan you may choose to do it, perhaps you ought to do it – but no one has a right to use your body to keep himself or herself alive.

Many written replies have been made to Thomson's essay. One strong, straightforward argument against Thomson's logic was by Gilbert Meilaender in his article "The Fetus as Parasite and Mushroom: Judith Jarvis Thomson's Defense of Abortion" (*Linacre Quarterly*, 46/2, May 1979, pp. 126–135).

Meilaender states that Thomson's analogy of the world famous violinist puts readers in a dilemma.

If readers believe innocent life should not be willfully ended, then they must agree that the hostage stay attached to the violinist. If readers believe such bondage should only occur on a voluntary basis (and thereby the hostage should have the right to be disconnected), then they agree that abortion is justified in cases of rape.

This dilemma fades, according to Meilaender, if Thomson's analogy is carefully criticized. An important difference between the violinist and the fetus is overlooked by Thomson. The violinist is not *created* through his attachment to the stranger's kidneys; he is *sustained*. The fetus is created *and* sustained within the mother – and the act of creation gives the fetus special human rights.

Meilaender believes that Thomson's comparison of the fetus to the violinist makes the fetus seem nothing more than a parasite attaching itself to a host, benefiting itself but draining the mother. This denies the fetus' status as a human being and ignores the fact that the parasite is not created by its host. "[P]arasitism is not a method of procreation" (Meilaender, 1979, p. 130).

The fetus is not a parasite but a human life developing in the environment natural to its early growth. As the fetus develops inside the mother, it moves toward independence; the parasite, in most cases, moves toward greater dependence the longer it associates with the host. The development of the fetus inside the woman's womb is natural to the process of human reproduction. The same cannot be said of the violinist and his hospital bedmate.

To reduce the fetus to the level of parasite is to deny our basic humanity and our particular means of procreation. There is no genetic relationship between the violinist and the person lying next to him on the hospital bed. They are not son and mother, sister and brother, or even cousins. If Thomson had used relatives in her analogy, the assumptions and conclusions drawn might have been different. The fetus, on the other hand, is a special part of the mother, composed of half her genetic material. It is possible that this genetic connection gives the mother a responsibility *not* to disconnect herself from her fetus, while the violinist's bedmate would not have a similar responsibility.

This discussion of Judith Jarvis Thomson's defense of abortion is not intended to provide any final answer but to show the complexity of this difficult ethical dilemma.

Callahan also lists four propositions that are the basis for the "Pro Choice" position:

1. Enforced maternities should not take place.
2. Unwanted children should not be brought into the world.
3. Male domination is responsible for stringent abortion laws.
4. Female freedom is ultimately dependent on a woman's full and free control of her procreative life. (Callahan, 1970, p. 450)

This line of reasoning can be expanded as follows:

> The laws that force a woman to bear a child against her will are the sickly heritage of feminine degradation and male supremacy. . . . The neglect of man-made laws to grant the choice of motherhood not only condemns women to the level of brood animals, but disfigures the sanctity of birth itself. . . . The complete legalization of abortion is the one just and inevitable answer to the quest for feminine freedom. (Lader, 1966, pp. 167-169)

Daniel Callahan himself illustrates the middle position by distinguishing between the legal and the moral problems. He concludes that in the absence of concrete evidence that abortion causes social harm, the law cannot presume to judge the validity of a woman's personal motivations and must step aside. However, in moral terms he sees both the "Pro Life" and "Pro Choice" arguments as one-dimensional and insufficiently cognizant of the variety of values at stake in any given abortion decision.

> To be sure this is to leave a matter of life and death in the hands of the woman herself. That is a grave weight to be borne. It gives the woman the unparalleled power of deciding the fate of an "other": whether that "other" is to live or die, to develop or not to develop. This is, and should always remain, a profoundly serious decision. . . . The wrestling should always be hard, whatever her conscience finally decides. (Callahan, 1970, pp. 479-480)

nant woman, the death of the fetus is not morally wrong because it is the unintended and indirect result of an action taken to save the woman's life. However, if the fetus itself is the cause of the danger to the mother's life, its destruction is not permissible because it would be a directly intended action.

Here is another statement summarizing the "Pro Life" viewpoint:

> Abortion is forbidden morally because it is an abuse of human power. It is a destruction of a human being by another human being, and as such it strikes at the heart of human dignity. . . . To give moral justification to abortion is to condemn all men to the level of expendable things. (Granfield, 1969, pp. 15-41)

Homosexuality

Homosexuality was once called "the love that dared not speak its name" but today it is a frequent topic of conversation and controversy. As public attitudes toward homosexuality have shifted, people are increasingly accepting the research that disproves it is an illness and are seeing homosexuality as a sexual orientation that develops for unknown reasons (see chapter 16). In keeping with this view, most religions take the position that it is not sinful to *be* homosexual (to have a homosexual orientation), although homosexual acts are still widely condemned. The underlying premise is that homosexuality as an orientation is not mainly a matter of free choice: thus, if the element of choice is weak or absent, it is unfair to assign moral responsibility. This perspective has been taken by the Vatican (Sacred Congregation for the Doctrine of the Faith, 1976) and by various Protestant denominations (Hiltner, 1980). The position of the Methodist General Conference of 1972 is a representative one:

Many gay congregations have appeared in the last decade to help homosexuals deal with their religious needs.

Religious and Ethical Perspectives on Sexuality

Homosexuals no less than heterosexuals are persons of sacred worth, who need the ministry and guidance of the church in their struggles for human fulfillment. . . . Further we insist that all persons are entitled to have their human and civil rights insured, though we do not condone the practice of homosexuality and consider this practice incompatible with Christian teaching.

There are, nevertheless, radically different appraisals of the morality of homosexual behavior. Most of the earlier laws that made homosexual acts a criminal offense, even between consenting adults, have been repealed although conservatives still try to limit the access of homosexuals to housing, certain kinds of jobs, custody of children, and election to public office. In addition to fighting for these rights, the increasingly numerous organized groups of homosexuals make it clear that they want to be recognized as different — but normal — and in no way inferior or mentally ill. Some heterosexual liberals support the latter position entirely. Most persons take a stand somewhere in between, with real concern for the civil rights of homosexuals but with some reservations about accepting homosexuals in exactly the same way as heterosexuals. The road is a little smoother now than a few years ago, but discrimination and rejection are still widespread.

The whole range of positions on homosexuality can be found in the churches (Hiltner, 1980). All religions agree that pastoral care should be available to homosexual persons, and nearly all want civil rights protected. However, there is some disagreement about whether homosexuals should be accepted as ministers, priests, or nuns. The orientation theory today has increasing acceptance. The number who believe that responsible homosexual expression between consenting adults is not immoral is growing, although this is still a minority opinion in most denominations. Churches fear that condoning

homosexuality would lend support to casual or nonmarital heterosexual relationships. The more liberal churches tend to be more open-minded about homosexuality, but groups working in favor of homosexuals also exist in most conservative churches. Catholicism is officially opposed to homosexual behavior, but some Catholic theologians argue that responsible sexual expression by homosexuals is moral (McNeill, 1976).

In 1981, the Universal Fellowship of Metropolitan Community Churches — a denomination formed in 1968 that openly endorses homosexuality and includes many gays among its 25,000 adherents — applied for membership in the National Council of Churches. After much controversy and discussion (including threats from various Eastern Orthodox churches of withdrawal from the Council if the request was approved), the Council's governing board refused to admit them by voting to postpone any action without making a final decision (*The New York Times*, November 10, 1983). Said one objective observer of the skirmishing: "For a group brought together by the Christian spirit, they're not exactly welcoming their brothers and sisters with open arms."

Jewish groups usually accept the idea of homosexuality as an orientation but tend to be conservative about the morality of sexual expression by homosexuals. American Jews generally do not get as impassioned about the question as do Catholics and Protestants (Hiltner, 1980).

Contraception

Several questions on birth control have recently been attracting a great deal of attention. First, there is the basic question of the morality of using different types of contraception. While all groups agree that contraception is morally justifiable, they debate over the exact ways in which contraception should be used. For example, the Catholic church opposes the use of "artificial" contraception, while permitting "natural" methods. According to the official church position, Catholics may use celibacy or periodic abstention (rhythm) to prevent conception since these are considered "natural" birth control methods. In Orthodox Judaism, males are prohibited from using any form of contraception, but female contraception is permissible (Franzblau, 1975; Schwartz, Jewelewicz, and VandeWiele, 1980).

A second question involves distinguishing between birth control methods that prevent conception and those that operate after conception occurs. The latter include the IUD, the "morning after" pill (both of which prevent implantation), and abortion, which some people regard as a backup contraceptive method. As it is difficult to decide exactly when a human life begins (at the moment of conception? at the end of the first trimester? at the time of quickening?), some people suggest that only types of birth control *preventing* conception (such as condoms, diaphragms, and vaginal foams or creams) are morally acceptable.

A third type of question involves the issue of which people should use contraception. For example: should contraceptives be made available to teenagers who want to use them? Some people believe that this would encourage "promiscuous" sexual behavior while others believe it is essential, given the high rates of unwanted teenage pregnancy. Should people from minority backgrounds be encouraged to use contraceptives? Some spokespersons for these groups believe that advocating contraception is a political-economic form of coercion and an attempt to selectively limit the growth of minority populations. Should contraceptives be used by people who are mentally retarded? And who makes the decision for them if they are not fully capable of making it themselves?

At a Vatican meeting in 1980, Archbishop John R. Quinn of San Francisco pointed out that in America more than 70 percent of churchgoing Catholic women of childbearing age use artificial contraceptives although the church condemns these methods. Perhaps more remarkably, less than 30 percent of U.S. Catholic priests consider this sinful (Murphy, 1981). This is just one sign of changing times and attitudes.

The various moral issues discussed in this chapter represent problems that involve individual and social judgments about the nature of responsible sexual behavior. In earlier eras, these issues were regarded as questions that had *one* right answer. Today, we understand these judgments to be relative because of our exposure to world religions, to different cultures, and to vastly differing points of view and sexual practices. No one can any longer be sure that what he or she prefers is right for everyone.

SUMMARY

1. Judaism accepts sexuality as a God-given gift and heartily endorses most forms of marital sex. Although the Orthodox Jewish tradition is sexually restrictive in certain ways — such as by opposing abortion and male contraception, and by banning sexual activity for at least twelve days after menstruation begins — Conservative and Reform Jews generally hold more liberal beliefs.

2. The official Catholic view of sexuality teaches that only marital sex with the potential for reproduction is permissible. All forms of premarital, extramarital, and solitary sexual activity are considered sinful by the church, which also bans "artificial" contraception, abortion, and divorce. However, many Catholic leaders in the U.S., Canada, and other Western nations have been urging that the Vatican reassess these positions in favor of a more permissive approach.

3. Protestant views on sexuality stretch

across the entire spectrum from very conservative positions that are almost identical to Catholicism to very liberal philosophies that endorse women's rights for abortion, permit homosexuals to be ordained ministers, and tolerate any sexual behavior that enhances personal relationships.

4. Many people find that the teachings of their church or synagogue about sexuality do not fit their own needs very well and move away from these "official" teachings. For example, more than 70 percent of American Catholic women of childbearing age use artificial methods of birth control.

5. Ethical analysis can be applied to situations in which one set of values conflicts with another. Abortion, homosexuality, and contraception are examples of sexual issues that currently provoke considerable controversy.

SUGGESTED READINGS

Callahan, Daniel. *Abortion: Law, Choice and Morality.* New York: Macmillan, 1970. A comprehensive, objective analysis of the abortion issue. Although now somewhat dated in its legal coverage, Callahan's discussion of the ethics of abortion is masterful.

Gordis, Robert. *Love and Sex: A Modern Jewish Perspective.* New York: Farrar Straus Giroux, 1978. A well-written and informative book that skillfully synthesizes historical and contemporary Jewish attitudes toward sexuality.

Gregory, Hamilton. (ed.). *The Religious Case for Abortion: Protestant, Catholic, and Jewish Perspectives.* Asheville, North Carolina: Madison & Polk, 1983. A slim, quick-reading, but provocative book that outlines the beliefs of representatives of three major faiths who feel that abortion need not be incompatible with religious commitment.

Kosnik, Anthony et al. *Human Sexuality: New Directions in American Catholic Thought.* New York: Paulist Press, 1977. Catholic teachings on sexuality are reexamined and reinterpreted in a modern perspective in this insightful discussion.

Matthews, Robert J. *The Human Adventure: A Study Course for Christians on Sexuality.* Lima, Ohio: C.S.S. Publishing Company, 1980. An overview of Christian teachings on sexual ethics and issues.

McNeill, John J. *The Church and the Homosexual.* Kansas City: Sheed Andrews and McMeel, Inc., 1976. A provocative discussion of homosexuality from a religious viewpoint.

Nugent, Robert. (ed.). *A Challenge to Love: Gay and Lesbian Catholics in the Church.* New York: Crossroad Publishing Company, 1983. A book by liberal Catholic theologians and academics that argues the case for greater acceptance of homosexuals by the Catholic Church. At times written in cumbersome language, the book is nevertheless an important indicator of an evolutionary direction within a segment of the Catholic community.

Parrinder, Geoffrey. *Sex in the World's Religions.* New York: Oxford University Press, 1980. A scholarly, comprehensive view of sexual attitudes and rules in religions around the world.

24 Sexuality in Cross-Cultural Perspective

by Paul H. Gebhard, Ph.D.

ANTHROPOLOGY, the study of humanity, is a vast museum with a wealth of information about human nature. More than a collection of curiosities, it is a science with value to us all. The cross-cultural study is one of anthropology's most significant contributions to analyzing human behavior. Thousands of socio-cultural experiments have been conducted in different times and places. By examining these experiments, we can get some ideas about the similarities and differences of patterns of behavior in various cultures and what may be common to all humanity.

THE STUDY OF SEX

Sex is particularly suited for cross-cultural studies since the sexual impulse is shared by virtually all humans. Cross-cultural studies can break through our culture-bound ideas and encourage us to examine objectively and reevaluate our previously unquestioned ideas and assumptions. In all cultures, people see life as they have been taught to see it: they assume that the norms

Dr. Gebhard was formerly Director of the Institute for Sex Research at Indiana University.

620

and values of their society must reflect the way things are or ought to be all over the world. Cross-cultural studies can dissolve such culture-bound thinking and help people see and appreciate the realities of life in other societies as well as in their own. Such objectivity is of the utmost importance to achieve truly effective individual decisions, social policies, and therapeutic procedures.

Learned Versus Instinctive

As we have seen throughout this book, human behavior is largely determined by learning and conditioning — especially by societal conditioning. However, we must not forget that both these processes operate within limits set by evolution, biology, and genetics. We all have some inherited sexual drive that is instinctive rather than learned. Similarly, we all have limits to our sexual capacities that are set by our genetically determined physiology and not by learning or conditioning. These limits, both floors and ceilings, are quite wide and consequently learning and conditioning can cause enormous differences in sexual behaviors and capacities.

It appears that differences in sexual behavior and capacity are greater than differences in other universal behaviors and capacities. For example, the differences in height between cultures are not great: the tallest people, the Watusi, are only about twice as tall as the shortest, the Pygmies. In physical strength, nearly all young male adults can lift fifty pounds over their heads, but only a few men can lift ten times that weight. Differences of these magnitudes are dwarfed by the differences commonly found in sex: some adults go without an orgasm for a year while others average an orgasm every day. With such vast individual variation possible, sex is an ideal subject for seeing how different cultures influence the attitudes and behaviors of their people.

Anthropology's Limits

Our anthropological record, however, is incomplete. Anthropology developed in Europe and the United States during the era of Victorian prudery, and consequently until recent years most anthropologists refrained from adequately studying their subjects' sexual attitudes and behaviors. Records of the sexual lives of women were especially incomplete because nearly all the early anthropologists were men. Furthermore, many anthropologists were reluctant to "risk their reputations" or to be "charged by their colleagues with being 'overly interested in sex'" if they published the data they gathered on sexual behavior (Suggs and Marshall, 1971, p. 221). Nevertheless, enough information has been collected to permit anthropologists to make important statements and generalizations.

SEXUAL ATTRACTION

Perceptions of sexual attractiveness generally depend on the values of a particular culture. Thus, in the United States, we esteem thin women; in parts of Africa where fat women are considered sexually attractive, American fashion models would be considered repulsive skeletons, and women are sometimes placed in a "fattening hut" before marriage, where they are fed high-calorie diets in order to put on weight and thus increase their attractiveness (Gregersen, 1983).

In the same way the sexual attractiveness of nudity is culturally determined. In general, the more clothing a society demands its members wear in daily life, the more nudity is considered sexually arousing. People who habitually go nude or nearly nude do not find nudity sexually stimulating.

Different parts of the body have erotic value in different societies: for example, in the United

Ideas of beauty vary from one culture to another.

States, the female breast is considered sexually important while in parts of China the breast is of interest only to hungry infants; in Samoa the navel is supposed to be kept covered, and the sight of a navel is sexually arousing; exposure of the female face is a sexual stimulus in certain Islamic tribes where women are usually veiled; and in the Celebes islands the sight of a knee is considered stimulating. However, all societies agree that the sight of exposed female genitals is sex-

ually arousing to males, and females are taught to conceal their genitals by clothing or (in nude societies) by position of the legs.

Interestingly, what is considered sexually stimulating to see is usually in terms of the male's response to female exposure. The unspoken message is that men become sexually aroused by certain kinds of female exposure and as a result cause trouble. In most societies, there is little concern that females will become sexually ex-

Sexuality in Cross-Cultural Perspective

cited by male genital exposure and commit some embarrassing or antisocial act; such a notion is simply unthinkable.

Of course, a great deal of sexual attractiveness stems not from physical appearance but from behavior. As this is the realm of the psychologist and psychiatrist, it will not be dealt with in any detail here. However, it appears that novelty is sexually stimulating. Animal experiments, as well as observation of humans, show that long-continued sexual relationships tend to reduce the strength of the sexual attractiveness of partners to one another, while a new sexual partner is perceived as more sexually stimulating (Bermant and Davidson, 1974; Hutchison, 1978). This fact, unpleasant as it may be to our ideas of monogamy and fidelity, is more noticeable in males than in females. There is also some evidence that being reared together diminishes sexual attractiveness between those thus reared. Israeli Kibbutz members seldom marry people in the same Kibbutz, and Chinese marriages in which the future bride and groom were brought up together as children seem less sexually exciting than marriages between persons who did not live together during childhood (Talmon, 1964; Shepher, 1971).

Male sexual attractiveness seems enhanced in all societies by behavior that indicates the male is socially successful — someone who has high status and is a good provider. Female attractiveness is enhanced by behavior that indicates she will be a good wife and mother (Ortner and Whitehead, 1981). In some countries, including the United States and Western Europe, female attractiveness is also enhanced by a suggestion of sexual availability. This must not be too blatant or the female will be condemned as promiscuous and her social value will decrease. At this point it is worth noting that while most societies condemn female promiscuity, some Australian tribes value it as evidence that the female is unusually

attractive, sought after, and obviously sexually experienced and expert. In these tribes the females brag about the number of sexual partners they accumulate.

EARLY SEXUAL ACTIVITY

Childhood

Childhood sexual activity is usually called "sex play" because we still, despite Freud, resist the idea that children are or can be sexual beings. If we label the behavior "play" we feel we are somehow excusing it or at least making it less threatening to our idea of children as sexually innocent. This unrealistic idea is shattered by the statement of two authorities, Cleland Ford and Frank Beach: "As long as the adult members of a society permit them to do so, immature males and females engage in practically every type of sexual behavior found in grown men and women" (Ford and Beach, 1951, p. 197).

Adult attitudes toward childhood sexual activity range from condemnation and punishment to amusement and pride. For example, among the Kwoma of New Guinea, boys are not permitted to touch their genitals (even while urinating!), and if an adult woman sees a boy with an erection, she will swat his penis with a stick (Ford and Beach, 1951). In contrast, Hopi Indian parents masturbate their children; the Chewa of Africa believe that childhood sexual activity is necessary for adult fertility; and the Lepcha of India believe that a girl must have coitus in order to mature (Ford and Beach, 1951).

Socially approved sexual contact between prepubertal children and adults is rare in human history — only a few societies permit it, generally in the form of child marriage. Where there are cases of adults masturbating fretful infants, the adults do not seem to consider this act as sexual but as a means of soothing the child and of obtaining peace and quiet. Evidence indicates that the overwhelming majority of adults are not sexually attracted to individuals below the age of puberty. However, among the Lepcha of India, sexual activity is encouraged between preadolescents and adults (Gorer, 1938).

Puberty

Recall from chapter 7 that puberty is a period of time during which females begin to menstruate and grow breasts, males begin to ejaculate, and both begin to grow pubic hair and become capable of reproduction. Since puberty is marked by such highly visible changes, all societies recognize it as an important transition point between childhood and adulthood.

A group circumcision ceremony in Cameroon.

Most societies have group ceremonies and rituals to mark the occasion of puberty, but as a matter of convenience, these ceremonies are only held several times a year. This tendency to have puberty rites at the convenience of society rather than geared to the physical development of the participants results in what one may call "social puberty" rather than actual physical puberty. In such cases a large puberty ceremony takes care of those just reaching puberty, of some who are not yet pubescent, and of others who reached puberty months or even years previously. However, one physical aspect of female puberty cannot be ignored — menstruation. The majority of societies regard menstrual blood as being magically powerful, often dangerous (Delaney, Lupton, and Toth, 1977). Consequently, girls usually are given an individual puberty ceremony at the onset of their first menstrual period, but a more lavish ceremony may be held later for a larger group.

Both male and female puberty rites frequently involve discomfort and pain, and often there are genital operations at or near puberty, particularly circumcision. This attention to the genitals shows that society now recognizes these organs are reproductively functional. Some puberty rites involve sexual acts serving symbolic and/or educative purposes. For instance, on the Polynesian island of Mangaia a boy is given a form of circumcision at puberty and two weeks later has intercourse with an experienced woman who teaches him about sexual techniques (Marshall, 1971). In a New Guinea tribe the male puberty rituals include homosexual activity (Herdt, 1981). While Western society does not have puberty ceremonies, we do commemorate puberty by allowing certain changes in dress and cosmetics and by regarding all subsequent male-female relationships among people of the same general age as being potentially sexual. "Playing together" becomes "dating."

Sexuality in Cross-Cultural Perspective

Genital Mutilation and Female Puberty Rites

In many African countries, females reaching puberty must undergo operations that mutilate their genitals as part of the ritual "rites of passage" that mark the transition to womanhood. These operations, which are sometimes mistakenly referred to as "female circumcision," are actually quite different from male circumcision as we know it in the Western world. In most cases, the operations are performed in poor circumstances: by illiterate older women with no medical training, without the use of anesthesia, with the struggling child held forcefully on the ground, and with no sterile precautions. Given these conditions, it is not surprising that numerous medical complications occur as a result of these practices, including many hundreds of deaths each year.

According to some estimates around 40 million African women have undergone these mutilative genital operations. There are actually three different operations that are performed:

(1) *Sunna circumcision* – "sunna" is the Arabic word for tradition, and in this traditional operation the hood of the clitoris is removed along with the excision (cutting off) of the glans of the clitoris.
(2) *Excision/clitoridectomy* – the removal of the entire shaft and glans of the clitoris along with much of the surrounding labia minora.
(3) *Excision/infibulation* – the excision of the entire clitoris and labia minora, after which the two remaining sides of the vulva are scraped raw and then sewn together so that they fuse with scar tissue during the healing process and block the opening to the vagina. After marriage, the sealed opening is reopened to permit intercourse, impregnation, and delivery. After birth, the woman is sometimes (but not always) reinfibulated.

Here is a more detailed description of the practice as it is performed in Egypt today:

> On the night before the operation [the girl] is adorned with gold and dressed in new clothes. ... With little fanfare or preparation, the midwife quickly performs the operation. As several women spread her legs, a bowl is placed beneath the girl to catch the blood, and the clitoris, labia minora, and part of the labia majora are excised with a razor or knife. The women meanwhile chant, "Come, you are now a woman," "You became a bride," ... "Bring her a penis, she is ready for intercourse," etc. ... According to some informants, this chanting and shouting serves partially to drown the screams of the child. ... After the ordeal, the mother and nearest female relatives serve dates, candy, popcorn and tea to the visiting women, and the hostess sprinkles them with perfume. ... Sometimes the child's legs remain tied together for forty days. More typically she is regarded

as healed seven to fifteen days after the operation. This healing process generally provides the scar tissue for complete closure of the vulva except for a small urination orifice which is kept open by a match or reed tube. (Kennedy, 1970)

Infibulation is practiced in order to make sexual intercourse impossible. In certain African societies, a serious male suitor often insists upon seeing the fused genitals of his potential wife before finalizing a marriage contract so that he can be assured of her virginity. In addition, these operations reduce female sexual responsivity and, especially in the case of infibulation, often cause painful sexual intercourse.

Although the primary rationales for continuing these procedures are that they are required for morality and are a custom decreed by ancestors, the operations have provoked great controversy in Western nations as their damaging effects and widespread use have become known. For instance, fatalities have occurred as a result of uncontrolled bleeding and infection from such operations, and subsequent long-range health consequences have included urinary disturbances due to chronic infection, possible infertility, and problems with childbirth. In fact, for women who have been infibulated, unless someone cuts away the scar tissue, vaginal delivery may be impossible for, or fatal to, the mother and baby.

Despite these health risks and the fact that these operations may seem barbaric or sexist to us, we should realize that they are seen in a completely different light in the societies that continue their use. Suggestions made by some Westerners to ban such operations entirely have been decried as a form of cultural imperialism – that is, our attempting to make others see things (and do things) *our* way. What are your feelings on this issue?

SOLITARY SEXUAL ACTIVITY

Since solitary sexual activity consists of masturbation and of orgasm in sleep, and since few anthropologists have paid any attention to either subject, little can be said from a cross-cultural perspective. Masturbation by children and adolescents seems widespread and generally tolerated, but masturbation by adults is usually regarded as an inferior form of sexual behavior, an admission of one's inability to obtain a sexual partner (Ford and Beach, 1951; Marshall and Suggs, 1971). In sexually permissive societies adult masturbation is rare, but attitudes toward masturbation vary enormously. Some societies condemn it severely, others consider it normal.

Orgasm in sleep, which occurs in both males and females, is almost never mentioned in anthropological literature. When it is described, it is usually thought to be due to spirits or ghosts who copulate with sleeping humans. This belief was also embedded in our European cultural heritage where *incubi* were male spirits who victimized women and *succubi* were female spirits who overtook males. These spirits were regarded not as desirable guests but as evil demons.

Despite the scarcity of data, one gains the impression that in all societies these solitary sexual activities were most important during childhood and adolescence and played only a minor role in the sex lives of most adults.

PREMARITAL HETEROSEXUALITY

Sexual activity before marriage is encouraged by some societies, condemned but never totally eradicated by others, while still others have a double standard of greater permissiveness for males and greater restrictiveness for females. All societies recognize that the sexual impulse doesn't conveniently wait for marriage but precedes it.

Petting

Usually the first heterosexual activity is what we would call petting — physical contact which does not involve insertion of the penis into the vagina. All humans need some affectional physical contact, especially during their formative years, and such contact with particular people is later perceived as sexually pleasurable. Our culture is unusual in that people often engage in petting as an end in itself; most people in the world regard petting as either (1) an attempt to sexually arouse someone so that they will agree to coitus, or (2) a prelude to already agreed upon coitus. In our European-American culture petting is important for allowing sexual expression while preserving virginity and avoiding pregnancy. This view is shared by only a few other societies, mainly those in parts of Black Africa (Ford, 1945; Laubscher, 1938).

Petting as a prelude to coitus (foreplay) is almost universal, but its duration and extent varies greatly, ranging from brief stimulation to lengthy and elaborate techniques. Both extremes of this range appear to be satisfactory to the participants; evidently what is important is not what you do but rather that you do what is socially expected.

Some Polynesians reverse this foreplay process. They feel that all males and females are interested in coitus and hence preliminaries are unnecessary. Marshall (1971, p. 119) reported that one Mangaian said: "Fooling around [with foreplay] would cut down the time that we could actually go in and out," and a man who "wastes" a woman's time with too much foreplay "is likely to be pushed away and called *ure paruparu*, 'limp penis.'" However, after coitus one feels affectionate toward the person who has given one pleasure and so then one expresses this by affectional petting.

Petting and foreplay techniques vary greatly from one group to another. While embracing seems universal, kissing is not. Some people such as the Thonga, Lepcha, and Balinese think of the mouth as a dangerous chewing and biting device not suited for expressing affection; such folk are more inclined to rub cheeks together (Ford and Beach, 1951). Stimulation of the female (but rarely the male) breast is common although a few societies think that any oral stimulation of the breast is ridiculous because it resembles infant suckling. Manual stimulation of the genitalia is nearly universal and is recognized as very effective in arousing the woman sexually, but a few societies consider female genital secretions to be filthy or magically dangerous and the males are careful not to contaminate their fingers (Devereux, 1936; Bryk, 1928). Not much information exists regarding mouth-genital contact, but it seems acceptable in some cultures (e.g., Asiatic civilizations) while in others (e.g., some Latin American cultures), it is regarded as disgusting and perverse. One curious cultural uniformity appears: a society that allows cunnilingus always allows fellatio, but the reverse is not always true. There are virtually no anthropological data regarding anal stimulation although the anus is physiologically an erogenous zone. In a considerable number of societies, scratching and biting is part of sexual activity, mostly done by the female.

Sexual Intercourse

Premarital coitus is permitted by nearly half of the societies of which we have record but is usually allowed only with certain persons and under certain conditions. If one adds to this societies that publicly deplore premarital coitus but secretly condone it, the percentage of permissive societies would rise to nearly 75 percent (Murdock, 1949). It is noteworthy that many societies are more permissive regarding males than females, presumably because only females become

pregnant, which causes social and economic complications. Thus, fathers in most societies attempt to protect the virginity of their unmarried daughters, sometimes enlisting the help of an extended kinship group in supervising their conduct and restricting the daughters' contacts with men.

In some societies, when premarital intercourse occurs the man is forced to marry the woman because she is now considered "damaged" (that is, she would command a much lower bride-price). In other societies, such as the Nuer, the father may demand payment from a man who seduces his daughter. There are also societies where premarital intercourse is dealt with by physical punishment. In still other societies, however, virginity is not considered important and a loss of virginity doesn't reduce a woman's marriage value but may actually increase it (Paige and Paige, 1981). In fact several African groups, such as the Masai and the Kipsigis, consider a premarital pregnancy an added value to the prospective bride's worth, as the future husband is recognized as having paternity rights to the child, and the child brings status and economic advantages to the parents.

The extent and duration of premarital coitus varies from societies such as ours where ten or more years of premarital life usually exist between puberty and marriage to nonindustrial societies where only a few years separate puberty and marriage.

In some societies premarital coitus was not simply allowed or expected but was demanded. For example, among the Rukuba of Nigeria a man could pay a girl's father for sexual rights to her for a period of at least six months although this did not usually lead to marriage (Muller, 1973).

In Polynesia, adolescent boys are encouraged to be as sexually active as possible. Because unmarried girls are under the control of their fathers, however, sex with the youths must be surreptitiously "stolen" — commonly done by a practice called "sleep crawling":

> Sleep crawling first entails stealthily and unexpectedly entering a girl's house at night and having sex with her, usually over her protest and resistance. In Mangaia it is called "motoro," and is seen as a sign of masculinity. A man who gains sexual access to a girl through formal engagement is seen as a weakling. The important thing is to sweet-talk her, rather than to use force, so that she will not scream and wake up her family.
> (Ortner and Whitehead, 1981, p. 373)

The great value some societies attach to female (but never male) virginity is the result of viewing females as property, of wanting one's children to be one's own, and of avoiding an experienced female who would not only have sexual expectations but who would be in a position to make comparisons between former lovers and her husband.

SEX AND MARRIAGE

The subject of sex and marriage is complicated not only by the various forms of marriage but by the problem of defining marriage. The Royal Anthropological Institute has what seems a complete definition: "Marriage is a union between a man and woman such that children born to the woman are recognized legitimate offspring of both parents" (Committee, 1951). As usual, humans refuse to be so easily classified. The Nuer of Africa and the Mohave of the Southwestern United States allowed women to marry women, and some North American Plains tribes allowed a man to marry a male transvestite. The Nayars of Southern India had a system so complex that some early anthropologists decided that they did not have marriage in the European sense. The simplest view is to regard marriage as a presumably sexual union between two or more persons which is recognized by society and the persons involved and which entails various legal obligations. With this definition one can say that all human societies of which we have knowledge have had some form of marriage.

Societal Regulations

Most societies are interested in having all their members ultimately marry except, in some cases, special persons such as priests and priestesses. However, all societies have rules as to whom one can or cannot marry.

INCEST

One cannot marry persons considered too closely related — this restriction is part of the incest taboo. Americans, for example, feel that parents, brothers, sisters, grandparents, aunts, uncles, nephews, nieces, sons, daughters, and first cousins are too closely related to one to permit marriage with any of them. This relatedness is not just genetic but social as well: the incest taboo also applies to people not genetically related, such as step-parents, adopted brothers and sisters, and others.

Much has been written as to why all peoples have some sort of incest taboo, but the simplest reason is that incest would make life unworkably complicated. Not only would it confuse kinship and inheritance unbearably, but it would also cause role conflicts.

Our definition of incest would seem shockingly liberal to the Chiricahua Apache who prohibit marriage between any persons known to be related in any way, no matter how remotely. On the other hand, our views would seem overly conservative to the Kubeo of South America, who require a boy to have intercourse with his mother to mark the beginning of his "official" sex life (Gregersen, 1983). Similarly,

Wedding ceremonies show great cultural variation. In the photo (top) of a Fiji Islands ceremony, the groom's clan has brought gifts of kerosene (in small metal drums) and the whale's teeth (lying on the mat attached to ropes) to the bride's clan. In America, gifts are traditionally given to the newlyweds, not to their families.

Sexuality in Cross-Cultural Perspective

brother-sister marriage was practiced by the royal families of ancient Egypt and Hawaii, and in Bali, a twin brother is permitted to marry his twin sister, although other forms of sibling incest are forbidden.

EXOGAMY AND ENDOGAMY

While societies prevent the marriages of persons deemed too closely related, they also try to prevent their members from marrying persons they consider too foreign. Usually one is urged to marry within one's race, religion, tribe, or neighborhood.

The tendency to marry outside one's relatives or group is called *exogamy;* the tendency to marry one's relatives or within one's group is called *endogamy.* Exogamy weakens group loyalty but allows new advantageous relationships and political power; endogamy strengthens group loyalty but isolates and politically weakens the group. All societies use various combinations of exogamy and endogamy. A good many have decided exactly how related and unrelated one's spouse should be and specify exactly whom one should marry. This is known as *preferential marriage,* and one's cousin is generally chosen as an ideal spouse. This cannot be any cousin, he or she must be a cross-cousin: one's father's sister's child or one's mother's brother's child.

MONOGAMY AND POLYGAMY

Although Western societies generally recognize only the form of marriage in which one man and one woman are married to each other at one time (a practice called *monogamy*), nearly half of the 862 societies listed in Murdock's *Ethnographic Atlas* regard *polygamy* (having more than one spouse) as the norm, and 39 percent permit it along with monogamy (Gregersen, 1983). The Pahaarii of northern India seem to be unique in having a society in which group marriage is the norm.

Types of Marriage

While all peoples have some form of marriage, attitudes toward it vary enormously. Figure 24-1 shows some of the varieties. Many cultures, unlike ours, believe that marriage should be based on practical reasons rather than romantic love. Such marriages are like a business partnership with sex added. In many cases real affection or love may develop, but this comes after, rather than before, marriage. A substantial number (and once probably a majority) of societies have marriages arranged by parents, and the husband and wife may be virtual strangers. Some groups in China formerly had a curious but rather logical form of marriage. In conventional marriages friction frequently arose between the husband's mother and the daughter-in-law who was viewed as an intruder who disrupted family routine and questioned the mother's authority. This problem was solved in advance by adopting a baby girl to be the young son's future wife. The girl and boy were reared like brother and sister until near puberty when they began to act more reserved toward one another — as fitting for an engaged couple. After puberty they were married in an inexpensive ceremony with a small bride-price and no dowry. Most of the brides and grooms were not especially sexually attracted to one another and would have preferred conventional (even if arranged) marriages.

The Gusii of Kenya, Africa, have a marriage ceremony which one would think would guarantee divorce, separation, or homicide. When the groom arrives for the ceremony the bride's kinfolk and friends insult him and prophesy he will be impotent. The bride, struggling and weeping, is dragged by the groom's people to the ceremony where the groom's female relatives insult her and try to keep her from entering the hut for the ceremony. After the marriage rites the bride vigorously resists coitus while the groom tries to penetrate her. If necessary, the groom calls in

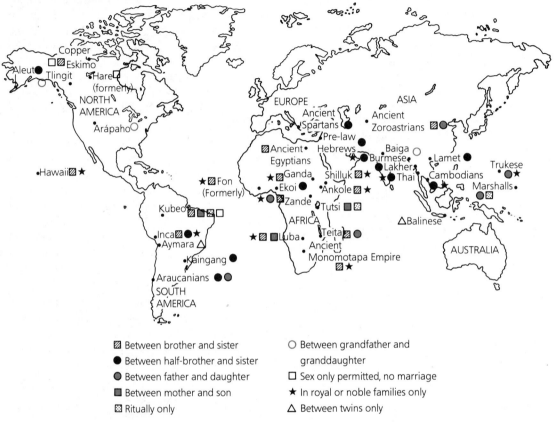

FIGURE 24–1
Various Cultural Rules About Sex and Marriage Between Close Relatives

Source: *Sexual Practices* by Edgar Gregersen. Copyright © 1982 by Mitchell Beazley Publishers Ltd. Used by permission of Franklin Watts, Inc.

male friends to hold her. A "real man" is supposed to hurt his wife by his penile thrusting, and she is supposed to cry out and complain. Yet despite all this, Gusii marriages are not fatally damaged — the participants do not feel as much hostility as they exhibit (Levine, 1959).

Frequencies of Marital Sexual Activity

In marriage where sexual access is not only permitted but usually encouraged by society, one would anticipate uniform and fairly high frequencies of coitus. However, this is not the case. In some societies where sexuality is regarded as basically nasty or evil, even marriage does not make it acceptable and, consequently, frequencies are low. For example, in the Irish community of Inis Beag, coitus in marriage was best measured in terms of per month or per year rather than per week (Messenger, 1971). In other societies sex is not considered bad, but there are various restrictions on when a couple can have coitus: the most extreme example is that of the Dani of New

Sexuality in Cross-Cultural Perspective

Guinea who delay the sexual consummation of marriage for two years and abstain from marital intercourse for five years after the birth of a child (Heider, 1976). In addition, it is not uncommon to find coitus discouraged just before certain important activities (going hunting or to war) or during certain activities or religious ceremonies. In general, this restriction is meant to focus undistracted attention on the special activity and to preserve a man's strength. (As a carryover from this practice, some American athletes continue to believe that sex before competition reduces their performance, although research has disproven this notion.)

In societies that have few or no such restrictions, the frequency of coitus in marriage averages once or twice a day during young adulthood and gradually decreases with age to about twice a week in middle age. For example, Marshall (1971) reported that the Mangaians of Polynesia had an average coital frequency of about twenty times per week at age eighteen, declining to two or three per week at age forty-eight. Not enough is known of coital frequencies in old age to make reliable cross-cultural estimates.

Extramarital Sex

If discovered, extramarital sexual activity frequently causes trouble ranging in severity from killing one or both of the offenders to verbal scolding. All societies are more inclined to allow or forgive extramarital activity by males and to be more harsh toward such behavior by females. This double standard of sexual morality probably stems from the realization that males tend to be more promiscuous than women, the fear that female adultery will result in the husband rearing some other man's child, the fact that it is harder to restrain or punish men, and the final fact that men make most of the social rules and are easier on themselves.

While most societies seemingly forbid and

punish extramarital activity, one finds on closer inspection that while forbidden in general, it is permitted in certain clearly defined circumstances. Sometimes extramarital coitus is allowed only with certain relatives — generally a brother-in-law (for wives) or sister-in-law (for husbands). In a few societies, such as the Eskimo, a husband may allow a friend or visitor sexual access to his wife as a gesture of hospitality. Lastly, societies may have special ceremonies when sexual rules are temporarily abandoned ("ceremonial license") and persons can have extramarital coitus without censure.

A minority of societies have built extramarital coitus into their normal living system. Among the Turu of Tanzania, wives are expected to have lovers but are supposed to conceal the fact from their husbands. The neighbors cooperate and abet these adulterous- liaisons (Schneider, 1971). The Rukuba of Nigeria generally betroth a girl at an early age to a man whom she seldom marries. Instead she marries someone else and her new husband then turns the bride over to her former betrothed for a period of one month at the end of which time she decides whether or not to stay with him or to return to her husband. The women of the Nayar of Southern India normally have a simultaneous mixture of husbands and casual sexual partners.

A different style of extramarital sex marks the Mehinaku, a tribe of Brazilian Indians. There it is accepted practice for a male suitor to hide behind a female's house waiting for her to come out so they can have sex (Gregor, 1977). The hiding is called "alligatoring" both because Mehinaku mythology portrays this animal as highly sexual and the alligator is famous for its ability to lie motionless while waiting for its prey. The Mehinaku male has several "alligator spots" in which he can hide; when his girlfriend finally appears, they rush down an "alligator path" to "alligator areas" where they quickly have intercourse.

In summary, all societies face the reality that marriage does not satisfy the sexual needs of all married couples all of the time. There are inevitably absences, illnesses, and incompatibilities, and humans accustomed to regular sexual gratification cannot be expected to endure long periods of abstinence. Consequently, a majority of societies permit or condone extramarital activity under well-defined circumstances.

Postmarital Sex

Preindustrial societies are generally arranged so that a widowed, separated, or divorced person is under great social and economic pressure to remarry. Consequently, postmarital sexual activity in such societies is usually confined to short periods of time. In cultures similar to the U.S., persons can maintain postmarital status indefinitely but most ultimately remarry (I. Reiss, 1980).

Societies allow postmarital persons far greater sexual freedom than that permitted to the never-married or married. It is as though society recognized the futility of trying to impose sexual abstinence on individuals accustomed through marriage to regular sexual gratification. We see this clearly in some segments of American society where there is great concern over premarital coitus by young people but virtually no concern over postmarital coitus. Indeed, we expect postmarital activity: note in our folklore the sexuality of the labels "merry widow" and the "gay divorcée" (before the word "gay" assumed another meaning).

Anthropologists have paid little attention to postmarital life, but we do know that in preindustrial societies when a female of marriageable age does not remarry she often becomes a concubine, semiprostitute, or prostitute. If a widow or divorcée is so elderly she cannot use her sexuality in one of these ways, she is generally supported by her children or relatives. Very little is known of elderly widowers; presumably if they do not remarry, they continue work until incapacity renders them dependent on children or relatives or until they die.

HOMOSEXUALITY

Male Homosexual Behavior

The majority of nonindustrial societies permit homosexual behavior, at least for certain individuals. Among males in these societies homosexuality generally occurs in three forms. The first might be called the ancient Greek form: a relationship between an older male and a younger adolescent male. The older male acts also as a teacher and guardian. Both have heterosexual relationships as well and the older male is usually married. When the younger male reaches manhood and marriage, the relationship breaks up and in time the now adult younger male seeks a boy of his own. The older male also obtains a new boy. This form of homosexuality is found around the Mediterranean, in many societies in the Middle East, Africa, and Asia, and in some Melanesian islands (Gregersen, 1983).

A second form of male homosexuality is associated with transvestism — wearing the clothing of the opposite gender. In some societies an occasional male finds the masculine role uncongenial and instead of vainly trying to live up to society's expectations of manhood, he adopts the role and dress of a woman. This change often involves engaging in homosexual behavior as well. Such transvestites are generally accepted and in the Plains of North America, where they were known as *bedarches* by American Indian tribes, they were often esteemed. The Navajo, Cheyenne, and Mohave tribes regarded bedarches as particularly good matchmakers and curers of sexually transmitted diseases (Whitehead, 1981). In Northern Asia some medicine men or shamans were both transvestites and partially homosexual, thereby gaining both male and female magic. In a variation on this theme, in Oman (a Middle Eastern, Arab country), about one out of fifty men live as *xaniths*, effeminate, homosexual prostitutes who dress in pastel-colored clothing (not women's clothes) and move freely among women without regard to ordinary social restrictions (Wikan, 1982).

Lastly, in some groups homosexual behavior is expected under specifically defined conditions. For example, in a primitive tribe in the Highlands of New Guinea, boys are expected to have homosexual experiences until marriage and then to be heterosexual for the rest of their lives (Herdt, 1981).

In some societies homosexuality is regarded as normal behavior for males. In the Melanesian society studied by Davenport he reported, ". . . at some time during his life, very nearly every male engages in extensive homosexual activities" (Davenport, 1965). At the other extreme are societies where homosexuality appears not only to be absent but beyond imagination.

Female Homosexual Behavior

Female homosexuality, which is less common than male homosexuality, lacks the Greek form, but occasional transvestism with homosexuality occurs. Most female homosexuality in preindustrial societies seems to be of a temporary and incidental nature such as might result when husbands or lovers were absent on lengthy trips or when one husband had more wives than he could satisfy. However, one must remember that most anthropologists have been male, reticent about studying sex, and very naive about female sexuality. Hence we know very little about female homosexuality in societies other than our European-American ones. This observation is confirmed by Gregersen (1983), who remarked that he could only find five societies in the world that specifically approve female homosexuality for at least some people.

We do find that where there is intolerance of homosexuality, the intolerance is far greater for males (Jensen, 1980). This is true in our Judaeo-Christian culture where the Bible and Talmud condemn male homosexuals and advocate their execution (Leviticus 20:13). There is no mention of female homosexuality, however, until one brief passage in the New Testament (Romans 1:26) where it is dismissed simply as a "vile affection." In the Judaic code lesbianism is punishable not by death but by being prohibited from marrying a priest.

Homosexuality and Anthropology's Perspective

Anthropology has contributed four important findings to our understanding of homosexuality. First, predominant or exclusive homosexuality as a lifetime pattern is very rare in preindustrial societies (Ford and Beach, 1951; Carrier, 1980). There seems to be something in well-developed civilizations conducive to predominant homosexuality.

Second, in many societies male homosexuality is divided into the penetrator and the penetrated. The latter is considered more feminine or at least submissive, and if there is intolerance it falls chiefly on the penetrated male. In some cultures the penetrated male is viewed as the "real homosexual" while the penetrator may escape the label completely. In Latin American countries there is the feeling that a person must be one or the other exclusively (Carrier, 1976). In the United States, however, this distinction between homosexual roles has little significance. Third, anthropology shows that heterosexuality and homosexuality are not mutually exclusive but can exist together in the same individual in noncompetitive fashion.

Fourth is a finding of profound significance for psychology: roles change as a result of culturally expected patterns, which is a powerful form of social conditioning. One striking example is found in Java where there are boys known as gimbalans who are kept as homosexual partners by rich men or by groups of less affluent men. Gimbalans appear to be exclusively or predominantly homosexual for years, but when they become adult and too old to be a gimbalan they turn heterosexual and usually marry. An equally dramatic example is seen in the "doce años" or twelve-year-old pseudohermaphrodite boys of the Dominican Republic, discussed in chapter 7. Another example of the power of expectation may be found in various societies where boys are taken from their homes and isolated in what could be called a boarding school for boys and adolescents. They are not allowed visits home and so spend their formative years in an all-male environment where, if they have sexual activity with another person, it must be homosexual. Yet when they attain a certain age they are sent back to their village where they develop a heterosexual life and marry.

RITUALIZED SEX

This behavior has been mentioned briefly at several points in this chapter but it merits more attention. Since humans always think in terms of their own experience, knowledge, and interests, it is not surprising that there has been a considerable amount of sexuality in religion, myth, ritual, and ceremony. Religions assign their deities gender: there are gods and goddesses that cop-

ulate and reproduce. Even in Christianity, a comparatively antisexual religion, God is a male who caused a human female to bear a son; and nuns are referred to as "brides of Christ." Many other religions have a strong sexual element with deities representing sexual desire and activity, and some of the rituals surrounding them are openly sexual. The sexual aspect of religion stemmed from human total dependence on the fertility of plant, animal, and human life, and some of the earliest religions featured fertility and mother goddesses. Lastly, some religious rites specified types of sexual activity, for example, temple prostitution.

Other forms of ritualized sex occur and these take precedence over the usual rules of social conduct. One arrangement is the *joking relationship* in which certain relatives are supposed to joke with one another in sexual terms. These relatives are chiefly those of appropriate age to be sexual partners: brothers' wives, wife's sisters, and cousins. This leads some anthropologists to think joking relationships represent society recognizing a potential sexual attraction and defusing it through humor. The other arrangement is *ceremonial license:* a brief time when ordinary sexual restraints become inoperative because of some ceremony, ritual, or celebration. Vestiges of such license persist in our culture in the form of the Mardi Gras and kissing under the mistletoe. License can be regarded as a sort of safety valve, a recognition that people should not be repressed sexually all of the time.

SUMMARY

1. All societies of which we have knowledge impose some restrictions on the sexual behavior of their members. Evidently some restrictions are necessary if social organization is to exist.

2. All societies have some form of marriage and define who can marry whom.

3. All societies prohibit sexual intercourse between certain persons because of their genetic and/or social relationship — the "incest taboo."

4. Human sexuality can be extremely modified by learning and conditioning; societies can have very different patterns of and attitudes toward sexual behavior.

5. No sexual act bears an inherent social or psychological value for good or evil — the value and meaning of an act is determined by the social context in which it occurs.

6. The effects of simple behavioral conditioning — the repetition of a certain sexual behavior — can be diluted or avoided by the expectations of the person involved which are partly derived from societal conditioning.

7. There must be a large degree of predictability of behavior for social organization to survive and function. Of greater importance than the sexual acts themselves is whether they constitute expected and understood patterns of behavior to which people know how to react. An unexpected or misunderstood act surprises and upsets people, and such acts are then labelled deviant.

SUGGESTED READINGS

Davenport, William H. "Sex in Cross-Cultural Perspective." In *Human Sexuality in Four Perspectives*, ed. Beach, F. A. Baltimore: The Johns Hopkins University Press, 1977, pp. 115-163. An outstanding discussion of cultural variance in sexual matters; readable and entertaining as well as enlightening.

Fisher, Lawrence E. "Relationships and Sexuality in Contexts and Culture: The Anthropology of Eros." In *Handbook of Human Sexuality*, eds. Wolman, B. B. and Money, J. Englewood Cliffs, New Jersey: Prentice-Hall, 1980, pp. 164-189. A balanced, up-to-date overview of the anthropological perspective on sex and sexuality.

Ford, Clellan, and Beach, Frank, eds. *Patterns of Sexual Behavior*. New York: Harper and Bros., 1951. A scholarly, comprehensive account of sexual behavior from a cross-cultural perspective. Dated but fascinating reading.

Gregersen, Edgar. *Sexual Practices*. New York: Franklin Watts, 1983. A fast-paced overview of cultural differences regarding sexual attitudes and behaviors. Profusely and interestingly illustrated.

Herdt, Gilbert H. *Guardians of the Flutes*. New York: McGraw-Hill, 1981. A detailed, thought-provoking study of a New Guinea tribe where ritualized male homosexual behavior precedes marriage.

Marshall, Donald, and Suggs, Robert, eds. *Human Sexual Behavior: Variations in the Ethnographic Spectrum*. New York: Basic Books, 1971. A collection of intriguing essays that provide an in-depth profile of sexual behavior in selected cultures.

Glossary

abortion Termination of a pregnancy before the fetus can survive outside the uterus. *Spontaneous* abortions occur naturally due to medical problems; *induced* abortions are done intentionally.

abstention (abstinence) Voluntarily not engaging in some act, e.g., sexual intercourse. A highly effective method of birth control, if practiced consistently.

acquired immune deficiency syndrome See *AIDS*.

acrosome (ak′ ro sōm) Chemical reservoir in the head of the spermatozoa.

adolescent growth spurt A period of fast bone growth usually occurring in the early or middle teens caused by the rising sex hormone levels of puberty.

adrenogenital syndrome (a drē′ nō jen′ i tul) An inherited disorder involving an enzyme block in the adrenal glands. Females born with this condition frequently have masculinized genitals because of excess androgen exposure prenatally. In males, genital appearance is usually unaffected.

adultery Sexual intercourse involving a married person with a partner other than his or her spouse.

ageism An attitude of prejudice against the elderly.

AIDS (acquired immune deficiency syndrome) A condition of increased susceptibility to unusual forms of cancer and infection due to disturbances of the body's immune defenses; a majority of cases have occurred in male homosexuals.

ambisexual (am′ bē sek shoo ul) Term used by Masters and Johnson to refer to men or women who have no preference over the gender of their sex partners and who accept or reject sexual opportunities based on their own physical need.

amniocentesis (am′ nē ō sen tē′ sis) Procedure used to obtain a sample of amniotic fluid from the uterus of a pregnant woman to analyze for a variety of genetic disorders and biochemical abnormalities in the fetus.

amnion (am′ nē on) The inner of the thin sacs of tissue (fetal membranes) that enclose the developing baby.

amniotic fluid (am′ nē ot′ ik) The liquid in which the developing fetus is suspended. It keeps the temperature constant and cushions shock.

anal stage According to Freud's theory of psychosexual development, the stage that occurs from about ages one to three when a child's sexual energies are focused on the anal zone and eliminative functions.

androgens (an′ dro jinz) Hormones such as testosterone that develop and maintain secondary sex characteristics in males and, if in large quantities, promote masculinization in females.

androgyny (an droj′ i nē) The combined presence of stereotyped feminine and masculine characteristics in one person.

anorgasmia (an′ or gaz′ mē uh) The inability of a woman to reach orgasm. Can be classified as primary (always existing), secondary (having been orgasmic in the past), situational (existing only in certain situations), coital (existing only during coitus) or random (existing on a frequent basis during different types of sexual activity).

aphrodisiac (af′ rō dēz′ ē ak) A substance that increases or is believed to increase a person's sexual powers or desire.

areola (a rē′ o luh) The circular area of dark skin around the nipple.

Long vowels are marked. Short vowels are left alone or changed to show the sound they make. Major (′) and minor (′) accents are marked.

639

assertiveness training (assertion training) A semi-structured teaching approach which emphasizes acquiring assertive skills through practice. It generally includes four basic procedures: (1) teaching people the difference between assertion and aggression and between nonassertion and politeness; (2) helping people identify and accept both their own personal rights and the rights of others; (3) reducing existing obstacles to acting assertively, e.g., irrational thinking, excessive anxiety, guilt, and anger; and (4) developing assertive skills through active practice methods.

atrophy (a′ truh fē) Reduction or wasting away of a cell, tissue, organ or part.

Bartholin's glands (bahr′ tō linz) Small glands adjacent to the vaginal opening. Although they produce minimal amounts of lubrication, their function is unknown.

basal body temperature (BBT) Temperature taken immediately after awakening and used to predict ovulation for the rhythm method of birth control. See *temperature method of birth control.*

bestiality (bēs′ tē al′ i tē) Engaging in sexual activity with an animal.

bipotential gonads The first stage of development of the embryonic gonads. At this point, the tissue can differentiate into either ovaries or testes.

bisexual (bī sek′ shoo ul) A person sexually attracted to both males and females.

blastocyst (blas′ tō sist) A spherical mass of cells with a hollow inner portion containing fluid produced by the cleavage of the fertilized egg.

bonding (parent-child) The emotional link partly created by cuddling, cooing, and physical and eye contact by the parent early in an infant's life.

Braxton-Hicks contractions Painless short episodes of muscle tightening sometimes mistaken for the onset of labor.

breech presentation In childbirth, when the buttocks or feet are the first part of the child to pass through the opening of the vagina.

bulbocavernosus (bul′ bō kav ur nō′ sus) A muscle encircling and supporting the entrance to the vagina.

calendar method of birth control A technique of determining the days in the menstrual cycle when the risk of pregnancy is low; a form of the rhythm method.

capacitation (kuh pas′ i tā′ shun) The process by which sperm become capable of penetrating an egg.

castration anxiety (kas trā′ shun) According to Freud, the unconscious fear in boys about the possible loss of their penis as a terrible form of punishment.

celibacy (sel′ uh buh sē) Abstention from sexual intercourse. Remaining unmarried as some members of the clergy.

cephalic presentation (se fal′ ik) In childbirth, when the head is the first part of the baby's body to pass through the birth canal.

cervical cap (ser′ vi kul kap) A small plastic or rubber contraceptive device worn on the cervix to provide a barrier to sperm.

cervical os (ser′ vi kul oss) The mouth or opening of the cervix.

cervix (ser′ viks) The cylindrical part of the uterus that protrudes into the vagina. The point where sperm cells enter the uterus and menstrual flow exits is called the cervical os.

cesarean section (seez air′ ee uhn) A surgical method of childbirth in which delivery occurs through an incision in the abdomen and uterus.

chancre (shan′ ker) A painless sore which appears in the primary stage of syphilis.

chloasma (klō as′ muh) Brown pigmented spots, usually on the face, caused either by birth control pills or hormones produced naturally during pregnancy.

chorion (kor ee on′) The outer sac of tissue that encloses the developing baby inside the uterus.

chromosomes (krō′ muh sōmz) The genetic material in the nucleus of every cell in the body. Sperm and eggs each have twenty-three chromosomes; all other cells normally have forty-six.

cilia (sil′ ē uh) The hair-like filaments on the inside of the Fallopian tubes which propel the egg along to the uterus.

circumcision (sur′ kum sizh′ un) Surgical removal of the foreskin.

climacteric (klī mak′ tur ik) Syndrome experienced by about 5 percent of men over sixty, marked by weakness, fatigue, poor appetite, decreased sexual drive, reduction or loss of potency, irritability and impaired ability to concentrate. See *menopause.*

clitoral glans (klit′ o rul) The tip or head and only visible part of the clitoris, resembling a small button.

clitoral hood The fold of skin covering the clitoral shaft. Sometimes referred to as the female foreskin.

clitoral shaft Part of the external female genitals; two small erectile bodies enclosed in a fibrous membrane and ending in a glans. Corresponds to the corpus cavernosa in the penis.

clitoris (klit′ o ris) Part of the external genitals of the female, situated at the anterior meeting of the labia minora and made up of two small erectile bodies, a glans and a hood. Its only known function is to focus and accumulate sexual sensations and erotic pleasure.

cohabitation An unmarried heterosexual couple living together.

coitus interruptus (kō′ i tus in tur rup′ tus) The removal of the penis from the vagina before ejaculation occurs.

colostrum (kohl ah′ strum) A thin, watery fluid secreted by the breasts late in pregnancy as a precursor to breast milk.

combination pill A birth control pill containing both estrogen and progesterone.

communal living Group cohabitation. Economic resources and personal energies are shared; emotional sharing and support are given. Can include sexual sharing, but not necessarily.

complementation The process of learning the gender-appropriate responses of one's own assigned sex by interacting with a member of the opposite sex.

congenital syphilis Syphilis contracted by the unborn fetus from an infected mother, causing various abnormalities in the unborn child.

coronal ridge (kor′ ō nul) The rim of tissue that separates the glans from the shaft of the penis.

corpora cavernosa (kor′ po ruh kav ur nō′ suh)

The two parallel cylindrical bodies of erectile tissue that make up the larger part of the shaft of the penis and the clitoris.

corpus luteum (kor′ pus lew′ tē um) The part of the capsule of the ovarian follicle left in the ovary after an egg is expelled. It secretes hormones and, if pregnancy does not occur, degenerates.

corpus spongiosum (kor′ pus spon′ jē ō′ sum) The cylinder of erectile tissue along the underside of the penis containing the urethra. The distal portion expands to form the glans.

cortisol (kor′ ti sol) A hormone secreted by the adrenal glands that influences a wide range of body functions.

couvade syndrome (koo vahd′) A condition in which a male experiences symptoms mimicking pregnancy.

Cowper's glands (kow′ perz) Two pea-sized structures connected to the urethra just below the prostate gland. They produce fluid before ejaculation but otherwise have no known function.

crowning In childbirth, the appearance of the baby's head at the opening of the vagina.

crura (kroo′ ruh) The internal branches of the clitoral shaft and the corpus cavernosa attached to the bony pelvis.

cryptorchid (krip tor′ kid) Undescended testes.

cunnilingus (kun′ i ling′ gus) Stimulation of the external genitals of the female by oral contact.

cystitis (sis tī′ tis) Inflammation of the bladder.

diaphragm (dī′ uh fram) A dome-shaped rubber contraceptive device that is positioned inside the vagina so that it blocks the cervix; it must be used with a spermicide to be effective.

differential socialization The ways in which parents and others react differently to boys and girls and reinforce different behaviors for the two sexes.

dihydrotestosterone (dī hī′ drō tes tos′ ter ōn) A hormone similar to testosterone which stimulates development of the penis, scrotum and prostate gland in the embryo.

dilatation (dil' uh tā' shun) Opening of the mouth of the cervix in preparation for birth.

dilatation and curettage (kyur e tazh') Process involving dilating the cervix and then gently scraping the lining of the uterus with a metal instrument. Sometimes used as a form of abortion.

douching (dūsh' ing) Using a liquid to flush the vagina.

Down's syndrome A chromosome disorder that causes mental retardation and defects of the heart, kidneys and intestines. Also known as trisomy 21 or mongolism.

dysfunctional (dis funk' shun ul) Abnormally impaired, as in sexual dysfunctions.

dysmenorrhea (dis men' or ē' uh) Painful menstruation, usually including backache, headache, cramps and a bloated feeling.

dyspareunia (dis' puh roo' nē uh) Painful intercourse.

eclampsia (e klamp' sē uh) A condition occurring during the latter half of pregnancy marked by high blood pressure, edema, protein in the urine and convulsions, sometimes resulting in coma or death. Also known as toxemia of pregnancy.

ectopic pregnancy (ek top' ik) A misplaced pregnancy. The implantation of the blastocyst occurs outside the uterus, for example in the tubes or abdomen.

edema (e dē' muh) Swelling due to fluid retention.

effacement (e fāce' munt) The thinning or flattening of the cervix during labor.

effleurage (ef' lu razh') The circular stroking movement used in massage of the abdomen during labor in the Lamaze method.

ejaculatory ducts (ē jak' you luh tō' rē) Paired tubelike structures that carry sperm from the vas deferens and fluid from the seminal vesicles into the prostatic urethra.

ejaculatory incompetence The inability to ejaculate within the vagina. Can be classified as primary (always existing) or secondary (having been able to ejaculate in the past).

ejaculatory inevitability The first stage of orgasm in men, a feeling of having passed the point where ejaculation can be controlled as the vas deferens, seminal vesicles, and prostate start contracting.

Electra complex In Freudian theory, the sexual attraction of a young girl toward her father, usually accompanied by hostility toward her mother. See also *Oedipus complex*.

embryo (em' brē ō) The unborn child during the first eight weeks after fertilization.

endocervical canal (en' dō ser' vi kul) Tubelike connection between the mouth of the cervix and the uterine cavity containing numerous secretory glands that produce mucus.

endometrium (en' dō mē' trē um) The inner lining of the uterus in which the egg implants and which is partially shed during menstruation.

engaging The settling of the fetal head into position against the pelvic bones for birth. It usually occurs during the last few weeks of pregnancy in women having their first child and during labor with subsequent pregnancies. Also called dropping or lightening.

epididymis (ep' i did' i mis) The tightly coiled tubing network folded against the back surface of each testis in which sperm cells spend several weeks maturing.

episiotomy (e piz' ē ot' uh mē) An incision in the mother's perineum that gives the baby's head more room to emerge.

erectile dysfunction The inability to have or maintain an erection firm enough for coitus. Can be classified as primary (always existing) or secondary (following a period of having functioned). See *impotence*.

estrogens (es' tro jinz) Hormones present in both sexes, but primarily considered female. Produced in the ovaries and adrenal glands in the female, they maintain the lining of the vagina and produce breast growth. Also important in controlling the menstrual cycle.

excitement phase First phase of the human sexual response cycle caused by physical and/or psychological stimulation. It is characterized by increasing levels of myotonia and vasocongestion.

exhibitionist A person who obtains sexual gratification by exposing the genitals to strangers. "Flasher" is slang term.

Fallopian tubes (fuh lō′ pē un) The tubes that transport eggs from the ovaries to the uterus. Also called oviducts.

false labor Irregular contractions which do not become regular. They are felt mainly in the lower abdomen and groin in contrast to true labor, which is felt in the back and abdomen.

fellatio (fe lā′ shē ō) Stimulation of the male genitals by oral contact.

fetal alcohol syndrome The effects on the unborn child of heavy use of alcohol by the pregnant woman, including growth deficiencies, nervous system damage, and facial abnormalities.

fetal membranes Two thin sacs of tissue, the inner amnion and the outer chorion, that enclose the developing baby.

fetal monitor Electronic equipment used during labor to check the progress of the baby, especially its heartbeat, and the duration, frequency and intensity of uterine contractions.

fetishism (fet′ ish iz um) A condition in which sexual arousal occurs principally in response to an inanimate object or body part rather than a partner.

fetus (fē′ tus) The unborn child from the ninth week after fertilization until birth.

fimbria (fim′ brē uh) Long, fingerlike extensions at the entrance to the Fallopian tubes.

follicle (fol′ i kul) A thin capsule of tissue surrounding immature eggs.

follicle stimulating hormone (FSH) A substance produced in the pituitary gland which prepares the ovary for ovulation and stimulates the production of sperm cells in the testes.

follicular phase (fol ik′ ū lar) The first phase of the menstrual cycle in which ovarian follicles begin to mature as a result of stimulation by FSH.

foreskin (for′ skin) The freely movable skin that covers the penis. Also the hood of the clitoris.

fornication (for′ nuh kā′ shun) Coitus between unmarried heterosexual adults. A crime in some states.

frenulum (fren′ ū lum) A small, triangular fold of skin on the underside of the penis connecting the glans with the foreskin.

frigidity (fri jid′ i tē) An outdated term that was used to describe female sexual difficulties.

FSH See *follicle stimulating hormone.*

gender identity The inner sense a person has of being male or female.

gender role Behavior that conveys to others that an individual is either male or female.

genital herpes (jen′ i tul her peez) Painful blisters of the genitals caused by infection with the herpes virus; outbreaks typically are recurrent and highly contagious.

genital stage In Freudian theory, the last stage of sexual development which begins at puberty because of internal biological forces. Characterized by growing independence and a final transition into adult genital sexuality.

genitals (jen′ i tulz) Sex organs in the pelvic region. Customarily refers to the penis, the testes and scrotum in the male and the vulva and vagina in the female.

glans (glanz) The tip or head of the penis or clitoris.

gonad Ovary or testicle.

gonadotropin releasing hormone (GnRH) (gō nad′ ō trō′ pin) A substance produced by the hypothalamus that controls the production and release of LH and FSH by the pituitary.

granulosa cells (gran′ ū lō′ suh) The cells lining the ovarian follicle which enlarge and form the corpus luteum.

G spot (Grafenberg spot) A proposed region of the front wall of the vagina claimed by some researchers to have a high degree of erotic sensitivity.

gynecomastia (jīn′ e kō mas′ tē uh) Enlargement of one or both male breasts.

hepatitis (hep ah tie′ tis) An infection or inflammation of the liver.

hermaphrodite (hur maf′ rō dīt) A person with both testicular and ovarian tissue.

heterosexual (het′ ur ō sek′ shoo ul) Person with sexual preference for partners of the opposite sex.

homophobia Obsessive hostility and fear toward homosexuals.

homosexual (hō′ mō sek′ shoo ul) Person with sexual preference for partners of his or her own sex.

hormone Chemical substance secreted by the endocrine system into the bloodstream to be carried directly to the tissue on which it acts.

hot flash Sudden sensations of warmth, blushing, and sweating, sometimes with dizziness, that occur commonly in menopausal women.

H-Y antigen The substance that controls the transformation of the primitive gonads into testes in the embryo. If it is not present, the primitive gonads develop into ovaries.

hymen (hī′ mun) A thin tissue membrane covering the opening of the vagina.

hypersexual Having an extraordinarily high sex drive. "Oversexed." Sometimes called nymphomania in women and satyriasis in men.

hypothalamus (hī′ pō thal′ uh mus) The portion of the brain that has primary control over most endocrine pathways. It reacts to the level of hormones in the blood supply which regulate many sexual responses and directs their production.

hysterectomy (his′ tur ek′ tuh mē) Partial or total removal of the uterus.

hysterotomy (his tur ot′ uh mē) Incision of the uterus. Infrequently used for abortion during the second trimester.

implantation The attachment of the blastocyst to the lining of the uterus.

impotence (im′ puh tence) The inability to have or maintain an erection firm enough for coitus. See *erectile dysfunction.*

incest Sexual activity between a person and a close relative.

induced labor Labor started artificially, usually by infusing oxytocin into a vein.

infertility The inability of a couple to have a baby, usually defined after a year or more of sexual intercourse without pregnancy.

inguinal canal (in′ gwuh nal) A passage about four cm long through which a nerve and the spermatic cord pass in the male and the round ligament of the uterus passes in the female.

inhibited sexual desire (ISD) A condition marked by very low interest in sexual behavior.

inner lips See *labia minora.*

intrauterine device (IUD) (in truh ū′ ter in) A small object, either plastic or metal, placed inside the uterus for birth control.

inverted nipples Congenital condition in which the nipples are not protuberant.

in vitro fertilization A procedure involving removing eggs from a woman's body and fertilizing them with sperm in a laboratory. After successful fertilization, the embryo is surgically implanted in the woman's uterus.

Klinefelter's syndrome A sex chromosome abnormality marked by an extra X chromosome in a genetic male, giving a 47, XXY pattern. Most of these men tend to be tall, with poor muscular development and small testes. Sexual desire is often low and impotence common.

labia majora (la′ bē uh muh jor′ uh) The two outer folds of skin on either side of the inner lips, the clitoris and the urethral and vaginal openings.

labia minora (la′ bē uh mi nor′ uh) The two inner folds of skin enclosing the urethral and vaginal openings.

labor The processes involved in giving birth, especially uterine contractions.

lactation (lak tā′ shun) The production of milk by the breasts, usually beginning a few days after birth.

laparotomy (lap uh rot′ uh mē) Any operation involving an incision through the abdominal wall. Now infrequently used for sterilization unless other surgery is required in the abdomen.

latency stage In Freudian theory, the period from about six years to puberty when sexual impulses are quiescent and are sublimated into non-sexual behaviors and interests.

latent stage (syphilis) Period in the course of syphilis when symptoms disappear and the disease is no longer contagious. During this stage infecting organisms burrow into most organs of the body.

Leydig cells (lī' dig) The cells in the testes where hormone production occurs.

libido (li bē' dō) In Freudian theory, psychic energy or drive, fundamentally of a sexual nature. Also used to mean level of sexual desire.

limerence Word coined by Dorothy Tennov to describe a blind, intense kind of love outside the person's rational control.

luteal phase (lū' tē ul) The third phase of the menstrual cycle, after ovulation. The corpus luteum produces large amounts of progesterone and estrogen which prepare the uterus to receive the fertilized egg.

luteinizing hormone (LH) (lū' tē in īz' ing) Produced by the pituitary gland, LH triggers ovulation and stimulates the Leydig cells to manufacture testosterone.

macho Aggressively male. The adjective form of *machismo*, which describes a set of masculine attitudes and behaviors orginally from South American and Mediterranean cultures.

macromastia (mak' rō mas' tē uh) Unusual enlargement of the breasts. Also known as mammary hyplasia.

masochism (mas' ō kiz um) The need for experiencing pain and humiliation in order to achieve sexual gratification.

mastectomy (mas tek' tuh mē) Surgical removal of the breast.

meiosis (mī ō' sis) The process by which each immature egg divides into four cells, only one of which is a mature egg.

menarche (me nar' kē) The onset of menses.

menopause (men' ō paws) The period during which menstruation gradually stops, usually occurring in the late forties.

menstruation (men stroo' ā' shun) A flow of blood from the lining of the uterus occurring about once a month in females from puberty until the late 40s or early 50s.

micropenis (mī' krō pē' nis) A penis which is correctly formed, but is less than 2 centimeters long.

minipill A contraceptive pill containing only progesterone in low dosage.

mongolism See *Down's syndrome*.

monilial vaginitis (mon il' ee all vaj in eye' tis) Infection of the vagina caused by a fungus; there is usually a thick, cheesy discharge with intense itching.

mons veneris (mōnz ven' e ris) The area over the pubic bone of the female which consists of a cushion of fatty tissue covered by skin and pubic hair. Also mons pubis or mound of Venus.

morula (more' u lah) A spherical mass of cells resulting from cleavage of the fertilized egg.

mucosa (mew kō' suh) Mucus membrane. The membrane lining of the body openings, especially of the vagina, kept moist by the secretions of various types of glands.

Müllerian duct (mew ler' ē un) One of two pairs of embryonic genital ducts. In females, this duct system develops into the Fallopian tubes, uterus, and inner part of the vagina. In males, a substance secreted by the embryonic testes causes the Müllerian duct system to shrink and practically disappear.

multiorgasmic (mul' tē or gaz' mik) The potential ability of women to have a series of identifiable orgasmic responses without dropping below the plateau level of arousal. Men do not share this capacity.

myometrium (mī' ō mē' trē um) The muscular component of the uterus, important in labor and delivery.

myotonia (mī' ō tō' nē uh) Involuntary contraction of muscle.

neuromuscular tension (new' rō mus' kew lur) Buildup of energy in the nerves and muscles sometimes caused by sexual arousal.

nipple Protuberance located at the tip of the breast consisting principally of smooth muscle fibers and a network of nerve endings and containing, in the female, the outlets of the milk ducts.

nocturnal emissions Involuntary male orgasm and

ejaculation during sleep (sometimes called "wet dreams").

nonspecific urethritis (NSU) Inflammation of the male's urethra not caused by gonorrhea.

nymphomania (nim′ fō mā′ nē uh) In females, compulsive sexual activity which gives only fleeting satisfaction. Male form is satyriasis.

obscenity Pictures or writing disgusting to the senses, abhorrent to morality or virtue and/or specifically designed to incite lust or depravity. Obscenity is illegal, pornography is not.

Oedipus complex (ed′ i pus) In Freudian theory, the sexual attraction of a young boy to his mother, accompanied by a mixture of fear and rivalry toward his father. See also *Electra complex*.

oral stage In Freudian theory, the first year of life, in which the sexual energies are focused in the region of the mouth.

orgasm (or′ gaz um) Third and shortest phase of the human sexual response cycle. A total body response involving the sudden discharge of accumulated sexual tension.

orgasmic dysfunction (or gaz′ mik) The inability of a female to reach orgasm. See also *anorgasmia*.

orgasmic platform The narrowing of the vagina during sexual excitement due to vasocongestion.

orgasmic reconditioning An approach used to condition a person away from an unsuitable sexual fantasy by instructing the person to begin masturbating using the unsuitable fantasy and to switch to a more appropriate fantasy at the moment of orgasm.

osteoporosis (ah stee oh pohr oh′ sis) A condition in which the bones become thin and brittle due to mineral loss; a common occurrence in postmenopausal women.

outer lips See *labia majora*.

ovariectomy (ō vuh′ rē ek′ tuh mē) Surgical removal of the ovaries.

ovaries (ō′ vur ēz) Paired structures located on each side of the uterus that contain and release eggs and secrete hormones such as estrogen and progesterone. The female gonads.

ovulation (ōv you lā′ shun) Second phase of the menstrual cycle; the release of the egg from the ovary.

ovulation method of birth control Depends on changes in the cervical mucus thought to indicate the time of ovulation. The mucus changes from cloudy, white and tacky to clear and stretchy at time of ovulation. Intercourse is thought to be safe four days after the ovulatory mucus begins and the mucus has returned to cloudy, tacky consistency. Failure rate is high.

ovum (ō′ vum) A mature egg cell which is capable, after maturation and fertilization, of becoming another member of the same species.

oxytocin (ahk′ sē to′ sin) A hormone made in the posterior pituitary thought to play a role in uterine contractions and lactation stimulation.

paraphilia (pair′ uh fil′ ē uh) A condition in which a person's sexual gratification is dependent on an unusual sexual experience (or fantasy). A neutral term for sexual alternatives which have been called deviant.

parent-child bonding The process of attachment and identification that usually occurs during early infancy.

pedophilia (ped ō fil′ ē uh) A sexual variation in which the preferred or exclusive method of achieving sexual excitement is by fantasizing or engaging in sexual activity with children.

penis (pē′ nis) The male organ of copulation. It consists primarily of three cylinders of spongy tissue, interspersed with many small, thin-walled blood vessels, and bound in a thick membrane sheath.

penis envy In Freudian theory, the girl's unconscious sense of inadequacy and jealousy at not having a penis.

perimenopausal years (perry men oh paws′ uhl) The years around menopause.

perineum (per i nē′ um) The hairless area of skin between the vagina and anus in the female and between the scrotum and anus in the male.

peristalsis (per′ i stal′ sis) Waves of contractions in the muscle fibers in the walls of tubes such as the Fallopian tubes. These contractions, along with the beating of the cilia, move the fertilized egg along the tubes to the uterus. In the male, peristaltic contractions of the urethra advance the ejaculate through the penis.

phallic stage In Freudian theory, the period from about three to five years of age when the child's sexual energies are focused on the genitals.

pituitary (pi tew′ i ter′ ē) An acorn-sized gland at the base of the brain which, at the direction of the hypothalamus, secretes several hormones important to sexual development and functioning. Once believed to control most of the endocrine system, it is now known to act only as a relay station.

placebo (pluh sē′ bō) An inert substance or treatment that may cause individuals to improve.

placenta (pluh sen′ tuh) The organ attached to the wall of the uterus that performs the functions of nutrition, respiration and excretion for the unborn child. It is also an endocrine organ secreting large amounts of several hormones.

plateau phase Phase of human sexual response following excitement, which presents a leveling off of sexual tensions. This phase can be short or long prior to reaching levels required to trigger orgasm.

polar bodies Cells that arise in the development of the ovum during meiosis.

pornography Books or pictures that depict erotic behavior with the intent of causing sexual excitement. Technically, pornography is not illegal, obscenity is.

postmenopausal years The period of a woman's life after the menses cease.

postpartum depression The letdown many women experience after giving birth. They are tearful and depressed and may have frightening dreams. Also "baby blues."

precocious puberty (pree koh′ shus pew′ burr tee) Physical changes of puberty occurring before age 8 in girls or age 10 in boys.

preeclampsia (prē′ e klamp′ sē uh) A condition occurring during the latter half of pregnancy characterized by high blood pressure, edema, and protein in the urine. May progress to eclampsia.

premature ejaculation Unintentional ejaculation during noncoital play, while the male is trying to

enter his partner, or soon after intercourse begins.

premenstrual syndrome Fatigue, irritability, depression and bloated feeling some women experience a few days before menstruation. Physical, psychological and social causes are debated.

prenatal care The combined efforts of doctor, nurse and mother to see that the pregnant woman stays healthy and the unborn child has everything needed to grow and develop.

prenatal period The time from conception to birth.

primary spermatocytes (spur mat′ ō sītz) The matured spermatogonia that have divided by meitotic division.

procreational sex (pro′ krē ā′ shun ul) Sexual intercourse solely for reproduction. Sometimes advocated as the only acceptable reason for sex.

progesterone (prō jes′ tur ōn) A hormone present in both sexes, but primarily known as a female hormone. Present in high levels during pregnancy.

prolapsed cord Condition whereby the umbilical cord is compressed until the blood supply to the baby is cut off.

prostate gland (pros′ tāt) Gland located directly below the bladder, surrounding the urethra as it exits the bladder. It secretes part of the seminal fluid and is a major site of the synthesis of prostaglandins.

prostatectomy (pros′ tuh tek′ tuh mē) Surgical removal of the prostate gland.

prostatitis (pros tuh tī′ tis) Inflammation of the prostate gland.

pseudohermaphrodite (sue′ dō hur maf′ rō dīt) An individual born with gonads matching the sex chromosomes but a genital appearance that resembles the opposite sex.

pubic lice Parasites that invade the pubic region, often transmitted during sexual intercourse.

pubococcygeus (pew′ bō kock sij′ ē us) A muscle encircling and supporting the vagina.

quadriplegia (kwahd ruh pleej′ ee ah) Paralysis of all limbs.

quickening The time during pregnancy when a woman can first feel the fetus moving.

recreational sex Sexual activity primarily for the pleasure it gives. Emotional involvement and intimacy are purposefully limited.

rectum (rek′ tum) The lower part of the large intestine.

refractory period In the male, the period immediately following ejaculation during which further orgasm is physiologically impossible. This period is not present in the female response cycle.

relational sex Sexual activity in the context of emotional involvement and intimacy in a relationship.

resolution phase Last phase of human sexual response following orgasm or maximum excitement in which the body returns to an unaroused state.

retarded ejaculation Condition in which ejaculation in the vagina occurs only after a lengthy time period and strenuous efforts.

retrograde ejaculation Condition in which the semen spurts backward into the bladder during orgasm because the bladder neck does not close off properly. It occurs in men with multiple sclerosis, diabetes and some types of prostate surgery.

Rh incompatibility Condition in which antibodies from the mother's bloodstream destroy red blood cells in the fetus, causing anemia, mental retardation or fetal death.

rubella (roo bel′ uh) German measles. If the virus crosses the placental barrier to the fetus, it can cause serious malformations including deafness, eye problems, and mental retardation.

Rubin's test A procedure to check for obstructed Fallopian tubes. Carbon dioxide is inserted into the uterus to see if it passes into the abdomen.

sadism (sā′ diz um) The intentional infliction of pain on another person to achieve sexual excitement.

satyriasis (sat′ i rī′ uh sis) In males, compulsive sexual activity which gives only fleeting satisfaction. Also called Don Juanism. Female form is nymphomania.

scrotum (skrō′ tum) The thin, loose sac of skin that contains the testes and has a layer of muscle fibers that contract involuntarily.

secondary spermatocytes (spur mat′ ō sītz) The product of the second division of the mature spermatogonia, which divide into spermatids.

seminal fluid (sem′ uh nul) The thick white, yellow or gray liquid portion of the male ejaculate.

seminal vesicles (sem′ uh nul ves′ e kulz) In the male, paired pouch-like bodies which empty into the ejaculatory ducts and provide the major part of fluid in the ejaculate.

seminiferous tubules (sem′ i nif′ ur us tū′ bewls) Microscopic tube-shaped structures in the testes where sperm is produced.

sensate focus Graduated touching experiences (not necessarily sexual) assigned to couples in therapy to reduce anxiety and teach nonverbal communication skills.

sex flush A temporary reddish, spotty, rashlike color change sometimes developing during sexual excitement. Usually on the abdomen and breasts, it can spread to any areas of the body.

sexual aversion A severe phobia (irrational fear) of sexual activity or the thought of sexual activity, which generally leads to avoidance of sexual situations.

sexual differentiation The process that begins at the moment of conception to create a normal male or female.

sexual dysfunction Conditions in which the ordinary physical responses of sexual excitement or orgasm are impaired. Can be classified as psychosocial (caused by psychological, interpersonal, environmental and cultural factors) or organic (caused by physical or medical factors such as illness, injury or drugs).

sexual orientation Preference for sexual partners of the same sex (homosexual), of the opposite sex (heterosexual) or of either sex (bisexual).

sexual psychopath Variously defined in law; most generally, a person exhibiting compulsive, repetitive and/or bizarre sexual behavior. This legal label, not a psychiatric diagnosis, permits people to be given jail sentences and implies they are a menace to society.

sexually transmitted disease (STD) Infection spread mainly by sexual contact.

smegma (smeg′ muh) Glandular secretions, dead

cells, dirt particles and bacteria which accumulate under the foreskin of the penis or the hood of the clitoris.

spermatids (spur' muh tids) The product of the third and last division of the male germ cell which mature into spermatozoa.

spermatogonia (spur' muh to gō' nē uh) Primitive male germ cells that mature into primary spermatocytes.

spermatozoa (spur' muh to zō' uh) The mature male germ cell.

squeeze technique Method for reducing the tendency for rapid ejaculation.

statutory rape Intercourse with a girl below the legal age of consent.

stereotypes Fixed, conventional beliefs based on oversimplified evidence or uncritical judgments.

sterilization Surgical procedure performed on men (vasectomy) or women (tubal ligation; hysterectomy) to prevent union of sperm and egg.

syphilis (sif' uh lis) A sexually transmitted disease caused by Treponema pallidum, whose stages consist of primary (characterized by chancres), secondary (characterized by rash, fever, aches and pains, weight loss and hair loss) and tertiary (characterized by serious heart problems and brain or spinal cord damage).

temperature method of birth control Technique of determining the part of the menstrual cycle when pregnancy is likely to occur so that intercourse can be avoided then. Involves daily recording of basal body temperature to pin-point ovulation. Intercourse is not allowed from the day menstrual flow stops until two to four days after the temperature rise. Failure rate is high.

teratogen (teh rat' ō jin) A substance, such as a drug or chemical, that causes birth defects.

testes (tes' tēz) The paired male reproductive glands contained in the scrotum. The male gonads.

testicular feminization syndrome An inherited condition in which tissues are insensitive to the effects of testosterone. The individual is born with a 46, XY chromosome pattern (male) but female genitals.

testosterone (tes tos' tur ŏn) The most important hormone in sexual function, present in both sexes. Often called the male hormone, it is secreted by the testes and adrenals in the male and the ovaries and adrenals in the female.

toxemia See *preeclampsia* and *eclampsia*.

toxic shock syndrome An illness of rapid onset caused by infection with the *Staphylococcus aureus* bacteria; symptoms include fever, vomiting, muscle pain, and a sunburn-like skin rash. Most, but not all, cases have occurred in menstruating women, and the syndrome is thought to be related to the use of high-absorbency vaginal tampons.

transsexualism A rare condition in which there is a persistent sense of discomfort and inappropriateness about one's anatomical sex accompanied by the desire to change one's sexual anatomy and live as a member of the opposite biological sex.

transudation (trans' ū dā' shun) The passing of a fluid through a membrane, especially the lubrication in the vagina during sexual arousal.

transverse position In childbirth, when the baby lies across the uterus and a shoulder or arm will first be seen at the opening of the vagina. A cesarean section is often necessary if the baby cannot be turned.

transvestite (trans ves' tīt) An individual who receives sexual gratification and release from anxiety by dressing in the clothing of the opposite sex. Unlike transsexuals, they are not interested in becoming a member of the opposite sex.

trichomonas vaginitis (trick o mōn' ess) An infection of the vagina caused by bacteria called trichomonas vaginalis. A frothy, thin, greenish or yellowish gray, foul-smelling discharge results, causing burning and itching.

trimester A three month period; generally used to describe the progression of pregnancy.

trisomy 21 (trī' sō mē) See *Down's syndrome*.

tubal ligation (tū' bull lī gā' shun) Literally, tying the tubes — cutting, cauterizing and blocking the Fallopian tubes to prevent conception.

Turner's syndrome A sex chromosome abnormality caused by a missing chromosome. The karyotype is 45, X. These individuals may appear fairly normal until puberty when non-functioning gonads prevent development of the secondary sex characteristics and the adolescent growth spurt. There may also be webbing of the neck, increased carrying angle of the elbow, heart defects and other abnormalities.

umbilical cord The cylindrical structure connecting the fetus to the placenta. It contains two arteries and a vein.

urethra (u rē′ thruh) A tube beginning at the bladder and ending at the urethral meatus, carrying urine in the female and urine or semen in the male.

urethral meatus (u rē′ thral mē ā′ tus) The urinary opening.

urinary stress incontinence A condition in which urine leaks from the urethra during coughing, laughing, and/or sexual arousal.

uterus (ū′ tur us) A hollow, pear-shaped muscular organ, part of the female internal genitals, in which the fertilized egg becomes embedded and the embryo and the fetus are nourished. Sometimes called a womb.

vacuum aspiration Method usually chosen for abortion during the first trimester. The cervix is dilated and the contents of the uterus removed through a plastic tube connected to a pump.

vagina (va jī′ nuh) The canal in the female which receives the penis in copulation, existing as a potential space capable of contraction and expansion. The opening is called the vaginal introitus.

vaginismus (vaj in iz′ mus) Involuntary spasms of the muscles around the vagina in response to attempts at penetration.

vaginitis (vaj in ī′ tis) Vaginal inflammation from infection or chemical irritation.

vas deferens (vas def′ ur enz) One of two long, tubelike structures that convey spermatozoa from the testes.

vasectomy (vas ek′ tuh mē) Surgical procedure for sterilization of the male consisting of cutting and tying each vas deferens. The operation does not stop sperm production, but blocks its passage from the testes.

vasocongestion (vas′ o kun jes′ chun) An increased amount of blood concentrated in body tissues, especially in the genitals and female breasts during sexual arousal. In the male it causes erection and in the female, an increase in the size of the clitoris and transudation of fluid in the vagina.

venereal warts Dry, usually painless, sexually-transmitted nodules that grow on or near the genitals and are caused by a virus.

vernix (vur niks) The cheeselike paste on the surface of the fetus during about the sixth month.

vertex presentation (vur′ teks) In childbirth, when the crown of the head is seen first at the opening of the vagina.

voyeurism (voi yur′ iz um) A sexual variation in which a person obtains sexual gratification by witnessing the sexual acts of others or by spying on them when they are undressing or nude.

vulva (vul′ vuh) The external sex organs of the female: the mons, labia, clitoris, and vaginal orifice.

wet dreams See *nocturnal emissions.*

withdrawal The removal of the penis from the vagina before ejaculation occurs. When used as a birth control method, failure rate is high. See *coitus interruptus.*

Wolffian duct (wool′ fē un) One of two primitive duct systems in the embryo. Develops in the male to form the epididymis, vas deferens, seminal vesicles and prostate and shrinks, in the female, to non-functioning remnants.

zona pellucida (zō′ nuh pe lew′ sē duh) The jellylike material surrounding the mature egg.

zoophilia (zō′ uh fil′ ē uh) A sexual variation in which the person prefers sexual activity with animals.

zygote (zī′ gōt) The single cell created by the penetration of an egg by the sperm. An organism produced by the union of two gametes.

References

Aarskog, D. "Maternal Progestins as a Possible Cause of Hypospadias." *New England Journal of Medicine* 300:75-78, 1979.

Abel, G. G., and Blanchard, E. B. "The Role of Fantasy in the Treatment of Sexual Deviation." *Archives of General Psychiatry* 30:467-75, 1974.

Abel, G. G., et al. "The Components of Rapists' Sexual Arousal." *Archives of General Psychiatry* 34:895-903, 1977.

———. "Women's Vaginal Responses During REM Sleep." *Journal of Sex and Marital Therapy* 5:5-14, 1979.

Abitbol, M. M., and Davenport, J. H. "Sexual Dysfunction After Therapy for Cervical Carcinoma." *American Journal of Obstetrics and Gynecology* 119:181-89, 1974.

Abramson, P. R. "The Relationship of the Frequency of Masturbation to Several Aspects of Behavior." *Journal of Sex Research* 9:132-42, 1973.

Abramson, P. R., and Mosher, D. L. "An Empirical Investigation of Experimentally Induced Masturbatory Fantasies." *Archives of Sexual Behavior* 8:27-39, 1979.

Adams, D. B.; Gold, A. R.; and Burt, A. D. "Rise in Female-Initiated Sexual Activity at Ovulation and Its Suppression by Oral Contraceptives." *New England Journal of Medicine* 299:1145-50, 1978.

Adams, G. R., and Huston, T. L. "Social Perception of Middle-Aged Persons Varying in Physical Attractiveness." *Developmental Psychology* II:657-58, 1975.

Addiego, F., et al. "Female Ejaculation: A Case Study." *Journal of Sex Research* 17(1):13-21, 1981.

Ainsworth, M. "The Effects of Maternal Deprivation: A Review of Finding and Controversy in the Context of Research Strategy." In *Deprivation of Maternal Care: A Reassessment of Its Effects.* Public Health Papers, no. 14. Geneva: World Health Organization, 1962.

Alan Guttmacher Institute. *Teenage Pregnancy: The Problem That Hasn't Gone Away.* New York: Alan Guttmacher Institute, 1981.

Alan Guttmacher Institute. *Safe and Legal: 10 Years' Experience with Legal Abortion in New York State.* New York: Alan Guttmacher Institute, 1980.

Alexander, L. "Treatment of Impotency and Anorgasmia by Psychotherapy Aided by Hypnosis." *American Journal of Clinical Hypnosis* 17:33-43, 1974.

Alington-MacKinnon, D., and Troll, L. E. "The Adaptive Function of the Menopause: A Devil's Advocate Position." *Journal of the American Geriatrics Society* 29:349-53, 1981.

Allen, D. M. "Young Male Prostitutes: A Psychosocial Study." *Archives of Sexual Behavior* 9:399-426, 1980.

Allen, J. A. "Premenstrual Frenzy." *New York Magazine,* pp. 37-42, 1 November 1982.

Altman, Dennis. *The Homosexualization of America.* Boston: Beacon Press, 1982.

Altman, I., Vinsel, A., and Brown, B. B. "Dialectic Conceptions in Social Psychology: An Application to Social Penetration and Privacy Regulation." *Advances in Experimental Social Psychology* 14:107-60, 1981.

Altschuler, M. "Cayapa Personality and Sexual Motivation." In Marshall, D., and Suggs, R. (eds.), *Human Sexual Behavior,* pp. 38-58. New York: Basic Books, 1971.

Alvior, G. T., Jr. "Pregnancy Outcome with Removal of Intrauterine Device." *Obstetrics and Gynecology* 41:894-96, 1973.

Alzate, H., and Londono, M. L. "Vaginal Erotic Sensitivity." *Journal of Sex & Marital Therapy* 10:49-56, 1984.

American Cancer Society. "Guidelines for the Cancer-Related Checkup." *Ca-A Cancer Journal for Clinicians* 30:194-240, 1980.

American Journal of Psychiatry. "Historical Notes: A Letter from Freud." 107:786-87, 1951.

American Psychiatric Association. *Diagnostic and Statistical Manual of Mental Disorders, 3rd ed. (DSM-III).* Washington, D.C.: American Psychiatric Association, 1980.

Amir, M. *Patterns in Forcible Rape.* Chicago: University of Chicago, 1971.

Anderson, B. G. *The Aging Game: Success, Sanity and Sex after 60.* New York: McGraw-Hill, 1979.

Anderson, T. P., and Cole, T. M. "Sexual Counseling of the Physically Disabled." *Postgraduate Medicine* 58:117-23, 1975.

Annon, J. S. *The Behavioral Treatment of Sexual Problems: Brief Therapy.* New York: Harper & Row, 1976.

Anthony, E. J.; Green, R.; and Kolodny, R. C. *Childhood Sexuality.* Boston: Little, Brown, 1982.

Antunes, C. M., et al. "Endometrial Cancer and Estrogen Use: Report of a Large Case-Control Study." *New England Journal of Medicine* 300:9-13, 1979.

Apfelbaum, B. "Why We Should Not Accept Sexual Fantasies." In Apfelbaum, B. (ed.), *Expanding the Boundaries of Sex Therapy,* rev. ed., pp. 101-8. Berkeley, Calif.: Berkeley Sex Therapy Group, 1980.

———. (Ed.). *Expanding the Boundaries of Sex Therapy.* Rev. ed. Berkeley, Calif.: Berkeley Sex Therapy Group, 1980a.

————. "Review of *The Hite Report on Male Sexuality.*" *Journal of Sex Research* 18:85-88, 1982.

————. *Expanding the Boundaries of Sex Therapy* (second edition). Berkeley, Calif.: Berkeley Sex Therapy Group, 1983.

Apuleius, L. *The Golden Ass.* New York: Pocket Books, 1954.

Arafat, I., and Cotton, W. L. "Masturbation Practices of Males and Females." *Journal of Sex Research* 10:293-307, 1974.

Arentewicz, G., and Schmidt, G., (Eds.). *The Treatment of Sexual Disorders.* New York: Basic Books, 1983.

Arms, S. *Immaculate Deception.* Boston: Houghton Mifflin, 1975.

Arthes, F. G., and Masi, A. T. "Myocardial Infarction in Younger Women: Associated Clinical Features and Relationship to Use of Oral Contraceptive Drugs." *Chest* 70:574-83, November 1976.

Ashford, J. *The Whole Birth Catalog.* Trumansburg, N.Y.: The Crossing Press, 1983.

Athanasiou, R. "A Review of Public Attitudes on Sexual Issues." In Zubin, J., and Money, J. (eds.), *Contemporary Sexual Behavior: Critical Issues in the 1970s,* pp. 361-90. Baltimore: Johns Hopkins University Press, 1973.

————. "Pornography: A Review of Research." In Wolman, B. B., and Money, J. (eds.), *Handbook of Human Sexuality,* pp. 251-65. Englewood Cliffs, N.J.: Prentice-Hall, 1980.

Athanasiou, R., and Sarkin, R. "Premarital Sexual Behavior and Postmarital Adjustment." *Archives of Sexual Behavior* 3:207-25, 1974.

Athanasiou, R., et al. "A Report to *Psychology Today* Readers on the Research Questionnaire on Sex." *Psychology Today* 4:37-52, 1970.

Atkinson, L., et al. "The Brightest Contraceptive Hopes for the 21st Century." *Sexual Medicine Today* 5(3):15-23, March 11, 1981.

Atwater, L. *The Extramarital Connection—Sex, Intimacy, and Identity.* New York: Irvington Publishers, 1982.

Averill, J. R. *Anger and Aggression.* New York: Springer-Verlag, 1982.

Ayalah, D., and Weinstock, I. J. *Breasts.* New York: Summit Books, 1979.

Azizi, F., et al. "Decreased Serum Testosterone Concentration in Male Heroin and Methadone Addicts." *Steroids* 22:467-72, 1973.

Babikian, H. M. "Abortion." In Freedman, A. M.; Kaplan, H. I.; and Sadock, B. J. (eds.), *Comprehensive Textbook of Psychiatry/II,* pp. 1496-1500. Baltimore: Williams & Wilkins, 1975.

Bach, G. R., and Wyden, P. *The Intimate Enemy.* New York: Aron Books, 1968.

Backhouse, C., and Cohen, L. *Sexual Harassment on the Job.* Englewood Cliffs, N.J.: Prentice-Hall, 1981.

Bahm, R. M. "The Influence of Nonsexual Cues, Sexual Explicitness, and Sex Guilt on Female's Erotic Response to Literature." Unpublished Ph.D. dissertation, University of Massachusetts, 1972.

Baker, C. D. "Preying on Playgrounds: The Sexploitation of Children in Pornography and Prostitution." In Schultz, L. (ed.), *The Sexual Victimology of Youth.* Springfield, Ill.: Charles C. Thomas, 1980.

Bakwin, H. "Erotic Feelings in Infants and Young Children." *Medical Aspects of Human Sexuality* 8(10):200-215, 1974.

Baldwin, W., and Cain, V. (Eds.). *Teenage Childbearing: Recent Research on the Determinants and Consequences.* Washington, D.C.: U.S. Government Printing Office, 1980.

Ballinger, C. B. "The Menopause and Its Syndromes." In J. G. Howells, ed., *Modern Perspectives in the Psychiatry of Middle Age,* pp. 279-303. New York: Brunner/Mazel, 1981.

Bancroft, J. *Deviant Sexual Behavior.* Oxford: Clarendon Press, 1974.

————. "The Behavioral Approach to Treatment." In Money, J., and Musaph, H. (eds.), *Handbook of Sexology,* pp. 1197-1225. Amsterdam: Elsevier/North-Holland, 1977.

————. "The Relationship Between Hormones and Sexual Behavior in Humans." In Hutchison, J. B. (ed.), *Biological Determinants of Sexual Behavior,* pp. 493-519. New York: Wiley, 1978.

————. "Hormones and Human Sexual Behavior." *Journal of Sex & Marital Therapy* 10:3-21, 1984.

Bancroft, J., et al. "Mood, Sexuality, Hormones and the Menstrual Cycle: III. Sexuality and the Role of Androgens." *Psychosomatic Medicine* 45:509-24, 1983.

Barbach, L. G. *For Yourself: The Fulfillment of Female Sexuality.* New York: Doubleday, 1975.

————. *Women Discover Orgasm.* New York: Free Press, 1980.

————. *For Each Other: Sharing Sexual Intimacy.* Garden City, N.Y.: Anchor Press, 1982.

Barbach, L. G., and Levine, L. *Shared Intimacies.* Garden City, N.Y.: Anchor Press/Doubleday, 1980.

Barbaree, H. E.; Marshall, W. L.; and Lanthier, R. D. "Deviant Sexual Arousal in Rapists." *Behavior Research & Therapy* 17:215-22, 1979.

Barber, T. Y. *Pitfalls in Human Research.* New York: Pergamon Press, 1976.

Barclay, A. M. "Sexual Fantasies in Men and Women." *Medical Aspects of Human Sexuality* 7(5):205-16, 1973.

Bardin, C., and Catterall, J. "Testosterone: A Major Determinant of Extragenital Sexual Dimorphism." *Science* 211(4488):1285-94, 1981.

Barlow, D. "Increasing Heterosexual Responsiveness in the Treatment of Sexual Deviation: A Review of the Clinical and Experimental Evidence." *Behavior Therapy* 4:655-71, 1973.

————. *Sexually Transmitted Diseases—The Facts.* New York: Oxford University Press, 1979.

Barocas, R., and Karoly, P. "Effects of Physical Appearance

on Social Responsiveness." *Psychology Review* 31:495–500, 1972.

Barrett, F. M. "Sexual Experience, Birth Control Usage, and Sex Education of Unmarried Canadian University Students: Changes Between 1968 and 1978." *Archives of Sexual Behavior* 9:367–90, 1980.

Bart, P. "Avoiding Rape: A Study of Victims and Avoiders." Final report to the National Institute of Mental Health, MH29311, Rockville, Md., 1980.

Bart, P. B., and Jozsa, M. "Dirty Books, Dirty Films, Dirty Data." In L. Lederer (ed.), *Take Back the Night*, pp. 204–17. New York: William Morrow, 1980.

Bart, P. B., and Grossman, M. "Menopause." In M. T. Notman and C. C. Nadelson (eds.), *The Woman Patient*, pp. 337–54. New York: Plenum Press, 1978.

Bartell, G. D. *Group Sex: A Scientist's Eyewitness Report on the American Way of Swinging*. New York: Wyden Books, 1971.

Bates, G. "On the Nature of the Hot Flash." *Clinical Obstetrics and Gynecology* 24(1):231–41, 1981.

Bauman, J. E. "Basal Body Temperature: Unreliable Method of Ovulation Detection." In press, 1981.

Bauman, J. E., et al. "Effectos Endocrinos Del Uso Cronico De La Marijuana En Mujeres." *Cuadernos Cientificos Cemesam* 10:85–97, July 1979.

Bayer, R. *Homosexuality and American Psychiatry: The Politics of Diagnosis*. New York: Basic Books, 1981.

Beach, F. (Ed.). *Sex and Behavior*. New York: Wiley, 1965.

———. *Human Sexuality in Four Perspectives*. Baltimore: Johns Hopkins University Press, 1977.

Becker, E. F. *Female Sexuality Following Spinal Cord Injury*. Bloomington, Ind.: Accent Special Publication, Cheever Publishing, 1978.

Becker, J. V., et al. "Incidence and Types of Sexual Dysfunctions in Rape and Incest Victims." *Journal of Sex & Marital Therapy* 8:65–74, 1983.

Beer, W. R. *Househusbands: Men and Housework in American Families*. New York: Praeger, 1983.

Beerthuizen, R. J., et al. "IUD and Salpingitis." *European Journal of Obstetrics, Gynecology, and Reproductive Biology* 13(1):31–41, 1982.

Bell, A. P., and Weinberg, M. S. *Homosexualities*. New York: Simon & Schuster, 1978.

Bell, A. P., Weinberg, M. S., and Hammersmith, S. K. *Sexual Preference—Its Development In Men and Women*. Bloomington, Ind.: Indiana University Press, 1981.

Bell, R., and Bell, P. "Sexual Satisfaction among Married Women." *Medical Aspects of Human Sexuality* 6(12):136–44, 1972.

Bell, R. T. "Friendships of Women and Men." *Psychology of Women Quarterly* 5:402–17, 1981.

Belliveau, F., and Richter, L. *Understanding Human Sexual Inadequacy*. New York: Bantam, 1970.

Belzer, E. "Orgasmic Expulsions of Women: A Review and Heuristic Inquiry." *Journal of Sex Research* 17:1–12, 1981.

Bem, S. L. "Psychology Looks at Sex Roles: Where Have All the Androgynous People Gone?" Paper presented at the UCLA Symposium on Women. Los Angeles: May 1972.

———. "The Measurement of Psychological Androgyny." *Journal of Consulting and Clinical Psychology* 42(2):155–62, 1974.

———. "Sex Role Adaptability: One Consequence of Psychological Androgyny." *Journal of Personality and Social Psychology* 31(4):634–43, 1975.

Bem, S. L.; Martyna, W.; and Watson, C. "Sex Typing and Androgyny: Further Explorations of the Expressive Domain." *Journal of Personality and Social Psychology* 34:1016–23, 1976.

Bender, L., and Blau, A. "The Reaction of Children to Sexual Relations with Adults." *American Journal of Orthopsychiatry* 7:500–518, 1937.

Bene, E. "On the Genesis of Male Homosexuality: An Attempt at Clarifying the Role of the Parents." *British Journal of Psychiatry* 111:803–13, 1965.

Benjamin, M. *The Transsexual Phenomenon*. New York: Julian Press, 1966.

Benson, P. L.; Karabenick, S. A.; and Lerner, R. M. "Pretty Pleases: The Effects of Physical Attractiveness, Race, and Sex on Receiving Help." *Journal of Experimental Social Psychology* 12:409–15, 1976.

Benson, R. C. *Current Obstetric & Gynecologic Diagnosis & Treatment*. Los Altos, Calif.: Lange Medical Publications, 1978.

Berger, Raymond M. *Gay and Gray: The Older Homosexual Male*. Urbana, Ill.: University of Illinois Press, 1982.

Bermant, G., and Davidson, J. M. (Eds.). *Biological Basis of Sexual Behavior*. New York: Harper & Row, 1974.

Berlin, F. S., and Meinecke, C. F. "Treatment of Sex Offenders with Antiandrogenic Medication." *American Journal of Psychiatry* 138:601–7, 1981.

Bernard, F. "Pedophilia: Psychological Consequences for the Child." In L. L. Constantine and F. M. Martinson (eds.), *Children and Sex: New Findings, New Perspectives*, pp. 189–99. Boston: Little, Brown, 1981.

Berne, E. *Sex in Human Loving*. New York: Pocket Books, 1971.

Berscheid, E., et al. "Physical Attractiveness and Dating Choice: A Test of the Matching Hypothesis." *Journal of Experimental Social Psychology* 7:173–89, 1971.

Bieber, I., et al. *Homosexuality: A Psychoanalytic Study*. New York: Basic Books, 1962.

Binkin, N. J., and Alexander, E. R. "Neonatal Herpes: How Can It Be Prevented?" *Journal of the American Medical Association* 250:3094–95, 1983.

Blood, R. O., and Wolfe, D. M. *Husbands and Wives*. Glencoe, Ill.: Free Press, 1960.

Blume, E. "Methodological Difficulties Plague PMS Research." *Journal of the American Medical Association* 249:2866, 1983.

Blumstein, P. W., and Schwartz, P. "Bisexuality in Women." *Archives of Sexual Behavior* 5:171–81, 1976.

Blumstein, P. W., and Schwartz, P. "Bisexuality: Some Social

Psychological Issues." *Journal of Social Issues* 33(2):30–45, 1977.

Blumstein, P. W., and Schwartz, P. *American Couples*. New York: William Morrow, 1983.

Boehm, D. "The Cervical Cap: Effectiveness as a Contraceptive." *Journal of Nurse-Midwifery* 28(1):3–6, 1983.

Bohlen, J. G. " 'Female Ejaculation' and Urinary Stress Incontinence." *Journal of Sex Research* 18:360–363, 1982.

Bohlen, J. G., et al. "Development of a Woman's Multiple Orgasm Pattern: A Research Case Report." *Journal of Sex Research* 18:130–45, 1982.

Bolton, F. G. *The Pregnant Adolescent: Problems of Premature Parenthood*. Beverly Hills, Calif.: Sage Publications, 1980.

Booth, A. "Sex and Social Participation." *American Sociological Review* 37:183–92, 1972.

Borneman, Ernest. "Progress in Empirical Research on Childhood Sexuality." Presented at the 6th World Congress of Sexology, Washington, D.C., 24 May 1983.

Bors, E., and Comarr, A. E. "Neurological Disturbances of Sexual Function with Special Reference to 529 Patients with Spinal Cord Injury." *Urological Survey* 10:191–222, 1960.

Boston Collaborative Drug Surveillance Programme. "Oral Contraceptives and Venous Thromboembolic Disease, Surgically Confirmed Gallbladder Disease, and Breast Tumors." *Lancet* 1:1399–1404, 1973.

Boston Women's Health Book Collective. *Our Bodies, Ourselves*. 2nd ed. New York: Simon & Schuster, 1976.

Boswell, J. *Christianity, Social Tolerance, and Homosexuality*. Chicago: University of Chicago Press, 1980.

Bower, D. W. "A Description and Analysis of a Cohabiting Sample in America." Unpublished master's thesis, University of Arizona, 1975.

Bower, D. W., and Christopherson, V. A. "University Student Cohabitation: A Regional Comparison of Selected Attitudes and Behaviors." *Journal of Marriage and the Family* 39:447–53, 1977.

Braen, G. R. "Examination of the Accused: The Heterosexual and Homosexual Rapist." In Warner, C. G. (ed.), *Rape and Sexual Assault*, pp. 85–91. Germantown, Md.: Aspens Systems Corp., 1980.

Bragonier, J. R. "Influence of Oral Contraception on Sexual Response." *Medical Aspects of Human Sexuality* 10(10):130–43, October 1976.

Branden, N. *The Psychology of Romantic Love*. Los Angeles: J. P. Tarcher, 1980.

Branden, N. *If You Could Hear What I Cannot Say*, New York: Bantam Books, 1983.

Brandt, E. N., Jr. "Physicians and Sexually Transmitted Disease: A Call to Action." *Journal of the American Medical Association* 248:2032, 1982.

Brashear, D. B. " 'Honk! If You Masturbate!' " *SIECUS Report* III(2): November 1974.

Brecher, E. *The Sex Researchers*. Boston: Little, Brown, 1969.

Brecher, E. M. "History of Human Sexual Research and Study." In Freedman, A. M.; Kaplan, H. I.; and Sadock, B. J. (eds.), *Comprehensive Textbook of Psychiatry/II*, pp. 1352–57. Baltimore: Williams & Wilkins, 1975.

———. "Women—Victims of the VD Ripoff." In M. Kirkpatrick (ed.), *Women's Sexual Experience—Explorations of the Dark Continent*, pp. 295–313. New York: Plenum Press, 1982.

Brecher, E. M., and the Editors of *Consumers Union Report*. *Love, Sex, and Aging*. Boston: Little, Brown, 1983.

Brecher, R., and Brecher, E. *An Analysis of Human Sexual Response*. New York: New American Library, 1966.

Breen, J. L. "A 21-Year Survey of 654 Ectopic Pregnancies." *American Journal of Obstetrics and Gynecology* 106:1004–19, 1970.

Brewer, M. B. "Further Beyond Nine to Five: An Integration and Future Directions." *Journal of Social Issues* 38(4):149–58, 1982.

Briddell, D., and Wilson, G. T. "Effects of Alcohol and Expectancy Set on Male Sexual Arousal." *Journal of Abnormal Psychology* 85:225–34, 1976.

Brindley, G. S., and Gillan, P. "Men and Women Who Do Not Have Orgasms." *British Journal of Psychiatry* 140:351–56, 1982.

Broderick, C. B. "Preadolescent Sexual Behavior." *Medical Aspects of Human Sexuality* 2(1):20–29, 1968.

Brodsky, A. M., and Hare-Mustin, R. (Eds.). *Women and Psychotherapy*. New York: Guilford Press, 1980.

Brooks-Gunn, J., and Ruble, D. N. "The Menstrual Attitude Questionnaire." *Psychosomatic Medicine* 42(5):503–11, 1980.

Broverman, I. K., et al. "Sex-Role Stereotypes: A Current Appraisal." *Journal of Social Issues* 28(2):59–78, 1972.

Brown, G. *The New Celibacy*. New York: McGraw-Hill, 1980.

Brown, J. *Nutrition for Your Pregnancy*. Minneapolis, Minn.: University of Minnesota Press, 1983.

Brown, J. M., and Chaves, J. F. "Hypnosis in the Treatment of Sexual Dysfunction." *Journal of Sex & Marital Therapy* 6(1):63–74, 1980.

Browning, D., and Boatman, B. "Incest: Children at Risk." *American Journal of Psychiatry* 134:69–72, 1977.

Brownmiller, S. *Against Our Will*. New York: Simon & Schuster, 1975.

Bry, A. *How to Get Angry Without Feeling Guilty*. New York: New American Library, 1977.

Bryk, F. *Neger-Eros. Ethnologische Studien über das Sexualleben bei Negern*. Berlin and Köln: A. Marcus & E. Weber Verlag, 1928.

Bryne, D., and Fisher, W. (Eds.) *Adolescents, Sex, and Contraception*. Hillsdale, N.J.: Laurence Erlbaum Associates, 1983.

Buchanan, R. "Breast-feeding: Aid to Infant Health and Fertility Control." *Population Reports*, Series J(4): July 1975.

Buckley, R. M., Jr., McGuckin, M., and MacGregor, R. R.

"Urine Bacterial Counts after Sexual Intercourse." *New England Journal of Medicine* 298:321-24, 1978.

Bullard, D. G., and Knight, S. E. (Eds.) *Sexuality and Physical Disability.* St. Louis, Mo.: C. V. Mosby, 1981.

Bullough, V. L. *Sexual Variance in Society and History.* New York: Wiley, 1976.

———. "Variant Life Styles: Homosexuality." In Murstein, B. I. (ed.), *Exploring Intimate Life Styles*, pp. 245-57. New York: Springer, 1978.

Bullough, V., and Bullough, B. *Sin, Sickness, and Sanity.* New York: New American Library, 1977.

Burchardt, C. J., and Serbin, L. A. "Psychological Androgyny and Personality Adjustment in College and Psychiatric Populations." *Sex Roles* 8:835-51, 1982.

Burgess, A. W., et al. *Sexual Assault of Children and Adolescents.* Lexington, Mass.: D. C. Heath, 1978.

Burgess, A. W., and Holmstrom, L. L. *Rape: Victims of Crisis.* Bowie, Md.: Robert J. Brady, 1974.

———. "Coping Behavior of the Rape Victim." *American Journal of Psychiatry* 133:413-18, 1976.

Burkhart, K. *Growing Into Love.* New York: Putnam, 1981.

Burton, R. *Anthropological Notes on the Sotadic Zone of Sexual Inversion Throughout the World.* New York: Falstaff Press, 1935.

Bush, P. *Drugs, Alcohol and Sex.* New York: Richard Marek Publishers, 1980.

Butler, R. M., and Lewis, M. I. *Sex After Sixty.* New York: Harper & Row, 1976.

Byrne, D. "The Imagery of Sex." In Money, J., and Musaph, H. (eds.), *Handbook of Sexology*, pp. 327-50. New York: Elsevier/North-Holland, 1977.

Cadden, V. "The Psychiatrists Versus Masters and Johnson." In LoPiccolo, J., and LoPiccolo, L., *Handbook of Sex Therapy*, pp. 485-90. New York: Plenum Press, 1978.

Caird, W., and Wincze, J. P. *Sex Therapy: A Behavioral Approach.* Hagerstown, Md.: Harper & Row, 1977.

Calderone, M. S. "Is Sex Education Preventative?" In Qualls, C. B.; Wincze, J. P.; and Barlow, D. H. (eds.), *The Prevention of Sexual Disorders*, pp. 139-55. New York: Plenum Press, 1978.

Calderone, M. "Fetal Erection and Its Message to Us." *SIECUS Report* XI (5/6):9-10, 1983.

Calderone, M., and Ramey, J. *Talking with Your Child about Sex.* New York: Random House, 1982.

Califia, P. "Lesbian Sexuality." *Journal of Homosexuality* 4(3):255-66, 1979.

Callahan, D. *Abortion: Law, Choice and Morality.* New York: Macmillan, 1970.

Calle, R., et al. "Conservative Management of Operable Breast Cancer: Ten Years Experience at the Foundation Curie." *Cancer* 42:2045-53, 1978.

Cardell, M., Finn, S., and Marecek, J. "Sex-role Identity, Sex-role Behavior, and Satisfaction in Heterosexual, Lesbian and Gay Male Couples." *Psychology of Women Quarterly* 5:488-94, 1981.

Carrier, J. "Cultural Factors Affecting Urban Mexican Male Homosexual Behavior." *Archives of Sexual Behavior* 5(2):103-24, 1976.

———. "Homosexual Behavior in Cross-Cultural Perspective." In Marmor, J. (ed.), *Homosexual Behavior*, pp. 100-122. New York: Basic Books, 1980.

Carter, C. S., and Greenough, W. T. "Sending the Right Sex Messages." *Psychology Today*, p. 112, September 1979.

Casper, R. F., Yen, S. S. C., and Wilkes, M. M. "Menopausal Flushes: A Neuroendocrine Link with Pulsatile Luteinizing Hormone Secretion." *Science* 205:823-25, 1979.

Cass, V. C. "Homosexual Identity Formation: A Theoretical Model." *Journal of Homosexuality* 4(3):219-35, 1979.

Catania, J. A., and White, C. B. "Sexuality in an Aged Sample: Cognitive Determinants of Masturbation." *Archives of Sexual Behavior* 11:237-45, 1982.

Cates, W., Jr., Weisner, P. J., and Curran, J. W. "Sex and Spermicides: Preventing Unintended Pregnancy and Infection." *Journal of the American Medical Association* 248:1636-37, 1982.

Catterall, R. D. *A Short Textbook of Venereology.* Philadelphia: Lippincott, 1974.

Cavero, C. "Modern Midwifery: Complicated Rebirth of an Ancient Art." *Family and Community Health* 2(3):29-39, November 1979.

Centers for Disease Control. *Abortion Surveillance 1978.* Atlanta, Ga.: U.S. Department of Health and Human Services/Public Health Service, November 1980.

Centers for Disease Control. "Gonorrhea: Recommended Treatment Schedules, 1979." *Annals of Internal Medicine* 90:809-11, 1979.

Centers for Disease Control. "Oral Contraceptive Use and the Risk of Ovarian Cancer." *Journal of the American Medical Association* 249:1596-99, 1983.

———. "Oral Contraceptive Use and the Risk of Endometrial Cancer." *Journal of the American Medical Association* 249:1600-1604, 1983a.

Chase, Allan. *The Truth about STD.* New York: William Morrow, 1983.

Chelune, G. A. "A Multidimensional Look at Sex and Target Differences in Disclosure." *Psychological Reports* 39:259-63, 1976.

Cherlin, A. J. *Marriage, Divorce, Remarriage.* Cambridge, Mass.: Harvard University Press, 1981.

Chesser, E. *The Sexual, Marital and Family Relationships of the English Woman.* London: Hutchinson's Medical Publications, 1956.

Chilman, C. *Adolescent Sexuality in a Changing American Society,* (no. NIH 79-1426). Bethesda, Md.: U.S. Department of Health, Education, and Welfare, 1979.

Chipouras, S., et al. *Who Cares? A Handbook on Sex Education and Counseling Services for Disabled People.* Washington, D.C.: George Washington University, 1979.

Chiriboga, D. A. "The Developmental Psychology of

Middle Age." In J. G. Howells (ed.), *Modern Perspectives in the Psychiatry of Middle Age*, pp. 3-25. New York: Brunner/Mazel, 1981.

Christensen, C. V., and Gagnon, J. H. "Sexual Behavior in a Group of Older Women." *Journal of Geriatrics* 20:351-56, 1965.

Christenson, C. V. *Kinsey: A Biography*. Bloomington, Ind.: Indiana University Press, 1971.

Cicero, T. J., et al. "Function of the Male Sex Organs in Heroin and Methadone Users." *New England Journal of Medicine* 292:882-87, 1975.

Clark, L. "Is There a Difference Between a Clitoral and a Vaginal Orgasm?" *Journal of Sex Research* 6:25-28, 1970.

Clarkson, T. B., and Alexander, N. J. "Long-Term Vasectomy: Effects on the Occurrence and Extent of Atherosclerosis in Rhesus Monkeys." *Journal of Clinical Investigation* 65(1):15-25, 1980.

Clarren, S. K., and Smith, D. W. "The Fetal Alcohol Syndrome." *New England Journal of Medicine* 298:1063-67, 1978.

Clayton, R. R., and Bokemeier, J. L. "Premarital Sex in the Seventies." *Journal of Marriage and the Family* 42:759-75, 1980.

Clayton, R. R., and Voss, H. L. "Shacking Up: Cohabitation in the 1970s." *Journal of Marriage and the Family* 39:273-83, 1977.

Clellan, F. S. *Comparative Study of Human Reproduction*. New Haven: Yale University Press, 1945.

Clendinen, D. "Throughout the Country, Homosexual Increasingly Flex Political Muscle." *New York Times*, 3 November 1983.

Clifford, R. E. "Subjective Sexual Experience in College Women." *Archives of Sexual Behavior* 7:183-97, 1978.

Clifford, R., and Kolodny, R. "Sex Therapy for Couples." In B. B. Wolman and G. Stricker (eds.), *Handbook of Family and Marital Therapy*, pp. 421-49. New York: Plenum Press, 1983.

Cochran, W. G.; Mosteller, F.; and Tukey, J. W. "Statistical Problems of the Kinsey Report." *Journal of the American Statistical Association* 48:673-716, 1953.

Cohen, H.; Rosen, R. C.; and Goldstein, L. "Electroencephalographic Laterality Changes During Human Sexual Orgasm." *Archives of Sexual Behavior* 5:189-99, 1976.

Cohen, M. L.; Seghorn, T.; and Calmas, W. "Sociometric Study of the Sex Offender." *Journal of Abnormal Psychology* 74:249-55, 1969.

Cohen, S. "The Volatile Nitrates." *Journal of the American Medical Association* 241:2077-78, 1979.

Coleman, E. "Developmental Stages of the Coming Out Process." *Journal of Homosexuality* 7(2/3):31-43, 1981/82.

Coleman, E. M., Hoon, P. W., and Hoon, E. F. "Arousability and Sexual Satisfaction in Lesbian and Heterosexual Women." *Journal of Sex Research* 19:58-73, 1983.

Coleman, S. "A Developmental Stage Hypothesis for Nonmarital Dyadic Relationships." *Journal of Marriage and Family Counseling* 3:71-76, 1977.

Coleman, S., and Piotrow, P. "Spermicides: Simplicity and Safety Are Major Assets." *Population Reports*, Series H(5): September 1979.

Coleman, S.; Piotrow, P. T.; and Rinehart, W. "Tobacco: Hazards to Health and Human Reproduction." *Population Reports*, Series L(1): March 1979.

Collins, E., and Turner, C. "Maternal Effects of Regular Salicylate Ingestion in Pregnancy." *Lancet* 2:335-39, 1975.

Collins, G. "New Studies of 'Girl Toys' and 'Boy Toys'." *New York Times*, 13 February 1984.

Collins, J. A., et al. "Treatment-independent Pregnancy among Infertile Couples." *New England Journal of Medicine* 309:1201-6, 1983.

Collu, R., et al. "Endocrine Effects of Chronic Administration of Psychoactive Drugs to Prepubertal Male Rats. I: Δ^9-tetrahydrocannabinol." *Life Sciences* 16:533-42, 1975.

Comfort, A. *The Joy of Sex*. New York: Crown, 1972.

Committee of the Royal Anthropological Institute of Great Britain and Ireland. 6th ed. London: Routledge and Kegan Paul, 1951.

Constantine, L. L. "Multilateral Relations Revisited: Group Marriage in Extended Perspective." In Murstein, B. I. (ed.), *Exploring Intimate Life Styles*, pp. 131-47. New York: Springer, 1978.

Constantine, L. L., and Constantine, J. M. *Group Marriage: A Study of Contemporary Multilateral Marriage*. New York: Macmillan, 1973.

Constantine, L. L., and Martinson, F. M. (Eds.). *Children and Sex*. Boston: Little, Brown, 1981.

Cook, M., and Wilson, G. (Eds.). *Love and Attraction*. New York: Pergamon, 1979.

Coombs, L. C. "Preferences for Sex of Children Among U.S. Couples." *Family Planning Perspectives* 9:259-65, 1977.

Cordero, J. F., and Layde, P. M. "Vaginal Spermicides, Chromosomal Abnormalities, and Limb Reduction Defects." *Family Planning Perspectives* 15(1):16-18, 1983.

Corey, L., et al. "Genital Herpes Simplex Virus Infections: Clinical Manifestations, Course, and Complications." *Annals of Internal Medicine* 98:958-72, 1983.

————. "Double-blind Controlled Trial of Topical Acyclovir in Genital Herpes Simplex Virus Infections." *American Journal of Medicine* 73:326-34, 1982.

Corey, L., and Holmes, K. K. "Sexual Transmission of Hepatitis A in Homosexual Men: Incidence and Mechanism." *New England Journal of Medicine* 302:435-38, 1980.

————. "Genital Herpes Simplex Virus Infections: Current Concepts in Diagnosis, Therapy, and Prevention." *Annals of Internal Medicine* 98:973-83, 1983.

Cotten-Huston, A. L., and Wheeler, K. A. "Preorgasmic Group Treatment: Assertiveness, Marital Adjustment and Sexual Function in Women." *Journal of Sex & Marital Therapy* 9:296-302, 1983.

Council on Scientific Affairs. "Estrogen Replacement in the Menopause." *Journal of the American Medical Association* 249:359-61, 1983.

Cowan, G. *See No Evil: The Backstage Battle Over Sex and Violence on Television.* New York: Simon & Schuster, 1979.

Crenshaw, T. L. "Counseling the Family and Friends." In S. Halpern (ed.), *Rape: Helping the Victim*, pp. 51-65. Ordell, N.J.: Medical Economics Books, 1978.

Crépault, C., and Couture, M. "Men's Erotic Fantasies." *Archives of Sexual Behavior* 9:565-81, 1980.

Crépault, C., et al. "Erotic Imagery in Women." In Gemme, R., and Wheeler, C. C. (eds.), *Progress in Sexology*, pp. 267-83. New York: Plenum Press, 1977.

Csikszentmihalyi, M. "Love and the Dynamics of Personal Growth." In Pope, K. S. (ed.), *On Love and Loving*, pp. 306-26. San Francisco: Jossey-Bass, 1980.

Culp, R. E., Cook, A. S., and Housley, P. C. "A Comparison of Observed and Reported Adult-infant Interactions: Effect of Perceived Sex." *Sex Roles* 9:475-79, 1983.

Cunningham, Susan. "Violent Pornography Said to Spur Aggression." *APA Monitor*, p. 30, March 1983.

Curran, J. W. "AIDS—Two Years Later." *New England Journal of Medicine* 309:609-11, 1983.

Currier, R. L. "Juvenile Sexuality in Global Perspective." In L. L. Constantine and F. M. Martinson (eds.), *Children and Sex: New Findings, New Perspectives*, pp. 9-19. Boston: Little, Brown, 1981.

Cushman, P., Jr. "Plasma Testosterone in Narcotic Addiction." *American Journal of Medicine* 55:452-58, 1973.

Cvetkovitch, G., and Grote, B. "Adolescent Development and Teenage Fertility." In D. Byrne and W. A. Fisher (eds.), *Adolescents, Sex and Contraception*, pp. 109-23. Hillsdale, N.J.: Laurence Erlbaum Associates, 1983.

Cvetkovitch, G., et al. "On the Psychology of Adolescents' Use of Contraception." *Journal of Sex Research* 11:256-70, 1975.

Dalton, K. "Menstruation and Acute Psychiatric Illness." *British Medical Journal*, pp. 148-49, 17 January 1959.

———. "Menstruation and Accidents." *British Medical Journal* 2:1425-26, 1960.

———. *The Premenstrual Syndrome.* Springfield, Ill.: Thomas, 1964.

———. "The Influence of Mother's Menstruation on Her Child." *Proceedings of the Royal Society of Medicine* 59:1014-16, 1966.

———. "Menstruation and Examinations." *Lancet* 2:1386-88, 1968.

———. "Children's Hospital Admissions and Mother's Menstruation." *British Medical Journal* 2:27-28, 1970.

———. "Cyclical Criminal Acts in Premenstrual Syndrome." *Lancet* 2:1070-71, 1980.

Dan, A. J. "Behavioral Variability and the Menstrual Cycle." Presented at the American Psychological Association Annual Convention. Washington, D.C.: 1976.

Dank, B. M. "Coming Out in the Gay World." *Psychiatry* 34:180-97, 1971.

Darrow, W. W. "Social and Psychological Aspects of Acquired Immune Deficiency Syndrome." Presented at the 26th Annual Meeting of the Society for the Scientific Study of Sex. Chicago, Ill.: 19 November 1983.

D'Augelli, J. F., and D'Augelli, A. R. "Moral Reasoning and Premarital Sexual Behavior: Toward Reasoning about Relationships." *Journal of Social Issues* 33(2):46-66, 1977.

Davenport, W. "Sexual Patterns and Their Regulation in a Society of the Southwest Pacific." In Beach, F. (ed.), *Sex and Behavior.* New York: Wiley, 1965.

———. "Sex in Cross-Cultural Perspective." In Beach, F. (ed.), *Human Sexuality in Four Perspectives*, pp. 115-63. Baltimore: Johns Hopkins University Press, 1977.

David. "The Commune Movement in the Middle 1970s." In Murstein, B. I. (ed.), *Exploring Intimate Life Styles*, pp. 69-82. New York: Springer, 1978.

David, H. P. "Abortion: A Continuing Debate." *Family Planning Perspectives* 10:313-16, 1978.

Davis, J. E., and Mininberg, D. T. "Prostatitis and Sexual Function." *Medical Aspects of Human Sexuality* 10(8):32-40, 1976.

Davis, K. B. *Factors in the Sex Life of Twenty-Two Hundred Women.* New York: Harper, 1929.

Davis, L. J., and Brody, E. M. *Rape and Older Women.* Rockville, Md.: U.S. Department of Health, Education, and Welfare, 1979.

DeCasper, A. J., and Fifer, W. P. "Of Human Bonding: Newborns Prefer Their Mothers' Voices." *Science* 208:1174-76, 1980.

DeGowin, E. L., and DeGowin, R. L. *Bedside Diagnostic Examination.* 3rd ed. New York: Macmillan, 1976.

DeLamater, J., and MacCorquodale, P. *Premarital Sexuality: Attitudes, Relationships, Behavior.* Madison, Wisc.: University of Wisconsin Press, 1979.

Delaney, J.; Lupton, M. J.; and Toth, E. *The Curse: A Cultural History of Menstruation.* New York: New American Library, 1977.

DeMartino, M. F. (Ed.). *Human Autoerotic Practices.* New York: Human Sciences Press, 1979.

Dennerstein, L., and Burrows, G. D. "Hormone Replacement Therapy and Sexuality in Women." *Clinics in Endocrinology and Metabolism* 11(3):661-79, November 1982.

Dennerstein, L.; Wood, C.; and Burrows, G. D. "Sexual Response Following Hysterectomy and Oophorectomy." *Obstetrics and Gynecology* 49:92-96, 1977.

Derenski, A., and Landsburg, S. B. *The Age Taboo: Older Women/Younger Men.* Boston: Little, Brown, 1981.

Dermer, M., and Thiel, D. L. "When Beauty May Fail." *Journal of Personality and Social Psychology* 31:1168-76, 1975.

Derogatis, L. R., and Kourlesis, S. M. "An Approach to Evaluation of Sexual Problems in the Cancer Patient." *Ca-A Cancer Journal for Clinicians* 31:46-50, 1981.

Deutsch, A. "Kinsey, the Man and His Project." In *Sex Habits of American Men*, pp. 1-39. New York: Prentice-Hall, 1948.

Devereux, G. *Sexual Life of the Mohave Indians*. Ph.D. dissertation, University of California at Berkeley, 1936.

Diagnostic and Statistical Manual of Mental Disorders (DSM-III). Washington, D.C.: American Psychiatric Association, 1980.

Diagram Group. *Man's Body: An Owner's Manual*. New York: Paddington Press, 1976.

Diamond, Irene. "Pornography and Repression: A Reconsideration of 'Who' and 'What'." In L. Lederer (ed.), *Take Back the Night*, pp. 187-203. New York: William Morrow, 1980.

Diamond, Milton. "Sexual Identity, Monozygotic Twins Reared in Discordant Sex Roles and a BBC Follow-up." *Archives of Sexual Behavior* 11:181-86, 1982.

Diamond, M. "Human Sexual Development." In Beach, F. (ed.), *Human Sexuality in Four Perspectives*, pp. 22-61. Baltimore: Johns Hopkins University Press, 1977.

Dickinson, P. A. *The Fires of Autumn: Sexual Activity in the Middle and Later Years*. New York: Drake Publishers, 1974.

Dick-Read, G. *Childbirth Without Fear*. New York: Harper & Row, 1932.

Dietz, P. E. "Social Factors in Rapist Behavior." In Rada, R. T. (ed.), *Clinical Aspects of the Rapist*, pp. 59-115. New York: Grune & Stratton, 1978.

Dion, K. K., and Berscheid, E. "Physical Attractiveness and Peer Perception Among Children." *Sociometry* 37:1-12, 1974.

Dion, K. K.; Berscheid, E.; and Walster, E. "What Is Beautiful Is Good." *Journal of Personality and Social Psychology* 24:285-90, 1972.

Dion, K. K., and Dion, K. L. "Self-Esteem and Romantic Love." *Journal of Personality* 43:39-57, 1975.

Dion, K. L.; and Dion, K. K. "Correlates of Romantic Love." *Journal of Consulting and Clinical Psychology* 41:51-56, 1973.

———. "Love, Liking and Trust in Heterosexual Relationships." *Personality and Social Psychology Bulletin*, 2:191-206, 1976.

Djerassi, C. *The Politics of Contraception*. New York: Norton, 1979.

Dodson, B. *Liberating Masturbation*. New York: Bodysex Designs, 1974.

Doe v. Kelley, reprinted in 6 FLR 3011(1980).

Doerr, P., et al. "Plasma Testosterone, Estradiol, and Semen Analysis in Male Homosexuals." *Archives of General Psychiatry* 29:829-33, 1973.

Donnerstein, E. "Massive Exposure to Sexual Violence and Desensitization to Violence and Rape." Presented at the 26th Annual Meeting of the Society for the Scientific Study of Sex. Chicago, Ill.: 20 November 1983.

Donnerstein, E., and Linz, D. "Sexual Violence in the Media: A Warning." *Psychology Today* 18(1):14-15, 1984.

Dorgan, M., Goebel, B. L., and House, A. E. "Generalizing About Sex Role and Self-Esteem: Results or Effects?" *Sex Roles* 9:719-24, 1983.

Dornblaser, C., and Landry, U. *The Abortion Guide: A Handbook for Women and Men*. New York: Berkley, 1982.

Dörner, G. "Hormonal Induction and Prevention of Female Homosexuality." *Journal of Endocrinology* 42:163-64, 1968.

———. *Hormones and Brain Differentiation*. Amsterdam: Elsevier Scientific Publishing Company, 1976.

Drew, W. L., et al. "Prevalence of Cytomegalovirus Infection in Homosexual Men." *Journal of Infectious Disease* 143:188-92, 1981.

Drill, V. A. "Oral Contraceptives: Relation to Mammary Cancer, Benign Breast Lesions, and Cervical Cancer." *Annual Review of Pharmacology* 15:367-85, 1975.

Duldt, B. W. "Sexual Harassment in Nursing." *Nursing Outlook*, pp. 336-43, June 1982.

Dullea, G. "Ads Seek Valentines All Year." *New York Times*, February 13, 1984, p. A18.

Dumm, J. J.; Piotrow, P. T.; and Dalsimer, I. A. "The Modern Condom—A Quality Product for Effective Contraception." *Population Reports*, Series H(2):May 1974.

Dunn, H. G., et al. "Maternal Cigarette Smoking during Pregnancy and the Child's Subsequent Development: II. Neurological and Intellectual Maturation to the Age of 6½ Years." *Canadian Journal of Public Health* 68:43-50, 1977.

Eddy, D. M. *Screening for Cancer: Theory, Analysis and Design*. Englewood Cliffs, N.J.: Prentice-Hall, 1980.

Edmiston, Susan. "Hers." *The New York Times*, p. Y20, 22 July 1982.

Ehrhardt, A. A., Evers, K.; and Money, J. "Influence of Androgen and Some Aspects of Sexual Dimorphic Behavior in Women with the Late-Treated Adrenogenital Syndrome." *Johns Hopkins Medical Journal* 123:115-22, 1968.

Ehrhardt, A. A.; Grisanti, G. C., and Meyer-Bahlburg, H. F. "Prenatal Exposure to Medroxyprogesterone Acetate (MPA) in Girls." *Psychoneuroendocrinology* 2:391-98, 1977.

Ehrhardt, A., and Meyer-Bahlburg, H. "Effects of Prenatal Sex Hormones on Gender-Related Behavior." *Science* 211(4488):1312-18, 1981.

Eidelberg, L. "A Contribution to the Study of Masturbation Fantasy." *International Journal of Psychoanalysis* 26:127-37, 1945.

Ekman, P., Levenson, R. W., and Friesen, W. V. "Autonomic Nervous System Activity Distinguishes Among Emotions." *Science* 221:1208-10, 1983.

Elias, J., and Gebhard, P. "Sexuality and Sexual Learning in Childhood." *Phi Delta Kappan*, pp. 401-5, March 1969.

Eliasson, R., and Lindholmer, C. "Functions of Male Accessory Genital Organs." In Hafez, E. S. (ed.), *Human Semen and Fertility Regulation in Men.* St. Louis, Mo.: C. V. Mosby, 1976.

Ellis, A. *Sex Without Guilt.* New York: Grove Press, 1965.

———. "Treatment of Erectile Dysfunction." In Leiblum, S. R. and Pervin, L. A. (eds.), *Principles and Practice of Sex Therapy*, pp. 235-62. New York: Guilford Press, 1980.

Ellis, A. *The American Sexual Tragedy.* New York: Twayne Publishers, 1959.

Englar, R. C., and Walker, C. E. "Male and Female Reactions to Erotic Literature." *Psychological Reports* 32:481-82, 1973.

Erikson, E. *Childhood and Society* (second edition). New York: Norton, 1963.

Erikson, E. *Identity: Youth and Crisis.* New York: Norton, 1968.

Erlik, Y., et al. "Association of Waking Episodes with Menopausal Hot Flushes." *Journal of the American Medical Association* 245:1741-44, 1981.

Ernst, M. L., and Loth, D. *American Sexual Behavior and the Kinsey Report.* New York: Greystone Press, 1948.

Ernster, V. L. "American Menstrual Expressions." *Sex Roles: A Journal of Research* 1:3-13, 1975.

Evans, D. R. "Exhibitionism." In Costello, C. G. (ed.), *Symptoms of Psychopathology.* New York: Wiley, 1970.

Eysenck, N., and Nias, D. K. B. *Sex, Violence, and the Media.* New York: St. Martin's Press, 1978.

Fabbri, R., Jr. "Hypnosis and Behavioral Therapy: A Coordinated Approach to the Treatment of Sexual Disorders." *American Journal of Clinical Hypnosis* 19:4-8, 1976.

Fairchild, B., and Hayward, N. *Now That You Know: What Every Parent Should Know About Homosexuality.* New York: Harcourt Brace Jovanovich, 1979.

Falicov, C. J. "Sexual Adjustment During First Pregnancy and Post-Partum." *American Journal of Obstetrics and Gynecology* 117:991-1000, 1973.

Family Planning Perspectives. "Depo-Provera May Be Linked to Uterine Cancer, Preliminary Data Imply." vol. 11:47, 1979.

Farber, B. A. "Adolescence." In Pope, K. S. (ed.), *On Love and Loving*, pp. 44-60. San Francisco: Jossey-Bass, 1980.

Farkas, G. M., and Rosen, R. C. "Effect of Alcohol on Elicited Male Sexual Response." *Journal of Studies on Alcohol* 37:265-72, 1976.

Farkas, G. M., Sine, L. F., and Evans, I. M. "Personality, Sexuality, and Demographic Differences Between Volunteers and Nonvolunteers for a Laboratory Study of Male Sexual Behavior." *Archives of Sexual Behavior* 7:513-20, 1978.

Fast, J. *Body Language.* New York: M. Evans, 1972.

Fauci, A. S. "The Acquired Immune Deficiency Syndrome: The Ever-Broadening Clinical Spectrum." *Journal of the American Medical Association* 249:2375-76, 1983.

Faust, B. *Women, Sex and Pornography.* New York: Macmillan, 1980.

Fawaz, K. A., and Matloff, D. S. "Viral Hepatitis in Homosexual Men." *Gastroenterology* 81:537-38, 1981.

Federation of Feminist Women's Health Centers. *A New View of a Woman's Body.* New York: Simon & Schuster, 1981.

Feldman, M. P., and MacCulloch, M. J. *Homosexual Behavior: Therapy and Assessment.* Oxford: Pergamon Press, 1971.

Feldman-Summers, S.; Gordon, P.; and Meagher, J. R. "The Impact of Rape on Sexual Satisfaction." *Journal of Abnormal Psychology* 88:101-5, 1979.

Felman, Y., and Nikitas, J. "Nongonococcal Urethritis." *Journal of the American Medical Association* 245(4):381-86, 1981.

Fertel, N. S., and Feuer, E. G. "Marital and Sexual Counseling in the Orthodox Jewish Community." *Journal of Sex Education and Therapy* 1(6):62-65, Winter 1979.

Fielding, J. E. "Adolescent Pregnancy Revisited." *New England Journal of Medicine* 299:893-96, 1978.

Finkel, M. I., and Finkel, D. J. "Sexual and Contraceptive Knowledge, Attitudes, and Behavior of Male Adolescents." *Family Planning Perspectives* 7:256-60, 1975.

Finkelhor, D. "Psychological, Cultural and Family Factors in Incest and Family Sexual Abuse." *Journal of Marriage and Family Counseling*, pp. 41-49, October 1978.

———. *Sexually Victimized Children.* New York: Free Press, 1979.

———. "Sex Among Siblings: A Survey on Prevalence, Variety, and Effects." *Archives of Sexual Behavior* 9:171-94, 1980.

Finkelhor, D. "Sex Between Siblings." In L. L. Constantine and F. M. Martinson (eds.), *Children and Sex: New Findings, New Perspectives.* Boston: Little, Brown, 1981, pp. 129-49.

Fiscella, K. "Relationship of Weight Change to Required Size of Vaginal Diaphragm." *Nurse Practitioner* 7(7):21,25, Jul.-Aug. 1982.

Fischer, J. L., and Narus, L. R., Jr. "Sex Roles and Intimacy in Same Sex and Other Sex Relationships." *Psychology of Women Quarterly* 5:444-55, 1981.

Fisher, L. E. "Relationships and Sexuality in Contexts and Culture: The Anthropology of Eros." In Wolman, B. B., and Money, J. (eds.), *Handbook of Human Sexuality*, pp. 164-89. Englewood Cliffs, N.J.: Prentice-Hall, 1980.

Fisher, S. *The Female Orgasm*. New York: Basic Books, 1973.

Fisher, W. A., Branscombe, N. R., and Lemery, C. R. "The Bigger the Better? Arousal and Attributional Responses to Erotic Stimuli That Depict Different Size Penises." *Journal of Sex Research* 19:337-96, 1983.

Fisher, W. A., and Byrne, D. "Sex Differences in Response to Erotica? Love vs. Lust." *Journal of Personality and Social Psychology* 36:117-25, 1978.

FitzGerald, M., and FitzGerald, D. "Deaf People are Sexual Too!" *SIECUS Report* 6(2):1, 13-15, 1977.

Forbes, G. B., and King, S. "Fear of Success and Sex-role: There are Reliable Relationships." *Psychological Reports* 53:735-38, 1983.

Ford, C. S. *Comparative Study of Human Reproduction*. New Haven: Yale University Press, 1945.

Ford, C. S., and Beach, F. A. *Patterns of Sexual Behavior*. New York: Harper & Brothers, 1951.

Ford, K. "Contraceptive Use in the United States, 1973-1976." *Family Planning Perspectives* 10(5):264-69, September/October 1978.

Forrest, J. D., and Henshaw, S. K. "What U.S. Women Think and Do About Contraception." *Family Planning Perspectives* 15:157-66, 1983.

Fortier, L. "Discussion." In *Contraception: Science, Technology and Application*, pp. 45-59. Washington, D.C.: National Academy of Sciences, 1979.

Foster, R. S., Jr., et al. "Breast Self-Exam Practices and Breast-Cancer Stage." *New England Journal of Medicine* 299:265-70, 1978.

Foucault, M. *The History of Sexuality. Volume 1: An Introduction*. Translated by Robert Hurley. New York: Random House, Vintage Books, 1980.

Fox, C. A. "Recent Studies in Human Coital Physiology." *Clinics in Endocrinology and Metabolism* 2:527-44, 1973.

Fox, C. A., and Fox, B. "Blood Pressure and Respiratory Patterns During Human Coitus." *Journal of Reproduction and Fertility* 19:405-15, 1969.

Francke, L. B. *The Ambivalence of Abortion*. New York: Random House, 1978.

Frank, D., et al. "Mastectomy and Sexual Behavior. A Pilot Study." *Sexuality and Disability* 1:16-26, 1978.

Frank, E.; Anderson, C.; and Rubinstein, D. "Frequency of Sexual Dysfunction in 'Normal' Couples." *New England Journal of Medicine* 299:111-15, 1978.

Frank, R. "The Hormonal Causes of Premenstrual Tension." *Archives of Neurology and Psychiatry* 26:1053-57, 1931.

Franklin, E. W., and Zeiderman, A. M. "Tubal Ectopic Pregnancy: Etiology and Obstetric and Gynaecologic Sequelae." *American Journal of Obstetrics and Gynecology* 117:220-25, 1973.

Franzblau, A. N. "Religion and Sexuality." In Freedman, A. M.; Kaplan, H. I.; and Sadock, B. J. (eds.), *Comprehensive Textbook of Psychiatry/II*, pp. 1599-1608. Baltimore: Williams & Wilkins, 1975.

Freud, S. *A General Introduction to Psychoanalysis*. Garden City, N.Y.: Garden City Publishing, 1943.

Freud, S. "Formulations Regarding Two Principles in Mental Functioning." In *Selected Papers* 4:13-21. London: Hogarth Press, 1946.

Friday, N. *My Secret Garden*. New York: Trident, 1973.
———. *Forbidden Flowers*. New York: Pocket Books, 1975.
———. *Men In Love*. New York: Delacorte, 1980.

Friedman, H. J. "The Divorced in Middle Age." In J. G. Howells (ed.), *Modern Perspectives in the Psychiatry of Middle Age*. New York: Brunner/Mazel, 1981, pp. 103-115.

Frieze, I. "Investigating the Causes and Consequences of Marital Rape." *Signs* 8:532-53, 1983.

Frieze, I. H., et al. *Women and Sex Roles: A Social Psychological Perspective*. New York: Norton, 1978.

Frisch, R. E., and McArthur, J. W. "Menstrual Cycles: Fatness as a Determinant of Minimum Weight for Height Necessary for Their Maintenance or Onset." *Science* 185:949-51, 1974.

Frisch, R. E.; Wyshak, G.; and Vincent, L. "Delayed Menarche and Amenorrhea in Ballet Dancers." *New England Journal of Medicine* 303:17-19, 1980.

Fromm, E. *The Art of Loving*. New York: Harper & Row, 1956.

Fuchs, E. *The Second Season: Life, Love and Sex for Women in the Middle Years*. Garden City, N.Y.: Anchor Books, 1978.

Fuchs, K., et al. "Vaginismus: The Hypno-Therapeutic Approach." *Journal of Sex Research* 11:39-45, 1975.

Fulford, R. "Notebook: The Politics of Homophobia." *Saturday Night*, pp. 9-10, April 1981.

Furstenberg, F. F., Jr. "The Social Consequences of Teenage Parenthood." *Family Planning Perspectives* 8:148-64, 1976.

Furstenberg, F., Jr., Mencken, J., and Lincoln, R. *Teenage Sexuality, Pregnancy, and Childbearing*. Philadelphia: University of Pennsylvania Press, 1981.

Gadpaille, W. J. *The Cycles of Sex*. New York: Scribner, 1975.

Gager, N., and Schurr, C. *Sexual Assault: Confronting Rape in America*. New York: Grosset & Dunlap, 1976.

Gagnon, J. H. *Human Sexualities*. Glenview, Ill.: Scott, Foresman, 1977.

Gagnon, J. H., and Simon, W. *Sexual Conduct: The Social Origins of Human Sexuality*. Chicago: Aldine, 1973.

Gambrell, R. D., Jr. "The Menopause: Benefits and Risks of Estrogen-Progestogen Replacement Therapy." *Fertility & Sterility* 37:457-64, 1982.

Gambrell, R. D., et al. "Changes in Sexual Drives of Patients on Oral Contraceptives." *Journal of Reproductive Medicine* 17(3):165-71, September 1976.

Gambrell, R. D., Jr., et al. "Reduced Incidence of Endometrial Cancer among Postmenopausal Women Treated with Progestogens." *Journal of the American Geriatrics Society* 27:389-98, 1979.

Gartrell, N. K.; Loriaux, D. L.; and Chase, T. N. "Plasma Testosterone in Homosexual and Heterosexual Women." *American Journal of Psychiatry* 134:117-19, 1977.

Gay, G. R., et al. "Drug-Sex Practice in the Haight-Ashbury or 'The Sensuous Hippie.'" In Sandler, M., and Gessa, G. L. (eds.), *Sexual Behavior: Pharmacology and Biochemistry*, pp. 63-79. New York: Raven Press, 1975.

Gay Liberation v. University of Missouri. 1977 [416 F. Supp. 1350 (W. D. Mo. 1976)].

Gay, P. *The Bourgeois Experience: Victoria to Freud.* Volume One: *Education of the Senses.* New York: Oxford Press, 1983.

Gebhard, P. H. "Factors in Marital Orgasm." *Journal of Social Issues* 22(4):88-95, 1966.

————. "Postmarital Coitus among Widows and Divorcees." In Bohannan, P. (ed.), *Divorce and After.* Garden City, N.Y.: Doubleday, 1968.

————. "Human Sexual Behavior: A Summary Statement." In Marshall, D., and Suggs, R. (eds.), *Human Sexual Behavior*, pp. 206-17. New York: Basic Books, 1971.

————. "The Acquisition of Basic Sex Information." *Journal of Sex Research* 13:148-69, 1977.

Gebhard, P., et al. *Sex Offenders: An Analysis of Types.* New York: Harper & Row, 1965.

Gebhard, P., and Johnson, A. B. *The Kinsey Data: Marginal Tabulations of the 1938-1963 Interviews Conducted by the Institute for Sex Research.* Philadelphia: Saunders, 1979.

Geer, J. H., Morokoff, P., and Greenwood, P. "Sexual Arousal in Women: The Development of a Measurement Device for Vaginal Blood Flow." *Archives of Sexual Behavior* 3:559-64, 1974.

Gellman, E., et al. "Vaginal Delivery After Cesarean Section." *Journal of the American Medical Association* 249:2935-37, 1983.

General Accounting Office. *Sexual Exploitation of Children — A Problem of Unknown Magnitude* (HRD-82-64). Washington, D.C.: U.S. General Accounting Office, 1982.

George, L. K., and Weiler, S. J. "Sexuality in Middle and Later Life." *Archives of General Psychiatry* 38:919-23, 1981.

Giallombardo, R. *The Social World of Imprisoned Girls.* New York: Wiley, 1974.

Gilbaugh, J. H., Jr., and Fuchs, P. C. "The Gonococcus and the Toilet Seat." *The New England Journal of Medicine* 301:91-93, 1979.

Gilgun, J. F. "Toward an Explanation of Child Sexual Abuse." Presented at the 26th Annual Meeting of the Society for the Scientific Study of Sex. Chicago, Ill.: 20 November 1983.

Gill, W. B., Schumacher, G. F. B., and Bibbo, M. "Pathological Semen and Anatomical Abnormalities of the Genital Tract in Human Male Subjects Exposed to Diethylstilbestrol In Utero." *Journal of Urology* 117:477-80, 1977.

Gillespie, Oscar. *Herpes: What To Do When You Have It.* New York: Grosset & Dunlap, 1982.

Gilmartin, B. G. "Sexual Deviance and Social Networks: A Study of Social, Family, and Marital Interaction Patterns Among Co-Marital Sex Participants." In Smith, J. R., and Smith, L. R. (eds.), *Beyond Monogamy*, pp. 291-322. Baltimore: Johns Hopkins University Press, 1974.

Glass, R., and Ericsson, R. *Getting Pregnant in the 1980s.* Berkeley, Calif.: University of California Press, 1982.

Goldberg, D. C., et al. "The Grafenberg Spot and Female Ejaculation: A Review of Initial Hypotheses." *Journal of Sex & Marital Therapy* 9:27-37, 1983.

Goldfoot, D. A., et al. "Lack of Effect of Vaginal Lavages and Aliphatic Acids on Ejaculating Responses in Rhesus Monkeys: Behavioral and Chemical Analyses." *Hormones and Behavior* 7:1-27, 1976.

Goldman, B. D. "Developmental Influences of Hormones on Neuroendocrine Mechanisms of Sexual Behavior: Comparisons with other Sexually Dimorphic Behaviors." In Hutchison, J. B. (ed.), *Biological Determinants of Sexual Behavior*, pp. 127-52. New York: Wiley, 1978.

Goldman, R., and Goldman, J. *Children's Sexual Thinking.* Boston: Routledge and Kegan Paul, 1982.

————. "Children's Sexual Thinking: Report of a Cross-national Study." *SIECUS Report* 10(3):3-7, January 1982a.

Goldstein, M. J. "Exposure to Erotic Stimuli and Sexual Deviance." *Journal of Social Issues* 29:197-220, 1973.

Goleman, D., and Bush, S. "The Liberation of Sexual Fantasy." *Psychology Today* 11:48-53, 104-7, October 1977.

Golub, S. "The Effect of Premenstrual Anxiety and Depression on Cognitive Function." *Journal of Personality and Social Psychology* 34:99-104, 1976.

————. (Ed.). *Menarche: The Transition from Girl to Woman.* Lexington, Mass.: Lexington Books (DC Heath), 1983.

Gomberg, E. S., and Franks, V. (Eds.). *Gender and Disordered Behavior: Sex Differences in Psychopathology.* New York: Brunner/Mazel, 1979.

González, E. R. "Premenstrual Syndrome: An Ancient Woe Deserving of Modern Scrutiny." *Journal of the American Medical Association* 245(14):1393-96, 1981.

Goode, E., and Troiden, R. R. "Amyl Nitrite Use Among Homosexual Men." *American Journal of Psychiatry* 136(8):1067-69, 1979.

Gordis, R. "Designated Discussion." In Masters, W. H., Johnson, V. E.; and Kolodny, R. C. (eds.), *Ethical Issues in Sex Therapy and Research*, pp. 32-38. Boston: Little, Brown, 1977.

————. *Love and Sex: A Modern Jewish Perspective.* New York: Farrar Straus Giroux, 1978.

Gordon, S. Speech at the Annual Meeting of the American Association for Sex Educators, Counselors, and Therapists, New York, N.Y., 13 March 1982. (Printed in

Impact 1982/83, Institute for Family Research and Education, Syracuse University.)

Gorer, G. "Justification by Numbers: A Commentary on the Kinsey Report." *The American Scholar,* pp. 280-86, Summer 1948.

————. *Himalayan Village.* London: Michael Joseph, 1938.

Gottlieb, B. "Incest: Therapeutic Intervention in a Unique Form of Sexual Abuse." In Warner, C. (ed.), *Rape and Sexual Assault,* pp. 121-40. Germantown, Md.: Aspen Systems Corp., 1980.

Gottman, J. M. *Marital Interaction: Experimental Investigations.* New York: Academic Press, 1979.

Gottman, J., et al. *A Couple's Guide to Communication.* Champaign, Ill.: Research Press, 1976.

Gould, R. L. "Men's Desires: *The Hite Report on Male Sexuality." New York Times Book Review,* pp. 8-9, 19, 12 July 1981.

Gove, W. R. "Sex Differences in the Epidemiology of Mental Disorder: Evidence and Explanations." In Gomberg, E. S., and Franks, V. (eds.), *Gender and Disordered Behavior,* pp. 23-68. New York: Brunner/Mazel, 1979.

Graber, B. (Ed.). *Circumvaginal Musculature and Sexual Function.* New York: Karger, 1982.

Graber, B., and Kline-Graber, G. "Clitoral Foreskin Adhesions and Female Sexual Function." *Journal of Sex Research* 15:205-12, 1979.

Grad, R., et al. *The Father Book—Pregnancy and Beyond.* Washington, D.C.: Acropolis Books, 1981.

Grafenberg, E. "The Role of the Urethra in Female Orgasm." *The International Journal of Sexology* 3:145-48, 1950.

Graham, S., et al. "Sex Patterns and Herpes Simplex Virus Type 2 in the Epidemiology of Cancer of the Cervix." *American Journal of Epidemiology* 115:729-35, 1982.

Granberg, D., and Granberg, B. W. "Abortion Attitudes, 1965-1980: Trends and Determinants." *Family Planning Perspectives* 12:250-61, 1980.

Granfield, D. *The Abortion Decision.* New York: Doubleday, 1969.

Green, A. W. "Sexual Activity and the Postmyocardial Infarction Patient." *American Heart Journal* 89:246-52, 1975.

Green, C. P., and Potteiger, K. "Teenage Pregnancy: A Major Problem for Minors." Washington, D.C.: Zero Population Growth, 1977.

Green, R. "Homosexuality as a Mental Illness." *International Journal of Psychiatry* 10(1):77-98, 1972.

————. "Pornography, Sexual Violence, and Censorship." *Sexual Medicine Today,* p. 32, April 1982.

————. *Sexual Identity Conflict in Children and Adults.* New York: Basic Books, 1974.

————. "Should Homosexuals Adopt Children?" In Brady, J. P., and Brodie, H. K. (eds.), *Controversy in Psychiatry,* pp. 813-28. Philadelphia: Saunders, 1978.

Green, R., and Money, J. (Eds.). *Transsexualism and Sex Reassignment.* Baltimore: Johns Hopkins University Press, 1969.

Green, R., and Wiener, J. (Eds.). *Methodology in Sex Research.* Rockville, Md.: U.S. Department of Health and Human Services (Publication Number [ADM] 80-766), 1980.

Green, T. H., Jr. *Gynecology: Essentials of Clinical Practice.* Boston: Little, Brown, 1977.

Greenblatt, C. S. "The Salience of Sexuality in the Early Years of Marriage." *Journal of Marriage and the Family* 45:289-99, 1983.

Greenblatt, D. R. "Semantic Differential Analysis of the 'Triangular System' Hypothesis in 'Adjusted' Overt Male Homosexuals." Ph.D. dissertation, University of California, 1966.

Greenblatt, R., et al. "Update on the Male and Female Climacteric." *American Geriatrics Society* 27(11):481-90, 1979.

Greenblatt, R. B., and Stoddard, L. D. "The Estrogen-Cancer Controversy." *Journal of the American Geriatrics Society* 26:1-8, 1978.

Greep, R. O., Koblinsky, M. A., and Jaffe, F. S. *Reproduction and Human Welfare: A Challenge to Research.* Cambridge, Mass.: MIT Press, 1976.

Greer, D. M., et al. "A Technique for Foreskin Reconstruction and Some Preliminary Results." *Journal of Sex Research* 18:324-30, 1982.

Greer, G. *The Female Eunuch.* New York: Bantam Books, 1972.

Gregersen, Edgar. *Sexual Practices.* New York: Franklin Watts, 1983.

Gregg, Carol H. "Sexuality Education: Who Should Be Teaching the Children?" *SIECUS Report* 11(5):1-4, September 1982.

Gregg, Charles. "Toxic Shock." In C. Gregg, *A Virus of Love and Other Tales of Medical Detection,* pp. 93-112. New York: Charles Scribner's Sons, 1983.

Gregor, T. *Mehinaku: The Drama of Daily Life in a Brazilian Indian Village.* Chicago: University of Chicago Press, 1977.

Griffin, S. *Pornography and Silence.* New York: Harper & Row, 1981.

Grimes, D. A., and Cates, W., Jr. "Abortions: Methods and Complications." In Hafez, E. S. (ed.), *Human Reproduction: Conception and Contraception,* pp. 796-813. Hagerstown, Md.: Harper & Row, 1980.

Grosskopf, D. *Sex and the Married Woman.* New York: Simon & Schuster, 1983.

Grossman, F.; Eichler, L.; and Winickoff, S. *Pregnancy, Birth and Parenthood.* San Francisco: Jossey-Bass, 1980.

Grossman, R., and Sutherland, J. (Eds.). *Surviving Sexual Assault.* New York: Congdon & Weed, 1982/83.

Groth, A. N. *Men Who Rape.* New York: Plenum Press, 1979.

Groth, A. N., and Burgess, A. W. "Male Rape: Offenders and Victims." *American Journal of Psychiatry* 137:806-10, 1980.

————. "Sexual Dysfunction During Rape." *The New England Journal of Medicine* 297:764-66, 1977.

Groth, A. N.; Burgess, A. W.; and Holmstrom, L. "Rape: Power, Anger, and Sexuality." *American Journal of Psychiatry* 134:1239-43, 1977.

Grumbach, M. "Genetic Mechanisms of Sexual Development." In Vallet, H., and Porter, I. (eds.), *Genetic Mechanisms of Sexual Development*, pp. 33-73. New York: Academic Press, 1979.

Grumbach, M. "The Neuroendocrinology of Puberty." *Hospital Practice*, pp. 51-60, March 1980.

Grundlach, R. "Sexual Molestation and Rape Reported by Homosexual and Heterosexual Women." *Journal of Homosexuality* 2:367-84, 1977.

Gurman, A. S., and Klein, M. "Marital and Family Conflicts." In Brodsky, A. M., and Hare-Mustin, R. (eds.), *Women and Psychotherapy*, pp. 159-88. New York: Guilford Press, 1980.

Hack, M.; Fanaroff, A. A.; and Merkatz, I. R. "The Low-Birth-Weight Infant: Evolution of a Changing Outlook." *New England Journal of Medicine* 301:1162-65, 1979.

Hacker, H. M. "Blabbermouths and Clams: Sex Differences in Self-disclosure in Same-sex and Cross-sex Friendship Dyads." *Psychology of Women Quarterly* 5:385-401, 1981.

Hahn, S. R., and Paige, K. E. "American Birth Practices: A Critical Review." In Parsons, J. E. (ed.), *The Psychobiology of Sex Differences and Sex Roles*, pp. 145-75. New York: McGraw-Hill, Hemisphere, 1980.

Halbreich, U., Endicott, J., and Nee, J. "Premenstrual Depressive Changes." *Archives of General Psychiatry* 40:535-42, 1983.

Hales, D., and Creasy, R. *New Hope for Problem Pregnancies.* New York: Harper & Row, 1982.

Halikas, J., Weller, R., and Morse, C. "Effects of Regular Marihuana Use on Sexual Performance." *Journal of Psychoactive Drugs* 14:59-70, 1982.

Haller, J. S., and Haller, R. M. *The Physician and Sexuality in Victorian America.* New York: Norton, 1977.

Hallstrom, T. "Sexuality of Women in Middle Age: The Goteborg Study." *Journal of Biosocial Sciences (Suppl.)* 6:165-75, 1979.

Halstead, M. M., and Halstead, L. S. "A Sexual Intimacy Survey of Former Nuns and Priests." *Journal of Sex & Marital Therapy* 4:83-90, 1978.

Harbison, R. D., and Mantilla-Plata, B. "Prenatal Toxicity, Maternal Distribution and Placental Transfer of Tetrahydrocannabinol." *Journal of Pharmacology and Experimental Therapeutics* 180:446-53, 1972.

Hariton, E. B., and Singer, J. L. "Women's Fantasies During Marital Intercourse: Normative and Theoretical Implications." *Journal of Consulting and Clinical Psychology* 42(3):313-22, 1974.

Harlap, S. "Gender of Infants Conceived on Different Days of the Menstrual Cycle." *New England Journal of Medicine* 300:1445-48, 1979.

Harlap, S., and Davies, A. M. *The Pill and Births: The Jerusalem Study.* Final Report. Bethesda, Md.: Department of Health, Education and Welfare; National Institute of Child Health and Development Center for Population Research, 1978.

Harlap, S., et al. "A Prospective Study of Spontaneous Fetal Losses After Induced Abortions." *New England Journal of Medicine* 301:677-81, 1979.

Harlow, H. F. "The Nature of Love." *American Psychologist*, 13:673-85, 1958.

Harlow, H., and Harlow M. "The Effect of Rearing Conditions on Behavior." *Bulletin of the Menninger Clinic* 26:213-24, 1962.

Harmon, J. W., et al. "Interference with Testicular Development with Δ^9-Tetrahydrocannabinol." *Surgical Forum* 27:350-52, 1976.

Harris, J. R.; Levene, M. B.; and Hellman, S. "The Role of Radiation Therapy in the Primary Treatment of Carcinoma of the Breast." *Seminars in Oncology* 5:403-16, 1978.

Harrison, F. *The Dark Angel—Aspects of Victorian Sexuality.* New York: Universe Books, 1977.

Harry, Joseph. *Gay Children Grown Up.* New York: Praeger, 1982.

Hartog, J., Audy, J. R., and Cohen, Y. A. (Eds.). *The Anatomy of Loneliness.* New York: International Universities Press, 1980.

Haseltine, F., and Ohno, S. "Mechanisms of Gonadal Differentiation." *Science* 211(4488):1272-78, 1981.

Haskett, R. F., et al. "Severe Premenstrual Tension: Delineation of the Syndrome." *Biological Psychiatry* 15:121-39, 1980.

Hass, A. *Teenage Sexuality.* New York: Macmillan, 1979.

Hatcher, R. A., et al. *Contraceptive Technology 1980-1981.* New York: Irvington Publishers, 1980.

Hatfield, E. "Passionate Love, Companionate Love, and Intimacy." In M. Fisher and G. Stricker (eds.), *Intimacy*, pp. 267-92. New York: Plenum Press, 1982.

Hatterer, L. J. *Changing Homosexuality in the Male.* New York: McGraw-Hill, 1970.

Hedgpeth, J. M. "Employment Discrimination Law and the Rights of Gay Persons." *Journal of Homosexuality* 5(1,2):67-78, 1979/1980.

Hegger, Susan. "Falling in Love Again . . . and Again . . . and Again." *The Riverfront Times (St. Louis)*, pp. 17-19, 26 January 1983.

Heider, K. G. "Dani Sexuality: A Low Energy System." *Man* 11:188-201, 1976.

Heilman, M. E. "Sex Discrimination." In Wolman, B. E., and Money, J. (eds.), *Handbook of Human Sexuality*, pp. 227-49. Englewood Cliffs, N.J.: Prentice-Hall, 1980.

Heiman, J. "A Psychophysiological Exploration of Sexual Arousal Patterns in Females and Males." *Psychophysiology* 14:266-74, 1977.

———. "Female Sexual Response Patterns." *Archives of General Psychiatry* 37:1311-16, 1980.

Heiman, J.; LoPiccolo, L.; and LoPiccolo, J. *Becoming Orgasmic: A Sexual Growth Program for Women.* Englewood Cliffs, N.J.: Prentice-Hall, 1976.

Heinlein, R. *Stranger in a Strange Land.* New York: Putnam, 1961.

Heinonen, O. P., et al. "Cardiovascular Birth Defects and Antenatal Exposure to Female Sex Hormones." *New England Journal of Medicine* 296:67-70, 1977.

Helsinga, K. *Not Made of Stone: The Sexual Problems of Handicapped People.* Springfield, Ill.: Charles C. Thomas, 1974.

Hembree, W. C.; Zeidenberg, P.; and Nahas, G. G. "Marihuana Effects Upon Human Gonadal Function." In Nahas, G. G. (ed.), *Marihuana: Chemistry, Biochemistry and Cellular Effects.* New York: Springer-Verlag, 1976.

Henshaw, S. K., and O'Reilly, K. "Characteristics of Abortion Patients in the United States, 1979 and 1980." *Family Planning Perspectives* 15(1):5-15, 1983.

Henson, C.; Rubin, H. B.; and Henson, D. E. "Women's Sexual Arousal Concurrently Assessed by Three Genital Measures." *Archives of Sexual Behavior* 8:459-79, 1979.

Henzl, M. R., et al. "The Treatment of Dysmenorrhea with Naproxen Sodium." *American Journal of Obstetrics and Gynecology* 127:818-23, 1977.

Herbst, A. L., Ulfelder, H., and Poskanzer, D. C. "Adenocarcinoma of the Vagina: Association of Maternal Stilbestrol Therapy with Tumor Appearance in Young Women." *New England Journal of Medicine* 284:878-81, 1971.

Herdt, G. *Guardians of the Flutes.* New York: McGraw-Hill, 1981.

Herman, J., and Hirschman, L. "Father-Daughter Incest." *Journal of Women in Culture and Society* 2:735-56, 1977.

Herzberg, B. N., et al. "Oral Contraceptives, Depression, and Libido." *British Medical Journal* 3:495-500, 1971.

Heston, L., and Shields, J. "Homosexuality in Twins." *Archives of General Psychiatry* 18:149-60, 1968.

Hier, D. B., and Crowley, W. F., Jr. "Spatial Ability in Androgen-deficient Men." *New England Journal of Medicine* 306:1202-5, 1982.

Higham, E. "Sexuality in the Infant and Neonate: Birth to Two Years." In Wolman, B. B., and Money, J. (eds.), *Handbook of Human Sexuality,* pp. 16-27. Englewood Cliffs, N.J.: Prentice-Hall, 1980.

Hilberman, E. "Rape: The Ultimate Violation of the Self." *American Journal of Psychiatry* 133:436, 1976.

———. "The Impact of Rape." In Notman, M., and Nadelson, C. (eds.), *The Woman Patient,* vol. 1, pp. 303-22. New York: Plenum Press, 1978.

Hill, C. T., Rubin, Z., and Peplau, L. A. "Breakups Before Marriage: The End of 103 Affairs." *Journal of Social Issues* 32:147-68, 1976.

Hill, L. M., Breckle, R., and Gehrking, W. C. "The Prenatal Detection of Congenital Malformations by Ultrasonography." *Mayo Clinic Proceedings* 58:805-26, 1983.

Hiltner, S. "Homosexuality and the Churches." In Marmor, J. (ed.), *Homosexual Behavior,* pp. 219-31. New York: Basic Books, 1980.

Hirsch, M. S., and Schooley, R. T. "Drug Therapy: Treatment of Herpesvirus Infections (second of two parts)." *New England Journal of Medicine* 309:1034-39, 1983.

Hitchens, D. "Social Attitudes, Legal Standards, and Personal Trauma in Child Custody Cases." *Journal of Homosexuality* 5(1,2):89-95, 1979/1980.

Hite, S. *The Hite Report.* New York: Dell, 1977.

Hite, S. *The Hite Report on Male Sexuality.* New York: Alfred A. Knopf, 1981.

Hjorth, N., and Schmidt, H. Edited by H. Maibach. *Venereology in Practice: The Sexually Committed Diseases.* Chicago: Year Book Medical Publishers, 1979.

Hoffman, M. "Homosexuality." In Beach, F. (ed.), *Human Sexuality in Four Perspectives,* pp. 164-89. Baltimore: Johns Hopkins University Press, 1977.

Hoffman, R. J. "Some Cultural Aspects of Greek Male Homosexuality." *Journal of Homosexuality* 5(3):217-26, 1980.

Hogan, D. R. "The Effectiveness of Sex Therapy: A Review of the Literature." In LoPiccolo, J., and LoPiccolo, L. (eds.), *Handbook of Sex Therapy,* pp. 57-84. New York: Plenum Press, 1978.

Holden, C. "House Chops Sex-Pot Probe." *Science* 192:450, 1976.

Hollender, M. H. "Women's Sexual Fantasies During Intercourse." *Archives of General Psychiatry* 8:86-90, 1963.

———. "Women's Wish to Be Held: Sexual and Nonsexual Aspects." *Medical Aspects of Human Sexuality* 5(10):12-26, 1971.

Hollender, M. H.; Brown, C. W.; and Roback, H. B. "Genital Exhibitionism in Women." *American Journal of Psychiatry* 134:436-38, 1977.

Holmes, K. K. "Syphilis." In Isselbacher, K. J., et al. (eds.), *Harrison's Principles of Internal Medicine,* 9th ed., pp. 716-26. New York: McGraw-Hill, 1980.

———. "The *Chlamydia* Epidemic." *Journal of the American Medical Association* 245:1718-23, 1981.

Holmes, K. K., et al. "Etiology of Nongonococcal Urethritis." *New England Journal of Medicine* 292:1199-1205, 1975.

Holmes, K. K., and Stamm, W. E. "Chlamydial Genital Infections: A Growing Problem." *Hospital Practice,* pp. 105-17, October 1979.

Hook, E. B., Cross, P. K., and Schreinemachers, D. "Chromosomal Abnormality Rates at Amniocentesis and in Live-born Infants." *Journal of the American Medical Association* 249:2034-38, 1983.

Hooker, E. "The Adjustment of the Male Overt Homosexual." *Journal of Projective Techniques* 21:18-31, 1957.

Hooper, R. R., et al. "Cohort Study of Venereal Disease. I.

The Risks of Gonorrhea Transmission from Infected Women to Men." *American Journal of Epidemiology* 108:136-44, 1978.

Hoover, R. N., Gray, L. A., and Fraumeni, J. D., Jr. "Stilbestrol (Diethylstilbestrol) and the Risk of Ovarian Cancer." *Lancet* 2:533-34, 1977.

Hopkins, J. R. "Sexual Behavior in Adolescence." *Journal of Social Issues* 33(2):67-85, 1977.

Horner, M. "Toward an Understanding of Achievement Related Conflicts in Women." *Journal of Social Issues* 28:157-75, 1972.

Horwitz, N. "Warning Memo to Women: Either Stop Pill or Smoking." *Medical Tribune*, p. 6, 4 May 1977.

Hosken, F. P. *The Hosken Report: Genital and Sexual Mutilation of Females,* 2nd ed. Lexington, Mass.: Women's International Network News, 1979.

Howard, M. "Postponing Sexual Involvement: A New Approach." *SIECUS Report* 10(4):5-8, March 1983.

Howells, J. G. (Ed.). *Modern Perspectives in the Psychiatry of Middle Age.* New York: Brunner/Mazel, 1981.

Huesmann, L. R. "Toward a Predictive Model of Romantic Behavior." In Pope, K. S. (ed.), *On Love and Loving,* pp. 152-71. San Francisco: Jossey-Bass, 1980.

Hume, E. "Gays See Election As Chance for Gains; May Be Main Political Force This Year." *The Wall Street Journal,* p. 60, 11 January 1984.

Humphreys, L. *Tearoom Trade: Impersonal Sex in Public Restrooms.* Chicago: Aldine, 1970.

Hunt, D. D.; Carr, J. E.; and Hampson, J. L. "Cognitive Correlates of Biologic Sex and Gender Identity in Transsexualism." *Archives of Sexual Behavior* 10:65-78, 1981.

Hunt, M. *The Natural History of Love.* New York: Funk & Wagnalls, Minerva Press, 1967.

————. *Sexual Behavior in the 1970s.* New York: Dell, 1975.

————. "The Future of Marriage." In DeBurger, J. E. (ed.), *Marriage Today,* pp. 683-98. New York: Wiley, 1977.

Huston, T. L., and Levinger, G. "Interpersonal Attraction and Relationships." *Annual Review of Psychology* 29:115-56, 1978.

Hutchison, J. B. (Ed.). *Biological Determinants of Sexual Behavior.* New York: Wiley, 1978.

Hymowitz, C. "More Men Infiltrating Professions Historically Dominated by Women." *The Wall Street Journal,* p. 27, 25 February 1981.

Imperato-McGinley, J., et al. "Androgens and the Evolution of Male-Gender Identity among Male Pseudohermaphrodites with 5α-Reductase Deficiency." *New England Journal of Medicine* 300(22):1233-37, 1979.

Imperato-McGinley, J., and Peterson, R. "Male Pseudohermaphroditism: The Complexities of Male Phenotypic Development." *American Journal of Medicine* 61:251-72, 1976.

Ingram, M. "Participating Victims: A Study of Sexual Offenses with Boys." In L. L. Constantine and F. M. Martinson (eds.), *Children and Sex: New Perspectives, New Findings,* pp. 177-87. Boston: Little, Brown, 1981.

Jacobelis v. Ohio. 378 U.S. 184 (1965).

Jaffe, J. H. "Drug Addiction and Drug Abuse." In Gilman, A. S.; Goodman, L. S.; and Gilman, A. (eds.), *The Pharmacological Basis of Therapeutics,* pp. 535-83. New York: Macmillan, 1980.

Jaffe, H. W. Bregman, D. J., and Selik, R. M. "Acquired Immune Deficiency Syndrome in the United States: The First 1,000 Cases." *Journal of Infectious Diseases* 148:339-45, 1983.

Jaffe, H. W., et al. "National Case-Control Study of Kaposi's Sarcoma and *Pneumocystis Carinii* Pneumonia in Homosexual Men: Part 1, Epidemiologic Results." *Annals of Internal Medicine* 99:145-51, 1983.

James, W. *The Principles of Psychology.* New York: Dover, 1950. (Originally published in 1890.)

James, W. H. "Coital Rates and the Pill." *Nature* 234:555-56, 1971.

Janerich, D. T.; Piper, J. M.; and Glebatis, D. M. "Oral Contraceptives and Congenital Limb-Reduction Defects." *NEJM* 291:697-700, 1974.

Jelliffe, D. B. "Community and Sociopolitical Considerations of Breast-Feeding." In Ciba Foundation Symposium 45 (new series), *Breast-Feeding and the Mother,* pp. 231-45. New York: Elsevier/North-Holland, 1976.

Jensen, G. D. "Childhood Sexuality." In Green, R. (ed.), *Human Sexuality: A Health Practitioner's Text,* 2nd ed., pp. 46-57. Baltimore: Williams & Wilkins, 1979.

————. "Cross-cultural Studies and Animal Studies of Sex." In Kaplan, H. I.; Freedman, A. M.; and Sadock, B. J. (eds.), *Comprehensive Textbook of Psychiatry/III,* pp. 1723-34. Baltimore: Williams & Wilkins, 1980.

Jessor, S. L., and Jessor, R. "Transition from Virginity to Nonvirginity among Youth: A Social-Psychological Study Over Time." *Developmental Psychology* 11:473-84, 1975.

————. *Problem Behavior and Psychosocial Development: A Longitudinal Study of Youth.* New York: Academic Press, 1977.

Jick, H., et al. "Myocardial Infarction and Other Vascular Diseases in Young Women: Role of Estrogens and Other Factors." *Journal of the American Medical Association* 240:2548-52, 1978.

————. "Oral Contraceptives and Nonfatal Stroke in Healthy Young Women." *Annals of Internal Medicine* 89:58-60, 1978a.

————. "Replacement Estrogens and Breast Cancer." *American Journal of Epidemiology* 112:586, 1980.

————. "Vaginal Spermicides and Congenital Disorders." *Journal of the American Medical Association* 245(13):1329-32, 1981.

————. "Vaginal Spermicides and Gonorrhea." *Journal of the American Medical Association* 248:1619-21, 1982.

Johnson, V. E., and Masters, W. H. "Intravaginal Contraceptive Study: Phase I. Anatomy." *Western Journal of Surgery, Obstetrics, and Gynecology* 70:202-7, 1962.

Jones, R. T. "Human Effects." In Petersen, R. C. (ed.), *Marihuana Research Findings: 1976*, pp. 128-78. NIDA. Dept. of HEW #(ADM) 78-501. Washington, D.C.: U.S. Government Printing Office, 1976.

Jones, W. H.; Chernovetz, M. E.; and Hansson, R. O. "The Enigma of Androgyny: Differential Implications for Males and Females?" *Journal of Consulting and Clinical Psychology* 46:298-313, 1978.

Jones, W., Freeman, J. E., and Goswick, R. "The Persistence of Loneliness: Self and Other Determinants." *Journal of Personality* 49:27-48, 1981.

Jong, E. *Fear of Flying.* New York: Signet, 1974.

Jost, A. "Problems of Fetal Endocrinology: The Gonadal and Hypophyseal Hormones." *Recent Progress in Hormone Research* 8:379-418, 1953.

———. "A New Look at Mechanisms Controlling Sex Differentiation in Mammals." *Johns Hopkins Medical Journal* 130:38-53, 1972.

Joyce, J. *Ulysses.* New York: Random House, 1961.

Kagan, J. "Psychology of Sex Differences." In Beach, F. (ed.), *Human Sexuality in Four Perspectives,* pp. 87-114. Baltimore: Johns Hopkins University Press, 1976.

Kallen, D. J., Stephenson, J. J., and Doughty, A. "The Need to Know: Recalled Adolescent Sources of Sexual and Contraceptive Information and Sexual Behavior." *Journal of Sex Research* 19:137-59, 1983.

Kallman, F. J. "Comparative Twin Study on the Genetic Aspects of Male Homosexuality." *Journal of Nervous and Mental Disease* 115:283-98, 1952.

Kanin, E. "Selected Dyadic Aspects of Male Sex Aggression." *Journal of Sex Research* 5:12-28, 1969.

Kantner, J. F., and Zelnik, M. "Sexual Experiences of Young Unmarried Women in the U.S." *Family Planning Perspectives* 4(4):9-17, 1972.

———. "Contraception and Pregnancy: Experience of Young Unmarried Women in the United States." *Family Planning Perspectives* 5:21-35, 1973.

Kaplan, A. "Clarifying the Concept of Androgyny: Implications for Therapy." *Psychology of Women Quarterly* 3:223-30, 1979.

Kaplan, A., and Sedney, M. A. *Psychology and Sex Roles: An Androgynous Perspective.* Boston: Little, Brown, 1980.

Kaplan, H. *The Evaluation of Sexual Disorders.* New York: Brunner/Mazel, 1983.

Kaplan, H. S. *The New Sex Therapy.* New York: Brunner/Mazel, 1974.

———. *The Illustrated Manual of Sex Therapy.* New York: Quadrangle/New York Times, 1975.

———. *Disorders of Sexual Desire.* New York: Brunner/Mazel, 1979.

Karlen, A. *Sexuality and Homosexuality: A New View.* New York: Norton, 1971.

———. "Homosexuality: The Scene and Its Students." In

Henslin, J. M., and Sagarin, E., *The Sociology of Sex,* pp. 223-48. New York: Schocken Books, 1978.

———. "Homosexuality in History." In Marmor, J. (ed.), *Homosexual Behavior,* pp. 75-99. New York: Basic Books, 1980.

Karmel, M. *Thank You, Dr. Lamaze.* Philadelphia: Lippincott, 1959.

Kasan, P. N., and Andrews, J. "Oral Contraception and Congenital Anomalies." *British Journal of Obstetrics and Gynaecology* 87:548-51, 1980.

Kassel, V. "Sex in Nursing Homes." *Medical Aspects of Human Sexuality* 10(3):129-31, March 1976.

Katchadourian, H. *The Biology of Adolescence.* San Francisco: W. H. Freeman, 1977.

Kaufman, D. W., et al. "Decreased Risk of Endometrial Cancer Among Oral Contraceptive Users." *New England Journal of Medicine* 303:1045-47, 1980.

Kegel, A. "Sexual Functions of the Pubococcygeus Muscle." *Western Journal of Surgery, Obstetrics, and Gynecology* 60:521-24, 1952.

Kelley, D. B., and Pfaff, D. W. "Generalizations from Comparative Studies on Neuroanatomical and Endocrine Mechanisms of Sexual Behavior." In Hutchison, J. B. (ed.), *Biological Determinants of Sexual Behavior,* pp. 225-54. New York: Wiley, 1978.

Kelly, G. F. *Good Sex: A Healthy Man's Guide to Sexual Fulfillment.* New York: Harcourt Brace Jovanovich, 1979.

Kempton, W. "Sex Education for the Mentally Handicapped." *Sex and Disability* 1(2):137-46, 1978.

Kennedy, J. G. "Circumcision and Excision in Egyptian Nubia." *Man* 5:175-91, 1970.

Kern, S. "Freud and the Discovery of Child Sexuality." *History of Childhood Quarterly* 1:117-41, 1973.

Kessler, I. I. "On the Etiology and Prevention of Cervical Cancer. A Status Report." *Obstetrics and Gynecological Survey* 34:790-94, 1979.

Key, W. B. *Media Sexploitation.* New York: Signet, 1977.

Keye, W. R. "Update: Premenstrual Syndrome." *Endocrine & Fertility Forum* 6(4):1-3, Fall 1983.

Keyserling, H. "Herpes Simplex: An Interview." *Urban Health* 11(7):30-32, 44, August 1982.

Kilmann, P. R. "The Treatment of Primary and Secondary Orgasmic Dysfunction: A Methodological Review of the Literature Since 1970." *Journal of Sex & Marital Therapy* 4:155-76, 1978.

Kilmann, P. R., et al. "The Treatment of Sexual Paraphilias: A Review of the Outcome Research." *Journal of Sex Research* 18:193-252, 1982.

Kilmann, P. R., and Auerbach, R. "Treatments of Premature Ejaculation and Psychogenic Impotence: A Critical Review of the Literature." *Archives of Sexual Behavior* 8:81-100, 1979.

Kimmel, D. "Adult Development and Aging: A Gay Perspective." *Journal of Social Issues* 34(3):113-30, 1978.

Kinsey, A. C., et al. *Sexual Behavior in the Human Female.* Philadelphia: Saunders, 1953.

Kinsey, A. C.; Pomeroy, W. B.; and Martin, C. E. *Sexual Behavior in the Human Male*. Philadelphia: Saunders, 1948.

Kirby, D., Alter, J., and Scales, P. *An Analysis of U.S. Sex Education Programs and Evaluation Methods*. Atlanta, Ga.: U.S. Department of Health, Education, and Welfare, Public Health Service, Center for Disease Control, Bureau of Health Education, Report #CDC-2021-79-DK-FR, 1979.

Kirkham, G. L. "Homosexuality in Prison." In Henslin, J. M. (ed.) *Studies in the Sociology of Sex*. New York: Appleton-Century-Crofts, 1971.

Klaus, M. H., et al. "Maternal Attachment: Importance of the First Post-Partum Days." *New England Journal of Medicine* 286:460-63, 1972.

Kline-Graber, G., and Graber, B. "Diagnosis and Treatment Procedures of Pubococcygeal Deficiencies in Women." In LoPiccolo, J., and LoPiccolo, L. (eds.), *Handbook of Sex Therapy*, pp. 227-39. New York: Plenum Press, 1978.

Klitsch, M. "Hormonal Implants: The Next Wave of Contraceptives." *Family Planning Perspectives* 15:239-43, 1983.

Klonoff, H. "Marijuana and Driving in Real-Life Situations." *Science* 186:317-24, 1974.

Knapp, J. J., and Whitehurst, R. N. "Sexually Open Marriage and Relationships: Issues and Prospects." In Murstein, B. I. (ed.), *Exploring Intimate Life Styles*, pp. 35-51. New York: Springer, 1978.

Knupfer, F.; Clark, W.; and Room, R. "The Mental Health of the Unmarried." *American Journal of Psychiatry* 122:841-51, 1966.

Knutson, D. C. (Ed.). "Introduction." *Journal of Homosexuality* 5(1,2):5-23, 1979/1980.

Koch, P. B. "College Students: The Concerns They Experience in Their Sexual Lives." Presented at the 15th Annual National Meeting of the American Association for Sex Educators, Counselors, and Therapists. New York, N.Y.: 13 March 1982.

Koeske, R. K. "Premenstrual Emotionality: Is Biology Destiny?" *Women and Health* 1:11-14, 1976.

Koeske, R. K.; and Koeske, G. F. "An Attributional Approach to Moods and the Menstrual Cycle." *Journal of Personality and Social Psychology* 31:474-78, 1975.

Kohlberg, L. "A Cognitive-Developmental Analysis of Children's Sex-Role Concepts and Attitudes." In Maccoby, E. E. (ed.), *The Development of Sex Differences*, pp. 82-172. Stanford, Calif.: Stanford University Press, 1966.

Kolata, G. B. "In Vitro Fertilization Goes Commercial." *Science* 221:1160-61, 1983.

———. "Math Genius May Have Hormonal Basis." *Science* 222:1312, 1983.

———. "Math and Sex: Are Girls Born with Less Ability?" *Science* 210:1234-35, 1980.

———. "NIH Panel Urges Fewer Cesarean Births." *Science* 210:176-77, 1980a.

Kolodny, R. C. "Sexual Dysfunction in Diabetic Females." *Diabetes* 20(8):557-59, 1971.

———. "Effects of Alpha-Methyldopa on Male Sexual Function." *Sexuality and Disability* 1:223-28, 1978.

———. "Ethical Issues in the Prevention of Sexual Problems." In Qualls, C. B., Wincze, J. P., and Barlow, D. H. (eds.), *The Prevention of Sexual Disorders*, pp. 183-96. New York: Plenum Press, 1978a.

———. "Adolescent Sexuality." Presented at the Michigan Personnel and Guidance Association Annual Convention. Detroit, November 1980.

———. "Effects of Marihuana on Sexual Behavior and Function." Paper presented at the Midwestern Conference on Drug Use. St. Louis, Mo.: 16 February 1981.

———. Unpublished observations, 1981.

———. "Evaluating Sex Therapy: Process and Outcome at the Masters & Johnson Institute." *Journal of Sex Research* 17:301-18, 1981.

———. Unpublished research. 1983.

———. "Sexual Issues in Mid-Adulthood." Presented at the Las Vegas Psychiatric Symposium. Las Vegas, Nev.: 23 January 1983.

———. "The Clinical Management of Sexual Problems in Substance Abusers." In T. E. Bratter and G. Forrest (eds.), *Current Management of Alcoholism and Substance Abuse*. New York: Free Press, 1985.

Kolodny, R. C., and Bauman, J. E. "Female Sexual Activity at Ovulation," (letter). *New England Journal of Medicine* 300:626, 1979.

Kolodny, R. C., et al. "Plasma Testosterone and Semen Analysis in Male Homosexuals." *New England Journal of Medicine* 285:1170-74, 1971.

———. "Depression of Plasma Testosterone Levels after Chronic Intensive Marihuana Use." *New England Journal of Medicine* 290:872-74, 1974.

———. "Sexual Dysfunction in Diabetic Men." *Diabetes* 23:306-09, 1974a.

———. "Depression of Plasma Testosterone with Acute Marihuana Administration." In Braude, M. C., and Szara, S. (eds.), *The Pharmacology of Marihuana*, pp. 217-25. New York: Raven Press, 1976.

———. "Endocrine Status of Men During Chronic Marihuana Use." Paper presented at Washington University Medical Center Research Seminar. St. Louis, Mo.: April 1979.

———. "Endocrine Effects of Chronic Marihuana Use by Women." Paper presented at the University of Rochester Medical School Endocrine Grand Rounds. Rochester, N.Y.: February 1980.

Kolodny, R. C.; Masters, W. H.; and Johnson, V. E. *Textbook of Sexual Medicine*. Boston: Little, Brown, 1979.

Kols, A., and Lewison, D. "Migration, Population Growth and Development." *Population Reports* Series M, Number 7, Sept.-Oct. 1983.

Kols, A., et al. "Oral Contraceptives in the 1980s." *Population Reports*, Series A, Number 6, May-June 1982.

Komarovsky, M. *Dilemmas of Masculinity*. New York: W. W. Norton, 1976.

Kornfeld, H., et al. "T-lymphocyte Subpopulations in Homosexual Men." *New England Journal of Medicine* 307:729-31, 1982.

Kosnik, A., et al. *Human Sexuality: New Directions in American Catholic Thought*. New York: Paulist Press, 1977.

Krane, R. J., and Siroky, M. B. "Neurophysiology of Erection." *Urologic Clinics of North America* 8:91-102, 1981.

Krebs, D., and Adinolfi, A. A. "Physical Attractiveness, Social Relations, and Personality Style." *Journal of Personality and Social Psychology* 31:245-53, 1975.

Kutchinsky, B. "Sex Crimes and Pornography in Copenhagen: A Study of Attitudes." *Technical Reports of the Commission on Obscenity and Pornography*, vol. 7. Washington, D.C.: U.S. Government Printing Office, 1970.

————. "The Effect of Easy Availability of Pornography on the Incidence of Sex Crimes." *Journal of Social Issues* 29:163-82, 1973.

Kutner, S. J.; Phillips, N. R.; and Hoag, E. J. "Oral Contraceptives, Personality, and Changes in Depression." In Ramcharan, S. (ed.), *The Walnut Creek Contraceptive Drug Study*, vol. II. Washington, D.C.: U.S. Government Printing Office, 1974.

Labovitz, S., and Hagedorn, R. *Introduction to Social Research*. New York: McGraw-Hill, 1976.

Lacoste-Utamsing, C., and Holloway, R. L. "Sexual Dimorphism in the Human Corpus Callosum." *Science* 216:1431-32, 1982.

Ladas, A. K., Whipple, B., and Perry, J. D. *The G Spot and Other Recent Discoveries About Human Sexuality*. New York: Holt, Rinehart & Winston, 1982.

Lader, L. *Abortion*. Indianapolis: Bobbs-Merrill, 1966.

Laino, C. "100 Thelarche Cases a Year in Puerto Rico—Why?" *Medical Tribune*, pp. 3, 19, 18 January 1984.

Lake, A. "Childbirth in America." *McCall's*, p. 128, January 1976.

Lamaze, F. *Painless Childbirth*. Chicago: Regnery, 1970.

Lamb, E. J., and Leurgans, S. "Does Adoption Affect Subsequent Fertility?" *American Journal of Obstetrics and Gynecology* 134:138-44, 1979.

Lamberti, J. "Sexual Adjustment after Radiation Therapy for Cervical Carcinoma." *Medical Aspects of Human Sexuality* 13(3):87-88, 1979.

Lane, H. C., et al. "Abnormalities of B-cell Activation and Immunoregulation in Patients with the Acquired Immunodeficiency Syndrome." *New England Journal of Medicine* 309:453-58, 1983.

Langfeldt, T. "Sexual Development in Children." In M. Cook and K. Howells (eds.), *Adult Sexual Interest in Children*. London: Academic Press, 1981.

Langston, Deborah. *Living with Herpes*. Garden City, N.Y.: Doubleday, 1983.

Larsen, B., and Galask, R. P. "Vaginal Microbial Flora: Composition and Influences of Host Physiology." *Annals of Internal Medicine* 96(Part 2):926-30, 1982.

Larson, T., and Bryson, Y. "Fomites and Herpes Simplex Virus: The Toilet Seat Revisited (abstract)." *Pediatric Research* 16:244, 1982.

Larzelere, R. E., and Huston, T. L. "The Dyadic Trust Scale: Toward Understanding Interpersonal Trust in Close Relationships." *Journal of Marriage and the Family* 42:595-604, 1980.

Lasater, M. "Sexual Assault: The Legal Framework." In Warner, C. (ed.), *Rape and Sexual Assault*, pp. 231-64. Germantown, Md.: Aspen Systems Corp., 1980.

Lattimer, J. K., et al. "The Optimum Time to Operate for Cryptorchidism." *Pediatrics* 53:96-99, 1974.

Laubscher, B. J. *Sex, Custom and Psychopathology: A Study of South African Pagan Natives*. New York: Robert McBride & Co., 1938.

Laurence, L. T. *Couple Constancy: Conversations with Today's Happily Married People*. Ann Arbor, Mich.: UMI Research Press, 1982.

Lawrence, D. H. *Lady Chatterley's Lover*. New York: Grove Press Black Cat Edition, 1962.

Lazarus, A. A. "Psychological Treatment of Dyspareunia." In Leiblum, S. R., and Pervin, L. A. (eds.), *Principles and Practice of Sex Therapy*, pp. 147-66. New York: Guilford Press, 1980.

LeBolt, S. A., Grimes, D. A., and Cates, W., Jr. "Mortality from Abortion and Childbirth." *Journal of the American Medical Association* 248:188-91, 1982.

Lebovitz, P. S. "Feminine Behavior in Boys: Aspects of Its Outcome." *American Journal of Psychiatry* 128:1283-89, 1972.

Leboyer, F. *Birth Without Violence*. New York: Knopf, 1975.

Lederer, L. (Ed.). *Take Back the Night*. New York: William Morrow, 1980.

Lee, A. L., and Scheurer, V. L. "Psychological Androgyny and Aspects of Self-image in Women and Men." *Sex Roles* 9:289-306, 1983.

Lee, J. A. *The Colours of Love*. Toronto: New Press, 1973.

————. *The Colors of Love*. Englewood Cliffs, N.J.: Prentice-Hall, 1976.

Lee, P. A. "The Relationship of Concentrations of Serum Hormones to Pubertal Gynecomastia." *Journal of Pediatrics* 86:212-15, 1975.

Leiblum, S., et al. "Vaginal Atrophy in the Postmenopausal Woman: The Importance of Sexual Activity and Hormones." *Journal of the American Medical Association* 249:2195-98, 1983.

Leiblum, S. R., and Pervin, L. A. *Principles and Practice of Sex Therapy*. New York: Guilford Press, 1980.

Lenton, E. A.; Weston, G. A.; and Cooke, I. D. "Problems in Using Basal Body Temperature Recordings in an Infertility Clinic." *British Medical Journal* 1:803-5, 1977.

Leo, J. "Stomping and Whomping Galore." *Time*, pp. 73-74, 4 May 1981.

668   References

————. "A New Fervor Over Pedophilia." *Time*, p. 47, 17 January 1983.

Lessing, D. *The Four-Gated City*. New York: Bantam Books, 1970.

Levin, A. A., et al. "Association of Induced Abortion with Subsequent Pregnancy Loss," *Journal of the American Medical Association* 243:2495-99, 1980.

Levin, R. J. "The Redbook Report on Premarital and Extramarital Sex: The End of the Double Standard?" *Redbook*, pp. 38-44, 190-192, October 1975.

Levin, R. J., and Levin, A. "Sexual Pleasure: The Surprising Preferences of 100,000 Women." *Redbook*, pp. 51-58, September 1975.

Levine, R. "Gusii Sex Offenses: A Study in Social Control." *American Anthropologist* 61(6):965-90, 1959.

Levine, S. B. "Marital Sexual Dysfunction: Introductory Concepts." *Annals of Internal Medicine* 84:448-53, 1976.

Levinger, G., and Raush, H. L. (Eds.). *Close Relationships: Perspectives on the Meaning of Intimacy* Amherst, Mass.: University of Massachusetts Press, 1977.

Levinson, D. J., et al. *The Seasons of a Man's Life*. New York: Ballantine, 1978.

Levy, N. L. "The Middle-aged Male and Female Homosexual." In J. G. Howells (ed.), *Modern Perspectives in the Psychiatry of Middle Age*, pp. 116-31. New York: Brunner/Mazel, 1981.

Lewis, M. "State as an Infant-Environment Interaction: An Analysis of Mother-Infant Interaction as a Function of Sex." *Merrill-Palmer Quarterly* 18:95-121, 1972.

Lewis, R. A. "Parents and Peers: Socialization Agents in the Coital Behavior of Young Adults." *Journal of Sex Research* 9:156-70, 1973.

Liang, A. P., et al. "Risk of Breast, Uterine Corpus and Ovarian Cancer in Women Receiving Medroxyprogesterone Injections." *Journal of the American Medical Association* 249:2909-12, 1983.

Liebowitz, M. R. *The Chemistry of Love*. Boston: Little, Brown, 1983.

Lief, H. I. "Inhibited Sexual Desire." *Medical Aspects of Human Sexuality* 11(7):94-95, 1977.

Lilius, H. G., Valtonen, E. J., and Wikström, J. "Sexual Problems in Patients Suffering from Multiple Sclerosis." *Journal of Chronic Diseases* 29:643-47, 1976.

Lincoln, G. A. "Luteinizing Hormone and Testosterone in Man." *Nature* 252:232-33, 1974.

Lindholm, F. B., et al. "Pituitary-Testicular Function in Patients with Chronic Alcoholism." *European Journal of Clinical Investigation* 8:269-72, 1978.

Lipkin, M., Jr., and Lamb, G. S. "The Couvade Syndrome: An Epidemiologic Study." *Annals of Internal Medicine* 96:509-11, 1982.

Lipsett, M. B. "Estrogen Use and Cancer Risk." *Journal of the American Medical Association* 237:1112-15, 1977.

Lipton, M. A. "The Problem of Pornography." In W. E. Fann et al. (eds.), *Phenomenology and Treatment of Psychosexual Disorders*, pp. 113-34. New York: Spectrum, 1983.

Liskin, L., Pile, J. M., and Quillin, W. F. "Vasectomy—Safe and Simple." *Population Reports* Series D, Number 4, Nov.-Dec. 1983.

Long Laws, J. *The Second X*. New York: Elsevier, 1979.

LoPiccolo, J. "Direct Treatment of Sexual Dysfunction in the Couple." In Money, J., and Musaph, H. (eds.), *Handbook of Sexology*, pp. 1227-44. Amsterdam: Elsevier/North-Holland, 1977.

LoPiccolo, J., and Heiman, J. "The Role of Cultural Values in the Prevention and Treatment of Sexual Problems." In Qualls, C. B.; Wincze, J. P.; and Barlow, D. H. (eds.), *The Prevention of Sexual Disorders*, pp. 43-71. New York: Plenum Press, 1978.

LoPiccolo, J., and Lobitz, W. C. "The Role of Masturbation in the Treatment of Orgasmic Dysfunction." *Archives of Sexual Behavior* 2:163-71, 1972.

LoPiccolo, J., and LoPiccolo, L. (Eds.). *Handbook of Sex Therapy*. New York: Plenum Press, 1978.

LoPiccolo, L. "Low Sexual Desire." In Leiblum, S. R., and Pervin, L. A. (eds.), *Principles and Practice of Sex Therapy*, pp. 29-64. New York: Guilford Press, 1980.

Loraine, J. A., et al. "Endocrine Function in Male and Female Homosexuals." *British Medical Journal* 4:406-08, 1970.

Lowry, T. P. "The Volatile Nitrites as Sexual Drugs: A User Survey." *Journal of Sex Education and Therapy* 1:8-10, 1979.

Lowry, T. P., and Williams, G. R. "Brachioproctic Eroticism." *Journal of Sex Education and Therapy* 9(1):50-52, 1983.

Lundberg, P. O. "Sexual Dysfunction in Patients with Neurological Disorders." In Gemme, R., and Wheeler, C. C. (eds.), *Progress in Sexology*, pp. 129-39. New York: Plenum Press, 1977.

Lundberg, P. O., and Wide, L. "Sexual Function in Males with Pituitary Tumors." *Fertility and Sterility* 29:175-79, 1978.

McBride, G. "Putting a Better Cap on the Cervix." *Journal of the American Medical Association* 243(16):1617-18, 1980.

McCandlish, B. M. "Therapeutic Issues with Lesbian Couples." *Journal of Homosexuality* 7(2-3):71-78, 1981/82.

McCarthy, B. W. "Sexual Dysfunctions and Dissatisfactions among Middle-years Couples." *Journal of Sex Education and Therapy* 8(2):9-12, 1982.

McCarthy, J., and Radish, E. S. "Education and Childbearing Among Teenagers." *Family Planning Perspectives* 14:154-55, 1982.

McClintock, M. "Menstrual Synchrony and Suppression." *Nature* (London) 229:244-45, 1971.

McCormick, M. C., Shapiro, S., and Starfield, B. "High Risk Young Mothers: Changes In Infant Mortality and Morbidity in Four Areas in the United States, 1973-1978." Presented at the Annual Meeting of the American Pediatric Association. San Francisco, Calif.: 30 April 1981.

Maccoby, E., and Jacklin, C. *The Psychology of Sex Differences.* Stanford: Stanford University Press, 1974.

McConaghy, N. "Penile Volume Responses to Moving and Still Pictures of Male and Female Nudes." *Archives of Sexual Behavior* 3:565-70, 1974.

McCrary, J., and Gutierrez, L. "The Homosexual Person in the Military and in National Security Employment." *Journal of Homosexuality* 5(1,2):115-46, 1979/1980.

McDougall, J. K., et al. "Cervical Carcinoma: Detection of Herpes Simplex Virus RNA in Cells Undergoing Neoplastic Change." *International Journal of Cancer* 25:1-8, 1980.

McEwen, B. "Neural Gonadal Steroid Actions." *Science* 211(4488):1303-11, 1981.

McGee, E. A. *Too Little, Too Late: Services for Teenage Parents.* New York: Ford Foundation, 1982.

McGhee, P. E., and Frueh, T. "Television Viewing and the Learning of Sex-role Stereotypes." *Sex Roles* 6:179-88, 1980.

McGuinness, D., and Pribram, K. "The Origins of Sensory Bias in the Development of Gender Differences in Perception and Cognition." In Bortner, M. (ed.), *Cognitive Growth and Development: Essays in Honor of Herbert G. Birch,* pp. 3-56. New York: Brunner/Mazel, 1978.

McGuire, L., and Wagner, N. "Sexual Dysfunction in Women Who Were Molested as Children: One Response Pattern and Suggestions for Treatment." *Journal of Sex & Marital Therapy* 4:11-15, 1978.

McGuire, R. J.; Carlisle, J. M.; and Young, B. G. "Sexual Deviations as Conditioned Behavior: A Hypothesis." *Behavioral Research and Therapy* 2:185-90, 1965.

McIntyre, J. "Victim Response to Rape: Alternative Outcomes." Final report to the National Institute of Mental Health, R01MH 29043, Rockville, Md., 1980.

Mack, T. M., et al. "Estrogens and Endometrial Cancer in a Retirement Community." *New England Journal of Medicine* 294:1262-67, 1976.

McKinley, H., and Drew, B. "The Nursing Home: Death of Sexual Expression." *Health and Social Work* 2(3):180-87, August 1977.

MacKinnon, C. A. *Sexual Harassment of Working Women.* New Haven: Yale University Press, 1979.

Macklin, E. D. "Unmarried Heterosexual Cohabitation on the University Campus." In Wiseman, J. P. (ed.), *The Social Psychology of Sex,* pp. 108-42. New York: Harper & Row, 1976.

————. "Review of Research on Nonmarital Cohabitation in the United States." In Murstein, B. I. (ed.), *Exploring Intimate Life Styles,* pp. 197-243. New York: Springer, 1978.

————. "Nontraditional Family Forms: A Decade of Research." *Journal of Marriage and the Family* 42:905-22, 1980.

McLane, M., Krop, H., and Mehta, J. "Psychosexual Adjustment and Counseling after Myocardial Infarction." *Annals of Internal Medicine* 92:514-19, 1980.

MacLusky, N., and Naftolin, F. "Sexual Differentiation of the Central Nervous System." *Science* 211(4488):1294-1303, 1981.

MacNamara, D. E. and Sagarin, E. *Sex, Crime, and the Law.* New York: Free Press, 1977.

McNeill, J. J. *The Church and the Homosexual.* Kansas City, Kan.: Sheed Andrews and McMeel, 1976.

McWhirter, D. P., and Mattison, A. M. *The Male Couple: How Relationships Develop.* N.J.: Prentice-Hall, 1984.

Macionis, J. J. "Intimacy, Structure and Process in Interpersonal Relationships." *Alternative Lifestyles* 1:113-30, 1978.

Maclean's, "Straight Talk in Gay Town." pp. 27-28, 23 February 1981.

Madore, C., et al. "A Study on the Effects of Induced Abortion on Subsequent Pregnancy Outcome." *American Journal of Obstetrics and Gynecology* 139(5):516-21, 1981.

Maine, D. "Depo: The Debate Continues." *Family Planning Perspectives* 10:342, 1978.

Malamuth, N. "Rape Proclivity among Males." *Journal of Social Issues* 37:138-57, 1981.

Malamuth, N., and Donnerstein, E. (Eds.). *Pornography and Sexual Aggression.* New York: Academic Press, 1984.

Malamuth, N., and Spinner, B. "A Longitudinal Content Analysis of Sexual Violence in the Best-Selling Erotic Magazines." *Journal of Sex Research* 16(3):226-37, 1980.

Malatesta, V. J. "Alcohol Effects on the Orgasmic-Ejaculatory Response in Human Males." *The Journal of Sex Research* 15:101-7, 1979.

Malatesta, V. J., et al. "Acute Alcohol Intoxication and Female Orgasmic Response." *Journal of Sex Research* 18:1-17, 1982.

Malinowski, B. *The Sexual Life of Savages.* New York: Harcourt, Brace & World, 1929.

Mann, J. I., and Inman, W. H. "Oral Contraceptives and Death from Myocardial Infarction." *British Medical Journal* 2:245-48, 1975.

Mannion, R. "Penile Laceration," (letter). *Journal of the American Medical Association* 224:1763, 1973.

Manno, J. E., et al. "Motor and Mental Performance with Marijuana: Relationship to Administered Dose of Δ^9-tetrahydrocannabinol and Its Interaction with Alcohol." In Miller, L. L. (ed.), *Marihuana: Effects on Human Behavior,* pp. 45-72. New York: Academic Press, 1974.

Marcus, I. M., and Francis, J. J. (Eds.). *Masturbation: From Infancy to Senescence.* New York: International Universities Press, 1975.

Marcus, S. *The Other Victorians.* New York: Bantam Books, 1967.

Margolin, G. "A Social Learning Approach to Intimacy." In M. Fisher and G. Stricker (eds.), *Intimacy,* pp. 175-201. New York: Plenum Press, 1982.

Marin, Peter. "A Revolution's Broken Promises." *Psychology Today*, pp. 50-57, July 1983.

Mark, E. W., and Alper, T. G. "Sex Differences in Intimacy Motivation." *Psychology of Women Quarterly* 5(2):164-69, 1980.

Markel, N., Long, J., and Saine, T. "Sex Effects on Conversational Interaction." *Human Communication Research* 2:356-64, 1976.

Markle, G. E. "Sex Ratio at Birth: Values, Variance and Some Determinants." *Demography* 11:131-42, 1974.

Marmor, J. " 'Normal' and 'Deviant' Sexual Behavior." *Journal of the AMA* 217:165-70, 1971.

———. (Ed.). *Homosexual Behavior*. New York: Basic Books, 1980.

———. "Clinical Aspects of Male Homosexuality." In Marmor, J. (ed.), *Homosexual Behavior*, pp. 267-79. New York: Basic Books, 1980a.

———. "Discussion of Paper by H. T. Engelhardt." In Masters, W. H., et al. (eds.), *Ethical Issues in Sex Therapy and Research*, Vol. 2, pp. 273-76. Boston: Little, Brown, 1980b.

Marshall, D. "Sexual Behavior on Mangaia." In Marshall, D., and Suggs, R. (eds.), *Human Sexual Behavior*, pp. 103-62. New York: Basic Books, 1971.

Marshall, D., and Suggs, R. (Eds). *Human Sexual Behavior*. New York: Basic Books, 1971.

Marshall, W. A. "Growth and Sexual Maturation in Normal Puberty." *Clinics in Endocrinology and Metabolism* 4:3-25, 1975.

———. *Human Growth and Its Disorders*. New York: Academic Press, 1977.

Marshall, W. A., and Tanner, J. M. "Variation in the Pattern of Pubertal Changes in Girls." *Archives of Disease in Childhood* 44:291-303, 1969.

———. "Variation in the Pattern of Pubertal Changes in Boys." *Archives of Disease in Childhood* 45:13-23, 1970.

Martin, C. E. "Sexual Activity in the Aging Male." In Money, J., and Musaph, H. (eds.), *Handbook of Sexology*, pp. 813-24. New York: Elsevier/North Holland Biomedical Press, 1977.

Martinez, G. A., and Dodd, D. A. "Milk Feeding Patterns in the U.S. During the First 12 Months of Life." *Pediatrics* 68:863-68, 1981.

Martinson, F. M. "Eroticism in Infancy and Childhood." *Journal of Sex Research* 12:251-62, 1976.

———. "Childhood Sexuality." In Wolman, B. B., and Money, J. (eds.), *Handbook of Human Sexuality*, pp. 29-59. Englewood Cliffs, N.J.: Prentice-Hall, 1980.

———. "Eroticism in Infancy and Childhood." In L. L. Constantine and F. M. Martinson (eds.), *Children and Sex: New Findings, New Perspectives*, pp. 23-35. Boston: Little, Brown, 1981.

Marx, J. L. "Dysmenorrhea: Basic Research Leads to a Rational Therapy." *Science* 205:175-76, 1979.

Mason, E. J., and Bramble, W. J. *Understanding and Conducting Research*. New York: McGraw-Hill, 1978.

Masters, W. H. "Update on Sexual Physiology." Paper presented at the Masters & Johnson Institute's Postgraduate Workshop on Human Sexual Function and Dysfunction. St. Louis, Mo.: 20 October 1980.

———. "Update on Sexual Physiology." Presented at the Masters & Johnson Institute's Advanced Workshop on Human Sexuality. St. Louis, Mo.: 12 June 1982.

Masters, W. H., et al. *Ethical Issues in Sex Therapy and Research*, Vol. 2. Boston: Little, Brown, 1980.

———. "Outcome Studies at the Masters & Johnson Institute." Presented at the 6th World Congress of Sexology. Washington, D.C.: 26 May 1983.

Masters, W. H., and Johnson, V. E. *Human Sexual Response*. Boston: Little, Brown, 1966.

———. *Human Sexual Inadequacy*. Boston: Little, Brown, 1970.

———. *The Pleasure Bond*. New York: Bantam Books, 1976.

———. *Homosexuality in Perspective*. Boston: Little, Brown, 1979.

———. "Facts and Fallacies in Sexual Physiology." Paper presented at the Fifth National Meeting of the American Association of Sex Educators, Counselors, and Therapists. San Francisco: 4 April 1981.

Masters, W. H.; Johnson, V. E.; and Kolodny, R. C. Unpublished observations, 1980.

Masur, F. T. "Resumption of Sexual Activity Following Myocardial Infarction." *Sexuality and Disability*. 2:98-114, 1979.

Matthews, R. J. *The Human Adventure: A Study Course for Christians on Sexuality*. Lima, Ohio: C.S.S. Publishing Co., 1980.

May, R. "Mood Shifts and the Menstrual Cycle." *Journal of Psychosomatic Research* 20:125-30, 1976.

Mayer, J. "Viewers' Objections May Block TV Ads for Contraceptives." *The Wall Street Journal*, p. 21, 21 January 1982.

Mehrabian, A. *Nonverbal Communication*. Chicago: Aldine Atherton, 1972.

Mehta, J., and Krop, H. "The Effect of Myocardial Infarction on Sexual Functioning." *Sexuality and Disability* 2:115-21, 1979.

Meilaender, G. "The Fetus as Parasite and Mushroom: Judith Jarvis Thomson's Defense of Abortion." *Linacre Quarterly* 46(2):126-35, May 1979.

Meiselman, K. C. *Incest*. San Francisco: Jossey-Bass, 1978.

Mendelson, J. H., et al. "Plasma Testosterone Levels Before, During, and After Chronic Marihuana Smoking." *New England Journal of Medicine* 291:1051-55, 1974.

Mendola, M. *The Mendola Report: A New Look at Gay Couples*. New York: Crown Publishers, 1980.

Meredith, N. "The Gay Dilemma." *Psychology Today* 18(1):56-62, January 1984.

Merriam, A. "Aspects of Sexual Behavior among the Bala (Basongye)." In Marshall, D., and Suggs, R. (eds.), *Hu-*

man *Sexual Behavior,* pp. 71–102. New York: Basic Books, 1971.

Merz, B. "Greater IUD Perforation Risk, Lactation Linked." *Journal of the American Medical Association* 249:3152, 1983.

Messenger, J. "Sex and Repression in an Irish Folk Community." In Marshall, D., and Suggs, R. (eds.), *Human Sexual Behavior,* pp. 3–37. New York: Basic Books, 1971.

Messenger, M. *The Breastfeeding Book.* New York: Von Nostrand Reinhold, 1982.

Metzger, D. "It Is Always the Woman Who Is Raped." *American Journal of Psychiatry* 133:405–8, 1976.

Meyer, J. K., and Hoopes, J. E. "The Gender Dysphoria Syndromes: A Position Statement on So-Called 'Transsexualism.'" *Plastic and Reconstructive Surgery* 54:444–51, 1974.

Meyer, J. K., and Reter, D. J. "Sex Reassignment." *Archives of General Psychiatry* 36:1010–15, 1979.

Meyer-Bahlburg, H. F. "Sex Hormones and Male Homosexuality in Comparative Perspective." *Archives of Sexual Behavior* 6:297–325, 1977.

———. "Behavioral Effects of Estrogen Treatment in Human Males." *Pediatrics* 62(Supplement):1171–77, 1978.

———. "Sex Hormones and Female Homosexuality: A Critical Examination." *Archives of Sexual Behavior* 8:101–20, 1979.

Meyers, Robert. *D.E.S.—The Bitter Pill.* New York: Seaview/Putnam, 1983.

Meyners, R., and Wooster, C. *Sexual Style.* New York and London: Harcourt Brace Jovanovich, 1979.

Michael, R. P., and Keverne, E. B. "Primate Sex Pheromones of Vaginal Origin." *Nature* (London) 225:84–85, 1970.

Michaud, S. G., and Aynesworth, H. *The Only Living Witness.* New York: LindenPress/Simon and Schuster, 1983.

Miller v. California. 413 U.S. 15 (1973).

Miller, C. W. "Survival and Ambulation Following Hip Fracture." *Journal of Bone and Joint Surgery* 60A:930–34, 1978.

Miller, D. B. "Sexual Practices and Administrative Policies in Long Term Care Institutions." In R. L. Solnick (ed.), *Sexuality and Aging* (revised), pp. 163–75. Los Angeles: University of Southern California Press, 1978.

Miller, H. *Tropic of Cancer.* New York: Grove Press, 1961.

———. *Tropic of Capricorn.* New York: Grove Press, 1961a.

Miller, J. (Ed.). *The Rolling Stone Illustrated History of Rock & Roll.* New York: Random House, 1980.

Miller, W. R., and Lief, H. I. "Masturbatory Attitudes, Knowledge and Experience: Data from the Sex Knowledge and Attitude Test (SKAT)." *Archives of Sexual Behavior* 5:447–67, 1976.

Millett, K. *Sexual Politics.* New York: Doubleday, 1970.

Mintz, J., et al. "Sexual Problems of Heroin Addicts." *Archives of General Psychiatry* 31:700–703, 1974.

Mirin, S., et al. "Opiate Use and Sexual Function." *American Journal of Psychiatry* 137:909–15, 1980.

Mishell, D. R., Jr. "Current Status of Contraceptive Steroids and the Intrauterine Device." *Clinical Obstetrics and Gynecology* 17(1):35–51, 1974.

———. "Contraception." *American Journal of Diseases of Children* 132:912–20, 1978.

———. "Noncontraceptive Health Benefits of Oral Steroidal Contraceptives." *American Journal of Obstetrics and Gynecology* 142:809–16, 1982.

Moghissi, K. S. "Accuracy of Basal Body Temperature for Ovulation Detection." *Fertility and Sterility* 27:1415–21, 1976.

Mohr, J. C. *Abortion in America: The Origins and Evolution of National Policy, 1800–1900.* New York: Oxford University Press, 1978.

Mohr, J. W.; Turner, R. E.; and Jerry, M. B. *Pedophilia and Exhibitionism.* Toronto: University of Toronto Press, 1964.

Monat, R. K. *Sexuality and the Mentally Retarded.* San Diego, Calif.: College-Hill Press, 1982.

Money, J. "Ablatio Penis: Normal Male Infant Sex-Reassigned as a Girl." *Archives of Sexual Behavior* 4:65–72, 1975.

———. "Childhood: The Last Frontier in Sex Research." *The Sciences,* 16(6):12–15 , 1976.

———. *Love and Love Sickness.* Baltimore: Johns Hopkins University Press, 1980.

Money, J., and Bohmer, C. "Prison Sexology: Two Personal Accounts of Masturbation, Homosexuality, and Rape." *Journal of Sex Research* 16:258–66, 1980.

Money, J., and Ehrhardt, A. E. *Man & Woman, Boy & Girl.* Baltimore: Johns Hopkins University Press, 1972.

Money, J.; Jobaris, R.; and Furth, G. "Apotemnophilia: Two Cases of Self-Demand Amputation as a Paraphilia." *Journal of Sex Research* 13:115–25, 1977.

Money, J., and Ogunro, C. "Behavioral Sexology: Ten Cases of Genetic Male Intersexuality with Impaired Prenatal and Pubertal Androgenization." *Archives of Sexual Behavior* 3:181–205, 1974.

Money, J., and Russo, A. J. "Homosexual Outcome of Discordant Gender Identity/Role in Childhood: Longitudinal Follow-Up." *Journal of Pediatric Psychology* 4(1):29–41, 1979.

Money, J., and Schwartz, M. "Dating, Romantic and Nonromantic Friendships, and Sexuality in 17 Early-Treated Adrenogenital Females, Aged 16–25." In Lee, P. A., et al. (eds.), *Congenital Adrenal Hyperplasia.* Baltimore: University Park Press, 1977.

Money, J., and Wiedeking, C. "Gender Identity/Role: Normal Differentiation and Its Transpositions." In Wolman, B. B., and Money, J. (eds.), *Handbook of Human Sexuality,* pp. 269–84. Englewood Cliffs, N.J.: Prentice-Hall, 1980.

Montagu, Ashley. *Touching—The Human Significance of the Skin.* New York: Harper & Row, 1977.

Moody, Lt. J., and Hayes, V. "Responsible Reporting: The Initial Step." In Warner, C. (ed.), *Rape and Sexual Assault.* Germantown, Md.: Aspen Systems Corp., 1980.

Mooney, T. O.; Cole, T. M.; and Chilgren, R. A. *Sexual Options for Paraplegics and Quadraplegics.* Boston: Little, Brown, 1975.

Moore, K. A., et al. *Teenage Motherhood: Social and Economic Consequences.* Washington, D.C.: The Urban Institute, 1979.

Moos, R. H. "Typology of Menstrual Cycle Symptoms." *American Journal of Obstetrics and Gynecology* 103:390-402, 1969.

Morgan, W. F. "Talks with Young Men on the Sexual Function." *New York Medical Times XXIV,* p. 334, 1896.

Morin, Jack. *Anal Pleasure and Health.* Burlingame, Calif.: Down There Press, 1981.

Morris, J. *Conundrum.* New York: New American Library, 1974.

Mott, F. L., and Maxwell, N. L. "School-age Mothers: 1968 and 1979." *Family Planning Perspectives* 13:287-92, 1981.

Moulton, R. "Divorce in the Middle Years: The Lonely Woman and the Reluctant Man." *American Journal of Psychoanalysis* 8:235-50, 1980.

Muller, J. "On Preferential/Prescriptive Marriage ..." *American Anthropologist* 75(5):1563-76, 1973.

Munjack, D. J., and Kanno, P. H. "Retarded Ejaculation: A Review." *Archives of Sexual Behavior* 8:139-50, 1979.

Munjack, D. J., and Oziel, L. J. *Sexual Medicine and Counseling in Office Practice.* Boston: Little, Brown, 1980.

Murdock, G. *Social Structure.* New York: Macmillan, 1949.

Murphy, F. X. "Of Sex and the Catholic Church." *Atlantic Monthly* 247(2):44-57, February 1981.

Murphy, W. D., et al. "Sexual Dysfunction and Treatment in Alcoholic Women." *Sexuality and Disability* 3:240-55, 1980.

Murstein, B. I. *Love, Sex and Marriage Through the Ages.* New York: Springer, 1974.

———. *Who Will Marry Whom? Theories and Research in Marital Choice.* New York: Springer, 1976.

———. (Ed.). *Exploring Intimate Life Styles.* New York: Springer, 1978.

———. "Swinging, or Comarital Sex." In Murstein, B. I. (ed.), *Exploring Intimate Life Styles,* pp. 109-30. New York: Springer, 1978a.

———. "Mate Selection in the 1970s." *Journal of Marriage and the Family* 42:777-92, 1980.

Muus, R. E. "Mental Health Implications of a Preventive Psychiatry Program in the Light of Research Findings." *Marriage and Family Living* 22:150-56, 1960.

Nabokov, V. *Lolita.* New York: McGraw-Hill, 1970.

Nadelson, C. C. "Rapist and Victim." *New England Journal of Medicine* 297:784-85, 1977.

———. "The Emotional Impact of Abortion." In Notman, M. T., and Nadelson, C. C. (eds.), *The Woman Patient, vol. 1,* pp. 173-79. New York: Plenum Press, 1978.

Nadelson, C. C., et al. "A Follow-up Study of Rape Victims." *American Journal of Psychiatry* 139:1266-70, 1982.

Naftolin, F. "Understanding the Bases of Sex Differences." *Science* 211(4488):1263-64, 1981.

Nahmias, A. J., et al. "Perinatal Risk Associated with Maternal Genital Herpes Simplex Virus Infection." *American Journal of Obstetrics and Gynecology* 110:825-32, 1971.

Nakashima, I., and Zakus, G. "Incest: Review and Clinical Experience." *Pediatrics* 60:696-701, 1977.

National Center for Health Statistics, U.S. Department of Health and Human Services, Vol. 30, Number 12, 18 March 1982.

National Coordinating Group for Male Contraceptives, Shanghai. "Gossypol: A New Male Contraceptive." *Chinese Medical Journal* 58:455-58, 1978.

Nelson, B. "Etan Patz Case Puts New Focus on a Sexual Disorder, Pedophilia." *New York Times,* 26 May 1983.

Nelson, C. "Victims of Rape: Who Are They?" In Warner, C. (ed.), *Rape and Sexual Assault,* pp. 9-26. Germantown, Md.: Aspen Systems Corp., 1980.

Nelson, J. B. *Embodiment.* Minneapolis, Minn.: Augsbury Publishing House, 1978.

Nelson, N. M. et al. "A Randomized Clinical Trial of the Leboyer Approach to Childbirth." *New England Journal of Medicine* 302:655-60, 1980.

Nemec, E. P.; Mansfield, L.; and Kennedy, J. W. "Heart Rate and Blood Pressure Response During Sexual Activity in Normal Males." *American Heart Journal* 92:274-77, 1976.

Nerurkar, L. S., et al. "Survival of Herpes Simplex Virus in Water Specimens Collected from Hot Tubs in Spa Facilities and on Plastic Surfaces." *Journal of the American Medical Association* 250:3081-83, 1983.

Newhouse, M. L., et al. "A Case Control Study of Carcinoma of the Ovary." *British Journal of Preventive and Social Medicine* 31(3):148-53, September 1977.

Newman, G., and Nichols, C. R. "Sexual Activities and Attitudes in Older Persons." *Journal of the American Medical Association* 173:117-19, 1960.

Newman, L. E. "Treatment for the Parents of Feminine Boys." *American Journal of Psychiatry* 133:683-87, 1976.

Newton, D. E. "Homosexual Behavior and Child Molestation: A Review of the Evidence." *Adolescence* 13:29-43, 1978.

New York Times, "Red Cross Barring Some For Blood." 7 March 1983.

Nillson, L., et al. *A Child Is Born.* New York: Delacorte/Seymour Lawrence, 1977.

Niswander, K. R.; Singer, J.; and Singer M. "Psychological Reaction to Therapeutic Abortion: II. Objective Response." *American Journal of Obstetrics and Gynecology* 114:29–33, 1972.

Nora, A. H., and Nora, J. J. "Maternal Exposure to Exogenous Progestogen/Estrogen as a Potential Cause of Birth Defects." *Advances in Planned Parenthood* 12(3):156–69, 1978.

Nora, J. J., and Nora, A. H. "Birth Defects and Oral Contraceptives." *Lancet* 1:941–42, 1973.

Norris, R. V., and Sullivan, C. *PMS—Premenstrual Syndrome.* New York: Rawson Wade, 1983.

Notman, M. T. "A Psychological Consideration of Mastectomy." In Notman, M. T., and Nadelson, C. C. (eds.), *The Woman Patient,* vol. 1, pp. 247–55. New York: Plenum Press, 1978.

Notman, M. T., and Nadelson, C. C. "The Rape Victim: Psychodynamic Considerations." *American Journal of Psychiatry* 133:408–13, 1976.

———. (Eds.). *The Woman Patient,* vol. 1. New York: Plenum Press, 1978.

Nutter, D. E., and Condron, M. K. "Sexual Fantasy and Activity Patterns of Females with Inhibited Sexual Desire Versus Normal Controls." *Journal of Sex & Marital Therapy* 9:276–82, 1983.

Offer, D., and Offer, J. *From Teenage to Young Manhood.* New York: Basic Books, 1975.

Offit, A. *The Sexual Self.* New York: Ballantine, 1977.

Olweus, D., et al. "Testosterone, Aggression, Physical and Personality Dimensions in Normal Adolescent Males." *Psychosomatic Medicine* 42:253–70, 1980.

O'Connor, J. J. "T.V.: 'Intimate Agony'." *New York Times,* 21 March 1983.

O'Neill, N. *The Marriage Premise.* New York: Bantam Books, 1978.

O'Neill, N., and O'Neill, G. *Open Marriage: A New Life Style for Couples.* New York: M. Evans and Company, 1972.

———. "Open Marriage: A Synergic Model." In DeBurger, J. E. (ed.), *Marriage Today: Problems, Issues and Alternatives,* pp. 287–96. New York: Wiley, 1977.

Oriel, J. D., et al. "Genital Yeast Infections." *British Medical Journal* 4:761–64, 1972.

Orr, M. T. "Sex Education and Contraceptive Education in U.S. Public High Schools." *Family Planning Perspectives* 14:304–13, 1982.

Ortner, S. B., and Whitehead, H. (Eds.). *Sexual Meanings — The Cultural Construction of Gender and Sexuality.* New York: Cambridge University Press, 1981.

Ory, H. W.; Rosenfeld, A.; and Landman, L. C. "The Pill at 20: An Assessment." *Family Planning Perspectives* 12:278–83, 1980.

Orzek, A. M. "Sexual Assault: The Female Victim, Her Male Partner, and Their Relationship." *Personnel & Guidance Journal* 62(3):143–46, Nov. 1983.

Osborne, N. G., Grubin, L., and Pratson, L. "Vaginitis in Sexually Active Women: Relationship To Nine Sexually Transmitted Organisms." *Obstetrics and Gynecology* 142:962–67, 1982.

Osofsky, J. D., et al. "Psychologic Effects of Legal Abortion." *Clinical Obstetrics and Gynecology* 14(1):215–34, 1971.

Ouellette, E. M., et al. "Adverse Effects on Offspring of Maternal Alcohol Abuse During Pregnancy." *New England Journal of Medicine* 297:528–30, 1977.

Paganini-Hill, A., et al. "Menopausal Estrogen Therapy and Hip Fractures." *Annals of Internal Medicine* 95:28–31, 1981.

Paige, K. "The Declining Taboo Against Menstrual Sex." *Psychology Today* 12(7):50–51, 1978.

Paige, K., and Paige, J. *The Politics of Reproductive Ritual.* Berkeley, Calif.: University of California Press, 1981.

Paige, K. E. "Woman Learn to Sing the Menstrual Blues." *Psychology Today,* pp. 41–46, April 1973.

Palmore, E. Published reactions to the Kinsey Report. *Social Forces* 31:165–70, December 1952.

Paludi, M. A., and Bauer, W. D. "Goldberg Revisited: What's in an Author's Name?" *Sex Roles* 9:387–90, 1983.

Pam, A.; Plutchik, R.; and Conte, H. R. "Love: A Psychometric Approach." *Psychological Reports* 37:83–88, 1975.

Parlee, M. B. "The Premenstrual Syndrome." *Psychological Bulletin* 80:454–65, 1973.

Parrinder, G. *Sex in the World's Religions.* New York: Oxford University Press, 1980.

Parsons, J. E. "Psychosexual Neutrality: Is Anatomy Destiny?" In Parsons, J. E. (ed.), *The Psychobiology of Sex Differences and Sex Roles,* pp. 3–29. New York: Hemisphere Publishing Corp., 1980.

Pauly, I. B. "Female Transsexualism: Part I." *Archives of Sexual Behavior* 3:487–507, 1974.

Peele, S. with Brodsky, A. *Love and Addiction.* New York: New American Library, 1976.

Peplau, L. A., and Gordon, S. L. "The Intimate Relationships of Lesbians and Gay Men." In E. R. Allgeier and N. B. McCormick (eds.), *Gender Roles and Sexual Behavior.* Palo Alto, Calif.: Mayfield, 1982.

Peplau, L. A., Padesky, C., and Hamilton, M. "Satisfaction in Lesbian Relationships." *Journal of Homosexuality* 8(2):23–35, 1982.

Perelman, M. A. "Treatment of Premature Ejaculation." In Leiblum, S. R., and Pervin, L. A. (eds.), *Principles and Practice of Sex Therapy,* pp. 199–233. New York: Guilford Press, 1980.

Perkins, R. P. "Sexual Behavior and Response in Relation to Complications of Pregnancy." *American Journal of Obstetrics and Gynecology* 134:498–505, 1979.

Perlmutter, J. F. "A Gynecological Approach to Menopause." In M. T. Notman and C. C. Nadelson (eds.), *The Woman Patient,* pp. 323–35. New York: Plenum Press, 1978.

Perry, J. D., and Whipple, B. "Pelvic Muscle Strength of Female Ejaculators: Evidence in Support of a New Theory of Orgasm." *Journal of Sex Research* 17(1):22-39, 1981.

Persky, H. "Reproductive Hormones, Moods and the Menstrual Cycle." In Friedman, R. C.; Richard, R. M.; and Vande Wiele, R. L. (eds.), *Sex Difference in Behavior*, pp. 455-66. New York: Wiley, 1974.

Persky, H., et al. "Plasma Testosterone Level and Sexual Behavior of Couples." *Archives of Sexual Behavior* 7:157-73, 1978.

Person, E., and Ovesey, L. "Transvestism: New Perspectives." *Journal of the American Academy of Psychoanalysis* 6:301-23, 1978.

Peterman, D. J.; Ridley, C. A.; and Anderson, S. M. "A Comparison of Cohabitating and Non-Cohabitating College Students." *Journal of Marriage and the Family* 36:344-54, 1974.

Peter, J. B., Bryson, Y., and Lovett, M. A. "Genital Herpes: Urgent Questions, Elusive Answers." *Diagnostic Medicine*, pp. 71-74, 76-88, March/April 1982.

Peters, J. "Children Who Are Victims of Sexual Assault and the Psychology of Offenders." *American Journal of Psychotherapy* 30:398-421, 1976.

Petersen, A. C. "Biopsychosocial Processes in the Development of Sex-related Differences." In Parsons, J. E. (ed.), *The Psychobiology of Sex Differences and Sex Roles*, pp. 31-55. New York: Hemisphere Publishing Corp., 1980.

Petersen, J. R. "Desire." *Playboy*, p. 180 , December 1980.

Petitti, D. B., and Wingerd, J. "Use of Oral Contraceptives, Cigarette Smoking, and Risk of Subarachnoid Hemorrhage." *Lancet* 2:234-35, 1978.

Petronius. *The Satyricon*. New York: New American Library, 1959.

Petty, J. A. "An Investigation of Factors Which Differentiate Between Types of Cohabitation." Unpublished master's thesis, Indiana University, 1975.

Pfeiffer, E., and Davis, G. C. "Determinants of Sexual Behavior in Middle and Old Age." *Journal of the American Geriatrics Society* 20:151-58, 1972.

Pfeiffer, E., Verwoerdt, A., and Davis, G. C. "Sexual Behavior in Middle Life." *American Journal of Psychiatry* 128:1262-67, 1972.

Pines, A. M., Aronson, E., and Kafry, D. *Burnout: From Tedium to Personal Growth*. New York: Free Press, 1981.

Piotrow, P. T.; Rinehart, W.; and Schmidt, J. C. "IUDs: An Update on Safety, Effectiveness, and Research." *Population Reports*, Series B(3): May 1979.

Pirke, K. M.; Kockott, G.; and Dittmar, F. "Psychosexual Stimulation and Plasma Testosterone in Man." *Archives of Sexual Behavior* 3:577-84, 1974.

Pivar, D. J. *Purity Crusade, Sexual Morality, and Social Control, 1868-1900*. Westport, Conn.: Greenwood Press, 1973.

Plapinger, L., and McEwen, B. S. "Gonadal Steroid-Brain Interactions in Sexual Differentiation." In Hutchison, J. B. (ed.), *Biological Determinants of Sexual Behavior*, pp. 153-218. New York: Wiley, 1978.

Platt, R., Rice, P. A., and McCormack, W. M. "Risk of Acquiring Gonorrhea and Prevalence of Abnormal Adnexal Findings among Women Recently Exposed to Gonorrhea." *Journal of the American Medical Association* 250:3205-09, 1983.

Platzker, A. C.; Lew, C. D.; and Stewart D. "Drug 'Administration' Via Breast Milk." *Hospital Practice*, pp. 111-22, September 1980.

Pleck, Joseph H. *The Myth of Masculinity*. Cambridge, Mass.: MIT Press, 1981.

Podolsky, S. "Erectile Impotence in the Diabetes Patient." *Practical Gastroenterology* 7(1):40-43, Jan./Feb. 1983.

Pogrebin, L. C. *Growing Up Free: Raising Your Child in the 80's*. New York: McGraw-Hill Book Co., 1980.

Pomeroy, W. B. "The Masters-Johnson Report and the Kinsey Tradition." In Brecher, R., and Brecher, E. (eds.), *An Analysis of Human Sexual Response*, pp. 111-23. New York: Signet Books, 1966.

———. *Your Child and Sex: A Guide for Parents*. New York: Delacorte, 1976.

Pomeroy, W. B., Flax, C. C., and Wheeler, C. C. *Taking a Sex History*. New York: Macmillan, 1982.

Pope, K. S. "Defining and Studying Romantic Love." In Pope, K. S. (ed.), *On Love and Loving*, pp. 1-26. San Francisco: Jossey-Bass, 1980.

Population Reports. Baltimore, Maryland: Population Information Program, Johns Hopkins University, 1983.

Postman, Neil. *The Disappearance of Childhood*. New York: Delacorte Press, 1982.

Powledge, T. M. "Unnatural Selection." In H. B. Holmes, B. B. Hoskins, and Michael Gross (eds.), *The Custom-Made Child? Women Centered Perspectives*. Clifton, N.J.: Humana Press, 1981.

Presser, H. B. "Guessing and Misinformation about Pregnancy Risk Among Urban Mothers." *Family Planning Perspectives* 9:111-15, 1977.

Priesand, Sally. *Judaism and the New Woman*. New York: Behrman House, 1975.

Pritchard, J. A., and MacDonald, P. C. *William's Obstetrics*, 16th ed. New York: Appleton-Century-Crofts, 1980.

Proctor, F.; Wagner, N.; and Butler, J. "The Differentiation of Male and Female Orgasm: An Experimental Study." In Wagner, N. (ed.), *Perspectives on Human Sexuality*. New York: Behavioral Publications, 1974.

Quigley, M., and Hammond, C. "Estrogen-replacement Therapy: Help or Hazard?" *New England Journal of Medicine* 301(12):646-49, 1979.

Rabin, B. *The Sensuous Wheeler: Sexual Adjustment for the Spinal Cord Injured*. San Francisco: Multi-Focus Resource Center, 1980.

Rachman, S. J., and Wilson, G. T. *The Effects of Psychologi-*

cal Therapy (second edition). New York: Pergamon Press, 1980.

Rada, R. T. "Alcoholism and the Child Molester." Annals of the New York Academy of Sciences 273:492–96, 1976.

————. (Ed.). Clinical Aspects of the Rapist. New York: Grune & Stratton, 1978.

Rainwater, L. "Marital Sexuality in Four 'Cultures of Poverty.' " In Marshall, D., and Suggs, R. (eds.), Human Sexual Behavior, pp. 187–205. New York: Basic Books, 1971.

Ramcharan, S. The Walnut Creek Contraceptive Drug Study: A Prospective Study of the Side Effects of Oral Contraceptives. Bethesda, Md.: U.S. Department of Health and Human Services, National Institutes of Health (publication #NIH 81-564), 1981.

Ramcharan, S., et al. "The Walnut Creek Contraceptive Study." Journal of Reproductive Medicine 25(Supp.):346–76, 1980.

Ramey, J. W. Intimate Friendships. Englewood Cliffs, N.J.: Prentice-Hall, 1976.

Reese, C. R. "Neurophysiological Studies of Cannabis in Human Subjects." Journal of Substance Use and Abuse 4:118–27, 1977.

Reichman, R. C., et al. "Treatment of Recurrent Genital Herpes Simplex Infections with Oral Acyclovir." Journal of the American Medical Association 251:2103–7, 1984.

Rein, M. F. "Epidemiology of Gonococcal Infections." In Roberts, R. B. (ed.), The Gonococcus, pp. 1–31. New York: Wiley, 1977.

Reiner, N. E., et al. "Asymptomatic Rectal Mucosal Lesions and Hepatitis B Surface Antigen at Sites of Sexual Contact in Homosexual Men with Persistent Hepatitis B Virus Infection." Annals of Internal Medicine 96:170–73, 1982.

Reingold, A. L. "Nonmenstrual Toxic Shock Syndrome: The Growing Picture." Journal of the American Medical Association 249:932, 1983.

Reingold, A. L., et al. "Toxic Shock Syndrome Surveillance in the United States, 1980 to 1981." Annals of Internal Medicine 96(Part 2):875–80, 1982.

Reinisch, J. M. "Fetal Hormones, the Brain, and Human Sex Differences: A Heuristic, Integrative Review of the Recent Literature." Archives of Sexual Behavior 3:51–90, 1974.

————. "Prenatal Exposure to Synthetic Progestins Increases Potential for Aggression in Humans." Science 211:1171–73, 1981.

Reiss, A. J. "The Social Integration of Queers and Peers." In Becker, H. S. (ed.), The Other Side: Perspectives on Deviance, pp. 181–210. New York: Free Press, 1967.

Reiss, B. F. "Psychological Tests in Homosexuality." In Marmor, J. (ed.), Homosexual Behavior, pp. 296–311. New York: Basic Books, 1980.

Reiss, I. L. "The Sexual Renaissance: A Summary and Analysis." Journal of Social Issues 22:123–37, 1966.

————. The Social Context of Premarital Sexual Permissiveness. New York: Holt, Rinehart and Winston, 1967.

————. Family Systems in America, 3rd ed. New York: Holt, Rinehart and Winston, 1980.

Reiss, I. L., et al. A Guide for Researching Heterosexual Relationships. University of Minnesota, Minnesota Family Study Center, 1980.

Rekers, G. A. "Sexual Problems: Behavior Modification." In Wolman, B. B., Egan, J., and Ross, A. O. (eds.), Handbook of Treatment of Mental Disorders in Childhood and Adolescence, pp. 268–96. Englewood Cliffs, N.J.: Prentice-Hall, 1978.

Rekers, G. A., et al. "Sex-role Stereotype and Professional Intervention For Childhood Gender Disturbance." Professional Psychology 9:127–36, 1978.

Rembar, C. The End of Obscenity. New York: Bantam Books, 1969.

Renshaw, D. Incest—Understanding and Treatment. Boston: Little, Brown, 1983.

————. "Inflatable Penile Prosthesis." Journal of the American Medical Association 241:2637–38, 1979.

Report of the Commission on Obscenity and Pornography. New York: Bantam Books, 1970.

Reynolds, W. "The Immigration and Nationality Act and the Rights of Homosexual Aliens." Journal of Homosexuality 5(1,2):79–87, 1979/1980.

Rheingold, H. L., and Cook, K. V. "The Contents of Boys' and Girls' Rooms as an Index of Parents' Behavior." Child Development 46:459–63, 1975.

Richart, R. M., and Barron, B. A. "Screening Strategies for Cervical Cancer and Cervical Intraepithileal Neoplasia." Presented at the American Cancer Society National Conference on Cancer Prevention and Detection. Chicago: 17–19 April 1980.

Rinehart, W. "Postcoital Contraception: An Appraisal." Population Reports, Series J(9):January 1976.

Rinehart, W., and Piotrow, P. T. "OCs: Update on Usage, Safety, and Side Effects." Population Reports, Series A(5):January 1979.

Rivenbark, W. H., III. "Self-disclosure among Adolescents." Psychological Reports 28:35–42, 1971.

Rizley, R. "Psychobiological Bases of Romantic Love." In Pope, K. S., et al., On Love and Loving, pp. 104–13. San Francisco: Jossey-Bass, 1980.

Roach, R. "One View of 'Certain Questions' In the Roman Catholic Community." SIECUS Report 5(3):1+, 1977.

Robbins, M., and Jensen, G. D. "Multiple Orgasm in Males." Journal of Sex Research 14:21–26, 1978.

Robboy, S. J., et al. Prenatal Diethylstilbestrol (DES) Exposure: Recommendations of the Diethylstilbestrol Adenosis (DESAD) Project for the Identification and Management of Exposed Individuals. Washington, D.C.: U.S. Department of Health and Human Services, NIH-Publication No. 81-2049, 1981.

Roberts, C. L., and Lewis, R. A. "The Empty Nest Syndrome." In J. G. Howells (ed.), *Modern Perspectives in the Psychiatry of Middle Age*, pp. 328–36. New York: Brunner/Mazel, 1981.

Robertson, D. H.; McMillan, A.; and Young, H. *Clinical Practice in Sexually Transmissible Diseases*. Kent, England: Pitman Medical, 1980.

Robinson, I., and Jedlicka, D. "Change in Sexual Attitude and Behavior of College Students from 1965 to 1980: A Research Note." *Journal of Marriage and the Family* 44:237–40, 1982.

Robinson, J. E., and Short, R. V. "Changes in Breast Sensitivity at Puberty, During the Menstrual Cycle, and at Parturition." *British Medical Journal* 1:1188–91, 1977.

Robinson, P. A. "What Liberated Males Do." *Psychology Today* 15:81–84, 1981.

Rodgers, D. A., and Ziegler, F. J. "Psychological Reactions to Surgical Contraception." In Fawcett, J. T. (ed.), *Psychological Perspectives on Population*, pp. 306–26. New York: Basic Books, 1973.

Roeske, N. C. "Hysterectomy and Other Gynecological Surgeries: A Psychological View." In Notman, M. T., and Nadelson, C. C. (eds.), *The Woman Patient*, vol. 1, pp. 217–32. New York: Plenum Press, 1978.

Rogers, C. R. *Becoming Partners*. New York: Delacorte Press, 1972.

Rommel, E. "Grade School Blues." *Ms. Magazine*, pp. 32–35, January 1984.

Rosenbaum, M. "When Drugs Come Into the Picture, Love Flies Out the Window: Women Addicts' Love Relationships." *International Journal of the Addictions* 16:1197–1206, 1981.

Rosenberg, L., et al. "Oral Contraceptive Use in Relation to Nonfatal Myocardial Infarction." *American Journal of Epidemiology* 111:59–66, 1980.

Rosenblatt, R. "The Baby in the Factory." *Time*, p. 90, 14 February 1983.

Rosenfeld, A. A., et al. "Parents Fears of Their Children's Developing Sexuality." *Medical Aspects of Human Sexuality* 16(10):96–102, October 1982.

Rosenfield, A., et al. "The Food and Drug Administration and Medroxyprogesterone Acetate: What Are the Issues?" *Journal of the American Medical Association* 249:2922–28, 1983.

Rosenheim, E. "Sexual Attitudes and Regulations in Judaism." In Money, J., and Musaph, H. (eds.), *Handbook of Sexology*, pp. 1315–23. New York: Elsevier/North-Holland, 1977.

Ross, C., and Piotrow, P. T. "Birth Control Without Contraceptives." *Population Reports*, Series I(1):June 1974.

Ross, M. W. "Retrospective Distortion in Homosexual Research." *Archives of Sexual Behavior* 9:523–32, 1980.

Ross, R. K., et al. "A Case-control Study of Menopausal Estrogen Therapy and Breast Cancer." *Journal of the American Medical Association* 243:1635–40, 1980.

Rossi, A. S., and Rossi, P. E. "Body Time and Social Time: Mood Patterns by Menstrual Cycle and Day of Week." *Social Science Research* 6:273–308, 1977.

Roth v. United States 354 U.S. 476 (1957).

Rotheram, M. J., and Weiner, N. "Androgyny, Stress, and Satisfaction." *Sex Roles* 9:151–58, 1983.

Rotkin, I. D. "A Comparison Review of Key Epidemiological Studies in Cervical Cancer Related to Current Searches for Transmissible Agents." *Cancer Research* 33:1353–67, 1973.

Rousseau, S., et al. "The Expectancy of Pregnancy for 'Normal' Infertile Couples." *Fertility & Sterility* 40:768–72, 1983.

Royal College of General Practitioners. *Oral Contraception and Health; An Interim Report from the Oral Contraception Study*. New York: Pitman, 1974.

Royal College of General Practitioners' Oral Contraception Study. "Mortality among Oral-Contraceptive Users." *Lancet* 2:727–31, 8 October 1977.

Rubenstein, C., and Shaver, P. *In Search of Intimacy*. New York: Random House, 1982.

Rubin, G. L. "Ectopic Pregnancy in the United States: 1970 Through 1978." *Journal of the American Medical Association* 249:1725–29, 1983.

Rubin, I. *Sexual Life After Sixty*. New York: Basic Books, 1965.

Rubin, J.; Provenzano, F.; and Luria, Z. "The Eye of the Beholder: Parents' Views on Sex of Newborns." *American Journal of Orthopsychiatry* 44:512–19, 1974.

Rubin, L. "Sex and Sexuality: Women at Midlife." In M. Kirkpatrick (ed.), *Women's Sexual Experiences — Explorations of the Dark Continent*, pp. 61–82. New York: Plenum Press, 1982.

————. *Intimate Strangers: Men and Women Together*. New York: Harper & Row, 1983.

Rubin, R.; Reinisch, J.; and Haskett, R. "Postnatal Gonadal Steroid Effects on Human Behavior." *Science* 211(4488):1318–24, 1981.

Rubin, T. I. *The Angry Book*. New York: Collier, 1970.

Rubin, Z. "Measurement of Romantic Love." *Journal of Personality and Social Psychology* 16(2):265–73, 1970.

————. *Liking and Loving: An Introduction to Social Psychology*. New York: Holt, Rinehart and Winston, 1973.

Rubin, Z., and Shenker, S. "Friendship, Proximity, and Self-disclosure." *Journal of Personality* 46:1–22, 1978.

Rubin, Z., et al. "Self-disclosure in Dating Couples: Sex-roles and the Ethic of Openness." *Journal of Marriage and the Family* 42:305–17, 1980.

Rubinstein, C. "The Modern Art of Courtly Love." *Psychology Today*, pp. 43–49, July 1983.

Ruble, D. N.; Brooks-Gunn, J.; and Clarke, A. "Research on Menstrual-Related Psychological Changes: Alternative Perspectives." In Parsons, J. E. (ed.), *The Psychobiology of Sex Differences and Sex Roles*, pp. 227–43. New York: McGraw-Hill, Hemisphere, 1980.

Ruddle, J., and Ruddle, F. "Mammalian Gonadal Determination and Gametogenesis." *Science* 211(4488):1265–71, 1981.

Rush, F. "The Sexual Abuse of Children: A Feminist Point

of View." In Connell, N., and Wilson, C. (eds.), *Rape: The First Sourcebook for Women*, pp. 65-75. New York: New American Library, 1974.

Russell, Diana E. H. *Rape in Marriage*. New York: Macmillan, 1982.

Ryback, R. S. "Chronic Alcohol Consumption and Menstruation" (letter). *Journal of the American Medical Association* 238:2143, 1977.

Ryder, N. B. "Contraceptive Failure in the United States." *Family Planning Perspectives* 5(3):133-42, 1973.

Saario, T.; Jacklin, C. N.; and Tittle, C. K. "Sex Role Stereotyping in the Public Schools." *Harvard Educational Review* 43:386-416, 1973.

Sacred Congregation for the Doctrine of the Faith. "Declaration on Certain Questions Concerning Sexual Ethics." Translated by the National Catholic News Service. *Origins* 5(31):485-94, 1976.

Sadoff, R. L. "Other Sexual Deviations." In Freedman, A. M.; Kaplan, H. I.; and Sadock, B. J. (eds.), *Comprehensive Textbook of Psychiatry/II*, pp. 1539-44. Baltimore: Williams & Wilkins, 1975.

Safran, C. "What Men Do to Women on the Job: A Shocking Look at Sexual Harassment." *Redbook*, pp. 148+, November 1976.

———. "Sexual Harassment: The View from the Top." *Redbook*, pp. 47-51, March 1981.

Sagarin, E. "Prison Homosexuality and Its Effect on Postprison Sexual Behavior." *Psychiatry* 39:245-57, 1976.

Sager, C. "A Typology of Intimate Relationships." *Journal of Sex & Marital Therapy* 3:83-112, 1977.

Sager, C., et al. *Treating the Remarried Family*. New York: Brunner/Mazel, 1983.

Saghir, M. T., and Robins, E. *Male and Female Homosexuality*. Baltimore: Williams & Wilkins, 1973.

Sairam, M. R., et al. "Isolation, Structure, and Synthesis of a Human Seminal Plasma Peptide with Inhibin-like Activity." *Science* 223:1199-1201, 1984.

Sandberg, E. C. "Psychological Aspects of Contraception." In Sadock, B. J.; Kaplan, H. I.; and Freedman, A. M. (eds.), *The Sexual Experience*, pp. 335-49. Baltimore: Williams & Wilkins, 1976.

Sanders, D., and Bancroft, J. "Hormones and the Sexuality of Women—The Menstrual Cycle." *Clinics in Endocrinology and Metabolism* 11:639-59, 1982.

Sanford, L. T. *Come Tell Me Right Away*. Fayetteville, N.Y.: Ed-U Press, 1982.

Sandfort, T. "Pedophile Relationships in the Netherlands: Alternative Lifestyle for Children?" *Alternative Lifestyles* 5(3):164-83, 1983.

Santen, R. J., et al. "Mechanism of Action of Narcotics in the Production of Menstrual Dysfunction in Women." *Fertility and Sterility* 26:538-48, 1975.

Sarafino, E. "An Estimate of Nationwide Incidence of Sexual Offenses against Children." *Child Welfare* 58:127-34, 1979.

Sarrel, L. J., and Sarrel, P. M. *Sexual Unfolding: Sexual Development and Sex Therapies in Late Adolescence*. Boston: Little, Brown, 1979.

Sarrel, P. "Male Rape." Paper presented at the Annual Meeting of the International Academy of Sex Research. Phoenix, Ariz.: November 1980.

Sarrel, P., and Masters, W. H. "Rape of Men by Men." Submitted for publication, 1981.

Sarrel, P. M., and Masters, W. H. "Sexual Molestation of Men by Women." *Archives of Sexual Behavior* 11:117-31, 1982.

Scacco, A. M., Jr. *Male Rape*. New York: AMS Press, 1982.

Scales, P. "Males and Morals: Teenage Contraceptive Behavior Amid the Double Standard." *Family Coordinator* 26:211-21, 1977.

Scanzoni, J., and Fox, G. L. "Sex Roles, Family and Society: The Seventies and Beyond." *Journal of Marriage and the Family* 42:743-58, 1980.

Schacter, J. "Chlamydial Infections." *New England Journal of Medicine* 298:428-35, 1978.

Schachter, S. "The Interaction of Cognitive and Physiological Determinants of Emotional State." In Berkowitz, L. (ed.), *Advances in Experimental Social Psychology*, vol. 1, pp. 49-80. New York: Academic Press, 1964.

Schaeffer, P. "Bishops' Study Data on Sexuality Published." *St. Louis Post-Dispatch*, p. 9D, 27 February 1981.

Schaffer, K. *Sex Roles and Human Behavior*. Cambridge, Mass.: Winthrop, 1981.

Schatten, G., and Schatten, H. "The Energetic Egg." *The Sciences* 23(5):28-34, 1983.

Schiff, I., and Ryan, K. H. "Benefits of Estrogen Replacement." *Obstetrics and Gynecology Survey* 35:400-411, 1980.

Schlech, W. F., III, et al. "Risk Factors for Development of Toxic Shock Syndrome." *Journal of the American Medical Association* 248:835-39, 1982.

Scholl, T. O., et al. "Effects of Vaginal Spermicides on Pregnancy Outcome." *Family Planning Perspectives* 15:244-50, 1983.

Schiller, P. *The Sex Profession*. Washington, D.C.: Shilmark House, 1981.

Schmidt, C. W., and Lucas, J. "The Short-Term, Intermittent, Conjoint Treatment of Sexual Disorders." In Meyer, J. K. (ed.), *Clinical Management of Sexual Disorders*. Baltimore: Williams & Wilkins, 1976.

Schmidt, G., and Sigusch, V. "Sex Differences in Responses to Psychosexual Stimulation by Films and Slides." *Journal of Sex Research* 6:268-83, 1970.

Schneider, E. L. (Ed.). *The Aging Reproductive System*. New York: Raven Press, 1978.

Schneider, H. "Romantic Love Among the Turu." In Marshall, D., and Suggs, R. (eds.), *Human Sexual Behavior*, pp. 59-70. New York: Basic Books, 1971.

Schofield, C. B. *Sexually Transmitted Diseases*. New York: Churchill Livingstone, 1979.

Schover, L. R., and LoPiccolo, J. "Treatment Effectiveness

for Dysfunctions of Sexual Desire." *Journal of Sex & Marital Therapy* 8:179–97, 1982.

Schover, L. R., et al. "The Multi-axial Problem-oriented Diagnostic System for the Sexual Dysfunctions: An Alternative to DSM-III." *Archives of General Psychiatry* 39:614–19, 1982.

Schreeded, M. T., et al. "Hepatitis B in Homosexual Men: Prevalence of Infection and Factors Related to Transmission." *Journal of Infectious Diseases* 146:7–15, 1982.

Schreiner-Engle, P., and Schiavi, R. "Sexual Arousability in Women." Paper presented at the Sixth Annual Meeting of the Society for Sex Therapy and Research. Cambridge, Mass.: 31 May 1980.

Schreiner-Engel, P., et al. "Sexual Arousability and the Menstrual Cycle." *Psychosomatic Medicine* 43:199–214, 1981.

Schulman, A. "Organs and Orgasms." In Gornick, V., and Moran, B. K. (eds.), *Women in Sexist Society*. New York: Basic Books, 1971.

Schultz, L. G. (Ed.). *The Sexual Victimology of Youth*. Springfield, Ill.: Charles C. Thomas, 1980.

Schumacher, S. "Effectiveness of Sex Therapy." In Gemme, R., and Wheeler, C. C., *Progress in Sexology*, pp. 141–51. New York: Plenum Press, 1977.

Schwartz, D. "Female Fecundity as a Function of Age." *New England Journal of Medicine* 306:404–6, 1982.

Schwartz, M. F. "Incest: Its Many Facets." Presentation at the Special Symposium on Incest of the Masters & Johnson Institute. St. Louis, Mo.: 4 June 1983.

Schwartz, M. F., and Masters, W. H. "Conceptual Factors in the Treatment of Paraphilias: A Preliminary Report." *Journal of Sex & Marital Therapy* 9:3–18, 1983.

Schwartz, M. F., and Bauman, J. E. "Hyperprolactinemia and Sexual Dysfunction in Men." Presented at the Seventh Annual Meeting of the Society for Sex Therapy and Research. New York: March 1981.

Schwartz, M.; Jewelewicz, R.; and Vande Wiele, R. L. "Application of Orthodox Jewish Law to Reproductive Medicine." *Fertility and Sterility* 33:471–74, 1980.

Schwartz, P., et al. "Type II Herpes Simplex Virus and Vulvar Carcinoma in Situ." *New England Journal of Medicine* 305:517–18, 1981.

Science. "News and Comments." *Science* 221:436, 1983.

Scott, J. F. *The Sexual Instinct: Its Use and Dangers as Affecting Heredity and Morals*, 3rd ed. Chicago: Login Brothers, 1930.

Sedney, M. A. "Sex-roles and Coping: Comparison of Feminine, Masculine and Androgynous Women's Responses to Stressful Life Events." Paper presented at the meeting of the Association for Women in Psychology. St. Louis, Mo.: February 1977.

Segal, S. J. "Methods of Fertility Regulation in Clinical Trial." In *Contraception: Science, Technology, and Application*, pp. 135–46. Washington, D.C.: National Academy of Sciences, 1979.

Seibel, M. M., Freeman, M., and Graves, W. "Carcinoma of the Cervix and Sexual Function." *Obstetrics & Gynecology* 55:484–87, 1980.

Semmens, J. P., and Wagner, G. "Estrogen Deprivation and Vaginal Function in Postmenopausal Women." *Journal of the American Medical Association* 248:445–48, 1982.

Senanayake, P., and Kramer, D. G. "Contraception and the Etiology of PID: New Perspectives." Paper presented at the International Symposium on Pelvic Inflammatory Disease. Atlanta: 1–3 April 1980.

Sevely, J., and Bennett, J. "Concerning Female Ejaculation and the Female Prostate." *Journal of Sex Research* 14:1–20, 1978.

Shah, F., and Zelnik, M. "Sexuality in Adolescence." In Wolman, B. B., and Money, J. (eds.), *Handbook of Human Sexuality*, pp. 83–92. Englewood Cliffs, N.J.: Prentice-Hall, 1980.

Shainess, N. "How 'Sex Experts' Debase Sex." *World* 2(1):21–25, 1973.

Shainess, N., and Greenwald, H. "Debate: Are Fantasies During Sexual Relations a Sign of Difficulty?" *Sexual Behavior* 1:38–54, 1971.

Shane, J. M.; Schiff, I.; and Wilson, E. A. *The Infertile Couple: Evaluation and Treatment. Clinical Symposia* 28(5), 1976.

Shanor, K. *The Fantasy Files*. New York: Dial Press, 1977.

Shapiro, S., et al. "Birth Defects and Vaginal Spermicides." *Journal of the American Medical Association* 247:2381–84, 1982.

Sheehy, G. *Prostitution: Hustling in Our Wide-Open Society*. New York: Delacorte, 1973.

———. *Passages: Predictable Crises of Adult Life*. New York: E. P. Dutton, 1976.

———. *Pathfinders*. New York: William Morrow, 1981.

Shepher, J. "Mate Selection among Second Generation Kibbutz Adolescents and Adults: Incest Avoidance and Negative Imprinting." *Archives of Sexual Behavior* 1(4):293–307, 1971.

Shereshefsky, P.; Liebenberg, B.; and Lockman, R. "Maternal Adaptation." In Shereshefsky, P., and Yarrow, L. (eds.), *Psychological Aspects of a First Pregnancy and Early Postnatal Adaptation*. New York: Raven Press, 1974.

Sherfey, M. J. *The Nature and Evolution of Female Sexuality*. New York: Random House, 1972.

Sherif, C. W. "A Social Psychological Perspective on the Menstrual Cycle." In Parsons, J. E. (ed.), *The Psychobiology of Sex Differences and Sex Roles*, pp. 245–68. New York: McGraw-Hill, Hemisphere, 1980.

Sherris, J. D., Lewison, D., and Fox, G. "Update on Condoms — Products, Protection, Promotion." *Population Reports* Series H, Number 6, 1982.

Sherris, J. D., Moore, S. H., and Fox, G. "New Developments in Vaginal Contraception." *Population Reports* Series H, Number 7, Jan./Feb. 1984.

Sherwin, R. V. "Law and Sex." In Money, J., and Musaph,

H. (eds.), *Handbook of Sexology*, pp. 1121–33. Amsterdam: Elsevier/North-Holland, 1977.

Shettles, L., and Rorvik, D., *Your Baby's Sex: Now You Can Choose*. New York: Dodd, Mead, 1970.

Shostak, A., McLouth, G., and Seng, L. *Men and Abortions: Lessons, Losses, and Love*. New York: Praeger, 1984.

Shope, D. F., and Broderick, C. B. "Level of Sexual Experience and Predicted Adjustment in Marriage." *Journal of Marriage and the Family* 29:424–27, 1967.

Shuckit, M. A., et al. "Premenstrual Symptoms and Depression in a University Population." *Diseases of the Nervous System* 36:516–17, 1975.

Siegel, R. K. "Cocaine and Sexual Dysfunction." *Journal of Psychoactive Drugs* 14:71–74, 1982.

Siegelman, M. "Parental Background of Male Homosexuals and Heterosexuals." *Archives of Sexual Behavior* 3:3–18, 1974.

Silber, S. *How to Get Pregnant*. New York: Scribner, 1980.

Silverberg, E. "Cancer Statistics, 1981." *Ca-A Cancer Journal for Clinicians* 31(1):13–28, 1981.

Silverstein, C. *Man to Man: Gay Couples in America*. New York: William Morrow, 1981.

Simenauer, J., and Carroll, D. *Singles: The New Americans*. New York: Simon and Schuster, 1982.

Simon, W., and Gagnon, J. "1967 Research Data." Cited in Gagnon, J. H. *Human Sexualities*, p. 157. Glenview, Ill.: Scott, Foresman, 1977.

Simons, M. "For Haiti's Tourism, the Stigma of AIDS Is Fatal." *New York Times*, 29 November 1983.

Singer, J. L. "Romantic Fantasy in Personality Development." In Pope, K. S. (ed.), *On Love and Loving*, pp. 172–94. San Francisco: Jossey-Bass, 1980.

Singer, J., and Singer, I. "Types of Female Orgasm." *Journal of Sex Research* 8:255–67, 1972.

Singh, B. K., Walton, B. L., and Williams, J. S. "Extramarital Sexual Permissiveness: Conditions and Contingencies." *Journal of Marriage and the Family* 38:701–12, 1976.

Singh, J., et al. "Sex Life and Psychiatric Problems after Myocardial Infarction." *Journal of the Association of Physicians of India* 18:503–07, 1970.

Slovenko, R. *Psychiatry and Law*, pp. 59–60. Boston: Little, Brown, 1973.

————. "Homosexuality and the Law: From Condemnation to Celebration." In Marmor, J. (ed.), *Homosexual Behavior*, pp. 194–218. New York: Basic Books, 1980.

Smith, B. *20th Century Masters of Erotic Art*. New York: Crown, 1980.

Smith, C. G., et al. "Effect of Delta-9 tetrahydrocannabinol (THC) on Secretion of Male Sex-Hormone in Rhesus Monkey." *Pharmacologist* 18:248, 1976.

Smith, D. W. "The Fetal Alcohol Syndrome." *Hospital Practice*, pp. 121–28, October 1979.

Smith, J., and Smith, L. "Co-marital Sex and the Sexual Freedom Movement." *Journal of Sex Research* 6:131–42, 1970.

Smith, P. B., and Mumford, D. M. (Eds.). *Adolescent Pregnancy: New Perspectives for the Health Professional*. Boston: G. K. Hall, 1980.

Smith, P. C. "Saving Lives with a Testicular Self-Examination." *Sexual Medicine Today* 4(6):11–12, 1980.

Smith, T. M. "Specific Approaches and Techniques in the Treatment of Gay Male Alcohol Abusers." *Journal of Homosexuality* 7(4):53–69, 1982.

Smukler, A. J., and Schiebel, D. "Personality Characteristics of Exhibitionists." *Diseases of the Nervous System* 36:600–603, 1975.

Socarides, C. W. "Homosexuality and Medicine." *Journal of the American Medical Association* 212:1199–1202, 1970.

Sokolov, J. J.; Harris, R. T.; and Hecker, M. R. "Isolation of Substances from Human Vaginal Secretions Previously Shown to Be Sex Attractant Pheromones in Higher Primates." *Archives of Sexual Behavior* 5:269–74, 1976.

Solberg, D. A., Butler, J., and Wagner, N. N. "Sexual Behavior in Pregnancy." *New England Journal of Medicine* 288:1098–1103, 1973.

Solomon, R. C. *Love—Emotion, Myth and Metaphor*. Garden City, N.Y.: Anchor Press, 1981.

Somers, A. "Sexual Harassment in Academe: Legal Issues and Definitions." *Journal of Social Issues* 38 (4):23–32, 1982.

Sorenson, R. C. *Adolescent Sexuality in Contemporary America*. New York: World Publishing Co., 1973.

Sorokin, P. A. *The American Sex Revolution*. Boston: Porter Sargent, 1956.

Soules, M. R., and Bremner, W. J. "The Menopause and Climacteric: Endocrinologic Basis and Associated Symptomatology." *Journal of the American Geriatrics Society* 30:547–61, 1982.

Spanier, G. B., and Cole, C. L. "Mate Swapping: Participation, Knowledge, and Values in a Midwestern Community." Presented at the Annual Meeting of the Midwest Sociological Society. Kansas City, Mo.: 21 April 1972.

Spanier, G. B., and Furstenberg, F. F., Jr. "Remarriage after Divorce: A Longitudinal Analysis of Well-being." *Journal of Marriage and the Family* 44:709–20, 1982.

Spaulding, D. "The Role of the Victim Advocate." In Warner, C. (ed.), *Rape and Sexual Assault*. Germantown, Md.: Aspen Systems Corp., 1980.

Spence, J. T., and Helmreich, R. L. *Masculinity & Femininity: Their Psychological Dimensions, Correlates, and Antecedents*. Austin, Tex.: Univ. of Texas Press, 1978.

Spence, J. T., Helmreich, R., and Stapp, J. "Ratings of Self and Peers on Sex-Role Attributes and Their Relation to Self-Esteem and Conceptions of Masculinity and Femininity." *Journal of Personality and Social Psychology* 32:29–39, 1975.

Speroff, L., Glass, R. H., and Kase, N. G. *Clinical Gynecologic Endocrinology and Infertility* (third edition). Baltimore: Williams & Wilkins, 1983.

Spitz, R. A. "Autoeroticism: Some Empirical Findings and Hypotheses on Three of Its Manifestations in the First Year of Life." In *The Psychoanalytic Study of the Child* 3(4):85-120. New York: International Universities Press, 1949.

Spring-Mills, E., and Hafez, E. S. "Male Accessory Sexual Organs." In Hafez, E. S. (ed.), *Human Reproduction*, pp. 60-90. New York: Harper & Row, 1980.

Stamm, W. E., et al. "Causes of the Acute Urethral Syndrome in Women." *New England Journal of Medicine* 303:409-15, 1980.

Stanley, J. P., and Wolfe, S. J. *The Coming Out Stories.* Watertown, Mass.: Persephone Press, 1980.

Starká, L., Sipová, I., and Hynie, J. "Plasma Testosterone in Male Transsexuals and Homosexuals." *Journal of Sex Research* 11:134-38, 1975.

Starr, B. D., and Weiner, M. B. *The Starr-Weiner Report on Sex & Sexuality in the Mature Years.* New York: Stein & Day, 1981.

Stearns, P. "Interpreting the Medical Literature on Aging." Presented at the Family and Community History Colloquia: The Physician and Social History. Chicago, Ill.: 30 October 1975 [cited in Bart and Grossman, 1978].

Steinam, G. "Erotica vs. Pornography." In G. Steinam, *Outrageous Acts and Everyday Rebellions.* New York: Holt, Rhinehart and Winston, 1983.

Stevens, F. A. "The Occurrence of *Staphyloccocus aureus* Infection with a Scarlatiniform Rash." *Journal of the American Medical Association* 88:1957-58, 1927.

Stewart, F., et al. *My Body, My Health: The Concerned Woman's Guide to Gynecology.* New York: Wiley, 1979.

Stock, W. E. "Effects of Exposure to Violent Pornography." Presented at the 26th Annual Meeting of the Society for the Scientific Study of Sex. Chicago, Ill.: 20 November 1983.

Stoenner, H. "Child Sexual Abuse Growing in the United States." In *Plain Talk about Child Abuse*, pp. 11-13. Denver: Denver Humane Society, 1972.

Stoller, R. "Erotic Vomiting." *Archives of Sexual Behavior* 11:361-65, 1982.

Stoller, R. J. "Etiological Factors in Female Transsexualism: A First Approximation." *Archives of Sexual Behavior* 2:47-64, 1972.

———. "Gender Identity." In Freedman, A. M.; Kaplan, H. I.; and Sadock, B. J. (eds.), *Comprehensive Textbook of Psychiatry/II*, pp. 1400-1408. Baltimore: Williams & Wilkins, 1975.

———. *Perversion: The Erotic Form of Hatred.* New York: Pantheon Books, 1975a.

———. "Sexual Deviations." In Beach, F. (ed.), *Human Sexuality in Four Perspectives*, pp. 190-214. Baltimore: Johns Hopkins University Press, 1977.

———. *Sexual Excitement.* New York: Pantheon Books, 1979.

Stuart, R. B. *Helping Couples Change.* New York: Guilford Press, 1980.

Sue, D. "Erotic Fantasies of College Students During Coitus." *Journal of Sex Research* 15:299-305, 1979.

Suggs, R. "Sex and Personality in the Marquesas: A Discussion of the Linton-Kardiner Report." In Marshall, D., and Suggs, R. (eds.), *Human Sexual Behavior*, pp. 163-86. New York: Basic Books, 1971.

Suggs, R., and Marshall, D. "Anthropological Perspectives on Human Sexual Behavior." In Marshall, D., and Suggs, R. (eds.), *Human Sexual Behavior*, pp. 218-43. New York: Basic Books, 1971.

Sullivan-Bolyai, J., et al. "Neonatal Herpes Simplex Virus Infection in King County, Washington." *Journal of the American Medical Association* 250:3059-62, 1983.

Sultan, F. E., and Chambles, D. L. "Pubococcygeal Function and Orgasm in a Normal Population." In B. Graber (ed.), *Circumvaginal Musculature and Sexual Function*, pp. 74-87. New York: Karger, 1982.

Sulloway, F. J. *Freud, Biologist of the Mind.* New York: Basic Books, 1979.

Summers, G. F., and Hammonds, A. D. "Toward a Paradigm of Respondent Bias in Survey Research." University of Wisconsin, 1965. Cited in Rosenthal, R. *Experimental Effects in Behavioral Research.* New York: Appleton-Century-Crofts, 1966.

Summit, R., and Kryso, J. "Sexual Abuse of Children: A Clinical Spectrum." *American Journal of Orthopsychiatry* 48:237-51, 1978.

Sussman, N. "Sex and Sexuality in History." In Sadock, B. J., Kaplan, H. I., and Freedman, A. M. (eds.), *The Sexual Experience*, pp. 7-70. Baltimore: Williams & Wilkins, 1976.

Sutherland, S., and Scherl, D. "Patterns of Response among Victims of Rape." *American Journal of Orthopsychiatry* 40:503-11, 1970.

Symons, D. *The Evolution of Human Sexuality.* New York: Oxford University Press, 1979.

Szasz, T. *Sex by Prescription.* New York: Anchor Press/Doubleday, 1980.

Talese, G. *Thy Neighbor's Wife.* New York: Doubleday, 1980.

Tallent, N. "Sexual Deviation as a Diagnostic Entity: A Confused and Sinister Concept." *Bulletin of the Menninger Clinic* 41:40-60, 1977.

Talmon, Y. "Mate Selection in Collective Settlements." *American Sociological Review* 29(4):491-508, 1964.

Tangri, S. S., Burt, M. R., and Johnson, L. B. "Sexual Harassment at Work: Three Explanatory Models." *Journal of Social Issues* 38(4):33-54, 1982.

Tannahill, R. *Sex in History.* New York: Stein & Day, 1980.

Tanner, J. M. "Sequence and Tempo in the Somatic Changes in Puberty." In Grumbach, M. M.; Grave, G. D.; and Mayer, F. E. (eds.), *Control of the Onset of Puberty.* New York: Wiley, 1974.

Tavris, C. *Anger — The Misunderstood Emotion*. New York: Simon and Schuster, 1982.

Tavris, C., and Offir, C. *The Longest War: Sex Differences in Perspective*. New York: Harcourt Brace Jovanovich, 1977.

Tavris, C., and Sadd, S. *The Redbook Report on Female Sexuality*. New York: Delacorte, 1977.

Taylor, G. R. *Sex in History*. New York: Vanguard, 1954.

Tennov, D. *Psychotherapy: The Hazardous Cure*. New York: Abelard-Schuman, 1975.

———. *Love and Limerence*. New York: Stein & Day, 1979.

Thin, R. N.; Leighton, M.; and Dixon, M. J. "How Often is Genital Yeast Infection Sexually Transmitted?" *British Medical Journal* 2:93-94, 1977.

Thomas, J. L. "The Catholic Tradition for Responsibility in Sexual Ethics." In Wynn, J. C. (ed.) *Sexual Ethics and Christian Responsibility*. New York: Association Press, 1970.

Thompson, A. P. "Extramarital Sex: A Review of the Research Literature." *Journal of Sex Research* 19:1-22, 1983.

Thompson, S. K. "Gender Labels and Early Sex Role Development." *Child Development* 46:339-47, 1975.

Thomson, J. J. "A Defense of Abortion." *Philosophy and Public Affairs* 1(1):47-66, 1971.

Thornton, C. E. "Sexuality Counseling of Women with Spinal Cord Injuries." *Sexuality and Disability* 2:267-77, 1979.

Tietze, C. "Induced Abortion." In Money, J., and Musaph, H. (eds.), *Handbook of Sexology*, pp. 605-20. New York: Elsevier/North-Holland, 1977.

———. "New Estimates on Mortality Associated with Fertility Control." *Family Planning Perspectives* 9, 1977a.

Tietze, C., and Lewit, S. "Legal Abortion." *Scientific American* 236:16, 21-27, 1977.

Todd, J., et al. "Toxic-shock Syndrome Associated with Phage-group-I Staphylococci." *Lancet* 2:1116-18, 1978.

Tollison, C. D., and Adams, H. E. *Sexual Disorders: Treatment, Theory, Research*. New York: Gardner Press, 1979.

Tolor, A., and DiGrazia, P. V. "Sexual Attitudes and Behavior Patterns During and Following Pregnancy." *Archives of Sexual Behavior* 5:539-51, 1976.

"Tong, S. M., Zhou, X. H., and Zhou, Y. X. "Human Antifertility effect of Gossypol: Cytologic Observation of Semen." *Chinese Medical Journal* 95(5):355-62, May 1982.

Tourney, G. "Hormones and Homosexuality." In Marmor, J. (ed.), *Homosexual Behavior*, pp. 41-58. New York: Basic Books, 1980.

Trause, M. A., Kennell, J., and Klaus, M. "Parental Attachment Behavior." In Money, J., and Musaph, H. (eds.), *Handbook of Sexology*, pp. 789-99. New York: Elsevier/North-Holland, 1977.

Trent, M. [Pseud.]. "On Being a Gay Teacher: My Problems — And Yours." *Psychology Today*, p. 136, April 1978.

Trilling, L. "The Kinsey Report." In Trilling, L., *The Liberal Imagination*. New York: Viking Press, 1948.

Tripp, C. A. *The Homosexual Matrix*. New York: McGraw-Hill, 1975.

Troiden, R. R., and Goode, E. "Variables Related to the Acquisition of a Gay Identity." *Journal of Homosexuality* 5(4):383-92, 1980.

Trudel, G., and Saint Laurent, S. "A Comparison Between the Effects of Kegel's Exercises and a Combination of Sexual Awareness Relaxation and Breathing on Situational Orgasmic Dysfunction in Women." *Journal of Sex & Marital Therapy* 9:204-9, 1983.

Trussell, J., and Westoff, C. F. "Contraceptive Practice and Trends in Coital Frequency." *Family Planning Perspectives* 12:246-49, 1980.

Turner, G., and Collins, E. "Fetal Effects of Regular Salicylate Ingestion in Pregnancy." *Lancet* 2:338-39, 1975.

Turner, R., et al. "Shedding and Survival of Herpes Simplex Virus from Fever Blisters." *Pediatrics* 70:547-49, 1982.

Tuttle, W. B., Cook, W. L., and Fitch, E. "Sexual Behavior in Postmyocardial Infarction Patients." *American Journal of Cardiology* 13:140-53, 1964.

Udry, J. R., and Cliquet, R. L. "A Cross-cultural Examination of the Relationship Between Ages at Menarche, Marriage, and First Birth." *Demography* 19:53-63, 1982.

Udry, J. R., and Morris, N. "Distribution of Coitus in the Menstrual Cycle." *Nature* 220:593-96, 1968.

———. "Effect of Contraceptive Pills on the Distribution of Sexual Activity in the Menstrual Cycle." *Nature* 227:502-3, 1970.

Unger, R. K. "Toward a Redefinition of Sex and Gender." *American Psychologist* 34(11):1085-94, 1979.

Updike, John, *Rabbit Redux*. Greenwich, Conn.: Fawcett Crest, 1972.

U.S. Bureau of the Census. "Fertility of American Women: June 1982 (Advance Report)." *Current Population Reports*, Series P-20, Number 379, 1983.

———. "Trends in Childspacing: June 1975." *Current Population Reports*, Series P-20(315): February 1978.

———. "Perspectives on American Husbands and Wives." *Current Population Reports*, Series P-23(77): December 1978a.

U.S. Department of Health, Education, and Welfare. *Age at Menarche in the United States*. DHEW Publication No. (HRA) 74-1615, p. 3, 1973.

U.S. Department of Justice. *Crime Statistics: 1975*. Washington, D.C.: U.S. Government Printing Office, 1976.

Utian, W. H. "Effect of Hysterectomy, Oophorectomy and Estrogen Therapy on Libido." *International Journal of Obstetrics and Gynaecology* 13:97-100, 1975.

Van Gelder, L. "Sex Bytes." *PC Magazine* 2:426-34, 1983.

Van Moffaert, M. "Social Reintegration of Sexual Delinquents by a Combination of Psychotherapy and

Anti-Androgen Treatment." *Acta Psychiatrica Scandinavica* 53:29-34, 1976.

Van Thiel, D. H. "Testicular Atrophy and Other Endocrine Changes in Alcoholic Men." *Medical Aspects of Human Sexuality* 10(6):153-54, 1976.

Vaughan, B., et al. "Contraceptive Failure among Married Women in the United States, 1970-73." *Family Planning Perspectives* 9:251-58, 1979.

Vermeulen, A. "Decline in Sexual Activity in Aging Men: Correlation with Sex Hormone Levels and Testicular Changes." *Journal of Biosocial Science* 6 (supp.):5-18, 1979.

Vessey, M., et al. "Outcome of Pregnancy in Women Using Intrauterine Device." *Lancet* 1:495-98, 1974.

———. "Fertility After Stopping Different Methods of Contraception." *British Medical Journal* 1:265-67, 1978.

Vessey, M., Lawless, M., and Yeates, D. "Efficacy of Different Contraceptive Methods." *Lancet* 1(8276):841-42, 1982.

Vessey, M., and Wiggins, P. "Use-effectiveness of the Diaphragm in a Selected Family Planning Clinic Population in the United Kingdom." *Contraception* 9:15-21, 1974.

Vessey, M. P., et al. "Pelvic Inflammatory Disease and the Intrauterine Device." *British Medical Journal* 282(6267):855-57, 1981.

Vetri, D. "The Legal Arena: Progress for Gay Civil Rights." *Journal of Homosexuality* 5(1,2):25-34, 1979/1980.

Voeller, B. "Society and the Gay Movement." In Marmor, J. (ed.), *Homosexual Behavior*, pp. 232-54. New York: Basic Books, 1980.

Vogel, S., Broverman, I., and Gardner, J. *Sesame Street and Sex-Role Stereotypes*. Pittsburgh: Know, 1970.

Voget, F. T. "Sex Life of American Indians." In Ellis, A., and Abarbanel, A. (eds.), *The Encyclopedia of Sexual Behavior*, pp. 90-109. New York: Hawthorn Books, 1961.

Vollman, R. F. *The Menstrual Cycle*. Philadelphia: Saunders, 1977.

Vontver, L. A., et al. "Recurrent Genital Herpes Simplex Virus Infection in Pregnancy: Infant Outcome and Frequency of Asymptomatic Recurrences." *American Journal of Obstetrics and Gynecology* 143:75-81, 1982.

Wachtel, S. S. "H-Y Antigen and Sexual Development." In Vallet, H., and Porter, I. (eds.), *Genetic Mechanisms of Sexual Development*, pp. 271-77. New York: Academic Press, 1979.

Walker, P. A. "The Role of Antiandrogens in the Treatment of Sex Offenders." In Qualls, C. B., Wincze, J. P., and Barlow, D. H. (eds.), *The Prevention of Sexual Disorders*, pp. 117-36. New York: Plenum Press, 1978.

Wallace, J. I., et al. "T-cell Ratios in New York City Prostitutes." *Lancet* 1:58-59, 1983.

Wallace, R. B., et al. "Vasectomy and Coronary Disease in Men Under 50: Absence of an Association." *Journal of Urology*, in press, 1981.

Walsh, F. M., et al. "Autoerotic Asphyxial Deaths: A Medicolegal Analysis of Forty-Three Cases." In Wecht, C. H. (ed.), *Legal Medicine Annual 1977*, pp. 157-82. New York: Appleton-Century-Crofts, 1977.

Walsh, R. N., et al. "The Menstrual Cycle, Sex and Academic Performance." *Archives of General Psychiatry* 38:219-21, 1981.

Walshok, M. L. "The Emergence of Middle Class Deviant Subcultures: The Case of Swingers." *Social Problems* 18:488-96, 1971.

Walster, E., et al. "'Playing Hard to Get': Understanding an Elusive Phenomenon." *Journal of Personality and Social Psychology* 26:113-21, 1973.

Walster, E., and Walster, G. W. *A New Look at Love*. Reading, Mass.: Addison-Wesley, 1978.

Walster, E.; Walster, G. W.; and Berscheid, E. *Equity: Theory and Research*. Boston: Allyn & Bacon, 1978.

Walum, L. R. *The Dynamics of Sex and Gender: A Sociological Perspective*. Chicago: Rand McNally College Publishing Co., 1977.

Wanderer, Z., and Cabot, T. *Letting Go*. New York: G. P. Putnam's Sons, 1978.

Warner, C. G. (Ed.). *Rape and Sexual Assault*. Germantown, Md.: Aspen Systems Corp., 1980.

Washburn, S. *Partners: How to Have a Loving Relationship after Women's Liberation*. New York: Atheneum, 1981.

Wasow, M., and Loeb, M. "Sexuality in Nursing Homes." *Journal of the American Geriatrics Society* 27:73-79, 1979.

Waterman, C. K., and Chiauzzi, E. J. "The Role of Orgasm in Male and Female Sexual Enjoyment." *Journal of Sex Research* 18:146-159, 1982.

Webster, S. K., Bauman, J. E., and Kolodny, R. C. "The Biochemistry of Dysmenorrhea: Failure to Validate the Distinction Between Spasmodic and Congestive Dysmenorrhea." Presented at the First Dysmenorrhea Symposium, St. Louis University. St. Louis, Mo.: 1978.

Weideger, P. *Menstruation and Menopause* (revised edition). New York: Delta Books, 1977.

Weinberg, S. K. *Incest Behavior*. New York: Citadel, 1955.

Weinberg, T. S. "On 'Doing' and 'Being' Gay: Sexual Behavior and Homosexual Male Self-Identity." *Journal of Homosexuality* 4:143-56, 1978.

Weiner, M. F. "Healthy and Pathological Love: Psychodynamic Views." In Pope, K. S. (ed.), *On Love and Loving*, pp. 114-32. San Francisco: Jossey-Bass, 1980.

Weiss, H. D. "The Physiology of Human Penile Erection." *Annals of Internal Medicine* 76:793-99, 1972.

Weiss, N. S., and Sayvetz, T. A. "Incidence of Endometrial Cancer in Relation to the Use of Oral Contraceptives." *New England Journal of Medicine* 302:551-54, 1980.

Weissman, M. "Depression." In Brodsky, A. M., and Hare-

Mustin, R. (eds.), *Women and Psychotherapy*, pp. 97–112. New York: Guilford Press, 1980.

Weissman, M. M., and Myers, J. K. "Affective Disorders in a U.S. Urban Community." *Archives of General Psychiatry* 35:1304–9, 1978.

Weitzman, L. J. "Sex-role Socialization." In Freeman, J. (ed.), *Women: A Feminist Perspective*. Palo Alto, Calif.: Mayfield, 1975.

Weitzman, L. J., et al. "Sex Role Socialization in Picture Books for Pre-School Children." *American Journal of Sociology* 77:1125–50, 1972.

Wellisch, D. K., Jamison, K. R., and Pasnau, R. O. "Psychosocial Aspects of Mastectomy: II. The Man's Perspective." *American Journal of Psychiatry* 135:543–46, 1978.

Wertz, R. W., and Wertz, D. C. *Lying-in: A History of Childbirth in America*. New York: Free Press, 1977.

Wesson, D. R. "Cocaine Use by Masseuses." *Journal of Psychoactive Drugs* 14:75–76, 1982.

Westoff, C. F., and McCarthy, J. "Sterilization in the United States." *Family Planning Perspectives* 11:147–52, 1979.

Westoff, C. F., and Rindfuss, R. R. "Sex Preselection in the U.S.: Some Implications." *Science* 184:633–36, 1974.

White, C. B. "Sexual Interest, Attitudes, Knowledge and Sexual History in Relation to Sexual Behavior in the Institutionalized Aged." *Archives of Sexual Behavior* 11:11–21, 1982.

Whitehead, H. "The Bow and the Burden Strap: A New Look at Institutionalized Homosexuality in Native North America." In B. Ortner and H. Whitehead (eds.), *Sexual Meanings — The Cultural Construction of Gender and Sexuality*, pp. 80–115. New York: Cambridge University Press, 1981.

Whitley, M. P., and Berke, P. A. "Sexual Response in Diabetic Women." *Journal of Sex Education and Therapy* 9(2):51–56, 1983.

Whitley, R. J., et al. "The Natural History of Herpes Simplex Virus Infection of Mother and Newborn." *Pediatrics* 66:489–94, 1980.

Whitman, W. *Leaves of Grass*. New York: New American Library, 1958.

Wickware, F. S. "Report on the Kinsey Report." *Life* 25:86–90, 2 August 1948.

Wiedeking C., et al. "Plasma Noradrenaline and Dopamine-Beta-Hydroxylase During Sexual Activity." *Psychosomatic Medicine* 39:143–48, 1977.

Wikan, U. *Behind the Veil in Arabia*. Baltimore: Johns Hopkins University Press, 1982.

Wilcox, D., and Hager, R. "Toward Realistic Expectation for Orgasmic Response in Women." *Journal of Sex Research* 16:162–79, 1980.

Wills, T. A., Weiss, R. L., and Patterson, G. R. "A Behavioral Analysis of the Determinants of Marital Satisfaction." *Journal of Consulting and Clinical Psychology* 42:802–11, 1974.

Wilson, C. "Pornography: The Emergence of a Social Issue

and the Beginning of a Psychological Study." *Journal of Social Issues* 29(3):7–17, 1973.

Wilson, E. O. *Sociobiology*. Cambridge, Mass.: Harvard University Press, 1975.

———. *On Human Nature*. Cambridge, Mass.: Harvard University Press, 1978.

Wilson, G. T., and Lawson, D. M. "Effects of Alcohol on Sexual Arousal in Women." *Journal of Abnormal Psychology* 85:489–97, 1976.

———. "Effects of Alcohol on Sexual Arousal in Male Alcoholics," *Journal of Abnormal Psychology* 87:609–16, 1978.

Wilson, J. "Sexual Differentiation." *Annual Review of Physiology* 40:279–306, 1978.

Wilson, J. G. "Embryotoxicity of Drugs in Man." In Wilson, J. G., and Fraser, F. C. (eds.), *Handbook Teratology*, vol. 1: *General Principles and Etiology*, pp. 309–55. New York: Plenum Press, 1977.

Wilson, J., George, F., and Griffin, J. "The Hormonal Control of Sexual Development." *Science* 211(4488):1278–84, 1981.

Wilson, W. C. "Can Pornography Contribute to the Prevention of Sexual Problems?" In Qualls, C. B., Wincze, J. P., and Barlow, D. H. (eds.), pp. 159–79. *The Prevention of Sexual Disorders*. New York: Plenum Press, 1978.

Wincze, J. P., et al. "The Effects of a Subjective Monitoring Task in the Physiological Measure of Genital Response to Erotic Stimulation." *Archives of Sexual Behavior* 9:533–45, 1980.

Wincze, J. P.; Hoon, E. F.; and Hoon, P. W. "Physiological Responsivity of Normal and Sexually Dysfunctional Women During Erotic Stimulus Exposure." *Journal of Psychosomatic Research* 20:445–51, 1976.

Winn, Marie. *Children Without Childhood*. New York: Pantheon Books, 1983.

Wise, T. "Urethral Manipulation: An Unusual Paraphilia." *Journal of Sex & Marital Therapy* 8:222–27, 1982.

Wise, T. N., and Meyer, J. K. "The Border Area Between Transvestism and Gender Dysphoria: Transvestitic Applicants for Sex Reassignment." *Archives of Sexual Behavior* 9(4):327–42, 1980.

Wish, P. A. "The Use of Imagery-Based Techniques in the Treatment of Sexual Dysfunction." *The Counseling Psychologist* 5:52–55, 1975.

Witkin, M. H. "Sex Therapy and Mastectomy." *Journal of Sex & Marital Therapy* 1:290–304, 1975.

Wolchik, S. A., Spencer, S. L., and Lisi, I. S. "Volunteer Bias in Research Employing Vaginal Measures of Sexual Arousal." *Archives of Sexual Behavior* 12:399–408, 1983.

Wolf, E. S. "Self-theory and Intimacy." In M. Fisher and G. Stricker (eds.), *Intimacy*, pp. 65–77. New York: Plenum Press, 1982.

Wolfe, J., and Baker, V. "Characteristics of Imprisoned Rapists and Circumstances of the Rape." In Warner, C.

(ed.), *Rape and Sexual Assault,* pp. 265–78. Germantown, Md.: Aspen Systems Corp., 1980.

Wolfe, L. "The Sexual Profile of that Cosmopolitan Girl." *Cosmopolitan,* pp. 254–65, September 1980.

Wolff, C. *Love Between Women.* New York: Harper & Row, 1971.

Wolpe, J. *Psychotherapy by Reciprocal Inhibition.* Stanford, Calif.: Stanford University Press, 1958.

———. *The Practice of Behavior Therapy.* Oxford: Pergamon, 1969.

Wong, H. "Typologies of Intimacy." *Psychology of Women Quarterly* 5:435–43, 1981.

World Health Organization. "A Prospective Multicentre Trial of the Ovulation Method of Natural Family Planning. II. The Effectiveness Phase." *Fertility & Sterility* 36:591–98, 1981.

———. *Special Programme of Research, Development and Research Training: Seventh Annual Report.* Geneva: November 1978.

Wortman, J. "Vasectomy: What Are the Problems?" *Population Reports,* Series D(2):January 1975.

———. "The Diaphragm and Other Intravaginal Barriers: A Review." *Population Reports,* Series H(4):January 1976.

Wortman, J., and Piotrow, P. T. "Laparoscopic Sterilization: II. What are the Problems?" *Population Reports,* Series C(2):March 1973.

Wright, N. H., et al. "Neoplasia and Dysplasia of the Cervix Uteri and Contraception: A Possible Protective Effect of the Diaphragm." *British Journal of Cancer* 38 (2):273–79, August 1978.

Wynn, J. C. (Ed.). *Sexual Ethics and Christian Responsibility.* New York: Association Press, 1970.

Yalom, I. D. "Aggression and Forbiddenness in Voyeurism." *Archives of General Psychiatry* 3:305–19, 1960.

Yalom, I. D., Green, R., and Fisk, N. "Prenatal Exposure to Female Hormones." *Archives of General Psychiatry* 28:554–61, 1973.

Yorukoglu, A., and Kemph, J. P. "Children Not Severely Damaged by Incest with a Parent." *Journal of the American Academy of Child Psychiatry* 5:111–24, 1966.

Zacharias, L., and Wurtman, R. J. "Age at Menarche: Genetic and Environmental Influences." *New England Journal of Medicine* 280:868–75, 1969.

Zamichow, N. "Is It Something in the Food?" *Ms. Magazine,* pp. 92–93, 141–143, October 1983.

Zeiss, A. M. "Expectation for the Effects of Aging on Sexuality in Parents and Average Married Couples." *Journal of Sex Research* 18:47–57, 1982.

Zelnik, M., and Kantner, J. F. "Attitudes of American Teenagers Towards Abortion." *Family Planning Perspectives* 7(2):89–91, 1975.

———. "Sexual and Contraceptive Experiences of Young Unmarried Women in the United States, 1976 and 1971." *Family Planning Perspectives* 9:55–71, 1977.

———. "Contraceptive Patterns and Premarital Pregnancy among Women Aged 15–19 in 1976." *Family Planning Perspectives* 10:135–42, 1978.

———. "Reasons for Nonuse of Contraception by Sexually Active Women Aged 15–19." *Family Planning Perspectives* 11:289–96, 1979.

———. "Sexual Activity, Contraceptive Use, and Pregnancy Among Metropolitan-Area Teenagers: 1971–1979." *Family Planning Perspectives* 12:230–37, 1980.

Zelnik, M., Kantner, J. F., and Ford, K. *Sex and Pregnancy in Adolescence.* Beverly Hills, Calif.: Sage Publications, 1981.

Zelnik, M., and Kim, Y. J. "Sex Education and Its Association with Teenage Sexual Activity, Pregnancy and Contraceptive Use." *Family Planning Perspectives* 14:117–26, 1982.

Zelnik, M., and Shah, F. K. "First Intercourse among Young Americans." *Family Planning Perspectives* 15:64–70, 1983.

Zilbergeld, B. *Male Sexuality: A Guide to Sexual Fulfillment.* Boston: Little, Brown, 1978.

———. "Alternatives to Couples Counseling for Sex Problems: Group and Individual Therapy." *Journal of Sex & Marital Therapy* 6(1):3–18, 1980.

Zilbergeld, B., and Ellison, C. R. "Social Skills Training as an Adjunct to Sex Therapy." *Journal of Sex & Marital Therapy* 5:340–50, 1979.

Zilbergeld, B., and Evans, M. "The Inadequacy of Masters and Johnson." *Psychology Today* 14:29–43, 1980.

Zimmer, D., Borchardt, E., and Fischle, C. "Sexual Fantasies of Sexually Distressed and Nondistressed Men and Women: An Empirical Comparison." *Journal of Sex & Marital Therapy* 9:38–50, 1983.

Zodhiates, K., Feinbloom, R., and Sagov, S. "Contraceptive Use of Cervical Caps" (letter). *New England Journal of Medicine* 304(15):915, 1981.

Zuckerman, A. J. "Viral Hepatitis." *Practical Gastroenterology* 6(6):16, 21–27, Nov./Dec. 1982.

Zuger, B. "Monozygotic Twins Discordant for Homosexuality: Report of a Pair and Significance of the Phenomenon." *Comprehensive Psychiatry* 17:661–69, 1976.

Zussman, J. U., Zussman, P. P., and Dalton, K. K. Abstract, Third Annual Meeting of the International Academy of Sex Research. Bloomington, Ind.: 1977.

———. "Post-pubertal Effect of Prenatal Administration of Progesterone." Paper presented at the Society for Research in Child Development. Denver: April 1975.

Zussman, L., et al. "Sexual Response after Hysterectomy-oophorectomy: Recent Studies and Reconsideration of Psychogenesis. *American Journal of Obstetrics and Gynecology* 140:725–29, 1981.

Zwerner, J. "Sexual Issues of Women with Spinal Cord Injury." *Sexuality and Disability* 5:158–171, 1982.

Index